Business Analysis & Valuation

Using Financial Statements

Third Edition · Text & Cases

Krishna G. Palepu, PhD

Ross Graham Walker Professor of Business Administration
Harvard University

Paul M. Healy, PhD, ACA

James R. Williston Professor of Business Administration
Harvard University

Victor L. Bernard, PhD, CPA

Late Price Waterhouse Professor of Accounting
University of Michigan

THOMSON
SOUTH-WESTERN

Australia · Canada · Mexico · Singapore · Spain · United Kingdom · United States

Business Analysis & Valuation: Using Financial Statements, 3e

Krishna G. Palepu, Paul M. Healy, and Victor L. Bernard

VP/Editorial Director:
Jack W. Calhoun

VP/Editor-in-Chief:
George Werthman

Acquisitions Editor:
Julie Lindsay

Developmental Editor:
Ken Martin

Marketing Manager:
Keith Chassé

Production Editor:
Chris Sears

Manufacturing Coordinator:
Doug Wilke

Media Developmental Editor:
Josh Fendley

Media Production Editor:
Kelly Reid

Production House:
Bay Island Books

Compositor:
John Richards

Cover Designer:
Bethany Casey

Cover Images:
© Corbis Corporation

Internal Designer:
Bethany Casey

Printer:
Quebecor World
Versailles, KY

For permission to use material
from this text or product, contact
us by
Tel (800) 730-2214
Fax (800) 730-2215
http://www.thomsonrights.com

For more information
contact South-Western,
5191 Natorp Boulevard,
Mason, Ohio, 45040.
Or you can visit our Internet site
at: http://www.swlearning.com.

PREFACE

Financial statements are the basis for a wide range of business analysis. Managers use them to monitor and judge their firms' performance relative to competitors, to communicate with external investors, to help judge what financial policies they should pursue, and to evaluate potential new businesses to acquire as part of their investment strategy. Securities analysts use financial statements to rate and value companies they recommend to clients. Bankers use them in deciding whether to extend a loan to a client and to determine the loan's terms. Investment bankers use them as a basis for valuing and analyzing prospective buyouts, mergers, and acquisitions. And consultants use them as a basis for competitive analysis for their clients. Not surprisingly, therefore, we find that there is a strong demand among business students for a course that provides a framework for using financial statement data in a variety of business analysis and valuation contexts. The purpose of this book is to provide such a framework for business students and practitioners.

The first two editions of this book have been successful well beyond our original expectations. The book has been used in Accounting and Finance departments in business schools in the U.S. and around the world.

CHANGES FROM THE SECOND EDITION

Many of our colleagues who used the second edition provided us with valuable feedback. Based on this feedback, we made the following changes:

- We rewrote the chapters dealing with accounting analysis to focus sharply on the task of the analyst. There are now two chapters on this topic. The first of these (Chapter 3) provides a conceptual approach to evaluating a firm's accounting choices and estimates with respect to assets, liabilities, entities, revenues, and expenses. The second chapter (Chapter 4) shows specific steps the analyst can take in examining assets, liabilities, revenues, and expenses, and in making adjustments to reported financial statements where needed. Our objective is that these two chapters will prepare students to identify questionable accounting practices, make adjustments, and produce a set of restated financials that are free of these accounting concerns.
- We revised the forecasting and valuation chapters (Chapters 6 and 7) to better prepare students for the task of making specific assumptions in the analysis steps. We use a real company example in both these chapters, so that students can use the material as a basis for studying the case applications.
- The chapter on management communication (Chapter 13) has been substantially revised. It now focuses heavily on the corporate governance role of financial reports and the role of key accounting institutions—auditors, audit committees of corporate boards, and top management of firms—in the governance process. The chapter is designed to address some of the issues raised in the aftermath of accounting and governance debacles at major corporations around the world.
- We included seven new cases in this edition. However, we also retained several popular cases from the previous edition because they have proved to be very effective for many instructors.

- This new edition is accompanied by a comprehensive software model, the **BAV Tool**, to implement the analytical framework and techniques discussed in this book. This companion software allows students to import a company's reported financial statements from any source, as long as they are in a Microsoft Excel spreadsheet format, and analyze them. The tool facilitates the following activities: (1) recasting the reported financial statements in a standard format for analysis; (2) performing accounting analysis as discussed in Chapters 3 and 4, making desired accounting adjustments, and producing restated financials; (3) computing ratios and free cash flows presented in Chapter 5; (4) producing forecasted income statement, balance sheet, and cash flow statements for as many as 15 years into the future, using the approach discussed in Chapter 6; and (5) valuing a company (either assets or equity) from these forecasts and preparing a terminal value forecast using the abnormal earnings method, the abnormal returns method, and discounted cash flow method discussed in Chapters 7 and 8. The tool also allows students to graph their assumptions and compare them with the historical performance of a large group of U.S. companies that are in the same performance range at the beginning of the forecasting period. This comparison is facilitated by a database consisting of key ratios for a comprehensive set of U.S. public companies listed on Standard & Poor's Compustat. We think that the BAV Tool will make it significantly easier for students to apply the framework and techniques discussed in the book in a real-world context.

- The third edition also includes access to ***Thomson Analytics–Business School Edition***, which is a web-based portal product that provides integrated access to Thomson financial content for the purpose of financial analysis. This new application delivers the most powerful and flexible tools available for turning critical market data into actionable intelligence for educational purposes. *Thomson Analytics–Business School Edition* is an educational version of the same financial resources used by Wall Street analysts on a daily basis.

Thomson Analytics–Business School Edition includes the following content sets:

I/B/E/S Consensus Estimate Includes consensus estimates—averages, means, and medians; analyst-by-analyst earnings coverage; analysts forecasts based on 15 industry standard measures; and current and historic coverage for the selected 500 companies that are drawn from a database of 60 established and emerging markets. Current history is five years forward and historic data is from 1976 for the U.S. and 1987 for international. Current data is <u>updated daily</u> and historic is <u>updated monthly</u>.

Worldscope Includes company profiles, financials and accounting results and market per-share data for the selected 500 companies drawn from a database of more than 55 established and emerging markets. Annual information and monthly prices going back to 1980 are all <u>updated daily</u>.

Disclosure SEC Database Includes company profiles, annual and quarterly company financials, pricing information, and earnings estimates for selected U.S. and Canadian companies. Annual information from 1987—quarterly data rolling 10 years—and monthly pricing are all <u>updated weekly</u>.

DataStream–International Equity and Index Daily Pricing Includes share price index and exchange rate data—<u>updated daily</u>.

ILX Systems Delayed Quotes Equities and indices, 20-minute-delayed quotes from domestic and international markets.

ComtexReal Time News Real-time feed of company and market news.

SEC Filings and *GlobalImage Source Filings* Regulatory and nonregulatory filings.

KEY FEATURES

This book differs from other texts in business and financial analysis in a number of important ways. We introduce and develop a framework for business analysis and valuation using financial statement data. We then show how this framework can be applied to a variety of decision contexts.

Framework for Analysis

We begin the book with a discussion of the role of accounting information and intermediaries in the economy, and how financial analysis can create value in well functioning markets. We identify four key components of effective financial statement analysis:

- Business Strategy Analysis
- Accounting Analysis
- Financial Analysis
- Prospective Analysis

The first of the components, business strategy analysis, involves developing an understanding of the business and competitive strategy of the firm being analyzed. Incorporating business strategy into financial statement analysis is one of the distinctive features of this book. Traditionally, this step has been ignored by other financial statement analysis books. However, we believe that it is critical to begin financial statement analysis with a company's strategy because it provides an important foundation for the subsequent analysis. The strategy analysis section discusses contemporary tools for analyzing a company's industry, its competitive position and sustainability within an industry, and the company's corporate strategy.

Accounting analysis involves examining how accounting rules and conventions represent a firm's business economics and strategy in its financial statements, and, if necessary, developing adjusted accounting measures of performance. In the accounting analysis section, we do not emphasize accounting rules. Instead we develop general approaches to analyzing assets, liabilities, entities, revenues, and expenses. We believe that such an approach enables students to effectively evaluate a company's accounting choices and accrual estimates, even if students have only a basic knowledge of accounting rules and standards. The material is also designed to allow students to make accounting adjustments rather than merely identify questionable accounting practices.

Financial analysis involves analyzing financial ratio and cash flow measures of the operating, financing, and investing performance of a company relative to either key competitors or historical performance. Our distinctive approach focuses on using financial analysis to evaluate the effectiveness of a company's strategy and to make sound financial forecasts.

Finally, under prospective analysis we show how to develop forecasted financial statements and how to use these to make estimates of a firm's value. Our discussion of valuation includes traditional discounted cash flow models as well as techniques that link value directly to accounting numbers. In discussing accounting-based valuation models, we integrate the latest academic research with traditional approaches such as earnings and book value multiples that are widely used in practice.

While we cover all four components of business analysis and valuation in the book, we recognize that the extent of their use depends on the user's decision context. For example, bankers are likely to use business strategy analysis, accounting analysis, financial analysis, and the forecasting portion of prospective analysis. They are less likely to be interested in formally valuing a prospective client.

Application of the Framework to Decision Contexts

The next section of the book shows how our business analysis and valuation framework can be applied to a variety of decision contexts:

- Securities Analysis
- Credit Analysis
- Corporate Financing Policies Analysis
- Merger and Acquisition Analysis
- Governance and Communication Analysis

For each of these topics we present an overview to provide a foundation for the class discussions. Where possible we discuss relevant institutional details and the results of academic research that are useful in applying the analysis concepts developed earlier in the book. For example, the chapter on credit analysis shows how banks and rating agencies use financial statement data to develop analysis for lending decisions and to rate public debt issues. This chapter also presents academic research on how to determine whether a company is financially distressed.

CASE APPROACH

We have found that teaching a course in business analysis and valuation is significantly enhanced, both for teachers and students, by using cases as a pedagogical tool. Students want to develop "hands-on" experience in business analysis and valuation so that they can apply the concepts in decision contexts similar to those they will encounter in the business world. Cases are a natural way to achieve this objective by presenting practical issues that might otherwise be ignored in a traditional classroom exercise. Our cases all present business analysis and valuation issues in a specific decision context, and we find that this makes the material more interesting and exciting for students.

To provide both guidance and flexibility in the choice of cases, we include one case at the end of each chapter, especially chosen for applying the concepts in that chapter. The multipurpose cases at the end of the book can be used with more than one chapter.

USING THE BOOK

We designed the book so that it is flexible for courses in financial statement analysis for a variety of student audiences—MBA students, Masters in Accounting students, Executive Program participants, and undergraduates in Accounting or Finance. Depending upon the audience, the instructor can vary the manner in which the conceptual materials in the chapters, end-of-chapter questions, and case examples are used.

Prerequisites

To get the most out of the book, students should have completed basic courses in financial accounting, finance, and either business strategy or business economics. The text provides a concise overview of some of these topics, primarily as background for preparing the cases. But it would probably be difficult for students with no prior knowledge in these fields to use the chapters as stand-alone coverage of them. We have integrated only a small amount of business strategy into each case and do not include any cases that focus exclusively on business strategy analysis.

The extent of accounting knowledge required for the cases varies considerably. Some require only a basic understanding of accounting issues, whereas others require a more detailed knowledge at the level of a typical intermediate financial accounting course. However, we have found it possible to teach even these more complex cases to students without a strong accounting background by providing additional reading on the topic. For some cases, the Teaching Manual includes a primer on the relevant accounting issue, which instructors can hand out to help students prepare the case.

How to Use the Text and Case Materials

The materials can be used in a variety of ways. If the book is used for students with prior working experience or for executives, the instructor can use almost a pure case approach, adding relevant lecture sections as needed. When teaching students with little work experience, a lecture class can be presented first, followed by an appropriate case. It is also possible to use the book primarily for a lecture course and include some of the cases as in-class illustrations of the concepts discussed in the book.

Alternatively, lectures can be used as a follow-up to cases to more clearly lay out the conceptual issues raised in the case discussions. This may be appropriate when the book is used in undergraduate capstone courses. In such a context, cases can be used in course projects that can be assigned to student teams.

We have designed the cases so that they can be taught at a variety of levels. For students who need more structure to work through a case, the Instructor's Manual includes a set of detailed questions that the instructor can hand out before class. For students who need less structure, there are recommended questions at the end of each case.

ACKNOWLEDGMENTS

We gratefully acknowledge the contributions of colleagues who co-authored several cases in this book: James Chang and Tarun Khanna (Korea Stock Exchange 1998) and Amy Hutton (America Online, The Upjohn Company: The Upjohn-Pharmacia Merger). We also wish to thank Jonathan Barnett for outstanding research assistance in the development of case material, in the revision of the text chapters, and especially in the development of the BAV Tool; Keith MacKay of Village Software for his help with the development of the BAV Tool; our assistants Christian Douglass and Kathy Cohrs for able assistance throughout the project; Chris Allen for assistance with data on financial ratios for U.S. companies; the Division of Research at the Harvard Business School for assistance in developing materials for this book; and our past and present MBA students for stimulating our thinking and challenging us to continually improve our ideas and presentation

We especially thank the following colleagues who gave us feedback as we wrote this edition: Jim Boatsman (Arizona State University), Wilfred Dellva (Villanova University), Frank Hodge (University of Washington), Paul Hriber (Cornell University), Duncan Kretovich (Portland State University), Thomas Omer (University of Illinois), Michael Sandretto (University of Illinois), David Shaffer (Villanova University), Billy Soo (Boston College), and Richard Willis (Duke University).

We are also very grateful to Laurie McKinzey and Deborah Marlino for their help and assistance throughout this project, to Julie Lindsay and Keith Chasse for their tireless efforts in promoting this revision, to our colleagues, and to Ken Martin, Chris Sears, and Julia Chitwood for their patient editorial and production help.

We would like to thank our parents and families for their strong support and encouragement throughout this project.

AUTHORS

Krishna G. Palepu is the Ross Graham Walker Professor of Business Administration and Senior Associate Dean and Director of Research at the Harvard Business School. During the past twenty years, Professor Palepu's research has focused on corporate strategy, governance, and disclosure. Professor Palepu is the winner of the American Accounting Association's Notable Contributions to Accounting Literature Award (in 1999) and the Wildman Award (in 1997).

Paul Healy is the James R. Williston Professor of Business Administration at the Harvard Business School and Co-Chair of the Doctoral Program. Professor Healy's research has focused on corporate governance and disclosure, mergers and acquisitions, earnings management, and management compensation. He has previously worked at the MIT Sloan School of Management, ICI Ltd., and Arthur Young in New Zealand. Professor Healy has won the Notable Contributions to Accounting Literature Award (in 1990 and 1999) and the Wildman Award (in 1997) for contributions to practice.

Vic Bernard, who passed away November 14, 1995, was a CPA and held a PhD from the University of Illinois. He was the Price Waterhouse Professor of Accounting and Director of the Paton Accounting Center at the University of Michigan and Director of Research for the American Accounting Association. His research examined issues in financial reporting, financial statement analysis, and financial economics. He received the Notable Contributions to Accounting Literature Award in 1991, 1993, and 1999, the Outstanding Accounting Educator Award in 1997, and the Wildman Award in 1997.

CONTENTS

PART 1

Framework

Chapter 1
**A Framework for Business Analysis and
Valuation Using Financial Statements**

A Framework for Business Analysis and Valuation Using Financial Statements

This chapter outlines a comprehensive framework for financial statement analysis. Because financial statements provide the most widely available data on public corporations' economic activities, investors and other stakeholders rely on financial reports to assess the plans and performance of firms and corporate managers.

A variety of questions can be addressed by business analysis using financial statements, as shown in the following examples:

- A security analyst may be interested in asking: "How well is the firm I am following performing? Did the firm meet my performance expectations? If not, why not? What is the value of the firm's stock given my assessment of the firm's current and future performance?"
- A loan officer may need to ask: "What is the credit risk involved in lending a certain amount of money to this firm? How well is the firm managing its liquidity and solvency? What is the firm's business risk? What is the additional risk created by the firm's financing and dividend policies?"
- A management consultant might ask: "What is the structure of the industry in which the firm is operating? What are the strategies pursued by various players in the industry? What is the relative performance of different firms in the industry?"
- A corporate manager may ask: "Is my firm properly valued by investors? Is our investor communication program adequate to facilitate this process?"
- A corporate manager could ask: "Is this firm a potential takeover target? How much value can be added if we acquire this firm? How can we finance the acquisition?"
- An independent auditor would want to ask: "Are the accounting policies and accrual estimates in this company's financial statements consistent with my understanding of this business and its recent performance? Do these financial reports communicate the current status and significant risks of the business?"

In the twentieth century, we have seen two distinct models for channeling savings into business investments. Communist and socialist market economies have used central planning and government agencies to pool national savings and to direct investments in business enterprises. The failure of this model is evident from the fact that most of these economies have abandoned it in favor of the second model—the market model. In almost all countries in the world today, capital markets play an important role in channeling financial resources from savers to business enterprises that need capital.

Financial statement analysis is a valuable activity when managers have complete information on a firm's strategies and a variety of institutional factors make it unlikely that they fully disclose this information. In this setting outside analysts attempt to create "inside information" from analyzing financial statement data, thereby gaining valuable insights about the firm's current performance and future prospects.

To understand the contribution that financial statement analysis can make, it is important to understand the role of financial reporting in the functioning of capital markets and the institutional forces that shape financial statements. Therefore we present first a brief description of these forces; then we discuss the steps that an analyst must perform to extract information from financial statements and provide valuable forecasts.

THE ROLE OF FINANCIAL REPORTING IN CAPITAL MARKETS

A critical challenge for any economy is the allocation of savings to investment opportunities. Economies that do this well can exploit new business ideas to spur innovation and create jobs and wealth at a rapid pace. In contrast, economies that manage this process poorly dissipate their wealth and fail to support business opportunities.

Figure 1-1 provides a schematic representation of how capital markets typically work. Savings in any economy are widely distributed among households. There are usually many new entrepreneurs and existing companies that would like to attract these savings to fund their business ideas. While both savers and entrepreneurs would like to do business with each other, matching savings to business investment opportunities is complicated for at least two reasons. First, entrepreneurs typically have better information than savers on the value of business investment opportunities. Second, communication by entrepreneurs to investors is not completely credible because investors know entrepreneurs have an incentive to inflate the value of their ideas.

These information and incentive problems lead to what economists call the "lemons" problem, which can potentially break down the functioning of the capital market.[1] It works like this. Consider a situation where half the business ideas are "good" and the other half are "bad." If investors cannot distinguish between the two types of business ideas, entrepreneurs with "bad" ideas will try to claim that their ideas are as valuable as the "good" ideas. Realizing this possibility, investors value both good and bad ideas at an average level. Unfortunately, this penalizes good ideas, and entrepreneurs with good ideas find the terms on which they can get financing to be unattractive. As these entrepreneurs leave the capital market, the proportion of bad ideas in the market increases. Over time, bad ideas "crowd out" good ideas, and investors lose confidence in this market.

Figure 1-1	Capital Markets

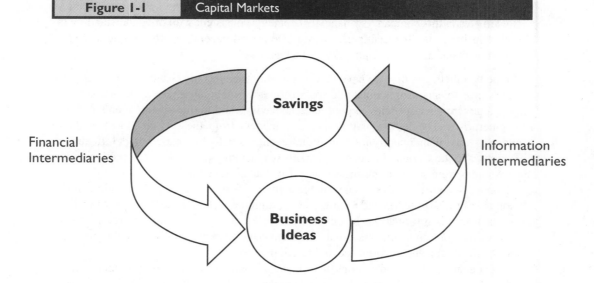

The emergence of intermediaries can prevent such a market breakdown. Intermediaries are like a car mechanic who provides an independent certification of a used car's quality to help a buyer and seller agree on a price. There are two types of intermediaries in the capital markets. Financial intermediaries, such as venture capital firms, banks, mutual funds, and insurance companies, focus on aggregating funds from individual investors and analyzing different investment alternatives to make investment decisions. Information intermediaries, such as auditors, financial analysts, bond-rating agencies, and the financial press, focus on providing information to investors (and to financial intermediaries who represent them) on the quality of various business investment opportunities. Both these types of intermediaries add value by helping investors distinguish "good" investment opportunities from the "bad" ones.

Financial reporting plays a critical role in the functioning of both the information intermediaries and financial intermediaries. Information intermediaries add value by either enhancing the credibility of financial reports (as auditors do), or by analyzing the information in the financial statements (as analysts and the rating agencies do). Financial intermediaries rely on the information in the financial statements to analyze investment opportunities, and supplement this information with other sources of information. In the following section, we discuss key aspects of the financial reporting system design that enable it to play effectively this vital role in the functioning of the capital markets.

FROM BUSINESS ACTIVITIES TO FINANCIAL STATEMENTS

Corporate managers are responsible for acquiring physical and financial resources from the firm's environment and using them to create value for the firm's investors. Value is created when the firm earns a return on its investment in excess of the cost of capital. Managers formulate business strategies to achieve this goal, and they implement them through business activities. A firm's business activities are influenced by its economic environment and its own business strategy. The economic environment includes the firm's industry, its input and output markets, and the regulations under which the firm operates. The firm's business strategy determines how the firm positions itself in its environment to achieve a competitive advantage.

As shown in Figure 1-2, a firm's financial statements summarize the economic consequences of its business activities. The firm's business activities in any time period are too numerous to be reported individually to outsiders. Further, some of the activities undertaken by the firm are proprietary in nature, and disclosing these activities in detail could be a detriment to the firm's competitive position. The firm's accounting system provides a mechanism through which business activities are selected, measured, and aggregated into financial statement data.

Intermediaries using financial statement data to do business analysis have to be aware that financial reports are influenced both by the firm's business activities and by its accounting system. A key aspect of financial statement analysis, therefore, involves understanding the influence of the accounting system on the quality of the financial statement data being used in the analysis. The institutional features of accounting systems discussed below determine the extent of that influence.

Accounting System Feature 1: Accrual Accounting

One of the fundamental features of corporate financial reports is that they are prepared using accrual rather than cash accounting. Unlike cash accounting, accrual accounting distinguishes between the recording of costs and benefits associated with economic activities and the actual payment and receipt of cash. Net income is the primary periodic performance

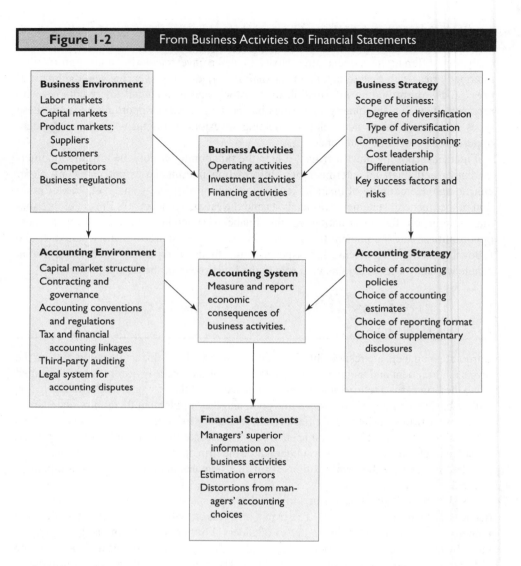

Figure I-2   From Business Activities to Financial Statements

Business Environment
Labor markets
Capital markets
Product markets:
    Suppliers
    Customers
    Competitors
Business regulations

Business Activities
Operating activities
Investment activities
Financing activities

Business Strategy
Scope of business:
    Degree of diversification
    Type of diversification
Competitive positioning:
    Cost leadership
    Differentiation
Key success factors and
    risks

Accounting Environment
Capital market structure
Contracting and
    governance
Accounting conventions
    and regulations
Tax and financial
    accounting linkages
Third-party auditing
Legal system for
    accounting disputes

Accounting System
Measure and report
economic
consequences of
business activities.

Accounting Strategy
Choice of accounting
    policies
Choice of accounting
    estimates
Choice of reporting format
Choice of supplementary
    disclosures

Financial Statements
Managers' superior
    information on
    business activities
Estimation errors
Distortions from man-
    agers' accounting
    choices

index under accrual accounting. To compute net income, the effects of economic transactions are recorded on the basis of *expected,* not necessarily *actual,* cash receipts and payments. Expected cash receipts from the delivery of products or services are recognized as revenues, and expected cash outflows associated with these revenues are recognized as expenses.

The need for accrual accounting arises from investors' demand for financial reports on a periodic basis. Because firms undertake economic transactions on a continual basis, the arbitrary closing of accounting books at the end of a reporting period leads to a fundamental measurement problem. Since cash accounting does not report the full economic consequence of the transactions undertaken in a given period, accrual accounting is designed to provide more complete information on a firm's periodic performance.

Accounting System Feature 2: Accounting Standards and Auditing

The use of accrual accounting lies at the center of many important complexities in corporate financial reporting. Because accrual accounting deals with *expectations* of future cash consequences of current events, it is subjective and relies on a variety of assumptions. Who should be charged with the primary responsibility of making these assumptions? A firm's managers are entrusted with the task of making the appropriate estimates and assumptions to prepare the financial statements because they have intimate knowledge of their firm's business.

The accounting discretion granted to managers is potentially valuable because it allows them to reflect inside information in reported financial statements. However, since investors view profits as a measure of managers' performance, managers have incentives to use their accounting discretion to distort reported profits by making biased assumptions. Further, the use of accounting numbers in contracts between the firm and outsiders provides another motivation for management manipulation of accounting numbers. Income management distorts financial accounting data, making them less valuable to external users of financial statements. Therefore, the delegation of financial reporting decisions to corporate managers has both costs and benefits.

A number of accounting conventions have evolved to ensure that managers use their accounting flexibility to summarize their knowledge of the firm's business activities, and not to disguise reality for self-serving purposes. For example, the measurability and conservatism conventions are accounting responses to concerns about distortions from managers' potentially optimistic bias. Both these conventions attempt to limit managers' optimistic bias by imposing their own pessimistic bias.

Accounting standards, called Generally Accepted Accounting Principles (GAAP), promulgated by the Financial Accounting Standards Board (FASB) and similar standard-setting bodies in other countries, also limit potential distortions that managers can introduce into reported numbers. Uniform accounting standards attempt to reduce managers' ability to record similar economic transactions in dissimilar ways, either over time or across firms.

Increased uniformity from accounting standards, however, comes at the expense of reduced flexibility for managers to reflect genuine business differences in their firm's financial statements. Rigid accounting standards work best for economic transactions whose accounting treatment is not predicated on managers' proprietary information. However, when there is significant business judgment involved in assessing a transaction's economic consequences, rigid standards which prevent managers from using their superior business knowledge would be dysfunctional. Further, if accounting standards are too rigid, they may induce managers to expend economic resources to restructure business transactions to achieve a desired accounting result.

Auditing, broadly defined as a verification of the integrity of the reported financial statements by someone other than the preparer, ensures that managers use accounting rules and conventions consistently over time, and that their accounting estimates are reasonable. Therefore auditing improves the quality of accounting data.

Third-party auditing may also reduce the quality of financial reporting because it constrains the kind of accounting rules and conventions that evolve over time. For example, the FASB considers the views of auditors in the standard-setting process. Auditors are likely to argue against accounting standards producing numbers that are difficult to audit, even if the proposed rules produce relevant information for investors.

The legal environment in which accounting disputes between managers, auditors, and investors are adjudicated can also have a significant effect on the quality of reported numbers. The threat of lawsuits and resulting penalties have the beneficial effect of improving the accuracy of disclosure. However, the potential for a significant legal liability might also discourage managers and auditors from supporting accounting proposals requiring risky forecasts, such as forward-looking disclosures.

Accounting System Feature 3: Managers' Reporting Strategy

Because the mechanisms that limit managers' ability to distort accounting data add noise, it is not optimal to use accounting regulation to eliminate managerial flexibility completely. Therefore real-world accounting systems leave considerable room for managers to influence financial statement data. A firm's reporting strategy, that is, the manner in which managers use their accounting discretion, has an important influence on the firm's financial statements.

Corporate managers can choose accounting and disclosure policies that make it more or less difficult for external users of financial reports to understand the true economic picture of their businesses. Accounting rules often provide a broad set of alternatives from which managers can choose. Further, managers are entrusted with making a range of estimates in implementing these accounting policies. Accounting regulations usually prescribe *minimum* disclosure requirements, but they do not restrict managers from *voluntarily* providing additional disclosures.

A superior disclosure strategy will enable managers to communicate the underlying business reality to outside investors. One important constraint on a firm's disclosure strategy is the competitive dynamics in product markets. Disclosure of proprietary information about business strategies and their expected economic consequences may hurt the firm's competitive position. Subject to this constraint, managers can use financial statements to provide information useful to investors in assessing their firm's true economic performance.

Managers can also use financial reporting strategies to manipulate investors' perceptions. Using the discretion granted to them, managers can make it difficult for investors to identify poor performance on a timely basis. For example, managers can choose accounting policies and estimates to provide an optimistic assessment of the firm's true performance. They can also make it costly for investors to understand the true performance by controlling the extent of information that is disclosed voluntarily.

The extent to which financial statements are informative about the underlying business reality varies across firms and across time for a given firm. This variation in accounting quality provides both an important opportunity and a challenge in doing business analysis. The process through which analysts can separate noise from information in financial statements, and gain valuable business insights from financial statement analysis, is discussed next.

FROM FINANCIAL STATEMENTS TO BUSINESS ANALYSIS

Because managers' insider knowledge is a source both of value and distortion in accounting data, it is difficult for outside users of financial statements to separate true information from distortion and noise. Not being able to undo accounting distortions completely, investors "discount" a firm's reported accounting performance. In doing so, they make a probabilistic assessment of the extent to which a firm's reported numbers reflect economic reality. As a result, investors can have only an imprecise assessment of an individual firm's performance. Financial and information intermediaries can add value by improving investors' understanding of a firm's current performance and its future prospects.

Effective financial statement analysis is valuable because it attempts to get at managers' inside information from public financial statement data. Because intermediaries do not have direct or complete access to this information, they rely on their knowledge of the firm's industry and its competitive strategies to interpret financial statements. Successful intermediaries have at least as good an understanding of the industry economics as do the firm's managers as well as a reasonably good understanding of the firm's competitive strategy. Although outside analysts have an information disadvantage relative to the firm's managers, they are more objective in evaluating the economic consequences of the firm's investment and operating decisions. Figure 1-3 provides a schematic overview of how business intermediaries use financial statements to accomplish four key steps: (1) business strategy analysis, (2) accounting analysis, (3) financial analysis, and (4) prospective analysis.

Analysis Step 1: Business Strategy Analysis

The purpose of business strategy analysis is to identify key profit drivers and business risks, and to assess the company's profit potential at a qualitative level. Business strategy analysis involves analyzing a firm's industry and its strategy to create a sustainable competitive advantage. This qualitative analysis is an essential first step because it enables the analyst to frame the subsequent accounting and financial analysis better. For example, identifying the key success factors and key business risks allows the identification of key accounting policies. Assessment of a firm's competitive strategy facilitates evaluating whether current profitability is sustainable. Finally, business analysis enables the analyst to make sound assumptions in forecasting a firm's future performance.

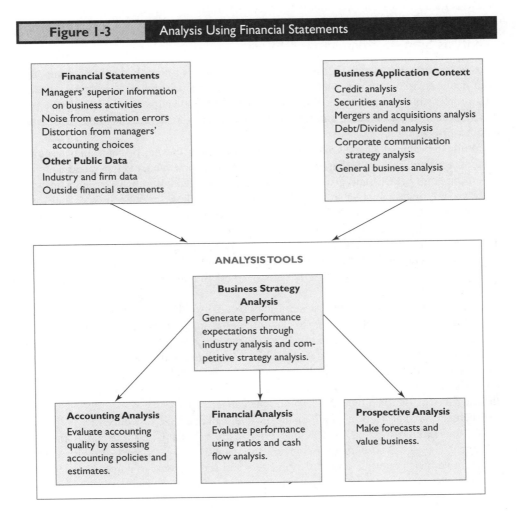

| **Figure 1-3** | Analysis Using Financial Statements |

Financial Statements

Managers' superior information on business activities
Noise from estimation errors
Distortion from managers' accounting choices

Other Public Data

Industry and firm data
Outside financial statements

Business Application Context

Credit analysis
Securities analysis
Mergers and acquisitions analysis
Debt/Dividend analysis
Corporate communication strategy analysis
General business analysis

ANALYSIS TOOLS

Business Strategy Analysis

Generate performance expectations through industry analysis and competitive strategy analysis.

Accounting Analysis

Evaluate accounting quality by assessing accounting policies and estimates.

Financial Analysis

Evaluate performance using ratios and cash flow analysis.

Prospective Analysis

Make forecasts and value business.

Analysis Step 2: Accounting Analysis

The purpose of accounting analysis is to evaluate the degree to which a firm's accounting captures the underlying business reality. By identifying places where there is accounting flexibility, and by evaluating the appropriateness of the firm's accounting policies and estimates, analysts can assess the degree of distortion in a firm's accounting numbers. Another important step in accounting analysis is to "undo" any accounting distortions by recasting a firm's accounting numbers to create unbiased accounting data. Sound accounting analysis improves the reliability of conclusions from financial analysis, the next step in financial statement analysis.

Analysis Step 3: Financial Analysis

The goal of financial analysis is to use financial data to evaluate the current and past performance of a firm and to assess its sustainability. There are two important skills related to financial analysis. First, the analysis should be systematic and efficient. Second, the analysis should allow the analyst to use financial data to explore business issues. Ratio analysis and cash flow analysis are the two most commonly used financial tools. Ratio analysis focuses on evaluating a firm's product market performance and financial policies; cash flow analysis focuses on a firm's liquidity and financial flexibility.

Analysis Step 4: Prospective Analysis

Prospective analysis, which focuses on forecasting a firm's future, is the final step in business analysis. Two commonly used techniques in prospective analysis are financial statement forecasting and valuation. Both these tools allow the synthesis of the insights from business analysis, accounting analysis, and financial analysis in order to make predictions about a firm's future.

While the value of a firm is a function of its future cash flow performance, it is also possible to assess a firm's value based on the firm's current book value of equity, and its future return on equity (ROE) and growth. Strategy analysis, accounting analysis, and financial analysis, the first three steps in the framework discussed here, provide an excellent foundation for estimating a firm's intrinsic value. Strategy analysis, in addition to enabling sound accounting and financial analysis, also helps in assessing potential changes in a firm's competitive advantage and their implications for the firm's future ROE and growth. Accounting analysis provides an unbiased estimate of a firm's current book value and ROE. Financial analysis allows you to gain an in-depth understanding of what drives the firm's current ROE.

The predictions from a sound business analysis are useful to a variety of parties and can be applied in various contexts. The exact nature of the analysis will depend on the context. The contexts that we will examine include securities analysis, credit evaluation, mergers and acquisitions, evaluation of debt and dividend policies, and assessing corporate communication strategies. The four analytical steps described above are useful in each of these contexts. Appropriate use of these tools, however, requires a familiarity with the economic theories and institutional factors relevant to the context.

There are several ways in which financial statement analysis can add value, even when capital markets are reasonably efficient. First, there are many applications of financial statement analysis whose focus is outside the capital market context—credit analysis, competitive benchmarking, analysis of mergers and acquisitions, to name a few. Second, markets become efficient precisely because some market participants rely on analytical tools such as the ones we discuss in this book to analyze information and make investment decisions.

SUMMARY

Financial statements provide the most widely available data on public corporations' economic activities; investors and other stakeholders rely on them to assess the plans and performance of firms and corporate managers. Accrual accounting data in financial statements are noisy, and unsophisticated investors can assess firms' performance only imprecisely. Financial analysts who understand managers' disclosure strategies have an opportunity to create inside information from public data, and they play a valuable role in enabling outside parties to evaluate a firm's current and prospective performance.

This chapter has outlined the framework for business analysis with financial statements, using the four key steps: business strategy analysis, accounting analysis, financial analysis, and prospective analysis. The remaining chapters in this book describe these steps in greater detail and discuss how they can be used in a variety of business contexts.

DISCUSSION QUESTIONS

1. John, who has just completed his first finance course, is unsure whether he should take a course in business analysis and valuation using financial statements since he believes that financial analysis adds little value, given the efficiency of capital markets. Explain to John when financial analysis can add value, even if capital markets are efficient.

2. Accounting statements rarely report financial performance without error. List three types of errors that can arise in financial reporting.

3. Joe Smith argues that "learning how to do business analysis and valuation using financial statements is not very useful, unless you are interested in becoming a financial analyst." Comment.

4. Four steps for business analysis are discussed in the chapter (strategy analysis, accounting analysis, financial analysis, and prospective analysis). As a financial analyst, explain why each of these steps is a critical part of your job and how they relate to one another.

NOTE

1. G. Akerlof, "The Market for 'Lemons': Quality Uncertainty and the Market Mechanism," *Quarterly Journal of Economics* (August 1970): 488–500.

The Role of Capital Market Intermediaries in the Dot-Com Crash of 2000

THE RISE AND FALL OF THE INTERNET CONSULTANTS

In the summer of 1999, a host of Internet consulting firms made their debut on the Nasdaq. Scient Corporation, which had been founded less than two years earlier in March 1997, went public in May 1999 at an IPO price of $20 per share ($10 on a pre-split basis). Its close on the first day of trading was $32.63. Other Internet consulting companies that went public that year included Viant Corporation, IXL Enterprises, and US Interactive (see Exhibit 1).

The main value proposition of these companies was that they would be able to usher in the new Internet era by lending their information technology and web expertise to traditional "old economy" companies that wanted to gain Web-based technology, as well as to the emerging dot-com sector. Other companies like Sapient Corporation and Cambridge Technology Partners had been doing IT consulting for years, but this new breed of companies was able to capitalize on the burgeoning demand for Internet expertise.

Over the following months, the stock prices of the Internet consultants rose dramatically. Scient traded at a high of $133.75 in March 2000. However, this was after a 2-1 split, so each share was actually worth twice this amount on a pre-split basis. This stock level represented a 1238 percent increase from its IPO price and a valuation of 62 times the company's revenues for the fiscal year 2000. Similar performances were put in by the other companies in this group. However, these valuation levels proved to be unsustainable. The stock prices of web consulting firms dropped sharply in April 2000 along with many others in the Internet sector, following what was afterwards seen as a general "correction" in the Nasdaq. The prices of the web consultants seemed to stabilize for a while, and many analysts continued to write favorably about their prospects and maintained buy ratings on their stocks. But starting early in September 2000, after some bad news from Viant Corporation and many subsequent analyst downgrades, the stocks went into a free-fall. All were trading in the single digits by February of 2001, representing a greater than 95 percent drop from their peak valuations (see Exhibit 2).

The dramatic rise and fall of the stock prices of the Web consultants, along with many others in the Internet sector, caused industry observers to wonder how this could have happened in a relatively sophisticated capital market like that of the United States. Several well-respected venture capitalists, investment banks, accounting firms, financial analysts, and money management companies were involved in bringing these companies to market and rating and trading their shares (see Exhibit 3). Who, if anyone, caused the Internet stock price bubble? What, if anything, could be done to avoid the recurrence of such stock market bubbles?

Gillian Elcock, MBA '01, prepared this case under the supervision of Professor Krishna Palepu. The case is intended solely as the basis for class discussion and is not intended to serve as an endorsement, source of primary data, or illustration of effective or ineffective management. Copyright © 2001 by the President and Fellows of Harvard College. HBS Case 9-103-083.

Context: The Technology Bull Market

The 1980s and 1990s marked the beginning of a global technology revolution that started with the personal computer (PC) and led to the Internet era. Companies like Apple, Microsoft, Intel, and Dell Computer were at the forefront of this new wave of technology that promised to enhance productivity and efficiency through the computerization and automation of many processes.

The capital markets recognized the value that was being created by these companies. Microsoft, which was founded in 1975, had a market capitalization of over $600 billion by the beginning of 2000, making it the world's most valuable company, and its founder, Bill Gates, one of the richest men in the world. High values were also given to many of the other blue-chip technology firms such as Intel and Dell (Exhibit 4).

The 1990s ushered in a new group of companies that were based on information networks. These included AOL, Netscape, and Cisco. Netscape was a visible symbol of the emerging importance of the Internet: its browser gave regular users access to the World Wide Web, whereas previously the Internet had been mostly the domain of academics and experts. In March 2000, Cisco Systems, which made the devices that routed information across the Internet, overtook Microsoft as the world's most valuable company (based on market capitalization). This seemed further evidence of the value shift that was taking place from PC-focused technologies and companies to those that were based on the global information network.

It appeared obvious that the Internet was going to profoundly change the world through greater computing power, ease of communication, and the host of technologies that could be built upon it. Opportunities to build new services and technologies were boundless, and they were global in scale. The benefits of the Internet were expected to translate into greater economic productivity through the lowering of communication and transaction costs. It also seemed obvious that someone would be able to capitalize upon these market opportunities and that "the next Microsoft" would soon appear. No one who missed out on the original Microsoft wanted to do so the second time around.

A phrase that became popularized during this time was the "new economy." New economy companies, as opposed to old economy ones (exemplified by companies in traditional manufacturing, retail, and commodities), based their business models around exploiting the Internet. They were usually small compared to their old economy counterparts, with little need for their real-world "bricks and mortar" structures, preferring to outsource much of the capital intensive parts of the business and concentrate on the higher value-added, information-intensive elements. Traditional companies, finding their market shares and business models attacked by a host of nimble, specialized dot-com start-ups, lived in danger of "being Amazoned." To many, the new economy was the future and old economy companies would become less and less relevant.

The capital markets seemed to think similarly. From July 1999 to February 2000, as the Nasdaq Composite Index (which was heavily weighted with technology and Internet stocks) rose by 74.4 percent, the Dow Jones Industrial Average (which was composed mainly of old economy stocks) fell by 7.7 percent. Investors no longer seemed interested in anything that was not new economy.

Internet gurus and economists predicted the far-reaching effects of the Internet. The following excerpts represent the mood of the time:

> *Follow the personal computer and you can reach the pot of gold. Follow anything else and you will end up in a backwater. What the Model T was to the industrial era . . . the PC is to the information age. Just as people who rode the wave of automobile technology—from tire makers to fast food franchisers—prevailed in the industrial era, so*

the firms that prey on the passion and feed on the force of the computer community will predominate in the information era.[1]

—George Gilder, 1992

* * * * *

Due to technological advances in PC-based communications, a new medium—with the Internet, the World Wide Web, and TCP/IP at its core—is emerging rapidly. The market for Internet-related products and services appears to be growing more rapidly than the early emerging markets for print publishing, telephony, film, radio, recorded music, television, and personal computers. . . . Based on our market growth estimates, we are still at the very early stages of a powerful secular growth cycle.[2]

—Mary Meeker, Morgan Stanley Dean Witter, February 1996

* * * * *

The easy availability of smart capital—the ability of entrepreneurs to launch potentially world-beating companies on a shoestring, and of investors to intelligently spread risk—may be the new economy's most devastating innovation. At the same time, onrushing technological change requires lumbering dinosaurs to turn themselves into clever mammals overnight. Some will. But for many others, the only thing left to talk about is the terms of surrender.[3]

—*The Wall Street Journal*, April 17, 2000

In the new economy, gaining market share was considered key because of the benefits of network effects. In addition, a large customer base was needed to cover the high fixed costs often associated with doing business. Profitability was of a secondary concern, and Netscape was one of the first of many Internet companies to go public without positive earnings. Some companies deliberately operated at losses because it was essential to spend a lot early to gain market share, which would presumably translate at a later point into profitability. This meant that revenue growth was the true measure of success for many Internet companies. Of course there were some dissenting voices, warning that this was just a period of irrational exuberance and the making of a classic stock market bubble. But for the most part, investors seemed to buy into the concept, as evidenced by the values given to several loss-making dot-coms (Exhibit 5).

Scient Corporation

The history of Scient, considered a leader in the Internet consulting space, is representative of what happened to the entire industry. The firm was founded in November 1997. Its venture capital backers included several leading firms such as Sequoia Capital and Benchmark Capital (see Exhibit 3).

Scient described itself as "a leading provider of a new category of professional services called eBusiness systems innovation" that would "rapidly improve a client's competitive

---

1. Mary Meeker and Chris DePuy, "U.S. Investment Research, Technology/New Media, The Internet Report" (Excerpt from Life After Television by George Gilder, 1992), Morgan Stanley Dean Witter, February 1996.

2. Mary Meeker and Chris DePuy, "U.S. Investment Research, Technology/New Media, The Internet Report," Morgan Stanley Dean Witter, February 1996.

3. John Browning and Spencer Reiss, "For the New Economy, the End of the Beginning," The Wall Street Journal, April 17, 2000.

position through the development of innovative business strategies enabled by the integration of emerging and existing technologies."[4] Its aim was to provide services in information technology and systems design as well as high-level strategy consulting, previously the domain of companies such as McKinsey and The Boston Consulting Group.

The company grew quickly to almost 2,000 people within three years, primarily organically. Its client list included AT&T, Chase Manhattan, Johnson & Johnson, and Homestore.com.[5] As with any consulting firm, its ability to attract and retain talented employees was crucial, since they were its main assets.

By the fiscal year ending in March 2000, Scient had a net loss of $16 million on revenues of $156 million (see financial statements in Exhibit 6). These revenues represented an increase of 653 percent over the previous year. Analysts wrote glowingly about the firm's prospects. In February 2000, when the stock was trading at around $87.25, a Deutsche Bank Alex Brown report stated:

We have initiated research coverage of Scient with a BUY investment rating on the shares. In our view Scient possesses several key comparative advantages: (1) an outstanding management team; (2) a highly scalable and leverageable operating model; (3) a strong culture, which attracts the best and the brightest; (4) a private equity portfolio, which enhances long-term relationships and improves retention; and (5) an exclusive focus on the high-end systems innovation market with eBusiness and industry expertise, rapid time-to-market and an integrated approach . . . . Scient shares are currently trading at roughly 27x projected CY00 revenues, modestly ahead of pure play leaders like Viant (24x) and Proxicom (25x), and ahead of our interactive integrator peer group average of just over 16x. Our 12-month price target is $120. It is a stock we would want to own.[6]

And in March 2000, when the stock was at $77.75, Morgan Stanley, which had given Scient an "outperform" rating, wrote:

All said we believe Scient continues to effectively execute on what is a very aggressive business plan. . . . While shares of SCNT trade at a premium valuation to its peer group, we continue to believe that such level is warranted given the company's high-end market focus, short but impressive record of execution, and deep/experienced management team. As well, in our view there is a high probability of meaningful upward revisions to Scient's model.[7]

Scient's stock reached a high of $133.75 in March 2000 but fell to $44 by June as part of the overall drop in valuation of most of the technology sector. In September the company announced it had authorized a stock repurchase of $25 million. But in December 2000 it lowered its revenue and earnings expectations for the fourth quarter due to the slowdown in demand for Internet consulting services. The company also announced plans to lay off 460 positions worldwide (over 20 percent of its workforce) as well as close two of its offices, and an associated $40–$45 million restructuring charge. By February 2001 the stock was trading at $2.94.

....

4. *Scient Corporation Prospectus, May 1999. Available from Edgar Online.*

5. *Scient Corporation website, <http://www.scient.com/non/content/clients/client_list/index.asp>*

6. *F. Mark D'Annolfo, William S. Zinsmeister, and Jeffrey A. Buchbinder, "Scient Corporation Premier Builder of eBusinesses," Deutsche Bank Alex Brown, February 14, 2000.*

7. *Michael A. Sherrick and Mary Meeker, "Scient Corporation Quarter Update," Morgan Stanley Dean Witter, March 2, 2000.*

The Dot-Com Crash

Most of the analysts that covered Scient had buy or strong buy ratings on the company as its stock rose to its peak and even after the Nasdaq correction in April 2000. Then in September a warning by Viant Corporation of results that would come in below expectations, due to a slowdown in e-business spending from large corporate clients, prompted many analysts to downgrade most of the companies in the sector, including Scient (see Exhibit 7). Several large mutual fund companies were holders of Scient as its stock rose, peaked, and fell (see Exhibit 8).

As the major technology indices continued their slump during late 2000 and early 2001, and the stock prices of the Internet consulting firms floundered in the single digits, they received increasing attention from the press:

> *Examining the downfall of the eConsultants provides an excellent case study of failed business models. Rose-colored glasses, a lack of a sustainable competitive advantage, and a "me too" mentality are just some of the mistakes these companies made. . . . The eConsultants failed to do the one thing that they were supposed to be helping their clients do—build a sustainable business model . . . many eConsultants popped up and expected to be able to take on the McKinseys and Booz Allens of the world. Now they are discovering that the relationships firmly established by these old economy consultants are integral to building a sustainable competitive advantage.*[8]

* * * * *

> *Seems like everything dot-com is being shunned by investors these days. But perhaps no other group has experienced quite the brutality that Web consultancies have. Once the sweethearts of Wall Street, their stocks are now high-tech whipping boys. Even financial analysts, who usually strive to be positive about companies they cover, seem to have given up on the sector. . . . Many of these firms were built on the back of the dot-com boom. Now these clients are gone. At the same time, pressure on bricks-and-mortar companies to build online businesses has lifted, leading to the cancellation or delay of Web projects.*[9]

The analysts who were formerly excited about Scient's prospects and had recommended the stock when it was trading at almost $80 per share now seemed much less enthusiastic. In January 2001, with the stock around $3.44, Morgan Stanley wrote:

> *We maintain our Neutral rating due to greater than anticipated market weakness, accelerating pricing pressure, the potential for increased turnover and management credibility issues. While shares of SCNT trade at a depressed valuation, we continue to believe that turnover and pricing pressure could prove greater than management's assumptions. While management indicated it would be "aggressive" to maintain its people, we still believe it will be difficult to maintain top-tier talent in the current market and company specific environment.*[10]

Performance of the Nasdaq

The performance of the stock prices of Scient and its peers mirrored that of many companies in the Internet sector. So dramatic was the drop in valuation of these companies that this period was subsequently often referred to as the "dot-com crash."

---

8. Todd N. Lebor, "The Downfall of Internet Consultants," Fool's Den, Fool.com, *December 11, 2000.*

9. Amey Stone, "Streetwise—Who'll Help the Web Consultants?" BusinessWeek Online, *February 15, 2001.*

10. Michael A. Sherrick, Mary Meeker, and Douglas Levine, "Scient Corporation. Outlook Remains Cloudy, Adjusting Forecasts," Morgan Stanley Dean Witter, *January 18, 2001.*

In the months following the crash, the equity markets essentially closed their doors to the Internet firms. Several once high-flying dot-coms, operating at losses and starved for cash, filed for bankruptcy or closed down their operations (see Exhibit 9).

The Nasdaq, which had reached a high of 5,132.52 in March of 2000 closed at 2470.52 in December 2000, a drop of 52 percent from its high. As of February 2001 it had not recovered, closing at 2151.83.

CAPITAL MARKET INTERMEDIARIES

The Role of Intermediaries in a Well Functioning Market

In a capitalist economy, individuals and institutions have savings that they want to invest, and companies need capital to finance and grow their businesses. The capital markets provide a way for this to occur efficiently. Companies issue debt or equity to investors who are willing to part with their cash now because they expect to earn an adequate return in the future for the risk they are taking.

However, there is an information gap between investors and companies. Investors usually do not have enough information or expertise to determine the good investments from the bad ones. And companies do not usually have the infrastructure and know-how to directly receive capital from investors. Therefore, both parties rely on intermediaries to help them make these decisions. These intermediaries include accountants, lawyers, regulatory bodies (such as the SEC in the United States), investment banks, venture capitalists, money management firms, and even the media (see Exhibit 10). The focus of this case is on the equity markets in the United States.

In a well functioning system, with the incentives of intermediaries fully aligned in accordance with their fiduciary responsibility, public markets will correctly value companies such that investors earn a normal "required" rate of return. In particular, companies that go public will do so at a value which will give investors this fair rate of investment.

The public market valuation will have a trickle down effect on all intermediaries in the investment chain. Venture capitalists, who typically demand a very high return on investment, and usually exit their portfolio companies through an IPO, will do their best to ensure these companies have good management teams and a sustainable business model that will stand the test of time. Otherwise, the capital markets will put too low a value on the companies when they try to go public. Investment bankers will provide their expertise in helping companies to go public or to make subsequent offerings, and introducing them to investors.

On the other side of the process, portfolio managers, acting on behalf of investors will only buy companies that are fairly priced, and will sell companies if they become overvalued, since buying or holding an overvalued stock will inevitably result in a loss. Sell-side analysts, whose clients include portfolio managers and therefore investors, will objectively monitor the performance of public companies and determine whether or not their stocks are good or bad investments at any point in time. Accountants audit the financial statements of companies, ensuring that they comply with established standards and represent the true states of the firms. This gives investors and analysts the confidence to make decisions based on these financial documents.

The integrity of this process is critical in an economy because it gives investors the confidence they need to invest their money into the system. Without this confidence, they would not plow their money back into the economy but instead keep it under the proverbial mattress.

The Dot-Com Crash

What happened during the dot-com bubble?

Many observers believed that something went wrong with the system during the dot-com bubble. In April 2001, *BusinessWeek* wrote about "The Great Internet Money Game. How America's top financial firms reaped billions from the Net boom, while investors got burned."[11] The following month, *Fortune* magazine's cover asked "Can we ever trust Wall Street again?"[12] referring to the way in which, in some people's opinions, Wall Street firms had led investors and companies astray before and after the dot-com debacle.

The implications of the Internet crash were far reaching. Many companies that needed to raise capital for investment found the capital markets suddenly shut to them. Millions of investors saw a large portion of their savings evaporate. This phenomenon was a likely contributor to the sharp drop in consumer confidence that took place in late 2000 and early 2001. In addition, the actual decrease in wealth threatened to dampen consumer spending. These factors, along with an overall slowing of the U.S. economy, threatened to put the United States into recession for the first time in over 10 years.

On a more macro level, the dot-coms used up valuable resources that could have been more efficiently allocated within the economy. The people who worked at failed Internet firms could have spent their time and energy creating lasting value in other endeavors, and the capital that funded the dot-coms could have been plowed into viable, lasting companies that would have benefited the overall economy. However, it could be argued that there were benefits as well, and that the large investment in the technology sector positioned the United States to be a world leader in the future.

Nevertheless, the question remained: how could the dot-com bubble occur in a sophisticated capital market system like that of the United States? Why did the market allow the valuations of many Internet companies to go so high? What was the role of the intermediaries in the process that gave rise to the stock market bubble? On a more macro level, the dot-coms used up valuable resources that could have been more efficiently allocated within the economy. The people who worked at failed Internet firms could have spent their time and energy creating lasting value in other endeavors, and the capital that funded the dot-coms could have been plowed into viable, lasting companies that would have benefited the overall economy. However, it could be argued that there were benefits as well, and that the large investment in the technology sector positioned the United States to be a world leader in the future.

Key Intermediaries

One way to try to answer some of these questions is to look more closely at some of the players in the investing chain. Much of the material in the following sections is derived from interviews with representatives from each sector.

Venture Capitalists

Venture capitalists (VCs) provided capital for companies in their early stages of development. They sought to provide a very high rate of return to their investors for the associated risk. This was typically accomplished by selling their stake in their portfolio companies either to the public through an IPO, or to another company in a trade sale.

---

11. Peter Elstrom, "The Great Internet Money Game. How America's top financial firms reaped billions from the Net boom while investors got burned," BusinessWeek e.biz, April 16, 2001.

12. Fortune, May 14, 2001.

The partners in a VC firm typically had a substantial percentage of their net worth tied up in their funds, which aligned their interests with their investors. Their main form of compensation was a large share of profits (typically 20 percent) in addition to a relatively low fee based on the assets under management.

A large part of a VC's job was to screen good business ideas and entrepreneurial teams from bad ones. Partners at a VC firm were typically very experienced, savvy business people who worked closely with their portfolio companies to both monitor and guide them to a point where they have turned a business idea into a well managed, fully functional company that could stand on its own. In a sense, their role was to nurture the companies until they reached a point where they were ready to face the scrutiny of the public capital markets after an IPO. Typically, companies would not go public until they had shown profits for at least three quarters.[13]

After the dot-com crash, some investors and the media started pointing fingers at the venture capitalists that had invested in many of the failed dot-coms. They blamed them for being unduly influenced by the euphoria of the market, and knowingly investing in and bringing public companies with questionable business models, or that had not yet proven themselves operationally. Indeed, many of the dot-coms went public within record time of receiving VC funding—a study of venture-backed initial public offerings showed that companies averaged 5.4 years in age when they went public in 1999, compared with 8 years in 1995.[14]

Did the venture capital investing process change in a way that contributed to the Internet bubble of 2000? According to a partner at a venture capital firm that invested in one of the Internet consulting companies, the public markets had a tremendous impact on the way VCs invested during the late 1990s.[15] He felt that, because of expectations of high stock market valuations, VC firms invested in companies during the late 1990s that they would not have invested in under ordinary circumstances. He also believed that the ready availability of money affected the business strategies and attitudes of the Internet companies: "If the [management] team knows $50 million is available, it acts differently, i.e., 'go for market share.' "

The VC partner acknowledged that VCs took many Internet companies public very early, but he felt that the responsibility of scrutinizing these companies lay largely with the investors that subscribed to the IPOs: "If a mutual fund wants to invest in the IPO of a company that has no track record, profitability, etcetera but sees it as a liquidity event, it has made a decision to become a VC. Lots of mutual funds thought 'VC is easy, I want a piece of it.' "

Investment Bank Underwriters

Entrepreneurs relied on investment banks (such as Goldman Sachs, Morgan Stanley Dean Witter and Credit Suisse First Boston) in the actual process of doing an initial public offering, or "going public." Investment banks provided advisory financial services, helped the companies price their offerings, underwrite the shares, and introduce them to investors, often in the form of a road show.

Investment banks were paid a commission based on the amount of money that the company manages to raise in its offering, typically on the order of 7 percent.[16] Several blue-

----

13. Peter Elstrom, "The Great Internet Money Game. How America's top financial firms reaped billions from the Net boom while investors got burned," BusinessWeek e.biz, April 16, 2001.

14. Shawn Neidorf, "Venture-Backed IPOs Make a Comeback," Venture Capital Journal, August 1, 1999.

15. Limited partners are the investors in a venture capital fund; the venture capital firm itself usually serves as the general partner.

16. Source: case writer interview.

chip firms were involved in the capital-raising process of the Internet consultants (see Exhibit 3), and they also received a share of the blame for the dot-com crash in the months that followed it. In an article entitled "Just Who Brought Those Duds to Market?," the *New York Times* wrote:

> . . . *many Wall Street investment banks, from top-tier firms like Goldman, Sachs . . . to newer entrants like Thomas Weisel Partners . . . have reason to blush. In one blindingly fast riches-to-rags story, Pets.com filed for bankruptcy just nine months after Merrill Lynch took it public.*
>
> *Of course, investment banks that took these underperforming companies public may not care. They bagged enormous fees, a total of more than $600 million directly related to initial public offerings involving just the companies whose stocks are now under $1.*
>
> . . . *How did investment banks, paid for their expert advice, pick such lemons?*[17]

Sell-Side Analysts

Sell-side analysts worked at investment banks and brokerage houses. One of their main functions was to publish research on public companies. Each analyst typically followed 15 to 30 companies in a particular industry, and his or her job involved forming relationships with and talking to the managements of the companies, following trends in the industry, and ultimately making buy or sell recommendations on the stocks. The recommendations analysts made could be very influential with investors. If a well respected analyst downgraded a stock, the reaction from the market could be severe and swift, resulting in a same-day drop in the stock price. Sell-side analysts typically interacted with buy-side analysts and portfolio managers at money management companies (the buy-side) to market or "sell" their ideas. In addition, they usually provided support during a company's IPO process, providing research to the buy-side before the company actually went public. Sell-side analysts were usually partly compensated based on the amount of trading fees and investment banking revenue they helped the firm to generate through their research.

In the months following the dot-com crash, sell-side technology and Internet analysts found themselves the target of criticism for having buy ratings on companies that had subsequently fallen drastically in price. Financial cable TV channel CNBC ran a report called "Analyzing the Analysts," addressing the issue of whether or not they were to blame for their recommendations of tech stocks. A March 2001 article in *The Wall Street Journal* raised similar issues after it was reported that J.P. Morgan Chase's head of European research sent out a memo requiring all the company's analysts to show their stock recommendation changes to the company involved and to the investment banking division.[18] The previously mentioned issue of *Forbes* featured an article criticizing Mary Meeker, a prominent Internet analyst.[19] And a *Financial Times* article entitled "Shoot all the analysts" made a sweeping criticism of their role in the market bubble:

> . . . *instead of forecasting earnings per share, they were now in the business of forecasting share prices themselves. And those prices were almost always very optimistic. Now, at last, they have had their comeuppance. Much of what many of them have done in the past several years has turned out to be worthless. High-flying stocks that*

17. Andrew Ross Sorkin, "Just Who Brought Those Duds to Market?" New York Times, April 15, 2001.

18. Wade Lambert and Jathon Sapsford, "J.P. Morgan Memo to Analysts Raises Eyebrows," The Wall Street Journal, March 22, 2001.

19. Peter Elkind, "Where Mary Meeker Went Wrong," Fortune, May 14, 2001.

a year ago were going to be cheap at twice the price have halved or worse—and some analysts have been putting out buy recommendations all the way down. . . . They should learn a little humility and get back to analysis.[20]

Responding to the media criticism of financial analysts, Karl Keirstead, a Lehman Brothers analyst who followed Internet consulting firms, stated:

It is too easy as they do on CNBC to slam the analysts for recommending stocks when they were very expensive. In the case of the Internet consulting firms, looking back before the correction in April 2000, the fundamentals were "nothing short of pristine." The companies were growing at astronomical rates, and it looked as though they would continue to do so for quite a while. Under these assumptions, if you modeled out the financials for these companies and discounted them back at a reasonable rate, they did not seem all that highly valued.[21]

Keirstead also pointed out that there were times when it was legitimate to have a buy rating on a stock that was "overvalued" based on fundamentals:

The future price of a stock is not always tied to the discounted value of cash flow or earnings, it is equal to what someone is willing to pay. This is especially true in periods of tremendous market liquidity and huge interest in young companies with illiquid stocks and steep growth curves that are difficult to project. The valuation may seem too high, but if the fundamentals are improving and Street psychology and hype are building, the stock is likely to rally. Stock pickers must pay as much attention to these factors as the company and industry fundamentals.

When asked his view on why the buy-side institutions went along with the high valuations that these companies were trading for, Keirstead commented, "A lot of buy-side analysts and portfolio managers became momentum investors in disguise. They claimed in their mutual fund prospectus that they made decisions based on fundamental analysis. Truth is, they played the momentum game as well."

Keirstead also commented on the criticism analysts had received for being too heavily influenced by the possibility of banking deals when making stock recommendations. He stated that this claim was "completely over-rated." Though there was some legitimacy to the argument and some of analysts' compensation did come from investment banking fees, it was a limited component. Analysts also got significant fees from the trading revenue they generated and from their published rankings.[22] He pointed out that critics' arguments were ludicrous because if analysts only made decisions based on banking fees, it would jeopardize their rankings and credibility with their buy-side clients. However, he did note that the potential deal flow could have distorted the view of some technology analysts during the boom.

Finally, Keirstead described the bias that was present on the sell side to be bullish:

To be negative when you are a sell-side analyst is to be a contrarian, to stick your neck out. You take a lot of heat, it's tough. And it would have been the wrong call for the last four years. Had I turned short in 1999 when these stocks seemed overvalued, I would have missed a 200 percent increase in the stocks. My view was: I can't be too

20. *"Shoot all the analysts,"* Financial Times, *March 20, 2001.*

21. *Source: case writer interview.*

22. *Several financial journals publish analyst rankings. The most prominent is* Institutional Investor *magazine, which publishes annual rankings of sell-side analysts by industry. These rankings are very influential in the analyst and investment community.*

The Dot-Com Crash

valuation-sensitive. The stocks are likely to rise as long as the fundamentals hold, and that's the position a lot of analysts took.

Consistent with this optimistic bias, there were very few sell recommendations from analysts during the peak of the Internet stock bubble. According to financial information company First Call, more than 70 percent of the 27,000 plus recommendations outstanding on some 6,000 stocks in November 2000 were strong buys or buys, while fewer than 1 percent were sells or strong sells.[23]

Buy-Side Analysts and Portfolio Managers

The "buy-side" refers to institutions that do the actual buying and selling of public securities, such as mutual fund companies, insurance companies, hedge funds, and other asset managers.

There were two main roles on the buy side: analysts and portfolio managers. Buy-side analysts had some of the same duties as their sell-side counterparts. They were usually assigned to a group of companies within a certain industry and were responsible for doing industry research, talking to the companies' management teams, coming up with earning estimates, doing valuation analysis, and ultimately rating the stock prices of the companies as either "buys" or "sells." The analyst's job was not yet complete, however. Though they did not publish their research, buy-side analysts needed to convince the portfolio managers within their company to follow their recommendations.

Portfolio managers were the ones who actually managed money, whether it was a retail mutual fund or an institutional account. Though they listened to the recommendations of the analysts, they were the ones who were ultimately responsible for buying or selling securities.

The compensation of the buy-side analysts was often linked to how well their stock recommendations did, and in the case of portfolio managers, compensation was determined by the performance of their funds relative to an appropriate benchmark return. These compensation schemes were designed to align the incentives of buy-side analysts and portfolio managers with the interests of investors.

Why then, did so many buy-side firms buy and hold on to the Internet consulting firms during the market bubble? Did they really believe the companies were worth what they were trading for? Or did they know they were overvalued, but invest in them anyway for other reasons?

According to a former associate at a large mutual fund company, many people within his company knew that most of the Internet companies were overvalued before the market correction, but they felt pressure to invest anyway:

My previous employer is known as a value investor, growth at a reasonable price. At first the general impression in the firm was that a lot of the Internet firms would blow up, that they didn't deserve these valuations. But articles were written about my company . . . that it was being left behind because it was not willing to invest in the Internet companies. Some of the analysts at the firm began to recommend companies simply because they knew that the stock prices would go up, even though they were clearly overvalued. And portfolio managers felt that if they didn't buy the stocks, they would lag their benchmarks and their competitors—they are rewarded on a one-year term horizon and three-year horizon. It is very important to meet their benchmark, it

----

23. Walter Updegrave, "The ratings game," Money, January 2001.

makes up a material part of their compensation. In addition, they compare against the performance of their peers for marketing purposes.[24]

THE ROLE OF INFORMATION

The Accounting Profession

Independent accountants audited the financial statements of public companies to verify their accuracy and freedom from fraud. If they were reasonably satisfied, they provided an unqualified opinion statement which was attached to the company's public filings. If auditors were not fully satisfied, this was noted as well. Investors usually took heed of the auditor's opinion as it provided an additional level of assurance of the quality of the information they were receiving from companies.

In the year 2000, the accounting profession in the United States was dominated by five major accounting firms, collectively referred to as "The Big Five" (PriceWaterhouse-Coopers, Deloitte & Touche, KPMG, Ernst & Young, and Arthur Andersen.) The top 100 accounting firms had roughly a 50 percent share of the market and the Big Five account for about 84 percent of the revenues of the top 100.[25] However, the Big Five made up an even larger percentage of the auditing activity of Internet IPOs. Of the 410 Internet services and software IPOs between January 1998 and December 2000, 373 of them, or 91 percent, were audited by one of the Big Five accountants.[26]

During the aftermath of the dot-com crash, these firms came under some criticism for not adequately warning investors about the precarious financial position of some of the companies. The *Wall Street Journal* wrote an article addressing the fact that many dot-coms that went bankrupt were not given "going concern" clauses by their auditors. A going concern clause was included by an auditor if it had a substantial doubt that the company would be able to remain in operation for another 12 months:

> *In retrospect, critics say, there were early signs that the businesses weren't sustainable, including their reliance on external financing, rather than money generated by their own operations, to stay afloat. You wonder where some of the skepticism was . . . critics say many auditors appear to have presumed the capital markets would remain buoyant. For anybody to have assumed a continuation of those aberrant, irrational conditions was in itself irrational and unjustifiable whether it was an auditor, a board member or an investor. . . .*[27]

However, in the same article, accountants defended their actions by noting that going concern judgments were subjective, and that they were not able to predict the future any better than the capital markets.

Dr. Howard Schilit, founder and CEO of CFRA, an independent financial research organization,[28] believed that accountants certainly had to take a part of the blame for what happened. In his opinion, they "looked the other way when they could have been more

....

24. *Source: case writer interview.*

25. *"Accounting Today Top 100 Survey Shows All Is Well,"* The CPA Journal, *May 1999.*

26. *Information extracted from IPO web site <http://www.ipo.com>.*

27. *Johnathan Weil, "'Going Concerns': Did Accountants Fail to Flag Problems at Dot-Com Casualties?"* The Wall Street Journal, *February 9, 2001.*

28. *CFRA's mission is to warn investors and creditors about companies experiencing operational problems and particularly those that employ unusual or aggressive accounting practices to camouflage such problems.*

rigorous in doing their work."[29] However, he noted that the outcome may not have been materially different even if they did.

One particular criticism he had was that many accountants didn't look closely enough at the substance of transactions and didn't do enough questioning of the circumstances surrounding sales contracts. His hope was that accountants "go back and learn what the basic rules are of when revenues should be booked. The rules haven't changed whether this is the new economy or old economy."

FASB—A Regulator

The Financial Accounting Standards Boards (FASB) was an independent regulatory body in the United States whose mission was to "establish and improve standards of financial accounting and reporting for the guidance and education of the public, including issuers, auditors, and users of financial information."[30] FASB standards were recognized by the Securities and Exchange Commission (SEC), which regulates the financial reporting of public companies in the United States.

The accounting practices of some new economy firms posed challenges for auditors and investors, and though some observers felt that the accountants were not doing a good enough job, others thought that the accounting rules themselves were too ambiguous, and this fact lent itself to exploitation by the companies.

Specific examples included the treatment of barter revenues in the case of companies that exchanged on-line advertising space, the practice of booking gross rather than net revenues in commission-based businesses (e.g., Priceline.com), and the issue of when to recognize revenues from long-term contracts (e.g., MicroStrategy Inc.) Given that the valuations of many Internet firms were driven by how quickly they grew revenues, there was a lot of incentive to inflate this number. In fact, the accounting practices of dot-coms became so aggressive that the SEC had to step in:

> The Securities & Exchange Commission's crackdown on the aggressive accounting practices that have taken off among many dot-com firms really began . . . when it quietly issued new guidelines to refocus corporate management and investors . . . . To rein in what it saw as an alarming trend in inflated revenue reports, the SEC required companies using lax accounting practices to restate financial results by the end of their next fiscal year's quarter. . . .
>
> The SEC has also directed the Financial Accounting Standards Board to review a range of Internet company accounting practices that could boost revenues or reduce costs unfairly. Under the scrutiny, more companies are likely to issue restatements of financial results . . . .[31]

In another spin on the issue, some questioned whether the accounting rules set out by the regulatory bodies had in fact become obsolete for the new economy. In July 2000, leaders in the accounting community told a Senate banking subcommittee that the United States needed "a new accounting model for the New Economy." A major concern of theirs was that the current rules did not allow companies to report the value of intangible assets on their balance sheets, such as customers, employees, suppliers and organization.[32] Others argued that the accounting rules caused Internet firms to appear unprofitable when they

29. Source: case writer interview.
30. FASB web site: <http://accounting.rutgers.edu/raw/fasb/>.
31. Catherine Yang, "Earth to Dot-Com Accountants," BusinessWeek, April 3, 2000.
32. Stephen Barlas, "New accounting model demanded," Strategic Finance, September 2000.

were actually making money. This was because old economy firms were allowed to capitalize their major investments such as factories, plants and equipment, whereas the rules did not allow capitalization of expenditures on R&D and marketing, which created value for many dot-com companies:

> *While Internet stocks may not be worth what they are selling for, the movement in their prices may not be as crazy as it seems. Many of these companies reporting losses actually make money—lots of it. It all has to do with accounting. Old-economy companies get to capitalize their most important investments, while new economy ones do not. While Amazon.com announces a loss almost every quarter, when it capitalizes its investments in intangibles that loss turns into a $400 million profit.*[33]

RETAIL INVESTORS

The role of the general public in the dot-com craze cannot be ignored. In addition to the people who poured money into mutual funds, many retail investors began trading on their own, often electronically. A group of avid day traders grew up, some of whom quit their regular jobs to devote all their time and energy to trading stocks. Analysts estimated that they made up almost 18 percent of the trading volume of the NYSE and Nasdaq in 2000.[34] Sites such as Yahoo Finance grew in popularity, while chat rooms devoted to stocks and trading proliferated.

The number of accounts of Internet stock brokers like Etrade and Ameritrade grew rapidly (Etrade grew from 544 thousand brokerage accounts in 1998 to 3 million in 2000 and Ameritrade grew from 98 thousand accounts in 1997 to 1.2 million in 2000) as they slashed their commissions, some to as low as $8/trade compared to the $50–$300[35] charged by traditional brokerage firms. These companies were dot-coms themselves and they were able to slash prices partly because they were operating at losses that they were not penalized for by the capital markets. This gave rise to an interesting positive feedback loop: the Etrades of the world, funded by the dot-com frenzied capital markets, slashed their prices and therefore encouraged more trading, which continued to fuel the enthusiasm of investors for the markets.

The financial press also became increasingly visible during this period. Several publications like *Barrons* and *The Wall Street Journal* had always been very influential in the financial community. However, a host of other information sources, often on the web, sprang up to support the new demand for information. CNBC and CNNfn, major network channels devoted to the markets, often featured analysts and portfolio managers making stock recommendations or giving their views on the market.

Many of the retail investors did not know much about finance or valuation, and often didn't understand much about the companies whose shares they were buying. They were therefore likely to be heavily influenced by some of the intermediaries previously described, especially the financial press, and the sell-side analysts that publicly upgraded and downgraded companies.

These investors were pointed to by some as having had a large role in driving Internet valuations to the levels they went to. The reasoning was that other more sophisticated buyers such as the institutional money managers may have bought overvalued companies

33. Geoffrey Colvin, "The Net's hidden profits," Fortune, April 17, 2000.
34. Amy S. Butte, "Day Trading and Beyond. A New Niche Is Emerging," Bear Stearns Equity Research, April 2000.
35. Lee Patterson, "If you can't beat 'em...," Forbes, August 23, 1999.

because they thought they could easily sell them later at even higher valuations to "dumb retail investors."

THE COMPANIES THEMSELVES

The entrepreneurs who founded the Internet consulting companies, and the management teams who ran them, could almost be described as bystanders to the process that took the stock prices of their companies to such lofty highs and then punishing lows. However, they were profoundly affected by these changes in almost every aspect of their businesses.

Obviously there were many benefits to having a high stock price. According to a managing director (MD) at one of the Internet consultants, the company was facing a very competitive labor market while trying to grow organically, and having a stock that was doing well helped with recruiting people since the option part of the compensation package was attractive.[36] He also explained that people were proud to be a part of the firm, partly because the stock was doing so well.

As the stock price of the company continued to rise higher and higher, the MD admitted that he did become afraid that the market was overvaluing the company, and that this doubt probably went all the way up to the CEO. As he put it, "We were trading at just absurd levels."

When asked about his thoughts on his firm's current stock price, the MD thought that the market had over-reacted and gone to the other extreme. He remarked that investors were worried that the Internet consulting firms were facing renewed competition from companies like IBM, the Big Five accounting firms, and the strategy consulting firms. Overall, though the rise and fall of the company's stock price was in many ways a painful experience, this MD thought that the market bubble presented a good opportunity that the company was able to capitalize upon. It was able to do a secondary offering at a high price and now had lots of cash on its balance sheet. His view was that "If you look at competitive sustainability [in this business], it could boil down to the company with the best balance sheet wins."

THE BLAME GAME

In the aftermath of the dot-com crash, many tried to pinpoint whose fault it was that the whole bubble occurred in the first place. As mentioned previously, sell-side analysts, often the most visible group in the investment community, came under frequent attack in the media, as did to some extent venture capitalists, investment bankers, and even the accounting industry. Company insiders (including the founder of Scient) were also scrutinized for selling large blocks of shares when the stock prices of their companies were near their peaks.[37]

A *Wall Street Journal* article entitled "Investors, Entrepreneurs All Play the Blame Game" described how these various players were trying to blame each other for what happened:

With the tech-heavy Nasdaq Composite Index dancing close to the 2,000 mark— down from over 5,000—Internet entrepreneurs and venture capitalists have stepped up their finger-pointing about just who's at fault for the technology meltdown, which

---

36. *Source: case writer interview.*

37. *Mark Maremont and John Hechinger, "If Only You'd Sold Some Stock Earlier—Say $100 Million Worth," The Wall Street Journal, March 22, 2001.*

continues to topple businesses and once-cushy lifestyles. . . . Fingers pointed right and left—from entrepreneurs to venture capitalists, from analysts to day traders to shareholders—and back around again.[38]

The Internet stock market bubble was certainly not the first to occur. Other notable instances include the Tulip Craze of the seventeenth century and the Nifty Fifty boom of the 1970s. In these cases market valuations went to unsustainably high levels and ended with a sharp decrease in valuation that left many investors empty-handed.

But the question of what happened in this latest bubble remained: who, if anyone, could be blamed for the dot-com rise and crash? How did the various intermediaries described here affect or cause what happened? Was there really a misalignment of incentives in the system? If so, could it be fixed so that this sort of thing did not happen in the future? Or were market bubbles an inevitable part of the way the economy functioned?

QUESTIONS

1. What is the intended role of each of the institutions and intermediaries discussed in the case for the effective functioning of capital markets?

2. Are their incentives aligned properly with their intended role? Whose incentives are most misaligned?

3. Who, if anyone, was primarily responsible for the Internet stock bubble?

4. What are the costs of such a stock market bubble? As a future business professional, what lessons do you draw from the bubble?

The Dot-Com Crash

---

38. Rebecca Buckman, "Investors, Entrepreneurs All Play the Blame Game," The Wall Street Journal, *March 5, 2001.*

EXHIBIT I

Timeline of the Internet Consultants—Founding and IPO

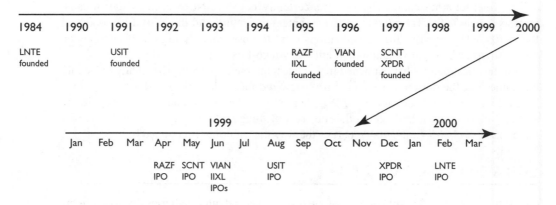

Sources: Edgar Online, Marketguide.com.

EXHIBIT 2

Internet Consultants—Stock Price Highs and Lows

Company	IPO Price[a]	Peak Price	% Change IPO to Peak	Date of Peak	Price at End of Feb 2001	% Change from Peak
Scient	10	133.75	1,238%	10-Mar-00	2.94	−97.8%
Viant	8	63.56	695%	14-Dec-99	3.06	−95.2%
IXL Enterprises	12	58.75	390%	20-Jan-00	1.25	−97.9%
Lante	20	87.50	338%	29-Feb-00	1.81	−97.9%
Razorfish	8	56.94	612%	14-Feb-00	1.16	−98.0%
US Interactive	10	83.75	738%	4-Jan-00	0.56[b]	−99.3%
Xpedior	19	34.75	83%	10-Jan-00	0.69	−98.0%

Sources: Yahoo! Finance, Marketguide.com.

a. Split adjusted.

b. Last trade on January 11, 2001. Filed for bankruptcy under Chapter 11 in January 2001.

The Dot-Com Crash

EXHIBIT 3

Intermediaries in the Capital-Raising Process of the Internet Consultants

Company	Venture Capital Stage Investors	Investment Bank Underwriters	Auditors[a]	Analyst Coverage	Selected Institutional Holders	Venture Funding ($M)	IPO Amount Raised ($M)[b]	IPO Underwriting Fee ($M)	Percent Institutional Ownership[c]
Scient	Sequoia Capital, Benchmark Capital, Stanford Univ., Capital Research, Morgan Stanley Venture Partners, Amerindo Investment Advisors, Palantir Capital	Morgan Stanley Dean Witter, Hambrecht & Quist, Thomas Weisel Partners	PWC	Merrill Lynch, Morgan Stanley Dean Witter, CSFB, Lehman Brothers, UBS Warburg, SG Cowen, others	Capital Research, Putnam, Janus, Vanguard, Wellington, State Street	31.2	60	4.2	34% (66% of float)
Viant	Kleiner Perkins Caufield & Byers, Mohr Davidow Ventures, Information Associates, Trident Capital, BancBoston Capital, General Motors, Technology Crossover Ventures	Goldman Sachs, Credit Suisse First Boston, WIT Capital Corporation	PWC	Goldman Sachs, Merrill Lynch, Lehman Brothers, CSFB, Wasserstein Perella, Bear Stearns, others	Fidelity, T Rowe Price, Putnam, Franklin, State Street, Vanguard, American Century, Goldman Sachs Asset Management	32.2	48	3.4	34% (67% of float)
IXL	Greylock Mgmt., Chase Capital Partners, Flatiron Partners, GE Capital, Kelso & Co., TTC Ventures, CB Capital, Portage Venture Partners, Transamerica Technology Finance	Merrill Lynch, BancBoston Robertson Stephens, DLJ, SG Cowen	PWC	Merrill Lynch, Robinson Humphrey, First Union Capital, others	Capital Research, State Street, Vanguard, Goldman Sachs Asset Management, GE Asset Management	91.0	72	5.0	29% (108% of float)
Lante	Frontenac Co., Dell Ventures, MSD Capital	Credit Suisse First Boston, Deutsche Bank Alex Brown, Thomas Weisel Partners	PWC	CSFB, Deutsche Bank, Thomas Weisel Partners, others	Fidelity, State Street, Vanguard, Goldman Sachs Asset Management	26.8	80	5.6	3% (21% of float)
Razorfish	N/A	Credit Suisse First Boston, BancBoston Robertson Stephens, Deutsche Bank Alex Brown, Lehman Brothers	AA, PWC	CSFB, Lehman Brothers, SG Cowen, others	Janus, Capital Research, Fidelity, Vanguard, Goldman Sachs Asset Management	N/A	48	3.4	8% (14% of float)
US Interactive	Safeguard Scientific, Technology Leaders	Lehman Brothers, Hambrecht & Quist, Adams Harkness & Hill	KPMG	Lehman Brothers, Hambrecht & Quist, Deutsche Bank Alex Brown, others	T Rowe Price, Prudential, JP Morgan Investment Management, Credit Suisse Asset Mgmt.	N/A	46	2.0	4% (6% of float)
Xpedior	N/A	DLJ, First Union Securities, JP Morgan, The Robinson-Humphrey Group	E&Y	DLJ, First Union Securities, Robinson-Humphrey, others	Capital Research, T Rowe Price, Franklin, Vanguard, John Hancock	N/A	162	11.4	2% (10% of float)

Sources: VentureSource, Edgar Online, Yahoo! Finance, Quicken.com, Lionshares.com.

a. PWC stands for PriceWaterhouseCoopers; AA for Arthur Anderson; E&Y for Ernst & Young.

b. Includes underwriting fee.

c. As of April 2001.

The Dot-Com Crash

EXHIBIT 4

Market Capitalization of Major Technology Companies, January 2000

Company	Market Capitalization ($ billions)[a]	Stock Price (January 3, 2000)
Microsoft	603	116.56
Intel	290	87.00
IBM	218	116.00
Dell Computer	131	50.88
Hewlett Packard	117	117.44
Compaq Computer	53	31.00
Apple Computer	18	111.94

Sources: Yahoo! Finance, Edgar Online.

a. Based on share price close on January 3, 2000, and reported shares outstanding.

EXHIBIT 5

Market Valuations Given to Loss-Making Dot-coms

Company	Net Income ('99/'00)[a] ($ millions)	Market Capitalization ($ billions)[b]	Stock Price (January 3, 2000)
Amazon.com	−720	30.8	89.38
DoubleClick	−56	30.1	268.00
Akamai Technologies	−58	29.7	321.25
VerticalNet	−53	12.4	172.63
Priceline.com	−1,055	8.4	51.25
E*Trade	−57	7.1	28.06
EarthLink	−174	5.2	44.75
Drugstore.com	−116	1.6	37.13

Sources: Yahoo! Finance, Edgar Online.

a. As of end of 1999 or early 2000, depending on fiscal year end.

b. Based on share price close on January 3, 2000, and reported shares outstanding.

The Dot-Com Crash

EXHIBIT 6

Scient—Consolidated Financial Statements

INCOME STATEMENT
(in thousands except per-share amounts)

	November 7, 1997 (inception) through March 31, 1998	Year Ended March 31,	
		1999	2000
Revenues	$179	$20,675	$155,729
Operating expenses:			
Professional services	102	10,028	70,207
Selling, general and administrative	1,228	15,315	90,854
Stock compensation	64	7,679	15,636
Total operating expenses	1,394	22,022	176,697
Loss from operations	(1,215)	(12,347)	(20,968)
Interest income and other, net	56	646	4,953
Net loss	$(1,159)	$(11,701)	$(16,015)
Net loss per share:			
Basic and diluted	$(0.10)	$(0.89)	$(0.29)
Weighted average shares	11,894	13,198	54,590

The Dot-Com Crash

The Dot-Com Crash

BALANCE SHEET
(in thousands except per-share amounts)

	March 31,	
	1999	2000
ASSETS		
Current Assets:		
Cash and cash equivalents	$11,261	$108,102
Short-term investments	16,868	121,046
Accounts receivable, net	5,876	56,021
Prepaid expenses	811	4,929
Other	318	4,228
Total Current Assets	35,134	294,326
Long-term investments	—	3,146
Property and equipment, net	3,410	16,063
Other	268	219
	$38,812	$313,754
LIABILITIES AND STOCKHOLDERS' EQUITY		
Current Liabilities:		
Bank borrowings, current	$413	$1,334
Accounts payable	832	5,023
Accrued compensation and benefits	2,554	33,976
Accrued expenses	2,078	9,265
Deferred revenue	524	6,579
Capital lease obligations, current	625	2,624
Total Current Liabilities	7,026	58,801
Capital lease obligations, long-term	680	2,052
	8,835	61,718
Commitments and contingencies (Note 5)		
Stockholders' equity:		
Convertible preferred stock; issuable in series, $.0001 par value; 10,000 shares authorized; 9,012 and no shares issued and outstanding, respectively	1	—
Common stock: $.0001 par value; 125,000 shares authorized; 33,134 and 72,491 shares issues and outstanding, respectively	3	7
Additional paid-in capital	70,055	297,735
Accumulated other comprehensive loss	—	(47)
Unearned compensation	(27,222)	(16,784)
Accumulated deficit	(12,860)	(28,875)
Total Stockholders' Equity	29,977	252,036
	$38,812	$313,754

Sources: Scient Corporation 10-K; Edgar Online <http://www.freedgar.com> (May 11, 2001).

EXHIBIT 7

Analyst Downgrades

The Internet Consultants

Company	Number of Analysts That Downgraded During August 30–September 8, 2000
Viant	13
Scient	7
IXL Enterprises	7
US Interactive	5
Xpedior	3
Lante	1
Razorfish	0

Scient Corporation, August 30–September 8, 2000

Institution	Previous Recommendation	New Recommendation	Date of Downgrade
Merrill Lynch	LT Buy	LT Accumulate	1-Sep-2000
Lehman Brothers	Buy	Outperform	1-Sep-2000
ING Barings	Buy	Hold	1-Sep-2000
SG Cowen	Buy	Neutral	1-Sep-2000
Legg Mason	Buy	Market Perform	1-Sep-2000
BB&T Capital Markets	Hold	Source of Funds	1-Sep-2000
First Union Securities	Strong Buy	Buy	31-Aug-2000

Source: Yahoo Finance.

EXHIBIT 8

Selected Institutional Holders of Scient Corporation, 1999–2000

Institution	Quarter Ended:						
	June 1999	September 1999	December 1999	March 2000	June 2000	September 2000	December 2000
Capital Research	—	—	—	265	1,079,911	586,442	586,706
Putnam Investments	5,000	—	625,900	2,209,200	4,800,800	5,749,200	—
Wellington Management	—	—	—	—	—	—	803,000
State Street	—	12,450	38,167	52,867	89,667	180,668	672,352
Janus	267,300	273,915	483,730	775,085	1,359,700	4,382,250	—

Source: Edgar Online (SEC).

EXHIBIT 9

Dot-coms That Filed for Bankruptcy or Closed Operations *(Selected List)*

August 2000

Auctions.com
Hardware.com
Living.com
SaviShopper.com
GreatCoffee

September 2000

Clickmango.com
Pop.com
FreeScholarships.com
RedLadder.com
DomainAuction.com
Gazoontite.com
Surfing2Cash.com
Affinia.com

October 2000

FreeInternet.com
Chipshot.com
Stockpower.com
The Dental Store
More.com
WebHouse
UrbanFetch.com
Boxman.com
RedGorilla.com
Eve.com
MyLackey.com
BigWords.com
Mortgage.com
MotherNature.com
Ivendor
TeliSmart.com

November 2000

Pets.com
Caredata.com
Streamline.com
Garden.com
Furniture.com
TheMan.com
Ibelieve.com
eSociety
UrbanDesign.com
HalfthePlanet.com
Productopia.com
BeautyJungle.com
ICanBuy.com
Bike.com
Mambo.com
Babystripes.com
Thirsty.com
Checkout.com

December 2000

Quepasa.com
Finance.com
BizBuyer.com
Desktop.com
E-pods.com
Clickabid.com
HeavenlyDoor.com
ShoppingList.com
Babygear.com
HotOffice.com
Goldsauction.com
AntEye.com
EZBid
Admart
I-US.com
Riffage.com

January 2001

MusicMaker.com
Mercata
Send.com
CompanyLeader.com
Zap.com
Savvio.com
News Digital Media
TravelNow.com
Foodline.com
LetsBuyIt.com
e7th.cm
CountryCool.com
Ibetcha.com
Fibermarket.com
Dotcomix
New Digital Media
GreatEntertaining.com
AndysGarage.com
Lucy.com
US Interactive

Sources: Johnathan Weil, "'Going Concerns': Did Accountants Fail to Flag Problems at Dot-Com Casualties?" *Wall Street Journal*, February 2001; Jim Battey, "Dot-com details: The numbers behind the year's e-commerce shake-out," *Infoworld*, March 2001.

EXHIBIT 10

Capital Flows from Investors to Companies

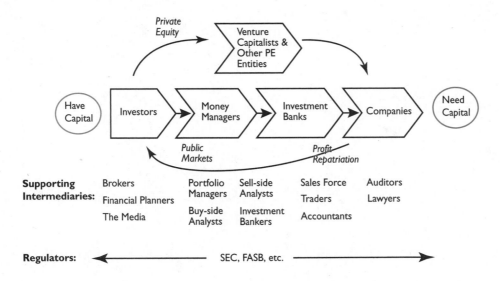

Source: created by case writer.

PART 2

Business Analysis and Valuation Tools

CHAPTER 2

Strategy Analysis

Strategy analysis is an important starting point for the analysis of financial statements. Strategy analysis allows the analyst to probe the economics of a firm at a qualitative level so that the subsequent accounting and financial analysis is grounded in business reality. Strategy analysis also allows the identification of the firm's profit drivers and key risks. This in turn enables the analyst to assess the sustainability of the firm's current performance and make realistic forecasts of future performance.

A firm's value is determined by its ability to earn a return on its capital in excess of the cost of capital. What determines whether or not a firm is able to accomplish this goal? While a firm's cost of capital is determined by the capital markets, its profit potential is determined by its own strategic choices: (1) the choice of an industry or a set of industries in which the firm operates (industry choice), (2) the manner in which the firm intends to compete with other firms in its chosen industry or industries (competitive positioning), and (3) the way in which the firm expects to create and exploit synergies across the range of businesses in which it operates (corporate strategy). Strategy analysis, therefore, involves industry analysis, competitive strategy analysis, and corporate strategy analysis.[1] In this chapter, we will briefly discuss these three steps and use the personal computer industry and Amazon.com, respectively, to illustrate the application of the steps.

INDUSTRY ANALYSIS

In analyzing a firm's profit potential, an analyst has to first assess the profit potential of each of the industries in which the firm is competing because the profitability of various industries differs systematically and predictably over time. For example, the ratio of earnings before interest and taxes to the book value of assets for all U.S. companies between 1981 and 1997 was 8.8 percent. However, the average returns varied widely across specific industries: for the bakery products industry, the profitability ratio was 43 percentage points greater than the population average, and for the silver ore mining industry it was 23 percentage points less than the population average.[2] What causes these profitability differences?

There is a vast body of research in industrial organization on the influence of industry structure on profitability.[3] Relying on this research, strategy literature suggests that the average profitability of an industry is influenced by the "five forces" shown in Figure 2-1.[4] According to this framework, the intensity of competition determines the potential for creating abnormal profits by the firms in an industry. Whether or not the potential profits are kept by the industry is determined by the relative bargaining power of the firms in the industry and their customers and suppliers. We will discuss each of these industry profit drivers in more detail below.

Degree of Actual and Potential Competition

At the most basic level, the profits in an industry are a function of the maximum price that customers are willing to pay for the industry's product or service. One of the key determinants of the price is the degree to which there is competition among suppliers of the same or similar products. At one extreme, if there is a state of perfect competition in the industry, micro-economic theory predicts that prices will be equal to marginal cost, and there will be

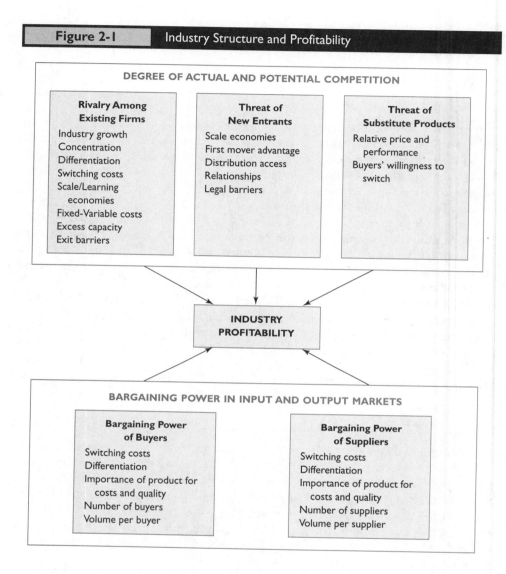

| Figure 2-1 | Industry Structure and Profitability |

DEGREE OF ACTUAL AND POTENTIAL COMPETITION

Rivalry Among Existing Firms

Industry growth
Concentration
Differentiation
Switching costs
Scale/Learning economies
Fixed-Variable costs
Excess capacity
Exit barriers

Threat of New Entrants

Scale economies
First mover advantage
Distribution access
Relationships
Legal barriers

Threat of Substitute Products

Relative price and performance
Buyers' willingness to switch

INDUSTRY PROFITABILITY

BARGAINING POWER IN INPUT AND OUTPUT MARKETS

Bargaining Power of Buyers

Switching costs
Differentiation
Importance of product for costs and quality
Number of buyers
Volume per buyer

Bargaining Power of Suppliers

Switching costs
Differentiation
Importance of product for costs and quality
Number of suppliers
Volume per supplier

few opportunities to earn supernormal profits. At the other extreme, if the industry is dominated by a single firm, there will be potential to earn monopoly profits. In reality, the degree of competition in most industries is somewhere in between perfect competition and monopoly.

There are three potential sources of competition in an industry: (1) rivalry between existing firms, (2) threat of entry of new firms, and (3) threat of substitute products or services. We will discuss each of these competitive forces in the following paragraphs.

Competitive Force 1: Rivalry Among Existing Firms

In most industries the average level of profitability is primarily influenced by the nature of rivalry among existing firms in the industry. In some industries firms compete aggressively, pushing prices close to (and sometimes below) the marginal cost. In other industries firms do not compete aggressively on price. Instead, they find ways to coordinate their pricing, or compete on nonprice dimensions such as innovation or brand image. Several factors determine the intensity of competition between existing players in an industry:

Industry Growth Rate   If an industry is growing very rapidly, incumbent firms need not grab market share from each other to grow. In contrast, in stagnant industries the only way existing firms can grow is by taking share away from the other players. In this situation one can expect price wars among firms in the industry.

Concentration and Balance of Competitors   The number of firms in an industry and their relative sizes determine the degree of concentration in an industry.[5] The degree of concentration influences the extent to which firms in an industry can coordinate their pricing and other competitive moves. For example, if there is one dominant firm in an industry (such as IBM in the mainframe computer industry in the 1970s), it can set and enforce the rules of competition. Similarly, if there are only two or three equal-sized players (such as Coke and Pepsi in the U.S. soft-drink industry), they can implicitly cooperate with each other to avoid destructive price competition. If an industry is fragmented, price competition is likely to be severe.

Degree of Differentiation and Switching Costs   The extent to which firms in an industry can avoid head-on competition depends on the extent to which they can differentiate their products and services. If the products in an industry are very similar, customers are ready to switch from one competitor to another purely on the basis of price. Switching costs also determine customers' propensity to move from one product to another. When switching costs are low, there is a greater incentive for firms in an industry to engage in price competition.

Scale/Learning Economies and the Ratio of Fixed to Variable Costs   If there is a steep learning curve or there are other types of scale economies in an industry, size becomes an important factor for firms in the industry. In such situations, there are incentives to engage in aggressive competition for market share. Similarly, if the ratio of fixed to variable costs is high, firms have an incentive to reduce prices to utilize installed capacity. The airline industry, where price wars are quite common, is an example of this type of situation.

Excess Capacity and Exit Barriers   If capacity in an industry is larger than customer demand, there is a strong incentive for firms to cut prices to fill capacity. The problem of excess capacity is likely to be exacerbated if there are significant barriers for firms to exit the industry. Exit barriers are high when the assets are specialized or if there are regulations which make exit costly.

Competitive Force 2: Threat of New Entrants

The potential for earning abnormal profits will attract new entrants to an industry. The very threat of new firms entering an industry potentially constrains the pricing of existing firms within it. Therefore the ease with which new firms can enter an industry is a key determinant of its profitability. Several factors determine the height of barriers to entry in an industry:

Economies of Scale   When there are large economies of scale, new entrants face the choice of having either to invest in a large capacity which might not be utilized right away or to enter with less than the optimum capacity. Either way, new entrants will at least initially suffer from a cost disadvantage in competing with existing firms. Economies of scale might arise from large investments in research and development (the pharmaceutical or jet engine industries), in brand advertising (soft-drink industry), or in physical plant and equipment (telecommunications industry).

First Mover Advantage   Early entrants in an industry may deter future entrants if there are first mover advantages. For example, first movers might be able to set industry standards, or enter into exclusive arrangements with suppliers of cheap raw materials. They may also acquire scarce government licenses to operate in regulated industries. Finally, if there are learning economies, early firms will have an absolute cost advantage over new entrants. First mover advantages are also likely to be large when there are significant switching costs for customers once they start using existing products. For example, switching costs faced by the users of Microsoft's DOS operating system make it difficult for software companies to market a new operating system.

Access to Channels of Distribution and Relationships   Limited capacity in the existing distribution channels and high costs of developing new channels can act as powerful barriers to entry. For example, a new entrant into the domestic auto industry in the U.S. is likely to face formidable barriers because of the difficulty of developing a dealer network. Similarly, new consumer goods manufacturers find it difficult to obtain supermarket shelf space for their products. Existing relationships between firms and customers in an industry also make it difficult for new firms to enter an industry. Industry examples of this include auditing, investment banking, and advertising.

Legal Barriers   There are many industries in which legal barriers such as patents and copyrights in research-intensive industries limit entry. Similarly, licensing regulations limit entry into taxi services, medical services, broadcasting, and telecommunications industries.

Competitive Force 3: Threat of Substitute Products

The third dimension of competition in an industry is the threat of substitute products or services. Relevant substitutes are not necessarily those that have the same form as the existing products but those that perform the same function. For example, airlines and car rental services might be substitutes for each other when it comes to travel over short distances. Similarly, plastic bottles and metal cans substitute for each other as packaging in the beverage industry. In some cases, threat of substitution comes not from customers' switching to another product but from utilizing technologies that allow them to do without, or use less of, the existing products. For example, energy-conserving technologies allow customers to reduce their consumption of electricity and fossil fuels.

The threat of substitutes depends on the relative price and performance of the competing products or services and on customers' willingness to substitute. Customers' perception of whether two products are substitutes depends to some extent on whether they perform the same function for a similar price. If two products perform an identical function, then it would be difficult for them to differ from each other in price. However, customers' willingness to switch is often the critical factor in making this competitive dynamic work. For example, even when tap water and bottled water serve the same function, many customers may be unwilling to substitute the former for the latter, enabling bottlers to charge a price premium. Similarly, designer label clothing commands a price premium even if it is not superior in terms of basic functionality because customers place a value on the image offered by designer labels.

While the degree of competition in an industry determines whether there is *potential* to earn abnormal profits, the *actual profits* are influenced by the industry's bargaining power with its suppliers and customers. On the input side, firms enter into transactions with suppliers of labor, raw materials and components, and finances. On the output side, firms either sell directly to the final customers or enter into contracts with intermediaries in the distribution chain. In all these transactions, the relative economic power of the two sides is important to the overall profitability of the industry firms.

Competitive Force 4: Bargaining Power of Buyers

Two factors determine the power of buyers: price sensitivity and relative bargaining power. Price sensitivity determines the extent to which buyers care to bargain on price; relative bargaining power determines the extent to which they will succeed in forcing the price down.[6]

Price Sensitivity Buyers are more price sensitive when the product is undifferentiated and there are few switching costs. The sensitivity of buyers to price also depends on the importance of the product to their own cost structure. When the product represents a large fraction of the buyers' cost (for example, the packaging material for soft-drink producers), the buyer is likely to expend the resources necessary to shop for a lower cost alternative. In contrast, if the product is a small fraction of the buyers' cost (for example, windshield wipers for automobile manufacturers), it may not pay to expend resources to search for lower-cost alternatives. Further, the importance of the product to the buyers' own product quality also determines whether or not price becomes the most important determinant of the buying decision.

Relative Bargaining Power Even if buyers are price sensitive, they may not be able to achieve low prices unless they have a strong bargaining position. Relative bargaining power in a transaction depends, ultimately, on the cost to each party of not doing business with the other party. The buyers' bargaining power is determined by the number of buyers relative to the number of suppliers, volume of purchases by a single buyer, number of alternative products available to the buyer, buyers' costs of switching from one product to another, and the threat of backward integration by the buyers. For example, in the automobile industry, car manufacturers have considerable power over component manufacturers because auto companies are large buyers with several alternative suppliers to choose from, and switching costs are relatively low. In contrast, in the personal computer industry, computer makers have low bargaining power relative to the operating system software producers because of high switching costs.

Competitive Force 5: Bargaining Power of Suppliers

The analysis of the relative power of suppliers is a mirror image of the analysis of the buyer's power in an industry. Suppliers are powerful when there are only a few companies and few substitutes available to their customers. For example, in the soft-drink industry, Coke and Pepsi are very powerful relative to the bottlers. In contrast, metal can suppliers to the soft drink industry are not very powerful because of intense competition among can producers and the threat of substitution of cans by plastic bottles. Suppliers also have a lot of power over buyers when the suppliers' product or service is critical to buyers' business. For example, airline pilots have a strong bargaining power in the airline industry. Suppliers also tend to be powerful when they pose a credible threat of forward integration. For example, IBM is powerful relative to mainframe computer leasing companies because of its unique position as a mainframe supplier and its own presence in the computer leasing business.

APPLYING INDUSTRY ANALYSIS: THE PERSONAL COMPUTER INDUSTRY

Let us consider the above concepts of industry analysis in the context of the personal computer (PC) industry.[7] The industry began in 1981 when IBM announced its PC with Intel's microprocessor and Microsoft's DOS operating system. By now personal computers are ubiquitous—over 136 million units were shipped worldwide in 2002 alone. Despite the spectacular growth in the sales volume in this industry, however, it was characterized by low profitability. Even the largest companies in the industry, such as IBM, Compaq, Dell, and Apple, reported poor performance in the early 1990s and were forced to undergo internal restructuring. What accounted for this low profitability? What was the computer industry's future profit potential?

Competition in the Personal Computer Industry

The competition was very intense for a number of reasons:

- The industry was fragmented, with many firms producing virtually identical products. Even though the computer market became more concentrated in the 1990s, with the top five vendors controlling close to 60 percent of the market, competition was intense, leading to routine price cuts on a monthly basis.
- Component costs accounted for more than 60 percent of total hardware costs of a personal computer, and volume purchases of components reduced these costs. Therefore there was intense competition for market share among competing manufacturers.
- Products produced by different firms in the industry were virtually identical, and there were few opportunities to differentiate the products. While brand name and service were dimensions that customers valued in the early years of the industry, they became less important as PC buyers became more informed about the technology.
- Switching costs across different brands of personal computers were relatively low because a vast majority of the personal computers used Intel microprocessors and Microsoft Windows operating systems.
- Access to distribution was not a significant barrier, as demonstrated by Dell Computers, which distributed its computers by direct mail through the 1980s and introduced Internet-based sales in the mid-1990s. The advent of computer superstores like CompUSA also mitigated this constraint, since these stores were willing to carry several brands.
- Since virtually all the components needed to produce a personal computer were available for purchase, there were very few barriers to entering the industry. In fact, Michael Dell started Dell Computer Company in the early 1980s by assembling PCs in his University of Texas dormitory room.
- Apple's Macintosh computers offered competition as a substitute product. Workstations produced by Sun and other vendors were also potential substitutes at the higher end of the personal computer market.

The Power of Suppliers and Buyers

Suppliers and buyers had significant power over firms in the industry for these reasons:

- Key hardware and software components for personal computers were controlled by firms with virtual monopoly. Intel dominated the microprocessor production for the personal computer industry, and Microsoft controlled the operating system market with its DOS and Windows operating systems.
- Buyers gained more power during the ten years from 1983 to 1993. Corporate buyers, who represented a significant portion of the customer base, were highly price sensitive since the expenditure on PCs represented a significant cost to their operations. Further, as they became knowledgeable about personal computer technology, customers were less influenced by brand name in their purchase decision. Buyers increasingly viewed PCs as commodities and used price as the most important consideration in their buying decision.

As a result of the intense rivalry and low barriers to entry in the personal computer industry, there was severe price competition among different manufacturers. Further, there was tremendous pressure on firms to spend large sums of money to introduce new products rapidly, maintain high quality, and provide excellent customer support. Both these factors led to a low profit potential in the industry. The power of suppliers and buyers reduced the profit potential further. Thus, while the personal computer industry represented a technologically dynamic industry, its profit potential was poor.

There were few indications of change in the basic structure of the personal computer industry, and there was little likelihood of viable competition emerging to challenge the domination of Microsoft and Intel in the input markets. Attempts by industry leaders like IBM to create alternative proprietary technologies have not succeeded. As a result, the profitability of the PC industry may not improve significantly any time in the near future.

Limitations of Industry Analysis

A potential limitation of the industry analysis framework discussed in this chapter is the assumption that industries have clear boundaries. In reality, it is often not easy to clearly demarcate industry boundaries. For example, in analyzing Dell's industry, should one focus on the IBM-compatible personal computer industry or the personal computer industry as a whole? Should one include workstations in the industry definition? Should one consider only the domestic manufacturers of personal computers or also manufacturers abroad? Inappropriate industry definition will result in incomplete analysis and inaccurate forecasts.

COMPETITIVE STRATEGY ANALYSIS

The profitability of a firm is influenced not only by its industry structure but also by the strategic choices it makes in positioning itself in the industry. While there are many ways to characterize a firm's business strategy, as Figure 2-2 shows, there are two generic competitive strategies: (1) cost leadership and (2) differentiation.[8] Both these strategies can potentially allow a firm to build a sustainable competitive advantage. Strategy researchers have traditionally viewed cost leadership and differentiation as mutually exclusive strategies. Firms that straddle the two strategies are considered to be "stuck in the middle" and are expected to earn low profitability.[9] These firms run the risk of not being able to attract price conscious customers because their costs are too high; they are also unable to provide adequate differentiation to attract premium price customers.[10]

Sources of Competitive Advantage

Cost leadership enables a firm to supply the same product or service offered by its competitors at a lower cost. Differentiation strategy involves providing a product or service that is distinct in some important respect valued by the customer. As an example in retailing, Nordstrom has succeeded on the basis of differentiation by emphasizing exceptionally high customer service. In contrast, Filene's Basement stores is a discount retailer competing purely on a low-cost basis.

Competitive Strategy 1: Cost Leadership

Cost leadership is often the clearest way to achieve competitive advantage. In industries where the basic product or service is a commodity, cost leadership might be the only way to achieve superior performance. There are many ways to achieve cost leadership, including

Figure 2-2	Strategies for Creating Competitive Advantage

Cost Leadership

Supply same product or service at a lower cost.

Economies of scale and scope
Efficient production
Simpler product designs
Lower input costs
Low-cost distribution
Little research and development or
  brand advertising
Tight cost control system

Differentiation

Supply a unique product or service at a cost lower than the price premium customers will pay.

Superior product quality
Superior product variety
Superior customer service
More flexible delivery
Investment in brand image
Investment in research and
  development
Control system focus on creativity
  and innovation

Competitive Advantage

- Match between firm's core competencies and key success factors to execute strategy
- Match between firm's value chain and activities required to execute strategy
- Sustainability of competitive advantage

economies of scale and scope, economies of learning, efficient production, simpler product design, lower input costs, and efficient organizational processes. If a firm can achieve cost leadership, then it will be able to earn above-average profitability by merely charging the same price as its rivals. Conversely, a cost leader can force its competitors to cut prices and accept lower returns, or to exit the industry.

Firms that achieve cost leadership focus on tight cost controls. They make investments in efficient scale plants, focus on product designs that reduce manufacturing costs, minimize overhead costs, make little investment in risky research and development, and avoid serving marginal customers. They have organizational structures and control systems that focus on cost control.

Competitive Strategy 2: Differentiation

A firm following the differentiation strategy seeks to be unique in its industry along some dimension that is highly valued by customers. For differentiation to be successful, the firm has to accomplish three things. First, it needs to identify one or more attributes of a product or service that customers value. Second, it has to position itself to meet the chosen customer need in a unique manner. Finally, the firm has to achieve differentiation at a cost that is lower than the price the customer is willing to pay for the differentiated product or service.

Drivers of differentiation include providing superior intrinsic value via product quality, product variety, bundled services, or delivery timing. Differentiation can also be achieved by investing in signals of value such as brand image, product appearance, or reputation. Differentiated strategies require investments in research and development, engineering skills, and marketing capabilities. The organizational structures and control systems in firms with differentiation strategies need to foster creativity and innovation.

While successful firms choose between cost leadership and differentiation, they cannot completely ignore the dimension on which they are not primarily competing. Firms that target differentiation still need to focus on costs so that the differentiation can be achieved at an acceptable cost. Similarly, cost leaders cannot compete unless they achieve at least a minimum level on key dimensions on which competitors might differentiate, such as quality and service.

Achieving and Sustaining Competitive Advantage

The choice of competitive strategy does not automatically lead to the achievement of competitive advantage. To achieve competitive advantage, the firm has to have the capabilities needed to implement and sustain the chosen strategy. Both cost leadership and differentiation strategy require that the firm make the necessary commitments to acquire the core competencies needed, and structure its value chain in an appropriate way. Core competencies are the economic assets that the firm possesses, whereas the value chain is the set of activities that the firm performs to convert inputs into outputs. The uniqueness of a firm's core competencies and its value chain and the extent to which it is difficult for competitors to imitate them determines the sustainability of a firm's competitive advantage.[11]

To evaluate whether a firm is likely to achieve its intended competitive advantage, the analyst should ask the following questions:

- What are the key success factors and risks associated with the firm's chosen competitive strategy?
- Does the firm currently have the resources and capabilities to deal with the key success factors and risks?
- Has the firm made irreversible commitments to bridge the gap between its current capabilities and the requirements to achieve its competitive advantage?
- Has the firm structured its activities (such as research and development, design, manufacturing, marketing and distribution, and support activities) in a way that is consistent with its competitive strategy?
- Is the company's competitive advantage sustainable? Are there any barriers that make imitation of the firm's strategy difficult?
- Are there any potential changes in the firm's industry structure (such as new technologies, foreign competition, changes in regulation, changes in customer requirements) that might dissipate the firm's competitive advantage? Is the company flexible enough to address these changes?

Applying Competitive Strategy Analysis

Let us consider the concepts of competitive strategy analysis in the context of Dell Computer Corporation. In 1998 Round Rock, Texas-based Dell Computer was the fourth largest computer maker, behind IBM, Hewlett-Packard, and Compaq. The company, founded by Michael Dell in his University of Texas dorm room, started selling "IBM clone" personal computers in 1984. From the beginning Dell sold its machines directly to end users rather than through retail outlets, at a significantly lower price than its competitors.

After rapid growth and some management hiccups, Dell firmly established itself in the personal computer industry by following a low-cost strategy. For the fiscal year ending January 31, 2003, Dell achieved $35.4 billion in revenues and $2.12 billion in net income. Dell's growth rates over the previous three years were extraordinary. Dell's stellar performance made it one of the most profitable personal computer makers in a highly competitive industry. How did Dell achieve such performance?

Dell's superior performance was based on a low-cost competitive strategy that consisted of the following key elements:

- *Direct selling.* Dell sold most of its computers directly to its customers, thus saving on retail markups. As computer users become sophisticated, and as computers become standardized on the Windows-Intel platform, the value of distribution through retailers declines. Dell was the first company to capitalize on this trend. In 1996 Dell began selling computers through its Internet web site. By 2003 the company was generating a very significant amount of its sales through on-line orders.
- *Made-to-order manufacturing.* Dell developed a system of flexible manufacturing that allowed the company to assemble and ship computers very quickly, usually within five days of receiving an order. This allowed the company to avoid large inventories of parts and assembled computers. Low inventories allowed Dell to save on working capital costs; it also reduced costly write-offs of obsolete inventories, a significant risk in the fast-changing computer industry.
- *Third-party service.* Dell used two low-cost approaches to after-sales service: telephone-based service and third-party maintenance service. Dell had several hundred technical support representatives accessible to customers by phone any time of the day. Using a comprehensive electronic maintenance system, the service representatives could diagnose problems and help customers to resolve them in the vast majority of cases. In the rare instance where on-site maintenance was required, Dell used third-party maintenance contracts with office equipment companies such as Xerox. Through this service strategy, Dell was able to avoid investing in an expensive field service network without compromising on service quality.
- *Low accounts receivable.* Dell was able to reduce its accounts receivable days to an industry minimum by encouraging its customers to pay by credit card at the time of the purchase or through electronic payment immediately after the purchase.
- *Focused investment in R&D.* Dell recognized that most of the basic innovations in the personal computer industry were led by the component suppliers and software producers. For example, two key suppliers, Intel and Microsoft, invested billions of dollars in developing new generation processors and software, respectively. Dell's innovations were primarily in creating a low-cost, high velocity organization that can respond quickly to these changes. By focusing its R&D innovations, Dell was able to minimize these costs and get high return on its investments.

As a result of the above strategy, Dell achieved a significant cost advantage over its competitors in the personal computer industry. This advantage resulted in a consistent pattern of rapid growth, increasing market share, and very high profitability in an industry that is characterized by rapid technological changes, significant supplier and buyer power, and intense competition. Further, because the strategy involved activities that are highly interrelated and involved continuous organizational innovations, Dell's business model was difficult to replicate, making its competitive advantage sustainable. In fact, Dell's success inspired several of its competitors, including Compaq and IBM, to attempt to replicate parts of its strategy. However no competitor to date has been able to replicate Dell's business model. The extraordinarily high earnings and book value multiples at which Dell's stock has been trading in recent years is evidence that investors are betting that Dell's competitive advantage and its superior profit performance is likely to be sustained for the foreseeable future.

CORPORATE STRATEGY ANALYSIS

So far in this chapter we have focused on the strategies at the individual business level. While some companies focus on only one business, many companies operate in multiple businesses. For example, the average number of business segments operated by the top 500 U.S. companies in 1992 is eleven industries.[12] In recent years, there has been an attempt by U.S. companies to reduce the diversity of their operations and focus on a relatively few "core" businesses. However, multibusiness organizations continue to dominate the economic activity in most countries in the world.

When analyzing a multibusiness organization, an analyst has to not only evaluate the industries and strategies of the individual business units but also the economic consequences—either positive or negative—of managing all the different businesses under one corporate umbrella. For example, General Electric has been very successful in creating significant value by managing a highly diversified set of businesses ranging from aircraft engines to light bulbs, but Sears has not been very successful in managing retailing together with financial services.

Sources of Value Creation at the Corporate Level

Economists and strategy researchers have identified several factors that influence an organization's ability to create value through a broad corporate scope. Economic theory suggests that the optimal activity scope of a firm depends on the relative transaction cost of performing a set of activities inside the firm versus using the market mechanism.[13] Transaction cost economics implies that the multiproduct firm is an efficient choice of organizational form when coordination among independent, focused firms is costly due to market transaction costs.

Transaction costs can arise out of several sources. They may arise if the production process involves specialized assets such as human capital skills, proprietary technology, or other organizational know-how that is not easily available in the marketplace. Transaction costs also may arise from market imperfections such as information and incentive problems. If buyers and sellers cannot solve these problems through standard mechanisms such as enforceable contracts, it will be costly to conduct transactions through market mechanisms.

For example, as discussed in Chapter 1, public capital markets may not work well when there are significant information and incentive problems, making it difficult for entrepreneurs to raise capital from investors. Similarly, if buyers cannot ascertain the quality of products being sold because of lack of information, or cannot enforce warranties because of poor legal infrastructure, entrepreneurs will find it difficult to break into new markets. Finally, if employers cannot assess the quality of applicants for new positions, they will have to rely more on internal promotions rather than external recruiting to fill higher positions in an organization. Emerging economies often suffer from these types of transaction costs because of poorly developed intermediation infrastructure.[14] Even in many advanced economies, examples of high transaction costs can be found. For example, in many countries other than the U.S., the venture capital industry is not highly developed, making it costly for new businesses in high technology industries to attract financing. Even in the U.S., transaction costs may vary across economic sectors. For example, until recently electronic commerce was hampered by consumer concerns regarding the security of credit card information sent over the Internet.

Transactions inside an organization may be less costly than market-based transactions for several reasons. First, communication costs inside an organization are reduced because confidentiality can be protected and credibility can be assured through internal mechanisms. Second, the headquarters office can play a critical role in reducing costs of enforcing agreements between organizational subunits. Third, organizational subunits can share valuable nontradable assets (such as organizational skills, systems, and processes) or nondivisible assets (such as brand names, distribution channels, and reputation).

There are also forces that increase transaction costs inside organizations. Top management of an organization may lack the specialized information and skills necessary to manage businesses across several different industries. This lack of expertise reduces the possibility of actually realizing economies of scope, even when there is potential for such economies. This problem can be remedied by creating a decentralized organization, hiring specialist managers to run each business unit, and providing these managers with proper incentives. However, decentralization will also potentially decrease goal congruence among subunit managers, making it difficult to realize economies of scope.

Whether or not a multibusiness organization creates more value than a comparable collection of focused firms is, therefore, context dependent.[15] Analysts should ask the following questions to assess whether an organization's corporate strategy has the potential to create value:

- Are there significant imperfections in the product, labor, or financial markets in the industries (or countries) in which a company is operating? Is it likely that transaction costs in these markets are higher than the costs of similar activities inside a well managed organization?
- Does the organization have special resources such as brand names, proprietary know-how, access to scarce distribution channels, and special organizational processes that have the potential to create economies of scope?
- Is there a good fit between the company's specialized resources and the portfolio of businesses in which the company is operating?
- Does the company allocate decision rights between the headquarters office and the business units optimally to realize all the potential economies of scope?
- Does the company have internal measurement, information, and incentive systems to reduce agency costs and increase coordination across business units?

Empirical evidence suggests that creating value through a multibusiness corporate strategy is hard in practice. Several researchers have documented that diversified U.S. companies trade at a discount in the stock market relative to a comparable portfolio of focused companies.[16] Studies also show that acquisitions of one company by another, especially when the two are in unrelated businesses, often fail to create value for the acquiring companies.[17] Finally, there is considerable evidence that value is created when multibusiness companies increase corporate focus through divisional spinoffs and asset sales.[18]

There are several potential explanations for the above diversification discount. First, managers' decisions to diversify and expand are frequently driven by a desire to maximize the size of their organization rather than to maximize shareholder value. Second, diversified companies often suffer from incentive misalignment problems leading to suboptimal investment decisions and poor operating performance. Third, capital markets find it difficult to monitor and value multibusiness organizations because of inadequate disclosure about the performance of individual business segments.

In summary, while companies can theoretically create value through innovative corporate strategies, there are many ways in which this potential fails to get realized in practice. Therefore, it pays to be skeptical when evaluating companies' corporate strategies.

Applying Corporate Strategy Analysis

Let us apply the concepts of corporate strategy analysis to Amazon.com, a pioneer in electronic commerce. Amazon started operations as an online bookseller in 1995 and went public in 1997 with a market capitalization of $561 million dollars. The company grew rapidly and began to pose a serious threat to the dominance of leading chain store booksellers like Barnes & Noble. Investors rewarded Amazon by increasing its market capitalization to a remarkable $36 billion dollars by April 1999.

Flush with his success in online book selling, Jeff Bezos, the founder and chief executive officer of Amazon, moved the company into many other areas of electronic commerce. Amazon claimed that its brand, its loyal customer base, and its ability to execute electronic commerce were valuable assets that can be exploited in a number of other online business areas. Through a series of acquisitions beginning in 1998, Amazon expanded into online selling of CDs, videos, gifts, prescription drugs, pet supplies, and groceries. In April 1999 Amazon announced plans to diversify into the online auction business by acquiring LiveBid.com. Bezos explained, "We are not a book company. We're not a music company. We're not a video company. We're not an auctions company. We're a customer company."[19]

Amazon's rapid expansion attracted controversy among the investment community. Some analysts argued that Amazon could create value through its broad corporate focus for the following reasons:

- Amazon has established a valuable brand name on the Internet. Given that electronic commerce is a relatively new phenomenon, customers are likely to rely on well known brands to reduce the risk of a bad shopping experience. Amazon's expansion strategy is sensible because it exploits this valuable resource.
- Amazon has been able to acquire critical expertise in flawless execution of electronic retailing. This is a general competency that can be exploited in many areas of electronic retailing.
- Amazon has been able to create a tremendous amount of loyalty among its customers through superior marketing and execution. As a result, a very high proportion of Amazon's sales comes from repeat purchases by its customers. Amazon's strategy exploits this valuable customer base.

There were also some skeptics who believed that Amazon was expanding too rapidly and that its diversification beyond book retailing was likely to fail. These skeptics questioned the value of Amazon's brand name. They argued that traditional retailers such as Barnes & Noble, Wal-Mart, and CVS, who are boosting their online efforts, also have valuable brand names, execution capabilities, and customer loyalty. Therefore these companies are likely to offer formidable competition to Amazon's individual business lines. Amazon's critics also pointed out that expanding rapidly into so many different areas is likely to confuse customers, dilute Amazon's brand value, and increase the chance of poor execution. Commenting on the fact that Amazon is losing money in all of its businesses while it is expanding rapidly, *Barron's* business weekly stated, "Increasingly, Amazon's strategy is looking like the dim-bulb businessman who loses money on every sale but tries to make it up by making more sales."[20]

Investor concerns about Amazon's corporate strategy began to affect its share price, which dropped from a high of $221 dollars in April 1999 to $118 dollars by the end of May 1999. Still, at a total market capitalization of about $19 billion dollars, many investors are betting that Amazon's corporate strategy is likely to yield rich dividends in the future.

An interesting question to examine is whether there are systematic reasons to believe that a company such as Amazon can succeed in pursuing a wide focus because its business model—on-line selling—somehow allows it to manage this diversity in a fundamentally different manner than a traditional retailer would be able to. Amazon's change in stock market fortunes from year 2000 on suggests that investors were reassessing in this respect. In response, Amazon's management was also making a series of changes in its business to make the company more cost-efficient, even though in 2003 the company was still in a wide range of product lines.

SUMMARY

Strategy analysis is an important starting point for the analysis of financial statements because it allows the analyst to probe the economics of the firm at a qualitative level. Strategy analysis also allows the identification of the firm's profit drivers and key risks, enabling the analyst to assess the sustainability of the firm's performance and make realistic forecasts of future performance.

Whether a firm is able to earn a return on its capital in excess of its cost of capital is determined by its own strategic choices: (1) the choice of an industry or a set of industries in which the firm operates (industry choice), (2) the manner in which the firm intends to compete with other firms in its chosen industry or industries (competitive positioning), and (3) the way in which the firm expects to create and exploit synergies across the range of businesses in which it operates (corporate strategy). Strategy analysis involves analyzing all three choices.

Industry analysis consists of identifying the economic factors which drive the industry profitability. In general, an industry's average profit potential is influenced by the degree of rivalry among existing competitors, the ease with which new firms can enter the industry, the availability of substitute products, the power of buyers, and the power of suppliers. To perform industry analysis, the analyst has to assess the current strength of each of these forces in an industry and make forecasts of any likely future changes.

Competitive strategy analysis involves identifying the basis on which the firm intends to compete in its industry. In general, there are two potential strategies that could provide a firm with a competitive advantage: cost leadership and differentiation. Cost leadership involves offering at a lower cost the same product or service that other firms offer. Differentiation involves satisfying a chosen dimension of customer need better than the competition, at an incremental cost that is less than the price premium that customers are willing to pay. To perform strategy analysis, the analyst has to identify the firm's intended strategy, assess whether the firm possesses the competencies required to execute the strategy, and recognize the key risks that the firm has to guard against. The analyst also has to evaluate the sustainability of the firm's strategy.

Corporate strategy analysis involves examining whether a company is able to create value by being in multiple businesses at the same time. A well crafted corporate strategy reduces costs or increases revenues from running several businesses in one firm relative to the same businesses operating independently and transacting with each other in the marketplace. These cost savings or revenue increases come from specialized resources that the firm has to exploit synergies across these businesses. For these resources to be valuable, they must be nontradable, not easily imitated by competition, and nondivisible. Even when a firm has such resources, it can create value through a multibusiness organization only when it is managed so that the information and agency costs inside the organization are smaller than the market transaction costs.

The insights gained from strategy analysis can be useful in performing the remainder of the financial statement analysis. In accounting analysis the analyst can examine whether a firm's accounting policies and estimates are consistent with its stated strategy. For example, a firm's choice of functional currency in accounting for its international operations should be consistent with the level of integration between domestic and international operations that the business strategy calls for. Similarly, a firm that mainly sells housing to low-income customers should have higher than average bad debts expenses.

Strategy analysis is also useful in guiding financial analysis. For example, in a cross-sectional analysis the analyst should expect firms with cost leadership strategy to have lower gross margins and higher asset turnover than firms that follow differentiated strategies. In a time series analysis, the analyst should closely monitor any increases in expense ratios and asset turnover ratios for low-cost firms, and any decreases in investments critical to differentiation for firms that follow differentiation strategy.

Business strategy analysis also helps in prospective analysis and valuation. First, it allows the analyst to assess whether, and for how long, differences between the firm's performance and its industry (or industries) performance are likely to persist. Second, strategy analysis facilitates forecasting investment outlays the firm has to make to maintain its competitive advantage.

DISCUSSION QUESTIONS

1. Judith, an accounting major, states, "Strategy analysis seems to be an unnecessary detour in doing financial statement analysis. Why can't we just get straight to the accounting issues?" Explain to Judith why she might be wrong?

2. What are the critical drivers of industry profitability?

3. One of the fastest growing industries in the last twenty years is the memory chip industry, which supplies memory chips for personal computers and other electronic devices. Yet the average profitability for this industry has been very low. Using the industry analysis framework, list all the potential factors that might explain this apparent contradiction.

4. Rate the pharmaceutical and lumber industries as high, medium, or low on the following dimensions of industry structure:

	Pharmaceutical Industry	Lumber Industry
Rivalry		
Threat of new entrants		
Threat of substitute products		
Bargaining power of buyers		
Bargaining power of suppliers		

Given your ratings, which industry would you expect to earn the highest returns?

5. Joe Smith argues, "Your analysis of the five forces that affect industry profitability is incomplete. For example, in the banking industry, I can think of at least three other factors that are also important; namely, government regulation, demographic trends, and cultural factors." His classmate Jane Brown disagrees and says, "These three factors are important only to the extent that they influence one of the five forces." Explain how, if at all, the three factors discussed by Joe affect the five forces in the banking industry.

6. Coca-Cola and Pepsi are both very profitable soft drinks. Inputs for these products include sugar, bottles/cans, and soft drink syrup. Coca-Cola and Pepsi produce the syrup themselves and purchase the other inputs. They then enter into exclusive contracts with independent bottlers to produce their products. Use the five forces framework and your knowledge of the soft drink industry to explain how Coca-Cola and Pepsi are able to retain most of the profits in this industry.

7. In the early 1980s, United, Delta, and American Airlines each started frequent flier programs as a way to differentiate themselves in response to excess capacity in the industry. Many industry analysts, however, believe that this move had only mixed success. Use the competitive advantage concepts to explain why.

8. What are the ways that a firm can create barriers to entry to deter competition in its business? What factors determine whether these barriers are likely to be enduring?

9. Explain why you agree or disagree with each of the following statements:
   a. It's better to be a differentiator than a cost leader, since you can then charge premium prices.
   b. It's more profitable to be in a high technology than a low technology industry.
   c. The reason why industries with large investments have high barriers to entry is because it is costly to raise capital.

10. There are very few companies that are able to be both cost leaders and differentiators. Why? Can you think of a company that has been successful at both?

11. Many consultants are advising diversified companies in emerging markets such as India, Korea, Mexico, and Turkey to adopt corporate strategies proven to be of value in advanced economies like the U.S. and the U.K. What are the pros and cons of this advice?

NOTES

1. The discussion presented here is intended to provide a basic background in strategy analysis. For a more complete discussion of the strategy concepts, see, for example, *Contemporary Strategy Analysis* by Robert M. Grant (Cambridge, MA: Blackwell Publishers, 1991); *Economics of Strategy* by David Besanko, David Dranove, and Mark Shanley (New York: John Wiley & Sons, 1996); *Strategy and the Business Landscape* by Pankaj Ghemawat (Reading, MA: Addison Wesley Longman, 1999); and *Corporate Strategy: Resources and the Scope of the Firm* by David J. Collis and Cynthia Montgomery (Burr Ridge, IL: Irwin/McGraw-Hill, 1997).

2. These data are taken from "Do Competitors Perform Better When They Pursue Different Strategies?" by Anita M. McGahan, Harvard Business School, working paper, May 12, 1999.

3. For a summary of this research, see *Industrial Market Structure and Economic Performance*, second edition, by F. M. Scherer (Chicago: Rand McNally College Publishing Co., 1980).

4. See *Competitive Strategy* by Michael E. Porter (New York: The Free Press, 1980).

5. The four-firm concentration ratio is a commonly used measure of industry concentration; it refers to the market share of the four largest firms in an industry.

6. While the discussion here uses the buyer to connote industrial buyers, the same concepts also apply to buyers of consumer products. Throughout this chapter we use the terms buyers and customers interchangeably.

7. The data on Dell and the PC industry discussed here and elsewhere in this chapter is drawn from "Dell Computer Corporation" by Das Narayandas and V. Kasturi Rangan, Harvard Business School Publishing Division, Case 9-596-058, and "Dell Online" by V. Kasturi Rangan and Marie Bell, Harvard Business School Publishing Division, Case 9-598-116.

8. For a more detailed discussion of these two sources of competitive advantage, see Michael E. Porter, *Competitive Advantage: Creating and Sustaining Superior Performance* (New York: The Free Press, 1985).

9. Ibid.

10. In recent years one of the strategic challenges faced by corporations is having to deal with competitors who achieve differentiation with low cost. For example, Japanese auto manufacturers have successfully demonstrated that there is no necessary trade-off between quality and cost. Similarly, in recent years several highly successful retailers like Wal-Mart and Home Depot have been able to combine high quality, high service, and low prices. These examples suggest that combining low cost and differentiation strategies is possible when a firm introduces a significant technical or business innovation. However, such cost advantage and differentiation will be sustainable only if there are significant barriers to imitation by competitors.

11. See *Competing for the Future* by Gary Hammel and C. K. Prahalad (Boston: Harvard Business School Press, 1994) for a more detailed discussion of the concept of core competencies and their critical role in corporate strategy.

12. Cynthia Montgomery, "Corporate Diversification," *Journal of Economic Perspectives*, Summer 1994.

13. The following works are seminal to the transaction cost economics: "The Nature of the Firm" by Ronald Coase, *Economica* 4 (1937): 386–405; *Markets and Hierarchies: Analysis and Antitrust Implications* by Oliver Williamson (New York: The Free Press, 1975); "Toward an Economic Theory of the Multi-product Firm" by David Teece, *Journal of Economic Behavior and Organization* 3 (1982): 39–63.

14. For a more complete discussion of these issues, see "Building Institutional Infrastructure in Emerging Markets" by Krishna Palepu and Tarun Khanna, *Brown Journal of World Affairs*, Winter/Spring 1998, and "Why Focused Strategies May Be Wrong for Emerging Markets," by Tarun Khanna and Krishna Palepu, *Harvard Business Review*, July/August 1997.

15. For an empirical study which illustrates this point, see "Is Group Affiliation Profitable in Emerging Markets? An Analysis of Diversified Indian Business Groups," by Tarun Khanna and Krishna Palepu, *Journal of Finance* (April 2000): 867–91.

16. See "Tobin's q, diversification, and firm performance" by Larry Lang and Rene Stulz, *Journal of Political Economy* 102 (1994): 1248–80, and "Diversification's Effect on Firm Value" by Phillip Berger and Eli Ofek, *Journal of Financial Economics* 37 (1994): 39–65.

17. See "Which Takeovers Are Profitable: Strategic or Financial?" by Paul Healy, Krishna Palepu, and Richard Ruback, *Sloan Management Review* 38 (Summer 1997): 45–57.

18. See "Effects of Recontracting on Shareholder Wealth: The Case of Voluntary Spinoffs" by Katherine Schipper and Abbie Smith, *Journal of Financial Economics* 12 (December 1983): 437–67; "Asset Sales, Firm Performance, and the Agency Costs of Managerial Discretion" by L. Lang, A. Poulsen, and R. Stulz, *Journal of Financial Economics* 37 (January 1995): 3–37.

19. "eBay vs. Amazon.com," *Business Week,* May 31, 1999.

20. "Amazon.Bomb" by Jacqueline Doherty, *Barron's,* May 31, 1999.

America Online, Inc.

When it comes to technology companies, the stock market's current mania, it's hard to top America Online, Inc. Technology stocks are hot, up about 50 percent on average this year, but AOL is positively scalding, up about 135 percent. In fact, AOL's stock has soared more than 2,000 percent from its initial public offering, in 1992. The Vienna-based company has 35 times the customers and 20 times the revenue it had five years ago. It's the nation's biggest on-line company and is building a recognized brand.

But look closely and you see that AOL is as much about accounting technology as it is about computer technology. So make sure you understand the numbers before rushing out to buy AOL, which is valued at about $4 billion.

The above report written by Allan Sloan appeared on October 24, 1995, in *Newsweek*'s business section.[1]

COMPANY BACKGROUND

Founded in Vienna, VA, America Online, Inc. (AOL) was a leader in the development of a new mass medium that encompassed online services, the Internet, multimedia, and other interactive technologies. Through its America Online service the company offered members a broad range of features including real-time talk, electronic mail, electronic magazines and newspapers, online classes and shopping, and Internet access. In addition to its online service, AOL's business had expanded during 1995 to include access software for the Internet, production and distribution of original content, interactive marketing and transactions capabilities, and networks to support the transmission of data.

AOL generated revenues principally from consumers through membership fees, as well as from content providers and merchandisers through advertising, commissions on merchandise sales and other transactions, and from other businesses through the sale of network and production services. Through continued investment in the growth of its existing online service, the pursuit of related business opportunities, its ability to provide a full range of interactive services, and its technological flexibility, the company positioned itself to lead the development of the evolving mass medium for interactive services.

Stephen Case and James Kimsey founded America Online's predecessor, Quantum Computer Services, in 1985. Quantum offered its Q-Link service for Commodore computers. In 1989 the service was extended to Apple computers. The company changed its name to America Online in 1991 and went public in 1992. That same year, AOL licensed its online technology to Apple for use in eWorld and NewtonMail services for which AOL continues to receive a usage-based royalty. In 1993 the company expanded its market with a Windows version of its software and began developing a version for palmtop computers. In 1994 AOL's subscription base surpassed those of CompuServe and Prodigy, two rival online service providers, making AOL the number one consumer online service in the

Professors Krishna Palepu and Amy Hutton prepared this case. The case is intended solely as the basis for class discussion and is not intended to serve as an endorsement, source of primary data, or illustration of effective or ineffective management. Copyright © 1997 by the President and Fellows of Harvard College. HBS Case 9-196-13.

1. Allan Sloan, "Look Beyond the High-Tech Accounting To Measure America Online's Market Risk," Newsweek, October 24, 1995.

United States. By the end of October 1995, AOL had a subscriber base of more than four million members.

AOL's Products

The broad range of features offered by the America Online service was designed to meet the varied needs of its four million members. A key feature of the online service was the ease with which members with related interests could communicate through real-time conferences, e-mail, and bulletin boards. Members used the interactive communications facilities to share information and ideas, exchange advice, and socialize. It was America Online's goal to continue developing and adding new sources of information and content in support of these member activities. The range of features offered by America Online included the following:

- *Online Community.* In addition to its e-mail service, AOL promoted real-time online communications by scheduling conferences and discussions on specific topics, offering interactive areas that served as "meeting rooms" for members to participate in lively interactive discussions with other members, and providing public bulletin boards on which members could share information and opinions on subjects of general or specialized interest.
- *Computing.* AOL provided its members access to tens of thousands of public domain and "shareware" software programs, to online help from 300 hardware and software developers, and to online computer shopping and online computer magazines such as *MacWorld, PC World,* and *Computer Life.*
- *Education and References.* AOL's online educational services allowed adults and children to learn without leaving their homes. AOL contracted with professional instructors to teach real-time interactive classes in subjects of both general academic interest and adult education (such as creative writing and gourmet cooking). Regular tutoring sessions were offered in English, biology, and math. Education and reference services included the Library of Congress, College Board, CNN, Smithsonian, *Consumer Reports*, and *Compton's Encyclopedia.*
- *News and Personal Finance.* AOL offered a broad range of information services, including domestic and international news, weather, sports, stock market prices, and personalized portfolio tracking. Members could search news wires for stories of interest, access mutual fund information through Fidelity Online and Morningstar, and execute brokered trades online through PC Financial Network. Subscribers had access to over 70 newspapers, periodicals, and wire services, including *The New York Times, Chicago Tribune, San Jose Mercury News, Time, Scientific American, Investors Business Daily,* and Reuters.
- *Travel and Shopping.* AOL members also had access to travel and shopping reference materials and transaction services. Subscribers could send customized greeting cards through Hallmark Corporation, send flowers through 1-800-Flowers, shop for CDs and tapes online at Tower Records, book vacation packages with Preview Vacations, and access account data and travel information and services with American Express-Net. Additionally, AOL had introduced its own interactive shopping service, 2Market, which featured goods and services from numerous catalogs and retailers.
- *Entertainment and Children's Programming.* AOL provided various clubs and forums for games and sports, multi-player games, and other related content for both adults and children. Specialized content was provided by such organizations as MusicSpace, the Games Channel, Disney Adventures, Comedy Clubs, Nintendo Power Source,

Kids Only, Hollywood Online, Warner-Reprise Records, American Association for Retired Persons, MTV, Cooking Club, Environment Club, and Baby Boomers' Forum.

Customer Acquisition and Retention

AOL's biggest expenditure was the cost of attracting new subscribers. AOL aggressively marketed its online service using both independent marketing efforts, such as direct mail packets with AOL software disks and television and print advertising featuring a toll-free telephone number for ordering the AOL software, as well as co-marketing efforts with computer magazine publishers and personal computer hardware and software producers. These companies bundled the AOL software with their computer products, facilitating easy trial use by their customers. With the AOL software in hand, the customer needed only a personal computer, a telephone line, and a computer modem to gain access to AOL's online service. Accompanying each program disk was a unique registration number and password that could be used to generate a new AOL account. Customers could activate their accounts by providing AOL with their credit card account number. The first ten hours of access by this new account were free, after which AOL automatically billed the customer's credit card account the standard monthly rate until the customer canceled the AOL account.

These types of promotions were expensive, costing more than $40 per new subscriber in 1994. Thus, to retain these new subscribers and increase customer loyalty and satisfaction, AOL invested in specialized retention programs including regularly scheduled online events and conferences, online promotions of upcoming events and new features, and the regular addition of new content, services, and software programs. AOL's goal was to maximize customer subscription life.

Critical to customer retention and usage rates was the content available on AOL. To build and create unique content, America Online participated in numerous joint ventures. During 1995 its alliances grew to include American Express, ABC, Reuters, Shoppers Express, Business Week, Fidelity, Vanguard, and the National Education Association. Also important to AOL were the newest stars of cyberspace, special-interest sites created by entrepreneurs such as Tom and David Gardner, who created Motley Fool and Follywood, two of the most popular sites offered on America Online. These hot special-interest sites kept customers on line, running up metered time and revenues. Traditionally, AOL had kept 80 percent or more of the revenues generated by these sites and had demanded exclusive contracts with the entrepreneurs creating them. However, content providers now had the option of setting up sites on the World Wide Web. While they could not yet collect fees from web browsers, this new distribution channel was changing the balance of power between AOL and its content providers.[2]

Compared to its competitors, AOL's rate structure was the easiest for consumers to understand and anticipate. A monthly fee of $9.95 provided access to all of America Online's services for up to five hours each month. Each additional hour was $2.95 and no additional downloading fees were charged. CompuServe and Prodigy offered the same standard pricing but charged additional fees for premium services and downloading. Microsoft Network (MSN), the newest entrant into the online services industry, offered a standard monthly plan of up to three hours for $4.95, with each additional hour costing $2.50. Content providers on MSN also applied charges to customers based on usage rates. The additional fees charged by AOL's competitors made it more difficult for their customers to anticipate their monthly spending.

....

2. Steven Lohr, "On-Line Stars Hear Siren Calls to Free Agency," New York Times, November 25, 1995.

Strategy for Future Growth

Through a tapestry of alliances and subsidiaries, AOL's goal was to establish a central and defining leadership position in the worldwide market for interactive services. Toward this end, AOL had signed new strategic partnerships with American Express, Business Week Online, and NTN Communications; shipped the 2Market CD-ROM shopping service with an online connection; and completed its acquisitions of Internet software developers BookLink Technologies, Inc., NaviSoft, Inc., and Internet backbone developer Advanced Network & Services (ANS). These deals, along with AOL's growing membership base, its enhanced look and feel, and its ability to program content to appeal to users, uniquely positioned America Online to lead the development of the new interactive services industry. In implementing its strategy, AOL pursued a number of initiatives:

- *Invest in Growth of Existing Service.* America Online planned to continue to invest in the rapid growth of its existing online service. AOL believed it could attract and retain new members by expanding the range of content and services it offered, continuing to improve the engaging multimedia context of its service and building a sense of community online. At the same time, by offering access to a large, growing, and demographically attractive audience, together with software tools and services to develop content and programming for that audience, AOL believed it would continue to appeal to content and service providers.
- *Exploit New Business Opportunities.* AOL intended to leverage its technology, management skills, and content packaging skills to identify and exploit new business opportunities, such as electronic commerce, entry into international markets, and the "consumerization" of the Internet with its highly graphical interface software and its World Wide Web browser, which used high-speed compression technology to improve access speed and graphic display performance.
- *Provide a Full Range of Interactive Services.* Through acquisitions and internal development, AOL had assembled content development, distribution capabilities, access software, and its own communications network to become a full service, vertically integrated provider of interactive services. As a result, AOL believed it was well positioned to influence the evolution of the interactive services market.
- *Maintain Technological Flexibility.* AOL recognized the need to provide its services over a diverse set of platforms. Its software worked on different types of personal computers and operating systems (including Macintosh, Windows 3.xx, and Windows 95) and supported a variety of different media, including online services, the Internet, and CD-ROM. AOL intended to adapt its products and services as new technologies became available.

While AOL currently generated revenues largely from membership fees, AOL's management believed that these initiatives would allow the company to increase the proportion of its revenues generated from other sources, such as advertising fees, commissions on merchandise sales to consumers, and revenues from the sale of production and network services to other enterprises.

INDUSTRY COMPETITION AND OUTLOOK

The online consumer services industry represented $1.1 billion in revenues in 1994 and was expected to grow by 30 percent to $1.4 billion in 1995. Eleven million customers subscribed to commercial online services worldwide and this number was expected to explode in the next five years. Industry leaders America Online, CompuServe, and Prodigy served about 8.5 million of the existing subscribers (4.0 million, 2.8 million, and 1.6 million, respectively). This oligopoly had very successfully acted as middlemen between thousands of content providers and millions of customers. They were the publishers, closely controlling the product and paying content providers, the writers, only modest royalties. However, with the advent of the Internet World Wide Web and the entrance of Microsoft Network, content providers now had alternative distribution channels which offered greater control over their products and potentially higher revenues.

Forbes discussed this topic in its August 28, 1995, issue:

> *Until recently the only way to reach cyberspace browsers was through one of the big three on-line services, America Online, CompuServe and Prodigy. That oligopoly is set to fade fast, and it's not just Microsoft that threatens. It's the whole Internet, the pulsating, undisciplined and rapidly expanding network of World Wide Web computers that contain public data bases.*[3]

While the big three acted as publishers, Microsoft had decided to act more like a bookstore, one in which every author (content provider) was his/her own publisher. Customers of MSN paid $4.95 per month for up to three hours (each additional hour was $2.50). Then each content provider charged whatever it wanted for its material, so much per hour, per page, or per picture. Microsoft kept a 30 percent commission out of the provider's fee and passed along the rest to the content provider. In addition to offering content providers a larger share of the revenues, MSN also offered content providers greater control over their own products. In contrast to the standardized screen displays and icons of the big three, MSN permitted content providers to use any font and format they wished. Thus, while Microsoft still acted as a middleman, it played a very limited and passive role in determining content and fees charged for that content.

Beyond Microsoft lurked the vast potential of the World Wide Web, where the middleman's role was shrunk still further. On the Internet, everyone with a computer was his/her own publisher. Customers would sign up for an Internet on-ramp service, of the sort offered by PST, Netcom, or MCI. Once on the net, the subscriber used browsing software like Netscape or Spyglass to roam the world's databases. While it remained difficult for self-publishers on the Internet to collect fees from browsers who read their pages, that was expected to change quickly as banks, Microsoft, and other intermediaries worked on systems to provide on-line currency.

Many content providers were beginning to take advantage of these alternative distribution channels. For example, *Wired* magazine, unwilling to settle for just 20 percent of the revenues from subscribers spending time on its pages on AOL, created HotWired on the Internet. Andrew Anker, chief technologist at *Wired*, believed that HotWired would soon be more lucrative than the America Online venture and he noted that on the Internet his firm had greater control of its own product. General Electric's NBC decided to switch from AOL to Microsoft Network. "While we had many users visiting us on America Online, we weren't making much revenue," explained Martin Yudkovitz, a senior vice-president at NBC.[4]

With the migration of proprietary services and content to web sites, the unique offerings of the big three services were declining. However, the online services were still better for interactive communications with full-fledged message boards and live chat. The web, on the other hand, was mainly a publication environment for reading. The question

---

3. Nikhil Hutheesing, "Who Needs the Middleman?," Forbes, August 28, 1995.
4. Ibid.

remained, what would be the role of online service providers in the future? Would they become just another Internet access provider with their own look and browsers or could they continue to offer something unique to users?

Some analysts were projecting that the U.S. online services market would grow 30–35 percent annually through the year 2000, and that the Internet market would grow even faster. These analysts expected America Online to retain about a 20 percent market share.[5] On the other hand, Forrester Research of Cambridge, Mass., predicted that the big three, America Online, CompuServe, and Prodigy, would continue to add subscribers only through 1997. After that, Forrester predicted, it would be all downhill for the big three.[6]

AOL'S RECENT PERFORMANCE

For the fourth quarter ended June 30, 1995, America Online announced that its earnings were $0.16, excluding $0.01 merger expenses and $0.02 amortization of goodwill. This was a significant improvement over 1994's fourth-quarter earnings, $0.02, and above analysts' estimate, $0.14. Service revenues surged to $139 million versus analysts' estimate of $132 million, and total revenues rose to $152 million versus $40.4 in the fourth quarter of 1994. For the fiscal year ended June 30, 1995, AOL reported a loss of $33.6 million on revenues of $394 million compared with a profit of $2.5 million on revenues of $116 million a year earlier. New charges recorded for the first time in 1995 included $50.3 million for acquired R&D, $1.7 million amortization of goodwill, and $2.2 million in merger expenses. (See Exhibit 3, America Online's 1995 Abridged Annual Report.)

New subscriber momentum continued to be strong, increasing 233 percent year-over-year and adding 691,000 new net subscribers during the fourth quarter. All major metrics used by analysts to evaluate AOL's franchise and gauge the "health" of its rapidly growing subscriber base also improved during the quarter: projected retention rates rose to 41 months from 39 months; paid usage grew to 2.93 hours from 2.73, and projected lifetime revenues per subscriber increased to $714 from $667. (See Exhibit 2 for the history of America Online's user metrics.) However, analysts were projecting lower gross margins in the future as subscribers continued to transition to higher-speed access and as AOL introduced a heavy-usage pricing plan in response to Microsoft's lower per-hour pricing.

On November 8, 1995, America Online announced its results for the first quarter of fiscal 1996, ended September 30, 1995. Even though revenues rose to $197.9 million from $56 million a year earlier, America Online reported a loss of $10.3 million compared with a profit of $1.5 million a year earlier. America Online took a $16.9 million charge to reflect research and development taking place at Ubique, a company it acquired on September 21, 1995, as well as to pay off other recently acquired assets. It took another charge of $1.7 million for amortization of goodwill. These charges were partially offset by AOL's decision to increase the period over which it amortized subscriber acquisition costs. Effective July 1, 1995, these costs would be amortized over 24 months rather than 12–18 months. The effect of the change in accounting estimates for the three months ended September 30, 1995, was to decrease the reported loss by $1.95 million. AOL also announced that it added 711,000 subscribers in the first quarter of 1996, bringing its total subscriber base to four million.[7]

....

5. A. Pooley, "America Online, Inc. — Company Report," The Chicago Corporation, April 18, 1995.

6. Hutheesing, op. cit.

7. "America Online Posts $10.3 Million Loss But Says Revenue Rose 250% in Quarter," The Washington Post, Nov. 8, 1995.

America Online

America Online's stock price had been on the move since the company's initial public offering (IPO) in March 1992. The stock price appreciated from the IPO price of $2.90 to $7.31, $14.63, and $28.00 at calendar year end 1992, 1993, and 1994, respectively. At its current price of $81.63 (dated November 8, 1995), the company's market value was around $4.0 billion. (See Exhibit 1 for the stock price history of America Online, its equity beta, and additional market-based data.)

THE CONTROVERSY SURROUNDING AOL

America Online's stock was one of the most controversial of this period. Some analysts promoted the stock's potential for price appreciation, while others recommended selling the shares short to profit from a decline in price. Bulls saw America Online as part of a revolution in communication, like cellular phones and cable television in the early days. They considered AOL's graphical interface software, its high-speed web browser, and Mr. Case's marketing genius (subscribership had quadrupled to over four million in a little over a year) to be major competitive advantages. Bears, on the other hand, anticipating new entrants competing in the online services industry and a migration of subscribers to the Internet, questioned whether AOL would continue to experience high growth in its subscriber base or be able to retain existing subscribers.

Shortsellers had sold around seven million America Online shares, betting that the stock's price would not go up forever. Shortsellers pointed to the recent hedging activities by Apple Computer to lock in profits on its 5.7 percent stake as an indication that AOL's stock was overvalued. Adding fuel to the shortsellers' fire, corporate insiders at AOL had sold some of their shareholdings. Between March 9 and March 15 of 1995, 17 insiders sold approximately 200,000 shares, including the company founders, President Steven Case (25,000 shares for $2.1 million) and Chairman James Kimsey (40,000 shares for $3.3 million).[8]

Adding to the controversy, some analysts labeled AOL's accounting "aggressive." AOL amortized its software development costs over five years, a long time in the fast-changing, uncertain online services industry, and AOL capitalized subscriber acquisition costs when its number one competitor, CompuServe, did not. Furthermore, effective July 1, 1995, AOL extended the amortization period for its subscriber acquisition costs from about 15 months to 24 months. Given the uncertainties surrounding AOL's subscriber retention rates and revenue growth as competition emerged in the young industry, analysts questioned the wisdom of AOL's accounting decisions. The big risk AOL faced was that eventually customers could switch online services as frequently as they moved among long-distance carriers.

While America Online expensed the free trial expenses (i.e., those charges incurred from the ten free hours given away in the initial month), it capitalized the marketing costs associated with acquiring a customer, including direct mail, advertising, start-up kits, and bundling costs. As indicated in its annual report, prior to July 1, 1995, the capitalization had occurred on two schedules depending on the acquisition method. Costs for subscribers acquired through direct marketing programs were amortized over a 12-month period. Costs for subscribers acquired through co-marketing efforts with personal computer producers and magazine publishers were amortized over an 18-month period, as these bundling campaigns had historically shown a longer response time. However, effective July 1,

....

8. As of August 15, 1995 all executive officers and directors as a group continued to own 3,729,547 shares. Steven Case owned 1,036,790 shares and James Kimsey owned 679,616 shares.

1995, AOL increased the period over which it amortized subscriber acquisition costs to 24 months for both acquisition methods.

Defending AOL's accounting choices, Lennert Leader, the Chief Financial Officer of America Online, Inc., said that the company was following standard accounting procedures in matching the timing of expenses with the period over which the revenues would be received. He argued that the company's marketing and software development expenses produced customer accounts that last a long time. Thus, he said, it was appropriate to write off the costs over a period of years, even though AOL had spent the cash.[9]

However, some analysts raised red flags about AOL's accounting choices. As noted in an October 24, 1995, *Newsweek* article:

> *One of AOL's hidden assets is the brilliant accounting decision it made to treat marketing and research and development costs as capital items rather than expenses. . . .*
>
> *AOL charges R&D expenses over a five-year period, a very long time in the on-line biz. In July, AOL began charging off marketing expenses over two years, up from about 15 months.*
>
> *Why change to 24 months from 15? Leader said it's because the average life of an AOL account has climbed to 41 months from 25 months in 1992. How many AOL customers have been around for 41 months? Almost none, as Leader concedes. That's understandable, considering that AOL has added virtually all its customers in the past 36 months. Leader says the 41-month average live number comes from projections. Of course, it will take years to find out if he's right. . . .*[10]

Analysts were also concerned about AOL's cash flow situation and the signal sent by the timing of its latest equity offering. The *Newsweek* article continued:

> *Accounting is terribly important to AOL. The better the numbers look, the more Wall Street loves it and the easier AOL can sell new shares to raise cash to pay its bills. . . . On October 10 [AOL] raised about $100 million by selling new shares. AOL sold the stock even though its shares had fallen to $58.37 from about $72 in September, when the sale plans were announced. Most companies would have delayed the offering, waiting for the price to snap back. AOL didn't, prompting cynics to think the company really needed the money. . . .*

Some analysts believed that AOL issued shares when its stock price was low because the company needed the cash immediately. Others argued that AOL was building a war chest needed because deep-pocketed rivals such as Microsoft were about to start an online price war and because information providers increasingly were going directly to the Internet rather than using middlemen such as AOL. Some analysts interpreted CompuServe's recent adoption of more aggressive accounting techniques as a sign that it too was readying for war. Beginning the first quarter of fiscal 1996, CompuServe would capitalize direct response advertising costs associated with customer acquisition activity.[11]

While AOL's stock price rebounded to $81.63 by November 8, 1995, there were many questions concerning AOL's future. How would the demand for AOL's services be affected by the entry of Microsoft Network and the growth of the Internet? Would AOL's accounting choices stand the test of time? What if AOL's subscription growth rates slowed or subscriber renewal rates fell? Did AOL have the financial flexibility to face these competitive pressures and accounting risks?

---

9. Sloan, op. cit.
10. Ibid.
11. Ibid.

QUESTIONS

1. Prior to 1995, why was America Online (AOL) so successful in the commercial online industry relative to its competitors CompuServe and Prodigy?

2. As of 1995, what are the key changes taking place in the commercial online industry? How are they likely to affect AOL's future prospects?

3. Was AOL's policy to capitalize subscriber acquisition costs justified prior to 1995?

4. Given the changes discussed in question 2, do you think AOL should change its accounting policy as of 1995? Is the company's response consistent with your view?

5. What would be the affect on AOL's 1994 and 1995 ending balance sheets if the company had followed the policy of expensing subscriber acquisition outlays instead of capitalizing them? What would be the effect of expensing subscriber acquisition costs on AOL's 1995 income statement?

EXHIBIT I

Stock Price History for America Online, Inc.

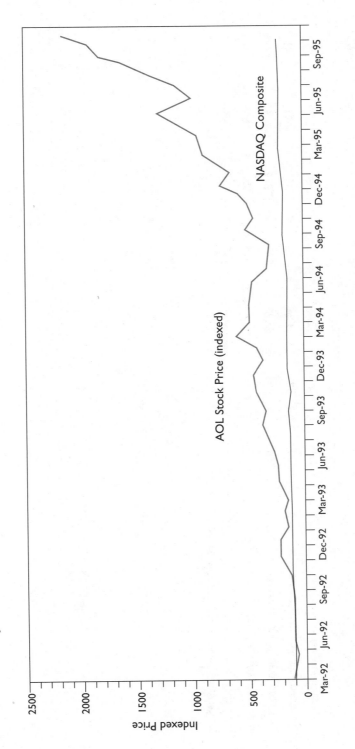

Additional market-based data:

America Online's equity beta	1.4
Moody's AAA corporate debt in November 1995 (%)	7.02
Treasury bills rate in November 1995 (%)	5.35
Government 30-year treasury rates in November 1995 (%)	6.26

Sources: Datastream International, Standard and Poor's Compustat, and the *Wall Street Journal*.

America Online

America Online

EXHIBIT 2
America Online, Inc. User Metrics to June 30, 1995

	Dec-93	Mar-94	Jun-94	Sep-94	Dec-94	Mar-95	Jun-95
Paid usage (hours)	1.85	2	2.1	2.27	2.46	2.73	2.93
Projected average months' retention	30	32	32+	34	36	39	41
Projected average lifetime revenue	$443	$496	$496	$551	$612	$667	$714
Internet usage (% time)		1%	3%	4%	5%	6%	9%

Source: Alex Brown & Sons, Inc., August 24, 1995.

EXHIBIT 3

America Online 1995 Abridged Annual Report

REPORT OF INDEPENDENT AUDITORS

Board of Directors and Stockholders
America Online, Inc.

We have audited the accompanying consolidated balance sheets of America Online, Inc., as of June 30, 1995 and 1994, and the related consolidated statements of operations, changes in stockholders' equity and cash flows for each of the three years in the period ended June 30, 1995. These financial statements are the responsibility of the Company's management. Our responsibility is to express an opinion on these financial statements based on our audits.

We conducted our audits in accordance with generally accepted auditing standards. Those standards require that we plan and perform the audit to obtain reasonable assurance about whether the financial statements are free of material misstatement. An audit includes examining, on a test basis, evidence supporting the amounts and disclosures in the financial statements. An audit also includes assessing the accounting principles used and significant estimates made by management, as well as evaluating the overall financial statement presentation. We believe that our audits provide a reasonable basis for our opinion.

In our opinion, the financial statements referred to above present fairly, in all material respects, the consolidated financial position of America Online, Inc. at June 30, 1995 and 1994, and the consolidated results of their operations and their cash flows for each of the three years in the period ended June 30, 1995, in conformity with generally accepted accounting principles.

As discussed in Note 9 to the consolidated financial statements, in fiscal 1994 the Company changed its method of accounting for income taxes. As discussed in Note 2 to the consolidated financial statements, in fiscal 1995 the Company changed its method of accounting for short-term investments in certain debt and equity securities.

Ernst & Young LLP

Vienna, Virginia
August 25, 1995

America Online

SELECTED CONSOLIDATED FINANCIAL AND OTHER DATA

(in thousands, except per share data)

	Year Ended June 30,				
	1995	1994	1993	1992	1991
Statements of Operations Data:					
Online service revenues	$358,498	$100,993	$38,462	$26,226	$19,515
Other revenues	35,792	14,729	13,522	12,527	10,646
Total Revenues	394,290	115,722	51,984	38,753	30,161
Income (loss) from operations	(19,294)	4,608	1,925	3,685	1,341
Income (loss) before extra-ordinary items	(33,647)	2,550	399	2,344	1,100
Net income (loss) [1]	(33,647)	2,550	1,532	3,768	1,761
Income (loss) per common share:					
Income (loss) before extra-ordinary item	$ (0.99)	$ 0.07	$ 0.01	$ 0.10	$ 0.06
Net income (loss)	$ (0.99)	$ 0.07	$ 0.05	$ 0.17	$ 0.09
Weighted average shares outstanding	33,986	34,208	29,286	22,828	19,304

	As of June 30,				
	1995	1994	1993	1992	1991
Balance Sheet Data:					
Working capital (deficiency)	$ (456)	$47,890	$10,498	$12,363	$ (966)
Total assets	406,464	154,584	39,279	31,144	11,534
Total debt	21,810	9,302	2,959	2,672	1,865
Stockholders' equity (deficiency)	217,944	98,297	23,785	21,611	(8,623)
Other data (at fiscal year end):					
Subscribers	3,005	903	303	182	131

(1) Net loss in the fiscal year ended June 30, 1995, includes charges of $50.3 million for acquired research and development and $2.2 million for merger expenses. See Note 3 of the Notes to Consolidated Financial Statements.

America Online

MANAGEMENT'S DISCUSSION AND ANALYSIS OF FINANCIAL CONDITIONS AND RESULTS OF OPERATIONS

Overview

The Company has experienced a significant increase in revenues over the past three fiscal years. The higher revenues have been principally produced by increases in the Company's subscriber base resulting from growth of the online services market, the introduction of a Windows version of America Online in the middle of fiscal 1993, which greatly increased the available market for the Company's service, as well as the expansion of its services and content. Additionally, revenues have increased as the average monthly revenue per subscriber has risen steadily during the past three years, primarily as a result of an increase in the average monthly paid hours of use per subscriber.

The Company's online service revenues are generated primarily from subscribers paying a monthly member's fee and hourly charges based on usage in excess of the number of hours of usage provided as part of the monthly fee. Through December 31, 1994, the Company's standard monthly membership fee, which includes five hours of service, was $9.95, with a $3.50 hourly fee for usage in excess of five hours per month. Effective January 1, 1995, the hourly fee for usage in excess of five hours per month decreased from $3.50 to $2.95, while the monthly membership fee remained unchanged at $9.95.

The Company's other revenues are generated primarily from providing new media and interactive marketing services, data network services, and multimedia and CD-ROM production services. Additionally, the Company generates revenues related to online transactions and advertising, as well as development and licensing fees.

In fiscal 1995 the Company acquired RCC, Navi-Soft, BookLink, ANS, WAIS, Medior and Global Network Navigator, Inc. Additionally, in August 1995, the Company entered into an agreement to acquire Ubique. For additional information relating to these acquisitions, refer to Notes 3 and 13 of the Notes to Consolidated Financial Statements.

The online services market is highly competitive. The Company believes that existing competitors, which include, among others, CompuServe, Prodigy and MSN, are likely to enhance their service offerings. In addition, new competitors have announced plans to enter the online services market, resulting in greater competition for the Company. The competitive environment could require new pricing programs and increased spending on marketing, content procurement and product development; limit the Company's opportunities to enter into and/or renew agreements with content providers and distribution partners; limit the Company's ability to grow its subscriber base; and result in increased attrition in the Company's subscriber base. Any of the foregoing events could result in an increase in costs as a percentage of revenues, and may have a material adverse effect on the Company's financial condition and operating results.

During September 1995, the Company modified the components of subscriber acquisition costs deferred and will be expensing certain subscriber acquisition cost as incurred, effective July 1, 1995. All costs capitalized before this change will continue to be amortized. The effect of this change for the year ended June 30, 1995 (including the amortization of amounts capitalized as of June 30, 1994) would have been to increase marketing costs by approximately $8 million. This change will have a greater impact on the Company's marketing costs in fiscal 1996, as the Company expects to significantly increase subscriber acquisition activity, including those subscriber acquisition expenditures which the Company will be expensing as incurred.

In addition, effective July 1, 1995, the Company changed the period over which it amortizes subscriber acquisition cost from twelve and eighteen months to twenty-four months. Based on the Company's historical average customer life experience, the change in amortization period is being made to more appropriately match subscriber acquisition costs with associated online service revenues. The effect of this change in accounting estimate for the year ended June 30, 1995 would have been to decrease the amount of the amortization of subscriber acquisition costs by approximately $27 million. While this change will thereby positively impact operating margins, the Company expects that any such positive impact will be partially offset by increased investments in marketing and other business activities during fiscal 1996 and the decision, effective July 1, 1995, to expense certain subscriber acquisition costs as incurred.

Results of Operations

Fiscal 1995 Compared to Fiscal 1994

Online Service Revenues. For fiscal 1995, online service revenues increased from $100,993,000 to $358,498,000, or 255%, over fiscal 1994. This increase was primarily attributable to a 289% increase in revenues from IBM-compatible subscribers and a 196% increase in revenues from Macintosh subscribers as a result of a 273% increase in the number of IBM-compatible subscribers and a 143% increase in the number of Macintosh subscribers. The percentage increase in online service revenues in fiscal 1995 was greater than the percentage increase in subscribers principally due to an increase in the average monthly online service revenue per subscriber, which increased from $15.00 in fiscal 1994 to $17.10 in fiscal 1995.

Other Revenues. Other revenues, consisting principally of new media and interactive marketing services, data network services, multimedia and CD-ROM production services, and development and licensing fees, increased from $14,729,000 in fiscal 1994 to $35,792,000 in fiscal 1995. This increase was primarily attributable to data network revenues and multimedia and CD-ROM production service revenues from companies acquired during fiscal 1995.

Cost of Revenues. Cost of revenues includes network-related costs, consisting primarily of data and voice communication costs, costs associated with operating the data center and providing customer support, royalties paid to information and service providers and other expenses related to marketing and production services. For fiscal 1995, cost of revenues increased from $69,043,000 to $229,724,000, or 233%, over fiscal 1994, and decreased as a percentage of total revenues from 59.7% to 58.3%.

The increase in cost of revenues was primarily attributable to an increase in data communication costs, customer support costs and royalties paid to information and service providers. Data communication costs increased primarily as a result of the larger customer base and more usage by customers. Customer support costs, which include personnel and telephone costs associated with providing customer support, were higher as a result of the larger customer base and a large number of new subscriber registrations. Royalties paid to information and service providers increased as a result of a larger customer base and more usage and the Company's addition of more service content to broaden the appeal of the America Online service.

The decrease in cost of revenues as a percentage of total revenues is primarily attributable to a decrease in expenses related to marketing services and personnel related costs as a percentage of total revenues, partially offset by an increase in data communication costs as a percentage of total revenues, primarily resulting from an increase in higher baud speed usage at a higher variable rate as well as lower hourly pricing for online service revenue which became effective January 1, 1995.

Marketing. Marketing expenses include the costs to acquire and retain subscribers and other general marketing expenses. Subscriber acquisition costs are deferred and charged to operations over a twelve or eighteen month period, using the straight-line method, beginning the month after such costs are incurred. For additional information regarding the accounting for deferred subscriber acquisition costs, refer to Note 2 of the Notes to Consolidated Financial Statements. For fiscal 1995, marketing expenses increased from $23,548,000 to $77,064,000, or 227%, over fiscal 1994, and decreased as a percentage of total revenues from 20.3% to 19.5%. The increase in marketing expenses was primarily due to an increase in the number and size of marketing programs to expand the Company's subscriber base. The decrease in marketing expenses as a percentage of total revenues is primarily attributable to a decrease as a percentage of total revenues in personnel related costs.

Product Development. Product development costs include research and development expenses, other product development costs and the amortization of software costs. For fiscal 1995, product development expenses increased from $4,961,000 to $12,842,000, or 159%, over fiscal 1994, and decreased as a percentage of total revenues from 4.3% to 3.3%. The increase in product development costs was primarily attributable to an increase in personnel costs related to an increase in the number of technical employees. The decrease in product development costs as a percentage of total revenues was principally a result of the substantial growth in revenues, which more than offset the additional product development costs. Product development costs, before capitalization and amortization, increased by 126% in fiscal 1995.

General and Administrative. Fiscal 1995 general and administrative costs increased from $13,562,000 to $41,966,000, or 209%, over fiscal 1994, and decreased as a percentage of total revenues from 11.7% to 10.6%. The increase in general and administrative expenses was principally attributable to higher office and personnel expenses related to an increase in the number of employees. The decrease in general and administrative costs as a percentage of total revenues was a result of the substantial growth in revenues, which more than offset the additional general and administrative costs, combined with the semi-variable nature of many of the general and administrative costs.

Acquired Research and Development. Acquired research and development costs, totaling $50,335,000, relate to in-process research and development purchased pursuant to the Company's acquisition of two early-stage Internet technology companies, BookLink and NaviSoft. The purchased research and development relating to the BookLink and NaviSoft acquisitions was the foundation of the development of the Company's Internet related products.

Amortization of Goodwill. Amortization of goodwill relates to the Company's acquisition of ANS, which resulted in approximately $44 million in goodwill. The goodwill related to the ANS acquisition is being amortized on a straight-line basis over a ten-year period.

Other Income. Other income consists primarily of investment and rental income net of interest expense. For fiscal 1995, other income increased from $1,774,000 to $3,023,000. This increase was primarily attributable to an increase in interest income generated by higher levels of cash available for investment, partially offset by a decrease in rental income and an increase in interest expense.

Merger Expenses. Non-recurring merger expenses totaling $2,207,000 were recognized in fiscal 1995 in connection with the mergers of the Company with RCC, WAIS and Medior.

Provisions for Income Taxes. The provision for income taxes was $3,832,000 and $15,169,000 in fiscal year 1994 and fiscal 1995, respectively. For additional information regarding income taxes, refer to Note 9 of the Notes to Consolidated Financial Statements.

Net Loss. The net loss in fiscal 1995 totaled $33,647,000. The net loss in fiscal 1995 included charges of $50,335,000 for acquired research and development and $2,207,000 for merger expenses.

Liquidity and Capital Resources

The Company has financed its operations through cash generated from operations, sale of its common stock and funding by third parties for certain product development activities. Net cash provided by operating activities was $2,205,000, $1,884,000 and $15,891,000 for fiscal 1993, fiscal 1994 and fiscal 1995, respectively. Included in operating activities were expenditures for deferred subscriber acquisition costs of $10,685,000, $37,424,000 and $111,761,000 in fiscal 1993, fiscal 1994 and fiscal 1995, respectively. Net cash used in investing activities was $8,915,000, $41,870,000 and $85,725,000 in fiscal 1993, fiscal 1994 and fiscal 1995, respectively. Investing activities included $20,523,000 in fiscal 1995 related to business acquisitions, substan-tially all of which were related to the acquisition of ANS.

In December 1993 the Company completed a public stock offering of 4,000,000 shares of common stock which generated net cash proceeds of approximately $62.7 million.

In April 1995 the company entered into a joint venture with Bertelsmann to offer interactive online services in Europe. In connection with the agreement, the Company received approximately $54 million through the sale of approximately 5% of its common stock to Bertelsmann.

The Company leases the majority of its equipment under noncancelable operating leases, and as part of its network portfolio strategy is building AOLnet, its data communications network. The buildout of this network requires a substantial investment in telecommunication equipment, which the Company plans to finance principally though leasing. In addition, the Company has guaranteed minimum commitments under certain data and voice communication agreements. The Company's future lease commitments and guaranteed minimums are discussed in Note 6 of the Notes to Consolidated Financial Statements.

The Company uses its working capital to finance ongoing operations and to fund marketing and content programs and the development of its products and services. The Company plans to continue to invest aggressively in acquisition marketing and content programs to expand its subscriber base, as well as in computing and support infrastructure. Additionally, the Company expects to use a portion of its cash for the acquisition and subsequent funding of technologies, products or businesses complementary to the Company's current business. Apart from its agreement to acquire Ubique, as discussed below, the Company has no agreements or understandings to acquire any businesses. The Company anticipates that available cash and cash provided by operating activities will be sufficient to fund its operations for the next fiscal year.

Various legal proceedings have arisen against the Company in the ordinary course of business. In the opinion of management, these proceedings will not have a material effect on the financial position of the Company.

The Company believes that inflation has not had a material effect on its results of operations.

On August 23, 1995, the Company entered into a stock purchase agreement to purchase Ubique, an Israeli company. The Company has agreed to pay approximately $15 million ($1.5 million in cash and

America Online

$13.5 million in common stock) in the transaction, which is to be accounted for as a purchase. Subject to the results of an in-process valuation, a substantial portion of the purchase price may be allocated to in-process research and development and charged to the Company's operations in the first quarter of fiscal 1996.

CONSOLIDATED STATEMENTS OF OPERATIONS
(Amounts in Thousands, Except Per Share Data)

	Year ended June 30,		
	1995	1994	1993
Revenues:			
Online service revenues	$358,498	$100,993	$ 38,462
Other revenues	35,792	14,729	13,522
Total revenues	394,290	115,722	51,984
Costs and expenses:			
Cost of revenues	229,724	69,043	28,820
Marketing	77,064	23,548	9,745
Product development	12,842	4,961	2,913
General and administrative	41,966	13,562	8,581
Acquired research and development	50,335	—	—
Amortization of goodwill	1,653	—	—
Total costs and expenses	413,584	111,114	50,059
Income (loss) from operations	(19,294)	4,608	1,925
Other income, net	3,023	1,774	371
Merger expenses	(2,207)	—	—
Income (loss) before provision for income taxes and extraordinary item	(18,478)	6,382	2,296
Provision for income taxes	(15,169)	(3,832)	(1,897)
Income (loss) before extraordinary item	(33,647)	2,550	399
Extraordinary item—tax benefit arising from net operating loss carryforward	—	—	1,133
Net income (loss)	$ (33,647)	$ 2,550	$ 1,532
Earnings (loss) per share:			
Income (loss) before extraordinary item	$ (0.99)	$ 0.07	$ 0.01
Net income (loss)	$ (0.99)	$ 0.07	$ 0.05
Weighted average shares outstanding	33,986	34,208	29,286

See accompanying notes.

America Online

CONSOLIDATED STATEMENTS OF CASH FLOWS
(Amounts in Thousands)

	Year ended June 30,		
	1995	1994	1993
Cash flows from operating activities:			
Net income (loss)	$ (33,647)	$ 2,550	$ 1,532
Adjustments to reconcile net income to net cash provided by operating activities:			
Depreciation and amortization	11,136	2,965	1,957
Amortization of subscriber acquisition costs	60,924	17,922	7,038
Loss/(Gain) on sale of property and equipment	37	5	(39)
Charge for acquired research and development	50,335	—	—
Changes in assets and liabilities:			
Trade accounts receivable	(14,373)	(4,266)	(936)
Other receivables	(9,057)	(681)	(966)
Prepaid expenses and other current assets	(19,641)	(2,867)	(1,494)
Deferred subscriber acquisition costs	(111,761)	(37,424)	(10,685)
Other assets	(8,432)	(2,519)	(89)
Trade accounts payable	60,824	10,204	2,119
Accrued personnel costs	1,846	367	336
Other accrued expenses and liabilities	5,703	9,526	1,492
Deferred revenue	7,190	2,322	1,381
Deferred income taxes	14,763	3,832	759
Deferred rent	44	(52)	(200)
Total adjustments	49,538	(666)	673
Net cash provided by operating activities	15,891	1,884	2,205
Cash flows from investing activities:			
Short-term investments	5,380	(18,947)	(5,105)
Purchase of property and equipment	(57,751)	(17,886)	(2,041)
Product development costs	(13,011)	(5,132)	(1,831)
Sale of property and equipment	180	95	62
Purchase costs of acquired businesses	(20,523)	—	—
Net cash used in investing activities	(85,725)	(41,870)	(8,915)
Cash flows from financing activities:			
Proceeds from issuance of common stock, net	61,253	67,372	609
Principal and accrued interest payments on line of credit and long-term debt	(3,298)	(7,716)	(6,924)
Proceeds from line of credit and issuance of long-term debt	13,741	14,200	7,181
Tax benefit from stock option exercises	—	—	6
Principal payments under capital lease obligations	(375)	(142)	(112)
Net cash provided by financing activities	71,321	73,714	760
Net increase (decrease) in cash and cash equivalents	1,487	33,728	(5,950)
Cash and cash equivalents at beginning of period	43,891	10,163	16,113
Cash and cash equivalents at end of period	$ 45,378	$ 43,891	$ 10,163

(continued)

CONSOLIDATED STATEMENTS OF CASH FLOWS (continued)

	Year ended June 30,		
	1995	1994	1993
Supplemental cash flow information			
Cash paid during the period for:			
Interest	1,067	575	193
Income taxes	—	—	15

See accompanying notes.

CONSOLIDATED BALANCE SHEETS
(Amounts in Thousands, Except Per Share Data)

	June 30,	
	1995	1994
ASSETS		
Current assets:		
Cash and cash equivalents	$ 45,378	$ 43,891
Short-term investments	18,672	24,052
Trade accounts receivable	32,176	8,547
Other receivables	11,103	2,036
Prepaid expenses and other current assets	25,527	5,753
Total current assets	132,856	84,279
Property and equipment at cost, net	70,466	20,306
Other assets:		
Product development costs, net	18,914	7,912
Deferred subscriber acquisition costs, net	77,229	26,392
License rights, net	5,537	53
Other assets	11,479	2,800
Deferred income taxes	35,627	12,842

America Online

CONSOLIDATED BALANCE SHEETS *(continued)*

	June 30,	
	1995	1994
LIABILITIES AND STOCKHOLDERS' EQUITY		
Current liabilities:		
Trade accounts payable	$ 84,639	$ 15,642
Accrued personnel costs	2,829	896
Other accrued expenses and liabilities	23,509	13,076
Deferred revenue	20,021	4,488
Line of credit	484	1,690
Current portion of long-term debt and capital lease obligations	1,830	597
Total current liabilities	133,312	36,389
Long-term liabilities:		
Notes payable	17,369	5,836
Capital lease obligations	2,127	1,179
Deferred income taxes	35,627	12,842
Deferred rent	85	41
Total liabilities	188,520	56,287
Stockholders' equity:		
Preferred stock, $.01 par value; 5,000,000 shares authorized, none issued	—	—
Common stock, $.01 par value; 100,000,000 shares authorized, 37,554,849 and 30,771,212 shares issued and outstanding at June 30, 1995 and 1994, respectively	375	308
Additional paid-in capital	251,539	98,836
Accumulated deficit	(33,970)	(847)
Total stockholders' equity	217,944	98,297
	$406,464	$154,584

See accompanying notes.

NOTES TO CONSOLIDATED FINANCIAL STATEMENTS

1. Organization

America Online, Inc. ("the Company") was incorporated in the State of Delaware in May 1985. The Company, based in Vienna, Virginia, is a leading provider of online services, offering its subscribers a wide variety of services, including e-mail, online conferences, entertainment, software, computing support, interactive magazines and newspapers, and online classes, as well as easy and affordable access to services of the Internet. In addition, the Company is a provider of data network services, new media and interactive marketing services, and multimedia and CD-ROM production services.

2. Summary of Significant Accounting Policies

Principles of Consolidation – The consolidated financial statements include the accounts of the Company and its subsidiaries. All significant intercompany accounts and transactions have been eliminated. Investments in affiliates owned twenty percent or more and corporate joint ventures are accounted for under the equity method. Other securities in companies owned less than twenty percent are accounted for under the cost method.

Business Combinations – Business combinations which have been accounted for under the purchase method of accounting include the results of operations of the acquired business from the date of acquisition. Net assets of the companies acquired are recorded at their fair value to the Company at the date of acquisition.

Other business combinations have been accounted for under the pooling of interests method of accounting. In such cases, the assets, liabilities, and stockholders' equity of the acquired entities were combined with the Company's respective accounts at recorded values. Prior period financial statements have been restated to give effect to the merger unless the effect of the business combination is not material to the financial statements of the Company.

Revenue and cost recognition – Online service revenue is recognized over the period services are provided. Other revenue, consisting principally of marketing, data network and multimedia production services, as well as development and royalty revenues, are recognized as services are rendered. Deferred revenue consists principally of third-party development

funding not yet recognized and monthly subscription fees billed in advance.

Property and equipment – Property and equipment are depreciated or amortized using the straight-line method over the estimated useful life of the asset, which ranges from 5 to 40 years, or over the life of the lease.

Property and equipment under capital leases are stated at the lower of the present value of minimum lease payments at the beginning of the lease term or fair value at inception of the lease.

Deferred subscriber acquisition costs – Subscriber acquisition costs are deferred and charged to operations over a twelve or eighteen month period (straight-line method) beginning the month after such costs are incurred. These costs, which relate directly to subscriber solicitations, principally include printing, production and shipping of starter kits and the costs of obtaining qualified prospects by various targeted direct marketing programs (i.e., direct marketing response cards, mailing lists) and from third parties, and are recorded separately from ordinary operating expenses. No indirect costs are included in subscriber acquisition costs. To date, all subscriber acquisition costs have been incurred for the solicitation of specific identifiable prospects. Costs incurred for other than those targeted at specific identifiable prospects for the Company's services, and general marketing, are expensed as incurred.

The Company's services are sold on a monthly subscription basis. Subscriber acquisition costs incurred to obtain new subscribers are recoverable from revenues generated by such subscribers within a short period of time after such costs are incurred.

Effective July 1, 1992, the Company changed, from twelve months to eighteen months, the period over which it amortizes the costs of deferred subscriber acquisition costs relating to marketing activities in which the Company's starter kit is bundled and distributed by a third-party marketing company. The change in accounting estimate was made to more accurately match revenues and expenses. Based on the Company's experience and the distribution channels used in such marketing activities, there is a greater time lag between the time the Company incurs the cost for the starter kits and the time the starter kits begin to generate new customers than with direct marketing activities. Also, the period over which new subscribers (and related revenues) are generated is longer than that experienced with the use of traditional independent, direct marketing activities. The effect of this change in accounting estimate for the year ended June 30, 1993 was to increase income before extraordinary item and net income by $264,000 ($.01 per share).

In the first quarter of fiscal 1995 the Company adopted the provisions of Statement of Position ("SOP") 93-7, "Reporting on Advertising Costs," which provides guidance on financial reporting on advertising costs. The adoption of SOP 93-7 had no effect on the Company's financial position or results of operations.

Product development costs – The Company capitalizes cost incurred for the production of computer software used in the sale of its services. Costs capitalized include direct labor and related overhead for software produced by the Company and the costs of software purchased from third parties. All costs in the software development process which are classified as research and development are expensed as incurred until technological feasibility has been established. Once technological feasibility has been established, such costs are capitalized until the software is commercially available. To the extent the Company retains the rights to software development funded by third parties, such costs are capitalized in accordance with the Company's normal accounting policies. Amortization is provided on a product-by-product basis, using the greater of the straight-line method or current year revenue as a percent of total revenue estimates for the related software product not to exceed five years, commencing the month after the date of product release.

Product development costs consist of the following:

	Year ended June 30,	
	1995	1994
	(in thousands)	
Balance, beginning of year	$ 7,912	$3,915
Cost capitalized	13,011	5,132
Cost amortized	(2,009)	(1,135)
Balance, end of year	$18,914	$7,912

The accumulated amortization of product development costs related to the production of computer software totaled $7,894,000, and $5,885,000 at June 30, 1995 and 1994, respectively.

Included in product development costs are research and development costs totaling $3,856,000, $2,126,000, and $1,130,000 and other product development costs totaling $6,977,000, $1,050,000 and $579,000 in the years ended June 30, 1995, 1994 and 1993, respectively.

License rights – The cost of acquired license rights is amortized using the straight-line method over the term of the agreement for such license rights, ranging from one to three years.

Goodwill – Goodwill consists of the excess of cost over the fair value of net assets acquired and certain other intangible assets relating to purchase transactions. Goodwill and intangible assets are amortized over periods ranging from 5–10 years.

Operating lease costs – Rent expense for operating leases is recognized on a straight-line basis over the lease term. The difference between rent expense incurred and rental payments is charged or credited to deferred rent.

Cash, cash equivalents and short-term investments – The Company considers all highly liquid investments with an original maturity of three months or less to be cash equivalents. In fiscal 1995, the Company adopted Statement of Financial Accounting Standards No. 115 ("SFAS 115"), "Accounting for Certain Investments in Debt and Equity Securities." The adoption was not material to the Company's financial position or results of operations. The Company has classified all debt and equity securities as available-for-sale. Available-for-sale securities are carried at fair value, with unrealized gains and losses reported as a separate component of stockholders' equity. Realized gains and losses and declines in value judged to be other-than-temporary on available-for-sale securities are included in other income. Available-for-sale securities at June 30, 1995, consisted of U.S. Treasury Bills and other obligations of U.S. Government agencies totaling $7,579,000 and U.S. corporate debt obligations totaling $11,093,000. At June 20, 1995, the estimated fair value of these securities approximated cost.

Net income (loss) per common share – Net income (loss) per share is calculated by dividing income (loss) before extraordinary item and net income (loss) by the weighted average number of common and, when dilutive, common equivalent shares outstanding during the period.

Reclassification – Certain amounts in prior years' consolidated financial statements have been reclassified to conform to the current year presentation.

3. Business Combination

Pooling Transactions

On August 19, 1994, Redgate Communications Corporation ("RCC") was merged with and into a subsidiary of the Company. The Company exchanged 1,789,300 shares of common stock for all of the outstanding common and preferred stock and warrants of RCC. Additionally, 401,148 shares of the Company's common stock were reserved for outstanding stock options issued by RCC and assumed by the Company. The merger was accounted for under the pooling of interests method of accounting, and accordingly, the accompanying consolidated financial statements have been restated for all periods prior to the acquisition to include the financial position, results of operations and cash flows of RCC. Effective August 1994, RCC's fiscal year-end has been changed from December 31 to June 30 to conform to the Company's fiscal year-end.

Revenues and net earnings (loss) for the individual entities are as follows:

	Three months ended September 30, 1994 (unaudited)	Year ended June 30, 1994	1993
	(in thousands)		
Total revenues:			
AOL	$50,783	$104,410	$40,019
RCC	3,813	11,312	11,965
Less intercompany sales	(173)	—	—
	$54,423	$115,722	$51,984
Net income (loss):			
AOL	$ 3,018	$ 6,210	$ 4,210
RCC	(42)	(3,660)	(2,678)
Merger expenses	(1,710)	—	—
	$ 1,266	$ 2,550	$ 1,532

In connection with the merger of the Company and RCC, merger expenses of $1,710,000 were recognized during 1995.

During fiscal 1995, Medior, Inc. and Wide Area Information Servers, Inc. were merged into subsidiaries of the Company. The Company issued 1,082,019 shares of its common stock in the transactions. The transactions were accounted for under the pooling of interests method of accounting. Prior year financial statements have not been restated for the transactions because the effect would not be material to the operations of the Company.

Purchase Transactions

During fiscal 1995, the Company acquired NaviSoft, Inc. ("NaviSoft"), BookLink Technologies, Inc. ("BookLink"), Advanced Network & Services, Inc. ("ANS") and Global Network Navigator, Inc., in transactions accounted for under the purchase method of accounting. The Company paid a total of $97,669,000, of which $75,697,000 was in stock and $21,972,000 was in cash for the acquisitions. Of the aggregate purchase price, approximately $50,335,000 was allocated to in-process

research and development and $55,314,000 was allocated to goodwill and other intangible assets.

The following unaudited pro forma information relating to the BookLink and ANS acquisitions is not necessarily an indication of the combined results that would have occurred had the acquisitions taken place at the beginning of the period, nor is necessarily an indication of the results that may occur in the future. Pro forma information for NaviSoft and Global Network Navigator, Inc. is immaterial to the operations of the consolidated entity. The amount of the aggregate purchase price allocated to in-process research and development for both the NaviSoft and BookLink acquisitions has been excluded from the pro forma information as it is a non-recurring item.

	Year ended June 30,	
	1995	1994
	(in thousands except per share data)	
Revenues	$410,147	$135,785
Income (loss) from operations	23,117	(5,465)
Pro forma income (loss)	11,205	(4,694)
Pro forma income (loss) per share	$ 0.25	$ (0.16)

4. Property and Equipment

Property and equipment consist of the following:

	June 30,	
	1995	1994
	(in thousands)	
Computer equipment	$49,167	$12,418
Furniture and fixtures	4,992	1,398
Buildings	13,800	5,648
Land	6,075	2,052
Building improvements	6,284	1,343
Property under capital leases	8,486	2,686
Leasehold improvements	3,059	306
	91,863	25,851
Less accumulated depreciation and amortization	(21,397)	(5,545)
Net property and equipment	$70,466	$20,306

5. License Rights

License rights consist of the following:

	June 30,	
	1995	1994
	(in thousands)	
License rights	$ 7,484	$ 954
Less accumulated amortization	(1,947)	(901)
	$ 5,537	$ 53

6. Commitments and Contingencies

The Company leases equipment under several long-term capital and operating leases. Future minimum payments under capital leases and noncancelable operating leases with initial terms of one year or more consist of the following:

Year ending June 30,	Capital Leases	Operating Leases
	(in thousands)	
1996	$1,654	$20,997
1997	1,236	21,264
1998	641	19,450
1999	310	8,711
2000	103	3,511
Thereafter	—	2,636
Total minimum lease payments	3,944	$76,569
Less amount representing interest	(402)	
Present value of net minimum capital lease payments, including current portion of $1,415	$3,542	

The Company's rental expense under operating leases in the years ended June 30, 1995, 1994 and 1993 totaled approximately $10,001,000, $2,889,000, and $2,155,000, respectively.

Communication networks – The Company has guaranteed monthly usage levels of data and voice communications with one of its vendors. The remaining commitments are $113,400,000, $59,000,000, $9,000,000 and $6,750,000 for the years ending June 30, 1996, 1997, 1998 and 1999, respectively. The related expense for the years ended June 30, 1995, 1994 and 1993 was $138,793,000, $40,315,000 and $11,226,000, respectively.

Contingencies – Various legal proceedings have arisen against the Company in the ordinary course of business. In the opinion of management, these proceedings will not have a material effect on the financial position of the Company.

7. Notes Payable

Notes payable at June 30, 1995 totaled approximately $18 million and consist primarily of amounts borrowed to finance the purchases of two office buildings. The notes are collateralized by the respective properties. The notes have a variable interest rate equal to 105 basis points above the 30 day London Interbank Offered Rate and a fixed interest rate of 8.48% per annum at June 30, 1995. Aggregate maturities of notes payable for the years ended June 30, 1996, 1997, 1998, 1999, 2000 and thereafter are $415,000, $429,000, $445,000, $462,000, $480,000 and $15,553,000, respectively.

8. Other Income

The following table summarizes the components of other income:

	Year ended June 30,		
	1995	1994	1993
	(in thousands)		
Interest income	$3,920	$1,646	$572
Interest expense	(1,054)	(575)	(172)
Other	157	703	(29)
	$3,023	$1,774	$371

9. Income Taxes

The provision for income taxes is attributable to:

	Year ended June 30,		
	1995	1994	1993
	(in thousands)		
Income before extraordinary item	$15,169	$3,832	$1,897
Tax benefit arising from net operating loss carryforward	—	—	(1,133)
	$15,169	$3,832	$ 764
Current	$ —	$ —	$ 5
Deferred	15,169	3,832	759
	$15,169	$3,832	$ 764

The provision for income taxes differs from the amount computed by applying the statutory federal income tax rate to income before provision for income taxes and extraordinary item. The sources and tax effects of the differences are as follows:

	Year ended June 30,		
	1995	1994	1993
	(in thousands)		
Income tax at the federal statutory rate of 34%	$(6,283)	$2,170	$ 781
State income tax, net of federal benefit	1,597	403	200
Losses relating to RCC	—	1,259	916
Nondeductible merger expenses	750	—	—
Nondeductible charge for purchased research and development	17,114	—	—
Loss, for which no tax benefit was derived	1,632	—	—
Other	359	—	—
	$15,169	$3,832	$1,897

Deferred income taxes arise because of differences in the treatment of income and expense items for financial reporting and income tax purposes, primarily relating to deferred subscriber acquisition and product development costs.

As of June 30, 1995, the Company has net operating loss carryforwards of approximately $109 million for tax purposes which will be available, subject to certain annual limitations, to offset future taxable income. If not used, these loss carryforwards will expire between 2001 and 2010. To the extent that net operating loss carryforwards, when realized, relate to stock option deductions, the resulting benefits will be credited to stockholders' equity.

The Company's income tax provision was computed on the federal statutory rate and the average state statutory rates, net of the related federal benefit.

Effective July 1, 1993 the Company changed its method of accounting for income taxes from the deferred method to the liability method required by FASB Statement No. 109, "Accounting for Income Taxes." As permitted under the new rules, prior years' financial statements have not been restated.

No increase to net income resulted from the cumulative effect of adopting Statement No. 109 as of July 1, 1993. The deferred tax asset increased by approximately $5,965,000 as a result of the adoption. Similarly, the deferred tax liability, stockholders' equity and the valuation allowance increased by approximately $3,173,000, $759,000 and $2,033,000, respectively.

Deferred income taxes reflect the net tax effects of temporary differences between the carrying amounts of assets and liabilities for financial reporting purposes and the amounts used for income tax purposes. Significant components of the Company's deferred tax liabilities and assets are as follows:

	Year ended June 30,	
	1995	1994
	(in thousands)	
Deferred tax liabilities:		
Capitalized software costs	$ 7,008	$ 2,962
Deferred member acquisition costs	28,619	9,880
Net deferred tax liabilities	$35,627	$12,842
Deferred tax assets:		
Net operating loss carryforwards	$39,000	$17,510
Total deferred tax assets	39,000	17,510
Valuation allowance for deferred assets	(3,373)	(4,668)
Net deferred tax assets	$35,627	$12,842

13. Subsequent Event

On August 23, 1995, the Company entered into a stock purchase agreement to purchase Ubique, Ltd., an Israeli company. The Company has agreed to pay approximately $15 million ($1.5 million in cash and $13.5 million in common stock) in the transaction, which is to be accounted for under the purchase method of accounting. Subject to the results of an in-process valuation, a substantial portion of the purchase price may be allocated to in-process research and development and charged to the Company's operations in the first quarter of fiscal 1996.

QUARTERLY INFORMATION (unaudited)

	Quarter Ended				
	September 30	December 31	March 31	June 30	Total
Fiscal 1995[a]					
Online service revenues	$50,056	$69,712	$99,814	$138,916	$358,498
Other revenues	6,880	6,683	9,290	12,939	35,792
Total revenues	56,936	76,395	109,104	151,855	394,290
Income (loss) from operations	4,623	(35,258)	233	11,108	(19,294)
Net income (loss)	1,481	(38,730)	(2,587)	6,189	(33,647)
Net income (loss) per share[b]	$ 0.04	$ (0.20)	$ (0.07)	$ 0.13	$ (0.99)
Fiscal 1994					
Online service revenues	$14,299	$20,292	$28,853	$37,549	$100,993
Other revenues	4,780	4,239	2,836	2,874	14,729
Total revenues	19,079	24,531	31,689	40,423	115,722
Income from operations	531	520	1,931	1,626	4,608
Net income	303	70	1,272	905	2,550
Net income per share[b]	$ 0.01	$ —	$ 0.03	$ 0.02	$ 0.07

a. Historical financial information for amounts previously reported in fiscal 1995 has been adjusted to account for pooling of interest transactions.

b. The sum of per-share earnings (loss) does not equal earnings (loss) per share for the year due to equivalent share calculations which are impacted by the Company's loss in 1995 and by fluctuations in the Company's common stock market prices.

America Online

CHAPTER 3

Overview of Accounting Analysis

The purpose of accounting analysis is to evaluate the degree to which a firm's accounting captures its underlying business reality.[1] By identifying places where there is accounting flexibility, and by evaluating the appropriateness of the firm's accounting policies and estimates, analysts can assess the degree of distortion in a firm's accounting numbers. Another important skill is adjusting a firm's accounting numbers using cash flow and footnote information to "undo" any accounting distortions. Sound accounting analysis improves the reliability of conclusions from financial analysis, the next step in financial statement analysis.

THE INSTITUTIONAL FRAMEWORK
FOR FINANCIAL REPORTING

There is typically a separation between ownership and management in public corporations. Financial statements serve as the vehicle through which owners keep track of their firms' financial situation. On a periodic basis, firms typically produce three financial reports: (1) an income statement that describes the operating performance during a time period, (2) a balance sheet that states the firm's assets and how they are financed, and (3) a cash flow statement (or in some countries, a funds flow statement) that summarizes the cash (or fund) flows of the firm. These statements are accompanied by footnotes that provide additional details on the financial statement line items, as well as by management's narrative discussion of the firm's performance in the Management Discussion and Analysis section.

To evaluate effectively the quality of a firm's financial statement data, the analyst needs to first understand the basic features of financial reporting and the institutional framework that governs them, as discussed in the following sections.

Accrual Accounting

One of the fundamental features of corporate financial reports is that they are prepared using accrual rather than cash accounting. Unlike cash accounting, accrual accounting distinguishes between the recording of costs and benefits associated with economic activities and the actual payment and receipt of cash. Net income is the primary periodic performance index under accrual accounting. To compute net income, the effects of economic transactions are recorded on the basis of *expected,* not necessarily *actual,* cash receipts and payments. Expected cash receipts from the delivery of products or services are recognized as revenues, and expected cash outflows associated with these revenues are recognized as expenses.

While there are many rules and conventions that govern a firm's preparation of financial statements, there are only a few conceptual building blocks that form the foundation of accrual accounting. The following definitions are critical to the income statement, which summarizes a firm's revenues and expenses[2]:

- **Revenues** are economic resources earned during a time period. Revenue recognition is governed by the realization principle, which proposes that revenues should be recognized when (a) the firm has provided all, or substantially all, the goods or services to be delivered to the customer and (b) the customer has paid cash or is expected to pay cash with a reasonable degree of certainty.

- **Expenses** are economic resources used up in a time period. Expense recognition is governed by the matching and the conservatism principles. Under these principles, expenses are (a) costs directly associated with revenues recognized in the same period, or (b) costs associated with benefits that are consumed in this time period, or (c) resources whose future benefits are not reasonably certain.
- **Profit** is the difference between a firm's revenues and expenses in a time period.[3]

The following fundamental relationship is therefore reflected in a firm's income statement:

Profit = Revenues − Expenses

In contrast, the balance sheet is a summary at one point in time. The principles that define a firm's assets, liabilities, equities, revenues, and expenses are as follows:

- **Assets** are economic resources owned by a firm that are (a) likely to produce future economic benefits and (b) measurable with a reasonable degree of certainty.
- **Liabilities** are economic obligations of a firm arising from benefits received in the past that (a) are required to be met with a reasonable degree of certainty and (b) whose timing is reasonably well defined.
- **Equity** is the difference between a firm's assets and its liabilities.

The definitions of assets, liabilities, and equity lead to the fundamental relationship that governs a firm's balance sheet:

Assets = Liabilities + Equity

Delegation of Reporting to Management

While the basic definitions of the elements of a firm's financial statements are simple, their application in practice often involves complex judgments. For example, how should revenues be recognized when a firm sells land to customers and also provides customer financing? If revenue is recognized before cash is collected, how should potential defaults be estimated? Are the outlays associated with research and development activities, whose payoffs are uncertain, assets or expenses when incurred? Are contractual commitments under lease arrangements or post-retirement plans liabilities? If so, how should they be valued?

Because corporate managers have intimate knowledge of their firms' businesses, they are entrusted with the primary task of making the appropriate judgments in portraying myriad business transactions using the basic accrual accounting framework. The accounting discretion granted to managers is potentially valuable because it allows them to reflect inside information in reported financial statements. However, since investors view profits as a measure of managers' performance, managers have an incentive to use their accounting discretion to distort reported profits by making biased assumptions. Further, the use of accounting numbers in contracts between the firm and outsiders provides a motivation for management manipulation of accounting numbers.

Earnings management distorts financial accounting data, making them less valuable to external users of financial statements. Therefore, the delegation of financial reporting decisions to managers has both costs and benefits. Accounting rules and auditing are mechanisms designed to reduce the cost and preserve the benefit of delegating financial reporting to corporate managers. The legal system is used to adjudicate disputes between managers, auditors, and investors.

Generally Accepted Accounting Principles

Given that it is difficult for outside investors to determine whether managers have used accounting flexibility to signal their proprietary information or merely to disguise reality, a number of accounting conventions have evolved to mitigate the problem. For example, in most countries financial statements are prepared using the historical cost convention, where assets and liabilities are recorded at historical exchange prices rather than fair values, replacement values, or values in use. This reduces managers' ability to overstate the value of the assets that they have acquired or developed, or to understate the value of liabilities. Of course, historical cost also limits the information that is available to investors about the potential of the firm's assets, since exchange prices are usually different from fair values or values in use.

Accounting standards and rules also limit management's ability to misuse accounting judgment by regulating how particular types of transactions are recorded. For example, accounting standards for leases stipulate how firms are to record contractual arrangements to lease resources. Similarly, pension and other post-employment benefit standards describe how firms are to record commitments to provide pensions and other retirement benefits for employees.

In the United States, the Securities and Exchange Commission (SEC) has the legal authority to set accounting standards. The SEC typically relies on private sector accounting bodies to undertake this task. Since 1973 accounting standards in the United States have been set by the Financial Accounting Standards Board (FASB). There are similar private sector or public sector accounting standard-setting bodies in many other countries. In addition, the International Accounting Standards Committee (IASC) has been attempting to set worldwide accounting standards, though IASC's pronouncements are not legally binding in the United States as of now.

Uniform accounting standards attempt to reduce managers' ability to record similar economic transactions in dissimilar ways either over time or across firms. Thus they create a uniform accounting language and increase the credibility of financial statements by limiting a firm's ability to distort them. Increased uniformity from accounting standards, however, comes at the expense of reduced flexibility for managers to reflect genuine business differences in a firm's accounting decisions. Rigid accounting standards work best for economic transactions whose accounting treatment is not predicated on managers' proprietary information. However, when there is significant business judgment involved in assessing a transaction's economic consequences, rigid standards are likely to be dysfunctional because they prevent managers from using their superior business knowledge. Further, if accounting standards are too rigid, they may induce managers to expend economic resources to restructure business transactions to achieve a desired accounting result.

External Auditing

Broadly defined as a verification of the integrity of the reported financial statements by someone other than the preparer, external auditing ensures that managers use accounting rules and conventions consistently over time, and that their accounting estimates are reasonable. In the U.S., all listed companies are required to have their financial statements audited by an independent public accountant. The standards and procedures to be followed by independent auditors are set by the American Institute of Certified Public Accountants (AICPA). These standards are known as Generally Accepted Auditing Standards (GAAS). While auditors issue an opinion on published financial statements, it is important to remember that the primary responsibility for the statements still rests with corporate managers.

Auditing improves the quality and credibility of accounting data by limiting a firm's ability to distort financial statements to suit its own purposes. However, as recent audit failures at companies such as Enron and Worldcom show, auditing is imperfect. Audits cannot review all of a firm's transactions. They can also fail because of lapses in quality, or because of lapses in judgment by auditors who fail to challenge management for fear of losing future business.

Third-party auditing may also reduce the quality of financial reporting because it constrains the kind of accounting rules and conventions that evolve over time. For example, the FASB considers the views of auditors in the standard-setting process. Auditors are likely to argue against accounting standards that produce numbers which are difficult to audit, even if the proposed rules produce relevant information for investors.

Legal Liability

The legal environment in which accounting disputes between managers, auditors, and investors are adjudicated can also have a significant effect on the quality of reported numbers. The threat of lawsuits and resulting penalties have the beneficial effect of improving the accuracy of disclosure. However, the potential for significant legal liability might also discourage managers and auditors from supporting accounting proposals requiring risky forecasts, for example, forward-looking disclosures. The U.S. auditing community often expresses this type of concern.

FACTORS INFLUENCING ACCOUNTING QUALITY

Because the mechanisms that limit managers' ability to distort accounting data themselves add noise, it is not optimal to use accounting regulation to eliminate managerial flexibility completely. Therefore, real-world accounting systems leave considerable room for managers to influence financial statement data. The net result is that information in corporate financial reports is noisy and biased, even in the presence of accounting regulation and external auditing.[4] The objective of accounting analysis is to evaluate the degree to which a firm's accounting captures its underlying business reality and to "undo" any accounting distortions. When potential distortions are large, accounting analysis can add considerable value.[5]

There are three potential sources of noise and bias in accounting data: (1) that introduced by rigidity in accounting rules, (2) random forecast errors, and (3) systematic reporting choices made by corporate managers to achieve specific objectives. Each of these factors is discussed below.

Noise from Accounting Rules

Accounting rules introduce noise and bias because it is often difficult to restrict management discretion without reducing the information content of accounting data. For example, the Statement of Financial Accounting Standards No. 2 issued by the FASB requires firms to expense research outlays when they are incurred. Clearly, some research expenditures have future value while others do not. However, because SFAS 2 does not allow firms to distinguish between the two types of expenditures, it leads to a systematic distortion of reported accounting numbers. Broadly speaking, the degree of distortion introduced by accounting standards depends on how well uniform accounting standards capture the nature of a firm's transactions.

Forecast Errors

Another source of noise in accounting data arises from pure forecast error, because managers cannot predict future consequences of current transactions perfectly. For example, when a firm sells products on credit, accrual accounting requires managers to make a judgment about the probability of collecting payments from customers. If payments are deemed "reasonably certain," the firm treats the transactions as sales, creating accounts receivable on its balance sheet. Managers then make an estimate of the proportion of receivables that will not be collected. Because managers do not have perfect foresight, actual defaults are likely to be different from estimated customer defaults, leading to a forecast error. The extent of errors in managers' accounting forecasts depends on a variety of factors, including the complexity of the business transactions, the predictability of the firm's environment, and unforeseen economy-wide changes.

Managers' Accounting Choices

Corporate managers also introduce noise and bias into accounting data through their own accounting decisions. Managers have a variety of incentives to exercise their accounting discretion to achieve certain objectives[6]:

- *Accounting-based debt covenants.* Managers may make accounting decisions to meet certain contractual obligations in their debt covenants. For example, firms' lending agreements with banks and other debt holders require them to meet covenants related to interest coverage, working capital ratios, and net worth, all defined in terms of accounting numbers. Violation of these constraints may be costly because it allows lenders to demand immediate payment of their loans. Managers of firms close to violating debt covenants have an incentive to select accounting policies and estimates to reduce the probability of covenant violation. The debt covenant motivation for managers' accounting decisions has been analyzed by a number of accounting researchers.[7]

- *Management compensation.* Another motivation for managers' accounting choice comes from the fact that their compensation and job security are often tied to reported profits. For example, many top managers receive bonus compensation if they exceed certain prespecified profit targets. This provides motivation for managers to choose accounting policies and estimates to maximize their expected compensation.[8]

- *Corporate control contests.* In corporate control contests, including hostile takeovers and proxy fights, competing management groups attempt to win over the firm's shareholders. Accounting numbers are used extensively in debating managers' performance in these contests. Therefore, managers may make accounting decisions to influence investor perceptions in corporate control contests.[9]

- *Tax considerations.* Managers may also make reporting choices to trade off between financial reporting and tax considerations. For example, U.S. firms are required to use LIFO inventory accounting for shareholder reporting in order to use it for tax reporting. Under LIFO, when prices are rising, firms report lower profits, thereby reducing tax payments. Some firms may forgo the tax reduction in order to report higher profits in their financial statements.[10]

- *Regulatory considerations.* Since accounting numbers are used by regulators in a variety of contexts, managers of some firms may make accounting decisions to influence regulatory outcomes. Examples of regulatory situations where accounting numbers are used include antitrust actions, import tariffs to protect domestic industries, and tax policies.[11]

- *Capital market considerations.* Managers may make accounting decisions to influence the perceptions of capital markets. When there are information asymmetries between managers and outsiders, this strategy may succeed in influencing investor perceptions, at least temporarily.[12]

- *Stakeholder considerations.* Managers may also make accounting decisions to influence the perception of important stakeholders in the firm. For example, since labor unions can use healthy profits as a basis for demanding wage increases, managers may make accounting decisions to decrease income when they are facing union contract negotiations. In countries like Germany, where labor unions are strong, these considerations appear to play an important role in firms' accounting policy. Other important stakeholders that firms may wish to influence through their financial reports include suppliers and customers.
- *Competitive considerations.* The dynamics of competition in an industry might also influence a firm's reporting choices. For example, a firm's segment disclosure decisions may be influenced by its concern that disaggregated disclosure may help competitors in their business decisions. Similarly, firms may not disclose data on their margins by product line for fear of giving away proprietary information. Finally, firms may discourage new entrants by making income-decreasing accounting choices.

In addition to accounting policy choices and estimates, the level of disclosure is also an important determinant of a firm's accounting quality. Corporate managers can choose disclosure policies that make it more or less costly for external users of financial reports to understand the true economic picture of their businesses. Accounting regulations usually prescribe minimum disclosure requirements, but they do not restrict managers from voluntarily providing additional disclosures. Managers can use various parts of the financial reports, including the Letter to the Shareholders, Management Discussion and Analysis, and footnotes, to describe the company's strategy, its accounting policies, and its current performance. There is wide variation across firms in how managers use their disclosure flexibility.[13]

STEPS IN DOING ACCOUNTING ANALYSIS

In this section we discuss a series of steps that an analyst can follow to evaluate a firm's accounting quality.

Step 1: Identify Key Accounting Policies

As discussed in the chapter on business strategy analysis, a firm's industry characteristics and its own competitive strategy determine its key success factors and risks. One of the goals of financial statement analysis is to evaluate how well these success factors and risks are being managed by the firm. In accounting analysis, therefore, the analyst should identify and evaluate the policies and the estimates the firm uses to measure its critical factors and risks.

Key success factors in the banking industry include interest and credit risk management; in the retail industry, inventory management is a key success factor; and for a manufacturer competing on product quality and innovation, research and development and product defects after the sale are key areas of concern. One of the key success factors in the leasing business is to make accurate forecasts of residual values of the leased equipment at the end of the lease terms. In each of these cases, the analyst has to identify the accounting measures the firm uses to capture these business constructs, the policies that determine how the measures are implemented, and the key estimates embedded in these policies. For example, the accounting measure a bank uses to capture credit risk is its loan loss reserves, and the accounting measure that captures product quality for a manu-facturer is its warranty expenses and reserves. For a firm in the equipment leasing indus-try, one of the most important accounting policies is the way residual values are recorded. Residual values influence the company's reported profits and its asset base. If residual values are overestimated, the firm runs the risk of having to take large write-offs in the future.

Step 2: Assess Accounting Flexibility

Not all firms have equal flexibility in choosing their key accounting policies and estimates. Some firms' accounting choice is severely constrained by accounting standards and con-ventions. For example, even though research and development is a key success factor for biotechnology companies, managers have no accounting discretion in reporting on this ac-tivity. Similarly, even though marketing and brand building are key to the success of con-sumer goods firms, they are required to expense all their marketing outlays. In contrast, managing credit risk is one of the critical success factors for banks, and bank managers have the freedom to estimate expected defaults on their loans. Similarly, software developers have the flexibility to decide at what points in their development cycles the outlays can be capitalized.

If managers have little flexibility in choosing accounting policies and estimates related to their key success factors (as in the case of biotechnology firms), accounting data are likely to be less informative for understanding the firm's economics. In contrast, if manag-ers have considerable flexibility in choosing the policies and estimates (as in the case of software developers), accounting numbers have the potential to be informative, depending upon how managers exercise this flexibility.

Regardless of the degree of accounting flexibility a firm's managers have in measuring their key success factors and risks, they will have some flexibility with respect to several other accounting policies. For example, all firms have to make choices with respect to depreciation policy (straight-line or accelerated methods), inventory accounting policy (LIFO, FIFO, or Average Cost), policy for amortizing goodwill (write-off over forty years or less), and policies regarding the estimation of pension and other post-employment ben-efits (expected return on plan assets, discount rate for liabilities, and rate of increase in wages and health care costs). Since all these policy choices can have a significant impact on the reported performance of a firm, they offer an opportunity for the firm to manage its reported numbers.

Step 3: Evaluate Accounting Strategy

When managers have accounting flexibility, they can use it either to communicate their firm's economic situation or to hide true performance. Some of the strategy questions one could ask in examining how managers exercise their accounting flexibility include the following:

- How do the firm's accounting policies compare to the norms in the industry? If they are dissimilar, is it because the firm's competitive strategy is unique? For example, consider a firm that reports a lower warranty allowance than the industry average. One explanation is that the firm competes on the basis of high quality and has invested con-siderable resources to reduce the rate of product failure. An alternative explanation is that the firm is merely understating its warranty liabilities.

- Do managers face strong incentives to use accounting discretion to manage earnings? For example, is the firm close to violating bond covenants? Or are the managers having difficulty meeting accounting-based bonus targets? Does management own significant stock? Is the firm in the middle of a proxy fight or union negotiations? Managers may also make accounting decisions to reduce tax payments or to influence the perceptions of the firm's competitors.

- Has the firm changed any of its policies or estimates? What is the justification? What is the impact of these changes? For example, if warranty expenses decreased, is it because the firm made significant investments to improve quality?

- Have the company's policies and estimates been realistic in the past? For example, firms may overstate their revenues and understate their expenses during the year by manipulating quarterly reports, which are not subject to a full-blown external audit. However, the auditing process at the end of the fiscal year forces such companies to make large fourth-quarter adjustments, providing an opportunity for the analyst to assess the quality of the firm's interim reporting. Similarly, firms that depreciate fixed assets too slowly will be forced to take a large write-off later. A history of write-offs may be, therefore, a sign of prior earnings management.

- Does the firm structure any significant business transactions so that it can achieve certain accounting objectives? For example, leasing firms can alter lease terms (the length of the lease or the bargain purchase option at the end of the lease term) so that the transactions qualify as sales-type leases for the lessors. Enron structured acquisitions of joint venture interests and hedging transactions with special purpose entities to avoid having to show joint venture liabilities, and to avoid reporting investment losses in its financial statements.[14] Such behavior may suggest that the firm's managers are willing to expend economic resources merely to achieve an accounting objective.

Step 4: Evaluate the Quality of Disclosure

Managers can make it more or less easy for an analyst to assess the firm's accounting quality and to use its financial statements to understand business reality. While accounting rules require a certain amount of minimum disclosure, managers have considerable choice in the matter. Disclosure quality, therefore, is an important dimension of a firm's accounting quality.

In assessing a firm's disclosure quality, an analyst could ask the following questions:

- Does the company provide adequate disclosures to assess the firm's business strategy and its economic consequences? For example, some firms use the Letter to the Shareholders in their annual report to clearly lay out the firm's industry conditions, its competitive position, and management's plans for the future. Others use the letter to puff up the firm's financial performance and gloss over any competitive difficulties the firm might be facing.

- Do the footnotes adequately explain the key accounting policies and assumptions and their logic? For example, if a firm's revenue and expense recognition policies differ from industry norms, the firm can explain its choices in a footnote. Similarly, when there are significant changes in a firm's policies, footnotes can be used to disclose the reasons.

- Does the firm adequately explain its current performance? The Management Discussion and Analysis section of the annual report provides an opportunity to help analysts understand the reasons behind a firm's performance changes. Some firms use this section to link financial performance to business conditions. For example, if profit margins went down in a period, was it because of price competition or because of increases in manufacturing costs? If the selling and general administrative expenses went up, was it because the firm is investing in a differentiation strategy, or because unproductive overhead expenses were creeping up?

- If accounting rules and conventions restrict the firm from measuring its key success factors appropriately, does the firm provide adequate additional disclosure to help outsiders understand how these factors are being managed? For example, if a firm invests in product quality and customer service, accounting rules do not allow the management to capitalize these outlays, even when the future benefits are certain. The firm's Management Discussion and Analysis can be used to highlight how these outlays are being managed and their performance consequences. For example, the firm can disclose physical indexes of defect rates and customer satisfaction so that outsiders can assess the progress being made in these areas and the future cash flow consequences of these actions.

- If a firm is in multiple business segments, what is the quality of segment disclosure? Some firms provide excellent discussion of their performance by product segments and geographic segments. Others lump many different businesses into one broad segment. The level of competition in an industry and management's willingness to share desegregated performance data influence a firm's quality of segment disclosure.

- How forthcoming is the management with respect to bad news? A firm's disclosure quality is most clearly revealed by the way management deals with bad news. Does it adequately explain the reasons for poor performance? Does the company clearly articulate its strategy, if any, to address the company's performance problems?

- How good is the firm's investor relations program? Does the firm provide fact books with detailed data on the firm's business and performance? Is the management accessible to analysts?

Step 5: Identify Potential Red Flags

In addition to the above analysis, a common approach to accounting quality analysis is to look for "red flags" pointing to questionable accounting quality. These indicators suggest that the analyst should examine certain items more closely or gather more information on them. Some common red flags are the following:

- *Unexplained changes in accounting, especially when performance is poor.* This may suggest that managers are using their accounting discretion to "dress up" their financial statements.[15]

- *Unexplained transactions that boost profits.* For example, firms might undertake balance sheet transactions, such as asset sales or debt for equity swaps, to realize gains in periods when operating performance is poor.[16]

- *Unusual increases in accounts receivable in relation to sales increases.* This may suggest that the company is relaxing its credit policies or artificially loading up its distribution channels to record revenues during the current period. If credit policies are relaxed unduly, the firm may face receivable write-offs in subsequent periods as a result of customer defaults. If the firm accelerates shipments to its distributors, it may either face product returns or reduced shipments in subsequent periods.

- *Unusual increases in inventories in relation to sales increases.* If the inventory build-up is due to an increase in finished goods inventory, it could be a sign that demand for the firm's products is slowing down, suggesting that the firm may be forced to cut prices (and hence earn lower margins) or write down its inventory. A build-up in work-in-progress inventory tends to be good news on average, probably signaling that managers expect an increase in sales. If the build-up is in raw materials, it could suggest manufacturing or procurement inefficiencies, leading to an increase in cost of goods sold (and hence lower margins).[17]

- *An increasing gap between a firm's reported income and its cash flow from operating activities.* While it is legitimate for accrual accounting numbers to differ from cash flows, there is usually a steady relationship between the two if the company's accounting policies remain the same. Therefore, any *change* in the relationship between reported profits and operating cash flows might indicate subtle changes in the firm's accrual estimates. For example, a firm undertaking large construction contracts might use the percentage-of-completion method to record revenues. While earnings and operating cash flows are likely to differ for such a firm, they should bear a steady relationship to each other. Now suppose the firm increases revenues in a period through an aggressive application of the percentage-of-completion method. Then its earnings will go up, but its cash flow remains unaffected. This change in the firm's accounting quality will be manifested by a *change* in the relationship between the firm's earnings and cash flows.

- *An increasing gap between a firm's reported income and its tax income.* Once again, it is quite legitimate for a firm to follow different accounting policies for financial reporting and tax accounting as long as the tax law allows it.[18] However, the relationship between a firm's book and tax accounting is likely to remain constant over time, unless there are significant changes in tax rules or accounting standards. Thus, an *increasing* gap between a firm's reported income and its tax income may indicate that financial reporting to shareholders has become more aggressive. For example, warranty expenses are estimated on an accrual basis for financial reporting, but they are recorded on a cash basis for tax reporting. Unless there is a big change in the firm's product quality, these two numbers bear a consistent relationship to each other. Therefore, a change in this relationship can be an indication either that product quality is changing significantly or that financial reporting estimates are changing.

- *A tendency to use financing mechanisms like research and development partnerships, special purpose entities, and the sale of receivables with recourse.* While these arrangements may have a sound business logic, they can also provide management with an opportunity to understate the firm's liabilities and/or overstate its assets.[19]

- *Unexpected large asset write-offs.* This may suggest that management is slow to incorporate changing business circumstances into its accounting estimates. Asset write-offs may also be a result of unexpected changes in business circumstances.[20]

- *Large fourth-quarter adjustments.* A firm's annual reports are audited by the external auditors, but its interim financial statements are usually only reviewed. If a firm's management is reluctant to make appropriate accounting estimates (such as provisions for uncollectable receivables) in its interim statements, it could be forced to make adjustments at the end of the year as a result of pressure from its external auditors. A consistent pattern of fourth-quarter adjustments, therefore, may indicate aggressive management of interim reporting.[21]

- *Qualified audit opinions or changes in independent auditors that are not well justified.* These may indicate a firm's aggressive attitude or a tendency to "opinion shop."

- *Related-party transactions or transactions between related entities.* These transactions may lack the objectivity of the marketplace, and managers' accounting estimates related to these transactions are likely to be more subjective and potentially self-serving.[22]

While the preceding list provides a number of red flags for potentially poor accounting quality, it is important to do further analysis before reaching final conclusions. Each of the red flags has multiple interpretations; some interpretations are based on sound business reasons, and others indicate questionable accounting. It is, therefore, best to use the red flag analysis as a starting point for further probing, not as an end point in itself.[23]

Step 6: Undo Accounting Distortions

If the accounting analysis suggests that the firm's reported numbers are misleading, analysts should attempt to restate the reported numbers to reduce the distortion to the extent possible. It is, of course, virtually impossible to perfectly undo the distortion using outside information alone. However, some progress can be made in this direction by using the cash flow statement and the financial statement footnotes.

A firm's cash flow statement provides a reconciliation of its performance based on accrual accounting and cash accounting. If the analyst is unsure of the quality of the firm's accrual accounting, the cash flow statement provides an alternative benchmark of its performance. The cash flow statement also provides information on how individual line items in the income statement diverge from the underlying cash flows. For example, if an analyst is concerned that the firm is aggressively capitalizing certain costs that should be expensed, the information in the cash flow statement provides a basis to make the necessary adjustment.

Financial statement footnotes also provide a lot of information that is potentially useful in restating reported accounting numbers. For example, when a firm changes its accounting policies, it provides a footnote indicating the effect of that change if it is material. Similarly, some firms provide information on the details of accrual estimates such as the allowance for bad debts. The tax footnote usually provides information on the differences between a firm's accounting policies for shareholder reporting and tax reporting. Since tax reporting is often more conservative than shareholder reporting, the information in the tax footnote can be used to estimate what the earnings reported to shareholders would be under more conservative policies.

In Chapter 4, we show how to make accounting adjustments for the some of the most common types of accounting distortions.

ACCOUNTING ANALYSIS PITFALLS

There are several potential pitfalls and common misconceptions in accounting analysis that an analyst should avoid.

1. Conservative accounting is not "good" accounting.

Some firms take the approach that it pays to be conservative in financial reporting and to set aside as much as possible for contingencies. This logic is commonly used to justify the expensing of R&D and advertising, and the rapid write-down of intangible assets such as goodwill. It is also used to support large loss reserves for insurance companies, for merger expenses, and for restructuring charges.

From the standpoint of a financial statement user, it is important to recognize that conservative accounting is not the same as "good" accounting. Financial statement users want to evaluate how well a firm's accounting captures business reality in an unbiased manner, and conservative accounting can be as misleading as aggressive accounting in this respect.

It is certainly true that it can be difficult to estimate the economic benefits from many in-tangibles. However, the intangible nature of some assets does not mean that they do not have value. Indeed, for many firms these types of assets are their most valued. For example, Merck's two most valued assets are its research capabilities that permit it to generate new drugs, and its sales force that enables it to sell those drugs to doctors. Yet neither is recorded on Merck's balance sheet. From the investors' point of view, accountants' reluctance to val-ue intangible assets does not diminish their importance. If they are not included in financial statements, investors have to look to alternative sources of information on these assets.

Further, conservative accounting often provides managers with opportunities for "income smoothing," which may prevent analysts from recognizing poor performance in a timely fashion. Finally, over time investors are likely to figure out which firms are conser-vative and may discount their management's disclosures and communications.

2. Not all unusual accounting is questionable.

It is easy to confuse unusual accounting with questionable accounting. While unusual ac-counting choices might make a firm's performance difficult to compare with other firms' performance, such an accounting choice might be justified if the company's business is un-usual. For example, firms that follow differentiated strategies or firms that structure their business in an innovative manner to take advantage of particular market situations may make unusual accounting choices to properly reflect their business. Therefore it is impor-tant to evaluate a company's accounting choices in the context of its business strategy.

Similarly, it is important not to necessarily attribute all *changes* in a firm's accounting policies and accruals to earnings management motives.[24] Accounting changes might be merely reflecting changed business circumstances. For example, as already discussed, a firm that shows unusual increases in its inventory might be preparing for a new product introduction. Similarly, unusual increases in receivables might merely be due to changes in a firm's sales strategy. Unusual decreases in the allowance for uncollectable receivables might be reflecting a firm's changed customer focus. It is therefore important for an ana-lyst to consider all possible explanations for accounting changes and investigate them using the qualitative information available in a firm's financial statements.

VALUE OF ACCOUNTING DATA AND ACCOUNTING ANALYSIS

What is the value of accounting information and accounting analysis? Given the incentives and opportunities for managers to affect their firms' reported accounting numbers, some have argued that accounting data and accounting analysis are not likely to be useful for investors.

Researchers have examined the value of accounting by estimating the return that could be earned by an investor with perfect earnings foresight one year prior to an earnings announcement.[25] The findings show that by buying stocks of firms with increased earnings and selling stocks of firms with decreased earnings each year, a hypothetical investor could earn an average portfolio return of 37.5 percent in the period 1954 to 1996. This is equivalent to 44 percent of the return that could have been earned if the investor had per-fect foresight of the stock price itself for one year and bought stocks with increased prices and sold stocks whose price decreased. Perfect foresight of ROE permits the investor to earn an even higher rate of return, 43 percent, than perfect earnings foresight. This is equivalent to 50 percent of the return that could be earned with perfect stock price fore-sight.

In contrast, cash flow data appear to be considerably less valuable than earnings or ROE information. Perfect foresight of cash flows from operations would permit the hypothetical investor to earn an average annual return of only 9 percent, equivalent to 11 percent of the return that could be earned with perfect foresight of stock prices.

Overall, this research suggests that the institutional arrangements and conventions cre-ated to mitigate potential misuse of accounting by managers are effective in providing assurance to investors. The research indicates that investors do not view earnings manage-ment as so pervasive as to make earnings data unreliable.

A number of research studies have examined whether superior accounting analysis is a valuable activity. By and large, this evidence indicates that there are opportunities for superior analysts to earn positive stock returns. Research findings indicate that companies criticized in the financial press for misleading financial reporting subsequently suffered an average stock price drop of 8 percent.[26] Firms where managers appeared to inflate reported earnings prior to an equity issue and subsequently reported poor earnings performance had more negative stock performance after the offer than firms with no apparent earnings man-agement.[27] Finally, firms subject to SEC investigation for earnings management showed an average stock price decline of 9 percent when the earnings management was first announced and continued to have poor stock performance for up to two years.[28]

These findings imply that analysts who are able to identify firms with misleading accounting are able to create value for investors. The findings also indicate that the stock market ultimately sees through earnings management. For all of these cases, earnings management is eventually uncovered and the stock price responds negatively to evidence that firms have inflated prior earnings through misleading accounting.

SUMMARY

In summary, accounting analysis is an important step in the process of analyzing corporate financial reports. The purpose of accounting analysis is to evaluate the degree to which a firm's accounting captures the underlying business reality. Sound accounting analysis im-proves the reliability of conclusions from financial analysis, the next step in financial state-ment analysis.

There are six key steps in accounting analysis. The analyst begins by identifying the key accounting policies and estimates, given the firm's industry and its business strategy. The second step is to evaluate the degree of flexibility available to managers, given the accounting rules and conventions. Next, the analyst has to evaluate how managers exercise their accounting flexibility and the likely motivations behind managers' accounting strat-egy. The fourth step involves assessing the depth and quality of a firm's disclosures. The analyst should next identify any red flags needing further investigation. The final account-ing analysis step is to restate accounting numbers to remove any noise and bias introduced by the accounting rules and management decisions.

The next chapter discusses how to implement these concepts and shows how to make some of the most common types of adjustments.

DISCUSSION QUESTIONS

1. A finance student states, "I don't understand why anyone pays any attention to accounting earnings numbers, given that a 'clean' number like cash from operations is readily available." Do you agree? Why or why not?

2. Fred argues, "The standards that I like most are the ones that eliminate all management discretion in reporting—that way I get uniform numbers across all companies and don't have to worry about doing accounting analysis." Do you agree? Why or why not?

3. Bill Simon says, "We should get rid of the FASB and SEC, since free market forces will make sure that companies report reliable information." Do you agree? Why or why not?

4. Many firms recognize revenues at the point of shipment. This provides an incentive to accelerate revenues by shipping goods at the end of the quarter. Consider two companies, one of which ships its product evenly throughout the quarter, and the second of which ships all its products in the last two weeks of the quarter. Each company's customers pay thirty days after receiving shipment. Using accounting ratios, how can you distinguish these companies?

5. a. If management reports truthfully, what economic events are likely to prompt the following accounting changes?
   • Increase in the estimated life of depreciable assets
   • Decrease in the uncollectibles allowance as a percentage of gross receivables
   • Recognition of revenues at the point of delivery rather than at the point cash is received
   • Capitalization of a higher proportion of software R&D costs
   b. What features of accounting, if any, would make it costly for dishonest managers to make the same changes without any corresponding economic changes?

6. The conservatism principle arises because of concerns about management's incentives to overstate the firm's performance. Joe Banks argues, "We could get rid of conservatism and make accounting numbers more useful if we delegated financial reporting to independent auditors rather than to corporate managers." Do you agree? Why or why not?

7. A fund manager states, "I refuse to buy any company that makes a voluntary accounting change, since it's certainly a case of management trying to hide bad news." Can you think of any alternative interpretation?

NOTES

1. Accounting analysis is sometimes also called quality of earnings analysis. We prefer to use the term accounting analysis since we are discussing a broader concept than merely a firm's earnings quality.

2. These definitions paraphrase those of the Financial Accounting Standards Board, Statement of Financial Accounting Concepts No. 6, "Elements of Financial Statements" (1985). Our intent is to present the definitions at a conceptual, not technical, level. For more complete discussion of these and related concepts, see the FASB's Statements of Financial Accounting Concepts.

3. Strictly speaking, the comprehensive net income of a firm also includes gains and losses from increases and decreases in equity from nonoperating activities or extraordinary items.

4. Thus, although accrual accounting is theoretically superior to cash accounting in measuring a firm's periodic performance, the distortions it introduces can make accounting data less valuable to

users. If these distortions are large enough, current cash flows may measure a firm's periodic performance better than accounting profits. The relative usefulness of cash flows and accounting profits in measuring performance, therefore, varies from firm to firm. For empirical evidence on this issue, see P. Dechow, "Accounting Earnings and Cash Flows as Measures of Firm Performance: The Role of Accounting Accruals," *Journal of Accounting and Economics* 18 (July 1994): 3–42.

5. For example, Abraham Briloff wrote a series of accounting analyses of public companies in *Barron's* over several years. On average, the stock prices of the analyzed companies changed by about 8 percent on the day these articles were published, indicating the potential value of performing such analysis. For a more complete discussion of this evidence, see G. Foster, "Briloff and the Capital Market," *Journal of Accounting Research* 17 (Spring 1979): 262–74.

6. For a complete discussion of these motivations, see *"Positive Accounting Theory,"* by R. Watts and J. Zimmerman, (Englewood Cliffs, NJ: Prentice-Hall, 1986). A summary of this research is provided by T. Fields, T. Lys, and L. Vincent in "Empirical Research on Accounting Choice," *Journal of Accounting & Economics* 31 (September 2001): 255–307.

7. The most convincing evidence supporting the covenant hypothesis is reported in a study of the accounting decisions by firms in financial distress: A. Sweeney, "Debt-Covenant Violations and Managers' Accounting Responses," *Journal of Accounting and Economics* 17 (May 1994): 281–308.

8. Studies that examine the bonus hypothesis generally report evidence supporting the view that managers' accounting decisions are influenced by compensation considerations. See, for example, P. Healy, "The Effect of Bonus Schemes on Accounting Decisions," *Journal of Accounting and Economics* 7 (April 1985): 85–107; R. Holthausen, D. Larcker, and R. Sloan, "Annual Bonus Schemes and the Manipulation of Earnings," *Journal of Accounting and Economics* 19 (February 1995): 29–74; and F. Guidry, A. Leone, and S. Rock, "Earnings-Based Bonus Plans and Earnings Management by Business Unit Managers," *Journal of Accounting and Economics*, 26 (January 1999): 113–42.

9. L. DeAngelo, "Managerial Competition, Information Costs, and Corporate Governance: The Use of Accounting Performance Measures in Proxy Contests," *Journal of Accounting and Economics* 10 (January 1988): 3–36.

10. The trade-off between taxes and financial reporting in the context of managers' accounting decisions is discussed in detail in *Taxes and Business Strategy* by M. Scholes and M. Wolfson (Englewood Cliffs, NJ: Prentice-Hall, 1992). Many empirical studies have examined firms' LIFO/FIFO choices.

11. Several researchers have documented that firms affected by such situations have a motivation to influence regulators' perceptions through accounting decisions. For example, J. Jones documents that firms seeking import protections make income-decreasing accounting decisions in "Earnings Management During Import Relief Investigations," *Journal of Accounting Research* 29, no. 2 (Autumn 1991): 193–228. A number of studies find that banks that are close to minimum capital requirements overstate loan loss provisions, understate loan write-offs, and recognize abnormal realized gains on securities portfolios (see S. Moyer, "Capital Adequacy Ratio Regulations and Accounting Choices in Commercial Banks," *Journal of Accounting and Economics* 12 (1990): 123–54; M. Scholes, G. P. Wilson, and M. Wolfson, "Tax Planning, Regulatory Capital Planning, and Financial Reporting Strategy for Commercial Banks," *Review of Financial Studies* 3 (1990): 625–50; A. Beatty, S. Chamberlain, and J. Magliolo, "Managing Financial Reports of Commercial Banks: The Influence of Taxes, Regulatory Capital and Earnings," *Journal of Accounting Research* 33, no. 2 (1995): 231–61; and J. Collins, D. Shackelford, and J. Wahlen, "Bank Differences in the Coordination of Regulatory Capital, Earnings and Taxes," *Journal of Accounting Research* 33, no. 2 (Autumn 1995): 263–91). Finally, Petroni finds that financially weak property-casualty insurers that risk regulatory attention understate claim loss reserves: K. Petroni, "Optimistic Reporting in the Property Casualty Insurance Industry," *Journal of Accounting and Economics* 15 (December 1992): 485–508.

12. P. Healy and K. Palepu "The Effect of Firms' Financial Disclosure Strategies on Stock Prices," *Accounting Horizons* 7 (March 1993): 1–11. For a summary of the empirical evidence, see P. Healy and J. Wahlen, "A Review of the Earnings Management Literature and Its Implications for Standard Setting," *Accounting Horizons* 13 (December 1999): 365–84.

13. Financial analysts pay close attention to managers' disclosure strategies; the Association for Investment Management and Research publishes an annual report evaluating them for U.S. firms.

For a discussion of these ratings, see M. Lang and R. Lundholm, "Cross-sectional Determinants of Analysts' Ratings of Corporate Disclosures," *Journal of Accounting Research* 31 (Autumn 1993): 246–71.

14. See P. Healy and K. Palepu, "The Fall of Enron," *Journal of Economic Perspectives* 17, no. 2 (Spring 2003): 3–26.

15. For a detailed analysis of a company that made such changes, see "Anatomy of an Accounting Change" by K. Palepu in *Accounting & Management: Field Study Perspectives*, edited by W. Bruns, Jr. and R. Kaplan (Boston: Harvard Business School Press, 1987).

16. An example of this type of behavior is documented by John Hand in his study, "Did Firms Undertake Debt-Equity Swaps for an Accounting Paper Profit or True Financial Gain?" *The Accounting Review* 64 (October 1989): 587–623.

17. For an empirical analysis of inventory build-ups, see V. Bernard and J. Noel, "Do Inventory Disclosures Predict Sales and Earnings?" *Journal of Accounting, Auditing, and Finance* (Fall 1991).

18. This is true by and large in the United States and in several other countries. However, in some countries, such as Germany and Japan, tax accounting and financial reporting are closely tied together and this particular red flag is not very meaningful.

19. For research on accounting and economic incentives in the formation of R&D partnerships, see A. Beatty, P. Berger, and J. Magliolo, "Motives for Forming Research and Development Financing Organizations" *Journal of Accounting & Economics* 19 (April 1995): 411–42. An overview of Enron's use of special purpose entities to manage earnings and window-dress its balance is provided by P. Healy and K. Palepu, "The Fall of Enron," *Journal of Economic Perspectives* 17, no. 2 (Spring 2003): 3–26.

20. For an empirical examination of asset write-offs, see J. Elliott and W. Shaw "Write-offs as Accounting Procedures to Manage Perceptions," *Journal of Accounting Research* 26, 1988: 91–119.

21. R. Mendenhall and W. Nichols report evidence consistent with managers taking advantage of their discretion to postpone reporting bad news until the fourth quarter. See R. Mendenhall and W. Nichols, "Bad News and Differential Market Reactions to Announcements of Earlier-Quarter versus Fourth-Quarter Earnings," *Journal of Accounting Research*, Supplement (1988): 63–86.

22. The role of insider transactions in the collapse of Enron are discussed by P. Healy and K. Palepu, "The Fall of Enron," *Journal of Economic Perspectives* 17, no. 2 (Spring 2003): 3–26.

23. This type of analysis is presented in the context of provisions for bad debts by M. McNichols and P. Wilson in their study, "Evidence of Earnings Management from the Provisions for Bad Debts," *Journal of Accounting Research*, Supplement (1988): 1–31.

24. This point has been made by several accounting researchers. For a summary of research on earnings management, see K. Schipper, "Earnings Management," *Accounting Horizons* (December 1989): 91–102.

25. See J. Chang, "The Decline in Value Relevance of Earnings and Book Values," unpublished dissertation, Harvard University, 1998. Evidence is also reported by J. Francis and K. Schipper, "Have Financial Statements Lost Their Relevance?" *Journal of Accounting Research* 37, no. 2 (Autumn 1999): 319–52; and W. E. Collins, E. Maydew, and I. Weiss, "Changes in the Value-Relevance of Earnings and Book Value over the Past Forty Years, *Journal of Accounting and Economics* 24 (1997): 39–67.

26. See G. Foster, "Briloff and the Capital Market," *Journal of Accounting Research* 17, no. 1 (Spring 1979): 262–74.

27. See S. H. Teoh, I. Welch, and T. J. Wong, "Earnings Management and the Long-Run Market Performance of Initial Public Offerings," *Journal of Finance* 53 (December 1998a): 1935–74; S. H. Teoh, I. Welch, and T. J. Wong, "Earnings Management and the Post-Issue Underperformance of Seasoned Equity Offerings," *Journal of Financial Economics* 50 (October 1998): 63–99; and S. Teoh, T. Wong, and G. Rao, "Are Accruals During Initial Public Offerings Opportunistic?" *Review of Accounting Studies* 3, no. 1-2 (1998): 175–208.

28. See P. Dechow, R. Sloan, and A. Sweeney, "Causes and Consequences of Earnings Manipulation: An Analysis of Firms Subject to Enforcement Actions by the SEC," *Contemporary Accounting Research* 13, no. 1 (1996): 1–36, and M. D. Beneish, "Detecting GAAP Violation: Implications for Assessing Earnings Management among Firms with Extreme Financial Performance," *Journal of Accounting and Public Policy* 16 (1997): 271–309.

Harnischfeger Corporation

In February 1985 Peter Roberts, the research director of Exeter Group, a small Boston-based investment advisory service specializing in turnaround stocks, was reviewing the 1984 annual report of Harnischfeger Corporation (Exhibit 4). His attention was drawn by the $1.28 per share net profit Harnischfeger reported for 1984. He knew that barely three years earlier the company had faced a severe financial crisis. Harnischfeger had defaulted on its debt and stopped dividend payments after reporting a hefty $7.64 per share net loss in fiscal 1982. The company's poor performance continued in 1983, leading to a net loss of $3.49 per share. Roberts was intrigued by Harnischfeger's rapid turnaround and wondered whether he should recommend purchase of the company's stock (see Exhibit 3 for selected data on Harnischfeger's stock).

COMPANY BUSINESS AND PRODUCTS

Harnischfeger Corporation was a machinery company based in Milwaukee, Wisconsin. The company had originally been started as a partnership in 1884 and was incorporated in Wisconsin in 1910 under the name Pawling and Harnischfeger. Its name was changed to the present one in 1924. The company went public in 1929 and was listed on the New York Stock Exchange.

The company's two major segments were the P&H Heavy Equipment Group, consisting of the Construction Equipment and the Mining and Electrical Equipment divisions, and the Industrial Technologies Group, consisting of the Material Handling Equipment and the Harnischfeger Engineers divisions. The sales mix of the company in 1983 consisted of: Construction Equipment 32 percent; Mining and Electrical Equipment 33 percent, Material Handling Equipment 29 percent, and Harnischfeger Engineers 6 percent.

Harnischfeger was a leading producer of construction equipment. Its products, bearing the widely recognized brand name P&H, included hydraulic cranes and lattice boom cranes. These were used in bridge and highway construction and for cargo and other material handling applications. Harnischfeger had market shares of about 20 percent in hydraulic cranes and about 30 percent in lattice boom cranes. In the 1980s the construction equipment industry in general was experiencing declining margins.

Electric mining shovels and excavators constituted the principal products of the Mining and Electrical Equipment Division of Harnischfeger. The company had a dominant share of the mining machinery market. The company's products were used in coal, copper, and iron mining. A significant part of the division's sales were from the sale of spare parts. Because of its large market share and the lucrative spare parts sales, the division was traditionally very profitable. Most of the company's future mining product sales were expected to occur outside the United States, principally in developing countries.

The Material Handling Equipment Division of Harnischfeger was the fourth largest supplier of automated material handling equipment, with a 9 percent market share. The division's products included overhead cranes, portal cranes, hoists, monorails, and components and parts. The demand for this equipment was expected to grow in the coming years as an increasing number of manufacturing firms emphasized cost reduction programs.

Professor Krishna Palepu prepared this case. The case is intended solely as the basis for class discussion and is not intended to serve as an endorsement, source of primary data, or illustration of effective or ineffective management. Copyright © 1985 by the President and Fellows of Harvard College. HBS Case 9-186-160.

Harnischfeger believed that the material handling equipment business would be a major source of its future growth.

Harnischfeger Engineers was an engineering services division engaged in design, custom software development, and project management for factory and distribution automation projects. The division engineered and installed complete automated material handling systems for a wide variety of applications on a fee basis. The company expected such automated storage and retrieval systems to play an increasingly important role in the "factory of the future."

Harnischfeger had a number of subsidiaries, affiliated companies, and licensees in a number of countries. Export and foreign sales constituted more than 50 percent of the total revenues of the company.

FINANCIAL DIFFICULTIES OF 1982

The machinery industry experienced a period of explosive growth during the 1970s. Harnischfeger expanded rapidly during this period, growing from $205 million in revenues in 1973 to $644 million in 1980. To fund this growth, the company relied increasingly on debt financing, and the firm's debt/equity ratio rose from 0.88 in 1973 to 1.26 in 1980. The worldwide recession in the early 1980s caused a significant drop in demand for the company's products starting in 1981 and culminated in a series of events that shook the financial stability of Harnischfeger.

Reduced sales and the high interest payments resulted in poor profit performance leading to a reported loss in 1982 of $77 million. The management of Harnischfeger commented on its financial difficulties:

> There is a persistent weakness in the basic industries, both in the United States and overseas, which have been large, traditional markets for P&H products. Energy-related projects, which had been a major source of business of our Construction Equipment Division, have slowed significantly in the last year as a result of lower oil demand and subsequent price decline, not only in the U.S. but throughout the world. Lack of demand for such basic minerals as iron ore, copper and bauxite have decreased worldwide mining activity, causing reduced sales for mining equipment, although coal mining remains relatively strong worldwide. Difficult economic conditions have caused many of our normal customers to cut capital expenditures dramatically, especially in such depressed sectors as the steel industry, which has always been a major source of sales for all P&H products.

The significant operating losses recorded in 1982 and the credit losses experienced by its finance subsidiary caused Harnischfeger to default on certain covenants of its loan agreements. The most restrictive provisions of the company's loan agreements required it to maintain a minimum working capital of $175 million, consolidated net worth of $180 million, and a ratio of current assets to current liabilities of 1.75. On October 31, 1982, the company's working capital (after reclassification of about $115 million long-term debt as a current liability) was $29.3 million, the consolidated net worth was $142.2 million, and the ratio of current assets to current liabilities was 1.12. Harnischfeger Credit Corporation, an unconsolidated finance subsidiary, also defaulted on certain covenants of its loan agreements, largely due to significant credit losses relating to the financing of construction equipment sold to a large distributor. As a result of these covenant violations, the company's long-term debt of $124.3 million became due on demand, the unused portion of the bank revolving credit line of $25.0 million became unavailable, and the unused short-term bank credit lines of $12.0 million were canceled. In addition, the $25.1 million debt of Harnischfeger Credit Corporation also became immediately due. The company was forced to stop paying dividends and began negotiations with its lenders to restructure its debt to permit operations to continue. Price Waterhouse, the company's audit firm, qualified its audit opinion on Harnischfeger's 1982 annual report with respect to the outcome of the company's negotiations with its lenders.

CORPORATE RECOVERY PLAN

Harnischfeger responded to the financial crisis facing the firm by developing a corporate recovery plan. The plan consisted of four elements: (1) changes in the top management, (2) cost reductions to lower the break-even point, (3) reorientation of the company's business, and (4) debt restructuring and recapitalization. The actions taken in each of these four areas are described below.

To deal effectively with the financial crisis, Henry Harnischfeger, then Chairman and Chief Executive Officer of the company, created the position of Chief Operating Officer. After an extensive search, the position was offered in August 1982 to William Goessel, who had considerable experience in the machinery industry. Another addition to the management team was Jeffrey Grade, who joined the company in 1983 as Senior Vice President of Finance and Administration and Chief Financial Officer. Grade's appointment was necessitated by the early retirement of the previous Vice President of Finance in 1982. The engineering, manufacturing, and marketing functions were also restructured to streamline the company's operations (see Exhibits 1 and 2 for additional information on Harnischfeger's current management).

To deal with the short-term liquidity squeeze, the company initiated a number of cost reduction measures. These included (1) reducing the workforce from 6,900 to 3,800; (2) eliminating management bonuses and reducing benefits and freezing wages of salaried and hourly employees; (3) liquidating excess inventories and stretching payments to creditors; and (4) permanent closure of the construction equipment plant at Escanaba, Michigan. These and other related measures improved the company's cash position and helped to reduce the rate of loss during fiscal 1983.

Concurrent with the above cost reduction measures, the new management made some strategic decisions to reorient Harnischfeger's business. First, the company entered into a long-term agreement with Kobe Steel, Ltd., of Japan. Under this agreement, Kobe agreed to supply Harnischfeger's requirements for construction cranes for sale in the United States as Harnischfeger phased out its own manufacture of cranes. This step was expected to significantly reduce the manufacturing costs of Harnischfeger's construction equipment, enabling it to compete effectively in the domestic market. Second, the company decided to emphasize the high technology part of its business by targeting for future growth the material handling equipment and systems business. To facilitate this strategy, the Industrial Technologies Group was created. As part of the reorientation, the company stated that it would develop and acquire new products, technology, and equipment and would expand its abilities to provide computer-integrated solutions to handling, storing, and retrieval in areas hitherto not pursued—industries such as distribution warehousing, food, pharmaceuticals, and aerospace.

While Harnischfeger was implementing its turnaround strategy, it was engaged at the same time in complex and difficult negotiations with its bankers. On January 6, 1984, the company entered into agreements with its lenders to restructure its debt obligations into three-year term loans secured by fixed as well as other assets, with a one-year extension option. This agreement required, among other things, specified minimum levels of cash and unpledged receivables, working capital, and net worth.

The company reported a net loss of $35 million in 1983, down from the $77 million loss the year before. Based on the above developments during the year, in the 1983 annual report the management expressed confidence that the company would return to profitability soon:

> We approach our second century with optimism, knowing that the negative events of the last three years are behind us, and with a firm belief that positive achievements will be recorded in 1984. By the time the corporation celebrates its 100th birthday on December 1, we are confident it will be operating profitably and attaining new levels of market strength and leadership.

During 1984 the company reported profits during each of the four quarters, ending the year with a pretax operating profit of $5.7 million, and a net income after tax and extraordinary credits of $15 million (see Exhibit 4). It also raised substantial new capital through a public offering of debentures and common stock. Net proceeds from the offering, which totaled $150 million, were used to pay off all of the company's restructured debt. In the 1984 annual report, management commented on the company's performance as follows:

> 1984 was the Corporation's Centennial year and we marked the occasion by re-dedicating ourselves to excellence through market leadership, customer service and improved operating performance and profitability.
>
> ⋮
>
> We look back with pride. We move ahead with confidence and optimism. Our major markets have never been more competitive; however, we will strive to take advantage of any and all opportunities for growth and to attain satisfactory profitability. Collectively, we will do what has to be done to ensure that the future will be rewarding to all who have a part in our success.

QUESTIONS

1. Identify all the accounting policy changes and accounting estimates that Harnischfeger made during 1984. Estimate, as accurately as possible, the effect of these on the company's 1984 reported profits.

2. What do you think are the motives of Harnischfeger's management in making the changes in its financial reporting policies? Do you think investors will see through these changes?

3. Assess the company's future prospects, given your insights from questions 1 and 2 and the information in the case about the company's turnaround strategy.

EXHIBIT I

Harnischfeger Corporation Board of Directions in 1984

		Director Since	Current Term	Shares Owned
Edward W. Duffy	Chairman of the Board and Chief Executive Officer of United States Gypsum Company, manufacturer of building materials and products used in industrial processes, since 1983; Vice Chairman from 1981 to 1983; President and Chief Operating Officer from 1971 to 1981. Director, American National Bank and Trust Company of Chicago, Walter E. Heller International Corporation, W. W. Grainger, Inc., and UNR Industries, Inc. Age 64.	1981	1985	100
Herbert V. Kohler, Jr.	Chairman, Chief Executive Officer, and Director of Kohler Company, manufacturer of plumbing and specialty products, engines, and generators, since 1972; President since 1974. Age 44.	1973	1985	700
Taisuke Mori	Executive Vice Chairman and Director of Kobe Steel, Ltd., a Japanese manufacturer of steel and steel products, industrial machinery, construction equipment, aluminum, copper and alloy products, and welding equipment and consumables. Age 63.	1981	1985	None
William W. Goessel	President and Chief Operating Officer of the Corporation since 1982. Executive Vice President of Beloit Corporation from 1978 to 1982. Director, Goulds Pumps, Inc. Age 56.	1982	1986	15,000
Henry Harnischfeger	Chairman of the Board and Chief Executive Officer of the Corporation since 1970; President from 1959 to 1982. Director, First Wisconsin Corporation and First Wisconsin National Bank of Milwaukee. Age 60.	1945	1986	611,362
Karl F. Nygren	Partner in Kirkland & Ellis, attorneys, since 1959. Age 56.	1964	1986	2,000
				(continued)

Harnischfeger Corporation

	Director Since	Current Term	Shares Owned
John P. Gallagher Senior lecturer, Graduate School of Business, University of Chicago. Director, IC Industries, Inc., Stone Container Corporation, UNR Industries, Inc., American National Bank and Trust Company of Chicago, and Walter E. Heller International Corporation. Age 67.	1979	1987	500
Jeffrey T. Grade Senior Vice President/Finance and Administration and Chief Financial Officer of the Corporation since August 1, 1983. Vice President Corporate Finance of IC Industries from 1981 to 1983; Assistant Vice President from 1976 to 1981. Age 40.	1983	1987	3,750
Donald Taylor President, Chief Operating Officer, and Director of Rexnord, Inc., a major manufacturer of industrial components and machinery, since 1978. Director, Johnson Controls, Inc., Marine Corporation, and Marine Bank, N.A. Age 56.	1979	1987	100
Frank A. Lee Director of Foster Wheeler Corporation since 1971; Chairman of the Board from 1981 to 1982; President and Chief Executive Officer from 1978 to 1981. Director, Belco Pollution Control Corporation, International General Industries, Inc., and Banker's Life Insurance Co. Age 59.	1983	1987	None

EXHIBIT 2

Executive Compensation, Harnischfeger Corporation

The following table sets forth all cash compensation paid to each of the Corporation's five most highly compensated executive officers and to all executive officers as a group for services rendered to the Corporation and its subsidiaries during fiscal 1984.

		Cash Compensation
Henry Harnischfeger	Chairman of the Board and Chief Executive Officer	$ 364,004
William W. Goessel	President and Chief Operating Officer	280,000
C. P. Cousland	Senior Vice President and group executive, P&H Heavy Equipment	210,000
Jeffrey T. Grade	Senior Vice President-Finance and Administration and Chief Financial Officer	205,336
Douglas E. Holt	President, Harnischfeger Engineers, Inc.	152,839
All persons who were executive officers during the fiscal year as a group (14 persons)		2,159,066

1985 Executive Incentive Plan

In December 1984, the board of directors established an Executive Incentive Plan for fiscal 1985 which provides an incentive compensation opportunity of 40% of annual salary for 11 senior executive officers only if the Corporation reaches a specific net after-tax profit objective; it provides an additional incentive compensation of up to 40% of annual salary for seven of those officers if the corporation exceeds the objective. The Plan covers the chairman, president, senior vice presidents; president, Harnischfeger Engineers, Inc.; vice president, P&H World Services; vice president; Material Handling Equipment; and secretary. Awards made in fiscal year 1984 are included in the compensation table above.

Harnischfeger Corporation

Harnischfeger Corporation

EXHIBIT 3

Harnischfeger Corporation, Selected Stock Price and Market Data

A. Stock Prices

	Harnischfeger's Stock Price			S&P 400 Industrials Index		
	High	Low	Close	High	Low	Close
January 4, 1985	9 1/8	8 6/8	9	186.4	181.8	182.2
January 11, 1985	10 6/8	8 7/8	10 5/8	188.2	182.2	182.8
January 18, 1985	11	10	10 4/8	191.9	186.9	191.3
January 25, 1985	11 2/8	10 1/8	11	199.7	191.3	198.6
February 1, 1985	11 5/8	10 7/8	11 2/8	201.8	198.6	200.0

Harnischfeger's stock beta = 0.95 (Value Line estimate)

B. Market Data

	February 1985
Median P/E ratio of Dow Jones Industrials	10.9
Median P/E ratio of Value Line stocks	11.3
Median P/E ratio of machinery industry (construction and mining equipment)	10.0
Prime rate	10.5%
91-day Treasury bill rate	8.4%
30-year Treasury bond yield	11.4%
Moody's Aaa corporate bond yield	12.0%

EXHIBIT 4

Harnischfeger Corporation 1984 Annual Report (abridged)

TO OUR SHAREHOLDERS

The Corporation recorded gains in each quarter during fiscal 1984, returning to profitability despite the continued depressed demand and intense price competition in the world markets it serves.

For the year ended October 31, net income was $15,176,000 or $1.28 per common share, which included $11,005,000 or 93¢ per share from the cumulative effect of a change in depreciation accounting. In 1983, the Corporation reported a loss of $34,630,000 or $3.49 per share.

Sales for 1984 improved 24% over the preceding year, rising to $398.7 million from $321 million a year ago. New orders totaled $451 million, a $101 million increase over 1983. We entered fiscal 1985 with a backlog of $193 million, which compared to $141 million a year earlier.

All Divisions Improved

All product divisions recorded sales and operating improvements during 1984.

Mining equipment was the strongest performer with sales up over 60%, including major orders from Turkey and the People's Republic of China. During the year we began the implementation of the training, engineering and manufacturing license agreement concluded in November, 1983 with the People's Republic of China, which offers the Corporation long-term potential in modernizing and mechanizing this vast and rapidly developing mining market.

Sales of material handling equipment and systems were up 10% for the year and the increasingly stronger bookings recorded during the latter part of the year are continuing into the first quarter of 1985.

Sales on construction equipment products showed some signs of selective improvement. In the fourth quarter, bookings more than doubled from the very depressed levels in the same period a year ago, although the current level is still far below what is needed to achieve acceptable operating results for this product line.

Financial Stability Restored

In April, the financial stability of the Corporation was improved through a public offering of 2.15 million shares of common stock, $50 million of 15% notes due April 15, 1994, and $100 million of 12% subordinated debentures due April 15, 2004, with two million common stock purchase warrants.

Net proceeds from the offering totaled $149 million, to which we added an additional $23 million in cash, enabling us to pay off all of our long-term debt. As a result of the refinancing, the Corporation gained permanent long-term capital with minimal annual cash flow requirements to service it. We now have the financial resources and flexibility to pursue new opportunities to grow and diversify.

Furthermore, should we require additional funds, they will be available through a $52 million unsecured three-year revolving credit agreement concluded in June with ten U.S. and Canadian banks. An $80 million product financing capability was also arranged through a major U.S. bank to provide financing to customers purchasing P&H products.

Outlook

Throughout 1985 we believe we will see gradual improvements in most of our U.S. and world markets.

For our mining excavator product line, coal and certain metals mining are expected to show a more favorable long-term outlook in selected foreign requirements and our capability to source equipment from the U.S., Japan or Europe places us in a strong marketing position. In the U.S., we see only a moderate strengthening in machinery requirements for coal, while metals mining will remain weak.

Continuing shipments of the Turkish order throughout 1985 will help to stabilize our plant utilization levels and improve our operating results for this product line.

In our material handling and systems markets, particularly in the U.S., we are experiencing a moderately strong continuation of the improved bookings which we began to see in the third and fourth quarters of last year.

In construction lifting equipment markets, we expect modest overall economic improvement in the U.S., which should help to absorb the large numbers of idle lifting equipment that have been manufacturer, distributor and customer inventories for the last three years. As this overhang on the market is reduced we will see gradual improvement in new sales.

Harnischfeger traditionally exports half of its U.S.-produced lifting products. However, as with mining equipment, the continued strength of the U.S. dollar severely restricts our ability to sell U.S.-built products in world markets.

In addition to the strong dollar and economic instability in many foreign nations, overcapacity in worldwide heavy equipment manufacturing remains a serious problem in spite of some exits from the market as well as consolidations within the industry.

The Corporation continues to respond to severe price competition through systematic cost reduction programs and through expanded sourcing of P&H equipment from our European operation and, most importantly, through our 30-year association with our Japanese partner, Kobe Steel, Ltd. P&H engineering and technology have established world standards for quality and performance for construction cranes and mining equipment, which customers can expect from every P&H machine regardless of its source. More than a dozen new models of foreign-sourced P&H construction cranes will be made available for the first time in the U.S. during 1985, broadening our existing product lines and giving competitive pricing to our U.S. distributors and customers.

To improve our future operating results, we restructured our three operating divisions into two groups. All construction and mining related activities are in the new "P&H Heavy Equipment Group." All material handling equipment and systems activities are now merged into the "Industrial Technologies Group." More information on these Groups is reported in their respective sections.

We are pleased to announce that John P. Moran was elected Senior Vice President and Group Executive, Industrial Technologies Group, and John R. Teitgen was elected Secretary and General Counsel.

In September Robert F. Schnoes became a member of our Board of Directors. He is President and Chief Executive Officer of Burgess, Inc. and of Ultrasonic Power Corporation, and a member of the Board of Signode Industries, Inc.

Beginning Our Second Century

1984 was the Corporation's Centennial year and we marked the occasion by rededicating ourselves to excellence through market leadership, customer service and improved operating performance and profitability.

Our first century of achievement resulted from the dedicated effort, support and cooperation of our employees, distributors, suppliers, lenders, and shareholders, and we thank all of them.

We look back with pride. We move ahead with confidence and optimism. Our major markets have never been more competitive; however, we will strive to take advantage of any and all opportunities for growth and to attain satisfactory profitability. Collectively, we will do what has to be done to ensure that the future will be rewarding to all who have a part in our success.

Henry Harnischfeger
Chairman of the Board

William W. Goessel
President

January 31, 1985

Harnischfeger Corporation

MANAGEMENT'S DISCUSSION & ANALYSIS

Results of Operations

1984 Compared to 1983

Consolidated net sales of $399 million in fiscal 1984 increased $78 million or 24% over 1983. Sales increases were 62% in the Mining and Electrical Equipment Segment, and 10% in the Industrial Technologies Segment. Sales in the Construction Equipment Segment were virtually unchanged reflecting the continued low demand for construction equipment world-wide.

Effective at the beginning of fiscal 1984, net sales include the full sales price of construction and mining equipment purchased from Kobe Steel, Ltd. and sold by the Corporation, in order to reflect more effectively the nature of the Corporation's transactions with Kobe. Such sales aggregated $28.0 million in 1984.

The $4.0 million increase in Other Income reflected a recovery of certain claims and higher license and technical service fees.

Cost of Sales was equal to 79.1% of net sales in 1984 and 81.4% in 1983; which together with the increase in net sales resulted in a $23.9 million increase in gross profit (net sales less cost of sales). Contributing to this increase were improved sales of higher-margin replacement parts in the Mining Equipment and Industrial Technologies Segments and a reduction in excess manufacturing costs through greater utilization of domestic manufacturing capacity and economies in total manufacturing costs including a reduction in pension expense. Reductions of certain LIFO inventories increased gross profit by $2.4 million in 1984 and $15.6 million in 1983.

Product development selling and administrative expenses were reduced, due to the funding of R&D expenses in the Construction Equipment Segment pursuant to the October 1983 Agreement with Kobe Steel, Ltd., to reductions in pension expenses and provision for credit losses, and to the absence of the corporate financial restructuring expenses incurred in 1983.

Net interest expense in 1984 increased $2.9 million due to higher interest rates on the outstanding funded debt and a reduction in interest income.

Equity in Earnings (Loss) of Unconsolidated Companies included 1984 income of $1.2 million of Harnischfeger Credit Corporation, an unconsolidated finance subsidiary, reflecting an income tax benefit of $1.4 million not previously recorded.

The preceding items, together with the cumulative effect of the change in depreciation method described in Financial Note 2, were included in net income of $15.2 million or $1.28 per common share, compared with net loss of $34.6 million or $3.49 per share in 1983.

The sales orders booked and unshipped backlogs of orders of the Corporation's three segments are summarized as follows (in million of dollars):

Orders Booked	1984	1983
Industrial Technologies	$132	$106
Mining and Electrical Equipment	210	135
Construction Equipment	109	109
	$451	$350

Backlogs at October 31		
Industrial Technologies	$ 79	$ 71
Mining and Electrical Equipment	91	50
Construction Equipment	23	20
	$193	$141

1983 Compared to 1982

Consolidated net sales of $321 million in fiscal 1983 were $126 million or 28% below 1982. This decline reflected, for the second consecutive year, the continued low demand in all markets served by the Corporation's products, with exports even more severely depressed due to the strength of the dollar. The largest decline was reported in the Construction Equipment Segment, down 34%; Mining and Electrical Equipment Segment shipments were down 27%, and the Industrial Technologies Segment, 23%.

Cost of Sales was equal to 81.4% of net sales in 1983 and 81.9% in 1982. The resulting gross profit was $60 million in 1983 and $81 million in 1982, a reduction equal to the rate of sales decrease.

The benefits of reduced manufacturing capacity and economies in total manufacturing costs were offset by reduced selling prices in the highly competitive markets. Reductions of certain LIFO inventories increased gross profits by $15.6 million in 1983 and $7.2 million in 1982.

Product development, selling and administrative expenses were reduced as a result of expense reduction measures in response to the lower volume of business and undertaken in connection with the Corporation's corporate recovery program, and reduced provisions for credit losses, which in 1982 included $4.0 million in income support for Harnischfeger Credit Corporation.

Net interest expense was reduced $9.1 million from 1982 to 1983, due primarily to increased interest income from short-term cash investments and an

Harnischfeger Corporation

accrual of $4.7 million in interest income on refundable income taxes not previously recorded.

The Credit for Income Taxes included a federal income tax benefit of $5 million, based upon the recent examination of the Corporation's income tax returns and refund claims. No income tax benefits were available for the losses of the U.S. operations in 1983.

The losses from unconsolidated companies recorded in 1983 included $0.5 million in Harnischfeger Credit Corporation; $2.1 million in Cranetex, Inc., a Corporation-owned distributorship in Texas; and $0.8 million in ASEA Industrial Systems Inc., then a 49%-owned joint venture between the Corporation and ASEA AB and now 19%-owned with the investment accounted for on the cost method.

The preceding items were reflected in a net loss of $34.6 million or $3.49 per share.

Liquidity and Financial Resources

In April 1984, the Corporation issued in public offerings 2,150,000 shares of Common Stock, $50 million principal amount of 15% Senior Notes due in 1994, and 100,000 Units consisting of $100 million principal amount of 12% Subordinated Debentures due in 2004 and 2,000,000 Common Stock Purchase Warrants.

The net proceeds from the sales of the securities of $149 million were used to prepay substantially all of the outstanding debt of the Corporation and certain of its subsidiaries.

During the year ended October 31, 1984, the consolidated cash balances increased $32 million to a balance of $96 million, with the cash activity summarized as follows (in million of dollars):

Funds provided by operations	$10
Funds returned to the Corporation upon restructuring of the Salaried Employees' Pension Plan	39
Debt repayment less the proceeds of sales of securities	(9)
Plant and equipment additions	(6)
All other changes—net	(2)
	$32

In the third quarter of fiscal 1984 the Corporation entered into a $52 million three-year revolving credit agreement with ten U.S. and Canadian banks. While the Corporation has adequate liquidity to meet its current working capital requirements, the revolver represents another step in the Corporation's program to strengthen its financial position and provide the required financial resources to respond to opportunities as they arise.

CONSOLIDATED STATEMENT OF OPERATIONS

(Dollar amounts in thousands except per share figures)	Year Ended October 31		
	1984	1983	1982
Revenues:			
Net sales	**$398,708**	$321,010	$447,461
Other income, including license and technical service fees	**7,067**	3,111	5,209
	405,775	324,121	452,670
Cost of Sales	**315,216**	261,384	366,297
Operating Income	**90,559**	62,737	86,373
Less:			
Product development, selling and administrative expenses	**72,196**	85,795	113,457
Interest expense—net	**12,625**	9,745	18,873
Provision for plant closing	**—**	—	23,700
Income (Loss) Before Provision (Credit) for Income Taxes, Equity Items and Cumulative Effect of Accounting Change	**5,738**	(32,803)	(69,657)
Provision (Credit) for Income Taxes	**2,425**	(1,400)	(1,600)
Income (Loss) Before Equity Items and Cumulative Effect of Accounting Change	**3,313**	(31,403)	(68,057)
Equity items:			
Equity in earnings (loss) of unconsolidated companies	**993**	(3,397)	(7,891)
Minority interest in (earnings) loss of consolidated subsidiaries	**(135)**	170	(583)
Income (Loss) Before Cumulative Effect of Accounting Change	**4,171**	(34,630)	(76,531)
Cumulative Effect of Change in Depreciation Method	**11,005**	—	—
Net Income (Loss)	**$ 15,176**	$ (34,630)	$ (76,531)
Earnings (Loss) per Common and Common Equivalent Share:			
Income (Loss) before cumulative effect of accounting change	**$ .35**	$(3.49)	$(7.64)
Cumulative effect of change in depreciation method	**.93**	—	—
Net income (loss)	**$1.28**	$(3.49)	$(7.64)
Pro forma Amounts Assuming the Changed Depreciation Method Had Been Applied Retroactively:			
Net (loss)		$ (33,918)	$ (76,695)
(Loss) per common share		$(3.42)	$(7.65)

(The accompanying notes are an integral part of the financial statements.)

Harnischfeger Corporation

Harnischfeger Corporation

CONSOLIDATED BALANCE SHEET

	October 31	
(Dollar amounts in thousands except per share figures)	1984	1983
Assets		
Current Assets:		
Cash and temporary investments	$ 96,007	$ 64,275
Accounts receivable	87,648	63,740
Inventories	144,312	153,594
Refundable income taxes and related interest	1,296	12,585
Other current assets	5,502	6,023
Prepaid income taxes	14,494	14,232
	349,259	314,449
Investments and Other Assets:		
Investments in and advances to:		
Finance subsidiary, at equity in net assets	8,849	6,704
Other companies	4,445	2,514
Other assets	13,959	6,411
	27,253	15,629
Operating Plants:		
Land and improvements	9,419	10,370
Buildings	59,083	60,377
Machinery and equipment	120,949	122,154
	189,451	192,901
Accumulated depreciation	(93,259)	(107,577)
	96,192	85,324
	$472,704	$415,402

(continued)

CONSOLIDATED BALANCE SHEET (continued)

	October 31	
(Dollar amounts in thousands except per share figures)	1984	1983
Liabilities and Shareholders' Equity		
Current Liabilities:		
Short-term notes payable to banks by subsidiaries	$ 9,090	$ 8,155
Long-term debt and capitalized lease obligations payable within one year	973	18,265
Trade accounts payable	37,716	21,228
Employee compensation and benefits	15,041	14,343
Accrued plant closing costs	2,460	6,348
Advance payments and progress billings	20,619	15,886
Income taxes payable	1,645	3,463
Account payable to finance subsidiary	—	3,436
Other current liabilities and accruals	29,673	32,333
	117,217	123,457
Long-Term Obligations:		
Long-term debt payable to:		
Unaffiliated lenders	128,550	139,092
Finance subsidiary	—	5,400
Capitalized lease obligations	7,870	8,120
	136,420	152,612
Deferred Liabilities and Income Taxes:		
Accrued pension costs	57,611	19,098
Other deferred liabilities	5,299	7,777
Deferred income taxes	6,385	134
	69,295	27,009
Minority Interest	2,400	2,405
Shareholders' Equity:		
Preferred stock $100 par value—authorized 250,000 shares:		
Series A $7.00 cumulative convertible preferred shares: authorized, issued and outstanding 117,500 shares in 1984 and 100,000 shares in 1983	11,750	10,000
Common stock, $1 par value—authorized 25,000,000 shares: issued and outstanding 12,283,563 shares in 1984 and 10,133,563 shares in 1983	12,284	10,134
Capital in excess of par value of shares	114,333	88,332
Retained earnings	19,901	6,475
Cumulative translation adjustments	(10,896)	(5,022)
	147,372	109,919
	$472,704	$415,402

(The accompanying notes are an integral part of the financial statements.)

Harnischfeger Corporation

CONSOLIDATED STATEMENT OF CHANGES IN FINANCIAL POSITION

(Dollar amounts in thousands)	Year Ended October 31,		
	1984	1983	1982
Funds Were Provided by (Applied to):			
Operations:			
Income (loss) before cumulative effect of accounting change	$ **4,171**	$(34,630)	$(76,531)
Cumulative effect of change in depreciation method	**11,005**	—	—
Net income (loss)	**15,176**	(34,630)	(76,531)
Add (deduct) items included not affecting funds:			
Depreciation	**8,077**	13,552	15,241
Unremitted (earnings) loss of unconsolidated companies	**(993)**	3,397	7, 891
Deferred pension contributions	**(500)**	4,834	—
Deferred income taxes	**6,583**	(3,178)	1,406
Reduction in accumulated depreciation resulting from change in depreciation method	**(17,205)**	—	—
Other—net	**(2,168)**	(67)	2,034
Decrease in operating working capital (see below)	**7,039**	11,605	72,172
Add (deduct) effects on operating working capital of:			
Conversion of export and factored receivable sales to debt	**—**	23,919	—
Reclassification to deferred liabilities:			
Accrued pension costs	**—**	14,264	—
Other liabilities	**—**	5,510	—
Foreign currency translation adjustments	**(6,009)**	(1,919)	(5,943)
Funds provided by operations	**10,000**	37,287	16,270
Financing, Investment and Other Activities:			
Transactions in debt and capitalized lease obligations —			
Long-Term debt and capitalized lease obligations:			
Proceeds from sale of 15% Senior Notes and 12% Subordinated Debentures, net of issue costs	**120,530**	—	—
Other increases	**1,474**	—	25,698
Repayments	**(161,500)**	(760)	(9,409)
Restructured debt	**—**	158,058	—
Debt replaced, including conversion of receivable sales of $23,919, and short-term bank notes payable of $9,028	**—**	(158,058)	—
	(39,496)	(760)	16,289
Net increase (repayment) in short-term bank notes payable	**2,107**	(3,982)	(2,016)
Net increase (repayment) in debt and capitalized lease obligations	**(37,389)**	(4,742)	14,273
Issuance of:			
Common stock	**21,310**	—	449
Common stock purchase warrants	**6,663**	—	—
Salaried pension assets reversion	**39,307**	—	—
Plant and equipment additions	**(5,546)**	(1,871)	(10,819)
Advances to unconsolidated companies	**(2,882)**	—	—

(continued)

Harnischfeger Corporation

CONSOLIDATED STATEMENT OF CHANGES IN FINANCIAL POSITION *(continued)*

(Dollar amounts in thousands)	Year Ended October 31,		
	1984	1983	1982
Other—net	269	1,531	848
Funds provided by (applied to) financing, investment and other activities	21,732	(5,082)	4,751
Increase in Cash and Temporary Investments Before Cash Dividends	$ 31,732	$ 32,205	$21,021
Cash Dividends	—	—	(2,369)
Increase in Cash and Temporary Investments	$ 31,732	$ 32,205	$ 18,652
Decrease (Increase) in Operating Working Capital (Excluding Cash Items, Debt and Capitalized Lease Obligations):			
Accounts receivable	$ (23,908)	$ (5,327)	$ 42,293
Inventories	9,282	56,904	26,124
Refundable income taxes and related interest	11,289	(2,584)	(6,268)
Other current assets	259	10,008	(439)
Trade accounts payable	16,488	(1,757)	(3,302)
Employee compensation and benefits	698	(15,564)	(3,702)
Accrued plant closing costs	(3,888)	(14,148)	20,496
Other current liabilities	(3,181)	(15,927)	(3,030)
Decrease in operating working capital	$ 7,039	$ 11,605	$ 72,172

(The accompanying notes are an integral part of the financial statements.)

Harnischfeger Corporation

Harnischfeger Corporation

CONSOLIDATED STATEMENT OF SHAREHOLDERS' EQUITY

(Dollar amounts in thousands except per share figures)	Preferred Stock	Common Stock	Capital in Excess of Par Value of Shares	Retained Earnings	Cumulative Translation Adjustments	Total
Balance at October 31, 1981	$10,000	$10,085	$ 87,932	$120,005	$ —	$228,022
Cumulative translation adjustments through October 31, 1981					(1,195)	(1,195)
Issuance of Common Stock:						
10,000 shares to Kobe Steel, Ltd.		10	91			101
38,161 shares under stock purchase and dividend reinvestment plans		39	309			348
Net (loss)				(76,531)		(76,531)
Cash dividends paid on:						
Preferred stock				(350)		(350)
Common stock $.20 per share				(2,019)		(2,019)
Translation adjustments, net of deferred income taxes of $128					(2,928)	(2,928)
Balance at October 31, 1982	10,000	10,134	88,332	41,105	(4,123)	145,448
Net (loss)				(34,630)		(34,630)
Translation adjustments, including deferred income taxes of $33					(899)	(899)
Balance at October 31, 1983	10,000	10,134	88,332	6,475	(5,022)	109,919
Issuance of:						
2,150,000 shares of common stock		2,150	19,160			21,310
2,000,000 common stock purchase warrants			6,663			6,663
17,500 shares of Series A $7.00 cumulative convertible preferred stock in discharge of dividends payable on preferred stock	1,750			(1,750)		—
Net income				15,176		15,176
Translation adjustments, net of deferred income taxes of $300					(5,874)	(5,874)
Other			178			178
Balance at October 31, 1984	$11,750	$12,284	$114,333	$ 19,901	$(10,896)	$147,372

(The accompanying notes are an integral part of the financial statements.)

FINANCIAL NOTES

Note 1

Summary of Significant Accounting Policies:

Consolidation—The consolidated financial statements include the accounts of all majority-owned subsidiaries except a wholly-owned domestic finance subsidiary, a subsidiary organized in 1982 as a temporary successor to a distributor, both of which are accounted for under the equity method, and a wholly-owned Brazilian subsidiary, which is carried at estimated net realizable value due to economic uncertainty. All related significant intercompany balances and transactions have been eliminated in consolidation.

Financial statements of certain consolidated subsidiaries, principally foreign, are included, effective in fiscal year 1984, on the basis of their fiscal years ending September 30; previously, certain of such subsidiaries had fiscal years ending July (See Note 2). Such fiscal periods have been adopted by the subsidiaries in order to provide for a more timely consolidation with the Corporation.

Inventories—The Corporation values its inventories at the lower of cost or market. Cost is determined by the last-in, first-out (LIFO) method for inventories located principally in the United States, and by the first-in, first-out (FIFO) method for inventories of foreign subsidiaries.

Operating Plants, Equipment and Depreciation—Properties are stated at cost. Maintenance and repairs are charged to expense as incurred and expenditures for betterments and renewals are capitalized. Effective in 1981, interest is capitalized for qualifying assets during their acquisition period. Capitalized interest is amortized on the same basis as the related asset. When properties are sold or otherwise disposed of, the cost and accumulated depreciation are removed from the accounts and any gain or loss is included in income.

Depreciation of plants and equipment is provided over the estimated useful lives of the related assets, or over the lease terms of capital leases, using, effective in fiscal year 1984, the straight-line method for financial reporting, and principally accelerated methods for tax reporting purposes. Previously, accelerated methods, where applicable, were also used for financial reporting purposes (See Note 2). For U.S. income tax purposes, depreciation lives are based principally on the Class Life Asset Depreciation Range for additions, other than buildings, in the years 1973 through 1980, and on the Accelerated Cost Recovery System for all additions after 1980.

Discontinued facilities held for sale are carried at the lower of cost less accumulated depreciation or estimated realizable value, which aggregated $4.9 million and $3.6 million at October 31, 1984 and 1983, respectively, and were included in Other Assets in the accompanying Balance Sheet.

Pension Plans—The Corporation has pension plans covering substantially all of its employees. Pension expenses of the principal defined benefit plans consist of current service costs of such plans and amortization of the prior service costs and actuarial gains and losses over periods ranging from 10 to 30 years. The Corporation's policy is to fund at a minimum the amount required under the Employee Retirement Income Security Act of 1974.

Income Taxes—The consolidated tax provision is computed based on income and expenses recorded in the Statement of Operations. Prepaid or deferred taxes are recorded for the difference between such taxes and taxes computed for tax returns. The Corporation and its domestic subsidiaries file a consolidated federal income tax return. The operating results of Harnischfeger GmbH are included in the Corporation's U.S. income tax returns.

Additional taxes are provided on the earnings of foreign subsidiaries which are intended to be remitted to the Corporation. Such taxes are not provided on subsidiaries' unremitted earnings which are intended to be permanently reinvested.

Investment tax credits are accounted for under the flow-through method as a reduction of the income tax provision, if applicable, in the year the related asset is placed in service.

Reporting Format—Certain previously reported items have been conformed to the current year's presentation.

Note 2

Accounting Changes:

Effective November 1, 1983, the Corporation includes in its net sales products puvThis change had the effect of increasing net sales by $5.4 million for the year ended October 31, 1984. The impact of these changes on net income was insignificant.

In 1984, the Corporation has computed depreciation expense on plants, machinery and equipment using the straight-line method for financial reporting purposes. Prior to 1984, the Corporation used principally accelerated methods for its U.S. operating plants.

The cumulative effect of this change, which was applied retroactively to all assets previously subjected to accelerated depreciation, increased net income for 1984 by $11.0 million or $.93 per common and common equivalent share. The impact of the new method on income for the year 1984 before the cumulative effect was insignificant.

As a result of the review of its depreciation policy, the Corporation, effective November 1, 1983, has changed its estimated depreciation lives on certain U.S. plants, machinery and equipment and residual values on certain machinery and equipment, which increased net income for 1984 by $3.2 million or $.27 per share. No income tax effect was applied to this change.

The changes in accounting for depreciation were made to conform the Corporation's depreciation policy to those used by manufacturers in the Corporation's and similar industries and to provide a more equitable allocation of the cost of plants, machinery and equipment over their useful lives.

Note 3

Cash and Temporary Investments:

Cash and temporary investments consisted of the following (in thousandvs of dollars):

	October 31, 1984	1983
Cash—in demand deposits	$ 2,155	$11,910
—in special accounts principally to support letters of credit	4,516	—
Temporary investments	89,336	52,365
	$96,007	$64,275

Temporary investments consisted of short-term U.S. and Canadian treasury bills, money market funds, time and certificates of deposit, commercial paper and bank repurchase agreements and bankers' acceptances. Temporary investments are stated at cost plus accrued interest, which approximates market value.

Note 4

Long-Term Debt, Bank Credit Lines and Interest Expense:

Outstanding long-term debt payable to unaffiliated lenders was as follows (in thousands of dollars):

	October 31, 1984	1983
Parent Company:		
15% Senior Notes due April 15, 1994	$ 47,700	$ —
12% Subordinated Debentures, with an effective interest rate of 16.3%; sinking fund redemption payments of $7,500 due annually on April 15 in 1994–2003, and final payment of $25,000 in 2004	100,000	—
Term Obligations— Insurance company debt:		
9% Notes	—	20,000
9 7/8 Notes	—	38,750
8 7/8 Notes	—	40,500
Bank debt, at 105% of prime	—	25,000
Paper purchase debt, at prime or LIBOR, plus 1 1/4%	—	18,519
9.23% Mortgage Note due monthly to April, 1998	4,327	4,481
	152,027	147,250
Consolidated Subsidiaries:		
Notes payable to banks in German marks	—	9,889
Contract payable in 1985–1989, in South African rands, with imputed interest rate of 12%	1,024	—
Other	—	36
	153,051	157,175
Less: Amounts payable within one year	644	17,799
Unamortized discounts	23,857	284
Long-Term Debt—excluding amounts payable within one year	$128,550	$139,092

Note 5

Harnischfeger Credit Corporation and Cranetex, Inc.:

Condensed financial information of Harnischfeger Credit Corporation ("Credit"), an unconsolidated wholly-owned finance subsidiary, accounted for under the equity method, was as follows (in thousands of dollars):

Balance Sheet	October 31, 1984	1983
Assets:		
Cash and temporary investments	$ 404	$19,824
Finance receivables—net	4,335	11,412
Factored account note and current account receivable from parent company	—	8,836
Other assets	4,181	661
	$8,920	$40,733
Liabilities and Shareholder's Equity:		
Debt payable	$ —	$32,600
Advances from parent company	950	—
Other liabilities	71	1,429
	1,021	34,029
Shareholder's equity	7,899	6,704
	$8,920	$40,733

Statement of Operations	Year Ended October 31,		
	1984	1983	1982
Revenues	**$1,165**	$2,662	$9,978
Less:			
Operating Expenses	1,530	3,386	14,613
Provision (credit) for income taxes	**(1,560)**	(222)	180
Net income (loss)	**$1,195**	$(502)	$(4,815)

Credit's purchases of finance receivables from the Corporation aggregated $1.1 million in 1984, $46.7 million in 1983 and $50.4 million in 1982. In 1982, Credit received income support of $4.0 million from the Corporation.

In 1982, the Corporation organized Cranetex, Inc. to assume certain assets and liabilities transferred by a former distributor of construction equipment, in settlement of the Corporation's and Credit's claims against the distributor and to continue the business on an interim basis until the franchise can be transferred to a new distributor. The Corporation recorded provisions of $2.5 million in 1983 and $2.3 million in 1982 and Credit recorded a provision of $6.7 million in 1982, for credit losses incurred in the financing of equipment sold to the former distributor.

The condensed balance sheet of Cranetex, Inc. was as follows (in thousand of dollars):

	October 31,	
	1984	1983
Assets:		
Cash	**$ 143**	$ 49
Accounts receivables	**566**	428
Inventory	**2,314**	3,464
Property and equipment	**1,547**	1,674
	$4,570	$5,615
Liabilities and Deficit:		
Loans payable	**$4,325**	$6,682
Other liabilities	**338**	620
	4,663	7,302
Shareholder's (deficit), net of accounts and advances payable to parent company	**(93)**	(1,687)
	$4,570	$5,615

The net losses of Cranetex, Inc. of $.2 million in 1984, $2.1 million in 1983 and $1.0 million in 1982 were included in Equity in Earnings (Loss) of Unconsolidated Companies in the Corporation's Statement of Operations.

Note 6

Transactions with Kobe Steel, Ltd. and ASEA Industrial Systems Inc.:

Kobe Steel, Ltd. of Japan ("Kobe"), has been a licensee for certain of the Corporation's products since 1955, and has owned certain Harnischfeger Japanese construction equipment patents and technology since 1981. As of October 31, 1984, Kobe held 1,030,000 shares or 8.4% of the Corporation's outstanding Common Stock (See Note 13). Kobe also owns 25% of the capital stock of Harnischfeger of Australia Pty. Ltd., a subsidiary of the Corporation. This ownership appears as the minority interest on the Corporation's balance sheet.

Under agreements expiring in December 1990, Kobe pays technical service fees on P&H mining equipment produced and sold under license from the Corporation, and trademark and marketing fees on sales of construction equipment outside of Japan. Net fee income received from Kobe was $4.3 million in 1984, $3.1 million in 1983, and $3.9 million in 1982; this income is included in Other Income in the accompanying Statement of Operations.

In October 1983, the Corporation entered into a ten-year agreement with Kobe under which Kobe agreed to supply the Corporation's requirements for construction cranes for sale in the United States as it phases out its own manufacture of cranes over the next several years, and to make the Corporation the exclusive distributor of Kobe-built cranes in the United States. The Agreement also involves a joint research and development program for construction equipment under which the Corporation agreed to spend at least $17 million over a three-year period and provided it does so, Kobe agreed to pay this amount to the Corporation. Sales of cranes outside the United States continue under the contract terms described in the preceding paragraph.

The Corporation's sales to Kobe, principally components for mining and construction equipment, excluding the R&D expenses discussed in the preceding paragraph, approximated $5.2 million, $10.5 million and $7.0 million during the three years ended October 31, 1984, 1983 and 1982, respectively. The purchases from Kobe of mining and construction equipment and components amounted to approximately $33.7 million, $15.5 million and $29.9 million during the three years ended October 31, 1984, 1983 and 1982, respectively, most of which were resold to customers (See Note 2).

The Corporation owns 19% of ASEA Industrial Systems Inc. ("AIS"), an electrical equipment company controlled by ASEA AB of Sweden. The Corporation's

Harnischfeger Corporation

purchases of electrical components from AIS aggregated $11.2 million in 1984 and $6.1 million in 1983 and its sales to AIS approximated $2.6 million in 1984 and $3.8 million in 1983.

The Corporation believes that its transactions with Kobe and AIS were competitive with alternative sources of supply for each party involved.

Note 7

Inventories:

Consolidated inventories consisted of the following (in thousand of dollars):

| | October 31, | |
	1984	1983
At lower of cost or market (FIFO method):		
Raw materials	$ 11,003	$ 11,904
Work in process and purchased parts	88,279	72,956
Finished goods	79,111	105,923
	178,393	190,783
Allowance to reduce inventories to cost on the LIFO method	(34,081)	(37,189)
	$144,312	$153,594

Inventories valued on the LIFO method represented approximately 82% of total inventories at both October 31, 1984 and 1983.

Inventory reductions in 1984, 1983 and 1982 resulted in a liquidation of LIFO inventory quantities carried at lower costs compared with the current cost of their acquisitions. The effect of these liquidations was to increase net income by 2.4 million or $.20 per common share in fiscal 1984, and to reduce the net loss by approximately $15.6 million or $1.54 per share in 1983, and by $6.7 million or $.66 per share in 1982; no income tax effect applied to the adjustment in 1984 and 1983.

Note 8

Accounts Receivable:

Accounts receivable were net of allowances for doubtful accounts of $5.9 million and $6.4 million at October 31, 1984 and 1983, respectively.

Note 9

Research and Development Expense:

Research and development expense incurred in the development of new products or significant improvements to existing products was $5.1 million in 1984 (net of amounts funded by Kobe Steel, Ltd.) $12.1 million in 1983 and $14.1 million in 1982.

Note 10

Foreign Operations:

The net sales, net income (loss) and net assets of subsidiaries located in countries outside the United States and Canada and included in the consolidated financial statements were as follows (in thousands of dollars):

| | Year Ended October 31, | | |
	1984	1983	1982
Net sales	$78,074	$45,912	$69,216
Net income (loss) after minority interests	828	(1,191)	3,080
Corporation's equity in total net assets	17,734	7,716	7,287

Foreign currency transaction losses included in Cost of Sales were $2.7 million in 1984, $1.2 million in 1983 and $1.3 million in 1982.

Note 11

Pension Plans and Other Postretirement Benefits:

Pension expense for all plans of the Corporation and its consolidated subsidiaries was $1.9 million in 1984, $6.5million in 1983 and $12.2 million in 1982.

Accumulated plan benefits and plan net assets for the Corporation's U.S. defined benefit plans, at the beginning of the fiscal years 1984 and 1983, with the data for the Salaried Employees' Retirement Plan as in effect on August 1, 1984, were as follows (in thousands of dollars):

	1984	1983
Actuarial present value of accumulated plan benefits:		
Vested	$52,639	$108,123
Nonvested	2,363	5,227
	$55,002	$113,350
Net assets available for benefits:		
Asset s of the Pension Trusts	$45,331	$112,075
Accrued contributions not paid to the Trusts	16,717	12,167
	$62,048	$124,242

The Salaried Employees' Retirement Plan, which covers substantially all salaried employees in the U.S., was restructured during 1984 due to overfunding of the Plan. Effective August 1, 1984, the Corporation terminated the existing plan and established a new plan which is substantially identical to the prior plan except for an improvement in the minimum pension benefit. All participants in the prior plan became fully vested upon its termination. All vested benefits earned through August 1, 1984 were covered through the purchase of individual annu-ities at a cost aggregating $36.7 million. The remaining plan assets, which totaled $39.3 million, reverted to the Corporation in cash upon receipt of regulatory approval of the prior plan termination from the Pension Benefit Guaranty Corporation. For financial reporting purposes, the new plan is considered to be a continuation of the terminated plan. Accordingly, the $39.3 million actuarial gain which resulted from the restructuring is included in Accrued Pension Costs in the accompanying Balance Sheet and is being amortized to income over a ten-year period commencing in 1984. For tax reporting purposes, the asset reversion will be treated as a fiscal 1985 transaction. The initial unfunded actuarial liability of the new plan, computed as of November 1, 1983, of $10.3 million is also included in Accrued Pension Costs.

In 1982 and 1983, the Pension Trusts purchased certain securities with effective yields of 13% and 12%, respectively, and dedicated these assets to the plan benefits of a substantial portion of the retired employees and certain terminated employees with deferred vested rights. These rates, together with 9% for active employees in 1984, 8% in 1983 and 7¼% in 1982, were the assumed rates of return used in determining the annual pension expense and the actuarial present value of accumulated plan benefits for the U.S. plans.

The effect of the changes in the investment return assumption rates for all U.S. plans, together with the 1984 restructuring of the U.S. Salaried Employees' Plan, was to reduce pension expense by approximately $4.0 million in 1984 and $2.0 million in 1983, and the actuarial present value of accumulated plan benefits by approximately $60.0 million in 1984. Pension expense in 1983 was also reduced $2.1 million from the lower level of active employees. Other actuarial gains, including higher than anticipated investment results, more than offset the additional pension costs resulting from plan changes and interest charges on balance sheet accruals in 1984 and 1983.

The Corporation's foreign pension plans do not determine the actuarial value of accumulated benefits or net assets available for retirement benefits as calculated and disclosed above. For those plans, the total of the plans' pension funds and balance sheet accruals approximated the actuarially computed value of vested benefits at both October 31, 1984 and 1983.

The Corporation generally provides certain health care and life insurance benefits for U.S. retired employees. Substantially all of the Corporation's current U.S. employees may become eligible for such benefits upon retirement. Life insurance benefits are provided either through the pension plans or separate group insurance arrangements. The cost of retiree health care and life insurance benefits, other than the benefits provided by the pension plans, is expensed as incurred; such costs approximated $2.6 million in 1984 and $1.7 million in 1983.

Note 12

Income Taxes:

Domestic and foreign income (loss) before income tax effects was as follows (in thousands of dollars):

	Year Ended October 31,		
	1984	1983	1982
Domestic	**$1,578**	$(35,412)	$(77,600)
Foreign:			
Harnischfeger GmbH	**432**	(2,159)	(475)
All other	**3,728**	4,768	8,418
	4,160	2,609	7,943
Total income (loss) before income tax effects, equity items and cumulative effect of accounting change	**$5,738**	$(32,803)	$(69,657)

Provision (credit) for income taxes, on income (loss) before income tax effects, equity items and cumulative effect of accounting change, consisted of (in thousands of dollars):

	1984	1983	1982
Currently payable (refundable):			
Federal	$ —	$(7,957))	$(9,736)
State	**136**	297	70
Foreign	**2,518**	3,379	5,376
	2,654	(4,281)	(4,290)
Deferred (prepaid):			
Federal	—	2,955	2,713
State and foreign	**(229)**	(74)	(23)
	(229)	2,881	2,690
Provision (credit) for income taxes	**$2,425**	$(1,400)	$(1,600)

During 1983 an examination of the Corporation's 1977–1981 federal income tax returns and certain refund claims was completed by the Internal Revenue Service, and as a result, a current credit for federal income taxes of $8.0 million was recorded in 1983, $3.0 million of which was applied to the reduction of prepaid income taxes.

In 1984, tax credits fully offset any federal income tax otherwise applicable to the year's income, and in 1983 and 1982, the relationship of the tax benefit to the pre-tax loss differed substantially from the U.S. statutory tax rate due principally to losses from the domestic operations for which only a partial federal tax benefit was available in 1982. Consequently, an

Harnischfeger Corporation

analysis of deferred income taxes and variance from the U.S. statutory rate is not presented.

Unremitted earnings of foreign subsidiaries which have been or are intended to be permanently reinvested were $19.1 million at October 31, 1984. Such earnings, if distributed, would incur income tax expense of substantially less than the U.S. income tax rate as a result of previously paid foreign income taxes, provided that such foreign taxes would become deductible as foreign tax credits. No income tax provision was made in respect of the tax-deferred income of a consolidated subsidiary that has elected to be taxed as a domestic international sales corporation. The Deficit Reduction Act of 1984 provides for such income to become nontaxable effective December 31, 1984.

At October 31, 1984, the Corporation had federal tax operating loss carry-forwards of approximately $70.0 million, expiring in 1998 and 1999, for tax return purposes, and $88.0 million for book purposes. In addition, the Corporation had for tax purposes, foreign tax credit carry-forwards of $3.0 million (expiring in 1985 through 1989), and investment tax credit carry-forwards of $1.0 million (expiring in 1997 through 1999). For book purposes, tax credit carry-forwards approximatevlidating eliminations for intercompany profits in inventories, and provisions, principally, for warranty, pension, compensated absences, product liability and plant closing costs.

REPORT OF INDEPENDENT ACCOUNTANTS

Milwaukee, Wisconsin
November 29, 1984

To the Directors and Shareholders of Harnischfeger Corporation:

In our opinion, the financial statements, which appear on pages 18 to 34 of this report, present fairly the consolidated financial position of Harnischfeger Corporation and its subsidiaries at October 31, 1984 and 1983, and the results of their operations and the changes in their financial position for each of the three years in the period ended October 31, 1984, in conformity with generally accepted accounting principles consistently applied during the period except for the change, with which we concur, in the method of accounting for depreciation expense as described in Note 2 on page 23 of this report. Our examinations of these statements were made in accordance with generally accepted auditing standards and accordingly included such tests of the accounting records and such other auditing procedures as we considered necessary in the circumstances.

Price Waterhouse

Implementing Accounting Analysis

We learned in Chapter 3 that accounting analysis requires the analyst to adjust a firm's accounting numbers using cash flow and footnote information to "undo" any accounting distortions. This entails recasting a firm's financial statements using standard reporting nomenclature and formats. Firms frequently use somewhat different formats and terminology for presenting their financial results. Recasting the financial statements using a standard template, therefore, helps ensure that performance metrics used for financial analysis are calculated using comparable definitions across companies and over time.

Once the financial statements have been standardized, the analyst is ready to identify any distortions in financial statements. The analyst's primary focus should be on those accounting estimates and methods that the firm uses to measure its key success factors and risks. If there are differences in these estimates and/or methods between firms or for the same firm over time, the analyst's job is to assess whether they reflect legitimate business differences and therefore require no adjustment, or whether they reflect differences in managerial judgment or bias and require adjustment. In addition, even if accounting rules are adhered to consistently, accounting distortions can arise because accounting rules themselves do a poor job of capturing firm economics, creating opportunities for the analyst to adjust a firm's financials in a way that presents a more realistic picture of its performance.

This chapter shows how to recast the firm's financial statements into a template that uses standard terminology and classifications, discusses the most common types of accounting distortions that can arise, and shows how to make adjustments to the standardized financial statements to undo these distortions.

A balance sheet approach is used to identify whether there have been any distortions to assets, liabilities, or owners' equity. Once any asset and liability misstatements have been identified, the analyst can make adjustments to the balance sheet at the beginning and/or end of the current year, as well as any needed adjustments to revenues and expenses in the latest income statement. This approach ensures that the most recent financial ratios used to evaluate a firm's performance and forecast its future results are based on financial data that appropriately reflect its business economics.

In some instances, information taken from a firm's footnotes and cash flow statement enables the analyst to make a precise adjustment for an accounting distortion. However, for many types of accounting adjustments the company does not disclose all of the information needed to perfectly undo the distortion, requiring the analyst to make an approximate adjustment to the financial statements.

RECASTING FINANCIAL STATEMENTS

Firms sometimes use different nomenclature and formats to present their financial results. For example, the asset goodwill can be reported separately using such titles as Goodwill, "Excess of cost over net assets of acquired companies," and "Cost in excess of fair value," or it can be included in the line item Other Intangible Assets. Interest Income can be reported as a subcategory of Revenues, shown lower down the income statement as part of Other Income and Expenses, or it is sometimes reported as Interest Expense, Net of Interest Income.

These differences in financial statement terminology, classifications, and formats can make it difficult to compare performance across firms, and sometimes to compare performance for the same firm over time. The first task for the analyst in accounting analysis is, therefore, to recast the financial statements into a common format. This involves designing a template for the balance sheet, income statement, and cash flow statement that can be used to standardize financial statements for any company. Tables 4-1, 4-2, and 4-3 present the format used throughout the book to standardize the income statement, balance sheet, and cash flow statement, respectively.

Table 4-1   Standardized Income Statement Format

Standard Income Statement Accounts	Sample Line Items Classified in Account
Sales	Revenues Membership fees Commissions Licenses
Cost of Sales	Cost of merchandise sold Cost of products sold Cost of revenues Cost of services Depreciation on manufacturing facilities
SG&A	General and administrative Marketing & sales Salaries and benefits Servicing and maintenance Depreciation on selling and administrative facilities
Other Operating Expense	Amortization of intangibles Product development Research & development Provision for losses on credit sales Pre-opening costs Special charges
Net Interest Expense (Income) 　Interest Income 　Interest Expense	
Investment Income	Equity income from associates Dividend income Rental income
Other Income	Gains on sale of investments/long-term assets Foreign exchange gains Pre-tax gains from accounting changes
Other Expense	Losses on sale of investments/long-term assets Foreign exchange losses Pre-tax losses from accounting changes Restructuring charges Merger expenses Asset impairments
Minority Interest	
Tax Expense	Provision for taxes
Unusual Items (after tax)	Any gains or losses reported on an after tax-basis, such as: 　Extraordinary items 　Non-recurring charges 　Effect of accounting changes

Table 4-2 Standardized Balance Sheet Format

Standard Balance Sheet Accounts	Sample Line Items Classified in Account
Assets	
Cash and Marketable Securities	Cash Short-term investments Time deposits
Accounts Receivable	Accounts/trade receivables Trade debtors
Inventory	Inventory Finished goods Raw materials Work-in-process Stocks
Deferred Taxes – Current Asset	
Other Current Assets	Prepaid expenses Taxes refundable Current assets of discontinued operations Due from affiliates Due from employees
Long-Term Tangible Assets	Plant, property & equipment Land Non-current assets of discontinued operations
Long-Term Intangible Assets	Goodwill Software development costs Deferred financing costs Deferred subscriber acquisition costs Deferred charges Trademarks License rights
Deferred Taxes – LT Asset	
Other Long-Term Assets	Long-term investments Long-term receivables Investment in sales-type or direct-financing leases

Standard Balance Sheet Accounts	Sample Line Items Classified in Account
Liabilities and Equity	
Short-Term Debt	Notes payable Current portion of long-term debt Current portion of capital lease obligation
Accounts Payable	Accounts/trade payables Trade creditors
Other Current Liabilities	Accrued expenses Accrued liabilities Taxes payable Dividends payable Deferred (unearned) revenue Customer advances
Deferred Taxes – Current Liability	
Long-Term Debt	Long-term debt Senior term notes Subordinated debt Capital lease obligations Convertible debt Pension/post-retirement benefit obligation
Deferred Taxes – Long-term Liability	
Other Long-Term Liabilities (non-interest bearing)	Non-current deferred (unearned) revenues Other non-current liabilities
Minority Interest	
Preferred Stock	Preferred stock Preferred convertible stock
Common Shareholders' Equity	Common stock Additional paid-in capital Capital in excess of par Treasury stock Retained earnings Cumulative foreign currency gains and losses Accumulated other comprehensive income

Table 4-3 Standardized Cash Flow Statement Format

Standard Cash Flow Statement Accounts	Sample Line Items Classified in Account
Net Income	
Non-operating Gains (Losses)	Gain (loss) on sale of investments/non-current assets
	Cumulative effect of accounting changes
	Gain (loss) on foreign exchange
	Extraordinary gains (losses)
Long-Term Operating Accruals	Depreciation and amortization
	Deferred revenues/costs
	Deferred income taxes
	Impairment of non-current assets
	Other non-cash charges to operations
	Equity earnings of affiliates/unconsolidated subs, net of cash received
	Minority interest
	Stock bonus awards
Net (Investments in) or Liquidation of Operating Working Capital	Changes in:
	Trade accounts receivable
	Other receivables
	Prepaid expenses
	Trade accounts payable
	Accrued expenses (liabilities)
	Due from affiliates
	Accounts payable and accrued expenses
	Refundable/payable income taxes
	Inventories
	Provision for doubtful accounts
	Other current liabilities
	Other current assets
Net (Investment in) or Liquidation of Operating Long-Term Assets	Purchase/sale of non-current assets
	Acquisition of research and development
	Acquisition/sale of business
	Capital expenditures
	Equity investments
	Acquisition of subsidiary stock
	Capitalization of computer software development costs
	Cost in excess of the fair value of net assets acquired
	Investment in sales-type and direct financing leases
Net Debt (Repayment) or Issuance	Principal payments on debt
	Borrowings (repayments) under credit facility
	Issuance (repayment) of long-term debt
	Net increase (decrease) in short-term borrowings
	Notes payable
Dividend (Payments)	Cash dividends paid on common stock
	Cash dividends paid on preferred stock
	Distributions
Net Stock (Repurchase) or Issuance	Proceeds from issuance of common stock
	Issue of common stock for services
	Issue (redemption) of preferred securities
	Issue of subsidiary equity
	Purchase (issue) of treasury stock

To create standardized financials for a particular company of interest, the analyst classifies each line item in that firm's financial statements using the appropriate account name from the above templates. This may require using information from the footnotes to ensure that accounts are classified appropriately. An example, applying the above template to standardize the 2002 financial statements for fashion retailer Nordstrom Inc., is shown in the appendix at the end of this chapter.

Once the financials have been standardized, the analyst can evaluate whether accounting adjustments are needed to correct for any distortions in assets, liabilities, or equity.

ASSET DISTORTIONS

Accountants define assets as resources that a firm owns or controls as a result of past business transactions, and which are expected to produce future economic benefits that can be measured with a reasonable degree of certainty. Assets can take a variety of forms, including cash, marketable securities, receivables from customers, inventory, fixed assets, long-term investments in other companies, and intangibles.

Distortions in asset values generally arise because there is ambiguity about whether

- The firm owns or controls the economic resources in question, or
- The economic resources are likely to provide future economic benefits that can be measured with reasonable certainty, or
- The fair value of assets fall below their book values.

Who owns or controls resources?

For most resources used by a firm, ownership or control is relatively straightforward: the firm using the resource owns the asset. However, some types of transactions make it difficult to assess who owns a resource. For example, who owns or controls a resource that has been leased? Is it the lessor or the lessee? Or consider a firm that discounts a customer receivable with a bank. If the bank has recourse against the firm should the customer default, is the real owner of the receivable the bank or the company?

Accountants frequently use mechanical rules to determine whether a company owns or controls an asset. While these rules make it easy for accountants to implement accounting standards, they also permit managers to "groom" transactions to satisfy their own financial reporting objectives. For example, U.S. rules on lease accounting permit two lease transactions with essentially the same terms to be structured so that one is reported as an asset by the lessee, and the other is shown as an asset by the lessor. Accounting analysis, therefore, involves assessing whether a firm's reported assets adequately reflect the key resources that are under its control, and whether adjustments are required to compare its performance with that of competitors.

Asset ownership issues also arise indirectly from the application of rules for revenue recognition. Firms are permitted to recognize revenues only when their product has been shipped or their service has been provided to the customer. Revenues are then considered "earned," and the customer has a legal commitment to pay for the product or service. As a result, for the seller, recognition of revenue frequently coincides with "ownership" of a receivable that is shown as an asset on its balance sheet. Accounting analysis that raises questions about whether or not revenues have been earned therefore often affects the valuation of assets.

Ambiguity over whether a company owns an asset creates a number of opportunities for accounting analysis:

- Despite management's best intentions, financial statements sometimes do a poor job of reflecting the firm's economic assets since it is difficult for accounting rules to capture all of the subtleties associated with ownership and control.

- Because accounting rules on ownership and control permit managers to groom transactions so that essentially similar transactions can be reported in very different ways, important assets may be omitted from the balance sheet even though the firm bears many of the economic risks of ownership.
- There may be legitimate differences in opinion between managers and analysts over residual ownership risks borne by the company, leading to differences in opinion over reporting for these assets.
- Aggressive revenue recognition, which boosts reported earnings, is also likely to affect asset values.

Can economic benefits be measured with reasonable certainty?

It is almost always difficult to accurately forecast the future benefits associated with capital outlays because the world is uncertain. A company does not know whether a competitor will offer a new product or service that makes its own obsolete. It does not know whether the products manufactured at a new plant will be the type that customers want to buy. A company does not know whether changes in oil prices will make the oil drilling equipment that it manufactures less valuable.

Accounting rules deal with these challenges by stipulating which types of resources can be recorded as assets and which cannot. For example, the economic benefits from research and development are generally considered highly uncertain: research projects may never deliver promised new products, the products they generate may not be economically viable, or products may be made obsolete by competitors' research. Accounting rules in most countries, therefore, require that R&D outlays be expensed.[1] In contrast, the economic benefits from plant acquisitions are considered less uncertain and are required to be capitalized.

Rules that require the immediate expensing of outlays for some key resources may be good accounting, but they create a challenge for the analyst—namely, they lead to less timely financial statements. For example, if all firms expense R&D, financial statements will reflect differences in R&D success only when new products are commercialized rather than during the development process. The analyst may attempt to correct for this distortion by capitalizing key R&D outlays and adjusting the value of the intangible asset based on R&D updates.[2]

Have fair values of assets declined below book value?

An asset is impaired when its fair value falls below its book value. In most countries accounting rules require that a loss be recorded for permanent asset impairments. U.S. rules (SFAS 144) specify that an impairment loss be recognized on a long-term asset when its book value exceeds the *undiscounted* cash flows expected to be generated from future use and sale. If this condition is satisfied, the firm is required to report a loss for the difference between the asset's fair value and its book value.

Of course markets for many long-term operating assets are illiquid and incomplete, making it highly subjective to infer their fair values. Consequently, considerable management judgement is involved in deciding whether an asset is impaired and determining the value of any impairment loss.

For the analyst, this raises the possibility that asset values are misstated. U.S. accounting rules themselves permit a certain amount of asset overstatement since the test for asset impairment compares the asset's book value to the expected value of *undiscounted* (rather than *discounted*) future cash flows associated with the asset. This can create situations where no financial statement loss is reported for an asset that is economically impaired.

In addition, the task of determining whether there has been an asset impairment and valuing the impairment is delegated to management, with oversight by the firm's auditors, potentially leaving opportunities for management bias in valuing assets and for legitimate differences in opinion between managers and analysts over asset valuations. In most cases, management bias will lead to overstated assets since managers will prefer not to recognize an impairment. However, managers can also bias asset values downward by "taking a bath," reducing future expenses and increasing future earnings.

In summary, distortions in assets are likely to arise when there is ambiguity about whether the firm owns or controls a resource, when there is a high degree of uncertainty about the value of the economic benefits to be derived from the resource, and when there are differences in opinion about the value of asset impairments. Opportunities for accounting adjustments can arise in these situations if

- Accounting rules do not do a good job of capturing the firm's economics, or
- Managers use their discretion to distort the firm's performance, or
- There are legitimate differences in opinion between managers and analysts about economic uncertainties facing the firm that are reflected in asset values.

OVERSTATED ASSETS

Asset overstatements are likely to arise when managers have incentives to increase reported earnings. Thus, adjustments to assets also typically require adjustments to the income statement in the form of either increased expenses or reduced revenues. The most common forms of asset (and earnings) overstatement are the following:

1. *Delays in writing down current assets.* If current assets become impaired, that is, their book values fall below their realizable values, accounting rules generally require that they be written down to their fair values. Current asset impairments also affect earnings since write-offs are charged directly to earnings. Deferring current asset write-downs is, therefore, one way for managers to boost reported profits.[3] Analysts that cover firms where management of inventories and receivables is a key success factor (e.g., the retail and manufacturing industries) need to be particularly cognizant of this form of earnings management. If managers over-buy or over-produce in the current period, they are likely to have to offer customers discounts to get rid of surplus inventories. In addition, providing customers with credit carries risks of default. Warning signs for delays in current asset write-downs include growing days' inventory and days' receivable, write-downs by competitors, and business downturns for a firm's major customers.

2. *Underestimated reserves (e.g., allowances for bad debts or loan losses).* Managers make estimates of expected customer defaults on accounts receivable and loans. If managers underestimate the value of these reserves, assets and earnings will be overstated. Warning signs of inadequate allowances include growing days receivable, business downturns for a firm's major clients, and growing loan delinquencies.

3. *Accelerated recognition of revenues (increasing receivables).* Managers typically have the best information on the uncertainties governing revenue recognition—whether a product or service has been provided to customers and whether cash collection is reasonably likely. However, managers may also have incentives to accelerate the recognition of revenues, boosting reported earnings for the period. Accounts

receivable and earnings will then be overstated. Aggressive revenue recognition is one of the most popular forms of earnings management cited by the SEC.

4. *Delayed write-downs of long-term assets.* Deteriorating industry or firm economic conditions can affect the value of long-term assets as well as current assets. Firms are required to recognize impairments in the values of long-term assets when they arise. However, since second-hand markets for long-term assets are typically illiquid and incomplete, estimates of asset valuations and impairment are inherently subjective. This is particularly true for intangible assets such as goodwill. As a result, managers can use their reporting judgment to delay write-downs on the balance sheet and avoid showing impairment charges in the income statement.[4] This issue is likely to be particularly critical for heavy asset-intensive firms in volatile markets (e.g., airlines) or for firms that follow a strategy of aggressive growth through acquisitions.[5] Warning signs of impairments in long-term assets include declining long-term asset turnover, declines in return on assets to levels lower than the weighted average cost of capital, write-downs by other firms in the same industry that have also suffered deteriorating asset use, and overpayment for or unsuccessful integration of key acquisitions.

5. *Overstated depreciation/amortization on long-term assets.* Managers make estimates of asset lives, salvage values, and amortization schedules for depreciable long-term assets. If these estimates are optimistic, long-term assets and earnings will be overstated. This issue is likely to be most pertinent for firms in heavy asset businesses (e.g., airlines, utilities).

Examples of How to Correct for Asset Overstatement

We illustrate some of the distortions that lead to overstated assets, and the types of corrections that the analyst can make to reduce bias in the financial statements.

Delaying Write-Downs of Current Assets   The dot-com stock market crash in April 2000 had a ripple effect on firms selling equipment to the telecommunications and Internet industries. One of the firms affected was Lucent Technologies. For Lucent the first sign of a downturn came in the June 2000 quarter, when earnings declined markedly over the same period one year earlier. This pattern persisted through the September and December 2000 quarters, when the company reported operating losses of $2.1 billion and $4.8 billion, respectively.

The decline in Lucent's performance and future prospects raised questions for analysts about whether the company's inventory was impaired. In December 2000 Lucent reported inventory valued at $6.9 billion, $1.5 billion higher than one year earlier. Yet sales for the December 2000 quarter ($5.8 billion) had declined precipitously relative to the same quarter in 1999 ($9.9 billion). As a result, Lucent's Day's Inventory increased from 58 days to 107 days. In the same period, the company's gross margins declined from 47 percent to 22 percent. Despite these significant declines in performance, Lucent recorded no inventory impairment charge for the December 2000 quarter.

Obviously it is difficult for an analyst to assess whether Lucent's inventory was impaired or to assess the severity of any impairment. By talking to Lucent's customers and by observing the performance of other firms in the industry, however, the analyst can judge whether the company's problems are likely to persist, whether there are serious technological risks for current inventory and, if so, the value of an appropriate impairment charge.

Having concluded that inventory was overstated, the analyst would have to revise the inventory level down, and show a decline in equity to reflect the after-tax cost of the impairment. In addition, the tax effect of the adjustment would be reflected in the company's Deferred Tax Liability, since the inventory write-down is assumed to only affect Lucent's financial reporting books. Its separate tax books are determined by IRS tax rules, which are assumed to be independent of financial reporting rules. For example, if an analyst concluded that Lucent's inventory was overstated by, say, $500 million, given the company's 35 percent marginal tax rate, the adjustment required to correct this overstatement in the December 31, 2000, financial statements would be as follows:

($ millions)	Adjustment	
	Assets	Liabilities & Equity
Balance Sheet		
Inventory	−500	
Deferred Tax Liability		−175
Common Shareholders' Equity		−325
Income Statement		
Cost of Sales		+500
Tax Expense		−175
Net Income		−325

In March 2001, following another quarter of deteriorating performance, Lucent announced that it would take a $536 million inventory write-down. This was followed by an additional write-down of $143 million at the end of June and $11 million in September.

Underestimating Reserves   Assets can also be overstated if reserve estimates are understated. For example, consider Lucent's accounts receivable allowances at the end of December 2000. As reported in its footnotes, allowances were increased from 5 percent in September 2000 to 7 percent in December of the same year. The challenge for the analyst is to assess whether this increase is adequate given the dramatic decline in the fortunes of Lucent's Internet and telecommunication customers. This requires a thorough review of the short-term cash generating potential of Lucent's major customers to judge how much of Lucent's receivables are likely to actually be collected.

If the analyst decides that receivable allowances are understated, adjustments have to be made to Accounts Receivable and to Equity for the after-tax cost of the incremental bad debt expense. For example, if the analyst decided that receivable allowances for Lucent should be 9 percent rather than 7 percent, Accounts Receivable would have to be reduced by $150 million. Given the company's marginal tax rate of 35 percent, this would reduce earnings and equity by $97.5 million, and reduce the Deferred Tax Liability by $52.5 million. The adjustment to the December 31, 2000, financial statements would, therefore, be as follows:

($ millions)	Adjustment	
	Assets	Liabilities & Equity
Balance Sheet		
Accounts Receivable	−150.0	
Deferred Tax Liability		−52.5
Common Shareholders' Equity		−97.5
Income Statement		
Cost of Sales		+150.0
Tax Expense		−52.5
Net Income		−97.5

Perhaps because it understated its receivables at the end of 2000, or perhaps because the problems facing the industry proved to be more serious than anyone could have anticipated, Lucent reported a steady increase in allowance estimates as a percent of gross receivables throughout 2001. Reported estimates were 8.7 percent in March, 11.2 percent in June, 12.5 percent in September, and 19.5 percent in December.

Accelerating Recognition of Revenues In November 1999 and January 2000, analysts at the Center for Financial Research and Analysis (CFRA) raised questions about the propriety of revenue recognition for MicroStrategy, a software company. MicroStrategy recognized revenues from the sale of licenses "after execution of a licensing agreement and shipment of the product, provided that no significant Company obligations remain and the resulting receivable is deemed collectible by management."[6] CFRA analysts were concerned about MicroStrategy's booking two contracts worth $27 million as quarterly revenues when the contracts were not announced until several days after the quarter's end. If the analysts decided to adjust for these distortions, the following changes would have to be made to Micro-Strategy's financial reports:

1. In the quarter that the contracts were booked, Sales and Accounts Receivable would both decline by $27 million.
2. Cost of Sales would decline and Inventory would increase to reflect the reduction in sales. The value of the Cost of Sales/Inventory adjustment can be estimated by multiplying the sales adjustment by the ratio of cost of sales to sales. For MicroStrategy, cost of license revenues is only 3 percent of license revenues, indicating that the adjustment would be modest ($0.8m). Also, since MicroStrategy does not have any inventory, the balance sheet adjustment would be to prepaid expenses, which are included in Other Current Assets on the standardized balance sheet.
3. The decline in pretax income would result in a lower Tax Expense in the company's financial reporting books (but presumably not in its tax books). Consequently, the Deferred Tax Liability would have to be reduced. MicroStrategy's marginal tax rate was 35 percent, implying that the decline in the Tax Expense and Deferred Tax Liability was $9.2 million [($27 − 0.8) × .35].

The full effect of the adjustment on the quarterly financial statements would therefore be as follows:

($ millions)	Adjustment	
	Assets	Liabilities & Equity
Balance Sheet		
Accounts Receivable	−27.0	
Other Current Assets	+0.8	
Deferred Tax Liability		−9.2
Common Shareholders' Equity		−17.0
Income Statement		
Sales		−27.0
Cost of Sales		−0.8
Tax Expense		−9.2
Net Income		−17.0

Of course, provided the contracts were legitimate transactions, the above adjustments imply that forecasts of next quarter's revenues should include the $27 million worth of contracts.

In March 2000 MicroStrategy confirmed that the CFRA analysts' suspicions about aggressive revenue recognition were founded. The company announced that it had "recorded revenue on certain contracts in one reporting period where customer signature and delivery had been completed, but where the contract may not have been fully executed by the Company in that reporting period."[7] After reviewing all licensing contracts near the end of the prior three years, MicroStrategy was forced to restate its financial statements to correct for the improprieties. The outcome was that accounts receivable for 1999 were reduced from $61.1 million to $37.6 million, leading to a dramatic drop in the company's stock price.

Delaying Write-Downs of Long-Term Assets Consider the widely acclaimed merger between AOL and Time Warner. The combination of the two companies was justified as enabling AOL to cross-sell Time Warner's content (film, news, etc.) to its large subscriber base, a win for both companies. As evidence of the value created from the merger, in its first annual report after the merger, in December 2001, the new company reported goodwill valued at $128 billion. Careful strategic analysis, however, would raise some questions about the merits of the deal. Earlier combinations of content providers and distributors in the entertainment industry (e.g., Disney's acquisition of ABC) had faced difficulties in realizing their potential. Why would the outcome of an AOL and Time Warner merger be any different? Also, it was not clear why AOL had to buy Time Warner to access its content. Why couldn't AOL simply sign a long-term licensing agreement for content with Time Warner? Finally, the merger raised questions about AOL and Time Warner relations with existing customers and suppliers. For example, would Time Warner still be able to sell its content to AOL's competitors (e.g., Microsoft), or would its own market be narrowed? Would AOL still be able to negotiate content deals with Time Warner's competitors? If Time Warner's content became stale, would AOL be committed to continue supplying it to its subscribers, leading to a decline in the value of both firms?

The questions about the economic benefits from the merger were quickly answered when Internet sector stocks crashed in mid-2000. AOL subsequently struggled to retain and grow its subscriber base and encountered more difficulty than expected in developing a successful business model to take advantage of Time Warner's content. As a result, in its December 31, 2001, report, the new company was forced to recognize that goodwill recorded under the merger was impaired and would have to be written down by $54 billion at the end of the following quarter (March 2002).

This raises several issues for analyzing AOL Time Warner. First, given the questionable strategic rationale for the merger in the first place, did the initial $128 billion of goodwill ever represent a true economic asset? If not, when would it make sense to recognize the impairment of goodwill—prior to December 31, 2000, in the December 31 financials, or when the company subsequently reported the decline in value (March 2002)? Second, was the $54 billion write-down adequate given the magnitude of the Internet stock market crash, which indicated that investors as a whole had radically lowered their expectations for Internet stocks such as AOL.

If an analyst decided to record the $54 billion write-down in the December 2001 financials, it would be necessary to make the following balance sheet adjustments:

1. Reduce Long-term Intangible Assets by $54 billion.
2. Reduce the Deferred Tax Liability for the tax effect of the write-down. Assuming a 35 percent tax rate, this amounts to $19 billion.
3. Reduce Common Shareholders' Equity for the after-tax effect of the write-down ($35 billion).

($ billions)	Adjustment	
	Assets	Liabilities & Equity
Balance Sheet		
Long-Term Intangible Assets	−54	
Deferred Tax Liability		−19
Common Shareholders' Equity		−35
Income Statement		
Other Expenses		+54
Tax Expense		−19
Net Income		−35

Note that the write-down of depreciable assets at the beginning of the year will require the analyst to also estimate the write-down's impact on depreciation and amortization expense for the year. For AOL Time Warner, since the asset is goodwill, which is no longer amortized (see SFAS 142), no such expense adjustment is required.

At the end of 2002, AOL announced the write-down of a further $45.5 billion of goodwill, and many of the top AOL managers that had advocated the merger in the first place were no longer with the company.

UNDERSTATED ASSETS

Asset understatements typically arise when managers have incentives to deflate reported earnings. This may occur when the firm is performing exceptionally well and managers decide to store away some of the current strong earnings for a rainy day. Income smoothing, as it has come to be known, can be implemented by overstating current period expenses (and understating the value of assets) during good times. Asset (and expense) understatements can also arise in a particularly bad year, when managers decide to "take a bath" by understating current period earnings to create the appearance of a turnaround in following years. Accounting analysis involves judging whether managers have understated assets (and also income) and, if necessary, adjusting the balance sheet and income statement accordingly.

Accounting rules themselves can also lead to the understatement of assets. In many countries accounting standards require firms to expense outlays for R&D and advertising because, even though they may create future value for owners, their outcomes are highly uncertain. Also, until recently some U.S. acquisitions were accounted for using the pooling of interests method, whereby the acquirer recorded the target's assets at their book value rather than their actual (higher) purchase price. In these cases the analyst may want to make adjustments to the balance sheet and income statement to ensure that they reflect the economic reality of the transactions.

Finally, asset understatements can arise when managers have incentives to understate liabilities. For example, if a firm records lease transactions as operating leases or if it discounts receivables with recourse, neither the assets nor the accompanying obligations are shown on its balance sheet. Yet in some instances this accounting treatment does not reflect the underlying economics of the transactions—the lessee may effectively own the leased assets, and the firm that sells receivables may still bear all of the risks associated with ownership. The analyst may then want to adjust the balance sheet (and also the income statement) for these effects.

The most common forms of asset (and earnings) understatement arise when there are the following:

1. *Overstated write-downs of current assets.* Managers potentially have an incentive to overstate current asset write-downs during years of exceptionally strong performance, or when the firm is financially distressed. By overstating current asset impairments and overstating expenses in the current period, managers can show lower future expenses, boosting earnings in years of sub-par performance or when a turnaround is needed. Overstated current asset write-downs can also arise when managers are less optimistic about the firm's future prospects than the analyst.

2. *Overestimated reserves (e.g., allowances for bad debts or loan losses).* If managers overestimate reserves for bad debts or loan losses, accounts receivable and loans will be understated.

3. *Overstated write-downs of long-term assets.* Overly pessimistic management estimates of long-term asset impairments reduce current period earnings and boost earnings in future periods.

4. *Overstated depreciation/amortization on long-term assets.* Firms that use tax depreciation estimates of asset lives, salvage values, or amortization rates are likely to amortize assets more rapidly than justifiable given the assets' economic usefulness, leading to long-term asset understatements.

5. *Excluded goodwill assets through the use of pooling accounting.* Recent changes in U.S. rules for merger accounting (SFAS 141 and 142) require that firms report mergers using the purchase method. Under this method the cost of the merger for the acquirer is the actual value of the consideration paid for the target firm's shares. The identifiable assets and liabilities of the target are then recorded on the acquirer's books at their fair values. If the value of the consideration paid for the target exceeds the fair value of its identifiable assets and liabilities, the excess is reported

as goodwill on the acquirer's balance sheet. The new rules require goodwill assets to be written off only if they become impaired in the future. However, as recently as 2001 many large acquisitions were reported using the pooling of interests method. Under the pooling of interests method, the purchase of target firm's shares is recorded at their historical book value rather than at their market value, so that no goodwill is recorded. Consequently, pooling does not reflect the true economic cost of the acquisition on the acquirer's books, making it more difficult for shareholders to understand the economic performance of the new firm after the merger.[8] This is likely to be a consideration for the analyst in evaluating the performance of serial stock-for-stock acquirers.[9]

6. *Lease assets off balance sheet.* Assessing whether a lease arrangement should be considered a rental contract (and hence recorded using the operating method) or equivalent to a purchase (and hence shown as a capital lease) is subjective. It depends on whether the lessee has effectively accepted most of the risks of ownership, such as obsolescence and physical deterioration. To standardize the reporting of lease transactions, U.S. accounting standards have created clear criteria for distinguishing between the two types. Under SFAS 13, a lease transaction is equivalent to an asset purchase if any of the following conditions hold: (1) ownership of the asset is transferred to the lessee at the end of the lease term, (2) the lessee has the option to purchase the asset for a bargain price at the end of the lease term, (3) the lease term is 75 percent or more of the asset's expected useful life, and (4) the present value of the lease payments is 90 percent or more of the fair value of the asset. However, because the criteria for reporting leases are objective, they create opportunities for management to circumvent the spirit of the distinction between capital and operating leases, potentially leading to the understatement of lease assets.[10] This is likely to be an important issue for the analysis of heavy asset industries where there are options for leasing (e.g., airlines).[11]

7. *Discounted receivables off balance sheet even though the firm still retains considerable collection risk.* Under current U.S. accounting rules (SFAS 140), receivables that are discounted with a financial institution are considered "sold" if the "seller" cedes control over the receivables to the financier. Control is surrendered if the receivables are beyond the reach of the seller's creditors should the seller file for bankruptcy, if the financier has the right to pledge or sell the receivables, and if the seller has no commitment to repurchase the receivables. The seller can then record the discount transaction as an asset sale. Otherwise it is viewed as a financing transaction that generates a liability for the "seller." However, just because a firm has "sold" receivables for financial reporting purposes does not necessarily mean that it is off the hook for credit risks. Financial institutions that discount receivables often have recourse against the "seller," requiring the seller to continue to estimate bad debt losses. In this event, U.S. rules permit the transaction to be reported as an asset sale only when the seller satisfies the above conditions for surrendering control of the receivables and has experience in estimating the value of the recourse liability (i.e., allowances for credit and refinancing risks). In extreme cases, where there is significant uncertainty about the value of the recourse liability, the analyst has to decide whether to restate the firm's financial statements by returning the "sold" receivables to the balance sheet. As discussed later in this chapter, this will also increase the firm's liabilities, and it will affect its income statement since any gains and losses on the sale need to be excluded, and interest income on the notes receivables and interest expense on the loan need to be recorded each year.

8. *Key intangible assets, such as R&D and brands, not reported on the balance sheet.* Some firms' most important assets are excluded from the balance sheet. Examples include investments in R&D, software development outlays, and brands and membership bases that are created through advertising and promotions. Accounting rules in most countries specifically prohibit the capitalization of R&D outlays and membership acquisition costs, primarily because it is believed that the benefits associated with such outlays are too uncertain.[12] New products or software may never reach the market due to technological infeasibility or to the introduction of superior products by competitors; new members that sign up for a service as a result of a promotions campaign may subsequently quit. Expensing the cost of intangibles has two implications for analysts. First, the omission of intangible assets from the balance sheet inflates measured rates of return on capital (either return on assets or return on equity).[13] For firms with key omitted intangible assets, this has important implications for forecasting long-term performance; unlike firms with no intangibles, competitive forces will not cause their rates of return to fully revert to the cost of capital over time. For example, pharmaceutical firms have shown very high rates of return over many decades, in part because of the impact of R&D accounting. A second effect of expensing outlays for intangibles is that it makes it more difficult for the analyst to assess whether the firm's business model works. Under the matching concept, operating profit is a meaningful indicator of the success of a firm's business model since it compares revenues and the expenses required to generate them. Immediately expensing outlays for intangible assets runs counter to matching and, therefore, makes it more difficult to judge a firm's operating performance. Consistent with this, research shows that investors view R&D and advertising outlays as assets rather than expenses.[14] Understated intangible assets are likely to be important for firms in pharmaceutical, software, branded consumer products, and subscription businesses.

Examples of How to Correct for Asset Understatement

We illustrate some of the types of distortions that understate assets, and show corrections that the analyst can make to ensure that assets are reflected appropriately.

Overstated Depreciation for Long-Term Assets. In 2001 Lufthansa, the German national airline, reported that it depreciated its aircraft over 12 years on a straight-line basis, with an estimated residual value of 15 percent of initial cost. In contrast, British Airways (BA), the UK national carrier, reported that its aircraft depreciation was also estimated using the straight-line method but assuming an average life of 20 years and an 8 percent salvage value.[15]

For the analyst these differences raise several questions. Do Lufthansa and BA fly different types of routes, potentially explaining the differences in their depreciation policies? Alternatively, do they have different asset management strategies? For example, does Lufthansa use newer planes to attract more business travelers, to lower maintenance costs, or to lower fuel costs? If there do not appear to be operating differences that explain the differences in the two firms' depreciation rates, the analyst may well decide that it is necessary to adjust the depreciation rates for one or both firms to ensure that their performance is comparable.

The difference in depreciation assumptions for BA and Lufthansa appears to at least partially reflect Lufthansa's decision to use similar depreciation rates for financial and tax reporting purposes, whereas BA uses different rates for these purposes. To adjust for this effect, the analyst could decrease Lufthansa's depreciation rates to match those of BA's. The following financial statement adjustments would then be required in Lufthansa's financial statements:

1. Increase the book value of the fleet at the beginning of the year to adjust for the relatively low depreciation rates that had been used in the past. This will also require an offsetting increase in equity (retained earnings), and in the deferred tax liability.

2. Reduce the depreciation expense (and increase the book value of the fleet) to reflect the lower depreciation for the current year. There will also be an increase in the tax expense, and on the balance sheet an increase in equity and deferred tax liability. In 2001 Lufthansa's marginal tax rate was 35 percent.

Note that these changes are designed to show Lufthansa's results as if it had always used the same depreciation assumptions as BA rather than to reflect a change in the assumptions for the current year going forward. This enables the analyst to be able to compare ratios that use assets (e.g., return on assets) for the two companies.

At the beginning of 2001, Lufthansa reported in its footnotes that its fleet of aircraft had originally cost 13,579.6m Euros, and that accumulated depreciation was 6,679.9m Euros. This implies that the average life of Lufthansa's fleet was 6.9 years, calculated as follows:

€ (millions unless otherwise noted)		
Aircraft cost, 1/1/2001	13,579.6	Reported
Depreciable cost	11,542.7	Cost × (1 − .15)
Accumulated depreciation, 1/1/2001	6,679.6	Reported
Accumulated depreciation/Depreciable cost	57.87%	
Depreciable life	12 years	Reported
Average age of aircraft	6.944 years	12 × .5787 years

If Lufthansa used the same life and salvage estimates as BA, the depreciable cost of its fleet would have been €12,493.2 [13,579.6 · (1 − .08)]. The annual depreciation rate would have been 5 percent, implying that given the average age of its fleet, Accumulated Depreciation would have been €4,337.6 (6.944 · .05 · 12,493.2) versus the reported €6,679.6. Consequently, the company's Long-term Tangible Assets would have increased by €2,341.9. Given the 35% marginal tax rate, this adjustment to Long-Term Tangible Assets would have required offsetting adjustments of €819.7 (.35 · 2,341.9) to the Deferred Tax Liability and €1,522.2 (.65 · 2,341.9) to Common Shareholders' Equity.

Assuming that €1,021.5m net new aircraft purchased in 2001 were acquired throughout the year, the depreciation expense for 2001 (included in Cost of Sales) would have been €648.2m {.05 · [12,493.2 + (1,021.5 · .92)/2]} versus the €865m reported by the company.[16] Thus Cost of Sales would decline by €216.8m. Given the 35 percent tax rate for 2001, the Tax Expense for the year would increase by €75.9m. On the balance sheet, these changes would increase Long-Term Tangible Assets by €216.8m, increase Deferred Tax Liability by €75.9m, and increase Common Shareholders' Equity by €140.9m.

In summary, if Lufthansa were using the same depreciation method as BA, its financial statements for the years ended December 31, 2000 and 2001, would have to be modified as follows:

(€ millions)	Adjustment Dec. 31, 2000		Adjustment Dec. 31, 2001	
	Assets	Liabilities & Equity	Assets	Liabilities & Equity
Balance Sheet				
Long-Term Tangible Assets	+2,341.9		+2,341.9 +216.8	
Deferred Tax Liability		+819.7		+819.7 +75.9
Common Shareholders' Equity		+1,522.2		+1,522.2 +140.9
Income Statement				
Cost of Sales				−216.8
Tax Expense				+75.9
Net Income				+140.9

Goodwill Excluded Through Use of Pooling Accounting.   In its June 2001 acquisition of ALZA, Johnson and Johnson (J&J) announced that it would use the pooling of interests method to record the transaction. Under the terms of the deal, J&J acquired ALZA's 234.3 million shares for 229.6 million J&J shares, valued at $12.2 billion. To adjust for the distortion from using pooling, the analyst can restate the acquirer's financial statements as follows:

1. Revalue the target's assets (and potentially its liabilities) to their fair values.
2. Recognize any goodwill from the transaction, computed as the difference between the purchase price and the fair value of the identifiable net assets of the target.
3. Record the consideration paid by the acquirer, usually acquirer shares, at its fair value.

For J&J's acquisition of ALZA, under pooling, the cost of acquiring ALZA's stock is shown at its book value of $1.6 billion, far below the actual purchase price of $12.2 billion. To record the acquisition under the purchase method, the analyst requires information on the fair value of ALZA's identifiable assets, which is not available. One solution is to assign the full $10.6 billion asset adjustment ($12.2 billion less $1.6 billion) to goodwill. This implicitly assumes that the book and fair values of ALZA's assets are roughly similar. The adjustment to the financial statements of the combined firm on July 31, 2001, immediately following the transaction, would therefore be as follows:

($ millions)	Adjustment	
	Assets	Liabilities & Equity
Balance Sheet		
Long-Term Intangible Assets	+10,600	
Common Shareholders' Equity		+10,600

Note that this adjustment includes in-process R&D as part of goodwill. While not in keeping with U.S. accounting standards, which require any in-process R&D to be expensed at the time of the acquisition, it does reflect the economics of the transaction—the price paid by J&J includes a premium for in-process R&D precisely because J&J expects that some of these projects will generate future benefits for shareholders.

Lease Assets Off Balance Sheet. Japan Airlines (JAL) rents part of its flight equipment and reports for these transactions using the operating method. These rented resources are therefore excluded from JAL's balance sheet, making it difficult for an analyst to compare JAL's financial performance to other airlines that either own their equipment or record leased resources using the capital method, and hence show their value on their balance sheet.

JAL notes that, even though it uses the operating method to report for leases, its leases actually qualify as capital leases. To correct this accounting, the analyst can use information on lease commitments presented in JAL's lease footnote to estimate the value of the assets and liabilities that are omitted from the balance sheet. The leased equipment is then depreciated over the life of the lease, and the lease payments are treated as interest and debt repayment. JAL estimates the present value of its future lease commitments for the years ended March 31, 2001 and 2002, as follows[17]:

(¥ millions)	March 31, 2002	March 31, 2001
Within 1 year	43,077	38,417
Over 1 year	148,777	212,871
	187,194	255,949

In addition, JAL indicates that its historical annual interest rate on outstanding interest-bearing debt is 3 percent, the lease life is 11 years, and the lease expense reported in 2002 is ¥48,816. Given this information, the analyst can make the following adjustments to JAL's beginning and ending balance sheets, and to its income statement for the year ended March 31, 2002:

1. Capitalize the present value of the lease commitments for March 31, 2001, increasing Long-Term Tangible Assets and Long-Term Debt by ¥255,949.

2. Calculate the value of any change in lease assets and lease liabilities during the year from new lease transactions or the return of leased equipment prior to the end of the contracted lease term. On March 31, 2001, JAL's liability for lease commitments in 2003 and beyond was ¥212,871. If there had been no changes in these commitments, one year later (on March 31, 2002), they would have been valued at ¥219,257 (¥212,871 · 1.03). Yet JAL's actual lease commitment on March 31, 2002, was only ¥187,194, indicating that the company reduced its leased aircraft equipment capacity following the economic downturn after September 11, 2001 by ¥32,063. JAL's Long-Term Tangible Assets and Long-Term Debt therefore declined by ¥32,063 during 2002 as a result of lease cancellations or sub-leases.

3. Reflect the change in lease asset value and expense from the depreciation during the year. The depreciation expense for 2002 (included in Cost of Sales) is the depreciation rate (1/11) multiplied by the beginning cost of leased equipment (¥255,949) less depreciation on the decline in leased equipment for 2002

(¥32,063), prorated throughout the year. The depreciation expense for 2002 is therefore ¥21,811 [¥255,949/11 − .5 · (¥32,063/11)].

4. Add back the lease expense in the income statement, included in Cost of Sales, and apportion the payment between Interest Expense and repayment of Long-Term Debt. As previously mentioned, the lease expense is ¥48,816. The portion of this that is shown as Interest Expense is calculated as follows:

Interest on beginning lease obligation (.03 · ¥255,949)	¥7,678
Less: interest on reduction in lease liability in 2002 from return on equipment, prorated throughout the year (.03 · .5 · ¥32,063)	(481)
Interest expense on lease debt	¥7,197

The Long-Term Debt repayment portion is then the remainder of the total lease payment, ¥41,619.

5. Make any needed changes to the Deferred Tax Liability to reflect differences in earnings under the capital and operating methods. JAL's expenses under the capital lease method are ¥29,008 (¥21,811 depreciation expense plus ¥7,197 interest expense) versus ¥48,816 under the operating method. JAL will not change its tax books, but for financial reporting purposes it will show higher earnings before tax and thus a higher Tax Expense through deferred taxes. Given its 33 percent tax rate, the Tax Expense will increase by ¥6,537 [.33 · (¥29,008 − ¥48,816)] and the Deferred Tax Liability will increase by the same amount.

In summary, the adjustments to JAL's financial statements on March 31, 2001 and 2002, are as follows:

(¥ millions)	Adjustment March 31, 2001 Assets	Adjustment March 31, 2001 Liabilities & Equity	Adjustment March 31, 2002 Assets	Adjustment March 31, 2002 Liabilities & Equity
Balance Sheet				
Long-Term Tangible Assets				
Beginning capitalization	+255,949		+255,949	
Lease cancellations			−32,063	
Annual depreciation			−21,811	
Long-Term Debt				
Beginning debt		+255,949		+255,949
Lease cancellations				−32,063
Debt repayment				−41,619
Deferred Tax Liability				+6,537
Common Shareholders' Equity				+13,271
Income Statement				
Cost of Sales:				
Lease expense			−48,816	
Depreciation expense			+21,811	
Interest Expense			+7,197	
Tax Expense			+6,537	
Net Income			+13,271	

These adjustments increase JAL's fixed assets by 24 percent in 2001 and 20 percent in 2002, reducing the company's asset turnover (sales/assets) from the reported value of 147 percent to 121 percent in 2001, and from 136 percent to 117 percent in 2002. There is also a difference in earnings, since the lease expense is replaced with the depreciation and interest expenses. This leads to an increase in operating earnings (before interest). As a result, the company's return on operating assets for 2002 actually increases from the reported value of –0.7 percent to 2.5 percent.

Key Intangible Assets Off Balance Sheet.   How should the analyst approach the omission of intangibles? One way is to leave the accounting as is, but to recognize that forecasts of long-term rates of return will have to reflect the inherent biases that arise from this accounting method. A second approach is to capitalize intangibles and amortize them over their expected lives.

For example, consider the case of Microsoft, the most valuable software company in the world. Microsoft does not capitalize any software R&D costs, even those arising after software products have passed the stage of technological feasibility. What adjustment would be required if the analyst decided to capitalize all of Microsoft's software R&D and to amortize the intangible asset using the straight-line method over the expected life of software (approximately three years)? Assume that R&D spending occurs evenly throughout the year, and that only half a year's amortization is taken on the latest year's spending. Given R&D outlays for the years 1999 to 2001, the R&D asset at the end of 2001 is $6.1 billion, calculated as follows:

Year	R&D Outlay	Proportion Capitalized 12/31/01	Asset 12/31/01	Proportion Capitalized 12/31/02	Asset 12/31/02
2002	$4.3b			$(1 - .33/2)$	$3.6b
2001	4.4	$(1 - .33/2)$	$3.7b	$(1 - .33/2 - .33)$	2.2
2000	3.8	$(1 - .33/2 - .33)$	1.9	$(1 - .33/2 - .67)$	0.6
1999	3.0	$(1 - .33/2 - .67)$	0.5		
Total			$6.1		$6.4

The R&D amortization expense (included in Other Operating Expenses) for 2001 and 2002 are $3.4 billion and $3.9 billion, respectively, and are calculated as follows:

Year	R&D Outlay	Proportion Amortized 12/31/01	Expense 12/31/01	Proportion Amortized 12/31/02	Expense 12/31/02
2002	$4.3b			.33/2	$0.7b
2001	4.4	.33/2	$0.7b	.33	1.5
2000	3.8	.33	1.2	.33	1.2
1999	3.0	.33	1.0	.33/2	0.5
1998	2.8	.33/2	0.5		
Total			$3.4		$3.9

Since Microsoft will continue to expense software R&D immediately for tax purposes, the change in reporting method will give rise to a Deferred Tax Liability. Given a marginal tax rate of 35 percent, this liability will equal 35 percent of the value of the Intangible Asset reported, with the balance increasing Common Shareholders' Equity.

In summary, the adjustments required to capitalize software R&D for Microsoft for the years 2001 and 2002 are as follows:

($ billions)	Adjustment Dec. 31, 2001		Adjustment Dec. 31, 2002	
	Assets	Liabilities & Equity	Assets	Liabilities & Equity
Balance Sheet				
Long-Term Intangible Assets	+6.1		+6.4	
Deferred Tax Liability		+2.2		+2.2
Common Shareholders' Equity		+3.9		+4.2
Income Statement				
Other Operating Expenses		−4.4 +3.4		−4.3 +3.9
Tax Expense		+0.3		+0.1
Net Income		+0.7		+0.3

LIABILITY DISTORTIONS

Liabilities are defined as economic obligations arising from benefits received in the past, and for which the amount and timing is known with reasonable certainty. Liabilities include obligations to customers that have paid in advance for products or services; commitments to public and private providers of debt financing; obligations to federal and local governments for taxes; commitments to employees for unpaid wages, pensions, and other retirement benefits; and obligations from court or government fines or environmental cleanup orders.

Distortions in liabilities generally arise because there is ambiguity about whether (1) an obligation has really been incurred and/or (2) the obligation can be measured.

Has an obligation been incurred?

For most liabilities there is little ambiguity about whether an obligation has been incurred. For example, when a firm buys supplies on credit, it has incurred an obligation to the supplier. However, for some transactions it is more difficult to decide whether there is any such obligation. For example, if a firm announces a plan to restructure its business by laying off employees, has it made a commitment that would justify recording a liability? Or, if a software firm receives cash from its customers for a five-year software license, should the firm report the full cash inflow as revenues, or should some of it represent the ongoing commitment to the customer for servicing and supporting the license agreement?

Can the obligation be measured?

Many liabilities specify the amount and timing of obligations precisely. For example, a 20-year $100 million bond issue with an 8 percent coupon payable semi-annually specifies that the issuer will pay the holders $100 million in twenty years, and it will pay out interest of $4 million every six months for the duration of the loan. However, for some liabilities it is difficult to estimate the amount of the obligation. For example, a firm that is responsible for an environmental cleanup clearly has incurred an obligation, but the amount is highly uncertain.[18] Similarly, firms that provide pension and post-retirement benefits for employees have incurred commitments that depend on uncertain future events, such as employee mortality rates, and on future inflation rates, making valuation of the obligation subjective. Future warranty and insurance claim obligations fall into the same category—the commitment is clear but the amount depends on uncertain future events.

Accounting rules frequently specify when a commitment has been incurred and how to measure the amount of the commitment. However, as discussed earlier, accounting rules are imperfect—they cannot cover all contractual possibilities and reflect all of the complexities of a firm's business relationships. They also require managers to make subjective estimates of future events to value the firm's commitments. Thus the analyst may decide that some important obligations are omitted from the financial statements or, if included, are understated, either because of management bias or because there are legitimate differences in opinion between managers and analysts over future risks and commitments. As a result, analysis of liabilities is usually with an eye to assessing whether the firm's financial commitments and risks are understated and/or its earnings overstated.

Understated Liabilities

Liabilities are likely to be understated when the firm has key commitments that are difficult to value and therefore not considered liabilities for financial reporting purposes. Understatements are also likely to occur when managers have strong incentives to overstate the soundness of the firm's financial position, or to boost reported earnings. By understating leverage, managers present investors with a rosy picture of the firm's financial risks. Earnings management also understates liabilities (namely deferred or unearned revenues) when revenues are recognized upon receipt of cash, even though not all services have been provided.

The most common forms of asset (and earnings) overstatement arise when the following conditions exist:

1. *Unearned revenues are understated through aggressive revenue recognition.* If cash has already been received but the product or service has yet to be provided, a liability (called unearned or deferred revenues) is created. This liability reflects the company's commitment to provide the service or product to the customer and is extinguished once that is accomplished. Firms that recognize revenues prematurely, after the receipt of cash but prior to fulfilling their product or service commitments to customers, understate deferred revenue liabilities and overstate earnings. Firms that bundle service contracts with the sale of a product are particularly prone to deferred revenue liability understatement since separating the price of the product from the price of the service is subjective.

2. *Loans from discounted receivables are off balance sheet.* As discussed earlier, receivables that are discounted with a financial institution are considered "sold" if the "seller" cedes control over the receivables to the financier. Yet if the sale permits the buyer to have recourse against the seller in the event of default, the seller continues to face collection risk. Given the management judgment involved in forecasting default and refinancing costs, as well as the incentives faced by managers to keep debt off the balance sheet, it will be important for the analyst to evaluate the firm's

estimates for default as well as the inherent commitments that it has for discounted receivables. Are the firm's estimates reasonable? Is it straightforward to forecast the costs of the default and prepayment risks? If not, does the analyst need to increase the value of the recourse liability? Or, in the extreme, does the analyst need to undo the sale and recognize a loan from the financial institution for the discounted value of the receivables.

3. *Long-term liabilities for leases are off balance sheet.* As discussed earlier in the chapter, key lease assets and liabilities can be excluded from the balance sheet if the company structures lease transactions to fit the accounting definition of an operating lease. Firms that groom transactions to avoid showing lease assets and obligations will have very different balance sheets from firms with virtually identical economics but which either use capital leases or borrow from the bank to actually purchase the equivalent resources. For firms that choose to structure lease transactions to fit the definition of an operating lease, the analyst can restate the leases as capital leases, as discussed in the Asset Understatement section. This will ensure that the firm's true financial commitments and risks will be reflected on its balance sheet, enabling comparison with peer firms.

4. *Pension and post-retirement obligations are not fully recorded.* Many firms make commitments to provide pension and retirement benefits to their employees. Accounting rules require managers to estimate and report the present value of the commitments that have been earned by employees over their years of working for the firm. This obligation is offset by any assets that the firm has committed to pension/retirement plans to fund future plan benefits. If the funds set aside in the retirement plan are greater (less) than the plan commitments, the plan is overfunded (underfunded). Several important issues arise for analyzing pension/post-retirement plan obligations. First, estimating the obligations themselves is subjective—managers have to make forecasts of future wage and benefit rates, worker attrition rates, the expected lives of retirees, and the discount rate.[19] If these forecasts are too low, the firm's benefit obligations (as well as the annual expenses for benefits reported in the income statement) will be understated.[20] Second, accounting rules require that incremental benefit commitments that arise from changes to a plan, and changes in plan funding status that arise from abnormal investment returns on plan assets, are smoothed over time rather than reflected immediately. As a result, for labor-intensive firms that offer attractive retirement benefits to employees, it is important that the analyst assess whether reported pension and retirement plan liabilities reflect the firms' true commitments.

Examples of How to Correct for Liability Understatement

We illustrate some of these types of liability understatements and the corrections that the analyst can make to reduce bias in the financial statements.

Unearned Revenues Understated Consider the case of MicroStrategy, the software company discussed earlier, which bundles customer support and software updates with its initial licensing agreements. This raises questions about how much of the contract price should be allocated to the initial license versus the company's future commitments. In March 2000 MicroStrategy conceded that it had incorrectly overstated revenues on contracts that involved significant future customization and consulting by $54.5 million. As a result, it would have to restate its financial statements for 1999 as well as for several earlier years. To undo the distortion to 1999 financials, the following adjustments would have to be made:

1. In the quarter that the contracts were booked by the company, Sales would decline and unearned revenues (included in Other Current Liabilities) would increase by $54.5 million.
2. Cost of Sales would decline and prepaid expenses (inventory for product companies) would increase to reflect the lower sales. As noted earlier, MicroStrategy's cost of license revenues is only 3 percent of license revenues, implying that the adjustment to prepaid expenses (included in Other Current Assets) and Cost of Sales is modest ($1.6m).
3. The decline in pretax income would result in a lower Tax Expense in the company's financial reporting books (but presumably not in its tax books). Given MicroStrategy's marginal tax rate of 35 percent, the decline in the Tax Expense as well as in the Deferred Tax Liability is $18.5 million [($54.5 − 1.6) · .35].

The full effect of the adjustment on the quarterly financial statements would, therefore, be as follows:

($ millions)	Adjustment	
	Assets	Liabilities & Equity
Balance Sheet		
Other Current Assets	+1.6	
Other Current Liabilities		+54.5
Deferred Tax Liability		−18.5
Common Shareholders' Equity		−34.4
Income Statement		
Sales		−54.5
Cost of Sales		−1.6
Tax Expense		−18.5
Net Income		−34.4

MicroStrategy's March 10 announcement that it had overstated revenues prompted the SEC to investigate the company. In the period when it announced its overstatements, MicroStrategy's stock price plummeted 94 percent, compared to the 37 percent drop by the NASDAQ in the same period.

Discounted Receivables Off Balance Sheet. Prior to 2000 Computer Associates (CA) discounted notes receivable from its long-term licensing contracts. In 2002 it reported a contingent liability of $218 million for receivables that had been discounted with recourse. The company did not provide information on the value of the recourse liability for these notes receivable, making it difficult to judge the adequacy of the allowance for credit and refinancing losses that potentially could arise on the discounted receivables. One way for the analyst to assess the impact of the financing is to reverse the sale and include a liability for the full $218 million on CA's balance sheet. This would require the following adjustments:

1. CA's Other Long-Term Assets would be increased by the receivable commitment ($218 million). In turn, Long-Term Debt would be recorded to reflect the value of the cash advanced to CA under the discount transaction. CA appears to charge its customers an annual interest rate of roughly 9 percent. Assuming customers repay the receivables in equal monthly installments over the next four years, and the bank charges a 10 percent interest rate, the receivable loan would be valued at $214.1 million.

2. The after-tax difference between the face value of the receivables and the loan, which would have been shown as a loss on sale under the reported accounting, needs to be reversed, increasing equity. Given the above assumptions and CA's 35 percent marginal tax rate, the adjustment would increase Common Shareholders' Equity by $2.5 million [3.9 · (1 − .35)].

3. The impact of the tax deduction from reporting a loss on sale, which would have reduced the Deferred Tax Liability, needs to be reversed. For CA, this amount would have resulted in a roughly $1.4 million (3.9 · .35) increase in the Deferred Tax Liability.

4. During the year ended March 31, 2003, customers are scheduled to make monthly payments on the discounted receivables, reducing the value of notes receivable under the adjusted accounting. For CA, these amounted to $54.5 million ($218 million · .25). Notes receivable would increase if any additional notes were discounted during the year. For CA, no new receivable discounts were undertaken since the company changed its sales strategy.

5. For 2003, CA's income statement would include Interest Income from notes receivable for $18.7 million {(218.0 · .09) − [(54.5 · .09) · .5]} and Interest Expense from the loan for roughly $17.2 million {(214.0 · .10) − [(54.5 · .10) · .5]} along with any tax effects.[21] The loan would decline by a smaller amount, since $1.6 million of the receivable repayments are allocated to covering the higher interest charged on the loan (exactly offsetting the wedge between the Interest Income and the Interest Expense for the year).

6. The value of the loan increases by the amount of any additional discounts undertaken during the year ($0), and declines by the value of receivable repayments by customers ($54.5 million) net of the portion of the repayment that represents incremental interest charged by the bank relative to the rate CA charged its customers ($1.5 million, or $18.7 million − $17.2 million).

The overall effect of these adjustments on CA's financial statements would, therefore, be as follows:

($ millions)	Adjustment for March 31, 2002		Adjustment for March 31, 2003	
	Assets	Liabilities & Equity	Assets	Liabilities & Equity
Balance Sheet				
Other Long-Term Assets	+218.0		+218.0 −54.5	
Long-Term Debt		+214.1		+214.1 −54.5 +1.5

(continued)

($ millions)	Adjustment for March 31, 2002		Adjustment for March 31, 2003	
	Assets	Liabilities & Equity	Assets	Liabilities & Equity
Balance Sheet (continued)				
Deferred Tax Liability		+1.4		+1.4
				−0.5
Common Shareholders' Equity		+2.5		+2.5
				−1.0
Income Statement				
Interest Income				+17.2
Interest Expense				+18.7
Tax Expense				−0.5
Net Income				−1.0

Pension/Post-Retirement Obligations Not Fully Recorded   Accounting rules require that firms estimate the value of pension and post-retirement commitments as the present value of future expected payouts under the plans. The obligation under pension plans is referred to as the Projected Benefit Obligation, and is the present value of plan commitments factoring in the impact of future increases in wage rates and salary scales on projected payouts.[22] For post-retirement plans, the firm's obligation is called the Expected Post-Retirement Benefit Obligation, and is calculated as the present value of expected future benefits for employees and their beneficiaries.

Each year the firm's pension and post-retirement obligations are adjusted to reflect the following factors:

- *Service Cost:* Defined benefit plans typically provide higher benefits for each additional year of service with the company. For example, in their 1996 agreement with the United Auto Workers, the three major U.S. auto manufacturers increased pension benefits for new employees by $4.55 a month for every year worked. The value of incremental benefits earned from another year of service is called the service cost, and increases the firm's obligation each year.
- *Interest Cost:* The passage of time increases the present value of the firm's obligation. The interest cost recognizes this effect, and it is calculated by multiplying the obligation at the beginning of the year by the discount rate.
- *Actuarial Gains and Losses:* Each year the actuarial assumptions used to estimate the firm's commitments are reviewed and, if appropriate, changes are made. The effect of these changes is shown as Actuarial Gains and Losses.
- *Benefits Paid:* The plan commitments are reduced as the plan makes payments to retirees each year.

For example, in its financial statement footnotes, General Motors (GM) provided the following information on its Expected Post-Retirement Benefit Obligation for the years ended December 31, 2001 and 2000:

($ millions)	2001	2000
Benefit Obligations		
Benefit obligation at beginning of year	$49,889	$44,683
Service cost	480	448
Interest cost	3,733	3,346
Actuarial losses	1,582	4,392
Benefits paid	(3,173)	(2,805)
Other	(22)	(175)
Benefit obligation at end of year	$52,489	$49,889

GM's obligation at the end of 2001 was $52.5 billion, a 5 percent increase over the prior year.

To meet their commitments under pension and other post-retirement plans, firms make contributions to the plans. These contributions are then invested in equities, debt, and other assets. Plan assets, therefore, are increased each year by new company (and employee) contributions. They are also increased or decreased by the returns generated each year from plan investments. Finally, plan assets decline when the plan pays out benefits to retirees. For the years ended December 31, 2001 and 2000, GM reported the following assets for post-retirement plans:

($ millions)	2001	2000
Plan assets		
Fair value of plan assets at beginning of year	$6,724	$6,291
Actual return on plan assets	(479)	421
Employer contributions	—	743
Plan participants' contributions	—	—
Benefits paid	(1,300)	(731)
Fair value of plan assets at end of year	$4,945	$6,724

In 2001 GM's plan assets declined significantly because they generated a negative return during the year. The difference between GM's post-retirement plan obligations and the plan assets, $47.5 billion, represents the company's unfunded obligation to employees under the plan. The company also reports that it has a $12.6 billion gap between its obligations under pension plans ($86.3 billion in 2001) and pension plan assets ($73.7 billion).

Of course, estimating pension and post-retirement obligations is highly subjective. It requires managers to forecast the future payouts under the plans, which in turn involves making projections of employees' service with the firm, retirement ages, and life expectancies, as well as future wage rates and health insurance costs. It also requires managers to select an interest rate to estimate the present value of the future benefits. For example, GM projected that health care costs would grow at 6 percent per year in 2002, 7.3 percent in 2004, and decline linearly to a steady state rate of 5 percent in 2008. It also assumed that the appropriate discount rate was 7.3 percent. GM reports that a 1 percent increase in the rate of health care inflation would increase the post-retirement obligation by $5.4 billion. Given the management judgment involved in making these forecasts and assumptions, analysts should question whether reported obligations adequately reflect the firm's true commitments.

So, given GM's unfunded post-retirement benefit obligation of $47.5 billion, it seems reasonable to expect that the company will report a liability on its balance sheet for $47.5 billion. Unfortunately, pension and post-retirement accounting is more complex than this. Financial reporting rules require that firms smooth out shocks to plan obligations and assets. For example, if GM agrees to increase its post-retirement or pension benefits for current workers, it will have to increase the value of its obligation. SFAS 87 requires this "prior period service obligation" to be amortized over employees' average expected remaining years of service rather than right away. Also, if the value of plan assets increases or decreases unexpectedly in a given year, or there needs to be adjustment in the actuarial assumptions made to estimate the obligation, the financial statement impact is reflected gradually rather than immediately. Thus, even though the actual gap between GM's post-retirement obligation and plan assets is $47.5 billion, this is not the value of the liability recorded on its balance sheet. GM provides a separate disclosure that reconciles the actual and the reported obligation:

($ millions)	2001	2000
Funded status	$(47,544)	$(43,165)
Unrecognized actuarial loss	8,902	6,444
Unrecognized prior service cost	249	207
Net amount recognized	$(38,393)	$(36,514)

The unrecognized actuarial loss arises because GM's earlier actuarial assumptions about parameters such as future health care costs, retirement rates, and assumed rates of return on plan assets have proven to be optimistic. These effects are recognized over time rather than right away. Similarly, prior service costs represent additional commitments from post-retirement plan changes that are recognized over time. Consequently, GM's reported post-retirement liability understates its real commitment by $9.1 billion ($47.5 billion less $38.4 billion). The company reports that its pension liability also understates it actual commitment by $28.3 billion.[23]

What does pension and post-retirement accounting imply for financial analysis? It is reasonable for the analyst to raise several questions about a firm's pension and post-retirement obligations, particularly for firms in labor-intensive industries.

1. Are the assumptions made by the firm to estimate its pension and post-retirement obligations realistic? These include assumptions about the discount rate, which is supposed to represent the current market interest rate for benefits, as well as assumptions about increases in wage and benefit costs. If these assumptions are optimistic, the obligations recorded on the books understate the firm's real economic commitment. As discussed above, GM notes that a 1 percent increase in expected health care costs increases its obligation by $5.4 billion. The analyst can use this information to adjust for any optimism in management's assumptions. For example, if the analyst decided that GM's forecasts of future healthcare costs were too low and needed to increase by 1 percent, the post-retirement obligation would have to be increased by $5.4 billion, with offsetting declines to equity (for the after-tax effect) and to the deferred tax liability. The adjustment to GM's 2001 balance sheet, assuming a 35 percent tax rate, would be as follows:

($ millions)	Adjustment	
	Assets	Liabilities & Equity
Balance Sheet		
Long-Term Debt		+$5,400
Deferred Tax Liability		−1,890
Common Shareholders' Equity		−$3,510

2. The process of smoothing prior service costs and differences between actual and forecasted parameters for pension and other benefit plans understates any obligations for pensions and post-retirement benefits. For GM this understatement is substantial. As noted above, GM reports a liability for unfunded post-retirement benefits that is $9.1 billion less than the actual obligations. The analyst can adjust for this distortion by increasing the firm's Long-Term Debt, and making offsetting adjustments to the Deferred Tax Liability (since the change would not affect the company's taxable income) and Common Shareholders' Equity. Assuming a 35 percent tax rate, the adjustment to GM's 2001 balance sheet would be as follows:

($ millions)	Adjustment	
	Assets	Liabilities & Equity
Balance Sheet		
Long-Term Debt		+$9,151
Deferred Tax Liability		−3,203
Common Shareholders' Equity		−$5,948

3. What effect do pension assumptions play in the income statement? The pension cost each year comprises (a) Service cost, plus (b) Interest cost, plus (c) Amortization of any prior period service costs, plus or minus (d) Amortization of actuarial gains and losses, minus (e) Expected return on plan assets (the expected long-term return multiplied by beginning assets under management). For example, GM shows that its post-retirement expenses for 2001 and 2000 are as follows:

($ millions)	2001	2000
Service cost	$480	$448
Interest cost	3,733	3,346
Expected return on plan assets	−542	−650
Amortization of prior service cost	−45	−42
Recognized net actuarial loss/(gain)	96	70
Net expense	$3,722	$3,172

This expense reflects the effect of smoothing actual asset returns, prior period service costs, and revisions in actuarial assumptions discussed earlier. For example, in 2001 the actual return on post-retirement plan assets was −$497 million, whereas the expected return reflected in the expense was $542 million. If the analyst used the actual return to compute the pension expense, an additional $1,039 million in post-retirement expenses, included in SG&A Expense, would be required. Since this adjustment would not change the firm's tax books, it would lower the Tax Expense by $364 million (.35 · $1,039m). The full income statement adjustment would therefore be as follows:

($ millions)	Adjustment
Income Statement	
SG&A Expense	+$1,039
Tax Expense	−364
Net Income	−$675

If desired, similar adjustments can be made to undo the income effects of smoothing changes in actuarial assumptions and prior-period service costs.

EQUITY DISTORTIONS

Accounting treats stockholders' equity as a residual claim on the firm's assets, after paying off the other claimholders. Consequently, equity distortions arise primarily from distortions in assets and liabilities. For example, distortions in assets or liabilities that affect earnings also lead to distortions in equity. However, there are two forms of equity distortions that would not typically arise in asset and liability analyses:

1. *Effect of hybrid securities.* Hybrid securities include convertible debt and debt with warrants attached. These securities are partially pure debt and partially equity. Current accounting rules do not separate these components, typically implying that the balance sheet overstates firm debt and understates its equity. Without adjusting for this distortion, it can be difficult to understand the real financial risks and returns for firms with different types of hybrids. New accounting rules proposed by the FASB are likely to address this issue by requiring securities such as convertible debt to be separated into two components on the balance sheet, a debt component and an equity component. Each would be valued at its fair value at the date of issue. This approach could be adopted by the analyst.

2. *Stock option expenses.* A stock option gives the holder the right to purchase a certain number of shares of stock at a predetermined price, called the exercise or strike price, for a specified period of time, termed the exercise period. In the 1980s and 1990s, stock options became the most significant component of compensation for many corporate executives. As a result, top management owned or had a claim to 13.2 percent of their company's shares in 1997, almost double the 1989 ownership percentage. Proponents of options argue that they provide managers with incentives to maximize shareholder value and make it easier to attract talented managers. In addition, many managers view options as a low-cost form of compensation, since no expense is typically recorded either when they are issued or when they are exercised.

   U.S. rules permit firms to report stock options using either the intrinsic value method (outlined in Accounting Principles Board [APB] 25) or the fair value method (discussed in SFAS 123). Under the intrinsic value method, no compensation expense is reported at the grant date for the vast majority of stock options awarded, where the exercise price is equal to the firm's current stock price. If the options are subsequently exercised, there is also no expense recorded, and the new stock that is issued is valued at the exercise price rather than its higher market value. In contrast, the fair value method requires firms to record an expense for stock option compensation when the options are issued. The value of the options issued is estimated using a recognized valuation model, such as the Black-Scholes model, and is then expensed over the vesting period.[24]

FASB's initial proposal that all companies use the fair value method met with considerable opposition from practitioners, particularly in the high-tech sector where stock options were most popular. Opponents of the proposal argued that Black-Scholes valuations are imprecise and overvalue nonmarketable management options. Consequently FASB backed down on its proposal and permitted companies to choose either the intrinsic or the fair value method. However, those that chose the intrinsic value method—and most did—were required to report in the footnotes the earnings effect from using the fair value method.[25]

Following the demise of Enron, there has been increased recognition that overuse of stock options can encourage managers to manage earnings to boost short-term stock prices. There has also been increased shareholder and political pressure to recognize some form of cost for stock option compensation, leading companies such as Coca-Cola, The Washington Post, and Amazon.com to voluntarily begin using the fair value method for reporting stock option awards. FASB has decided to revisit stock options in the coming years, and it may well mandate some form of fair value method.

The net effect of the debate over stock option accounting is that many firms still show no expense for stock option awards. While Black-Scholes valuations are imperfect, there is no question that they present a more accurate reflection of the economic cost of stock option awards to the firm's shareholders than the zero cost reported under the intrinsic value method. Consequently, for firms that rely heavily on stock options, such as high-technology firms, it is important for the analyst to understand how the firm accounts for management stock options and whether an adjustment is required.

Examples of How to Correct for Equity Distortions

We illustrate these types of equity distortions and the corrections that the analyst can make to reduce bias in the financial statements.

Hybrid Securities   On February 3, 1999, Amazon.com completed an offering of $1.25 billion of 4.75 percent Convertible Subordinated Notes due in 2009. Several months earlier Amazon had issued senior notes with an annual interest rate of 10 percent. The conversion premium was therefore significant—if the notes had not included a conversion option, Amazon would probably have had to pay a coupon rate in excess of 10 percent. The value of the $1.25 billion convertible issue at a 10 percent discount rate is only $0.87 billion, implying that the convertibility premium was worth roughly $0.38 billion. One way to adjust for this effect is to record the debt component at $0.87 billion and to show the $0.38 conversion premium as part of Common Shareholders' Equity. Interest on the debt would then be based on the 10 percent coupon rate rather than the 4.75 percent (which reflects the conversion premium).

The effect of this adjustment on Amazon's financial statements at March 31, 2002, would be as follows:

($ billions)	Adjustment for March 31, 2002	
	Assets	Liabilities & Equity
Balance Sheet		
Long-Term Debt		−0.38
Common Shareholders Equity		+0.38

Stock Option Expenses To adjust for the effective cost to the company from providing stock option compensation, the analyst must first recognize the fair value of options earned in the period as an expense and as an increase in Common Shareholders' Equity (reflecting the option grants). The second step is to adjust the firm's tax expense to reflect the deferred tax impact of expensing the fair value of options awarded. Given the footnote disclosures required under SFAS 123, it is relatively easy to determine these effects.

For example, consider the case of Microsoft, which uses stock options extensively and reports using the intrinsic value method. In its June 30, 2001, financial statement footnotes, Microsoft noted that earnings before taxes using fair value accounting would have been $8.148 billion versus $11.525 billion reported earnings, a difference of $3.377 billion. Of this amount, $0.32 billion is allocated to Cost of Sales, $1.727 billion is allocated to R&D Expense, and the remaining $1.33 is reported as Selling and Administrative expenses. In addition, the lower fair value method earnings would have lowered the Tax Expense by $1.115 billion (indicating a 33 percent tax rate), with an offset on the balance sheet to Deferred Tax Liability. Finally, stock options, included in equity, would be reported at a value of $3.337 billion. The overall effect of the adjustment on Microsoft's financial statements would, therefore, be as follows:

($ billions)	Adjustment	
	Assets	Liabilities & Equity
Balance Sheet		
Deferred Tax Liability		−1.115
Common Shareholders Equity		−2.262
		+3.377
Income Statement		
Cost of Sales		+0.320
SG&A Expense		+1.330
Other Operating Expenses		+1.727
Tax Expense		−1.115
Net Income		−2.262

SUMMARY

To implement accounting analysis, the analyst must first recast the financial statements into a common format so that financial statement terminology and formatting is comparable between firms and across time. A standard template for recasting the financials, presented in this chapter, is used throughout the remainder of the book.

Once the financial statements are standardized, the analyst can determine what accounting distortions exist in the firm's assets, liabilities, and equity. Common distortions that overstate assets include delays in recognizing asset impairments, underestimated reserves, aggressive revenue recognition leading to overstated receivables, and optimistic assumptions on long-term asset depreciation. Asset understatements can arise if managers overstate asset write-offs, use operating leases to keep assets off the balance sheet, or make conservative assumptions for asset depreciation. They can also arise because accounting rules require outlays for key assets (e.g., R&D and brands) to be immediately expensed. For liabilities, the primary concern for the analyst is whether the firm understates its real commitments. This can arise from off-balance liabilities (e.g., operating lease obligations), from questionable management judgment and limitations in accounting rules for estimating pension and benefit plan liabilities, and from aggressive revenue recognition that understates unearned revenue obligations. Equity distortions frequently arise when there are distortions in assets and liabilities. However, they can also arise if no expense is reported for stock option compensation, or for firms that issue hybrid securities.

Adjustments for distortions can, therefore, arise because accounting standards, although applied appropriately, do not reflect a firm's economic reality. They can also arise if the analyst has a different point of view than management about the estimates and assumptions made in preparing the financial statements. Once distortions have been identified, the analyst can use footnote and cash flow statement information to make adjustments to the balance sheet at the beginning and/or end of the current year, as well as any needed adjustments to revenues and expenses in the latest income statement. This ensures that the most recent financial ratios used to evaluate a firm's performance and to forecast its future results are based on financial data that appropriately reflect its business economics.

Several points are worth remembering when doing accounting analysis. First, the bulk of the analyst's time and energy should be focused on evaluating and adjusting accounting policies and estimates that describe the firm's key strategic value drivers. Of course this does not mean that management bias is not reflected in other accounting estimates and policies, and the analyst should certainly examine these. But given the importance of evaluating how the firm is managing its key success factors and risks, the bulk of the accounting analysis should be spent examining those policies that describe these factors and risks.

It is also important to recognize that many accounting adjustments can only be approximations rather than precise calculations, since much of the information necessary for making precise adjustments is not disclosed. The analyst should, therefore, try to avoid worrying about being overly precise in making accounting adjustments. By making even crude adjustments, it is usually possible to mitigate some of the limitations of accounting standards and problems of management bias in financial reporting.

DISCUSSION QUESTIONS

1. Use the templates shown in Tables 4-1, 4-2, and 4-3 to recast the following financial statements for Amazon.com.

Amazon.com Inc. Consolidated Balance Sheet at December 31, 2002
($ thousands)

	12/31/02	12/31/01
ASSETS		
Current assets:		
Cash and cash equivalents	$738,254	$540,282
Marketable securities	562,715	456,303
Inventories	202,425	143,722
Accounts receivable, net and other current assets	112,282	67,613
Total current assets	$1,615,676	$1,207,920
Fixed assets, net	239,398	271,751
Goodwill, net	70,811	45,367
Other intangibles, net	3,460	34,382
Other equity investments	15,442	28,359
Other assets	45,662	49,768
Total assets	$1,990,449	$1,637,547
LIABILITIES AND STOCKHOLDERS' DEFICIT		
Current liabilities:		
Accounts payable	618,128	444,748
Accrued expenses and other current liabilities	314,935	305,064
Unearned revenue	47,916	87,978
Interest payable	71,661	68,632
Current portion of long-term debt and other	13,318	14,992
Total current liabilities	$1,065,958	$921,414
Long-term debt and other	2,277,305	2,156,133
Shareholders' deficit:		
Common stock, $0.01 par value: Authorized shares 5,000,000 ; Issued and outstanding shares—387,906 and 373,218 shares, respectively	3,879	3,732
Additional paid-in capital	$1,649,946	$1,462,769
Deferred stock-based compensation	(6,591)	(9,853)
Accumulated other comprehensive income (loss)	9,662	(36,070)
Accumulated deficit	(3,009,710)	(2,860,578)
Total stockholders' deficit	$(1,352,814)	$(1,440,000)
Total liabilities and stockholders' deficit	1,990,449	1,637,547

Amazon.com Inc. Consolidated Income Statement for the Year Ended December 31, 2002 ($ thousands)

	12/31/02	12/31/01	12/31/00
Net sales	$3,932,936	$3,122,433	$2,761,983
Cost of sales	2,940,318	2,323,875	2,106,206
Gross profit	992,618	798,558	655,777

(continued)

	12/31/02	12/31/01	12/31/00
Operating expenses:			
Fulfillment	392,467	374,250	414,509
Marketing	125,383	138,283	179,980
Technology and content	215,617	241,165	269,326
General and administrative	79,049	89,862	108,962
Stock-based compensation	68,927	4,637	24,797
Amortization of goodwill and other intangibles	5,478	181,033	321,772
Restructuring-related and other	41,573	181,585	200,311
Total operating expenses	$928,494	$1,210,815	$1,519,657
Income (loss) from operations	64,124	(412,257)	(863,880)
Interest income	23,687	29,103	40,821
Interest expense	(142,925)	(139,232)	(130,921)
Other income (expense), net	5,623	(1,900)	(10,058)
Other gains (losses), net	(96,273)	(2,141)	(142,639)
Total non-operating expenses, net	$(209,888)	$(114,170)	$(242,797)
Loss before equity in losses of equity-method investees	(145,764)	(526,427)	(1,106,677)
Equity in losses of equity-method investees, net	(4,169)	(30,327)	(304,596)
Loss before change in accounting principle	$(149,933)	$(556,754)	$(1,411,273)
Cumulative effect of change in accounting principle	801	(10,523)	
Net loss	$(149,132)	$(567,277)	$(1,411,273)

Amazon.com Inc. Consolidated Cash Flow Statement for the Year Ended December 31, 2002 ($ thousands)

	12/31/02	12/31/01	12/31/00
OPERATING ACTIVITIES:			
Net loss	$(149,132)	$(567,277)	$(1,411,273)
Adjustments to reconcile net loss to net cash provided by (used in) operating activities:			
Depreciation of fixed assets and other amortization	82,274	84,709	84,460
Stock-based compensation	68,927	4,637	24,797
Equity in losses of equity-method investees, net	4,169	30,327	304,596
Amortization of goodwill and other intangibles	5,478	181,033	321,772
Non-cash restructuring-related and other	3,470	73,293	200,311
Gain on sale of marketable securities, net	(5,700)	(1,335)	(280)
Other losses (gains), net	96,273	2,141	142,639
Non-cash interest expense and other	29,586	26,629	24,766
Cumulative effect of change in accounting principle	(801)	10,523	
Changes in operating assets and liabilities:			
Inventories	(51,303)	30,628	46,083
Accounts receivable, net and other current assets	(32,948)	20,732	(8,585)
Accounts payable	156,542	(44,438)	22,357
Accrued expenses and other current liabilities	4,491	50,031	93,967
Unearned revenue	95,404	114,738	97,818
Amortization of previously unearned revenue	(135,466)	(135,808)	(108,211)
Interest payable	3,027	(345)	34,341
Net cash provided by (used in) operating activities	$174,291	$(119,782)	$(130,442)

(continued)

	12/31/02	12/31/01	12/31/00
INVESTING ACTIVITIES:			
Sales/maturities of marketable securities and investments	553,289	370,377	545,724
Purchases of marketable securities	(635,810)	(567,152)	(184,455)
Purchases of fixed assets, including internal-use software	(39,163	(50,321)	(134,758)
Investments (including equity-method investees)		(6,198)	(62,533)
Net cash provided by (used in) investing activities	$(121,684)	$(253,294)	$163,978
FINANCING ACTIVITIES:			
Proceeds from exercise of stock options and other	121,689	16,625	44,697
Proceeds from issuance of common stock, net of issue costs		99,831	
Proceeds from long-term debt and other		10,000	681,499
Repayment of capital lease obligations and other	(14,795)	(19,575)	(16,927)
Financing costs			(16,122)
Net cash provided by financing activities	$106,894	$106,881	$693,147
Effect of exchange-rate changes on cash and cash equivalents	38,471	(15,958)	(37,557)
Net increase (decrease) in cash and cash equivalents	$197,972	$(282,153)	$689,126

2. Refer to the Lucent example on delaying write-downs of current assets (page 4-9). How much excess inventory do you estimate Lucent is holding in December 2000 if the firm's optimal Days' Inventory is 58 days? Calculate the inventory impairment charge for Lucent if 50 percent of this excess inventory is deemed worthless? Record the changes to Lucent's financial statements from adjusting for this impairment.

3. Acceptance Insurance Companies Inc. underwrites and sells specialty property and casualty insurance. The company is the third largest writer of crop insurance products in the United States. In its 1998 10-K report to the SEC, it discloses the following information on the loss reserves created for claims originating in 1990:

Percentage of claim liability arising in 1990 paid as of:	
One year later	40.6%
Two years later	70.8
Three years later	88.5
Four years later	101.2
Five years later	107.5
Six years later	109.7
Seven years later	111.4
Eight years later	111.8
Net reserves for 1990 obligations reestimated as of:	
One year later	100.3%
Two years later	102.3
Three years later	107.4
Four years later	110.7
Five years later	112.7
Six years later	112.0
Seven years later	112.5
Eight years later	113.4
Net cumulative deficiency	−13.4

Was the initial estimate for loss reserves originating in 1990 too low or too high? How has the firm updated its estimate of this obligation over time? What percentage of the original liability remains outstanding for 1990 claims at the end of 1998? As a financial analyst, what questions would you have for the CFO on its 1990 liability?

4. AMR, the parent of American Airlines, provides the following footnote information on its capital and operating leases:

> AMR's subsidiaries lease various types of equipment and property, primarily aircraft and airport facilities. Lease terms vary but are generally 10 to 25 years for aircraft. The future minimum lease payments required under capital leases, together with the present value of such payments, and future minimum lease payments required under operating leases that have initial or remaining non-cancelable lease terms in excess of one year as of December 31, 2001, were (in millions):

Year Ending December 31,	Capital Leases	Operating Leases
2002	$326	$1,336
2003	243	1,276
2004	295	1,199
2005	229	1,138
2006	231	1,073
2007 and subsequent years	1,233	11,639
	2,557	$17,661
Less amount representing interest	817	
Present value of net minimum lease payments	$1,740	

What interest rate does AMR use to capitalize its capital leases? Use this rate to capitalize AMR's operating leases at December 31, 2001. Record the adjustment to AMR's balance sheet to reflect the capitalization of operating leases. How would this reporting change affect AMR's Income Statement in 2002?

5. What approaches would you use to estimate the value of brands? What assumptions underlie these approaches? As a financial analyst, what would you use to assess whether the brand value of £1.575 billion reported by Cadbury Schweppes in 1997 was a reasonable reflection of the future benefits from these brands? What questions would you raise with the firm's CFO about the firm's brand assets?

6. As the CFO of a company, what indicators would you look at to assess whether your firm's long-term assets were impaired? What approaches could be used, either by management or an independent valuation firm, to assess the dollar value of any asset impairment? As a financial analyst, what indicators would you look at to assess whether a firm's long-term assets were impaired? What questions would you raise with the firm's CFO about any charges taken for asset impairment?

7. The cigarette industry is subject to litigation for health hazards posed by its products. The industry has been negotiating a settlement of these claims with state and federal governments. As the CFO for Philip Morris, one of the larger firms in the industry, what information would you report to investors in the annual report on the firm's litigation risks? How would you assess whether the firm should record a liability for this risk, and if so, how would you assess the value of this liability? As a financial analyst following Philip Morris, what questions would you raise with the CEO over the firm's litigation liability?

8. Refer to the General Motors example on post-retirement benefits (page 4-27). Show the adjustments that would be required to record the full amount of the unfunded post-retirement benefit on December 31, 2000. What factors account for the difference between the adjustments to Common Shareholders' Equity on December 31, 2000 and 2001?

9. Intel reports the following information on its stock options incentive programs in its December 31, 2001, financial statement footnotes.

> The company's stock option plans are accounted for under the intrinsic value recognition and measurement principles of APB Opinion No. 25, "Accounting for Stock Issued to Employees," and related interpretations. As the exercise price of all options granted under these plans was equal to the market price of the underlying common stock on the grant date, no stock-based employee compensation cost, other than acquisition-related compensation, is recognized in net income. The following table illustrates the effect on net income and earnings per share if the company had applied the fair value recognition provisions of SFAS No. 123, "Accounting for Stock-Based Compensation," to employee stock benefits, including shares issued under the stock option plans and under the company's Stock Participation Plan, collectively called "options."

($ millions)	2002	2001	2000
Net income, as reported	$ 3,117	$ 1,291	$ 10,535
Less: Total stock-based employee compensation expense determined under the fair value method for all awards, net of tax	1,170	1,037	836
Pro-forma net income	$ 1,947	$ 254	$ 9,699

Record the adjustments to the financial statements required to show an expense for stock options under the fair value method for 2001 and 2002. Intel reports that its marginal tax rate is 35 percent.

10. Refer to the Lufthansa example on asset depreciation estimates (pages 4-16 and 4-17). What adjustments would be required if Lufthansa's aircraft depreciation were computed using an average life of 25 years and salvage value of 5 percent (instead of the reported values of 12 years and 15 percent)? Show the adjustments to the 2000 and 2001 balance sheets, and to the 2001 income statement.

11. In early 2003 Bristol-Myers Squibb announced that it would have to restate its financial statements as a result of stuffing as much as $3.35 billion worth of products into wholesalers' warehouses from 1999 through 2001. The company's sales and cost of sales during this period was as follows:

	2001	2000	1999
Net sales	$18,139	$17,695	$16,502
Cost of products sold	5,454	4,729	4,458

The company's marginal tax rate during the three years was 35 percent. What adjustments are required to correct Bristol-Myers Squibb's balance sheet for December 31, 2001? What assumptions underlie your adjustments? How would you expect the adjustments to affect Bristol-Myers Squibb's performance in the coming few years?

NOTES

1. A notable exception in the U.S. is the requirement that software development costs be capitalized once the software reaches the stage of technological feasibility (see SFAS 86).

2. See P. Healy, S. Myers, and C. Howe, "R&D Accounting and the Tradeoff Between Relevance and Objectivity," *Journal of Accounting Research* 40 (June 2002): 677–711, for analysis of the value of capitalizing R&D and then annually assessing impairment.

3. J. Elliott and D. Hanna find that the market anticipates large write-downs by about one quarter, consistent with managers being reluctant to take write-downs on a timely basis. See "Repeated Accounting Write-Offs and the Information Content of Earnings," *Journal of Accounting Research* 34, Supplement, 1996.

4. J. Francis, D. Hanna, and L. Vincent find that management is more likely to exercise judgment in its self-interest for goodwill write-offs and restructuring charges than for inventory or PP&E write-offs. See "Causes and Effects of Discretionary Asset Write-Offs," *Journal of Accounting Research* 34, Supplement, 1996.

5. P. Healy, K. Palepu, and R. Ruback find that acquisitions add value for only one third of the 50 largest acquisitions during the early 1980s, suggesting that acquirers frequently do not recover goodwill. See "Which Takeovers Are Profitable—Strategic or Financial?" *Sloan Management Review*, Summer 1997.

6. MicroStrategy 1998 10-K, Footnote 1.

7. Ibid.

8. Recent evidence indicates that there are negative stock price effects for acquirers that use pooling. See J. Weber, "Shareholder Wealth Effects of Pooling-of-Interests Accounting: Evidence from the SEC's Restriction on Share Repurchases Following Pooling Transactions," working paper, MIT Sloan School of Management, October 2000, and A. Martinez-Jarad, "Interaction Between Accounting and Corporate Governance: Evidence from Business Combinations," working paper, Harvard Business School, February 2003.

9. Several studies indicate that some firms are willing to go to considerable lengths, including paying an additional premium, to be able to use the pooling method for recording an acquisition. See J. Robinson and P. Shane, "Acquisition Accounting Method and Bid Premia for Target Firms," *The Accounting Review* 65 (January 1990): 25–49, and T. Lys and L. Vincent, "An Analysis of Value Destruction in AT&T's Acquisition of NCR," *Journal of Financial Economics* 39 (October/November 1995): 353–79.

10. Research indicates that some firms responded to the adoption of SFAS 13, which changed the rules for lease capitalization, by grooming transactions to avoid having to capitalize leases. See E. Imhoff and J. Thomas, "Economic Consequences of Accounting Standards: The Lease Disclosure Rule Change," *Journal of Accounting & Economics,* 10 (December 1988): 277–311, and S. El-Gazzar, S. Lilien, and V. Pastena, "Accounting for Leases by Lessees," *Journal of Accounting & Economics* 8 (October 1986): 217–38.

11. E. Imhoff, R. Lipe, and D. Wright show that adjustments to capitalize operating leases have a significant impact on leverage and other key financial ratios. See "Operating Leases: Impact of Constructive Capitalization," *Accounting Horizons* 5 (March 1991): 51–64.

12. Accounting rules in the U.S., the U.K., Canada, and Germany require expensing R&D outlays. Expensing is the norm in Japan and France, even though capitalization is permitted.

13. P. Healy, S. Myers, and C. Howe, "R&D Accounting and the Tradeoff Between Relevance and Objectivity," *Journal of Accounting Research* 40 (June 2002): 677–711, show that the magnitude of this bias is sizable.

14. See B. Bublitz and M. Ettredge, "The Information in Discretionary Outlays: Advertising, Research and Development," *The Accounting Review* 64 (1989): 108–124; S. Chan, J. Martin, and J. Kensinger, "Corporate Research and Development Expenditures and Share Value," *Journal of Financial Economics* 26 (1990): 255–76; R. Dukes, "An Investigation of the Effects of Expensing Research and Development Costs on Security Prices," in proceedings of the conference on topical research in accounting (New York University, 1976); J. Elliott, G. Richardson, T. Dyckman, and R. Dukes, "The Impact of SFAS No. 2 on Firm Expenditures on Research and Development:

Replications and Extensions," *Journal of Accounting* 22 (1984): 85–102; M. Hirschey and J. Weygandt, "Amortization Policy for Advertising and Research and Development Expenditures," *Journal of Accounting Research* 23 (1985): 326–35; C. Wasley and T. Linsmeier, "A Further Examination of the Economic Consequences of SFAS No. 2," *Journal of Accounting Research* 30 (1992): 156–64; E. Eccher, "The Value Relevance of Capitalized Software Development Costs," working paper, MIT Sloan School of Management, Cambridge, MA, 1997; B. Lev and T. Sougiannis, "The Capitalization, Amortization, and Value-Relevance of R&D," *Journal of Accounting and Economics* 21 (1996): 107–138; and D. Aboody and B. Lev, "The Value-Relevance of Intangibles: The Case of Software Capitalization," working paper, University of California, 1998.

15. See BA versus Lufthansa case, Lakshmanan Shivakumar, London Business School.

16. It is interesting to note that Lufthansa's depreciation expense for the year 2001 is significantly lower than expected given its 12 year life and 15 percent salvage estimates. The reported depreciation under these assumptions would have been 994m $(.083 \cdot \{11{,}542.7 + [(1{,}021.5 \cdot .85)/2]\})$. The company provides no explanation for the difference.

17. JAL actually shows the present value of its lease commitments. However, most companies report the value of future lease payments for the next five years and then show a lump sum value for all payments beyond five years. To estimate the value of the lease liability, the analyst must decide how to allocate this lump sum over year six and beyond, and estimate a suitable interest rate on the lease debt. It is then possible to compute the present value of the lease payments.

18. Mary E. Barth and Maureen McNichols discuss ways for investors to estimate the value of environmental liabilities. See "Estimation and Market Valuation of Environmental Liabilities Relating to Superfund Sites," *Journal of Accounting Research* 32, Supplement, 1994.

19. Defined contribution plans, where companies agree to contribute fixed amounts today to cover future benefits, require very little forecasting to estimate their annual cost since the firm's obligation is limited to its annual obligation to contribute to the employees' retirement funds.

20. E. Amir and E. Gordon show that firms with larger postretirement benefit obligations and more leverage tend to make more aggressive estimates of postretirement obligation parameters. See "A Firm's Choice of Estimation Parameters: Empirical Evidence from SFAS No. 106," *Journal of Accounting, Auditing & Finance* 11, no. 3, Summer 1996.

21. The interest expense is only a rough approximation of the amount that would be reported by CA, since it does not adjust for the portion of the customer payments that were effectively interest for the bank given the premium rate charged.

22. In their footnotes firms also report the Accumulated Benefit Obligation for the pension plan, which is the present value of plan commitments using current wage rates and salary scales.

23. M. Barth finds that investors regard these footnote disclosures as more useful than the liability reported in the financial statements. See "Relative Measurement Errors Among Alternative Pension Asset and Liability Measures," *The Accounting Review* 66, no. 3, 1991.

24. The Black-Scholes option-pricing model estimates the value of an option as a nonlinear function of the exercise price, the remaining time to expiration, the estimated variance of the underlying stock, and the risk-free interest rate. Studies of the valuation of executive stock options include T. Hemmer, S. Matsunaga, and T. Shevlin, "Optimal Exercise and the Cost of Granting Employee Stock Options with a Reload Provision," *Journal of Accounting Research* 36, no. 2, 1998; C. Cuny and P. Jorion, "Valuing Executive Stock Options with Endogenous Departure," *Journal of Accounting and Economics* 20 (September 1995): 193–206; and S. Huddart, "Employee Stock Options," *Journal of Accounting and Economics* 18 (September 1994): 207–32.

25. P. Dechow, A. Hutton, and R. Sloan find that lobbying against SFAS 123 was motivated by concerns about reporting higher levels of executive compensation. See "Economic Consequences of Accounting for Stock-Based Compensation," *Journal of Accounting Research*, Supplement, 1996.

APPENDIX: RECASTING FINANCIAL STATEMENTS INTO STANDARDIZED TEMPLATES

The following tables show the financial statements for Nordstrom, Inc. for the year ended December 31, 2002. The first column in each statement presents the recast financial statement classifications that are used for each line item. Note that the classifications are not applied to subtotal lines such as Total current assets or Net income. The recast financial statements for Nordstrom are prepared by simply totaling the balances of line-items with the same standard classifications. For example, on the recast balance sheet there are two line items classified as Other Current Assets: Prepaid expenses and Other current assets.

Nordstrom Reported Balance Sheet ($ 000's)

Classifications	Fiscal Year Ended December 31,	2002	2001
	ASSETS		
	Current assets:		
Cash and Marketable Securities	Cash and cash equivalents	$331,327	$25,259
Accounts Receivable	Accounts receivable, net	698,475	721,953
Inventory	Merchandise inventories	888,172	945,687
Other Current Assets	Prepaid expenses	34,375	28,760
Other Current Assets	Other current assets	102,249	91,323
	Total current assets	2,054,598	1,812,982
Long-Term Tangible Assets	Land, buildings and equipment, net	1,761,082	1,599,938
Long-Term Intangible Assets	Intangible assets, net	138,331	143,473
Other Long-Term Assets	Other assets	94,768	52,110
	TOTAL ASSETS	$4,048,779	$3,608,503
	LIABILITIES AND SHAREHOLDERS' EQUITY		
	Current liabilities:		
Short-Term Debt	Notes payable	$148	$83,060
Accounts Payable	Accounts payable	490,988	466,476
Other Current Liabilities	Accrued salaries, wages and related benefits	236,373	234,833
Other Current Liabilities	Income taxes and other accruals	142,002	153,613
Short-Term Debt	Current portion of long-term debt	78,227	12,586
	Total current liabilities	947,738	950,568
Long-Term Debt	Long-term debt	1,351,044	1,099,710
Other Long-Term Liabilities (non-interest-bearing)	Deferred lease credits	342,046	275,252
Other Long-Term Liabilities (non-interest-bearing)	Other liabilities	93,463	53,405
	Shareholders' equity:		
Common Shareholders' Equity	Common stock, no par: 250,000,000 shares authorized; 134,468,608 and 133,797,757 shares issued and outstanding	341,316	330,394
Common Shareholders' Equity	Unearned stock compensation	(2,680)	(3,740)
Common Shareholders' Equity	Retained earnings	975,203	900,090
Common Shareholders' Equity	Accumulated other comprehensive earnings	649	2,824
	Total shareholders' equity	1,314,488	1,229,568
	TOTAL LIABILITIES AND SHAREHOLDERS' EQUITY	$4,048,779	$3,608,503

Nordstrom Reported Income Statement ($ 000's)

Classifications	Fiscal-Year Ended December 31,	2002	2001	2000
Sales	Net sales	$5,634,130	$5,528,537	$5,149,266
Cost of Sales	Cost of sales and related buying and occupancy	(3,765,859)	(3,649,516)	(3,359,760)
	Gross profit	1,868,271	1,879,021	1,789,506
SG&A	Selling, general and administrative	(1,722,635)	(1,747,048)	(1,523,836)
	Operating income	145,636	131,973	265,670
Net Interest Expense (Income)	Interest expense, net	(75,038)	(62,698)	(50,396)
Other Expense	Write-down of investment	0	(32,857)	0
Other Income	Service charge income and other, net	133,890	130,600	116,783
	Earnings before income taxes	204,488	167,018	332,057
Tax Expense	Income taxes	−79,800	−65,100	−129,500
	NET EARNINGS	$124,688	$101,918	$202,557

Nordstrom Reported Cash Flow Statement ($ 000's)

Classifications	Fiscal-Year Ended December 31,	2002	2001	2000
	OPERATING ACTIVITIES			
Net Income	Net earnings	$124,688	$101,918	$202,557
	Adj. to reconcile net earnings to net cash provided by operating activities:			
Long-Term Operating Accruals	Depreciation and amortization of buildings and equipment	213,089	203,048	193,718
Long-Term Operating Accruals	Amortization of intangible assets	4,630	1,251	0
Long-Term Operating Accruals	Amortization of deferred lease credits and other, net	(8,538)	(12,349)	(6,387)
Long-Term Operating Accruals	Stock-based compensation expense	3,414	6,480	3,331
Long-Term Operating Accruals	Deferred income taxes, net	15,662	(3,716)	(22,859)
Long-Term Operating Accruals	Write-down of investment	0	32,857	0
	Change in operating assets and liabilities, net of effects from acquisition of business:			
Net (Investment) Liquidation of Oper. WC.	Accounts receivable, net	22,556	(102,945)	(29,854)
Net (Investment) Liquidation of Oper. WC.	Merchandise inventories	215,731	6,741	79,894
Net (Investment) Liquidation of Oper. WC.	Prepaid expenses	(1,684)	(173)	(6,976)
Net (Investment) Liquidation of Oper. WC.	Other assets	(16,770)	(3,821)	(8,880)
Net (Investment) Liquidation of Oper. WC.	Accounts payable	(159,636)	(67,924)	(76,417)
Net (Investment) Liquidation of Oper. WC.	Accrued salaries, wages and related benefits	(203)	17,850	14,942
Net (Investment) Liquidation of Oper. WC.	Income tax liabilities and other accruals	(11,310)	3,879	965
Net (Investment) Liquidation of Oper. WC.	Other liabilities	12,088	(7,184)	25,212
	Net cash provided by operating activities	413,717	175,912	369,246
	INVESTING ACTIVITIES			
Net (Investment) Liquidation of Oper. LT Assets	Capital expenditures	($390,138)	($321,454)	(305,052)
Net (Investment) Liquidation of Oper. LT Assets	Additions to deferred lease credits	$126,383	$92,361	114,910
Net (Investment) Liquidation of Oper. LT Assets	Payment for acquisition, net of cash acquired	$0	($83,828)	0
Net (Investment) Liquidation of Oper. LT Assets	Other, net	($3,309)	($1,781)	(452)
	Net cash used in investing activities	(267,064)	(314,702)	(190,594)
	FINANCING ACTIVITIES			
Net Debt (Repayment) or Issuance	Proceeds (payments) from notes payable	(82,912)	12,126	(7,849)
Net Debt (Repayment) or Issuance	Proceeds from issuance of long-term debt	300,000	308,266	0
Net Debt (Repayment) or Issuance	Principal payments on long-term debt	(18,640)	(58,191)	(63,341)
Net Stock (Repurchase) or Issuance	Capital contribution to subsidiary from minority shareholders	0	0	16,000
Net Stock (Repurchase) or Issuance	Proceeds from issuance of common stock	10,542	6,250	9,577
Dividend (Payments)	Cash dividends paid	(48,265)	(45,935)	(44,463)
Net Stock (Repurchase) or Issuance	Purchase and retirement of common stock	(1,310)	(85,509)	(302,965)
	Net cash provided by (used in) financing activities	159,415	137,007	(393,041)
	Net increase (decrease) in cash and cash equivalents	306,068	(1,783)	(214,389)
	Cash and cash equivalents at beginning of year	25,259	27,042	241,431
	CASH AND CASH EQUIVALENTS AT END OF YEAR	$331,327	$25,259	$27,042

The standardized financial statements for Nordstrom Inc. are as follows:

Nordstrom Standardized Balance Sheet ($ 000's)

Fiscal Year Ending December 31,	2001	2002
Balance Sheet		
Assets		
Cash and Marketable Securities	25,259	331,327
Accounts Receivable	721,953	698,475
Inventory	945,687	888,172
Other Current Assets	120,083	136,624
Total Current Assets	**1,812,982**	**2,054,598**
Long-Term Tangible Assets	1,599,938	1,761,082
Long-Term Intangible Assets	143,473	138,331
Other Long-Term Assets	52,110	94,768
Total Long-Term Assets	**1,795,521**	**1,994,181**
Total Assets	**3,608,503**	**4,048,779**
Liabilities		
Accounts Payable	466,476	490,988
Short-Term Debt	95,646	78,375
Other Current Liabilities	388,446	378,375
Total Current Liabilities	**950,568**	**947,738**
Long-Term Debt	1,099,710	1,351,044
Deferred Taxes	0	0
Other Long-Term Liabilities (non-interest bearing)	328,657	435,509
Total Long-Term Liabilities	**1,428,367**	**1,786,553**
Total Liabilities	**2,378,935**	**2,734,291**
Minority Interest	0	0
Shareholders' Equity		
Preferred Stock	0	0
Common Shareholders' Equity	1,229,568	1,314,488
Total Shareholders' Equity	**1,229,568**	**1,314,488**
Total Liabilities and Shareholders' Equity	**3,608,503**	**4,048,779**

Nordstrom Standardized Income Statement ($ 000's)

Fiscal Year Ending December 31,	2000	2001	2002
Sales	**5,149,266**	**5,528,537**	**5,634,130**
Cost of Sales	3,359,760	3,649,516	3,765,859
Gross Profit	**1,789,506**	**1,879,021**	**1,868,271**
SG&A	1,523,836	1,747,048	1,722,635
Other Operating Expense	0	0	0
Operating Income	**265,670**	**131,973**	**145,636**
Investment Income	0	0	0
Other Income, net of Other Expense	116,783	97,743	133,890
Other Income	116,783	130,600	133,890
Other Expense	0	32,857	0
Net Interest Expense (Income)	−50,396	−62,698	−75,038
Interest Income	na	na	na
Interest Expense	na	na	na
Minority Interest	na	na	na
Pre-Tax Income	**432,849**	**292,414**	**354,564**
Tax Expense	129,500	65,100	79,800
Unusual Items (after tax)	0	0	0
Net Income	**303,349**	**227,314**	**274,764**
Preferred Dividends	0	0	0
Net Income to Common	**303,349**	**227,314**	**274,764**

Nordstrom Standardized Cash Flow Statement ($ 000's)

	2000	2001	2002
Net Income	**202,557**	**101,918**	**124,688**
After-tax net interest expense (income)	30,742	38,260	45,755
Non-operating losses (gains)	0	0	0
Long-term operating accruals	167,803	227,571	228,257
Operating cash flow before working capital investments	**401,102**	**367,749**	**398,700**
Net (investments in) or liquidation of operating working capital	(1,114)	(153,577)	60,772
Operating cash flow before investment in long-term assets	**399,988**	**214,172**	**459,472**
Net (investment in) or liquidation of operating long-term assets	(190,594)	(314,702)	(267,064)
Free cash flow available to debt and equity	**209,394**	**(100,530)**	**192,408**
After-tax net interest expense (income)	30,742	38,260	45,755
Net debt (repayment) or issuance	(71,190)	262,201	198,448
Free cash flow available to equity	**107,462**	**123,411**	**345,101**
Dividend (payments)	(44,463)	(45,935)	(48,265)
Net stock (repurchase) or issuance	(277,388)	(79,259)	9,232
Net increase (decrease) in cash balance	**(214,389)**	**(1,783)**	**306,068**

Pre-Paid Legal Services, Inc.

*Pre-Paid Legal plans are designed to help middle-income Americans have afford-
able access to quality legal assistance.*

Pre-Paid Legal Services Corporate Vision

Harland C. Stonecipher founded Pre-Paid Legal Services, Inc. (PPLS) in 1972 after an expensive encounter with lawyers stemming from an automobile accident. PPLS sold legal expense insurance that provided for partial payment of legal fees in connection with the defense of certain civil and criminal actions. The company went public in 1979 and grew rapidly throughout the 1980s as an increasing number of Americans subscribed to legal service insurance (see Exhibit 1). In 1998 the company had membership revenues of $110 million, earnings of $30.2 million, and end-of-year book equity of $101.1 million. In May 1999 it began trading on the New York Stock Exchange and in August 1999 its market capitalization reached $738 million, an increase of 101 percent over the previous year.

Despite its strong financial performance, opinions about the future of Pre-Paid Legal Services varied widely among U.S. equity analysts in the period late 1997 to mid-1999. The company was highly recommended by a number of analysts, but there was also persistent short selling of the stock.[1] Short sellers' primary concern about the company was outlined in a *Fortune* article in late 1997. The business publication alleged that the company was using an inappropriate method of accounting for sales commissions. As a result of this uncertainty, the company's stock price fluctuated widely from a high of $40.50 to a low of $13.50 between late 1997 and mid-1999 (see Exhibit 2).

BUSINESS DESCRIPTION[2]

PPLS offered its customers (termed members) a wide range of legal insurance. The most popular plan, the Family Plan, accounted for 94 percent of all memberships in 1998. This plan provided reimbursement for a broad range of legal expenses incurred by members and their spouses, including will and testament preparation, document review and letter writing, and some of the legal costs associated with employment-related trial defense, traffic violations, and Internal Revenue Service audits.[3] The Family Plan specified limits on the number of hours of attorney time that a member was entitled to receive for many of these services. It also provided a 25 percent discount on attorney rates for the purchase of any legal services over and above those provided under the insurance contract.

PPLS's membership premiums in 1998 averaged $19.08 per month (or $229 per year). Premiums were typically paid on a monthly basis either by automatic charges to the

Professor Paul M. Healy and Teaching Fellow Jacob Cohen J.D. prepared this case. The case is intended solely as the basis for class discussion and is not intended to serve as an endorsement, source of primary data, or illustration of effective or ineffective management. Copyright © 2002 by the President and Fellows of Harvard College. HBS Case 9-100-037.

1. Short sellers borrow stock certificates from a brokerage firm and sell the stocks on the open market. If the stock price declines, short sellers can buy back stock, cover their loan from the brokerage firm, and earn a profit. Of course, if the price increases, short sellers make a loss.

2. The material in this section is from Pre-Paid Legal Services, Inc.'s 1998 10-K Statement.

3. Legal services specifically excluded from coverage included domestic matters, bankruptcy, deliberate criminal acts, alcohol or drug-related matters, business matters, and pre-existing conditions.

member's credit card or through employee payroll deductions. The premiums were generally guaranteed renewable and non-cancelable except for fraud, nonpayment of premiums, or upon written request by a member. The annual membership persistency rate in 1998 was high; approximately 75 percent of members at the beginning of the year and new members during the year continued to be enrolled in the program at the end of the year. At March 31, 1999, PPLS had 648,475 active members, and membership had been increasing at about 40 percent per year.

PPLS marketed its memberships through a multi-level program that encouraged buyers to become salespeople. Members that sought to become sales associates paid the company a fee, typically $65, to cover the cost of training materials, training meetings, and home office support services. Registered sales associates sold the company's services to their friends and business associates. The most successful even recruited and developed their own sales force. In 1998 PPLS generated 76 percent of its annual sales from the roughly 150,000 members registered as sales associates. The remaining 24 percent of sales were generated through arrangements with insurance and service companies with established sales forces, such as CNA and Primerica Financial Services.

Sales associates were compensated on a commission basis (see Exhibit 3). Prior to 1995, associates that signed up a new member received a commission of 70 percent of the first year premium, and a 16 percent commission for subsequent year renewals. First year commissions were paid in advance whereas renewal commissions were paid as premiums were received. For example, if a new member signed up at a premium of $229 per year, the associate responsible for the sale received a first year commission of $160 (0.70 × $229) at sign-up. If the member renewed in subsequent years, the sales associate received a monthly commission of $3.04 (0.16 × $19).

After 1995 PPLS modified its commission formula to a flat 25 percent commission for both initial year and subsequent renewal memberships. To retain and attract sales associates, PPLS advanced the sales associate three years of commission on every new membership sold. If a membership lapsed before the advances had been recovered, PPLS deducted 50 percent of any unearned advances from future commissions to the relevant associate. For example, if a new member signed up at a premium of $229, the associate received a commission advance of $171.75 (25 percent × 3 × $229). If one year later the member cancelled the policy, PPLS sought to recover $57.25, equal to 50 percent of the second and third year commissions (50 percent of $229 × 2 × 0.25).

PPLS had historically offered two forms of legal services, each with very different implications for managing legal claim costs. The first form of service, termed open panel, allowed members to use their own attorney to provide legal services available under their policy. Member's attorneys were reimbursed for their services using a payment schedule that reflected "usual, reasonable and customary fees" for a particular service and geographic area.

The second form of service, closed panel memberships, required members to access legal services through a network of independent attorneys that were under contract with PPLS. These provider attorneys were paid a fixed monthly fee on a per capita basis to provide services to plan members living within the state in which the attorney was licensed to practice. PPLS contracted with one large, highly rated legal firm in each of its 36 major markets. Provider attorneys are typically rated "AV" by Martindale-Hubbell, its highest rating. They were selected after a detailed review by PPLS management.

Average costs of membership benefits in 1998 were 33 percent of membership premiums and management reported that these costs were expected to remain at around 35 percent in the future.

FINANCIAL PERFORMANCE

PPLS reported record financial performance in 1997 and 1998 (see Exhibit 4 for summary financial data and Exhibit 5 for 1998 financial statements and excerpted footnotes.). Membership revenues during this period grew by an average of 59 percent per year, net income grew by 71 percent per year, and operating cash flows grew 500 percent per year. The firm's financial performance for the first six months of 1999 continued to be impressive. Membership revenues grew by 20 percent, earnings by 54 percent, and operating cash flows by 138 percent (from $2.4 million to $5.7 million).

As a result of the company's growth performance, a number of equity analysts that followed the stock recommended it to their clients. For example, David Strasser of Salomon Brothers issued strong buy recommendations for PPLS in August 1997 and commented on the stock as follows:

> We reiterate our Strong Buy recommendation on the shares of Pre-Paid Legal Services, Inc. . . . We have recently increased our one-year price to $34 from $26. We did this for several reasons. First, the company continues to demonstrate consistent earnings growth, in line with Wall Street estimates, which gives us greater visibility of our projected 36 percent growth rate. . . . We are also encouraged by the company's ability to generate positive operating cash flow while still growing revenues 53 percent. This positive cash flow is indicative of the seasoned membership base that generates cash in spite of the company's policy of paying commission advances to its associates for new sales. We continue to believe that the company will announce an alliance with a major insurance company to sell the company's products. This would essentially double the size of the company's productive sales force and increase overall visibility of the prepaid legal product.

ACCOUNTING DISPUTE

Despite its strong financial performance, in late 1997 PPLS was a target of short selling. On November 24, 1997, *Fortune* published an article titled "Will Pre-Paid Keep Growing?" The article cited short seller Robert Olstein of Olstein's Financial Alert Fund, who explained that his concern arose because "PPLS's accounting for commissions is unrealistic and not in accordance with economic reality."[4] The *Fortune* article noted:

> Rather than record the commissions as an instant hit to earnings, Pre-Paid spreads them out over a three-year period. Such deferrals, the shorts argue, make today's earnings growth look stronger than it really is. In the first half of this year, for example, if the company had swallowed commissions when they were paid, it would have shown little if any earnings growth—certainly not a level of growth to justify the stock's trading at nearly 40 times earnings.
>
> Plus, trouble could emerge if the company's cancellation rate on its policies increases and it can't somehow recover the commissions it has already paid. Pre-Paid shrugs this off, arguing that its historic cancellation rate is a manageable 24 percent. And, Harp (PPLS's CEO) boasts, "I can predict this business more precisely than anybody you want to mention."
>
> Maybe so, but the company's own figures, disclosed in SEC filings, show that the rate is on an upward trend. The filings also state that Pre-Paid's cancellation rate will

---

4. Herb Greenberg, "Will Pre-Paid Keep Growing? A Company's HMO-Style Approach to Legal Services Has Won It Plenty of Fans—And a Soaring Price. But Shortsellers Say The Numbers Don't Add Up," Fortune, November 24, 1997.

rise if newly written policies make up a greater portion of its business, and the company warns (deep in its 10-K annual report) that it experienced a "significant increase" in sales of new contracts last year. Unless this shift is offset by "other factors," the 10-K says, financial performance could be severely hurt. In other words, Olstein contends, Pre-Paid may face a big write-off at some point.

MANAGEMENT RESPONSE

PPLS argued that its policy of accounting for commissions resulted in a commission expense that was more consistent with the collection of the premiums generated by the sale of such contracts. Exhibit 6 shows management's discussion of commissions and membership persistency in the firm's 10-K statement. In addition, between October 1998 and June 1999 management acquired 1,384,440 of the firm's shares on the open market at an average price of $28 per share.[5]

Nonetheless, concern over the company's accounting persisted. In late June 1999, short sales were 6.5 percent of outstanding shares, more than four times the level of typical companies.[6] The company's stock traded at $26.63, well off its yearly high of $39.25 and the all-time high of $40.50.

Rick Nelson, an analyst at Furman Selz, summed up the market sentiment this way: "insiders feel they've got a company that's trading well off its high where the operating fundamentals are going gangbusters. But the shorts have caught on the notion that from a cash flow standpoint, the company just can't handle the growth, and that their business model itself will come back to haunt them."[7]

QUESTIONS

1. How does PPLS create value for its customers? What are the critical risks that it has to manage well?

2. How did the pre-1995 commission formula work? Why do you think the company changed its policy?

3. Based on the post-1995 commission formula and information in the case on pricing and commission rates, calculate the cash inflows for premiums and cash outflows for commissions for years 1 to 3 that would arise from the sign-up of 1000 new members at the beginning of year 1. Assume that (a) actual member renewal rates are 75 percent for both years 2 and 3 and (b) 25 percent of recoverable commission advances in each of years 2 and 3 prove uncollectable.

4. How does Pre-Paid Legal account for the transactions described in question 3?

5. Do you agree with *Fortune*'s criticism of PPLS's method of reporting for commissions? Why or why not?

6. What actions could PPLS's management take to reduce the unease among key investors about the firm's accounting and its business model?

5. Quicken.com, *Insider Trading in Pre-Paid Legal Services.*

6. "Uncovered Short Positions Rise on Big Board and Amex," *The New York Times*, June 22, 1999.

7. See discussion in "The Long and Short of It" by Ian Mount, SmartMoney.com, May 25, 1999.

EXHIBIT I

Number of Subscribers to Legal Service Plans in the U.S., 1981 to 1997

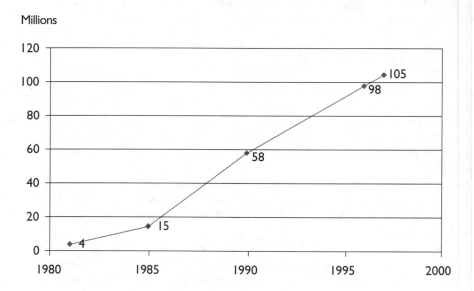

The above estimates were developed by The National Resources Center for Consumer LegaServices (NRC) and report-ed by PPLS in its 1998 10-K Report. NRC estimates included free member plans sponsored by labor unions, the Amer-ican Association for Retired Persons, the National Education Association and military services, as well as employer-paid plans. PPLS estimated that 10 percent of the total legal insurance market was covered by plans comparable to those provided by PPLS. The other major companies servicing this market were Hyatt Legal Services, ARAG Group, LawPhone, National Legal Plan, and the Signature Group. The NRC estimated that in 1997 the market share of these firms (and PPLS) was 79 percent. The market share of PPLS alone was estimated at 15 percent.

Source: Pre-Paid Legal Services Annual Report, 1998.

EXHIBIT 2

Stock Performance for Pre-Paid Legal Services Versus Dow Jones Industrial Average, August 1997 to July 1999

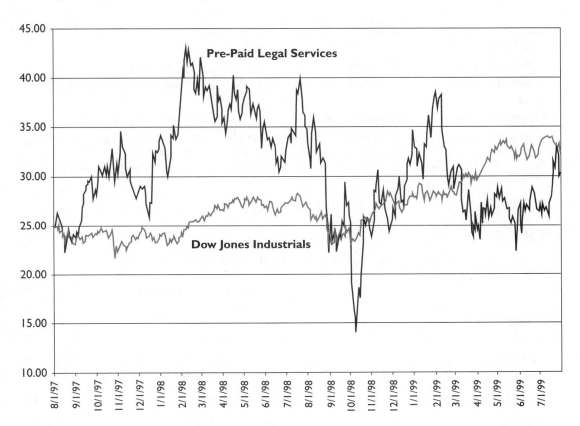

Source: Datastream International.

EXHIBIT 3

Summary of Commission Rates and Timing of Payment for Pre-Paid Legal Services

	First-Year Commission	Subsequent Year Commissions
Pre-1995:		
Commission rate	70% of subscription	16% of subscription
Timing of payment	At customer sign-up	Monthly
1995:		
Commission rate	25% of subscription	25% of subscription
Timing of payment	Advance of three years' worth of commissions at customer sign-up	None for first three years, then monthly

EXHIBIT 4

Summary Financial Information for Pre-Paid Legal Services

(in $000)	Year ended December 31			
	1998	1997	1996	1995
Membership revenues	$110,003	$76,688	$50,582	$31,290
Net income	30,210	18,790	12,470	7,312
Cash from operations	$9,895	$7,733	$942	$548
Total assets	$167,903	$91,912	$57,532	$35,629
Book value of equity	101,304	70,511	45,474	29,740
New memberships sold	391,827	283,723	194,483	109,922
Period-end memberships in force	603,017	425,381	294,151	203,535
Commission advances current	$21,224	$15,705	$9,108	$3,923
Noncurrent commission advances, net	60,661	38,038	21,744	8,548

Source: Annual Reports, 1995–98.

EXHIBIT 5

Financial Statements and Selected Footnotes for Pre-Paid Legal Services, December 31, 1998

BALANCE SHEET

($000)	December 31, 1998	December 31, 1997
ASSETS		
Current assets:		
Cash and cash equivalents	$8,604	$27,722
Available-for-sale investments, at fair value	2,368	0
Held-to-maturity investments	0	4,242
Accrued Membership income	3,595	2,399
Inventories	2,588	2,116
Prepaid product commissions	1,384	2,136
Amount due from coinsurer	12,498	0
Membership commission advances - current portion	21,224	15,705
Total current assets	52,261	54,320
Available-for-sale investments, at fair value	36,207	0
Held-to-maturity investments	0	650
Investments pledged	2,922	2,772
Membership commission advances, net	60,661	38,038
Property and equipment, net	7,678	5,226
Production costs, net	1,373	1,008
Other	6,801	3,702
Total assets	$167,903	$105,716
LIABILITIES AND STOCKHOLDERS' EQUITY		
Current liabilities:		
Membership benefits	$3,808	$2,649
Deferred product sales revenue	3,932	4,737
Accident and health reserves	12,498	0
Life insurance reserves	970	0
Current portion of capital lease obligation	487	142
Accounts payable and accrued expenses	9,386	12,009
Total current liabilities	31,081	19,537
Deferred income taxes	27,148	16,471
Life insurance reserves	7,711	0
Capital lease obligation, net of current portion	659	238
Total liabilities	66,599	36,246
Stockholders' equity:		
Preferred stock, $1 par value; authorized 400 shares; 3 issued and outstanding as follows: $3.00 Cumulative Convertible Preferred Stock, 3 shares authorized, issued and outstanding at December 31, 1998 and 1997, respectively; liquidation value of	3	3
Special preferred stock, $1 par value; authorized 500 shares, issued and outstanding in one series designated as follows: $1.00 Non-Cumulative Special Preferred Stock, 18 and 23 shares authorized, issued and outstanding at December 31, 1998 and 1997, respectively; liquidation value of $240 and $304 at December 31, 1998 and 1997, respectively	18	23

(continued)

Pre-Paid Legal Services

BALANCE SHEET *(continued)*

($000)	December 31, 1998	December 31, 1997
Common stock, $.01 par value; 100,000 shares authorized; 24,321 and 24,151 issued at December 31, 1998 and 1997, respectively	243	242
Capital in excess of par value	55,241	52,051
Retained earnings	49,528	19,328
Accumulated other comprehensive income:		
Unrealized gains (losses) on investments	(24)	0
Less: Treasury stock at cost; 797 and 747 shares held at December 31, 1998 and 1997, respectively	(3,705)	(2,177)
Total stockholders' equity	101,304	69,470
Total liabilities and stockholders' equity	$167,903	$105,716

Source: This data was extracted from Pre-Paid Legal Services Inc.'s 10-K Statement and downloaded from the SEC's EDGAR database using PricewaterhouseCoopers Global Technology Centre Edgarscan. Please read the on-line disclaimer at <http://edgarscan.pwcglobal.com/EdgarScan/edgarscan_disclaimer.html>.

Pre-Paid Legal Services

INCOME STATEMENT

($000)	December 31, 1998	December 31, 1997	December 31, 1996
Revenues:			
Membership premiums	$110,003	$76,688	$50,582
Product sales	27,779	41,070	26,425
Associate services	17,255	12,143	5,646
Interest income	2,576	1,689	1,303
Other	2,840	1,814	1,678
	160,453	133,404	85,634
Costs and expenses:			
Membership benefits	36,103	25,132	16,871
Product costs	17,967	27,017	20,568
Commissions	24,261	16,717	11,476
General and administrative	21,902	20,311	15,150
Associate services and direct marketing	14,738	11,431	4,544
Depreciation	2,944	2,026	533
Premium taxes	1,206	866	372
	119,121	103,500	69,514
Income before income taxes	41,332	29,904	16,120
Provision for income taxes	11,122	12,381	5,857
Net income	30,210	17,523	10,263
Less dividends on preferred shares	10	13	15
Net income applicable to common stockholders	$30,200	$17,510	$10,248
Basic earnings per common share	$1.29	$0.76	$0.46
Diluted earnings per common share	$1.26	$0.74	$0.44
Comprehensive Income:			
Net income	$30,210	$17,523	$10,263
Other comprehensive income (loss):			
Unrealized gains (losses) on investments			
Unrealized holding gains (losses) arising during period	(24)	0	0
Other comprehensive income	(24)	0	0
Comprehensive income	$30,186	$17,523	$10,263

Source: This data was extracted from Pre-Paid Legal Services Inc.'s 10-K Statement and downloaded from the SEC's EDGAR database using PricewaterhouseCoopers Global Technology Centre Edgarscan. Please read the on-line disclaimer at <http://edgarscan.pwcglobal.com/EdgarScan/edgarscan_disclaimer.html>.

Pre-Paid Legal Services

CASH FLOW STATEMENT

($000)	December 31, 1998	December 31, 1997	December 31, 1996
Cash flows from operating activities:			
Net income	$30,210	$17,523	$10,263
Adjustments to reconcile net income to net cash provided by operating activities:			
Provision for stock grant, stock transfer and associate stock options	0	644	1,122
Provision for deferred income taxes	11,122	12,293	5,857
Depreciation and amortization	2,944	2,026	533
Net changes in asset and liability accounts, net of effects of purchase of UFL:			
Increase in accrued Membership income	(1,196)	(689)	(672)
Increase in commission advances	(28,142)	(22,891)	(18,381)
Increase in other assets	(304)	(678)	(1,360)
Increase in inventories	(472)	(489)	(1,270)
Decrease (increase) in prepaid product commissions	752	(513)	(622)
(Decrease) increase in deferred revenue	(805)	771	1,390
Increase in Membership benefits	1,159	787	315
(Decrease) increase in accounts payable and accrued expenses	(5,373)	5,688	1,914
Net cash provided by (used in) operating activities	9,895	14,472	(911)
Cash flows from investing activities:			
Acquisition of UFL, net of cash acquired	(18,995)	0	0
Additions to property and equipment and production costs	(4,926)	(3,619)	(1,592)
Purchases of held-to-maturity investments	(36,116)	(3,035)	(1,374)
Proceeds from sales of held-to-maturity investments	23,718	0	0
Maturities of held-to-maturity investments	4,892	400	111
Net cash used in investing activities	(31,427)	(6,254)	(2,855)
Cash flows from financing activities:			
Proceeds from sale of common and preferred stock	3,186	3,229	4,904
Increase in capital lease obligations	766	248	84
Purchase of treasury stock	(1,528)	0	0
Dividends paid on preferred stock	(10)	(13)	(15)
Net cash provided by financing activities	2,414	3,464	4,973
Net (decrease) increase in cash and cash equivalents	(19,118)	11,682	1,207
Cash and cash equivalents at beginning of year	27,722	16,040	14,833
Cash and cash equivalents at end of year	$ 8,604	$27,722	$16,040
Supplemental disclosure of cash flow information:			
Cash paid for interest	47	36	28
Purchases of property and equipment under capital leases	1,104	445	63
Assets acquired in acquisition of UFL	44,598		
Liabilities assumed in acquisition of UFL	23,929		

Pre-Paid Legal Services (side margin text)

Source: This data was extracted from Pre-Paid Legal Services Inc.'s 10-K Statement and downloaded from the SEC's EDGAR database using PricewaterhouseCoopers Global Technology Centre Edgarscan. Please read the on-line disclaimer at <http:// edgarscan.pwcglobal.com/EdgarScan/edgarscan_disclaimer.html>.

SELECTED FOOTNOTE INFORMATION

Note 1 - Nature of Operations and Summary of Significant Accounting Policies

Estimates

The preparation of financial statements in conformity with generally accepted accounting principles requires management to make estimates and assumptions that affect the reported amounts of assets and liabilities and disclosure of contingent assets and liabilities at the date of the financial statements and the reported amounts of revenues and expenses during the reporting period. Actual results could differ from those estimates.

Commissions

Effective March 1, 1995, the Company implemented a level membership commission schedule of approximately 25% of annual premium revenue for all Membership years. This commission schedule results in the Company incurring commission expense related to the sale of its legal expense plans on a basis consistent with the collection of the premiums generated by the sale of such Memberships. The Company currently advances the equivalent of three years of commissions on new Membership sales. In January 1997, the Company implemented a new policy whereby associates receive only earned commissions on the first three Memberships submitted unless the associate successfully completes a training program which includes an intensive one-day training seminar, produces three Memberships and recruits one associate within 15 business days from their training date. Prior to March 1, 1995, first year commissions payable on the sale of a Membership, and earned in the first Membership year, were approximately 70% of annual Membership premiums while renewal commissions (payable as earned after the first Membership year) were approximately 16% of annual premiums.

Revenue Recognition

Membership premiums are recognized in income when due in accordance with Membership terms which generally require the holder of the Membership to remit premiums on a monthly basis. Memberships are canceled for nonpayment of premium after ninety days. Premiums due but not collected at the end of an accounting period are recorded as accrued Membership income; a provision for uncollectible premiums, if any, is recorded currently. Revenues from Associates' training program fees and sales of marketing supplies are recognized as income when cash is received. Revenues for product sales are recognized when products are shipped or services provided.

Commission Advances

Commission advances represent the unearned portion of commissions advanced to Associates on sales of Memberships. Commissions are earned as premiums are collected, usually on a monthly basis. The Company reduces Commission advances as premiums are paid and commissions earned. Unearned commission advances on lapsed Memberships are recovered through collection of premiums on an associate's active Memberships. At December 31, 1998 and 1997, the Company had an allowance of $4.0 million and $3.7 million, respectively, to provide for estimated uncollectible balances. The Company charges interest at the prime rate on unearned commission advances relating to Memberships that canceled subsequent to the advance being made.

Membership Benefit Liability

The Membership benefit liability represents claims reported but not paid and actuarially estimated claims incurred but not reported on open panel Memberships and per capita amounts due provider attorneys on closed panel Memberships. The Company calculates the benefit liability costs on open panel Memberships based on completion factors that consider historical claims experience based on the dates that claims are incurred, reported to the Company and subsequently paid. Processing costs related to these claims are accrued based on an estimate of expenses to process such claims.

Life Insurance Reserves

Incurred but not reported claim estimates are actuarially estimated based on life insurance in force and estimated claims occurrences.

Source:This data was extracted from Pre-Paid Legal Services Inc.'s 10-K Statement and downloaded from the SEC's EDGAR database using PricewaterhouseCoopers Global Technology Centre Edgarscan. Please read the on-line disclaimer at <http://edgarscan.pwcglobal.com/EdgarScan/edgarscan_disclaimer.html>.

EXHIBIT 6

Excerpts from Management's Discussion and Analysis of Financial
Condition and Results, Pre-Paid Legal Services 10-K, December 31,
1998

COMMISSIONS AND MEMBERSHIP PERSISTENCY

Commissions

Beginning with new Memberships written after March 1, 1995, the Company implemented a
level commission schedule which results in the Company incurring commission expense
related to the sale of its legal expense plans on a basis more consistent with the collection of
the premiums generated by the sale of such Memberships. Prior to March 1, 1995, the Company had incurred much higher commissions (approximately 70%) during the first year of the
Membership with substantially lower commissions (approximately 16%) in all subsequent
years. The level commission structure results in the Company incurring commissions at the
rate of approximately 25% per year for all Membership years.

Prior to January 1997 the Company advanced commissions at the time of sale of all new
Memberships. In January 1997, the Company implemented a policy whereby the associate
receives only earned commissions on the first three sales unless the associate has successfully
completed the new training program that was implemented at the same time. For all sales
beginning with the fourth Membership or all sales made by an associate successfully completing the new training program, the Company currently advances commissions at the time of
sale of a new Membership. The amount of cash potentially advanced upon the sale of a new
Membership, prior to the recoupment of any charge-backs (described below), represents an
amount equal to up to three years commission earnings. Although the average number of
marketing associates receiving an advance commission payment on a new Membership is 11,
the overall initial advance may be paid to more than 20 different individuals, each at a different
level within the overall commission structure. This commission advance immediately increases
an associate's account with the Company and represents prepaid commissions on active Memberships.

Should a Membership lapse before the advances have been recovered for each commission
level, the Company immediately generates a "charge-back" to the applicable sales associate to
recapture 50% of any unearned advance. This charge-back is immediately deducted from any
future advances that would otherwise be payable to the associate for additional new Memberships. The Company historically has been able to immediately recover the majority of such
charge-backs. Any remaining unrecovered advance on a Membership that has lapsed represents a receivable from the associate and is reflected as commission advances and is catego-
rized as current or non-current based on the expected recovery period. Additionally, even
though a commission advance may have been fully recovered on a particular Membership, no
additional commission earnings from any Membership will be paid to an associate until all previous advances on all Memberships, both active and lapsed, have been recovered. During 1998,
22% of all associates submitting new Memberships accounted for 75% of all such new Memberships produced thereby further enhancing the recovery of commission advances.

The Company's commission advance policy exposes the Company to the risk of uncollectible commission advances, particularly for associates who do not receive commissions on a
large number of Memberships or who experience below average Membership persistency.
The Company closely monitors such commission advances to ensure maximum recoverability
and maintains a recoverability reserve which at December 31, 1998 and 1997, was $4.0 mil-
lion and $3.7 million, respectively.

Associates also receive compensation when associates sponsored by them or other associates that they have sponsored in their organization successfully complete the new training program implemented by the Company on January 4, 1997. In order to successfully qualify, the new associate going through the training program must produce 3 new Memberships and recruit 1 new associate within 15 days of receiving the training.

Membership Persistency

One of the major factors affecting the Company's profitability and cash flow is Membership persistency, which represents the ability of the Company to retain a Membership, and therefore receive premiums, once it has been written. The Company monitors its overall Membership persistency rate, as well as the persistency rates with respect to Memberships sold by individual associates and agents and persistency rates with respect to Membership sales by geographic region and payment method. The Company's Membership persistency rate measures the number of Memberships in force at the end of a year as a percentage of the total of (i) Memberships in force at the beginning of such year, plus (ii) new Memberships sold during such year. From 1981 through the year ended December 31,1998, the Company's annual Membership persistency rates, using the foregoing method, have averaged approximately 75%. The annual Membership persistency rates were 73.8%, 73.6% and 73.9% for 1998, 1997 and 1996, respectively. The Company's overall Membership persistency rate varies based on, among other factors, the relative age of total Memberships in force. The Company's overall Membership persistency rate could be lower when the Memberships in force include a higher proportion of newer Memberships. During the last three years, the Company has experienced significant increases in new Membership sales and, as a result, the percentage of newer Memberships in its total Memberships in force has increased. Unless offset by other factors, this increase could result in a decline in the Company's overall Membership persistency rate as determined by the formula described above, but does not necessarily indicate that the new Memberships written are less persistent, only that the ratio of new Memberships to total Memberships is higher than it averaged during the 1981 through 1998 period. The Company's financial condition and results of operations may be materially adversely affected if the persistency rates of existing and new Memberships are materially lower than the Company's historical experience.

Source: This data was extracted from Pre-Paid Legal Services Inc.'s 10-K Statement and downloaded from the SEC's EDGAR database using PricewaterhouseCoopers Global Technology Centre Edgarscan. Please read the on-line disclaimer at <http://edgarscan.pwcglobal.com/EdgarScan/edgarscan_disclaimer.html>.

Financial Analysis

The goal of financial analysis is to assess the performance of a firm in the context of its stated goals and strategy. There are two principal tools of financial analysis: ratio analysis and cash flow analysis. Ratio analysis involves assessing how various line items in a firm's financial statements relate to one another. Cash flow analysis allows the analyst to examine the firm's liquidity, and how the firm is managing its operating, investment, and financing cash flows.

Financial analysis is used in a variety of contexts. Ratio analysis of a company's present and past performance provides the foundation for making forecasts of future performance. As we will discuss in later chapters, financial forecasting is useful in company valuation, credit evaluation, financial distress prediction, security analysis, mergers and acquisitions analysis, and corporate financial policy analysis.

RATIO ANALYSIS

The value of a firm is determined by its profitability and growth. As shown in Figure 5-1, the firm's growth and profitability are influenced by its product market and financial market strategies. The product market strategy is implemented through the firm's competitive strategy, operating policies, and investment decisions. Financial market strategies are implemented through financing and dividend policies.

Thus the four levers managers can use to achieve their growth and profit targets are (1) operating management, (2) investment management, (3) financing strategy, and (4) dividend policies. The objective of ratio analysis is to evaluate the effectiveness of the firm's policies in each of these areas. Effective ratio analysis involves relating the financial numbers to the underlying business factors in as much detail as possible. While ratio analysis may not give all the answers to an analyst regarding the firm's performance, it will help the analyst frame questions for further probing.

In ratio analysis, the analyst can (1) compare ratios for a firm over several years (a time-series comparison), (2) compare ratios for the firm and other firms in the industry (cross-sectional comparison), and/or (3) compare ratios to some absolute benchmark. In a time-series comparison, the analyst can hold firm-specific factors constant and examine the effectiveness of a firm's strategy over time. Cross-sectional comparison facilitates examining the relative performance of a firm within its industry, holding industry-level factors constant. For most ratios there are no absolute benchmarks. The exceptions are measures of rates of return, which can be compared to the cost of the capital associated with the investment. For example, subject to distortions caused by accounting, the rate of return on equity (ROE) can be compared to the cost of equity capital.

In the discussion below, we will illustrate these approaches using the example of Nordstrom, Inc., a prominent U.S. retailer. We will compare Nordstrom's ratios for the fiscal year ending January 31, 2002, with its own ratios for the fiscal year ending January 31, 2001, and with the ratios for TJX Companies, Inc., another U.S. retailer, for the fiscal year ending January 31, 2002.[1]

Nordstrom is in the middle of implementing a restructuring and turnaround strategy, so analyzing its performance over time allows us to assess how well the strategy is working in terms of financial performance. Comparison of Nordstrom with TJX allows

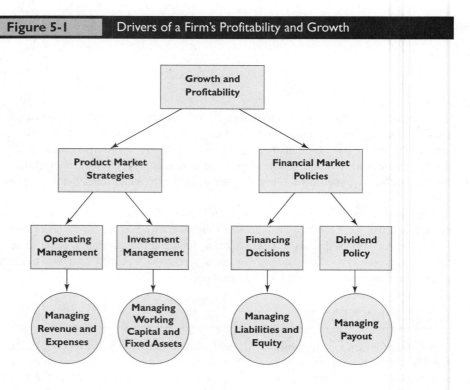

| **Figure 5-1** | Drivers of a Firm's Profitability and Growth |

us to see the impact of different strategies on financial ratios. While pursuing different competitive strategies, Nordstrom and TJX also follow different investment and financing strategies. Nordstrom makes significant investment in its stores whereas TJX leases its stores. Nordstrom has a credit card operation whereas TJX does not. We will illustrate how these differences between the two companies affect their ratios. We will also try to see which strategy is delivering better performance for shareholders.

In order to facilitate replication of the ratio calculations presented below, we present financial statements of both these companies in the appendix to this chapter. Three versions of these companys' financials are presented in the appendix. The first version is the one reported by the two companies in their SEC filings. The second set of financial statements are presented in the standardized format described in Chapter 4. These "standardized financial statements" put both companies' financials in one standard format to facilitate direct comparison. We also present the two companies' financial statements in a third format in the appendix. These statements, labeled "Condensed Financial Statements," are essentially a recasting of the standardized financial statements to facilitate the calculation of several ratios discussed in the chapter. We will discuss later in the chapter how this recasting process works.

Background Information on Nordstrom and TJX

Nordstrom

Nordstrom is a leading fashion specialty retailer, offering a wide variety of high-end apparel, shoes, and accessories for men, women, and children. As of January 31, 2002, the company operated 156 stores, including 80 full-line Nordstrom stores, 45

Nordstrom Rack stores, two free-standing Nordstrom shoe stores, and one Last Chance clearance store. Following the acquisition of Faconnable, S.A. of Nice, France, in October 2000, Nordstrom also operated 24 Faconnable boutiques in Europe and 4 in the U.S.*

Dissatisfied with inconsistent earnings performance in recent years, Nordstrom introduced a new management team in August of 2000, which again put Nordstrom family members at the helm.† Shortly thereafter management announced a turnaround plan aimed at improving the company's profit performance. Central to the plan were several key promises including improving inventory control, expense control, and merchandising, as well as the implementation of new information systems.

Nordstrom management also had to contend with shifting consumers' perceptions of the brand. Since its founding as a single shoe store in 1901, Nordstrom's strategy consistently emphasized the breadth and depth of its quality offerings. In recent years an aggressive expansion plan that included opening bigger and more glamorous stores coupled with an unbalanced merchandising strategy that favored stocking the highest quality product, rather than matching the quality of offerings to key price points, resulted in an increase in Nordstrom's average price point and the erosion of the company's value proposition. In the process, Nordstrom alienated a portion of its core customer base as the brand became increasingly associated with premium pricing. The need to subdue the company's elitist image was recognized by management and securities analysts alike.

By 2002 management had begun to deliver on its promises. The rollout of a new perpetual inventory management system was on track to be fully implemented by the second quarter. Additionally, alterations to the company's merchandising strategy provided more price balance to the product mix.

Analysts were intrigued by management's accomplishments, yet a string of past disappointments engendered ample skepticism. Citing these improvements, a number of analysts issued buy ratings during the first half of 2002. Among them were Wayne Hood and Laura Macedo of Prudential Financial who believed that "Nordstrom is finally in the midst of a sustainable earnings recovery."‡ Other analysts including Michael Exstein and Jennifer Justynski of Credit Suisse First Boston were less sanguine about the company's strategy. Though Exstein and Justynski upgraded their stock rating from Hold to Buy, in the company analysis section of their report the analysts profess "we are somewhat confused by the message Nordstrom is trying to convey to the customer . . . [asking, but not answering the question] Is Nordstrom a high-end retailer?"§

TJX

TJX Companies pursues a strategy quite different from Nordstrom's. TJX is the leading off-price apparel and home fashions retailer in the U.S. and worldwide.** As of

---

Faconnable, S.A. is a designer, wholesaler and retailer of high quality women's and men's clothing and accessories.

† Nordstrom's management restructuring eliminated the company's copresidency structure adopted in 1995 when six fourth-generation members of the Nordstrom family were named copresidents. This restructuring also entailed replacing CEO John Whitacre with Bruce Nordstrom, after five years of retirement.

‡ Wayne Hood and Laura Macedo, "Nordstrom Inc.," Prudential Financial, May 10, 2002.

§ Michael Exstein and Jennifer Justynski, "Nordstrom Inc.," Credit Suisse First Boston, September 6, 2002.

***The TJX Companies, Inc., 2001 Annual Report.*

January 31, 2002, the company operated 1,665 retail outlets through its T.J. Maxx, T.K. Maxx (Europe), Marshall's, HomeGoods, HomeSense (Canada), A.J. Wright, and Winners stores. TJX's divisions are united by the same strategy: offer a rapidly changing assortment of quality, brand-name merchandise at 20–60 percent below department and specialty store regular prices. The company sought to accomplish this by buying opportunistically and by operating with a highly efficient distribution network and a low cost structure.

Regarding competitive advantage, TJX management asserted, "Among TJX's most valuable assets is the equity built into our brands . . . for our customers, these brands are synonymous with value . . . [B]ecause our brands are so strong, TJX is able to spend far less than the industry average on advertising specials or promotions. Instead, advertising campaigns keep stores at the top of customers' minds as places to find great bargains on quality merchandise."* TJX also benefits from its pursuit of continuous improvement in its approach to inventory management. Recent enhancements to TJX's distribution network allowed buyers to further delay purchase decisions, getting better deals in the process, while maintaining confidence that goods will arrive in stores in a timely manner.

During fiscal 2001 (ended January 31, 2002), TJX management reported solid results despite a challenging economic environment. In that year TJX expanded the store base for each of its concepts, launched a new business, and expanded its distribution network. Despite the financing requirements from this ambitious growth strategy, the company also pursued an aggressive share buyback program.

TJX analysts generally maintained a positive outlook. For example, early in 2002 UBS Warburg analysts Richard Jaffe and Corinna Freedman upgraded their stock rating from Buy to Strong Buy with the comment, "maintain[ing] an overall positive view, as we believe TJX is a long-term growth story with an attractive inventory and new business concepts that are expected to perform well."[†]

---

* Ibid.

† Richard Jaffe and Corinna Freedman, "The TJX Companies, Inc.," UBS Warburg, March 5, 2002.

Measuring Overall Profitability

The starting point for a systematic analysis of a firm's performance is its return on equity (ROE), defined as

$$\text{ROE} = \frac{\text{Net income}}{\text{Shareholder's equity}}$$

ROE is a comprehensive indicator of a firm's performance because it provides an indication of how well managers are employing the funds invested by the firm's shareholders to generate returns. On average over long periods, large publicly traded firms in the U.S. generate ROEs in the range of 11 to 13 percent.

In the long run, the value of the firm's equity is determined by the relationship between its ROE and its cost of equity capital.[2] That is, those firms that are expected over the long run to generate ROEs in excess of the cost of equity capital should have market values in excess of book value, and vice versa. (We will return to this point in more detail in the chapter on valuation.)

A comparison of ROE with the cost of capital is useful not only for contemplating the value of the firm but also in considering the path of future profitability. The generation of consistent supernormal profitability will, absent significant barriers to entry, attract competition. For that reason ROEs tend over time to be driven by competitive forces toward a "normal" level—the cost of equity capital. Thus one can think of the cost of equity capital as establishing a benchmark for the ROE that would be observed in a long-run competitive equilibrium. Deviations from this level arise for two general reasons. One is the industry conditions and competitive strategy that cause a firm to generate supernormal (or subnormal) economic profits, at least over the short run. The second is distortions due to accounting.

Table 5-1 shows the ROE based on reported earnings for Nordstrom and TJX.

Table 5-1 Return on Equity for Nordstrom and TJX

Ratio	Nordstrom 2001	Nordstrom 2000	TJX 2001
Return on equity	10.1%	8.6%	41.1%

Nordstrom's ROE showed an improvement, from 8.6 percent to 10.1 percent, between 2000 and 2001. This indicates that Nordstrom's strategy of focusing on profit improvement is beginning to show positive results. Compared to historical trends of ROE in the economy, Nordstrom's 2000 performance can be viewed as being below average. Further, its ROE in 2000 is not adequate to cover reasonable estimates of its equity cost of capital. The 1.5 percentage points increase in ROE in 2001 allowed Nordstrom to get closer to both these benchmarks.[3]

Despite the improvement in 2001, Nordstrom's performance was still far behind TJX's ROE of 41.1 percent. At that performance TJX was earning excess returns relative to both the historical trends in ROE in the U.S. economy, as well as to its own cost of equity.

TJX's superior performance relative to Nordstrom is reflected in the difference in the two companies' ratio of market value of equity to book value. As we will discuss in Chapter 7, ROE is a key determinant of a company's market to book ratio. As of January 31, 2002, Nordstrom's market value to book value ratio was 2.6, while the same ratio for TJX was 8.4.

Decomposing Profitability: Traditional Approach

A company's ROE is affected by two factors: how profitably it employs its assets and how big the firm's asset base is relative to shareholders' investment. To understand the effect of these two factors, ROE can be decomposed into return on assets (ROA) and a measure of financial leverage, as follows:

$$\text{ROE} = \text{ROA} \times \text{Financial leverage}$$

$$= \frac{\text{Net income}}{\text{Assets}} \times \frac{\text{Assets}}{\text{Shareholders' equity}}$$

ROA tells us how much profit a company is able to generate for each dollar of assets invested. Financial leverage indicates how many dollars of assets the firm is able to deploy for each dollar invested by its shareholders.

The return on assets itself can be decomposed as a product of two factors:

$$\text{ROA} = \frac{\text{Net income}}{\text{Sales}} \times \frac{\text{Sales}}{\text{Assets}}$$

The ratio of net income to sales is called net profit margin or return on sales (ROS); the ratio of sales to assets is known as asset turnover. The profit margin ratio indicates how much the company is able to keep as profits for each dollar of sales it makes. Asset turnover indicates how many sales dollars the firm is able to generate for each dollar of its assets.

Table 5-2 displays the three drivers of ROE for our retail firms: net profit margins, asset turnover, and financial leverage. In 2001 Nordstrom's ROE is largely driven by increases in its net profit margin and in its financial leverage. In fact, its return on equity in 2001 was hurt by a decline in its asset turnover. TJX's superior ROE seems to be driven by higher profit margins and better asset utilization; TJX was able to achieve higher ROE than Nordstrom even though it has a lower financial leverage ratio. In other words, TJX's superior performance is attributable to its superior operating performance, as indicated by its high ROA relative to Nordstrom's ROA. And Nordstrom's inferior operating performance is cushioned by its more aggressive financial management relative to TJX.

Table 5-2 Traditional Decomposition of ROE

Ratio	Nordstrom 2001	Nordstrom 2000	TJX 2001
Net profit margin (ROS)	2.2%	1.8%	4.67%
Asset turnover	1.56	1.81	3.71
= Return on assets (ROA)	3.4%	3.3%	17.3%
× Financial leverage	2.93	2.58	2.37
= Return on equity (ROE)	10.1%	8.6%	41.1%

Decomposing Profitability: Alternative Approach

Even though the above approach is popularly used to decompose a firm's ROE, it has several limitations. In the computation of ROA, the denominator includes the assets claimed by all providers of capital to the firm, but the numerator includes only the earnings available to equity holders. The assets themselves include both operating assets and financial assets such as cash and short-term investments. Further, net income includes income from operating activities, as well as interest income and expense, which are consequences of financing decisions. Often it is useful to distinguish between these two sources of performance. Finally, the financial leverage ratio used above does not recognize the fact that a firm's cash and short-term investments are in essence "negative debt" because they can be used to pay down the debt on the company's balance sheet.[4] These issues are addressed by an alternative approach to decomposing ROE discussed below.[5]

Before discussing this alternative ROE decomposition approach, we need to define some terminology used in this section as well as in the rest of this chapter. This terminology is given in Table 5-3.

Table 5-3 Definitions of Accounting Items Used in Ratio Analysis

Item	Definition
Net interest expense after tax	(Interest expense − Interest income) × (1 − Tax rate)[a]
Net operating profit after taxes (NOPAT)	Net income + Net interest expense after tax
Operating working capital	(Current assets − Cash and marketable securities) − (Current liabilities − Short-term debt and current portion of long-term debt)
Net long-term assets	Total long-term assets − Non-interest-bearing long-term liabilities
Net debt	Total interest bearing liabilities − Cash and marketable securities
Net assets	Operating working capital + Net long-term assets
Net capital	Net debt + Shareholders' equity

a. *The calculation of net interest expense treats interest expense and interest income as absolute values, independent of how these figures are reported in the income statement.*

We use the terms defined above to recast the financial statements of Nordstrom and TJX. These recasted financial statements, which are shown in the appendix, are used to decompose ROE in the following manner:

$$
\begin{aligned}
\text{ROE} \;=\;& \frac{\text{NOPAT}}{\text{Equity}} - \frac{(\text{Net interest expense after tax})}{\text{Equity}} \\[2mm]
=\;& \frac{\text{NOPAT}}{\text{Net assets}} \times \frac{\text{Net assets}}{\text{Equity}} - \frac{\text{Net interest expense after tax}}{\text{Net debt}} \times \frac{\text{Net debt}}{\text{Equity}} \\[2mm]
=\;& \frac{\text{NOPAT}}{\text{Net assets}} \times \left(1 + \frac{\text{Net debt}}{\text{Equity}}\right) - \frac{\text{Net interest expense after tax}}{\text{Net debt}} \times \frac{\text{Net debt}}{\text{Equity}} \\[2mm]
=\;& \text{Operating ROA} + (\text{Operating ROA} - \text{Effective interest rate after tax}) \\
& \times \text{Net financial leverage} \\[2mm]
=\;& \text{Operating ROA} + \text{Spread} \times \text{Net financial leverage}
\end{aligned}
$$

Operating ROA is a measure of how profitably a company is able to deploy its operating assets to generate operating profits. This would be a company's ROE if it were financed with all equity. Spread is the incremental economic effect from introducing debt into the capital structure. This economic effect of borrowing is positive as long as the return on operating assets is greater than the cost of borrowing. Firms that do not earn adequate operating returns to pay for interest cost reduce their ROE by borrowing. Both the positive and negative effect is magnified by the extent to which a firm borrows relative to its equity base. The ratio of net debt to equity provides a measure of this net financial leverage. A firm's spread times its net financial leverage, therefore, provides a measure of the financial leverage gain to the shareholders.

Operating ROA can be further decomposed into NOPAT margin and operating asset turnover as follows:

$$\text{Operating ROA} = \frac{\text{NOPAT}}{\text{Sales}} \times \frac{\text{Sales}}{\text{Net assets}}$$

NOPAT margin is a measure of how profitable a company's sales are from an operating perspective. Operating asset turnover measures the extent to which a company is able to use its operating assets to generate sales.

Table 5-4 presents the decomposition of ROE for Nordstrom and TJX. The ratios in this table show that there is a significant difference between Nordstrom's ROA and its operating ROA. In 2001, for example, Nordstrom's ROA was 3.4 percent, while its operating ROA was 7.1 percent.

This difference in ROA and operating ROA is even more remarkable for TJX: its ROA in 2001 was 17.3 percent whereas the operating ROA was 35.7 percent. Because TJX had a large amount of non-interest-bearing liabilities and short-term investments, its operating ROA is dramatically larger than its ROA. This shows that, for at least some firms, it is important to adjust the simple ROA to take into account interest expense, interest income, and financial assets.

Table 5-4 Distinguishing Operating and Financing Components in ROE Decomposition

Ratio	Nordstrom 2001	Nordstrom 2000	TJX 2001
Net operating profit margin	3.0%	2.5%	4.8%
× Net operating asset turnover	2.35	2.75	7.41
= Operating ROA	7.1%	7.0%	35.7%
Spread	3.2%	2.3%	28.7%
× Net financial leverage	0.95	0.69	0.19
= Financial leverage gain	3.0%	1.6%	5.3%
ROE = Operating ROA + Financial leverage gain	10.1%	8.6%	41.1%

The appropriate benchmark for evaluating operating ROA is the weighted average cost of debt and equity capital, or WACC. In the long run, the value of the firm's assets is determined by where operating ROA stands relative to this norm. Moreover, over the long run and absent some barrier to competitive forces, operating ROA will tend to be pushed toward the weighted average cost of capital. Since the WACC is lower than the cost of equity capital, operating ROA tends to be pushed to a level lower than that to which ROE tends.

The average operating ROA for large firms in the U.S., over long periods of time, is in the range of 9 to 11 percent. Nordstrom's operating ROA in 2000 and 2001 is beneath this range, indicating that its operating performance is below average. At 35.7 percent, TJX's operating ROA is far larger than Nordstrom's and also the U.S. industrial average and any reasonable estimates of TJX's weighted average cost of capital. This dramatic superior operating performance of TJX would have been obscured by using the simple ROA measure.[6]

TJX dominates Nordstrom in terms of both operating drivers of ROE—it has a better NOPAT margin and a dramatically higher operating asset turnover. TJX's higher operating asset turnover is primarily a result of its strategy of renting its stores, unlike Nordstrom, which owns many of its stores. What is surprising is discount retailer TJX's higher NOPAT margin, given that Nordstrom is supposed to be the firm with the premium pricing strategy. Nordstrom's inferior NOPAT margin suggests that the company is unable to price its merchandise high enough to recoup the cost of its high service strategy.

Nordstrom is able to create shareholder value through its financing strategy. In 2000 the spread between Nordstrom's operating ROA and its after-tax interest cost was 2.3 percent; its net debt as a percent of its equity was 69 percent. Both these factors contributed to a net increment of 1.6 percent to its ROE. Thus, while Nordstrom's operating ROA in 2000 was 7 percent, its ROE was 8.6 percent. In 2001 Nordstrom's spread increased to 3.2 percent, its net financial leverage went up to 95 percent, leading to a 3 percent net increment to ROE due to its debt policy. With an operating ROA of 7.1 percent in that year, its ROE went up to 10.1 percent.

TJX had a very high spread in 2001, to the tune of 28.7 percent. As a result, even though it had only a modest financial leverage of 18.5 percent, it had a high financial leverage gain of 5.3 percent. This financial leverage gain added to its already higher operating ROA to produce a high ROE of 41.1 percent. In fact, TJX appears not to have exploited its financial leverage potential fully. With a higher level of leverage, it could have exploited its spread to produce an even higher ROE.

Assessing Operating Management: Decomposing Net Profit Margins

A firm's net profit margin or return on sales (ROS) shows the profitability of the company's operating activities. Further decomposition of a firm's ROS allows an analyst to assess the efficiency of the firm's operating management. A popular tool used in this analysis is the common-sized income statement in which all the line items are expressed as a ratio of sales revenues.

Common-sized income statements make it possible to compare trends in income statement relationships over time for the firm, and trends across different firms in the industry. Income statement analysis allows the analyst to ask the following types of questions: (1) Are the company's margins consistent with its stated competitive strategy? For example, a differentiation strategy should usually lead to higher gross margins than a low-cost strategy. (2) Are the company's margins changing? Why? What are the underlying business causes—changes in competition, changes in input costs, or poor overhead cost management? (3) Is the company managing its overhead and administrative costs well? What are the business activities driving these costs? Are these activities necessary?

To illustrate how the income statement analysis can be used, common-sized income statements for Nordstrom and TJX are shown in Table 5-5. The table also shows some commonly used profitability ratios. We will use the information in Table 5-5 to investigate why Nordstrom had a net income margin (or return on sales) of 2.2 percent in 2001 and 1.8 percent in 2000, while TJX had a net margin of 4.7 percent in 2001.

Gross Profit Margins

The difference between a firm's sales and cost of sales is gross profit. Gross profit margin is an indication of the extent to which revenues exceed direct costs associated with sales, and it is computed as

$$\text{Gross profit margin} \quad = \quad \frac{\text{Sales} - \text{Cost of sales}}{\text{Sales}}$$

Gross margin is influenced by two factors: (1) the price premium that a firm's products or services command in the marketplace and (2) the efficiency of the firm's procurement

Table 5-5 Common-Sized Income Statement and Profitability Ratios

	Nordstrom 2001	Nordstrom 2000	TJX 2001
Line Items as a Percent of Sales			
Sales	100%	100%	100%
Cost of sales	(66.8)	(66.0)	(75.9)
Selling, general, and admin. expense	(30.6)	(31.6)	(15.7)
Other income/expense	2.4	2.4	0
Net interest expense/income	(1.3)	(1.1)	(.24)
Income taxes	(1.4)	(1.2)	(3.1)
Unusual gains/losses, net of taxes			(0.4)
Net income	2.2%	1.8%	4.7%
Key Profitability Ratios			
Gross profit margin	33.2%	34.0%	24.1%
EBITDA margin	5.0%	4.2%	8.4%
NOPAT margin	3.0%	2.5%	4.8%
Net Income Margin	2.2%	1.8%	4.7%

and production process. The price premium a firm's products or services can command is influenced by the degree of competition and the extent to which its products are unique. The firm's cost of sales can be low when it can purchase its inputs at a lower cost than competitors and/or run its production processes more efficiently. This is generally the case when a firm has a low-cost strategy.

Table 5-5 indicates that Nordstrom's gross margin in 2001 decreased slightly to 33.2 percent, reflecting pricing pressure as a result of increased competition and a weakened economy. This brings into question whether the new merchandising strategy of the company is indeed effective in shoring up its margins.

Consistent with Nordstrom's premium price strategy, its gross margins in both 2001 and 2000 were significantly higher than TJX's gross margin in 2001, which stood at 24.1 percent.

Selling, General, and Administrative Expenses

A company's selling, general, and administrative (SG&A) expenses are influenced by the operating activities it has to undertake to implement its competitive strategy. As discussed in Chapter 2, firms with differentiation strategies have to undertake activities to achieve differentiation. A company competing on the basis of quality and rapid introduction of new products is likely to have higher R&D costs relative to a company competing purely on a cost basis. Similarly, a company that attempts to build a brand image, distribute its products through full-service retailers, and provide significant customer service is likely to have higher selling and administration costs relative to a company that sells through warehouse retailers or direct mail and does not provide much customer support.

A company's SG&A expenses are also influenced by the efficiency with which it manages its overhead activities. The control of operating expenses is likely to be especially important for firms competing on the basis of low cost. However, even for differentiators, it is important to assess whether the cost of differentiation is commensurate with the price premium earned in the marketplace.

Several ratios in Table 5-5 allow us to evaluate the effectiveness with which Nordstrom and TJX were managing their SG&A expenses. First, the ratio of SG&A expense to sales shows how much a company is spending to generate each sales dollar. We see that Nordstrom has a significantly higher ratio of SG&A to sales than does TJX. This should not be surprising given that TJX pursues a low-cost off-price strategy whereas Nordstrom pursues a high service strategy. In accordance with its stated goal to manage its profitability better, Nordstrom improved its cost management: its SG&A expense as a percent of sales decreased from 31.6 percent in 2000 to 30.6 percent in 2001.

Given that Nordstrom and TJX are pursuing radically different pricing, merchandising, and service strategies, it is not surprising that they have very different cost structures. As a percent of sales, Nordstrom's cost of sales is lower, and its SG&A expense is higher. The question is, when both these costs are netted out, which company is performing better? Two ratios provide useful signals here: net operating profit margin (NOPAT margin) ratio and EBITDA margin:

$$\text{NOPAT margin} \quad = \quad \frac{\text{NOPAT}}{\text{Sales}}$$

$$\text{EBITDA margin} \quad = \quad \frac{\text{Earnings before interest, taxes, depreciation, and amortization}}{\text{Sales}}$$

NOPAT margin provides a comprehensive indication of the operating performance of a company because it reflects all operating policies and eliminates the effects of debt policy. EBITDA margin provides similar information, except that it excludes depreciation and amortization expense, a significant noncash operating expense. Some analysts prefer to use EBITDA margin because they believe that it focuses on "cash" operating items. While this is to some extent true, it can be potentially misleading for two reasons. EBITDA is not a strictly cash concept because sales, cost of sales, and SG&A expenses often include non-cash items. Also, depreciation is a real operating expense, and it reflects to some extent the consumption of resources. Therefore, ignoring it can be misleading.

From Table 5-5 we see that Nordstrom's NOPAT margin has improved between 2000 and 2001. Even with this improvement, in 2001 the company is able to retain only 3 cents in net operating profits for each dollar of sales, whereas TJX is able to retain 4.8 cents.

Recall that in Table 5-3 we define NOPAT as net income plus net interest expense. Therefore, NOPAT is influenced by any unusual or nonoperating income (expense) items included in net income. We can calculate a "recurring" NOPAT margin by eliminating these items. For Nordstrom, recurring NOPAT margin was 1.46 percent in 2000 and 1.53 percent in 2001. These numbers are significantly lower than the NOPAT margin numbers we discussed above, suggesting that a significant portion of the company's NOPAT is derived from sources other than its core retailing operations. These sources include a significant amount of investment income that Nordstrom reported in its financial statements. In contrast, the recurring NOPAT margin for TJX is 5.2 percent, which is higher than its NOPAT margin discussed above since the company reported a one-time loss due to discontinued operations. Recurring NOPAT may be a better benchmark to use when one is extrapolating current performance into the future since it reflects margins from the core business activities of a firm.

TJX also has a better EBITDA margin than Nordstrom. However, this comparison is potentially misleading because TJX leases most of its stores while Nordstrom owns its stores; TJX's leasing expense is included in the EBITDA calculation, but Nordstrom's store depreciation is excluded. This is an example of how EBITDA margin can sometimes be misleading.

Tax Expense

Taxes are an important element of firms' total expenses. Through a wide variety of tax planning techniques, firms can attempt to reduce their tax expenses.[7] There are two measures one can use to evaluate a firm's tax expense. One is the ratio of tax expense to sales, and the other is the ratio of tax expense to earnings before taxes (also known as the average tax rate). The firm's tax footnote provides a detailed account of why its average tax rate differs from the statutory tax rate.

When evaluating a firm's tax planning, the analyst should ask two questions: (1) Are the company's tax policies sustainable, or is the current tax rate influenced by one-time tax credits? (2) Do the firm's tax planning strategies lead to other business costs? For example, if the operations are located in tax havens, how does this affect the company's profit margins and asset utilization? Are the benefits of tax planning strategies (reduced taxes) greater than the increased business costs?

Table 5-5 shows that Nordstrom's tax rate did not change significantly between 2000 and 2001. Nordstrom's taxes as a percent of sales were somewhat lower than TJX's. An important reason for this is that TJX's pretax profits as a percent of sales were higher. In fact, the average tax rate (ratio of tax expense to pretax profits) for both Nordstrom and TJX were nearly the same, at 39 percent and 38 percent, respectively.

In summary, we conclude that Nordstrom's small improvement in return on sales is primarily driven by a reduction in its selling, general, and administrative costs. In all other areas, Nordstrom's performance either stayed the same or worsened a bit. TJX is able to earn a superior return on its sales despite following an off-price strategy because it is able to save significantly on its SG&A expenses.

Evaluating Investment Management: Decomposing Asset Turnover

Asset turnover is the second driver of a company's return on equity. Since firms invest considerable resources in their assets, using them productively is critical to overall profitability. A detailed analysis of asset turnover allows the analyst to evaluate the effectiveness of a firm's investment management.

There are two primary areas of asset management: (1) working capital management and (2) management of long-term assets. Working capital is defined as the difference between a firm's current assets and current liabilities. However, this definition does not distinguish between operating components (such as accounts receivable, inventory, and accounts payable) and the financing components (such as cash, marketable securities, and notes payable). An alternative measure that makes this distinction is operating working capital, as defined in Table 5-3:

Operating working capital = (Current assets − cash and marketable securities)
− (Current liabilities − Short-term and current portion of long-term debt)

Working Capital Management

The components of operating working capital that analysts primarily focus on are accounts receivable, inventory, and accounts payable. A certain amount of investment in working capital is necessary for the firm to run its normal operations. For example, a firm's credit policies and distribution policies determine its optimal level of accounts receivable. The nature of the production process and the need for buffer stocks determine the optimal level of inventory. Finally, accounts payable is a routine source of financing for the firm's working capital, and payment practices in an industry determine the normal level of accounts payable.

The following ratios are useful in analyzing a firm's working capital management: operating working capital as a percent of sales, operating working capital turnover, accounts receivable turnover, inventory turnover, and accounts payable turnover. The turnover ratios can also be expressed in number of days of activity that the operating working capital (and its components) can support. The definitions of these ratios are given below.

$$\text{Operating working capital to sales ratio} \quad = \quad \frac{\text{Operating working capital}}{\text{Sales}}$$

$$\text{Operating working capital turnover} \quad = \quad \frac{\text{Sales}}{\text{Operating working capital}}$$

$$\text{Accounts receivable turnover} \quad = \quad \frac{\text{Sales}}{\text{Accounts receivable}}$$

$$\text{Inventory turnover} \quad = \quad \frac{\text{Cost of goods sold}}{\text{Inventory}}$$

$$\text{Accounts payable turnover} \quad = \quad \frac{\text{Purchases}}{\text{Accounts payable}} \quad or \quad \frac{\text{Cost of goods sold}}{\text{Accounts payable}}$$

$$\text{Days' receivables} \quad = \quad \frac{\text{Accounts receivable}}{\text{Average sales per day}}$$

$$\text{Days' inventory} \quad = \quad \frac{\text{Inventory}}{\text{Average cost of goods sold per day}}$$

$$\text{Days' payables} \quad = \quad \frac{\text{Accounts payable}}{\text{Average purchases (or cost of goods sold) per day}}$$

Operating working capital turnover indicates how many dollars of sales a firm is able to generate for each dollar invested in its operating working capital. Accounts receivable turnover, inventory turnover, and accounts payable turnover allow the analyst to examine how productively the three principal components of working capital are being used. Days' receivables, days' inventory, and days' payables are another way to evaluate the efficiency of a firm's working capital management.[8]

Long-Term Assets Management

Another area of investment management concerns the utilization of a firm's long-term assets. It is useful to define a firm's investment in long-term assets as follows:

Net long-term assets = (Total long-term assets
            − Non-interest-bearing long-term liabilities)

Long-term assets generally consist of net property, plant, and equipment (PP&E), intangible assets such as goodwill, and other assets. Non-interest-bearing long-term liabilities include such items as deferred taxes. We define net long-term assets and net working capital in such a way that their sum, net operating assets, is equal to the sum of net debt and equity, or net capital. This is consistent with the way we defined operating ROA earlier in the chapter.

The efficiency with which a firm uses its net long-term assets is measured by the following two ratios: net long-term assets as a percent of sales and net long-term asset turnover. Net long-term asset turnover is defined as

$$\text{Net long-term asset turnover} \quad = \quad \frac{\text{Sales}}{\text{Net long-term assets}}$$

Property plant and equipment (PP&E) is the most important long-term asset in a firm's balance sheet. The efficiency with which a firm's PP&E is used is measured by the ratio of PP&E to sales, or by the PP&E turnover ratio:

$$\text{PP\&E turnover} = \frac{\text{Sales}}{\text{Net property, plant, and equipment}}$$

The ratios listed above allow the analyst to explore a number of business questions in four general areas:

1. How well does the company manage its inventory? Does the company use modern manufacturing techniques? Does it have good vendor and logistics management systems? If inventory ratios are changing, what is the underlying business reason? Are new products being planned? Is there a mismatch between the demand forecasts and actual sales?
2. How well does the company manage its credit policies? Are these policies consistent with its marketing strategy? Is the company artificially increasing sales by loading the distribution channels?
3. Is the company taking advantage of trade credit? Is it relying too much on trade credit? If so, what are the implicit costs?
4. Are the company's investment in plant and equipment consistent with its competitive strategy? Does the company have a sound policy of acquisitions and divestitures?

Table 5-6 shows the asset turnover ratios for Nordstrom and TJX. Nordstrom experienced an erosion in its working capital management between 2000 and 2001, as can be seen from an increase of operating working capital as a percent of sales and a decrease in operating working capital turnover. This erosion is attributable to an increase in accounts receivable and a downturn in inventory management. There was also an extension in its accounts payable days, which favorably impacted the company's working capital management ratios. In addition, Nordstrom's long-term asset utilization did not improve in 2001: its net long-term asset turnover and PP&E turnover show declines. In its annual report, Nordstrom acknowledges that the sales from stores that it operated for more than a year

Table 5-6 Asset Management Ratios

Ratio	Nordstrom 2001	Nordstrom 2000	TJX 2001
Operating working capital/Sales	19.3%	16.5%	3.7%
Net long-term assets/Sales	23.3%	19.9%	9.8%
PP&E/Sales	28.6%	25.6%	8.5%
Operating working capital turnover	5.2	6.1	26.8
Net long-term assets turnover	4.3	5.0	10.2
PP&E turnover	3.5	3.9	11.8
Accounts receivable turnover	7.8	9.0	173.2
Inventory turnover	4.0	4.6	5.6
Accounts payable turnover	8.1	9.3	12.6
Days' accounts receivable	46.8	40.7	2.1
Days' inventory	91.7	79.8	65.3
Days' accounts payable	45.2	39.1	29.0

(also called same-store sales) showed a small decline in 2001 because management was focusing on controlling costs.

TJX achieved dramatically better asset utilization ratios in 2001 relative to Nordstrom. TJX was able to invest a negligible amount of money in its operating working capital by taking full advantage of trade credit from its vendors and by delaying payment of some of its operating expenses. Also, because TJX has no credit card operations of its own, it is able to collect its receivables in 2.1 days, in contrast to Nordstrom's 46.8 receivable days. TJX is also managing its inventory more efficiently, perhaps because of its more focused merchandising strategy. Finally, because TJX uses operating leases to rent its stores, it has significantly lower capital tied up in its stores. As a result, its PP&E turnover is more than three times as much as Nordstrom's. One should, however, be cautious in interpreting this difference between the two companies because, as TJX discloses in its footnotes, it owes a substantial amount of money in the coming years on noncancelable operating leases. TJX's financial statements do not fully recognize its investment in its stores through these non-cancelable leases, potentially inflating its operating asset turns.

Evaluating Financial Management: Financial Leverage

Financial leverage enables a firm to have an asset base larger than its equity. The firm can augment its equity through borrowing and the creation of other liabilities like accounts payable, accrued liabilities, and deferred taxes. Financial leverage increases a firm's ROE as long as the cost of the liabilities is less than the return from investing these funds. In this respect it is important to distinguish between interest-bearing liabilities such as notes payable, other forms of short-term debt and long-term debt that carry an explicit interest charge, and other forms of liabilities. Some of these other forms of liability, such as accounts payable or deferred taxes, do not carry any interest charge at all. Other liabilities, such as capital lease obligations or pension obligations, carry an implicit interest charge. Finally, some firms carry large cash balances or investments in marketable securities. These balances reduce a firm's net debt because conceptually the firm can pay down its debt using its cash and short-term investments.

While financial leverage can potentially benefit a firm's shareholders, it can also increase their risk. Unlike equity, liabilities have predefined payment terms, and the firm faces risk of financial distress if it fails to meet these commitments. There are a number of ratios to evaluate the degree of risk arising from a firm's financial leverage.

Current Liabilities and Short-Term Liquidity

The following ratios are useful in evaluating the risk related to a firm's current liabilities:

$$\text{Current ratio} = \frac{\text{Current assets}}{\text{Current liabilities}}$$

$$\text{Quick ratio} = \frac{\text{Cash} + \text{Short-term investments} + \text{Accounts receivable}}{\text{Current liabilities}}$$

$$\text{Cash ratio} = \frac{\text{Cash} + \text{Marketable securities}}{\text{Current liabilities}}$$

$$\text{Operating cash flow ratio} = \frac{\text{Cash flow from operations}}{\text{Current liabilities}}$$

All the above ratios attempt to measure the firm's ability to repay its current liabilities. The first three compare a firm's current liabilities with its short-term assets that can be used to repay those liabilities. The fourth ratio focuses on the ability of the firm's operations to generate the resources needed to repay its current liabilities.

Since both current assets and current liabilities have comparable duration, the current ratio is a key index of a firm's short-term liquidity. Analysts view a current ratio of more than one to be an indication that the firm can cover its current liabilities from the cash realized from its current assets. However, the firm can face a short-term liquidity problem even with a current ratio exceeding one when some of its current assets are not easy to liquidate. Quick ratio and cash ratio capture the firm's ability to cover its current liabilities from liquid assets. Quick ratio assumes that the firm's accounts receivable are liquid. This is true in industries where the credit-worthiness of the customers is beyond dispute, or when receivables are collected in a very short period. When these conditions do not prevail, cash ratio, which considers only cash and marketable securities, is a better indication of a firm's ability to cover its current liabilities in an emergency. Operating cash flow is another measure of the firm's ability to cover its current liabilities from cash generated from operations of the firm.

The liquidity ratios for Nordstrom and TJX are shown in Table 5-7. Nordstrom's liquidity situation in 2001 was comfortable when measured in terms of current ratio or quick ratio. Both these ratios improved in 2001. All this was good news for Nordstrom's short-term creditors. TJX also had a comfortable liquidity position, thanks to its large cash balance and a sound operating cash flow. Because of its tight management of operating working capital, however, TJX's current and quick ratios are smaller than Nordstrom's.

Table 5-7 Liquidity Ratios

Ratio	Nordstrom 2001	Nordstrom 2000	TJX 2001
Current ratio	2.28	2.14	1.40
Quick ratio	0.94	0.92	0.16
Cash ratio	0.03	0.07	0.11
Operating cash flow ratio	0.58	0.29	0.75

Debt and Long-Term Solvency

A company's financial leverage is also influenced by its debt financing policy. There are several potential benefits from debt financing. First, debt is typically cheaper than equity because the firm promises predefined payment terms to debt holders. Second, in most countries, interest on debt financing is tax deductible whereas dividends to shareholders are not tax deductible. Third, debt financing can impose discipline on the firm's management and motivate it to reduce wasteful expenditures. Fourth, it is often easier for management to communicate their proprietary information on the firm's strategies and prospects to private lenders than to public capital markets. Such communication can potentially reduce a firm's cost of capital. For all these reasons, it is optimal for firms to use at least some debt in their capital structure. Too much reliance on debt financing, however, is potentially costly to the firm's shareholders. The firm will face financial distress if it defaults on the interest and principal payments. Debt holders also impose covenants on the firm, restricting the firm's operating, investment, and financing decisions.

The optimal capital structure for a firm is determined primarily by its business risk. A firm's cash flows are highly predictable when there is little competition or there is little threat of technological changes. Such firms have low business risk and hence they can rely heavily on debt financing. In contrast, if a firm's operating cash flows are highly volatile and its capital expenditure needs are unpredictable, it may have to rely primarily on equity financing. Managers' attitude towards risk and financial flexibility also often determine a firm's debt policies.

There are a number of ratios which help the analyst in this area. To evaluate the mix of debt and equity in a firm's capital structure, the following ratios are useful:

$$\text{Liabilities-to-equity ratio} = \frac{\text{Total liabilities}}{\text{Shareholders' equity}}$$

$$\text{Debt-to-equity ratio} = \frac{\text{Short-term debt} + \text{Long-term debt}}{\text{Shareholders' equity}}$$

$$\text{Net-debt-to-equity ratio} = \frac{\text{Short-term debt} + \text{Long-term debt} - \text{Cash and marketable securities}}{\text{Shareholders' equity}}$$

$$\text{Debt-to-capital ratio} = \frac{\text{Short-term debt} + \text{Long-term debt}}{\text{Short-term debt} + \text{Long-term debt} + \text{Shareholders' equity}}$$

$$\text{Net-debt-to-net-capital ratio} = \frac{\text{Interest bearing liabilities} - \text{Cash and marketable securities}}{\text{Interest bearing liabilities} - \text{Cash and marketable securities} + \text{Shareholders' equity}}$$

The first ratio restates the assets-to-equity ratio (one of the three primary ratios underlying ROE) by subtracting one from it. The second ratio provides an indication of how many dollars of debt financing the firm is using for each dollar invested by its shareholders. The third ratio uses net debt, which is total debt minus cash and marketable securities, as the measure of a firm's borrowings. The fourth and fifth ratios measure debt as a proportion of total capital. In calculating all the above ratios, it is important to include all interest-bearing obligations, whether the interest charge is explicit or implicit. Recall that examples of line items which carry an implicit interest charge include capital lease obligations and pension obligations. Analysts sometimes include any potential off-balance-sheet obligations that a firm may have, such as noncancelable operating leases, in the definition of a firm's debt.

The ease with which a firm can meet its interest payments is an indication of the degree of risk associated with its debt policy. The interest coverage ratio provides a measure of this construct:

$$\text{Interest coverage (earnings basis)} = \frac{\text{Net income} + \text{Interest expense} + \text{Tax expense}}{\text{Interest expense}}$$

$$\text{Interest coverage (cash flow basis)} = \frac{\text{Cash flow from operations} + \text{Interest expense} + \text{Taxes paid}}{\text{Interest expense}}$$

One can also calculate coverage ratios that measure a firm's ability to measure all fixed financial obligations, such as interest payment, lease payments, and debt repayments, by appropriately redefining the numerator and denominator in the above ratios. In doing so it is important to remember that while some fixed charge payments, such as interest and lease rentals, are paid with pretax dollars while others, such as debt repayments, are made with after-tax dollars.

The earnings-based coverage ratio indicates the dollars of earnings available for each dollar of required interest payment; the cash-flow-based coverage ratio indicates the dollars of cash generated by operations for each dollar of required interest payment. In both these ratios, the denominator is the interest expense. In the numerator we add taxes back because taxes are computed only after interest expense is deducted. A coverage ratio of one implies that the firm is barely covering its interest expense through its operating activities, which is a very risky situation. The larger the coverage ratio, the greater the cushion the firm has to meet interest obligations.

Key Analysis Questions

Some of the business questions to ask when the analyst is examining a firm's debt policies follow:

- Does the company have enough debt? Is it exploiting the potential benefits of debt—interest tax shields, management discipline, and easier communication?
- Does the company have too much debt given its business risk? What type of debt covenant restrictions does the firm face? Is it bearing the costs of too much debt, risking potential financial distress and reduced business flexibility?
- What is the company doing with the borrowed funds? Investing in working capital? Investing in fixed assets? Are these investments profitable?
- Is the company borrowing money to pay dividends? If so, what is the justification?

We show debt and coverage ratios for Nordstrom and TJX in Table 5-8. Nordstrom recorded an increase in its liabilities-to-equity and debt-to-equity ratios. Nordstrom also increased its net financial leverage even after taking into account a significant increase in its cash balance in 2001. The company's interest coverage also remained at comfortable levels. All these ratios suggest that Nordstrom has been following a fairly conservative debt policy.

TJX's debt ratios confirm that it is primarily relying on non-interest-bearing liabilities such as accounts payable and accrued expenses to finance its operations. Its interest

Table 5-8 Debt and Coverage Ratios

Ratio	Nordstrom 2001	Nordstrom 2000	TJX 2001
Liabilities to equity	1.94	1.58	1.37
Debt to equity	0.97	0.74	0.29
Net debt to equity	0.95	0.69	.19
Debt to capital	0.49	0.43	0.23
Net debt to net capital	0.49	0.41	.16
Net debt to equity, including operating lease obligations	not available	not available	2.23
Interest coverage (earnings based)	3.35	3.33	21.54
Interest coverage (cash flow based)	7.02	5.26	31.04
Fixed charges coverage, including lease payments (earnings based)	2.44	2.40	2.71
Fixed charges coverage, including lease payments (cash flow based)	4.69	3.57	3.50

coverage ratios are extraordinarily high. But this picture changes when one considers the fact that TJX relies heavily on operating leases for its stores. If the present value of minimum lease rental obligations is added to TJX's net debt, its net-debt-to-equity ratio increases dramatically. Similarly, when one includes both interest and minimum rental payments in the coverage ratio, TJX's coverage drops dramatically relative to when only interest is included. This illustrates the importance of considering off-balance-sheet obligations in analyzing a company's financial management.

Ratios of Disaggregated Data

So far we have discussed how to compute ratios using information in the financial statements. Analysts often probe the above ratios further by using disaggregated financial and physical data. For example, for a multibusiness company, one could analyze the information by individual business segments. Such an analysis can reveal potential differences in the performance of each business unit, allowing the analyst to pinpoint areas where a company's strategy is working and where it is not. It is also possible to probe financial ratios further by computing ratios of physical data pertaining to a company's operations. The appropriate physical data to look at varies from industry to industry. As an example in retailing, one could compute productivity statistics such as sales per store, sales per square foot, customer transactions per store, and amount of sale per customer transactions; in the hotel industry, room occupancy rates provide important information; in the cellular telephone industry, acquisition cost per new subscriber and subscriber retention rate are important. These disaggregated ratios are particularly useful for young firms and young industries such as Internet firms, where accounting data may not fully capture the business economics due to conservative accounting rules.

Putting It All Together: Assessing Sustainable Growth Rate

Analysts often use the concept of sustainable growth as a way to evaluate a firm's ratios in a comprehensive manner. A firm's sustainable growth rate is defined as

$$\text{Sustainable growth rate} = \text{ROE} \times (1 - \text{Dividend payout ratio})$$

We already discussed the analysis of ROE in the previous four sections. The dividend payout ratio is defined as

$$\text{Dividend payout ratio} = \frac{\text{Cash dividends paid}}{\text{Net income}}$$

A firm's dividend payout ratio is a measure of its dividend policy. As we discuss in detail in Chapter 12, firms pay dividends for several reasons. Dividends are a way for the firm to return to its shareholders any cash generated in excess of its operating and investment needs. When there are information asymmetries between a firm's managers and its shareholders, dividend payments can serve as a signal to shareholders about managers' expectation of the firm's future prospects. Firms may also pay dividends to attract a certain type of shareholder base.

Sustainable growth rate is the rate at which a firm can grow while keeping its profitability and financial policies unchanged. A firm's return on equity and its dividend payout policy determine the pool of funds available for growth. Of course the firm can grow at a rate different from its sustainable growth rate if its profitability, payout policy, or financial leverage changes. Therefore, the sustainable growth rate provides a benchmark against which a firm's growth plans can be evaluated. Figure 5-2 shows how a firm's sustainable

Figure 5-2	Sustainable Growth Rate Framework for Financial Ratio Analysis

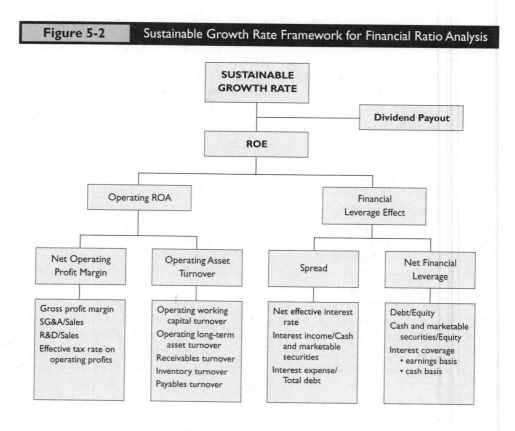

growth rate can be linked to all the ratios discussed in this chapter. These linkages allow an analyst to examine the drivers of a firm's current sustainable growth rate. If the firm intends to grow at a higher rate than its sustainable growth rate, one could assess which of the ratios are likely to change in the process. This analysis can lead to asking business questions such as these: Where is the change going to take place? Is management expecting profitability to increase? Or asset productivity to improve? Are these expectations realistic? Is the firm planning for these changes? If the profitability is not likely to go up, will the firm increase its financial leverage or cut dividends? What is the likely impact of these financial policy changes?

Table 5-9 shows the sustainable growth rate and its components for Nordstrom and TJX. Nordstrom had a lower ROE and a higher dividend payout ratio relative to TJX, leading to a significantly lower sustainable growth rate in both 2001 and 2000. However, Nordstrom improved its sustainable growth rate because of its improved ROE and a marginal decline in its payout ratio.

Table 5-9 Sustainable Growth Rate

Ratio	Nordstrom 2001	Nordstrom 2000	TJX 2001
ROE	10.1%	8.6%	41.1%
Dividend payout ratio	39%	45%	9.7%
Sustainable growth rate	6.2%	4.7%	37.1%

Nordstrom's actual growth rates in 2001 in sales, assets, and liabilities were different from its sustainable growth rate in 2000. In 2001 Nordstrom's sales declined by 7 percent, net operating assets increased by 18.7 percent, and its net debt grew by 42 percent. These differences in Nordstrom's sustainable growth rate and its actual growth rates in sales, net assets, and net debt are reconciled by the fact that Nordstrom reduced its equity base through significant stock repurchases. Nordstrom has the room to grow in future years at about 6 percent without altering its operating and financial policies. In contrast, TJX has a significantly higher sustainable growth rate of 37.1 percent, implying that it can grow at a much faster rate than Nordstrom without altering its operating and financial policies.

Historical Patterns of Ratios for U.S. Firms

To provide a benchmark for analysis, Table 5-10 reports historical values of the key ratios discussed in this chapter. These ratios are calculated using financial statement data for all publicly listed U.S. companies. The table shows the values of ROE, its key components, and the sustainable growth rate for each of the years 1983 to 2002, and the average for this twenty-year period. The data in the table show that the average ROE during this period has been 11.2 percent, average operating ROA has been 7.8 percent, and the average spread between operating ROA and net borrowing costs after tax has been 2.6 percent. Average

Table 5-10 Historical Values of Key Financial Ratios

Year	ROE	NOPAT Margin	Operating Asset Turnover	Operating ROA	Spread	Net Financial Leverage	Sustainable Growth Rate
1984	12.2%	6.1%	1.71	9.4%	3.8%	0.52	6.3%
1985	10.6%	5.7%	1.66	8.7%	1.9%	0.63	4.3%
1986	10.2%	5.9%	1.54	7.9%	1.6%	0.74	3.7%
1987	11.2%	6.9%	1.55	9.5%	2.7%	0.81	4.6%
1988	13.7%	7.0%	1.61	11.0%	6.9%	0.84	6.8%
1989	12.1%	6.9%	1.54	9.8%	4.6%	1.07	5.5%
1990	10.6%	6.7%	1.53	9.2%	2.4%	1.17	4.0%
1991	7.5%	6.4%	1.45	6.6%	−0.8%	1.19	1.1%
1992	5.1%	4.6%	1.47	5.4%	−1.7%	1.13	−1.5%
1993	9.6%	5.1%	1.48	5.7%	−0.2%	1.16	2.8%
1994	14.4%	7.0%	1.50	9.1%	2.7%	1.18	8.1%
1995	14.3%	5.8%	1.54	6.8%	6.3%	1.13	7.8%
1996	15.1%	6.5%	1.53	7.6%	6.3%	1.17	8.8%
1997	14.3%	7.1%	1.54	8.5%	3.7%	1.14	8.6%
1998	13.6%	7.5%	1.49	8.3%	3.1%	1.26	7.8%
1999	14.0%	7.5%	1.42	8.3%	4.0%	1.28	8.7%
2000	10.7%	6.5%	1.45	6.4%	2.4%	1.34	5.9%
2001	1.6%	3.7%	1.24	2.3%	−3.2%	1.29	−3.0%
2002	2.1%	3.4%	1.13	−1.0%	−5.7%	1.34	−2.4%
Average	11.2%	6.3%	1.51	7.8%	2.6%	1.06	5.0%

Because Table 5-10 ratios are based on beginning balance sheet data, the ratios for 1983 are not computed.

Source: Financial statement data for all companies publicly traded in the U.S. from 1983 to 2002, listed in the Compustat files.

sustainable growth rate for U.S. companies during this period has been 5.0 percent. Of course an individual company's ratios might depart from these economy-wide averages for a number of reasons, including industry effects, company strategies, and management effectiveness. Nonetheless, the average values in the table serve as useful benchmarks in financial analysis.

CASH FLOW ANALYSIS

The ratio analysis discussion focused on analyzing a firm's income statement (net profit margin analysis) or its balance sheet (asset turnover and financial leverage). The analyst can get further insights into the firm's operating, investing, and financing policies by examining its cash flows. Cash flow analysis also provides an indication of the quality of the information in the firm's income statement and balance sheet. As before, we will illustrate the concepts discussed in this section using Nordstrom's and TJX's cash flows.

Cash Flow and Funds Flow Statements

All U.S. companies are required to include a statement of cash flows in their financial statements under Statement of Financial Accounts Standard No. 95 (SFAS 95). In the reported cash flow statement, firms classify their cash flows into three categories: cash flow from operations, cash flow related to investments, and cash flow related to financing activities. Cash flow from operations is the cash generated by the firm from the sale of goods and services after paying for the cost of inputs and operations. Cash flow related to investment activities shows the cash paid for capital expenditures, intercorporate investments, acquisitions, and cash received from the sales of long-term assets. Cash flow related to financing activities shows the cash raised from (or paid to) the firm's stockholders and debt holders.

Firms use two cash flow statement formats: the direct format and the indirect format. The key difference between the two formats is the way they report cash flow from operating activities. In the direct cash flow format, which is used by only a small number of firms in practice, operating cash receipts and disbursements are reported directly. In the indirect format, firms derive their operating cash flows by making adjustments to net income. Because the indirect format links the cash flow statement with the firm's income statement and balance sheet, many analysts and managers find this format more useful. As a result, the FASB required firms using the direct format to report operating cash flows in the indirect format as well.

Recall from Chapter 3 that net income differs from operating cash flows because revenues and expenses are measured on an accrual basis. There are two types of accruals embedded in net income. First, there are current accruals like credit sales and unpaid expenses. Current accruals result in changes in a firm's current assets (such as accounts receivable, inventory, prepaid expenses) and current liabilities (such as accounts payable and accrued liabilities). The second type of accruals included in the income statement is noncurrent accruals such as depreciation, deferred taxes, and equity income from unconsolidated subsidiaries. To derive cash flow from operations from net income, adjustments have to be made for both these types of accruals. In addition, adjustments have to be made for nonoperating gains included in net income such as profits from asset sales.

Most firms outside the U.S. report a funds flow statement rather than a cash flow statement of the type described above. Prior to SFAS 95, U.S. firms also reported a similar statement. Funds flow statements show working capital flows, not cash flows. It is useful for analysts to know how to convert a funds flow statement into a cash flow statement.

Funds flow statements typically provide information on a firm's working capital from operations, defined as net income adjusted for noncurrent accruals, and gains from the sale of long-term assets. As discussed above, cash flow from operations essentially involves a third adjustment, the adjustment for current accruals. Thus it is relatively straightforward to convert working capital from operations to cash flow from operations by making the relevant adjustments for current accruals related to operations.

Information on current accruals can be obtained by examining changes in a firm's current assets and current liabilities Typically, operating accruals represent changes in all the current asset accounts other than cash and cash equivalents, and changes in all the current liabilities other than notes payable and the current portion of long-term debt.[9] Cash from operations can be calculated as follows:

Working capital from operations
− Increase (or + decrease) in accounts receivable
− Increase (or + decrease) in inventory
− Increase (or + decrease) in other current assets excluding cash and cash equivalents
+ Increase (or − decrease) in accounts payable
+ Increase (or − decrease) in other current liabilities excluding debt.

Funds flow statements also often do not classify investment and financing flows. In such a case, the analyst has to classify the line items in the funds flow statement into these two categories by evaluating the nature of the business transactions that give rise to the flow represented by the line items.

Analyzing Cash Flow Information

Cash flow analysis can be used to address a variety of questions regarding a firm's cash flow dynamics:

- How strong is the firm's internal cash flow generation? Is the cash flow from operations positive or negative? If it is negative, why? Is it because the company is growing? Is it because its operations are unprofitable? Or is it having difficulty managing its working capital properly?
- Does the company have the ability to meet its short-term financial obligations, such as interest payments, from its operating cash flow? Can it continue to meet these obligations without reducing its operating flexibility?
- How much cash did the company invest in growth? Are these investments consistent with its business strategy? Did the company use internal cash flow to finance growth, or did it rely on external financing?
- Did the company pay dividends from internal free cash flow, or did it have to rely on external financing? If the company had to fund its dividends from external sources, is the company's dividend policy sustainable?
- What type of external financing does the company rely on? Equity, short-term debt, or long-term debt? Is the financing consistent with the company's overall business risk?
- Does the company have excess cash flow after making capital investments? Is it a long-term trend? What plans does management have to deploy the free cash flow?

While the information in reported cash flow statements can be used to answer the above questions directly in the case of some firms, it may not be easy to do so always for a number of reasons. First, even though SFAS 95 provides broad guidelines on the format of a cash flow statement, there is still significant variation across firms in how cash flow data are disclosed. Therefore, to facilitate a systematic analysis and comparison across firms, analysts often recast the information in the cash flow statement using their own cash flow model. Second, firms include interest expense and interest income in computing their cash flow from operating activities. However, these two items are not strictly related to a firm's operations. Interest expense is a function of financial leverage, and interest income is derived from financial assets rather than operating assets. Therefore it is useful to restate the cash flow statement to take this into account.

Analysts use a number of different approaches to restate the cash flow data. One such model is shown in Table 5-11. This presents cash flow from operations in two stages. The first step computes cash flow from operations before operating working capital investments. In computing this cash flow, the model excludes interest expense and interest income. To compute this number starting with a firm's net income, an analyst adds back three types of items: (1) after-tax net interest expense because this is a financing item that will be considered later, (2) nonoperating gains or losses typically arising out of asset disposals or asset write-offs because these items are investment related and will be considered later, and (3) long-term operating accruals such as depreciation and deferred taxes because these are noncash operating charges.

Table 5-11   Cash Flow Analysis

Line Item	Nordstrom 2001	Nordstrom 2000	TJX 2001
Net income (dollars in millions)	124.7	101.9	500.4
After-tax net interest expense (income)	45.8	38.3	15.9
Nonoperating losses (gains)	0	32.9	70.6
Long-term operating accruals	228.3	194.7	239.3
Operating cash flow before working capital investments	**398.7**	**367.7**	**826.2**
Net (investments in) or liquidation of operating working capital	60.8	(153.6)	95.3
Operating cash flow before investment in long-term assets	**459.5**	**214.2**	**921.5**
Net (investment in) or liquidation of operating long-term assets	(267.1)	(314.7)	(442.6)
Free cash flow available to debt and equity	**192.4**	**(100.5)**	**478.9**
After-tax net interest (expense) or income	(45.8)	(38.3)	(15.9
Net debt (repayment) or issuance	198.5	262.2	302.1
Free cash flow available to equity	**345.1**	**123.4**	**765.1**
Dividend (payments)	(48.3)	(45.9)	(48.3)
Net stock (repurchase) or issuance	9.2	(79.3)	(359.0
Net increase (decrease) in cash balance	**306.1**	**(1.8)**	**357.9**

Several factors affect a firm's ability to generate positive cash flow from operations. Healthy firms that are in a steady state should generate more cash from their customers than they spend on operating expenses. In contrast, growing firms—especially those investing cash in research and development, advertising and marketing, or building an organization to sustain future growth—may experience negative operating cash flow. Firms' working capital management also affects whether they generate positive cash flow from operations. Firms in the growing stage typically invest some cash flow in operating working capital items like accounts receivable, inventories, and accounts payable. Net investments in working capital are a function of firms' credit policies (accounts receivable), payment policies (payables, prepaid expenses, and accrued liabilities), and expected growth in sales (inventories). Thus, in interpreting firms' cash flow from operations after working capital, it is important to keep in mind their growth strategy, industry characteristics, and credit policies.

The cash flow analysis model next focuses on cash flows related to long-term investments. These investments take the form of capital expenditures, intercorporate investments, and mergers and acquisitions. Any positive operating cash flow after making operating working capital investments allows the firm to pursue long-term growth opportunities. If the firm's operating cash flows after working capital investments are not sufficient to finance its long-term investments, it has to rely on external financing to fund its growth. Such firms have less flexibility to pursue long-term investments than those that can fund their growth internally. There are both costs and benefits from being able to fund growth internally. The cost is that managers can use the internally generated free cash flow to fund unprofitable investments. Such wasteful capital expenditures are less likely if managers are forced to rely on external capital suppliers. Reliance on external capital markets may make it difficult for managers to undertake long-term risky investments if it is not easy to communicate to the capital markets the benefits from such investments.

Any excess cash flow after these long-term investments is free cash flow that is available for both debt holders and equity holders. Payments to debt holders include interest payments and principal payments. Firms with negative free cash flow have to borrow additional funds to meet their interest and debt repayment obligations, or cut some of their investments in working capital or long-term investments, or issue additional equity. This situation is clearly financially risky for the firm.

Cash flow after payments to debt holders is free cash flow available to equity holders. Payments to equity holders consist of dividend payments and stock repurchases. If firms pay dividends despite negative free cash flow to equity holders, they are borrowing money to pay dividends. While this may be feasible in the short term, it is not prudent for a firm to pay dividends to equity holders unless it has a positive free cash flow on a sustained basis. On the other hand, firms that have a large free cash flow after debt payments run the risk of wasting that money on unproductive investments to pursue growth for its own sake. An analyst, therefore, should carefully examine the investment plans of such firms.

The model in Table 5-11 suggests that the analyst should focus on a number of cash flow measures: (1) cash flow from operations before investment in working capital and interest payments, to examine whether or not the firm is able to generate a cash surplus from its operations, (2) cash flow from operations after investment in working capital, to assess how the firm's working capital is being managed and whether or not it has the flexibility to invest in long-term assets for future growth, (3) free cash flow available to debt and equity holders, to assess a firm's ability to meet its interest and principal payments, and (4) free cash flow available to equity holders, to assess the firm's financial ability to sustain its dividend policy and to identify potential agency problems from excess free cash flow. These measures have to be evaluated in the context of the company's business, its growth strategy, and its financial policies. Further, changes in these measures from year to year provide valuable information on the stability of the cash flow dynamics of the firm.

Key Analysis Questions

The cash flow model in Table 5-11 can be also used to assess a firm's earnings quality, as discussed in Chapter 3. The reconciliation of a firm's net income with its cash flow from operations facilitates this exercise. Following are some of the questions an analyst can probe in this respect:

- Are there significant differences between a firm's net income and its operating cash flow? Is it possible to clearly identify the sources of this difference? Which accounting policies contribute to this difference? Are there any one-time events contributing to this difference?
- Is the relationship between cash flow and net income changing over time? Why? Is it because of changes in business conditions or because of changes in the firm's accounting policies and estimates?
- What is the time lag between the recognition of revenues and expenses and the receipt and disbursement of cash flows? What type of uncertainties need to be resolved in between?
- Are the changes in receivables, inventories, and payables normal? If not, is there adequate explanation for the changes?

Finally, as we will discuss in Chapter 7, free cash flow available to debt and equity and free cash flow available to equity are critical inputs into the cash-flow-based valuation of firms' assets and equity, respectively.

Analysis of Nordstrom's Cash Flow

Nordstrom and TJX reported their cash flows using the indirect cash flow statement. Table 5-11 recasts these statements using the approach discussed above so that we can analyze the two companies' cash flow dynamics.

Cash flow analysis presented in Table 5-11 shows Nordstrom had an operating cash flow before working capital investments of $398.7 million in 2001, an improvement from $367.7 million in 2000. The difference between earnings and these cash flows is primarily attributable to the depreciation and amortization charge included in the company's income statement.

In 2001 Nordstrom managed to squeeze an additional $60.8 million from its operating working capital, primarily by reducing its investment in accounts receivable and inventory. This contrasts with a net operating working capital investment of $153.6 million in 2000. As a result of this improvement in working capital management, the company had an operating cash flow before long-term investments to the tune of $459.5 million in 2001, a significant improvement over the 2000 figure of $214.2 million. As a result, unlike in 2000, Nordstrom generated more than adequate cash flow from operations in 2001 to meet its total investment in long-term assets. Nordstrom thus had $192.4 million of free cash flow available to debt and equity holders in 2001, compared to a deficit of $100.5 million in 2000.

Both in 2000 and 2001, Nordstrom was a net borrower. As a result, there was considerable free cash flow available to equity holders in both years. The company utilized this free cash flow to pay its regular dividends and also buy back stock in 2000. The difference between the two years, however, is that in 2001 Nordstrom had adequate internal cash flow to make distributions to shareholders, while in 2000 the company could not have made these payments to equity holders either without borrowing or without cutting its long-term investments. Clearly, Nordstrom's cash flow improved significantly in 2001.

TJX also had a very strong cash flow situation in 2001. It had $826.2 million in operating cash flow before working capital investments. TJX was also able to reduce its investments in operating working capital. There is, however, a significant difference between the way investments in working capital appear to have been managed by TJX and Nordstrom. While Nordstrom reduced its investments in inventory and accounts receivable, TJX stretched its payables and accrued expenses. Similar to Nordstrom, TJX was able to fund all its long-term investments in operating assets from its own operating cash flow. As a result, TJX had $478.9 million in free cash flow available to debt and equity holders. From this, the company paid out $15.9 million in interest (net of taxes). The company was a net borrower to the tune of $302.1 million, leaving it with a whopping $765.1 million in free cash flow available to equity holders. The company distributed close to half of it to its shareholders—$48.3 million in dividends and $359 million in stock repurchases—leaving a cash increase of about $357.9 million.

SUMMARY

This chapter presents two key tools of financial analysis: ratio analysis and cash flow analysis. Both these tools allow the analyst to examine a firm's performance and its financial condition, given its strategy and goals. Ratio analysis involves assessing the firm's income statement and balance sheet data. Cash flow analysis relies on the firm's cash flow statement.

The starting point for ratio analysis is the company's ROE. The next step is to evaluate the three drivers of ROE, which are net profit margin, asset turnover, and financial leverage. Net profit margin reflects a firm's operating management, asset turnover reflects its investment management, and financial leverage reflects its liability management. Each of these areas can be further probed by examining a number of ratios. For example, common-sized income statement analysis allows a detailed examination of a firm's net margins. Similarly, turnover of key working capital accounts like accounts receivable, inventory, and accounts payable, and turnover of the firm's fixed assets allow further examination of a firm's asset turnover. Finally, short-term liquidity ratios, debt policy ratios, and coverage ratios provide a means of examining a firm's financial leverage.

A firm's sustainable growth rate—the rate at which it can grow without altering its operating, investment, and financing policies—is determined by its ROE and its dividend policy. The concept of sustainable growth provides a way to integrate the ratio analysis and to evaluate whether or not a firm's growth strategy is sustainable. If a firm's plans call for growing at a rate above its current sustainable rate, then the analyst can examine which of the firm's ratios is likely to change in the future.

Cash flow analysis supplements ratio analysis in examining a firm's operating activities, investment management, and financial risks. Firms in the U.S. are currently required to report a cash flow statement summarizing their operating, investment, and financing cash flows. Firms in other countries typically report working capital flows, but it is possible to use this information to create a cash flow statement.

Since there are wide variations across firms in the way cash flow data are reported, analysts often use a standard format to recast cash flow data. We discussed in this chapter one such cash flow model. This model allows the analyst to assess whether a firm's operations generate cash flow before investments in operating working capital, and how much cash is being invested in the firm's working capital. It also enables the analyst to calculate the firm's free cash flow after making long-term investments, which is an indication of the firm's ability to meet its debt and dividend payments. Finally, the cash flow analysis shows how the firm is financing itself, and whether its financing patterns are too risky.

The insights gained from analyzing a firm's financial ratios and its cash flows are valuable in forecasts of the firm's future prospects.

DISCUSSION QUESTIONS

1. Which of the following types of firms do you expect to have particularly high or low asset turnover? Explain why.
   - a supermarket
   - a pharmaceutical company
   - a jewelry retailer
   - a steel company

2. Which of the following types of firms do you expect to have high or low sales margins? Why?
   - a supermarket
   - a pharmaceutical company
   - a jewelry retailer
   - a software company

3. James Broker, an analyst with an established brokerage firm, comments: "The critical number I look at for any company is operating cash flow. If cash flows are less than earnings, I consider a company to be a poor performer and a poor investment prospect." Do you agree with this assessment? Why or why not?

4. In 1995 Chrysler has a return on equity of 20 percent, whereas Ford's return is only 8 percent. Use the decomposed ROE framework to provide possible reasons for this difference.

5. Joe Investor asserts, "A company cannot grow faster than its sustainable growth rate." True or false? Explain why.

6. What are the reasons for a firm having lower cash from operations than working capital from operations? What are the possible interpretations of these reasons?

7. ABC Company recognizes revenue at the point of shipment. Management decides to increase sales for the current quarter by filling all customer orders. Explain what impact this decision will have on
   - Days' receivable for the current quarter
   - Days' receivable for the next quarter
   - Sales growth for the current quarter
   - Sales growth for the next quarter
   - Return on sales for the current quarter
   - Return on sales for the next quarter

8. What ratios would you use to evaluate operating leverage for a firm?

9. What are the potential benchmarks that you could use to compare a company's financial ratios? What are the pros and cons of these alternatives?

10. In a period of rising prices, how would the following ratios be affected by the accounting decision to select LIFO, rather than FIFO, for inventory valuation?
- Gross margin
- Current ratio
- Asset turnover
- Debt-to-equity ratio
- Average tax rate

NOTES

1. We will call the fiscal year ending January 2002 as the year 2001, and the fiscal year ending January 2001 as the year 2000.

2. In computing ROE, one can either use the beginning equity, ending equity, or an average of the two. Conceptually, the average equity is appropriate, particularly for rapidly growing companies. However, for most companies, this computational choice makes little difference as long as the analyst is consistent. Therefore, in practice most analysts use ending balances for simplicity. This comment applies to all ratios discussed in this chapter where one of the items in the ratio is a flow variable (items in the income statement or cash flow statement) and the other item is a stock variable (items in the balance sheet). Throughout this chapter we use the beginning balances of the stock variables.

3. We discuss in greater detail in Chapter 8 how to estimate a company's cost of equity capital. The equity beta for both Nordstrom and TJX was close to one in 1999, and the yield on long-term treasury bonds was approximately 6 percent. If one assumes a risk premium of 6 percent, the two firms' cost of equity is 12 percent; if the risk premium is assumed to be 8 percent, then their cost of equity is 14 percent. Lower assumed risk premium will, of course, lead to lower estimates of equity capital.

4. Strictly speaking, part of a cash balance is needed to run the firm's operations, so only the excess cash balance should be viewed as negative debt. However, firms do not provide information on excess cash, so we subtract all cash balance in our definitions and computations below. An alternative possibility is to subtract only short-term investments and ignore the cash balance completely.

5. See Doron Nissim and Stephen Penman, "Ratio Analysis and Valuation: From Research to Practice," *Review of Accounting Studies* 6 (2001): 109–154, for a more detailed description of this approach.

6. TJX has a small amount of debt and a cash balance larger than its debt. Therefore its weighted average cost of capital is likely to be similar to its cost of equity. We will discuss in Chapter 8 how to estimate a company's weighted average cost of capital.

7. See *Taxes and Business Strategy* by Myron Scholes and Mark Wolfson (Englewood Cliffs, NJ: Prentice-Hall, 1992).

8. There are a number of issues related to the calculation of these ratios in practice. First, in calculating all the turnover ratios, the assets used in the calculations can either be beginning of the year values, year-end values or an average of the beginning and ending balances in a year. We use the beginning of the year values in our calculations. Second, strictly speaking, one should use credit sales to calculate accounts receivable turnover and days' receivables. But since it is usually difficult to obtain data on credit sales, total sales are used instead. Similarly, in calculating accounts payable turnover or days' payables, cost of goods sold is substituted for purchases for data availability reasons.

9. Changes in cash and marketable securities are excluded because this is the amount being explained by the cash flow statement. Changes in short-term debt and the current portion of long-term debt are excluded because these accounts represent financing flows, not operating flows.

APPENDIX
PART A: NORDSTROM, INC. FINANCIAL STATEMENTS

CONSOLIDATED STATEMENTS OF EARNINGS ($ 000's)

Fiscal Year Ended January 31,	2000	2001	2002
Net sales	**5,149,266**	**5,528,537**	**5,634,130**
Cost of sales and related buying and occupancy	(3,359,760)	(3,649,516)	(3,765,859)
Gross profit	**1,789,506**	**1,879,021**	**1,868,271**
Selling, general, and administrative	(1,523,836)	(1,747,048)	(1,722,635)
Operating income	265,670	131,973	145,636
Interest expense, net	(50,396)	(62,698)	(75,038)
Write-down of investment	0	(32,857)	0
Service charge income and other, net	116,783	130,600	133,890
Earnings before income taxes	**332,057**	**167,018**	**204,488**
Income taxes	(129,500)	(65,100)	(79,800)
NET EARNINGS	**202,557**	**101,918**	**124,688**
Basic earnings per share	$1.47	$0.78	$0.93
Diluted earnings per share	$1.46	$0.78	$0.93
Cash dividends paid per share	$0.32	$0.35	$0.36

Source: Edgarscan.

CONSOLIDATED BALANCE SHEETS ($ 000's)

Fiscal Year Ended January 31,	2000	2001	2002
ASSETS			
Current assets:			
Cash and cash equivalents	52,569	25,259	331,327
Accounts receivable, net	616,989	721,953	698,475
Merchandise inventories	797,845	945,687	888,172
Prepaid expenses	97,245	28,760	34,375
Other current assets	0	91,323	102,249
Total current assets	1,564,648	1,812,982	2,054,598
Land, buildings, and equipment, net	1,429,492	1,599,938	1,761,082
Intangible assets, net	0	143,473	138,331
Other assets	67,941	52,110	94,768
TOTAL ASSETS	3,062,081	3,608,503	4,048,779
LIABILITIES AND SHAREHOLDERS' EQUITY			
Current liabilities:			
Notes payable	70,934	83,060	148
Accounts payable	390,688	466,476	490,988
Accrued salaries, wages, and related benefits	211,308	234,833	236,373
Income taxes and other accruals	135,388	153,613	142,002
Current portion of long-term debt	58,191	12,586	78,227
Total current liabilities	866,509	950,568	947,738
Long-term debt	746,791	1,099,710	1,351,044
Deferred lease credits	194,995	275,252	342,046
Other liabilities	68,172	53,405	93,463
Shareholders' equity:			
Common stock, no par: 250,000,000 shares authorized; 134,468,608 and 133,797,757 shares issued and outstanding	247,559	330,394	341,316
Unearned stock compensation	(8,593)	(3,740)	(2,680)
Retained earnings	929,616	900,090	975,203
Accumulated other comprehensive earnings	17,032	2,824	649
Total shareholders' equity	1,185,614	1,229,568	1,314,488
TOTAL LIABILITIES AND SHAREHOLDERS' EQUITY	3,062,081	3,608,503	4,048,779

Source: Edgarscan.

CONSOLIDATED STATEMENTS OF CASH FLOWS ($ 000's)

Fiscal Year Ended January 31,	2000	2001	2002
OPERATING ACTIVITIES			
Net earnings	202,557	101,918	124,688
Adjustments to reconcile net earnings to net cash provided by operating activities:			
Depreciation and amortization of buildings and equipment	193,718	203,048	213,089
Amortization of intangible assets	0	1,251	4,630
Amortization of deferred lease credits and other, net	(6,387)	(12,349)	(8,538)
Stock-based compensation expense	3,331	6,480	3,414
Deferred income taxes, net	(22,859)	(3,716)	15,662
Write-down of investment	0	32,857	0
Change in operating assets and liabilities, net of effects from acquisition of business:			
Accounts receivable, net	(29,854)	(102,945)	22,556
Merchandise inventories	79,894	6,741	215,731
Prepaid expenses	(6,976)	(173)	(1,684)
Other assets	(8,880)	(3,821)	(16,770)
Accounts payable	(76,417)	(67,924)	(159,636)
Accrued salaries, wages, and related benefits	14,942	17,850	(203)
Income tax liabilities and other accruals	965	3,879	(11,310)
Other liabilities	25,212	(7,184)	12,088
Net cash provided by operating activities	369,246	175,912	413,717
INVESTING ACTIVITIES			
Capital expenditures	(305,052)	(321,454)	(390,138)
Additions to deferred lease credits	114,910	92,361	126,383
Payment for acquisition, net of cash acquired	0	(83,828)	0
Other, net	(452)	(1,781)	(3,309)
Net cash used in investing activities	(190,594)	(314,702)	(267,064)
FINANCING ACTIVITIES	0	0	0
Proceeds (payments) from notes payable	(7,849)	12,126	(82,912)
Proceeds from issuance of long-term debt	0	308,266	300,000
Principal payments on long-term debt	(63,341)	(58,191)	(18,640)
Capital contribution to subsidiary from minority shareholders	16,000	0	0
Proceeds from issuance of common stock	9,577	6,250	10,542
Cash dividends paid	(44,463)	(45,935)	(48,265)
Purchase and retirement of common stock	(302,965)	(85,509)	(1,310)
Net cash provided by (used in) financing activities	(393,041)	137,007	159,415
Net increase (decrease) in cash and cash equivalents	(214,389)	(1,783)	306,068
Cash and cash equivalents at beginning of year	241,431	27,042	25,259
CASH AND CASH EQUIVALENTS AT END OF YEAR	27,042	25,259	331,327

Source: Edgarscan.

STANDARDIZED STATEMENTS OF EARNINGS ($ 000's)

Fiscal Year Ended January 31,	2000	2001	2002
Sales	5,149,266	5,528,537	5,634,130
Cost of goods sold	3,359,760	3,649,516	3,765,859
Gross Profit	1,789,506	1,879,021	1,868,271
SG&A	1,523,836	1,747,048	1,722,635
Depreciation & amortization	0	0	0
Other operating expense	0	32,857	0
Operating Income	265,670	99,116	145,636
Investment income	0	0	0
Other income, net of other expense	116,783	130,600	133,890
Other income	116,783	130,600	133,890
Other expense	0	0	0
Net interest expense (income)	50,396	62,698	75,038
Interest income	0	0	0
Interest expense	0	0	0
Minority interest	0	0	0
Pretax Income	332,057	167,018	204,488
Tax expense	129,500	65,100	79,800
Unusual items (after tax)	0	0	0
Net Income	202,557	101,918	124,688
Preferred dividends	0	0	0
Net Income to Common	202,557	101,918	124,688

Source: BAV Model (v.2.0).

STANDARDIZED BEGINNING BALANCE SHEETS ($ 000's)

Fiscal Year Beginning February 1,	2000	2001	2002
Assets			
Cash and marketable securities	52,569	25,259	331,327
Accounts receivable	616,989	721,953	698,475
Inventory	797,845	945,687	888,172
Other current assets	97,245	120,083	136,624
Total current assets	**1,564,648**	**1,812,982**	**2,054,598**
Long-term tangible assets	1,429,492	1,599,938	1,761,082
Long-term intangible assets	0	143,473	138,331
Other long-term assets	67,941	52,110	94,768
Total long-term assets	**1,497,433**	**1,795,521**	**1,994,181**
Total Assets	**3,062,081**	**3,608,503**	**4,048,779**
Liabilities			
Accounts payable	390,688	466,476	490,988
Short-term debt	129,125	95,646	78,375
Other current liabilities	211,308	234,833	236,373
Total current liabilities	**731,121**	**796,955**	**805,736**
Long-term debt	746,791	1,099,710	1,351,044
Deferred taxes	135,388	153,613	142,002
Other long-term liabilities (non-interest-bearing)	263,167	328,657	435,509
Total long-term liabilities	**1,145,346**	**1,581,980**	**1,928,555**
Total Liabilities	**1,876,467**	**2,378,935**	**2,734,291**
Minority interest	0	0	0
Shareholders' equity			
Preferred stock	0	0	0
Common shareholders' equity	1,185,614	1,229,568	1,314,488
Total shareholders' equity	**1,185,614**	**1,229,568**	**1,314,488**
Total Liabilities and Shareholders' Equity	**3,062,081**	**3,608,503**	**4,048,779**

Source: BAV Model (v.2.0).

STANDARDIZED STATEMENTS OF CASH FLOWS ($ 000's)

Fiscal Year Ended January 31,	2000	2001	2002
Net income	202,557	101,918	124,688
After-tax net interest expense (income)	30,742	38,260	45,755
Non-operating losses (gains)	0	32,857	0
Long-term operating accruals	167,803	194,714	228,257
Operating cash flow before working capital investments	401,102	367,749	398,700
Net (investments in) or liquidation of operating working capital	(1,114)	(153,577)	60,772
Operating cash flow before investment in long-term assets	399,988	214,172	459,472
Net (investment in) or liquidation of operating long-term assets	(190,594)	(314,702)	(267,064)
Free cash flow available to debt and equity	209,394	(100,530)	192,408
After-tax net interest expense (income)	30,742	38,260	45,755
Net debt (repayment) or issuance	(71,190)	262,201	198,448
Free cash flow available to equity	107,462	123,411	345,101
Dividend (payments)	(44,463)	(45,935)	(48,265)
Net stock (repurchase) or issuance	(277,388)	(79,259)	9,232
Net increase (decrease) in cash balance	(214,389)	(1,783)	306,068

Source: BAV Model (v.2.0).

CONDENSED STATEMENTS OF EARNINGS ($ 000's)

Fiscal Year Ended January 31,	2000	2001	2002
Sales	5,149,266	5,528,537	5,634,130
Net Operating Profit after Tax	233,299	140,178	170,443
Net income	202,557	101,918	124,688
+ Net interest expense after tax	30,742	38,260	45,755
= Net Operating Profit after Tax	233,299	140,178	170,443
− Net Interest Expense after Tax	30,742	38,260	45,755
Interest expense	0	0	0
− Interest income	0	0	0
= Net interest expense (income)	50,396	62,698	75,038
× (1 − Tax expense/pre-tax income)	.6098	.6102	.6100
= Net Interest Expense after Tax	30,742	38,260	45,755
= Net Income	202,557	101,918	124,688
− Preferred stock dividends	0	0	0
= Net Income to Common	202,557	101,918	124,688

Source: BAV Model (v.2.0).

CONDENSED BEGINNING BALANCE SHEETS ($ 000's)

Fiscal Year Beginning February 1,	2000	2001	2002
Beginning Net Working Capital	910,083	1,086,414	995,910
Accounts receivable	616,989	721,953	698,475
+ Inventory	797,845	945,687	888,172
+ Other current assets	97,245	120,083	136,624
− Accounts payable	390,688	466,476	490,988
− Other current liabilities	211,308	234,833	236,373
= Beginning Net Working Capital	**910,083**	**1,086,414**	**995,910**
+ Beginning Net Long-Term Assets	1,098,878	1,313,251	1,416,670
Long-term tangible assets	1,429,492	1,599,938	1,761,082
+ Long-term intangible assets	0	143,473	138,331
+ Other long-term assets	67,941	52,110	94,768
− Minority interest	0	0	0
− Deferred taxes	135,388	153,613	142,002
− Other long-term liabilities (non-interest-bearing)	263,167	328,657	435,509
= Beginning Net Long-Term Assets	**1,098,878**	**1,313,251**	**1,416,670**
= Total Assets	**2,008,961**	**2,399,665**	**2,412,580**
Beginning Net Debt	823,347	1,170,097	1,098,092
Short-term debt	129,125	95,646	78,375
+ Long-term debt	746,791	1,099,710	1,351,044
− Cash	52,569	25,259	331,327
= Beginning Net Debt	**823,347**	**1,170,097**	**1,098,092**
+ Beginning Preferred Stock	0	0	0
+ Beginning Shareholders' Equity	1,185,614	1,229,568	1,314,488
= Total Net Capital	**2,008,961**	**2,399,665**	**2,412,580**

Source: BAV Model (v.2.0).

APPENDIX
PART B: THE TJX COMPANIES, INC. FINANCIAL STATEMENTS

CONSOLIDATED STATEMENTS OF INCOME ($ 000's)

Fiscal Year Ended January 31,	2000	2001	2002
Net sales	**8,795,347**	**9,579,006**	**10,708,998**
Cost of sales, including buying and occupancy costs	6,579,400	7,188,124	8,122,922
Selling, general, and administrative expenses	1,354,665	1,503,036	1,686,389
Interest expense, net	7,345	22,904	25,643
Income from continuing operations before income taxes and cumulative effect of accounting change	**853,937**	**864,942**	**874,044**
Provision for income taxes	327,115	326,876	333,647
Income from continuing operations before cumulative effect of accounting change	526,822	538,066	540,397
(Loss) from discontinued operations, net of income taxes	0	0	(40,000)
Income before cumulative effect of accounting change	526,822	538,066	500,397
Cumulative effect of accounting change, net of income taxes	(5,154)	0	0
Net income	**521,668**	**538,066**	**500,397**
Basic earnings per share:			
Income from continuing operations before cumulative effect of accounting change	$1.67	$1.87	$1.96
Net income	$1.66	$1.87	$1.82
Weighted average common shares—basic	314,577,145	287,440,637	275,323,741
Diluted earnings per share:			
Income from continuing operations before cumulative effect of accounting change	$1.66	$1.86	$1.94
Net income	$1.64	$1.86	$1.80
Weighted average common shares—diluted	317,790,764	289,196,228	278,133,862
Cash dividends declared per share	$0.14	$0.16	$0.18

Source: Edgarscan.

CONSOLIDATED BALANCE SHEETS ($ 000's)

Fiscal Year Ended January 31,	2000	2001	2002
ASSETS			
Current assets:			
Cash and cash equivalents	371,759	132,535	492,776
Accounts receivable, net	55,461	61,845	69,209
Merchandise inventories	1,229,587	1,452,877	1,456,976
Prepaid expenses and other current assets	43,758	74,690	84,962
Current deferred income taxes, net	0	43,997	12,003
Total current assets	**1,700,565**	**1,765,944**	**2,115,926**
Property at cost:			
Land and buildings	116,005	133,714	144,958
Leasehold costs and improvements	622,962	704,011	880,791
Furniture, fixtures, and equipment	849,932	984,848	1,210,366
	1,588,899	1,822,573	2,236,115
Less accumulated depreciation and amortization	754,314	914,590	1,076,196
	834,585	907,983	1,159,919
Property under capital lease, net of accumulated amortization of $1,489	0	0	31,083
Other assets	55,826	69,976	83,139
Non-current deferred income taxes, net	23,143	3,394	26,575
Goodwill and trade name, net of amortization	190,844	184,986	179,101
Total Assets	**2,804,963**	**2,932,283**	**3,595,743**
LIABILITIES			
Current liabilities:			
Current installments of long-term debt	100,359	73	0
Obligation under capital lease due within one year	0	0	1,244
Short-term debt	0	39,000	0
Accounts payable	615,671	645,672	761,546
Accrued expenses and other current liabilities	471,159	544,014	552,220
Total current liabilities	**1,187,189**	**1,228,759**	**1,315,010**
Other long-term liabilities	179,179	165,440	237,656
Obligation under capital lease, less portion due within one year	0	0	30,336
Long-term debt, exclusive of current installments	319,367	319,372	672,043
Commitments and contingencies	0	0	0
Shareholders' Equity			
Common stock, authorized 1,200,000,000 shares, par value $1, issued and outstanding 271,537,653 and 280,378,675 shares, respectively	299,979	280,379	271,538
Additional paid-in capital	0	0	0
Accumulated other comprehensive income (loss)	(1,433)	(3,288)	(6,755)
Retained earnings	820,682	941,621	1,075,915
Total shareholders' equity	**1,119,228**	**1,218,712**	**1,340,698**
Total Liabilities and Shareholders' Equity	**2,804,963**	**2,932,283**	**3,595,743**

Source: Edgarscan.

CONSOLIDATED STATEMENTS OF CASH FLOWS ($ 000's)

Fiscal Year Ended January 31,	2000	2001	2002
Cash flows from operating activities:			
Net income	521,668	538,066	500,397
Adjustments to reconcile net income to net cash provided by operating activities:			
Loss from discontinued operations, net of tax	0	0	40,000
Cumulative effect of accounting change	5,154	0	0
Depreciation and amortization	160,466	175,781	204,081
Property disposals and impairments	4,624	4,559	6,832
Tax benefit of employee stock options	11,736	15,941	30,644
Deferred income tax provision (benefit)	1,790	(24,235)	35,230
Changes in assets and liabilities:			
(Increase) in accounts receivable	(8,137)	(6,501)	(7,615)
(Increase) in merchandise inventories	(26,856)	(232,031)	(13,292)
(Increase) in prepaid expenses and other current assets	(15,519)	(12,083)	(1,273)
Increase (decrease) in accounts payable	(2,747)	34,158	120,770
Increase (decrease) in accrued expenses and other liabilities	(35,673)	69,134	16,054
Other, net	(21,282)	(6,026)	(19,382)
Net cash provided by operating activities	595,224	556,763	912,446
Cash flows from investing activities:			
Property additions	(238,569)	(257,005)	(449,444)
Issuance of note receivable	(5,848)	(23,100)	(5,402)
Proceeds from sale of other assets	0	9,183	0
Net cash (used in) investing activities	(244,417)	(270,922)	(454,846)
Cash flows from financing activities:			
Proceeds from borrowings of short-term debt, net	0	39,000	0
Proceeds from borrowings of long-term debt	198,060	0	347,579
Principal payments on long-term debt	(695)	(100,203)	(73)
Payments on short-term debt	0	0	(39,000)
Payments on capital lease obligation	0	0	(992)
Proceeds from sale and issuance of common stock, net	9,312	26,101	65,202
Cash payments for repurchase of common stock	(604,560)	(444,105)	(424,163)
Cash dividends paid	(42,739)	(44,693)	(48,290)
Net cash (used in) financing activities	(440,622)	(523,900)	(99,737)
Effect of exchange rate changes on cash	330	(1,165)	2,378
Net increase (decrease) in cash and cash equivalents	(89,485)	(239,224)	360,241
Cash and cash equivalents at beginning of year	461,244	371,759	132,535
Cash and cash equivalents at end of year	371,759	132,535	492,776

Source: Edgarscan.

STANDARDIZED STATEMENTS OF INCOME ($ 000's)

Fiscal Year Ended January 31,	2000	2001	2002
Sales	**8,795,347**	**9,579,006**	**10,708,998**
Cost of goods sold	6,579,400	7,188,124	8,122,922
Gross Profit	**2,215,947**	**2,390,882**	**2,586,076**
SG&A	1,354,665	1,503,036	1,686,389
Depreciation & amortization	0	0	0
Other operating expense	0	0	0
Operating Income	**861,282**	**887,846**	**899,687**
Investment income	0	0	0
Other income, net of other expense	0	0	0
Other income	0	0	0
Other expense	0	0	0
Net interest expense (income)	7,345	22,904	25,643
Interest income	0	0	0
Interest expense	0	0	0
Minority interest	0	0	0
Pretax Income	**853,937**	**864,942**	**874,044**
Tax expense	327,115	326,876	333,647
Unusual items (after tax)	(5,154)	0	(40,000)
Net Income	**521,668**	**538,066**	**500,397**
Preferred dividends	0	0	0
Net Income to Common	**521,668**	**538,066**	**500,397**

Source: BAV Model (v.2.0).

STANDARDIZED BEGINNING BALANCE SHEETS ($ 000's)

Fiscal Year Beginning February 1,	2000	2001	2002
ASSETS			
Cash and marketable securities	371,759	132,535	492,776
Accounts receivable	55,461	61,845	69,209
Inventory	1,229,587	1,452,877	1,456,976
Other current assets	43,758	74,690	84,962
Total current assets	**1,700,565**	**1,721,947**	**2,103,923**
Long-term tangible assets	834,585	907,983	1,191,002
Long-term intangible assets	190,844	184,986	179,101
Other long-term assets	55,826	69,976	83,139
Total long-term assets	**1,081,255**	**1,162,945**	**1,453,242**
Total Assets	**2,781,820**	**2,884,892**	**3,557,165**
LIABILITIES			
Accounts payable	615,671	645,672	761,546
Short-term debt	100,359	39,073	1,244
Other current liabilities	471,159	544,014	552,220
Total current liabilities	**1,187,189**	**1,228,759**	**1,315,010**
Long-term debt	319,367	319,372	702,379
Deferred taxes	−23,143	−47,391	−38,578
Other long-term liabilities (non-interest-bearing)	179,179	165,440	237,656
Total long-term liabilities	**475,403**	**437,421**	**901,457**
Total Liabilities	**1,662,592**	**1,666,180**	**2,216,467**
Minority interest	0	0	0
Shareholders' Equity			
Preferred stock	0	0	0
Common shareholders' equity	1,119,228	1,218,712	1,340,698
Total shareholders' equity	**1,119,228**	**1,218,712**	**1,340,698**
Total Liabilities and Shareholders' Equity	**2,781,820**	**2,884,892**	**3,557,165**

Source: BAV Model (v.2.0).

STANDARDIZED STATEMENTS OF CASH FLOWS ($ 000's)

Fiscal Year Ended January 31,	2000	2001	2002
Net Income	521,668	538,066	500,397
After-tax net interest expense (income)	4,531	14,248	15,854
Non-operating losses (gains)	16,890	15,941	70,644
Long-term operating accruals	162,256	151,546	239,311
Operating cash flow before working capital investments	705,345	719,801	826,206
Net (investments in) or liquidation of operating working capital	(110,214)	(153,349)	95,262
Operating cash flow before investment in long-term assets	595,131	566,452	921,468
Net (investment in) or liquidation of operating long-term assets	(233,945)	(243,263)	(442,612)
Free cash flow available to debt and equity	361,186	323,189	478,856
After-tax net interest expense (income)	4,531	14,248	15,854
Net debt (repayment) or issuance	191,517	(84,303)	302,112
Free cash flow available to equity	548,172	224,638	765,114
Dividend (payments)	(42,739)	(44,693)	(48,290)
Net stock (repurchase) or issuance	(595,248)	(418,004)	(358,961)
Net increase (decrease) in cash balance	(89,815)	(238,059)	357,863

Source: BAV Model (v.2.0).

CONDENSED STATEMENTS OF INCOME ($ 000's)

Fiscal Year Ended January 31,	2000	2001	2002
Sales	8,795,347	9,579,006	10,708,998
Net Operating Profit after Tax	526,199	552,314	516,251
Net income	521,668	538,066	500,397
+ Net interest expense after tax	4,531	14,248	15,854
= **Net Operating Profit after Tax**	526,199	552,314	516,251
− **Net Interest Expense after Tax**	4,531	14,248	15,854
Interest expense	0	0	0
− Interest income	0	0	0
= Net interest expense (income)	7,345	22,904	25,643
× (1 − Tax expense/pre-tax income)	.6098	.6102	.6100
= **Net Interest Expense after Tax**	4,531	14,248	15,854
= **Net Income**	521,668	538,066	500,397
− Preferred stock dividends	0	0	0
= **Net Income to Common**	521,668	538,066	500,397

Source: BAV Model (v.2.0).

CONDENSED BEGINNING BALANCE SHEET ($ 000's)

Fiscal Year Beginning February 1,	2000	2001	2002
Beginning Net Working Capital	241,976	399,726	297,381
Accounts receivable	55,461	61,845	69,209
+ Inventory	1,229,587	1,452,877	1,456,976
+ Other current assets	43,758	74,690	84,962
− Accounts payable	615,671	645,672	761,546
− Other current liabilities	471,159	544,014	552,220
= **Beginning Net Working Capital**	241,976	399,726	297,381
+ **Beginning Net Long-Term Assets**	925,219	1,044,896	1,254,164
Long-term tangible assets	834,585	907,983	1,191,002
+ Long-term intangible assets	190,844	184,986	179,101
+ Other long-term assets	55,826	69,976	83,139
− Minority interest	0	0	0
− Deferred taxes	−23,143	−47,391	−38,578
− Other long-term liabilities (non-interest-bearing)	179,179	165,440	237,656
= **Beginning Net Long-Term Assets**	925,219	1,044,896	1,254,164
= **Total Assets**	1,167,195	1,444,622	1,551,545
Beginning Net Debt	47,967	225,910	210,847
Short-term debt	100,359	39,073	1,244
+ Long-term debt	319,367	319,372	702,379
− Cash	371,759	132,535	492,776
= **Beginning Net Debt**	47,967	225,910	210,847
+ **Beginning Preferred Stock**	0	0	0
+ **Beginning Shareholders' Equity**	1,119,228	1,218,712	1,340,698
= **Total Net Capital**	1,167,195	1,444,622	1,551,545

Source: BAV Model (v.2.0).

The Home Depot, Inc.

The difference between a company with a concept and one without is the difference between a stock that sells for 20 times earnings and one that sells for 10 times earnings. The Home Depot is definitely a concept stock, and it has the multiple to prove it — 27–28 times likely earnings in the current fiscal year ending this month. On the face of it, The Home Depot might seem like a tough one for the concept-mongers to work with. It's a chain of hardware stores. But, as we noted in our last visit to the company in the spring of '83, these hardware stores are huge warehouse outlets — 60,000 to 80,000 feet in space. You can fit an awful lot of saws in these and still have plenty of room left over to knock together a very decent concept.

And in truth, the warehouse notion is the hottest thing in retailing these days. The Home Depot buys in quantum quantities, which means that its suppliers are eager to keep within its good graces and hence provide it with a lot of extra service. The company, as it happens, is masterful in promotion and pricing. The last time we counted, it had 22 stores, all of them located where the sun shines all the time.

Growth has been sizzling. Revenues, a mere $22 million in fiscal '80, shot past the quarter billion mark three years later. As to earnings, they have climbed from two cents in fiscal '80 to an estimated 60 cents in the fiscal year coming to an end [in January 1985].

Its many boosters in the Street, moreover, anticipate more of the same as far as the bullish eye can see. They're confidently estimating 30% growth in the new fiscal year as well. Could be. But while we share their esteem for the company's merchandising skills and imagination, we're as bemused now as we were the first time we looked at The Home Depot by its rich multiple. Maybe a little more now than then.[1]

The above report appeared on January 21, 1985, in "Up & Down Wall Street," a regular column in *Barron's* financial weekly.

COMPANY BACKGROUND

Bernard Marcus and Arthur Blank founded The Home Depot in 1978 to bring the warehouse retailing concept to the home center industry. The company operated retail "do-it-yourself" (DIY) warehouse stores which sold a wide assortment of building materials and home improvement products. Sales, which were on a cash-and-carry basis, were concentrated in the home remodeling market. The company targeted as its customers individual homeowners and small contractors.

The Home Depot's strategy had several important elements. The company offered low and competitive prices, a feature central to the warehouse retailing concept. The Home Depot's stores, usually in suburbs, were also the warehouses, with inventory stacked over merchandise displayed on industrial racks. The warehouse format of the stores kept the overhead low and allowed the company to pass the savings to customers. Costs were further reduced by emphasizing higher volume and lower margins with a high inventory

Professor Krishna Palepu prepared this case. The case is intended solely as the basis for class discussion and is not intended to serve as an endorsement, source of primary data, or illustration of effective or ineffective management. Copyright © 1988 by the President and Fellows of Harvard College. HBS Case 9-188-148.

1. Reprinted with permission from Barron's, January 21, 1985.

turnover. While offering low prices, The Home Depot was careful not to sacrifice the depth of merchandise and the quality of products offered for sale.

To ensure that the right products were stocked at all times, each Home Depot store carried approximately $4,500,000 of inventory, at retail, consisting of approximately 25,000 separate stock-keeping units. All these items were kept on the sales floor of the store, thus increasing convenience to the customer and minimizing out-of-stock occurrences. The company also assured its customers that the products sold by it were of the best quality. The Home Depot offered nationally advertised brands as well as lesser known brands carefully chosen by the company's merchandise managers. Every product sold by The Home Depot was guaranteed by either the manufacturer or by the company itself.

The Home Depot complemented the above merchandising strategy with excellent sales assistance. Since the great majority of the company's customers were individual homeowners with no prior experience in their home improvement projects, The Home Depot considered its employees' technical knowledge and service orientation to be very important to its marketing success. The company pursued a number of policies to address this need. Approximately 90% of the company's employees were on a full-time basis. To attract and retain a strong sales force, the company maintained salary and wage levels above those of its competitors. All the floor sales personnel attended special training sessions to gain thorough knowledge of the company's home improvement products and their basic applications. This training enabled them to answer shoppers' questions and help customers in choosing equipment and material appropriate for their projects. Often, the expert advice the sales personnel provided created a bond that resulted in continuous contact with the customer throughout the duration of the customer's project.

Finally, to attract customers, The Home Depot pursued an aggressive advertising program utilizing newspapers, television, radio, and direct mail catalogues. The company's advertising stressed promotional pricing, the broad assortment and depth of its merchandise, and the assistance provided by its sales personnel. The company also sponsored in-store demonstrations of do-it-yourself techniques and product uses. To increase customers' shopping convenience, The Home Depot's stores were open seven days a week, including weekday evenings.

Fortune magazine commented on The Home Depot's strategy as follows:

> *Warehouse stores typically offer shoppers deep discounts with minimal service and back-to-basics ambiance. The Home Depot's outlets have all the charm of a freight yard and predictably low prices. But they also offer unusually helpful customer service. Although warehouse retailing looks simple, it is not: As discounting cuts into gross profit margins, the merchant must carefully control buying, merchandising, and inventory costs. Throwing in service, which is expensive and hard to systematize, makes the job even tougher. In the do-it-yourself (DIY) segment of the industry – which includes old-style hardware stores, building supply warehouses, and the everything-under-one-roof home centers – The Home Depot is the only company that has successfully brought off the union of low prices and high service.*[2]

The Home Depot's strategy was successful in fueling an impressive growth in the company's operations. The first three Home Depot stores, opened in Atlanta in 1979, were a quick success. From this modest beginning, the company grew rapidly and went public in 1981. The company's stock initially traded over-the-counter and was listed on the New York Stock Exchange in April 1984. Several new stores were opened in markets

2. Reprinted with permission from Fortune, February 1988, p. 73.

The Home Depot

throughout the Sunbelt, and the number of stores operated by The Home Depot grew from 3 in 1979 to 50 by the end of fiscal 1985. As a result, sales grew from $7 million in 1979 to $700 million in 1985. Exhibit 1 provides a summary of the growth in the company's operations. The company's stock price performance during 1985 is summarized in Exhibit 2.

INDUSTRY AND COMPETITION

The home improvement industry was large and growing during the 1980s. The industry sales totaled approximately $80 billion in 1985 and strong industry growth was expected to continue, especially in the do-it-yourself (DIY) segment, which had grown at a compounded annual rate of 14 percent over the last 15 years. With the number of two-wage-earner households growing, there was an increase in families' average disposable income, making it possible to increase the frequency and magnitude of home improvement projects. Further, many homeowners were undertaking these projects by themselves rather than hiring a contractor. Research conducted by the Do-It-Yourself Institute, an industry trade group, showed that DIY activities had become America's second most popular leisure-time activity after watching television.

The success of warehouse retailing pioneered by The Home Depot attracted a number of other companies into the industry. Among the store chains currently operating in the industry were Builders Square (a division of K Mart), Mr. HOW (a division of Service Merchandise), The Home Club (a division of Zayre Corp.), Payless Cashways (a division of W.R. Grace), and Hechinger Co. Most of these store chains were relatively new and not yet achieving significant profitability.

Among The Home Depot's competitors, the most successful was Hechinger, which had operated hardware stores for a long time and recently entered the do-it-yourself segment of the industry. Using a strategy quite different from The Home Depot's, Hechinger ran gleaming upscale stores and aimed at high profit margins. As of the end of fiscal 1985, the company operated 55 stores, located primarily in southeastern states. Hechinger announced that it planned to expand its sales by 20 to 25 percent a year by adding 10 to 14 stores a year. A summary of Hechinger's recent financial performance is presented in Exhibit 3.

THE HOME DEPOT'S FUTURE

While The Home Depot had achieved rapid growth every year since its inception, fiscal 1985 was probably the most important in the company's seven-year history. During 1985 the company implemented its most ambitious expansion plan to date by adding 20 new stores in eight new markets. Nine of these stores were acquired from Bowater, a competing store chain which was in financial difficulty. As The Home Depot engaged in major expansion, its revenues rose 62 percent from $432 million in fiscal 1984 to $700 million in 1985. However, the company's earnings declined in 1985 from the record levels achieved during the previous fiscal year. In fiscal 1985, The Home Depot earned $8.2 million, or $0.33 per share, as compared with $14.1 million or $0.56 per share in fiscal 1984.

Bernard Marcus, The Home Depot's chairman and chief executive officer, commented on the company's performance as follows:

Fiscal 1985 was a year of rapid expansion and continued growth for The Home Depot. Feeling the time was ripe for us to enhance our share of the do-it-yourself market, we seized the opportunity to make a significant investment in our long-term future. At the same time, we recognized that our short-term profit growth would be affected.

The Home Depot's 1985 annual report (Exhibit 4) provided more details on the firm's financial performance during the year.

As fiscal 1985 came to a close, The Home Depot faced some critical issues. The competition in the do-it-yourself industry was heating up. The fight for market dominance was expected to result in pressure on margins, and industry analysts expected only the strongest and most capable firms in the industry to survive. Also, The Home Depot had announced plans for further expansion that included the opening of nine new stores in 1986. The company estimated that site acquisition and construction would cost about $6.6 million for each new store, and investment in inventory (net of vendor financing) would require an additional $1.8 million per store. The company needed significant additional financing to implement these plans.

Home Depot relied on external financing—both debt and equity—to fund its growth in 1984 and 1985. However, the significant drop in its stock price in 1985 made further equity financing less attractive. While the company could borrow from its line of credit, it had to make sure that it could satisfy the interest coverage requirements (see Note 3 in Exhibit 4 for a discussion of debt covenant restrictions). Clearly, generating more cash from its own operations would be the best way for Home Depot to invest in its growth on a sustainable basis.

QUESTIONS

1. Evaluate Home Depot's business strategy. Do you think it is a viable strategy in the long run?

2. Analyze Home Depot's financial performance during the fiscal years 1983–1985. Compare Home Depot's performance in this period with Hechinger's performance. (You may use the ratios and the cash flow analysis in Exhibit 3 in this summary.)

3. How productive were Home Depot's stores in the fiscal years 1983–1985? (You may use the statistics in Exhibit 1 in this analysis.)

4. Home Depot's stock price dropped by 23 percent between January 1985 and February 1986, making it difficult for the company to rely on equity capital to finance its growth. Covenants on existing debt (discussed in Note 3 of Exhibit 4) restrict the magnitude of the company's future borrowing. Given these constraints, what specific actions should Home Depot take with respect to its current operations and growth strategy? How can the company improve its operating performance? Should the company change its strategy? If so, how?

The Home Depot

EXHIBIT I

The Home Depot, Inc. – Summary of Performance During Fiscal Years 1981–1985

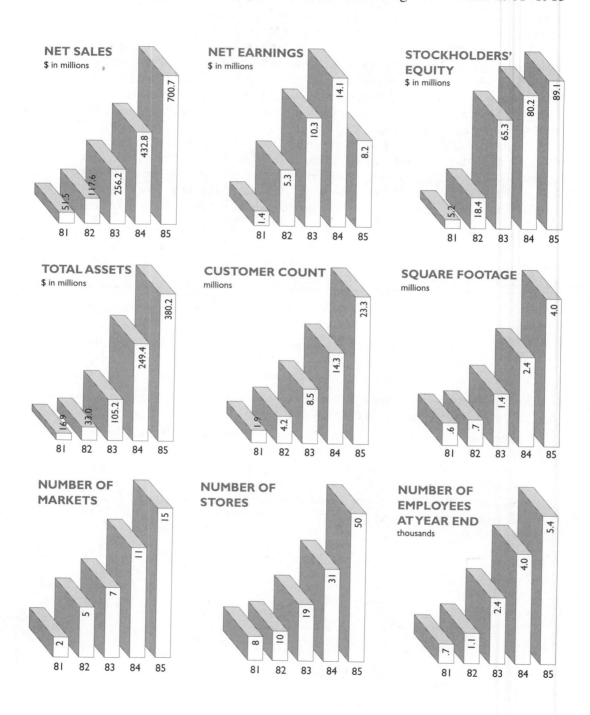

NET SALES
$ in millions

51.5 · 117.6 · 256.2 · 432.8 · 700.7
81 82 83 84 85

NET EARNINGS
$ in millions

1.4 · 5.3 · 10.3 · 14.1 · 8.2
81 82 83 84 85

STOCKHOLDERS' EQUITY
$ in millions

5.2 · 18.4 · 65.3 · 80.2 · 89.1
81 82 83 84 85

TOTAL ASSETS
$ in millions

16.9 · 33.0 · 105.2 · 249.4 · 380.2
81 82 83 84 85

CUSTOMER COUNT
millions

1.9 · 4.2 · 8.5 · 14.3 · 23.3
81 82 83 84 85

SQUARE FOOTAGE
millions

.6 · .7 · 1.4 · 2.4 · 4.0
81 82 83 84 85

NUMBER OF MARKETS

2 · 5 · 7 · 11 · 15
81 82 83 84 85

NUMBER OF STORES

8 · 10 · 19 · 31 · 50
81 82 83 84 85

NUMBER OF EMPLOYEES AT YEAR END
thousands

.7 · 1.1 · 2.4 · 4.0 · 5.4
81 82 83 84 85

EXHIBIT 2

The Home Depot's Common Stock Price and Standard & Poor's 500
Composite Index from January 1985 to February 1986

Date	Home Depot Stock Price	S&P 500 Composite Index
1/2/85	$17.125	165.4
2/1/85	16.375	178.6
3/1/85	19.000	183.2
4/1/85	17.000	181.3
5/1/85	18.000	178.4
6/3/85	16.125	189.3
7/1/85	13.000	192.4
8/1/85	12.625	192.1
9/2/85	11.875	197.9
10/1/85	11.375	185.1
11/1/85	10.750	191.5
12/2/85	11.000	200.5
1/2/86	12.625	209.6
2/3/86	13.125	214.0
Cumulative Return:	−23.4%	29.4%

*The Home Depot's ß = 1.3 (*Value Line *estimate).*

EXHIBIT 3

The Home Depot, Inc. – Summary of Financial Performance of Hechinger Company

I. Hechinger's Financial Ratios

	Year Ending		
	February 1, 1986	February 2, 1985	January 28, 1984
Profit Before Taxes/Sales (%)	7.80	9.40	9.80
× Sales/Average Assets	1.48	1.72	2.02
× Average Assets/Average Equity	2.21	2.12	1.79
× (1 − Average Tax Rate)	0.62	0.55	0.54
= Return on Equity (%)	15.80	18.90	19.10
× (1 − Dividend Payout Ratio)	0.93	0.95	0.95
= Sustainable Growth Rate (%)	14.70	18.00	18.10
Gross Profit/Sales (%)	29.30	30.10	32.10
Selling, General and Administrative Expenses/Sales (%)	21.60	21.10	22.90
Interest Expenses/Sales (%)	2.10	1.30	0.70
Interest Income/Sales (%)	2.20	1.70	1.30
Inventory Turnover	4.50	4.50	4.40
Average Collection Period[a] (Days)	32.00	33.00	35.00
Average Accounts Payable Period[b] (Days)	58.00	61.00	63.00

a. Assumed 365 days in the fiscal year.

b. Payables also include accrued wages and expenses. Purchases are computed as cost of sales plus increase in inventory during the year. Assumed 365 days in the fiscal year.

The Home Depot

II. Hechinger's Cash Flow

	Year Ending		
(Dollars in Thousands)	February 1, 1986	February 2, 1985	January 28, 1984
Cash Provided from Operations			
Net earnings	$23,111	$20,923	$16,243
Items not requiring the use of cash or marketable securities:			
Depreciation and amortization	6,594	4,622	3,429
Deferred income taxes	1,375	2,040	1,515
Deferred rent expense	2,321	2,064	1,463
	33,401	**29,649**	**22,650**
Cash Invested in Operations			
Accounts receivable	4,657	7,905	7,954
Merchandise inventories	17,998	8,045	20,596
Other current assets	4,891	3,760	1,304
Accounts payable and accrued expenses	(6,620)	(12,099)	(9,767)
Taxes on income – current	285	3,031	(575)
	21,211	**10,642**	**19,512**
Net Cash Provided from Operations	**12,190**	**19,007**	**3,138**
Cash Used for Investment Activities			
Expenditures for property, furniture and equipment, net of disposals, and other assets	**(36,037)**	**(25,531)**	**(16,346)**
Cash Used to Pay Dividends to Shareholders	**(1,550)**	**(1,091)**	**(868)**
Cash Provided from Financing Activities			
Proceeds from public offering of 8½% converted subordinated debentures, net of expenses	—	85,010	—
Proceeds from public offering of common stock net of expenses	28,969	—	13,439
Proceeds from sale and leaseback transactions under operating leases	—	8,338	6,874
Increase (decrease) in long-term debt	—	(4,750)	6,366
Decrease in short-term debt	—	—	(318)
Exercise of stock options including income tax benefit	180	674	611
Decrease in capital lease obligations	(311)	(280)	(254)
	28,838	**88,992**	**26,718**
Increase in Cash and Marketable Securities	**$ 3,441**	**$81,377**	**$12,642**

The Home Depot

The Home Depot

EXHIBIT 4

The Home Depot, Inc.—Abridged Annual Report for Fiscal Year 1985

A Letter to Our Shareholders:

Fiscal 1985 was a year of rapid expansion and continued growth for The Home Depot. Feeling the time was ripe for us to enhance our share of the do-it-yourself market, we seized the opportunity to make a significant investment in our long-term future. At the same time, we recognized that our short-term profit growth would be affected.

The Home Depot intends to be the dominant factor in every market we serve. The key to our success has been that upon entering a new market, we make a substantial commitment—opening multiple stores, providing excellent customer service, creating highly visible promotions, and growing the entire market. We turn the novice into a do-it-yourselfer and enable the expert to do more for less money.

From shortly before the end of fiscal 1984 to the close of fiscal 1985, The Home Depot entered eight new markets—Dallas, Houston, Jacksonville, San Diego, Los Angeles, Shreveport, Baton Rouge and Mobile—in a period of approximately 13 months. In that time, the number of Home Depot stores rose dramatically, from 22 to 50, including 9 stores acquired in the Bowater acquisition which had not been in our original plan. Twenty of these stores were opened during the past fiscal year alone. During this time span, we have become the only national warehouse retailing chain serving markets across the Sunbelt.

This expansion program required a tremendous investment of capital expenditures and inventory, as well as in personnel. As a result, our net earnings declined from record levels achieved during the previous fiscal year. In fiscal 1985, The Home Depot earned $8,219,000, or $.33 per share, as compared with $14,122,000, or $.56 per share, in fiscal 1984. However, as The Home Depot engaged in this major thrust forward, it also increased its market share and market presence as revenues rose 62% from $432,779,000 in fiscal 1984 to $700,729,000 in fiscal 1985.

Despite our significant investments, we still continue to be in a very strong financial condition. In December, The Home Depot replaced a prior $100 million bank credit line with an eight-year decreasing revolving credit agreement of $200 million. In addition, we are pursuing sale-and-leaseback negotiations for an aggregate of approximately $50 million for ten of our stores. These sources of additional funds, along with internally generated cash flow, will provide us with an ample financial foundation to continue to underwrite our growth over the next several years.

We are also quite proud that The Home Depot achieved its substantial gain in sales and market share in what turned out to be a very difficult year for our industry and retailing in general. The do-it-yourself "warehouse" industry, which we pioneered only a few short years ago, has recently attracted many competitors, some of whom have already fallen by the wayside, having mistaken our dramatic success as a path towards easy profits. Now the industry is faced with a situation when only the strongest and most capable will survive. As this process continues, we expect to encounter additional cost competition in the fight for market dominance. However, with our strengths—both financial and our successful ability to develop a loyal customer base—we are confident that The Home Depot will emerge an even stronger company.

We have never doubted The Home Depot's ability to be a leader in our business. We have the market dominance, the superior retailing concepts and the necessary foundation of experienced management. Further, we have the determination to maintain our position.

Looking at some of our markets individually, clearly our most difficult environment has been in Houston, where the oil-related economy is undergoing painful contractions combined with particularly fierce industry competition. This has caused our newly-opened stores to operate at a sub par level. In Dallas/Fort Worth, the stores we acquired at the end of fiscal 1984 have not yet generated the profits we expect. Such difficult market conditions demand a flexible reaction both in merchandising and operations. Recognizing the future potential of both of these markets, our management team is addressing the issues and feels confident that the final outcome will be positive.

In the other markets entered this year, the situation has been considerably more positive. There, our stores are experiencing growth much closer to our historical patterns.

In support of our California and Arizona operations, a West Coast division was inaugurated to facilitate a timely response to the demands of that marketplace. With management personnel in place, this division is now responsible for the merchandising and operations of all stores in the western states.

Other highlights of the past year's activities include the progress we have made in expanding our management team, and the computer systems we installed into our operations to enhance our efficiency.

During the year, we completed the store price look-up phase of our management information system. This facilitates tracking individual items' sales through our registers, resulting in a more concise method of inventory reorder and margin management with the information now available.

During the coming year we will be testing a perpetual inventory tie-in with our price look-up system, eliminating pricing of our merchandise at the store level. The latter is being tested in several stores presently and hopefully will be expanded to include all of our stores by year end. This will have a significant effect on labor productivity at the store level.

The Home Depot is always looking for ways in which to do things better, priding ourselves on our flexibility and ability to innovate and to react to changing conditions. Whether it is a matter of developing state-of-the-art computer systems, reevaluating our store layouts or adapting to fast-changing markets and new types of merchandising, flexibility has always been a Home Depot characteristic.

In fiscal 1986, The Home Depot will continue to expand, but at a much more moderate pace. We plan to open nine new stores. These stores will be in existing markets except for two locations in the new market of San Jose, California.

When we open stores in existing markets, sharing advertising costs and operational expenses, we achieve a faster return than stores in new markets. With this in mind, in January 1986, we withdrew from the Detroit market and delayed the opening of stores in San Francisco. These stores were targeted for a substantial initial loss in earnings that would have been necessary to achieve market dominance. From our standpoint, these new markets would have had the combined effect of diluting our personnel and negatively affecting our earnings.

It has always been Home Depot's philosophy to maintain orderly growth and achieve market dominance as we expand to new markets. Indeed, growth for growth's sake has never been and never will be our objective. We intend to invest prudently and expand aggressively in our business and our markets only when such expenditures meet our criteria for long-term profitability.

We are quite optimistic about our company's future—both for fiscal 1986 and for the years to follow. Essential to this optimism is the fact that The Home Depot has consistently proven that we can grow the market in every geographical area we enter. Simply, this means that we do not have to take business away from hardware stores and other existing home-improvement outlets, but rather, to create new do-it-yourselfers out of those who have never done their own home improvements.

Our philosophy is to educate our customers on how to be do-it-yourselfers. Our customers have come to expect The Home Depot's knowledgeable sales staff to guide them through any project they care to undertake, whether it be installing kitchen cabinets, constructing a deck, or building an entire house. Our sales staff knows how to complete each project, what tools and material to include, and how to sell our customers everything they need.

The Home Depot traditionally holds clinics for its customers in such skills as electrical wiring, carpentry, and plumbing, to name a few. Upon the successful completion of such clinics, our customers are confident in themselves and in The Home Depot. This confidence allows them to attempt increasingly advanced and complex home improvements.

Concerning our facilities, Home Depot's warehouse retailing concept allows us to carry a truly fantastic selection of merchandise and offer it at the lowest possible prices. Each of our stores ranges from about 65,000 to over 100,000 square feet of selling space, with an additional 4,000 to 10,000 square feet of outdoor selling area. In these large stores, we are able to stock all the materials and tools needed to build a house from scratch, and to landscape its grounds. With each store functioning as its own warehouse, with a capacity of over 25,000 different items, we are able to keep our prices at a minimum while providing the greatest selection of building materials and name brand merchandise.

For the majority of Americans, their home is their most valuable asset. It is an asset that consistently appreciates. It is also an asset in need of ongoing care and maintenance. By becoming do-it-yourselfers, homeowners can significantly enhance the value of their homes. We at The Home Depot have found that by successfully delivering this message, we have created loyal and satisfied customers. And by maintaining leadership in our markets, we have established a sound basis on which to build a future of growth with profitability.

The Home Depot

The Home Depot management and staff are dedicated
to the proposition that we are—and will remain—
America's leading do-it-yourself retailer.

Bernard Marcus
Chairman and
Chief Executive Officer

Arthur M. Blank
President and
Chief Operating Officer

CONSOLIDATED STATEMENTS OF EARNINGS

	Fiscal Year Ended		
	February 2, 1986 **(52 weeks)**	February 3, 1985 (53 weeks)	January 29, 1984 (52 weeks)
Net Sales (note 2)	**$700,729,000**	$432,779,000	$256,184,000
Cost of Merchandise Sold	**519,272,000**	318,460,000	186,170,000
Gross Profit	**181,457,000**	114,319,000	70,014,000
Operating Expenses:			
Selling and store operating expenses	**134,354,000**	74,447,000	43,514,000
Preopening expenses	**7,521,000**	1,917,000	2,456,000
General and administrative expenses	**20,555,000**	12,817,000	7,376,000
Total Operating Expenses	**162,430,000**	89,181,000	53,346,000
Operating Income	**19,027,000**	25,138,000	16,668,000
Other Income (Expense):			
Net gain on disposition of property and equipment (note 7)	**1,317,000**	—	—
Interest income	**1,481,000**	5,236,000	2,422,000
Interest expense (note 3)	**(10,206,000)**	(4,122,000)	(104,000)
	(7,408,000)	1,114,000	2,318,000
Earnings Before Income Taxes	**11,619,000**	26,252,000	18,986,000
Income Taxes (note 4)	**3,400,000**	12,130,000	8,725,000
Net Earnings	**$ 8,219,000**	$ 14,122,000	$ 10,261,000
Earnings per Common and Common **Equivalent Share (note 5)**	**$ .33**	$ .56	$ .41
Weighted Average Number of Common **and Common Equivalent Shares**	**25,247,000**	25,302,000	24,834,000

CONSOLIDATED BALANCE SHEETS

	February 2, 1986	February 3, 1985
ASSETS		
Current Assets:		
Cash, including time deposits of $43,374,000 in 1985	$ 9,671,000	$ 52,062,000
Accounts receivable, net (note 7)	21,505,000	9,365,000
Refundable income taxes	3,659,000	—
Merchandise inventories	152,700,000	84,046,000
Prepaid expenses	2,526,000	1,939,000
Total current assets	190,061,000	147,412,000
Property and Equipment, at Cost (note 3):		
Land	44,396,000	30,044,000
Buildings	38,005,000	3,728,000
Furniture, fixtures, and equipment	34,786,000	18,162,000
Leasehold improvements	23,748,000	11,743,000
Construction in progress	27,694,000	14,039,000
	168,629,000	77,716,000
Less accumulated depreciation and amortization	7,813,000	4,139,000
Net property and equipment	160,816,000	73,577,000
Cost in Excess of the Fair Value of Net Assets Acquired, net of accumulated amortization of $730,000 in 1985 and $93,000 in 1984 (note 2)	24,561,000	25,198,000
Other	4,755,000	3,177,000
	$380,193,000	$249,364,000
LIABILITIES AND STOCKHOLDERS' EQUITY		
Current Liabilities:		
Accounts payable	$ 53,881,000	$ 32,356,000
Accrued salaries and related expenses	5,397,000	3,819,000
Other accrued expenses	13,950,000	10,214,000
Income taxes payable (note 4)	—	626,000
Current portion of long-term debt (note 3)	10,382,000	287,000
Total current liabilities	83,610,000	47,302,000
Long-Term Debt, Excluding Current Installments (note 3):		
Convertible subordinated debentures	100,250,000	100,250,000
Other long-term debt	99,693,000	17,692,000
	$199,943,000	$117,942,000
Other Liabilities	861,000	1,320,000
Deferred Income Taxes (note 4)	6,687,000	2,586,000

(continued)

The Home Depot

CONSOLIDATED BALANCE SHEETS *(continued)*

	February 2, 1986	February 3, 1985
Stockholders' Equity (note 5):		
Common stock, par value $.05. Authorized: 50,000,000 shares; issued and outstanding — 25,150,063 shares at February 2, 1986 and 25,055,188 shares at February 3, 1985	1,258,000	1,253,000
Paid-in capital	48,900,000	48,246,000
Retained earnings	38,934,000	30,715,000
Total stockholders' equity	89,092,000	80,214,000
Commitments and Contingencies (notes 5, 6 and 8)	$380,193,000	$249,364,000

CONSOLIDATED STATEMENTS OF CHANGES IN FINANCIAL POSITION

	Fiscal Year Ended		
	February 2, 1986	February 3, 1985	January 29, 1984
Sources of Working Capital:			
Net earnings	$8,219,000	$14,122,000	$ 10,261,000
Items which do not use working capital:			
Depreciation and amortization of property and equipment	4,376,000	2,275,000	903,000
Deferred income taxes	3,612,000	1,508,000	713,000
Amortization of cost in excess of the fair value of net assets required	637,000	93,000	—
Net gain on disposition of property and equipment	(1,317,000)	—	—
Other	180,000	77,000	59,000
Working capital provided by operations	15,707,000	18,075,000	11,936,000
Proceeds from disposition of property and equipment	9,469,000	861,000	3,000
Proceeds from long-term borrowings	92,400,000	120,350,000	4,200,000
Proceeds from sale of common stock, net	659,000	814,000	36,663,000
	$118,235,000	$140,100,000	$ 52,802,000
Uses of Working Capital:			
Additions to property and equipment	$ 99,767,000	$50,769,000	$ 16,081,000
Current installments and repayments of long-term debt	10,399,000	6,792,000	52,000
Acquisition of Bowater Home Center, Inc., net of working capital of $9,227,000 (note 2):			
Property and equipment	—	4,815,000	—
Cost in excess of the fair value of net assets acquired	—	25,291,000	—
Other assets, net of liabilities	—	(913,000)	—

(continued)

CONSOLIDATED STATEMENTS OF CHANGES IN FINANCIAL POSITION *(continued)*

	Fiscal Year Ended		
	February 2, 1986	February 3, 1985	January 29, 1984
Other, net	1,728,000	2,554,000	252,000
Increase in working capital	6,341,000	50,792,000	36,417,000
	$118,235,000	$140,100,000	$ 52,802,000

Changes in Components of Working Capital:

Increase (decrease) in current assets:

Cash	(42,391,000)	$29,894,000	$ 13,917,000
Receivables, net	15,799,000	7,170,000	1,567,000
Merchandise inventories	68,654,000	25,334,000	41,137,000
Prepaid expenses	587,000	1,206,000	227,000
	42,649,000	63,604,000	56,848,000

Increase (decrease) in current liabilities:

Accounts payable	21,525,000	10,505,000	17,150,000
Accrued salaries and related expenses	1,578,000	(93,000)	2,524,000
Other accrued expenses	3,736,000	2,824,000	341,000
Income taxes payable	(626,000)	(657,000)	406,000
Current portion of long-term debt	10,095,000	233,000	10,000
	36,308,000	12,812,000	20,431,000
Increase in Working Capital	$ 6,341,000	$ 50,792,000	$ 36,417,000

The Home Depot

SELECTED FINANCIAL DATA

	Fiscal Year Ended				
	February 2, 1986	February 3, 1985[a]	January 29, 1984	January 30, 1983	January 31, 1982
Selected Consolidated Statement of Earnings Data:					
Net sales	$700,729,000	$432,779,000	$256,184,000	$117,645,000	$51,542,000
Gross profit	181,457,000	114,319,000	70,014,000	33,358,000	14,735,000
Earnings before income taxes and extraordinary item	11,619,000	26,252,000	18,986,000	9,870,000	1,963,000
Earnings before extraordinary item	8,219,000	14,122,000	10,261,000	5,315,000	1,211,000
Extraordinary item-reduction of income taxes arising from carryforward of prior years' operating losses	—	—	—	—	234,000
Net earnings	$ 8,219,000	$ 14,122,000	$10,261,000	$5,315,000	$1,445,000
Per Common and Common Equivalent Share:					
Earnings before extraordinary item	$ .33	$ .56	$ .41	$ .24	$.06
Extraordinary item	—	—	—	—	.01
Net earnings	$ .33	$ .56	$ .41	$ .24	$ .07
Weighted average number of common and common equivalent shares	25,247,000	25,302,000	24,834,000	22,233,000	21,050,000
Selected Consolidated Balance Sheet Data:					
Working capital	$106,451,000	$100,110,000	$ 49,318,000	$ 12,901,000	$ 5,502,000
Total assets	380,193,000	249,364,000	105,230,000	33,014,000	16,906,000
Long-term debt	199,943,000	117,942,000	4,384,000	236,000	3,738,000
Stockholders' equity	89,092,000	80,214,000	65,278,000	18,354,000	5,024,000

a. *53-week fiscal year; all others were 52-week fiscal years.*

The Home Depot

MANAGEMENT'S DISCUSSION AND ANALYSIS OF RESULTS OF OPERATIONS AND FINANCIAL CONDITION

The data below reflect the percentage relationship between sales and major categories in the Consolidated Statements of Earnings and selected sales data of the percentage change in the dollar amounts of each of the items.

	Fiscal Year[a]			Percentage Increase (Decrease) of Dollar Amounts	
	1985	1984	1983	**1985 v. 1984**	1984 v. 1983
Selected Consolidated Statements of Earnings Data:					
Net sales	**100.0%**	100.0%	100.0%	**61.9%**	68.9%
Gross profit	**25.9**	26.4	27.3	**58.7**	63.3
Cost and expenses:					
Selling and store operating	**19.2**	17.2	17.0	**80.5**	71.1
Preopening	**1.1**	.4	.9	**292.3**	(21.9)
General and administrative	**2.9**	3.0	2.9	**60.4**	73.8
Net gain on disposition of property and equipment	**(.2)**	—	—	**—**	—
Interest income	**(.2)**	(1.2)	(.9)	**(71.7)**	116.2
Interest expense	**1.4**	.9	—	**147.6**	3,863.5
	24.2	20.3	19.9	**92.9**	72.6
Earnings before income taxes	**1.7**	6.1	7.4	**(55.7)**	38.3
Income taxes	**.5**	2.8	3.4	**(72.0)**	39.0
Net earnings	**1.2%**	3.3%	4.0%	**(41.8%)**	37.6%
Selected Consolidated Sales Data:					
Number of customer transactions	**23,324,000**	14,256,000	8,479.000	**63.6%**	68.1%
Average amount of sale per transaction	**$30.04**	$30.36	$30.21	**(1.1)**	.5
Weighted average weekly sales per operating store	$ **342,500**	$ 365,500	$ 360,300	**(6.3)**	1.4

a. Fiscal years 1985, 1984 and 1983 refer to the fiscal years ended February 2, 1986, February 3, 1985 and January 29, 1984, respectively. Fiscal 1984 consisted of 53 weeks while 1985 and 1983 each consisted of 52 weeks.

Results of Operations

For an understanding of the significant factors that influenced the Company's performance during the past three fiscal years, the following discussion should be read in conjunction with the consolidated financial statements appearing elsewhere in this annual report.

Fiscal Year Ended February 2, 1986 Compared to February 3, 1985

Net sales in fiscal year 1985 increased 62% from $432,779,000 to $700,729,000. The growth is attributable to several factors. First, the Company opened 20 new stores during 1985 and closed one store. Second, second-year sales increases were realized from the three new stores opened in 1984 and from the nine former Bowater Home Center stores acquired during 1984. Third, comparable store sales increases of 2.3% were achieved despite comparing the 52-week 1985 fiscal year to the sales of the 53-week 1984 fiscal year, due in part to the number of customer transactions increasing by 64%. Finally, the weighted average weekly sales per operating store declined 6% in 1985 due to the significant increase in the ratio of the number of new stores to total stores in operation—new stores have a lower sales rate than mature stores until they establish market share.

The Home Depot

Gross profit in 1985 increased 59% from $114,319,000 to $181,457,000. This increase was due to the increased sales and was partially offset by a reduction in the gross profit margin from 26.4% to 25.9%. The reduction is primarily due to lower margins achieved while establishing market presence in new markets.

Cost and expenses increased 93% during 1985 and, as a percent of sales, increased from 20.3% to 24.2%. The increase in selling and store operating, preopening expenses and net interest expense is due to the opening of 20 new stores, the costs associated with the former Bowater Home Center stores, and the related cost of building market share. The large percentage of new stores which have lower sales but fixed occupancy and certain minimum operating expenses tends to cause the percentage of selling and store operating costs to increase as a percentage of sales. The net gain on disposition of property and equipment is discussed fully in note 7 to the financial statements.

Earnings before income taxes decreased 56% from $26,252,000 to $11,619,000 resulting from the increase in operating expenses to support the Company's expansion program. The Company's effective income tax rate declined from 46.2% to 29.3% resulting from an increase in investment and other tax credits as a percentage of the total tax provision. As a percentage of sales, earnings decreased from 3.3% in 1984 to 1.2% in 1985 due to the increase in operating expenses as discussed above.

Fiscal Year Ended February 3, 1985 Compared to January 29, 1984

Net sales in fiscal 1984 increased 69% from $256,184,000 to $432,779,000. The growth was attributable to several factors. First, the company opened three new stores during fiscal 1984. Second, the Company had sales of $9,755,000 from the nine former Bowater Home Center stores acquired on December 3, 1984. Third, second-year sales increases were realized from the nine stores opened during fiscal 1983. Fourth, comparable store sales increases of 14% were due in part to 53 weeks in fiscal 1984 compared to 52 weeks in fiscal 1983 and in part to the number of customer transactions increasing by 63%. Finally, excluding the sales of the former Bowater Home Center stores, the weighted average weekly sales per operating store increased 6% to $383,500 in fiscal 1984.

Gross profit in fiscal 1984 increased 63% from $70,014,000 to $114,319,000. This net increase was due to the increased sales and was partially offset by a reduction in the gross profit margin from 27.3% to 26.4%. The reduction in the gross profit percentage is largely the result of the purchase of a high proportion of promoted merchandise by customers in the second quarter.

Costs and expenses increased 73% during fiscal 1984. As a percent of sales, costs and expenses increased from 19.9% to 20.3% due to increased selling, store operating, general and administrative expenses. This planned increase was in preparation of the Company's future expansion. Interest expense increased significantly as a result of the issuance of substantial debt during fiscal 1984 to fund the Company's expansion. These increases were partially offset by reduced preopening expenses and increased interest income resulting from temporary investment of the proceeds of the debt financing.

Earnings before income taxes increased 38% from $18,986,000 to $26,252,000 resulting from the factors discussed above. Such pretax earnings, however, were reduced by a loss from the Bowater stores of approximately $1,900,000 from date of acquisition (December 1984) to year end. The Company's effective income tax rate increased slightly from 46.0% to 46.2% resulting principally from less investment and other tax credits as a percentage of the total tax provision. As a percentage of sales, earnings decreased from 4.0% in fiscal 1983 to 3.3% in fiscal 1984. The decline is a result of the company's reduced gross profit percentage and increases in the operating expenses discussed above.

Impact of Inflation and Changing Prices

Although the Company cannot accurately determine the precise effect of inflation on its operations, it does not believe inflation has had a material effect on sales or results of operations. The Company has complied with the reporting requirements of the Financial Accounting Standards Board Statement No. 33 in note 10 to the financial statements. Due to the experimental techniques, subjective estimates and assumptions, and the incomplete presentation required by this accounting pronouncement, the Company questions the value of the required reporting.

Liquidity and Capital Resources

Cash flow generated from existing store operations provided the Company with a significant source of liquidity since sales are on a cash-and-carry basis. In addition, a significant portion of the Company's inventory is financed under vendor credit terms. The Company has supplemented its operating cash flow from time to time with bank credit and equity and debt financing. During fiscal 1985, $88,000,000 of working capital was provided by the revolving bank credit line, $4,400,000 from industrial revenue bonds, and approximately $15,707,000 from operations. In addition, during fiscal 1985, the Company entered into a new credit agreement for a $200,000,000 revolving credit facility with a group of banks.

The Company has announced plans to open nine new stores during fiscal 1986, two in the new market of northern California and the balance in existing markets. The cost of this store expansion program will depend upon, among other factors, the extent to which the Company is able to lease second-use store space as opposed to acquiring leases or sites and having stores constructed to its own specifications. The Company estimates that approximately $6,600,000 per store will be required to acquire sites and construct facilities to the Company's specifications and that approximately $1,700,000 will be required to open a store in leased space plus any additional costs of acquiring the lease. These estimates include costs for site acquisition, construction expenditures, fixtures and equipment, and in-store minicomputers and point-of-sale terminals. In addition, each new store will require approximately $1,800,000 to finance inventories, net of vendor financing. The Company believes it has the ability to finance these expenditures through existing cash resources, current bank lines of credit which include a $200,000,000 eight-year revolving credit agreement, funds generated from operations, and other forms of financing, including but not limited to various forms of real estate financing and unsecured borrowings.

The Home Depot

NOTES TO CONSOLIDATED FINANCIAL STATEMENTS

1. Summary of Significant Accounting Policies

Fiscal Year

The Company's fiscal year ends on the Sunday closest to the last day of January and usually consists of 52 weeks. Every five or six years, however, there is a 53-week year. The fiscal year ended February 2, 1986 (1985) consisted of 52 weeks, the year ended February 3, 1985 (1984) consisted of 53 weeks and the year ended January 29, 1984 (1983) consisted of 52 weeks.

Principles of Consolidation

The consolidated financial statements include the accounts of the Company and its wholly owned subsidiary. All significant intercompany transactions have been eliminated in consolidation. Certain reclassifications were made to the 1984 balance sheet to conform to current year presentation.

Merchandise Inventories

Inventories are stated at the lower of cost (first-in, first-out) or market, as determined by the retail inventory method.

Depreciation and Amortization

The Company's buildings, furniture, fixtures, and equipment are depreciated using the straight-line method over the estimated useful lives of the assets. Improvements to leased premises are amortized on the straight-line method over the life of the lease or the useful life of the improvement, whichever is shorter.

Investment Tax Credit

Investment tax credits are recorded as a reduction of Federal income taxes in the year the credits are realized.

Store Preopening Costs

Non-capital expenditures associated with opening new stores are charged to expense as incurred.

Earnings Per Common and Common Equivalent Share

Earnings per common and common equivalent share are based on the weighted average number of shares and equivalents outstanding. Common equivalent shares used in the calculation of earnings per share represent shares granted under the Company's employee stock option plan and employee stock purchase plan.

Shares issuable upon conversion of the 8½% convertible subordinated debentures are also common stock equivalents. Shares issuable upon conversion of the 9% convertible subordinated debentures would only be included in the computation of fully diluted earnings per share. However, neither shares issuable upon conversion of the 8½% nor the 9% convertible debentures were dilutive in any year presented, and thus neither were considered in the earnings per share computations.

2. Acquisition

On December 3, 1984 the Company acquired the outstanding capital stock of Bowater Home Center, Inc. (Bowater) for approximately $38,420,000 including costs incurred in connection with the acquisition. Bowater operated nine retail home center stores primarily in the Dallas, Texas metropolitan area. The acquisition was accounted for by the purchase method and, accordingly, results of operations have been included with those of the Company from the date of acquisition. Cost in excess of the fair value of net assets acquired amounted to approximately $25,291,000, which is being amortized over forty years from date of acquisition using the straight-line method.

The following table summarizes, on a pro forma, unaudited basis, the estimated combined results of operations of the Company and Bowater for the years ended February 3, 1985 and January 29, 1984, as though the acquisition were made at the beginning of fiscal year 1983. This pro forma information does not purport to be indicative of the results of operations which would have actually been obtained if the acquisition had been effective on the dates indicated.

	Fiscal Year Ended	
	February 3, 1985	January 29, 1984*
	(Unaudited)	
Net sales	$482,752,000	$274,660,000
Net earnings	9,009,000	6,913,000
Earnings per common and common equivalent share	.36	.28

Includes the operations and pro forma adjustments from the date of inception of Bowater's operations in August 1983.

3. Long-Term Debt and Lines of Credit

Long-term debt consists of the following:

	February 2, 1986	February 3, 1985
8½% convertible subordinated debentures, due July 1, 2009, convertible into shares of common stock of the Company at a conversion price of $26.50 per share. The debentures are redeemable by the Company at a premium from July 1, 1986 to July 1, 1995, will retire 70% of the issue prior to maturity. Interest is payable semi-annually.	$86,250,000	$86,250,000
9% convertible subordinated debentures, due December 15, 1999, convertible into shares of common stock of the Company at a conversion price of $16.90 per share. The debentures are redeemable by the Company at a premium from December 15, 1986 to December 15, 1994. An annual mandatory sinking fund of $2,000,000 per year is required from 1994 to 1998. Interest is payable semi-annually.	14,000,000	14,000,000
Total convertible subordinated debentures	100,250,000	100,250,000
Revolving credit agreement. Interest may be fixed for any portion outstanding for up to 180 days, at the Company's option, based on a CD rate plus ¾%, the LIBOR rate plus ½% or at the prime rate.	88,000,000	—
*Variable Rate Industrial Revenue Bond (see note 7)	10,100,000	10,100,000
*Variable Rate Industrial Revenue Bond, secured by a letter of credit, payable in sinking fund installments from December 1, 1991 through December 1, 2010	4,400,000	—
9⅝% Industrial Revenue Bond, secured by a letter of credit, payable on December 1, 1993, with interest payable semi-annually	4,200,000	4,200,000

(continued)

	February 2, 1986	February 3, 1985
*Variable Rate Industrial Revenue Bond, secured by land, payable in annual installments of $233,000 with interest payable semi-annually	3,267,000	3,500,000
Other	108,000	179,000
Total long-term debt	210,325,000	118,229,000
Less current portion	10,382,000	287,000
Long-term debt, excluding current portion	$199,943,000	$117,942,000

The interest rates on the variable rate industrial revenue bonds are related to various short-term municipal money market composite rates.

Maturities of long-term debt are approximately $10,382,000 for fiscal 1986 and $234,000 for each of the next four subsequent years.

During the fiscal year ended February 2, 1986, the Company entered into a new unsecured revolving line of credit for a maximum of $200,000,000, subject to certain limitations, of which $88,000,000 is outstanding at year-end. Commitment amounts under the agreement decrease by $15,000,000 on July 31, 1990, by $20,000,000 each six months from that date through January 31, 1993, by $35,000,000 on July 31, 1993, and with the remaining $50,000,000 commitment expiring on January 31, 1994. Maximum borrowings outstanding within the commitment limits may not exceed specified percentages of inventories, land and buildings, and fixtures and equipment, all as defined in the Agreement. Under certain conditions, the commitments may be extended and/or increased. An annual commitment fee of ¼% to ⅜% is required to be paid on the unused portion of the revolving line of credit. Interest rates specified may be increased by a maximum of ⅜ of 1% based on specified ratios of interest rate coverage and debt to equity.

Under the revolving credit agreement, the Company is required, among other things, to maintain during fiscal year 1985 a minimum tangible net worth (defined to include the convertible subordinated debentures) of $150,000,000 (increasing annually to $213,165,000 by January 3, 1989), a debt to tangible net worth ratio of no more than 2 to 1, a current ratio of not less than 1.5 to 1, and a ratio of earnings before interest expense and income taxes to interest expense, net, of not less than 2 to 1. The Company was in compliance with all restrictive covenants as of February 2, 1986. The restrictive covenants related to the letter of credit agreements securing the industrial revenue bonds and the convertible subordinated debentures are no more restrictive than those under the revolving line of credit agreement.

Interest expense in the accompanying consolidated statements of earnings is net of interest capitalized of $3,429,000 in fiscal 1985 and $1,462,000 in fiscal 1984.

4. Income Taxes

The provision for income taxes consists of the following:

	Fiscal Year Ended		
	February 1, 1986	February 3, 1985	January 29, 1984
Current:			
Federal	**$(578,000)**	$9,083,000	$6,916,000
State	**366,000**	1,539,000	1,096,000
	(212,000)	10,622,000	8,012,000
Deferred:			
Federal	**3,306,000**	1,464,000	713,000
State	**306,000**	44,000	—
	3,612,000	1,508,000	713,000
Total	**$3,400,000**	$12,130,000	$8,725,000

The effective tax rates for fiscal 1985, 1984, and 1983 were 29.3%, 46.2%, and 46.0%, respectively. A reconciliation of income tax expense at Federal statutory rates to actual tax expense for the applicable fiscal years follows:

	Fiscal Year Ended		
	February 2, 1986	February 3, 1985	January 29, 1984
Income taxes at Federal statutory rate, net of surtax exemption	**$5,345,000**	$12,076,000	$8,734,000
State income taxes, net of Federal income tax benefit	**363,000**	855,000	592,000
Investment and targeted jobs tax credits	**(2,308,000)**	(800,000)	(747,000)
Other, net	**—**	(1,000)	146,000
	$3,400,000	$12,130,000	$8,725,000

Deferred income taxes arise from differences in the timing of reporting income for financial statement and income tax purposes. The sources of these differences and the tax effect of each are as follows:

	Fiscal Year Ended		
	February 2, 1986	February 3, 1985	January 29, 1984
Accelerated depreciation	**$2,526,000**	$1,159,000	$713,000
Interest capitalization	**855,000**	349,000	—
Other, net	**231,000**	—	—
	$3,612,000	$1,508,000	$713,000

5. Leases

The Company leases certain retail locations, office, and warehouse and distribution space, equipment, and vehicles under operating leases. All leases will expire within the next 25 years; however, it can be expected that in the normal course of business, leases will be renewed or replaced. Total rent expense, net of minor sublease income for the fiscal years ended February 2, 1986, February 3, 1985 and January 29, 1984 amounted to approximately $12,737,000, $6,718,000 and $4,233,000, respectively. Under the building leases, real estate taxes, insurance, maintenance, and operating expenses applicable to the leased property are obligations of the Company. Certain of the store leases provide for contingent rentals based on percentages of sales in excess of specified minimums. Contingent rentals for fiscal years ended February 2, 1986, February 3, 1985 and January 29, 1984 were approximately $650,000, $545,000 and $111,000.

The approximate future minimum lease payments under operating leases at February 2, 1986 are as follows:

Fiscal Year

1986	**$ 16,093,000**
1987	16,668,000
1988	16,345,000
1989	16,086,000
1990	16,129,000
Thereafter	171,455,000
	$252,776,000

7. Disposition of Property and Equipment

During the fourth quarter of fiscal year 1985, the Company disposed of certain properties and equipment at a net gain of $1,317,000. The properties represented real estate located in Detroit, Houston and Tucson, and the equipment represented the trade-in of cash registers of current generation point of sale equipment. Under the terms of the Detroit real estate sale, the purchaser will either assume the bond obligations of the Company of $10,100,000 after February 2, 1986 or pay the Company the funds disbursed under the bonds in order for the Company to prepay the total amount outstanding. Included in accounts receivable at February 2, 1986 is $13,800,000 related to these transactions.

8. Commitments and Contingencies

At February 2, 1986, the Company was contingently liable for approximately $5,300,000 under outstanding letters of credit issued in connection with purchase commitments.

The Company has litigation arising from the normal course of business. In management's opinion, this litigation will not materially affect the Company's financial condition.

9. Quarterly Financial Data (Unaudited)

The following is a summary of the unaudited quarterly results of operations for fiscal years ended February 2, 1986 and February 3, 1985:

The Home Depot

	Net Sales	Gross Profit	Net Earnings	Net Earnings per Common and Common Equivalent Share
Fiscal year ended February 2, 1986:				
First Quarter	$145,048,000	$ 36,380,000	$ 1,945,000	$ .08
Second Quarter	174,239,000	45,572,000	2,499,000	.10
Third Quarter	177,718,000	46,764,000	1,188,000	.05
Fourth Quarter	203,724,000	52,741,000	2,587,000	.10
	$700,729,000	$181,457,000	$ 8,219,000	$ .33
Fiscal year ended February 3, 1985:				
First Quarter	$ 95,872,000	$ 25,026,000	$ 3,437,000	$ .14
Second Quarter	119,068,000	29,185,000	3,808,000	.15
Third Quarter	100,459,000	27,658,000	3,280,000	.13
Fourth Quarter	117,380,000	32,450,000	3,597,000	.14
	$432,779,000	$114,319,000	$14,122,000	$ .56

AUDITORS' REPORT

The Board of Directors and Stockholders,
The Home Depot, Inc.:

We have examined the consolidated balance sheets of The Home Depot, Inc. and subsidiary as of February 2, 1986 and February 3, 1985 and the related consolidated statements of earnings, stockholders' equity, and changes in financial position for each of the years in the three-year period ended February 2, 1986. Our examinations were made in accordance with generally accepted auditing standards, and, accordingly, included such tests of the accounting records and such other auditing procedures as we considered necessary in the circumstances.

In our opinion, the aforementioned consolidated financial statements present fairly the financial position of The Home Depot, Inc. and subsidiary at February 2, 1986 and February 3, 1985, and the results of their operations and the changes in their financial position for each of the years in the three-year period ended February 2, 1986, in conformity with generally accepted accounting principles applied on a consistent basis.

PEAT, MARWICK, MITCHELL & CO.
Atlanta, Georgia
March 24, 1986

The Home Depot

Prospective Analysis: Forecasting

Most financial statement analysis tasks are undertaken with a forward-looking decision in mind—and much of the time, it is useful to summarize the view developed in the analysis with an explicit forecast. Managers need forecasts for planning and to provide performance targets; analysts need forecasts to help communicate their views of the firm's prospects to investors; bankers and debt market participants need forecasts to assess the likelihood of loan repayment. Moreover, there are a variety of contexts (including but not limited to security analysis) where the forecast is usefully summarized in the form of an estimate of the firm's value—an estimate that, after all, can be viewed as the best attempt to reflect in a single summary statistic the manager's or analyst's view of the firm's prospects.

Prospective analysis includes two tasks—forecasting and valuation—that together represent approaches to explicitly summarizing the analyst's forward-looking views. In this chapter we focus on forecasting; valuation is the topic of the next two chapters. The key concepts discussed in this chapter are again illustrated using analysts' forecasts for Nordstrom.

RELATION OF FORECASTING TO OTHER ANALYSES

Forecasting is not so much a separate analysis as it is a way of summarizing what has been learned through business strategy analysis, accounting analysis, and financial analysis. For example, a projection of the future performance of TJX as of early fiscal year 2002 must be grounded ultimately in an understanding of questions such as these:

- *From business strategy analysis:* How long will TJX's strategy and competitive advantage yield the type of spectacular performance it reported in prior years? At what rate can the company grow both in the short term and in the long term without sacrificing its superior margins? Will competition be able to replicate TJX's retailing model?
- *From accounting analysis:* Are there any aspects of TJX's accounting that suggest past earnings and assets are overstated, or expenses or liabilities are understated? If so, what are the implications for future accounting statements?
- *From financial analysis:* What are the sources of TJX's superior performance? Is it sustainable?

The upshot is that a forecast can be no better than the business strategy analysis, accounting analysis, and financial analysis underlying it. However, there are certain techniques and knowledge that can help a manager or analyst to structure the best possible forecast, conditional on what has been learned in the previous steps. Below we summarize an approach to structuring the forecast, offer information useful in getting started, and give detailed steps to forecast earnings, balance sheet data, and cash flows.

THE TECHNIQUES OF FORECASTING

The Overall Structure of the Forecast

The best way to forecast future performance is to do it comprehensively—producing not only an earnings forecast, but a forecast of cash flows and the balance sheet as well. A comprehensive approach is useful, even in cases where one might be interested primarily in a single facet of performance, because it guards against unrealistic implicit assumptions. For example, if an analyst forecasts growth in sales and earnings for several years without explicit consideration of the required increases in working capital and plant assets and the associated financing, the forecast might possibly imbed unreasonable assumptions about asset turnover, leverage, or equity capital infusions.

A comprehensive approach involves many forecasts, but in most cases they are all linked to the behavior of a few key "drivers." The drivers vary according to the type of business involved, but for businesses outside the financial services sector, the sales forecast is nearly always one of the key drivers; profit margin is another. When asset turnover is expected to remain stable—often a realistic assumption—working capital accounts and investment in plant should track the growth in sales closely. Most major expenses also track sales, subject to expected shifts in profit margins. By linking forecasts of such amounts to the sales forecast, one can avoid internal inconsistencies and unrealistic implicit assumptions.

In some contexts the manager or analyst is interested ultimately in a forecast of cash flows, not earnings per se. Nevertheless, even forecasts of cash flows tend to be grounded in practice on forecasts of accounting numbers, including sales, earnings, assets, and liabilities. Of course it would be possible in principle to move *directly* to forecasts of cash flows—inflows from customers, outflows to suppliers and laborers, and so forth—and in some businesses this is a convenient way to proceed. In most cases, however, the growth prospects, profitability, and investment and financing needs of the firm are more readily framed in terms of accrual-based sales, operating earnings, assets, and liabilities. These amounts can then be converted to cash flow measures by adjusting for the effects of non-cash expenses and expenditures for working capital and plant.

The most practical approach to forecasting a company's financial statements is to focus on projecting "condensed" financial statements, as used in the ratio analysis in Chapter 5, rather than attempting to project detailed financial statements that the company reports. There are several reasons for this recommendation. First, this approach involves making a relatively small set of assumptions about the future of the firm, so the analyst will have more ability to think about each of the assumptions carefully. A detailed line-item forecast is likely to be very tedious, and an analyst may not have a good basis to make all the assumptions necessary for such forecasts. Further, for most purposes condensed financial statements are all that are needed for analysis and decision making. We therefore approach the task of financial forecasting with this framework.

Recall that the condensed income statement that we used in Chapter 5 consists of the following elements: sales, net operating profits after tax (NOPAT), net interest expense after tax, taxes, and net income. The condensed balance sheet consists of: net operating working capital, net long-term assets, net debt, and equity. Also recall that we start with a balance sheet at the beginning of the forecasting period. Assumptions about how we use the beginning balance sheet and run the firm's operations will lead to the income statement for the forecasting period; assumptions about investment in working capital and long-term assets, and how we finance these assets, results in a balance sheet at the end of the forecasting period.

To forecast the condensed income statement, one needs to begin with an assumption about next period's sales. Beyond that, assumptions about NOPAT margin, interest rate on beginning debt, and tax rate are all that are needed to prepare the condensed income statement for the period.

To forecast the condensed balance sheet for the end of the period (or the equivalent, the beginning of the next period), we need to make the following additional assumptions: the ratio of operating working capital to the sales to estimate the level of working capital needed to support those sales, the ratio of net operating long-term assets to the following year's sales to calculate the expected level of net operating long-term assets, and the ratio of net debt to capital to estimate the levels of debt and equity needed to finance the estimated amount of assets in the balance sheet.

Once we have the condensed income statement and balance sheet, it is relatively straightforward to compute the condensed cash flow statement, including cash flow from operations before working capital investments, cash flow from operations after working capital investments, free cash flow available to debt and equity, and free cash flow available to equity.

Below we discuss how best to make the necessary assumptions to forecast the condensed income statement, balance sheet, and cash flow statements.

Getting Started: Points of Departure

Every forecast has, at least implicitly, an initial "benchmark" or point of departure—some notion of how a particular amount, such as sales or earnings, would be expected to behave in the absence of detailed information. For example, in beginning to contemplate fiscal 2002 profitability for TJX, one must start somewhere. A possibility is to begin with the 2001 performance. Another starting point might be 2001 performance adjusted for recent trends. A third possibility that might seem reasonable—but one that generally turns out not to be very useful—is the average performance over several prior years.

By the time one has completed a business strategy analysis, an accounting analysis, and a detailed financial analysis, the resulting forecast might differ significantly from the original point of departure. Nevertheless, simply for purposes of having a starting point that can help anchor the detailed analysis, it is useful to know how certain key financial statistics behave "on average."

In the case of some key statistics, such as earnings, a point of departure based only on prior behavior of the number is more powerful than one might expect. Research demonstrates that some such benchmarks for earnings are not much less accurate than the forecasts of professional security analysts, who have access to a rich information set. (We return to this point in more detail below.) Thus the benchmark is often not only a good starting point but also close to the amount forecast after detailed analysis. Large departures from the benchmark could be justified only in cases where the firm's situation is demonstrably unusual.

Reasonable points of departure for forecasts of key accounting numbers can be based on the evidence summarized below. Such evidence may also be useful for checking the reasonableness of a completed forecast.

The Behavior of Sales Growth

Sales growth rates tend to be "mean-reverting": firms with above-average or below-average rates of sales growth tend to revert over time to a "normal" level (historically in the range of 7 to 9 percent for U.S. firms) within three to ten years. Figure 6-1 documents this effect for 1984 through 2001 for all the publicly traded U.S. firms covered by the COMPSTAT database. All firms are ranked in terms of their sales growth in 1984 (year 1) and formed into five portfolios based on the relative ranking of their sales growth in that year. Firms in portfolio 1 have the top 20 percent of rankings in terms of their sales growth in 1984, and those in portfolio 2 fall into the next 20 percent; those in portfolio 5 have the bottom 20 percent sales growth ranks. The sales growth rates of firms in each of these five portfolios are traced from 1984 through the subsequent nine years (years 2 to 10). The same experiment is repeated with 1988 and then 1992 as the base year (year 1). The results are averaged over the three experiments and the resulting sales growth rates of each of the five portfolios for years 1 through 10 plotted in Figure 6-1.

The figure shows that the group of firms with the highest growth initially—sales growth rates of just over 60 percent—experience a decline to about 13 percent growth rate within two years and are never above 16 percent in the next seven years. Those with the lowest initial sales growth rates, minus 17 percent, experience an increase to about a 6 percent growth rate by year 5, and average about 8 percent annual growth in years 6 through 10. One explanation for the pattern of sales growth seen in Figure 6-1 is that as industries and companies mature, their growth rate slows down due to demand saturation and intra-industry competition. Therefore, even when a firm is growing rapidly at present, it is generally unrealistic to extrapolate the current high growth indefinitely. Of course, how quickly a firm's growth rate reverts to the average depends on the characteristics of its industry and its own competitive position within an industry.

| Figure 6-1 | Behavior of Sales Growth for U.S. Firms over Time, 1984–2001 |

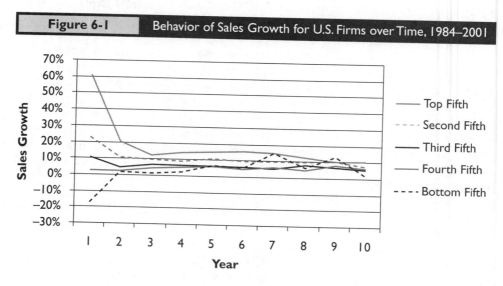

The Behavior of Earnings

Earnings have been shown on average to follow a process that can be approximated by a "random walk" or "random walk with drift." Thus the prior year's earnings is a good starting point in considering future earnings potential. As will be explained, it is reasonable to adjust this simple benchmark for the earnings changes of the most recent quarter (that is, changes relative to the comparable quarter of the prior year after controlling for the long-run trend in the series). Even a simple random walk forecast—one that predicts next year's earnings will be equal to last year's earnings—is surprisingly useful. One study documents that professional analysts' year-ahead forecasts are only 22 percent more accurate, on average, than a simple random walk forecast.[1] Thus a final earnings forecast will *usually* not differ dramatically from a random walk benchmark.

The implication of the evidence is that, in beginning to contemplate future earnings possibilities, a useful number to start with is last year's earnings; the average level of earnings over several prior years is not useful. Long-term trends in earnings tend to be sustained on average, and so they are also worthy of consideration. If quarterly data are also included, then some consideration should usually be given to any departures from the long-run trend that occurred in the most recent quarter. For most firms, these most recent changes tend to be partially repeated in subsequent quarters.[2]

The Behavior of Returns on Equity

Given that prior earnings serves as a useful benchmark for future earnings, one might expect the same to be true of rates of return on investment, like ROE. That, however, is not the case for two reasons. First, even though the *average* firm tends to sustain the current earnings level, this is not true of firms with unusual levels of ROE. Firms with abnormally high (low) ROE tend to experience earnings declines (increases).[3]

Second, firms with higher ROEs tend to expand their investment bases more quickly than others, which causes the denominator of the ROE to increase. Of course if firms could earn returns on the new investments that match the returns on the old ones, then the level of ROE would be maintained. However, firms have difficulty pulling that off. Firms with higher ROEs tend to find that, as time goes by, their earnings growth does not keep pace with growth in their investment base, and ROE ultimately falls.

The resulting behavior of ROE and other measures of return on investment is characterized as "mean-reverting": firms with above-average or below-average rates of return tend to revert over time to a "normal" level (for ROE, historically in the range of 10 to 15 percent for U.S. firms) within no more than ten years.[4] Figure 6-2 documents this effect for U.S. firms from 1984 through 2001. All firms are ranked in terms of their ROE in 1984 (year 1) and formed into five portfolios. Firms in portfolio 1 have the top 20 percent ROE rankings in 1984, those in portfolio 2 fall into the next 20 percent, and those in portfolio 5 have the bottom 20 percent. The average ROE of firms in each of these five portfolios is then traced through nine subsequent years (years 2 to 10). The same experiment is repeated with 1988 and 1992 as the base year (year 1), and the subsequent years as years +2 to +10. Figure 6-2 plots the average ROE of each of the five portfolios in years 1 to 10 averaged across these three experiments.

Though the five portfolios start out in year 1 with a wide range of ROEs (−49 percent to +29 percent), by year 10 the pattern of mean-reversion is clear. The most profitable group of firms initially—with average ROEs of 29 percent—experience a decline to 19.8 percent within three years. By year 10 this group of firms has an ROE of 16 percent. Those with the lowest initial ROEs (−49 percent) experience a dramatic increase in ROE and then level off at 7.5 percent in year 10.

| Figure 6-2 | Behavior of ROE for U.S. Firms over Time, 1984–2001 |

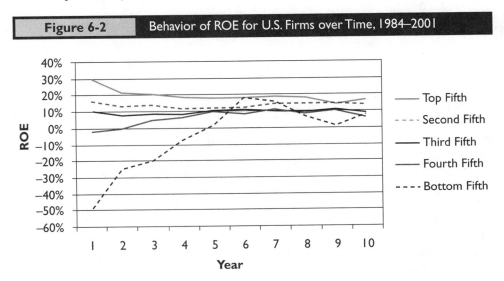

The pattern in Figure 6-2 is not a coincidence; it is exactly what the economics of competition would predict. The tendency of high ROEs to fall is a reflection of high profitability attracting competition; the tendency of low ROEs to rise reflects the mobility of capital away from unproductive ventures toward more profitable ones.

Despite the general tendencies documented in Figure 6-2, there are some firms whose ROEs may remain above or below normal levels for long periods of time. In some cases the phenomenon reflects the strength of a sustainable competitive advantage (e.g., Wal-Mart), but in other cases it is purely an artifact of conservative accounting methods. A good example of the latter phenomenon in the U.S. is pharmaceutical firms, whose major economic asset, the intangible value of research and development, is not recorded on the balance sheet and is therefore excluded from the denominator of ROE. For those firms, one could reasonably expect high ROEs—in excess of 20 percent—over the long run, even in the face of strong competitive forces.

The Behavior of Components of ROE

The behavior of rates of return on equity can be analyzed further by looking at the behavior of its key components. Recall from Chapter 5 that ROEs and profit margins are linked as follows:

$$\begin{aligned} \text{ROE} \quad &= \quad \text{Operating ROA} + (\text{Operating ROA} - \text{Net interest rate after tax}) \\ &\quad \times \text{Net financial leverage} \\ &= \quad \text{NOPAT margin} \times \text{Operating asset turnover} + \text{Spread} \\ &\quad \times \text{Net financial leverage} \end{aligned}$$

The time-series behavior of the components of ROE for U.S. companies for 1984 through 2001 are shown in a series of figures in the appendix to this chapter. Some major conclusions can be drawn from these figures: (1) Operating asset turnover tends to be rather stable, in part because it is so much a function of the technology of the industry. The only exception to this is the set of firms with very high asset turnover, which tends to decline somewhat over time before stabilizing. (2) Net financial leverage also tends to be stable, simply because management policies on capital structure aren't often changed. (3) NOPAT margin and spread stand out as the most variable component of ROE; if the forces of competition drive abnormal ROEs toward more normal levels, the change is most likely to arrive in the form of changes in profit margins and the spread. The change in spread is itself driven by changes in NOPAT margin, since the cost of borrowing is likely to remain stable if leverage remains stable.

To summarize, profit margins, like ROEs, tend to be driven by competition to "normal" levels over time. What constitutes normal varies widely according to the technology employed within an industry and the corporate strategy pursued by the firm, both of which influence turnover and leverage.[5] In a fully competitive equilibrium, profit margins should remain high for firms that must operate with a low turnover, and vice versa.

The above discussion of rates of return and margins implies that a reasonable point of departure for forecasting such a statistic should consider more than just the most recent observation. One should also consider whether that rate or margin is above or below a normal level. If so, then absent detailed information to the contrary, one would expect some movement over time to that norm. Of course this central tendency might be overcome in some cases—for example, where the firm has erected barriers to competition that can protect margins, even for extended periods. The lesson from the evidence, however, is that such cases are unusual.

In contrast to rates of return and margins, it is reasonable to assume that asset turnover, financial leverage, and net interest rate remain relatively constant over time. Unless there is an explicit change in technology or financial policy being contemplated for future periods, a reasonable point of departure for assumptions for these variables is the current period level. The only exceptions to this appear to be firms with either very high asset turns that experience some decline in this ratio before stabilizing, or those firms with very low (usually negative) net debt to capital that appear to increase leverage before stabilizing.

As we proceed with the steps involved in producing a detailed forecast, the reader will note that we draw on the above knowledge of the behavior of accounting numbers to some extent. However, it is important to keep in mind that a knowledge of *average* behavior will not fit all firms well. The art of financial statements analysis requires not only knowing what the "normal" patterns are but also having expertise in identifying those firms that will *not* follow the norm.

MAKING FORECASTS

Here we summarize steps that could be followed in producing a comprehensive forecast. The discussion assumes that the firm being analyzed is among the vast majority for which the forecast would reasonably be anchored by a sales forecast. We use the example of TJX, the discount retailer discussed in Chapter 5, to illustrate the mechanics of forecasting. In Chapter 5 we analyzed the performance of TJX during the fiscal year ending January 31, 2002 (fiscal 2001). We begin our forecasting exercise using this as the point of departure.

Table 6-1 shows the forecasting assumptions for fiscal years 2002 to 2011. Table 6-2 shows the forecasted income statements for these same fiscal years, and beginning of the year balance sheets for fiscal years 2003 to 2011 (that for fiscal 2002 is the actual balance sheet reported by the company for the year ending January 31, 2002). We discuss below the logic behind the forecasting assumptions.

One Year Ahead Forecasts

As mentioned above, we have the actual balance sheet for the beginning of the year in fiscal 2002, so there is no need to forecast this. In general, making a short-term income statement forecast, such as a one year ahead forecast, is often a straightforward extrapolation of recent performance. This is a particularly valid approach for an established company such as TJX for several reasons. First, the company is unlikely to effect major changes in its operating and financing policies in the short term, unless it is in the middle of a restructuring program. Second, the beginning of the year balance sheet for any given year will put constraints on operating activities during that fiscal year. For example, inventories at the beginning of the year will determine to some extent the sales activities during the year; stores in operation at the beginning of the year also determine to some extent the level of sales achievable during the year. To put it another way, since our discussion above shows that asset turns for a company do not usually change significantly over time, sales in any period are to some extent constrained by the beginning of the period assets in place in the company's balance sheet. Of course it is possible to achieve some flexibility in this regard if there are explicit plans to either expand assets significantly during the year (for example, through new store openings in the case of TJX), or through a change in the asset utilization (for example, a change in the same-store sales in the case of TJX).

With this framework in mind, our assumptions for TJX for fiscal 2002 are the following: We assume that sales will grow at 12 percent. This sales growth rate is essentially the same as the actual growth rate achieved in fiscal year 2001, and it is based on the assumption that the company built up its assets during 2001 with an expectation of achieving a similar

Table 6-1 Forecasting Assumptions for TJX

For fiscal year	2002	2003	2004	2005	2006	2007	2008	2009	2010	2011	2012
Sales growth	12%	11.5%	11%	10.5%	10%	9.5%	9%	8.5%	8%	8%	8%
NOPAT margin	4.5%	4%	3.5%	3%	2.5%	2%	1.9%	1.8%	1.7%	1.6%	1.6%
After-tax net interest rate	7%	7%	7%	7%	7%	7%	7%	7%	7%	7%	7%
Beginning net working capital to sales ratio	2.5%	2.5%	2.5%	2.5%	2.5%	2.5%	2.5%	2.5%	2.5%	2.5%	2.5%
Beginning net long term assets to sales ratio	10.5%	10.5%	10.5%	10.5%	10.5%	10.5%	10.5%	10.5%	10.5%	10.5%	10.5%
Beginning net debt to capital ratio	13.6%	13.6%	13.6%	13.6%	13.6%	13.6%	13.6%	13.6%	13.6%	13.6%	13.6%

Note: In addition to these assumptions, we also assume that sales will continue to grow at 8 percent in 2012 and all the balance sheet ratios remain constant, to compute the beginning balance sheet for 2012 and cash flows for 2011.

growth rate as in the previous year. This growth rate leads to an expected sales level in fiscal 2002 of $11.994 billion. The implied ratio of beginning net working capital to sales is 2.5 percent, and beginning long-term assets to sales ratio is 10.5 percent, or a total of net operating assets to sales ratio of 13 percent. This is in line with the company's net operating assets to sales ratios for the two previous years, which were 12.2 percent and 13.5 percent, respectively.

Notice that a beginning of year balance sheet at the start of the forecasting horizon is a given. Therefore, we are starting with a given level of assets to work with. So we can either make an assumption about sales growth rate and check the implied ratio of beginning net assets to sales for reasonableness, or make an assumption of the beginning net assets to sales ratio for the year, and check for the reasonableness of the implied sales growth rate. In other words, we are free to make only one of the two assumptions—either sales growth or net asset turns. In subsequent years in the forecast horizon, we relax this constraint because we can build up both a desired beginning balance sheet and income statement for the following years.

Another assumption we make for TJX for fiscal 2002 is that its NOPAT margin will be 4.5 percent, slightly lower than the extraordinarily high margin the company achieved in the previous two years (5.8 percent and 4.8 percent, respectively). Notice that the time-series trends in NOPAT margins discussed earlier suggest that companies with very high margins tend to experience a gradual decline in margins over time. Our assumption for fiscal 2002 begins to reflect this trend.

The third assumption we make to forecast TJX's income statement for fiscal 2002 relates to the after-tax cost of debt. We know the company's beginning level of debt and its beginning debt to capital ratio for fiscal 2002, based on the company's actual balance sheet at that time. These ratios are somewhat similar to the ratios at the beginning of the previous fiscal year. Therefore, it is reasonable to assume that the company's interest rate on its debt will be somewhat similar to the effective interest during the previous year, which was about 10.8 percent. With an assumed tax rate of 35 percent, the after-tax interest rate is 7 percent.

These assumptions together lead to a projected $524.9 million net income in fiscal year 2002 compared with a reported net income of $500.4 million in fiscal 2001.

Forecasts for Years Two to Ten

In making longer-term forecasts, such as for years two to ten, we can rely on the time-series behavior of various performance ratios we discussed earlier in the chapter. We will assume that the relatively high sales growth rate of TJX will decline from 12 percent in 2002 gradually over time, by half a percentage point per year, reaching a level of 8 percent in year 2011. Beyond 2011, we assume that the sales growth rate will stabilize at 8 percent per year.

We assume a similar pattern of declining NOPAT margins over time, again consistent with the time-series trend we documented earlier in the chapter for firms with initially high NOPAT. While TJX clearly has a great deal of competitive advantage over its rivals, it is prudent to assume, given the history of U.S. firms, that this advantage will decline over time. So we assume that the company's NOPAT margin will decline by half a percentage point per year, from 4.5 percent in 2002 to 2.0 percent in 2007. Thereafter, we assume that the margin decline will be slower, by 0.1 percent per year, to reach a level of 1.6 percent in 2010. At that point we will assume that the NOPAT margin will have reached steady state and will remain at that level in subsequent years.

Since asset turns generally show a flat time series trend, and because TJX is known for its excellent asset utilization skills (inventory management and sales-per-store performance), we will assume that the ratio of beginning operating working capital to sales and beginning long-term assets to sales will remain unchanged during the entire forecasting period. Thus we assume that the beginning operating working capital to sales ratio will remain at 2.5 percent from 2003 to 2011 and beyond; we also assume that the beginning long-term assets to sales ratio will remain at 10.5 percent throughout this period.

We make a similar assumption for the company's capital structure policy. The company has a relatively conservative financing policy with 13.6 percent debt to net capital ratio at the beginning of 2002. We assume that it will remain at this level during the entire forecasting period. This assumption of a constant capital structure policy is consistent with the general pattern observed in historical data discussed earlier in the chapter. Since we hold the capital structure constant, we can assume that the company's borrowing rate also remains unchanged, at 10.8 percent before tax, or 7 percent after tax.

With these assumptions it is a straightforward task to derive the forecasted income statements for fiscal years 2002 to 2011, and beginning balance sheets for years 2003 to 2011, as shown in Table 6-2. Under these forecasts TJX's sales will grow to 27.3 billion dollars by 2011. By the beginning of 2011, TJX will have a net asset base of $3.54 billion. Its return on beginning equity will be at 34.5 percent in 2002. It will gradually decline from this high level to 13.1 percent in 2011, a level somewhat above its cost of equity.

Cash Flow Forecasts

Once we have forecasted income statements and balance sheets, deriving cash flows for the years 2002 to 2011 is straightforward. Note that we need to forecast the beginning balance sheet for 2012 to compute the cash flows for 2011. This balance sheet is not shown in Table 6-2. For the purpose of illustration, we assume that all the sales growth and all the balance sheet ratios remain the same in 2012 as in 2011. Based on this we project a beginning balance sheet for 2012 and compute the cash flows for 2011. Cash flow to capital is equal to NOPAT minus increases in net working capital and net long-term assets. Cash flow to equity is cash flow to capital minus net interest after tax plus increase in net debt. These two sets of forecasted cash flows are shown in Table 6-2.

Table 6-2 Forecasted Financial Statements for TJX

Fiscal Year	2002	2003	2004	2005	2006	2007	2008	2009	2010	2011	2012
Beginning Balance Sheet ($mm)											
Beg. Net Working Capital	297.4	334.3	371.1	410.1	451.1	493.9	538.4	584.2	630.9	681.4	735.9
+ Beg. Net Long-Term Assets	1,254.2	1,404.2	1,558.7	1,722.3	1,894.6	2,074.5	2,261.3	2,453.5	2,649.7	2,861.7	3,090.7
= **Net Operating Assets**	**1,551.5**	**1,738.5**	**1,929.8**	**2,132.4**	**2,345.6**	**2,568.5**	**2,799.6**	**3,037.6**	**3,280.6**	**3,543.1**	**3,826.5**
Net Debt	210.8	236.3	262.2	289.8	318.8	349.0	380.5	412.8	445.8	481.5	520.0
+ Preferred Stock	0.0	0.0	0.0	0.0	0.0	0.0	0.0	0.0	0.0	0.0	0.0
+ Shareholders' Equity	1,340.7	1,502.3	1,667.5	1,842.6	2,026.9	2,219.4	2,419.2	2,624.8	2,834.8	3,061.6	3,306.5
= **Net Capital**	**1,551.5**	**1,738.5**	**1,929.8**	**2,132.4**	**2,345.6**	**2,568.5**	**2,799.6**	**3,037.6**	**3,280.6**	**3,543.1**	**3,826.5**
Income Statement ($mm)											
Sales	11,994.1	13,373.4	14,844.5	16,403.1	18,043.5	19,757.6	21,535.8	23,366.3	25,235.6	27,254.5	29,434.8
Net Operating Profits After Tax	539.7	534.9	519.6	492.1	451.1	395.2	409.2	420.6	429.0	436.1	471.0
− Net Interest Expense After Tax	14.8	16.6	18.4	20.3	22.4	24.5	26.7	29.0	31.3	33.8	36.5
= **Net Income**	**524.9**	**518.4**	**501.1**	**471.8**	**428.7**	**370.6**	**382.5**	**391.6**	**397.7**	**402.3**	**434.5**
Operating ROA	34.8%	30.8%	26.9%	23.1%	19.2%	15.4%	14.6%	13.8%	13.1%	12.3%	12.3%
ROE	39.2%	34.5%	30.1%	25.6%	21.2%	16.7%	15.8%	14.9%	14.0%	13.1%	13.1%
BV of Assets Growth Rate	7.4%	12.1%	11.0%	10.5%	10.0%	9.5%	9.0%	8.5%	8.0%	8.0%	8.0%
BV of Equity Growth Rate	10.0%	12.1%	11.0%	10.5%	10.0%	9.5%	9.0%	8.5%	8.0%	8.0%	8.0%
Net Operating Asset Turnover	7.7	7.7	7.7	7.7	7.7	7.7	7.7	7.7	7.7	7.7	7.7
Free Cash Flow to Capital	352,737	343,696	316,929	278,853	228,250	163,988	171,209	177,584	166,555	152,625	164,835
Free Cash Flow to Equity	312,524	301,122	270,984	229,532	175,590	108,071	112,162	115,582	99,593	80,306	86,730

Note: We do not show the beginning balance sheet forecasted for 2012 here, but it is implicit in the calculation of cash flows for 2011. As stated in Table 6-1, we assume that sales continue to grow in 2012 and that all the balance sheet ratios continue to be the same, to derive the beginning balance sheet for 2012.

SENSITIVITY ANALYSIS

The projections discussed thus far represent nothing more than a "best guess." Managers and analysts are typically interested in a broader range of possibilities. For example, in considering the likelihood that short-term financing will be necessary, it would be wise to produce projections based on a more pessimistic view of profit margins and asset turnover. Alternatively, an analyst estimating the value of TJX should consider the sensitivity of the estimate to the key assumptions about sales growth, profit margins, and asset utilization. What if TJX is able to retain its competitive advantage better than assumed in the above forecasts? What if TJX is unable to maintain its high levels of asset utilization assumed?

There is no limit to the number of possible scenarios that can be considered. One systematic approach to sensitivity analysis is to start with the key assumptions underlying a set of forecasts and then examine the sensitivity to the assumptions with greatest uncertainty in a given situation. For example, if a company has experienced a variable pattern of gross margins in the past, it is important to make projections using a range of margins. Alternatively, if a company has announced a significant change in its expansion strategy, asset utilization assumptions might be more uncertain. In determining where to invest one's time in performing sensitivity analysis, it is therefore important to consider historical patterns of performance, changes in industry conditions, and changes in a company's competitive strategy.

Seasonality and Interim Forecasts

Thus far we have concerned ourselves with annual forecasts. However, especially for security analysts in the U.S., forecasting is very much a quarterly game. Forecasting quarter by quarter raises a new set of questions. How important is seasonality? What is a useful point of departure—the most recent quarter's performance? The comparable quarter of the prior year? Some combination of the two? How should quarterly data be used in producing an annual forecast? Does the item-by-item approach to forecasting used for annual data apply equally well to quarterly data? Full consideration of these questions lies outside the scope of this chapter, but we can begin to answer some of them.

Seasonality is a more important phenomenon in sales and earning behavior than one might guess. It is present for more than just the retail sector firms that benefit from holiday sales. Seasonality also results from weather-related phenomena (e.g., for electric and gas utilities, construction firms, and motorcycle manufacturers), new product introduction patterns (e.g., for the automobile industry), and other factors. Analysis of the time series behavior of earnings for U.S. firms suggests that at least some seasonality is present in nearly every major industry.

The implication for forecasting is that one cannot focus only on performance of the most recent quarter as a point of departure. In fact the evidence suggests that, in forecasting earnings, if one had to choose only one quarter's performance as a point of departure, it would be the comparable quarter of the prior year, not the most recent quarter. Note how this finding is consistent with the reports of analysts or the financial press; when they discuss a quarterly earnings announcement, it is nearly always evaluated relative to the performance of the comparable quarter of the prior year, not the most recent quarter.

Research has produced models that forecast sales, earnings, or EPS based solely on prior quarters' observations. Such models are not used by many analysts, since analysts have access to much more information than such simple models contain. However, the models are useful for helping those unfamiliar with the behavior earnings data to understand how it tends to evolve through time. Such an understanding can provide useful general background, a point of departure in forecasting that can be adjusted to reflect details not revealed in the history of earnings, or a "reasonableness" check on a detailed forecast.

Using Q_t to denote earnings (or EPS) for quarter t, and $E(Q_t)$ as its expected value, one model of the earnings process that fits well across a variety of industries is the so-called Foster model[7]:

$$E(Q_t) \ = \ Q_{t-4} + \delta + \phi(Q_{t-1} - Q_{t-5})$$

Foster shows that a model of the same form also works well with sales data.

The form of the Foster model confirms the importance of seasonality because it shows that the starting point for a forecast for quarter t is the earnings four quarters ago, Q_{t-4}. It states that, when constrained to using only prior earnings data, a reasonable forecast of earnings for quarter t includes the following elements:

the earnings of the comparable quarter of the prior year (Q_{t-4});

a long-run trend in year-to-year quarterly earnings increases (δ); and

a fraction (ϕ) of the year-to-year increase in quarterly earnings experienced most recently ($Q_{t-1} - Q_{t-5}$).

The parameters δ and ϕ can easily be estimated for a given firm with a simple linear regression model available in most spreadsheet software.[8] For most firms the parameter ϕ tends to be in the range of .25 to .50, indicating that 25 to 50 percent of an increase in quarterly earnings tends to persist in the form of another increase in the subsequent quarter. The parameter δ reflects in part the average year-to-year change in quarterly earnings over past years, and it varies considerably from firm to firm.

Research indicates that the Foster model produces one-quarter-ahead forecasts that are off, on average, by $.30 to $.35 per share. Such a degree of accuracy stacks up surprisingly well with that of security analysts, who obviously have access to much information ignored in the model. As one would expect, most of the evidence supports analysts' being more accurate, but the models are good enough to be "in the ball park" in most circumstances. While it would certainly be unwise to rely completely on such a naïve model, an understanding of the typical earnings behavior reflected by the model is useful.

SUMMARY

Forecasting represents the first step of prospective analysis and serves to summarize the forward-looking view that emanates from business strategy analysis, accounting analysis, and financial analysis. Although not every financial statement analysis is accompanied by such an explicit summarization of a view of the future, forecasting is still a key tool for managers, consultants, security analysts, investment bankers, commercial bankers and other credit analysts, and others.

The best approach to forecasting future performance is to do it comprehensively—producing not only an earnings forecast but a forecast of cash flows and the balance sheet as well. Such a comprehensive approach provides a guard against internal inconsistencies and unrealistic implicit assumptions. The approach described here involves line-by-line analysis, so as to recognize that different items on the income statement and balance sheet are influenced by different drivers. Nevertheless, it remains the case that a few key projections—such as sales growth and profit margin—usually drive most of the projected numbers.

The forecasting process should be embedded in an understanding of how various financial statistics tend to behave on average, and what might cause a firm to deviate from that average. Absent detailed information to the contrary, one would expect sales and earnings numbers to persist at their current levels, adjusted for overall trends of recent years. However, rates of return on investment (ROEs) tend, over several years, to move from abnormal to normal levels—close to the cost of equity capital—as the forces of competition come into play. Profit margins also tend to shift to normal levels, but for this statistic "normal" varies widely across firms and industries, depending on the levels of asset turnover and leverage. Some firms are capable of creating barriers to entry that enable them to fight these tendencies toward normal returns, even for many years, but such firms are the unusual cases.

For some purposes, including short-term planning and security analysis, forecasts for quarterly periods are desirable. One important feature of quarterly data is seasonality; at least some seasonality exists in the sales and earnings data of nearly every industry. An understanding of a firm's within-year peaks and valleys is a necessary ingredient of a good forecast of performance on a quarterly basis.

There are a variety of contexts (including but not limited to security analysis) where the forecast is usefully summarized in the form of an estimate of the firm's value—an estimate that, after all, can be viewed as the best attempt to reflect in a single summary statistic the manager's or analyst's view of the firm's prospects. That process of converting a forecast into a value estimate is labeled valuation. It is to that topic that we turn in the following chapter.

DISCUSSION QUESTIONS

1. Merck is one of the largest pharmaceutical firms in the world, and over an extended period of time in the recent past, it consistently earned higher ROEs than the pharmaceutical industry as a whole. As a pharmaceutical analyst, what factors would you consider to be important in making projections of future ROEs for Merck? In particular, what factors would lead you to expect Merck to continue to be a superior performer in its industry, and what factors would lead you to expect Merck's future performance to revert to that of the industry as a whole?

2. John Right, an analyst with Stock Pickers Inc., claims, "It is not worth my time to develop detailed forecasts of sales growth, profit margins, etcetera, to make earnings projections. I can be almost as accurate, at virtually no cost, using the random walk model to forecast earnings." What is the random walk model? Do you agree or disagree with John Right's forecast strategy? Why or why not?

3. Which of the following types of businesses do you expect to show a high degree of seasonality in quarterly earnings? Explain why.
   - a supermarket
   - a pharmaceutical company
   - a software company
   - an auto manufacturer
   - a clothing retailer

4. What factors are likely to drive a firm's outlays for new capital (such as plant, property, and equipment) and for working capital (such as receivables and inventory)? What ratios would you use to help generate forecasts of these outlays?

5. How would the following events (reported this year) affect your forecasts of a firm's future net income?
   - an asset write-down
   - a merger or acquisition
   - the sale of a major division
   - the initiation of dividend payments

6. Consider the following two earnings forecasting models:

   Model 1: $E_t(EPS_{t+1}) = EPS_t$

   Model 2: $E_t(EPS_{t+1}) = \frac{1}{5}\sum_{t=1}^{5} EPS_t$

   $E_t(EPS)$ is the expected forecast of earnings per share for year $t+1$, given information available at t. Model 1 is usually called a random walk model for earnings, whereas Model 2 is called a mean-reverting model. The earnings per share for Ford Motor Company for the period 1990 to 1994 are as follows:

Year	1	2	3	4	5
EPS	$0.93	$(2.40)	$(0.73)	$2.27	$4.97

   a. What would be the year 6 forecast for earnings per share for each model?
   b. Actual earnings per share for Ford in 6 were $3.58. Given this information, what would be the year 7 forecast for earnings per share for each model? Why do the two

models generate quite different forecasts? Which do you think would better describe earnings per share patterns? Why?

7. Joe Fatcat, an investment banker, states, "It is not worth my while to worry about detailed long-term forecasts. Instead, I use the following approach when forecasting cash flows beyond three years. I assume that sales grow at the rate of inflation, capital expenditures are equal to depreciation, and that net profit margins and working capital to sales ratios stay constant." What pattern of return on equity is implied by these assumptions? Is this reasonable?

NOTES

1. See Patricia O'Brien, "Analysts' Forecasts as Earnings Expectations," *Journal of Accounting and Economics* (January 1988): 53–83.

2. See George Foster, "Quarterly Accounting Data: Time Series Properties and Predictive Ability Results," *The Accounting Review* (January 1977): 1–21.

3. See Robert Freeman, James Ohlson, and Stephen Penman, "Book Rate-of-Return and Prediction of Earnings Changes: An Empirical Investigation," *Journal of Accounting Research* (Autumn 1982): 639–53.

4. See Stephen H. Penman, "An Evaluation of Accounting Rate-of-Return," *Journal of Accounting, Auditing, and Finance* (Spring 1991): 233–56; Eugene Fama and Kenneth French, "Size and Book-to-Market Factors in Earnings and Returns," *Journal of Finance* (March 1995): 131–56; and Victor Bernard, "Accounting-Based Valuation Methods: Evidence on the Market-to-Book Anomaly and Implications for Financial Statements Analysis," University of Michigan, working paper (1994). Ignoring the effects of accounting artifacts, ROEs should be driven in a competitive equilibrium to a level approximating the cost of equity capital.

5. A "normal" profit margin is that which, when multiplied by the turnover achievable within an industry and with a viable corporate strategy, yields a return on investment that just covers the cost of capital. However, as mentioned above, accounting artifacts can cause returns on investment to deviate from the cost of capital for long periods, even in a competitive equilibrium.

6. See Foster, op. cit. A somewhat more accurate model is furnished by Brown and Rozeff, but it requires interactive statistical techniques for estimation—Lawrence D. Brown and Michael Rozeff, "Univariate Time Series Models of Quarterly Accounting Earnings per Share," *Journal of Accounting Research* (Spring 1979): 179–89.

7. To estimate the model, we write in terms of realized earnings (as opposed to expected earnings) and move Q_{t-4} to the left-hand side:

$$Q_t - Q_{t-4} = \delta + \phi(Q_{t-1} - Q_{t-5}) + e_t$$

We now have a regression where $(Q_t - Q_{t-4})$ is the dependent variable, and its lagged value— $(Q_{t-1} - Q_{t-5})$—is the independent variable. Thus, to estimate the equation, prior earnings data must first be expressed in terms of year-to-year changes; the change for one quarter is then regressed against the change for the most recent quarter. The intercept provides an estimate of δ, and the slope is an estimate of ϕ. The equation is typically estimated using 24 to 40 quarters of prior earnings data.

8. See O'Brien, op. cit.

APPENDIX: THE BEHAVIOR OF COMPONENTS OF ROE

In Figure 6-2 we show that ROEs tend to be mean-reverting. In this appendix we show the behavior of the key components of ROE—operating ROA, operating margin, operating asset turnover, spread, and net financial leverage. These ratios are computed using the same portfolio approach described in the chapter, based on the data for all U.S. firms for the time period 1984 through 2001.

| **Figure A-1** | Behavior of Operating ROA for U.S. Firms, 1984–2001 |

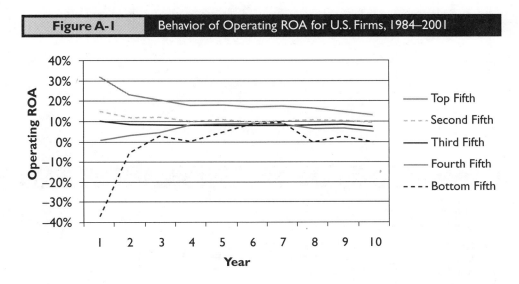

| **Figure A-2** | Behavior of NOPAT Margin for U.S. Firms, 1984–2001 |

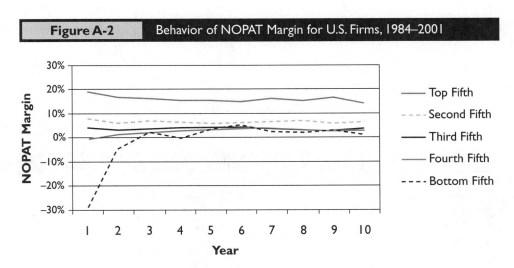

| Figure A-3 | Behavior of Operating Asset Turnover for U.S. Firms, 1984–2001 |

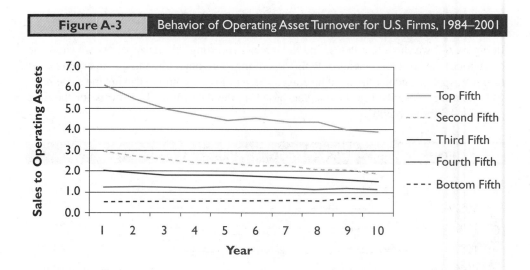

| Figure A-4 | Behavior of Spread for U.S. Firms, 1984–2001 |

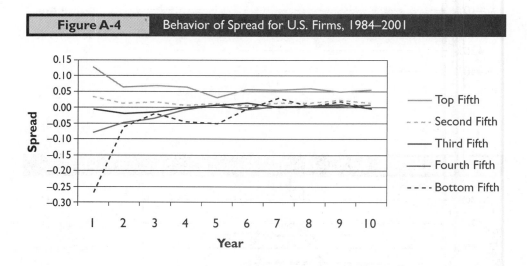

| Figure A-5 | Behavior of Net Financial Leverage for U.S. Firms, 1984–2001 |

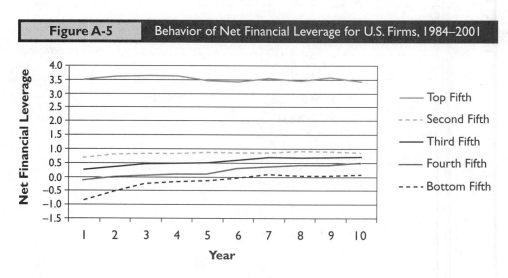

Krispy Kreme Doughnuts

Krispy Kreme is a one of a kind phenomenon, in our view, boasting a combination of a powerful consumer brand, a multi-channel distribution channel and a business model that produces best-in-class financial returns. . . . Krispy Kreme is still an attractive growth story, in our view, and represents a well established brand still early in its growth trajectory.

> CIBC World Markets analysts John Glass and Jeffrey Farmer, June 3, 2002

Krispy Kreme Doughnuts completed its initial public offering on April 5, 2000. By the end of the first day of trading, its stock had soared 76 percent from the $5.50 offering price to $9.25 (adjusted for two 2-for-1 stock splits). In the following two years, Krispy Kreme's stock price reached a high of $45.66 (in late December 2001) and was trading at around $37 in late May 2002. (Exhibit 1 shows Krispy Kreme's stock performance relative to the S&P 500 from the IPO date to May 30, 2002.)

During the two years following the IPO, Krispy Kreme reported strong growth and financial performance. For example, for the year ended February 3, 2002, revenue growth was 31 percent, earnings growth was 80 percent, and the company's return on beginning equity was 21 percent. (Financial statements for Krispy Kreme for the year ended February 3, 2002, and the first quarter of 2003 are shown in Exhibit 2.)

A key challenge for CIBC World Markets' John Glass and Jeffrey Farmer was to forecast the company's financial performance for the next few years. Would Krispy Kreme be able to sustain its recent revenue and earnings growth? What working capital and other resources would the company require? How would it finance its growth? To answer these questions, Glass and Farmer would have to understand Krispy Kreme's growth strategy, the basis for its recent financial performance, and the nature of competition in the doughnut industry.

KRISPY KREME'S BUSINESS[1]

In 1937 Vernon Rudolph purchased a secret recipe for yeast-raised doughnuts from a French chef from New Orleans, rented a building in Winston-Salem, North Carolina, and began selling Krispy Kreme doughnuts to local grocery stores. Within a year, he had knocked a hole in the wall of his production facility and begun selling "hot original glazed" doughnuts to customers directly.

The company's reputation for making tasty, high-quality doughnuts grew steadily throughout the southeastern United States in the 1960s and 1970s. New stores were added either as company-owned outlets or as franchise operations (known as franchise associates). In the mid-1990s the company's management decided to pursue a strategy of geographic expansion using a new area developer franchise model. Under this model a

1. *Information on Krispy Kreme's history, operations, and financing strategy are from the company's 10-K statement for the fiscal year ended February 3, 2002.*

developer for a metropolitan region was granted a license to develop a specified number of new Krispy Kreme stores. New area developer stores soon appeared in Washington and Baltimore. In 1996 the first New York City store was opened; in 1999 stores were opened in California; and in 2001 the first international store was added, in Toronto, Canada. In the years ended January 2001 and January 2002, area developer store openings accounted for 72 percent and 83 percent of systemwide store growth, respectively.

By April 2002 the Krispy Kreme network comprised 222 factory stores in 34 states and produced 5 million doughnuts a day, or 2 billion doughnuts a year. Systemwide sales were $621.7 million in the year ended February 3, 2002, and $183.1 million for the first quarter of 2002 (a 30.4 percent increase over the first quarter for the prior year). Comparable store sales grew by 11.7 percent in the year ended February 3, 2002, and 10.5 percent in the first quarter of 2002.

Krispy Kreme generated revenues from three sources. First, it owned and operated doughnut stores. Second, it received royalties from franchise associates and area developers. Finally, it received revenues from the sale of doughnut mixes and doughnut-making equipment to franchise associates and area developers.

In April 2002, 75 of the Krispy Kreme network stores were company owned, an increase of 12 over the prior year. These stores baked and sold doughnuts and complementary products on-site. They also sold to grocery stores and supermarkets under either the Krispy Kreme brand or under the retailer's label.

Franchise associates owned and operated 53 of the 222 network stores in April 2002. Associate agreements with Krispy Kreme were typically for 15 years and required franchise owners to pay royalties of 3 percent for on-premises sales and 1 percent for all other sales (excluding private-label sales). Associates were not required to contribute to company advertising. Krispy Kreme anticipated that it would not add any further stores under this model, preferring instead to use the new area developer model.

Area developers had opened 94 stores by April 2002. Under the terms of the area developer agreements, Krispy Kreme received a one-time franchise fee between $20,000 and $40,000 for each new store opening, a 4.5 percent royalty fee on all sales, and a 1 percent contribution toward company advertising. These agreements had a 15-year term and could be renewed at Krispy Kreme's discretion. Krispy Kreme typically did not provide financing to area developers.

Finally, Krispy Kreme received revenues from the sale of proprietary doughnut mixes and doughnut-making equipment, both produced in Winston-Salem, to franchise associates and area developers. The revenues generated from these sales were attributed to Krispy Kreme Manufacturing and Distribution (KKM&D). (Exhibit 3 shows the breakdown of revenues and operating expenses for KKM&D as well as for the company store and franchise business segments.)

COMPETITORS

The doughnut industry was highly fragmented. The second-largest retailer after Krispy Kreme, Dunkin Donuts, was owned by the British food and spirits conglomerate Allied Domecq. Dunkin Donuts operated 4,736 franchise stores in 43 states and 20 countries and sold 4.4 million doughnuts a day, or 1.6 billion doughnuts per year.[2] Other competitors were regional operators. Winchell's was located primarily on the West Coast and operated

2. See Allied Domecq financial report for 2002.

200 stores[3]; Donut Connection had 140 stores in 13 states, primarily in the mid-Atlantic region[4]; and Honeydew Donuts operated 100 stores in New England.[5] Finally, there were hundreds of regional bakeries that sold doughnuts through supermarkets, convenience stores, restaurants, and retail stores.

Growth Plans[6]

Krispy Kreme expected to open 62 new stores in 2003, mostly franchise stores. Area developers were contractually obligated to open 200 stores in the period 2003 to 2006. In addition to domestic growth, the company indicated that it was exploring long-term opportunities for growth in Japan, South Korea, Australia, Spain, and the United Kingdom.

On average, the development of a new store required an initial investment of $800,000 for a building of around 4,600 square feet, plus $625,000 for equipment, furniture, and fixtures. In February 2002 company-owned stores generated average weekly sales per store of $72,000 versus $53,000 for franchise stores. This difference reflected significantly lower sales for older associate stores. Area developer franchise stores showed similar sales patterns to those of company-owned stores. (Average weekly sales per store for company-owned and franchise stores in the period 1998 to 2002 are shown in Exhibit 4.)

In addition to growth through opening new stores, Krispy Kreme planned to increase the sale of complementary products through existing stores. In February 2001 it acquired Digital Java, a small Chicago-based coffee company, to enable the addition of enhanced espresso and coffee offerings at Krispy Kreme stores.

In fall 2000 Krispy Kreme announced the development of a smaller hot doughnut machine that produced the same quality doughnuts as existing larger machines. The new machine was being tested in three doughnut and coffee shops in 2002 and was to be added to 10 to 12 more stores in 2003. If successful, the smaller machine would enable Krispy Kreme to begin offering hot doughnuts in small coffee shops and malls, allowing it to expand into smaller markets and into dense urban areas that were more costly to reach under the larger factory store model.

The growth in franchise operations required Krispy Kreme to invest heavily in plants, property, and equipment. For example, in the year ended February 2002 the company spent $37 million to construct and equip new company-owned factory stores, to remodel older company stores, to acquire and upgrade equipment-manufacturing facilities, to install coffee-roasting operations in stores, and to construct doughnut and coffee shops. The company's management anticipated that to achieve its planned growth it would have to continue to invest aggressively in both long-term assets and working capital.

Krispy Kreme had historically used a combination of debt and equity to finance its growth. In 2002 it raised funds through a $17.2 million stock offering (for 10.4 million shares), increased its revolving credit facility from $28 million to $40 million, and agreed to a $35 million bank loan to fund the construction of a new mix and distribution facility.[7] Kripsy Kreme's management anticipated that, as of February 2002, the company's capital needs for the next 24 months could be covered by "the proceeds from the initial public

Krispy Kreme Doughnuts

3. See Winchell's Web site.

4. See Donut Connection's Web site.

5. See Honeydew Donuts Web site.

6. Information on Krispy Kreme's growth plans is from the company's 10-K statement for the fiscal year ended February 3, 2002.

7. Under the terms of the revolving credit agreement, the company would pay interest at the lower of the prime rates less 110 basis points and one-month LIBOR plus 100 basis points.

offering completed in April 2000 and our follow-on public offering completed in early February 2001, cash flow generated from operations and our borrowing capacity under lines of credit. . . . If additional capital is needed, we may raise such capital through public or private equity or debt financing."

Analyst Forecasts

An important function performed by the analysts who followed Krispy Kreme was to forecast the company's financial performance for the coming two years. As shown in Exhibit 5, which contains excerpts from their June 2, 2002 report on Krispy Kreme, Glass and Farmer approached this task by first forecasting systemwide revenues (for company-owned stores and stores owned by franchise associates and area developers). These forecasts reflected the company's plans for new store growth and growth in sales from existing stores given the company's business model and competitive pressures. From these forecasts, Glass and Farmer were able to forecast Krispy Kreme's revenues and margins for its three core businesses (store sales, franchise operations, and sales of mix and equipment). Based on this analysis, they predicted that Krispy Kreme would report earnings per share of $0.64 for the year ended January 2003 and $0.83 for the January 2004 year. These forecasts represented projected earnings growth of 42 percent and 33 percent for the next two years, respectively, virtually identical to consensus predictions for all analysts covering Krispy Kreme.[8]

QUESTIONS

1. Analysts are predicting that Krispy Kreme will be able to perform highly effectively and continue to grow rapidly in the coming two years. Do you agree with their analysis? If so, why? If not, why not?

2. What factors did the CIBC analysts examine to forecast sales growth for KKD in the years ended January 2003 and 2004? What assumptions did they implicitly make about number of new stores and weekly sales per store (for both company and franchise stores)? What are their implicit assumptions about revenue growth from franchise operations and KKM&D? Do you agree with these forecasts?

3. What are the NOPAT margins that the CIBC analysts have forecasted for KKD for the years ended January 2003 and 2004? What assumptions were made about specific expense items (e.g. margins, G&A, D&A, taxes)? Do you agree with these forecasts?

4. The CIBC analysts do not forecast KKD's balance sheet for the following year (ended January 2003). Make your own balance sheet forecasts.

5. In general, do you expect analysts' forecasts for a company like KKD to be optimistic, pessimistic or unbiased? Why?

---

8. See First Call consensus earnings forecasts at June 1, 2002. A total of eight firms followed Krispy Kreme at the end of May 2002. In addition to CIBC World Markets, they included BB&T Capital Markets (Andrew Wolf), Brean Murray & Co. (Kathleen Heaney), Dain Rauscher Wessels (David Geraty), JP Morgan & Co. (John Ivankoe and David Linsen), Merrill Lynch (Peter Oakes), Thomas Weisel Partners (Skip Carpenter), and Deutsche Bank (Alex Brown). Source: Krispy Kreme Doughnuts Investors Relations Web site.

EXHIBIT 1

Stock Price Performance for Krispy Kreme and the S&P 500, April 2000 to May 2002

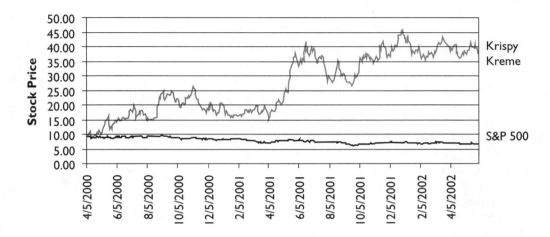

Source: Chart created from information found on Standard & Poor's Research Insight.

Note: Krispy Kreme's equity beta was 1.4 (source: SmartMoney.com). The long-term government bond rate on May 30, 2002, was 5.79 percent (source: Federal Reserve Statistical Release).

Krispy Kreme Doughnuts

EXHIBIT 2

Financial Statements for Krispy Kreme Doughnuts for the Fiscal Years
Ended January 30, 2000, to February 3, 2002, and for the Quarters Ended
April 29, 2001, and May 5, 2002

CONSOLIDATED BALANCE SHEETS
(in thousands)

	YEAR ENDED			QUARTER ENDED	
	JAN. 30, 2000	JAN. 28, 2001	FEB. 3, 2002	APR. 29, 2001	MAY 5, 2002
ASSETS					
CURRENT ASSETS:					
Cash and cash equivalents	$ 3,183	$ 7,026	$ 21,904	$ 21,326	$ 21,601
Short-term investments	—	18,103	15,292	24,738	22,073
Accounts receivable, net	17,965	19,855	26,894	20,202	29,232
Accounts receivable, affiliates	1,608	2,599	9,017	5,028	8,443
Other receivables	794	2,279	2,771	2,498	1,919
Inventories	9,979	12,031	16,159	11,511	21,118
Prepaid expenses	3,148	1,909	2,591	1,796	2,700
Income taxes refundable	861	—	2,534	34	—
Deferred income taxes	3,500	3,809	4,607	4,775	5,741
Total current assets	41,038	67,611	101,769	91,908	112,827
Property and equipment, net	60,584	78,340	112,577	85,464	151,152
Deferred income taxes	1,398	—	—	—	—
Long-term investments	—	17,877	12,700	11,319	6,058
Investment in unconsolidated joint ventures	—	2,827	3,400	4,921	4,382
Intangible assets	—	—	16,621	—	16,508
Other assets	1,938	4,838	8,309	6,578	7,387
Total assets	$104,958	$171,493	$255,376	$200,190	$298,314
LIABILITIES AND SHAREHOLDERS' EQUITY					
CURRENT LIABILITIES:					
Accounts payable	$13,106	$8,211	$12,095	$ 15,671	$ 14,763
Book overdraft		5,147	9,107	—	8,074
Accrued expenses	14,080	21,243	26,729	16,941	20,832
Revolving line of credit	—	3,526	3,871	4,400	4,171
Current maturities of long-term debt	2,400	—	731	—	2,382
Income taxes payable	—	41	—	—	303
Total current liabilities	29,586	38,168	52,533	37,012	50,525
Deferred income taxes	—	579	3,930	2,113	727
Compensation deferred (unpaid)	990	1,106	727	954	35,133
Long-term debt, net of current portion	20,502	—	3,912	—	5,957
Accrued restructuring expenses	4,259	3,109	1,919	2,855	1,653
Other long-term obligations	1,866	1,735	2,197	1,641	2,883
Total long-term liabilities	27,617	6,529	12,685	7,563	46,353
Minority interest	—	1,117	2,491	1,059	2,703

(continued)

CONSOLIDATED BALANCE SHEETS (continued)

	YEAR ENDED			QUARTER ENDED	
	JAN. 30, 2000	JAN. 28, 2001	FEB. 3, 2002	APR. 29, 2001	MAY 5, 2002
SHAREHOLDERS' EQUITY:					
Common stock, no par value, 100,000 shares authorized; issued and outstanding — 51,832 (2001) and 54,271 (2002)	—	85,060	121,052	108,741	123,777
Common stock, $10 par value, 1,000 shares authorized; issued and outstanding — 467 (2000) and 0 (2001)	15,475	—	—	—	—
Unearned compensation	—	(188)	(186)	(176)	(169)
Notes receivable, employees	(2,547)	(2,349)	(2,580)	(2,958)	(2,556)
Nonqualified employee benefit plan assets	—	−126	−138	(126)	(339)
Nonqualified employee benefit plan liability	—	126	138	126	339
Accumulated other comprehensive income	—	609	456	683	(105)
Retained earnings	34,827	42,547	68,925	48,266	77,786
Total shareholders' equity	47,755	125,679	187,667	154,556	198,733
Total liabilities and shareholders' equity	$104,958	$171,493	$255,376	$200,190	$298,314

STATEMENT OF OPERATIONS
(in thousands, except per share data)

	YEAR			THREE MONTHS	
	JAN. 30, 2000	JAN. 28, 2001	FEB. 3, 2002	APR. 29, 2001	MAY 5, 2002
Total revenues	$220,243	$300,715	$394,354	$87,921	$111,059
Operating expenses	190,003	250,690	316,946	71,195	86,362
General and administrative expenses	14,856	20,061	27,562	6,222	7,623
Depreciation and amortization expenses	4,546	6,457	7,959	1,872	2,546
Income (loss) from operations	10,838	23,507	41,887	8,632	14,528
Interest expense (income), net, and other	1,232	(1,698)	(2,408)	(976)	(495
Equity loss in joint ventures	—	706	602	(171)	(198)
Minority interest	—	716	1,147	(175)	(533)
Loss on sale of property and equipment	—	—	—	(39)	—
Income (loss) before income taxes	9,606	23,783	42,546	9,223	14,292
Provision (benefit) for income taxes	3,650	9,058	16,168	3,504	5,431
Net income (loss)	$5,956	$14,725	$26,378	$5,719	$8,861
Net income (loss) per share:					
Basic	$0.16	$0.30	$0.49	$0.11	$0.16
Diluted	0.15	0.27	0.45	$0.10	$0.15
Shares used in calculation of net income (loss) per share:					
Basic	37,360	49,184	53,703	51,991	55,381
Diluted	39,280	53,656	58,443	57,190	59,073

CONSOLIDATED STATEMENTS OF CASH FLOWS
(in thousands)

	YEAR ENDED			QUARTER ENDED	
	JAN. 30, 2000	JAN. 28, 2001	FEB. 3, 2002	APR. 29, 2001	MAY 5, 2002
CASH FLOW FROM OPERATING ACTIVITIES:					
Net income	$5,956	$14,725	$26,378	$5,719	$8,861
Items not requiring (providing) cash:					
Depreciation and amortization	4,546	6,457	7,959	1,872	2,546
Deferred income taxes	258	1,668	2,553	568	893
Loss on disposal of property and equipment, net	—	20	235	39	—
Compensation expense related to restricted stock awards	—	22	52	12	17
Tax benefit from exercise of nonqualified stock options	—	595	9,772	2,944	1,689
Provision for restructuring	(127)	—	—		
Provision for store closings and impairment	1,139	318	—		
Minority interest	—	716	1,147	175	533
Equity loss in joint ventures	—	706	602	171	198
Change in assets and liabilities:					
Receivables	(4,760)	(3,434)	(13,317)	(2,127)	(912)
Inventories	(93	(2,052)	(3,977)	520	(4,846)
Prepaid expenses	(1,619)	1,239	(682)	113	(109)
Income taxes, net	(2,016)	902	(2,575)	(75)	2,837
Accounts payable	540	2,279	3,884	(450)	2,668
Accrued expenses	4,329	7,966	4,096	(3,165)	(6,255)
Deferred compensation and other long-term obligations	345	(15)	83	(246)	319
Net cash provided by operating activities	8,498	32,112	36,210	6,070	8,439
CASH FLOW FROM INVESTING ACTIVITIES:					
Purchase of property and equipment	(11,335)	(25,655)	(37,310)	(8,956)	(40,954)
Proceeds from disposal of property and equipment	—	1,419	3,196	9	—
Proceeds from disposal of assets held for sale	830	—	—		
Acquisition of associate and area developer markets, net of cash acquired	—	—	(20,571)		
Investments in unconsolidated joint ventures	—	(4,465)	(1,218)	(1,265)	(1,187)
(Increase) decrease in other assets	479	(3,216)	(4,237)	(3,696)	755
(Purchase) sale of investments, net	—	(35,371)	7,877	(3)	(235)
Net cash used for investing activities:	(10,026)	(67,288)	(52,263)	(13,911)	(41,621)

(continued)

CONSOLIDATED STATEMENTS OF CASH FLOWS *(continued)*

	YEAR ENDED			QUARTER ENDED	
	JAN. 30, 2000	JAN. 28, 2001	FEB. 3, 2002	APR. 29, 2001	MAY 5, 2002
CASH FLOW FROM FINANCING ACTIVITIES:					
Repayment of long-term debt	$(2,400)	$(3,600)	$ —	$ —	$(128)
Net (repayments) borrowings from revolving line of credit	—	(15,775)	345	874	300
Borrowings of long-term debt	4,282	—	4,643	—	33,000
Proceeds from stock offering	—	65,637	17,202	17,202	—
Proceeds from exercise of stock options	—	104	3,906	2,656	1,036
Minority interest	—	401	227	(233)	(321)
Book overdraft	482	(941)	3,960	1,372	(1,033
Cash dividends paid	(1,518)	(7,005)	—	—	—
Issuance of notes receivable	(674)	—	—	—	—
Collection of notes receivable	226	198	648	270	25
Net cash provided by financing activities:	398	39,019	30,931	22,141	32,879
Net increase (decrease) in cash and cash equivalents	(1,130)	3,843	14,878	14,300	(303
Cash and cash equivalents at beginning of year	4,313	3,183	7,026	7,026	21,904
Cash and cash equivalents at end of year	$3,183	$7,026	$21,904	$21,326	$21,601
Supplemental schedule of non-cash investing and financing activities					
Issuance of stock to Krispy Kreme Profit-Sharing Stock Ownership Plan	—	$3,039	—	—	—
Issuance of restricted common shares	—	210	50	—	—
Issuance of stock in conjunction with acquisition of associate market	—	—	4,183	—	—
Issuance of stock in exchange for employee notes receivable	—	—	879	—	—
Unrealized gain (loss) on investments	—	609	(111)	74	(94)
Foreign currency translation adjustment	—	—	—	—	(8)
Change in fair value of cash flow hedge	—	—	—	—	459

Source: Krispy Kreme Doughnut's Annual Report for February 3, 2002 and the quarterly report for May 5, 2002.

Krispy Kreme Doughnuts

EXHIBIT 3

Business Segment Data for Krispy Kreme Doughnuts for the Fiscal Years
Ended January 30, 2000, to February 3, 2002

	YEAR ENDED		
(in thousands)	JAN. 30, 2000	JAN. 28, 2001	FEB. 3, 2002
REVENUES BY BUSINESS SEGMENT:			
Company Store Operations	$164,230	$213,677	$266,209
Franchise Operations	5,529	9,445	14,008
KKM&D	50,484	77,593	114,137
Total revenues	$220,243	$300,715	$394,354
OPERATING EXPENSES BY BUSINESS SEGMENT:			
Company Store Operations	$142,925	$181,470	$217,419
Franchise Operations	4,012	3,642	4,896
KKM&D	43,066	65,578	94,631
Total operating expenses	$190,003	$250,690	$316,946

Source: Krispy Kreme Doughnut's Annual Report, February 3, 2002.

EXHIBIT 4

Operating Data for Krispy Kreme Doughnuts for the Fiscal Years Ended
February 1, 1998, to February 3, 2002

	FEB. 1, 1998	JAN. 31, 1999	JAN. 30, 2000	JAN. 28, 2001	FEB. 3, 2002
Systemwide sales ($000)	$203,439	$240,316	$318,854	$448,129	$621,665
Number of stores at end of period:					
Company	58	61	58	63	75
Franchised	62	70	86	111	143
Systemwide	120	131	144	174	218
Average weekly sales per store ($000)					
Company	$42	$47	$54	$69	$72
Franchised	23	28	38	43	53
Operating cash flow/store revenues	NA	20.3%	23.2%	26.1%	28.6%

Source: Krispy Kreme Doughnut's 10-K, February 3, 2002

EXHIBIT 5

Excerpts from the CIBC World Markets Equity Research Report on Krispy Kreme Doughnuts, Inc.*
Prepared by John S. Glass and Jeffrey D. Farmer

Company Overview

For both investors and consumers, Krispy Kreme is a one of a kind phenomenon, in our view, boasting a combination of a powerful consumer brand, a multi-channel distribution channel and a business model that produces best-in-class financial returns. What's more, the company is vertically integrated, not only retailing doughnuts, but also manufacturing and distributing high-margin doughnut mix as well as manufacturing proprietary doughnut-making equipment.

Krispy Kreme is still an attractive growth story, in our view, and represents a well-established brand still early in its growth trajectory. The company is just one-third of the way through the rollout of their large-format factory stores—not including the substantial incremental growth prospects of its prototype smaller-format units.

These prospects have not gone unnoticed. Since its IPO in April 2000 priced at a split-adjusted $5.50, the stock has risen over 600% in the last 26 months, making it the most successful public offering in recent years. That performance has been fueled by substantial sales and earnings outperformance—as well as a fair amount of publicity. The key components to the Krispy Kreme business model follow.

TABLE A

Company-Operated and Systemwide Unit Same-Store Sales (1999–2002E)

Company Stores	1999	2000	2001	2002
1Q	7.1%	23.3%	13.1%	10.5%
2Q	9.7%	24.4%	11.9%	10.0%E
3Q	14.0%	23.6%	11.1%	8.0%E
4Q	17.1%	20.6%	10.7%	8.0%E
Year	12.0%	22.9%	11.7%	9.0%E

Systemwide Stores	1999	2000	2001	2002
1Q	9.8%	19.1%	11.4%	12.9%
2Q	13.4%	19.4%	13.1%	10.5%E
3Q	15.9%	15.5%	13.6%	8.5%E
4Q	16.6%	14.9%	13.1%	8.5%E
Year	14.1%	17.1%	12.8%	10.0%E

Source: CIBC World Markets and company information.

....

*John S. Glass and Jeffrey D. Farmer, "Krispy Kreme Doughnuts Inc. Doughnuts to Dollars: Initiating Coverage," CIBC World Markets Equity Research Report, June 3, 2002. © 2002 CIBC World Markets Corp. Reprinted with permission. All rights reserved.

Company-Owned Retail Stores

Company-owned stores, most of which are in the Deep South, are referred to internally as the "heritage markets," representing about 60% of Krispy Kreme's profits. Although the company has focused most of its growth in franchised markets and has owned few new stores of its own, sales and profit trends have nonetheless been healthy due to a combination of strong comp store sales, driven by a combination of retail and wholesale business. While management has designated franchising in new markets as its primary growth driver, there is nonetheless substantial opportunity for growth in the heritage markets to develop underpenetrated markets as well as increase same-store sales through more efficient wholesale distribution and new wholesale accounts.

TABLE B

Systems and Operating Margin Leverage

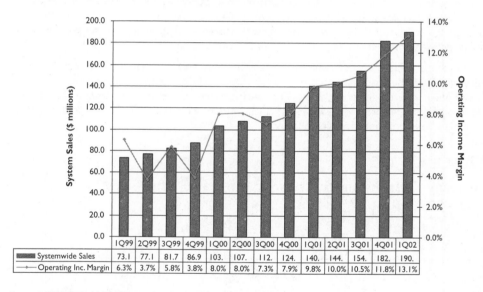

	1Q99	2Q99	3Q99	4Q99	1Q00	2Q00	3Q00	4Q00	1Q01	2Q01	3Q01	4Q01	1Q02
Systemwide Sales	73.1	77.1	81.7	86.9	103.	107.	112.	124.	140.	144.	154.	182.	190.
Operating Inc. Margin	6.3%	3.7%	5.8%	3.8%	8.0%	8.0%	7.3%	7.9%	9.8%	10.0%	10.5%	11.8%	13.1%

Source: CIBC World Markets and company information.

In addition, management has from time to time elected to repurchase older franchised markets—particularly those where there is still significant growth potential. Markets recently acquired include Charleston, SC, Savannah, GA, Cleveland and Akron, OH, and Baltimore, MD. In many cases, the company will resell a stake in these markets but retain the majority.

Margin expansion in the company-owned markets has been substantial, up 500 bp to 16% in 2001 as the company leveraged fixed costs through volume increases and focused on operation, particularly better labor cost management. Best-in-class store margins (including D&A) run into the high teens, particularly given that average weekly sales at company units were $72,000 in 2001, or $3.7 million annualized.

TABLE C

Average Weekly Sales per Store (1999–2001)

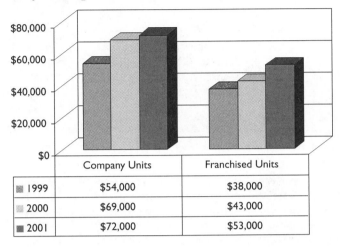

	Company Units	Franchised Units
1999	$54,000	$38,000
2000	$69,000	$43,000
2001	$72,000	$53,000

Source: CIBC World Markets and company information.

Franchise Income

While the company has always had a close-knit group of original franchisees—known as the Associates—its real franchising growth came in the mid-1990s when the company began committing to area developer agreements outside its heritage markets. These new agreements are more profitable—4.5% royalties vs. 3% for Associates—and the income stream is much faster growing as the area developers rapidly roll out new units. In 2001, the area developer store base grew at a 68% clip to 143 units. Franchise income now represents 16% of profits, but given its inherent high-margin nature (current profit flow through is 65% on its way to 75% to 80%) and growth rate (franchise profits grew by nearly 60% in 2001) we expect the franchise income will continue to be a margin and earnings driver over the next several years as area developers continue to grow sales faster than the company-owned units.

In part, the growth in franchise income has been driven by massive new store openings as the company enters new markets. In fact, Krispy Kreme's new store openings follow an inverse store maturation curve, often producing peak volumes in a new store the first few weeks and then slowly settling over the next 12 months to a normalized level. *Typically, new stores retain about 40% of opening week sales. However, given the unusually strong first week sales recently, in some cases the retention rate is likely to be closer to 15% to 25%.* For example, new stores opened recently in Denver, Seattle, and Minneapolis have produced opening week volumes of $400,000 to $480,000. Over time, average weekly volume may settle around $75,000 to $100,000.

TABLE D

Krispy Kreme's Record Opening Week Sales

Date	Location	Opening Week Sales
May 2002	Minneapolis, MN	$480,693
December 2001	Toronto, ON	$465,003*
November 2001	Seattle, WA	$454,125
April 2001	Denver, CO	$369,000

*Toronto opening in Canadian dollars

Source: CIBC World Markets and company information.

This honeymoon phenomenon could negatively impact systemwide comp store sales. If sales do not stabilize within 18 months (the point when stores enter the comp base), systemwide comp store sales will be negatively impacted—the magnitude depends on the number of units coming into the comp base, but could be as great as a 5% to 10% negative impact in some quarters. *Big-store openings also give rise to another phenomenon: 70% of franchisee sales are not in the comp base, so comp store sales are not yet a key driver of franchise income and KKM&D sales.* Since the company itself is not opening new stores, the above *has no impact* on company-owned comp store sales.

TABLE E

Hypothetical Weekly Sales Trends

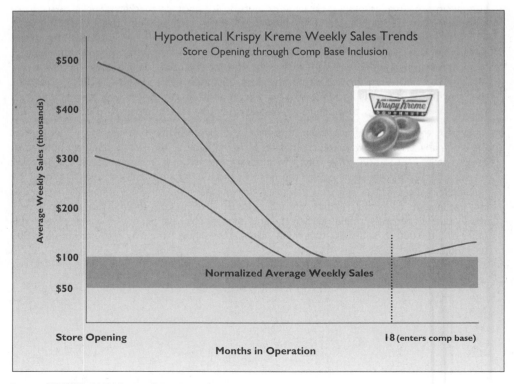

Source: CIBC World Markets and company information.

Krispy Kreme Manufacturing and Distribution (KKM&D)

KKM&D is the company's captive manufacturing and distribution arm. The manufacturing—primarily of doughnut mix which must be purchased by franchisees and machinery—is the higher-margin business, while the distribution margins are cost plus an estimated 2% to 3% markup. Blended margins for KKM&D run 16.6% of sales and are rising at a 100bp clip per year due to greater capacity utilization. The company opened a second distribution facility on the West Coast last year, and will open a second manufacturing facility in Effingham, IL shortly, helping to reduce shipping costs (both in and out) and raising margins. Sales growth for KKM&D should keep lock step with top-line growth of franchises.

Incremental Sales/Earnings Drivers

Embedded in each of these three lines, we think there are at least four incremental earnings drivers beyond the current base business. Those are:

1. **Hot Doughnut Shop** Late in 2001, the company announced it had developed a prototype small-format unit (1,000–1,500 square feet), complete with a much smaller doughnut machine which reheats and glazes doughnuts. The implication on growth and unit potential is profound, in our view, allowing Krispy Kreme to enter urban centers, malls, and a variety of other locations that could not be reached through the factory store model. These small units also facilitate the sale of coffee, which has a much tighter draw radius than a traditional doughnut shop. Data on these new units is scare as only a handful exist. But, based on the number of Starbucks (4,000) and Dunkin Donuts (3,600) in the U.S., the opportunity for high-quality coffee and doughnuts given the Krispy Kreme brand is substantial. Unit sales potential for these smaller units could range from $750,000 to 1.5 million, in our view, based on what similar concepts are able to produce. We note that there is no empirical data at this time.

2. **Coffee sales** Currently, beverage sales are a distant second to doughnuts at Krispy Kreme, running 10% of sales, and coffee just half of that. We think through a combination of more focus on the beverage program and the smaller more conventional markets, coffee sales are likely to grow in proportion to overall sales. Coffee is also where the repeat business is in this segment, in our view.

3. **Equity stakes in franchises** In most new franchise agreements, Krispy has taken an equity stake—anywhere from 20% to 70%. As franchisees become profitable, these equity stakes will become profit contributors. Currently, they run at a modest loss.

4. **International** We believe the brand has significant international potential and is natural in places such as the U.K., Japan, and potentially other European countries. International expansion is not currently in our forecast.

Financial Outlook

Over the next three years, we expect Krispy Kreme to grow its earnings by 35%, driven by a combination of:

- Top-line growth of 25% to 30%, including systemwide square footage growth of 25% to 30% and mid-single digit comp sales.

- Margin expansion of 75 bp to 100 bp per year due to 1) mix shift toward higher margin KKM&D and franchise income, and 2) margin improvements in each of these categories.

The company's track record of exceeding earnings expectations is strong, with outperformance in each of the eight quarters since the company has come public. Earnings per share grew 65% in 2001. Our current forecast calls for 36% EPS growth in 2002.

An element for continued earnings growth at Krispy Kreme will be margin expansion. As Table F shows, the company now is already at its original long-term operating margin goal of 10%. Given the revenue mix shift toward higher profit income streams, operating efficiency improvements in company stores, and increased capacity utilization and lower shipping costs for the distribution and manufacturing operations, we believe operating profit margins can reach 15% over the next three to five years, well ahead of the original 10% goal.

TABLE F

Upward Revision of Margin Guidance

	CY 1998	CY 2001	Long-Term at IPO	Long-Term Today
Company Stores	9.0%	16.0%	13–14%	16–18%
Franchise Ops	13.5%	65.0%	70–75%	70–75%
Support Ops	13.0%	16.6%	16–17%	17–18%
G & A	6.0%	7.0%	6–7%	6–7%
EBIT	3.0%	10.6%	9–10%	14–16%

Source: CIBC World Markets and company information.

Financial Condition

Given the company's primary focus on the franchising and strong cash flow, to date the company has been able to fund its own expansion internally. In 2001, cash from operations of $30.5 million financed the company's $25.6 million cap-ex budget and $6.3 million in investments in joint ventures. However, Krispy Kreme's financing needs are likely to be greater in the near future given the addition of more manufacturing and distribution assets and more joint venture investment opportunities. In 2002, we expect that cap-ex will be $43 million plus an additional $35 million from the recently canceled synthetic lease program, which is likely now to be funded by debt. We expect cash from operations to be around $35 million to $40 million.

Recent Trends

Business trends for the last three quarters have been very consistent with systemwide comp store sales around 11% to 13% and company stores at about 10%; these results were achieved despite challenging comparisons from 2000 of 17% on a systemwide basis. In the F1Q, EPS grew 51%, driven by 26% top line and over 300 bp of operating margin expansion. Although store development was modest—a net of four units—the company is still committed to operating 62 new units, or 28% systemwide square footage growth.

Our current forecast for 2002 calls for 26% revenue growth, driven by 9% to 10% systemwide comps and 62 new units, as well as 100 bp of operating margin expansion (to 12+%).

Risk and Uncertainties

- **Decelerating comp store sales** Decelerating comp store sales, particularly due to large new store openings entering the comp base, could negatively impact comp store sales—a metric widely used in valuing retail stocks. We note as before that 70% of franchisee revenues are still noncomp, therefore a comp deceleration in the franchise base would not materially impact earnings near term.

- **Increasing capital costs** Given the need for new production and distribution capacity, capital intensity is rising, as described earlier in this report. New unit costs have risen to $1.3 million to $1.5 million from an initial $1 million cost (ex-land) due to increased equipment and building costs. This primarily impacts franchisees as company new unit development has been limited.

- **Limited operating history with small-format units** While we are highly optimistic about the company's new smaller-format units, there is limited operating history to date and no public information on the unit economics.

- **Competition** Although we are less concerned about competition in the doughnut category, Krispy Kreme will encounter competition as it enters the coffee segment. Still, it is our view that its existing brand and customer loyalty will mitigate that risk.

- **Fad risk** Although Krispy Kreme is about 65 years old, its initial reception in many markets is unlikely to be sustained over time. We expect some cannibalization as the brand becomes better established. Offsetting this, we believe, will be the positive impact of the more convenience-oriented small-format units.

TABLE G

Krispy Kreme Income Statement (FY01–FY04E)

Fiscal Year Ends: January	FY 2001A	FY 2002A	FY 2003E	FY 2004E
Company Stores	213,677	266,209	303,206	334,624
Franchised Stores	234,452	355,456	533,968	779,888
Systemwide Sales	$448,129	$621,655	$837,174	$1,114,512
Company Stores	213,677	266,209	303,206	334,624
Franchise Operations	9,445	14,963	22,615	32,128
Support Sales	77,516	114,137	169,507	239,445
Net Sales	$300,638	$394,354	$494,818	$606,197
Company Store Expenses	181,469	217,418	245,065	270,026
Franchise Expenses	3,643	4,896	6,771	9,780
Support Operations Expenses	65,512	94,631	138,413	194,058
Operating Expenses	250,624	316,946	390,249	473,864
D & A	6,458	7,959	10,121	12,081
General & Admin. Expense	20,061	27,562	33,959	40,918
Operating Profit	29,953	41,887	60,489	79,334
Interest/Other Expense (Income)	(1,593)	(2,408)	(1,395)	(1,400)
Joint Venture Income (Loss)	(600)	(602)	(198	450
Minority Interest	(717)	(1,147)	(1,183)	(850)
Earnings Before Taxes	23,771	42,546	60,503	80,334
Income Taxes	9,058	16,168	22,991	30,527
Net Income	14,713	26,378	37,512	49,807
EPS	$0.27	$0.45	$0.63	$0.84
Avg. Shs. Outs. (FD)	53,656	58,434	59,174	59,574
Sales Ratios				
Operating Expenses	83.36%	80.37%	78.87%	78.17%
Contribution Profit (Bef. G & A)	16.64%	19.63%	21.13%	21.83%
D & A	2.15%	2.02%	2.05%	1.99%
General Administrative Exp.	6.67%	6.99%	6.86%	6.75%
Operating Income	9.96%	10.62%	12.22%	13.09%
Tax Rate	38.10%	38.00%	38.00%	38.00%
Net Income	4.89%	6.69%	7.58%	8.22%
Year-Over-Year % Change:				
Systemwide Sales	40.6%	38.7%	34.7%	33.1%
Company Sales	36.5%	31.2%	25.5%	22.5%
Operating Expenses	29.6%	26.5%	23.1%	21.4%
Selling General & Admin. Expense	27.5%	37.4%	23.2%	20.5%
Operating Profit	167.5%	39.8%	44.4%	31.2%
Net Income	147.0%	79.3%	42.2%	32.8%
EPS	81.1%	64.6%	40.4%	31.9%

Source: CIBC World Markets and company information.

TABLE H

Krispy Kreme Balance Sheet (FY2000–FY2002)
(dollars in thousands)

Fiscal Year Ended: January	FY 2000A	FY 2001A	FY2002A
Assets			
Cash/S-T investments	$3,183	$25,129	$37,196
Receivables (net)	20,367	24,733	38,682
Inventory	9,979	12,031	16,159
Other	7,509	5,718	9,732
Total Current Assets	41,038	67,611	101,769
Net Plant, Property, & Equipment	60,584	78,340	112,577
Other Assets	3,336	25,542	41,030
Total Long-term assets	63,920	103,882	153,607
Total Assets	**$104,958**	**$171,493**	**$255,376**
Liabilities & Stockholders' Equity			
Accounts Payable	$13,106	$14,697	$21,202
Accrued Liabilities	14,080	19,904	26,729
Current Mat. of Debt	2,400	0	0
Other		3,567	4,602
Total current liabilities	29,586	38,168	52,533
Long-term debt	20,502	0	3,912
Other long-term liabilities	7,115	6,529	8,773
Total long-term liabilities	27,617	6,529	12,685
Total liabilities	57,203	44,697	65,218
Minority interest		1,117	2,491
Total Stockholders' Equity	47,755	125,679	187,667
TOTAL LIABILITIES & EQUITY	**$104,958**	**$171,493**	**$255,376**

Source: CIBC World Markets and company information.

Krispy Kreme Doughnuts

Prospective Analysis: Valuation Theory and Concepts

The previous chapter introduced forecasting, the first stage of prospective analysis. In this and the following chapter we describe the second and final stage of prospective analysis, valuation. This chapter focuses on valuation theory and concepts, and the following chapter discusses implementation issues.

Valuation is the process of converting a forecast into an estimate of the value of the firm or some component of the firm. At some level, nearly every business decision involves valuation (at least implicitly). Within the firm, capital budgeting involves consideration of how a particular project will affect firm value. Strategic planning focuses on how value is influenced by larger sets of actions. Outside the firm, security analysts conduct valuation to support their buy/sell decisions, and potential acquirers (often with the assistance of their investment bankers) estimate the value of target firms and the synergies they might offer. Valuation is necessary to price an initial public offering and to inform parties to sales, estate settlements, and divisions of property involving ongoing business concerns. Even credit analysts, who typically do not explicitly estimate firm value, must at least implicitly consider the value of the firm's equity "cushion" if they are to maintain a complete view of the risk associated with lending activity.

In practice, a wide variety of valuation approaches are employed. For example, in evaluating the fairness of a takeover bid, investment bankers commonly use five to ten different methods of valuation. Among the available methods are the following:

- *Discounted dividends.* This approach expresses the value of the firm's equity as the present value of forecasted future dividends.
- *Discounted abnormal earnings.* Under this approach the value of the firm's equity is expressed as the sum of its book value and discounted forecasts of abnormal earnings.
- *Valuation based on price multiples.* Under this approach a current measure of performance or single forecast of performance is converted into a value through application of some price multiple for other presumably comparable firms. For example, firm value can be estimated by applying a price-to-earnings ratio to a forecast of the firm's earnings for the coming year. Other commonly used multiples include price-to-book ratios and price-to-sales ratios.
- *Discounted cash flow (DCF) analysis.* This approach involves the production of detailed, multiple-year forecasts of cash flows. The forecasts are then discounted at the firm's estimated cost of capital to arrive at an estimated present value.

All of the above approaches can be structured in two ways. The first is to directly value the equity of the firm, since this is usually the variable the analyst is directly interested in estimating. The second is to value the assets of the firm, that is, the claims of equity and net debt, and then to deduct the value of net debt to arrive at the final equity estimate. Theoretically, both approaches should generate the same values. However, as we will see in the following chapter, there are implementation issues in reconciling the approaches. In this chapter we illustrate valuation using an all-equity firm to simplify the discussion. Where appropriate we discuss the theoretical issues in valuing the firm's assets.

From a theoretical perspective, shareholder value is the present value of future dividend payoffs. This definition can be implemented by forecasting and discounting future dividends directly. Alternatively, it can be framed by recasting dividends in terms of earnings and book values, or in terms of free cash flows to shareholders. These methods are developed throughout the chapter, and their pros and cons discussed.

Valuation using multiples is also discussed. Multiples are a popular method of valuation because, unlike the discounted dividend, discounted abnormal earnings, and discounted cash flow methods, they do not require analysts to make multiyear forecasts. However, the identification of comparable firms is a serious challenge in implementing the multiples approach. The chapter discusses how the discounted abnormal earnings valuation approach can be recast to generate firm-specific estimates of two popular multiples, value-to-book and value-earnings ratios. Value-to-book multiples are shown to be a function of future abnormal ROEs, book value growth, and the firm's cost of equity. Value-earnings multiples are driven by the same factors and also the current ROE.

DEFINING VALUE FOR SHAREHOLDERS

How should shareholders think about the value of their equity claims on a firm? Finance theory holds that the value of any financial claim is simply the present value of the cash payoffs that its claimholders receive. Since shareholders receive cash payoffs from a company in the form of dividends, the value of their equity is the present value of future dividends (including any liquidating dividend).

Equity value   =   PV of expected future dividends

If we denote the expected future dividend for a given year as DIV and r_e as the cost of equity capital (the relevant discount rate), the stock value is as follows:

$$\text{Equity value} \quad = \quad \frac{DIV_1}{(1 + r_e)} + \frac{DIV_2}{(1 + r_e)^2} + \frac{DIV_3}{(1 + r_e)^3} + \dots$$

Notice that the valuation formula views a firm as having an indefinite life. But in reality firms can go bankrupt or get taken over. In these situations shareholders effectively receive a terminating dividend on their stock.

If a firm had a constant dividend growth rate (g^d) indefinitely, its value would simplify to the following formula:

$$\text{Equity value} \quad = \quad \frac{DIV_1}{r_e - g^d}$$

To better understand how the discounted dividend approach works, consider the following example. At the beginning of year 1, Down Under Company raises $60 million of equity and uses the proceeds to buy a fixed asset. Operating profits before depreciation (all received in cash) and dividends for the company are expected to be $40 million in year 1, $50 million in year 2, and $60 million in year 3, at which point the company terminates. The firm pays no taxes. If the cost of equity capital for this firm is 10 percent, the value of the firm's equity is computed as follows:

Year	Dividend	PV Factor	PV of Dividend
1	$40m	0.9091	$36.4m
2	50	0.8264	41.3
3	60	0.7513	45.1
Equity value			$122.8m

The above valuation formula is called the dividend discount model. It forms the basis for most of the popular theoretical approaches for stock valuation. The remainder of the chapter discusses how this model can be recast to generate the discounted abnormal earnings, discounted cash flow, and price multiple models of value.

THE DISCOUNTED ABNORMAL EARNINGS VALUATION METHOD

As discussed in Chapter 3, there is a link between dividends and earnings. If all equity effects (other than capital transactions) flow through the income statement,[1] the expected book value of equity for existing shareholders at the end of year 1 (BVE_1) is simply the book value at the beginning of the year (BVE_0) plus expected net income (NI_1) less expected dividends (DIV_1).[2] This relation can be rewritten as follows:

$$DIV_1 = NI_1 + BVE_0 - BVE_1$$

By substituting this identity for dividends into the dividend discount formula and rearranging the terms, stock value can be rewritten as follows[3]:

$$\text{Equity value} = \text{Book value of equity} + \text{PV of expected future abnormal earnings}$$

Abnormal earnings are net income adjusted for a capital charge computed as the discount rate multiplied by the beginning book value of equity. Abnormal earnings therefore make an adjustment to reflect the fact that accountants do not recognize any opportunity cost for equity funds used. Thus, the discounted abnormal earnings valuation formula is

$$\text{Equity value} = BVE_0 + \frac{NI_1 - r_e \cdot BVE_0}{(1 + r_e)} + \frac{NI_2 - r_e \cdot BVE_1}{(1 + r_e)^2} + \frac{NI_3 - r_e \cdot BVE_2}{(1 + r_e)^3} + \cdots$$

As noted earlier, equity values can also be estimated by valuing the firm's assets and then deducting its net debt. Under the earnings-based approach, this implies that the value of the assets is

$$\text{Asset value} = BVA_0 + \frac{NOPAT_1 - WACC \cdot BVA_0}{(1 + WACC)} + \frac{NOPAT_2 - WACC \cdot BVA_1}{(1 + WACC)^2} + \cdots$$

BVA is the book value of the firm's assets, NOPAT is net operating profit (before interest) after tax, and WACC is the firm's weighted-average cost of debt and equity. From this asset value the analyst can deduct the market value of net debt to generate an estimate of the value of equity.

The earnings-based formulation has intuitive appeal. It implies that if a firm can earn only a normal rate of return on its book value, then investors should be willing to pay no more than book value for the stock. Investors should pay more or less than book value if earnings are above or below this normal level. Thus the deviation of a firm's market value from book value depends on its ability to generate "abnormal earnings." The formulation also implies that a firm's stock value reflects the cost of its existing net assets (that is, its book equity) plus the net present value of future growth options (represented by cumulative abnormal earnings).

To illustrate the earnings-based valuation approach, let's return to the Down Under Company example. Since the company is an all-equity firm, the value of the firm's equity and its assets (debt plus equity) are the same. If the company depreciates its fixed assets using the straight-line method, its beginning book equity, earnings, abnormal earnings, and valuation will be as follows:

Year	Beginning Book Value	Earnings	Abnormal Earnings	PV Factor	PV of Abnormal Earnings
1	$60m	$20m	$14m	0.9091	$12.7m
2	40	30	26	0.8264	21.5
3	20	40	38	0.7513	28.6
Cumulative PV of abnormal earnings					62.8
+ Beginning book value					60.0
= Equity value					$122.8m

This stock valuation of $122.8 million is identical to the value estimated when the expected future dividends are discounted directly.

Key Analysis Questions

Valuation of equity (debt plus equity) under the discounted abnormal earnings method requires the analyst to answer the following questions:

- What are expected future net income (NOPAT) and book values of equity (assets) over a finite forecast horizon (usually 5 to 10 years)?
- What are expected future abnormal earnings (NOPAT), after deducting a capital charge from forecasts of net income (NOPAT)? The capital charge is the firm's cost of equity (WACC) multiplied by beginning book equity (assets).
- What is expected future abnormal net income (NOPAT) beyond the final year of the forecast horizon (called the "terminal year") based on some simplifying assumption?
- What is the present value of abnormal earnings (NOPAT) discounted at the cost of equity capital (WACC)?
- What is the estimated value of equity, computed by adding the current book value of equity (assets) to the cumulated present value of future abnormal earnings (NOPAT)? Are there nonoperating assets held by the firm that have been ignored in the previous abnormal earnings (NOPAT) forecasts (e.g., marketable securities or real estate held for sale)? If so, their values should be included in the equity estimate.

Recent research shows that abnormal earnings estimates of value outperform traditional multiples, such as price-earnings ratios, price-to-book ratios, and dividend yields, for predicting future stock movements.[4] Firms with high abnormal earnings model estimates of value relative to current price show positive abnormal future stock returns, whereas firms with low estimated value-to-price ratios have negative abnormal stock performance.

Accounting Methods and Discounted Abnormal Earnings

It may seem odd that firm value can be expressed as a function of accounting numbers. After all, accounting methods per se should have no influence on firm value (except as those choices influence the analyst's view of future real performance). Yet the valuation approach used here is based on numbers—earnings and book value—that vary with accounting method choices. How then can the valuation approach deliver correct estimates?

It turns out that because accounting choices affect *both* earnings *and* book value, and because of the self-correcting nature of double-entry bookkeeping (all "distortions" of accounting must ultimately reverse), estimated values based on the discounted abnormal earnings method will not be affected by accounting choices per se. For example, assume that Down Under Company's managers choose to be conservative and expense some unusual costs that could have been capitalized as inventory at year 1, causing earnings and ending book value to be lower by $10 million. This inventory is then sold in year 2. For the time being, let's say the accounting choice has no influence on the analyst's view of the firm's real performance.

Managers' choice reduces abnormal earnings in year 1 and book value at the beginning of year 2 by $10 million. However, future earnings will be higher, for two reasons. First, future earnings will be higher (by $10 million) when the inventory is sold in year 2 at a lower cost of sales. Second, the benchmark for normal earnings (based on book value of equity) will be lower by $10 million. The $10 million decline in abnormal earnings in year 1 is perfectly offset (on a present value basis) by the $11 million higher abnormal earnings in year 2. As a result, the value of Down Under Company under conservative reporting is identical to the value under the earlier accounting method ($122.8 million).

Year	Beginning Book Value	Earnings	Abnormal Earnings	PV Factor	PV of Abnormal Earnings
I	$60m	$10m	$4m	0.9091	$3.6m
2	30	40	37	0.8264	30.6
3	20	40	38	0.7513	28.6
Cumulative PV of abnormal earnings					62.8
+ Beginning book value					60.0
= Equity value					$122.8m

Provided the analyst is aware of biases in accounting data as a result of the use of aggressive or conservative accounting choices by management, abnormal earnings-based valuations are unaffected by the variation in accounting decisions. This implies that strategic and accounting analyses are critical precursors to abnormal earnings valuation. The strategic and accounting analysis tools help the analyst to identify whether abnormal earnings arise from sustainable competitive advantage or from unsustainable accounting manipulations. For example, consider the implications of failing to understand the reasons for a decline in earnings from a change in inventory policy for Down Under Company. If the analyst mistakenly interpreted the decline as indicating that the firm was having difficulty moving its inventory, rather than that it had used conservative accounting, she might reduce expectations of future earnings. The estimated value of the firm would then be lower than that reported in our example.

VALUATION USING PRICE MULTIPLES

Valuations based on price multiples are widely used by analysts. The primary reason for their popularity is their simplicity. Unlike the discounted abnormal earnings, discounted dividend, and discounted cash flow methods, they do not require detailed multiple-year forecasts about a variety of parameters, including growth, profitability, and cost of capital.

Valuation using multiples involves the following steps:

Step 1: Select a measure of performance or value (e.g., earnings, sales, cash flows, book equity, book assets) as the basis for multiple calculations.

Step 2: Estimate price multiples for comparable firms using the measure of performance or value.

Step 3: Apply the comparable firm multiple to the performance or value measure of the firm being analyzed.

Under this approach, the analyst relies on the market to undertake the difficult task of considering the short- and long-term prospects for growth and profitability and their implications for the values of the comparable firms. Then the analyst *assumes* that the pricing of those other firms is applicable to the firm at hand.

On the surface, using multiples seems straightforward. Unfortunately, in practice it is not as simple as it would appear. Identification of "comparable" firms is often quite difficult. There are also some choices to be made concerning how multiples will be calculated. Finally, explaining why multiples vary across firms, and how applicable another firm's multiple is to the one at hand, requires a sound understanding of the determinants of each multiple.

Selecting Comparable Firms

Ideally, price multiples used in a comparable firm analysis are those for firms with similar operating and financial characteristics. Firms within the same industry are the most obvious candidates. But even within narrowly defined industries, it is often difficult to find multiples for similar firms. Many firms are in multiple industries, making it difficult to identify representative benchmarks. In addition, firms within the same industry frequently have different strategies, growth opportunities, and profitability, creating comparability problems.

One way of dealing with these issues is to average across *all* firms in the industry. The analyst implicitly hopes that the various sources of noncomparability cancel each other out, so that the firm being valued is comparable to a "typical" industry member. Another approach is to focus on only those firms within the industry that are most similar.

For example, consider using multiples to value Nordstrom. OneSource classifies the company in the Retail: Apparel industry. OneSource reported that Nordstrom's competitors could be narrowed to the following firms: Ann Taylor, Charming Shoppes, Dayton Hudson (now Target), Dillard's, Federated Department Stores, The Gap, The Limited, May Department Stores, Neiman Marcus, J C Penney, Saks, and TJX Companies. The average price-earnings ratio for these direct competitors was 223.76 and the average price-to-book ratio was 2.64.

Multiples for Firms with Poor Performance

Price multiples can be affected when the denominator variable is performing poorly. This is especially common when the denominator is a flow measure, such as earnings or cash flows. For example, Sak's Inc., one of Nordstrom's competitors, had earnings of only 0.3 million in 2001 and a price-earnings ratio of 4,443.4. Similarly, the Gap had negative earnings in 2001, making the price-earnings ratio negative.

What are analysts' options for handling the problems for multiples created by transitory shocks to the denominator? One option is to simply exclude firms with large transitory effects from the set of comparable firms. If Sak's Inc. and the Gap are excluded from Nordstrom's peer set, the average industry price-earnings ratio declines from 223.76 to

6.32. This dramatic change in the industry average shows the sensitivity of price-earnings multiples to transitory shocks.

As an alternative to excluding some firms from the industry comparison group, if the poor performance is due to a transitory shock such as a write-off or special item, the effect can be excluded from computation of the multiple. Finally, the analyst can use a denominator that is a forecast of future performance rather than a past measure. Multiples based on forecasts are termed *leading* multiples, whereas those based on historical data are called *trailing* multiples. Leading multiples are less likely to include one-time gains and losses in the denominator, simply because such items are difficult to anticipate.

Adjusting Multiples for Leverage

Price multiples should be calculated in a way that preserves consistency between the numerator and denominator. Consistency is an issue for those ratios where the denominator reflects performance *before* servicing debt. Examples include the price-to-sales multiple and any multiple of operating earnings or operating cash flows. When calculating these multiples, the numerator should include not just the market value of equity but the value of debt as well.

Determinants of Value-to-Book and Value-Earnings Multiples

Even across relatively closely related firms, price multiples can vary considerably. Careful analysis of this variation requires consideration of factors that might explain why one firm's multiples should be higher than those of benchmark firms. We therefore return to the abnormal earnings valuation method and show how it provides insights into differences in value-to-book and value-to-earnings multiples across firms

If the abnormal earnings formula is scaled by book value, the left-hand side becomes the equity value-to-book ratio as opposed to the equity value itself. The right-hand side variables are now earnings deflated by book value, or our old friend return on equity (ROE), discussed in Chapter 5.[5] The valuation formula becomes

$$\text{Equity value-to-book ratio} \;=\; 1 + \frac{ROE_1 - r_e}{(1 + r_e)} + \frac{(ROE_2 - r_e)(1 + gbve_1)}{(1 + r_e)^2}$$

$$+ \; \frac{(ROE_3 - r_e)(1 + gbve_1)(1 + gbve_2)}{(1 + r_e)^3} \; + \; \dots$$

where $gbve_t$ = growth in book value (*BVE*) from year t-1 to year t or

$$\frac{BVE_t - BVE_{t-1}}{BVE_{t-1}}$$

The formulation implies that a firm's equity value-to-book ratio is a function of three factors: its future abnormal ROEs, its growth in book equity, and its cost of equity capital. Abnormal ROE is defined as ROE less the cost of equity capital (ROE – r_e). Firms with positive abnormal ROE are able to invest their net assets to create value for shareholders and have price-to-book ratios greater than one. Firms that are unable to generate returns greater than the cost of capital have ratios below one.

The magnitude of a firm's value-to-book multiple also depends on the amount of growth in book value. Firms can grow their equity base by issuing new equity or by reinvesting profits. If this new equity is invested in positive valued projects for shareholders, that is, projects with ROEs that exceed the cost of capital, the firm will boost its equity value-to-book multiple. Of course for firms with ROEs that are less than the cost of capital, equity growth further lowers the multiple.

The valuation task can now be framed in terms of two key questions about the firm's "value drivers":

- How much greater (or smaller) than normal will the firm's ROE be?
- How quickly will the firm's investment base (book value) grow?

If desired, the equation can be rewritten so that future ROEs are expressed as the product of their components: profit margins, sales turnover, and leverage. Thus the approach permits us to build directly on projections of the same accounting numbers utilized in financial analysis (see Chapter 9) without the need to convert projections of those numbers into cash flows. Yet in the end, the estimate of value should be the same as that from the dividend discount model.[6]

It is also possible to structure the multiple valuation as the debt plus equity value-to-book assets ratio by scaling the abnormal NOPAT formula by book value of net operating assets. The valuation formula then becomes

$$\text{Debt plus equity value-to-book ratio} = 1 + \frac{ROA_1 - WACC}{(1 + WACC)} + \frac{(ROA_2 - WACC)(1 + gbva)}{(1 + WACC)^2}$$
$$+ \frac{(ROA_3 - WACC)(1 + gbva_1)(1 + gbva_2)}{(1 + WACC)^3} + \ldots$$

where ROA = operating return on assets = NOPAT/(Operating working capital + Net long-term assets)

$WACC$ = weighted average cost of debt and equity

$gbva_n$ = growth in book value of assets (BVA) from year t-1 to year t or

$$\frac{BVA_t - BVA_{t-1}}{BVA_{t-1}}$$

The value of a firm's debt and equity to net operating assets multiple therefore depends on its ability to generate asset returns that exceed its WACC, and on its ability to grow its asset base. The value of equity under this approach is then the estimated multiple times the current book value of assets less the market value of debt.

Returning to the Down Under Company example, the implied equity value-to-book multiple can be estimated as follows:

	Year 1	Year 2	Year 3
Beginning book value	$60m	$40m	$20m
Earnings	$20m	$30m	$40m
ROE	0.33	0.75	2.00
− Cost of capital	0.10	0.10	0.10
= Abnormal ROE	0.23	0.65	1.90
× (1+ cumulative book value growth)	1.00	0.67	0.33
= Abnormal ROE scaled by book value growth	0.23	0.43	0.63
× PV factor	0.9091	0.8264	0.7513
= PV of abnormal ROE scaled by book value growth	0.212%	0.358%	0.476%

	Year 1	Year 2	Year 3
Cumulative PV of abnormal ROE scaled by book value growth	1.046		
+ 1.00	1.000		
= Equity value-to-book multiple	2.046		

The equity value-to-book multiple for Down Under is therefore 2.046, and the implied stock value is $122.8 ($60 times 2.046), once again identical to the dividend discount model value. Recall that Down Under is an all-equity firm, so that the abnormal ROE and abnormal ROA structures for valuing the firm are the same.

The equity value-to-book formulation can also be used to construct the equity value-earnings multiple as follows:

$$\text{Equity value-to-earnings multiple} \quad = \quad \text{Equity value-to-book multiple} \times \frac{\text{Book value of equity}}{\text{Earnings}}$$

$$= \quad \frac{\text{Equity value-to-book multiple}}{\text{ROE}}$$

In other words, the same factors that drive a firm's equity value-to-book multiple also explain its equity value-earnings multiple. The key difference between the two multiples is that the value-earnings multiple is affected by the firm's current level of ROE performance, whereas the value-to-book multiple is not. Firms with low current ROEs therefore have very high value-earnings multiples and vice versa. If a firm has a zero or negative ROE, its PE multiple is not defined. Value-earnings multiples are therefore more volatile than value-to-book multiples.

The following data for a subset of firms in the Retail: Apparel industry illustrate the relation between ROE, equity growth, the price-to-book ratio, and the price-earnings ratio:

Company	ROE	Book Value Growth	Price-to-Book Ratio	Price-Earnings Ratio
Dillard's	2.73%	1.47%	0.43	15.96
J C Penney	1.67%	−1.60%	1.14	66.95
Target	20.98%	20.57%	5.10	29.31
TJX	41.06%	10.01%	8.41	22.53

Both the price-to-book and price-earnings ratios are high for Target. Investors therefore expect that in the future Target will generate even higher ROEs than its current high level (21 percent). In contrast, TJX has a high price-to-book ratio (8.41) but a low price-earnings ratio (22.53). This indicates that investors expect that TJX will continue to generate positive abnormal ROEs but that the current level of ROE (41 percent) is not sustainable. J C Penney has a price-to-book ratio of 1.14, indicating that investors expect it to earn about normal ROEs. However it has a high price-earnings multiple (66.95), suggesting that the current low ROE (1.67) is considered temporary. Finally, Dillard's has a relatively low price-to-book ratio, 0.43, and a low price-earnings multiple. Investors apparently do not expect Dillard's to significantly improve its poor performance.

Key Analysis Questions

To value a firm using multiples, an analyst has to assess the quality of the variable used as the multiple basis, and to determine the appropriate peer firms to include in the benchmark multiple. Analysts are therefore likely to be interested in answering the following questions:

- What is the expected future growth in the variable to be used as the basis for the multiple? For example, if the variable is earnings, has the firm made conservative or aggressive accounting choices that are likely to unwind in the coming years? If the multiple is book value, what is the sustainability of the firm's growth and ROE? What is the dynamics of the firm's industry and product market? Is it a market leader in a high growth industry, or is it in a mature industry with fewer growth prospects? How is the firm's future performance likely to be affected by competition or potential new entry in the industry?
- Which are the most suitable peer companies to include in the benchmark multiple computation? Have these firms had comparable growth (earnings or book values), profitability, and quality of earnings as the firm being analyzed? Do they have the same risk characteristics?

SHORTCUT FORMS OF EARNINGS-BASED VALUATION

The discounted abnormal earnings valuation formula can be simplified by making assumptions about the relation between a firm's current and future abnormal earnings. Similarly, the equity value-to-book formula can be simplified by making assumptions about long-term ROEs and growth.

1. Relation Between Current and Future Abnormal Earnings

Several assumptions about the relation between current and future net income are popular for simplifying the abnormal earnings model. First, abnormal earnings are assumed to follow a random walk. The random walk model for abnormal earnings implies that an analyst's best guess about future expected abnormal earnings are current abnormal earnings. The model assumes that past shocks to abnormal earnings persist forever, but that future shocks are random or unpredictable. The random walk model can be written as follows:

$$\text{Forecasted } AE_1 = AE_0$$

Forecasted AE_1 is the forecast of next year's abnormal earnings and AE_0 is current period abnormal earnings. Under the model, forecasted abnormal earnings for two years ahead are simply abnormal earnings in year one, or once again current abnormal earnings. In other words, the best guess of abnormal earnings in any future year is just current abnormal earnings.[7]

How does the above assumption about future abnormal earnings simplify the discounted abnormal earnings valuation model? If abnormal earnings follow a random walk, all future forecasts of abnormal earnings are simply current abnormal earnings. It is then possible to rewrite value as follows:

$$\text{Stock value} = BVE_0 + \frac{AE_0}{r_e}$$

The stock value is the book value of equity at the end of the year plus current abnormal earnings divided by the cost of capital.

In reality of course, shocks to abnormal earnings are unlikely to persist forever. Firms that have positive shocks are likely to attract competitors that will reduce opportunities for future abnormal performance. Firms with negative abnormal earnings shocks are likely to fail or to be acquired by other firms that can manage their resources more effectively. The persistence of abnormal performance will therefore depend on strategic factors such as barriers to entry and switching costs, discussed in Chapter 2. To reflect this, analysts frequently assume that current shocks to abnormal earnings decay over time. Under this assumption, abnormal earnings are said to follow an autoregressive model. Forecasted abnormal earnings are then

$$\text{Forecasted } AE_1 \quad = \quad \beta AE_0$$

β is a parameter that captures the speed with which abnormal earnings decay over time. If there is no decay, β is one and abnormal earnings follow a random walk. If β is zero, abnormal earnings decay completely within one year. Estimates of β using actual company data indicate that for a typical U.S. firm, β is approximately 0.6. However, it varies by industry, and is smaller for firms with large accruals and one-time accounting charges.[8]

The autoregressive model implies that stock values can again be written as a function of current abnormal earnings and book values[9]:

$$\text{Stock value} \quad = \quad BVE_0 \; + \; \frac{\beta AE_0}{1 + r_e - \beta}$$

This formulation implies that stock values are simply the sum of current book value plus current abnormal earnings weighted by the cost of equity capital and persistence in abnormal earnings.

2. ROE and Growth Simplifications

It is also possible to make simplifications about long-term ROEs and equity growth to reduce forecast horizons for estimating the equity value-to-book multiple. Firms' long-term ROEs are affected by such factors as barriers to entry in their industries, change in production or delivery technologies, and quality of management. As discussed in Chapter 6, these factors tend to force abnormal ROEs to decay over time. One way to model this decay is to assume that ROEs follow a mean reverting process. Forecasted ROE in one period's time then takes the following form:

$$\text{Forecasted } ROE_1 \quad = \quad ROE_0 \; + \; \beta (ROE_0 \; - \; \overline{ROE})$$

$\overline{ROE}$ is the steady state ROE (either the firm's cost of capital or the long-term industry ROE) and β is a "speed of adjustment factor" that reflects how quickly it takes the ROE to revert to its steady state.[10]

Growth rates are affected by several factors. First, the size of the firm is important. Small firms can sustain very high growth rates for an extended period, whereas large firms find it more difficult to do so. Second, firms with high rates of growth are likely to attract competitors, which reduces their growth rates. As discussed in Chapter 10, book value growth rates for real firms exhibit considerable reversion to the mean.

The long-term patterns in ROE and book equity growth rates imply that for most companies there is limited value in making forecasts for valuation beyond a relatively short horizon, three to five years. Powerful economic forces tend to lead firms with superior or inferior performance early in the forecast horizon to revert to a level that is comparable to that of other firms in the industry or the economy. For a firm in steady state, that is, expected to have a stable ROE and book equity growth rate (*gbve*), the value-to-book multiple formula simplifies to the following:

$$\text{Equity value-to-book multiple} = 1 + \frac{ROE_0 - r_e}{r_e - gbve}$$

Consistent with this simplified model, there is a strong relation between price-to-book ratios and current ROEs. Figure 7-1 shows the relation between these variables for firms in the Retail: Apparel industry we discussed earlier.

Figure 7-1	Relation Between ROE and Price-to-Book Multiples

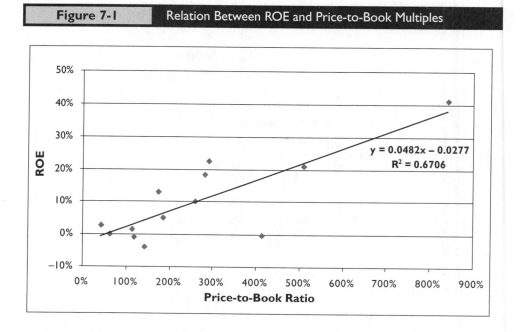

The correlation between the two variables is 0.82.

Of course, analysts can make a variety of simplifying assumptions about a firm's ROE and growth. For example, they can assume that they decay slowly or rapidly to the cost of capital and the growth rate for the economy. They can assume that the rates decay to the industry or economy average ROEs and book value growth rates. The valuation formula can easily be modified to accommodate these assumptions

THE DISCOUNTED CASH FLOW MODEL

The final valuation method discussed here is the discounted cash flow approach. This is the valuation method taught in most finance classes. Like the abnormal earnings approach, it is derived from the dividend discount model. It is based on the insight that dividends can be recast as free cash flows,[11] that is

$$\text{Dividends} = \text{Operating cash flow} - \text{Capital outlays} + \text{Net cash flows from debt owners}$$

As discussed in Chapter 5, operating cash flows to equity holders are simply net income plus depreciation less changes in working capital accruals. Capital outlays are capital expenditures less asset sales. Finally, net cash flows from debt owners are issues of new debt less retirements less the after-tax cost of interest. By rearranging these terms, the free cash flows to equity can be written as follows:

$$\text{Dividends} \;=\; \text{Free cash flows to equity} \;=\; NI - \Delta BVA + \Delta BVND$$

where NI is net income, ΔBVA is the change in book value of operating net assets (including changes in working capital plus capital expenditures less depreciation expense), and $\Delta BVND$ is the change in book value of net debt (interest-bearing debt less excess cash).

The dividend discount model can therefore be written as the present value of free cash flows to equity. Under this formulation firm value is estimated as follows:

$$\text{Equity value} \;=\; \text{PV of free cash flows to equity claim holders}$$

$$= \frac{NI_1 - \Delta BVA_1 + \Delta BVND_1}{(1 + r_e)} + \frac{NI_2 - \Delta BVA_2 + \Delta BVND_2}{(1 + r_e)^2} + \ldots$$

Alternatively, the free cash flow formulation can be structured by estimating the value of claims to net debt and equity and then deducting the market value of net debt. This approach is more widely used in practice because it does not require explicit forecasts of changes in debt balances.[12] The value of debt plus equity is then

$$\text{Debt plus equity value} \;=\; \text{PV of free cash flows to net debt and equity claim holders}$$

$$= \frac{NOPAT_1 - \Delta BVA_1}{(1 + WACC)} + \frac{NOPAT_2 - \Delta BVA_2}{(1 + WACC)^2} + \ldots$$

Valuation under the discounted cash flow method therefore involves the following steps:

Step 1: Forecast free cash flows available to equity holders (or to debt and equity holders) over a finite forecast horizon (usually 5 to 10 years).

Step 2: Forecast free cash flows beyond the terminal year based on some simplifying assumption.

Step 3: Discount free cash flows to equity holders (debt plus equity holders) at the cost of equity (weighted average cost of capital). The discounted amount represents the estimated value of free cash flows available to equity (debt and equity holders as a group).

Returning to the Down Under Company example, there is no debt, so that the free cash flows to owners are simply the operating profits before depreciation. Since Down Under is an all-equity firm, its WACC is the cost of equity (10 percent), and the present value of the free cash flows is as follows:

Year	Free Cash Flows	PV Factor	PV of Free Cash Flows
1	$40m	0.9091	$36.4m
2	50	0.8264	41.3
3	60	0.7513	45.1
Equity value			$122.8m

COMPARING VALUATION METHODS

We have discussed three methods of valuation derived from the dividend discount model: discounted dividends, discounted abnormal earnings (or abnormal ROEs), and discounted cash flows. What are the pluses and minuses of these approaches? Since the methods are all derived from the same underlying model, no one version can be considered superior to the others. As long as analysts make the same assumptions about firm fundamentals, value estimates under all four methods will be identical.

However, there are several important differences between the models that are worth noting:

- they focus the analyst's task on different issues;
- they require different levels of structure for valuation analysis; and
- they have different implications for the estimation of terminal values.

Focus on Different Issues

The methods frame the valuation task differently and can in practice focus the analyst's attention on different issues. The earnings-based approaches frame the issues in terms of accounting data such as earnings and book values. Analysts spend considerable time analyzing historical income statements and balance sheets, and their primary forecasts are typically for these variables.

Defining values in terms of ROEs has the added advantage that it focuses analysts' attention on ROE, the same key measure of performance that is decomposed in a standard financial analysis. Further, because ROEs control for firm scale, it is likely to be easier for analysts to evaluate the reasonableness of their forecasts by benchmarking them with ROEs of other firms in the industry and the economy. This type of benchmarking is more challenging for free cash flows and abnormal earnings.

Differences in Required Structure

The methods differ in the amount of analysis and structure required for valuation. The discounted abnormal earnings and ROE methods require analysts to construct both pro forma income statements and balance sheets to forecast future earnings and book values. In contrast, the discounted cash flow method requires analysts to forecast income statements and changes in working capital and long-term assets to generate free cash flows. Finally, the discounted dividend method requires analysts to forecast dividends.

The discounted abnormal earnings, ROE, and free cash flow models all require more structure for analysis than the discounted dividend approach. They therefore help analysts to avoid structural inconsistencies in their forecasts of future dividends by specifically allowing for firms' future performance and investment opportunities. Similarly, the discounted abnormal earnings/ROE method requires more structure and work than the discounted cash flow method to build full pro forma balance sheets. This permits analysts to avoid inconsistencies in the firm's financial structure.

Differences in Terminal Value Implications

A third difference between the methods is in the effort required for estimating terminal values. Terminal value estimates for the abnormal earnings and ROE methods tend to represent a much smaller fraction of total value than under the discounted cash flow or dividend methods. On the surface, this would appear to mitigate concerns about the aspect of valuation that leaves the analyst most uncomfortable. Is this apparent advantage real? As explained below, the answer turns on how well value is already reflected in the accountant's book value.

The abnormal earnings valuation does not eliminate the discounted cash flow terminal value problem, but it does reframe it. Discounted cash flow terminal values include the present value of *all* expected cash flows beyond the forecast horizon. Under abnormal earnings valuation, that value is broken into two parts: the present values of *normal* earnings and *abnormal* earnings beyond the terminal year. The terminal value in the abnormal earnings technique includes only the *abnormal* earnings. The present value of *normal* earnings is already reflected in the original book value or growth in book value over the forecast horizon.

The abnormal earnings approach, then, recognizes that current book value and earnings over the forecast horizon already reflect many of the cash flows expected to arrive after the forecast horizon. The approach builds directly on accrual accounting. For example, under accrual accounting book equity can be thought of as the minimum recoverable future benefits attributable to the firm's net assets. In addition, revenues are typically realized when earned, not when cash is received. The discounted cash flow approach, on the other hand, "unravels" all of the accruals, spreads the resulting cash flows over longer horizons, and then reconstructs its own "accruals" in the form of discounted expectations of future cash flows. The essential difference between the two approaches is that abnormal earnings valuation recognizes that the accrual process may already have performed a portion of the valuation task, whereas the discounted cash flow approach ultimately moves back to the primitive cash flows underlying the accruals.

The usefulness of the accounting-based perspective thus hinges on how well the accrual process reflects future cash flows. The approach is most convenient when the accrual process is "unbiased," so that earnings can be abnormal only as the result of economic rents and not as a product of accounting itself.[13] The forecast horizon then extends to the point where the firm is expected to approach a competitive equilibrium and earn only normal earnings on its projects. Subsequent abnormal earnings would be zero, and the terminal value at that point would be zero. In this extreme case, *all* of the firm's value is reflected in the book value and earnings projected over the forecast horizon.

Of course accounting rarely works so well. For example, in most countries research and development costs are expensed, and book values fail to reflect any research and development assets. As a result, firms that spend heavily on research and development— such as pharmaceuticals—tend on average to generate abnormally high earnings even in the face of stiff competition. Purely as an artifact of research and development accounting, abnormal earnings would be expected to remain positive indefinitely for such firms, and the terminal value could represent a substantial fraction of total value.

If desired, the analyst can alter the accounting approach used by the firm in his or her own projections. "Better" accounting would be viewed as that which reflects a larger fraction of the firm's value in book values and earnings over the forecast horizon.[14] This same view underlies analysts' attempts to "normalize" earnings; the adjusted numbers are intended to provide better indications of value, even though they reflect performance only over a short horizon.

Recent research has focused on the performance of earnings-based valuation relative to discounted cash flow and discounted dividend methods. The findings indicate that over relatively short forecast horizons, ten years or less, valuation estimates using the abnormal earnings approach generate more precise estimates of value than either the discounted dividend or discounted cash flow models. This advantage for the earnings-based approach persists for firms with conservative or aggressive accounting, indicating that accrual accounting in the U.S. does a reasonably good job of reflecting future cash flows.[15]

Key Analysis Questions

The above discussion on the trade-offs between different methods of valuing a company raises several questions for analysts about how to compare methods and to consider which is likely to be most reliable for their analysis:

- What are the key performance parameters that the analyst forecasts? Is more attention given to forecasting accounting variables, such as earnings and book values, or to forecasting cash flow variables?
- Has the analyst linked forecasted income statements and balance sheets? If not, is there any inconsistency between the two statements, or in the implications of the assumptions for future performance? If so, what is the source of this inconsistency and does it affect discounted earnings-based and discounted cash flow methods similarly?
- How well does the firm's accounting capture its underlying assets and obligations? Does it do a good enough job that we can rely on book values as the basis for long-term forecasts? Alternatively, does the firm rely heavily on off-balance-sheet assets, such as R&D, which make book values a poor lower bound on long-term performance?
- Has the analyst made very different assumptions about long-term performance in the terminal value computations under the different valuation methods? If so, which set of assumptions is more plausible given the firm's industry and its competitive positioning?

SUMMARY

Valuation is the process by which forecasts of performance are converted into estimates of price. A variety of valuation techniques are employed in practice, and there is no single method that clearly dominates others. In fact, since each technique involves different advantages and disadvantages, there are gains to considering several approaches simultaneously.

For shareholders, a stock's value is the present value of future dividends. This chapter described three valuation techniques directly based on this dividend discount definition of value: discounted dividends, discounted abnormal earnings/ROEs, and discounted free cash flows. The discounted dividend method attempts to forecast dividends directly. The abnormal earnings approach expresses the value of a firm's equity as book value plus discounted expectations of future abnormal earnings. Finally, the discounted cash flow method represents a firm's stock value by expected future free cash flows discounted at the cost of capital.

Although these three methods were derived from the same dividend discount model, they frame the valuation task differently. In practice they focus the analyst's attention on different issues and require different levels of structure in developing forecasts of the underlying primitive, future dividends.

Price multiple valuation methods were also discussed. Under these approaches, analysts estimate ratios of current price to historical or forecasted measures of performance for comparable firms. The benchmarks are then used to value the performance of the firm being analyzed. Multiples have traditionally been popular, primarily because they do not require analysts to make multiyear forecasts of performance. However it can be difficult to identify comparable firms to use as benchmarks. Even across highly related firms, there are differences in performance that are likely to affect their multiples.

The chapter discussed the relation between two popular multiples, value-to-book and value-earnings ratios, and the discounted abnormal earnings valuation. The resulting formulations indicate that value-to-book multiples are a function of future abnormal ROEs, book value growth, and the firm's cost of equity. The value-earnings multiple is a function of the same factors and also the current ROE.

DISCUSSION QUESTIONS

1. Joe Watts, an analyst at EMH Securities, states: "I don't know why anyone would ever try to value earnings. Obviously, the market knows that earnings can be manipulated and only values cash flows." Discuss.

2. Explain why terminal values in accounting-based valuation are significantly less than those for DCF valuation.

3. Manufactured Earnings is a "darling" of Wall Street analysts. Its current market price is $15 per share, and its book value is $5 per share. Analysts forecast that the firm's book value will grow by 10 percent per year indefinitely, and the cost of equity is 15 percent. Given these facts, what is the market's expectation of the firm's long-term average ROE?

4. Given the information in question 3, what will be Manufactured Earnings' stock price if the market revises its expectations of long-term average ROE to 20 percent?

5. Analysts reassess Manufactured Earnings' future performance as follows: growth in book value increases to 12 percent per year, but the ROE of the incremental book value is only 15 percent. What is the impact on the market-to-book ratio?

6. How can a company with a high ROE have a low PE ratio?

7. What types of companies have
   a. a high PE and a low market-to-book ratio?
   b. a high PE ratio and a high market-to-book ratio?
   c. a low PE and a high market-to-book ratio?
   d. a low PE and a low market-to-book ratio?

8. Free cash flows (FCF) used in DCF valuations discussed in the chapter are defined as follows:

   FCF to debt and equity = Earnings before interest and taxes × (1 − tax rate)
   　　　　　　　　　　　　　+ Depreciation and deferred taxes − Capital
   　　　　　　　　　　　　　expenditures −/+ Increase/decrease in working capital

   FCF to equity = Net income + Depreciation and deferred taxes − Capital
   　　　　　　　　　expenditures −/+ Increase/decrease in working capital
   　　　　　　　　　+/− Increase/decrease in debt

   Which of the following items affect free cash flows to debt and equity holders? Which affect free cash flows to equity alone? Explain why and how.
   - An increase in accounts receivable
   - A decrease in gross margins
   - An increase in property, plant, and equipment

- An increase in inventory
- Interest expense
- An increase in prepaid expenses
- An increase in notes payable to the bank

9. Starite Company is valued at $20 per share. Analysts expect that it will generate free cash flows to equity of $4 per share for the foreseeable future. What is the firm's implied cost of equity capital?

10. Janet Stringer argues that "the DCF valuation method has increased managers' focus on short-term rather than long-term performance, since the discounting process places much heavier weight on short-term cash flows than long-term ones." Comment.

NOTES

1. The incorporation of all noncapital equity transactions into income is called clean surplus accounting. It is analogous to comprehensive income, the concept defined in FAS 130.

2. Changes in book value also include new capital contributions. However the dividend discount model assumes that new capital is issued at fair value. As a result, any incremental book value from capital issues is exactly offset by the discounted value of future dividends to new shareholders. Capital transactions therefore do not affect firm valuation.

3. The appendix to this chapter provides a simple proof of the earnings-based valuation formula.

4. See C. Lee and J. Myers, "What is the Intrinsic Value of the Dow?" Cornell University, working paper, 1997.

5. There is an important difference between the way ROE is defined in the value-to-book formulation and the way it is defined in Chapter 9. The valuation formula defines ROE as return on beginning equity, whereas in our ratio discussion we used return on ending or return on average equity.

6. It may seem surprising that one can estimate value with no explicit attention to two of the cash flow streams considered in DCF analysis, investments in working capital and capital expenditures. The accounting-based technique recognizes that these investments cannot possibly contribute to value without impacting abnormal earnings, and that therefore only their earnings impacts need be considered. For example, the benefit of an increase in inventory turnover surfaces in terms of its impact on ROE (and thus, abnormal earnings), without the need to consider explicitly the cash flow impacts involved.

7. It is also possible to include a drift term in the model, allowing earnings to grow by a constant amount, or at a constant rate each period.

8. See P. M. Dechow, A. P. Hutton, and R. G. Sloan, "An empirical assessment of the residual income valuation model," *Journal of Accounting and Economics* 23, January 1999.

9. This formulation is a variant of a model proposed by James Ohlson, "Earnings, book values, and dividends in security valuation," *Contemporary Accounting Research* 11, Spring 1995. Ohlson includes in his forecasts of future abnormal earnings a variable that reflects relevant information other than current abnormal earnings. This variable then also appears in the stock valuation formula. Empirical research by Dechow, Hutton, and Sloan, "An empirical assessment of the residual income valuation model," *Journal of Accounting and Economics* 23, January 1999, indicates that financial analysts' forecasts of abnormal earnings do reflect considerable information other than current abnormal earnings, and that this information is useful for valuation.

10. This specification is similar to the model for dividends developed by J. Lintner, "Distribution of incomes of corporations among dividends, retained earnings, and taxes," *American Economic Review* 46 (May 1956): 97–113.

11. In practice, firms do not have to pay out all of their free cash flows as dividends; they can retain surplus cash in the business. The conditions under which a firm's dividend decision affects its

value are discussed by M. H. Miller and F. Modigliani in "Dividend Policy, Growth and the Valuation of Shares," *Journal of Business* 34 (October 1961): 411–33.

12. A good forecast, however, would be grounded in an understanding of these changes as well as all other key elements of the firm's financial picture. The changes in financing cash flows are particularly critical for firms that anticipate changing their capital structure.

13. Unbiased accounting is that which, in a competitive equilibrium, produces an expected ROE equal to the cost of capital. The actual ROE thus reveals the presence of economic rents. Market-value accounting is a special case of unbiased accounting that produces an expected ROE equal to the cost of capital, even when the firm is *not* in a competitive equilibrium. That is, market-value accounting reflects the present value of future economic rents in book value, driving the expected ROEs to a normal level. For a discussion of unbiased and biased accounting, see G. Feltham and J. Ohlson, "Valuation and Clean Surplus Accounting for Operating and Financial Activities," *Contemporary Accounting Research* 11, No. 2 (Spring 1995): 689–731.

14. In Bennett Stewart's book on EVA valuation, *The Quest for Value* (New York: HarperBusiness, 1999), he recommends a number of accounting adjustments, including the capitalization of research and development.

15. S. Penman and T. Sougiannis, "A Comparison of Dividend, Cash Flow, and Earnings Approaches to Equity Valuation," *Contemporary Accounting Research* (Fall 1998): 343–83, compares the valuation methods using actual realizations of earnings, cash flows, and dividends to estimate prices. J. Francis, P. Olsson, and D. Oswald, "Comparing Accuracy and Explainability of Dividend, Free Cash Flow and Abnormal Earnings Equity Valuation Models," *Journal of Accounting Research* 38 (Spring 2000): 45–70, estimates values using *Value Line* forecasts.

APPENDIX: RECONCILING THE DISCOUNTED DIVIDENDS AND DISCOUNTED ABNORMAL EARNINGS MODELS

To derive the earnings-based valuation from the dividend discount model consider the following two-period valuation:

$$\text{Equity value} = \frac{DIV_1}{(1 + r_e)} + \frac{DIV_2}{(1 + r_e)^2}$$

With clean surplus accounting, dividends (DIV) can be expressed as a function of net income (NI) and the book value of equity (BVE):

$$DIV_t = NI_t + BVE_{t-1} - BVE_t$$

Substituting this expression into the dividend discount model yields the following:

$$\text{Equity value} = \frac{NI_1 + BVE_0 - BVE_1}{(1 + r_e)} + \frac{NI_2 + BVE_1 - BVE_2}{(1 + r_e)^2}$$

This can be rewritten as follows:

$$\text{Equity value} = \frac{NI_1 - r_e BVE_0 + BVE_0(1 + r_e) - BVE_1}{(1 + r_e)}$$

$$+ \frac{NI_2 - r_e BVE_1 + BVE_1(1 + r_e) - BVE_2}{(1 + r_e)^2}$$

$$= BVE_0 + \frac{NI_1 - r_e BVE_0}{(1 + r_e)} + \frac{NI_2 - r_e BVE_1}{(1 + r_e)^2} - \frac{BVE_2}{(1 + r_e)^2}$$

The value of equity is therefore the current book value plus the present value of future abnormal earnings. As the forecast horizon expands, the final term (the present value of liquidating book value) becomes inconsequential.

Valuation Ratios in the Airline Industry

In mid-2001 the U.S. airline industry appeared to be headed into its first cyclical downturn in ten years. In May air travel fell in the United States for the first time in a decade and ticket prices softened.[1] In addition, profitability in the industry, as measured by return on equity (ROE), had declined from 25 percent in 1997 to 12 percent in 2000. Analysts forecasted that ROE would decline further to 2.3 percent in 2001.[2]

The downturn also affected industry valuation ratios. For example, price-to-book ratios declined from 2.8 in 1997 to 2.0 in 2000,[3] while price-to-earnings ratios, which were 8.3 in 1997, were not meaningful in mid-2001 since aggregate earnings for the industry were negative.[4] However these ratios varied widely across firms. In mid-2001 price-to-book ratios ranged from a low of 0.4 to a high of 3.7, and price-to-earnings ratios for firms with positive earnings ranged from 8 to 22.

INDUSTRY OVERVIEW

The deregulation of the U.S. domestic airlines market in 1978 was a turning point for domestic air travel. The 20 years following this event saw real fares decline by 50 percent and air traffic triple.[5] The period was also marked by turbulence for many firms that had pioneered air travel in the United States, with Pan Am, Eastern, and TWA being forced into bankruptcy. By mid-2001 the industry was dominated by a relatively small number of long-haul national-international carriers, while dozens of regional and commuter carriers competed for "point-to-point" (or nonstop) short-haul routes.[6]

National Carriers

Six national carriers—United Air Lines, American Airlines, Delta Air Lines, Northwest Airlines, US Airways, and Continental Airlines—provided both long-haul domestic and international service for U.S.-based passengers. Using "hub-and-spoke" networks, long-haul carriers or their regional "spoke" affiliates shuttled passengers from lightly traveled markets to central hubs where they could connect to longer flight-legs. In addition to enabling long-haul carriers to take advantage of economies of scale on their long flights, the

Professors Paul Healy and Krishna Palepu and Research Associate Jonathan Barnett prepared this case. The case is intended solely as the basis for class discussion and is not intended to serve as an endorsement, source of primary data, or illustration of effective or ineffective management. Copyright © 2003 by the President and Fellows of Harvard College. HBS case 9-103-002.

1. Airline traffic growth was predicted to increase 3.5 percent in 2001, a marked decline from the 4.7 percent and 5.2 percent increases in 1999 and 2000. Yield (or average revenue per passenger) was forecast to grow 4 percent in 2001. Stephen Klein and Richard Stice, "Airlines," Standard & Poor's (S&P) Industry Surveys, March 29, 2001.

2. Stephen Sanborn, "The Air Transport Industry," Value Line Investment Survey, June 15, 2001.

3. S&P Research Insight.

4. The airline industry's average beta was 0.89. Given the long-term government bond rate in June 2001 of 5.7 percent and the long-term risk premium of 7.6 percent, the average cost of equity for the industry was therefore 12.5 percent. S&P Research Insight.

5. "Air Travel, Air Trouble," The Economist, July 7, 2001.

6. In 2000 the ten largest U.S. airlines accounted for 92.3 percent of total U.S. traffic. Stephen Klein and Richard Stice, "Airlines," S&P Industry Surveys, March 29, 2001.

hub-and-spoke system had reduced competition in many of the smaller hub cities, where the hub carrier owned a dominant share of the terminal gates.

Long-haul carriers had little control over the pricing of key inputs, including aircraft and jet fuel. Two suppliers, Boeing and Airbus, controlled the development and production of large-scale jet aircraft, and the price of jet fuel was heavily influenced by the impact of OPEC's oil production policies on global supply. Labor costs, the other major airline operating cost, were typically determined through intense and protracted negotiations between each carrier and the more than one dozen unions that represented distinct groups of airline personnel (e.g., pilots, attendants, mechanics, baggage handlers, etc.).

The economics of the airline business made it difficult for operators to pass on production-cost increases to passengers. Given their high fixed costs and low marginal costs, airline carriers had frequently resorted to fare reductions to boost flight capacity and yield (defined as average revenue per passenger). But competing airlines were quick to match or undercut rivals' fare reductions, resulting in periodic fare wars. Thus the continual threat of intense price competition dampened the industry's prospects for revenue growth.

Long-haul carriers developed a number of responses to the challenges of price competition and yield management. In the 1980s frequent flyer programs were introduced to increase customer loyalty and mitigate the effect of fare wars. In the 1990s the industry was quick to take advantage of the Internet to improve the booking and ticketing process. The results were mixed: while online reservation systems helped airlines to improve yield management, the broad dissemination of information on competing flight schedules and fares enabled price-sensitive consumers to search for the lowest possible fares.

In response to growth opportunities in international travel in the mid-1990s, long-haul carriers had used alliances to strengthen their international presence. Alliances took advantage of "open skies" treaties between the United States and other governments that permitted code-sharing and partial ownership between international airlines. In mid-2001 there were four global airline alliances involving U.S. carriers.[7] However, allegiance within the alliances had proven weak, with a number of carriers switching alliance memberships.

Regional Carriers

U.S. regional carriers, such as America West, ComAir, Frontier Airlines, Mesa Air, and Sky-West Airlines, typically provided nonstop short-haul service. Many of these airlines were affiliated with long-haul carriers. Affiliations typically permitted regional carriers to schedule flights under a code-sharing arrangement, meaning that each carrier could sell seats for flights on joint routes. To schedule these trips, regional affiliates, operating under the major carrier's designator code, were granted access to that carrier's computer reservation system.

Regional carriers were subject to many of the same economic forces as their long-haul counterparts. They, too, had little control over fuel prices and were forced to negotiate with a small number of aircraft manufacturers.[8] However, some of the newer regional carriers did not have a unionized labor force, making it easier to design flexible work arrangements and to manage labor costs.

....

7. The four major global airline alliances included the Star Alliance (anchored by United Air Lines and Lufthansa), the OneWorld alliance (anchored by American Airlines and British Airways), the SkyTeam alliance (anchored by Delta Air Lines and Air France), and Wings (anchored by KLM and Northwest Airlines). Each alliance also included a number of smaller carriers.

8. While long-haul and regional carriers could not directly influence the price of jet fuel, both types of carriers frequently hedged their fuel-price risk using futures as part of a comprehensive risk-management strategy.

Recent technological advances in the design of smaller regional jets had opened up new opportunities for carriers in under-served domestic markets. Although jet aircraft were first introduced to U.S. passenger service in 1958, they had proved uneconomical for small markets. However, following the 1995 introduction of new low-cost jet aircraft by Brazil's Embraer and Canada's Bombardier, regional jet operations proliferated as the short-haul markets that were previously abandoned by major airlines became viable destinations.[9] In addition to opening new markets, the seating capacity and travel range of regional jets continued to expand. As a result, regional jets were increasingly used not only to feed passengers to and from hub airports but also to provide point-to-point competition against carriers employing full-sized jets. Having recognized the value of regional carriers, major airlines had recently taken steps to increase their control over such operators, primarily through acquiring equity positions.

STRATEGY AND PERFORMANCE FOR FOUR AIRLINE CARRIERS

The following brief sketches of two long-haul carriers (American Airlines and Delta Air Lines), one regional carrier (SkyWest Airlines), and one hybrid carrier (Southwest Airlines) illustrate the differences in business strategy and performance experienced by firms in the airline industry. See Exhibits 1 and 2 for a comparison of the recent financial performance of these carriers.

American Airlines

American Airlines ("American"), the principal operating subsidiary of parent AMR Corporation, traced its roots back to the Embry-Riddle Company in the early 1920s. Later renamed the Aviation Corporation (AVCO), American became one of the first U.S. airline giants through the acquisition of 82 smaller airlines.

In 2000 American was the largest U.S. airline based on revenues. It operated hubs in Dallas-Fort Worth, Chicago O'Hare, Miami, and San Juan (Puerto Rico), and provided service to 169 destinations throughout North America, Europe, the Caribbean, Latin America, and the Pacific Rim.[10] The company owned two regional airlines operating as "American Eagle," American Eagle Airlines and Executive Airlines, which provided connecting service from eight of American's high-traffic hubs to smaller markets in the United States, Canada, the Caribbean, and the Bahamas. American was also a member of the global OneWorld alliance, which linked the operations of American, British Airways, Canadian Airlines, Cathay Pacific Airways, Qantas Airways, Finnair, Iberia, and LanChile. In addition to its passenger services, American was one of the largest air freight carriers in the world, providing a full range of freight and mail services to shippers throughout its system.[11]

On most of its nonstop domestic routes, American faced competition from one or more of the other U.S. long-haul carriers, regional airlines, and other cargo-service firms. As

9. Breakeven capacity for a regional jet was approximately 50 percent, versus 63 percent for larger jet aircraft. In 2000 there were an estimated 529 regional jets in service in the United States versus 137 in 1997. Stephen Klein and Richard Stice, "Airlines," S&P Industry Surveys, March 29, 2001.

10. In its 2000 10-K Report, American reported that domestic and foreign operations comprised 71 percent and 29 percent of total revenues, respectively.

11. As reported in American's 2000 10-K Report, its revenue mix consisted of 90 percent passenger service and 10 percent cargo and other.

many as nine airlines provided service on American's most competitive routes. Its pricing decisions were affected in part by competition from other airlines, some of which had cost structures significantly lower than American's and could therefore operate profitably at lower fare levels. On international routes American competed with state-owned carriers, foreign investor-owned carriers, international cargo service providers, and U.S. airlines that had been granted authority to provide international passenger service.[12]

American touted several sources of competitive advantage. First, its fleet of aircraft, one of the youngest in the United States, was relatively efficient and quiet. Second, in 2000 the company began aggressively deploying its American Eagle regional jet fleet. Third, by operating a comprehensive domestic and international route network anchored by efficient hubs, the company expected to be able to benefit from whatever traffic growth occurred. The firm's chairman, Donald Carty, reported in his 2000 Letter to Shareholders that American would continue to expand its domestic and international network in Boston, New York, Los Angeles, San Jose (California), Paris, and Taipei. Finally, through its AAdvantage frequent flyer program, the largest in the industry, its More Room Throughout Coach program, and its continuing efforts to provide superior service, American sought to enhance its position in the industry.

During 2000 American's revenues increased by 11 percent. Net income for the year declined by 17 percent, although profits before special items and discontinued operations rose nearly 19 percent.[13] Despite 4 percent revenue growth for the three months ended March 31, 2001, American reported a net loss from continuing operations of $43 million, versus a net gain of $89 million in the same quarter for 2000.[14] These results primarily reflected an increase in fares, offset by higher fuel costs. To mitigate the financial impact of the downturn in air travel in mid-2001, American retired older aircraft, cancelled options to purchase new jets, imposed a management hiring freeze, and deferred spending on capital projects. Despite these changes, analysts predicted that American would show a loss for 2001.[15] For 2002 analysts expected that American would show revenue growth of 8 percent and return to profitability, with an expected return on equity of 8.5 percent.[16]

Delta Air Lines

Delta Air Lines ("Delta") was founded as the world's first crop-dusting service in 1924 (then named Huff Daland Dusters). In 1928 the company began to diversify by securing air-mail contracts, and in 1929 it inaugurated passenger service between Dallas and Jackson, Mississippi. Following World War II and throughout the 1950s and 1960s, Delta prospered as a major regional airline. During the 1970s and 1980s, the company expanded its domestic network, largely by acquiring other regional carriers (including Northeast Airlines and Western Airlines). In 1991 it made a major push into international markets.

In 2001 Delta operated four hubs located in Atlanta, Cincinnati, Dallas-Fort Worth, and Salt Lake City. The company was the largest U.S. airline in terms of aircraft departures and number of passengers served, and the third largest U.S. airline in terms of operating revenues.[17] Including its wholly owned regional subsidiaries Atlantic Southeast Airlines

12. AMR Corp. 10-K Report, December 31, 2000.

13. Ibid.

14. AMR Corp. 10-Q Report, March 31, 2001.

15. Thompson Financial, FirstCall estimates.

16. Stephen Sanborn, "AMR Corporation," Value Line Investment Survey, June 15, 2001.

17. Rankings are based on calendar year-end data. Delta Air Lines 2000 10-K Report.

and ComAir, Delta served 201 U.S. cities in 45 states, the District of Columbia, the U.S. Virgin Islands, and Puerto Rico, as well as 50 cities in 32 countries in Europe, Asia, Latin America, the Caribbean, and Canada.[18] The company also operated a cargo service.[19]

Delta's services included the Delta Shuttle, Delta Express, the Delta Connection Program, and its international alliances. The Delta Shuttle was a high-frequency service providing hourly nonstop service between New York's La Guardia Airport and both Washington, D.C.'s Ronald Reagan National Airport and Boston's Logan International Airport. Delta Express was a low-fare, leisure-oriented service providing flights from select cities in the Northeast and Midwest to five destinations in Florida. The Delta Connection Program was Delta's regional carrier serving passengers in small and medium-sized cities. Finally, the company's international alliance agreements included code-sharing, frequent flyer benefits, shared or reciprocal access to passenger lounges, joint advertising, and other marketing arrangements with Aeromexico, Aeropostal, Air France, Air Jamaica, CSA Czech Airlines, Korean Air, China Southern, Royal Air Maroc, South African Airways, and Transbrasil.

Despite its prominent industry rankings, Delta sustained several years of heavy losses in the early 1990s, and in 1994 it announced a drastic cost-cutting plan dubbed the Leadership 7.5 program.[20] The restructuring initiative, which included a 20 percent reduction in the company's workforce, a realignment of its domestic route system, and the discontinuation of less profitable European routes, was designed to eliminate $2 billion in operating expenses over a three-year period, and to reduce the cost of flying to 7.5 cents per mile, per seat. Though the company was successful in engineering a quick financial comeback, posting a profit in the fourth quarter of fiscal 1995, the accompanying reduction in the company's customer service team resulted in a significant increase in passenger complaints, and by 1997 Delta had dropped to last place in on-time rankings among the ten leading U.S. airlines.[21]

In 2000 Delta also struggled with a number of labor issues. In May its mainline pilots' contract expired and months of unproductive negotiations followed. When the impasse dragged into December, the pilots retaliated by refusing voluntary overtime during one of the airline's busiest seasons, forcing Delta to cancel 3,500 flights over the course of the month and an additional 1,700 flights during the first ten days of 2001.[22] Although Delta reached an agreement with its mainline pilots in April 2001, granting them substantial pay raises, it continued to be negatively impacted by the ComAir pilots' strike announced on March 26, 2001. ComAir was the second largest regional airline in the United States and some analysts believed that the outcome of these negotiations would be an "industry-defining event . . . likely to affect regional pilot pay scales throughout the industry."[23] By mid-June of 2001, the dispute remained unresolved and was estimated to be costing Delta 3–4 million dollars per day in lost revenues.

During 2000 Delta's revenues increased 12 percent, yet profits fell by 31 percent. Excluding extraordinary items and discontinued operations, profits fell 25 percent.[24] In an

18. Delta acquired Atlantic Southeast Airlines and ComAir in 1999.

19. In 2000 cargo and other revenues accounted for 6 percent of total revenues; passenger revenues represented the remaining 94 percent.

20. Delta Air Lines Annual Report, June 30, 1994.

21. For additional background information, see Thomas Derdack, The International Directory of Company Histories, vol. 39.

22. Ibid.

23. Caglar Somek, "Delta Air Lines," Credit Suisse First Boston, May 22, 2001.

24. Delta Air Lines Annual Report, June 30, 2000.

The Airline Industry

effort to improve the bottom line, Delta reduced advertising costs, retired aircraft, released employees, and implemented a new management structure. The company's Chairman and CEO, Leo F. Mullin, also announced the industry's largest regional jet order ever, designed to "cement [Delta's] competitive advantage in this important market." [25]

Analysts predicted that the current difficult economic climate and the accompanying slowing in demand for air transport would result in a net loss for Delta for 2001, followed by a moderate rebound in 2002. Consensus forecasts called for an 8 percent return on equity in 2002, growing to 13 percent between 2004 and 2006. [26]

SkyWest Airlines

In 1972 attorney J. Ralph Atkin founded SkyWest Airlines (then named Inter American Aviation) so that he and four friends could own a plane for fun. That same year Atkin decided to offer commercial flights. Since then SkyWest Airlines ("SkyWest"), the principal operating subsidiary of SkyWest Inc., had grown to become one of the larger regional airlines in the United States. The company operated a fleet of 108 aircraft from six hubs located in Los Angeles, Salt Lake City, San Francisco, Portland, and Seattle/Tacoma. It offered passenger and air freight service with over 1,000 daily departures to 68 destinations in 14 western states and Canada.

Nearly 70 percent of SkyWest flights were jointly coded with Delta Air Lines and United Airlines flights under long-term revenue code-sharing relationships.[27] Under the terms of these relationships, on SkyWest-controlled flights, SkyWest oversaw scheduling, ticketing, pricing, and seat inventories, and received a prorated portion of passenger fares. On contract routes, where SkyWest's major airline partner handled these functions, SkyWest received negotiated payments per flight departure and incentives based on passenger volumes and levels of customer satisfaction.[28] SkyWest first became a code-sharing partner with Delta Air Lines in Salt Lake City in 1987, and it teamed up with United Air Lines in Los Angeles in 1997.

Skywest management attributed the carrier's success in securing these contracts to its delivery of high-quality customer service and argued that these relationships provided important benefits for SkyWest. First, they enabled the carrier to "reduce reliance on any single major airline [designator] code and to enhance and stabilize operating results through a mixture of SkyWest-controlled flying and contract flying."[29] They also provided SkyWest with opportunities to grow the airline. Based on its existing Delta Connection and United Express code-sharing contracts, which were to be in place until 2008 and 2010, SkyWest had committed to acquire an additional 113 regional jets with options on another 119 aircraft. However this commitment was not without risk, since both Delta and United could terminate the code-sharing arrangements "for any or no reason" with 180 days' advance notice.[30]

SkyWest primarily competed with other regional airlines, some of which were owned by, or were operated as code-sharing partners of, major airlines. On certain routes

25. Ibid.

26. Damon Churchwell, "Delta Air Lines," *Value Line Investment Survey*, June 15, 2001.

27. SkyWest operated as the Delta Connection in Salt Lake City and as United Express in Los Angeles, San Francisco, Denver, and the Pacific Northwest. SkyWest's contract business was nearly evenly distributed between United Air Lines (55%) and Delta Air Lines (45%). Caglar Somek, "Delta Airlines," *Credit Suisse First Boston*, May 22, 2001.

28. SkyWest 10-K Report, March 31, 2001.

29. SkyWest Annual Report, March 31, 2001.

30. Ibid.

SkyWest also competed with low-fare carriers and major airlines. While SkyWest's joint affiliations with Delta and United distinguished it from the majority of its competitors, so too did the carrier's strong relationship with its wholly nonunionized workforce.

For the year ended March 31, 2001, SkyWest reported that revenues grew 12 percent, versus 22 percent in 2000. Profits were flat due to a nearly 17 percent increase in operating expenses, primarily from increased fuel costs and, to a lesser extent, from increased salaries and wages as the airline continued to add personnel.[31] Despite the slowdown in revenue growth, analysts forecasted that SkyWest's sales would grow at a compound annual growth rate of more than 30 percent between 2002 and 2005, while earnings were forecasted to grow 32 percent in 2002 and 22 percent in 2003. Based on these forecasts, the company was expected to generate a return on equity of nearly 23 percent in 2002 and 2003.[32]

Southwest Airlines

Founded in 1971 with three Boeing 737 aircraft serving just three destinations in Texas, Southwest Airlines ("Southwest") rapidly grew to become a major domestic airline. Based on data for the second quarter of 2001, Southwest operated 344 aircraft, provided scheduled service to 57 destinations in 29 states, and was the largest U.S. airline based on domestic departures and the fourth largest based on number of domestic passengers served.[33]

Southwest had achieved its rapid growth by positioning itself as a cost leader in the industry. To accomplish this position, Southwest offered its customers "no-frills" service at a low price. It had elected not to develop the costly hub-and-spoke networks used by United, American, Delta, and the other major domestic carriers. Instead, the company provided frequent flights to conveniently located, but typically less congested, satellite airports such as Dallas Love Field, Chicago Midway, and T.F. Green in Providence, Rhode Island. In so doing Southwest was able to develop a record for reliable on-time performance and achieved high asset utilization. High asset utilization and tight control over operating expenses were maintained through operating only a single type of aircraft, the Boeing 737, which simplified scheduling, maintenance, flight operations, and training activities. As a result of these and other activities, Southwest reduced the amount of time an aircraft sat idle at a gate to approximately 25 minutes (less than half the industry average), which reduced the number of aircraft and gate facilities that would otherwise be required.

There were other notable differences between Southwest and other major U.S. carriers. For example, Southwest did not enter into code-sharing relationships with other airlines, nor did it maintain any commuter feeder relationships. Southwest also eschewed both a ticket reservation system (to avoid paying fees to travel agents) and the commonly used multi-tier pricing strategy, in favor of a simple fare structure that featured low, unrestricted everyday coach fares. Being majority-owned by its employees, Southwest had enjoyed strong relationships with its predominantly nonunionized workforce, yielding further cost savings and labor flexibility. Finally, Southwest's frequent flyer program also differed from those of the other major airlines, with travel awards based on the number of trips taken rather than on the number of miles accrued. All told, management estimated that the

The Airline Industry

---

31. *SkyWest 10-K Report, March 31, 2001.*

32. *Thompson Financial FirstCall and case writer estimates.*

33. *Southwest Airlines 10-K Report, December 31, 2000.*

company's strategy resulted in its providing approximately 90 percent of all low-fare air-line service in the United States.[34]

Fiscal 2000 was Southwest's twenty-second consecutive year of profitability and ninth consecutive year of increased profits. During 2000 Southwest's revenues and profits increased by 19 percent and 27 percent, respectively, and the company earned a 22 percent return on equity.[35] For the three months ended March 31, 2001, revenues and profits increased 15 percent and 25 percent, respectively, compared to the same quarter one year earlier.[36] 2001 and 2002 consensus forecasts for revenue and earnings growth were 11 percent and 19 percent, and 12 percent and 24 percent, respectively. Based on these estimates, analysts predicted a ROE of 17 percent in 2001 and 17.5 percent in 2002.[37]

QUESTIONS

1. Match the valuation multiples below with each of the four airlines discussed in the case. What is your reasoning for the matches you selected?

VALUATION MULTIPLES [*]

Airline	Price / Earnings	Price / Book Value
A	7.5	0.8
B	6.8	1.2
C	16.8	3.1
D	26.8	4.9

(*) The ratios were calculated using fiscal 2000 year-end figures.
Source: Case writer estimates.

2. What is the general relationship between a company's strategy, its current performance, and price-to-book and price-to-earnings ratios?

34. Southwest Airlines Annual Report, December 31, 2000.
35. Ibid.
36. Southwest Airlines 10-Q Report, March 31, 2001.
37. Warren Thorpe, "Southwest Airlines," Value Line Investment Survey, June 15, 2001.

EXHIBIT I

Financial Performance Comparison for American Airlines, Delta Air Lines, SkyWest Airlines, and Southwest Airlines

American Airlines	2000	1999	1998	1997	1996
Net operating profit margin	0.05	0.07	0.08	0.06	0.07
Net operating asset turnover	1.74	1.96	2.34	2.03	2.16
Operating ROA = product of above	0.09	0.13	0.18	0.12	0.16
Spread	0.05	0.05	0.11	0.08	0.10
Net financial leverage	0.65	0.35	0.32	0.58	1.16
Financial leverage gain	0.03	0.02	0.03	0.05	0.12
ROE = Operating ROA + Financial leverage gain	0.12	0.15	0.21	0.17	0.27
5-year compound annual growth rates (CAGR):					
Revenues	3.1				
Assets	6.0				
Equity	14.6				
Beta	1.16				

Delta Air Lines	2000	1999	1998	1997	1996
Net operating profit margin	0.06	0.09	0.08	0.07	0.02
Net operating asset turnover	2.25	3.33	3.46	4.12	4.30
Operating ROA = product of above	0.13	0.29	0.26	0.29	0.09
Spread	0.07	0.01	0.19	0.15	−0.01
Net financial leverage	0.51	0.07	0.29	0.23	0.59
Financial leverage gain	0.04	0.00	0.06	0.03	−0.01
ROE = Operating ROA + Financial leverage gain	0.17	0.29	0.32	0.32	0.08
5-year compound annual growth rates (CAGR):					
Revenues	6.1				
Assets	12.4				
Equity	18.3				
Beta	0.76				

SkyWest Airlines	2000	1999	1998	1997	1996
Net operating profit margin	0.09	0.11	0.11	0.08	0.04
Net operating asset turnover	2.64	2.88	3.75	2.18	1.87
Operating ROA = product of above	0.24	0.32	0.40	0.18	0.07
Spread	0.16	0.28	0.39	0.17	0.09
Net financial leverage	−0.35	−0.35	−0.51	−0.02	0.14
Financial leverage gain	−0.06	−0.10	−0.20	0.00	0.01
ROE = Operating ROA + Financial leverage gain	0.18	0.22	0.20	0.18	0.08
5-year compound annual growth rates (CAGR):					
Revenues	16.1				
Assets	20.1				
Equity	17.2				
Beta	0.70				

Southwest Airlines	2000	1999	1998	1997	1996
Net operating profit margin	0.11	0.10	0.11	0.09	0.07
Net operating asset turnover	1.71	1.78	1.95	2.21	1.91
Operating ROA = product of above	0.19	0.19	0.21	0.19	0.13
Spread	0.15	0.12	0.09	−0.01	0.07
Net financial leverage	0.16	0.11	0.06	0.05	0.25
Financial leverage gain	0.02	0.01	0.01	0.00	0.02
ROE = Operating ROA + Financial leverage gain	0.21	0.20	0.22	0.19	0.15
5-year growth rates (CAGR):					
Revenues	14.5				
Assets	15.4				
Equity	18.5				
Beta	0.72				

Sources: OneSource, Dow Jones Interactive, and case writer estimates.

The Airline Industry

EXHIBIT 2

Definitions of Ratios and Corresponding Accounting Items

Definitions of Ratios

Ratio	Definition
Net operating profit margin	Net operating profit after taxes (NOPAT) / Sales
Net operating asset turnover	Sales / Net assets
Operating ROA	Net operating profit margin × Net operating asset turnover
Net financial leverage	Net debt / Equity
Spread	Operating ROA − Effective interest rate after tax
Financial leverage gain	Spread × Net financial leverage
ROE	Operating ROA + Spread × Net financial leverage

Definitions of Accounting Items Used in Ratio Analysis

Item	Definition
Net interest expense after tax	(Interest expense − Interest income) × (1 − Tax rate)
Net operating profit after taxes (NOPAT)	Net income + Net interest expense after tax
Operating working capital	(Current assets − Cash and marketable securities) − (Current liabilities − Short-term debt and current portion of long-term debt)
Net long-term assets	Total long-term assets − Non-interest-bearing long-term liabilities
Net debt	Total interest bearing liabilities − Cash and marketable securities
Net assets	Operating working capital + Net long-term assets
Net capital	Net debt + Shareholders' equity

Prospective Analysis: Valuation Implementation

To move from the valuation theory discussed in the previous chapter to the actual task of valuing a company, one has to deal with a number of issues. First, the analyst needs to make forecasts of financial performance stated in terms of abnormal earnings and book values, or free cash flows over the life of the firm. As a practical matter, the forecasting task is often divided into two subcomponents—detailed forecasts over a finite number of years and a forecast of "terminal value," which represents a summary forecast of performance beyond the period of detailed forecasts. Second, the analyst needs to estimate the cost of capital to discount these forecasts. We discuss these issues in this chapter, and provide guidance on how to deal with them.

DETAILED FORECASTS OF PERFORMANCE

The horizon over which detailed forecasts are to be made is itself a choice variable. We will discuss later in this chapter how the analyst might make this choice. Once it is made, the next step is to consider the set of assumptions regarding a firm's performance that are needed to arrive at the forecasts. We described in Chapter 6 the general framework of financial forecasting. Since valuation involves forecasting over a long time horizon, it is not practical to forecast all the line items in a company's financial statements. Instead, the analyst has to focus on the key elements of a firm's performance.

The key to sound forecasts, of course, is that the underlying assumptions are grounded in a company's business reality. Strategy analysis provides a critical understanding of a company's value proposition, and whether current performance is likely to be sustainable in future. Accounting analysis and ratio analysis provide a deep understanding of a company's current performance, and whether the ratios themselves are reliable indicators of performance. It is, therefore, important to see the valuation forecasts as a continuation of the earlier steps in business analysis rather than as a discreet and unconnected exercise from the rest of the analysis.

Recall that we used the discount retailer TJX to illustrate ratio analysis and financial forecasting in Chapters 5 and 6. Specifically, we forecasted in Chapter 6 TJX's condensed income statement, beginning balance sheet, and free cash flows for a period of ten years starting in fiscal year 2002 (year beginning in February 2002). We will use these same forecasting assumptions and financial forecasts, which are shown in Tables 6-1 and 6-2, as a starting point to value TJX as of February 1, 2002.

The key forecasts required to use the formulas discussed in Chapter 7 for valuing a firm's equity are: abnormal earnings, abnormal ROE, and free cash flows to equity. If one is valuing a firm's assets, the corresponding variables of interest are abnormal NOPAT, abnormal operating ROA, and free cash flows to debt and equity. To calculate abnormal earnings and abnormal returns, we can begin with the forecasts in Table 6-2 for TJX, but we also need estimates of its cost of capital. So let us begin our discussion with a framework for estimating a firm's cost of capital. Then we will try to convert the financial forecasts in Table 6-2 into estimates of value.

COMPUTING A DISCOUNT RATE

To value a company's assets, the analyst discounts abnormal NOPAT, abnormal operating ROA, or cash flows available to both debt and equity holders. The proper discount rate to use is therefore the weighted average cost of capital (WACC). The WACC is calculated by weighting the costs of debt and equity capital according to their respective market values:

$$\text{WACC} = \frac{V_d}{V_d + V_e} r_d (1 - T) + \frac{V_e}{V_d + V_e} r_e$$

where V_d = the market value of debt and V_e = the market value of equity
r_d = the cost of debt capital
r_e = the cost of equity capital
T = the tax rate reflecting the marginal tax benefit of interest

Weighting the Costs of Debt and Equity

The weights assigned to debt and equity represent their respective fractions of total capital provided, measured in terms of market values. Computing a market value for debt should not be difficult. It is reasonable to use book values if interest rates have not changed significantly since the time the debt was issued. Otherwise, the value of the debt can be estimated by discounting the future payouts at current market rates of interest applicable to the firm.

What is included in debt? Should short-term as well as long-term debt be included? Should payables and accruals be included? The answer is revealed by considering how we calculated free cash flows. Free cash flows are the returns to the providers of the capital to which the WACC applies. The cash flows are those available *before* servicing short-term and long-term debt—indicating that both short-term and long-term debt should be considered a part of capital when computing the WACC. Servicing of other liabilities, such as accounts payable or accruals, should already have been considered as we computed free cash flows. Thus internal consistency requires that operating liabilities not be considered a part of capital when computing the WACC.

The tricky problem we face is assigning a market value to equity. That is the very amount we are trying to estimate in the first place! How can the analyst possibly assign a market value to equity at this intermediate stage, given that the estimate will not be known until all steps in the DCF analysis are completed?

One common approach to the problem is to insert at this point "target" ratios of debt to capital $[V_d/(V_d + V_e)]$ and equity to capital $[V_e/(V_d + V_e)]$. For example, one might expect that a firm will, over the long run, maintain a capital structure that is 40 percent debt and 60 percent equity. The long-run focus is reasonable because we are discounting cash flows over a long horizon.

Another way around the problem is to start with book value of equity as a weight for purposes of calculating an initial estimate of the WACC, which in turn can be used in the discounting process to generate an initial estimate of the value of equity. That initial estimate can then be used in place of the guess to arrive at a new WACC, and a second estimate of the value of equity can be produced. This process can be repeated until the value used to calculate the WACC and the final estimated value converge.

Estimating the Cost of Debt

The cost of debt (r_d) is the interest rate on the debt. If the assumed capital structure in future periods is the same as the historical structure, then current interest rate on debt will be a good proxy for this. However, if the analyst assumes a change in capital structure, then it is important to estimate the expected interest rate given the new level of debt ratio. One approach to this would be to estimate the expected credit rating of the company at the new level of debt and use the appropriate interest rates for that credit category.

The cost of debt should be expressed on a net-of-tax basis because it is after-tax cash flows that are being discounted. In most settings the market rate of interest can be converted to a net-of-tax basis by multiplying it by one minus the marginal corporate tax rate.

Estimating the Cost of Equity

Estimating the cost of equity (r_e) can be difficult, and a full discussion of the topic lies beyond the scope of this chapter. At any rate, even an extended discussion would not supply answers to all the questions that might be raised in this area because the field of finance is in a state of flux over what constitutes an appropriate measure of the cost of equity.

One possibility is to use the capital asset pricing model (CAPM), which expresses the cost of equity as the sum of a required return on riskless assets plus a premium for systematic risk:

$$r_e = r_f + \beta [E(r_m) - r_f]$$

where r_f is the riskless rate;

$[E(r_m) - r_f]$ is the risk premium expected for the market as a whole, expressed as the excess of the expected return on the market index over the riskless rate;

and β is the systematic risk of the equity.

To compute r_e, one must estimate three parameters: the riskless rate, r_f, the market risk premium $[E(r_m) - r_f]$, and systematic risk, β. For r_f, analysts often use the rate on intermediate-term treasury bonds, based on the observation that it is cash flows beyond the short term that are being discounted.[1] When r_f is measured in that way, then average common stock returns (based on the returns to the Standard and Poor's 500 index) have exceeded that rate by 7.0 percent over the 1926–2002 period.[2] This excess return constitutes an estimate of the market risk premium $[E(r_m) - r_f]$. Finally, systematic risk (β) reflects the sensitivity of the firm's value to economy-wide market movements.[3]

Although the above CAPM is often used to estimate the cost of capital, the evidence indicates that the model is incomplete. Assuming stocks are priced competitively, stock returns should be expected just to compensate investors for the cost of their capital. Thus long run average returns should be close to the cost of capital and should (according to the CAPM) vary across stocks according to their systematic risk. However, factors beyond just systematic risk seem to play some role in explaining variation in long-run average returns. The most important such factor is labeled the "size effect": smaller firms (as measured by market capitalization) tend to generate higher returns in subsequent periods. Why this is so is unclear. It could mean either that smaller firms are riskier than indicated by the CAPM or that they are underpriced at the point their market capitalization is measured, or some combination of both. Average stock returns for U.S. firms (including NYSE, AMEX, and NASDAQ firms) varied across size deciles from 1926 to 2002 as shown in Table 8-1.

The table shows that, historically, investors in firms in the top two deciles of the size distribution have realized returns of only 11.2 to 12.9 percent. In contrast, firms in the smallest two size deciles have realized significantly higher returns, ranging from 17.1 to 20.8 percent. Note, however, that if we use firm size as an indicator of the cost of capital, we are implicitly assuming that large size is indicative of lower risk. Yet finance theorists have not developed a well-accepted explanation for why that should be the case.

One method for combining the cost of capital estimates is based on the CAPM and the "size effect." The approach calls for adjustment of the CAPM-based cost of capital, based

Table 8-1 Stock Returns and Firm Size

Size decile	Market value of largest company in decile, in 2002 (millions of dollars)	Average annual stock return, 1926–2002 (%)	Fraction of total NYSE value represented by decile (in 2002, %)
1-small	141.5	20.8	0.89
2	314.0	17.1	1.28
3	521.3	16.2	1.48
4	791.3	15.2	1.91
5	1,143.8	14.9	2.24
6	1,691.2	14.5	3.07
7	2,680.6	14.0	3.74
8	5,012.7	13.5	6.35
9	11,628.7	12.9	12.76
10-large	293,137.3	11.2	66.27

Source: Ibbotson and Associates, *Stocks, Bonds, Bills, and Inflation* (2003).

on the difference between the average return on the market index used in the CAPM (the Standard and Poor's 500) and the average return on firms of size comparable to the firm being evaluated. The resulting cost of capital is

$$r_e = r_f + \beta [E(r_m) - r_f] + r_{size}$$

In light of the continuing debate on how to measure the cost of capital, it is not surprising that managers and analysts often consider a range of estimates. In particular, there has been considerable debate in recent times about whether or not the historical risk premium of 7 percent is valid today. Many analysts argue that a variety of changes in the U.S. economy make the historical risk premium an invalid basis for forecasting expected risk premium going forward. Some recent academic research has provided evidence that suggests that the expected risk premium in the market in recent years has declined substantially, to the range of 3 to 4 percent.[4] Since this debate is still unresolved, it is prudent for analysts to use a range of risk premium estimates in computing a firm's cost of capital.

Adjusting Cost of Equity for Changes in Leverage

Both cost of debt and cost of equity change as a function of a firm's leverage. As the leverage increases, debt and equity become more risky so they become more costly. If an analyst is contemplating changing capital structure during the forecasting time period relative to the historical capital structure of the firm, or changing the capital structure over time during the forecasting period, it is important to reestimate the cost of debt and equity to take these changes into account. We describe below a simple approach to this task.

We begin with the observation that the beta of a firm's assets is equal to the weighted average of its debt and equity betas, weighted by the proportion of debt and equity in its capital structure. A firm's equity beta can be estimated directly using its stock returns and the capital asset pricing model. Its debt beta can be inferred from the capital asset pricing model if we have information on the current interest rate and risk-free rate. From these estimated equity and debt betas at the current capital structure, we can infer the firm's asset beta.

When the firm's capital structure changes, its equity and debt betas will change, but its asset beta remains the same. We can take advantage of this fact to estimate the expected equity beta for the new capital structure. We first have to get an estimate of the interest rate on debt at the new capital structure level. Once we have this information, we can estimate the implied debt beta using the capital asset pricing model and the risk-free rate. Now we can estimate the equity beta for the new capital structure using the identity that the new equity beta and the new debt beta, weighted by the new capital structure weights, have to add up to the asset beta estimated earlier.

Estimating TJX's Cost of Capital

To estimate the cost of capital for TJX, we start with the assumption that its after-tax cost of debt is 7 percent, based on the ratio of the net interest expense after tax to beginning net debt in fiscal 2001 (with an assumed tax rate of 35 percent, this translates into a pre-tax cost of debt of 10.8 percent). The company's equity beta estimated in February 2002 was 0.90. The ten-year treasury bond rate at that time was 5.04 percent. Using the historical risk premium for equities of 7 percent, we can calculate its cost of equity to be 11.3 percent. Clearly this estimate is only a starting point, and the analyst can change the estimate by changing the assumed market risk premium or by adjusting for the size effect.

TJX's equity market value in February 2002 was $11,275 million; its net book debt was $210.8 million. Using these numbers we can calculate the "market value" weights of debt and equity in the company's capital structure as 2 percent and 98 percent respectively. Based on these weights and the above estimates of costs equity and debt, our estimate of TJX's weighted average cost of capital (WACC) in February 2002 is 11.3 percent (which is essentially the same as cost of equity since the company uses so little debt).

Since we keep the capital structure of TJX constant throughout the forecasting period, we will use these estimates of cost of equity and cost of capital.

Making Performance Forecasts for Valuing TJX

Recall that we made income statement, balance sheet, and cash flow forecasts for TJX for fiscal years 2002 to 2011 in Chapter 6 (Tables 6-1 and 6-2). Tables 8-2 and 8-3 present these same forecasts. Table 8-4 shows the performance forecasts implied by these financial statement forecasts for the ten-year period 2002 to 2011. Six performance forecasts, which can be used as input into the valuation exercise, are shown in the table. Abnormal earnings, abnormal ROE, and free cash flows to equity are inputs to value TJX's equity. Abnormal NOPAT, abnormal operating ROA, and free cash flows to debt and equity holders are three alternative inputs to value TJX's assets.

Table 8-2 Forecasting Assumptions for TJX

Fiscal year	2002	2003	2004	2005	2006	2007	2008	2009	2010	2011
Sales growth	12%	11.5%	11%	10.5%	10%	9.5%	9%	8.5%	8%	8%
NOPAT margin	4.5%	4%	3.5%	3%	2.5%	2%	1.9%	1.8%	1.7%	1.6%
After-tax net interest rate	7%	7%	7%	7%	7%	7%	7%	7%	7%	7%
Beginning net working capital to sales ratio	2.5%	2.5%	2.5%	2.5%	2.5%	2.5%	2.5%	2.5%	2.5%	2.5%
Beginning net long-term assets to sales ratio	10.5%	10.5%	10.5%	10.5%	10.5%	10.5%	10.5%	10.5%	10.5%	10.5%
Beginning net debt to capital ratio	13.6%	13.6%	13.6%	13.6%	13.6%	13.6%	13.6%	13.6%	13.6%	13.6%

Table 8-3 Forecasted Financial Statements for TJX

Fiscal year	2002	2003	2004	2005	2006	2007	2008	2009	2010	2011
Beginning Balance Sheet ($mm)										
Beg. Net Working Capital	297.4	334.3	371.1	410.1	451.1	493.9	538.4	584.2	630.9	681.4
+ Beg. Net Long-Term Assets	1,254.2	1,404.2	1,558.7	1,722.3	1,894.6	2,074.5	2,261.3	2,453.5	2,649.7	2,861.7
= Net Operating Assets	**1,551.5**	**1,738.5**	**1,929.8**	**2,132.4**	**2,345.6**	**2,568.5**	**2,799.6**	**3,037.6**	**3,280.6**	**3,543.1**
Net Debt	210.8	236.3	262.2	289.8	318.8	349.0	380.5	412.8	445.8	481.5
+ Preferred Stock	0.0	0.0	0.0	0.0	0.0	0.0	0.0	0.0	0.0	0.0
+ Shareholders' Equity	1,340.7	1,502.3	1,667.5	1,842.6	2,026.9	2,219.4	2,419.2	2,624.8	2,834.8	3,061.6
= Net Capital	**1,551.5**	**1,738.5**	**1,929.8**	**2,132.4**	**2,345.6**	**2,568.5**	**2,799.6**	**3,037.6**	**3,280.6**	**3,543.1**
Income Statement ($mm)										
Sales	11,994.1	13,373.4	14,844.5	16,403.1	18,043.5	19,757.6	21,535.8	23,366.3	25,235.6	27,254.5
Net operating profits after tax	539.7	534.9	519.6	492.1	451.1	395.2	409.2	420.6	429.0	436.1
− Net interest expense after tax	14.8	16.6	18.4	20.3	22.4	24.5	26.7	29.0	31.3	33.8
= Net income	**524.9**	**518.4**	**501.1**	**471.8**	**428.7**	**370.6**	**382.5**	**391.6**	**397.7**	**402.3**
Operating ROA	34.8%	30.8%	26.9%	23.1%	19.2%	15.4%	14.6%	13.8%	13.1%	12.3%
ROE	39.2%	34.5%	30.1%	25.6%	21.2%	16.7%	15.8%	14.9%	14.0%	13.1%
BV of Assets Growth Rate	7.4%	12.1%	11.0%	10.5%	10.0%	9.5%	9.0%	8.5%	8.0%	8.0%
BV of Equity Growth Rate	10.0%	12.1%	11.0%	10.5%	10.0%	9.5%	9.0%	8.5%	8.0%	8.0%
Net Operating Asset Turnover	7.7	7.7	7.7	7.7	7.7	7.7	7.7	7.7	7.7	7.7
Free Cash Flow to Capital	352,737	343,696	316,929	278,853	228,250	163,988	171,209	177,584	166,555	152,625
Free Cash Flow to Equity	312,524	301,122	270,984	229,532	175,590	108,071	112,162	115,582	99,593	80,306

The cash flows in 2011 are based on a forecasted beginning balance sheet for 2012, not shown here. To make this forecast, we assume that sales growth and all the beginning balance sheet ratios in 2012 remain at the same level as in 2011.

The calculations of performance forecasts in Table 8-4 use the following definitions: (1) abnormal earnings is net income less shareholders' equity at the beginning of the year times cost of equity; (2) abnormal ROE is the difference between ROE and cost of equity; (3) free cash flow to equity is net income less the increase in operating working capital less the increase in net long-term assets plus the increase in net debt; (4) abnormal NOPAT is NOPAT less total net capital at the beginning of the year times the weighted average cost of capital; (5) abnormal operating ROA is the difference between operating ROA and the weighted average cost of capital (WACC); and (6) free cash flow to capital is NOPAT less the increase in operating working capital less the increase in net long-term assets.

As discussed earlier, to derive cash flows in 2011, we need to make assumptions about sales growth rate and balance sheet ratios in 2012. We discuss below three different sets of assumptions in this regard. The cash flow forecasts shown in Table 8-4 are based on the simple assumption that the sales growth and beginning balance sheet ratios in 2012 remain the same as in 2011. We relax this assumption later.

Table 8-4 Performance Forecasts for TJX for the fiscal years 2002 to 2011

Fiscal year	2002	2003	2004	2005	2006	2007	2008	2009	2010	2011
Equity Valuation ($000's)										
Abnormal Earnings	372,897	347,992	312,048	262,798	198,860	118,964	108,135	93,960	76,242	55,086
Abnormal ROE	27.8%	23.2%	18.7%	14.3%	9.8%	5.4%	4.5%	3.6%	2.7%	1.8%
Free Cash Flow to Equity	363,347	353,099	326,056	287,489	236,155	170,899	176,840	181,629	170,924	157,344
Asset Valuation ($000's)										
Abnormal NOPAT	365,129	339,287	302,387	252,122	187,116	106,105	94,118	78,752	59,817	37,347
Abnormal Operating ROA	23.5%	19.5%	15.7%	11.8%	8.0%	4.1%	3.4%	2.6%	1.8%	1.1%
Free Cash Flow to Capital	352,737	343,696	316,929	278,853	228,250	163,988	171,209	177,584	166,555	152,625
Discount rates:										
Equity	0.898	0.807	0.725	0.651	0.584	0.525	0.471	0.423	0.380	0.342
Assets	0.899	0.808	0.726	0.653	0.587	0.527	0.474	0.426	0.383	0.344
Growth factors*:										
Equity	1.000	1.121	1.244	1.374	1.512	1.655	1.804	1.958	2.114	2.284
Assets	1.000	1.121	1.244	1.374	1.512	1.655	1.804	1.958	2.114	2.284

*The growth factor is relevant only for calculating the present value for abnormal ROA and ROE.

TERMINAL VALUES

The forecasts in Tables 8-3 and 8-4 extend only through the year 2011, and thus we label 2011 the "terminal year." (Selection of an appropriate terminal year is discussed later.) Terminal value is essentially the present value of either abnormal earnings or free cash flows occurring beyond the terminal year. Since this involves forecasting performance over the remainder of the firm's life, the analyst must adopt some assumption that simplifies the process of forecasting. Below we discuss a variety of alternative approaches to this task.

Terminal Values with the Competitive Equilibrium Assumption

Table 8-2 projects a sales growth rate and return on equity declining gradually over time during the period 2002 to 2011 before stabilizing sometime during that period. What should we assume beyond 2011? Is it reasonable to assume a continuation of the same stable 2011 performance in 2012 and beyond? Is some other pattern more reasonable?

One thing that seems clear is that continuation of a sales growth that is significantly greater than the average growth rate of the economy is unrealistic over a very long horizon. That rate would likely outstrip inflation in the dollar and the real growth rate of the world economy. Over many years, it would imply that TJX would grow to a size greater than that of all other firms in the world combined. But what would be a suitable alternative assumption? Should we expect the firm's sales growth rate to ultimately settle down to the rate of inflation? Or to a higher rate, such as the nominal GDP growth rate? Or to something else?

Ultimately, to answer these questions, one must consider how much longer the rate of growth in industry sales can outstrip the general growth in the world economy, and how long TJX's competitive advantages can enable it to grow faster than the overall industry. Clearly, looking eleven or more years into the future, any forecasts of sales growth rates are likely to be subject to considerable error.

Fortunately, in many if not most situations, how we deal with the seemingly imponderable questions about long-range growth in sales simply *does not matter very much!* In fact, under plausible economic assumptions, there is no practical need to consider sales growth beyond the terminal year. Such growth may be *irrelevant*, so far as the firm's current value is concerned!

How can long-range growth in sales *not* matter? The reasoning revolves around the forces of competition. Competition tends to constrain a firm's ability to identify, on a consistent basis, growth opportunities that generate supernormal profits. (Recall the evidence in Chapter 6 concerning the reversion of ROEs to normal levels over horizons of five to ten years.) Certainly a firm may at a point in time maintain a competitive advantage that permits it to achieve returns in excess of the cost of capital. When that advantage is protected with patents or a strong brand name, the firm may even be able to maintain it for many years, perhaps indefinitely. With hindsight, we know that some such firms—like Coca-Cola and Wal-Mart—were able not only to maintain their competitive edge but to expand it across dramatically increasing investment bases. But in the face of competition, one would typically not expect a firm to extend its supernormal profitability to new *additional* projects *year after year*. Ultimately, we would expect high profits to attract enough competition to drive the firm's return down to a normal level. Each new project would generate cash flows with a present value no greater than the cost of the investment—the investment would be a "zero net present value" project. Since the benefits of the project are offset by its costs, it does nothing to enhance the current value of the firm, and the associated growth can be ignored.

Of course, terminal value estimation does not necessarily *require* this "competitive equilibrium assumption." If the analyst expects that supernormal margins can be extended to new markets for many years, it can be accommodated within the context of a valuation analysis. At a minimum, as we will discuss in the next section, the analyst may expect that supernormal margins can be maintained on the existing sales base, or on markets that grow at the rate of inflation. However, the important lesson here is that the rate of growth in *sales* beyond the forecast horizon is *not* a relevant consideration *unless* the analyst believes that the growth can be achieved while generating supernormal margins—and competition may make that a difficult trick to pull off.

Assumption Only on Incremental Sales

An alternative version of the competitive equilibrium assumption is to assume that TJX will continue to earn abnormal earnings forever on the sales it had in 2011, but there will be no abnormal earnings on any incremental sales beyond that level. If we invoke the competitive equilibrium assumption on incremental sales for years beyond 2011, then it does not matter what sales growth rate we use beyond that year, and we may as well simplify our arithmetic by treating sales *as if* they will be constant at the year 2011 level. Then operating ROA, ROE, NOPAT, net income, free cash flow to debt and equity, and free cash flow to equity will all remain constant at the year 2011 level.

Under this scenario, it is simple to estimate the terminal value by dividing the 2011 level of each of the variables by the appropriate discount rate. As one would expect, terminal values in this scenario will be higher than those with no abnormal returns on all sales in years 2012 and beyond. This is entirely due to the fact that we are now assuming that TJX can retain its superior performance on its existing base of sales indefinitely.

Terminal Value with Persistent Abnormal Performance and Growth

Each of the approaches described above appeals in some way to the "competitive equilibrium assumption." However, there are circumstances where the analyst is willing to assume that the firm may defy competitive forces and earn abnormal rates of return on new projects for many years. If the analyst believes supernormal profitability can be extended to larger markets for many years, one possibility is to project earnings and cash flows over a longer horizon, until the competitive equilibrium assumption can reasonably be invoked. In the case of TJX, for example, we could assume that the supernormal profitability will continue for five years beyond 2011 (for a total forecasting horizon of 15 years from the beginning of the forecasting period), but after that period, the firm's ROE and Operating ROA will be equal to its cost of equity and its weighted average cost of capital.

Another possibility is to project growth in abnormal earnings or cash flows at some constant rate. Consider the following. By treating TJX as if its competitive advantage can be maintained only on the *nominal* sales level achieved in the year 2011, we will be assuming that in *real* terms its competitive advantage will shrink. Let's say that the analyst expects TJX to maintain its advantage (through supplies of new and more advanced products to a similar customer base) on a sales base that remains constant in *real* terms—that grows beyond the year 2011 at the expected long-run inflation rate of 3.5 percent. The computations implied by these assumptions are described below. The approach is more aggressive than the one described earlier, but it may be more realistic. After all, there is no obvious reason why the *real* size of the investment base on which TJX earns abnormal returns should depend on inflation rates.

The approach just described still relies to some extent on the competitive equilibrium assumption. The assumption is now invoked to suggest that supernormal profitability can be extended only to an investment base that remains constant in real terms. However, there is nothing about the valuation method that requires *any* reliance on the competitive equilibrium assumption. The calculations described below could be used with *any* rate of growth in sales. The question is not whether the arithmetic is available to handle such an approach, but rather how realistic it is.

Let's stay with the approach that assumes TJX will extend its supernormal margins to sales that grow beyond 2011 at the rate of inflation. How would abnormal earnings and free cash flows beyond 2011 behave?

Beyond our terminal year, 2011, as the sales growth rate remains constant at 3.5 percent, abnormal earnings, free cash flows, and book values of assets and equity also grow at a constant rate of 3.5 percent. This is simply because we held all other performance ratios constant in this period. As a result, abnormal operating ROA and abnormal ROE remain constant at the same rate as in the terminal year.

The above exercise shows that, when we assume that the abnormal performance persists at the same level as in the terminal year, projecting abnormal earnings and free cash flows is a simple matter of growing them at the assumed sales growth rate. Since the rate of abnormal earnings and cash flows growth is constant starting in 2012, it is also straightforward to discount those flows. For a given discount rate r, any flow stream growing at the constant rate g can be discounted by dividing the flows in the first year by the amount $(r-g)$.

Terminal Value Based on a Price Multiple

A popular approach to terminal value calculation is to apply a multiple to abnormal earnings, cash flows, or book values of the terminal period. The approach is not as ad hoc as it might at first appear. Note that under the assumption of no sales growth, abnormal earnings or cash flows beyond 2011 remain constant. Capitalizing these flows in perpetuity by dividing by the cost of capital is equivalent to multiplying them by the inverse of the cost of capital. For example, capitalizing free cash flows to equity at 11.3 percent is equivalent to assuming a terminal cash flow multiple of 8.84. Thus applying a multiple in this range is similar to discounting all free cash flows beyond 2011 while invoking the competitive equilibrium assumption on incremental sales.

The mistake to avoid here is to capitalize the future abnormal earnings or cash flows using a multiple that is too high. The earnings or cash flow multiples might be high currently because the market anticipates abnormally profitable growth. However, once that growth is realized, the PE multiple should fall to a normal level. It is that normal PE, applicable to a stable firm or one that can grow only through zero net present value projects, that should be used in the terminal value calculation. Thus multiples in the range of 7 to 10—close to the reciprocal of cost of equity and WACC—should be used here. Higher multiples are justifiable only when the terminal year is closer and there are still abnormally profitable growth opportunities beyond that point. A similar logic applies to the estimation of terminal values using book value multiples.

Selecting the Terminal Year

A question begged by the above discussion is how long to make the detailed forecast horizon. When the competitive equilibrium assumption is used, the answer is whatever time is required for the firm's returns on incremental investment projects to reach that equilibrium—an issue that turns on the sustainability of the firm's competitive advantage. As indicated in Chapter 6, historical evidence indicates that most firms in the U.S. should expect ROEs to revert to normal levels within five to ten years. But for the typical firm, we can justify ending the forecast horizon even earlier—note that the return on *incremental* investment can be normal even while the return on *total* investment (and therefore ROE) remains abnormal. Thus a five- to ten-year forecast horizon should be more than sufficient for most firms. Exceptions would include firms so well insulated from competition (perhaps due to the power of a brand name) that they can extend their investment base to new markets for many years and still expect to generate supernormal returns. In 1999 the Wrigley Company, producer of chewing gum, was still extending its brand name to untapped markets in other nations, and appears to be such a firm.

Estimates of TJX's Terminal Value

Choosing Terminal Year In the case of TJX, the terminal year used is ten years beyond the current one. Table 8-3 shows that the ROE (and operating ROA) is forecasted to decline only gradually over these ten years, from the unusually high 39.2 percent in 2002 to 13.1 percent by 2011. At this level the company will earn an abnormal return on equity of 1.8 percent, since its cost of equity is estimated to be 11.3 percent.

If NOPAT margins could be maintained at the projected 1.6 percent on ever-increasing sales, this abnormal ROE could be achieved even on new investment in 2012 and beyond. But even a slight decline in the NOPAT margin to about 1.5 percent would, in the face of continued sales growth, be enough to cause the return on the *incremental* investment to be very close to the cost of capital. Thus the performance we have already projected for the terminal year 2011 is not far removed from a competitive equilibrium, and extending the forecast horizon by a few more years would have little impact on the calculated value. Even if we project continuation of the 1.6 percent NOPAT margin through 2017 with 8 percent annual sales increases (and with the competitive equilibrium assumption invoked thereafter), the final estimated firm value would increase only marginally. Large changes in the value estimate would arise only if the analyst is willing to assume abnormal rates of return on investments well into the twenty-first century. In light of historical patterns for corporate performance, such an assumption would have to be based on a strong belief in TJX's continued competitive advantage. The upshot is that an analyst could argue that the terminal year used for TJX should be extended from the tenth year to, say, the fifteenth year, depending on the perceived sustainability of its competitive advantage. However, this becomes more of a significant issue only if the analyst assumes that TJX will have a significantly large competitive advantage in 2011 relative to what was assumed in the forecasts in Table 8-3. Based on this logic, we will fix the terminal year for TJX as 2011 and attempt to estimate its terminal value at that time.

Terminal Value Under Varying Assumptions   Table 8-5 shows TJX's terminal value under the three scenarios we discussed above. Scenario one of this table shows the terminal value if we assume that TJX will continue to grow its sales at 8 percent beyond fiscal year 2011, and that it will continue to earn the same level of abnormal returns as in 2011 (that is, we assume that all the other forecasting assumptions will be the same as in 2011). Scenario 2 shows the terminal value if we assume that TJX will grow at a lower rate, closer to the historical growth rate of U.S. GDP, at 4 percent in 2012 and beyond, but will maintain its competitive advantage and therefore its level of abnormal returns in 2011 forever. Scenario 3 shows the terminal value if we assume that the company will grow at 4 percent and will not have any significant abnormal returns in 2012 and beyond. In this scenario we are assuming that NOPAT margins will decline to 1.5 percent in 2012 and will remain at that level; all the remaining assumptions except sales level and NOPAT margins will remain unchanged from 2011.

COMPUTING ESTIMATED VALUES

Table 8-5 shows the estimated value of TJX's assets and equity, each using three different methods. Value of assets is estimated using abnormal operating ROA, abnormal NOPAT, and free cash flows to debt and equity. Value of equity is estimated using operating ROE, abnormal NOPAT, and free cash flow to equity. These values are computed using the financial forecasts in Table 8-4 and the terminal value forecasts under different scenarios we discussed earlier.

Note that the cash flow forecasts in Table 8-4 are based on scenario 1 for 2012. When we change these assumptions, the cash flow forecasts for 2011 change. Therefore the present values of cash flows for years 2002 to 2011 also vary across the three scenarios.

In Table 8-5, present values of abnormal NOPAT and free cash flow to capital are computed using a WACC of 11.3 percent; present values of abnormal earnings and free cash flow to equity are computed using a cost of equity of 11.3 percent. To calculate the present values of abnormal operating ROA and abnormal ROE, the values for each year are first multiplied by the corresponding growth factor, as shown in the formulae in Chapter 7, and then they are discounted using a WACC of 11.3 percent and cost of equity of 11.3 percent.

Value estimates presented in each scenario show that the abnormal returns method, abnormal earnings method, and the free cash flow method result in the same value, as

Table 8-5 Valuation Summary for TJX Under Varying Scenarios*

Scenario 1	Beginning Book Value	Value from Forecasts for 2002–2011	Value from Forecasts Beyond 2011 (Terminal Value)	Total Value	Value per Share ($)
Equity Value ($000s)					
Abnormal Earnings	1,340,698	1,329,973	608,428	3,279,098	11.91
Abnormal ROE	1,340,698	1,329,973	608,428	3,279,098	11.91
Free Cash Flows to Equity	N/A	1,541,241	1,737,857	3,279,098	11.91
Asset Value ($000s)					
Abnormal NOPAT	1,551,545	1,266,154	426,755	3,244,454	N/A
Abnormal ROA	1,551,545	1,266,154	426,755	3,244,454	N/A
Free Cash Flows to Capital	N/A	1,500,462	1,743,992	3,244,454	N/A

Scenario 2	Beginning Book Value	Value from Forecasts for 2002–2011	Value from Forecasts Beyond 2011 (Terminal Value)	Total Value	Value per Share ($)
Equity Value ($000s)					
Abnormal Earnings	1,340,698	1,329,973	266,605	2,937,276	10.67
Abnormal ROE	1,340,698	1,329,973	266,605	2,937,276	10.67
Free Cash Flows to Equity	N/A	1,583,072	1,354,204	2,937,276	10.67
Asset Value ($000s)					
Abnormal NOPAT	1,551,545	1,266,154	184,331	3,002,030	N/A
Abnormal ROA	1,551,545	1,266,154	184,331	3,002,030	N/A
Free Cash Flows to Capital	N/A	1,549,248	1,452,782	3,002,030	N/A

Scenario 3	Beginning Book Value	Value from Forecasts for 2002–2011	Value from Forecasts Beyond 2011 (Terminal Value)	Total Value	Value per Share ($)
Equity Value ($000s)					
Abnormal Earnings	1,340,698	1,329,973	134,700	2,805,371	10.19
Abnormal ROE	1,340,698	1,329,973	134,700	2,805,371	10.19
Free Cash Flows to Equity	N/A	1,583,072	1,222,299	2,805,371	10.19
Asset Value ($000s)					
Abnormal NOPAT	1,551,545	1,266,154	49,814	2,867,513	N/A
Abnormal ROA	1,551,545	1,266,154	49,814	2,867,513	N/A
Free Cash Flows to Capital	N/A	1,549,248	1,318,265	2,867,513	N/A

*Scenario 1: Sales growth and NOPAT/Sales of 8% and 1.6%, respectively.
Scenario 2: Sales growth and NOPAT/Sales of 4% and 1.6%, respectively.
Scenario 3: Sales growth and NOPAT/Sales of 4% and 1.5%, respectively.

claimed in Chapter 7. Note also that TJX's terminal value represents a significantly larger fraction of the total value of assets and equity under the free cash flow method relative to the other methods. As discussed in Chapter 7, this is due to the fact that the abnormal returns and earnings methods rely on a company's book value of assets and equity, so the terminal value estimates are estimates of incremental values over book values. In contrast, the free cash flow approach ignores the book values, so the terminal value forecasts are estimates of total value during this period.

The primary calculations in the above estimates treat all flows as if they arrive at the end of the year. Of course, they are likely to arrive throughout the year. If we assume for the sake of simplicity that cash flows will arrive mid-year, then we should adjust our value estimates upward by the amount $\left[1 + \left(\dfrac{r}{2} \right) \right]$, where r is the discount rate.

Value Estimates Versus Market Values

As the discussion above shows, valuation involves a substantial number of assumptions by analysts. Therefore the estimates of value will vary from one analyst to the other. The only way to ensure that one's estimates are reliable is to make sure that the assumptions are grounded in the economics of the business being valued. It is also useful to check the assumptions against the time-series trends for performance ratios discussed in Chapter 6. While it is quite legitimate for an analyst to make assumptions that differ markedly from these trends in any given case, it is important for the analyst to be able to articulate the business and strategy reasons for making such assumptions.

When a company being valued is publicly traded, it is possible to compare one's own estimated value with the market value of a company. When an estimated value differs substantially from a company's market value, it is useful for the analyst to understand why such differences arise. A way to do this is to redo the valuation exercise and figure out what valuation assumptions are needed to arrive at the observed stock price. One can then examine whether the market's assumptions are more or less valid relative to one's own assumptions. As we discuss in the next chapter, such an analysis can be invaluable in using valuation to make buy or sell decisions in the security analysis context.

For example in the case of TJX, our estimated value of the firm's equity is significantly smaller than the observed value at the beginning of fiscal 2002. Our estimated value per share under the most optimistic terminal value assumptions was about $12 per share, while the company's stock price at that time was $20.67. Clearly the market was making more optimistic assumptions than our own. The differences in the two sets of assumptions might be related either to growth rates, NOPAT margins, asset turns, or discount rates (primarily due to differences in assumed equity risk premium or capital structure). One could run different scenarios regarding each of these variables and test the sensitivity of the estimated value to these assumptions.

Other Practical Issues in Valuation

The above discussion provides a blueprint for doing valuation. In practice, the analyst has to deal with a number of other issues that have an important effect on the valuation task. We discuss below three frequently encountered complications—accounting distortions, negative book values, and excess cash.

Dealing with Accounting Distortions

We know from the discussion in Chapter 7 that accounting methods per se should have no influence on firm value (except as those choices influence the analyst's view of future real performance). Yet the abnormal returns and earnings valuation approaches used here are based on numbers—earnings and book value—that vary with accounting method choices. How, then, can the valuation approach deliver correct estimates?

Because accounting choices must affect both earnings *and* book value, and because of the self-correcting nature of double-entry bookkeeping (all "distortions" of accounting must ultimately reverse), estimated values will not be affected by accounting choices, *as long as the analyst recognizes the accounting distortions*.[5] As an example, let's assume that managers are aggressive in their accounting choices, choosing to provide for a lower allowance for uncollected receivables even though they have information to the contrary, thus causing the current period's abnormal earnings and the ending book value to be higher by $100. For the time being, let's say the accounting choice has no influence on the analyst's view of the firm's real performance. That is, the analyst is assumed to recognize that management's current estimate of future customer defaults is artificially lower and can make accurate forecasts of future defaults.

Our accounting-based valuation approach starts with the current period's abnormal earnings, which are $100 higher as a result of the accounting choice. However, the choice also causes future abnormal earnings to be lower for two reasons. First, future earnings will be lower (by $100) in a later period, when the customer actually defaults on the payments and receivables will have to be written off. Second, in the meantime the benchmark for normal earnings, the book value of equity, will be higher by $100. Let's say the accounts receivable are not written off until two years after the current period. Then assuming a discount rate of 13 percent and the impact of the current aggressive accounting, the subsequent write-down on our calculation of value is as follows:

	Dollar Impact	Present Value
Increase in current abnormal earnings (and book value)	$100	$100.00
Decrease in abnormal earnings of year 1, due to higher book value (.13 × $100)	−13	÷ 1.13 = −11.50
Decrease in abnormal earnings of year 2, due to higher book value (.13 × $100) due to lower earnings from accounts receivable write-off	−13 −100 −113	÷ 1.13^2 = −88.50
Impact of accounting choice on present value		$0.00

The impact of the higher current abnormal earnings and the lower future abnormal earnings offset exactly, leaving no impact of the current underestimation of the allowance for uncollected receivables on estimated firm value.

The above discussion makes it appear as if the analyst would be indifferent to the accounting methods used. There is an important reason why this is not necessarily true. When a company uses "biased" accounting—either conservative or aggressive—the analyst is forced to expend resources doing accounting analyses of the sort described in Chapter 3. These additional analysis costs are avoided for firms with unbiased accounting.

If a thorough analysis is not performed, a firm's accounting choices can, in general, influence analysts' perceptions of the real performance of the firm and hence the forecasts of future performance. In the above example, the managers' allowance and receivables estimates, if taken at face value, will influence the analyst's forecasts of future earnings and cash flows. If so, the accounting choice per se would affect expectations of future earnings and cash flows in ways beyond those considered above. The estimated value of the firm would presumably be higher—but it would still be the same regardless of whether the valuation is based on DCF or discounted abnormal earnings.[6]

An analyst who encounters biased accounting has two choices—either to adjust current earnings and book values to eliminate managers' accounting biases, or to recognize these biases and adjust future forecasts accordingly. Both approaches lead to the same estimated firm value. For example, in the above illustration a simple way to deal with managers' underestimation of current default allowance is to increase the allowance and to decrease the current period's abnormal earnings by $100. Alternatively, as shown above, the analyst could forecast the write-off two periods from now. Which of the two approaches is followed will have an important impact on what fraction of the firm's value is captured within the forecast horizon, and what remains in the terminal value.

Holding forecasting horizon and future growth opportunities constant, higher accounting quality allows a higher fraction of a firm's value to be captured by the current book value and the abnormal earnings within the forecasting horizon. Accounting can be of low quality either because it is unreliable or because it is extremely conservative. If accounting reliability is a concern, the analyst has to expend resources on "accounting adjustments." If accounting is conservative, the analyst is forced to increase the forecasting horizon to capture a given fraction of a firm's value, or to rely on relatively more uncertain terminal values estimates for a large fraction of the estimated value.

Dealing with Negative Book Values

A number of firms have negative earnings and book values of book equity. Firms in the start-up phase have negative equity, as do those in high technology industries. These firms incur large investments whose payoff is uncertain. Accountants write off these investments as a matter of conservatism, leading to negative book equity. Examples of firms in this situation include biotechnology firms, Internet firms, telecommunication firms, and other high technology firms. A second category of firms with negative book equity are those that are performing poorly, resulting in cumulative losses exceeding the original investment by the shareholders.

Negative book equity makes it difficult to use the accounting-based approach to value a firm's equity. There are several possible ways to get around this problem. The first approach is to value the firm's assets (using, for example, abnormal operating ROA or abnormal NOPAT) rather than equity. Then, based on an estimate of the value of the firm's debt, one can estimate the equity value. Another alternative is to "undo" accountants' conservatism by capitalizing the investment expenditures written off. This is possible if the analyst is able to establish that these expenditures are value creating. A third alternative, feasible for publicly traded firms, is to start from the observed stock and work backwards. Using reasonable estimates of cost of equity and steady-state growth rate, the analyst can calculate the average long-term level of abnormal earnings needed to justify the observed stock price. Then the analytical task can be framed in terms of examining the feasibility of achieving this abnormal earnings "target."

It is important to note that the value of firms with negative book equity often consists of a significant option value. For example, the value of high-tech firms is not only driven by the expected earnings from their current technologies but also the payoff from technology options embedded in their research and development efforts. Similarly, the value of troubled companies is driven to some extent by the "abandonment option"—shareholders with limited liability can put the firm to debt holders and creditors. One can use the options theory framework to estimate the value of these "real options."

Dealing with Excess Cash and Excess Cash Flow

Firms with excess cash balances, or large free cash flows, also pose a valuation challenge. In our projections in Table 8-2, we implicitly assumed that cash beyond the level required to finance a company's operations will be paid out to the firm's shareholders. Excess cash flows are assumed to be paid out to shareholders either in the form of dividends or stock repurchases. Notice that these cash flows are already incorporated into the valuation process when they are earned, so there is no need to take them into account when they are paid out.

It is important to recognize that both the accounting-based valuation and the discounted cash flow valuation assume a dividend payout that can potentially vary from period to period. This dividend policy assumption is required as long as one wishes to assume a constant level of financial leverage, a constant cost of equity, and a constant level of weighted average cost of capital used in the valuation calculations. As discussed in a later chapter, firms rarely have such a variable dividend policy in practice. However, this in itself does not make the valuation approaches invalid, as long as a firm's dividend policy does not affect its value. That is, the valuation approaches assume that the well known Modigliani-Miller theorem regarding the irrelevance of dividends holds.

A firm's dividend policy can affect its value if managers do not invest free cash flows optimally. For example, if a firm's managers are likely to use excess cash to undertake value-destroying acquisitions, then our approach overestimates the firm's value. If the analyst has these types of concerns about a firm, one approach is to first estimate the firm according to the approach described earlier and then adjust the estimated value for whatever agency costs the firm's managers may impose on its investors. One approach to evaluating whether or not a firm suffers from severe agency costs is to examine how effective its corporate governance processes are.

SUMMARY

We illustrate in this chapter how to apply the valuation theory discussed in Chapter 7. The chapter explains the set of business and financial assumptions one needs to make to conduct the valuation exercise. It also illustrates the mechanics of making detailed valuation forecasts and terminal values of earnings, free cash flows, and accounting rates of return. We also discuss how to compute cost of equity and the weighted average cost of capital. Using a detailed example, we show how a firm's equity values and asset values can be computed using earnings, cash flows, and rates of return. Finally, we offer ways to deal with some commonly encountered practical issues, including accounting distortions, negative book values, and excess cash balances.

DISCUSSION QUESTIONS

1. How will the forecasts in Table 8-3 for TJX change if the assumed growth rate in sales from 2002 to 2011 remains at 12 percent (and all the other assumptions are kept unchanged)?

2. Recalculate the forecasts in Table 8-3 assuming that the NOPAT profit margin declines by 0.1 percentage points per year between fiscal 2002 and 2011 (keeping all the other assumptions unchanged).

3. Recalculate the forecasts in Table 8-4 assuming that the ratio of net operating working capital to sales is 3 percent, and the ratio of net long-term assets to sales is 15 percent for all the years from fiscal 2003 to fiscal 2011. Keep all the other assumptions unchanged.

4. Calculate TJX's cash payouts to its shareholders in the years 2002–2011 that are implicitly assumed in the projections in Table 8-3.

5. How will the abnormal earnings calculations in Table 8-4 change if the cost of equity assumption is changed to 15 percent?

6. How will the terminal values in Table 8-5 change if the sales growth in years 2012 and beyond is 12 percent, and the company keeps forever its abnormal returns at the same level as in fiscal 2011 (keeping all the other assumptions in the table unchanged)?

7. Calculate the proportion of terminal values to total estimated values of equity under the abnormal earnings method and the discounted cash flow method. Why are these proportions different?

8. What will be TJX's cost of equity if the equity market risk premium is 5 percent?

9. Assume that TJX changes its capital structure so that its market value weight of debt to capital increases to 30 percent, and its after-tax interest rate on debt at this new leverage level is 8 percent. Assume that the equity market risk premium is 7 percent. What will be the cost of equity at the new debt level? What will be the weighted average cost of capital?

10. Nancy Smith says she is uncomfortable making the assumption that TJX's dividend payout will vary from year to year. If she makes a constant dividend payout assumption, what changes does she have to make in her other valuation assumptions to make them internally consistent with each other?

NOTES

1. See T. Copeland, T. Koller, and J. Murrin, *Valuation: Measuring and Managing the Value of Companies*, 2nd edition (New York: John Wiley & Sons, 1994). Theory calls for the use of a short-term rate, but if that rate is used here, a difficult practical question rises: how does one reflect the premium required for expected inflation over long horizons? While the premium could, in principle, be treated as a portion of the term $[E(r_m) - r_f]$, it is probably easier to use an intermediate- or long-term riskless rate that presumably reflects expected inflation.

2. The average return reported here is the arithmetic mean as opposed to the geometric mean. Ibbotson and Associates explain why this estimate is appropriate in this context (see *Stocks, Bonds, Bills, and Inflation*, 2002 Yearbook, Chicago).

3. One way to estimate systematic risk is to regress the firm's stock returns over some recent time period against the returns on the market index. The slope coefficient represents an estimate of β. More fundamentally, systematic risk depends on how sensitive the firm's operating profits are to shifts in economy-wide activity, and the firm's degree of leverage. Financial analysis that assesses these operating and financial risks should be useful in arriving at reasonable estimates of β.

4. See "Toward an Implied Cost of Capital" by William R. Gebhardt, Charles M. C. Lee, and Bhaskaran Swaminathan, Cornell University, working paper, 1999; and "The Equity Premium Is Much Lower Than You Think It Is: Empirical Estimates from a New Approach" by James Claus and Jacob Thomas, Columbia University, working paper, 1999.

5. Valuation based on discounted abnormal earnings does require one property of the forecasts: that they be consistent with "clean surplus accounting." Such accounting requires the

following relation:

End-of-period book value =

Beginning book value + earnings − dividends ± capital contributions/withdrawals

Clean surplus accounting rules out situations where some gain or loss is excluded from earnings but is still used to adjust the book value of equity. For example, under U.S. GAAP, gains and losses on foreign currency translations are handled this way. In applying the valuation technique described here, the analyst would need to deviate from GAAP in producing forecasts and treat such gains/losses as a part of earnings. However, the technique does *not* require that clean surplus accounting has been applied *in the past*—so the existing book value, based on U.S. GAAP or any other set of principles, can still serve as the starting point. All the analyst needs to do is apply clean surplus accounting in his/her forecasts. That much is not only easy but is usually the natural thing to do anyway.

6. It is important to recognize that when the analyst uses the "indirect" cash flow forecasting method, undetected accounting biases can influence not only future earnings forecasts but also future free cash flow forecasts. In the current example, since accounts receivables are overstated, the analyst will assume that they will be collected as cash in some future period, leading to a higher future cash flow estimate.

Home Depot, Inc. in the New Millennium

On October 12, 2000, Home Depot, the largest retailer of home improvement products and the third largest retailer of any sort in the United States, shocked many investors by announcing that earnings in the third and fourth quarters of 2000 would be a good deal lower than expected. In response, the company's stock price experienced its largest one-day drop ever, falling 28 percent (to $35), which erased $33 billion from its market value.

Arthur Blank, Home Depot's CEO, said that the earnings shortfall was primarily the result of a slowing economy. In fact, retail stocks generally had been down all year, and when Home Depot made its announcement, other retail stocks fell as well. To many analysts, however, Home Depot had competencies that very few other retailers had. It was one of the most successful retailers in American history. From the fall of 1981, when the company went public, to the end of 1999, its stock had risen at a compound annual rate of 52 percent. During the decade of the 1990s, its diluted earnings per share had risen at a compound annual rate of 29 percent. On October 12, however, the company said that it expected earnings for the third quarter (ending at the end of October) to be only $.28 per share, compared to $.25 in the third quarter of 1999. For the fourth quarter (ending in January), it expected earnings to be $.26 or $.25, compared to $.25 in the fourth quarter of the previous year. For the full year, it expected earnings to be $1.16 or $1.17, compared to $1.00 in 1999.

The U.S. economy had experienced uninterrupted growth since 1992. Between June 1999 and May 2000, however, the Federal Reserve had raised interest rates six times—for a total of 1.75 percentage points—in an effort to slow the economy, and economists had been noticing some softening of overall consumer demand.

Because of the nature of Home Depot's business, many observers regarded it as, if not recession proof, fairly protected from the vicissitudes of the economy. It was primarily involved in selling materials that ordinary people use for home improvement projects. The company, however, was undertaking several significant growth initiatives, and it wasn't clear whether the decline in the stock price was primarily a function of a slowing economy, a reaction to an overvaluation of the stock, or a reflection of possible problems with the company's strategy for the future.

HISTORY

Bernard Marcus and Arthur Blank founded Home Depot in 1978 in Atlanta, Georgia. They had been managing a chain of Handy Dan home improvement stores but thought that if they had to compete against a no-frills warehouse, they would be in trouble. So they started such a company themselves.

The company they founded revolutionized the do-it-yourself home improvement market in the United States. They opened stores that contained a huge assortment of building materials and home improvement products and that targeted as customers individual homeowners and small contractors. The stores *were* the warehouses, and they sold large volumes of goods at low prices. The really distinctive feature of Home Depot, however,

Research Associate Jeremy Cott prepared this case under the supervision of Professor Krishna Palepu. The case is intended solely as the basis for class discussion and is not intended to serve as an endorsement, source of primary data, or illustration of effective or ineffective management. Copyright © 2001 by the President and Fellows of Harvard College. HBS Case 9-101-117.

was that it also provided knowledgeable customer service. Many salespeople had themselves worked in the building trades, and in any case they were all required to attend product knowledge training classes. Thus in 1988 *Fortune* magazine viewed Home Depot as "the only company that has successfully brought off the union of low prices and high service."[1] The company was thus able to make home improvement projects both less expensive and more understandable for many people.

Financial and Operating Performance

Over the years the company's financial and operating performance had been extraordinary. Exhibit 1 shows its return on book equity, and the decomposition of that return on equity, from 1986 through 1999. Exhibit 2 shows various measures of operating performance over the same period.

The company's stock price had risen dramatically over the years. There were, however, significant variations in stock returns from year to year. Exhibit 3 shows annual changes in returns on the company's stock for the1990s, along with comparable data for the S&P 500. It also shows annual earnings per share figures and the number of common shares outstanding. Finally, Exhibit 4 provides detailed income statements, balance sheets, and cash flow statements for the last few years of the decade. (Home Depot's fiscal year ends in January, and when it referred to fiscal year 1999, for example, it meant the twelve-month period ending at the end of January 2000.)

As of the end of 1999 the company was by far the largest home improvement retailer in the country. (The second largest, Lowe's, was about half Home Depot's size.) It operated 930 stores, almost all of them in the United States and Canada. Most of the U.S. stores were clustered in large metropolitan areas. The company was planning on 21–22 percent annual growth in stores over the next several years, so that the number of stores by the end of 2003 would total over 1,900.

Macroeconomic Factors

During the period in which Home Depot had existed, the home improvement industry in the U.S. had grown at an annual rate of about 6 percent, or slightly slower than the U.S. economy as a whole. In 1998, however, the industry grew about 10.4 percent and in 1999 about 7.3 percent—which exceeded the economy as a whole. In June 2000, with the expectation of some slowing in the economy, the Home Improvement Research Institute projected average nominal growth in the industry of about 4.5 percent a year over the next several years (see Exhibit 5).

The home improvement industry was generally thought to have benefited in recent years from low interest rates, strong housing turnover, rising home ownership, and increases in discretionary income. During the recession of 1990–1991 Home Depot experienced only a small decline in same-store sales, but at that point it occupied a far smaller share of the market. In 1995 macroeconomic factors evidently had a greater impact. From March 1994 through February 1995, 30-year mortgage interest rates increased by an average of 24 percent. By contrast, in full years 1990, 1991, 1992, 1993, 1996, 1997, and 1998, they declined. In October 1998 rates reached a 31-year low of 6.5 percent. In May 2000, however, they had climbed to 8.6 percent, before falling a bit below 8 percent in the fall.

----

1. Bill Saporito, "The Fix Is In at Home Depot," Fortune, February 29, 1988.

Management Change

Over the years, Bernard Marcus and Arthur Blank had generally worked closely together. To some people they seemed, in terms of the decisions they made, almost interchangeable. In 1997, however, Blank succeeded Marcus as CEO of the company, with Marcus remaining as chairman. (Marcus was 68 years old in 1997; Blank was 13 years younger.) Blank commented in 1999: "My role is certainly very different than Bernie's was in the earlier days of our company. Back then, we were just trying to open the stores. Now the role is much more complex because we're thinking about how to drive deeper into the industry and how to serve customers differently in other segments of the industry."[2]

STYLE OF OPERATING

The company never seemed to regard the way it operated as settled. It spoke fairly often of "reexamining" or "reviewing" certain procedures and practices, and "testing" or "experimenting" with new ones. It would typically try out new products or procedures in a small number of stores, and only after it saw the results there would it extend them to many more stores.

Decision making regarding the location of new stores also had a distinctive character. Stores existed in almost all states in the U.S. as well as in all Canadian provinces. Some of the new stores were opened in new markets for the company (new regions or metropolitan areas). However, in recent years about two-thirds of new stores were opened in existing markets. Company management had specific reasons for this:

> In existing markets, we believe a number of Home Depot stores are operating at or above their optimum capacity. To increase customer service levels and enhance long-term market penetration, we often open new stores near the edge of the market areas served by existing stores. While these openings may initially have a negative impact on comparable store-for-store sales, we believe this "cannibalization" strategy increases customer satisfaction and overall market share by reducing delays in shopping, increasing utilization by existing customers and attracting new customers to more convenient locations.[3]

The company had for years offered special services in its stores closely related to the products it sold. For example, there were brief courses—"how-to clinics"—to help customers in carrying out projects (e.g., installing tile, organizing closets). There were also longer, four-week courses that were part of what the company called Home Depot University. (About 50,000 customers took these longer courses in 1999.) Through a closely related operation, customers could also rent trucks on an hourly basis if they had bulky purchases that they needed to transport. The company also offered proprietary credit cards, which accounted for 17 percent of all sales. During 1999 it also began testing a program that would allow customers to apply for unsecured loans to make large purchases in its stores.

COMPETITION

Among home improvement retailers that sold primarily to do-it-yourself customers, Home Depot's principal competitor was Lowe's, which had annual sales of $16 billion. Lowe's

---

2. Patti Bond, "Executive Pushes New Concepts," Cox News Service, August 9, 1999.

3. 1999 10-K.

operated 576 stores at the end of 1999 and planned to add 78 new ones in 2000. Lowe's began its 1999 Annual Report by stating that it was "the world's second largest home improvement retailer competing in a highly fragmented . . . industry." Lowe's began in 1946 with small stores in rural towns. In the mid-1990s, however, it began to copy Home Depot's model, opening huge, warehouse-type stores in metropolitan markets, complete with how-to clinics for its customers. Lowe's sold some product lines that Home Depot didn't and also tried to appeal more to women shoppers, with wider aisles and brighter lighting than Home Depot. In certain markets Lowe's and Home Depot went head to head with each other. Some of their stores were virtually within eyesight of each other. (Exhibit 6 shows summary data for Lowe's for the last three years.)

The next largest competitors—Menards and HomeBase—were far smaller, but they were geographically more focused. Menards, which had annual sales of about $4 billion, operated solely in several midwestern states and was said to have a loyal customer base. In the greater Milwaukee area, for instance, Menards' share of the home improvement market in 1998 was 35 percent; Home Depot's was 15 percent. HomeBase, which had annual sales of about $1.5 billion, operated solely in several western states. Its stores were as large as Home Depot's—averaging over 100,000 square feet—and 50 of them were located in California (where Home Depot had 122 sites).

When Home Depot began growing in the 1980s its most important competitor was Hechinger, which was considered "the premium home-improvement chain by which Wall Street measured every other chain."[4] Hechinger had historically operated a chain of upscale community hardware and building-supply stores that were known for very good customer service, but when it tried to follow Home Depot into the "big box" warehouse format, it lost out in market after market. In 1999, after years of declining performance, it went out of business. A customer visiting one of its stores during the waning days of the company said: "It's obvious they don't put anything into employee training. There are good people there who are just not prepared. If I needed anything serious I'd go to Home Depot."[5]

REDEFINITION OF THE MARKET

Home Depot reports noted that the company's name was "synonymous" with home improvement. Total home improvement product sales in the United States totaled $159 billion in 1999. That would make Home Depot's market share close to 24 percent, and that is roughly what some analysts said its market share was.

In 1997, however, the company engaged in what it called a "redefinition" of its industry. Most of its sales came from do-it-yourself customers. Product sales for that market, it said, totaled about $100 billion in the United States in 1997. However, product sales to professional customers (e.g., contractors, electricians, plumbers, landscapers, property maintenance managers) represented an even larger market. It totaled approximately $265 billion in the U.S. in 1997. Excluding the "heavy industrial" sector, which the company said it didn't serve, the professional market totaled about $215 billion. Of that market, the company said its share was less than 4 percent.

Thereafter the company would refer to its relevant market as something a lot broader than the market with which it had historically been associated—residential home repair and remodeling by do-it-yourself customers. It now said its market consisted of "all sales

4. Erica Johnston, "The Region in Review," Washington Post, September 12, 1999.
5. Stephanie Stoughton, "Hechinger Files for Bankruptcy Protection," Washington Post, June 12, 1999.

of home improvement and other housing and building-related products for new and existing homes." And it said that it was developing long-term strategies with this view of the market in mind.[6]

At the end of 1998 the company said its total market was $365 billion. This included the "heavy industrial" sector. At the end of 1999 it said that, although it couldn't measure its market share precisely, it estimated it was about 8.9 percent. It also said that it expected to increase its North American market share to 18 percent by the end of 2003.

GROWTH INITIATIVES

The company had a variety of growth initiatives in the works. It was pursuing growth in terms of customer groups, product categories, store formats, store location, and sales channels.

Customer Groups

The customer group with which Home Depot had for years been associated was nonprofessional, do-it-yourself (DIY) customers. In recent years, however, it had shifted to a triple-customer strategy.

Buy-It-Yourself Customers The company was making increased efforts to serve the needs of what it called buy-it-yourself (BIY) customers, people who wanted to select the materials that would go into their homes but who wanted someone else to actually install them. The company already offered a number of installation services and was in the process of adding new services of this sort for roofing, vinyl siding, and replacement windows. (The company arranged for these services through approximately 6,200 third-party contractors, from whom it collected a fee.) "As the population ages," the company said, "we expect more customers will want products installed for them." The total market for installation services in the U.S. was about $75 billion. The company said that it was about to surpass Sears Roebuck as the largest installer of home improvement products but that it still had less than 2 percent of the installation market. It therefore regarded this as a terrific opportunity. It expected its installation services to increase at least 40 percent a year over the next few years.

Professional Customers The company was also working hard on expanding its share of the market for professional customers (e.g., contractors, electricians, plumbers, landscapers, property maintenance managers). The market for professional customers was huge, and it also involved a greater propensity for repeat business. Thus, for example, the company was increasing the availability in its stores of products packaged in "job lot" quantities; it was providing customer service geared specifically to professionals through a "Pro Service Desk" in many of its stores; it was doing mass mailings of catalogues containing over 15,000 products of particular interest to facility maintenance managers and the building trades. In addition, in late 1999 it acquired a company named Apex Supply, which was a wholesaler of plumbing, air conditioning, and related products geared to professional customers. "Through this acquisition," the company said, "we believe we will increase our penetration of the professional plumbing trades and be able to handle special orders for plumbing products more efficiently in Home Depot stores."

Home Depot in the New Millennium

....

6. *Home Depot 1998 Annual Report.*

Company management recognized that the needs of professional customers were quite different from the needs of its do-it-yourself customers. Thus it claimed that it "experimented" with certain changes geared to professional customers in its stores before fully implementing them in order "to ensure that the do-it-yourself customer is not disadvantaged." National "rollout" of the "pro initiative" was expected to take place over the next three years. At the start of 2000 it was operating in 110 stores.

In 1999 the analyst at Deutsche Bank Alex Brown, Dan Wewer, thought that "the pro business will probably influence [Home Depot's] sales and profitability more than any of the other initiatives." At the same time, the professional segment of the business was apt to be more cyclical than the DIY segment.

Product Categories

The store was always in the process of reviewing and revising its product offerings. Occasionally, however, it made some significant changes. In 1999, for example, the company began selling major appliances (e.g., ovens, refrigerators, dishwashers) at 135 of its stores and said that it expected to be selling them in all of its stores by the end of 2000. (The stores actually stocked only the "more popular" items but provided computer kiosks at which customers could special-order many more items.) It said that it regarded appliances as a natural extension of the products and services it was already selling and a way of "extending the trusting relationship" it had with customers.

In 1999 Home Depot acquired a company named Georgia Lighting, a specialty lighting designer, distributor, and retailer. Management believed that the acquisition would "strengthen our sourcing, training, and merchandising in lighting" in its stores.

In an appeal to both do-it-yourself and professional customers, the company was also expanding a tool rental service. It already had ten different categories of tools that it rented on an hourly, weekly, or monthly basis. Company management believed that this service "increased the sales of related merchandise without reducing the sales of equipment similar to that available for rental." This service was growing fast. At the end of 1998 the tool rental service existed in 46 stores; at the end of 1999, 150 stores; and the company expected the service to be available in 350 stores by the end of 2000. (It expected the service would ultimately exist in 60 percent of all of its stores.)

Store Formats

The store format with which Home Depot was primarily associated was the warehouse-type store that carried a huge assortment of home improvement products. The company was now, however, about to move forward with a very different store format. This was the Expo Design Center, which targeted customers interested in carrying out major home decorating projects.

Expo Design Center stores were often located right next to a warehouse store and were almost as large. Expo, however, sold higher-end products and services. They carried much less inventory than the warehouse stores. About 80 percent of the floor space consisted of sample displays of how different rooms (e.g., a kitchen or bedroom or bathroom) might look when remodeled. If a customer was interested in a major home decorating project, he or she would pay a retainer fee to get started, and store employees would work with the

7. *Home Depot 1997 Annual Report.*

8. Patti Bond, *"Executive Pushes New Concepts,"* Cox News Service, August 9, 1999.

customer to handle every aspect of the remodeling process. The goal was for each project to generate $10,000 or more worth of products and services. As a business model, the Expo stores involved—compared to the warehouse stores—less inventory, higher gross margins, higher payroll expense, and probably a greater sensitivity to cyclical changes in discretionary income.

Home Depot opened its first Expo Design store in 1991 and added a few more in the next few years. They were initially treated as a kind of laboratory, and over the years the company made many changes in their size and format. By the end of 1998 there were eight of these stores. Then in 1999 the company added seven more, and it said it planned to be operating about 200 of them within five to six years.

The company had also begun testing a much smaller store format, one that was meant to satisfy customers' needs for smaller projects. These stores would be about one-third the size of the big stores, would be in more "convenient" locations, and would operate not under the Home Depot name but under the name Villager's Hardware. (They would compete with neighborhood hardware stores like TrueValue and Ace Hardware.) In 1999 the company opened two of these smaller stores in New Jersey and planned to open two more in 2000. Blank said that this store concept would be in "test mode" for an unspecified period of time.

International Growth

The company was beginning to expand internationally. In 1998 it opened two stores in Chile and one in Puerto Rico. In 1999 it added two more in Chile and another in Puerto Rico.[9] (The Chilean stores were operated as a joint venture with a Chilean department store. Home Depot controlled two-thirds of the equity.) Over the next few years it planned to open several additional stores in Chile and Argentina. "Every day," Blank said in March of 1999, "we learn more about serving the diverse needs of customers in other areas of the world. We are also learning that the Home Depot culture is, indeed, transferable, and customer service is valued around the world."[10]

How far the company would go with international expansion, however, wasn't clear. In August of 1999 Blank said that "international growth is going to be very important in the next five to fifteen years. We'll be planting seeds in the next five years, maybe in the Far East, or it could be in Europe." He noted some potential problems with this, however. "There are challenges in all of our growth initiatives, but the international realm is the most complex because of real estate and the logistics of the supply chain. Obviously, there are language and cultural differences to overcome, too."[11]

Internet Sales

The company was in the process of developing its Internet site. The site was meant primarily to provide people with information about home improvement projects (e.g., a calculator to estimate the amount of material a person would need). The company was also going to sell products over the Internet, but it was moving into this only gradually, and it regarded the Internet not as an alternative sales channel but as a sales channel that would be additional

....

9. For an extended account of Home Depot's considerations in opening its first stores in Chile, see Clifford Krauss, "Foreign Expansion: Well-Planned or Ill-Timed?" New York Times, September 6, 1998.

10. Home Depot 1998 Annual Report.

11. Patti Bond, "Executive Pushes New Concepts," Cox News Service, August 9, 1999.

or complementary to its physical stores. So far its e-commerce was in operation only in a few metropolitan markets: orders placed over the Internet were being fulfilled from the company's physical stores, and customers could choose to pick them up at the stores or have them delivered. Arthur Blank claimed, however, that the web site would eventually be the "world's largest e-commerce site in our industry."[12]

POTENTIAL PROBLEMS

The company's growth plans involved some risks. The following describes a few of them:

Market Saturation   One risk was the possibility of over-saturation of certain big-city markets. Home Depot and Lowe's were both planning on opening a lot of new stores in the U.S. in the next few years, and many of them would be in markets that they were already in. These markets were seen as extremely attractive, but there was a question of how many stores they could support. In the Atlanta, Georgia, area, for example, there were 43 Home Depot, Lowe's, Ace Hardware, and True Value stores within twenty miles of each other. In Portland, Oregon, Home Depot was planning in 2000 to increase the number of stores it had from 7 to 13. Lowe's was in the process of constructing two large stores there. HomeBase wasn't planning any additions but already had four stores there. In the Dallas/Fort Worth area, Home Depot had 30 stores while Lowe's had 14. Lowe's had been in the Dallas market for just a few years, and observers noted that when it moved in, prices at home improvement stores fell.

Different Customer Groups   Home Depot was a "category killer," but there were components of its product mix that other companies addressed in a more focused way. For example, national and regional wholesalers of electrical products, who sold to professional customers, believed that they could offer more than Home Depot—in terms of a broader and deeper inventory, more knowledgeable sales help with technical questions, and reliable delivery. In their view, "Home Depot, for all its high-profile positioning as a source of supply for professional contractors, still focuses primarily on the fastest-moving items." Some of these wholesalers found that "their customers still needed more than that."

The example of one company demonstrated the problems in pursuing a "dual customer" strategy. A regional seller of home improvement products named National Home Centers opened stores in the late 1970s that were geared primarily to professional contractors. In 1983 it began marketing to both professional contractors and do-it-yourself customers. In 1998, however, it shifted its focus back to professional contractors, saying that it couldn't adequately compete in both markets.[13]

Appliances   Home Depot's chairman, Bernard Marcus, said that the company planned to eventually be number one in the retail market for major appliances. At the moment, Sears had about 30 percent, or $6 billion, of the market; it offered on its premises a broad product assortment; and it also maintained an extensive service network. Circuit City had recently given up on selling appliances, which freed up about 5 percent of the market. Wal-Mart, however, had announced that it was entering the market along with Home Depot, and both of those companies intended to sell most appliances through computer kiosks in their stores. (Home Depot's current market share was about 3 percent.)

....

12. Debbie Howell, "Home Depot Touts Pro, E-Tail Initiatives," National Home Center News, June 19, 2000.

13. Jim Lucy, "The Super Influentials," Broadcast Engineering, May 1999.

Cross-Selling   There was also a question of how much cross-selling, or bundling of products and services, Home Depot could successfully handle. Its big stores were already, in a sense, department stores (what people in the past might have bought at the lumber shop, the paint shop, the wallpaper shop, and so on), but the company was now taking this concept much further (e.g., providing installation services, selling appliances). Huge financial corporations like Citicorp were basing much of their strategy on cross-selling. In order to be successful at cross-selling, however, companies had to be able to truly integrate different products within a given organizational structure. In addition, the increasing availability of information through the Internet made it easier for consumers to locate providers of different products and services on their own.

Employees   Home Depot ended 1999 with 201,000 employees. It had long regarded high-quality customer service as one of the keys to its success. The company planned, however, on more than doubling the number of stores over the next four years. It claimed that attracting good "associates" wasn't difficult, but the challenges of maintaining high levels of customer service over a far larger market base could be substantial.

Macroeconomy   Naturally, the macroeconomy was a wild card. The company had historically claimed that its fortunes were relatively insulated from changes in the macroeconomy, but the record suggested that that might not be the case. (See Exhibit 2.)

THE VIEW OF STOCK ANALYSTS

In the previous year or two, sell-side analysts had generally been supportive of Home Depot's various growth initiatives (e.g., going after more professional customers, expanding the Expo Design Center format, adding to its product line, opening some sites in other countries, developing Internet business). They generally cited these initiatives approvingly, but occasionally there were expressions of concern about the possible saturation of certain big-city markets, particularly given the competition from Lowe's. However, large parts of the country weren't remotely near any Home Depot or Lowe's store, and analysts were aware that Home Depot and Lowe's generally took a certain amount of market share away from other businesses and that they helped to actually expand the market (by making home-improvement projects less expensive and more understandable for many people).[14]

In the previous ten months, however, there had been very different views among analysts about the appropriate valuation of the company's stock. The following provide some examples:

- Raymond James report on 12/29/99, when the stock price had just reached its all-time high of $68: The price was at that point 70 times trailing earnings and 56 times the analyst's estimated earnings for the year 2000. He expected an earnings growth rate of 25 percent over the next several years. He said that, in his view, Home Depot was the best managed retailer in the country, if not the world. It continued to have, he believed, great fundamentals. But at the current stock price, he essentially regarded it as overvalued. Interestingly, he also noted that company management had "conditioned the Street to expect it to beat [estimated] numbers."
- CreditSuisse/First Boston report on 2/25/00, when the stock was trading at $54: The analyst noted that the market had just had a "tepid" reaction to the company's announcement of fourth quarter results, even though they exceeded consensus

---

14. *SalomonSmithBarney's report on Home Depot, dated December 2, 1998, contains some good discussion of the possibility of market saturation.*

estimates by a bit. He said that this reflected a general concern over interest rates and the Federal Reserve's intent to slow consumer spending, which would hurt most retailers. He thought that Home Depot's ability to continue to gain market share and increase margins would, however, offset some of the slowdown in consumer spending. He had positive comments about all of the company's growth initiatives. He regarded the "pro initiative" (the effort to increase sales to professional customers) as the company's most important growth initiative and thought that it could eventually increase sales by 7 to 10 percent in each store where it was operating, but he also believed that it wasn't yet operating in enough stores to have a material impact on earnings growth. He expected an earnings growth rate of 23 percent over the next several years, an EPS of $1.25 in 2000, and a 25 percent increase in the stock price over the next twelve months.

- Morgan Stanley Dean Witter report on 3/1/00, when the stock was trading at $55: The analyst expected earnings growth rate over the next several years of 22 percent. Her EPS estimate for 2000 was $1.25. She had positive comments on all of the company's growth initiatives. She thought that rising interest rates would have some impact on the company. Nevertheless, she thought the current P/E of 44 (relative to 2000 estimated earnings) would be maintained, and she expected an 18 percent increase in the stock price over the next twelve months.

- CIBC World Markets report on 4/12/00, when the stock was trading at $66: The analyst noted that the stock was at that point trading at 66 times trailing earnings and 53 times his estimated earnings for the year 2000 (which was $1.25). He noted that the latter was twice the multiple for the S&P 500 (which was 26 times estimated earnings). He expected an earnings growth rate of 25 percent over the next few years—although, given the strength of the company's growth initiatives, he felt that it might exceed that. He noted that the Fed had been raising interest rates in an effort to slow the economy down. He disputed the analogy, however, to the last period of rising interests (1994–1995) and the negative impact that that evidently had on Home Depot's performance. Things were different now, in his view. For example, the company's growth initiatives had a lot of potential; consumer spending remained strong; the company's greater purchasing clout now would help it maintain gross margins; the company's competitive position had improved with the weakening of smaller competitors. Thus he was bullish on the stock, with a twelve-month price target roughly 30 percent higher than its current price.

- Lehman Brothers report on 5/16/00, when the stock was trading at $56: Like other analysts, he expected an earnings growth rate of 25 percent over the next few years. He noted that the stock was currently trading at 45 times his estimated EPS for 2000 (which was $1.25) He noted that the P/E multiple of 45 represented a 79 percent premium to the S&P 500 and an 81 percent premium to his long-term estimated growth rate for the company of 25 percent. He regarded this valuation as "attractive."

- A.G. Edwards report on 8/22/00, when the stock was trading at $50: This analyst was cautious about the stock, even though he regarded Home Depot as a great company. He noted that the annual growth rate in the company's earnings over the last ten years had averaged about 30 percent, and he now expected a more moderate growth rate of about 25 percent a year. He therefore anticipated a contraction of the then-current P/E multiple of 41 (based on his estimated EPS for 2000, which was $1.25).

- SalomonSmithBarney report on 8/23/00, when the stock was trading at $50: This analyst was also cautious about the stock, even though he also regarded Home Depot as a great company. He expected a deceleration in the company's earnings growth to about 25 percent a year. He thought this would occur primarily because of the macroeconomic environment—higher interest rates and a slowing economy. He noted that the stock was currently trading at a P/E multiple of 41 (based on his estimated EPS for 2000, which was $1.25) but that the average multiple for the company during the 1990s had been about 32. He also noted that the company's P/E-to-growth ratio was currently about 1.5 (based on earnings for the next twelve months and assuming a long-term earnings growth rate of 25 percent) but that, over the last ten years, the company's P/E-to-growth ratio had averaged about 1.2. The lowest such ratio for the company occurred in late 1995, when it was 0.7. He thought that the current economic environment for housing-oriented businesses like Home Depot was similar to that in 1995 (e.g., a lagging effect from rising mortgage interest rates), and he noted that in 1995 Home Depot experienced a sharp deceleration in same-store sales increases. He was confident that the stock would not move down to the valuation level reached in late 1995. The company's business was, in his view, too outstanding for that. Nevertheless, he was cautious about the stock's near-term prospects. He added that he wasn't downgrading Lowe's stock as well because Lowe's stock didn't have nearly as high a valuation.

On October 12 the company's stock price dropped to $35. Exhibit 7 provides a graph of Home Depot's stock from January 1 through October 12 of 2000. Exhibit 8 compares changes in Home Depot's stock to those of the S&P 500 and the S&P Retail Stores index (a composite of thirty-five retail stocks) for the same period.

MANAGEMENT'S PREDICTION

Several months earlier, in the spring of 2000, Arthur Blank acknowledged that the company's share price had already suffered to some extent because of concerns about rising interest rates, but he said he wasn't concerned about these short-term dips. He continued to expect 23 to 25 percent growth in earnings per share over the next several years. "At the end of the day," he said, "we feel our prospects are very good. Essentially what we've done for the last twenty-one years is what we'll continue to do."[15]

QUESTIONS

1. What is your estimate of the intrinsic value of Home Depot's stock as of February 1, 2001?

2. What set of assumptions regarding Home Depot's future growth rate, return on equity, and cost of equity are consistent with its observed stock price of $48.20 on February 1, 2001?

15. Patti Bond, "Home Depot: Retailer Plans to Stick to Usual Winning Script," Atlanta Journal and Constitution, May 21, 2000.

Home Depot in the New Millennium

EXHIBIT I

Home Depot, Decomposition of ROE, 1986–1999

	1986	1987	1988	1989	1990	1991	1992	1993	1994	1995	1996	1997	1998	1999
ROE	26.8%	33.2%	'23.9%	29.2%	31.9%	36.5%	21.5%	19.9%	21.5%	21.3%	18.8%	19.5%	22.7%	26.5%
Decomposition														
NOPAT ($ millions)	30	56	77	114	167	240	346	439	609	722	932	1,159	1,618	2,315
NOPAT margin	2.9%	3.8%	3.9%	4.1%	4.4%	4.7%	4.8%	4.7%	4.9%	4.7%	4.8%	4.8%	5.4%	6.0%
Net assets ($ millions)	290	263	347	475	681	1,079	1,568	2,735	3,267	4,390	5,602	6,647	8,235	10,258
Operating asset turnover	3.5	5.5	5.8	5.8	5.6	4.8	4.6	3.4	3.8	3.5	3.5	3.6	3.7	3.7
Operating ROA	10.2%	21.1%	22.3%	23.9%	24.5%	22.3%	22.1%	16.0%	18.6%	16.4%	16.6%	17.4%	19.7%	22.6%
Net debt ($ millions)	201	100	27	92	169	395	(123)	431	453	948	614	691	1,137	1,518
Net financial leverage	2.25	0.61	0.08	0.24	0.33	0.58	(0.07)	0.19	0.16	0.28	0.12	0.12	0.16	0.17
Net interest expense after tax ($ millions)	5.7	1.5	0.6	1.6	3.7	(9.1)	(16.7)	(18.7)	4.6	(9.5)	(5.8)	(1.2)	4.3	(5.5)
Net interest rate after tax	2.8%	1.5%	2.2%	1.8%	2.2%	-2.3%	13.6%	4.3%	1.0%	-1.0%	-0.9%	-0.2%	0.4%	-0.4%
Spread	7.4%	19.6%	20.1%	22.2%	22.4%	24.6%	8.4%	20.4%	17.6%	17.4%	17.6%	17.6%	19.3%	22.9%
Financial leverage effect	16.6%	12.0%	1.7%	5.3%	7.4%	14.2%	-0.6%	3.8%	2.8%	4.8%	2.2%	2.0%	3.1%	4.0%

Notes:
• Explanation of terms appears on following page.
• Years indicated end in January of the following year. Thus 1999 data is for the twelve-month period ending at the end of January 2000.

Sources: Compustat and case writer's calculations.

Home Depot, Decomposition of ROE (*continued*)

Explanation of Terms

ROE = Net income / Equity
     = Operating ROA + Financial leverage effect

NOPAT (net operating profit after taxes) = Net income + Net interest expense after tax

NOPAT margin = NOPAT / Sales

Net assets = Operating working capital + Net long-term assets
     Operating working capital = (Current assets − Cash and marketable securities) − (Current liabilities − Short-term debt and current portion of long-term debt)
     Net long-term assets = Total long-term assets − Non-interest-bearing long-term liabilities

Operating asset turnover = Sales / Net assets

Operating ROA = NOPAT / Net assets
     = NOPAT margin × Operating assets turnover

Net debt = Total interest-bearing liabilities − Cash and marketable securities

Net financial leverage = Net debt / Equity

Net interest expense after tax = (Interest expense − Interest income) × (1 − effective tax rate)

Net interest rate after tax = (Net interest expense after tax) / Net debt

Net pretax interest rate = (Interest expense − interest and investment income) / Net debt

Net after-tax interest rate = Net pretax interest rate × (1 − Effective tax rate)

Spread = Operating ROA − Net interest rate after tax

Financial leverage effect = Net financial leverage × Spread

Source: Palepu, Healy, and Bernard, *Business Analysis and Valuation*, second edition.

Home Depot in the New Millennium

Home Depot in the New Millennium

EXHIBIT 2

Home Depot, Operational Data, 1986–1999

	1986	1987	1988	1989	1990	1991	1992	1993	1994	1995	1996	1997	1998	1999
Sales (millions)	$1,011	$1,454	$2,000	$2,758	$3,815	$5,137	$7,148	$9,239	$12,477	$15,470	$19,535	$24,156	$30,219	$38,434
Number of stores	60	75	96	118	145	174	214	264	340	423	512	624	761	930
Total square footage at year-end (000)	5,000	6,000	8,000	10,000	13,000	16,000	21,000	26,000	35,000	44,000	54,000	66,000	81,000	100,000
Increase in square footage	20.6%	27.6%	33.4%	26.9%	27.4%	24.1%	26.8%	26.3%	33.2%	26.3%	21.6%	23.1%	22.8%	23.5%
Average square footage per store (000)	80	82	86	88	92	95	98	100	103	105	105	106	107	108
Same-store sales increase	7%	18%	13%	13%	10%	11%	15%	7%	8%	3%	7%	7%	7%	10%
Weekly sales per store (000)	$355	$418	$464	$515	$566	$633	$724	$764	$802	$787	$803	$829	$844	$876
Sales per square foot	$230	$265	$282	$303	$322	$348	$387	$398	$404	$390	$398	$406	$410	$423
Number of customer transactions (millions)	34	48	64	84	112	146	189	236	302	370	464	550	665	797
Average sale per transaction	$29.73	$30.24	$31.13	$32.65	$33.92	$35.13	$37.72	$39.13	$41.29	$41.78	$42.09	$43.63	$45.05	$47.87
GMROI	179%	219%	219%	233%	246%	255%	254%	236%	238%	227%	232%	224%	227%	243%
Number of employees at year-end	6,600	9,100	13,000	17,500	21,500	28,000	38,900	50,600	67,300	80,800	98,100	124,400	156,700	201,400

Notes:
- Years indicated end in January of the following year. Thus 1999 data is for the twelve-month period ending at the end of January 2000.
- GMROI = gross margin return on inventory investment = gross margin dollars divided by average inventory balance times 100. The GMROI captures the combined impact of gross margin and inventory turnover.

Sources: Company annual reports; Compustat; case writer's calculations.

EXHIBIT 3

Home Depot EPS and Stock Data, 1990–1999

	1990	1991	1992	1993	1994	1995	1996	1997	1998	1999
Diluted EPS	$0.10	$0.13	$0.18	$0.22	$0.29	$0.34	$0.43	$0.55	$0.71	$1.00
Diluted EPS increase	43%	30%	38%	22%	32%	17%	26%	28%	29%	41%
Weighted number of shares o/s assuming dilution (millions)	1,824	1,985	2,096	2,132	2,142	2,151	2,195	2,287	2,320	2,342
Total return on stock:										
Home Depot	54%	167%	48%	–20%	19%	6%	6%	81%	111%	77%
S&P 500	–5%	32%	8%	10%	2%	38%	22%	34%	28%	21%

Sources: Company Annual Report; Bloomberg.

EXHIBIT 4

Home Depot Consolidated Financial Statements

INCOME STATEMENTS
($ millions, except earnings per share)

	Years Ending January		
	2000	1999	1998
Net Sales	38,434	30,219	24,156
Cost of Merchandise Sold	27,023	21,614	17,375
Gross Profit	11,411	8,605	6,781
Operating Expenses			
Selling and Store Operating	6,832	5,341	4,303
Pre-Opening	113	88	65
General and Administrative	671	515	413
Non-Recurring Charge	—	—	104
Total Operating Expenses	7,616	5,944	4,885
Operating Income	3,795	2,661	1,896
Interest and Investment Income	37	30	44
Interest Expense	(28)	(37)	(42)
Interest, net	9	(7)	2
Earnings Before Income Taxes	3,804	2,654	1,898
Income Taxes	1,484	1,040	738
Net Earnings	2,320	1,614	1,160
Basic Earnings Per Share	1.03	0.73	0.53
Diluted Earnings Per Share	1.00	0.71	0.52

Note: Cost of merchandise sold includes all of the company's depreciation and amortization expense, which totaled $463, $373, and $283 million in years ending January 2000, 1999, and 1998, respectively. By contrast, Lowe's does not include depreciation and amortization in its cost of merchandise sold figures; it has a separate operating expense line for them.

Source: Company 10-K

Home Depot in the New Millennium

BALANCE SHEETS ($ millions)

	As of End of January	
	2000	1999
ASSETS		
Cash and Cash Equivalents	168	62
Short-Term Investments	2	—
Receivables, net	587	469
Merchandise Inventories	5,489	4,293
Other Current Assets	144	109
Total Current Assets	6,390	4,933
Property and Equipment:		
Land	3,248	2,739
Buildings	4,834	3,757
Furniture, Fixtures and Equipment	2,279	1,761
Leasehold Improvements	493	419
Construction in Progress	791	540
Capital Leases	245	206
	11,890	9,422
Less Accumulated Depreciation and Amortization	1,663	1,262
Net Property and Equipment	10,227	8,160
Cost in Excess of the Fair Value of Net Assets Acquired	311	268
Other	153	104
Total Assets	17,081	13,465
LIABILITIES AND STOCKHOLDERS' EQUITY		
Accounts Payable	1,993	1,586
Accrued Salaries and Related Expenses	541	395
Sales Taxes Payable	269	176
Other Accrued Expenses	763	586
Income Taxes Payable	61	100
Current Installments of Long-Term Debt	29	14
Total Current Liabilities	3,656	2,857
Long-Term Debt, excluding current installments	750	1,566
Other Long-Term Liabilities	237	208
Deferred Income Taxes	87	85
Minority Interest	10	9
Stockholders' Equity:		
Common Stock	115	111
Paid-In Capital	4,319	2,817
Retained Earnings	7,941	5,876
Other	(34)	(64)
Total Stockholders' Equity	12,341	8,740
Total Liabilities and Stockholders' Equity	17,081	13,465

Source: Company 10-K.

Home Depot in the New Millennium

CASH FLOW STATEMENTS ($ millions)

| | Years Ending January | | |
	2000	1999	1998
Cash Flows from Operating Activities			
Net Earnings	2,320	1,614	1,160
Depreciation and Amortization	463	373	283
(Increase) Decrease in Receivables, net	(85)	85	(166)
Increase in Merchandise Inventories	(1,142)	(698)	(885)
Increase in Accounts Payable and Accrued Expenses	820	423	577
Increase in Income Taxes Payable	93	59	83
Other	(23)	61	(23)
	2,446	1,917	1,029
Cash Flows from Investing Activities			
Capital Expenditures	(2,581)	(2,053)	(1,420)
Purchase of Remaining Interest in The Home Depot Canada	—	(261)	—
Payments for Businesses Acquired, net	(101)	(6)	(61)
Proceeds from Sales of Property and Equipment	87	45	85
Purchases of Investments	(32)	(2)	(194)
Proceeds from Maturities of Investments	30	4	599
Advances Secured by Real Estate, net	(25)	2	20
	(2,622)	(2,271)	(971)
Cash Flows from Financing Activities			
(Repayments) Issuance of Commercial Paper Obligations, net	(246)	246	—
Proceeds from Long-Term Borrowings, net	522	—	15
Repayments of Long-Term Debt	(14)	(8)	(40)
Proceeds from Sale of Common Stock, net	267	167	122
Cash Dividends Paid to Stockholders	(255)	(168)	(139)
Minority Interest Contributions to Partnership	7	11	10
	281	248	(32)
Effect of Exchange Rate Changes	1	(4)	—
Increase (Decrease) in Cash and Cash Equivalents	106	(110)	26
Cash and Cash Equivalents at Beginning of Year	62	172	146
Cash and Cash Equivalents at End of Year	168	62	172

Note: At the end of 1999 the company said it owned 77% of its stores and leased 23% of them. In recent years it had increased the relative percentage of stores that were owned because it felt that doing so provided greater operating control and flexibility and generally lower occupancy costs. It noted that the cost of new stores to be constructed and owned by the company averaged $13.2 million. The cost to fix up stores to be leased averaged $4.3 million. The cost of inventory for new stores averaged $3.2 million, net of vendor financing.

Source: Company 10-K.

Home Depot in the New Millennium

EXHIBIT 5

Projected Growth in U.S. Market for Home
Improvement Products, as of June 2000

Year	Percent Change over Previous Year
2000	6.3%
2001	3.2%
2002	4.0%
2003	4.4%
2004	4.6%

Source: Home Improvement Research Institute.

EXHIBIT 6

Summary Data for Lowe's ($ millions)

	1999	1998	1997
Sales	$15,905	$13,330	$11,108
NOPAT	$727	$530	$398
NOPAT margin	4.6%	4.0%	3.6%
Net assets	$4,961	$3,545	$2,810
Operating ROA (NOPAT/Net assets)	14.7%	15.0%	14.2%
Number of stores at year-end	576	520	477
Comparable store sales increase	6%	6%	4%
Sales per square foot	$303	$273	$302
GMROI	169%	173%	162%

Note: GMROI = gross margin return on inventory investment = gross margin dollars divided by average inventory balance times 100. The GMROI captures the combined impact of gross margin and inventory turnover.

Sources: Company Annual Report and 10-K; case writer's calculations.

Home Depot in the New Millennium

EXHIBIT 7

Home Depot's Stock Price

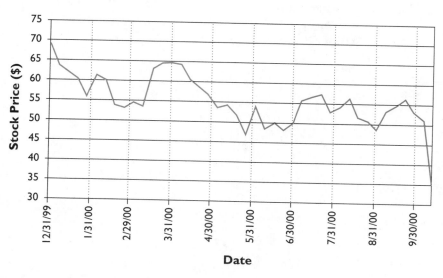

Data as of early October 2000:
Home Depot's beta: 1.09
Yields on Treasury securities:
30-day–6.00%; 90-day–6.18%; 1-year–6.13%; 10-year–5.80%; 30-year–5.83%

Sources: Bloomberg; Federal Reserve; *Wall Street Journal.*

EXHIBIT 8

Return on Home Depot's Stock Compared to S&P Retail Index and S&P 500

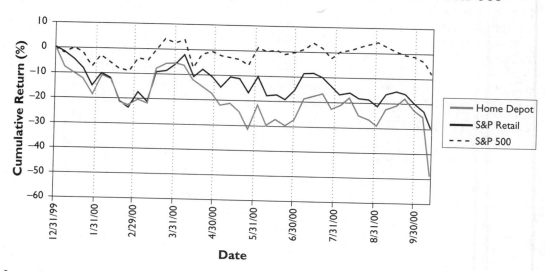

Source: Bloomberg.

P A R T 3

Business Analysis and Valuation Applications

CHAPTER 9

Equity Security Analysis

Equity security analysis is the evaluation of a firm and its prospects from the perspective of a current or potential investor in the firm's stock. Security analysis is one step in a larger investment process that involves (1) establishing the objectives of the investor, (2) forming expectations about the future returns and risks of individual securities, and then (3) combining individual securities into portfolios to maximize progress toward the investment objectives.

Security analysis is the foundation for the second step, projecting future returns and assessing risk. Security analysis is typically conducted with an eye toward identification of mispriced securities in hopes of generating returns that more than compensate the investor for risk. However, that need not be the case. For analysts who do not have a comparative advantage in identifying mispriced securities, the focus should be on gaining an appreciation for how a security would affect the risk of a given portfolio, and whether it fits the profile that the portfolio is designed to maintain.

Security analysis is undertaken by individual investors, by analysts at brokerage houses (sell-side analysts), and by analysts that work at the direction of funds managers for various institutions (buy-side analysts). The institutions employing buy-side analysts include mutual funds, pension funds, insurance companies, universities, and others.

A variety of questions are dealt with in security analysis:

- A sell-side analyst asks: How do my forecasts compare to those of the analysts' consensus? Is the observed market price consistent with that consensus? Given my expectations for the firm, does this stock appear to be mispriced? Should I recommend this stock as a buy, a sell, or a hold?
- A buy-side analyst for a "value stock fund" asks: Does this stock possess the characteristics we seek in our fund? That is, does it have a relatively low ratio of price to earnings, low price-to-book value, and other fundamental indicators? Do its prospects for earnings improvement suggest good potential for high future returns on the stock?
- An individual investor asks: Does this stock offer the risk profile that suits my investment objectives? Does it enhance my ability to diversify the risk of my portfolio? Is the firm's dividend payout rate low enough to help shield me from taxes while I continue to hold the stock?

As the above questions underscore, there is more to security analysis than estimating the value of stocks. Nevertheless, for most sell-side and buy-side analysts, the key goal remains the identification of mispriced stocks.

INVESTOR OBJECTIVES

The investment objectives of individual savers in the economy are highly idiosyncratic. For any given saver they depend on such factors as income, age, wealth, tolerance for risk, and tax status. For example, savers with many years until retirement are likely to prefer to have a relatively large share of their portfolio invested in equities, which offer a higher expected return but high short-term variability. Investors in high tax brackets are likely to prefer to have a large share of their portfolio in stocks that generate tax-deferred capital gains rather than stocks that pay dividends or interest-bearing securities.

Mutual funds (or unit trusts as they are termed in some countries) have become popular investment vehicles for savers to achieve their investment objectives. Mutual funds sell shares in professionally managed portfolios that invest in specific types of stocks and/or fixed income securities. They therefore provide a low-cost way for savers to invest in a portfolio of securities that reflects their particular appetite for risk.

The major classes of mutual funds include (1) money market funds that invest in CDs and treasury bills, (2) bond funds that invest in debt instruments, (3) equity funds that invest in equity securities, (4) balanced funds that hold money market, bond, and equity securities, and (5) real estate funds that invest in commercial real estate. Within the bond and equities classes of funds, however, there are wide ranges of fund types. For example, bond funds include:

- *Corporate bond funds* that invest in investment-grade rated corporate debt instruments
- *High yield funds* that invest in non-investment-grade rated corporate debt
- *Mortgage funds* that invest in mortgage-backed securities
- *Municipal funds* that invest in municipal debt instruments and which generate income that can be nontaxable

Equity funds include:

- *Income funds* that invest in stocks that are expected to generate dividend income
- *Growth funds* that invest in stocks expected to generate long-term capital gains
- *Income and growth funds* that invest in stocks that provide a balance of dividend income and capital gains
- *Value funds* that invest in equities that are considered to be undervalued
- *Short funds* that sell short equity securities that are considered to be overvalued
- *Index funds* that invest in stocks that track a particular market index, such as the S&P 500
- *Sector funds* that invest in stocks in a particular industry segment, such as the technology or health sciences sectors
- *Regional funds* that invest in equities from a particular country or geographic region, such as Japan, Europe, or the Asia-Pacific region

The focus of this chapter is on analysis for equity securities.

EQUITY SECURITY ANALYSIS AND MARKET EFFICIENCY

How a security analyst should invest his or her time depends on how quickly and efficiently information flows through markets and becomes reflected in security prices. In the extreme, information would be reflected in security prices fully and immediately upon its release. This is essentially the condition posited by the *efficient markets hypothesis*. This hypothesis states that security prices reflect all available information, as if such information could be costlessly digested and translated immediately into demands for buys or sells without regard to frictions imposed by transactions costs. Under such conditions, it would be impossible to identify mispriced securities on the basis of public information.

In a world of efficient markets, the expected return on any equity security is just enough to compensate investors for the unavoidable risk the security involves. Unavoidable risk is that which cannot be "diversified away" simply by holding a portfolio of many securities. Given efficient markets, the investor's strategy shifts away from the search for mispriced securities and focuses instead on maintaining a well diversified portfolio. Aside from this, the investor must arrive at the desired balance between risky securities and short-term government bonds. The desired balance depends on how much risk the investor is willing to bear for a given increase in expected returns.

The above discussion implies that investors who accept that stock prices already reflect available information have no need for analysis involving a search for mispriced securities. If all investors adopted this attitude, of course no such analysis would be conducted, mispricing would go uncorrected, and markets would no longer be efficient![1] This is why the efficient markets hypothesis cannot represent an equilibrium in a strict sense. In equilibrium there must be just enough mispricing to provide incentives for the investment of resources in security analysis.

The existence of some mispricing, even in equilibrium, does not imply that it is sensible for just anyone to engage in security analysis. Instead, it suggests that securities analysis is subject to the same laws of supply and demand faced in all other competitive industries: it will be rewarding only for those with the strongest comparative advantage. How many analysts are in that category depends on a number of factors, including the liquidity of a firm's stock and investor interest in the company.[2] For example, there are about 40 sell-side professional analysts who follow IBM, a company with a highly liquid stock and considerable investor interest. There are many other buy-side analysts who track the firm on their own account without issuing any formal reports to outsiders. For the smallest publicly traded firms in the U.S., there is typically no formal following by analysts, and would-be investors and their advisors are left to themselves to conduct securities analysis.

Market Efficiency and the Role of Financial Statement Analysis

The degree of market efficiency that arises from competition among analysts and other market agents is an empirical issue addressed by a large body of research spanning the last three decades. Such research has important implications for the role of financial statements in security analysis. Consider for example the implications of an extremely efficient market, where information is fully impounded in prices within minutes of its revelation. In such a market, agents could profit from digesting financial statement information in two ways. First, the information would be useful to the select few who receive newly announced financial data, interpret it quickly, and trade on it within minutes. Second, and probably more important, the information would be useful for gaining an understanding of the firm, so as to place the analyst in a better position to interpret other news (from financial statements as well as other sources) as it arrives.

On the other hand, if securities prices fail to reflect financial statement data fully, even days or months after its public revelation, there is a third way in which market agents could profit from such data. That is to create trading strategies designed to exploit any systematic ways in which the publicly available data are ignored or discounted in the price-setting process.

Market Efficiency and Managers' Financial Reporting Strategies

The degree to which markets are efficient also has implications for managers' approaches to communicating with their investment communities. The issue becomes most important when the firm pursues an unusual strategy, or when the usual interpretation of financial statements would be misleading in the firm's context. In such a case, the communication avenues managers can successfully pursue depend not only on management's credibility, but also on the degree of understanding present in the investment community. We will return to the issue of management communications in more detail in Chapter 13.

Evidence of Market Efficiency

There is an abundance of evidence consistent with a high degree of efficiency in the primary U.S. securities markets.[3] In fact, during the 1960s and 1970s, the evidence was so one-sided that the efficient markets hypothesis gained widespread acceptance within the academic community and had a major impact on the practicing community as well.

Evidence pointing to very efficient securities markets comes in several forms:

- When information is announced publicly, the markets react *very* quickly.
- It is difficult to identify specific funds or analysts who have consistently generated abnormally high returns.
- A number of studies suggest that stock prices reflect a rather sophisticated level of fundamental analysis.

While a large body of evidence consistent with efficiency exists, recent years have witnessed a re-examination of the once widely accepted thinking. A sampling of the research includes the following:

- On the issue of the speed of stock price response to news, a number of studies suggest that even though prices react quickly, the initial reaction tends to be incomplete.[4]
- A number of studies point to trading strategies that could have been used to outperform market averages.[5]
- Some related evidence—still subject to ongoing debate about its proper interpretation—suggests that, even though market prices reflect some relatively sophisticated analyses, prices still do not fully reflect all the information that could be garnered from publicly available financial statements.[6]

The controversy over the efficiency of securities markets is unlikely to end soon. However, there are some lessons that are accepted by most researchers. First, securities markets not only reflect publicly available information, they also anticipate much of it before it is released. The open question is what fraction of the response remains to be impounded in price once the day of the public release comes to a close. Second, even in most studies that suggest inefficiency, the degree of mispricing is relatively small for large stocks.

Finally, even if some of the evidence is currently difficult to align with the efficient markets hypothesis, it remains a useful benchmark (at a minimum) for thinking about the behavior of security prices. The hypothesis will continue to play that role unless it can be replaced by a more complete theory. Some researchers are developing theories that encompass the existence of market agents who are forced to trade for unpredictable "liquidity" reasons, and prices that differ from so-called "fundamental values," even in equilibrium. Also, behavioral finance models recognize that cognitive biases can affect investor behavior.[7]

APPROACHES TO FUND MANAGEMENT AND SECURITIES ANALYSIS

Approaches used in practice to manage funds and analyze securities are quite varied. One dimension of variation is the extent to which the investments are actively or passively managed. Another variation is whether a quantitative or a traditional fundamental approach is used. Security analysts also vary considerably in terms of whether they produce formal or informal valuations of the firm.

Active Versus Passive Management

Active portfolio management relies heavily on security analysis to identify mispriced securities. The passive portfolio manager serves as a price taker, avoiding the costs of security analysis and turnover while typically seeking to hold a portfolio designed to match some overall market index or sector performance. Combined approaches are also possible. For example, one may actively manage 20 percent of a fund balance while passively managing the remainder. The widespread growth of passively managed funds in the U.S. over the past twenty years serves as testimony to many fund managers' belief that earning superior returns is a difficult thing to do.

Quantitative Versus Traditional Fundamental Analysis

Actively managed funds must depend on some form of security analysis. Some funds employ "technical analysis," which attempts to predict stock price movements on the basis of market indicators (prior stock price movements, volume, etc.). In contrast, "fundamental analysis," the primary approach to security analysis, attempts to evaluate the current market price relative to projections of the firm's future earnings and cash-flow generating potential. Fundamental analysis involves all the steps described in the previous chapters of this book: business strategy analysis, accounting analysis, financial analysis, and prospective analysis (forecasting and valuation).

In recent years, some analysts have supplemented traditional fundamental analysis, which involves a substantial amount of subjective judgment, with more quantitative approaches. The quantitative approaches themselves are quite varied. Some involve simply "screening" stocks on the basis of some set of factors, such as trends in analysts' earnings revisions, price-earnings ratios, price-book ratios, and so on. Whether such approaches are useful depends on the degree of market efficiency relative to the screens.

Quantitative approaches can also involve implementation of some formal model to predict future stock returns. Longstanding statistical techniques such as regression analysis and probit analysis can be used, as can more recently developed, computer-intensive techniques such as neural network analysis. Again, the success of these approaches depends on the degree of market efficiency and whether the analysis can exploit information in ways not otherwise available to market agents as a group.

Quantitative approaches play a more important role in security analysis today than they did a decade or two ago. However, by and large, analysts still rely primarily on the kind of fundamental analysis involving complex human judgments, as outlined in our earlier chapters.

Formal Versus Informal Valuation

Full-scale, formal valuations based on the methods described in Chapter 7 have become more common, especially in recent years. However, less formal approaches are also possible. For example, an analyst can compare his or her long-term earnings projection with the consensus forecast to generate a buy or sell recommendation. Alternatively, an analyst might recommend a stock because his or her earnings forecast appears relatively high in comparison to the current price. Another possible approach might be labeled "marginalist." This approach involves no attempt to value the firm. The analyst simply assumes that if he or she has unearthed favorable (or unfavorable) information believed not to be recognized by others, the stock should be bought (or sold).

Unlike many security analysts, investment bankers produce formal valuations as a matter of course. Investment bankers, who estimate values for purposes of bringing a private firm to the public market, for evaluating a merger or buyout proposal, or for purposes of periodic managerial review, must document their valuation in a way that can readily be communicated to management and, if necessary, to the courts.

THE PROCESS OF A COMPREHENSIVE SECURITY ANALYSIS

Given the variety of approaches practiced in security analysis, it is impossible to summarize all of them here. Instead, we briefly outline steps to be included in a comprehensive security analysis. The amount of attention focused on any given step varies among analysts.

Selection of Candidates for Analysis

No analyst can effectively investigate more than a small fraction of the securities on a major exchange, and thus some approach to narrowing the focus must be employed. Sell-side analysts are often organized within an investment house by industry or sector. Thus they tend to be constrained in their choices of firms to follow. However, from the perspective of a fund manager or an investment firm as a whole, there is usually the freedom to focus on any firm or sector.

As noted earlier, funds typically specialize in investing in stocks with certain risk profiles or characteristics (e.g., growth stocks, "value" stocks, technology stocks, cyclical stocks). Managers of these types of funds seek to focus the energies of their analysts on identifying stocks that fit their fund objective In addition, individual investors who seek to maintain a well diversified portfolio without holding many stocks also need information about the nature of a firm's risks.

An alternative approach to stock selection is to screen firms on the basis of some hypothesis about mispricing—perhaps with follow-up detailed analysis of stocks that meet the specified criteria. For example, one fund managed by a large U.S. insurance company screens stocks on the basis of recent "earnings momentum," as reflected in revisions in the earnings projections of sell-side and buy-side analysts. Upward revisions trigger investigations for possible purchase. The fund operates on the belief that earnings momentum is a positive signal of future price movements. Another fund complements the earnings momentum screen with one based on recent short-term stock price movements, in the hopes of identifying earnings revisions not yet reflected in stock prices.

Key Analysis Questions

Depending on whether fund managers follow a strategy of targeting stocks with specific types of characteristics, or of screening stocks that appear to be mispriced, the following types of questions are likely to be useful:

- What is the risk profile of a firm? How volatile is its earnings stream and stock price? What are the key possible bad outcomes in the future? What is the upside potential? How closely linked are the firm's risks to the health of the overall economy? Are the risks largely diversifiable, or are they systematic?

- Does the firm possess the characteristics of a growth stock? What is the expected pattern of sales and earnings growth for the coming years? Is the firm reinvesting most or all of its earnings?
- Does the firm match the characteristics desired by "income funds"? Is it a mature or maturing company, prepared to "harvest" profits and distribute them in the form of high dividends?
- Is the firm a candidate for a "value fund"? Does it offer measures of earnings, cash flow, and book value that are high relative to the price? What specific screening rules can be implemented to identify misvalued stocks?

Inferring Market Expectations

If the security analysis is conducted with an eye toward the identification of mispricing, it must ultimately involve a comparison of the analyst's expectations with those of "the market." One possibility is to view the observed stock price as the reflection of market expectations and to compare the analyst's own estimate of value with that price. However, a stock price is only a "summary statistic." It is useful to have a more detailed idea of the market's expectations about a firm's future performance, expressed in terms of sales, earnings, and other measures. For example, assume that an analyst has developed new insights about a firm's near-term sales. Whether those insights represent new information for the stock market, and whether they indicate that a "buy" recommendation is appropriate, can be easily determined if the analyst knows the market consensus sales forecast.

Around the world a number of agencies summarize analysts' forecasts of sales and earnings. Forecasts for the next year or two are commonly available, and for many firms, a "long-run" earnings growth projection is also available—typically for three to five years. Some agencies in the U.S provide continuous on-line updates to such data, so if an analyst revises a forecast, that can be made known to fund managers and other analysts within seconds.

As useful as analysts' forecasts of sales and earnings are, they do not represent a complete description of expectations about future performance, and there is no guarantee that consensus analyst forecasts are the same as those reflected in market prices. Further, financial analysts typically forecast performance for only a few years, so that even if these do reflect market expectations, it is helpful to understand what types of long-term forecasts are reflected in stock prices. Armed with the model in Chapters 7 and 8 that expresses price as a function of future cash flows or earnings, an analyst can draw some educated inferences about the expectations embedded in stock prices.

For example, consider the valuation of IBM. On March 19, 2003, IBM's stock price was $81.50. For the year ended December 31, 2002, the company reported that earnings per share declined from $4.58 the prior year to $2.10, reflecting losses on discontinued operations and an economic downturn that hit the IT sector particularly severely. By mid-March analysts were forecasting that IBM would show a turnaround in 2003, with earnings projected to grow by 105 percent to $4.31. More modest growth was projected for following years: 14 percent in 2004 ($4.92) and 9.7 percent per year for 2004 to 2007.[8]

How do consensus forecasts by analysts reconcile with the market valuation of IBM? What are the market's implicit assumptions about the short-term and long-term earnings growth for the company? By altering the amounts for key value drivers and arriving at combinations that generate an estimated value equal to the observed market price, the analyst can infer what the market might have been expecting for IBM in mid-March 2003. Table 9-1 summarizes the combinations of earnings growth, book value growth, and cost of capital that generate prices comparable to the market price of $81.50.

IBM has an equity beta of 1.5. Given long-term government bond rates of 5 percent and a market risk premium of 3–4 percent, IBM's cost of equity capital probably lies between 10 and 11 percent. In addition, the company's growth in book value has been stable at 4 percent for the last three years, which is close to the historical long-term book value growth rate for the economy. Critical questions for judging the market valuation of IBM are (1) how quickly will the company's earnings return to the level reported in 2002, and (2) how quickly will earnings growth revert to the same level as average firms in the economy, historically around 4 percent. The analysis reported in Table 9-1 assumes that IBM's superior earnings growth persists for five years, through 2007, and then reverts to the economy average.

Table 9-1 Alternative Assumptions About Value Drivers for IBM Consistent with Observed Market Price of $81.50

Assumed equity cost of capital of 10%:	2003	2004	2005	2006	2007	Implied earnings per share in 2007
Earnings growth: Scenario 1	100%	12%	12%	12%	12%	$6.48
Scenario 2	50%	21.5%	21.5%	21.5%	21.5%	$6.73
Scenario 3	25%	28%	28%	28%	28%	$6.91
Assumed equity cost of capital of 11%:						
Earnings growth: Scenario 1	100%	17%	17%	17%	17%	$7.72
Scenario 2	50%	27%	27%	27%	27%	$8.04
Scenario 3	25%	33.5%	33.5%	33.5%	33.5%	$8.18

Table 9-1 shows the implications for IBM's earnings growth if the economic turnaround is slower than analysts anticipate. This analysis indicates that with a 10 percent cost of equity and a rapid return to pre-2002 performance (i.e., 100 percent growth in 2003), earnings need to grow by 12 percent per year between 2004 and 2007 to justify the $81.50 stock price. However, if 2003 growth is 50 percent, earnings have to increase by 21.5 percent per year for the next four years, and if 2003 growth is only 25 percent (due to, say, a longer downturn in the IT sector than expected), earnings growth from 2004 to 2007 will have to be 28 percent per year. The impact of a slow turnaround in 2003 is even more pronounced if IBM's cost of equity is 11 percent. In this case earnings growth from 2004 to 2007 needs to be 27 percent per year if there is a 50 percent recovery in 2003, and 33.5 percent per year if the recovery is only 25 percent. This type of scenario analysis provides the analyst with insights about investors' expectations for IBM, and is useful for judging whether the stock is correctly valued.

Security analysis need not involve such a detailed attempt to infer market expectations. However, whether the analysis is made explicit or not, a good analyst understands what economic scenarios could plausibly be reflected in the observed price.

Key Analysis Questions

By using the discounted abnormal earnings/ROE valuation model, analysts can infer the market's expectations for a firm's future performance. This permits analysts to ask whether the market is over- or undervaluing a company. Typical questions that analysts might ask from this analysis include the following:

- What are the market's assumptions about long-term ROE and growth? For example, is the market forecasting that the company can grow its earnings without a corresponding level of expansion in its asset base (and hence equity)? If so, how long can this persist?
- How do changes in the cost of capital affect the market's assessment of the firm's future performance? If the market's expectations seem to be unexpectedly high or low, has the market reassessed the company's risk? If so, is this change plausible?

Developing the Analyst's Expectations

Ultimately, a security analyst must compare his or her own view of a stock with the view embedded in the market price. The analyst's own view is generated using the same tools discussed in Chapters 2 through 8: business strategy analysis, accounting analysis, financial analysis, and prospective analysis. The final product of this work is, of course, a forecast of the firm's future earnings and cash flows and an estimate of the firm's value. However, that final product is less important than the understanding of the business and its industry that the analysis provides. It is such understanding that enables the analyst to interpret new information as it arrives and to infer its implications.

Key Analysis Questions

In developing expectations about the firm's future performance using the financial analysis tools discussed throughout this book, the analyst is likely to ask the following types of questions:

- How profitable is the firm? In light of industry conditions, the firm's corporate strategy, and its barriers to competition, how sustainable is that rate of profitability?
- What are the opportunities for growth for this firm?
- How risky is this firm? How vulnerable are operations to general economic downturns? How highly levered is the firm? What does the riskiness of the firm imply about its cost of capital?
- How do answers to the above questions compare to the expectations embedded in the observed stock price?

The Final Product of Security Analysis

For financial analysts, the final product of security analysis is a recommendation to buy, sell, or hold the stock (or some more refined ranking). The recommendation is supported by a set of forecasts and a report summarizing the foundation for the recommendation.

Analysts' reports often delve into significant detail and include an assessment of a firm's business as well as a line-by-line income statement, balance sheet, and cash flow forecasts for one or more years.

In making a recommendation to buy or sell a stock, the analyst has to consider the investment time horizon required to capitalize on the recommendation. Are anticipated improvements in performance likely to be confirmed in the near-term, allowing investors to capitalize quickly on the recommendation? Or do expected performance improvements reflect long-term fundamentals that will take several years to play out? Longer investment horizons impose greater risk on investors that the company's performance will be affected by changes in economic conditions that cannot be anticipated by the analyst, reducing the value of the recommendation. Consequently, thorough analysis requires not merely being able to recognize whether a stock is misvalued, but being able to anticipate when a price correction is likely to take place.

Because there are additional investment risks from following recommendations that require long-term commitments, security analysts tend to focus on making recommendations that are likely to pay off in the short-term. This potentially explains why so few analysts recommended selling dot-com and technology stocks during the late 1990s when their prices would be difficult to justify on the basis of long-term fundamentals. It also explains why analysts recommended Enron's stock at its peak, even though the kind of analysis performed in this chapter would have shown that the future growth and ROE performance implied by this price would be extremely difficult to achieve. It also implies that to take advantage of long-term fundamental analysis can often require access to patient, long-term capital.

PERFORMANCE OF SECURITY ANALYSTS AND FUND MANAGERS

There has been extensive research on the performance of security analysts and fund managers during the last two decades. We summarize a few of the key findings.

Performance of Security Analysts

Despite the recent failure of security analysts to foresee the dramatic price declines for dot-com and telecommunications stocks, and to detect the financial shenanigans and overvaluation of companies such as Enron and Worldcom, research shows that analysts generally add value in the capital market. Analyst earnings forecasts are more accurate than those produced by time series models that use past earnings to predict future earnings.[9] Of course this should not be too surprising since analysts can update their earnings forecasts between quarters to incorporate new firm and economy information, whereas time-series models cannot. In addition, stock prices tend to respond positively to upward revisions in analysts' earnings forecasts and recommendations, and negatively to downward revisions.[10] Finally, recent research finds that analysts play a valuable role in improving market efficiency. For example, stock prices for firms with higher analyst following more rapidly incorporate information on accruals and cash flows than prices of less followed firms.[11]

Several factors seem to be important in explaining analysts' earnings forecast accuracy. Not surprisingly, forecasts of near-term earnings are much more accurate than those of long-term performance.[12] This probably explains why analysts typically make detailed forecasts for only one or two years ahead. Studies of differences in earnings forecast accuracy across analysts find that analysts that are more accurate tend to specialize by industry and work for large well-funded firms that employ other analysts who follow the same industry.[13]

Although analysts perform a valuable function in the capital market, research shows that their forecasts and recommendations tend to be biased. Early evidence on bias indicated that analyst earnings forecasts tended to be optimistic and that their recommendations were almost exclusively for buys.[14] Several factors potentially explain this finding. First, security analysts at brokerage houses are typically compensated on the basis of the trading volume that their reports generate. Given the costs of short selling and the restrictions on short selling by many institutions, brokerage analysts have incentives to issue optimistic reports that encourage investors to buy stocks rather than to issue negative reports that create selling pressure. Second, analysts that work for investment banks are rewarded for promoting public issues by current clients and for attracting new banking clients, creating incentives for optimistic forecasts and recommendations. Studies show that analysts that work for lead underwriters make more optimistic long-term earnings forecasts and recommendations for firms raising equity capital than unaffiliated analysts.[15]

More recent evidence indicates that during the late 1990s there was a marked decline in analyst optimism for forecasts of near-term earnings.[16] One explanation offered for this change is that during the late 1990s analysts relied heavily on private discussions with top management to make their earnings forecasts. Management allegedly used these personal connections to manage analysts' short-term expectations downward so that the firm could subsequently report earnings that beat analysts' expectations. In response to concerns about this practice, in October 2000 the SEC approved Regulation Fair Disclosure, which prohibits management from making selective disclosures of non-public information.

Performance of Fund Managers

Measuring whether mutual and pension fund managers earn superior returns is a difficult task for several reasons. First, there is no agreement about how to estimate benchmark performance for a fund. Studies have used a number of approaches—some have used the Capital Asset Pricing Model (CAPM) as a benchmark, others have used multi-factor pricing models. For studies using the CAPM, there are questions about what type of market index to use. For example, should it be an equal- or value weighted index, a NYSE index or a broader market index? Second, many of the traditional measures of fund performance abstract from market-wide performance, which understates fund abnormal performance if fund managers can time the market by reducing portfolio risk prior to market declines and increasing risks before a market run-up. Third, given the overall volatility of stock returns, statistical power is an issue for measuring fund performance. Finally, tests of fund performance are likely to be highly sensitive to the time period examined. Value or momentum investing could therefore appear to be profitable depending on when the tests are conducted.

Perhaps because of these challenges, there is no consistent evidence that actively managed mutual funds generate superior returns for investors. While some studies find evidence of positive abnormal returns for the industry, others conclude that returns are generally negative.[17] Of course even if mutual fund managers on average can only generate "normal" returns for investors, it is still possible for the best managers to show consistently strong performance. Some studies do in fact document that funds earning positive abnormal returns in one period continue to outperform in subsequent periods. However, more recent evidence suggests that these findings are caused by general momentum in stock returns and fund expenses rather than superior fund manager ability.[18] Researchers have also examined which, if any, investment strategies are most successful. However, no clear consensus appears—several studies have found that momentum and high turnover strategies generate superior returns, whereas others conclude that value strategies are better.[19]

Finally, recent research has examined whether fund managers tend to buy and sell many of the same stocks at the same time. They conclude that there is evidence of "herding" behavior, particularly by momentum fund managers.[20] This could arise because managers have access to common information, because they are affected by similar cognitive biases, or because they have incentives to follow the crowd.[21] For example, consider the calculus of a fund manager who holds a stock but who, through long-term fundamental analysis, estimates that it is misvalued. If the manager changes the fund's holdings accordingly and the stock price returns to its intrinsic value in the next quarter, the fund will show superior relative portfolio performance and will attract new capital. However, if the stock continues to be misvalued for several quarters, the informed fund manager will underperform the benchmark and capital will flow to other funds. In contrast, a risk-averse manager who simply follows the crowd will not be rewarded for detecting the misvaluation, but neither will this manager be blamed for a poor investment decision when the stock price ultimately corrects, since other funds made the same mistake.

There has been considerably less research on the performance of pension fund managers. Overall, the findings show little consistent evidence that pension fund managers either over- or under-perform traditional benchmarks.[22]

SUMMARY

Equity security analysis is the evaluation of a firm and its prospects from the perspective of a current or potential investor in the firm's stock. Security analysis is one component of a larger investment process that involves (1) establishing the objectives of the investor or fund, (2) forming expectations about the future returns and risks of individual securities, and then (3) combining individual securities into portfolios to maximize progress toward the investment objectives.

Some security analysis is devoted primarily to assuring that a stock possesses the proper risk profile and other desired characteristics prior to inclusion in an investor's portfolio. However, especially for many professional buy-side and sell-side security analysts, the analysis is also directed toward the identification of mispriced securities. In equilibrium, such activity will be rewarding for those with the strongest comparative advantage. They will be the ones able to identify any mispricing at the lowest cost and exert pressure on the price to correct the mispricing. What kinds of efforts are productive in this domain depends on the degree of market efficiency. A large body of evidence exists that is supportive of a high degree of efficiency in the U.S. market, but recent evidence has reopened the debate on this issue.

In practice, a wide variety of approaches to fund management and security analysis are employed. However, at the core of the analyses are the same steps outlined in Chapters 2 through 8 of this book: business strategy analysis, accounting analysis, financial analysis, and prospective analysis (forecasting and valuation). For the professional analyst, the final product of the work is, of course, a forecast of the firm's future earnings and cash flows, and an estimate of the firm's value. But that final product is less important than the understanding of the business and its industry, which the analysis provides. It is such understanding that positions the analyst to interpret new information as it arrives and infer its implications.

DISCUSSION QUESTIONS

1. Despite many years of research, the evidence on market efficiency described in this chapter appears to be inconclusive. Some argue that this is because researchers have been unable to link company fundamentals to stock prices precisely. Comment.

2. Geoffrey Henley, a professor of finance, states: "The capital market is efficient. I don't know why anyone would bother devoting their time to following individual stocks and doing fundamental analysis. The best approach is to buy and hold a well-diversified portfolio of stocks." Do you agree? Why or why not?

3. What is the difference between fundamental and technical analysis? Can you think of any trading strategies that use technical analysis? What are the underlying assumptions made by these strategies?

4. Investment funds follow many different types of investment strategies. Income funds focus on stocks with high dividend yields, growth funds invest in stocks that are expected to have high capital appreciation, value funds follow stocks that are considered to be undervalued, and short funds bet against stocks they consider to be overvalued. What types of investors are likely to be attracted to each of these types of funds? Why?

5. Intergalactic Software Company went public three months ago. You are a sophisticated investor who devotes time to fundamental analysis as a way of identifying mispriced stocks. Which of the following characteristics would you focus on in deciding whether to follow this stock?
   - The market capitalization
   - The average number of shares traded per day
   - The bid–ask spread for the stock
   - Whether the underwriter that brought the firm public is a Top Five investment banking firm
   - Whether its audit company is a Big Four firm
   - Whether there are analysts from major brokerage firms following the company
   - Whether the stock is held mostly by retail or institutional investors

6. There are two major types of financial analysts: buy-side and sell-side. Buy-side analysts work for investment firms and make stock recommendations that are available only to the management of funds within that firm. Sell-side analysts work for brokerage firms and make recommendations that are used to sell stock to the brokerage firms' clients, which include individual investors and managers of investment funds. What would be the differences in tasks and motivations of these two types of analysts?

7. Many market participants believe that sell-side analysts are too optimistic in their recommendations to buy stocks and too slow to recommend sells. What factors might explain this bias?

8. Joe Klein is an analyst for an investment banking firm that offers both underwriting and brokerage services. Joe sends you a highly favorable report on a stock that his firm recently helped go public and for which it currently makes the market. What are the potential advantages and disadvantages in relying on Joe's report in deciding whether to buy the stock?

9. Intergalactic Software Company's stock has a market price of $20 per share and a book value of $12 per share. If its cost of equity capital is 15 percent and its book value is expected to grow at 5 percent per year indefinitely, what is the market's assessment of

its steady state return on equity? If the stock price increases to $35 and the market does not expect the firm's growth rate to change, what is the revised steady state ROE? If instead the price increase was due to an increase in the market's assessments about long-term book value growth rather than long-term ROE, what would the price revision imply for the steady state growth rate?

10. Joe states, "I can see how ratio analysis and valuation help me do fundamental analysis, but I don't see the value of doing strategy analysis." Can you explain to him how strategy analysis could be potentially useful?

NOTES

1. P. Healy and K. Palepu, "The Fall of Enron," *Journal of Economic Perspectives* 17, no. 2 (Spring 2003): 3–26, discuss how weak money manager incentives and long-term analysis contributed to the stock price run-up and subsequent collapse for Enron. A similar discussion on factors affecting the rise and fall of dot-com stocks is provided in "The Role of Capital Market Intermediaries in the Dot-Com Crash of 2000," Harvard Business School Case 9-101-110, 2001.

2. See R. Bhushan, "Firm characteristics and analyst following," *Journal of Accounting and Economics* 11 (2/5), July 1989: 255–75, and P. O'Brien and R. Bhushan, "Analyst following and institutional ownership," *Journal of Accounting Research* 28, Supplement (1990): 55–76.

3. Recent reviews of evidence on market efficiency are provided by E. Fama, "Efficient Capital Markets: II," *Journal of Finance* 46 (December 1991): 1575–1617; S. Kothari, "Capital Markets Research in Accounting," *Journal of Accounting and Economics* 31 (September 2001):105–231; and C. Lee, "Market Efficiency in Accounting Research," *Journal of Accounting and Economics* 31 (September 2001): 233–53.

4. For example, see V. Bernard and J. Thomas, "Evidence That Stock Prices Do Not Fully Reflect the Implications of Current Earnings for Future Earnings," *Journal of Accounting and Economics* 13 (December 1990): 305–41.

5. Examples of studies that examine a "value stock" strategy include J. Lakonishok, A. Shleifer, and R. Vishny, "Contrarian Investment, Extrapolation, and Risk," *Journal of Finance* 49 (December 1994): 1541–78, and R. Frankel and C. Lee, "Accounting Valuation, Market Expectation, and Cross-Sectional Stock Returns," *Journal of Accounting & Economics* 25 (June 1998): 283–319.

6. For example, see J. Ou and S. Penman, "Financial Statement Analysis and the Prediction of Stock Returns," *Journal of Accounting and Economics* 11 (November 1989): 295–330; R. Holthausen and D. Larcker, "The Prediction of Stock Returns Using Financial Statement Information," *Journal of Accounting and Economics* 15 (June/September 1992): 373–412; and R. Sloan, "Do Stock Prices Fully Reflect Information in Accruals and Cash Flows about Future Earnings?" *The Accounting Review* 71 (July 1996): 298–325.

7. For an overview of research in behavioral finance, see R. Thaler, *Advances in Behavioral Finance* (New York: Russell Sage Foundation, 1993), and A. Shleifer, *Inefficient Markets: An Introduction to Behavioral Finance* (Oxford: Oxford University Press, 2000).

8. These forecasts were taken from multexinvestor.com.

9. Time series model forecasts of future annual earnings are the most recent annual earnings (with or without some form of annual growth), and forecasts of future quarterly earnings are a function of growth in earnings for the latest quarter relative to both the last quarter and the same quarter one year ago. See L. Brown and M. Rozeff "The Superiority of Analyst Forecasts as Measures of Expectations: Evidence from Earnings," *Journal of Finance* 33 (1978): 1–16; L. Brown, P. Griffin, R. Hagerman, and M. Zmijewski, "Security Analyst Superiority Relative to Univariate Time-Series Models in Forecasting Quarterly Earnings," *Journal of Accounting and Economics* 9 (1987): 61–87; and D. Givoly, "Financial Analysts' Forecasts of Earnings: A Better Surrogate for Market Expectations," *Journal of Accounting and Economics* 4, no. 2 (1982): 85–108.

10. See D. Givoly and J. Lakonishok, "The Information Content of Financial Analysts' Forecasts of Earnings: Some Evidence on Semi-Strong Efficiency," *Journal of Accounting and Economics* 2 (1979): 165–86; T. Lys and S. Sohn, "The Association Between Revisions of Financial Analysts' Earnings

Forecasts and Security Price Changes," *Journal of Accounting & Economics* 13 (1990): 341–64; and J. Francis and L. Soffer, "The Relative Informativeness of Analysts' Stock Recommendations and Earnings Forecast Revisions," *Journal of Accounting Research* 35, no. 2 (1997): 193–212.

11. See M. Barth and A. Hutton, "Information Intermediaries and the Pricing of Accruals," working paper, Stanford University, 2000.

12. See P. O'Brien, "Forecasts Accuracy of Individual Analysts in Nine Industries." *Journal of Accounting Research* 28 (1990): 286–304.

13. See M. Clement, "Analyst Forecast Accuracy: Do Ability, Resources, and Portfolio Complexity Matter?" *Journal of Accounting and Economics* 27 (1999): 285–304; J. Jacob, T. Lys, and M. Neale, "Experience in Forecasting Performance of Security Analysts." *Journal of Accounting and Economics* 28 (1999): 51–82; and S. Gilson, P. Healy, C. Noe, and K. Palepu, "Analyst Specialization and Conglomerate Stock Breakups," *Journal of Accounting Research* 39 (December 2001): 565–73.

14. See L. Brown, G. Foster, and E. Noreen, "Security Analyst Multi-Year Earnings Forecasts and the Capital Market," Studies in Accounting Research, No. 23, American Accounting Association (Sarasota, FL), 1985. M. McNichols and P. O'Brien, in "Self-Selection and Analyst Coverage," *Journal of Accounting Research,* Supplement (1997): 167–208, find that analyst bias arises primarily because analysts issue recommendations on firms for which they have favorable information and withhold recommending firms with unfavorable information.

15. See H. Lin and M. McNichols, "Underwriting Relationships, Analysts' Earnings Forecasts and Investment Recommendations," *Journal of Accounting and Economics* 25, no. 1 (1998): 101–28; R. Michaely and K. Womack, "Conflict of Interest and the Credibility of Underwriter Analyst Recommendations," *Review of Financial Studies* 12, no. 4 (1999): 653–86; and P. Dechow, A. Hutton, and R. Sloan, "The Relation Between Analysts' Forecasts of Long-Term Earnings Growth and Stock Price Performance Following Equity Offerings," *Contemporary Accounting Research* 17, no. 1 (2000):1–32.

16. See L. Brown, "Analyst Forecasting Errors: Additional Evidence," *Financial Analysts' Journal* (November/December 1997): 81–88, and D. Matsumoto, "Management's Incentives to Avoid Negative Earnings Surprises," *The Accounting Review* 77 (July 2002): 483–515.

17. For example, evidence of superior fund performance is reported by M. Grinblatt and S. Titman, "Mutual Fund Performance: An Analysis of Quarterly Holdings, *Journal of Business* 62 (1994), and by D. Hendricks, J. Patel, and R. Zeckhauser, "Hot Hands in Mutual Funds: Short-Run Persistence of Relative Performance," *The Journal of Finance* 48 (1993): 93–130. In contrast, negative fund performance is shown by M. Jensen, "The Performance of Mutual Funds in the Period 1945–64," *The Journal of Finance* 23 (May 1968): 389–416, and B. Malkiel, "Returns from Investing in Equity Mutual Funds from 1971 to 1991," *Journal of Finance* 50 (June 1995): 549–73.

18. M. Grinblatt and S. Titman, "The Persistence of Mutual Fund Performance," *Journal of Finance* 47 (December 1992): 1977–86, and D. Hendricks, J. Patel, and R. Zeckhauser, "Hot Hands in Mutual Funds: Short-Run Persistence of Relative Performance," *Journal of Finance* 48 (March 1993): 93–130, find evidence of persistence in mutual fund returns. However, M. Carhart, "On Persistence in Mutual Fund Performance," *The Journal of Finance* 52 (March 1997): 57–83, shows that much of this is attributable to momentum in stock returns and to fund expenses; B. Malkiel, "Returns from Investing in Equity Mutual Funds from 1971 to 1991," *The Journal of Finance* 50 (June 1995): 549–73, shows that survivorship bias is also an important consideration.

19. See M. Grinblatt, S. Titman, and R. Wermers, "Momentum Investment Strategies, Portfolio Performance, and Herding: A Study of Mutual Fund Behavior," *The American Economic Review* 85 (December 1995): 1088–1105.

20. For example, J. Lakonishok, A. Shleifer, and R. Vishny, "Contrarian Investment, Extrapolation, and Risk," *Journal of Finance* 49 (December 1994): 1541–79, find that value funds show superior performance, whereas M. Grinblatt, S. Titman, and R. Wermers, "Momentum Investment Strategies, Portfolio Performance, and Herding: A Study of Mutual Fund Behavior," *The American Economic Review* 85 (December 1995): 1088–1105, find that momentum investing is profitable.

21. See D. Scharfstein and J. Stein, "Herd Behavior and Investment," *The American Economic Review* 80 (June 1990): 465–80, and P. Healy and K. Palepu, "The Fall of Enron," *Journal of Economic Perspectives* 17, no. 2 (Spring 2003): 3–26.

22. For evidence on performance by pension fund managers, see J. Lakonishok, A. Shleifer, and R. Vishny, "The Structure and Performance of the Money Management Industry," Brookings Papers on Economic Activity, Washington, DC (1992): 339–92; T. Coggin, F. Fabozzi, and S. Rahman, "The Investment Performance of U.S. Equity Pension Fund Managers: An Empirical Investigation," *The Journal of Finance* 48 (July 1993): 1039–56; and W. Ferson and K. Khang, "Conditional Performance Measurement Using Portfolio Weights: Evidence for Pension Funds," *Journal of Financial Economics* 65 (August 2002): 249–282.

United Parcel Service's IPO

This is an historic step for UPS. We intend to remain the preeminent company in our industry and expand our role as an enabler of global commerce. A publicly traded stock will build on our financial strength as a triple A-rated company and give us more flexibility to pursue strategic opportunities around the world. This will allow us to better meet the changing needs of our customers for innovative new products and services.

James Kelly, UPS chairman and CEO, July 21, 1999

In July of 1999, United Parcel Service (UPS) surprised both Wall Street and Main Street with the announcement that, after more than 90 years as a private, employee-owned operation, it was planning an initial public offering that would transform "Big Brown" into a publicly traded company. UPS was a company with $1.7 billion of net income and almost a century-long track record of financial performance, a marked contrast to the Internet and technology-related IPOs launched in the late 1990s. Although pricing for the shares had yet to be announced, the offering looked likely to be the largest IPO in U.S. history.

Determining an appropriate price for the new shares was a central concern of the joint Morgan Stanley Dean Witter & Co.-UPS deal team that had been charged with launching the offering. The actual price per share would be set only hours before the first trading day for the new stock. In the weeks before the listing, the deal team would be expected to consider a variety of factors in fixing the offer price, including current and future trends in the package delivery industry, UPS's strengths and weaknesses relative to other competitors, UPS's recent financial performance, and the valuation of comparable companies.

THE PACKAGE DELIVERY INDUSTRY

In 1999 package delivery in the United States was a $43 billion industry serving a broad array of distinct customer segments—individuals sending overnight letters, small to medium-sized enterprises demanding affordable shipment of time-critical parcels, and large corporations moving heavy freight between facilities.

The industry offered two basic products—air and ground. Ground traditionally referred to deliveries made within one to six business days using surface transportation such as cars, vans, trucks, and trains. For much of the century, ground was the only reliable option for moving letters and parcels. Air delivery enabled customers to request overnight service, which was expedited using complex air networks. Two- and three-day air products, a segment that rapidly expanded in the 1980s and 1990s given its substantially lower price compared to overnight products and faster delivery time relative to traditional ground services, were often referred to as "time-deferred" or "deferred" service. Although the lines between air express and ground had blurred somewhat as ground networks improved to the point where overnight and "two-day air" deliveries could be made on the ground, industry analysts continued to segment the market in these terms. As of 1999, the domestic

Professor Paul Healy and Brett Laschinger and Ajay Shroff (MBAs '02) prepared this case. The case is intended solely as the basis for class discussion and is not intended to serve as an endorsement, source of primary data, or illustration of effective or ineffective management. Copyright © 2002 by the President and Fellows of Harvard College. HBS Case 2-103-015.

air industry (including overnight and deferred) comprised 60 percent of the market by revenue and 46 percent by volume, compared to 40 percent of revenue and 54 percent of volume for ground.[1] (See Exhibits 1 to 3 for historical market size and growth data.)

The asset-intensive and highly complex nature of both the domestic air and ground industries had resulted in intense competition among three very large competitors: Atlanta-based UPS (51 percent share of market by revenue), Memphis-based Federal Express (26 percent), and the U.S. Postal Service (17 percent).[2] (See Exhibit 4 for overnight, deferred, and ground market share data.) UPS was the market leader in the $17 billion ground segment, with competition coming from FedEx and the USPS as well as private delivery fleets of individual companies, courier services, regional delivery services, less than a truckload (LTL) trucking firms, and third-party logistics companies. UPS was the number two player to the USPS in the deferred segment and number two to FedEx in the overnight express market.

U.S. Postal Service

The U.S. Postal Service (USPS) was a quasi-government entity that moved more than four times as many deliveries each day as UPS and FedEx combined[3] and operated a delivery network that reached every household and commercial address in the country, six days a week. The USPS offered a number of delivery products that competed directly with UPS's offerings. The most prominent of these was Priority Mail, which offered ground shipment of packages in one to three business days to any destination in the United States. Priority Mail was generally considered to be less expensive but also less reliable than either UPS's or FedEx's two- and three-day offerings. The USPS also lacked the premier logistics and package-tracking information systems that both FedEx and UPS had developed. However, rumor had it that Lockheed Martin had been hired to help the USPS create a comparable tracking system to be completed in 2001.[4]

Observers pointed out that with e-mail and other forms of electronic communication cutting deeply into the USPS's traditional regular mail monopoly, the service was especially eager to allocate resources to other segments of the package delivery market, which would mean more frequent competition with UPS and FedEx.[5]

FedEx

FedEx, a $17 billion global transportation and logistics enterprise, was credited with single-handedly pioneering the concept of overnight delivery in the early 1970s. By the late 1990s, FedEx moved over 3 million packages each day, with the ability to reach virtually every business address in the United States and almost every country around the world within 24 hours. Federal Express, the overnight delivery arm of FedEx Corp., was by far its largest and most important operating unit, accounting for 84 percent of total revenues and 83 percent of operating income in 1998. FedEx also controlled a variety of other related businesses. FedEx Custom Critical was a time-critical carrier, FedEx Logistics provided logistics

1. SJ Consulting estimates.

2. SJ Consulting estimates.

3. USPS Web site. Includes first-class mail in addition to parcel volume. First-class mail represents about 90 percent of USPS's total shipment volume.

4. Brian O'Reilly, "UPS vs. FedEx: They've Got Mail," Fortune, February 7, 2000.

5. Deutsche Bank Alex Brown, UPS Equity Research Report, December 1, 1999.

solutions and assistance to other businesses, and Viking Freight operated as a less-than-truckload West Coast regional carrier. FedEx's operating philosophy with respect to these various companies was to "operate independently, compete collectively,"[6] and hence each operating company remained a separate operating entity with discrete management and its own trucks, sorting hubs, and other assets.

With the 1998 acquisition of Roadway Package System (RPS), the second-largest ground delivery business-to-business (B2B) small-package shipper in the nation (after UPS), FedEx also developed a presence in the ground business. Prior to the acquisition, RPS employed 22,000 direct and contract employees, operated 365 sorting and other facilities in North America, and reported revenues of $1.3 billion. It was estimated that RPS served 10–12 percent of the U.S. B2B ground delivery market in 1998.[7] RPS had achieved its considerable success in part by selectively targeting some of UPS's most valuable accounts—high-volume customers in high-density locations. RPS had also developed the premier package logistics and tracking software in the ground delivery industry. Following the acquisition, FedEx renamed RPS as FedEx Ground to take advantage of its own strong brand.

Other Competitors

Smaller players in the U.S. market included Airborne Freight, CNF, and DHL. Airborne Freight, with 1998 revenues of just over $3 billion, was the third largest U.S. express delivery carrier and had achieved significant growth over the 1990s by positioning itself as the low-cost overnight delivery alternative for B2B customers. CNF focused on ground delivery and heavyweight airfreight. DHL, a European international express-mail carrier, was active in U.S. international shipping. In 1998 the German government-backed Deutsche Post AG acquired a 25 percent stake in DHL and was expected to compete more aggressively for U.S. domestic business.

Industry Outlook

In July 1999 the outlook for the package industry was mixed. Robust gross domestic product (GDP) growth and ever-increasing demands for faster delivery suggested continued strong growth potential for the air-express segment, which had enjoyed double-digit expansion through the 1980s and high single-digit growth in the 1990s. However, the digitization of documents and emergence of electronic signatures threatened the significant overnight letter business. As for the ground industry, which had grown at a rate somewhat in excess of U.S. GDP, the rapid expansion of Internet shopping hinted at a potential boost for the business-to-consumer (B2C) ground business, while industry rivalry threatened intense price competition.[8]

In terms of international delivery, the large integrated carriers had constructed global delivery networks that could reach over 90 percent of the world's population. International revenue was derived from the export needs of U.S.-based customers as well as intracountry operations in other parts of the world. As saturation occurred in the U.S. market, industry observers anticipated that this market would provide an attractive growth opportunity.

6. FedEx web site.

7. "RPS Adopts a New Name as Parent FedEx Shifts its Marketing Strategy," Pittsburgh Business Times Journal, January 21, 2000.

8. SJ Consulting estimates.

UNITED PARCEL SERVICE (UPS)

With over 340,000 employees, 149,000 delivery vehicles, 500 planes, and $25 billion in annual revenues, UPS was the largest parcel delivery company in the world. The company delivered nearly 13 million packages each business day (9,000 packages every minute) to over 200 countries worldwide. Each year UPS moved some 6 percent of U.S. GDP. In addition to air and ground package delivery, UPS helped its customers with supply chain management, logistics, and financial services. The company had daily contact with 1.8 million customers (including every company in the *Fortune* 1000) and made deliveries to 6 million business and residential addresses. In 1999, *Fortune* magazine recognized UPS as the "World's Most Admired Global Mail, Package and Freight Delivery Company," and *Forbes* magazine named UPS "Company of the Year."[9]

History

Using $100 borrowed from a friend, 19-year old James "Jim" Casey founded the American Messenger Company in Seattle, Washington, in 1907. The company provided private messenger and delivery services—such as the transportation of letters, hand baggage, and trays of food—by bicycle, foot, and streetcar.[10]

In the 1920s the company, renamed United Parcel Service, shifted its focus to package delivery for retailers who sought to outsource that function. UPS grew quietly alongside the retail industry for the next three decades, slowly expanding its geographical reach and breadth of services. During this period, the company pioneered the concept of consolidated delivery—combining packages for a particular neighborhood within one delivery vehicle—and developed the first-ever mechanical sorter and conveyor belt system.

Gradual innovation and expansion continued until the 1950s when UPS realized that its growth options would be limited if it remained solely focused on package delivery for retailers. As of 1954 UPS only had operations in 16 cities. To expand its geographic reach and scope of operations, UPS had to petition state and federal authorities for broader business activity rights. Over the next 30 years, UPS fought dozens of legal and regulatory battles to gain the right to operate delivery vehicles within each state and between any two states, known in the industry as "common carrier" rights. By 1980 UPS achieved national coverage and had become a direct and formidable competitor to the USPS. By the early 1980s, UPS's ground business had grown so rapidly that it quickly surpassed the USPS's in terms of parcel (i.e., nonletter) volume. Over the next two decades UPS went on to become the largest player in the ground delivery segment.[11]

UPS grew its air network in parallel with its ground infrastructure. Blue Label Air, a two-day service between major cities, began in 1953 and reached national coverage by 1978. During the 1970s, despite the rapid growth of the overnight express market that newly formed Federal Express pioneered, UPS stuck to two- to three-day air service at a rate one-tenth that of FedEx's overnight service.[12] In August 1982, however, "in response

---

9. UPS 1999 Annual Report, filed March 30, 2000.

10. "United Parcel Service (A)," Harvard Business School Case 488-016, 1992, p. 3.

11. John D. Williams, "The Brown Giant: UPS Delivers Profits By Expanding Its Area," The Wall Street Journal, August 25, 1980, p. 1.

12. Ibid.

to customer demand," UPS finally announced its entry into the next-day air-express arena, nine years after FedEx.[13]

The 1980s and early 1990s were pivotal for UPS as it was forced to play "catch-up" to FedEx in the air-express segment and respond to market share gains by RPS and the USPS on the ground. The company's responses included a major technology upgrade, changes in pricing, and a change in marketing strategy. Between 1988 and 1999, UPS spent more than $1 billion per year upgrading its infrastructure to track packages precisely, deliver electronic proof of delivery, and manage shipments online. The new systems included electronic scanners, bar codes on packages, and computerized clipboards for all UPS drivers.[14] In addition, the company hired thousands of programmers and technicians to manage its information needs and develop innovative applications and services for its customers. By 1999, UPS could handle six times as many online tracking requests as FedEx,[15] leading *Forbes* magazine to declare, "UPS used to be a trucking company with technology. Now it's a technology company with trucks."[16]

UPS also responded to competitive challenges by changing its pricing and marketing strategies. It began transitioning away from using standard rates to allowing prices to vary across markets and customers based on cost differences. It also introduced a widely aired new ad campaign that touted "We run the tightest ship in the shipping business,"[17] a marked change from its prior policy of shying away from publicity.

Throughout the 1990s UPS steadily captured market share in the express arena, reaching an estimated 32 percent share by 1998, and its ground business returned to a pace of moderate growth despite cost-cutting and targeted sales efforts by competitors.[18] Reflecting on UPS's transformation during the 1990s, UPS CEO Jim Kelly proclaimed, "Truth is, we're not your father's UPS anymore!"[19]

UPS chose to expand the scope of its business in 1993 with the formation of UPS Logistics Group, which provided supply chain management solutions and consulting services to UPS's customer base. Typical service contracts included back-end fulfillment for Sprint PCS, the timely delivery of fresh ingredients to all Papa John's Pizza locations, and the distribution of vehicles from Ford's manufacturing plants to automobile dealerships nationwide. By 1999 the Logistics Group generated nearly $1 billion in incremental revenue for the company.[20]

Operations

UPS coordinated and managed the pickup of 13 million packages each day from 2 million addresses for delivery to over 6 million commercial and residential addresses worldwide. To do so, it relied on a carefully designed network of vehicles, sorting facilities, and hubs as well as the support of a sophisticated IT system. The system had been developed and refined over the last decade and was continually enhanced to ensure the highest levels of reliability, efficiency, and speed.

Drivers followed precisely defined routes to pick up packages from customers at preset times. Those packages were taken to hubs where they were consolidated and sorted at speeds of upwards

13. Sharen Kindel, "When Elephants Dance," Financial World, June 9, 1992, p. 76.

14. Kenneth Labich, "Big Changes at Big Brown," Fortune, January 18, 1988, p. 60.

15. Fedex.com and UPS.com company web sites.

16. From www.ups.com, "Speeches," Mike Eskew, March 29, 2000.

17. Kenneth Labich, "Big Changes at Big Brown," Fortune, January 18, 1988, p. 57.

18. SJ Consulting.

19. James Kelly, speech at the Robert C. Goizueta Global Leadership Award breakfast, December 14, 2001 (available at www.ups.com, "Speeches").

20. 1999 UPS Annual Report.

of hundreds of thousands of packages per hour. Packages for the same zip code or delivery area were loaded onto the appropriate conveyor belt and then onto the familiar brown trucks in the order in which they would be delivered. This allowed drivers to deliver their packages in sequence, "from one address to the next closest address . . . as quickly and productively as possible."[21]

Unlike FedEx, UPS made no distinction between the operating facilities for air and ground operations. All facilities were shared, including the single fleet of trucks that handled the pickup and delivery of all UPS shipments. The integration of its air and ground operations gave UPS the ability to optimize use of its assets while still meeting customer service requirements. For example, the same fleet of UPS trucks was used to pick up and deliver ground and air packages. Also, because the operations were integrated, a package marked for "Next Day Air" delivery could be transported by truck if that method of transportation was deemed less expensive and just as reliable (see Exhibit 5). UPS's sophisticated IT systems coordinated this process.[22]

Human Resource Management

Since its inception, UPS enjoyed a loyal workforce with an operational and service-excellence culture. Employees were recruited through part-time positions and educational assistance programs. They were trained in carefully studied work methods and educated about UPS's time-tested policies and procedures at a cost of over $300 million annually.[23] These educational programs, combined with on-the-job training and role modeling, helped UPS command one of the lowest turnover rates in the industry (less than 5 percent annually) and succeeded in developing a portion of its workforce for management positions each year. UPS took pride in this "promote from within" policy, which was epitomized by the fact that Kelly, UPS chairman and CEO, started his career as a package delivery driver.

The company's unique culture emphasized accountability and efficient execution at every level of the organization. Operating employees adhered to fairly rigid operational guidelines developed by industrial engineers and rooted in time-motion studies. Drivers, for example, were instructed on how to best perform their jobs from the moment they started work until the end of their day. A lengthy and detailed guide precisely defined how a driver should start the delivery vehicle's engine, greet customers, scan packages, and even buckle and unbuckle his or her safety belt between stops. Within corporate headquarters, employees faced similar policies that focused on efficiency, "such as no coffee at desks, and two 15-minute breaks during the work day."[24] These and other operating features were captured in the company's *Policy Book,* which had guided the company since 1929.

Since 1919, union issues were a way of life at UPS. Over 200,000 of UPS's 340,000 employees belonged to the International Brotherhood of Teamsters, making UPS the largest single constituency for that union. Labor relations had generally been harmonious. The only exception had arisen during a 15-day work stoppage in 1997 that cost UPS several hundred million dollars in lost revenues and an immeasurable loss of goodwill among certain customers. Management and the unions were able to strike flexible work arrangements when needed to allow UPS to offer customers a greater range of services. In return, UPS drivers and other unionized personnel enjoyed the highest pay in the industry.

Experts believed UPS's combination of "controls, rules, a detailed union contract, and carefully studied work methods . . . helped guarantee the customer reliable, low-cost service."[25]

....

21. UPS web site, www.ups.com.

22. Ibid.

23. Ibid.

24. "United Parcel Service (A)," Harvard Business School Case 488-016, 1992, p. 15.

25. David E. Bowen and Edward E. Lawler, "The Empowerment of Service Workers: What, Why, How, and When," Sloan Management Review (Spring 1992): 32.

VALUATION BENCHMARKS

The IPO team considered several potential benchmarks for valuing UPS. The first potential benchmark was the trucking industry. Industry analysts typically included package delivery firms in the trucking industry, making it a natural comparison. However, the team decided that the fragmented trucking industry, with its low barriers to entry and poor profitability, was of limited value as a benchmark for UPS. Instead, the investment banking members of the team favored using Federal Express as a benchmark, whereas UPS's management argued that UPS was better compared to "best-of-breed" companies in other industries.

Federal Express

UPS's foremost publicly listed competitor, particularly in the overnight-express segment of the market, was Tennessee-based FedEx Corporation. FedEx operated a fleet of 634 aircraft and 41,000 pickup and delivery vehicles and employed 88,000 permanent full-time and 50,000 permanent part-time employees. On November 1, 1999, FedEx's stock price closed at $41.50, representing a price-to-earnings multiple of 19.8 and a price-to-book value of 2.7 (see Exhibit 6).

Although FedEx had been created as an overnight air-express carrier and UPS had focused on multiday ground delivery, over time their business models had converged. This had been accelerated by FedEx's acquisition of RPS. FedEx Chairman Fred Smith noted the newly merged company transformed FedEx into a "global transportation and logistics powerhouse. Customers increasingly demand a complete, seamless solution to supply chain management needs on a global basis, and the [Federal Express] companies will be able to offer it."[26]

In an effort to keep ground delivery operating costs below those of UPS, FedEx was planning to use contracted drivers and trucks, which were significantly cheaper than its rival's Teamster-organized delivery workforce. FedEx also planned to invest in RPS's existing ground network to expand its reach and capacity[27] and to increase RPS's customer service levels through enhancing technology and training.[28]

UPS and FedEx also both looked to the international delivery business as a key source of growth. In 1999, FedEx's international services represented 25 percent of total revenues and had been growing at an annual rate of almost 10 percent. For UPS, international operations for the nine months ended September 30, 1999, accounted for $2.56 billion (or 13 percent) of revenues and $147 million (or 5 percent) of operating profits.

However, there were also important differences between the two companies that could be relevant in using FedEx multiples for valuing UPS. UPS's recent financial performance was superior to FedEx's. Over the three years from 1997 to 1999, UPS reported average net profit margins of 6.5 percent and a return on equity (ROE) of 25.2 percent, versus 2.8 percent and 10.6 percent, respectively, for FedEx. (Financial statements for UPS and FedEx are shown in Exhibits 7 and 8.)

The differences in FedEx's and UPS's financial and nonfinancial performance reflected several underlying factors. UPS relied to a greater degree than FedEx on the ground delivery business, which had a different cost structure than the air-express delivery business (see Exhibits 9 and 10). Further, UPS's ground delivery business took advantage of much higher daily package volumes and customer density than FedEx's operations, which meant

....

26. "RPS Greets World with New Parent Federal Express," Pittsburgh Post-Gazette, January 29, 1998.

27. "FedEx Hits the Ground Running," Modern Materials Handling, July 2001.

28. "They've Got Mail," Fortune, February 7, 2000.

that UPS drivers would on average pick up and deliver significantly more packages per hour than FedEx drivers could. Finally, some observers believed that UPS's decision to operate its ground and express businesses as one integrated company sharing the same trucks and sorting centers gave it an operating advantage over FedEx, which maintained separate operating units for express and ground delivery.[29]

Superior customer service was one of the distinguishing hallmarks of FedEx, and for this reason FedEx was generally seen as competing most effectively at the higher-end, high-service segment of the package delivery market. FedEx's commitment to high customer service was reflected in its best-in-industry on-time reliability record and the flexibility it offered customers in pickup and delivery times. For example, it had even been known to keep trucks idling outside a customer's business to help deliver an unforeseen order on time.

Finally, there were differences in financial management policies at the two companies. UPS maintained an AAA credit rating, whereas FedEx's rating was BBB.[30] FedEx used operating leases to finance much of its aircraft fleet, whereas UPS financed its fleet with operating cash flow, public debt, or long-term capital leases. (Exhibits 11 and 12 present footnote information on lease obligations for the two companies.)

Best-of-Breed Industry Leaders

UPS's management believed that the company's stock price should be valued at a premium to reflect its superior performance over other firms in the industry. It noted that there was support for this approach in the market, where other companies with comparable dominant positions in their industry commanded significant best-of-breed stock price premiums over their competitors. For example, Coca-Cola's price-to-earnings and market-to-book multiples were 39 and 15, respectively, versus 25 and 8 for PepsiCo. Wal-Mart commanded a price-to-earnings multiple of 46 and a market-to-book multiple of 11.6, versus 27 and 6 for Target. (Exhibit 13 presents a comparison of price premiums and financial performance for selected companies considered best-of-breed industry leaders.)

UPS'S IPO

Industry Trends and Opportunities

UPS management had decided by the late 1990s to focus on three emerging trends that it believed would define the package delivery industry of the future and present the company with opportunities for continued growth. These were the emerging trends of globalization, e-commerce, and supply chain management.

Globalization By the late 1990s, international trade represented over one-quarter of total U.S. GDP, up from only 11 percent in 1970. While UPS had not expanded globally as quickly or forcefully as other companies, by 1998 it was generating over $3 billion in global revenues, with 37,000 non-U.S. UPS employees delivering almost 1 million packages a day to, from, and within over 200 countries. John Alden, vice chairman of UPS, noted, "In the package delivery industry, globalization means that we must knit together worldwide

---

29. *Bear Stearns UPS Equity Research Report, November 24, 1999.*

30. *On August 31, 1999, the yield for 20-year U.S. Treasury bonds was 6.5 percent, the yield for AAA-rated debt was 6.9 percent, and the yield for BBB-rated debt was 8.0 percent. Source: Standard & Poor's, Inc.*

distribution networks that match our customers' geographic operations. If we don't, our competitors will."[31] As a result, one of UPS's major strategic growth initiatives was building capacity in non-U.S. markets, first in Europe and more recently in Asia and Latin America.[32]

E-Commerce UPS projected that by 2003 online B2C sales in the United States would surpass the $100 billion spent annually on catalog sales.[33] Already the preferred shipper for online commerce, UPS was moving to strengthen its position in this new market through a number of initiatives. For instance, it was aggressively pursuing partnerships with online retailers and other e-commerce players like e-Bay, and by 1999 UPS functionality was being offered on over 10,000 business Web sites.[34] The company was also working on UPS Returns on the Web, a service that, when unveiled, would allow customers to print a return label from their home PC to ease the process of customer returns of online purchases to the retailer of origin.[35]

Supply Chain Management UPS managers likened the supply chain of the future to a moving conveyor belt: "A supply chain in constant motion means minimal inventory, lower costs, and faster time to market. The inventory, if you could call it that, is always in transit."[36] Increasingly, UPS was forging partnerships with supplier companies, from auto manufacturer suppliers to electronic component producers, which involved UPS's handling the continuous flow of shipments to down-market corporate customers. Additionally, through its UPS Logistics Group, UPS began offering suppliers a portfolio of financial services and logistics technology software applications designed to help them better manage their inventory and shipping logistics.

UPS's management anticipated that the company would be able to fund much of these growth opportunities through operating cash flows. The primary benefit from the IPO would, therefore, not be the funds raised from the stock offering—indeed, management committed that it would use the IPO proceeds to repurchase its own stock. Instead, the IPO would provide UPS with publicly traded stock, an attractive tax-efficient medium of exchange, to fund any subsequent acquisitions. In explaining the change in strategy, management noted:

> *As we enter the 21st century, we face a rapidly changing competitive and operating environment. The package delivery industry is globalizing and consolidating at an unprecedented rate. We face new competitive challenges from postal monopolies, which have considerable resources and infrastructures. We believe that we should have a publicly traded equity security that we could use when appropriate for strategic alliances and acquisitions in order to maintain our pre-eminent position.*[37]

Impact on Current Owners and UPS Culture

In 1999 approximately two-thirds of UPS's equity was held by current and retired employees; the remaining third was owned by founding families and foundations. Under the

----

31. *"What in the World Drives UPS?"* International Business, *March/April 1998.*
32. *As of October 1999, UPS, unlike FedEx, had not received rights to fly to China.*
33. *Jim Kelly, speech to the Economic Club of Detroit, January 19, 1999.*
34. *Ibid.*
35. *UPS 2000 Annual Report.*
36. *Jim Kelly, speech to the Houston Forum, October 6, 1999.*
37. *UPS Form S-4 Registration Statement, July 21, 1999, p. 63.*

company's Management Incentive Plan, in place since the mid-1940s, 15 percent of profits were set aside each year for stock awards to supervisors and managers. Employees who received stock awards were encouraged to hold the stock as long as they remained with the company, and most chose to do so. For those employees who wished to sell, typically after retirement, the company would buy back the stock at a price set each quarter by the board of directors. In mid-1999, the price set by the board was $25.50.

UPS's employee ownership had served the company well. It had enabled the company to grow a capital-intensive business without needing to incur the costs of outside financing. Its employees were extremely loyal; many had joined the firm as part-time workers while at college and then stayed after graduation. It was not uncommon for employees to spend their entire working career at UPS. Virtually all of the seven executives who served on the firm's board began their careers "tossing boxes in the warehouse, driving trucks through the streets or handling paperwork in the back office."[38] As a result, experts on corporate culture and resource management observed that the company succeeded by "promoting a 'we all win together, we all fail together' kind of mentality. . . . The common experience of getting packages delivered creates tremendous loyalty among UPS employees. . . . Senior management understands what it means to be a regular person, because they once were that."[39]

To ensure that the IPO preserved the company's culture and control by employees, the offering created two classes of shares. Class A shares, for existing owners, would carry 10 votes each, whereas Class B shares, to be issued to the public, would carry only one vote each. The funds raised in the IPO would then be used to repurchase shares from Class A shareholders, enabling them to divest up to 10 percent of their holdings. For the following 18 months, Class A shares would gradually become available to be sold in the market, at which point they would become Class B shares. As a result of this arrangement, it was anticipated that after the IPO current UPS shareowners would own 90 percent of the firm's equity and control about 99 percent of the vote. Considerable time at UPS was devoted to educating management owners about the reasons for becoming a public company, the details of the share changes, and company policy on employee share ownership and trading.

Offer Pricing

As the IPO date approached, the Morgan Stanley Dean Witter & Co.-UPS deal team considered what price to recommend for the offer. What were UPS's future business and financial prospects given its positioning in the package delivery industry? Were FedEx multiples reasonable benchmarks for valuing UPS stock? Or, given its consistently strong financial returns, should UPS be benchmarked relative to best-in-breed industry leaders?

QUESTIONS

1. What are the key success factors and risks for UPS given its business strategy?

2. How is UPS performing? What factors are driving this performance? Is the current performance likely to be sustained? Why or why not?

---

38. Jerry Knight, "Managers Are No Strangers To the Brown-Collar World," The Washington Post, August 13, 1997.
39. Ibid.

3. How is FedEx performing? How, if at all, do its performance and plans affect your assessment of the sustainability of UPS's current performance?

4. Given your assessment of the company's strategy and the sustainability of its performance, forecast the key factors for UPS's stock value.

5. What is your estimate of UPS's value and its multiples?

6. How do your estimates of UPS's PE and PB multiples compare with those for FedEx? How do they compare with those for the "best of breed" companies' multiples?

EXHIBIT I

Size of U.S. Overnight, Deferred, and Ground Markets, 1990–1999

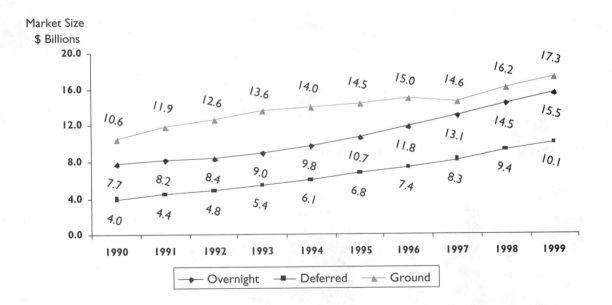

Source: SJ Consulting Group.

United Parcel Service's IPO

EXHIBIT 2

Package Volume in U.S. Overnight, Deferred, and Ground Markets, 1990–1999

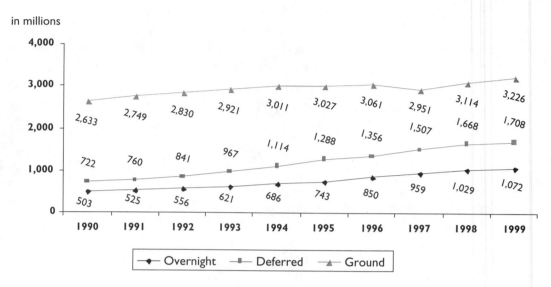

Source: SJ Consulting Group.

EXHIBIT 3

Air Express and Ground Market Growth Rates, 1990–2005E

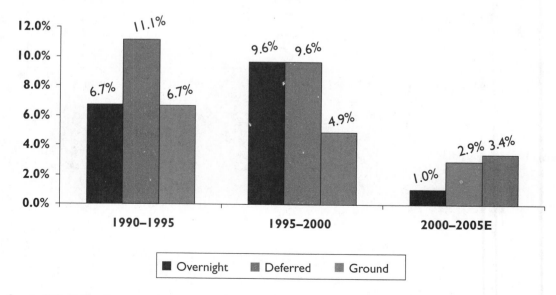

Source: SJ Consulting Group.

United Parcel Service's IPO

EXHIBIT 4

Overnight, Deferred, and Ground Market Shares, 1990–1999

	By Revenue										By Volume
	1990	1991	1992	1993	1994	1995	1996	1997	1998	1999	1999
Overnight											
UPS Next Day Air	31%	30%	30%	30%	30%	30%	32%	31%	32%	34%	25%
FDX Overnight	51%	51%	50%	50%	50%	49%	49%	48%	47%	46%	46%
ABF Next Day	10%	11%	12%	13%	13%	14%	13%	15%	15%	14%	23%
USPS Express Mail	8%	8%	8%	7%	7%	7%	6%	6%	6%	6%	6%
Deferred	1990	1991	1992	1993	1994	1995	1996	1997	1998	1999	1999
UPS Deferred	40%	38%	35%	34%	32%	30%	30%	28%	26%	27%	13%
FDX Deferred (E2, ES)	16%	17%	16%	18%	18%	19%	18%	20%	23%	22%	13%
ABF Second Day	5%	5%	6%	6%	6%	6%	7%	6%	6%	6%	4%
USPS Priority Mail	39%	40%	43%	42%	44%	45%	45%	46%	45%	45%	70%
Ground	1990	1991	1992	1993	1994	1995	1996	1997	1998	1999	1999
UPS Ground	87%	87%	85%	85%	83%	82%	82%	81%	80%	80%	79%
FedEx Ground without RPS	0%	0%	0%	0%	0%	0%	0%	0%	0%	0%	0%
With RPS*	5%	5%	6%	7%	8%	8%	8%	9%	10%	10%	11%
USPS Parcel Post	8%	8%	9%	8%	9%	10%	10%	10%	10%	10%	10%

* RPS acquired by FedEx in 10/97.

Note: Ground market shares are based on the revenues and volume of the largest providers in the industry. They do not include data for private delivery fleets of individual companies, courier services, regional delivery services, LTL trucking firms, and third-party logistics companies

Source: SJ Consulting Group.

EXHIBIT 5

UPS Versus FedEx Process Flow

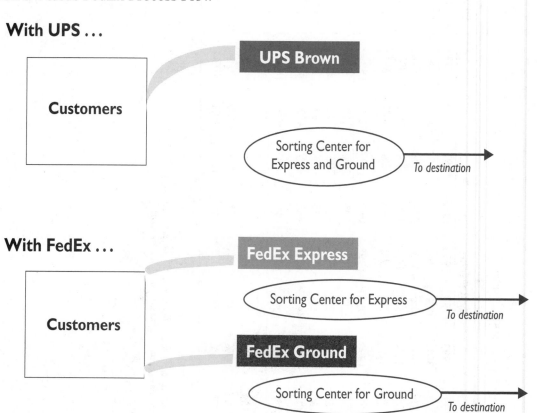

Source: Derived by case writers.

EXHIBIT 6

FedEx Stock Price Performance and Valuation Multiples

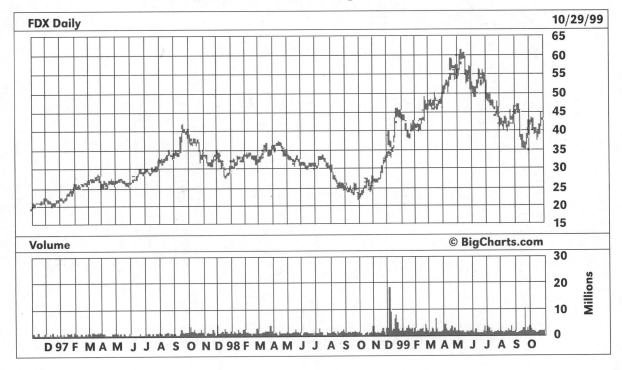

Source: Copyright © 1998–2002 MarketWatch.com, Inc. Historical and current end-of-day data provided by FT Interactive Data. Intraday data provided by S&P Comstock.

Market Data and Multiples—November 1, 1999

Shares outstanding (weighted average, diluted)	300.6 million
Share price	$41.50
Price/Earnings[a]	19.8
Price/Total revenue[b]	0.74
Market/Book value[c]	2.68
Equity Beta[d]	1.16

a. Total market capitalization/net income.

b. Total market capitalization/total revenue.

c. Total market capitalization/shareholders' equity.

d. Salomon Smith Barney Equity Research report on FedEx, June 22, 1999.

Source: FedEx company filings.

United Parcel Service's IPO

EXHIBIT 7

United Parcel Service's IPO

UPS Financial Statements, 1994–1999

STATEMENT OF INCOME (year ended December 31)

($ millions, except per share amounts)	1994	1995	1996	1997	1998	Nine Months Ended September 30, 1998	Nine Months Ended September 30, 1999
REVENUE							
U.S. domestic package	16,943	17,773	18,881	18,868	20,650	15,129	16,239
International package	2,346	2,886	2,989	2,934	3,237	2,342	2,562
Nonpackage	2287	386	498	656	901	653	805
TOTAL REVENUES	19,576	21,045	22,368	22,458	24,788	18,124	19,606
Operating expenses:							
Compensation and benefits	11,727	12,401	13,326	13,289	14,346	10,587	11,226
Other	6,293	6,478	7,013	7,461	7,352	5,315	5,522
Restructuring charge	—	372	—	—	—	—	—
TOTAL OPERATING EXPENSES	18,020	19,251	20,339	20,760	21,698	15,902	16,748
OPERATING PROFIT (LOSS)							
U.S. domestic package	1,821	1,937	2,181	1,654	2,899	2,098	2,522
International package	(390)	(250)	(281)	(67)	56	19	147
Nonpackage	125	107	129	111	135	105	85
Corporate	—	—	—	—	—	—	104
TOTAL OPERATING PROFIT	1,556	1,794	2,029	1,698	3,090	2,222	2,858
Other income (expense):							
Investment income	13	26	39	70	84	56	115
Interest expense	(29)	(77)	(95)	(187)	(227)	(169)	(170)
Tax assessment	—	—	—	—	—	—	(1,786)
Miscellaneous, net	35	(35)	(63)	(28)	(45)	(3)	(30)
INCOME BEFORE INCOME TAXES	1,575	1,708	1,910	1,553	2,902	2,106	987
Income taxes	632	665	764	644	1,161	847	765
NET INCOME	943	1,043	1,146	909	1,741	1,259	222
Per share amounts:							
Basic earnings per share	0.84	0.93	1.03	0.82	1.59	1.16	0.20
Diluted earnings per share	0.82	0.92	1.01	0.81	1.57	1.14	0.20
Dividends declared per share	0.28	0.32	0.34	0.35	0.43	0.20	0.28
Net income before impact of tax assessment	943	1,043	1,146	909	1,741	1,259	1,664
As a percentage of revenue	4.8%	5.0%	5.1%	4.0%	7.0%	7.0%	8.5%

BALANCE SHEET

($ millions, except where noted) As of December 31,	1997	1998
ASSETS		
CURRENT ASSETS		
Cash and cash equivalents	460	1,240
Marketable securities and short-term investments	—	389
Accounts receivable	2,405	2,713
Prepaid employee benefit costs	669	703
Materials, supplies, and other prepaid expenses	417	380
Common stock held for stock plans	526	—
Total Current Assets	4,477	5,425
PROPERTY, PLANT, AND EQUIPMENT		
Vehicles	3,519	3,482
Aircraft (including aircraft under capitalized leases)	6,771	7,739
Land	654	651
Buildings	1,433	1,478
Leasehold improvements	1,734	1,803
Plant equipment	4,063	4,144
Construction in progress	328	257
	18,502	19,554
Less accumulated depreciation and amortization	7,495	8,170
Net Property, Plant, and Equipment	11,007	11,384
Other Assets	428	258
TOTAL ASSETS	15,912	17,067
LIABILITIES AND SHAREOWNERS' EQUITY		
CURRENT LIABILITIES		
Accounts payable	1,207	1,322
Accrued wages and withholdings	1,194	1,092
Dividends payable	191	247
Deferred income taxes	140	—
Current maturities of long-term debt	41	410
Other current liabilities	625	646
Total Current Liabilities	3,398	3,717
Long-Term Debt (including capitalized lease obligations)	2,583	2,191
Accumulated Postretirement Benefit Obligation	911	969
Deferred Taxes, Credits, and Other Liabilities	2,933	3,017
SHAREOWNERS' EQUITY		
Preferred stock, no par value, authorized 200,000,000 shares, none issued	—	—
Common stock, par value $.01 per share, authorized 4,600,000,000 shares, issued 1,124,000 and 1,118,000,000 in 1999 and 1998	56	56
Additional paid-in capital	—	325
Retained earnings	6,112	7,325
Accumulated other comprehensive loss	(81)	(63)
Unrealized loss on marketable securities	—	—
	6,087	7,598
Treasury stock, at cost (0 and 23, 211,904 shares in 1997 and 1998)	—	(425)
	6,087	7,173
TOTAL LIABILITIES AND SHAREOWNERS' EQUITY	15,912	17,067

United Parcel Service's IPO

Balance Sheet Data at end of period ($ millions):	Year Ended December 31					6 Months Ended
	1994	1995	1996	1997	1998	June 30, 1999
Working capital	$ 120	$ 261	$ 1,097	$ 1,079	$ 1,708	$ 434
Long-term debt	$ 1,127	$ 1,729	$ 2,573	$ 2,583	$ 2,191	$ 2,138
Total assets	$11,182	$12,645	$14,954	$15,912	$17,067	$18,302
Shareowner's equity	$ 4,647	$ 5,151	$ 5,901	$ 6,087	$ 7,173	$ 6,122

Excerpts from Management's Discussion and Analysis of Financial Condition and Results of Operations, June 30, 1999

1999 Compared to 1998

Net income for 1999 decreased by $858 million from 1998, resulting in a decrease in diluted earnings per share from $1.57 in 1998 to $0.77 in 1999. These results reflect the charge we recorded during the second quarter of 1999, resulting from an unfavorable ruling of the U.S. Tax Court. Excluding the impact of this one-time charge of $1.442 billion, our net income for 1999 would have been $2.325 billion, with an associated diluted earnings per share of $2.04.

On August 9, 1999, the U.S. Tax Court issued an opinion unfavorable to us regarding a Notice of Deficiency asserting that we are liable for additional tax for the 1983 and 1984 tax years. The Court held that we are liable for tax on income of Overseas Partners Ltd., a Bermuda company, which had reinsured excess value package insurance purchased by our customers beginning in 1984.

The Court held that for the 1984 tax year we are liable for taxes of $31 million on income reported by OPL, penalties and penalty interest of $93 million and interest for a total after-tax exposure estimated at approximately $246 million. In February 2000, the Court entered a decision in accord with its opinion.

In addition, during the first quarter of 1999, the IRS issued two Notices of Deficiency asserting that we are liable for additional tax for the 1985 through 1987 tax years, and the 1988 through 1990 tax years. The primary assertions by the IRS relate to the reinsurance of excess value package insurance, the issue raised for the 1984 tax year. The IRS has based its assertions on the same theories included in the 1983-1984 Notice of Deficiency.

We anticipate that the IRS will take similar positions for tax years subsequent to 1990. Based on the Tax Court opinion, we currently estimate that our total after-tax exposure for the tax years 1984 through 1999 could be as high as $2.353 billion. We believe that a number of aspects of the Tax Court decision are incorrect, and we intend to appeal the decision to the U.S. Court of Appeals for the Eleventh Circuit.

In the second quarter 1999 financial statements, we recorded a tax assessment charge of $1.786 billion, which included an amount for related state tax liabilities. The charge included taxes of $915 million and interest of $871 million. This assessment resulted in a tax benefit of $344 million related to the interest component of the assessment. As a result, our net charge to net income for the tax assessment was $1.442 billion, increasing our total after-tax reserve at that time with respect to these matters to $1.672 billion. The tax benefit of deductible interest is included in income taxes; however, since none of the income on which this tax assessment is based is our income, we have not classified the tax charge as income taxes.

We determined the size of our reserve with respect to these matters in accordance with generally accepted accounting principles based on our estimate of our most likely liability. In making this determination, we concluded that it was more likely that we would be required to pay taxes on income reported by OPL and interest, but that it was not probable that we would be required to pay any penalties and penalty interest. If penalties and penalty interest ultimately are determined to be payable, we would have to record an additional charge of up to $681 million.

On August 31, 1999, we deposited $1.349 billion with the IRS related to these matters for the 1984 through 1994 tax years. We included the profit of the excess value package insurance program, using the IRS's methodology for calculating these amounts, for both 1998 and 1999 in filings we made with the IRS in the fourth quarter of 1999. In February 2000, we deposited $339 million with the IRS related to these matters for the 1995 through 1997 tax years.

These deposits and filings were made in order to stop the accrual of interest, where applicable, on that amount of the IRS's claim, without conceding the IRS's position or giving up our right to appeal the Tax Court's decision.

1998 Compared to 1997

Net income increased by $832 million in 1998 over 1997. Approximately $496 million of this improvement was due primarily to higher revenue per piece on U.S. domestic products, improved product mix, improved international operating results and the containment of operating expense growth. The remaining increase of $336 million resulted from the change in net income for August 1998 as compared to August 1997, the period in which the Teamsters strike occurred.

Source: UPS company filings.

United Parcel Service's IPO

EXHIBIT 8

FedEx Financial Statements, 1996–1999

CONSOLIDATED STATEMENTS OF INCOME

(in thousands, except earnings per share) Years ended May 31,	1996	1997*	1998	1999
REVENUES	$10,273,619	$14,237,892	S15,872,810	$16,773,47
OPERATING EXPENSES:				
Salaries and employee benefits	4,619,990	6,150,247	6,647,140	7,087,72
Purchased transportation	370,650	1,252,901	1,481,590	1,537,78
Rentals and landing fees	959,055	1,138,690	1,304,296	1,396,694
Depreciation and amortization	719,609	928,833	963,732	1,035,11
Maintenance and repairs	617,657	773,765	874,400	958,873
Fuel	578,614	734,722	726,776	604,929
Merger expenses	—	—	88,000	—
Restructuring and impairment charges (credits)	—	225,036	(16,000)	—
Other	1,784,220	2,526,696	2,792,216	2,989,25
	9,649,795	13,730,890	14,862,150	15,610,38
OPERATING INCOME	623,824	507,002	1,010,660	1,163,08
OTHER INCOME (EXPENSE):				
Interest, net	(95,599)	(104,195)	(124,413)	(98,191
Other, net	11,734	23,058	13,271	(3,831
	(83,865)	(81,137)	(111,142)	(102,022
INCOME FROM CONTINUING OPERATIONS BEFORE INCOME TAXES	539,959	425,865	899,518	1,061,064
PROVISION FOR INCOME TAXES	232,182	229,761	401,363	429,731
INCOME FROM CONTINUING OPERATIONS	307,777	196,104	498,155	631,333
INCOME FROM DISCONTINUED OPERATIONS, NET OF INCOME TAXES	—	—	4,875	—
NET INCOME	$307,777	$196,104	$503,030	$631,333
EARNINGS PER COMMON SHARE				
Continuing operations	$2.69	$.67	$1.70	$2.13
Discontinued operations	—	.02		—
	$2.69	$.67	$1.72	$2.13
EARNINGS PER COMMON SHARE, ASSUMING DILUTION				
Continuing operations	$2.69	$.67	$1.67	$2.10
Discontinued operations	—	—	.02	—
	$2.69	$.67	$1.69	$1.69

a. Financial results for 1997 and subsequent years are consolidated to include the acquisition of Caliber System Inc.

CONSOLIDATED BALANCE SHEETS

(in millions) Years ended May 31,	1995	1996	1997*	1998	1999
ASSETS					
CURRENT ASSETS					
Cash and cash equivalents	357.6	93.5	160.9	229.6	325.3
Receivables, less allowances	1,130.3	1,271.6	1,878.0	1,943.4	2,153.2
Spare parts, supplies and fuel	193.3	222.1	339.4	364.7	291.9
Deferred income taxes	115.8	92.6	197.0	232.8	290.7
Prepaid expenses and other	72.2	48.5	68.6	109.6	79.9
Total current assets	1,869.1	1,728.3	2,643.7	2,880.1	3,141.0
PROPERTY AND EQUIPMENT, AT COST					
Flight equipment	3,006.7	3,372.6	3,741.4	4,056.5	4,556.7
Package handling and ground support equipment and vehicles	1,841.1	2,148.5	3,131.1	3,425.3	3,858.8
Computer and electronic equipment	1,224.0	1,439.9	1,957.9	2,162.6	2,363.6
Other	1,625.9	1,717.5	2,557.6	2,819.4	2,940.7
	7,697.7	8,678.5	11,387.9	12,463.9	13,719.9
Less accumulated depreciation and amortization	3,982.5	4,561.9	5,917.5	6,528.8	7,160.7
Net property and equipment	3,715.2	4,116.6	5,470.4	5,935.1	6,559.2
OTHER ASSETS					
Goodwill	397.3	380.7	370.3	356.3	344.0
Equipment deposits and other assets	451.8	473.4	559.8	514.6	604.0
Total other assets	849.0	854.1	930.2	870.9	948.0
	6,433.4	6,699.0	9,044.3	9,686.1	10,648.2
LIABILITIES AND STOCKHOLDERS' INVESTMENT					
CURRENT LIABILITIES					
Current portion of long-term debt	255.4	8.0	356.7	257.5	14.9
Accounts payable	618.6	705.5	999.8	1,145.4	1,134.0
Accrued expenses	904.5	904.9	1,223.0	1,400.9	895.4
Other Liabilities	—	—	—	—	740.5
Total current liabilities	1,778.5	1,618.4	2,579.5	2,803.8	2,784.8
LONG-TERM DEBT, LESS CURRENT PORTION	1,324.7	1,325.3	1,598.0	1,385.2	1,359.7
DEFERRED INCOME TAXES	56.0	64.0	181.8	274.1	293.5
OTHER LIABILITIES	1,028.6	1,115.1	1,183.9	1,261.7	1,546.6
COMMITMENTS AND CONTINGENCIES (NOTES 5, 13 and 14)					
COMMON STOCKHOLDERS' INVESTMENT					
Common Stock, $.10 par value	5.6	5.7	14.8	14.7	29.8
Additional paid-in capital	775.3	815.1	938.0	992.8	1,061.3
Retained earnings	1,466.4	1,766.6	2,621.5	2,999.4	3,615.8
Accumulated other comprehensive income	0.0	0.0	0.0	(27.3)	(24.7)
	2,247.3	2,587.4	3,574.3	3,979.6	4,682.2
Less treasury stock, at cost, and deferred compensation	1.7	11.3	73.1	18.4	18.5
Total common stockholders' investment	2,245.6	2,576.1	3,501.2	3,961.2	4,663.7
	6,433.4	6,699.0	9,044.3	9,686.1	10,648.2

a. Financial results for 1997 and subsequent years are consolidated to include the acquisition of Caliber System Inc.

The accompanying Notes to Consolidated Financial Statements are an integral part of these balance sheets.

Source: FedEx company filings.

United Parcel Service's IPO

EXHIBIT 9

Selected UPS Operating Statistics (financial data in millions)

	Year Ended December 31,			
	1995	1996	1997	1998
Operating Data:				
Delivery volume (in millions of packages)	3,094	3,153	3,038	3,137
Average daily package volume (in thousands)				
U.S. domestic:				
Next Day Air	668	760	822	938
Deferred	716	763	771	783
Ground	9,949	10,015	9,521	9,645
Total U.S. domestic	11,333	11,538	11,114	11,366
International				
Domestic	722	683	678	730
Export	175	194	217	256
Total International	897	877	895	986
Total average daily package volume	12,230	12,415	12,009	12,352
Average revenue per piece:				
U.S. domestic:				
Next Day Air	$19.34	$19.34	$19.49	$19.69
Deferred	11.27	11.39	11.86	12.39
Ground	4.95	5.09	5.19	5.51
Total U.S. domestic	6.20	6.44	6.71	7.15
International				
Domestic	6.22	6.10	5.36	5.14
Export	37.18	37.32	35.01	33.46
Total International	12.26	13.01	12.55	12.49
Total average revenue per piece	$ 6.64	$ 6.91	$ 7.15	$ 7.58
Revenue:				
U.S. domestic:				
Next Day Air	$3,269	$3,734	$4,054	$4,690
Deferred	2,041	2,207	2,314	2,464
Ground	12,463	12,940	12,500	13,496
Total U.S. domestic	17,773	18,881	18,868	20,650
International				
Domestic	1,136	1,058	919	953
Export	1,646	1,839	1,922	2,176
Cargo	176	177	226	270
Total International	2,958	3,074	3,067	3,399
Nonpackage	314	413	523	739
Total revenue	$21,045	$22,368	$22,458	$24,788
Operating weekdays	253	254	253	254
Capital expenditures (in millions)	$2,096	$2,333	$1,984	$1,645

Source: UPS prospectus filing, September 1999.

United Parcel Service's IPO

EXHIBIT 10

Summary of FedEx and UPS Operating Statistics

	UPS	FedEx
Calendar 1998 Average Daily Package Volume (thousands of packages)		
• U.S. Express	938	1,957
• U.S. Deferred	783	894
• U.S. Ground	9,645	1,385
• Total U.S.	11,366	4,236
• Total International	986	282
• Total packages	12,352	4,518
Calendar 1998 Average U.S. Revenue per package[a]		
• Express	$19.69	$14.34
• Deferred	$12.39	$9.93
• Ground	$5.51	$5.36
Number of Employees (full-time and contract positions)	340,000	156,386
Total on-balance-sheet assets	$23.0 billion	$10.6 billion
Number of jet and small aircraft owned and leased	536	634
Number of vehicles	149,000	46,000

a. *Revenues per package (yield) is a function of both average package weight and distance.*

Source: Derived by case writers using UPS and FedEx company filings.

United Parcel Service's IPO

EXHIBIT 11

FedEx Note on Leases

The company utilizes certain aircraft, land, facilities and equipment under capital and operating leases that expire at various dates through 2027. In addition, supplemental aircraft are leased under agreements that generally provide for cancellation upon 30 days' notice.

The components of property and equipment recorded under capital leases were as follows:

May 31, 1999 ($ thousands)

Package handling and ground support equipment and vehicles	$245,041
Facilities	134,442
Computer and electronic equipment and other	6,496
	385,979
Less accumulated depreciation	268,696
	$117,283

Rent expense under operating leases for the years ended May 31 was as follows:

($ thousands)

Minimum rentals	$1,246,259
Contingent rentals	59,839
	$1,306,098

Contingent rentals are based on hours flown under supplemental aircraft leases.

A summary of future minimum lease payments under capital leases and noncancelable operating leases (principally aircraft and facilities) with an initial or remaining term in excess of one year at May 31, 1999 is as follows:

($ thousands)	Capital Leases	Operating Leases
2000	$15,023	$1,011,957
2001	15,023	933,339
2002	15,023	876,055
2003	15,023	809,770
2004	14,894	764,550
Thereafter	302,502	8,717,952
	$377,488	$13,113,623

At May 31, 1999, the present value of future minimum lease payments for capital lease obligations including certain tax-exempt bonds was $200,077,000.

FedEx makes payments under certain leveraged operating leases that are sufficient to pay principal and interest on certain pass-through certificates. The pass-through certificates are not direct obligations of, or guaranteed by, the Company or FedEx.

Source: 1999 FedEx Annual Report, Notes to Consolidated Statements.

EXHIBIT 12

UPS Note on Leases

UPS has capitalized lease obligations for certain aircraft, which are included in property, plant, and equipment at December 31 as follows:

1998 ($ millions)	
Aircraft	$614
Accumulated amortization	(38)
	$576

UPS leases certain aircraft, facilities, equipment, and vehicles under operating leases, which expire at various dates through 2034. Total aggregate minimum lease payments under capitalized leases and under operating leases are as follows (in millions):

($ millions)	Capitalized Leases	Operating Leases
1999	$ 67	$ 211
2000	67	146
2001	67	115
2002	67	94
2003	67	77
After 2003	526	477
Total minimum lease payments	$861	$1,120
Less inputted interest	(263)	
Present value of minimum capitalized lease payments	598	
Less current portion	(39)	
Long-term capitalized lease obligations	$559	

Source: UPS prospectus filing, September 1999, Notes to Financial Statements.

EXHIBIT 13

Selected "Best-of-Breed" Ratios Versus Industrial Comparables

	Stock Price[a]	Market Cap (billions)	Net Income[b] (millions)	ROE	Price to Earnings	Market to Book
Home Depot	$68.50	100.8	1,979	25%	50.9	12.7
Lowe's	$49.31	18.9	556	17%	34.1	5.8
Coca-Cola	$49.94	124.7	3,174	40%	39.3	15.6
PepsiCo	$32.19	48.9	1,921	31%	25.5	7.9
Wal-Mart	$50.81	227.4	4,927	25%	46.1	11.6
Target	$64.31	28.4	1,052	22%	27.0	6.0

a. As of close of trading, October 15, 1999.

b. Latest 12 months.

Source: Derived by caseworkers using SEC filings and market data from bigcharts.com., accessed on June 23, 2002.

United Parcel Service's IPO

Credit Analysis and Distress Prediction

Credit analysis is the evaluation of a firm from the perspective of a holder or potential holder of its debt, including trade payables, loans, and public debt securities. A key element of credit analysis is the prediction of the likelihood a firm will face financial distress.

Credit analysis is involved in a wide variety of decision contexts:

- A potential supplier asks: Should I sell products or services to this firm? The associated credit will be extended only for a short period, but the amount is large and I should have some assurance that collection risks are manageable.
- A commercial banker asks: Should we extend a loan to this firm? If so, how should it be structured? How should it be priced?
- If the loan is granted, the banker must later ask: Are we still providing the services, including credit, that this firm needs? Is the firm still in compliance with the loan terms? If not, is there a need to restructure the loan, and if so, how? Is the situation serious enough to call for accelerating the repayment of the loan?
- A pension fund manager, insurance company, or other investor asks: Are these debt securities a sound investment? What is the probability that the firm will face distress and default on the debt? Does the yield provide adequate compensation for the default risk involved?
- An investor contemplating purchase of debt securities in default asks: How likely is it that this firm can be turned around? In light of the high yield on this debt relative to its current price, can I accept the risk that the debt will not be repaid in full?

Although credit analysis is typically viewed from the perspective of the financier, it is obviously important to the borrower as well:

- A manager of a small firm asks: What are our options for credit financing? Would the firm qualify for bank financing? If so, what type of financing would be possible? How costly would it be? Would the terms of the financing constrain our flexibility?
- A manager of a large firm asks: What are our options for credit financing? Is the firm strong enough to raise funds in the public market? If so, what is our debt rating likely to be? What required yield would that rating imply?

Finally, there are third parties—those other than borrowers and lenders—who are interested in the general issue of how likely it is that a firm will avoid financial distress:

- An auditor asks: How likely is it that this firm will survive beyond the short run? In evaluating the firm's financials, should I consider it a going concern?
- An actual or potential employee asks: How confident can I be that this firm will be able to offer employment over the long term?
- A potential customer asks: What assurance is there that this firm will survive to provide warranty services, replacement parts, product updates, and other services?
- A competitor asks: Will this firm survive the current industry shakeout? What are the implications of potential financial distress at this firm for my pricing and market share?

THE MARKET FOR CREDIT

An understanding of credit analysis requires an appreciation for the various players in the market for credit. We describe those players briefly here.

Suppliers of Credit

The major suppliers in the market for credit are described below.

Commercial Banks

Commercial banks are very important players in the market for credit. Since banks tend to provide a range of services to a client, and have intimate knowledge of the client and its operations, they have a comparative advantage in extending credit in settings where (1) knowledge gained through close contact with management reduces the perceived riskiness of the credit and (2) credit risk can be contained through careful monitoring of the firm.

A constraint on bank lending operations is that the credit risk be relatively low so that the bank's loan portfolio will be of acceptably high quality to bank regulators. Because of the importance of maintaining public confidence in the banking sector and the desire to shield government deposit insurance from risk, governments have incentives to constrain banks' exposure to credit risk. Banks also tend to shield themselves from the risk of shifts in interest rates by avoiding fixed-rate loans with long maturities. Since banks' capital mostly comes from short-term deposits, such long-term loans leave them exposed to increases in interest rates, unless the risk can be hedged with derivatives. Thus, banks are less likely to play a role when a firm requires a very long-term commitment to financing. However, in some such cases they assist in providing a placement of the debt with, say, an insurance company, a pension fund, or a group of private investors.

Other Financial Institutions

Banks face competition in the commercial lending market from a variety of sources. In the U.S., there is competition from savings and loans, even though the latter are relatively more involved in financing mortgages. Finance companies compete with banks in the market for asset-based lending (i.e., the secured financing of specific assets such as receivables, inventory, or equipment). Insurance companies are involved in a variety of lending activities. Since life insurance companies face obligations of a long-term nature, they often seek investments of long duration (e.g., long-term bonds or loans to support large, long-term commercial real estate and development projects). Investment bankers are prepared to place debt securities with private investors or in the public markets (discussed below). Various government agencies are another source of credit.

Public Debt Markets

Some firms have the size, strength, and credibility necessary to bypass the banking sector and seek financing directly from investors, either through sales of commercial paper or through the issuance of bonds. Such debt issues are facilitated by the assignment of a debt rating. In the U.S., Moody's and Standard and Poor's are the two largest rating agencies. A firm's debt rating influences the yield that must be offered to sell the debt instruments. After the debt issue, the rating agencies continue to monitor the firm's financial condition. Changes in the rating are associated with fluctuation in the price of the securities.

Banks often provide financing in tandem with a public debt issue or other source of financing. In highly levered transactions, such as leveraged buyouts, banks commonly provide financing along with public debt that has a lower priority in case of bankruptcy. The bank's "senior financing" would typically be scheduled for earlier retirement than the public debt, and it would carry a lower yield. For smaller or startup firms, banks often provide credit in conjunction with equity financing from venture capitalists. Note that in the case of both the leveraged buyout and the startup company, the bank helps provide the cash needed to make the deal happen, but it does so in a way that shields it from risks that would be unacceptably high in the banking sector.

Sellers Who Provide Financing

Another sector of the market for credit are manufacturers and other suppliers of goods and services. As a matter of course, such firms tend to finance their customers' purchases on an unsecured basis for periods of 30 to 60 days. Suppliers will, on occasion, also agree to provide more extended financing, usually with the support of a secured note. A supplier may be willing to grant such a loan in the expectation that the creditor will survive a cash shortage and remain an important customer in the future. However the customer would typically seek such an arrangement only if bank financing is unavailable because it could constrain flexibility in selecting among and/or negotiating with suppliers.

THE CREDIT ANALYSIS PROCESS

At first blush, credit analysis might appear less difficult than the valuation task discussed in Chapters 7 and 8. After all, a potential creditor ultimately cares only about whether the firm is strong enough to pay its debts at the scheduled times. The firm's exact value, its upside potential, or its distance from the threshold of credit-worthiness may not appear so important. Viewed in that way, credit analysis may seem more like a "zero-one" decision: either the credit is extended, or it is not.

It turns out, however, that credit analysis involves more than just establishing credit-worthiness. First, there are ranges of credit-worthiness, and it is important to understand where a firm lies within that range for purposes of pricing and structuring a loan. Moreover, if the creditor is a bank or other financial institution with an expected continuing relationship with the borrower, the borrower's upside potential is important, even though downside risk must be the primary consideration in credit analysis. A firm that offers growth potential also offers opportunities for future income-generating financial services.

Given this broader view of credit analysis, it should not be surprising that it involves most of the same issues already discussed in the prior chapters on business strategy analysis, accounting analysis, financial analysis, and prospective analysis. Perhaps the greatest difference is that credit analysis rarely involves any explicit attempt to estimate the value of the firm's equity. However, the determinants of that value are relevant in credit analysis because a larger equity cushion translates into lower risk for the creditor.

Below we describe one series of steps that is used by commercial lenders in credit analysis. Of course not all commercial lenders follow the same process, but the steps are representative of typical approaches. The approach used by commercial lenders is of interest in its own right and illustrates a comprehensive credit analysis. However, analysis by others who grant credit often differs. For example, even when a manufacturer conducts some credit analysis prior to granting credit to a customer, it is typically much less extensive than the analysis conducted by a banker because the credit is very short-term and the manufacturer is willing to bear some credit risk in the interest of generating a profit on the sale.

We present the steps in a particular order, but they are in fact all interdependent. Thus, analysis at one step may need to be rethought depending on the analysis at some later step.

Step 1: Consider the Nature and Purpose of the Loan

Understanding the purpose of a loan is important not just for deciding whether it should be granted but also for structuring the loan. Loans might be required for only a few months, for several years, or even as a permanent part of a firm's capital structure. Loans might be used for replacement of other financing, to support working capital needs, or to finance the acquisition of long-term assets or another firm.

The required amount of the loan must also be established. In the case of small and medium-sized companies, a banker would typically prefer to be the sole financier of the business, in which case the loan would have to be large enough to retire existing debt. The preference for serving as the sole financier is not just to gain an advantage in providing a menu of financial services to the firm. It also reflects the desirability of not permitting another creditor to maintain a superior interest that would give it a higher priority in case of bankruptcy. If other creditors are willing to subordinate their positions to the bank, that would of course be acceptable so far as the bank is concerned.

Often the commercial lender deals with firms that may have parent-subsidiary relations. The question of to whom one should lend then arises. The answer is usually the entity that owns the assets that will serve as collateral (or that could serve as such if needed in the future). If this entity is the subsidiary and the parent presents some financial strength independent of the subsidiary, a guarantee of the parent could be considered.

Step 2: Consider the Type of Loan and Available Security

The type of loan considered is a function of not only its purpose but also the financial strength of the borrower. Thus, to some extent, the loan type will be dictated by the financial analysis described in the following step in the process. Some of the possibilities are as follows:

- *Open line of credit.* An open line of credit permits the borrower to receive cash up to some specified maximum on an as-needed basis for a specified term, such as one year. To maintain this option, the borrower pays a fee (e.g., ⅜ of 1 percent) on the unused balance in addition to the interest on any used amount. An open line of credit is useful in cases where the borrower's cash needs are difficult to anticipate.
- *Revolving line of credit.* When it is clear that a firm will need credit beyond the short run, financing may be provided in the form of a "revolver." Sometimes used to support working capital needs, the borrower is scheduled to make payments as the operating cycle proceeds and inventory and receivables are converted to cash. However it is also expected that cash will continue to be advanced so long as the borrower remains in good standing. In addition to interest on amounts outstanding, a fee is charged on the unused line.
- *Working capital loan.* Such a loan is used to finance inventory and receivables, and it is usually secured. The maximum loan balance may be tied to the balance of the working capital accounts. For example, the loan may be allowed to rise to no more than 80 percent of receivables less than 60 days old.
- *Term loan.* Term loans are used for long-term needs and are often secured with long-term assets such as plant or equipment. Typically, the loan will be amortized, requiring periodic payments to reduce the loan balance.
- *Mortgage loan.* Mortgages support the financing of real estate, have long terms, and require periodic amortization of the loan balance.

- *Lease financing.* Lease financing can be used to facilitate the acquisition of any asset but is most commonly used for equipment, including vehicles. Leases may be structured over periods of 1 to 15 years, depending on the life of the underlying asset.

Much bank lending is done on a secured basis, especially with smaller and more highly levered companies. Security will be required unless the loan is short-term and the borrower exposes the bank to minimal default risk. When security is required, one consideration is whether the amount of available security is sufficient to support the loan. The amount that a bank will lend on given security involves business judgment, and it depends on a variety of factors that affect the liquidity of the security in the context of a situation where the firm is distressed. The following are some rules of thumb often applied in commercial lending to various categories of security:

- *Receivables.* Accounts receivable are usually considered the most desirable form of security because they are the most liquid. One large regional bank allows loans of 50 to 80 percent of the balance of nondelinquent accounts. The percentage applied is lower when (1) there are many small accounts that would be costly to collect in the case the firm is distressed; (2) there are a few very large accounts, such that problems with a single customer could be serious; and/or (3) the customer's financial health is closely related to that of the borrower, so that collectibility is endangered just when the borrower is in default. On the latter score, banks often refuse to accept receivables from affiliates as effective security.
- *Inventory.* The desirability of inventory as security varies widely. The best-case scenario is inventory consisting of a common commodity that can easily be sold to other parties if the borrower defaults. More specialized inventory, with appeal to only a limited set of buyers, or inventory that is costly to store or transport is less desirable. The large regional bank mentioned above lends up to 60 percent on raw materials, 50 percent on finished goods, and 20 percent on work in process.
- *Machinery and equipment.* Machinery and equipment is less desirable as collateral. It is likely to be used, and it must be stored, insured, and marketed. Keeping the costs of these activities in mind, banks typically will lend only up to 50 percent of the estimated value of such assets in a forced sale such as an auction.
- *Real estate.* The value of real estate as collateral varies considerably. Banks will often lend up to 80 percent of the appraised value of readily salable real estate. On the other hand, a factory designed for a unique purpose would be much less desirable.

When security is required to make a loan viable, a commercial lender will estimate the amounts that could be lent on each of the assets available as security. Unless the amount exceeds the required loan balance, the loan would not be extended.

Even when a loan is not secured initially, a bank can require a "negative pledge" on the firm's assets—a pledge that the firm will not use the assets as security for any other creditor. In that case, if the borrower begins to experience difficulty and defaults on the loan, and if there are no other creditors in the picture, the bank can demand the loan become secured if it is to remain outstanding.

Step 3: Analyze the Potential Borrower's Financial Status

This portion of the analysis involves all the steps discussed in our chapters on business strategy analysis, accounting analysis, and financial analysis. The emphasis, however, is on the firm's ability to service the debt at the scheduled rate. The focus of the analysis depends on the type of financing under consideration. For example, if a short-term loan is considered to support seasonal fluctuations in inventory, the emphasis would be on the ability of the firm to convert the inventory into cash on a timely basis. In contrast, a term loan to support plant and equipment must be made with confidence in the long-run earnings prospects of the firm.

Key Analysis Questions

Some of the questions to be addressed in analyzing a potential borrower's financial status include the following:

- *Business strategy analysis*: How does this business work? Why is it valuable? What is its strategy for sustaining or enhancing that value? How well qualified is the management to carry out that strategy effectively? Is the viability of the business highly dependent on the talents of the existing management team?
- *Accounting analysis*: How well do the firm's financial statements reflect its underlying economic reality? Are there reasons to believe that the firm's performance is stronger or weaker than reported profitability would suggest? Are there sizable off-balance-sheet liabilities (e.g., operating leases) that would affect the potential borrower's ability to repay the loan?
- *Financial analysis*: Is the firm's level of profitability unusually high or low? What are the sources of any unusual degree of profitability? How sustainable are they? What risks are associated with the operating profit stream? How highly levered is the firm? What is the firm's funds flow picture? What are its major sources and uses of funds? Are funds required to finance expected growth? How great are fund flows expected to be relative to the debt service required? Given the possible volatility in those fund flows, how likely is it that they could fall to a level insufficient to service debt and meet other commitments?

Ultimately, the key question in the financial analysis is how likely it is that cash flows will be sufficient to repay the loan. With that question in mind, lenders focus much attention on solvency ratios: the magnitude of various measures of profits and cash flows relative to debt service and other requirements. To the extent such a ratio exceeds 1, it indicates the "margin of safety" the lender faces. When such a ratio is combined with an assessment of the variance in its numerator, it provides an indication of the probability of nonpayment.

Ratio analysis from the perspective of a creditor differs somewhat from that of an owner. For example, there is greater emphasis on cash flows and earnings available to *all* claimants (not just owners) *before* taxes (since interest is tax-deductible and paid out of pretax dollars). To illustrate, the creditor's perspective is apparent in the following solvency ratio, called the "funds flow coverage ratio":

$$\text{Funds flow coverage} = \frac{\text{EBIT} + \text{Depreciation}}{\text{Interest} + \dfrac{\text{Debt repayment}}{(1 - \text{tax rate})} + \dfrac{\text{Preferred dividends}}{(1 - \text{tax rate})}}$$

We see earnings before both interest and taxes in the numerator. This measures the numerator in a way that can be compared directly to the interest expense in the denominator, because interest expense is paid out of pretax dollars. In contrast, any payment of principal scheduled for a given year is nondeductible and must be made out of after-tax profits. In essence, with a 50 percent tax rate, one dollar of principal payment is "twice as expensive" as a one-dollar interest payment. Scaling the payment of principal by (1   tax rate) accounts for this. The same idea applies to preferred dividends, which are not tax deductible.

The funds flow coverage ratio provides an indication of how comfortably the funds flow can cover unavoidable expenditures. The ratio excludes payments such as common dividends and capital expenditures on the premise that they could be reduced to zero to make debt payments if necessary.[1] Clearly, however, if the firm is to survive in the long run, funds flow must be sufficient to not only service debt but also maintain plant assets. Thus, long-run survival requires a funds flow coverage ratio well in excess of 1.[2]

It would be overly simplistic to establish any particular threshold above which a ratio indicates a loan is justified. However, a creditor clearly wants to be in a position to be repaid on schedule, even when the borrower faces a reasonably foreseeable difficulty. That argues for lending only when the funds flow coverage is expected to exceed 1, even in a recession scenario—and higher if some allowance for capital expenditures is prudent.

The financial analysis should produce more than an assessment of the risk of nonpayment. It should also identify the nature of the significant risks. At many commercial banks it is standard operating procedure to summarize the analysis of the firm by listing the key risks that could lead to default and factors that could be used to control those risks if the loan were made. That information can be used in structuring the detailed terms of the loan so as to trigger default when problems arise, at a stage early enough to permit corrective action.

Step 4: Utilize Forecasts to Assess Payment Prospects

Already implicit in some of the above discussion is a forward-looking view of the firm's ability to service the loan. Good credit analysis should also be supported by explicit forecasts. The basis for such forecasts is usually management, but, not surprisingly, lenders do not accept such forecasts without question.

In forecasting, a variety of scenarios should be considered—including not just a "best guess" but also a "pessimistic" scenario. Ideally, the firm should be strong enough to repay the loan even in the latter scenario. Ironically, it is not necessarily a decline in sales that presents the greatest risk to the lender. If managers can respond quickly to a sales dropoff, it should be accompanied by a liquidation of receivables and inventory, which enhances cash flow for a given level of earnings. The nightmare scenario is one that involves large negative profit margins, perhaps because managers are caught by surprise by a downturn in demand and are forced to liquidate inventory at substantially reduced prices.

At times it is possible to reconsider the structure of a loan so as to permit it to "cash flow." That is, the term of the loan might be extended or the amortization pattern changed. Often a bank will grant a loan with the expectation that it will be continually renewed, thus becoming a permanent part of the firm's financial structure. (Such a loan is labeled an "evergreen.") In that case the loan will still be written as if it is due within the short term, and the bank must assure itself of a viable "exit strategy." However, the firm would be expected to service the loan by simply covering interest payments.

Step 5: Assemble the Detailed Loan Structure, Including Loan Covenants

If the analysis thus far indicates that a loan is in order, it is then time to pull together the detailed structure: type of loan, repayment schedule, loan covenants, and pricing. The first two items were discussed above. Here we discuss loan covenants and pricing.

Writing Loan Covenants

Loan covenants specify mutual expectations of the borrower and lender by specifying actions the borrower will and will not take. Some covenants require certain actions (such as regular provision of financial statements); others preclude certain actions (such as undertaking an acquisition without the permission of the lender); still others require maintenance of certain financial ratios. Violation of a covenant represents an event of default that could cause immediate acceleration of the debt payment, but in most cases the lender uses the default as an opportunity to re-examine the situation and either waive the violation or renegotiate the loan.

Loan covenants must strike a balance between protecting the interests of the lender and providing the flexibility management needs to run the business. The covenants represent a mechanism for ensuring that the business will remain as strong as the two parties anticipated at the time the loan was granted. Thus, required financial ratios are typically based on the levels that existed at that time, perhaps with some allowance for deterioration but often with some expected improvement over time.

The particular covenants included in the agreement should contain the significant risks identified in the financial analysis, or to at least provide early warning that such risks are surfacing. Some commonly used financial covenants include:

- *Maintenance of minimum net worth.* This covenant assures that the firm will maintain an "equity cushion" to protect the lender. Covenants typically require a level of net worth rather than a particular level of income. In the final analysis, the lender may not care whether that net worth is maintained by generating income, cutting dividends, or issuing new equity. Tying the covenant to net worth offers the firm the flexibility to use any of these avenues to avoid default.
- *Minimum coverage ratio.* Especially in the case of a long-term loan, such as a term loan, the lender may want to supplement a net worth covenant with one based on coverage of interest or total debt service. The funds flow coverage ratio presented above would be an example. Maintenance of some minimum coverage helps assure that the ability of the firm to generate funds internally is strong enough to justify the long-term nature of the loan.
- *Maximum ratio of total liabilities to net worth.* This ratio constrains the risk of high leverage and prevents growth without either retaining earnings or infusing equity.
- *Minimum net working capital balance or current ratio.* Constraints on this ratio force a firm to maintain its liquidity by using cash generated from operations to retire current liabilities (as opposed to acquiring long-lived assets).
- *Maximum ratio of capital expenditures to earnings before depreciation.* Constraints on this ratio help prevent the firm from investing in growth (including the illiquid assets necessary to support growth) unless such growth can be financed internally, with some margin remaining for debt service.

In addition to such financial covenants, loans sometimes place restrictions on other borrowing activity, pledging of assets to other lenders, selling of substantial parts of assets, engaging in mergers or acquisitions, and payment of dividends.

Covenants are included not only in private lending agreements with banks, insurance companies, and others, but also in public debt agreements. However, public debt agreements tend to have less restrictive covenants for two reasons. First, negotiations resulting from a violation of public debt covenants are costly (possibly involving not just the trustee, but also bondholders), and so they are written to be triggered only in serious circumstances. Second, public debt is usually issued by stronger, more credit-worthy firms.

(The primary exception would be high-yield debt issued in conjunction with leveraged buyouts.) For the most financially healthy firms with strong debt ratings, very few covenants will be used—only those necessary to limit dramatic changes in the firm's operations, such as a major merger or acquisition.

Loan Pricing

A detailed discussion of loan pricing falls outside the scope of this text. The essence of pricing is to assure that the yield on the loan is sufficient to cover (1) the lender's cost of borrowed funds; (2) the lender's costs of administering and servicing the loan; (3) a premium for exposure to default risk; and (4) at least a normal return on the equity capital necessary to support the lending operation. The price is often stated in terms of a deviation from a bank's prime rate—the rate charged to stronger borrowers. For example, a loan might be granted at prime plus 1½ percent. An alternative base is LIBOR, or the London Interbank Offer Rate, the rate at which large banks from various nations lend large blocks of funds to each other.

Banks compete actively for commercial lending business, and it is rare that a yield includes more than 2 percentage points to cover the cost of default risk. If the spread to cover default risk is, say, 1 percent, and the bank recovers only 50 percent of amounts due on loans that turn out bad, then the bank can afford only 2 percent of their loans to fall into that category. This underscores how important it is for banks to conduct a thorough analysis and to contain the riskiness of their loan portfolio.

FINANCIAL STATEMENT ANALYSIS AND PUBLIC DEBT

Fundamentally, the issues involved in analysis of public debt are no different from those of bank loans and other private debt issues. Institutionally, however, the contexts are different. Bankers can maintain very close relations with clients so as to form an initial assessment of their credit risk and monitor their activities during the loan period. In the case of public debt, the investors are distanced from the issuer. To a large extent, they must depend on professional debt analysts, including debt raters, to assess the riskiness of the debt and monitor the firm's ongoing activities. Such analysts and debt raters thus serve an important function in closing the information gap between issuers and investors.

The Meaning of Debt Ratings

The two major debt rating agencies in the U.S. are Moody's and Standard and Poor's. Using the Standard and Poor's labeling system, the highest possible rating is AAA. Proceeding downward from AAA, the ratings are AA, A, BBB, BB, B, CCC, CC, C, and D, where "D" indicates debt in default. Table 10-1 presents examples of firms in rating categories AAA through CCC, as well as average yields across all firms in each category. Only about 1 percent of the public industrial companies rated by Standard & Poor's have the financial strength to merit an AAA rating. Among the few are General Electric, Johnson & Johnson, Merck, and Nestlé—all among the largest, most profitable firms in the world. AA firms are also very strong and include Microsoft and Wal-Mart. Firms rated AAA and AA have the lowest costs of debt financing; in January 2002 their average yields were roughly 3.5 percent over the 12 month LIBOR rate.

To be considered investment grade, a firm must achieve a rating of BBB or higher. Many funds are precluded by their charters from investing in any bonds below that grade. Even to achieve a grade of BBB is difficult. AT&T, the largest long-distance telephone carrier in the U.S., was rated as "only" BBB—barely investment grade—in 2003. Apple Computer and Delta Air Lines were in the BB category. Delta was the third largest airline carrier in the U.S. However, it had suffered from the dramatic decline in demand following September 11, 2001. The B category includes Continental Airlines, Lucent Technologies, and Northwest Airlines, all of which were facing financial difficulty. An example of a CCC rated firm is AMR, the parent of American Airlines, which was close to bankruptcy following the massive financial problems faced by the industry. UAL, the parent of United Airlines, was rated as D, since it had filed for bankruptcy in 2003.

Table 10-1 shows that the cost of debt financing rises markedly once firms' debt falls below investment grade. For example, in January 2002 yields for BBB rated debt issues were 4.4 percent over the 12 month LIBOR rate; yields for B rated issues were 7.3 percent above LIBOR rates; and yields for firms with CCC rated debt, which were close to bankruptcy, were 20.5 percent over LIBOR.

Table 10-1 Debt Ratings: Example Firms and Average Yields by Category

S&P debt rating	Example firms in 2003	Percentage of public industrials given same rating by S&P	Average yield, January 2002	Average spread over 12 month LIBOR rate
AAA	General Electric Johnson & Johnson Merck and Co. Nestlé S.A.	0.9%	5.95%	3.51%
AA	Microsoft GlaxoSmithKline Wal-Mart Stores, Inc.	3.6	5.98	3.54
A	American Express Coca-Cola Enterprises McDonald's Corp. Sony Corp.	20.0	6.23	3.79
BBB	AT&T British Airways Ford Motor Company General Motors Sears Roebuck & Co.	29.0	6.80	4.36
BB	Apple Computer Delta Air Lines	22.6	8.53	6.09
B	Continental Airlines Lucent Technologies Northwest Airlines	20.9	9.75	7.31
CCC	American Airlines (AMR)	3.0	22.90	20.46
D	United Air Lines (UAL)			

Source: Standard and Poor's 2003, and Standard and Poor's Compustat 2002.

Table 10-2 shows median financial ratios for firms by debt rating category. Firms with AAA and AA ratings have very strong earnings and cash flow performance as well as minimal leverage. Firms in the BBB class are only moderately leveraged, with about 37 percent of long- term capitalization coming in the form of debt. Earnings tend to be relatively strong, as indicated by a pretax interest coverage (EBIT/interest) of 2.8 and a cash flow debt coverage (cash flow from operations/total debt) of nearly 27 percent. Firms with B and CCC ratings, however, face significant risks: they typically report losses, have high leverage, and have interest coverage ratios less than 1.

Table 10-2 Debt Ratings: Median Financial Ratios by Category

Median ratios for overall category in January 2002
(industrials only)

S&P debt rating	Pretax return on long-term capital	Pretax interest coverage	Cash flow from operations to total debt	Long-term debt to total capital
AAA	27.6%	21.9 times	45.1%	8%
AA	17.4	7.4	52.1	20
A	10.9	4.2	29.2	34
BBB	7.1	2.8	26.7	37
BB	3.6	1.7	18.4	48
B	–3.9	0.5	8.1	64
CCC	–16.0	–0.9	1.4	59

Source: Standard and Poor's Compustat, 2002.

Factors That Drive Debt Ratings

Research demonstrates that some of the variation in debt ratings can be explained as a function of selected financial statement ratios, even as used within a quantitative model that incorporates no subjective human judgment. Some debt rating agencies rely heavily on quantitative models, and such models are commonly used by insurance companies, banks, and others to assist in the evaluation of the riskiness of debt issues for which a public rating is not available.

Table 10-3 lists the factors used by three different firms in their quantitative debt-rating models. The firms include one insurance company and one bank, which use the models in their private placement activities, and an investment research firm, which employs the model in evaluating its own debt purchases and holdings. In each case profitability and leverage play an important role in the rating. One firm also uses firm size as an indicator, with larger size associated with higher ratings.

Table 10-3 Factors Used in Quantitative Models of Debt Ratings

	Firm 1	Firm 2	Firm 3
Profitability measures	Return on long-term capital	Return on long-term capital	Return on long-term capital
Leverage measures	Long-term debt to capitalization	Long-term debt to capitalization Total debt to total capital	Long-term debt to capitalization
Profitability and leverage	Interest coverage Cash flow to long-term debt	Interest coverage Cash flow to long-term debt	Fixed charge coverage Coverage of short-term debt and fixed charges
Firm size	Sales	Total assets	
Other		Standard deviation of return Subordination status	

Several researchers have estimated quantitative models used for debt ratings. Two of these models, developed by Kaplan and Urwitz and shown in Table 10-4, highlight the relative importance of the factors.[3] Model 1 has the greater ability to explain variation in bond ratings. However, it includes some factors based on stock market data, which are not available for all firms. Model 2 is based solely on financial statement data.

The factors in Table 10-4 are listed in the order of their statistical significance in Model 1. An interesting feature is that the most important factor explaining debt ratings is not a financial ratio at all—it is simply firm size! Large firms tend to get better ratings than small firms. Whether the debt is subordinated or unsubordinated is next most important, followed by a leverage indicator. Profitability appears less important, but in part that reflects the presence in the model of multiple factors (ROA and interest coverage) that capture profitability. It is only the explanatory power that is *unique* to a given variable that is indicated by the ranking in Table 10-4. Explanatory power common to the two variables is not considered.

When applied to a sample of bonds that were not used in the estimation process, the Kaplan-Urwitz Model 1 predicted the rating category correctly in 44 of 64 cases, or 63 percent of the time. Where it erred, the model was never off by more than one category, and in about half of those cases its prediction was more consistent with the market yield on the debt than was the actual debt rating. The discrepancies between actual ratings and those estimated using the Kaplan-Urwitz model indicate that rating agencies incorporate factors other than financial ratios in their analysis. These are likely to include the types of strategic, accounting, and prospective analyses discussed throughout this book.

Given that debt ratings can be explained reasonably well in terms of a handful of financial ratios, one might question whether ratings convey any *news* to investors—anything that could not already have been garnered from publicly available financial data. The answer to the question is yes, at least in the case of debt rating downgrades. That is, downgrades are greeted with drops in both bond and stock prices.[4] To be sure, the capital markets anticipate much of the information reflected in rating changes. But that is not surprising, given that the changes often represent reactions to recent known events and that the rating agencies typically indicate in advance that a change is being considered.

Table 10-4 Kaplan-Urwitz Models of Debt Ratings

Firm or debt characteristic	Variable reflecting characteristic	Coefficients	
		Model 1	Model 2
	Model intercept	5.67	4.41
Firm size	Total assets[a]	.0011	.0014
Subordination status of debt	1 = subordinated; 0 = unsubordinated	−2.36	−2.56
Leverage	Long-term debt to total assets	−2.85	−2.72
Systematic risk	Market model beta, indicating sensitivity of stock price to market-wide movements (1 = average)[b]	−.87	—
Profitability	Net income to total assets	5.13	6.40
Unsystematic risk	Standard deviation of residual from market model (average = .10)[b]	−2.90	—
Riskiness of profit stream	Coefficient of variation in net income over 5 years (standard deviation/mean)	—	−.53
Interest coverage	Pretax funds flow before interest to interest expense	.007	.006

The score from the model is converted to a bond rating as follows:
If score > 6.76, predict AAA
   score > 5.19, predict AA
   score > 3.28, predict A
   score > 1.57, predict BBB
   score < 0.00, predict BB

a. The coefficient in the Kaplan-Urwitz model was estimated at .005 (Model 1) and .006 (Model 2). Its scale has been adjusted to reflect that the estimates were based on assets measured in dollars from the early 1970s. Given that $1 from 1972 is approximately equivalent to $4.40 in 2003, the original coefficient estimate has been divided by 4.4

b. Market model is estimated by regressing stock returns on the market index, using monthly data for the prior 5 years.

PREDICTION OF DISTRESS AND TURNAROUND

The key task in credit analysis is assessing the probability that a firm will face financial distress and fail to repay a loan. A related analysis, relevant once a firm begins to face distress, involves considering whether it can be turned around. In this section we consider evidence on the predictability of these states.

The prediction of either distress or turnaround is a complex, difficult, and subjective task that involves all of the steps of analysis discussed throughout this book: business strategy analysis, accounting analysis, financial analysis, and prospective analysis. Purely quantitative models of the process can rarely serve as substitutes for the hard work the analysis involves. However, research on such models does offer some insight into which financial indicators are most useful in the task. Moreover, there are some settings where extensive credit checks are too costly to justify, and where quantitative distress prediction models are useful. For example, the commercially available "Zeta" model is used by some manufacturers and other firms to assess the credit-worthiness of their customers.[5]

Several distress prediction models have been developed over the years.[6] They are similar to the debt rating models, but instead of predicting ratings, they predict whether a firm will face some state of distress within one year, typically defined as bankruptcy. One study suggests that the factors most useful (on a stand-alone basis) in predicting bankruptcy one year in advance are[7]:

1. Profitability $= \left[\dfrac{\text{Net income}}{\text{Net worth}} \right]$

2. Volatility $= \left[\text{Standard deviation of} \left(\dfrac{\text{Net income}}{\text{Net worth}} \right) \right]$

3. Financial leverage $= \left[\dfrac{\text{Market value of equity}}{(\text{Market value of equity} + \text{Book value of debt})} \right]$

The evidence indicates that the key to whether a firm will face distress is its level of profitability, the volatility of that profitability, and how much leverage it faces. Interestingly, liquidity measures turn out to be much less important. Current liquidity won't save an unhealthy firm if it is losing money at a fast pace.

Of course if one were interested in predicting distress, there would be no need to restrict attention to one variable at a time. A number of multi-factor models have been designed to predict financial distress. One such model, the Altman Z-score model, weights five variables to compute a bankruptcy score.[8] For public companies the model is as follows[9]:

$$Z = 1.2(X_1) + 1.4(X_2) + 3.3(X_3) + 0.6(X_4) + 1.0(X_5)$$

where X_1 = net working capital/total assets
X_2 = retained earnings/total assets
X_3 = EBIT/total assets
X_4 = market value of equity/book value of total liabilities
X_5 = sales/total assets

The model predicts bankruptcy when $Z < 1.81$. The range between 1.81 and 2.67 is labeled the "gray area."

The following table presents calculations for two companies, Lucent Technologies and Merck:

	Model Coefficient	Lucent Technologies		Merck	
		Ratios	Score	Ratios	Score
Net working capital/assets	0.717	0.16	0.19	0.05	0.06
Retained earnings/Total assets	0.847	−1.24	−1.73	0.75	1.04
EBIT/Total assets	3.11	−0.38	−1.24	0.21	0.71
Market value of equity/Book value of total liabilities	0.42	0.26	0.16	4.37	2.62
Sales/Total assets	0.998	0.69	0.69	1.09	1.09
			−1.93		5.53

With the fall of the dot-com sector in 2000, Lucent Technologies experienced a dramatic decline in revenues and profits that persisted for the next two years. In the year ended December 31, 2002, Lucent earned a loss before interest and taxes, its retained earnings were negative, and its market value of equity was only $5.9 billion. It is not surprising to see that the model rates Lucent's likelihood of failure as high. Merck, an AAA rated company, has much stronger financial performance and a much higher market valuation ($128.4 billion) than Lucent. Merck's score indicates that it has a very low likelihood of failure.

Such models have some ability to predict failing and surviving firms. Altman reports that when the model was applied to a holdout sample containing 33 failed and 33 non-failed firms (the same proportion used to estimate the model), it correctly predicted the outcome in 63 of 66 cases. However, the performance of the model would degrade substantially if applied to a holdout sample where the proportion of failed and nonfailed firms was not forced to be the same as that used to estimate the model.

Simple distress prediction models like the Altman model cannot serve as a replacement for in-depth analysis of the kind discussed throughout this book. But they do provide a useful reminder of the power of financial statement data to summarize important dimensions of the firm's performance. In addition, they can be useful for screening large numbers of firms prior to more in-depth analysis of corporate strategy, management expertise, market position, and financial ratio performance.

SUMMARY

Credit analysis is the evaluation of a firm from the perspective of a holder or potential holder of its debt. Credit analysis is important to a wide variety of economic agents—not just bankers and other financial intermediaries but also public debt analysts, industrial companies, service companies, and others.

At the heart of credit analysis lie the same techniques described in Chapters 2 through 8: business strategy analysis, accounting analysis, financial analysis, and portions of prospective analysis. The purpose of the analysis is not just to assess the likelihood that a potential borrower will fail to repay the loan. It is also important to identify the nature of the key risks involved, and how the loan might be structured to mitigate or control those risks. A well structured loan provides the lender with a viable "exit strategy," even in the case of default. A key to this structure is properly designed accounting-based covenants.

Fundamentally, the issues involved in analysis of public debt are no different from those involved in evaluating bank loans or other private debt. Institutionally, however, the contexts are different. Investors in public debt are usually not close to the borrower and must rely on other agents, including debt raters and other analysts, to assess credit-worthiness. Debt ratings, which depend heavily on firm size and financial measures of performance, have an important influence on the market yields that must be offered to issue debt.

The key task in credit analysis is the assessment of the probability of default. The task is complex, difficult, and to some extent, subjective. A small number of key financial ratios can help predict financial distress with some accuracy. The most important financial indicators for this purpose are profitability, volatility of profits, and leverage. However, the models cannot replace the in-depth forms of analysis discussed in this book.

DISCUSSION QUESTIONS

1. What are the critical performance dimensions for (a) a retailer and (b) a financial services company that should be considered in credit analysis? What ratios would you suggest looking at for each of these dimensions?

2. Why would a company pay to have its public debt rated by a major rating agency (such as Moody's or Standard and Poor's)? Why might a firm decide not to have its debt rated?

3. Some have argued that the market for original-issue junk bonds developed in the late 1970s as a result of a failure in the rating process. Proponents of this argument suggest that rating agencies rated companies too harshly at the low end of the rating scale, denying investment grade status to some deserving companies. What are proponents of this argument effectively assuming were the incentives of rating agencies? What economic forces could give rise to this incentive?

4. Many debt agreements require borrowers to obtain the permission of the lender before undertaking a major acquisition or asset sale. Why would the lender want to include this type of restriction?

5. Betty Li, the CFO of a company applying for a new loan, states, "I will never agree to a debt covenant that restricts my ability to pay dividends to my shareholders because it reduces shareholder wealth." Do you agree with this argument?

6. Cambridge Construction Company follows the percentage-of-completion method for reporting long-term contract revenues. The percentage of completion is based on the cost of materials shipped to the project site as a percentage of total expected material costs. Cambridge's major debt agreement includes restrictions on net worth, interest coverage, and minimum working capital requirements. A leading analyst claims that "the company is buying its way out of these covenants by spending cash and buying materials, even when they are not needed." Explain how this may be possible.

7. Can Cambridge improve its Z score by behaving as the analyst claims in Question 6? Is this change consistent with economic reality?

8. A banker asserts, "I avoid lending to companies with negative cash from operations because they are too risky." Is this a sensible lending policy?

9. A leading retailer finds itself in a financial bind. It doesn't have sufficient cash flow from operations to finance its growth, and it is close to violating the maximum debt-to-assets ratio allowed by its covenants. The Vice-President for Marketing suggests, "We can raise cash for our growth by selling the existing stores and leasing them back. This source of financing is cheap since it avoids violating either the debt-to-assets or interest coverage ratios in our covenants." Do you agree with his analysis? Why or why not? As the firm's banker, how would you view this arrangement?

NOTES

1. The same is true of preferred dividends. However, when preferred stock is cumulative, any dividends missed must be paid later, when and if the firm returns to profitability.

2. Other relevant coverage ratios are discussed in Chapter 5.

3. Robert Kaplan and G. Urwitz, "Statistical Models of Bond Ratings: A Methodological Inquiry," *Journal of Business* (April 1979): 231–61.

4. See Robert Holthausen and Richard Leftwich, "The Effect of Bond Rating Changes on Common Stock Prices," *Journal of Financial Economics* (September 1986): 57–90; and John Hand, Robert Holthausen, and Richard Leftwich, "The Effect of Bond Rating Announcements on Bond and Stock Prices," *Journal of Finance* (June 1992): 733–52.

5. See Edward Altman, *Corporate Financial Distress* (New York: John Wiley, 1993).

6. See Edward Altman, "Financial Ratios, Discriminant Analysis, and the Prediction of Corporate Bankruptcy," *Journal of Finance* (September 1968): 589–609; Altman, *Corporate Financial Distress,* op. cit.; William Beaver, "Financial Ratios as Predictors of Distress," *Journal of Accounting Research,* Supplement (1966): 71–111; James Ohlson, "Financial Ratios and the Probabilistic Prediction of Bankruptcy," *Journal of Accounting Research* (Spring 1980): 109–131; and Mark Zmijewski,

"Predicting Corporate Bankruptcy: An Empirical Comparison of the Extant Financial Distress Models," working paper, SUNY at Buffalo, 1983.

7. Zmijewski, op. cit.

8. Altman, *Corporate Financial Distress,* op. cit.

9. For private firms, Altman, ibid., adjusts the public model by changing the numerator for the variable X_4 from the market value of equity to the book value. The revised model follows:

$$Z = .717(X_1) + .847(X_2) + 3.11(X_3) + 0.420(X_4) + .998(X_5)$$

where X_1 = net working capital/total assets
X_2 = retained earnings/total assets
X_3 = EBIT/total assets
X_4 = book value of equity/book value of total liabilities
X_5 = sales/total assets

The model predicts bankruptcy when $Z < 1.20$. The range between 1.20 and 2.90 is labeled the "gray area."

Amazon.com in the Year 2000

On June 22, 2000, Ravi Suria, a credit analyst at Lehman Brothers, issued a report sounding an alarm about the convertible debt of Amazon.com. When he looked at the company's financials, he saw a "weak balance sheet, poor working capital management, and massive negative operating cash flow." He regarded the debt as "extremely weak and deteriorating" and strongly advised investors to avoid it.

> Amazon.com was, he noted, "the pioneering and best-established brand" among Internet retailers. Nevertheless, he was convinced that the company was going to run out of cash in less than a year because of its poor operating performance, reflecting basic weaknesses in its business model. Amazon, he said, had really evolved from a "virtual" retailer to something more like a "real world" retailer, and was encountering the same kinds of cash flow problems and problems related to management of working capital that had spelled disaster for many retailers in the past. In February 1999 the company had issued $1.25 billion in convertible debt. A year later, it completed a second offering of convertible debt, this time for $680 million. As Suria saw things, however, the company was burning cash up fast, and if it was not able to start generating positive free cash flows soon, it would be in dire straits. "The party is over," he said, "and the February round of financing seems to have been the last call."[1]

In response to Suria's report, the price of Amazon's convertible debt dropped 15 percent and its stock price dropped 19 percent in one day after the report became public.

BACKGROUND

Jeff Bezos—Amazon's founder, chairman, and CEO—knew a good deal about the worlds of both technology and finance. After earning a degree in computer science and electrical engineering at Princeton, he worked for two years in commercial banking; then four years in investment banking in New York, managing a hedge fund. Then, fascinated by the possibilities of selling consumer goods over the Internet, he started Amazon.com.[2] The company was founded in 1994, began selling books online in 1995, and went public in 1997.

Bezos initially considered a number of possible retailing businesses for the Internet. He regarded book selling as especially attractive for several reasons:

- The number of products that customers might want was far larger than any physical store could carry. There were over a million books in print—and many more that were out of print. (The largest physical book stores, so-called "superstores," carried about 150,000 titles. Mall stores and small independent stores carried a small fraction of that.)

Research Associate Jeremy Cott prepared this case under the supervision of Professor Krishna Palepu. The case is intended solely as the basis for class discussion and is not intended to serve as an endorsement, source of primary data, or illustration of effective or ineffective management. Copyright © 2001 by the President and Fellows of Harvard College. HBS Case 9-101-045.

1. Ravi Suria, "Amazon.com, Inc.: Credit Analysis of the Convertible Bonds," Lehman Brothers, June 22, 2000.

2. For a detailed description of Amazon's business and its competitive strategy during its early years, see "Leadership Online: Barnes & Noble vs. Amazon.com," Harvard Business School Case 798-063.

- The existing market was large. Annual retail sales of books were about $25 billion in the United States and about $80 billion worldwide.
- The book publishing and retailing industries were relatively fragmented. No book publisher controlled more than 15 percent of the U.S. market, and the two largest land-based book retailers, Barnes & Noble and Borders, controlled about 25 percent of the market. (Barnes & Noble and Borders, however, had been expanding significantly in recent years.)

Bezos' decision to locate the company in Seattle, Washington, was also deliberate. The Seattle area had a lot of computer-technical talent (e.g., Microsoft was located nearby); it was near one of the largest book wholesalers in the country; and it would provide, he felt, a time-zone advantage in making shipments to customers around the country.[3]

EVOLUTION OF CORPORATE STRATEGY

As the company developed, it made two major changes in strategy: (1) it began doing more self-distribution, and (2) it expanded the product line from books to other products.

Self-Distribution

During the first few years of its existence, Amazon pursued a "sell all, carry few" strategy. In the fall of 1997, for example, it billed itself as the world's largest bookstore, offering a selection of 2.5 million different titles. It actually stocked, however, only a few thousand. Generally, it ordered books from its suppliers (primarily wholesalers) only after making the sale to a customer. About 95 percent of Amazon's sales were handled that way.

Competition from Barnes & Noble, the largest land-based book retailer in the country, prompted a change in this approach. When Barnes & Noble opened its online store in May 1997, it said that it would use the distribution strength of its land-based operation to gain a competitive advantage in its online selling. Barnes & Noble operated a large distribution center in New Jersey where it stocked about 400,000 titles and from which it shipped books to its many physical stores around the country. Barnes & Noble said that it would also use this distribution center to fill many of the individual orders that it received from online customers.[4] There were two advantages to this approach.

- First, it reduced the cost of goods. Most of the books that Barnes & Noble stocked in its distribution center were ordered direct from publishers rather than wholesalers. Books ordered from publishers cost less than books ordered from wholesalers. The difference was several additional percentage points in discount, which, in a low-margin business like book retailing, was significant. (The cost of holding inventory was of course an offsetting cost factor.) Amazon had been ordering most of its books from wholesalers because wholesalers delivered books much faster than publishers. In the fall of 1997, however, the Chief Operating Officer of Barnes & Noble, Steve Riggio, said, "The cost advantages of self-distribution are tremendous." He said that 40 percent of the books it sold were supplied by its own distribution complex, and he

3. Ibid.

4. "Barnes & Noble Drops Names, Disses Amazon.com as Web Site Launches," *Book Publishing Report, May 19, 1997.*

Amazon.com in 2000

planned to get to 50 percent within a year. Jeff Bezos said, "The logistics of distribution are the iceberg below the waterline of online bookselling."[5]

- Second, having greater control over the order fulfillment process could provide greater assurance of the quality of a key element of customer service. In 1999, for example, Toys "R" Us, in planning to go online to challenge eToys, concluded that it needed to handle the fulfillment operation itself. "The minute you outsource," the CEO of Toys "R" Us said, "it's just something that's out of your hands. What happens at Christmas time when you're using [a certain third-party fulfillment operation]? They're servicing [someone else]. How do you get your service priorities to the top of the list?"[6]

The move to self-distribution changed the competitive landscape. When Barnes & Noble opened its online store in May 1997, it said that it would offer "the lowest everyday prices of any online bookseller."[7] It began by announcing discounts on a lot of books that were greater than what Amazon at that point was offering, and stiffer price competition was thus set in motion.

In response, in the fall of 1997 Amazon announced that it would enlarge its Seattle warehouse by 70 percent, open a new one on the East Coast, in Delaware, and buy a much larger portion of its books direct from publishers.

Then in 1999 Amazon made a dramatic move. It increased the number of distribution centers it had from two to ten, thus giving it over four million square feet of warehouse and distribution space. In its 1999 10-K it said that it carried "increased levels of inventory in order to be able to meet customer demand and ship products to customers on a timely basis," and that in 1999 it "increased our direct purchasing from manufacturers." It didn't disclose, however, what percentage of customer orders it filled from its own stock.

Selling Other Products

When Amazon first went online in 1995, it sold only books. When it went public in May 1997 it was selling books and a small number of tapes and CDs related to books.

In 1998, however, Amazon began to significantly expand its product offerings, and by mid-2000 it had established, and was operating on its web site, businesses that sold not only books but also music CDs, videotapes, DVDs, computer games, toys, software, consumer electronics, tools and hardware, lawn and patio products, and kitchen products. All of these products it sold itself: that is, it bought the actual inventory, and it sold it directly to customers. The company also set itself up as a middleman for, or strategic partner to, a number of other businesses that were allowed to use space on Amazon's web site to sell their own products to Amazon's customers.

....

5. Quotations come from Anthony Bianco, "Virtual Bookstores Start to Get Real," Business Week, October 27, 1997. The economics of order fulfillment in e-tailing could take a few different forms. At one extreme, Buy.com—a multi-product e-tailer that opened for business in 1997—outsourced almost everything having to do with inventory: it didn't maintain any inventory on its balance sheet, and wholesalers fulfilled all of the orders that it received. Buy.com said that this was the most efficient way of handling things, but it paid the wholesalers' markup on the goods as well as a fee that wholesalers charged for carrying out the fulfillment function. Many e-tailers outsourced some, but not all, of their order fulfillment. When Musicland—the successful, land-based retailer of CDs, tapes, DVDs, and books—went online in 1999, it said that it would do its own order fulfillment. It claimed that, by using its existing distribution infrastructure, it would save 10 percent of sales compared with e-tailers who outsourced the order fulfillment function. It would save about 5 percent, it said, by ordering direct from manufacturers, thereby avoiding the wholesaler's markup; and about 5 percent by using its own distribution system, which was what it said other companies paid third-party distributors. (The source for the information about Musicland is Jim McCartney, "Launching Web Site Is More Than Defensive Strategy for Some Retailers," Saint Paul Pioneer Press, June 16, 1999.)

6. Abigail Goldman, "E-Commerce Gets an F Without the D Word," Los Angeles Times, July 25, 1999.

7. "Barnes & Noble Drops Names … ," op. cit.

Marketplace Services In these arrangements the company provided space on its web site to auction businesses and thousands of small, non-auction businesses so that consumers could eventually come to the Amazon web site and—as Jeff Bezos put it—"find and discover anything they want to buy. That's anything with a capital 'A.'"[8] He ruled out only animals, porn, and contraband.

One auction business involved the famous art auction house Sothebys. The large assemblage of small, non-auction businesses was named "zShops." As Bezos said when announcing the zShops program in the fall of 1999, the "z" stands for zero. "What we're trying to do is create a shopping environment that has zero risk, zero hassles, and zero products you can't find." For example, he said that Amazon would guarantee up to $1,000 of any customer's purchase from these zShops. That is, the customer would get up to $1,000 of his or her money back if the merchant didn't fulfill the order.[9]

From these small, non-auction businesses Amazon would receive monthly subscription fees ($9.99) and sales commissions (up to 5 percent of the sale). Amazon wouldn't own or manage any of their inventories. Bezos characterized this as a low-top-line, high-margin business. When asked, however, whether he had any sense of how much of Amazon's revenue would come from this service, Bezos said he didn't.

Strategic Partnerships Amazon was also making minority investments in many e-commerce companies.[10] These companies were given distinct, co-branded sections on the Amazon web site where they sold their products or services, and Amazon received advertising revenues from them for allowing them to do so. Thus, for example, the "health and beauty products" section was co-branded with the company Drugstore.com, in which Amazon had made a minority investment; the "pet products" section was co-branded with the company Pets.com, in which Amazon had also made a minority investment. Amazon considered these strategic partnerships (of which there were, in 2000, about a dozen) part of the "Amazon Commerce Network" (ACN). The company had high hopes for them. In a press release in February 2000, the company said that these equity-method partnerships/investments "represent more than $500 million in revenue commitments to Amazon.com over the next five years." In the first quarter of 2000, Amazon recorded $20 million of ACN revenues, and analysts believed that the direct cost of those revenues was negligible.

These strategic partnerships had been attracting both admiration and skepticism from analysts. To some, Amazon was partly adopting the role of a venture capitalist, investing in various early-stage e-commerce companies that it viewed as especially promising. As a principal at Chase Capital Partners said, "If you can lock up the best of breed corporate partners, you can effectively block out the competition."[11] To other analysts, however, there was an illusory quality to these relationships. Amazon had begun to record high-margin advertising revenues from these companies, but the companies as a whole were losing a lot of money.[12] (As the income statements in Exhibit 1 show, Amazon's share of the losses of its equity-method investees in 1999 was $77 million; in the first quarter of 2000, $88 million.)

....

8. Helen Jung, "Amazon Opens Site to Other Merchants," Seattle Times, September 29, 1999.

9. Ibid.

10. Most of these companies were identified in Amazon's financial statements as "equity-method investees." Equity-method accounting applied to investments that gave the investor "significant influence," but not outright control, over an investee. (This was normally assumed to involve ownership of between 20 percent and 50 percent of the investee's common stock.) Once the investment was made, the investing company would record in its financial statements its proportional share of the investee's profit or loss.

11. Stephen Lacey, "Amazon.com: Venture Capital on Steriods," IPO Reporter, March 27, 2000.

12. Gretchen Morgenson, "Bond Market Seems Wary of Amazon," New York Times, February 9, 2000; Herb Greenberg, "More on the Bear Case for Amazon," TheStreet.com, April 27, 2000.

Rationale   What was the business rationale for this dramatic expansion in product offerings? Bezos said that it would allow the company to leverage its "Internet platform." By this he meant the company's growing customer base and brand name, the innovative technology it was developing, and its distribution capabilities. "We believe," the company's Annual Report stated, "that this platform allows us to launch new e-commerce businesses quickly, with a high quality of customer experience, economical incremental cost, and good prospects for success."

Implications of Amazon's Strategy

Bezos said repeatedly that he was committed to placing growth ahead of profitability during the first few years of the company's existence. The key to Amazon's appeal, he believed, would be the high level of customer service it provided, involving huge product selection, easy-to-use search and browse features, personalized shopping services, secure payment protection, and reliable and timely delivery.

Amazon's expansion was also geographic. It could ship products almost anywhere, but in 1999 it also established distinct web sites and distribution facilities in England and Germany.

Thus in mid-2000 Amazon was the largest Internet retailer in the world, with $1.9 billion in trailing twelve-month revenues and 20 million customers in over 150 countries. It claimed to offer for sale 18 million different products (SKUs). And its brand was very well known.

Some observers, however, believed that Amazon was badly overextending itself. In trying to be all things to all people, some people felt, the company was taking on more than it could handle. Al Ries, the author of a book on Internet branding, said:

> *The most powerful brands in the world stand for something simple. Volvo stands for safety. Dell is a personal computer. Even Microsoft is software. Now Amazon is going to stand for books and charcoal grills. This makes no sense to me.* [13]

Since the web was indifferent to distance and place, it was, in the view of some people, better suited to specialist retailers, to "category killers," than to generalists. (For example, eToys specialized in selling toys; CDNow specialized in selling CDs, Outpost.com specialized in selling computers and other electronic products.) Specialist retailers would, in this view, know more about particular categories of products and would be better able to develop the merchandising skills necessary to make their particular businesses successful.

Customer Service

In Jeff Bezos' view, however, what Amazon.com "stood for" was high-quality customer service. And part of the reason why it could provide that, he believed, was that people at Amazon knew more about e-commerce than anyone else. In 1998 the chairman of Putnam/Penguin, one of the largest book publishers in the world, said, "When you talk to Amazon, you realize it's a technology company, not a merchant." [14] Such was the sophistication of the company's software, Bezos claimed, that "coming to Amazon will not be like entering the halls of a huge, soulless department store. It will be more like stopping by at a local shop where your every taste and preference is known." [15] The company had in fact been developing many information-rich features for its web site—for example, product reviews by both outside

13. Quoted in Robert Hof, "Can Amazon Make It?" *Business Week*, July 10, 2000.
14. David Streitfeld, "Booking the Future," *Washington Post*, July 10, 1998.
15. "Amazon's Delta," *The Economist*, November 20, 1999.

Amazon.com in 2000

experts and other Amazon customers, the customer's own purchasing history, "collaborative filtering" software that aimed to provide a kind of electronic word-of-mouth among people with similar tastes, e-mails to alert customers to the release of new products they had asked about, and a means for customers to track the shipment of products they ordered.

Pricing

An academic study, published in April 2000, seemed to support Bezos' view of things.[16] Amazon often engaged in aggressive pricing in order to attract customers, but the academic study found that pricing differences among Internet retail businesses, even for commodity-type products like books and CDs, were as pronounced as they were for conventional retailers and that Internet sites with the lowest prices didn't necessarily have the largest market shares. Amazon, for example, was the leader in online book and CD sales but, this study found, didn't necessarily have the lowest prices. The level of customer satisfaction and customer service it provided was evidently key to its ability to attract customers.

Amazon itself, however, regarded the pricing issue as a threat. "New and expanded web technologies," it said in its 1999 10-K, "may increase the competitive pressures on online retailers. For example, 'shopping agent' technologies permit customers to quickly compare our prices with those of our competitors. This increased competition may reduce our operating margins, diminish our market share, or impair the value of our brand."

A professor of operations and information management, Eric Clemons, writing in the *Financial Times* in June 2000 about particular kinds of risk in the e-commerce world, noted that Amazon, like most e-commerce businesses, was continuing to spend significant amounts of money to acquire new customers, but he wasn't at all sure that that made sense.

> *It is too early to determine if consumers will remain loyal to these sites, allowing these retailers time to harvest profits and cover the costs of their acquisition, or whether the web's empowerment of consumer choice will mean that customers constantly migrate to the lowest-cost online seller. If the web is as liberating and empowering as most accounts have led us to believe, all business models based on paying to acquire share are flawed.[17]*

FINANCING STRATEGY

Amazon had started with private equity financing of about $1 million. It sold $8 million of convertible preferred in 1996 (which was converted to common the following year). The IPO in May 1997 brought in about $50 million. The company had also been receiving cash from employees when they exercised their stock options.

The company had issued debt on three occasions:

- In May 1998 the company sold 10 percent senior discount notes due in 2008. They sold for $326 million, but their value at maturity would be $530 million. They accreted interest until 2003 and paid cash interest after that. (During 1999 the company repurchased $266 million principal amount of this issue [representing $178 million accreted value]. Thus as of year-end 1999, the accreted amount outstanding was $191 million.)
- In February 1999 the company sold $1.25 billion par value of 4.75 percent convertible subordinated notes due in 2009.

---

16. Erik Brynjolfsson, "Frictionless Commerce?" Management Science, *March 2000.*
17. Eric Clemons, "Managing Risk," Financial Times, *June 13, 2000.*

- In February 2000 the company sold €690 ($680 million) par value of 6.875 percent euro-denominated convertible subordinated notes due in 2010.

When this second set of convertibles was issued, observers noted the much higher interest rate that Amazon had to offer compared to the 4.75 percent interest rate it offered on the convertibles it had sold just a year earlier. Some observers also suggested that Amazon had taken the offering to Europe because it had been a tough sell in the United States. The company denied this. It said that it sold this second set of convertibles in Europe because it wanted to broaden its market recognition there. It also said that it intended to use some of the proceeds from the issue to support growth in its European operations. Exhibit 5 shows the company's cash obligations for interest and principal for all of its debt securities over the next ten years.

Thus at the end of the first quarter of 2000, Amazon had $2.15 billion in debt outstanding (including some capital leases), of which about $1.9 billion consisted of the convertibles. The convertibles were rated triple C by both Standard & Poor's and Moody's. A summary of the terms of the two convertible issues is provided in Exhibit 6.

FINANCIAL PERFORMANCE

Exhibit 1 shows Amazon.com's Income Statements, Balance Sheets, and Cash Flow Statements for the last few years. Exhibit 2 gives some data about customers that analysts referred to a fair amount. Exhibit 3 shows segment information for the company for the last three years and for the first quarter of 2000. Exhibit 4 provides information about its fixed assets.

Since its inception the company had recorded total sales of about $3 billion and total losses of $1.2 billion (of which about $350 million was amortization of goodwill and other intangibles). Total cash flows from operations had been a negative $380 million. The stock went public in May 1997 at about $2 a share (split adjusted), peaked at $106 in late 1999, and had declined to $42 just before the Lehman analyst issued his critical report.

Some components of the Income Statement involved accounting policies or had meanings that were somewhat different from what one would expect in most businesses.

Sales

Most of Amazon's sales were product sales. The sales figures also included, however, revenue that the company had begun to record from its "Amazon Commerce Network" partners. Most of the revenue from these companies wasn't coming in the form of cash, however; it was coming in the form of the companies' stock. (As Exhibit 1 cash flow statements show, $18 million of the $20 million of ACN revenues that Amazon recorded during the first quarter of 2000 was non-cash.) What happened essentially was that Amazon would receive a certain amount of these companies' stock when the partnership agreements were signed. The stock would be valued as of that date, recorded initially as unearned revenue, and then later credited to revenue as Amazon provided the related services (space on its web site). If the value of the stock declined, that would be reflected in Amazon's financial statements only when Amazon marked it down as a "permanent impairment."

Marketing and Sales Expense

This included not only standard kinds of marketing and sales expense (e.g., advertising and promotional expenditures and payroll for those functions) but also fulfillment expense. Fulfillment expense, the company said, represented "those costs incurred in operating and staffing distribution and customer service centers, including costs attributable to receiving, inspecting, and warehousing inventories; picking, packaging, and preparing customers' orders for shipment; and responding to inquiries from customers." All of the company's distribution centers were leased, and almost all of them were accounted for as operating leases.

Another key component of Amazon's marketing expenses was what it called its "Associates Program." Many companies were agreeing to place on their web sites a link to Amazon.com—involving, say, a product recommendation—and for every sale that Amazon made as a result of that link, Amazon would pay a referral fee of between 5 and 15 percent. Many Internet businesses were developing this kind of "associate" or "affiliate" marketing, but Amazon had the largest such program, involving (as of early 2000) 430,000 web sites.

Technology and Content

Technology and content expenses consisted primarily of payroll and related expenses for the development of computer software and telecommunications systems, as well as for the acquisition of certain editorial content such as freelance reviews. Technology and content costs, it said, "are generally expensed as incurred, except for certain costs relating to the development of internal-use software that are capitalized and depreciated over estimated useful lives."

In Bezos's view, certain expenditures on technology could reduce fulfillment costs. For example, he said that a lot of customers had been calling the customer service department regarding problems that the company had now enabled them to handle themselves by means of an online software tool.[18]

Amortization of Goodwill and Other Intangibles

Amazon had acquired a number of companies; the acquisitions were generally accounted for as "purchases"; and most of the purchase prices had been allocated to goodwill and other intangible assets. Amazon said that it was amortizing those assets over a period of only two to four years.

Stock Options

Amazon didn't record the cost of stock options in its income statements—which was acceptable under generally accepted accounting standards. However, it disclosed that, had it recorded the fair value of stock options granted (using the Black-Scholes option pricing model), its net profit in 1999 and 1998 would have been $312 million and $70 million lower, respectively.

BUSINESS MODEL

Amazon's business plan, of course, was premised on the expectation that it would ultimately perform better than comparable land-based retailers. Exhibit 7a shows some key operating data for Barnes & Noble and Borders, the two largest land-based book retailers in the United States. (Both of these companies were involved in online bookselling businesses, but those businesses were structured as separate entities. Therefore the data in Exhibit 7a

18. "Newsmaker Q&A," BusinessWeek Online, "Daily Briefing" <http//www.businessweek.com >, June 30, 2000.

Amazon.com in 2000

should reasonably represent the performance of their land-based bookselling operations.) Amazon's aggressive pricing resulted in relatively low gross margins, and Exhibit 7b shows some key operating data for two very successful, land-based retailers that operated with low gross margins. (Wal-Mart was the largest retailer in the world. Costco was the largest operator of discount warehouse stores in the United States.)

Company Guidance

In April, when it reported first quarter 2000 results, the company told analysts that it expected to have positive cash flows from operations for the balance of the calendar year. It said it also expected that its cash flows from operations would fully cover its planned capital expenditures of approximately $250–$300 million and that its cash balance at the end of the calendar year would be about $1 billion. It said that it hoped to reduce fulfillment expense as a percentage of sales from 17 percent in the first quarter to the low teens by the fourth quarter. It also said it expected its operating margin loss (excluding amortization, stock-based compensation, and other special charges) to fall from 21 percent in 1999 to single digits for all of 2000. In addition, Bezos reiterated his intention to continue to invest in new product lines and to expand further in international markets.

ANALYSTS' ASSESSMENT OF AMAZON'S STOCK AND DEBT

During the first few years of Amazon's existence, stock analysts had been groping for ways to value the company's stock. Some analysts assumed certain multiples of sales or earnings for a company of this sort, forecasted sales or earnings figures for Amazon a number of years down the road, and then discounted those values back to the present. Some analysts attempted to calculate the present value of each of Amazon's customers (which involved an extraordinary array of assumptions). Most analysts gave very little attention to cash flows.[19]

An equity analyst at Prudential Securities, however, argued in February 1999 that "one of the appeals of Amazon.com's business model is its cash flow." She pointed out that, since its inception, the company had generated positive cash flow from operations of $30 million, had spent $37 million on capital expenditures, and therefore had had cumulative cash outflow of under $10 million. Thus, she said, the company "has essentially built its business with a net cash outlay of less than $10 million."[20]

Lehman Brothers Report

When a Lehman Brothers analyst, Ravi Suria, sounded his alarm about Amazon's debt in June 2000, he focused almost exclusively on cash flows. He was a debt analyst, and although the upside potential of the debt securities he was dealing with was tied to their convertibility into common stock, he focused his analysis on the company's credit risk.[21]

....

19. For example, in her first report on Amazon in September 1997, Mary Meeker, the soon-to-be very influential analyst of Internet stocks at Morgan Stanley Dean Witter, recommended the stock, but more or less said that it was almost impossible to do a valuation of it. She put together a matrix indicating a whole range of possible valuations based on a variety of assumptions about price-to-sales ratios, net margins, discount rates, and sales figures for the year 2001. She stated, "We have learned that too much focus on valuation can often lead to short-sighted investment errors." (Mary Meeker, "Amazon.com: Initiating Coverage," September 22, 1997.)

20. Amy Ryan, "Amazon.com," Prudential Securities, February 1, 1999.

21. Ravi Suria, op. cit.

"In a best-case scenario," he said, "we believe that the current cash balances will last the company through the first quarter of 2001." "Despite [the company's] much-touted brand identity, first mover advantage, virtual storefronts, hits and visits," he found the company "woefully lacking from an operational aspect."

Suria noted that the company, since it opened for business, had recorded $1.2 billion in accounting losses. More important from his point of view, however, was the fact that its operating cash flows had been negative almost every quarter. Add its capital expenditures to that, and total free cash flows from the fourth quarter of 1997 through the first quarter of 2000 had been a minus $718 million. (Exhibit 8 shows information that he put together.)

So far the company had been supported, in his view, by an extremely forgiving capital market. For every $1 of revenue that the company had generated from the start of 1997 through the first quarter of 2000, he claimed, it had raised $.95 from the capital markets. The total figures he cited were $2.9 billion in revenue during that period and $2.8 billion raised from the capital markets. He defined money raised from the capital markets as consisting of money from the IPO in 1997, cash received from the three debt securities, and cash received from employees' exercise of stock options.

The component of Amazon's financial performance that Suria emphasized more than anything else in his report was what he called "cash flow per unit of product sold." He said, "We believe that the fundamental problem with the operations lies in the fact that Amazon does not generate positive net cash flow per unit of product it sells." The first few times he referred to this he didn't define what he meant, but then later in his report he said, "Our favorite metric for measuring success of a company is to look at its operating cash flow. . . . It is the best measurement of the ability of a retailing business to make money per unit sold." By this measurement, he said, Amazon's performance had been getting worse as time went on. Suria felt there was "a clear correlation between [Amazon's] cash outflows and [its] revenues—indicating operational inefficiencies at the unit sales level."

From his point of view, the most important ingredient in Amazon's cash flow was its management of working capital. Thus he focused on accounts receivable, accounts payable, and inventory.

- *Accounts receivable.* Amazon didn't have any (because customers paid with credit cards). This, he said, was the strongest operating characteristic of the company.
- *Accounts payable.* Amazon, he thought, had become fairly savvy in stretching payables. However, payment of accounts payable in the first quarter of 2000 increased cash outflow by $207 million, and he thought that payables flexibility was likely to decrease for the company.
- *Inventory.* Suria thought this was the biggest problem Amazon faced. The critical period for most retailers, he said, was the fourth and first quarters, the periods tied to peak seasonal sales. Suria calculated Amazon's inventory turnover quarter by quarter, and he also used sales in the numerator (rather than cost of goods) because, he said, of the different accounting conventions used by companies to determine expense classifications. Exhibit 9 shows the inventory turnover figures that he calculated. They had decreased steadily, from 8.5 in the first quarter of 1998 to a low of 2.9 in the first quarter of 2000. More important than the absolute level of inventory turnover, Suria said, was its steady deterioration. This showed that the company wasn't managing its sales growth well.

Then there were, in his view, other problems on the horizon as well: the fact that the company was now selling greater numbers of toys and electronics, which he said were logistically more difficult to handle than books; the presence of an increasing number of old-world retailers in the e-tailing space; Amazon's intention to continue to establish new businesses; a probable slowdown in the economy.

Suria's pessimistic view of Amazon's prospects had to do largely with its business model:

> As the e-tailing model begins to look more and more like standard retailers, the cash flow cycle of the business will track that of an Old Economy retailer. Thus, depending upon the season, working capital either sucks in cash or spins out cash. But, net-net for a successful retailer, the annualized operating cash flow should be consistently positive, especially when the operating costs are not burdened by startup costs that many expanding retailers face in opening new physical locations.[22]

Finally, he pointed out that Amazon had very little financial flexibility. As of the end of the first quarter of 2000, the company's debt to capital ratio was 99 percent. The ratio of debt to tangible capital, however—that is, netting out the large amount of goodwill and other intangibles—was 141 percent. "Going into what is arguably its most challenging holiday season," he said, "we believe that the combination of negative cash flow, poor working capital management, and high debt load in a hyper competitive environment will put the company under extremely high risk."

The company, he said, had to do either one of two things—start becoming cash sufficient, or keep raising capital until it became cash sufficient. He was doubtful about the prospects for either of these two things.

Reactions to the Report

The financial markets reacted immediately to the Lehman Brothers report. The day after it was issued, the prices of the two convertible debt securities dropped 15 percent. The common stock dropped 19 percent, thus losing about $2.8 billion of its market value. Exhibit 10 shows graphs of the prices of Amazon's two convertible debt issues from their issue date through the end of June 2000. Exhibit 11 shows, for the period from the beginning of 1999 through the end of June 2000, the return on Amazon's stock compared to the return on the Nasdaq index.

Amazon's Reaction   A company spokesperson called the Lehman Brothers report "pure hogwash," although he didn't identify any specific facts or assumptions that were wrong. "We are nowhere near running out of cash," he said, "and anybody who understands the cash flow dynamics of our company understands that."[23]

Bezos said the report was "baloney." When asked why the company, then, wasn't profitable, Bezos said that the books, music, and video segment was now showing an operating profit but that, at the same time, the company was investing in a lot of young businesses. "It would have been easy to make the business profitable at much lower revenue levels," he said, "but we wouldn't have had the opportunity to build an important and lasting company." Bezos said the argument had been made innumerable times that the company was buying products for a dollar and selling them for 90 cents. He said that wasn't the case. He said the company was selling dollar bills for $1.20 but that the reason it wasn't profitable was that it was investing in a lot of new things.[24]

---

22. *Ibid.*
23. "Irrational Over-reaction," Business Line, July 5, 2000.
24. "Newsmaker Q&A," BusinessWeek Online, "Daily Briefing" <http//www.businessweek.com >, June 30, 2000.

Barron's Alan Abelson, in his "Up and Down Wall Street" column in *Barron's* on June 26, called the Lehman Brothers report "brilliant, thorough, and very well crafted." He also said it was "miraculously free of the gibberish and webbygook that ooze from virtually all the brokerage stuff churned out on anything tech and everything Internet." Abelson noted that "Amazon has inspired comment in [*Barron's*] on a number of occasions in the past few years, and we have been consistently underwhelmed by the company and its prospects . . . . Indeed, the first truly penetrating dissection of Amazon appeared in [*Barron's*] in January 1999." (The article was entitled "Bubble Trouble" and the byline for it was "Alan Abelson and Rhonda Brammer.") He said that the thrust of that article was that "the company's fabled business plan had been anticipated by the pig farmer who lost 50 bucks on every pig he sold but was confident of making it up in volume." The article, he said, had essentially argued that "it was a reasonably safe bet that Amazon would never make any money." And he said that that, in a sense, was the core of the Lehman Brothers report.[25]

Business Week *Business Week* ran a long article providing a more mixed reaction.[26] It restated the key arguments and figures that the Lehman analyst had presented, said that this was "scary stuff," and noted that timing now was critical. The sharp downturn that had occurred in the stocks of many Internet companies "means that Amazon's access to new capital will likely be cut off now, so the clock is ticking." The article also raised questions about Amazon's whole "one-stop shopping mentality" (selling everything from books to charcoal grills) and what some people considered the over-extension of its brand.

   On the other hand, it pointed out various positive trends. The company's operating losses (excluding special items like amortization and stock-based compensation) declined from 26 percent in the fourth quarter of 1999 to 17 percent in the first quarter of 2000. The company, it said, was evidently able to move customers quickly to new product offerings—for example, the company became the largest seller of CDs after only four months—and both its repeat business as a percentage of total business and the average dollar sale per customer were increasing (see Exhibit 2). It also noted the view of some people that the Lehman analyst made the mistake of "focusing on the one year of Amazon's greatest expansion and projecting those costs forward into the future."

Other Analysts Mary Meeker, the influential analyst of Internet stocks at Morgan Stanley Dean Witter, reiterated her "buy" recommendation but sounded a note of caution. She said she thought the year-end holiday season could be a make-or-break time for the company.[27] Most stock analysts reiterated their "buy" recommendation. That included the equity analyst at Lehman Brothers.

   The analyst at Salomon Smith Barney, Tim Albright, said he thought the concerns about Amazon's running out of cash were way overblown. He projected revenues for the company of $3.0 billion in 2000 and $4.9 billion in 2001. He also expected the company to lose $342 in cash from March 2000 through March 2001 but to generate $93 million in cash flow from March 2001 through March 2002, thus ending the March 2001 and 2002 quarters with $666 million and $757 million in cash, respectively. He said that even when he stress-tested his cash flow model for lower inventory turnover and higher payables turnover, the company would still have plenty of cash on hand at the end of both periods.[28]

   The chief executive of an e-commerce company based in Seattle said in early July that he thought Amazon had the best chance of surviving the e-tailing shakeout but that it

25. Alan Abelson, "Virtual Disaster," Barron's, June 26, 2000.

26. Robert Hof, op. cit.

27. Frances Katz, "Fear Spurs Amazon Drop," Atlanta Journal and Constitution, June 24, 2000.

28. Tim Albright, "Amazon.com," Salomon Smith Barney, July 13, 2000.

might have to drastically revise its business model in the face of competition from real-world retailers like Wal-Mart. "The economics haven't proven their way out yet," he said. "It's a tough issue. I come down on either side of it on any given day. It's going to be a wait and see thing."[29]

LATER DEVELOPMENTS

Exhibit 12 shows Amazon's income statements, balance sheets, and cash flow statements through the first quarter of 2001. Ravi Suria's claim in June 2000 that "in a best-case scenario…the current cash balances will last the company through the first quarter of 2001" didn't pan out. At the end of the first quarter of 2001 Amazon had total cash and marketable securities of $643 million.

In August 2000 Amazon transferred much of the management and risk of its toys business to Toys "R" Us—an established bricks and mortar retailer that had entered the online world the previous year. Amazon sold all of its toys inventory to Toys "R" Us (for $29 million). The web site for Toys "R" Us, however, became part of Amazon's web site. Per an agreement that the two companies reached, Toys "R" Us would purchase and own all of the inventory for the toys business, and Amazon would provide the necessary customer service, order fulfillment, and warehousing, for which it would receive from Toys "R" Us a combination of fixed payments and variable payments related to sales volume.

In the second half of 2000, two of the online retailers with which Amazon had had "strategic relationships" closed down. One was Living.com, which had been selling furniture and other home products and in which Amazon had invested about $10 million. The other was Pets.com, which had been selling pet supplies and in which Amazon had invested $58 million. Both companies had attempted to raise additional capital to keep going but were unable to do so.

In January 2001 Amazon indicated that although 2000 sales were 68 percent higher than prior year's sales, they had fallen short of expectations, and it announced the closure of one of its distribution facilities in the U.S. and the partial closure of another. (Prior to the announcement the company had been operating eight distribution centers in the U.S.) It also announced the streamlining of various departments, which involved laying off about 1,300 employees. (At the end of 2000 it had employed about 9,000 people.) These moves produced restructuring charges in the first quarter of 2001 of $114 million (classified as "Impairment-related and other" in its income statement).

The company's securities continued to decline. From the end of June 2000 to the end of April 2001, its stock price fell about 58 percent, and the prices of its convertible debt issues fell about 20 percent (to about 50 percent of par). Market analysts were divided on whether Amazon would fall prey to the ongoing Internet retailing shakeout, or would be an exception to the trend and emerge as a winner.

QUESTIONS

1. What is your assessment of the long-term viability of Amazon's business model?

2. Do you agree with Ravi Suria's analysis of the credit risks associated with Amazon's bonds?

3. Why did the markets (both bond and stock) react so significantly to Suria's report?

---

29. Scott Hillis, "Amazon Turns 5, But Some Doubt It Will Survive," Toronto Star, July 17, 2000.

EXHIBIT 1

Amazon.com Financial Statements

INCOME STATEMENTS
($ millions)

	1997 Full year	1998 Full year	1999 Full year	2000 1st qtr.
Sales[a]	148	610	1,640	574
Cost of sales[b]	(119)	(476)	(1,349)	(446)
Gross profit	29	134	291	128
Operating expenses				
Marketing and sales[c]	(40)	(133)	(413)	(140)
Technology & content	(14)	(46)	(160)	(61)
General & administrative	(7)	(16)	(70)	(26)
Stock-based compensation	(1)	(2)	(31)	(14)
Amortization of goodwill and other intangibles	0	(42)	(215)	(83)
Merger, acquisition, & invest-ment-related costs	0	(4)	(8)	(2)
Operating loss	(33)	(109)	(606)	(198)
Interest expense	—	(27)	(84)	(27)
Interest income	2	14	45	10
Other income (expense), net	0	0	2	(5)
	(31)	(122)	(643)	(220)
Equity in losses of equity-method investees	—	(3)	(77)	(88)
Net loss	(31)	(125)	(720)	(308)
Average number of shares o/s (millions)	261	296	327	344

a. Revenues consisted primarily of sales to customers. However, beginning in 2000 a portion represented advertising revenue from the Amazon.com Commerce Network (ACN) ($20 million in the first quarter of 2000).

b. Cost of sales consisted of the cost of merchandise sold, the cost of inbound and outbound shipping charges, and the cost of packaging materials. One special charge was an inventory writedown of $39 million in the 4th quarter of 1999.

c. The two largest components were advertising and fulfillment expenses. Advertising expense in full-year 1999, 1998, and 1997 was $141 million, $60 million, and $21 million respectively. Fulfillment expense in full-year 1999, 1998, and 1997 was $188 million, $50 million, and $12 million, respectively. During the first quarters of 2000 and 1999 it was $100 million and $34 million, respectively.

Source: Company 10-Ks and 10-Qs.

Amazon.com in 2000

Amazon.com in 2000

BALANCE SHEETS
($ millions)

	1997	1998	1999	2000
	31-Dec	31-Dec	31-Dec	31-Mar
Current assets				
Cash & marketable securities	125	373	706	1,009
Inventories	9	30	221	172
Prepaid expenses etc.	3	21	85	90
Cash & marketable securities	137	424	1,012	1,271
Fixed assets	10	30	318	335
Goodwill & other purchased intangibles		179	730	647
Investments		7	371	422
Other	2	8	40	55
Total assets	149	648	2,471	2,730
Current liabilities				
Accounts payble	33	113	463	256
Accrued expenses & other current liabilities	10	48	207	161
Unearned revenue	—	—	55	134
Current portion of long-term debt	1	1	14	16
	44	162	739	567
Long-term debt	77	348	1,466	2,137
Stockholders' equity				
Common stock	66	300	1,148	1,216
Accumulated deficit	(38)	(162)	(882)	(1,190)
	28	138	266	26
Total liabilities & stockholders equity	149	648	2,471	2,730

Source: Company 10-Ks and 10-Qs.

CASH FLOW STATEMENTS
($ millions)

	1997	1998	1999		2000
	Full year	Full year	4th qtr.	Full year	1st qtr.
Operating activities					
Net loss	(31)	(125)	(324)	(720)	(308)
Depreciation & amortization of fixed assets	3	10		37	18
Amort. of deferred stock-based compensation	2	2		31	14
Equity in losses of equity-method investees	—	3		77	88
Amortization of goodwill and other intangibles	—	43		215	83
Non-cash interest expense	—	24		29	6
Non-cash revenue for advertising & promotional services	—	—		(6)	(18)
Other	—	2		17	(1)
	(26)	(41)	(171)	(320)	(118)
Changes in operating assets and liabilities, net of effects from acquisitions					
Inventories	(8)	(21)	(83)	(172)	48
Prepaid expenses and other current assets	(3)	(17)	(27)	(60)	3
Accounts payable	30	79	208	330	(207)
Accrued expenses and other current liabilities	8	31	90	107	(37)
Interest payable	—	—	15	25	(9)
	27	72	203	230	(202)
Net cash provided (used) in operating activities	1	31	31	(90)	(320)
Investing activities					
Sales of marketable securities	4	332		4,025	1,014
Purchases of marketable securities	(122)	(547)		(4,290)	(1,333)
Purchase of fixed assets	(8)	(28)		(287)	(27)
Acquisitions and investments in businesses, net of cash acquired	—	(19)		(370)	(47)
Net cash used in investing activities	(126)	(262)		(922)	(393)

(continued)

CASH FLOW STATEMENTS *(continued)*

	1997 Full year	1998 Full year	1999 4th qtr.	1999 Full year	2000 1st qtr.
Financing activities					
Proceeds from long-term debt	75	326		1,264	679
Repayment of long-term debt	—	(78)		(189)	(4)
Financing costs and other	(2)	(8)		(35)	(16)
Proceeds from issuance of capital stock and exercise of stock options[a]	53	14		64	21
Net cash provided by financing activities	126	254		1,104	680
Net increase (decrease) in cash	1	23		92	(33)
Cash at beginning of period	1	2		25	117
Cash at end of period	2	25		117	84
Supplemental cash flow information:					
Stock issued in connection with business acquisitions	—	217		774	—
Equity securities for unearned Amazon Commerce Network services	—	—		54	98
Cash paid for interest	—	27		60	—

a. *Proceeds from the exercise of stock options were $68 million and $6 million in 1999 and 1998, respectively. In 1997 the company received approximately $50 million through its IPO.*

Source: Company 10-Ks and 10-Qs.

Amazon.com in 2000

EXHIBIT 2

Amazon.com Customer Data

	1997	1998	1999					2000
	Full year	Full year	1st qtr.	2nd qtr	3rd qtr.	4th qtr.	Full year	1st qtr.
No. of customer accounts	1,510,000	6,200,000	8,400,000	10,700,000	13,100,000	16,900,000	16,900,000	20,000,000
No. of new customers	1,375,000	4,690,000	2,200,000	2,300,000	2,400,000	3,800,000	10,700,000	3,100,000
Average sale per customer in trailing 12-month period			$108			$116		$121
Orders from repeat customers as percent of all orders			66%			73%		76%
Customer acquisition cost[a]			$13	$19	$14	$19		$13

a. Customer acquisition cost was a metric used by a good many analysts of e-commerce businesses. For Amazon, analysts calculated it by dividing total sales and marketing costs (excluding fulfillment costs) by the number of new customers acquired during a given period of time. (This assumes that sales and marketing costs relate solely to new customers.) Studies done by The Boston Group and Forrester Research concluded that the average customer acquisition cost in the e-commerce world in 1999 was about $40.

Sources: Company reports; estimates by Morgan Stanely Dean Witter, Merrill Lynch, Robertson Stephens; various press reports.

Amazon.com in 2000

Amazon.com in 2000

EXHIBIT 3

Amazon.com Segment Information

($ millions)	U.S. books, music, and DVD/video	Inter-national	Early-stage businesses and other	Consoli-dated
2000 (first quarter)				
Revenues from external customers	401	75	97	574
Gross profit (loss)	83	16	29	128
Segment loss	(2)	(27)	(69)	(99)
Other operating expenses	—			(99)
Net interest expense and other	—	—	—	(22)
Equity in losses of equity-method investees	—	—	—	(88)
Net loss				(308)
1999				
Revenues from external customers	1,308	168	164	1,640
Gross profit (loss)	263	35	(8)	291
Segment loss	(31)	(79)	(242)	(352)
Other operating expenses	—	—	—	(253)
Net interest expense and other	—	—	—	(38)
Equity in losses of equity-method investees	—	—	—	(77)
Net loss				(720)
1998				
Revenues from external customers	588	22	—	610
Gross profit	129	5	—	134
Segment loss	(35)	(25)	—	(61)
Other operating expenses	—	—	—	(48)
Interest expense, net	—	—	—	(12)
Equity in losses of equity-method investees	—	—	—	(3)
Net loss				(125)
1997				
Revenues from external customers	148	—	—	148
Gross profit	29	—	—	29
Segment loss	(31)	—	—	(31)
Other operating expenses	(1)	—	—	(1)
Interest income, net	1	—	—	1
Equity in losses of equity-method investees	—	—	—	—
Net loss				(31)

Notes:

• *"Early-stage businesses" includes electronics, software, video games, toys, home improvement products, "market-place services," and the "Amazon Commerce Network."*

• *"Other operating expenses" include amortization of goodwill and other intangibles, acquisition- and investment-related costs, and stock-based compensation.*

Source: Company 10-K and 10-Q.

EXHIBIT 4

Amazon.com: Fixed Assets

($ millions)	Dec. 31	
	1999	1998
Computers, equipment, and software[a]	187	36
Leasehold improvements	44	6
Leased assets	52	—
Construction in progress	83	2
	366	44
Less accumulated depreciation and amortization	(49)	(14)
Fixed assets, net	317	30

a. *Consists mostly of servers, storage, and telecom systems.*

Source: Company 10-K.

EXHIBIT 5

Cash Obligations for Debt: Interest plus Repayment of Principal

Year	10% discount notes due 2008	4.75% convertible notes due 2009	6.875% convertible notes due 2010	Total ($ millions)
2000	0	59	0	59
2001	0	59	47	106
2002	0	59	47	106
2003	26	59	47	132
2004	26	59	47	132
2005	26	59	47	132
2006	26	59	47	132
2007	26	59	47	132
2008	290	59	47	396
2009		1,309	47	1,356
2010			727	727

Note: The 6.875% notes are euro-denominated. Dollar proceeds from the issue in 2000 were $680, and the above interest and repayment amounts assume that the exchange rate between the Euro and dollar is unchanged. The indenture of the issue, however, doesn't fix the exchange rate.

Source: 10-K and 10-Qs.

EXHIBIT 6

Summary of Terms of Amazon's Convertible Notes

Terms Common to Both Issues

- Rank equally, but are subordinate to all existing and future senior debt, including trade payables of subsidiaries. "As of December 31, 1999, we had approximately $901 million of indebtedness that constituted senior indebtedness."

- Unsecured.

- "The indenture does not contain any financial covenants and does not restrict us from paying dividends, incurring indebtedness, or issuing or repurchasing our other securities. The indenture does not protect you in the event of a highly leveraged transaction or a change in control except in limited circumstances."

- "We may from time to time reduce the conversion price [by any amount]...if our board of directors has made a determination that this reduction would be in our best interests."

Terms Specific to 4.75% Convertible Notes

- Pay interest semi-annually.

- Convertible to 12.816 common shares; the conversion price was therefore $78.03.

- Redeemable by the company after 2002 at fairly standard redemption prices involving small premiums. Prior to 2002 the company could redeem them at par if the company's average stock price for a certain number of days exceeded 150% of the conversion price. If the company did so, however, it would have to pay a significant penalty (approximately $208 for every $1,000 note).

Terms Specific to 6.875% Convertible Notes

- Pay interest annually.

- Convertible to 9.529 common shares; the conversion price was therefore €104.94. Included a sweetener—reset provisions that would lower the conversion price in February 2001 and February 2002 if the company's stock price fell. (Specifically, the conversion price would be lowered if the euro-equivalent of the average stock price for a certain number of days was below €104.94. The conversion price couldn't, however, be reset below €84.883.)

- Redeemable by the company after 2003 at par. Prior to 2003 the company could withdraw the conversion rights altogether if the company's average stock price for a certain number of days exceeded 160% of the initially stated conversion price (thus €167.92). If the company did so, however, it would have to pay a significant penalty (approximately €200 for every €1,000 note).

- Exchange ratio between the euro and the dollar not fixed.

Sources: Form S-3, dated 3/15/99; Form 8-K, dated 2/14/00.

EXHIBIT 7

Key Operating Data for Leading Retailers

A. THE TWO LARGEST LAND-BASED BOOK RETAILERS

	1999	1998	1997
Barnes & Noble			
Total sales (billions)	$3.5	$3.0	$2.8
Total selling space in retail stores (millions of square feet)	15.1	13.8	
Gross margin	39%	39%	39%
Ordinary overhead expenses as percent of sales	33%	33%	33%
ROE	16%	15%	
ROE excluding goodwill	22%	18%	
Inventory turnover	2.1	2.0	
Ratio of inventory to accounts payable (year-end)	1.8	1.9	
Borders			
Total sales (billions)	$3.0	$2.6	$2.3
Total selling space in retail stores (millions of square feet)	11.6	9.5	
Gross margin	39%	39%	39%
Ordinary overhead expenses as percent of sales	34%	33%	33%
ROE	12%	14%	
ROE excluding goodwill	14%	16%	
Inventory turnover	1.7	1.7	
Ratio of inventory to accounts payable (year-end)	1.9	1.7	

Notes:
- Inventory turnover is an annualized figure calculated in the customary way: cost of goods sold divided by the average of beginning and ending inventory balances.
- Gross margin, overhead expense, and inventory turnover involve estimates made by the casewriter to make those figures comparable to Amazon. The problem is that Barnes & Noble and Borders include "occupancy costs" (i.e., rent, CAM charges, etc.) with cost of goods sold, and the estimates reassign occupancy costs to ordinary overhead expense.
- In addition to selling space in retail stores, Barnes & Noble and Borders each had about 1 million square feet of space in its distribution centers (from which it shipped merchandise to retail stores).

Source: Company 10-Ks.

Amazon.com in 2000

B. TWO FINANCIALLY SUCCESSFUL COMPANIES WITH LOW GROSS MARGINS

	1999	1998	1997
Wal-Mart			
Total sales (billions)	$165	$138	$118
Gross margin	21%	21%	21%
Ordinary overhead expenses as percent of sales	16%	16%	16%
ROE	24%	22%	
Inventory turnover	7	6	
Ratio of inventory to accounts payable (year-end)	1.5	1.7	
Costco			
Total sales (billions)	$27	$24	$22
Gross margin	12%	12%	12%
Ordinary overhead expenses as percent of sales	9%	9%	9%
ROE	16%	17%	
Inventory turnover	12	12	
Ratio of inventory to accounts payable (year-end)	1.2	1.2	

Notes:

• *Inventory turnover is an annualized figure calculated in the customary way: cost of goods sold divided by the average of beginning and ending inventory balances.*

• *Neither of these companies had any significant amount of goodwill on their balance sheets.*

Source: Company 10-Ks.

EXHIBIT 8

Lehman Brothers Information: Amazon's Cash Flows

| | $ millions | | |
Quarter	Operating Cash Flow	Capital Expenditures	Free Cash Flows
Dec-97	7	(3)	4
Mar-98	(7)	(2)	(9)
Jun-98	2	(6)	(4)
Sep-98	(3)	(11)	(14)
Dec-98	39	(10)	29
Mar-99	(17)	(19)	(36)
Jun-99	(30)	(92)	(122)
Sep-99	(75)	(71)	(146)
Dec-99	31	(105)	(74)
Mar-00	(320)	(27)	(347)
	(373)	(346)	(719)

Source: Ravi Suria (Lehman Brothers), op. cit.

EXHIBIT 9

Lehman Brothers Information: Amazon's Inventory Turnover

Quarter	Inventory Turnover
Mar-98	8.5
Jun-98	8.1
Sep-98	8.3
Dec-98	10.3
Mar-99	7.9
Jun-99	6.0
Sep-99	4.0
Dec-99	4.0
Mar-00	2.9

Source: Ravi Suria (Lehman Brothers), op. cit.

Amazon.com in 2000

EXHIBIT 10

Amazon's Convertible Notes

A. 4.75% NOTE

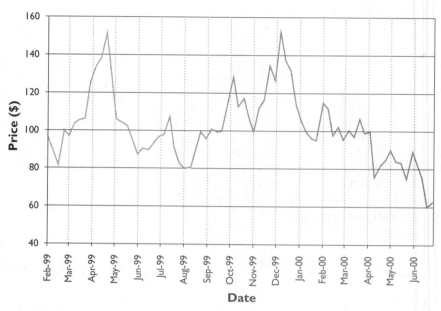

Source: Bloomberg.

B. 6.875% NOTE

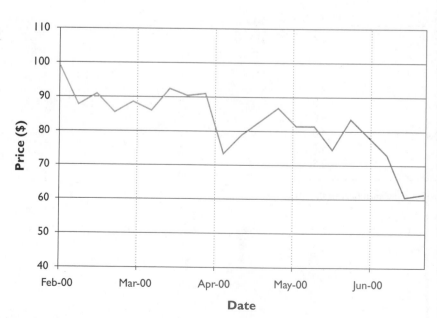

Source: Bloomberg.

EXHIBIT 11

Return on Amazon's Stock Compared to Nasdaq Index

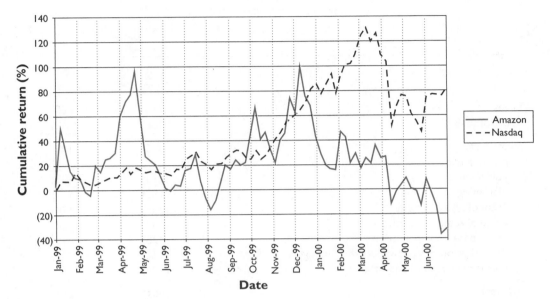

Source: Bloomberg.

EXHIBIT 12

Amazon.com Financial Statements

INCOME STATEMENTS
($ millions)

	2000 Full year	2001 1st qtr.
Sales	2,762	700
Cost of sales	(2,106)	(518)
Gross profit	656	182
Operating expenses		
Fulfillment	(415)	(98)
Marketing	(180)	(37)
Technology & content	(269)	(70)
General & administrative	(109)	(26)
Stock-based compensation	(25)	(3)
Amortization of goodwill & other intangibles	(322)	(51)
Impairment-related and other	(200)	(114)
Operating loss	(864)	(217)
Interest expense	(131)	(34)
Interest income	41	10
Other income (expense), net	(10)	(4)
Non-cash gains and losses, net	(142)	34
Net interest expense and other	(242)	6
Loss before equity in losses of equity-method investees	(1,106)	(211)
Equity in losses of equity-method investees	(305)	(13)
Loss before change in accounting	(1,411)	(224)
Cumulative effect of change in accounting principle	—	(10)
Net loss	(1,411)	(234)
Average number of shares o/s (millions)	351	357

Source: Company 10-Ks and 10-Qs.

BALANCE SHEETS
($ millions)

	2000 Dec. 31	2001 31-Mar
Current assets		
Cash	823	447
Marketable securities	278	196
Inventories	174	156
Prepaid expenses etc.	86	57
	1,361	856
Fixed assets	367	304
Goodwill & other purchased intangibles	255	204
Investments in equity-method investees	52	23
Other equity investments	40	29
Other	60	54
Total assets	2,135	1,470
Current liabilities		
Accounts payble	485	257
Accrued expenses & other current liabilities	342	234
Unearned revenue	131	94
Current portion of long-term debt	17	19
	975	604
Long-term debt	2,127	2,119
Stockholders' equity		
Common stock	1,326	1,274
Accumulated deficit	(2,293)	(2,527)
	(967)	(1,253)
Total liabilities & stockholders equity	2,135	1,470

Source: Company 10-Ks and 10-Qs.

Amazon.com in 2000

CASH FLOW STATEMENTS
($ millions)

	2000	2001
	Full year	1st qtr.
Operating activities		
Net loss	(1,411)	(234)
Depreciation and amortization of fixed assets	84	23
Amort. of deferred stock-based compensation	25	3
Equity in losses of equity-method investees	305	13
Amortization of goodwill and other intangibles	322	51
Impairment-related and other	200	62
Amortization of previously unearned revenue	(108)	(33)
Non-cash investment gains and losses, net	143	(34)
Non-cash interest expense and other	25	7
Cumulative effect of change in accounting principle	—	10
	(415)	(132)
Changes in operating assets and liabilities		
Inventories	46	20
Prepaid expenses and other current assets	(9)	27
Accounts payable	22	(230)
Accrued expenses and other current liabilities	94	(58)
Unearned revenue	98	18
Interest payable	34	(52)
	285	(275)
Net cash provided (used) in operating activities	(130)	(407)
Investing activities		
Sales of marketable securities	546	94
Purchases of marketable securities	(184)	(30)
Purchase of fixed assets	(135)	(19)
Investments in equity-method investees and other investments	(63)	—
Net cash used in investing activities	164	45
Financing activities		
Proceeds from long-term debt	681	10
Repayment of long-term debt	(17)	(5)
Financing costs and other	(16)	—
Proceeds from issuance of capital stock and exercise of stock options	45	6
Net cash provided by financing activities	693	11
Effect of exchange-rate changes on cash	(38)	(24)
Net increase (decrease) in cash	689	(375)
Cash at beginning of period	133	822
Cash at end of period	822	447
Supplemental cash flow information:		
Stock issued in connection with business acqs.	32	—
Fixed assets acquired under financing agreements	9	2
Equity securities received for commercial agreements	107	—
Cash paid for interest	92	86

Source: Company 10-Ks and 10-Qs.

CHAPTER 11

Mergers and Acquisitions

Mergers and acquisitions have long been a popular form of corporate investment, particularly in countries with Anglo-American forms of capital markets. There is no question that these transactions provide a healthy return to target stockholders. However, their value to acquiring shareholders is less understood. Many skeptics point out that given the hefty premiums paid to target stockholders, acquisitions tend to be negative-valued investments for acquiring stockholders.[1]

A number of questions can be examined using financial analysis for mergers and acquisitions:

- Securities analysts can ask: Does a proposed acquisition create value for the acquiring firm's stockholders?
- Risk arbitrageurs can ask: What is the likelihood that a hostile takeover offer will ultimately succeed, and are there other potential acquirers likely to enter the bidding?
- Acquiring management can ask: Does this target fit our business strategy? If so, what is it worth to us, and how can we make an offer that can be successful?
- Target management can ask: Is the acquirer's offer a reasonable one for our stockholders? Are there other potential acquirers that would value our company more than the current bidder?
- Investment bankers can ask: How can we identify potential targets that are likely to be a good match for our clients? And how should we value target firms when we are asked to issue fairness opinions?

In this chapter we focus primarily on the use of financial statement data and analysis directed at evaluating whether a merger creates value for the acquiring firm's stockholders. However, our discussion can also be applied to these other merger contexts. The topic of whether acquisitions create value for acquirers focuses on evaluating motivations for acquisitions, the pricing of offers, and the methods of financing, as well as assessing the likelihood that an offer will be successful. Throughout the chapter we use Exxon's merger with Mobil in 1999 to illustrate how financial analysis can be used in a merger context.[2]

MOTIVATION FOR MERGER OR ACQUISITION

There are a variety of reasons that firms merge or acquire other firms. Some acquiring managers may want to increase their own power and prestige. Others, however, realize that business combinations provide an opportunity to create new economic value for their stockholders. New value can be created in the following ways:

1. *Taking advantage of economies of scale.* Mergers are often justified as a means of providing the two participating firms with increased economies of scale. Economies of scale arise when one firm can perform a function more efficiently than two. For example, Exxon and Mobil are both major oil firms with considerable overlap in production and administrative facilities. The merger was expected to provide operating synergies from eliminating duplicate facilities and excess capacity, and from reducing general and administrative costs. At the time of the merger, management estimated that it would save $730 million by cutting roughly 9,000 jobs and closing offices,

an additional $1.15 billion by trimming business overlap, and that sharing exploration, procurement budgets, and technology could save another $780 million. All told, the management stated that it could realize cost savings of about $2.8 billion per year through the merger.

2. *Improving target management.* Another common motivation for acquisition is to improve target management. A firm is likely to be a target if it has systematically underperformed its industry. Historical poor performance could be due to bad luck, but it could also be due to the firm's managers making poor investment and operating decisions, or deliberately pursuing goals which increase their personal power but cost stockholders.

3. *Combining complementary resources.* Firms may decide that a merger will create value by combining complementary resources of the two partners. For example, a firm with a strong research and development unit could benefit from merging with a firm that has a strong distribution unit. In the Exxon-Mobil merger, the two firms appeared to have complementary capabilities and resources. Exxon had a reputation for conservative financial management, reflected in successful cost-cutting efforts and modest financial leverage. However, its oil reserves had been growing only modestly, with an average five-year reserve replacement ratio of only 102 percent. In contrast, Mobil was touted as one of the leading exploration firms, with a five-year reserve replacement ratio of 147 percent, a 25 percent stake in the important Tengiz oil field, and extensive reserves elsewhere in the world.

4. *Capturing tax benefits.* In the U.S. the 1986 Tax Reform Act eliminated many of the tax benefits from mergers and acquisitions. However, several merger tax benefits remain. The major benefit is the acquisition of operating tax losses. If a firm does not expect to earn sufficient profits to fully utilize operating loss carryforward benefits, it may decide to buy another firm which is earning profits. The operating losses and loss carryforwards of the acquirer can then be offset against the target's taxable income.[3] A second tax benefit often attributed to mergers is the tax shield that comes from increasing leverage for the target firm. This was particularly relevant for leveraged buyouts in the 1980s.[4]

5. *Providing low-cost financing to a financially constrained target.* If capital markets are imperfect, perhaps because of information asymmetries between management and outside investors, firms can face capital constraints. Information problems are likely to be especially severe for newly formed, high-growth firms. These firms can be difficult for outside investors to value since they have short track records, and their financial statements provide little insight into the value of their growth opportunities. Further, since they typically have to rely on external funds to finance their growth, capital market constraints for high-growth firms are likely to affect their ability to undertake profitable new projects. Public capital markets are therefore likely to be costly sources of funds for these types of firms. An acquirer that understands the business and is willing to provide a steady source of finance may therefore be able to add value.[5]

6. *Increasing product-market rents.* Firms also can have incentives to merge to increase product-market rents. By merging and becoming a dominant firm in the industry, two smaller firms can collude to restrict their output and raise prices, thereby increasing their profits. This circumvents problems that arise in cartels of independent firms, where firms have incentives to cheat on the cartel and increase their output.

While product-market rents make sense for firms as a motive for merging, the two partners are unlikely to announce their intentions when they explain the merger to their investors, since most countries have antitrust laws which regulate mergers between two firms in the same industry. For example, in the U.S. there are three major antitrust statutes—The Sherman Act of 1890, The Clayton Act of 1914, and The Hart Scott Rodino Act of 1976.

Anti-competitive concerns were significant for the Exxon-Mobil merger since Exxon and Mobil were the largest and second-largest U.S. oil producers, respectively. Merger approval was required by both the U.S. Federal Trade Commission (FTC) and the European Commission. Both did eventually approve the merger but required the new firm to sell assets in certain businesses and regions to preserve competition.

While many of the motivations for acquisitions are likely to create new economic value for shareholders, some are not. Firms that are flush with cash but have few new profitable investment opportunities are particularly prone to using their surplus cash to make acquisitions. Stockholders of these firms would probably prefer that managers pay out any surplus or "free" cash flows as dividends, or use the funds to repurchase their firm's stock. However, these options reduce the size of the firm and the assets under management's control. Management may therefore prefer to invest the free cash flows to buy new companies, even if they are not valued by stockholders. Of course managers will never announce that they are buying a firm because they are reluctant to pay out funds to stockholders. They may explain the merger using one of the motivations discussed above, or they may argue that they are buying the target at a bargain price.

Another motivation for mergers that is valued by managers but not stockholders is diversification. Diversification was a popular motivation for acquisitions in the 1960s and early 1970s. Acquirers sought to dampen their earnings volatility by buying firms in unrelated businesses. Diversification as a motive for acquisitions has since been widely discredited. Modern finance theorists point out that in a well functioning capital market, investors can diversify for themselves and do not need managers to do so for them. In addition, diversification has been criticized for leading firms to lose sight of their major competitive strengths and to expand into businesses where they do not have expertise.[6]

Key Analysis Questions

In evaluating a proposed merger, analysts are interested in determining whether the merger creates new wealth for acquiring and target stockholders, or whether it is motivated by managers' desires to increase their own power and prestige. Key questions for financial analysis are likely to include:

- *What is the motivation(s) for an acquisition and any anticipated benefits disclosed by acquirers or targets?*
- *What are the industries of the target and acquirer?* Are the firms related horizontally or vertically? How close are the business relations between them? If the businesses are unrelated, is the acquirer cash-rich and reluctant to return free cash flows to stockholders?
- *What are the key operational strengths of the target and the acquirer?* Are these strengths complementary? For example, does one firm have a renowned research group and the other a strong distribution network?
- *Is the acquisition a friendly one, supported by target management, or hostile?* A hostile takeover is more likely to occur for targets with poor-performing management who oppose the acquisition to preserve its job. However, as discussed below, this typically reduces acquirer management's access to information about the target, increasing risk of overpayment.

- *What is the premerger performance of the two firms?* Performance metrics are likely to include ROE, gross margins, general and administrative expenses to sales, and working capital management ratios. On the basis of these measures, is the target a poor performer in its industry, implying that there are opportunities for improved management? Is the acquirer in a declining industry and searching for new directions?
- *What is the tax position of both firms?* What are the average and marginal current tax rates for the target and the acquirer? Does the acquirer have operating loss carryforwards and the target taxable profits?

This analysis should help the analyst understand what specific benefits, if any, the merger is likely to generate.

Motivation for the Exxon-Mobil Merger

Several industry factors influenced Exxon and Mobil to merge. Since the OPEC oil embargo of 1973, the oil industry had been subjected to wide price fluctuations that increased exploration risks. For example, real prices per barrel increased from $11.83 in 1973 to $50.94 in 1981 and then declined precipitously to $16.61 per barrel in 1986. Between 1987 and 1998, prices continued to fluctuate wildly, with a low of $10.53 in 1998 and a high of $23.15 in 1990. In addition to pricing risks, oil companies faced significant political risks in exploration since much of their reserves were located in politically volatile countries, where private property rights were subject to change.

The industry responded to these challenges by adopting cost reduction programs. From 1980 to 1992, employment at eight major oil companies declined by 63 percent, from 800,000 to 300,000. Headquarters staff at six of the largest firms declined from 3,000 to 800 in the period 1988 to 1992. In addition, companies sought to increase flexibility by leasing rather than owning tankers. But as prices continued to plummet in the late 1990s, oil companies sought other ways to increase efficiency.

The outcome was a series of large mergers and acquisitions that transformed the industry: BP merged with Amoco in 1998 and acquired Arco the following year; Total, a French oil firm, acquired the large Belgian oil firm Petrofina in late 1998 and subsequently purchased Elf Acquitaine in a $49 billion hostile takeover; Texaco was acquired by Chevron in 2000; and Phillips Petroleum acquired Tosco in early 2001, and late during the same year agreed to merge with Conoco.

The management of Exxon and Mobil argued that a merger would provide the new company with three significant benefits. First, as noted above, the combined firm would be able to reduce costs by $2.8 billion per year through efficiency improvements such as streamlining administrative overhead, eliminating excess capacity and duplicate facilities, using purchasing power to reduce raw material costs, and coordinating exploration in regions where the two firms operated separately. These savings were expected to be fully realized by the third year after the merger. Second, management noted that the two companies had complementary assets that would help increase productivity. For example, Exxon was a leader in deepwater exploration in West Africa, which complemented Mobil's production and exploration activities in Nigeria and Equatorial Guinea. In the Caspian, Exxon's presence in Azerbaijan complemented Mobil's strength in Kazakhstan, including a significant interest in the Tengiz field and its presence in Turkmenistan. Complementary exploration and production operations also existed in South America, Russia, and Eastern Canada. Finally, management argued that the merger provided the company with the scale required to manage the risks associated with very sizeable investments involved in new exploration projects.

Analysts and the financial media concurred with management's assessments of the economic benefits that potentially would be derived from the merger. Some analysts nevertheless expressed concern that differences in the cultures of the two companies might make it difficult for them to actually achieve these synergies. Exxon had a reputation for being "tight-lipped and conservative" whereas Mobil was viewed as "more open, both to the public and to new ideas."[7]

ACQUISITION PRICING

A well thought-out economic motivation for a merger or acquisition is a necessary but not sufficient condition for it to create value for acquiring stockholders. The acquirer must be careful to avoid overpaying for the target. Overpayment makes the transaction highly desirable and profitable for target stockholders, but it diminishes the value of the deal to acquiring stockholders. A financial analyst can use the following methods to assess whether the acquiring firm is overpaying for the target.

Analyzing Premium Offered to Target Stockholders

One popular way to assess whether the acquirer is overpaying for a target is to compare the premium offered to target stockholders to premiums offered in similar transactions. If the acquirer offers a relatively high premium, the analyst is typically led to conclude that the transaction is less likely to create value for acquiring stockholders.

Premiums differ significantly for friendly and hostile acquisitions. Premiums tend to be about 30 percent higher for hostile deals than for friendly offers, implying that hostile acquirers are more likely to overpay for a target.[8] There are several reasons for this. First, a friendly acquirer has access to the internal records of the target, making it much less likely that it will be surprised by hidden liabilities or problems once it has completed the deal. In contrast, a hostile acquirer does not have this advantage in valuing the target and is forced to make assumptions that may later turn out to be false. Second, the delays that typically accompany a hostile acquisition often provide opportunities for competing bidders to make an offer for the target, leading to a bidding war.

Comparing a target's premium to values for similar types of transactions is straightforward to compute, but it has several practical problems. First, it is not obvious how to define a comparable transaction. Figure 11-1 shows the mean and median premiums paid for U.S. targets between 1992 and 2001. Average premiums have risen from around 40 percent through the mid-1990s to between 50 and 60 percent in 1999–2001. Median premiums also increased during this period, from around 30 percent to 40 percent. However, mean and median premiums have to be interpreted with caution since there is considerable variation across transactions, making it difficult to use these estimates as a benchmark.

A second problem in using premiums offered to target stockholders to assess whether an acquirer overpaid is that measured premiums can be misleading if an offer is anticipated by investors. The stock price run-up for the target will then tend to make estimates of the premium appear relatively low. This limitation can be partially offset by using target

| **Figure 11-1** | Premium Paid for Mergers and Acquisitions, 1992–2001 |

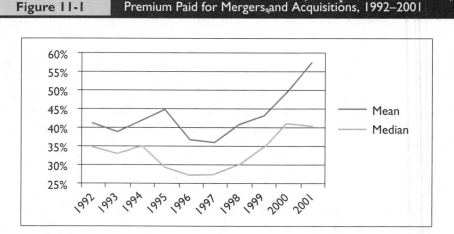

Source: *Mergerstat Review* (W.T. Grimm & Co., Chicago, 2002).

stock prices one month prior to the acquisition offer as the basis for calculating premiums. However, in some cases offers may have been anticipated for even longer than one month.

Finally, using target premiums to assess whether an acquirer overpaid ignores the value of the target to the acquirer after the acquisition. This value can be viewed as

Value of target after acquisition = Value as independent firm +
Value of merger benefits

The value of the target before acquisition is the present value of the free cash flows for the target if it were to remain an independent entity. This is likely to be somewhat different from the firm's stock price prior to any merger announcement since the pre-takeover price is a weighted average of the value of the firm as an independent unit and its value in the event of a takeover. The benefits of the merger include such effects as improvements in target operating performance from economies of scale, improved management, and tax benefits, as well as any spillover benefits to the acquirer from the acquisition. Clearly, acquirers will be willing to pay higher premiums for targets which are expected to generate higher merger benefits. Thus, examining the premium alone cannot determine whether the acquisition creates value for acquiring stockholders.

Analyzing Value of the Target to the Acquirer

A second and more reliable way of assessing whether the acquirer has overpaid for the target is to compare the offer price to the estimated value of the target to the acquirer. This latter value can be computed using the valuation techniques discussed in Chapters 7 and 8. The most popular methods of valuation used for mergers and acquisitions are earnings multiples and discounted cash flows. Since a comprehensive discussion of these techniques is provided earlier in the book, we focus here on implementation issues that arise for valuing targets in mergers and acquisitions. We recommend first computing the value of the target as an independent firm. This provides a way of checking whether the valuation assumptions are reasonable, since for publicly listed targets we can compare our estimate with pre-merger market prices. It also provides a useful benchmark for thinking about how the target's performance, and hence its value, is likely to change once it is acquired.

Earnings Multiples

To estimate the value of a target to an acquirer using earnings multiples, we have to forecast earnings for the target and decide on an appropriate earnings multiple, as follows:

Step 1: Forecasting earnings. Earnings forecasts are usually made by first forecasting next year's net income for the target assuming no acquisition. Historical sales growth rates, gross margins, and average tax rates are useful in building a pro forma income model. Once we have forecasted the income for the target prior to an acquisition, we can incorporate into the pro forma model any improvements in earnings performance that we expect to result from the acquisition. Performance improvements can be modeled as

- Higher operating margins through economies of scale in purchasing, or increased market power;
- Reductions in expenses as a result of consolidating research and development staffs, sales forces, and/or administration; or
- Lower average tax rates from taking advantage of operating tax loss carryforwards.

Step 2: Determining the price-earnings multiple. How do we determine the earnings multiple to be applied to our earnings forecasts? If the target firm is listed, it may be tempting to use the preacquisition price-earnings multiple to value postmerger earnings. However, there are several limitations to this approach. First, for many targets earnings growth expectations are likely to change after a merger, implying that there will be a difference between the pre- and postmerger price-earnings multiples. Postmerger earnings should then be valued using a multiple for firms with comparable growth and risk characteristics. (See discussion in Chapter 7.) A second problem is that premerger price-earnings multiples are unavailable for unlisted targets. Once again it becomes necessary to decide which types of listed firms are likely to be good comparables. Finally, if a premerger price-earnings multiple is appropriate for valuing postmerger earnings, care is required to ensure that the multiple is calculated prior to any acquisition announcement since the price will increase in anticipation of the premium to be paid to target stockholders.

The following table summarizes how price-earnings multiples are used to value a target firm before an acquisition (assuming it will remain an independent entity), and to estimate the value of a target to a potential acquirer:

Summary of Price-Earnings Valuation for Targets

Value of target as an independent firm	Target earnings forecast for the next year, assuming no change in ownership, multiplied by its *premerger* PE multiple.
Value of target to potential acquirer	Target *revised* earnings forecast for the next year, incorporating the effect of any operational changes made by the acquirer, multiplied by its *postmerger* PE multiple.

Limitations of Price-Earnings Valuation

As explained in Chapter 7, there are serious limitations to using earnings multiples for valuation. In addition to these limitations, the method has two more that are specific to merger valuations:

1. PE multiples assume that merger performance improvements come either from an immediate increase in earnings or from an increase in earnings growth (and hence an increase in the postmerger PE ratio). In reality, improvements and savings can come

in many forms—gradual increases in earnings from implementing new operating policies, elimination of overinvestment, better management of working capital, or paying out excess cash to stockholders. These types of improvements are not naturally reflected in PE multiples.

2. PE models do not easily incorporate any spillover benefits from an acquisition for the acquirer since they focus on valuing the earnings of the target.

Discounted Abnormal Earnings or Cash Flows

As discussed in Chapters 7 and 8, we can also value a company using the discounted abnormal earnings and discounted free cash flow methods. These require us to first forecast the abnormal earnings or free cash flows for the firm and then discount them at the cost of capital, as follows.

Step 1: Forecast abnormal earnings/free cash flows. A pro forma model of expected future income and cash flows for the firm provides the basis for forecasting abnormal earnings/free cash flows. As a starting point, the model should be constructed under the assumption that the target remains an independent firm. The model should reflect the best estimates of future sales growth, cost structures, working capital needs, investment and research and development needs, and cash requirements for known debt retirements, developed from financial analysis of the target. The abnormal earnings method requires that we forecast abnormal earnings or net operating profit after tax (NOPAT) for as long as the firm expects new investment projects to earn more than their cost of capital. Under the free cash flow approach, the pro forma model will forecast free cash flows to either the firm or to equity, typically for a period of five to ten years. Once we have a model of the abnormal earnings or free cash flows, we can incorporate any improvements in earnings/free cash flows that we expect to result from the acquisition. These will include the cost savings, cash received from asset sales, benefits from eliminating overinvestment, improved working capital management, and paying out excess cash to stockholders.

Step 2: Compute the discount rate. If we are valuing the target's postacquisition abnormal NOPAT or cash flows to the firm, the appropriate discount rate is the weighted average cost of capital for the target, using its expected *postacquisition* capital structure. Alternatively, if the target equity cash flows are being valued directly or if we are valuing abnormal earnings, the appropriate discount rate is the target's *postacquisition cost of equity* rather than its weighted average cost of capital (WACC). Two common mistakes are to use the acquirer's cost of capital or the target's *preacquisition* cost of capital to value the postmerger abnormal earnings/cash flows from the target.

The computation of the target's postacquisition cost of capital can be complicated if the acquirer plans to make a change to the target's capital structure after the acquisition, since the target's costs of debt and equity will change. As discussed in Chapter 8, this involves estimating the asset beta for the target, calculating the new equity and debt betas under the modified capital structure, and finally computing the revised cost of equity capital or weighted cost of capital. As a practical matter, the effect of these changes on the weighted average cost of capital is likely to be quite small unless the revision in leverage has a significant effect on the target's interest tax shields or its likelihood of financial distress.

The following table summarizes how the discounted abnormal earnings/cash flow methods can be used to value a target before an acquisition (assuming it will remain an independent entity), and to estimate the value of a target firm to a potential acquirer.

Summary of Discounted Abnormal Earnings/Cash Flow Valuation for Targets

Value of target without an acquisition	(a) Present value of abnormal earnings/free cash flows to target equity assuming no acquisition, discounted at *premerger* cost of equity; or
	(b) Present value of abnormal NOPAT/free cash flows to target debt and equity assuming no acquisition, discounted at *premerger* WACC, less value of debt.
Value of target to potential acquirer	(a) Present value of abnormal earnings/free cash flows to target equity, *including benefits from merger,* discounted at *postmerger* cost of equity; or
	(b) Present value of abnormal NOPAT/free cash flows to target, *including benefits from merger,* discounted at *postmerger* WACC, less value of debt.

Step 3: Analyze sensitivity. Once we have estimated the expected value of a target, we will want to examine the sensitivity of our estimate to changes in the model assumptions. For example, answering the following questions can help the analyst assess the risks associated with an acquisition:

- What happens to the value of the target if it takes longer than expected for the benefits of the acquisition to materialize?
- What happens to the value of the target if the acquisition prompts its primary competitors to respond by also making an acquisition? Will such a response affect our plans and estimates?

Key Analysis Questions

To analyze the pricing of an acquisition, the analyst is interested in assessing the value of the acquisition benefits to be generated by the acquirer relative to the price paid to target stockholders. Analysts are therefore likely to be interested in answers to the following questions:

- What is the premium that the acquirer paid for the target's stock? What does this premium imply for the acquirer in terms of future performance improvements to justify the premium?
- What are the likely performance improvements that management expects to generate from the acquisition? For example, are there likely to be increases in the revenues for the merged firm from new products, increased prices, or better distribution of existing products? Alternatively, are there cost savings as a result of taking advantage of economies of scale, improved efficiency, or a lower cost of capital for the target?
- What is the value of any performance improvements? Values can be estimated using multiples or discounted abnormal earnings/cash flow methods.

Exxon's Pricing of Mobil

Exxon's $74.2 billion price for Mobil represented a 26.4 percent premium to target stockholders over the market value on November 20, 1998, when rumors of a merger first reached Wall Street. This was below the mean and median premiums reported for all acquisitions during that year (41 percent and 30 percent, respectively). However, it was toward the high end of estimates made by J. P. Morgan, Exxon's financial advisor, who reviewed 38 large comparable acquisitions and concluded that a 15–25 percent premium was justified. In comparison, BP had paid a 35 percent premium for Amoco during the same period.

In terms of traditional multiple forms of valuation, Exxon's pricing of Mobil appears to be reasonable. For example, at the time of the announcement of Exxon's offer, the PE value for other firms in the oil industry that were comparable to Mobil ranged from 19.3 to 23.8. Exxon's offer valued Mobil at 22.7 times current earnings.

The market reaction to the acquisition announcement suggests that analysts initially believed that the deal was marginal for Exxon's stockholders—Exxon's stock price dropped by 1.5 percent (adjusted for market-wide changes), or $2.6 billion, during the 11 days prior to the announcement through to the actual announcement day. However, by the tenth trading day after the announcement, Exxon's stock was up 3.6 percent, or $6.3 billion. Given the $15.5 billion premium that Exxon paid for Mobil, investors believed that the merger would create value of $21.8 billion.

Subsequent short-term financial results for Exxon-Mobil support the market's optimism about the merger synergies. In August 2000 Exxon-Mobil announced that merger synergies had reached $4.6 billion, far ahead of projections at the time of the merger. Analysts projected that they would reach $7 billion by 2002.

ACQUISITION FINANCING

Even if an acquisition is undertaken to create new economic value and is priced judiciously, it may still destroy shareholder value if it is inappropriately financed. Several financing options are available to acquirers, including issuing stock or warrants to target stockholders, or acquiring target stock using surplus cash or proceeds from new debt. The trade-offs between these options from the standpoint of target stockholders usually hinge on their tax and transaction cost implications. For acquirers, they can affect the firm's capital structure and provide new information to investors.

As we discuss below, the financing preferences of target and acquiring stockholders can diverge. Financing arrangements can therefore increase or reduce the attractiveness of an acquisition from the standpoint of acquiring stockholders. As a result, a complete analysis of an acquisition will include an examination of the implications of the financing arrangements for the acquirer.

Effect of Form of Financing on Target Stockholders

As noted above, the key financing considerations for target stockholders are the tax and transaction cost implications of the acquirer's offer.

Tax Effects of Different Forms of Consideration

Target stockholders care about the after-tax value of any offer they receive for their shares. In the U.S., whenever target stockholders receive cash for their shares, they are required to pay capital gains tax on the difference between the takeover offer price and their original purchase price. Alternatively, if they receive shares in the acquirer as consideration and the acquisition is undertaken as a tax-free reorganization, they can defer any taxes on the capital gain until they sell the new shares.

U.S. tax laws appear to cause target stockholders to prefer a stock offer to a cash one. This is certainly likely to be the case for a target founder who still has a significant stake in the company. If the company's stock price has appreciated over its life, the founder will face a substantial capital gains tax on a cash offer and will therefore probably prefer to receive stock in the acquiring firm. However, cash and stock offers can be tax-neutral for some groups of stockholders. For example, consider the tax implications for risk arbitrageurs, who take a short-term position in a company that is a takeover candidate in the hope that other bidders will emerge and increase the takeover price. They have no intention of holding stock in the acquirer once the takeover is completed and will pay ordinary income tax on any short-term trading gain. Cash and stock offers therefore have identical after-tax values for risk arbitrageurs. Similarly, tax-exempt institutions are likely to be indifferent to whether an offer is in cash or stock.

Transaction Costs and the Form of Financing

Transaction costs are another factor related to the form of financing that can be relevant to target stockholders. Transaction costs are incurred when target stockholders sell any stock received as consideration for their shares in the target. These costs will not be faced by target stockholders if the bidder offers them cash. Transaction costs are unlikely to be significant for investors who intend to hold the acquirer's stock following a stock acquisition. However they may be relevant for investors who intend to sell, such as risk arbitrageurs.

Effect of Form of Financing on Acquiring Stockholders

For acquiring stockholders the costs and benefits of different financing options usually depend on how the offer affects their firm's capital structure and any information effects associated with different forms of financing.

Capital Structure Effects of Form of Financing

In acquisitions where debt financing or surplus cash are the primary form of consideration for target shares, the acquisition increases the net financial leverage of the acquirer. This increase in leverage may be part of the acquisition strategy, since one way an acquirer can add value to an inefficient firm is to lower its taxes by increasing interest tax shields. However, in many acquisitions an increase in postacquisition leverage is a side effect of the method of financing and not part of a deliberate tax-minimizing strategy. The increase in leverage can then potentially reduce shareholder value for the acquirer by increasing the risk of financial distress.

To assess whether an acquisition leads an acquirer to have too much leverage, financial analysts can assess the acquirer's financial risk following the proposed acquisition by these methods:

- Assessing the pro forma financial risks for the acquirer under the proposed financing plan. Popular measures of financial risk include debt-to-equity and interest-coverage ratios, as well as projections of cash flows available to meet debt repayments. The ratios can be compared to similar performance metrics for the acquiring and target firms' industries. Do postmerger ratios indicate that the firm's probability of financial distress has increased significantly?
- Examining whether there are important off-balance-sheet liabilities for the target and/ or acquirer which are not included in the pro forma ratio and cash flow analysis of postacquisition financial risk.

- Determining whether the pro forma assets for the acquirer are largely intangible and therefore sensitive to financial distress. Measures of intangible assets include such ratios as market to book equity and tangible assets to the market value of equity.

Information Problems and the Form of Financing

As we discuss in Chapter 12, information asymmetries between managers and external investors can make managers reluctant to raise equity to finance new projects. Managers' reluctance arises from their fear that investors will interpret the decision as an indication that the firm's stock is overvalued. In the short term, this effect can lead managers to deviate from the firm's long-term optimal mix of debt and equity. As a result, acquirers are likely to prefer to use internal funds or debt to finance an acquisition, since these forms of consideration are less likely to be interpreted negatively by investors.[9]

The information effects imply that firms forced to use stock financing are likely to face a stock price decline when investors learn of the method of financing.[10] From the viewpoint of financial analysts, the financing announcement may, therefore, provide valuable news about the preacquisition value of the acquirer. On the other hand, it should have no implications for analysis of whether the acquisition creates value for acquiring shareholders, since the news reflected in the financing announcement is about the *preacquisition* value of the acquirer and not about the *postacquisition* value of the target to the acquirer.

A second information problem arises if the acquiring management does not have good information about the target. Stock financing then provides a way for acquiring stockholders to share the information risks with target shareholders. If the acquirer finds out after the acquisition that the value of the target is less than previously anticipated, the accompanying decline in the acquirer's equity price will be partially borne by target stockholders who continue to hold the acquirer's stock. In contrast, if the target's shares were acquired in a cash offer, any postacquisition loss would be fully borne by the acquirer's original stockholders. The risk-sharing benefits from using stock financing appears to be widely recognized for acquisitions of private companies, where public information on the target is largely unavailable.[11] In practice it appears to be considered less important for acquisitions of large public corporations.

Key Analysis Questions

The form of financing has important tax and transaction cost implications for target stockholders. It can also have important capital structure and information effects for acquirers. From the perspective of the analyst, the effect of any corporate tax benefits from debt financing should already be reflected in the valuation of the target. Information effects are not relevant to the value of the acquisition. However, the analyst does need to consider whether demands by target stockholders for consideration in cash lead the acquirer to have a postacquisition capital structure which increases the risk of financial distress to a point that is detrimental for stockholders. Thus, part of the analyst's task is to determine how it affects the acquirer's capital structure and its risks of financial distress by asking the following questions:

- What is the leverage for the newly created firm? How does this compare to leverage for comparable firms in the industry?

- What are the projected future cash flows for the merged firm? Are these sufficient to meet the firm's debt commitments? How much of a cushion does the firm have if future cash flows are lower than expected? Is the firm's debt level so high that it is likely to impair its ability to finance profitable future investments if future cash flows are below expectations?

Exxon's Financing of Mobil

Exxon offered Mobil shareholders 1.32 Exxon shares for each Mobil share. Given Mobil's 780 million shares outstanding, Exxon issued 1,030 million shares, which at $72 per share implied a total offer of $74.2 billion.

The merger was structured as a "tax-free reorganization" for federal income tax purposes. This implied that Mobil shareholders would not recognize any gain or loss for federal income tax purposes from exchanging their Mobil stock for Exxon Mobil stock in the merger.

By using stock to finance the acquisition, Exxon actually reduced its financial leverage. However, initially the market reacted negatively to the offer, lowering Exxon's stock price by 1.5 percent (adjusting for marketwide returns) on the announcement date (December 1, 1998). This reaction could have occurred because investors interpreted Exxon's stock offer as indicating that its stock was overvalued. Yet in the following ten days, Exxon's stock staged a recovery, increasing by 3.6 percent.

It is also worth noting that, under accounting rules in force at the time of the Exxon-Mobil merger, the form of financing had an effect on the acquirer's financial statements following the acquisition. In 1999, when the merger was completed, two methods of reporting for an acquisition were permitted under U.S. accounting—purchase and pooling of interests. Under the *purchase method,* the acquirer wrote up the assets of the target to their market value and recorded the difference between the purchase price and the market value of the target's tangible net assets as goodwill. Goodwill was subsequently amortized to earnings over a period of from 5 to 40 years. The *pooling-of-interests method* of accounting for mergers, which was rarely used outside the U.S., required acquirers to show the target's assets, liabilities, and equity at their original book values. Thus no goodwill was recorded, and subsequent earnings did not need to be reduced by the amortization of goodwill.

An acquirer's decision on a method of financing an acquisition largely determined its method of accounting for the transaction. The pooling-of-interests method was typically used if the acquirer issued voting common shares (not cash) in exchange for at least 90 percent of the voting common shares of the target, and if the acquisition occurred in a single transaction. The acquisition of Mobil satisfied these criteria, and Exxon announced that it therefore would use the pooling-of-interests method.

However SFAS 141 and 142 require that, as of July 2001, the purchase method be used to record all acquisitions no matter how they are financed. In contrast to the old purchase accounting rules, goodwill is no longer to be amortized unless there is evidence of impairment. Under these rules the financial statements of Exxon Mobil would look markedly different from those reported under the pooling-of-interests method. Mobil's equity would be valued at the $74.2 billion purchase price rather than its $19 billion premerger book value. The ROEs for the new firm would therefore seriously overstate the returns to Exxon shareholders from the acquisition. As discussed in Chapter 4, one way for the analyst to deal with this problem is to adjust the financial statements to reflect purchase accounting.

ACQUISITION OUTCOME

The final question of interest to the analyst evaluating a potential acquisition is whether it will indeed be completed. If an acquisition has a clear value-based motive, the target is priced appropriately, and its proposed financing does not create unnecessary financial risks for the acquirer, it may still fail because the target receives a higher competing bid or because of opposition from entrenched target management. Therefore, to evaluate the likelihood that an offer will be accepted, the financial analyst has to understand whether there are potential competing bidders who could pay an even higher premium to target stockholders than is currently offered. They also have to consider whether target managers are entrenched and, to protect their jobs, likely to oppose an offer.

Other Potential Acquirers

If there are other potential bidders for a target, especially ones who place a higher value on the target, there is a strong possibility that the bidder in question will be unsuccessful. Target management and stockholders have an incentive to delay accepting the initial offer to give potential competitors time to also submit a bid. From the perspective of the initial bidder, this means that the offer could potentially reduce stockholder value by the cost of making the offer (including substantial investment banking and legal fees). In practice, a losing bidder can usually recoup these losses and sometimes even make healthy profits from selling to the successful acquirer any shares it has accumulated in the target.

Key Analysis Questions

The financial analyst can determine whether there are other potential acquirers for a target and how they value the target by asking the following questions:

- Are there other firms that could also implement the initial bidder's acquisition strategy? For example, if this strategy relies on developing benefits from complementary assets, look for potential bidders who also have assets complementary to the target. If the goal of the acquisition is to replace inefficient management, what other firms in the target's industry could provide management expertise?

- Who are the acquirer's major competitors? Could any of these firms provide an even better fit for the target?

Target Management Entrenchment

If target managers are entrenched and fearful for their jobs, it is likely that they will oppose a bidder's offer. Some firms have implemented "golden parachutes" for top managers to counteract their concerns about job security at the time of an offer. Golden parachutes provide top managers of a target firm with attractive compensation rewards should the firm get taken over. However, many firms do not have such schemes, and opposition to an offer from entrenched management is a very real possibility.

While the existence of takeover defenses for a target indicates that its management is likely to fight a bidding firm's offer, defenses have typically not prevented an acquisition from taking place. Instead, they tend to cause delays, which increase the likelihood that there will be competing offers made for the target, including offers by friendly parties solicited by target management, called "white knights." Takeover defenses therefore increase the likelihood that the bidder in question will be outbid for the target, or that it will have to increase its offer significantly to win a bidding contest. Given these risks, some have argued that acquirers are now less likely to embark on a potentially hostile acquisition.

Key Analysis Questions

To assess whether the target firm's management is entrenched and therefore likely to oppose an acquisition, analysts can ask the following questions:

- Does the target firm have takeover defenses designed to protect management? Many such defenses were used during the turbulent 1980s, when hostile acquisitions were at their peak. Some of the most widely adopted include poison pills, staggered boards, super-majority rules, dual-class recapitalizations, fair-price provisions, ESOP plans, and changes in firms' states of incorporation to states with more restrictive anti-takeover laws.
- Has the target been a poor performer relative to other firms in its industry? If so, management's job security is likely to be threatened by a takeover, leading it to oppose any offers.
- Is there a golden parachute plan in place for target management? Golden parachutes provide attractive compensation for management in the event of a takeover to deter opposition to a takeover for job security reasons.

Analysis of Outcome of Exxon's Offer for Mobil

Analysts covering Mobil had little reason to question whether Mobil would be sold to Exxon. The offer was a friendly one that had received the approval of Mobil's management and board of directors. There probably was some risk of another major oil company entering the bidding for Mobil. For example, BP had shown an appetite for making major acquisitions with its purchase of Amoco in August 1998. In early 1999 BP also acquired Arco in a second mega-deal. Chevron was also rumored to be open to an acquisition, and in October 2000 it acquired Texaco. In the end, none of these competitors made a bid for Mobil. The acquisition was completed on December 1, 1999, twelve months after announcement of the initial agreement.

SUMMARY

This chapter summarizes how financial statement data and analysis can be used by financial analysts interested in evaluating whether an acquisition creates value for an acquiring firm's stockholders. Obviously, much of this discussion is also likely to be relevant to other merger participants, including target and acquiring management and their investment banks.

For the external analyst, the first task is to identify the acquirer's acquisition strategy. We discuss a number of strategies. Some of these are consistent with maximizing acquirer value, including acquisitions to take advantage of economies of scale, improve target management, combine complementary resources, capture tax benefits, provide low-cost financing to financially constrained targets, and increase product-market rents.

Other strategies appear to benefit managers more than stockholders. For example, some unprofitable acquisitions are made because managers are reluctant to return free cash flows to shareholders, or because managers want to lower the firm's earnings volatility by diversifying into unrelated businesses.

The financial analyst's second task is to assess whether the acquirer is offering a reasonable price for the target. Even if the acquirer's strategy is based on increasing shareholder value, it can overpay for the target. Target stockholders will then be well rewarded but at the expense of acquiring stockholders. We show how the ratio, pro forma, and valuation techniques discussed earlier in the book can all be used to assess the worth of the target to the acquirer.

The method of financing an offer is also relevant to a financial analyst's review of an acquisition proposal. If a proposed acquisition is financed with surplus cash or new debt, it increases the acquirer's financial risk. Financial analysts can use ratio analysis of the acquirer's postacquisition balance sheet and pro forma estimates of cash flow volatility and interest coverage to assess whether demands by target stockholders for consideration in cash lead the acquirer to increase its risk of financial distress.

Finally, the financial analyst is interested in assessing whether a merger is likely to be completed once the initial offer is made, and at what price. This requires the analyst to determine whether there are other potential bidders, and whether target management is entrenched and likely to oppose a bidder's offer.

DISCUSSION QUESTIONS

1. During the early 1990s there was a noticeable increase in mergers and acquisitions between firms in different countries (termed cross-border acquisitions). What factors could explain this increase? What special issues can arise in executing a cross-border acquisition and in ultimately meeting your objectives for a successful combination?

2. In the 1980s leveraged buyouts (LBOs) were a popular form of acquisition. Under a leveraged buyout, a buyout group (which frequently includes target management) makes an offer to buy the target firm at a premium over its current price. The buyout group finances much of the acquisition with debt capital, leading the target to become a highly leveraged private company following the acquisition.
   a. What types of firms would make ideal candidates for LBOs? Why?
   b. How might the acquirer add sufficient value to the target to justify a high buyout premium?

3. Kim Silverman, CFO of the First Public Bank Company, notes: "We are fortunate to have a cost of capital of only 10 percent. We want to leverage this advantage by acquiring other banks that have a higher cost of funds. I believe that we can add significant value to these banks by using our lower cost financing." Do you agree with Silverman's analysis? Why or why not?

4. The Boston Tea Company plans to acquire Hi Flavor Soda Co. for $60 per share, a 50 percent premium over current market price. John E. Grey, the CFO of Boston Tea, argues that this valuation can easily be justified, using a price-earnings analysis. "Boston Tea has a price-earnings ratio of 15, and we expect that we will be able to generate long-term earnings for Hi Flavor Soda of $5 per share. This implies that Hi Flavor is worth $75 to us, well below our $60 offer price." Do you agree with this analysis? What are Grey's key assumptions?

5. You have been hired by GS Investment Bank to work in the merger department. The analysis required for all potential acquisitions includes an examination of the target for

any off-balance-sheet assets or liabilities that have to be factored into the valuation. Prepare a checklist for your examination.

6. Company T is currently valued at $50 in the market. A potential acquirer, A, believes that it can add value in two ways: $15 of value can be added through better working capital management, and an additional $10 of value can be generated by making available a unique technology to expand T's new product offerings. In a competitive bidding contest, how much of this additional value will A have to pay out to T's shareholders to emerge as the winner?

7. In 1995 Disney acquired ABC television at a significant premium. Disney's management justified much of this premium by arguing that the acquisition would guarantee access for Disney's programs on ABC's television stations. Evaluate the economic merits of this claim.

8. A leading oil exploration company decides to acquire an Internet company at a 50 percent premium. The acquirer argues that this move creates value for its own stockholders because it can use its excess cash flows from the oil business to help finance growth in the new Internet segment. Evaluate the economic merits of this claim.

9. Under current U.S. accounting standards, acquirers are required to capitalize goodwill and report any subsequent declines in value as an impairment charge. What performance metrics would you use to judge whether goodwill is impaired?

NOTES

1. In a review of studies of merger returns, Michael Jensen and Richard Ruback, "The Market for Corporate Control: The Scientific Evidence," *Journal of Financial Economics* 11, (April 1983): 5–50, conclude that target shareholders earn positive returns from takeovers, but that acquiring shareholders only break even.

2. Much of our discussion is based on analysis of the acquisition presented by F. Weston, "The Exxon-Mobil Merger: An Archetype," *Journal of Applied Finance* 12, no. 1, Spring/Summer 2002.

3. Of course another possibility is for the profitable firm to acquire the unprofitable one. However, in the U.S. the IRS will disallow the use of tax loss carryforwards by an acquirer if it appears that an acquisition was tax-motivated.

4. See Steven Kaplan, "Management Buyouts: Evidence on Taxes as a Source of Value," *Journal of Finance* 44 (1989): 611–32.

5. Krishna Palepu, "Predicting takeover targets: A methodological and empirical analysis," *Journal of Accounting and Economics* 8 (March 1986): 3–36.

6. Chapter 2 discusses the pros and cons of corporate diversification and evidence on its implications for firm performance.

7. See S. Liesman and A. Sullivan, "Tight-Lipped Exxon, Outspoken Mobil Face Major Image, Cultural Differences," *Wall Street Journal,* December 2, 1998.

8. See Paul Healy, Krishna Palepu, and Richard Ruback, "Which Mergers Are Profitable—Strategic or Financial?," *Sloan Management Review* 38, no. 4 (Summer 1997): 45–58.

9. See Stewart Myers and Nicholas Majluf, "Corporate Financing and Investment Decisions When Firms Have Information That Investors Do Not," *Journal of Financial Economics* (June 1984): 187–221.

10. For evidence see Nicholas Travlos, "Corporate takeover bids, methods of payments, and bidding firms' stock returns," *Journal of Finance* 42 (1987): 943–63.

11. See S. Datar, R. Frankel, and M. Wolfson, "Earnouts: The Effects of Adverse Selection and Agency Costs on Acquisition Techniques," *Journal of Law, Economics, and Organization* 17 (2001): 201–238.

Schneider and Square D

In late January 1991, Didier Pineau-Valencienne, CEO and Chairman of the French firm Groupe Schneider, was frustrated at his lack of success in building a closer working relationship between his company and Square D, Schneider's American counterpart in the electrical equipment industry. Convinced that a global market was developing for electrical equipment, Pineau-Valencienne believed that Schneider needed to become a major player in the U.S. market to maintain its future competitive position. Given the lack of success in partnering with Square D, he was considering the option of acquiring the company.

THE ELECTRICAL EQUIPMENT INDUSTRY

The electrical equipment industry generates revenue from new construction as well as from the maintenance of existing equipment. Demand for both closely follows general economic conditions. The 1990 economic slump hit the electrical manufacturing segment in the United States severely. However, by early 1991 analysts expected prospects for the industry to brighten with the predicted upturn in the economy and the construction market.

Two related trends dominated the industry in 1990: globalization and industry concentration. The first of these has led many U.S. firms to expand internationally to take advantage of market growth in Western Europe and Pacific Rim countries. These international opportunities have been enhanced by the globalization of product standards in the industry. The most widely accepted standards in the U.S. were developed by the National Electrical Manufacturers Association (NEMA). European products conformed to a different set of standards, developed by the International Electrical Commission (IEC) in Geneva. However, many in the industry expected that the move toward a unified Europe, set for 1992, would ultimately lead IEC standards to become dominant in the world.

The second major trend in the industry, concentration of manufacturing and research capabilities, resulted from increasing costs of development and production as well as from globalization. The development of a new product line costs between $46 million and $74 million (FF 250 million to FF 400 million). Globalization of markets and product standards enabled firms to take advantage of economies of scale, using their expertise and technologies to create common products for domestic and international markets.

SQUARE D COMPANY

Square D is a major supplier of electrical equipment, services, and systems in the U.S. (see Exhibit 1 for Square D's U.S. market shares). The company was incorporated in 1903 and has grown steadily since then. It currently owns and operates 18 manufacturing plants in 11 foreign countries. Operations are concentrated in two segments: electrical distribution and industrial control. The electrical distribution segment manufactures products and systems used to transmit electricity from power lines to outlets for residential, commercial,

Edouard De Vitry D'Avaucourt prepared this case under the supervision of Professor Paul Healy. Additional comments and information were provided by Professors Paul Asquith from the MIT Sloan School of Management and Anant Sundaram from the Amos Tuck School. The case is intended solely as the basis for class discussion and is not intended to serve as an endorsement, source of primary data, or illustration of effective or ineffective management.

industrial, or other types of buildings. The industrial control segment manufactures products and provides services to control power used by electrical devices or processes.

One of Square D's strengths is its network of independent electrical distributors, or wholesalers, which market its products. Individual distributors, selected by Square D, provide products and services to all types of clients (contractors, utilities, industrial users, and original equipment manufacturers). This extensive network is the result of many years of relationship building, and is the envy of most of Square D's competitors.

Square D's major competitors include ABB, Westinghouse, Siemens, Allen Bradley, General Electric, and Schneider (through its subsidiaries Télémécanique and Merlin Gerin). These companies compete across a number of segments. In late 1990 *US Industrial Outlook* ranked Square D second in the U.S. industrial control business after Allen Bradley. In electrical distribution, the company ranks third in the U.S. market behind Westinghouse and General Electric.

Square D has had an impressive financial track record—it has been profitable for each of the last 59 years. In the mid-1980s, however, company performance indicators began to deteriorate, prompting the Board to make a change in top management. Jerre Stead joined Square D as president and COO in 1987, was elected CEO in 1988, and was appointed Chairman of the Board in 1989. Stead led a revitalization plan to restore the company's performance and help it face the new industry challenges. Under the plan the following restructuring changes were made:

- Some facilities in the U.S. and Canada were closed, and others were consolidated.
- The firm's businesses were reorganized into three externally focused sectors serving industrial control, electrical distribution, and international markets.
- The resources generated by redeployments and disposal of operations not closely related to the core were used to strengthen core businesses.

Thanks to these efforts, Square D weathered the 1990 recession better than many of its competitors. In 1990 Square D's sales were $1.7 billion (see Exhibit 2 for financial statements), 71 percent in the electrical distribution segment (85 percent of operating earnings) and 29 percent in the industrial control segment (15 percent of operating earnings). By early 1991 analysts were expressing optimism about the industry's prospects for late 1991 and 1992, especially those for Square D. *Value Line* noted that "a stronger economy, a rebound in housing, and positive operating leverage . . . could enable earnings per share to surge to $5.50 or so in 1992 (from $4.73 in 1990)."

GROUPE SCHNEIDER

Schneider was founded in October 1886 as a partnership and was transformed into a corporation (*société anonyme*) in 1966. It is one of the largest industrial groups in France and is ranked 184 in Fortune's 500 (worldwide ranking).

In 1981, with the arrival of Pineau-Valencienne as chairman and CEO of the group, Schneider embarked on an ambitious restructuring program. The first stage of the program was to divest all loss-making businesses (shipbuilding, railways, and telephone equipment), which had historically generated much of the firm's sales. Selling these businesses allowed the group to simplify its operational structure and to strengthen its finances. In the second stage of the restructuring Schneider focused on two core businesses:

- Electrical equipment manufacturing for power distribution and automation of industrial complexes (56 percent of sales, 85 percent of operating profits in 1990)

- Electrical building contracting (44 percent of sales, 15 percent of operating profits in 1990)

As a result of the restructuring efforts, Schneider transformed itself from a diversified holding company into an industrial group focused on electrical equipment, engineering, and contracting. The company was organized around four major industrial subsidiaries:

- *Merlin Gerin*—Manufacturer of high-, medium-, and low-voltage equipment, as well as process control systems
- *Télémécanique*—Manufacturer of automation systems and equipment
- *Jeumont Schneider*—Manufacturer of electrical and electronic engineering equipment
- *Spie Batignolles*—Provider of electrical contracting and civil engineering services

With sales of 51 billion francs (financial statements are presented in Exhibit 3) and 85,000 employees throughout the world in 1990, Schneider ranked second or third in most segments of the global electrical equipment industry.

In the late 1980s, Pineau-Valencienne became convinced that the industry was moving more toward a global industry. In his communications with analysts, he emphasized that IEC standards would gain influence in the U.S. and would become the worldwide standard. In addition, he believed that increasing R&D and manufacturing costs would encourage international concentration. Consequently, Schneider began a third restructuring stage— geographical diversification. This move was initiated with two major acquisitions in 1989:

- Spie Batignolles acquired 15 percent of DAVY, the leading British engineering company.
- Schneider acquired a controlling interest in Federal Pioneer, the leading Canadian electrical equipment manufacturer.

The Relationship Between Schneider and Square D

Schneider became interested in Square D in 1988. In September 1988, Pineau-Valencienne arranged a meeting between the top executives of the two companies, during which Schneider presented its vision of a possible joint venture. After this presentation, operational meetings were scheduled from fall 1988 to spring 1989 to determine the product lines most suitable for such a joint venture. To protect the information exchanged, the companies entered into a confidentiality agreement in late October 1988. This restricted the use and public disclosure of confidential information received during the discussions, but it did not contain any "standstill" provisions limiting purchase of securities or business combination proposals.

Very early in the negotiations it became clear that the two CEOs diverged in their understanding of the nature of the relationship. Pineau-Valencienne had hoped that Schneider would acquire an equity position in Square D to cement the relationship. Stead, however, made it very clear that he did not welcome this, and requested that Square D's independence be respected. In correspondence on September 25, 1989, Pineau-Valencienne made his views very clear, connecting the future of the joint venture discussions to Square D's agreeing to Schneider acquiring a 20 percent interest in Square D. As a result, joint venture discussions between the two firms terminated. Frustrated over this standstill, in September 1990 Pineau-Valencienne indicated to Stead that Schneider's interests in Square D had changed from a joint venture to a "friendly cash merger transaction." Square D's Board subsequently became increasingly hostile to Schneider's proposals.

At the same time that Schneider was making overtures to Square D, Square D was organizing legal defenses against hostile takeovers. In 1989 it moved to Delaware, where state laws require hostile bidders to have a minimum of 85 percent of the shares tendered to effect a takeover. In addition, it created poison pill amendments to fight potential unsolicited bids, including a Common Stock Purchase Plan (see Exhibit 4 for details).

During November 1990, unusual activity was noticeable in Square D's stock. Rumors of a takeover led to a jump in volume and increased the share price from $36.50 on October 22 to $49.75 on November 7 (see Exhibit 5). On November 6, 1990, Stead discussed the unusual activity in a phone conversation with Pineau-Valencienne, who expressed an interest in having the opportunity to propose a transaction to Square D if any other parties were given such an opportunity.

On February 1, 1991, *Value Line Investments Survey* made the following comments:

Square D stock is trading on takeover speculation, as it has for the past three months. Square D has several attractions (including positions in selected electrical equipment markets), and could well be a tempting takeover target, especially to a foreign company trying to establish or to enlarge a market presence in the U.S. An acquirer might be willing to pay $70 a share or more for the company. But after three months of unusually heavy trading in the stock, during which time all of its outstanding shares theoretically have changed hands, no evidence of a pending buyout attempt has appeared. If none is eventually forthcoming, we'd expect the stock to gradually drift lower, perhaps to the range of $40–$45 a share. At this juncture, only speculative investors should be holding these shares.

Potential Acquisition of Square D

One option that Pineau-Valencienne was considering was to make a bid for Square D. After two years of contacts with Square D, he had a number of ideas for synergies and sources of value that could result from a full combination of the two companies. These included:

- Rationalizing R&D efforts between the two companies and sharing the benefits of existing technologies;
- Providing access to larger distribution channels for both companies;
- Rationalizing manufacturing capabilities; and
- Expanding Square D's product lines by selling products developed by Télémécanique or Merlin Gerin.

Lazard Frères, the financial advisor of Schneider, was asked to analyze the stand-alone value of Square D as well as its value to Schneider. To determine Square D's stand-alone value, Lazard Frères prepared a set of base assumptions for the firm's future performance as an independent entity. They projected that (a) sales would grow 3.5 percent in 1991 and 7 percent per year thereafter; (b) EBIT would be 15–16 percent of sales; (c) net working capital would continue to be 11–13 percent of sales; (d) projected capital expenditures would be 5 percent of sales; and (e) depreciation expenses would remain at 4 percent of sales between 1991 and 1997, and 4.3 percent thereafter. Based on the synergies between Schneider and Square D, Lazard Frères estimated that Square D could save approximately $60 million per year in expenses (after tax) if it were combined with Schneider. In addition, the disposal of some of Square D's unrelated assets could generate $150 million in cash. Other data relevant to the valuation of Square D is presented in Exhibit 6.

One other issue that Pineau-Valencienne was concerned about in a possible acquisition of Square D was its effect on Schneider's income. Under French accounting, Schneider would have to amortize goodwill, regardless of whether the offer was cash or stock-financed. Lazard Frères estimated that asset and liability revaluations under an acquisition would be minimal, implying that there would be significant goodwill amortization charges, even if the maximum period of 40 years was chosen. Pineau-Valencienne expected that many analysts would react negatively to the resulting dilution of earnings.

Didier Pineau-Valencienne felt he had to make a quick decision. There were rumors that Square D already had been approached by a number of other companies about a business combination. Pineau-Valencienne was very concerned that other competitors could gain control of Square D, leaving Schneider with few opportunities to gain access to the U.S. market.

QUESTIONS

1. Assess and discuss the strategic fit between Square D and Schneider. What are the economic pros and cons of a combination?

2. Evaluate the base assumptions Lazard Frères made for valuing Square D. What is the company worth to Schneider under these assumptions?

3. Use your own assumptions to estimate the value of Square D as an independent company. What is the company worth to Schneider?

4. What would be the effect of the acquisition on Schneider's future earnings, assuming that it was forced to pay the full value of Square D? Should Schneider be concerned about this effect?

5. If you were Mr. Pineau-Valencienne in late January 1991, what would you do? Would you offer a bid for Square D? If so, how much would you bid, and would you make your offer friendly or hostile?

EXHIBIT 1

Schneider and Square D Market Shares, U.S. and Europe

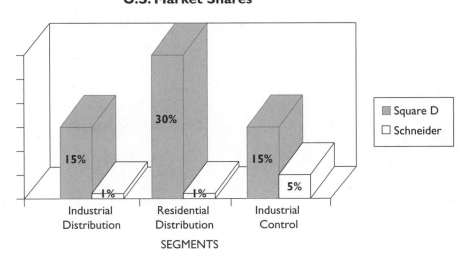

U.S. Market Shares

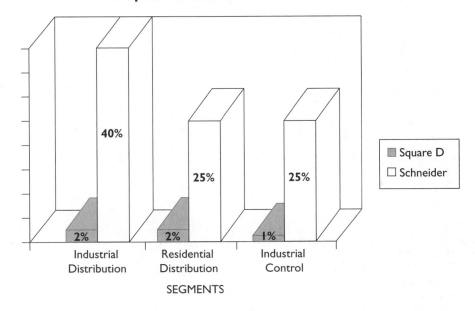

European Market Shares

EXHIBIT 2

Selected Pages from Square D's 1990 Annual Report

CONSOLIDATED FINANCIAL STATEMENTS

CONSOLIDATED STATEMENTS OF NET EARNINGS

	Year Ended December 31		
(Amounts in thousands, except per share)	1990	1989	1988
Net Sales	$1,653,319	$1,598,688	$1,497,772
Costs and Expenses:			
Cost of products sold	1,088,977	1,027,348	979,591
Selling, administrative and general	385,903	369,726	338,962
Restructuring charge	—	26,320	—
Operating Earnings	178,439	175,294	179,219
Non-Operating Income	34,740	17,106	17,255
Interest Expense	(28,760)	(31,438)	(22,082)
Earnings from Continuing Operations before Income Taxes	184,419	160,962	174,392
Provision for Income Taxes	67,773	59,856	63,310
Earnings from Continuing Operations	116,646	101,106	111,082
Discontinued Operations:			
(Loss) earnings from operations, net of income tax (benefit) expense: 1990—$(1,188); 1989—$(1,086); 1988—$3,831	(312)	798	7,852
Gain on disposal, net of other provisions; net of income taxes of $1,865	4,391	—	—
Earnings from Discontinued Operations	4,079	798	7,852
Net Earnings	120,725	101,904	118,934
Preferred Dividend, Net of Income Taxes	6,176	3,300	—
Net Earnings Available for Common Shareholders	$ 114,549	$ 98,604	$ 118,934
Earnings per Common Share:			
Primary:			
Continuing operations	$ 4.76	$ 3.95	$ 4.15
Discontinued operations	.18	.03	.29
Net Earnings	$ 4.94	$ 3.98	$ 4.44
Fully Diluted:			
Continuing operations	$ 4.57	$ 3.88	$ 4.13
Discontinued operations	.16	.03	.29
Net Earnings	$ 4.73	$ 3.91	$ 4.42
Weighted Average Number of Common Shares Outstanding:			
Primary	23,181	24,763	26,776
Fully diluted	25,088	25,809	27,016

Schneider and Square D

CONSOLIDATED BALANCE SHEETS

	December 31,	
(Dollars in thousands, except per share)	1990	1989

ASSETS

Current Assets:		
Cash and short-term investments	$ 244,933	$ 66,348
Receivables, less allowances (1990—$23,759; 1989—$18,556)	305,241	314,123
Inventories	159,109	151,316
Prepaid expenses	12,664	15,206
Prepaid income taxes	4,714	—
Deferred income tax benefit	34,988	26,459
Net assets of discontinued operation	—	117,116
Total Current Assets	761,649	690,568
Investment in Leveraged Leases	137,182	133,344
Property, Plant and Equipment:		
Land	24,477	22,216
Buildings and improvements	222,105	212,992
Equipment	552,785	501,531
Property, Plant and Equipment—at cost	799,367	736,739
Less accumulated depreciation	349,265	318,261
Property, Plant and Equipment—net	450,102	418,478
Net Assets of Discontinued Operations	36,681	52,949
Excess of Purchase Price Over Net Assets of Businesses Acquired, Less Amortization (1990—$13,769; 1989— $12,978)	51,391	50,528
Other Assets	22,744	26,718
Total Assets	$1,459,749	$1,372,585

LIABILITIES AND COMMON SHAREHOLDERS' EQUITY

Current Liabilities:		
Short-term debt	$ 123,871	$ 263,730
Current maturities of long-term debt	15,067	10,174
Accounts payable and accrued expenses	220,575	200,686
Income taxes	—	10,327
Dividends payable	12,633	11,893
Total Current Liabilities	372,146	496,810
Long-Term Debt	244,820	123,420
Deferred Income Taxes	82,381	74,464
Deferred Income Taxes—Leveraged Leases	127,699	112,473
Other Liabilities	14,000	—
Minority Interest	10,941	9,295
Preferred Stock, No Par Value, Authorized 6,000,000 Shares; Issued 1,709,402 Shares, Outstanding 1,701,822 Shares, Cumulative Series A ESOP Convertible Preferred Stock	$ 124,568	$ 125,000
Note Receivable from ESOP Trust	(25,000)	(125,000)
Unearned ESOP Compensation	(95,400)	—
Common Shareholders' Equity:		
Common stock, par value $1.66⅔, authorized 100,000,000 shares	49,601	49,409

(continued)

Schneider and Square D

CONSOLIDATED BALANCE SHEET (continued)

(Dollars in thousands, except per share)	December 31, 1990	1989
Additional paid-in capital	130,401	120,211
Retained earnings	773,126	713,225
Cumulative translation adjustments	3,262	(8,788)
Treasury stock—at cost	(352,796)	(317,934)
Total Common Shareholders' Equity	603,594	556,123
Total Liabilities and Common Shareholders' Equity	$1,459,749	$1,372,585

CONSOLIDATED STATEMENTS OF CASH FLOWS

(Dollars in thousands)	Year Ended December 31, 1990	1989	1988
Cash and Short-Term Investments at January 1	$ 66,348	$ 65,855	$ 94,488
Cash and Short-Term Investments Were Provided from (Used for):			
Operating Activities:			
Earnings from Continuing Operations	116,646	101,106	111,082
Add (deduct) non-cash items included in earnings from continuing operations:			
Depreciation and amortization	59,300	49,443	45,174
Deferred income taxes	1,707	(25,147)	(8,506)
Deferred income taxes—leveraged leases	15,226	23,445	25,683
(Gain) loss on sale of property, plant and equipment	(1,011)	1,936	657
(Gain) loss on foreign exchange	(2,222)	964	(52)
Minority interest	1,646	985	1,047
Other credits to earnings—net	—	(15)	(63)
Current Items (net of effects of purchase of businesses):			
Receivables	13,501	(58,515)	(20,789)
Inventories	(1,285)	26,568	(52,795)
Prepaid expenses	2,769	12,027	1,635
Accounts payable and accrued expenses	(7,312)	16,736	20,316
Income taxes	(15,253)	(3,319)	8,243
Net cash provided from continuing operations	183,712	146,214	131,632
Net cash (used for) provided from discontinued operations	(484)	2,971	721
Net cash provided from operating activities	183,228	149,185	132,353
Investing Activities:			
Increase in investment in leveraged leases	$ (3,838)	$ (2,876)	$ (4,829)
Purchase of businesses, net of $103 of cash acquired	—	(9,271)	—
Property additions	(83,117)	(80,024)	(70,419)

(continued)

CONSOLIDATED STATEMENTS OF CASH FLOWS *(continued)*

	Year Ended December 31,		
(Dollars in thousands)	1990	1989	1988
Proceeds from sale of business	175,476	—	—
Proceeds from sale of property, plant and equipment	21,774	6,186	14,222
Decrease (increase) in other investments	1,281	(12,794)	24,692
Net cash provided from (used for) investing activities	111,576	(98,779)	(36,334)
Financing Activities:			
Net (decrease) increase in short-term debt	(143,983)	142,262	44,430
Increase in long-term debt	27,883	614	11,066
Reductions in long-term debt	(14,412)	(21,580)	(17,910)
Proceeds of note receivable from ESOP trust	125,000	—	—
Loan to ESOP trust	(25,000)	—	—
Cash dividends paid on common stock	(50,128)	(50,590)	(54,601)
Cash dividends paid on preferred stock	(9,956)	(5,000)	—
Common stock issued	6,602	8,929	6,349
Purchase of treasury stock	(34,916)	(126,778)	(111,394)
Redemption of preferred stock	(432)	—	—
Treasury stock issued	54	114	256
Net cash used for financing activities	(119,288)	(52,029)	(121,804)
Effect of exchange rate changes on cash	3,069	2,116	(2,848)
Net Increase (Decrease) in Cash and Short-Term Investments	178,585	493	(28,633)
Cash and Short-Term Investments at December 31	$244,933	$ 66,348	$ 65,855

See accompanying notes to consolidated financial statements.

Schneider and Square D

NOTES TO CONSOLIDATED FINANCIAL STATEMENTS
(Dollars in thousands, except per share)

A. Summary of Significant Accounting Policies

Principles of Consolidation
The financial statements include the accounts of the company and all majority-owned subsidiaries. Investments in unconsolidated affiliates are accounted for by the equity method. All significant intercompany accounts and transactions have been eliminated. The statements are based on years ended December 31, except for substantially all international subsidiaries whose fiscal years end November 30.

Cash and Short-Term Investments
Cash consists of cash in banks and time deposits. Short-term investments consist of a variety of highly liquid short-term instruments with purchased maturities of generally three months or less. Short-term investments are carried at cost, which approximates market.

Inventories
Inventories are stated at the lower of cost or market. Cost of inventories is determined using the last-in, first-out (LIFO) method for substantially all domestic inventories and certain international inventories. The first-in, first-out (FIFO) method is used for substantially all international inventories.

Property, Plant and Equipment
Depreciation of property, plant and equipment is provided on a straight-line basis over the estimated useful lives of the assets. Accelerated methods are used for income tax purposes.

Businesses Acquired
The excess of purchase price over net assets of businesses acquired is amortized on a straight-line basis over not more than forty years.

Income Taxes
Income taxes are accounted for in accordance with APB No. 11. The Financial Accounting Standards Board has issued Statement No. 96, which will change the accounting for income taxes; the company will adopt this statement no later than January 1, 1992.

Off-Balance Sheet Financial Instruments
The company enters into a variety of financial instruments in the management of its exposure to changes in interest rates and foreign currency rates. These instruments include interest rate swap agreements and foreign exchange contracts. These financial instruments do not represent a material off-balance sheet risk in relation to the financial statements.

Earnings per Common Share
Primary earnings per common share are determined by dividing the weighted average number of common shares outstanding during the year into net earnings after deducting after-tax dividends attributable to preferred shares. Common share equivalents in the form of stock options and convertible debt are excluded from the calculation since they do not have a material dilutive effect on per share figures. Fully diluted earnings per share reflect the conversion of all convertible preferred stock and common stock equivalents into common stock.

Reclassifications
Certain amounts in the 1989 and 1988 financial statements have been reclassified to conform to the current year's financial statement presentation.

B. Discontinued Operations

As of June 30, 1990, the company reported its General Semiconductor Industries (GSI) business as a discontinued operation, and as of September 30, 1989, the company reported its Yates Industries (Yates) copper foil business as a discontinued operation. Accordingly, the consolidated financial statements of the company have been reclassified to report separately the net assets and operating results of these discontinued operations. Financial results for periods prior to the dates of discontinuance have been restated to reflect continuing operations.

In January 1990, the company concluded the sale of its Yates operations in Europe and its 50 percent joint venture interest in Japan. In April 1990, the company completed the sale of its Yates operation in Bordentown, N.J. Total gross proceeds from the sale of all Yates operations were $175,476. The proceeds from the sale of Yates operations and the associated costs approximated management's original estimates. Management is actively pursuing the sale of the GSI business.

A gain from the sale of Yates, offset by provisions for a loss on the prospective sale of GSI and costs associated with other previously discontinued businesses, resulted in a gain of $4,391, net of income taxes, in the second quarter of 1990 from discontinued operations. The gain on the sale of Yates is net of a $14,000 provision for long-term environmental costs. The gain from the sale of Yates' foreign locations included a gain of $6,895 from the recognition of cumulative translation adjustments.

Net assets of discontinued operations were $36,681 and $170,065 at December 31, 1990 and 1989, respectively. These amounts consist of current assets; property, plant and equipment; other noncurrent assets; and current and concurrent liabilities.

Sales applicable to the discontinued operations prior to the dates of discontinuance were $16,158, $124,121 and $159,000 in 1990, 1989 and 1988, respectively. Interest expense of $249, $2,730 and $2,246, net of income taxes, was allocated to the discontinued operations prior to dates of discontinuance based on net assets for 1990, 1989 and 1988, respectively. The operating results of GSI from the date of discontinuance to December 31, 1990 were immaterial.

C. Restructuring Charge

In 1989, a restructuring charge of $17,511 net of taxes, or $.71 per share, was incurred by the company as a part of a plan to rationalize and improve profitability of several businesses and product lines both in the United States and abroad. The charge is principally comprised of costs associated with product, facility and organizational rationalization of the electrical distribution segment; product rationalization of the industrial control segment; plant consolidation and organizational restructuring in Canada; reorganization in Europe; and marketing restructuring.

D. Acquisitions

In 1989, the company acquired Crisp Automation, Inc. of Dublin, Ohio. Crisp Automation is a designer of process controls and factory automation systems and operates as part of the Square D Automation Products business. Also in 1989, the company acquired Electrical Specialty Products (ESP) of Montevallo, Alabama. ESP is a manufacturer of electrical connectors and operates as part of the Square D Connectors business. These acquisitions were accounted for as purchases; their sales and net earnings for the periods prior to the dates of acquisition were not material.

G. Inventories

Inventories valued by the last-in, first-out (LIFO) method aggregated $83,941 and $65,017 at December 31, 1990 and 1989, respectively. If the first-in, first-out (FIFO) method had been used, inventories would have been $138,120 and $140,076 higher than reported in the accompanying consolidated balance sheets at December 31, 1990 and 1989, respectively.

Schneider and Square D

Inventories are maintained by element of cost; therefore, it is not practical to determine major classes such as finished goods, work in process and raw materials.

H. Lease Commitments

The company rents various warehouse and office facilities and certain equipment, principally computers and vehicles, under lease arrangements classified as operating leases.

Future minimum rental payments under noncancelable operating leases with initial terms of one year or more as of December 31, 1990 are:

1991	$10,160
1992	7,266
1993	5,520
1994	4,473
1995	975
Remainder	1,224
Total	$29,618

J. Debt

Long-term debt consists of:

	1990	1989
ESOP Notes, 7.7%, due on various dates to 2004	$120,400	$ —
Senior Notes, 10.0%, due 1995	75,000	75,000
Industrial Revenue Bonds, 5.6% to 8.8%, due on various dates to 2004	25,715	26,610
First Mortgage Notes, 9.0% to 9.2%, due on various dates to 2009	10,825	11,119
Subordinated Convertible Notes, 9.0%, due 1992 (net of unamortized discount at 13.0%: 1990—$220, 1989—$376)	2,787	4,096
Payable to banks; average rate 1990—13.8%, 1989—10.3%; due on various dates to 1996	1,114	2,423
Other debt: average rate 1990—14.4%, 1989—12.7%; due on various dates to 2000	24,046	14,346
Subtotal	259,887	133,594
Less current maturities	15,067	10,174
Total	$244,820	$123,420

The aggregate annual maturities of long-term debt for the years 1991 through 1995 are $15,067, $14,642, $14,968, $13,877 and $82,187, respectively.

The Employee Stock Ownership Plan (ESOP) Notes include $25,000 of direct borrowings by the company, the proceeds from which have been advanced in the form of a loan to the company's ESOP. Direct borrowings of the ESOP, aggregating $95,400 as of December 31, 1990, have been guaranteed by the company and accordingly, are reported as long-term debt of the company. See Note Q for further discussion.

Industrial Revenue Bonds of $9,115 and the First Mortgage Notes are secured by the property and equipment acquired with the proceeds of the financings.

The Subordinated Convertible Notes are convertible at a rate of 28.57 shares for each one thousand dollars of principal. The company has reserved 85,934 shares of common stock for the conversion.

The company has entered into revolving credit agreements in which twelve of its principal banks participate. The agreements provide for up to $180,000 of revolving credit through 1994. The credit is available in both the domestic and euro markets.

Short-term debt includes bank borrowings of $33,611 and $19,438 and commercial paper of $70,260 and $214,292 at December 31, 1990 and 1989, respectively. Additionally, short-term debt includes a master note agreement of $20,000 and $30,000 at December 31, 1990 and 1989, respectively.

The company has additional unused short-term lines of credit which aggregated $69,501 at December 31, 1990.

K. Income Taxes

Pre-tax income from continuing operations is as follows:

	1990	1989	1988
United States	$163,674	$142,855	$155,453
International	20,745	18,107	18,939
Total	$184,419	$160,962	$174.392

Income tax provisions for continuing operations are as follows:

	1990	1989	1988
Current:			
U.S. Federal	$ 33,452	$ 46,784	$ 35,261
International	7,999	4,752	3,989
State	9,037	9,902	6,625
	50,488	61,438	45,875
Deferred:			
U.S. Federal	17,189	(1,375)	17,475
International	(869)	1,479	228
State	965	(1,686)	(268)
	17,285	(1,582)	17,435
Total	$ 67,773	$ 59,856	$ 63,310

The components of the deferred income tax provision are as follows:

	1990	1989	1988
Leasing subsidiary income	$ 17,077	$ 22,502	$ 25,256
401(k) contributions	4,383	—	—
State tax	965	(1,686)	(268)
Tax over book depreciation	2,535	1,301	751
Deferred taxable income on installment sales	—	(13,006)	(5,615)

(continued)

Schneider and Square D

	1990	1989	1988
Alternative minimum tax	—	8,484	1,634
Funding of group health insurance trust	—	(6,863)	(11,634)
Restructuring charge	—	(4,510)	—
Other	(7,675)	(7,804)	7,311
Deferred Income Tax Expense (Benefit)	$ 17,285	$ (1,582)	$ 17,435

A reconciliation between the statutory and effective tax rates for continuing operations is as follows:

	1990	1989	1988
U.S. Federal statutory rate	34.0%	34.0%	34.0%
State income taxes, net of Federal benefit	3.6	3.4	2.4
Rate reduction	—	—	(2.5)
U.S. tax on international dividend	0.4	0.3	4.2
International rate differential	0.1	(0.9)	(2.6)
Leasing subsidiary	(0.1)	(0.2)	(0.8)
Restructuring charge	—	0.6	—
Other	(1.3)	—	1.6
Effective tax rate	36.7%	37.2%	36.3%

No provisions have been made for possible international withholding and U.S. income taxes payable on the distribution of approximately $120,009 of undistributed earnings which have been or will be reinvested abroad or are expected to be returned to the United States in tax-free distributions. Provisions for taxes have been made for all earnings which the company presently plans to repatriate.

L. Supplementary Earnings Statement Information

	1990	1989	1988
Non-Operating Income:			
Interest income	$25,501	$14,497	$9,666
Settlement of lawsuit	5,695	—	—
Income from leveraged leases	5,273	6,694	8,219
Gain (loss) on sale of property, plant and equipment	1,005	(1,933)	(673)
Other non-operating (expense) income	(2,734)	(2,152)	43
Total	$34,740	$17,106	$17,255
Research and Development	$55,384	$44,720	$46,533
Maintenance and Repairs	47,328	49,572	47,131
Advertising	26,584	25,933	19,586
Rents	22,857	23,238	19,958
Foreign Currency Transaction (Loss) Gain	(1,423)	292	2,343

O. Pension Plans

The company's domestic operations maintain several pension plans, primarily defined benefit pension plans covering substantially all employees for normal retirement benefits at age 65. Defined benefits for salaried employees are based on a final average compensation formula and hourly plans are based on an amount per year of service formula. The company makes annual contributions to the plans in accordance with ERISA and IRS regulations, including amortization of past service cost over the average remaining service life of active employees.

In 1989 the company adopted SFAS No. 87 for its significant international pension plans. For the company's international pension plans that have not adopted SFAS No. 87, the excess of vested benefits over fund assets is insignificant. The company makes annual contributions to the plans in accordance with the laws and regulations of the respective international taxing jurisdictions in which the company operates.

Components of net periodic pension cost for the company's domestic and international pension plans consist of the following:

	1990	1989	1988
Service cost—benefits earned during period	$12,409	$11,039	$9,515
Net deferral and amortization	(42,253)	24,976	(11,621)
Interest on projected benefit obligation	28,547	25,796	25,414
Actual return on plan assets	10,809	(55,795)	(14,388)
Net periodic pension cost	$ 9,512	$ 6,016	$ 8,920

The net periodic pension cost attributable to the company's significant international pension plans was $843 and $1,000 in 1990 and 1989, respectively.

The following tables set forth the company's domestic and international pension plans' funded status and amounts recognized in the company's balance sheet at December 31:

	Overfunded Plans		Underfunded Plans	
	1990	1989	1990	1989
Actuarial present value of benefit obligations:				
Vested employees	$(193,615)	$(194,793)	$(96,325)	$(90,466)
Non-vested employees	(12,169)	(6,073)	(15,407)	(3,251)
Total accumulated benefit obligation	(205,784)	(200,866)	(111,732)	(93,717)
Additional amounts related to projected salary increases	(35,705)	(45,637)	(3,949)	(3,095)
Projected benefit obligation	(241,489)	(246,503)	(115,681)	(96,812)
Fair value of plan assets (primarily common equities and fixed income instruments)	245,953	267,184	75,493	68,884
Projected benefit obligation less than (in excess of) plan assets	4,464	20,681	(40,188)	(27,928)
Unrecognized net (gain) loss	(7,583)	(15,018)	9,451	8,442
Unrecognized prior service cost	(6,374)	(6,934)	17,281	4,673
Unrecognized net liability existing at the date of initial adoption of SFAS No. 87	6,604	1,682	1,378	4,569
(Accrued) Prepaid Pension Cost	$ (2,889)	$ 411	$(12,078)	$(10,244)

The economic assumptions used in determining the actuarial present value of the projected benefit obligation of the domestic plans were:

	1990	1989
Weighted average discount rate	9.0%	8.3%
Rate of increase in future compensation levels	5.3	5.3
Rate of return on plan assets	10.0	10.0

The assumed rates for the company's international plans, which reflect the economic conditions of each plan, generally varied from U.S. rates by 1.0 percent to 2.0 percent.

Total pension expense for all plans was $10,914, $8,073 and $12,962 for 1990, 1989 and 1988, respectively. Actuarial assumptions were revised in 1990, 1989 and 1988 principally to update the investment return and rates of pay increase to levels more reflective of current economic conditions. These and other changes increased pension expense in 1990 by approximately $920 and reduced pension expense in 1989 and 1988 by approximately $5,838 and $1,218, respectively.

P. Post-Retirement Benefits

The company provides health plan coverage and life insurance benefits for retired employees of substantially all of its domestic operations. Substantially all of the company's employees may become eligible for these benefits when they retire from active employment with the company. The cost of retiree health coverage is recognized as an expense when claims are paid. The cost of life insurance benefits is recognized as an expense as premiums are paid. These costs totaled $6,165 in 1990, $5,075 in 1989 and $3,982 in 1988.

The Financial Accounting Standards Board has issued Statement of Financial Accounting Standards No. 106, "Employers' Accounting for Post-Retirement Benefits Other Than Pensions." This Statement will require accrual of post-retirement benefits during the years an employee provides services. While the impact of this new standard has not been fully determined, the change will result in significantly greater expense being recognized for these benefits. The company plans to adopt this Statement in 1993.

T. Segment and Geographic Information

The company is engaged in the manufacture and sale of electrical distribution products, systems and services and industrial control products, systems and services, and operates in virtually every major marketing area in the world. Major manufacturing plants are located throughout the United States and in Europe, Latin America, Canada, Australia and Thailand.

The electrical distribution segment primarily consists of the manufacture and sale of products, systems and services used in the distribution of electricity. Distribution equipment is used principally in distributing electricity from the end of transmission lines to points of utilization within residential, commercial, industrial or other types of buildings. Distribution products include industrial molded case circuit breakers, miniature circuit breakers, load centers, safety switches, metering devices, switchboards, panelboards, motor control centers, low and medium voltage switchgear, busways and raceways, dry type transformers and power and cast resin transformers.

The industrial control segment mainly consists of the manufacture and sale of control products, systems and services that control the electricity used in the operation of power utilization devices or processes. Control equipment includes motor starters, contactors, push buttons, adjustable frequency motor controllers and sensors. Other products in this segment include programmable controllers, cell controllers, electronic computerized control and data-gathering systems, uninterruptible power systems, power protection equipment, infrared radiation thermometers and pyrometers and snap dome switches and keyboards.

Substantially all products of the electrical distribution and industrial control segments are marketed through the company's own marketing organization and distributed through a system of strategically located warehouses. The majority of all sales are made directly to authorized electrical distributors who, in turn, market the products to electrical contractors, electrical utilities, large industrial plants and other classes of trade.

Sales between geographic areas and industry segments are based on prices approximating current market values. Net sales to a group of customers under common control, for both industry segments, were $161,015 in 1990, $161,156 in 1989 and $176,700 in 1988.

Financial information by industry segment for the three years ended December 31, 1990 is summarized as follows:

Industry Segments	1990	1989	1988
Sales			
Electrical Distribution:			
Unaffiliated customers	$1,170,420	$1,117,619	$1,057,359
Intercompany	18,203	13,083	10,484
	1,188,623	1,130,702	1,067,843
Industrial Control:			
Unaffiliated customers	482,899	481,069	440,413
Intercompany	63,919	51,923	49,244
	546,818	532,992	489,657
Eliminations	(82,122)	(65,006)	(59,728)
Consolidated	$1,653,319	$1,598,688	$1,497,772
Operating Earnings			
Electrical Distribution	$ 152,280	$ 143,541	$ 138,229
Industrial Control	26,302	31,614	40,046
Eliminations	(143)	139	944
Consolidated	$ 178,439	$ 175,294	$ 179,219
Identifiable Assets			
Electrical Distribution	$ 920,781	$ 755,253	$ 701,973
Industrial Control	503,079	447,913	418,247
Eliminations	(792)	(646)	(835)
Identifiable Assets of Continuing Operations	$1,423,068	$1,202,520	$1,119,385
Net Assets of Discontinued Operations	36,681	170,065	181,338
Consolidated	$1,459,749	$1,372,585	$1,300,723
Depreciation and Amortization Expense			
Electrical Distribution	$ 36,688	$ 29,815	$ 26,345
Industrial Control	22,612	19,628	18,829
Capital Additions			
Electrical Distribution	$ 54,763	$ 50,323	$ 43,980
Industrial Control	39,125	30,125	27,975

Effective September 30, 1989, the company changed its reportable segments from Electrical Equipment and Electronic Products to Electrical Distribution Products, Systems and Services and Industrial Control Products, Systems and Services.

Schneider and Square D

Schneider and Square D

Financial information by geographic area for the three years ended December 31, 1990, is summarized as follows:

Geographic Areas	1990	1989	1988
Sales			
United States:			
Unaffiliated customers	$1,332,390	$1,321,769	$1,256,009
Intercompany	73,646	62,253	47,479
	1,406,036	1,384,022	1,303,488
Europe:			
Unaffiliated customers	138,836	115,678	105,471
Intercompany	22,617	23,691	25,207
	161,453	139,369	130,678
Latin America:			
Unaffiliated customers	78,867	68,178	53,242
Intercompany	1,300	1,217	1,761
	80,167	69,395	55,003
Other International:			
Unaffiliated customers	103,226	93,063	83,050
Intercompany	447	256	620
	103,673	93,319	83,670
Eliminations	(98,010)	(87,417)	(75,067)
Consolidated	$1,653,319	$1,598,688	$1,497,772
Operating Earnings			
United States	$ 164,155	$ 163,202	$ 156,791
Europe	3,555	212	4,098
Latin America	10,445	12,547	11,212
Other International	650	(463)	3,942
Eliminations	(366)	(204)	3,176
Consolidated	$ 178,439	$ 175,294	$ 179,219
Identifiable Assets			
United States	$1,131,085	$ 952,865	$ 883,334
Europe	158,637	120,483	109,297
Latin America	65,847	62,171	62,924
Other International	70,203	69,357	64,886
Eliminations	(2,704)	(2,356)	(1,056)
Identifiable Assets of Continuing Operations	1,423,068	1,202,520	1,119,385
Net Assets of Discontinued Operations	36,681	170,065	181,338
Consolidated	$1,459,749	$1,372,585	$1,300,723

SELECTED FINANCIAL DATA

	1990	1989	1988	1987	1986	1985
Summary of Operations						
Net sales	$1,653,319	$1,598,688	$1,497,772	$1,330,784	$1,274,932	$1,223,193
Cost of products sold	1,088,977	1,027,348	979,591	838,749	820,457	787,310
Selling, administrative and general expenses	385,903	369,726	338,962	287,386	267,066	237,790
Restructuring charge	—	26,320	—	11,192	—	—
Non-operating income	34,740	17,106	17,255	17,590	26,670	14,486
Interest expense	28,760	31,438	22,082	19,699	24,977	21,191
Earnings from continuing operations before income taxes	184,419	160,962	174,392	191,348	189,102	191,388
Provision for income taxes	67,773	59,856	63,310	75,736	85,191	89,465
Earnings from continuing operations	116,646	101,106	111,082	115,612	103,911	101,923
Earnings (loss) from discontinued operations, net of income taxes	4,079	798	7,852	(5,611)	(4,983)	(14,735)
Net earnings	120,725	101,904	118,934	110,001	98,928	87,188
Financial Information						
Working capital	$ 389,503	$ 193,758	$ 178,399	$ 192,693	$ 204,083	$ 202,076
Property, plant and equipment—at cost	799,367	736,739	673,946	630,754	606,757	570,538
Total assets	1,459,749	1,372,585	1,300,723	1,252,819	1,178,826	1,118,473
Long-term debt	244,820	123,420	135,467	141,085	166,389	201,028
Common shareholders' equity	603,594	556,123	636,029	679,711	670,789	606,139
Capital additions	93,888	80,448	71,955	35,356	71,617	61,880
Depreciation and amortization	59,300	49,443	45,174	42,277	38,548	32,430
Share Data						
Earnings per common share:						
Primary:						
Continuing operations	$4.76	$3.95	$4.15	$4.01	$3.59	$3.53
Discontinued operations	.18	.03	.29	(.19)	(.17)	(.51)
Net earnings	4.94	3.98	4.44	3.82	3.42	3.02
Fully diluted:						
Continuing operations	4.57	3.88	4.13	3.98	3.56	3.50
Discontinued operations	.16	.03	.29	(.19)	(.17)	(.50)
Net earnings	4.73	3.91	4.42	3.79	3.39	3.00
Cash dividends declared per common share	2.20	2.00	1.94	1.86	1.84	1.84
Common shares outstanding at December 31	22,886	23,489	25,691	27,660	28,966	28,864
Common shareholders' equity per share	$26.37	$23.68	$24.76	$24.57	$23.16	$21.00

(continued)

Schneider and Square D

SELECTED FINANCIAL DATA (continued)

	1990	1989	1988	1987	1986	1985
Key Financial Relationships						
Gross profit	34.1%	35.7%	34.6%	37.0%	35.6%	35.6%
Current ratio	2.0:1	1.4:1	1.5:1	1.7:1	1.9:1	1.8:1
Average total debt to average total equity	66.2%	55.7%	38.2%	29.0%	39.2%	40.5%
Average long-term debt to average capital	23.3%	13.6%	15.6%	16.7%	22.0%	19.8%

All financial data for the periods prior to 1990 have been restated for discontinued operations.

All financial data for the periods prior to 1988 have been restated for the consolidation of a majority-owned subsidiary.

EXHIBIT 3

Schneider Financial Statements and Accounting Policies

STATEMENT OF INCOME

(in FF million for the year ended December 31)	1990	1989	1988
Net sales	**49,884**	**45,127**	**40,493**
Cost of goods sold, personnel and administrative expenses	(44,978)	(41,008)	(36,766)
Depreciation and amortization	(1,565)	(1,166)	(1,272)
Operating expenses	**(46,543)**	**(42,174)**	**(38,038)**
Operating income	**3,341**	**2,953**	**2,455**
Interest expense – net	(832)	(757)	(182)
Income before non-recurring items, amortization of goodwill, taxes and minority interest	**2,509**	**2,196**	**2,273**
Non-recurring items:			
Gains on disposition of assets – net	419	550	484
Other non-recurring income and expense – net	(367)	(343)	(642)
Income before taxes, employee profit-sharing, amortization of goodwill and minority interests	**2,561**	**2,403**	**2,115**
Employee profit-sharing	(158)	(130)	(126)
Income taxes	(802)	(912)	(701)
Net income of fully consolidated companies before amortization of goodwill	**1,601**	**1,361**	**1,288**
Amortization of goodwill	(236)	(235)	(345)
Net income of fully consolidated companies	**1,365**	**1,126**	**943**
Group's share of income of companies accounted for by the equity method	**4**	**17**	**(53)**
Minority interests	(445)	(266)	(330)
Net income (Schneider SA share)	**924**	**877**	**560**
Net income (Schneider SA share) per share – in FF	62.96	63.06	48.85
Net income (Schneider SA share) per share after dilution – in FF	61.65	60.53	N/A

BALANCE SHEET

(in FF million for the year ended December 31)	1990	1989	1988
ASSETS			
Current Assets			
Cash and equivalents	1,841.3	3,400.3	1,579.6
Marketable securities	3,020.9	1,924.3	1,243.7
Accounts receivable – trade	14,597.4	14,987.3	13,998.5
Other receivables and prepaid expenses	4,738.1	3,876.5	4,054.9
Deferred taxes	407.5	290.2	236.9
Inventories and work in process	7,712.6	7,159.0	29,715.3
Total current assets	**32,317.8**	**31,637.6**	**50,828.9**
Non-Current Assets			
Property, plant and equipment	14,293.9	13,107.5	12,019.7
Accumulated depreciation	(6,691.5)	(6,365.6)	(6,409.5)
Property, plant and equipment – net	7,602.4	6,741.9	5,610.2
Investments accounted for by the equity method	175.9	135.7	244.9
Other equity investments	1,727.9	571.3	684.6
Other investments	573.0	618.3	909.8
Total investments	2,476.8	1,325.3	1,839.3
Intangible assets – net	147.5	153.5	115.0
Goodwill – net	7,032.8	6,087.8	5,596.8
Total non-current assets	**17,259.5**	**14,308.5**	**13,161.3**
Total assets	**49,577.3**	**45,946.1**	**63,990.2**
LIABILITIES AND SHAREHOLDERS' EQUITY			
Current Liabilities			
Accounts payable – trade	9,867.9	9,614.6	8,440.8
Taxes and benefits payable	4,822.5	4,795.8	3,748.4
Other payables and accrued liabilities	5,230.4	4,332.2	3,405.5
Short-term debt	3,120.5	3,165.8	3,081.3
Customer prepayments	2,505.9	3,848.3	27,606.1
Total current liabilities	**25,547.2**	**25,756.7**	**46,282.1**
Long-term debt	9,958.4	7,345.9	7,712.1
Provisions for contingencies	3,942.6	3,890.0	3,758.8
Shareholder's Equity			
Capital stock	1,414.4	1,397.2	1,146.3
Retained earnings	6,091.1	5,344.6	3,046.6
Total Shareholders' Equity	**7,505.5**	**6,741.8**	**4,192.9**
Minority interests	2,623.6	2,211.7	2,044.3
Total shareholders' equity and minority interests	**10,129.1**	**8,953.5**	**6,237.2**
Total liabilities and shareholders' equity	**49,577.3**	**45,946.1**	**63,990.2**

Schneider and Square D

STATEMENT OF CASH FLOWS

(in FF million for the year ended December 31)	1990	1989
I. Operating activities		
Net income of fully consolidated companies	1,368.5	1,143.7
Depreciation, amortization and provisions, net of recoveries	2,164.0	2,283.0
(Gains) on disposals of assets	(418.7)	(550.1)
Others	(0.8)	(28.7)
Net cash provided by operating activities before changes in operating assets and liabilities	**3,113.0**	**2,847.9**
Decrease (increase) in accounts receivable	(944.4)	1,170.4
Inventories and work in process	675.4	(1,708.6)
Increase (decrease) in accounts payable	578.7	(16.3)
Other current assets and liabilities	(1,681.4)	736.0
Net change in operating assets and liabilities	**(1,371.7)**	**181.5**
Net cash provided by operating activities	**1,741.3**	**3,029.4**
II. Investing activities		
Disposals of fixed assets	712.9	1,394.8
Purchases of property, plant and equipment and intangible assets	(2,589.5)	(2,154.3)
Financial investments	(2,788.2)	(1,068.8)
Other long-term investments	125.5	13.4
Net cash used in investing activities	**(4,539.3)**	**(1,814.9)**
III. Financing activities		
Reduction in long-term debt	(1,626.4)	(3,045.2)
New borrowings	1,508.7	2,435.1
Convertible bonds issued	2,655.6	634.7
Common stock issued	71.9	1,877.0
Dividends paid:		
Schneider SA shareholders	(174.6)	(126.1)
Minority interests	(116.5)	(69.7)
Net cash provided by financing activities	**2,318.7**	**1,705.8**
IV. Net effect of exchange rate and other changes	**13.8**	**178.5**
Net increase (decrease) in cash and cash equivalents (I + II + III + IV)	**(465.5)**	**3,098.8**
Cash and cash equivalents at beginning of year	**3,424.9**	**326.1**
at end of year	**2,959.4**	**3,424.9**

The following notes are an integral part of these financial statements.

Schneider and Square D

SELECTED NOTES TO FINANCIAL STATEMENTS

1. Accounting Principles

The consolidated financial statements of Schneider SA have been prepared in accordance with French generally accepted accounting principles and with the international accounting principles recommended by the International Accounting Standards Committee (I.A.S.C.). The differences between these principles and U.S. GAAP are explained in Note I.m), below.

The financial statements of consolidated subsidiaries, which are prepared in accordance with accounting principles generally accepted in the countries in which they operate, have been restated in accordance with the principles applied by the Group.

a) Consolidation principles

All significant companies that are controlled directly or indirectly by Schneider SA have been fully consolidated.

Companies over which Schneider SA exercises significant influence have been accounted for by the equity method.

As an exception to the above principles, Banque Morhange, in which the Group holds a majority interest but whose operations are not material in relation to the Group as a whole, has also been consolidated by the equity method.

In accordance with French generally accepted accounting principles, joint ventures in which the Group is the managing partner are fully consolidated by Schneider SA, after deducting the other partners' share in the income or loss of the joint venture. In cases where the Group is not the managing shareholder, only Schneider SA's share of the income or loss is accounted for, except for two contracts which are consolidated by the proportional method.

Goodwill is amortized out of income over a maximum of forty years based on estimated useful life.

b) Translation of the financial statements of foreign subsidiaries

The financial statements of foreign subsidiaries are translated into French francs as follows:

–Assets and liabilities are translated at year-end exchange rates;

–Income statement and cash flow items are translated at average exchange rates.

Differences arising on translation are recorded under shareholders' equity.

c) Translation of foreign currency transactions

With the exception of the transactions described below, foreign currency debts and receivables are translated into French francs at year-end exchange rates. As allowed under French law, translation differences are recorded in the income statement under interest income and expense.

Exchange gains as well as carrybacks and carryforwards related to forward purchases and sales of foreign currency used to hedge the Group's trading commitments are deferred and recognized at the same time as the gain or loss on the underlying transaction.

Gains and losses on unhedged forward currency transactions are credited or charged to income. The gain or loss corresponds to the difference between the forward exchange rate provided for in the contract and the exchange rate prevailing at year end for purchases and sales made in the same currency and according to the same term.

In cases where a speculative currency position is considered to exist due to the future interest on fixed to variable currency swaps, the interest is discounted on the basis of the fixed rate and stated at the exchange rate prevailing at year end for cash transactions. The translation difference is credited or charged to income.

d) Financial instruments based on exchange and interest rates

The Group uses financial instruments based on exchange and interest rates. The methods used to account for these instruments are described above.

e) Long-term contracts

Income from long-term contracts is recognized by the percentage-of-completion method, based on the financial status of the contract. Probable losses upon completion of a given contract are provided for in full as soon as they become known. The cost of work in process includes costs relating directly to the contracts and a percentage of overheads.

The estimated cost of the remaining work on contracts expected to generate a loss does not take account of any income from claims, except where such claims have been accepted by the customer and the latter has no major financing problems. Contracts in progress are therefore stated at the lower of cost or realizable value.

In accordance with the logic underlying the percentage-of-completion method, work in process is matched with customer prepayments received upon presentation of a schedule of work performed to date. However, prepayments in connection with the work in process include:

—Prepayments to finance production;

—Prepayments for work in process on contracts which are still in the early stages and for which it is not possible to make any estimate of probable income or losses; and

—Contracts scheduled to last less than twelve months.

f) Research and development expenditures

Internally-financed research and development expenditures are charged to income for the period.

g) Deferred taxes

Deferred taxes corresponding to timing differences between the recognition of income and expenses in the consolidated financial statements and for tax purposes are accounted for by the liability method.

h) Provisions for retirement bonuses

The Group's liability for retirement bonuses is calculated taking into account projected future compensation levels. The method used is in accordance with the Financial Accounting Standards Board (FASB) Statement of Financial Accounting Standards No. 87.

Part of the Group's liability for retirement bonuses is provided for and part is funded by an insured plan. The provisions are calculated for all eligible employees and the same discount and indexation rates are used for all Group companies that have adopted this method. For the insured plan, the current value of the plan assets has been calculated and provision has been made for any unfunded liability.

i) Marketable securities

Almost all marketable securities represent conventional short-term instruments (commercial paper, mutual funds and related securities). They are stated at cost. In the case of bonds and other debt instruments, cost includes accrued interest.

j) Inventories and work in process

Inventories and work in process are stated at weighted average cost. Any difference between cost and realizable value is provided for.

The cost of work in process, semi-finished and finished products includes direct materials and labor costs, sub-contracting costs incurred up to the balance sheet date and a percentage of production overheads

k) Property, plant and equipment

Land, buildings and equipment are stated at cost. Assets held at the time of a legal revaluation are stated at revalued cost. An equivalent amount is recorded in shareholders' equity, under retained earnings or revaluation reserve, and is written back to income in an amount matching the corresponding depreciation and disposals, so that the revaluation has no impact on income.

In the case of subsidiaries operating in high-inflation countries, the impact of legal revaluations is eliminated on consolidation and the resulting translation differences are recorded in retained earnings.

Property, plant and equipment is depreciated on a straight-line basis over the estimated useful lives of the assets.

Property, plant and equipment acquired under a capital lease is capitalized on the basis of the cost of the asset concerned and depreciated in accordance with the above principles. An obligation in the same amount is recorded on the liabilities side of the balance sheet.

l) Non-consolidated equity investments and other investments

Non-consolidated equity investments and other investments are stated at cost, except for investments held at the time of the 1977 legal revaluation. Each year, the carrying value is compared to fair value and any difference is provided for. Fair value is determined by reference to the Group's share in the underlying net assets, the expected future profitability and business prospects of the investee company, and – in the case of listed securities – the market value of the stock.

m) Differences between Schneider SA accounting principles and U.S. GAAP

The main differences between the accounting principles described above and U.S. GAAP are as follows:

Write-ups

As mentioned in Note l.k. above, the Company has performed certain write-ups which are contrary to U.S. GAAP. The write-ups have no impact on income but do affect shareholders' equity.

Consolidation

As indicated in Note a, Banque Morhange, whose operations are not material in relation to the Group as a whole, has been accounted for by the equity method.

Provisions for contingencies

In U.S. GAAP, the part of these provisions related to operating cycles would be considered as accrued liabilities.

Customer prepayments

In the consolidated financial statements, customer prepayments are recorded as a separate component of current liabilities. Under U.S. GAAP, work in process in an amount equal to the cost of the work performed for which no income or loss has been recognized.

Deferred taxes

In December 1987, the FASB issued a new standard concerning the accounting treatment of deferred taxes. The application of this standard is not compulsory in 1990. The Company has not yet decided the date at which it will start applying this standard and, in view of the complexity of the new rules, has not determined the impact that its application would have had on the 1990 financial statements as presented.

Non-recurring income and expense

Non-recurring income and expense includes items that the Company considers to be non-recurring but that would be treated as operating income and expense under U.S. GAAP. In addition, under U.S. GAAP, the amortization of goodwill would have been accounted for under income from continuing operations.

These reclassifications would have the following impact on income from continuing operations:

(in FF million)	1990	1989
Income from continuing operations, before tax	**2,509**	2,196
Non-recurring income other than extraordinary items	**(237)**	85
Amortization of goodwill	**(236)**	(235)
Income from continuing operations, before tax, according to U.S. GAAP	**2,036**	2,046

Schneider and Square D

EXHIBIT 4

Square D Common Stock Purchase Plan

The firm's Articles of Incorporation were modified in August 1988 as follows:

The Company adopted a new Share Purchase Rights Plan and declared a dividend distribution of one new common purchase right on each outstanding share of Square D common stock. The rights are exercisable only if someone acquires 20 percent or more of the company's common stock or announces a tender offer. At any time a person or group acquires 20 percent or more of the company's outstanding common stock and prior to that person acquiring 50 percent or more of the company's common stock, the company may exchange the rights (other than rights owned by such 20 percent or greater shareholder) in whole or in part for one share of common stock per right. If a person or group acquires 20 percent or more of the common stock, or certain events occur, each right not owned by the 20 percent or greater shareholder becomes exercisable for the number of shares of the company having a market value of twice the exercise price of the right. If the company is acquired in a merger or other business combination transaction or 50 percent or more of its assets or earning power are sold at any time after the rights become exercisable, the rights entitle a holder to buy a number of shares of common stock of the acquiring company having a market value of twice the exercise price of each right.

EXHIBIT 5

Selected Square D Stock Data for the Fourth Quarter 1990[a]

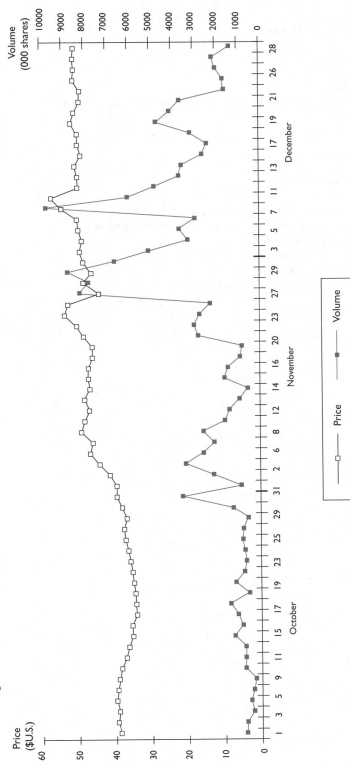

a. In late 1990, approximately 23 million shares were outstanding.

Schneider and Square D

EXHIBIT 6

Valuation Data for Square D

Square D equity beta	0.95
Moody's corporate bond average yield in February 1991 for major ratings:	
Aaa	8.83%
Aa	9.16%
A	9.38%
Ba	10.07%
Prime rate in February 1991	8.8%
Treasury bills rates in February 1991 (3 months)	6.0%
Government 30-year treasuries rates in February 1991	8.25%
Square D commercial paper rating in February 1991 (on a scale from P3 to P1, P1 being the best rating)	P1
Square D corporate bonds rating in February 1991	Aa3
U.S. federal statutory tax rate in 1990	34.0%
State income tax rate, net of federal benefit in 1990	3.6%

Corporate Financing Policies

In this chapter, we discuss how firms set their capital structure and dividend policies to maximize shareholder value. There is a strong relation between these two decisions. For example, a firm's decision to retain internally-generated funds rather than paying them out as a dividend can also be thought of as a financing decision. It is not surprising, therefore, to find that many of the factors that are important in setting capital structure (such as taxes, costs of financial distress, agency costs, and information costs) are also relevant for dividend policy decisions. We examine how these factors affect capital structure and dividend policy, as well as how the financial analysis tools, discussed in Part 2 of this book, can be used to evaluate capital structure and dividend policy decisions.

A variety of questions are dealt with in analysis of corporate financing policies:

- Securities analysts can ask: Given its capital structure and dividend policy, how should we position a firm in our fund—as a growth or income stock?
- Takeover specialists can ask: Can we improve stockholder value for a firm by changing its financial leverage or by increasing dividend payouts to owners?
- Management can ask: Have we selected a capital structure and dividend policy which supports our business objectives?
- Credit analysts can ask: What risks do we face in lending to this company, given its business and current financial leverage?

Throughout our discussion we take the perspective of an external analyst who is evaluating whether a firm has selected a capital structure and dividend policy that maximize shareholder value. The topic obviously also applies to management's decisions about what debt and dividend policies it should implement.

FACTORS THAT DETERMINE FIRMS' DEBT POLICIES

As discussed in Chapter 5, a firm's debt policy can be represented by comparing its net debt, defined as interest-bearing debt less excess cash and marketable securities, and its equity. In practice, since it is difficult to estimate excess cash and marketable securities, analysts typically use total cash and marketable securities as a proxy. For example, consider the debt policies for Pfizer Inc., a large pharmaceutical company, and Duke Energy Corporation, a large public utility, for the year ended December 31, 2001, reported in Table 12-1.

Table 12-1 Net Interest-Bearing Debt for Pfizer and Duke Energy for the Year Ended December 31, 2001

($ millions, except for net debt to equity ratio)	Pfizer	Duke Energy
Interest-bearing debt	$9,461	$14,198
Less: cash and short-term investments	8,615	290
Net debt	846	13,908
Book shareholders' equity	18,293	12,689
Net interest-bearing debt to book equity	5%	110%

Pfizer's liquid assets (cash and marketable securities) are comparable to its interest-bearing debt. As a result, its net debt is only 5 percent of its book equity. In contrast, Duke Energy has a ratio of net debt to book equity of 110 percent. Throughout the chapter we will examine factors that are relevant to the financing differences for these firms.

When financial analysts evaluate a firm's capital structure, two related questions typically emerge. First, in the long term, what is the best mix of debt and equity for creating stockholder value? And second, if managers are considering new investment initiatives in the short term, what type of financing should they use? Two popular models of capital structure provide help in thinking about these questions. The static model of capital structure examines how trade-offs between the benefits and costs of debt determine a firm's long-term optimal mix of debt and equity. And the dynamic model examines how information effects can lead a firm to deviate from its long-term optimal capital structure as it seeks financing for new investments. We discuss both models, since they have somewhat different implications for thinking about capital structure.

THE OPTIMAL LONG-TERM MIX OF DEBT AND EQUITY

To determine the best long-term mix of debt and equity capital for a firm, we need to consider the benefits and costs of financial leverage. By trading off these benefits and costs, we can decide whether a firm should be financed mostly with equity or mostly with debt.

Benefits of Leverage

The major benefits of financial leverage typically include corporate tax shields on interest and improved incentives for management.

Corporate Interest Tax Shields

In the U.S., and in many other countries for that matter, tax laws provide a form of government subsidy for debt financing which does not exist for equity financing. This arises from the corporate tax deductibility of interest against income. No such corporate tax shield is available for dividend payments or for retained earnings. Debt financing therefore has an advantage over equity, since the interest tax shields under debt provide additional income to debt and equity holders. This higher income translates directly into higher firm values for leveraged firms in relation to unleveraged firms.

Some practitioners and theorists have pointed out that the corporate tax benefit from debt financing is potentially offset by a personal tax disadvantage of debt.[1] That is, since the holders of debt must pay relatively high tax rates on interest income, they require that corporations offer high pretax yields on debt. This disadvantage is particularly severe when interest income is taxed at a higher rate than capital gains on equity. Under current U.S. tax laws, personal tax rates on interest income are higher than on long-term capital gains, implying that personal tax effects at least partially offset the corporate tax benefits of debt. However, most financial managers and financial economists believe that there is a corporate tax advantage to debt financing.

Therefore, the corporate tax benefits from debt financing should encourage firms with high effective tax rates and few forms of tax shield other than interest to have highly leveraged capital structures. In contrast, firms that have tax shield substitutes for interest, such as depreciation, or that have operating loss carryforwards and hence do not expect to pay taxes, should have capital structures that are largely equity.

Key Analysis Questions

To evaluate the tax effects of additional debt, analysts can use accounting, financial ratio, and prospective analysis to answer the following types of questions:

- What is a firm's average income tax rate? How does this rate compare with the average tax rate and financial leverage for its major competitors?
- What portion of a firm's tax expense is deferred taxes versus current taxes?
- What is the firm's marginal corporate tax rate likely to be?
- Does the firm have tax loss carryforwards or other tax benefits? How long are they expected to continue?
- What noninterest tax shields are currently available to the firm? For example, are there sizeable tax shields from accelerated depreciation?
- Based on pro forma income and cash flow statements, what are estimates for the firm's taxable income for the next five to ten years? What noninterest tax shields are available to the firm? Finally, what would be the tax savings from using some debt financing?

Management Incentives for Value Creation

A second benefit of debt financing is that it focuses management on value creation, thus reducing conflicts of interest between managers and shareholders. Conflicts of interest can arise when managers make investments that are of little value to stockholders and/or spend the firm's funds on perks, such as overly spacious office buildings and lavish corporate jets. Firms are particularly prone to these temptations when they are flush with cash but have few promising new investment opportunities, often referred to as "free cash flow" situations. These firms' stockholders would generally prefer that their managers pay out any free cash flows as dividends or use the funds to repurchase stock. However, these payouts reduce the size of the firm and the assets under management's control. Management may therefore invest the free cash flows in new projects, even if they are not valued by stockholders, or spend the cash flows on management perks.

How can debt help reduce management's incentives to overinvest and to overspend on perks? The primary way is by reducing resources available to fund these types of outlays, since firms with relatively high leverage face pressures to generate cash flows to meet payments of interest and principal.

The debt introduced as a result of the 1988 leveraged buyout of RJR Nabisco was viewed by many as an example of debt creating pressure for management to refocus on value creation for stockholders. Under this view, the incentive problems facing the company stemmed from the high cash flows it generated in the tobacco business and the low investment opportunities in this line of business given the decline in popularity of smoking in the U.S. The increased debt taken with the LBO forced RJR Nabisco's management to eliminate unnecessary perks, such as corporate jets and parties with famous sports stars, to slow diversification into the food industry, and to cancel unprofitable projects such as the smokeless cigarette.

Key Analysis Questions

Financial ratio and prospective analysis can help analysts assess whether there are currently free cash flow inefficiencies at a firm as well as risks of future inefficiencies.

Symptoms of excessive management perks and investment in unprofitable projects include the following:

- *High ratios of general and administrative expenses and overhead to sales.* If a firm's ratios are higher than those for its major competitors, one possibility is that management is wasting money on perks.
- *Significant new investments in unrelated areas.* If it is difficult to rationalize these new investments, there might be free cash flow problems.
- *High levels of expected operating cash flows (net of essential capital expenditures and debt retirements) from pro forma income and cash flow statements.*
- *Poor management incentives to create additional shareholder value,* evidenced by a weak linkage between management compensation and firm performance.

Costs of Leverage: Financial Distress

As a firm increases its leverage, it increases the likelihood of financial distress, where it is unable to meet interest or principal repayment obligations to creditors. This may force the firm to declare bankruptcy or to agree to restructure its financial claims.

Financial distress can be expensive, since restructurings of a firm's ownership claims typically involve costly legal negotiations. It can also be difficult for distressed firms to raise capital to undertake profitable new investment opportunities. Finally, financial distress can intensify conflicts of interest between stockholders and the firm's debtholders, increasing the cost of debt financing.

Legal Costs of Financial Distress

When a firm is in serious financial distress, its owners' claims are likely to be restructured. This can take place under formal bankruptcy proceedings or out of bankruptcy. Restructurings are likely to be costly, since the parties involved have to hire lawyers, bankers, and accountants to represent their interests, and they have to pay court costs if there are formal legal proceedings. These are often called the *direct* costs of financial distress.

Costs of Foregone Investment Opportunities

When a firm is in financial distress and particularly when it is in bankruptcy, it may be very difficult for it to raise additional capital for new investments, even though they may be profitable for all the firm's owners. In some cases bankrupt firms are run by court-appointed trustees, who are unlikely to take on risky new investments—profitable or not. Even for a firm whose management supports new investment, the firm is likely to be capital constrained. Creditors are unlikely to approve the sale of nonessential assets unless the proceeds are used to first repay their claims. Potential new investors and creditors will be wary of the firm because they do not want to become embroiled in the legal disputes themselves. Thus, in all likelihood the firm will be unable to make significant new investments, potentially diminishing its value.

Costs of Conflicts Between Creditors and Stockholders

When a firm is performing well, both creditors' and stockholders' interests are likely to coincide. Both want the firm's managers to take all investments which increase the value of the firm. But when the firm is in financial difficulty, conflicts can arise between different classes of owners. Creditors become concerned about whether the firm will be able to meet its interest and principal commitments. Shareholders become concerned that their equity will revert to the creditors if the firm is unable to meet its outstanding obligations. Thus managers are likely to face increased pressure to make decisions which serve the interests of only one form of owner, typically stockholders, rather than making decisions in the best interests of all owners. For example, managers have incentives to issue additional debt with equal or higher priority, to invest in riskier assets, or to pay liquidating dividends, since these actions reduce the value of outstanding creditors' claims and benefit stockholders. When it is costly to completely eliminate this type of game playing, creditors will simply reduce the amount they are willing to pay the firm for the debt when it is issued, increasing the costs of borrowing for the firm's stockholders.

Overall Effects of Financial Distress

The costs of financial distress discussed above offset the tax and monitoring benefits of debt. As a result, firms that are more likely to fall into financial distress or for which the costs of financial distress are especially high should have relatively low financial leverage. Firms are more likely to fall into financial distress if they have high business risks, that is, if their revenues and earnings before interest are highly sensitive to fluctuations in the economy. Financial distress costs are also likely to be relatively high for firms whose assets are easily destroyed in financial distress. For example, firms with human capital and brand intangibles are particularly sensitive to financial distress since dissatisfied employees and customers can leave or seek alternative suppliers. In contrast, firms with tangible assets can sell their assets if they get into financial distress, providing additional security for lenders and lowering the costs of financial distress. Firms with intangible assets are therefore less likely to be highly leveraged than firms whose assets are mostly tangible.

These factors probably largely explain why Pfizer and Duke Energy, the two companies discussed at the beginning of the chapter, have such different financing policies. Pfizer probably keeps its leverage low because many of its core assets are intangibles, such as research staff and sales force representatives. These types of assets can easily be lost if Pfizer gets into financial difficulty as a result of too much leverage. In all likelihood, management would be forced to cut back on R&D and marketing, allowing their most talented researchers and sales representatives to be subject to offers from competitors. Pfizer can reduce these risks by having very low leverage.

In contrast, Duke Energy is a utility. It has very stable cash flows since its revenues are largely regulated. In addition, its major asset is its physical plant, which is less likely to diminish in value if it gets into financial distress. If the debtholders ended up as the new owners of the firm following financial distress, they could continue to use the existing assets. Duke Energy can therefore take advantage of the tax benefits from corporate debt without bearing a high cost of financial distress.

Key Analysis Questions

The above discussion implies that a firm's optimal financial leverage will depend on its underlying business risks and asset types. If the firm's business risks are relatively high or its assets can be easily destroyed by financial distress, changing the mix of debt and equity toward more debt may actually destroy shareholder value. Analysts can use ratio, cash flow, and pro forma analysis to assess a firm's business risks and whether its assets are easily destroyed by financial distress. Their analysis should focus on these activities:

- *Comparing indicators of business risk for the firm and other firms in its industry with the economy.* Popular indicators of business risk include the ratio of fixed operating expenses (such as depreciation on plant and equipment) to sales, the volatility of return on assets, as well as the relation between indicators of the firm's performance and indicators of performance for the economy as a whole.
- *Examining competition in the industry.* For firms in a highly competitive industry, performance is very sensitive to changes in strategy by competitors.
- *Determining whether the firm's assets are largely intangible and therefore sensitive to financial distress,* using such ratios as market-to-book equity.

Determining the Long-Term Optimal Mix of Debt and Equity

The above discussion implies that the optimal mix of debt and equity for a firm can be estimated by trading off the corporate interest tax shield and monitoring benefits of debt against the costs of financial distress. As the firm becomes more highly leveraged, the costs of leverage presumably begin to outweigh the tax and monitoring benefits of debt.

However there are several practical difficulties in trying to estimate a firm's optimal financial leverage. One difficulty is quantifying some of the costs and benefits of leverage. For example, it is not easy to value the expected costs of financial distress or any management incentive benefits from debt. There are no easy answers to this problem. The best that we can do is to qualitatively assess whether the firm faces free cash flow problems, and whether it faces high business risks and has assets that are easily destroyed by financial distress. These qualitative assessments can then be used to adjust the more easily quantified tax benefits from debt to determine whether the firm's financial leverage should be relatively high, low, or somewhere in between.

A second practical difficulty in deciding on a firm's level of financial leverage is quantifying what we mean by high, low, and medium. One way to resolve this question is to use indicators of financial leverage, such as debt-to-equity ratios, for the market as a whole as a guide on leverage ranges.

To provide a rough sense of what companies usually consider to be high and low financial leverage, Table 12-2 shows median debt-to-market equity and debt-to-book equity ratios for selected U.S. industries for the year ended December 31, 2001. Median ratios are reported for all listed companies and for NYSE companies.

Median debt-to-book equity ratios are highest for the electric services and water supply industries. The core assets for firms in these industries include physical equipment and property that are readily transferable to debt holders in the event of financial distress. In addition, firms in the electric power and water supply industries are typically not highly sensitive to economy risk. In contrast, the software and pharmaceutical industries' core assets are their research staffs. Ownership of these types of assets cannot be easily transferred to debt holders if the firm is in financial distress. Researchers are likely to leave for greener pastures if their budgets are cut. As a result, firms in this industry have relatively conservative capital structures. Petroleum refining and hotel firms have leverage in between these extremes, reflecting the need to balance the impact of having extensive physical assets and being subject to more volatile revenue streams.

It is also interesting to note that NYSE firms tend to have higher leverage than non-NYSE firms in the same industries. This probably reflects the fact that larger NYSE firms tend to have more product offerings and to be more diversified geographically, reducing

Table 12-2 Median Net Interest-Bearing Debt-to-Book Equity and Net Interest-Bearing Debt-to-Market Equity for Selected U.S. Industries in 2001

Industry	Net Interest-Bearing Debt-to-Book Equity		Net Interest-Bearing Debt-to-Market Equity	
	All Listed Firms	NYSE Firms	All Listed Firms	NYSE Firms
Prepackaged Computer Software	−64%	−25%	−17%	−7%
Pharmaceutical	−54%	−5%	−8%	−1%
Hotels & Motels	46%	64%	111%	68%
Petroleum Refining	52%	49%	29%	23%
Water Supply	96%	101%	40%	52%
Electric Services	124%	125%	67%	71%

their vulnerability to negative events for a single product or market, and enabling them to take on more debt.

The net debt-to-market equity ratios by and large tell a similar story to the debt-to-book equity ratios. They reflect the fact that most firms have market-to-book equity ratios greater than 1 because companies generally invest in projects that add value for stockholders and because some types of assets, such as R&D, are typically not reflected in book equity.

THE FINANCING OF NEW PROJECTS

The second model of capital structure focuses on how firms make new financing decisions. Proponents of this dynamic model argue that there can be short-term frictions in capital markets which cause deviations from long-run optimal capital structure. One source of friction arises when managers have better information about their firm's future performance than outside investors. This could lead managers to deviate from their long-term optimal capital structure as they seek financing for new investments.

To see how information asymmetries between outside investors and management can create market imperfections and potentially affect short-term capital structure decisions, consider management's options for financing a proprietary new project that it expects to be profitable. One financing option is to use retained earnings to cover the investment outlay. However, what if the firm has no retained earnings available today? If it pays dividends, it could perhaps cut dividends to help pay for the project. But as we see later, investors usually interpret a dividend cut as an indication that the firm's management anticipates poor future performance. A dividend cut is therefore likely to lead to a stock price decline, which management would probably prefer to avoid. Also, many firms do not pay dividends.

A second financing option is to borrow additional funds to finance the project. However, if the firm is already highly leveraged, the tax shield benefits from debt are likely to be relatively modest and the potential costs of financial distress relatively high, making additional borrowing unattractive.

The final financing option available to the firm is to issue new equity. However, if investors know that management has superior information on the firm's value, they are likely to interpret an equity offer as an indication that management believes that the firm's stock price is higher than the intrinsic value of the firm.[2] The announcement of an equity offer is therefore likely to lead to a drop in the price of the firm's stock, raising the firm's cost of capital, and potentially leading management to abandon a perfectly good project.

This discussion implies that if the firm has internal cash flows available or is not already highly leveraged, it is relatively straightforward for it to arrange financing for the new project. Otherwise, management has to decide whether undertaking the new project is worthwhile given the costs of cutting dividends, issuing additional debt, or issuing equity to finance the project. The information costs of raising funds by these means lead to a "pecking order" for new financing. Managers first use internal cash to fund investments, and only if this is unavailable do they resort to external financing. Further, if they have to use external financing, managers first use debt financing. New equity issues are used only as a last resort because of the difficulties that investors have in interpreting these issues.[3]

One way for management to mitigate the information problems of using external financing is to ensure that the firm has financial slack. Management can create financial slack by reinvesting free cash flows in marketable securities so that it doesn't have to go to the capital market to finance a new project. It could also choose to have relatively low levels of debt, so that the firm can borrow easily in the future.

In summary, information asymmetries between managers and external investors can make managers reluctant to raise equity to finance new projects. Managers' reluctance arises from their fear that investors will interpret the decision as an indication that the firm's stock is overvalued. In the short term, this effect can lead managers to deviate from the firm's long-term optimal mix of debt and equity.

Key Analysis Questions

The above discussion implies that in the short term management should attempt to finance new projects primarily with retained earnings. Further, it suggests that management would be well advised to maintain financial slack to ensure that it is not forced to use costly external financing. To assess a firm's financing options, we would ask the following types of questions:

- What is the value of current cash reserves (not required for day-to-day working capital needs) that could be used for new capital outlays? What operating cash resources are expected to become available in the coming few years? Do these internal resources cover the firm's expected cash needs for new investment and working capital?
- How do the firm's future cash needs for investment change as its operating performance deteriorates or improves? Are its investment opportunities relatively fixed, or are they related to current operating cash flow performance? Investment opportunities for many firms decline during a recession and increase during booms, enabling them to consistently use internal funds for financing. Therefore firms with stable investment needs should build financial slack during booms so that they can support investment during busts.
- If internal funds are not readily available, what opportunities does the firm have to raise low-cost debt financing? Normally, a firm which has virtually zero debt could do this without difficulty. However, if it is in a volatile industry or has mostly intangible assets, debt financing may be costly.
- If the firm has to raise costly equity capital, are there ways to focus investors on the value of the firm's assets and investment opportunities to lower any

> information asymmetries between managers and investors? For example, manage-ment might be able to disclose additional information about the value of existing assets, and the uses and expected returns from the new funds.

Summary of Debt Policy

There are no easy ways to quantify the best mix of debt and equity for a firm and its best financing options. However, some general principles are likely to be useful in thinking about these questions. We have seen that the benefits from debt financing are likely to be highest for firms with

- high marginal tax rates and few noninterest tax shields, making interest tax shields from debt valuable;
- high, stable income/cash flows and few new investment opportunities, increasing the monitoring value of debt and reducing the likelihood that the firm will fall into financial distress or require costly external financing for new projects; and
- high tangible assets that are not easily destroyed by financial distress.

The financial analysis tools developed in Part 2 of the book are useful in rating a firm's interest tax shield benefits, its business risk and investment opportunities, and its major asset types. This information can then be used to judge whether there are benefits from debt or whether the firm would be better off using equity financing to support its business strategies.

FACTORS THAT DETERMINE DIVIDEND POLICIES

To assess a firm's dividend policy, analysts typically examine its dividend payout, its dividend yield, and any stock repurchases. Dividend payout is defined as cash dividends as a percentage of income available to common shareholders, and it reflects the extent to which a company pays out profits or retains them for reinvestment. Dividend yield is dividends per share as a percentage of the current stock price, and indicates the current dividend return earned by shareholders. Finally, stock repurchases are relevant because many companies use repurchases of their own stock as an alternative way of returning cash to shareholders. Table 12-3 provides information on these variables for Pfizer and Duke Energy.

Table 12-3 Dividend Policy for Pfizer and Duke Energy for the Year Ended December 31, 2001

	Pfizer	Duke Energy
Dividend payout	35%	64%
Dividend yield	1.1%	3.9%
Cash common dividends	$2,715m	$1,200m
Stock repurchases	$3,603m	$0m

Pfizer appears to be following a more conservative dividend policy. It has a lower payout than Duke Energy and a lower dividend yield. However, in 2001 Pfizer returned

$3.6 billion to shareholders through stock repurchases, whereas Duke Energy made no stock repurchases. If this distribution is included with dividends, Pfizer actually paid out 81 percent of income in 2001.

What factors should a firm consider when setting its dividend policy? Do investors prefer firms to pay out profits as dividends or to retain them for reinvestment? As we noted above, many of the factors that affect dividends are similar to those examined in the section on capital structure decisions. This should not be too surprising, since a firm's dividend policy also affects its financing decisions. Thus, dividends provide a means of reducing free cash flow inefficiencies. They also have tax implications for investors and can reduce a firm's financial slack. Finally, lending contracts that are designed to protect lenders' interests can affect a firm's dividend payouts.

Below we discuss the factors that are relevant to managers' dividend decisions and how financial analysis tools can be used in this decision process.

Dividends as a Way of Reducing Free Cash Flow Inefficiencies

As we discussed earlier, conflicts of interest between managers and shareholders can affect a firm's optimal capital structure; they also have implications for dividend policy decisions. Stockholders of a firm with free cash flows and few profitable investment opportunities want managers to adopt a dividend policy with high payouts. This will deter managers from growing the firm by reinvesting the free cash flows in new projects that are not valued by stockholders or from spending the free cash flows on management perks. In addition, if managers of a firm with free cash flows wish to fund a new project, most stockholders would prefer that they do so by raising new external capital rather than cutting dividends. Stockholders can then assess whether the project is genuinely profitable or simply one of management's pet projects.

Key Analysis Questions

Earlier we discussed how ratio and cash flow analysis can help analysts assess whether a firm faces free cash flow inefficiencies, and how pro forma analysis can help indicate the likelihood of future free cash flow problems. The same analysis and questions can be used to decide whether a firm should initiate dividends.

Tax Costs of Dividends

What are the implications for dividend policy if dividends and capital gains are taxed, particularly at different rates? Classical models of the tax effects of dividends predict that if the capital gains tax rate is less than the rate on dividend income, investors will prefer that the firm either pay no dividends, so that they subsequently take gains as capital accumulation, or that the firm undertakes a stock repurchase, which qualifies as a capital distribution. Even if capital gains are slightly higher than dividend tax rates, investors may prefer capital gains to dividends since they do not actually have to realize their capital gains. They can delay selling their shares and thereby defer paying the taxes on any capital appreciation. Of course, if capital gains tax rates are substantially higher than the rates on ordinary income, investors are likely to favor dividend distributions over capital gains.

Today many practitioners and theorists believe that taxes play only a minor role in determining a firm's dividend policy since a firm can attract investors with various tax preferences. Thus a firm that wishes to pay high dividend rates will attract stockholders that are tax-exempt institutions, which do not pay taxes on dividend income. In contrast, a firm that prefers to pay low dividend rates will attract stockholders who have high marginal tax rates and prefer capital gains to dividend income.

Dividends and Financial Slack

We discussed earlier how managers' information advantage over dispersed investors can increase a firm's cost of external funds. One way to avoid having to raise costly external funds is to have a conservative dividend policy which creates financial slack in the organization. By paying only a small percentage of income as dividends and reinvesting the free cash flows in marketable securities, management reduces the likelihood that the firm will have to go to the capital market to finance a new project.

Managers of firms with high intangible assets and growth opportunities are particularly likely to have an information advantage over dispersed investors, since accounting information for these types of firms is frequently a poor indicator of future performance. Accountants, for example, do not attempt to value R&D, intangibles, or growth opportunities. These types of firms are therefore more likely to face information problems and capital market constraints. To compound this problem, high-growth firms are typically heavily dependent on external financing since they are not usually able to fund all new investments internally. Any capital market constraints are therefore likely to affect their ability to undertake profitable new projects.

Because paying dividends reduces financial slack and is thus costly, a firm's dividend policy can help management communicate effectively with external investors. Investors recognize that managers will only increase their firm's dividend rate if they anticipate that the payout does not have a serious effect on the firm's future financing options. Thus, the decision to increase dividends can help investors appreciate management's optimism about the firm's future performance and its ability to finance growth.[4]

Key Analysis Questions

As noted earlier for debt policy, the financial analysis tools discussed in Part 2 of the book can help analysts assess how much financial slack a firm should maintain. The same analysis and questions are relevant to dividend policy analysis. Based on the answers to the earlier questions, analysts can assess whether the firm's projected cash needs for new investments are stable in relation to its operating cash flows. If so, it makes sense for management not to pursue too high a dividend payout and to build financial slack during boom periods to help fund investments during busts. Similarly, if the firm's ability to raise low-cost debt is limited because it is in a volatile industry or has mostly intangible assets, management is likely to avoid high dividend payouts to reduce the risk that it will have to raise high-cost external capital in the future or even forego a profitable new project.

Lending Constraints and Dividend Policy

One of the concerns of a firm's creditors is that when the firm is in financial distress, managers will pay a large dividend to stockholders. This problem is likely to be particularly severe for a firm with highly liquid assets, since its managers can pay a large dividend without selling assets. To limit these types of ploys, managers agree to restrict dividend payments to stockholders. Such dividend covenants usually require the firm to maintain certain minimum levels of retained earnings and current asset balances, which effectively limit dividend payments in times of financial difficulty. However these constraints on dividend policy are unlikely to be severe for a profitable firm.

Determining Optimal Dividend Payouts

One question that arises in using the above factors to determine dividend policy is defining what we mean by high, low, and medium dividend payouts. To provide a rough sense of what companies usually consider to be high and low dividend payouts and yields, Table 12-4 shows median dividend payout ratios and dividend yields for selected U.S. industries for the year ended December 31, 2001. Median ratios are reported for all listed companies and for NYSE companies.

Table 12-4 Median Dividend Payout Ratio and Dividend Yield for Selected U.S. Industries in 2001

Industry	Dividend Payout Ratio		Dividend Yield	
	All Listed Firms	NYSE Firms	All Listed Firms	NYSE Firms
Prepackaged Computer Software	0%	0%	0.0%	0.0%
Pharmaceutical	0%	1%	0.0%	0.8%
Hotels & Motels	0%	0%	0.0%	0.0%
Petroleum Refining	0%	12%	0.9%	1.9%
Electric Services	47%	49%	4.2%	4.3%
Water Supply	58%	61%	3.0%	3.0%

It is interesting to note that many U.S. listed companies do not pay any dividends. This is particularly true for non-NYSE firms, which probably have more attractive growth opportunities. The highest payouts tend to be made by public utilities, such as natural gas, water, and electric services. For these firms the median payouts tend to be roughly 45–60 percent and yields are between 3 and 4.3 percent. In contrast, firms in highly competitive industries with substantial reinvestment opportunities, such as software and pharmaceutical, tend to have very low dividend payouts and dividend yields.

Returning to the cases of Pfizer and Duke Energy, it is interesting to see that Pfizer has a higher dividend payout ratio than its industry median (35 percent versus 0 percent). When stock repurchases are included, Pfizer actually paid out 81 percent of its 2001 profits. Apparently the company believes that it does not have to reinvest all of its profits to maintain its high rate of success in drug development. It is also interesting to note that Pfizer uses stock repurchases as an important way to return funds to shareholders. One potential explanation for this is that Pfizer does not want to commit to the current high rate of payout indefinitely. Its dividend payout therefore represents its long-term payout commitment, and repurchases are used for temporary increases in that rate. Also, Pfizer's use of stock repurchases is probably tax effective for its shareholders since capital gains rates on repurchased stock gains are lower than ordinary income rates on dividends.

A Summary of Dividend Policy

Just as it is difficult to provide a simple formula to compute a firm's optimal capital structure, it is difficult to formalize the optimal dividend policy. However, we can identify several factors that appear to be important:

- High-growth firms should have low dividend payout ratios, and they should use their internally generated funds for reinvestment. This minimizes any costs from capital market constraints on financing growth options.
- Firms with high and stable operating cash flows and few investment opportunities should have high dividend payouts to reduce managers' incentives to reinvest free cash flows in unprofitable ventures.
- Firms should probably not be too concerned about tax factors in setting dividend policy. Whatever their policy, they will be able to attract a clientele of investors. Firms that select high dividend payouts will attract tax-exempt institutions or corporations, and firms that pay low or no dividends will attract individuals in high tax brackets.
- Firms' financial covenants can have an impact on their dividend policy decisions. Firms will try to avoid being too close to their constraints in order to minimize the possibility of cutting their dividend.

SUMMARY

This chapter examined how firms make optimal capital structure and dividend decisions. We show that a firm's optimal long-term capital structure is largely determined by its expected tax status, business risks, and types of assets. The benefits from debt financing are expected to be highest for firms with (1) high marginal tax rates and few non-interest tax shields, making interest tax shields valuable; (2) high, stable income/cash flows and few new investment opportunities, increasing the monitoring value of debt and reducing the likelihood that the firm will fall into financial distress; and (3) high tangible assets that are not easily destroyed by financial distress.

We also show that, in the short term, managers can deviate from their long-term optimal capital structure when they seek financing for new investments. In particular, managers are reluctant to raise external financing, especially new equity, for fear that outside investors will interpret their action as meaning that the firm is overvalued. This information problem has implications for how much financial slack a firm is likely to need to avoid facing these types of information problems.

Optimal dividend policy is determined by many of the same factors—firms' business risks and their types of assets. Thus, dividend rates should be highest for firms with high and stable cash flows and few investment opportunities. By paying out relatively high dividends, these firms reduce the risk of managers investing free cash flows in unprofitable projects. Conversely, firms with low, volatile cash flows and attractive investment opportunities, such as start-up firms, should have relatively low dividend payouts. By reinvesting operating cash flows and reducing the amount of external financing required for new projects, these firms reduce their costs of financing.

Financial statement analysis can be used to better understand a firm's business risks, its expected tax status, and whether its assets are primarily assets in place or growth opportunities. Useful tools for assessing whether a firm's current capital structure and dividend policies maximize shareholder value include accounting analysis to determine off-balance-sheet liabilities, ratio analysis to help understand a firm's business risks, and cash flow and pro forma analysis to explore current and likely future investment needs.

DISCUSSION QUESTIONS

1. Financial analysts typically measure financial leverage as the ratio of debt to equity. However, there is less agreement on how to measure debt, or even equity. How would you treat the following items in computing this ratio? Justify your answers.
   - Revolving credit agreement with bank
   - Cash and marketable securities
   - Deferred tax liabilities
   - Preferred stock
   - Convertible debt

2. Until 1987 Master Limited Partnerships (MLPs) were treated as partnerships for tax purposes. This meant that no corporate taxes were paid by the entity. Instead, taxes were paid by partners (at their individual tax rates) on entity profits (both distributed and undistributed). The marginal tax rate for corporations in 1987 was 34 percent, compared to 33 percent for individuals in the highest tax bracket.
   a. If an entity distributes all after-tax earnings as dividends and generates before-tax earnings of $10 million, what would be the distribution to owners (after entity and personal taxes) if it is organized as (1) a corporation and (2) an MLP?
   b. What would be the optimal capital structure for the MLP discussed in (a)? Justify your answer.
   c. What types of dividend policy do you expect the MLP to follow? Why?

3. Finance theory implies that the debt-to-equity ratio should be computed using the market values of debt and equity. However, most financial analysts use book values of debt and equity to compute a firm's financial leverage. What are the limitations of using book values rather than market values for comparing leverage across industries or firms? For what types of industries/firms are book values likely to be most misleading?

4. One important driver of a firm's capital structure and dividend policy decisions is its business risk. What ratios would you look at to assess business risk? Name two industries with very high business risk and two industries with very low business risk.

5. U.S. public companies with "low" leverage have an interest-bearing net debt-to-equity ratio of 0 percent or less, firms with "medium" leverage have a ratio between 1 and 62 percent, and "high" leverage firms have a ratio of 63 percent or more. Given these data, how would you classify the following firms in terms of their optimal debt-to-equity ratio (high, medium, or low)?
   - a successful pharmaceutical company
   - an electric utility
   - a manufacturer of consumer durables
   - a commercial bank
   - a start-up software company

6. A rapidly growing Internet company, recently listed on NASDAQ, needs to raise additional capital to finance new research and development. What financing options are available, and what are the trade-offs between each?

7. The following table reports (in millions) earnings, dividends, capital expenditures, and R&D for Intel for the period 1990–95:

Year	Net Income	Dividends	Capital Expenditures	R&D
1990	$650	$0	$680	$517
1991	819	0	948	618
1992	1,067	43	1,228	780
1993	2,295	88	1,933	970
1994	2,288	100	2,441	1,111
1995	3,566	133	3,550	1,296

What are the dividend payout rates for Intel during these years? Is this payout policy consistent with the factors expected to drive dividend policy discussed in the chapter? What factors do you expect would lead Intel's management to increase its dividend payout? How do you expect the stock market to react to such a decision?

8. U.S. public companies with low dividend payouts have payout ratios of 0 percent or less, firms with medium payouts have ratios between 1 and 48 percent, and high payout firms have a ratio of 49 percent or more. Given these data, how would you classify the following firms in terms of their optimal payout policy (high, medium, or low)?
   • a successful pharmaceutical company
   • an electric utility
   • a manufacturer of consumer durables
   • a commercial bank
   • a start-up software company

9. It is frequently argued that Japanese and German companies can afford to have more financial leverage and to follow lower dividend payout policies than U.S. companies because they are largely owned by financial institutions that have long-term horizons. Does this argument make economic sense? If so, explain why, and if not, why not. What other factors might explain differences in capital structure and dividend policy across countries?

10. In 1990 U.S. tax law increased capital gains rates from 20 percent to the same level as ordinary income rates, between 28 and 34 percent. What implications does this change have for corporate dividend policy and capital structure?

NOTES

1. See Merton Miller, "Debt and Taxes," *Journal of Finance* 32 (May 1977): 261–76.

2. Paul Healy and Krishna Palepu in "Earnings and Risk Changes Surrounding Primary Stock Offers," *Journal of Accounting Research* 28 (Spring 1990): 25–49, find that announcements of stock issues are interpreted by investors as a signal from management that the firm is riskier than investors expected.

3. These issues are discussed by Stewart Myers and Nicholas Majluf in "Corporate Financing and Investment Decisions When Firms Have Information That Investors Do Not Have," *Journal of Financial Economics* (June 1984): 187–221.

4. Findings by Paul Healy and Krishna Palepu in "Earnings Information Conveyed by Dividend Initiations and Omissions," *Journal of Financial Economics* 21 (September 1988): 149–75, indicate that investors interpret announcements of dividends initiations and omissions as managers' forecasts of future earnings performance.

CUC International, Inc. (A)

In March 1989 Stuart Bell, Executive Vice President and CFO of CUC International, Inc., was concerned that the company's stock was seriously undervalued. He attributed the undervaluation to the investment community's concern about the quality of CUC's earnings:

> I am afraid our accounting is misunderstood by many investors. Recently, we have been forced to spend a lot of top management time and energy defending our policy in analysts' meetings. As a result we have been unable to focus investors' attention on our innovative business strategy and the tremendous cash-flow generating potential of our business. Concerns about our earnings quality are scaring new institutional investors from investing in our business. Many money managers tell me that they love our business concept but are afraid to buy our stock because they are worried about our accounting. The accounting is also giving short sellers an excuse to scare our current investors and drive down the stock price.

While Bell was convinced that CUC's accounting was appropriate, he wondered whether it was actually hurting, rather than helping, the company. What, if anything, should CUC do to shore up investors' confidence in the company?

BUSINESS HISTORY AND OPERATIONS

CUC International, located in Stamford, Connecticut, was a membership-based consumer services company. CUC marketed its membership programs to credit cardholders of major financial, retailing, and oil companies, including Chase Manhattan, Citibank, Sears, JC Penney, and Amoco. The company was formed in 1973 as Comp-U-Card of America, went public in 1983, and was renamed CUC International in 1987. As a result of its strong performance, the company was included in *Inc.* magazine's list of the fastest growing public companies in 1984 and 1986.

CUC's most popular product was Shoppers Advantage, introduced in 1981. Consumers paid an annual membership fee for this service, which entitled them to call the company's operators on a toll-free line, or to use on-line computer access seven days a week to inquire about, price, and/or buy brand-name products. Shoppers Advantage offered more than 250,000 brand-name and specialty items. Many members used the service principally as a reference for comparison pricing, not necessarily to purchase items directly. The company's large membership base allowed it to negotiate attractive discounts on the products offered in its catalog. As a result, the company guaranteed its subscribers the lowest prices available on goods it sold. If a member, after purchasing merchandise through CUC, sent an advertisement from an authorized dealer with a lower price within 30 days of placing an order, the company agreed to refund the difference. Members' purchase orders were executed through independent vendors who shipped the merchandise directly to customers, enabling the company to carry no inventory.

The firm acquired a large share of its new members through agreements with major credit card issuers, who provided CUC access to its list of cardholders. These individuals

Professor Paul Healy and Professor Krishna Palepu prepared this case. The case is intended solely as the basis for class discussion and is not intended to serve as an endorsement, source of primary data, or illustration of effective or ineffective management. Copyright © 1992 by the President and Fellows of Harvard College. HBS Case 9-192-099.

were solicited by three direct marketing approaches: billing statement inserts, solo mailings, and telemarketing. In billing statement insert programs, membership applications were enclosed in the monthly billing statements of credit card issuers. Solo mailings were membership offers mailed directly. Telemarketing involved following up mailings with telephone calls to explain membership offers further. CUC paid 10 to 20 percent of initial and renewal membership fees as a commission to the credit card company.

CUC incurred a large one-time cost for new member solicitations. Because only a small fraction of people reached through direct mail solicitations purchased the service, membership acquisition costs typically exceeded membership fees in the first year. For example, in 1989 the annual membership fee for Shoppers Advantage was $39, the average solicitation cost per new member was $29.37, commissions to the credit card companies were $6.63, and the average operating service cost per member was $5.00. Thus on average for each new member acquired, CUC incurred a cash outflow of $2 in the first year.

Members subscribed to Shoppers Advantage for a single year at a time. Renewals were automatically billed each year through the credit card company, and members could elect to cancel the service. There were thus no direct solicitation costs for renewing members. In 1989 CUC had a net cash inflow of $27.37 for each renewing member—membership fees were $39, and the commissions to the credit card companies and operating service costs totaled $11.63.[1] Membership renewal rates were therefore a key determinant of the profitability of the Shoppers Advantage program. The average annual renewal rate for Shoppers Advantage in recent years was 71 percent, making the program very profitable. This average was based on eight years' experience with the product since 1981.

CUC capitalized on its Shoppers Advantage experience by introducing a variety of other membership-based products. These included: (1) Travellers Advantage—a travel membership created in 1988 to provide subscribers access to database information and reservations on discount airline travel, hotels and auto rental, tours, and cruises; (2) AutoVantage—provided subscribers with new car price and performance summaries, used car valuations, and parts and service discounts; and (3) Premier Dining—a service introduced in 1989 that offered subscribers two-for-one dining at mid- to upscale restaurants in major U.S. cities. The company made large marketing investments to build memberships in these new programs.

CUC's management explained the key elements of its business strategy as follows:

The company's expansion has been built on a foundation of creating, developing, and marketing a broad array of valuable services to consumers. . . . Aggressive marketing is an important strength. We sell our goods and services directly to millions of customers of major credit card issuers. Because our consumer services are a natural enhancement to personal financial services, more than 40 of the top 50 money center banks and a growing number of retailers and oil companies find it advantageous to work with CUC. . . . As competition heats up in the financial services industry, demand for CUC's services is likely to increase. Credit card issuers rely upon our services to draw new customers, increase card use, and raise average balances. They also use our services to differentiate their cards from others, and to tailor what they offer to appeal to different life-style and geographic preferences. Finally, card issuers benefit from the stream of membership commissions they receive from CUC.[2]

1. The figures in this and the previous paragraph are from an analyst report by Brian E. Stack of Advest, Inc. dated October 30, 1989.

2. Source: CUC's 1988 Annual Report.

By December 1988, CUC had approximately 12 million members enrolled in its programs. Revenues had grown from $45 million in the year ending January 31, 1984 (fiscal year 1984) to $198 million in the year ending January 31,1988 (fiscal 1988), and earnings had grown from $3 million to $17 million during this period. Exhibits 3 and 4 present the financial statements for the year ended January 31, 1988, and for the nine months ended October 31, 1988. Management expected the company to continue its rapid growth in the future, with revenues for the fiscal year ending January 31, 1989 projected to be approximately $270 million.

THE FINANCIAL REPORTING CONTROVERSY

CUC's management decided that because current marketing outlays provided significant future benefits, the company should capitalize membership solicitation costs in its financial statements, and amortize them over three years at rates of 40 percent, 30 percent, and 30 percent. This choice was endorsed by Ernst & Whinney, the company's auditors, and by the Securities and Exchange Commission when the company went public.

While it was unusual to capitalize marketing costs, CUC's managers believed that this decision was justified given the nature of the company's business and their confidence in future renewal rates. Bell explained the rationale behind CUC's accounting choice:

> *Many companies spend money on acquiring plant and equipment, and they capitalize these costs. Our business does not require major investments in plant and equipment. Instead, it requires investments in membership acquisitions. Because our membership renewal rates are so high and steady, I believe that it is important for accounting to reflect future benefits from spending money on membership acquisition in the current period. While expensing these costs is conservative, it fails to reflect their true nature.*

In its accounting choice, CUC's management could not obtain much guidance from other companies' practices. Magazine publishers typically expensed costs of acquiring new subscribers, whereas insurance companies capitalized policy acquisition costs. Safecard Services, Inc., a credit-card registration company which also incurred large outlays for membership acquisition, capitalized its membership acquisition costs and amortized them over a ten-year period.

When CUC made the initial public stock offering, it had only a limited following among analysts and institutional investors. As the company grew larger, it sought to broaden its investor base. Some analysts, however, were concerned that capitalized marketing costs would subsequently have to be written off as losses because of high uncertainty about future renewal rates. They argued that deferring current marketing costs lowered the firm's earnings quality.

Analysts' concerns about the firm's accounting for marketing costs may have arisen from their experience with Safecard Services Inc. Safecard's capitalization of membership acquisition costs had been the subject of considerable controversy in the financial press. Safecard's decision to write off deferred marketing costs in 1987 may have heightened analysts' concerns about the value of CUC's capitalized marketing costs.

By early 1989 the company's stock had become a target of short sellers and its price began to suffer. As shown in Exhibit 1, short positions in the company rose from approximately 157,000 in November 1988 to more than 2,000,000 in March 1989.[3] While the

---

3. *Source:* Barron's Financial Weekly *(Dow Jones News Service).*

stock market was generally on the upswing, CUC's stock price declined from $19.3 at the beginning of January 1988 to $16.3 at the beginning of March 1989. Exhibit 2 shows the stock price performance for CUC relative to the performance of the value-weighted OTC market index between January 1, 1988, and March 1, 1989. During this period CUC's stock price declined by 50 percent relative to the market. *Value Line Investment Survey* commented in its report on CUC dated March 17, 1989:

> *CUC International shares have taken a beating. The stock has fallen more than 35% since our last report three months ago. Wall Street's concern over the company's accounting methods . . . contributed to the stock price decline.*

Management believed that the decline in CUC's stock performance could not be explained by either disappointing current operating performance or by forecasts of slower growth. Quarterly revenues and earnings grew steadily throughout 1988, and were consistent with *Value Line* analyst forecasts. In its March 18, 1988, report, *Value Line* forecasted that the company would have earnings of $5.5 million, $6 million, and $6.6 million in the quarters ending in April 1988, July 1988, and October 1988. Actual earnings in these quarters were $6 million, $6.6 million, and $6.9 million, respectively. The company projected that its growth would continue in the future—sales were projected to grow by 30 percent per year and operating cash flows would grow by 60 percent per year during the next five years. Finally, the firm was able to fund its substantial marketing outlays solely from operating cash flows during this period.

POSSIBLE MANAGEMENT RESPONSES

At least three options were available to CUC's management in responding to investors' concerns. One approach would be to adopt a more conservative policy to account for membership acquisition costs. By writing off previously capitalized expenses and adopting a policy of expensing future outlays as incurred, the firm would eliminate the major source of analysts' criticisms. However, such a move would seriously affect the company's balance sheet and income statement. More important, the accounting change would be unlikely to help management convince investors that current marketing outlays have future benefits.

An alternative strategy would be to provide expanded disclosure to justify the firm's capitalization of membership acquisition costs. This approach would involve identifying what type of information is likely to be most relevant and credible to investors. Further, it would require assessing whether the additional disclosures would provide proprietary information to competitors.

Finally, CUC could use corporate finance policies to enhance its stock price. Investors typically interpret cash payouts in the form of dividends and share repurchases as an indication of management's optimism about the firm's future cash flows. Such payouts, however, need to be planned in the context of the firm's investment needs for membership acquisitions.

One of the items on the agenda of CUC's upcoming board meeting was to consider proposals for dealing with the firm's communication challenge. Stu Bell was wondering which of the above options he should recommend.

QUESTIONS

1. Evaluate CUC's business model. What are the key value drivers and risks in this business?

2. Why do you think the investors are so concerned about CUC?

3. CUC's CFO Stu Bell was considering a large stock repurchase or one-time dividend payment, financed by debt, as a way to improve investor confidence. Do you think this is a good idea? What is the maximum amount the company can borrow to finance this initiative without taking undue financial risk? Under your recommendation, what will CUC's interest coverage and cash flow available for servicing interest and principal payments on the debt be for the next two years?

4. Assuming CUC implements the stock repurchase or dividend payment plan, should the company do anything with respect to its accounting for membership acquisition costs?

EXHIBIT 1

CUC International Shares Sold Short from January 1988 to March 1989

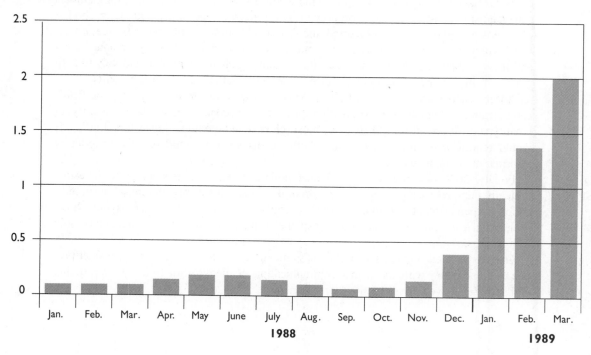

No. of Shares in Millions

EXHIBIT 2

Cumulative Difference in Stock Returns for CUC International and the OTC Market
Index in the Period January 4, 1988, to March 9, 1989

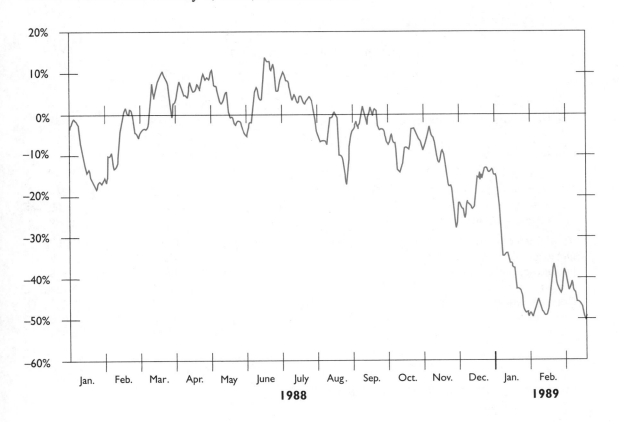

EXHIBIT 3

CUC International, Abridged Annual Report for the Year Ended January 31, 1988

CONSOLIDATED FINANCIAL STATEMENTS

CONSOLIDATED BALANCE SHEET

	January 31	
(Dollar amounts in thousands)	1988	1987
ASSETS		
Current Assets		
Cash and cash equivalents	$ 25,953	$ 14,810
Receivables, less allowance of $613 and $405	33,201	24,209
Prepaid expenses and other	3,468	3,288
Total Current Assets	62,622	42,307
Deferred membership charges, net	22,078	13,112
Prepaid solicitation costs	17,089	4,915
Prepaid commissions	6,267	8,127
Contract renewal rights, net	27,944	30,443
Excess of cost over net assets acquired, net	33,301	19,066
Properties, net	16,048	10,074
Other	1,519	4,416
Total Assets	$186,868	$132,460
LIABILITIES AND SHAREHOLDERS' EQUITY		
Current Liabilities		
Members' deposits	$ 4,997	$ 4,340
Accounts payable and accrued expenses	36,063	16,446
Federal and state income taxes	423	
Current portion of long-term obligations	1,404	5,011
Total Current Liabilities	42,887	25,797
Convertible subordinated debentures	12,000	22,000
Long-term obligations	3,767	5,120
Deferred income taxes	14,624	6,073
Other	1,229	1,268
Total Liabilities	74,507	60,258
Shareholders' Equity		
Common stock-par value $.01 per share; authorized 50 million shares; issued 19,683,567 and 17,820,338	197	178
Additional paid-in capital	82,271	59,550
Retained earnings	32,420	14,997
Treasury stock—398,230 and 398,091 shares, at cost	(2,527)	(2,523)
Total Shareholders' Equity	112,361	72,202
Total Liabilities and Shareholders' Equity	$186,868	$132,460

CONSOLIDATED STATEMENT OF INCOME

(Dollar amounts in thousands, except per share amounts)	Year Ended January 31		
	1988	1987	1986
Revenues			
Membership and service fees	$195,277	$138,149	$84,123
Other	3,180	3,610	3,342
Total Revenues	198,457	141,759	87,465
Expenses			
Operating	64,092	43,248	26,729
Marketing	68,937	56,496	35,042
General and administrative	31,729	23,342	14,572
Interest	2,259	2,663	1,507
Total Expenses	167,017	125,749	77,850
Operating Income	31,440	16,010	9,615
Acquisition costs			2,348
Income Before Income Taxes and Extraordinary Credit	31,440	16,010	7,267
Provision for income taxes	14,017	7,350	4,435
Income Before Extraordinary Credit	17,423	8,660	2,832
Extraordinary credit-utilization of tax loss carryforwards		1,041	3,589
Net Income	$ 17,423	$ 9,701	$ 6,421
Income Per Common Share			
Income before extraordinary credit	$.90	$.49	$.18
Extraordinary credit		.06	.23
Net Income Per Common Share	$.90	$.55	$.41

CUC International

CONSOLIDATED STATEMENT OF CASH FLOWS

(Dollar amounts in thousands)	Year Ended January 31		
	1988	1987	1986
Operating Activities			
Net income	$17,423	$ 9,701	$ 6,421
Adjustments to reconcile net income to net cash provided by operating activities:			
Amortization of membership acquisition costs	44,641	35,501	20,237
Amortization of prepaid commissions	1,860	2,029	2,081
Amortization of contract rights and excess cost	3,423	2,199	
Deferred income taxes	11,712	5,553	442
Depreciation	2,506	2,582	1,969
Extraordinary credit and loss from discontinued operations			(1,475)
Change in operating assets and liabilities, net of acquisitions:			
Net (increase) decrease in receivables	(8,049)	(6,747)	3,795
Net increase (decrease) in members' deposits, accounts payable and accrued expenses and federal and state income taxes	12,755	(3,649)	(586)
Deferred membership income	9,629	14,366	9,052
Membership acquisition costs	(63,236)	(43,720)	(42,564)
Prepaid solicitation costs	(12,174)	(4,915)	
Prepaid commissions			(409)
Other, net	2,576	(1,748)	39
Net cash from (used in) operating activities	23,066	11,152	(998)
Investing Activities			
Acquisitions, net of cash acquired	(4,625)	(18,341)	
Acquisitions of properties	(7,586)	(5,078)	(4,345)
Proceeds from disposal of properties net of $3.2 million note receivable		783	
Disposals of marketable securities		1,933	2,724
Other, net			240
Net cash from (used in) investing activities	(12,211)	(20,703)	(1,381)
Financing Activities			
Issuance of Common Stock	5,326	6,220	613
Issuance of convertible subordinated debentures			15,000
Purchase of treasury stock		(2,377)	
Repayments of long-term obligations	(4,960)	(2,955)	(795)
Other, net	(78)		
Net cash from financing activities	288	888	14,818
Net Increase (Decrease) in Cash and Cash Equivalents	11,143	(8,663)	12,439
Cash and cash equivalents at beginning of year	14,810	23,473	11,034
Cash and cash equivalents at end of year	$25,953	$14,810	$23,473

CUC International

NOTES TO CONSOLIDATED FINANCIAL STATEMENTS

Note 1. Summary of Significant Accounting Policies

Principles of Consolidation: The consolidated financial statements include the accounts of CUC International Inc. (formerly Comp-U-Card International Incorporated) and its wholly-owned subsidiaries. The Company operates in one business segment, providing a variety of services through individual, financial institution, credit union and group memberships. All significant intercompany transactions have been eliminated in consolidation.

Deferred Membership Charges, Net: Deferred membership charges is comprised of (in thousands):

January 31,	1988	1987
Deferred membership income	$(52,834)	$(43,205)
Unamortized membership acquisition costs	74,912	56,317
Deferred membership charges, net	$ 22,078	$ 13,112

The related membership fees and membership acquisition costs have been between $30 and $39 per individual member during the years ended January 31, 1988 and 1987. In addition, the annual renewal costs have remained between ten and twenty percent of annual membership fees for the same period.

Renewal costs consist principally of charges from sponsoring institutions and are amortized over the renewal period. Individual memberships are principally for a one-year period. These membership fees are recorded, as deferred membership income, upon acceptance of membership, net of estimated cancellations, and pro-rated over the membership period. The related initial membership acquisition costs are recorded as incurred and charged to operations as membership fees are recognized, allowing for renewals, over a three-year period. Such costs are amortized commencing with the beginning of the membership period, at the annual rate of 40%, 30% and 30%, respectively. Membership renewal rates are dependent upon the nature of the benefits and services provided by the Company in its various membership programs. Through January 31, 1988, membership renewal rates have been sufficient to generate future revenue in excess of deferred membership acquisition costs over the remaining amortization period.

Amortization of membership acquisition costs, including deferred renewal costs, amounted to $44.6 million, $35.5 million and $20.2 million for the years ended January 31, 1988, 1987, and 1986, respectively.

Prepaid Solicitation Costs: Prepaid solicitation costs consist of initial membership acquisition costs pertaining to membership solicitation programs that were in process at year end. Accordingly, no membership fees had been received or recognized at year end.

Prepaid Commissions: Prepaid commissions consist of the amount to be paid in connection with the termination of contracts with the Company's field sales force ($4.9 million and $5.8 million at January 31, 1988 and 1987, respectively) and the termination of special compensation agreements with an officer and former officer ($1.3 million and $1.6 million at January 31, 1988 and 1987, respectively). The amount relating to the termination of the field sales force is being amortized, using the straight-line method, over eight years and the amount relating to the termination of the special compensation agreement is being amortized ratably over ten years.

Contract Renewal Rights: Contract renewal rights represent the value assigned to contracts acquired in acquisitions and are being amortized over 9 to 16 years using the straight-line method.

CUC International

Excess of Cost Over Net Assets Acquired: The excess of cost over net assets acquired is being amortized over 15 to 25 years using the straight-line method.

Earnings Per Share: Amounts per share have been computed using the weighted average number of common and common equivalent shares outstanding. The weighted average number of common and common equivalent shares outstanding was 19.4 million, 17.8 million and 15.8 million for the years ended January 31, 1988, 1987, and 1986, respectively. Fully diluted earnings per share did not differ significantly from primary earnings per share in any year.

Statement of Cash Flows: The Company adopted Financial Accounting Standards Board (FASB) "Statement of Cash Flows" in its fiscal 1988 financial statements and restated previously reported statements of changes in financial position for fiscal years 1987 and 1986. For purposes of the consolidated statement of cash flows, the Company considers all investments with a maturity of three months or less to be cash equivalents.

FINANCIAL HIGHLIGHTS

(In thousands, except per share amounts)

Year Ended January 31	1988	1987	1986	1985	1984
Total Revenues	$198,457	$141,759	$87,465	$65,947	$45,468
Net Income	17,423	9,701	6,421	4,214	3,184
Per Common Share:					
Net Income	$ .90	$ .55	$ .41	$ .28	$ .23
Book Value	5.83	4.14	2.33	1.94	1.70
Shareholders' Equity	$112,361	$ 72,202	$34,859	$28,673	$24,806
Number of Active Members	10,000	8,400	4,700	1,200	450

REPORT OF INDEPENDENT AUDITORS

Ernst & Whinney

Six Landmark Square, Suite 500
Stamford, Connecticut 06901

Board of Directors and Shareholders
CUC International Inc.
Stamford, Connecticut

We have examined the consolidated balance sheet of CUC International Inc. as of January 31, 1988 and 1987, and the related consolidated statements of income, shareholders' equity and cash flows for each of the three years in the period ended January 31, 1988. Our examinations were made in accordance with generally accepted auditing standards and, accordingly, included such tests of the accounting records and such other auditing procedures as we considered necessary in the circumstances.

In our opinion, the consolidated financial statements referred to above present fairly the consolidated financial position of CUC International Inc. at January 31, 1988 and 1987, and the consolidated results of operations and cash flows for each of the three years in the period ended January 31, 1988, in conformity with generally accepted principles applied on a consistent basis.

Ernst & Whinney

Stamford, Connecticut
March 30, 1988

CUC International

EXHIBIT 4

CUC International, Abridged Interim Financial Statements for Nine Months Ended October 31, 1988

CONSOLIDATED BALANCE SHEET

(Dollar amounts in thousands)	October 31, 1988 (unaudited)	January 31, 1988
ASSETS		
Current Assets		
Cash and cash equivalents	$ 32,003	$ 25,953
Receivables	38,118	33,201
Other	4,164	3,468
Total Current Assets	74,285	62,622
Deferred membership charges, net	37,223	22,078
Prepaid solicitation costs	25,538	17,089
Prepaid commissions	5,397	6,267
Contract renewal rights and intangible assets, net	64,419	61,245
Properties, net	19,805	16,048
Other	2,040	1,519
Total Assets	$228,707	$186,868
LIABILITIES AND SHAREHOLDERS' EQUITY		
Current Liabilities		
Members' deposits	$ 4,485	$ 4,997
Accounts payable and accrued expenses	50,017	36,063
Federal and state income taxes	1,264	423
Current portion of long-term obligations	1,494	1,404
Total Current Liabilities	57,260	42,887
Convertible subordinated debentures	12,000	12,000
Long-term obligations	2,673	3,767
Deferred income taxes	16,844	14,624
Other	1,402	1,229
Total Liabilities	90,179	74,507
Shareholders' Equity		
Common Stock	203	197
Other shareholders' equity	138,325	112,164
Total Shareholders' Equity	138,528	112,361
Total Liabilities and Shareholders' Equity	$228,707	$186,868

CONSOLIDATED INCOME STATEMENT
(unaudited)

(In thousands, except per share amounts)	Three Months Ended October 31		Nine Months Ended October 31	
	1988	1987	1988	1987
Revenues				
Membership and service fees	$70,131	$50,696	$192,016	$143,409
Other	938	386	2,297	1,693
Total Revenues	71,069	51,082	194,313	145,102
Expenses				
Operating	24,320	16,258	64,123	47,608
Marketing	23,524	17,761	65,647	50,625
General and administrative	11,787	8,721	32,363	25,097
Total Expenses	59,631	42,740	162,133	123,330
Operating Income	11,438	8,342	32,180	21,772
Provision for income taxes	4,577	3,672	12,854	9,591
Net Income	$ 6,861	$ 4,670	$ 19,326	$ 12,181
Net Income Per Common Share	$.33	$.24	$.93	$.63
Weighted Average Number of Common and Common Equivalent Shares Outstanding	20,752	19,665	20,870	19,231

CUC International

Communication and Governance

Corporate governance has become an increasingly important issue in capital markets throughout the world following financial market meltdowns in the Asian and U.S. markets. These market collapses exposed problems of accounting misstatements and lack of corporate transparency, as well as governance problems and conflicts of interest among the intermediaries charged with monitoring management and corporate disclosures.

The breakdowns have increased the challenge for managers in communicating credibly with skeptical outside investors, making it more difficult than ever for new (and in some cases even established) firms to raise capital. Financial reports, the traditional platform for management to communicate with investors, are viewed with increased skepticism following a number of widely publicized audit failures and the demise of Arthur Andersen.

The market crashes have also raised questions about improving the quality of governance by information and financial intermediaries. New regulations, such as the Sarbanes-Oxley Act in the U.S., attempt to increase accountability and financial competence for audit committees and external auditors, who are charged with reviewing the financial reporting and disclosure process.

This chapter discusses how many of the financial analysis tools developed in Chapters 2 through 8 can be used by managers to develop a coherent disclosure strategy, and by corporate board members and external auditors to improve the quality of their work. The following types of questions are dealt with:

- Managers ask: Is our current communication strategy effective in helping investors understand the firm's business strategy and expected future performance, thereby ensuring that our stock price is not seriously over- or undervalued?
- Audit committee members ask: What are the firm's key business risks? Are they reflected appropriately in the financial statements? How is management communicating on important risks that cannot be reflected in the financial statements? Is information on the firm's performance presented to the board consistent with that provided to investors in the financial report and firm disclosures?
- External auditors ask: What are the firm's key business risks, and how are they reflected in the financial statements? Where should we focus our audit tests? Is our assessment of the firm's performance consistent with that of external investors and analysts? If not, are we overlooking something, or is management misrepresenting the firm's true performance in disclosures?

Throughout this book we have focussed primarily on showing how financial statement data can be helpful for analysts and outside investors in making a variety of decisions. In this chapter we change our emphasis and focus primarily on management and governance agents. Of course an understanding of the management communication process and corporate governance is also important for security analysts and investors. The approach taken here, however, is more germane to insiders since most of the types of analyses we discuss are not available to outsiders.

GOVERNANCE OVERVIEW

As we discuss throughout this book, outside investors require access to reliable information on firm performance, both to value their debt and equity claims and to monitor the performance of management. Investors require that managers provide information on their company's performance and future plans when they agree to provide capital to the firm.

However, left to their own devices, managers are likely to paint a rosy picture of the firm's performance in their disclosures. There are three reasons for manager optimism in reporting. First, most managers are genuinely positive about their firms' prospects, leading them to unwittingly emphasize the positive and downplay the negative.

A second reason for management optimism in reporting arises because firm disclosures play an important role in mitigating "agency" problems between managers and investors.[1] Investors use firm disclosures to judge whether managers have run the firm in investors' best interests or, on the other hand, have abused their authority and control over firm resources. Reporting consistently poor earnings increases the likelihood that top management will be replaced, either by the board of directors or by an acquirer who takes over the firm to improve its management.[2] Of course managers are aware of this and have incentives to show positive performance.

Finally, managers are also likely to make optimistic disclosures prior to issuing new equity. Recent evidence indicates that entrepreneurs tend to take to their firms public after disclosure of strong reported, but frequently unsustainable, earnings performance. Also, seasoned equity offers typically follow strong, but again unsustainable, stock and earnings performance. The strong earnings performance prior to IPOs and seasoned offers appears to be at least partially due to earnings management.[3] Of course rational outside investors recognize management's incentives to manage earnings and downplay any bad news prior to a new issue. They respond by discounting the stock, demanding a hefty new issue discount, and in extreme cases refusing to purchase the new stock. This raises the cost of capital and potentially leaves some of the best new ventures and projects unfunded.[4]

Financial and information intermediaries help reduce agency and information problems that face outside investors by evaluating the quality of management representations in the firm's disclosures, providing their own analysis of firms' (and managers') performance and making investment decisions on investors' behalf. As presented in Figure 13-1, these intermediaries include internal governance agents, assurance professionals, information analyzers, and professional investors. The importance of these intermediaries is underscored by the magnitude of the fees that they collectively receive from investors and entrepreneurs.

Internal governance agents, such as corporate boards, are responsible for monitoring a firm's management. Their functions include reviewing business strategy, evaluating and rewarding top management, and assuring the flow of credible information to external parties. Assurance professionals, such as external auditors, enhance the credibility of financial information prepared by managers. Information analyzers, such as financial analysts and ratings agencies, are responsible for gathering and analyzing information to provide performance forecasts and investment recommendations to both professional and retail individual investors. Finally, professional investors (such as banks, mutual funds, insurance, and venture capital firms) make investment decisions on behalf of dispersed investors. They are therefore responsible for valuing and selecting investment opportunities in the economy.

In this framework, management, internal governance agents, and assurance professionals are charged with supplying information; individual and professional investors and

Figure 13-1	The Intermediation Chain Between Managers and Investors

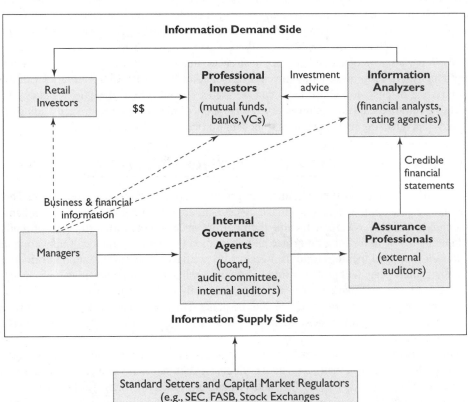

information analyzers make up the demand side. Both the supply and demand sides are governed by a variety of regulatory institutions. These include public regulators, such as the Securities and Exchange Commission and the bank regulators, as well as private sector bodies, such the Financial Accounting Standards Board, the American Institute of Certified Public Accountants, and stock exchanges.

The level and quality of information and residual information and agency problems in capital markets are determined by the organizational design of these intermediaries and regulatory institutions. Key organizational design questions include the following: What are the optimal incentive schemes for rewarding top managers? What should be the composition and charter of corporate boards? Should auditors assure that financial reports comply with accounting standards or represent a firm's underlying economics? Should there be detailed accounting standards or a few broad accounting principles? What should be the organizational form and business scope of auditors and analysts? What incentive schemes should be used for professional investors to align their interests with individual investors?

A variety of economic and institutional factors are likely to influence the answers to these design questions. Examples include the ability to write and enforce optimal contracts, proprietary costs that might make disclosure costly for investors, and regulatory imperfections. The spectacular rise and fall of Enron suggests that these limitations could have a first-order effect on the functioning of capital markets.

While it is interesting to speculate on how to improve the functioning of capital markets through changes in organizational design, that issue goes beyond the scope of this chapter. Instead, we discuss how the financial analysis tools developed in Chapters 2 through 8 can be used to improve the performance of some of the information intermediaries who have been widely criticized following revelations of financial reporting fraud and misstatements at companies such as Enron, Worldcom, Tyco, Xerox, Global Crossing, and Lucent.[5]

We have already discussed the application of financial analysis tools to equity and credit analysts and to professional investors in Chapters 9 and 10. In the remainder of this chapter, we discuss how these tools can be used by managers to develop a strategy for effective communication with investors, by members of boards of directors and audit committees in overseeing management and the audit process, and by audit professionals.

MANAGEMENT COMMUNICATION WITH INVESTORS

Some managers argue that communication problems are not worth worrying about. They maintain that as long as managers make investment and operating decisions that enhance shareholder value, investors will value their performance and the firm's stock accordingly. While this is true in the long run, since all information is eventually public, it may not hold in the short or even medium term. If investors do not have access to the same information as management, they will probably find it difficult to value new and innovative investments. In an efficient capital market, they will not consistently over- or undervalue these new investments, but their valuations will tend to be noisy. This can make stock prices relatively noisy, leading management at various times to consider their firms to be either seriously over- or undervalued.

Does it matter if a firm's stock is over- or undervalued for a period? Most managers would prefer to not have their stock undervalued, since it makes it more costly to raise new financing. They may also worry that undervaluation is likely to increase the chance of a takeover by a hostile acquirer, with an accompanying reduction in their job security. Managers of firms that are overvalued may also be concerned about the market's assessment, since they are legally liable for failing to disclose information relevant to investors.[6] They may therefore not wish to see their stock seriously overvalued, even though overvaluation provides opportunities to issue new equity at favorable rates.

A Word of Caution

As noted above, it is natural that many managers believe that firms are undervalued by the capital market. This frequently occurs because it is difficult for managers to be realistic about their company's future performance. After all, it is part of their job to sell the company to new employees, customers, suppliers, and investors. In addition, forecasting the firm's future performance objectively requires them to judge their own capabilities as managers. Thus many managers may argue that investors are uninformed and that their firm is undervalued. Only some can back that up with solid evidence.

If management decides that the firm does face a genuine information problem, it can begin to consider whether and how this could be redressed. Is the problem potentially serious enough that it is worth doing something to alter investors' perceptions? Or is the problem likely to resolve itself within a short period? Does the firm have plans to raise new equity or to use equity to acquire another company? Is management's job security threatened? As we discuss below, management has a wide range of options in this situation.

Key Analysis Questions

We recommend that before jumping to the conclusion that their firms are under-valued, managers should analyze their firms' performance and compare their own forecasts of future performance with those of analysts, using the following approach:

- *Is there a significant difference between internal management forecasts of future earnings and cash flows and those of outside analysts?*
- *Do any differences between managers' and analysts' forecasts arise because of different expectations about economy-wide performance?* Managers may understand their own businesses better than analysts, but they may not be any better at forecasting macroeconomic conditions.
- *Can managers identify any factors that might explain a difference between analysts' and managers' forecasts of future performance?* For example, are analysts unaware of positive new R&D results, do they have different information about customer responses to new products and marketing campaigns, etc.? These types of differences could indicate that the firm faces an information problem.

Example: Communication Issues for FPIC Insurance Group

FPIC Insurance Group Inc. is the largest provider of liability insurance for doctors and hospitals in Florida. In the period 1996 to 1998, FPIC reported stable returns on equity of 13.8 percent, average growth in both revenues and net income of 28 percent, and growth in book equity of 2.8 percent. On December 31, 1998, the firm had a book value per share of $15.85, a price-to-book value of 2.23, a price to earnings multiple of 15.9, and an equity beta of 1.57.

In August 1999 the firm's stock price declined from $45.25 to $14.25. The stock decline began on August 10, the day the company reported a 48 percent jump in second-quarter profits to $7.4 million. The earnings increase was in part attributable to the FPIC's Florida Physicians unit releasing $8.1 million in reserves it had set aside against future claims, compared with $4 million in the year-ago quarter. In addition, the company reported higher-than-expected claims in a health insurance plan offered to Florida Dental Association members.

Reuters reported that the stock price decline reflected investors' concern about the quality of the firm's earnings. In response, FPIC spokeswoman Amy D. Ryan stated, "As far as we're concerned, we had a great quarter." The company's chief operating officer, John Byers, argued that the company's decision to release the unit's reserves was normal business practice and based on its expectations of future claims. In response to the higher than expected dental claims, the company announced that it had increased its rates for this insurance.

The sharp decline in its price raises questions about the valuation of the company's stock. On September 9, 1999, the price-to-book ratio was less than 1, and the price-to-earnings multiple was 6.0. The market therefore expected that the company would generate a return on equity somewhat lower than its cost of capital. FPIC's management appeared to be puzzled by the sharp drop in price and argued that the market was under-valuing the firm. However, before this can be concluded, a number of questions need to be answered:

- Was the firm previously overvalued? If so, what forces were behind the market's high valuation of the company? If the market expected the company to continue to grow at 2.8 percent, to generate a 13.8 percent return on equity, and the firm's cost of capital is 11.3 percent (consistent with a market risk premium of 4 percent and a risk-free rate of 5 percent), FPIC would be worth around $20.50. Why then was the stock valued at $45 early in August? Had management been painting too rosy a picture for the company's future in its meetings with analysts?
- What events explain the company's sudden drop in stock value? As noted above, the primary question for analysts was the quality of the firm's earnings. However management needs to have a deeper understanding of these issues.
- If management believes that the firm is actually undervalued, what options are available to correct the market's view of the company?

COMMUNICATION THROUGH FINANCIAL REPORTING

Financial reports are the most popular format for management communication. Below we discuss the role of financial reporting as a means of investor communication, the institutions that make accounting information credible, and when it is likely to be ineffective.

Accounting As a Means of Management Communication

As we discussed in Chapters 3 and 4, financial reports are an important medium for management communication with external investors. Reports provide investors with an explanation of how their money has been invested, a summary of the performance of those investments, and a discussion of how current performance fits within the firm's overall philosophy and strategy.

Accounting reports not only provide a record of past transactions, they also reflect management estimates and forecasts of the future. For example, they include estimates of bad debts, forecasts of the lives of tangible assets, and implicit forecasts that outlays will generate future cash flow benefits that exceed their cost. Since management is likely to be in a position to make forecasts of these future events that are more accurate than those of external investors, financial reports are a potentially useful way of communicating with investors. However, as discussed above, investors are also likely to be skeptical of reports prepared by management.

Factors That Increase the Credibility of Accounting Communication

A number of mechanisms mitigate conflicts of interest in financial reporting and increase the credibility of accounting information that is communicated to stockholders. These include accounting standards, auditing, monitoring of management by financial analysts, and management reputation.

Accounting Standards and Auditing

Accounting standards, such as those promulgated by the Financial Accounting Standards Board (FASB) and the Securities Exchange Commission (SEC) in the U.S., provide guidelines for managers on how to make accounting decisions and provide outside investors with a way of interpreting these decisions. Uniform accounting standards attempt to reduce managers' ability to record similar economic transactions in different ways, either over time or across firms. Compliance with these standards is enforced by external auditors who attempt to ensure that managers' estimates are reasonable. Auditors therefore reduce the likelihood of earnings management.

Monitoring by Financial Analysts

Financial intermediaries such as analysts also limit management's ability to manage earnings. Financial analysts specialize in developing firm- and industry-specific knowledge, enabling them to assess the quality of a firm's reported numbers and to make any necessary adjustments. Analysts evaluate the appropriateness of management's forecasts implicit in accounting method choices and reported accruals. This requires a thorough understanding of the firm's business and the relevant accounting rules used in the preparation of its financial reports. Superior analysts adjust reported accrual numbers, if necessary, to reflect economic reality, perhaps by using the cash flow statement and the footnote disclosures.

Analysts' business and technical expertise as well as their legal liability and incentives differ from those of auditors. Consequently, analyst reports can provide information to investors on whether the firm's accounting decisions are appropriate or whether managers are overstating the firm's economic performance to protect their jobs.[7]

Management Reputation

A third factor that can counteract external investors' natural skepticism about financial reporting is management reputation. Managers that expect to have an ongoing relation with external investors and financial intermediaries may be able to build a track record for unbiased financial reporting. By making accounting estimates and judgments that are supported by subsequent performance, managers can demonstrate their competence and reliability to investors and analysts. As a result, managers' future judgments and accounting estimates are more likely to be viewed as credible sources of information.

Limitations of Financial Reporting for Investor Communication

While accounting standards, auditing, monitoring of management by financial analysts, and management concerns about its reputation increase the credibility and informativeness of financial reports, these mechanisms are far from perfect. Consequently there are times when financial reporting breaks down as a means for management to communicate with external investors. These breakdowns can arise when (1) there are no accounting rules to guide practice or the existing rules do not distinguish between poor and successful performers, (2) auditors and analysts do not have the expertise to judge new products or business opportunities, or (3) management faces credibility problems.

Accounting Rule Limitations

Despite the rapid increase in new accounting standards, accounting rules frequently do not distinguish between good and poor performers. For example, current accounting rules do not permit managers to show on their balance sheets in a timely fashion the benefits of investments in quality improvements, human resource development programs, research and development (with the exception of software development costs), and customer service.

Some of the problems with accounting standards arise because it takes time for standard setters to develop appropriate standards for many new types of economic transactions. Other difficulties arise because standards are the result of compromises between different interest groups (e.g., auditors, investors, corporate managers, and regulators).

Auditor and Analyst Limitations

While auditors and analysts have access to proprietary information, they do not have the same understanding of the firm's business as managers. The divergence between managers' and auditors'/analysts' business assessments is likely to be most severe for firms with distinctive business strategies, or firms that operate in emerging industries. In addition, auditors' decisions in these circumstances are likely to be dominated by concerns about legal liability, hampering management's ability to use financial reports to communicate effectively with investors.

Finally, conflicts of interest faced by auditors and analysts make their analysis imperfect. Conflicts can potentially induce auditors to side with management to retain the audit, or to enable the audit firm to sell profitable non-audit services to the client. They can also arise for analysts who provide favorable ratings and research on companies to support investment banking services, or to increase trading volume among less informed investors.

Limited Management Credibility

When is management likely to face credibility problems with investors? There is very little evidence on this question. However, managers of new firms, firms with volatile earnings, firms in financial distress, and firms with poor track records in communicating with investors should expect to find it difficult to be seen as credible reporters.

If management has a credibility problem, financial reports are likely to be viewed with considerable skepticism. Investors will see financial reporting estimates that increase income as evidence that management is padding earnings. This makes it very difficult for management to use financial reports to communicate positive news about future performance.

Example: Accounting Communication for FPIC Insurance Group

FPIC Insurance Group's key financial reporting estimates are for loss reserves for insurance claims using actuarial analysis of its own and other insurers' claims histories. At the end of fiscal year 1998, FPIC reported a loss reserve of $242.3 million. In its 10-K, management warned that "the uncertainties inherent in estimating ultimate losses on the basis of past experience have grown significantly in recent years, principally as a result of judicial expansion of liability standards and expansive interpretations of insurance contracts. These uncertainties may be further affected by, among other factors, changes in the rate of inflation and changes in the propensities of individuals to file claims. The inherent uncertainty of establishing reserves is relatively greater for companies writing long-tail casualty insurance."

To help investors assess its track record in making loss estimates, FPIC is required to provide a detailed breakdown of changes in loss estimates from prior years given actual claim losses. These data indicate that FPIC has actually been quite conservative in prior years' forecasts and has historically incurred fewer losses than it had initially predicted.

It is interesting to note that the area that raised questions for investors about FPIC's record was precisely its conservative estimation of loss reserves and their subsequent reversal. By being conservative, management may have raised questions about its ability to forecast losses reliably in the future, or given investors the impression that it had been managing earnings.

Key Analysis Questions

For management interested in understanding how effectively the firm's financial reports help it communicate with outside investors, the following questions are likely to provide a useful starting point:

- What are the key business risks that have to be managed effectively? What processes and controls are in place to manage these risks? How are the firm's key business risks reflected in the financial statements? For example, credit risks are reflected in the bad debt allowance, and product quality risks are reflected in allowances for product returns and the method of revenue recognition. For these types of risks, what message is the firm sending on the management of these risks through its estimates or choices of accounting methods? Has the firm been unable to deliver on the forecasts underlying these choices? Alternatively, does the market seem to be ignoring the message underlying the firm's financial reporting choices, indicating a lack of credibility?
- How does the firm communicate about key risks that cannot be reflected in accounting estimates or methods? For example, if technological innovation risk is critical for a company, it is unable to reflect how well it is managing this risk through research and development in its financial statements. But investors will still have questions about this business issue.

OTHER FORMS OF COMMUNICATING WITH INVESTORS

Given the limitations of accounting standards, auditing, and monitoring by financial analysts, as well as the reporting credibility problems faced by management, firms that wish to communicate effectively with external investors are often forced to use alternative media. Below we discuss three alternative ways that managers can communicate with external investors and analysts: meetings with analysts to publicize the firm, expanded voluntary disclosure, and using financing policies to signal management expectations. These forms of communication are typically not mutually exclusive.

Analyst Meetings

One popular way for managers to help mitigate communication problems is to meet regularly with financial analysts that follow the firm. At these meetings management will field questions about the firm's current financial performance as well discuss its future business plans. In addition to holding analyst meetings, many firms appoint a director of public relations, who provides further regular contact with analysts seeking more information on the firm.

In the last ten years, conference calls have become a popular forum for management to communicate with financial analysts. Recent research finds that firms are more likely to host calls if they are in industries where financial statement data fail to capture key business fundamentals on a timely basis.[8] In addition, conference calls themselves appear to provide new information to analysts about a firm's performance and future prospects.[9]

While firms continue to meet with analysts, new SEC rules, called Regulation Fair Disclosure (or Reg FD), have changed the nature of these interactions. Under these new rules, which became effective in the U.S. in October 2000, firms that provide material nonpublic information to security analysts or professional investors must simultaneously (or promptly thereafter) disclose the information to the public. This has reduced the information that managers are willing to disclose in conference calls and private meetings, making these less effective forums for resolving information problems.

Voluntary Disclosure

Another way for managers to improve the credibility of their financial reporting is through voluntary disclosure. Accounting rules usually prescribe minimum disclosure requirements, but they do not restrict managers from voluntarily providing additional information. These could include an articulation of the company's long-term strategy, specification of nonfinancial leading indicators which are useful in judging the effectiveness of the strategy implementation, explanation of the relation between the leading indicators and future profits, and forecasts of future performance. Voluntary disclosures can be reported in the firm's annual report, in brochures created to describe the firm to investors, in management meetings with analysts, or in investor relations responses to information requests.[10]

One constraint on expanded disclosure is the competitive dynamics in product markets. Disclosure of proprietary information on strategies and their expected economic consequences may hurt the firm's competitive position. Managers then face a trade-off between providing information that is useful to investors in assessing the firm's economic performance, and withholding information to maximize the firm's product market advantage.

A second constraint in providing voluntary disclosure is management's legal liability. Forecasts and voluntary disclosures can potentially be used by dissatisfied shareholders to bring civil action against management for providing misleading information. This seems ironic, since voluntary disclosures should provide investors with additional information. Unfortunately, it can be difficult for courts to decide whether managers' disclosures were good-faith estimates of uncertain future events which later did not materialize, or whether management manipulated the market. Consequently many corporate legal departments recommend against management providing much voluntary disclosure.

Finally, management credibility can limit a firm's incentives to provide voluntary disclosures. If management faces a credibility problem in financial reporting, any voluntary disclosures it provides are also likely to be viewed skeptically. In particular, investors may be concerned about what management is not telling them, particularly since such disclosures are not audited.

Selected Financial Policies

Managers can also use financing policies to communicate effectively with external investors. Financial policies that are useful in this respect include dividend payouts, stock repurchases, financing choices, and hedging strategies. One important difference between this type of communication and additional disclosure is that the firm does not provide potentially proprietary information to competitors. The signal therefore indicates to competitors that a firm's management is bullish on its future, but it does not provide any details.

Dividend Payout Policies

As we discussed in Chapter 12, a firm's cash payout decisions can provide information to investors on managers' assessments of the firm's future prospects. This arises because dividend payouts tend to be sticky, in the sense that managers are reluctant to cut dividends. Thus, managers will only increase dividends when they are confident that they will be able to sustain the increased rate in future years. Consequently, investors interpret dividend increases as signals of managers' confidence in the quality of current and future earnings.[11]

Stock Repurchases

In some countries, such as the U.S. and the U.K., managers can use stock repurchases to communicate with external investors. Under a stock repurchase, the firm buys back its own stock, either through a purchase on the open market, through a tender offer, or through a negotiated purchase with a large stockholder. Of course a stock repurchase, particularly a tender offer repurchase, is an expensive way for management to communicate with outside investors. Firms typically pay a hefty premium to acquire their shares in tender offer repurchases, potentially diluting the value of the shares that are not tendered or not accepted for tender. In addition, the fees to investment banks, lawyers, and share solicitation fees are not trivial. Given these costs, it is not surprising that research findings indicate that stock repurchases are effective signals to investors about the level and risk of future earnings performance.[12] Research findings also suggest that firms that use stock repurchases to communicate with investors have accounting assets that reflect less of firm value and have high general information asymmetry.[13]

Financing Choices

Firms that have problems communicating with external investors may be able to use financing choices to reduce them. For example, a firm that is unwilling to provide proprietary information to help dispersed public investors value it may be willing to provide such information to a knowledgeable private investor—which can become a large stockholder/creditor—or a bank that agrees to provide the company with a significant new loan. A firm with credibility problems in financial reporting can sell stock or issue debt to an informed private investor such as a large customer who has superior information about the quality of its product or service.

Such changes in financing and ownership can mitigate communication problems in two ways. First, the terms of the new financing arrangement and the credibility of the new lender or stockholder can provide investors with information to reassess the value of the firm. Second, the accompanying increased concentration of ownership and the role of large block holders in corporate governance can have a positive effect on valuation. If investors are concerned about management's incentives to increase shareholder value, the presence of a new block shareholder or significant creditor on the board can be reassuring. This type of monitoring arises in leveraged buyouts, start-ups backed by venture capital firms, and in firms with equity partnership investments. In Japanese and German corporations, it may also arise because large banks own both debt and equity and have close working relationships with firms' managers.

Of course, in the extreme, management can decide that the best option for a firm is to no longer operate as a public company. This can be accomplished by a management buyout, where a buyout group (including management) leverages its own investment (using bank or public debt finance), buys the firm, and takes it private. The buyout group hopes to run the firm for several years and then take the company public again, hopefully with a track record of improved performance that enables investors to value the firm more effectively.

Hedging

An important source of mispricing arises if investors are unable to distinguish between unexpected changes in reported earnings due to management performance and transitory shocks that are beyond managers' control (e.g., foreign currency translation gains and losses). Managers can counteract these effects by hedging such "accounting" risks. Even though hedging is costly, it may be valuable if it reduces information problems that potentially lead to misvaluation.

Example: Other Communications for FPIC Insurance Group

On August 12, 1999, FPIC Insurance Group announced that it would immediately begin purchasing shares of its common stock. As many as 429,000 shares were to be repurchased under the program. The company argued that the dramatic drop in its stock price was unwarranted and that its stock was now greatly undervalued. William R. Russell, president and chief executive officer of FPIC stated: "We believe the recent drop in our stock price may be linked to certain changes in our reserving policy that were described in our earnings release. We believe that our reserving policy is now and has always been appropriate. We believe that the market has overreacted and that FPIC continues to be an excellent long-term investment. Our repurchases . . . reflect our commitment to enhance shareholder value." (Reuters, August 12, 1999)

The repurchase temporarily arrested FPIC's stock price slide. The price recovered from $21 to around $26 during the repurchase period. However this effect was temporary, and the price subsequently fell further to $14.25.

Key Analysis Questions

For management considering whether to use financing policies to communicate more effectively with investors, the following questions are likely to provide a useful starting point for analysis:

- Have other potentially less costly actions, such as expanded disclosure or accounting communication, been considered? If not, would these alternatives provide a lower cost means of communication? Alternatively, if management is concerned about providing proprietary information to competitors, or has low credibility, these alternatives may not be effective.
- Does the firm have sufficient free cash flow to be able to implement a share repurchase program or to increase dividends? If so, these may be feasible options. If the firm has excess cash available today but expects to be constrained in the future, a stock repurchase may be more effective. Alternatively, if management expects to have some excess cash available each year, a dividend increase may be in order.
- Is the firm cash constrained and unable to increase disclosure for proprietary reasons? If so, management may want to consider changing the mix of owners as a way of indicating to investors that another informed outsider is bullish on the company. Of course another possibility is for management itself to increase its stake in the company.

AUDITOR ANALYSIS

In the U.S. the auditor is responsible for providing investors with assurance that the financial statements are prepared in accordance with Generally Accepted Accounting Procedures (or GAAP). This requires the auditor to evaluate whether transactions are recorded in a way that is consistent with the rules produced by regulators (including the FASB, AICPA, and SEC) and whether management estimates reflected in the financial statements are reasonable. The results of the audit are disclosed in the audit report, which is part of the financial statements. If the firm's financial statements conform to GAAP, the auditor issues an unqualified report. However, if the financials do not conform to GAAP, the auditor is required to issue a qualified or an adverse report that provides information to investors on the discrepancies. Finally, if the auditor is uncertain about whether the firm can survive during the coming year, a going concern report is issued that points out the firm's survival risks.

In contrast, in the UK and countries that have adopted the UK system, such as Australia, New Zealand, Singapore, Hong Kong, and India, auditors undertake a broader review than their U.S. counterparts. UK audits are required to not only assess whether the financial statements are prepared in accordance with UK GAAP, but also to judge whether they fairly reflect the client's underlying economic performance. This additional assurance requires more judgment on the part of the auditor but also increases the value of the audit to outside investors.

The key procedures involved in a typical audit include (1) understanding the client's business and industry to identify key risks for the audit, (2) evaluating the firm's internal control system to assess whether it is likely to produce reliable information, (3) performing preliminary analytic procedures to identify unusual events and possible errors, and (4) collecting specific evidence on controls, transactions, and account balance details to form the basis for the auditor's opinion. In most cases client management is willing to respond to issues raised by the audit to ensure that the company receives an unqualified audit opinion. Once the audit is completed, the auditor presents a summary of audit scope and findings to the Audit Committee of the firm's Board of Directors.

It is worth noting that in both the U.S. and UK systems, the audit is not intended to detect fraud. Of course in some cases it may do so, but that is not its purpose. The detection of fraud is the domain of the internal audit.

Challenges Facing Audit Industry[14]

To understand the current problems facing the audit industry, it is necessary to go back to the mid-1970s, when two critical events created pressures on audit firms to cut costs and seek alternative revenue sources. The first of these was a decision by the Federal Trade Commission, concerned with a potential oligopoly by the large audit firms, to pressure the major firms to compete aggressively with each other for clients. The second was a shift in legal standards that enabled investors of companies with accounting problems to seek legal redress against the auditor without having to show that they had specifically relied on questionable accounting information in making their investment decisions. Instead, they could assert that they had relied on the stock price itself, which has been affected by the misleading disclosures. This change, along with increasing litigiousness, dramatically increased the lawsuit risk for auditors.

Audit firms responded to the new business environment in several ways. They lobbied for mechanical accounting and auditing standards and developed standard operating procedures to reduce the variability in audits. This approach reduced the cost of audits and provided a defense in the case of litigation. But it also meant that auditors were more likely to view their role narrowly, rather than as matters of broader business judgment.

Furthermore, while mechanical standards make auditing easier, they do not necessarily increase corporate transparency.[15] Audit firms decided that profit margins would be thin in a world of mechanized, standardized audits, and they responded in two ways. One way was by aggressively pursuing a high volume strategy, and so audit partner compensation and promotion became more closely linked to a cordial relationship with top management that attracted new audit clients and retained existing clients. This made it difficult for partners to be effective watchdogs. The large audit firms also responded to challenges to their core business by developing new higher margin, higher growth consulting services. This diversification strategy deflected top management energy and partner talent from the audit side of the business to the more profitable consulting part.

The Enron debacle dramatically illustrated many of the problems facing the industry. The use of mechanical, standardized audits encouraged Enron's auditors to take a narrow perspective on their role as financial report watchdogs. Even though they may have believed that Enron's reports met GAAP, they failed to ask big picture questions about their client's strategy, core risks, and the company's overall transparency. Mechanical standards also made it easier for Enron's unscrupulous managers to meet the letter of GAAP (although in the end they did not even do that), but to skirt their spirit, concealing important obligations and overstating profits. Finally, the pressure on Enron's auditors to retain their clients and to grow their firms' consulting businesses reduced their independence, leading them to approve questionable accounting decisions and to work closely with management to meet Enron's financial reporting objectives.

Several recent regulatory changes have been passed to correct the structural problems facing the industry. The SEC has banned audit firms from providing certain types of consulting services to their clients. The Sarbanes-Oxley Act requires the Audit Committee of the Board of Directors to become more active in appointing and reviewing the audit. It also requires the CEO and CFO to sign off that the financials fairly represent the financial performance of the company. These are all likely to improve the dynamics of the industry. It remains to be seen whether they will be sufficient once the current anxiety dies down.

Role of Financial Analysis Tools for Auditing

How can the financial analysis tools discussed in this book be used by audit professionals? The four steps in financial analysis are strategy analysis, accounting analysis, financial analysis, and prospective analysis. We discuss how each of these is relevant to the audit.

Strategy Analysis

One of the fundamental challenges facing auditors is how to narrow the scope of their work. Large corporations undertake millions of transactions each year. It is not possible for any audit to review all of these. So the auditor has to decide where to focus attention and time.

Strategy analysis can help identify those few key areas of the business that are critical to the organization's survival and future success. These are the areas that investors want to understand so that they can evaluate the firm's value proposition and how well it is managing key success factors. They are also likely to be areas worth further testing and analysis by the auditor, to assess their impact on the financial statements. For example, the key success factor for Tyco, a conglomerate that pursued a strategy of acquisitions to consolidate small players in a variety of industries, was managing acquisitions. The key success factor for a financial services firm is managing loan risks, and the key risk for Intel is its product innovation.

Strategy analysis is critical to the first stage to the audit, understanding the client's business, industry, and risks. It is important that the auditor develop the expertise to be able to identify the one or two key risks facing their clients.

Accounting Analysis

For the auditor, accounting analysis involves two steps. First, the auditor must understand how the key success factors and risks are reflected in the financial statements. For Tyco, for example, they are reflected in the valuation of goodwill. If Tyco fails to manage its acquisitions successfully, it will have to take a write-down of goodwill. For financial services companies the key success factors and risks are reflected in loan loss reserves. If a firm fails to manage its loan process properly, it will begin making loans to more risky clients, leading to higher future default rates and requiring higher loan loss estimates. In contrast, for Intel, accounting rules treat its key success factor, product innovation, in a mechanical way by requiring that it expense all R&D when it is incurred. While this probably makes the audit easier to perform, it implies that Intel's financial statements are not a very timely source of information on the company's innovation, and the auditor's service is less valuable. Intel's management will have to use other ways of providing credible information to investors on its product innovation.

The second step in accounting analysis is for the auditor to evaluate management judgment reflected in the key financial statements items. For example, for a financial services company where loan loss reserves are critical, the auditor will need to design tests and collect evidence to evaluate management's forecasts of future loan losses implicit in the reserve. The auditor must assess whether these forecasts are reasonable given the company's historical performance, the current economic climate, and the credit review and collection process in place in the firm. For a firm such as Tyco, where goodwill valuations are critical, the auditor must judge whether the current performance of acquired companies meets forecasts made by Tyco's management at the time of the acquisition and is reflected in the price Tyco paid for the target.

Financial Analysis

Auditors use financial ratio analysis as part of their analytic review. Financial ratios help auditors judge whether there are any unusual performance changes for their client, either relative to past performance or relative to their competitors. Such changes merit further investigation to ensure that the reasons for the change can be fully explained, and to determine what additional tests are required to satisfy the auditor that the reported changes in performance are justified.

For example, financial ratio analysis of Worldcom's financial performance should have revealed a significant decline in the company's cost structure that was not matched by any of its competitors. Such analysis should have been a red flag for the auditor that prompted a detailed examination of Worldcom's costs and capitalization policies, and might have led the auditor to detect the massive fraudulent change in capitalization of network costs at Worldcom.

Careful ratio analysis can also reveal whether clients are facing business problems that might induce management to conceal losses or keep key obligations off the balance sheet. Such information should alert auditors that extra care and additional detailed tests are likely to be required to reach a conclusion on the client's financial statements.

Prospective Analysis

Auditors use prospective analysis to assess whether estimates and forecasts made by management are consistent with the firm's economic position. They typically do not concern themselves with the stock market's valuation of their client. Yet there is valuable information for auditors in the market's valuation. The market's perception of a client's future performance provides a useful benchmark for affirming or disconfirming the auditor's assessment of the client's propsects. If the auditor reaches a different conclusion about a client than the market, it is worth exploring reasons for the differences. Is the client failing to disclose some critical information known to the auditor? Or is the auditor too optimistic or pessimistic?

If the auditor concludes that the market is overly optimistic about a client, is additional disclosure required to help investors get a more realistic view of the company's prospects? Are the estimates and forecasts made by management in preparing the financial statements realistic, or do they seek to avoid disappointing the market?

Alternatively, if the auditors decide that the market is overly pessimistic about their client's prospects, what additional information, if any, can be disclosed to increase transparency? Is the company too conservative in its financial statement estimates and forecasts?

Key Analysis Questions

The following questions are likely to provide a useful starting point for auditors in their analysis of a client's financial statements:

- What are the key business risks facing the firm? How well are these risks managed?
- What are the key accounting policies and estimates that reflect the firm's key risks? What tests and evidence are required to evaluate management judgment that is reflected in these accounting decisions?
- Do key ratios indicate any unusual changes in client performance? What tests and evidence are required to understand the causes of such changes?
- Has firm performance deteriorated, creating pressure on management to manage earnings or record off-balance-sheet transactions? If so, what additional tests and evidence are required to provide assurance that the financial statements are consistent with GAAP and (for UK system auditors) fairly represent the firm's financial position?
- How is the market assessing the client's prospects? If different from the auditor, what is the reason for the difference? If the market is overly optimistic or pessimistic, are there implications for client disclosure or accounting estimates?

Example: Auditing FPIC Insurance Group

For FPIC Insurance Group, how well the company manages claim risk is its most critical success factor. Not surprisingly, the stock market volatility appears to be largely driven by changing perceptions of this risk. In the financial statements, claim risk is reflected in the reserves set aside for future claims. This should be a key focus of the audit.

Questions for the auditor include the following.

- Why did the company change its reserve policy this period? Does the change reflect a change in its business model, such as an attempt to reduce insurance sales for more risky customers? If so, is there evidence of a change in customer demographics and claim patterns?
- Does the change reflect excessive over-reserving by the client in earlier periods? If so, why did the auditors approve this earlier policy? Why did management select this year to release those reserves?
- Is the change in reserve policy justifiable, or is management simply responding to pressure to meet unrealistic market expectations?
- What information is available about a representative sample of outstanding claims? Are estimates of the cost of settling these claims realistic given prior settlements and experiences for other firms in the same industry?

- If the change in claim reserves appears to be reasonable, what additional information can the firm provide to investors to address their concerns? Will this information need to be audited?

AUDIT COMMITTEE REVIEWS

Audit committees are responsible for overseeing the work of the auditor, for ensuring that the financial statements are properly prepared, and for reviewing the internal controls at the company. Audit committees, which are mandated by many stock exchanges, typically comprise three to four outside directors who meet regularly before or after their full board meetings.

In the last few years requirements for audit committee have been beefed up and formalized. In December 1999, the SEC, the national stock exchange(s), and the Auditing Standards Board issued new audit committee rules based largely on recommendations of the Blue Ribbon Committee (BRC) on Improving the Effectiveness of Corporate Audit Committees. The new rules defined best practices for judging audit committee members' independence and their qualifications.

Following the collapse of Enron, additional audit committee requirements have been created under the Sarbanes-Oxley Act. This requires that audit committees take formal responsibility for appointing, overseeing, and negotiating fees with external auditors. Audit committee members are required to be independent directors with no consulting or other potentially compromising relation to management. It is recommended that at least one member of the committee have financial expertise, such as being a CFO or CEO, or being a retired audit partner.

Ideally the audit committee is expected to be independent of management and to take an active role in reviewing the propriety of the firm's financial statements. Committee members are expected to question management and the auditors about the quality of the firm's financial reporting, the scope and findings of the external audit, and the quality of internal controls.

In reality, however, the audit committee has to rely extensively on information from management as well as internal and external auditors. Given the ground that it has to cover, its limited available time, and the technical nature of accounting standards, audit committees are not in a position to catch management fraud or auditors' failures on a timely basis.

How then can the audit committee add value?[16] We believe that many of the financial analysis tools discussed in this book can provide a useful way for audit committees to approach their tasks. Many of the applications of the financial analysis steps discussed for auditors also apply for audit committees.

In its scrutiny of financial statements, the committee should use the 80-20 rule, devoting most of its time to assessing the effectiveness of those *few* policies and decisions that have the *most* impact on investors' perceptions of the company's critical performance indicators. This should not require any additional work for committee members, since they should already have a good understanding of the firm's key success factors and risks from discussions of the full board.

Audit committee members should also have sufficient financial background to identify where in the financial statements the key risks are reflected. Their discussions with management and external auditors should focus on these risks. How well are they being managed? How are the auditors planning their work to focus on these areas? What evidence have they gathered to judge the adequacy of key financial statement estimates?

The audit committee also receives regular reviews of company performance from management as part of their regular board duties. Committee members should be especially proactive in requesting information that helps them evaluate how the firm is managing its key risks, since this information can also help them judge the quality of the financial statements. Audit committee members need to ask: Is information on company performance we are receiving in our regular board meetings consistent with the picture portrayed in the financial statements? If not, what is missing? Are additional disclosures required to ensure that investors are well informed about the firm's operations and performance?

Finally, audit committees need to focus on capital market expectations, not just statutory financial reports. In today's capital markets, the game begins when companies set expectations via analyst meetings, press releases, and other forms of investor communications. Indeed, the pressure to manage earnings is often a direct consequence of Wall Street's unrealistic expectations, either deliberately created by management or sustained by their inaction. Thus it is also important for audit committees to oversee the firm's investor relations strategy and ensure that management sets realistic expectations for both the short and long term.

Key Analysis Questions

The following questions are likely to provide a useful starting point for audit committees in their discussions with management and auditors over the firm's financial statements:

- How are the key business risks facing the firm reflected in its financial statements? How are these risks being managed?
- How are the firm's key risks reflected in the financial statements—what are the key accounting policies and estimates? What was the basis for the external auditor's assessment of these items?
- Is information on the key value drivers and firm performance presented to the full board consistent with the picture of the firm reflected in the financial statements and MD&A?
- What expectations are management creating in the capital market? Are these likely to create undue pressure to manage earnings?

SUMMARY

This chapter discussed how many of the financial analysis tools developed in Chapters 2 through 8 can be used by managers to develop a coherent disclosure strategy, and by corporate board members and external auditors to improve the quality of their work.

By communicating effectively with investors, management can potentially reduce information problems for outside investors, lowering the likelihood that the stock will be mispriced or unnecessarily volatile. This can be important for firms that wish to raise new capital, avoid takeovers, or whose management is concerned that its true job performance is not reflected in the firm's stock.

The typical way for firms to communicate with investors is through financial reporting. Accounting standards and auditing make the reporting process a way for managers to not only provide information about the firm's current performance, but to indicate, through accounting estimates, where they believe the firm is headed in the future. However, financial reports are not always able to convey the types of forward-looking information that investors need. Accounting standards often do not permit firms to capitalize outlays, such as R&D, that provide significant future benefits to the firm.

A second way that management can communicate with investors is through non-accounting means. We discussed several such mechanisms, including meeting with financial analysts to explain the firm's strategy, current performance, and outlook; disclosing additional information, both quantitative and qualitative, to provide investors with similar information as management's; and using financial policies (such as stock repurchases, dividend increases, and hedging) to help signal management's optimism about the firm's future performance.

In this chapter we have stressed the importance of communicating effectively with investors. But firms also have to communicate with other stakeholders, including employees, customers, suppliers, and regulatory bodies. Many of the same principles discussed here can also be applied to management communication with these other stakeholders.

Finally, we examined the capital market role of governance agents, such as external auditors and audit committees. Both have recently faced considerable public scrutiny following a spate of financial reporting meltdowns in the U.S. Much has been done to improve the governance and independence of these intermediaries. We focus on how the financial analysis tools developed in the book can be used to improve the quality of audit and audit committee work. The tools of strategy analysis, accounting analysis, financial analysis, and prospective analysis can help auditors and audit committee members to identify the key issues in the financial statements to focus on and provide commonsense ways of assessing whether there are potential reporting problems that merit additional testing and analysis.

DISCUSSION QUESTIONS

1. Apple's inventory increased from $1 billion on December 29, 1994, to $1.95 billion one year later. In contrast, sales for the fourth quarter in each of these years increased from $2 billion to $2.6 billion. What is the implied annualized inventory turnover for Apple for these years? What different interpretations about future performance could a financial analyst infer from this change? What information could Apple's management provide to investors to clarify the change in inventory turnover? What are the costs and benefits to Apple from disclosing this information? What issues does this change raise for the auditor? What additional tests would you want to conduct as Apple's auditor?

2. a. What are likely to be the long-term critical success factors for the following types of firms?
   - a high technology company such as Microsoft
   - a large low-cost retailer such as Kmart

   b. How useful is financial accounting data for evaluating how well these two companies are managing their critical success factors? What other types of information would be useful in your evaluation? What are the costs and benefits to these companies from disclosing this type of information to investors?

3. Management frequently objects to disclosing additional information on the grounds that it is proprietary. Consider the recent FASB proposals on expanding disclosures on (a) executive stock compensation and (b) business segment performance. Many

corporate managers expressed strong opposition to both proposals. What are the potential proprietary costs from expanded disclosures in each of these areas? If you conclude that proprietary costs are relatively low for either, what alternative explanations do you have for management's opposition?

4. Financial reporting rules in many countries outside the U.S. (e.g., the UK, Australia, New Zealand, and France) permit management to revalue fixed assets (and in some cases even intangible assets) which have increased in value. Revaluations are typically based on estimates of realizable value made by management or independent valuers. Do you expect that these accounting standards will make earnings and book values more or less useful to investors? Explain why or why not. How can management make these types of disclosures more credible?

5. Under a management buyout, the top management of a firm offers to buy the company from its stockholders, usually at a premium over its current stock price. The management team puts up its own capital to finance the acquisition, with additional financing typically coming from a private buyout firm and private debt. If management is interested in making such an offer for its firm in the near future, what are its financial reporting incentives? How do these differ from the incentives of management that are not interested in a buyout? How would you respond to a proposed management buyout if you were the firm's auditor? What about if you were a member of the audit committee?

6. You are approached by the management of a small start-up company that is planning to go public. The founders are unsure about how aggressive they should be in their accounting decisions as they come to the market. John Smith, the CEO, asserts, "We might as well take full advantage of any discretion offered by accounting rules, since the market will be expecting us to do so." What are the pros and cons of this strategy? As the partner of a major audit firm, what type of analysis would you perform before deciding to take on a new start-up that is planning to go public?

7. Two years after a successful public offering, the CEO of a biotechnology company is concerned about stock market uncertainty surrounding the potential of new drugs in the development pipeline. In his discussion with you, the CEO notes that even though they have recently made significant progress in their internal R&D efforts, the stock has performed poorly. What options does he have to help convince investors of the value of the new products? Which of these options are likely to be feasible?

8. Why might the CEO of the biotechnology firm discussed in Question 7 be concerned about the firm being undervalued? Would the CEO be equally concerned if the stock were overvalued? Do you believe that the CEO would attempt to correct the market's perception in this overvaluation case? How would you react to company concern about market under- or overvaluation if you were the firm's auditor? Or if you were a member of the audit committee?

9. When companies decide to shift from private to public financing by making an initial public offering for their stock, they are likely to face increased costs of investor communications. Given this additional cost, why would firms opt to go public?

10. German firms are traditionally financed by banks, which have representatives on the companies' boards. How would communication challenges differ for these firms relative to U.S. firms, which rely more on public financing?

NOTES

1. M. Jensen and W. Meckling, "Theory of the Firm: Managerial Behavior, Agency Costs, and Capital Structure," *Journal of Financial Economics* 3 (October 1976): 305–360, analyzed agency problems between managers and outside investors. Subsequent work by B. Holmstrom and others examined how contracts between managers and outside investors could mitigate the agency problem.

2. Kevin J. Murphy and Jerold L. Zimmerman, "Financial Performance Surrounding CEO Turnover," *Journal of Accounting and Economics* 16 (January/April/July 1993): 273–315, find a strong relation between CEO turnover and earnings-based performance.

3. See S. Teoh, I. Welch, and T. Wong, "Earnings Management and the Long-Run Market Performance of Initial Public Offerings, *The Journal of Finance* 63 (December 1998): 1935–74, and S. Teoh, I. Welch, and T. Wong, "Earnings Management and the Underperformance of Seasoned Equity Offerings," *Journal of Financial Economics* 50 (October 1998): 63–99.

4. This market imperfection is often referred to as a "lemons" or "information" problem. It was first discussed by G. Akerlof in relation to the used car market (see "The Market for 'Lemons': Quality Uncertainty and the Market Mechanism," *Quarterly Journal of Economics* 90 (1970): 629–50. Akerlof recognized that the seller of a used car knew more about the car's value than the buyer. This meant that the buyer was likely to end up overpaying, since the seller would accept any offer that exceeded the car's true value and reject any lower offer. Car buyers recognized this problem and would respond by only making low-ball offers for used cars, leading sellers with high quality cars to exit the market. As a result, only the lowest quality cars (the "lemons") would remain in the market. Akerlof pointed out that qualified independent mechanics could correct this market breakdown by providing buyers with reliable information on a used car's true value.

5. Of course improved analysis alone is unlikely to be sufficient to improve market intermediation if the structural reforms implemented by the Sarbanes-Oxley Act and the stock exchanges fail to correct the serious conflicts of interest for intermediaries that we have witnessed in the last few years.

6. Douglas J. Skinner, "Earnings disclosures and stockholder lawsuits," *Journal of Accounting and Economics* (November 1997): 249–83, finds that firms with bad earnings news tend to predisclose this information, perhaps to reduce the cost of litigation that inevitably follows bad news quarters.

7. For example, G. Foster, "Briloff and the Capital Market," *Journal of Accounting Research* 17, no. 1 (Spring 1979): 262–74, finds firms that are criticized for their accounting by Abraham J. Briloff on average suffer an 8 percent decline in their stock price.

8. See Sarah Tasker, "Bridging the Information Gap: Quarterly Conference Calls as a Medium for Voluntary Disclosure." *Review of Accounting Studies* 3, no. 1-2 (1998): 137–67.

9. See Richard Frankel, Marilyn Johnson, and Douglas Skinner, "An Empirical Examination of Conference Calls as a Voluntary Disclosure Medium," *Journal of Accounting Research* 37, no. 1 (Spring 1999): 133–50.

10. Recent research on voluntary disclosure includes Mark Lang and Russell Lundholm, "Cross-Sectional Determinants of Analysts' Ratings of Corporate Disclosures," *Journal of Accounting Research* 31 (Autumn 1993): 246–71; Lang and Lundholm, "Corporate Disclosure Policy and Analysts," *The Accounting Review* 71 (October 1996): 467–92; M. Welker, "Disclosure Policy, Information Asymmetry and Liquidity in Equity Markets," *Contemporary Accounting Research* (Spring 1995); Christine Botosan, "The Impact of Annual Report Disclosure Level on Investor Base and the Cost of Capital," *The Accounting Review* (July 1997): 323–50; and Paul Healy, Amy Hutton, and Krishna Palepu, "Stock Performance and Intermediation Changes Surrounding Sustained Increases in Disclosure," *Contemporary Accounting Research* 16, no. 3 (Fall 1999): 485–521. This research finds that firms are more likely to provide high levels of disclosure if they have strong earnings performance, issue securities, have more analyst following, and have less dispersion in analyst forecasts. In addition, firms with high levels of disclosure policies tend to have a lower cost of capital and bid-ask spread. Finally, firms that increase disclosure have accompanying increases in stock returns, institutional ownership, analyst following, and stock liquidity. In "The Role of Supplementary Statements with Management's Earnings Forecasts," working paper, Harvard Business School, 2003, A. Hutton, G. Miller, and D. Skinner examine the market response to management earnings forecasts

and find that bad news forecasts are always informative but that good news forecasts are informative only when they are supported by verifiable forward-looking statements.

11. Findings by Paul Healy and Krishna Palepu in "Earnings Information Conveyed by Dividend Initiations and Omissions," *Journal of Financial Economics* 21 (1988): 149–75, indicate that investors interpret announcements of dividend initiations and omissions as managers' forecasts of future earnings performance.

12. See Larry Dann, Ronald Masulis, and David Mayers, "Repurchase Tender Offers and Earnings Information," *Journal of Accounting & Economics* (September 1991): 217–52, and Michael Hertzel and Prem Jain, "Earnings and Risk Changes Around Stock Repurchases," *Journal of Accounting & Economics* (September 1991): 253–76.

13. See Mary Barth and Ron Kasznik, "Share Repurchases and Intangible Assets," *Journal of Accounting & Economics* 28 (December 1999): 211–41.

14. See P. Healy and K. Palepu, "The Fall of Enron," *Journal of Economic Perspectives,* forthcoming; and P. Healy and K. Palepu, "How the Quest for Efficiency Undermined the Market," *Harvard Business Review,* forthcoming.

15. For example, M. Nelson, J. Eliott, and R. Tarpley, in "Evidence from Auditors About Managers' and Auditors' Earnings Management Decisions," *The Accounting Review* 77 (2002 Supplement): 175–202, show that mechanical accounting rules for structured finance transactions lead to more earnings management.

16. See P. Healy and K. Palepu, "Audit the Audit Committees: After Enron Boards Must Change the Focus and Provide Greater Financial Transparency," *Financial Times,* June 10, 2002, p. 14.

Computer Associates International, Inc.: Governance and Investor Communication Challenge

In the first six months of 2002, Computer Associates announced the appointment of six new members to its board of directors. The changes in board composition followed a period in which the company had made significant changes to its business model and its financial reporting. Commenting on the four new director changes announced on July 16, 2002, Sanjay Kumar, CA's CEO, noted:

> Our business model, which was implemented in October 2000, is delivering sustainable competitive advantage and—as evidenced by today's announcements, the April additions of Jay Lorsch, a noted governance expert from Harvard, and Walter Schuetze, the former chief accountant to the Securities and Exchange Commission, and last year's addition of lead independent director Lewis Ranieri—we have continued to make excellent progress in attracting highly qualified independent directors to CA's board."

Despite management's belief that the company had made good progress in improving its business model and governance, there remained considerable skepticism about CA in the stock market. The company's stock price dropped by about 60 percent during the first half of 2002 (see Exhibit 1 for a comparison of the stock's performance versus that of the S&P 500). Investors were confused about the company's new accounting, and were skeptical of the "pro forma" numbers the company was disclosing as a way to help investors assess the impact of the accounting change. In addition, Sam Wyly, a Texas entrepreneur who had sold his company, Sterling Software, to CA in 2001, was continuing his efforts to challenge management through a protracted proxy fight.

Kumar was convinced that the business and accounting changes that the company made were absolutely the right things to have done. He was pleased to see that the new business model the company had implemented was producing exactly the type of results he had hoped to achieve. And he thought the company was doing its best to communicate with Wall Street. He was, therefore, surprised by the skepticism with which investors viewed the company and its financial reports.

As Kumar prepared for the upcoming board meeting, he wondered how the company should respond to the skepticism in the market, and how the company's new board could help him restore investor confidence.

COMPUTER ASSOCIATES

Charles Wang founded Computer Associates in 1976 as a joint venture with Swiss-owned Computer Associates (CA) to sell software in the United States. The company's first product, a file organizer for IBM storage systems, was highly successful, and in 1980 Wang

Professors Paul Healy and Krishna Palepu prepared this case. The case is intended solely as the basis for class discussion and is not intended to serve as an endorsement, source of primary data, or illustration of effective or ineffective management. Copyright © 2002 by the President and Fellows of Harvard College. HBS Case 9-103-007.

bought out his Swiss partners.[1] Wang sought to provide CA customers with higher quality products than they could buy from IBM and to develop a strong distribution network to sell these products.

During the 1980s and 1990s, Wang recognized the importance of increasing the range of software products that could be offered and supported through CA's extensive distribution and service network. Acquisitions of existing software, which reduced the risk of in-house development and moved products to market sooner, became CA's favorite means of growth (see Exhibit 2 for a list of major acquisitions). To integrate its acquisitions, CA would interview and subsequently rank all new employees, and then either assign them new positions or let them go.

Wang stepped down as CEO in 2000 to become chairman, and Kumar, who had joined the company through the acquisition of UCCEL in 1987 and had been CA's president since 1994, became CEO.

By 2002 CA had become the third-largest independent software company in the world (after Microsoft and Oracle). The company had expanded beyond mainframe utilities into PC software, database and banking applications, and network software. For the year ended March 31, 2002, CA reported annual sales of $3.0 billion, operating cash flow of $1.3 billion, and ending assets of $12.2 billion. (Financial statements and selected footnote information for the year ended March 31, 2002, are presented in Exhibit 3.)

CA's Old Business Model and Accounting

Under a typical licensing arrangement customers agreed to pay a license fee to CA for the right to use software for a period of three to ten years. CA based license fees on either the aggregate capacity of all machines that used the software, or on the processing power of individual licensed machines. The license fees also reflected the number of years of the license—the longer the license period, the higher the fee. However, the incremental fee for additional years of licensing declined over time at a rate of roughly 30 percent per year to reflect obsolescence. Despite the fact that licenses were for multiple years, current financial reporting rules required CA to report the licensing fee as revenue once a customer had signed a contract, the software had been delivered, and collection of fees was reasonably assured.

CA also charged customers an annual maintenance fee of roughly 10 to 20 percent of the initial license fee. Annual renewal rates for CA maintenance contracts typically exceeded 85 percent. Maintenance fees, whether bundled with product licenses or priced separately, were required to be recognized ratably over the maintenance period.

Unlike other independent software firms, CA provided its customers with the option of financing the initial license fee. As a result, CA's financial statements looked very different from those of its major competitors. Its balance sheet included sizeable receivables—on March 31, 1999, 60 percent of its assets were short- or long-term receivables. Its income statement included effective interest from financing its customers—for 1999, effective interest amounted to $408 million, 9 percent of total licensing revenues. Also, its cash inflows were steadier, since revenues were collected over time rather than at the time of sale.

Problems with the Old Business Model

Despite being the standard for the software industry, the old business model had generated a number of problems. The primary problem was that customers had learned that pressure

----

1. For more information on Computer Associates International, please see Amy Hutton, "Computer Associates International," Harvard Business School Case 102-061, 2002.

on sales representatives for CA (as well as for other software firms) to meet quarterly sales targets intensified toward the end of each quarter. By waiting until the last week of the quarter to sign a license agreement, savvy customers were able to negotiate attractive licensing-fee discounts. Consequently, CA recorded a significant portion of its sales for a given quarter in the last week of the quarter.

This selling pattern was primarily driven by the incentives of CA's sales representatives and top management. Sales representatives were compensated on a commission basis, with commissions computed quarterly as a percentage of the present value of the annual license fees for contracts sold. Sales representatives' financial incentives were therefore tied to quarterly sales targets, and pressure to meet these targets intensified as the quarter end approached. CA's top management faced similar pressures, in their case to meet Wall Street quarterly revenue and earnings expectations. Management pressure to increase sales each quarter reinforced the incentives of sales representatives, particularly since the full effect of multi-year licenses was recorded as revenue when the contract was signed and the software delivered.

Sales representatives would therefore agree to deep discounts on licenses signed in the last week of the quarter. Discounts were particularly significant for the later years of a contract, when obsolescence risk was high and the present-value implications for sales representatives' commissions were small. Top management went along with the discounting to boost reported revenues and earnings. Because the incremental costs of software production were negligible, reducing license fees for the later contract years could be argued to still be profitable for shareholders, since even minimal revenues in those years contributed toward recovering the costs of software development.

However, there were a number of negative consequences to the pattern in sales over the quarter. First, it made it very difficult for firms in the software industry to maintain margins. There was constant pressure to lower prices. For example, it was difficult for sales representatives to deny discounts offered to customers negotiating contracts in the last week of the quarter to other customers who negotiated new contracts the following quarter. More important, customers who had succeeded in negotiating attractive discounts on licenses in the later years of a contract used these low rates as a base for negotiating subsequent license fees when the contract was up for renewal.

The sales pattern also made it difficult for CA to forecast revenues and earnings for any given quarter. Since most of the quarter's sales arose in the last week, management found it difficult to warn analysts and investors of any drop in revenues until after the quarter was actually over. As a result, it was difficult for analysts to forecast earnings, leading to wide stock price swings at the time of earnings announcements. CA was particularly sensitive to this problem—in July 2000 the company saw its stock price fall by 42 percent when it announced a quarterly earnings shortfall that was partially caused by delays in "several large contracts, previously expected to close in the final days of the quarter."[2]

Finally, the current business model had several other negative implications for CA. Sales representatives tended to focus heavily on clients who were considering buying or renewing their long-term licenses. However, once a license agreement was signed, they had little incentive to follow up during the contract period, which often ran several years; their time was better spent focusing on new customers or customers whose licenses were about to expire. As a result, there was considerable customer dissatisfaction with CA. This dissatisfaction, coupled with reluctance by customers to experiment with new software

2. Laura Johannes, "Computer Associates Says Latest Results Will Be Hurt by Delays in Big Contracts," The Wall Street Journal, July 5, 2000, p A14.

that required another multi-year license, reduced opportunities for follow-up sales of new software products to existing customers.

Change in Business Model

In October 2000, CA announced changes in its business model, including reducing software license lives, changing the method of compensating sales representatives, and revamping customer support.

By reducing software license lives from seven years to a minimum of one month and a maximum of three years, CA's management anticipated that sales representatives would have to meet regularly with customers and offer good service. This would be needed to ensure that customers renewed existing contracts but could also be used as an opportunity to sell new software products. Under the new arrangement customers could experiment with new products for a minimum of one month. If they did not find them valuable, they could simply fail to renew them the following month. Also, shorter contracts were expected to reduce the opportunity for sales representatives to agree to discounts on license fees as they had in the sixth and seventh years of a long-term contract. CA was confident that the shorter contract lives would not adversely affect its economics because the renewal rates historically had been very high.

Under the new sales representative compensation arrangement, sales representatives were given monthly sales quotas. Commission rates were made variable, with the highest rates reserved for sales of new products to new customers, lower rates for sales of new products to existing customers, and the lowest rate being the extension of a license for an existing customer. In addition, sales representatives' training focused on improving customer service and satisfaction, and 20 percent of commissions were assigned on the basis of customer satisfaction. To ensure that the sales representatives did not oppose the business model change, or worse still, leave the organization, CA's management promised that their total compensation under the new scheme would not be lower than current compensation.

Finally, CA revamped its customer service organization by unifying all post-sales customer groups under a common organizational structure. In addition, the company hired 625 new staff for its customer relations organization so that customers could "have a single point of contact for all their needs."

Change in Revenue Recognition

At the same time that it changed its business model, CA changed its method of reporting for revenues. Instead of recognizing the present value of multi-year license fees in the year the contract was signed and software delivered, the company began to recognize revenues ratably over the life of the contract.

CA's management argued that the accounting change would benefit both customers and shareholders:

> *Ratable recognition will help* CA *move away from the end-of-quarter customer "dance" that leaves both* CA *and our customers unhappy—a situation that is obviously inconsistent with a business model that stresses partnership. It is well known in the software industry that the majority of deals are signed at the end of the quarter, as vendors try to make their quarterly numbers. This end-of-quarter flurry of deals—the proverbial "hockey stick effect"—creates an unnecessarily adversarial relationship between customers and vendors in which both parties rush to sign any deal rather than the right deal.*
>
> *Ratable recognition provides shareholders with greater transparency and lower volatility in quarterly revenue and earnings. Because a majority of our contracts*

*have historically been closed in the last few days of the quarter, CA, like other soft-
ware companies, has had difficulty providing guidance on quarterly earnings.*[3]

However, since CA could not retroactively change its method of accounting, the reporting change posed a short-term challenge for investors in comparing the company's performance over time. Under the new method, license-fee revenues for 2001 were only $3.7
billion versus $5.6 billion for 2000, in part because 2001 revenues included only the
license fees for that year and not the multi-year effect of new licensing contracts shown in
2000. As a result, CA reported a loss of $591 million in 2001, compared with a profit of
$696 million in 2000.

MANAGEMENT AND BOARD THINKING ABOUT THE CHANGES

Kumar, the CEO, summed up CA's perspective on the new business model:

*The new business model is one of our most important steps in unlocking the value of
CA for our customers, shareholders, and employees. We are taking the lead in adopting a model that improves our ability to partner with our customers to realize value
and that creates the transparency and consistency in financial results desired by
investors. Our employees are highly energized by the changes we are making.*

Citing a study by the consulting firm McKinsey & Company, Sanjay Kumar stated that
"given all the benefits the new business model offers, we expect to see more software companies following our lead."

The company's board was fully involved in the business model and accounting change.
While the board members strongly supported both moves, they expressed concern that
investors might not fully understand the potential benefits of the proposed changes. Of
particular concern to the board was the potential problem investors might face in comparing the company's past and future performance, given the change in accounting policy.
The board's concern was reinforced by advice from investment bankers who indicated that
time-series comparability of reported numbers was of critical importance to investors.

To help investors compare performance across years, CA provided "pro forma pro rata"
revenues and earnings for the current year (2001) and the year before (2000) under the
new accounting method and under the assumption that it had always owned two companies acquired in 1999 and 2000. This information was presented in the management discussion and analysis section of the company's annual report. Thus, unlike the pro forma
information provided by many companies in their press releases, this information was subject to attestation by the company's auditor, KPMG. (Pro forma information is presented in
Exhibit 4.) Pro forma total revenues were $5.8 billion and $5.6 billion for 2002 and 2001,
and earnings were $1,542 million and $951 million, respectively.

CA also used the pro forma numbers in its communication with analysts and Wall
Street, in its press releases, and in the information provided on the company's web site.
The company felt that this approach would make it easier for investors to understand the
benefits of the change in business model, and not misinterpret the decline in reported
revenues and profits in the current year as a result of the changed generally accepted
accounting principles (GAAP) accounting statements.

---

3. *"How our new business model delivers value to customers, shareholders, and employees," company document, Computer Associates International, Inc., 2001.*

Computer Associates International

REACTIONS TO THE CHANGES

Reactions to CA's business and accounting changes were mixed. An article in *Fortune* was positive about the changes:

> *The most immediate result is higher profit margins, because software companies no longer have to make concessions on price. It should also mean an end to those nasty earnings misses, as substantially more revenue gets locked in at the beginning of the quarter rather than the end. . . . And negotiations for big deals should go a lot smoother. At the last minute, the software company can tell haggling customers to take a hike (or at least to come back next quarter). "Assuming there's a real need on the customer's part, they'll have to get the deal done in the normal course of business rather than waiting until the 11th hour of the next quarter," says John Barr of Robertson Stephens. Adds Jack Ciesielski, publisher of* The Analysts Accounting Observer: *"Its just a cleaner, more realistic way of recognizing revenue. They're looking at having more numbers we can trust."* [4]

IDC also supported the moves, citing the improved incentives between CA and its customers and the opportunities for the company to sell new products to its existing customers. In a bulletin, IDC concluded:

> *Computer Associates (CA) has taken a market-leading position with respect to software payments, moving from an annuity model to one in which it will accept payments for software licenses on a month to month basis and recognize revenue the same way, regardless of how customers buy the software. . . . The move should also take the bumps out of* CA's *revenue stream by removing incentives for customers to wait till the end of a quarter or year to close a deal in the hopes of throttling CA salespeople into providing bigger discounts. Additionally,* CA *is better positioned to get access to new and competitive accounts, as well as emerging partners that need to finance nascent business models.* [5]

However, not all the responses were as supportive. On April 29, 2001, *The New York Times* published a piece on CA titled "A Software Company Runs Out of Tricks; The Past May Haunt Computer Associates." Among other things, the article challenged CA's pro forma financial information:

> *As measured by standard accounting rules, Computer Associates' sales have fallen almost two-thirds over the last six months. To cover that, the company has begun presenting its financial results in a way that confuses even the Street analysts who follow it."*
>
> :
> :
>
> *On April 16, Computer Associates reported another banner quarter. "New Business Model Rules; Q4 Rocks," it said proudly in a news release outlining its results for the three months ended March 31. The company appeared untouched by the slowdown in technology spending that hurt other big software companies like Oracle.*
>
> *Computer Associates said that on a "pro forma, pro rata" basis, its revenues had risen to $1.44 billion for the quarter, from $1.39 billion in the period a year earlier. Profits were 47 cents a share, it said, up from 39 cents a share.*
>
> :
> :

---

4. Herb Greenberg, "Against the grain: Software makers get freed by an accounting change," Fortune, June 1, 2001

5. Steve McHale and Kevin Restivo, International Data Corporation, Document #23533, November 2000.

> *But the last line of the April 16 news release told a different story. There, Computer Associates reported its revenue and income according to "generally accepted accounting principles," the standard that companies are required to use in filings with the Securities and Exchange Commission to calculate results. By those rules, revenue fell almost 60%, to $732 million, from $1.91 billion. After earning a profit of $1.13 a share, or about $700 million, last year, the company lost 29 cents a share, or about $175 million, this year.[6]*

Analysts and investors, who viewed the company's accounting change and pro forma disclosure with suspicion, cited several concerns. First, they wondered whether the new revenue recognition policy meant that the company's previous policy was overly aggressive. Did the company overstate its revenues and earnings in previous years? This was especially troubling because top management was awarded close to $1 billion in stock compensation based on the past reported performance. Second, were the pro forma disclosures, which showed significantly better results than those reported under the current accounting policy, meant to divert investors' attention from the company's poor performance? Third, were the new business model and accounting changes really motivated by the reasons stated by management or merely to hide that the company was no longer in a position to achieve dramatic growth acquisitions as in the past?

PROXY FIGHT AND CORPORATE GOVERNANCE CHANGES

Close on the heels of the accounting and business model controversy, the company found itself in the middle of a proxy fight. In June 2001 Sam Wyly, a Texas entrepreneur who had sold his company, Sterling Software, to CA a year earlier for $3.91 billion, launched a proxy fight requesting CA's shareholders to vote out CA's current management team and the board. Wyly was attempting to capitalize on the controversy surrounding the company's accounting and investors' prior concerns regarding CA's top management compensation and corporate governance. Wyly alleged that "the company has abused and alienated customers, employees and shareholders alike. Management's use of accounting gimmicks and its excessive compensation for lackluster performance have strained credibility with the financial community."[7]

After a bruising fight, CA's management won the proxy fight in August 2001 after promising shareholders that it would make the board more independent and share more strategic information with investors. Specifically, the company promised to add two independent directors to its board, in addition to the two independent directors it had added just after the proxy fight began. The company also promised to share with shareholders information on customer satisfaction from its own surveys, disclose specific growth targets, and generally pursue a friendlier investor relations strategy. In return, all ten incumbent directors won more than 75 percent of the votes cast in the proxy fight.

Subsequent to the proxy fight, the company initiated a number of significant board and corporate governance changes. In March 2002 the company announced the appointment of two new directors, Walter P. Schuetze and Jay W. Lorsch. Schuetze was a charter member of the Financial Accounting Standards Board, a member of the Financial Accounting

6. Alex Besensen, "A Software Company Runs Out of Tricks: The Past May Haunt Computer Associates," The New York Times, April 29, 2001, section 3.

7. Stephanie Kirchaessner, "Texan seeks to oust CA board," Financial Times, June 22, 2001.

Computer Associates International

Standards Advisory Council, and a member and chair of the Accounting Standards Executive Committee of the American Institute of Certified Public Accountants. He had been the chief accountant to the SEC from January 1992 to March 1995 and the chief accountant of the commission's Division of Enforcement from November 1997 until February 2000. Lorsch was a Harvard Business School professor and a renowned governance expert.

In May 2002 the company adopted a set of new governance policies. Under these policies, the company appointed one of its directors and the former vice chairman of Salomon Brothers, Lewis Ranieri, as the "lead independent director." Schuetze was appointed as the chairman of the company's audit committee. Other governance changes adopted included an annual board evaluation of the company's CEO, adoption of New York Stock Exchange (NYSE) guidelines for deciding which directors qualified as independent, reducing the number of insiders on the board to three (out of a total of 12 directors), and limiting the terms of the independent directors.

In July 2002 CA named four new directors: Kenneth Cron, CEO of Vivendi Universal Games, a division of Vivendi Universal; Robert E. La Blanc, former vice chairman of Continental Telecom Corporation and a former general partner of Salomon Brothers Inc.; Alex Serge Vieux, an international technology and software entrepreneur; and Thomas H. Wyman, the former chairman and CEO of CBS, Inc.[8] These four directors replaced Willem F.P. de Vogel, a private investor and director since 1991; Shirley Strum Kenny, president of the State University of New York at Stony Brook and director since 1994; Richard Grasso, the chairman of the NYSE and director since 1994; and Roel Pieper, an executive in the hi-tech field. The first three of these were retiring as a result of the new director term-limit policy that the company had adopted; Pieper stepped down as a result of other business commitments. In addition to the newly appointed six board members, the company had five other continuing members. (A list of the other members of CA's board, their length of tenure, and their affiliations is shown in Exhibit 5.)

The Investor Communication Challenge

As Kumar reviewed the events of the last 15 months, he was pleased with the progress that had been made. He was convinced that the company's new business model was not only the right model for the company and its customers, but one that all software companies were likely to adopt sooner or later. Internal data clearly showed that the new business model was producing all the benefits that he had hoped to achieve. As intended, there was a significant decline in end-of-quarter contract-closing frenzy, with all its associated dysfunctional financial and organizational consequences that the company had had to deal with prior to the business model change. New sales contracts were shorter and more profitable. Internal surveys indicated that customer satisfaction was increasing as sales representatives were interacting more frequently with customers, both to renew existing contracts and to explore the sale of new products to existing customers. The new approach to revenue recognition was not only conservative, but also made revenues and earnings more predictable.

However, the company still faced a significant challenge in convincing investors and Wall Street analysts that the new business model and accounting were beneficial. Despite all the efforts that Kumar and his chief financial officer, Ira Zar, had made during the past year, investors and analysts still seemed to be skeptical. Further, the decision to release the "pro forma, pro rata" numbers, intended to help investors compare performance over time, seemed to have created suspicion and confusion.

---

8. Jerry Guidera, "Computer Associates Names Directors Before Proxy Battle," The Wall Street Journal, July 17, 2002.

Investor concerns intensified when the company announced in February 2002 that the SEC was investigating its past accounting practices.[9] Short sellers, capitalizing on this investigation, spread rumors that the company had adopted the new accounting method to disguise past accounting abuses that had overstated revenues and earnings. Even though the company strongly denied these allegations, investor confidence was clearly damaged. Wyly, the company's dissident investor, announced yet another challenge to the company's management by filing a slate of five nominees to replace incumbent directors at a vote at the company's annual shareholder meeting on August 28, 2002.

Kumar felt that the recent dramatic changes made to the company's board and governance would be a strong foundation on which to rebuild investor trust and confidence. He wondered what changes, if any, the company should make to its investor communication strategy as part of this effort. Should the company rethink its decision to release the "pro forma, pro rata" numbers? If these numbers were not reported, should they be replaced with some other information? Given all the supplementary information that the company was already reporting, would more disclosure help or hurt? How could the company convince investors that the business and accounting changes were truly in their long-term interest? What role should the board play in crafting this strategy?

QUESTIONS

1. What was CA trying to accomplish by the change in business model? How did the changes accomplish these goals? What risks does the new model create?

2. How does the change in accounting fit with the new business model?

3. Do you agree with the company's decision to produce pro forma earnings numbers?

4. What action plan would you recommend for Sanjay Kumar?

9. Alex Berenson, "Computer Associates Says U.S. Is Seeking Data on Accounting," The New York Times, May, 2002, p.4.

Computer Associates International

EXHIBIT I

Computer Associates International Relative Stock Price Performance

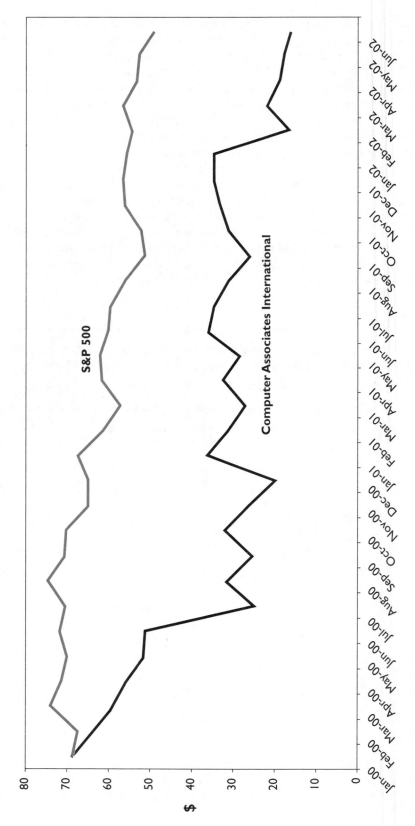

Source: Datastream International.

EXHIBIT 2

Major Acquisitions by Computer Associates International, Inc.

Acquisition Date	Acquisition Cost	Company Acquired	Products Acquired
1982		Capex Software	MVS operating systems
1984		Supercalc	Spreadsheet software
1987	$780m	UCCEL	Utilities software
1989	$320m	Cullinet	Database and banking applications
1994	$309m	ASK	Network software Systems software
1995	$1.7b	Legent	Client/server solutions
1996	$1.2b	Cheyenne Software	Network solutions
1999	$3.5b	PLATINUM Technology International Inc	Portals, business intelligence, application development, and infrastructure management
2000	$4.0b	Sterling Software	Business software

Sources: CA web site, <http://ca.com/about/history.htm>, and press releases from *The Wall Street Journal* and *Financial Times*.

Computer Associates International

EXHIBIT 3

Financial Statements and Selected Footnotes, Computer Associates International, Inc. and Subsidiaries

CONSOLIDATED BALANCE SHEETS

(dollars in millions)	Year Ended March 31, 2002	2001
ASSETS		
CURRENT ASSETS		
Cash and cash equivalents	$1,093	$763
Marketable securities	87	87
Trade and installment accounts receivable, net	1,825	1,788
Deferred income taxes	0	106
Other current assets	56	65
TOTAL CURRENT ASSETS	3,061	2,809
INSTALLMENT ACCOUNTS RECEIVABLE, due after one year, net	1,566	2,883
PROPERTY AND EQUIPMENT		
Land and buildings	531	524
Equipment, furniture and improvements	857	839
	1,388	1,363
Accumulated depreciation and amortization	670	569
TOTAL PROPERTY AND EQUIPMENT, net	718	794
PURCHASED SOFTWARE PRODUCTS, net of accumulated amortization of $2,648 and $2,193, respectively	1,836	2,328
GOODWILL AND OTHER INTANGIBLE ASSETS, net of accumulated amortization of $1,524 and $1,023, respectively	4,835	5,400
OTHER ASSETS	210	222
TOTAL ASSETS	$12,226	$14,436
LIABILITIES AND STOCKHOLDERS' EQUITY		
CURRENT LIABILITIES		
Loans payable and current portion of long-term debt	$508	$816
Accounts payable	208	272
Salaries, wages and commissions	236	196
Accrued expenses and other current liabilities	474	613
Deferred subscription revenue (collected)—current	577	166
Taxes payable, other than income taxes payable	116	132
Federal, state and foreign income taxes payable	195	257
Deferred income taxes	7	0
TOTAL CURRENT LIABILITIES	2,321	2,452
LONG-TERM DEBT, net of current portion	3,334	3,629
DEFERRED INCOME TAXES	1,267	1,900
DEFERRED SUBSCRIPTION REVENUE (COLLECTED)—NONCURRENT	208	127
DEFERRED MAINTENANCE REVENUE	456	538
OTHER NONCURRENT LIABILITIES	23	10

(continued)

(dollars in millions)	Year Ended March 31,	
	2002	2001
STOCKHOLDERS' EQUITY		
Common stock, $.10 par value, 1,100,000,000 shares authorized, 630,920,576 shares issued	63	63
Additional paid-in capital	3,878	3,936
Retained earnings	2,335	3,483
Accumulated other comprehensive loss	(361	(388)
Treasury stock, at cost—53,739,842 shares for 2002 and 55,223,485 shares for 2001	(1,298)	(1,314)
TOTAL STOCKHOLDERS' EQUITY	4,617	5,780
TOTAL LIABILITIES AND STOCKHOLDERS' EQUITY	$12,226	$14,436

CONSOLIDATED STATEMENT OF OPERATIONS

(in millions except per share amounts)	Year Ended March 31,		
	2002	2001	2000
REVENUE:			
Subscription revenue	$827	$59	$ —
Software fees and other	432	1,881	4,179
Maintenance	958	1,087	877
Financing fees	444	638	529
Professional services	303	525	509
TOTAL REVENUE	2,964	4,190	6,094
OPERATING EXPENSES:			
Amortization of capitalized software costs	487	492	271
Cost of professional services	283	463	446
Selling, general and administrative	1,790	2,120	1,462
Product development and enhancements	678	695	568
Commissions and royalties	275	308	300
Depreciation and amortization	609	618	323
Purchased research and development	—	—	795
1995 Stock Plan	—	(184)	—
TOTAL OPERATING EXPENSES	4,122	4,512	4,165
(Loss) income before other expenses	(1,158)	(322)	1,929
Interest expense, net	227	344	339
(Loss) income before income taxes	(1,385)	(666)	1,590
Income taxes	(283)	(75)	894
NET (LOSS) INCOME	(1,102)	(591)	696
BASIC (LOSS) EARNINGS PER SHARE	($1.91)	($1.02)	$1.29
Basic weighted-average shares used in computation	577	582	539
DILUTED (LOSS) EARNINGS PER SHARE	($1.91)	($1.02)	$1.25
Diluted weighted-average shares used in computation	577	582	557

Computer Associates International

CONSOLIDATED STATEMENT OF CASH FLOWS

(in millions)	Year Ended March 31, 2001	2000	1999
OPERATING ACTIVITIES:			
Net (loss) income	($1,102)	($591)	$696
Adjustments to reconcile net (loss) income to net cash provided by operating activities:			
Depreciation and amortization	(1,096	1,110	594
Provision for deferred income taxes	(544)	(350)	412
Charge for purchased research and development	0	0	795
Compensation expense (gain) related to stock and pension plans	24	(146)	30
Decrease (increase) in noncurrent installment accounts receivable, net	1,316	828	(1,039)
Increase in deferred subscription revenue (collected)—noncurrent	81	127	0
(Decrease) increase in deferred maintenance revenue	(81)	(3)	113
Foreign currency transaction loss—before taxes	6	14	5
Impairment charge	59	0	50
Gain on sale of property and equipment	0	0	(5)
Changes in other operating assets and liabilities, net of effect of acquisitions:			
(Increase) decrease in trade and installment receivables, net—current	(45)	253	83
Increase in deferred subscription revenue (collected)—current	415	166	0
Other changes in operating assets and liabilities	26	(25)	(168)
NET CASH PROVIDED BY OPERATING ACTIVITIES	1,251	1,383	1,566
INVESTING ACTIVITIES:			
Acquisitions, primarily purchased software, marketing rights and intangibles, net of cash acquired	(2)	(174)	(3,049)
Settlements of purchase accounting liabilities	(59)	(367)	(429)
Purchases of property and equipment	(25)	(89)	(198)
Proceeds from sale of property and equipment	0	5	12
Disposition of businesses	0	158	0
Purchases of marketable securities	(38)	(48)	(95)
Sales of marketable securities	36	40	189
Increase in capitalized development costs and other	(53)	(49)	(36)
NET CASH USED IN INVESTING ACTIVITIES	(141)	(524)	(3,606)
FINANCING ACTIVITIES:			
Dividends paid	(46)	(47)	(43)
Purchases of treasury stock	(95)	(449)	0
Proceeds from borrowings	3,387	1,049	3,672
Repayments of borrowings	(3,967)	(1,981)	(776)
Purchase of a call spread option	(95)	0	0
Exercise of common stock options and other	0	0	96
NET CASH (USED IN) PROVIDED BY FINANCING ACTIVITIES	(40)	(50)	2,949
INCREASE (DECREASE) IN CASH AND CASH EQUIVALENTS BEFORE EFFECT OF EXCHANGE RATE CHANGES ON CASH	334	(519)	909
Effect of exchange rate changes on cash	(4)	(25)	(1)
INCREASE (DECREASE) IN CASH AND CASH EQUIVALENTS	330	(544)	908
CASH AND CASH EQUIVALENTS—BEGINNING OF YEAR	763	1,307	399
CASH AND CASH EQUIVALENTS—END OF YEAR	$1,093	0	$1,307

Computer Associates International

Selected Notes to Consolidated Financial Statements

NOTE 1—SIGNIFICANT ACCOUNTING POLICIES

Basis of Revenue Recognition

The Company derives revenue from licensing software products and providing post-contract customer support (hereafter referred to as "maintenance") and professional services, such as consulting and education services. The Company licenses its software products to end users primarily through the Company's direct sales force.

The Company licenses to customers the right to use its software products pursuant to software license agreements (hereafter referred to as a "license arrangement"). The license arrangement generally restricts the customer's right to use the Company's enterprise software products as specified in the license arrangement. The license arrangements' original terms generally range from one to ten years for license arrangements prior to December 2000 and one to five years for license arrangements beginning in December 2000. In addition, customers can subscribe to software arrangements under month-to-month licenses beginning in December 2000. The timing and amount of license revenue recognized during an accounting period is determined by the nature of the contractual provisions included in the license arrangement with customers.

Beginning in December 2000, the Company began executing software license arrangements that include flexible contractual provisions that, among other things, allow customers to receive unspecified future software products within designated product lines. Under these arrangements (referred to as the "new Business Model"), the Company is required to recognize revenue attributable to the software products ratably over the term of the license arrangement commencing upon delivery of the currently available software products.

The Company recognizes revenue pursuant to the requirements of the American Institute of Certified Public Accountants ("AICPA") Statement of Position No. 97-2 "Software Revenue Recognition" ("SOP 97-2"), issued in October 1997, as amended by AICPA Statement of Position No. 98-4 and No. 98-9. SOP 97-2 was effective for the Company April 1, 1998. Amendment 98-4 deferred for one year to April 1, 1999, the effective date of certain SOP 97-2 provisions pertaining to multiple-element arrangements. SOP 98-9 amended SOP 97-2 and requires recognition of revenue under the "residual method" when certain criteria are met and was effective for the Company April 1, 1999. These statements set forth GAAP for recognizing revenue on software transactions and establish four criteria necessary in order to recognize revenue—persuasive evidence of an arrangement exists, delivery has occurred, the fee is fixed or determinable and collectibility is probable. Under the residual method, revenue is recognized in a multiple element arrangement when company-specific objective evidence of fair value exists for all of the undelivered elements in the arrangement, but does not exist for one or more of the delivered elements in the arrangement. At the outset of the arrangement with the customer, the Company defers revenue for the fair value of its undelivered elements (e.g., maintenance, consulting, education services) and recognizes revenue for the remainder of the arrangement fee attributable to the elements initially delivered in the arrangement when the criteria in SOP 97-2 have been met. For license arrangements prior to December 2000 (referred to as the "old Business Model"), once the four criteria in SOP 97-2 were met, revenue was recognized up-front for such delivered elements. Under the new Business Model, once the four criteria are met, revenue attributable to license and maintenance fees is recognized ratably over the arrangement term as the terms of such arrangements provide for flexible contractual provisions, such as "unspecified future deliverables."

Subscription Revenue

Subscription revenue represents the ratable recognition of revenue by the Company attributable to license arrangements under the new Business Model.

Deferred subscription revenue, in general, represents the aggregate portion of all undiscounted contractual and committed license and maintenance fees pursuant to all new Business

Computer Associates International

Model arrangements that has not yet been recognized as revenue on a ratable basis over the life of the license arrangement.

Beginning in fiscal year 2002, the Company has disaggregated the total deferred subscription revenue into two components, the amount of cash collected in excess of the amount recognized as revenue and the amount that has not yet been collected that has not been recognized as revenue. Each appear within the Company's Consolidated Balance Sheets as "Deferred subscription revenue (collected)," and as "Deferred subscription revenue," a component of installment accounts receivable, respectively. The components of installment accounts receivables are detailed in Note 5. Each of these components is further classified as either current or non-current. Balances applicable to fiscal year 2001 have been reclassified for comparability purposes.

Software Fees and Other

Prior to December 2000, the Company executed software license arrangements that included contractual provisions that resulted in the recognition of revenue attributable to the software products upon delivery of the software products, provided that the arrangement fee was fixed or determinable, collectibility of the fee was probable and persuasive evidence of an arrangement existed.

The Company has a standard business practice of entering into long term installment contracts with customers. The Company has a history of enforcing the contract terms and successfully collecting under such arrangements, and therefore considers such fees fixed or determinable.

The Company also enters into license arrangements with distribution partners whereby revenue is recognized upon sell-through to the end user by the distribution partner.

Maintenance

For arrangements executed under the old Business Model, maintenance was bundled for a portion of the term of the license arrangement. Under these arrangements, the fair value of the maintenance, which was based on optional annual renewal rates stated in the arrangement, initially was deferred and subsequently amortized into revenue over the initial contractual term of the arrangement. Maintenance renewals have been recognized ratably over the term of the renewal arrangement. The Company has recently experienced maintenance renewal rates on such contracts of approximately 80%.

The "Deferred maintenance revenue" line item on the Company's Consolidated Balance Sheets principally represents payments received in advance of services rendered as of the balance sheet dates.

For arrangements executed under the new Business Model, maintenance is bundled for the entire term of the license arrangement. Under these arrangements, maintenance revenue is included in subscription revenue and is recognized ratably over the term of the license arrangement, along with the license fee, commencing upon delivery of the currently available software products.

Financing Fees

Accounts receivable resulting from old Business Model product sales with extended payment terms are discounted to present value at prevailing market rates. In subsequent periods, the receivable is increased to the amount due and payable by the customer through the accretion of financing revenue on the unpaid receivables due in future years.

Professional Services

Professional services revenue is derived from the Company's consulting services and educational programs. The fair value of the professional services, which is based on fees charged to customers when the related services are sold separately or under time and materials contracts, initially is deferred and subsequently recognized as revenue when the services are performed. For professional services rendered pursuant to a fixed-price contract, revenue is recognized on the percentage-of-completion method.

Source: Computer Associates International, Inc., 10-K Statement, March 31, 2002.

EXHIBIT 4

Computer Associates International, Inc. Pro Forma Results of Operations

To provide comparable financial results, management's discussion and analysis is supplemented with separate pro forma financial information. This pro forma information is presented in order to give effect to the purchase of PLATINUM and Sterling under the assumption that the Company, PLATINUM and Sterling operated under the new Business Model since their inception. Pro forma operating results are calculated by adjusting prior period revenue recorded under the old Business Model to revenue recognized on a ratable basis under the new Business Model, exclusive of acquisition amortization and special items. Reconciliations of GAAP results to pro forma operating results are provided below. While these results may not be indicative of operations had these acquisitions actually occurred on that date and had the Company historically been operating under the new Business Model, the Company believes they provide a basis for comparison at the outset of the transition to the new Business Model. Professional services revenue and total expenses are identical under both the new and old Business Models; therefore, management's discussion and analysis of these captions has not been repeated under the pro forma results of operations. The following pro forma measures may not be comparable to similarly titled measures reported by other companies.

(in millions, except per share amts)	Fiscal Year Ended March 31, 2002			Fiscal Year Ended March 31, 2001		
	GAAP Results	Adjustments	Pro Forma Operating Results	GAAP Results	Adjustments	Pro Forma Operating Results
Revenue[8]	$2,964	$2,837[1]	$5,801	$4,190	$1,368[2]	$5,558
Total expenses[8]	4,349	(1,015)[3]	3,334	4,856	(820)[4]	4,036
Pretax (loss) income	(1,385)	3,852[5]	2,467	(666)	2,188[5]	1,522
Income tax (benefit) provision	(283)	1,208[6]	925	(75)	646[6]	571
Net loss	(1,102)		N/A	(591)		N/A
Net operating income	N/A		1,542	N/A		951
Diluted EPS	($1.91)		N/A	($1.02)		N/A
Shares used	577		N/A	582		N/A
Diluted operating EPS	N/A		$2.61	N/A		$1.61
Shares used	577	14[7]	591	582	10[7]	592

(1) Represents amortization of revenue recognized at contract signing from direct product sales in prior fiscal years for CA ($2,513), Sterling ($161) and PLATINUM ($163) as if revenue had been ratably recognized since their inception.

(2) Represents amortization of revenue recognized at contract signing from direct product sales in prior fiscal years for CA ($2,317), Sterling ($228) and PLATINUM ($252) as if revenue had been ratably recognized since their inception, offset by revenue recognized up-front ($1,429) under the old Business Model.

(3) Represents the elimination of acquisition amortization ($956) and a charge associated with the impairment of assets for sale ($59).

(4) Represents the elimination of acquisition amortization ($973), a gain associated with the 1995 Stock Plan ($184) and a charge related to the Inacom bankruptcy ($31).

(5) Represents the effect on pre-tax loss resulting from the adjustments to revenue and expenses reflected in footnotes (1), (2), (3) and (4).

(6) Represents the tax effect of adjustments. The assumed effective tax rate approximated 37.5%.

(7) Represents the inclusion of common stock equivalents since they are no longer antidilutive.

(8) Prior period adjusted to conform with current period presentation. See Note 1 of the Consolidated Financial Statements for additional information.

Total pro forma revenue for the fiscal year ended March 31, 2002 was $5.801 billion, an increase of 4%, or $243 million, over the prior year pro forma revenue of $5.558 billion. The increase was attributable to the ratable recognition of revenue on contracts transacted during the prior fiscal year, partially offset by a reduction in professional services revenue ($222 million), which was primarily the result of the divestiture of FSG in the third quarter of fiscal year 2001, which generated $94 million of revenue in that fiscal year and the Company's decision to reduce professional services associated with non-CA products. North America and international pro forma revenue represented 64% and 36%, respectively, of overall pro forma revenue in both fiscal years 2002 and 2001. The international pro forma revenue was unfavorably impacted by the effect of exchange rates on the U.S. dollar versus foreign currencies.

On a pro forma basis, pre-tax income excluding acquisition amortization and special charges was $2.467 billion for fiscal year 2002, an increase of 62%, or $945 million, over prior year's pre-tax income of $1.522 billion, exclusive of acquisition amortization and special items. Pro forma net income, excluding acquisition amortization and special items, was $1.542 billion for the fiscal year ended March 31, 2002, an increase of $591 million, or 62%, over fiscal year 2001. The increase was largely attributable to the Company's emphasis on overall cost control measures related to a reduction in the Company's headcount of approximately 3,000 over the prior fiscal year. The Company's consolidated annual effective tax rate, excluding acquisition amortization and special items, was assumed to be 37.5% for both fiscal years 2002 and 2001.

Source: Computer Associates 10-K Statement, March 31, 2002.

EXHIBIT 5

Continuing Members of Board of Directors, Computer Associates International, Inc.

Name	Age	Director Since	Share Ownership
Russell M. Artzt (1) Executive Vice President—Research and Development since April 1987 and the Senior Development Officer of the Company since 1976	52	1980	0.6%
Alfonse M. D'Amato (2) (4) Partner in Park Strategies LLP, a business consulting firm, since January 1999. United States Senator from January 1981 until January 1999. During his tenure, he served as Chairman of the Senate Committee on Banking, Housing and Urban Affairs, and Chairman of the Commission on Security and Cooperation in Europe. He is also a director of Avis Rent-a-Car, Inc. and NRT Incorporated.	61	1999	
Lewis Ranieri (1) (3) Founder and prime originator of Hyperion Partners L.P. and Hyperion Partners II L.P. (collectively "Hyperion"). He is also Vice Chairman and Director of Hyperion Capital Management, Inc. and chairman or director of various Hyperion entities. Since June 26, 2001, Mr. Ranieri has served as a director of the Company. From July 1968 to December 1987, he was Vice Chairman of Salomon Brothers, Inc. He also serves as Chairman and Chief Executive Officer of Ranieri & Co., Inc., a private investment corporation. He is also a director of Delphi Financial Group, Inc., Reckson Associates Realty Corp., and Transworld Healthcare, Inc.	54	2001	
Sanjay Kumar (1) President and Chief Operating Officer since January 1994. He was Executive Vice President-Operations from January 1993 to December 1993, Senior Vice President-Planning from April 1989 to December 1992, Vice President-Planning from November 1988 to March 1989. He joined the Company with the acquisition of UCCEL in August 1987.	37	1994	1.1%
Charles B. Wang (1) Chief Executive Officer of the Company since 1976 and Chairman of the Board since April 1980. He is also a director of Symbol Technologies, Inc.	54	1976	6.4%

(1) Member Executive Committee.

(2) Member Audit Committee.

(3) Member Stock Option and Compensation Committee.

(4) Member Nominating Committee.

Source: Computer Associates International, Inc., Proxy Statement, 2001.

Computer Associates International

PART 4

Additional Cases

Anacomp, Inc.

On September 10, 1982, Anacomp, Inc., a computer software company, released its first annual report after being listed on the New York Stock Exchange. Prior to 1982, the company's stock was traded on the over-the-counter market. In the annual report Anacomp's management outlined the company's strategy for new software systems development:

Anacomp is committed to being the world's leading supplier of software and services to the banking industry. Anacomp and its subsidiaries have licensed software products, sold data processing services, or entered into software consulting agreements with more than 200 billion-dollar financial institutions around the world. But the bank marketplace is changing rapidly. Regulatory and technological changes are blurring the distinctions between banks and other financial institutions. Bank customers—both retail and wholesale—are becoming more sophisticated and more demanding. Bankers require computer systems which encourage total customer relationships, adapt quickly to product changes, and meet requirements of round-the-clock banking.

Since 1979, Anacomp has been developing a totally new generation of banking computer software systems to serve those evolving needs. Anacomp's software development effort is one the most substantial ever undertaken by an independent computer services vendor. It is based on an Anacomp innovation—the software R&D partnership—and on the philosophy of getting prospective customers involved in developing the software products they will eventually use.

In 1979, when its net worth was $10 million, Anacomp recognized the opportunity to develop at a cost of $12 million a major new IBM-based real-time retail banking system. The development was expected to take several years to complete. Anacomp selected the limited partnership alternative to buffer the company's stockholders from the financial risks involved. To help assure the development of a superior product, Anacomp also sought the participation of a cross-section of major financial institutions—the ultimate users of the bank product. To induce these banks to become co-developers, it was necessary to show that the required funding was in place and that Anacomp's commitment was firmly established. A limited partnership was the best way to induce four "primary development banks" to contribute collectively $6 million and 24 software development people for two years to the project.

The same considerations were present in each of the four subsequent partnerships—BANKSERV 10000, CEFT, CDA, and CIBS. Each partnership assumed development risks; except for BANKSERV 10000, each project involved several major banks acting as co-developers with Anacomp. Any product developed becomes the property of the partnership. Anacomp has the option to purchase the products but is under no obligation to exercise this option; Anacomp did purchase the CIS and BANKSERV 10000 systems in 1982. In total, more than $60 million has been raised since 1979 for investment in the development of new wholesale and retail banking software products.

Professor Krishna Palepu prepared this case. The case is intended solely as the basis for class discussion and is not intended to serve as an endorsement, source of primary data, or illustration of effective or ineffective management. Copyright © 1987 by the President and Fellows of Harvard College. HBS Case 9-187-153.

1

COMPANY BACKGROUND

Anacomp, based in Indianapolis, Indiana, began as a computer and data services company in 1969. The company was founded by Ronald Palamara, a Ph.D. in computer sciences. Among the computer services offered by the company were the design and implementation of computer software systems and the management of customers' computer facilities. The company also operated customers' data centers, offered data processing and microfilming services, and sold micrographic equipment. The company saw its future growth coming primarily from the design and development of software for the banking industry.

Prior to 1980, the company's principal proprietary software system for commercial banks and thrift institutions was the Customer Integrated/Reference File (CI/RF) system. CI/RF integrated a customer's banking relationships—such as checking, savings, loans, etc.—and incorporated them into a single record. The system was utilized by banks in 20 states throughout the United States, including Manufacturers Hanover Trust and Sumitomo Bank of California. The system and software primarily used a computer language designed for computers manufactured by NCR Corporation.

Beginning in 1980 Anacomp announced plans to develop a number of new software systems for the banking and financial services industry. For the retail banking industry the company was developing two new products: the Continuous Integrated System (CIS) and the BANKSERVE 10000 system. CIS was claimed to be the first on-line real-time retail banking transactions processing system designed for IBM computers. The BANKSERVE 10000 system would allow banks to share networks of point-of-sale terminals or automated teller machines on a national or regional basis.

Anacomp had also announced plans to develop a full line of software systems to help banks deal more efficiently with their wholesale customers—companies, institutions, and other banks. The Corporate Electronic Funds Transfer (CEFT) system was expected to combine three banking functions: an electronic funds transfer mechanism that would take payments from external sources, a money transfer component which would automate the bank's internal paying and receiving functions, and a corporate funds control component which would allow the bank to monitor its own cash position and the cash position of each customer. The Corporate Deposit and Analysis (CDA) system, another wholesale banking product that Anacomp targeted for development, was expected to automate the bank's depository relationships with large corporations and other banks.

In August 1982 the company announced that it was initiating the development of yet another new software system, Corporate International Banking System (CIBS). CIBS was the most complex system the company planned to date, and was intended to help a large international bank automate certain internal treasury operations, generate complete information on the bank's foreign currency positions, and automate the processing of letters of credit and documentary credit collections.

Anacomp's management believed that the above software systems, if successfully developed and implemented, would enable the company to become a leading supplier of software and services to the banking industry.

INDUSTRY AND COMPETITION[1]

The computer services industry was marked by very rapid growth. In 1981 computer service revenues totaled $18.9 billion, up 23 percent from $15.4 billion a year, according to

---

1. Material in this section is drawn from Standard and Poor's industry surveys on office equipment systems and services, October 21, 1982.

INPUT, a leading international consulting firm. INPUT had estimated that the industry growth rate between 1981 and 1986 would be approximately 23 percent per annum.

There were three major segments of the computer services industry: processing services, professional services, and software products. The companies in the processing area offered customers access to a large computer facility in which batch processing, remote computing services, and facilities management services were performed. This segment accounted for 57 percent of total computer services revenues in 1981 and was expected to grow at a compound annual rate of 17 percent between 1981 and 1986. The companies in the professional services segment provided customers alternatives to in-house data processing. These services included custom-made computer systems and programming to perform specialized tasks, as well as the management of data processing facilities. The professional services segment, which accounted for 23 percent of total computer services industry revenues in 1981, was expected to grow 29 percent annually from 1981 to 1986. Software products, the third segment of the software services industry, was the fastest-growing sector. Software products consist of instructions that guide computer equipment through tasks. This segment was expected to grow at an annual compound growth rate of 33 percent between 1981 and 1986.

The high growth rates of the computer services industry were being fueled by the large number of computers installed and customers' realization of the value computer services can have in lifting their productivity. Hardware, the premiere growth area of the 1960s and 1970s, had since taken on a commodity-like status as a result of progressively lower manufacturing costs. Computer services, on the other hand, increased in value and in price.

The computer services industry in 1982 consisted of some 5,000 companies ranging from small software operations to giants such as IBM and Control Data Corporation. Smaller companies in the industry generally concentrated on serving particular market niches; their performance depended on factors influencing these small sectors.

There was active competition in each of the areas of services provided by Anacomp. In the computer service area, Anacomp competed with other computer service companies, manufacturers of mainframe computers, and companies developing in-house computer service capabilities. In the data center service business, Anacomp competed with other data processing and micrographic service companies. Anacomp believed that the services performed by it represented only a small portion of the market in each of the fields it operated.

The computer services industry was subject to rapid technological change requiring constant adaptation to provide competitive service. Competition in the computer services industry was based primarily on technical capability and expertise, pricing, quality of work, and ability to meet system development deadlines. In the other areas of Anacomp's business, competition was based upon the reliability and timeliness of the services and products provided.

TOP MANAGEMENT

The names, ages, and current and former positions of Anacomp's executive officers in September 1982 were as follows:

Ronald D. Palamara, Ph.D., age 42, has served as Chairman and President for more than the past five years.

Stanley E. Hirschfeld, age 47, became Senior Vice President of Corporate Development during 1981. For more than the prior five years, he served as Vice President-Finance and Secretary of Anacomp.

Ralph C. McAuley, age 47, became President of Anacomp's Computer Services group during 1981. For more than the five prior years, he served as Vice President of Data Processing Services.

John J. Flanigan, age 42, became Group Vice President of Data Services in 1981. During the prior five-year period, he served as Vice President of Data Processing Services.

Christopher Duffy, age 44, became Vice President and Chief Administrative Officer during 1981. For more than the five prior years, he served as Vice President and General Manager of an Indianapolis television station.

Myles Hannan, age 44, became Vice President-Finance, General Counsel and Secretary during 1981. During 1979 and 1980, he served as Vice President-Law and Administration for Delaware North Companies, Incorporated. For more than the prior two years he served as Vice President-Legal and Staff Divisions of the Stop & Shop Companies, Inc.

William C. Ater, age 40, became Vice President of Administration during 1981. During 1979 and 1980, he served as Anacomp's Vice President of Bank Data Processing. For more than the prior two years, he served in various computer management positions with NCR Corporation.

As of the end of fiscal 1981, all officers and directors as a group owned 15.1 percent of Anacomp's common stock and were paid $2.9 million in cash and cash equivalent forms of remuneration during the year.

NEW SOFTWARE SYSTEMS DEVELOPMENT

Anacomp organized and financed its new software development in a unique manner. During the fiscal year ended June 30, 1980, Anacomp initiated the development of a major new computer software system called Continuous Integrated System (CIS) to be marketed to major financial institutions. According to Anacomp's management, CIS would represent a major advance over the company's current CI/RF system.

Anacomp stated that, in view of the anticipated significant development expenditure for the CIS system, the company had entered into an agreement in November 1979 with a limited partnership, RTS Associates. Under this agreement, Anacomp agreed to develop the CIS system on behalf of the partnership. In return, RTS agreed to pay a development fee of $6 million, of which $2.2 million was paid in 1980. Upon completion of the development of the CIS system, Anacomp agreed to market CIS for five years on a commission basis. Anacomp also had the option to acquire all rights to the CIS system at the greater of its appraised fair market value or RTS's investment plus a fixed profit. RTS had the right to extend Anacomp's five-year marketing agreement an additional five years or to cancel it if Anacomp did not use its best efforts to market CIS.

RTS Associates' payments for the CIS development expenses were financed by (1) an investment of $1.444 million by the partners, (2) a $3.25 million bank loan to RTS, secured by bank letters of credit and personal guarantees of the limited partners, and (3) a $2.2 million loan to RTS, personally guaranteed by the limited partners, from Anacomp, with interest at 11 percent per annum payable quarterly through December 31, 1981, and with principal and interest payable thereafter in 84 equal monthly installments. In addition, if the CIS development expenses exceeded $6 million and therefore RTS was required to pay further development fees, Anacomp agreed to loan RTS, without recourse to the limited partners, up to $1.5 million to complete the CIS system.

Several officers and directors of Anacomp were affiliated with the corporate general partner of RTS, and were also investors in the limited partnership arrangement. Ronald

Palamara, Chairman of the Board and President of Anacomp, and three other directors of Anacomp, were also directors and officers of the corporate general partner of RTS. The ownership interest of Anacomp's officers and directors in the limited partnership amounted to 38.5 percent of the total.

During the fiscal year 1981, thirteen major banks, including the National Bank of North America in New York, the Shawmut National Bank in Boston, Provident National Bank in Philadelphia, and the First National Bank in Kansas City, contracted with Anacomp to participate as advisory banks in the CIS project for a nonrefundable fee of $150,000 each. The arrangement permitted each bank to review the project during development and provide input regarding changes to enhance the ultimate marketability of CIS.

In June 1982 Anacomp announced that the CIS system development was completed. The company also announced that it purchased the system from RTS Associates for $16 million.

FINANCIAL PERFORMANCE

After reporting a strong increase in revenues and profits from 1978 to 1981, Anacomp reported a slower revenue growth and a decline in profits in fiscal 1982. Dr. Palamara commented that the 1982 performance was a short-term aberration, and that the company's long-term strategy and prospects were sound:

> *Fiscal 1982 marked the beginning of one era and the end of another for Anacomp. A new era began with five events having tremendous long-term significance for Anacomp: the purchase of two major software products, the completion of our most significant acquisition, an offering of $50 million in convertible debentures, the formation of history's largest software research and development partnership, and Anacomp's listing on the New York Stock Exchange. Thus, despite a difficult fourth quarter which was affected by several non-recurring items and resulted in lower earnings for the year, fiscal 1982 was perhaps the most significant year of achievements in Anacomp's history.*
>
> *Judged solely by the numbers, of course, 1982 does not seem especially memorable. . . . In terms of positioning the company for future growth, however, 1982 may well be remembered as the most significant year in Anacomp's history. . . .*
>
> *We believe that Anacomp's performance in future years will demonstrate that the company is well along in its evolution from a small, explosive-growth firm to a nationally recognized market leader.*

Dr. Palamara projected record financial results in fiscal 1983. He also assured investors that Anacomp would place renewed emphasis on improving the company's profitability and reducing its financial leverage.

Exhibit 1 shows Anacomp's stock price data around the time of its 1982 results. An abridged version of the company's annual report is presented in Exhibit 2.

QUESTIONS

1. Evaluate Anacomp's new product development strategy. What are the risks and benefits of this strategy for Anacomp's shareholders?

2. How is Anacomp's accounting influenced by the way the company organizes and finances its new product development?

Anacomp

3. Compare Anacomp's cash flow performance with its accounting performance. What is your evaluation of the company's financial condition?

4. What is your assessment of Anacomp's future?

EXHIBIT 1

Anacomp—Stock Price and Trading Volume Data

Trading	Anacomp Trading Volume (thousands)	Anacomp Closing Price (dollars)	S&P 500 Composite Closing
9/1/82	109	10.875	118.25
9/2/82	92	10.875	120.38
9/3/82	437	11.125	122.68
9/7/82	120	10.875	121.37
9/8/82	231	11.000	122.20
9/9/82	230	10.750	121.97
9/10/82	417	10.625	120.97
9/13/82	284	10.375	122.24

Anacomp's common stock beta = 1.3 (Value Line estimate)

Stock Trading Information

	Stock Price		
	High	Low	Cash Dividends
Fiscal Year 1981			
First quarter	$15.63	$10.63	$.026
Second quarter	19.88	13.75	.026
Third quarter	16.50	12.75	.026
Fourth quarter	18.38	15.13	.030
Fiscal Year 1982			
First quarter	16.63	11.25	.030
Second quarter	14.00	11.88	.030
Third quarter	12.25	10.00	.030
Fourth quarter	13.38	10.88	.030

Other Information

Interest rate on 3-month Treasury bills:	8.2%
Interest rate on 20-year government bonds:	12.2%
P/E ratio for Standard & Poor's 400 Industrials:	23.2

EXHIBIT 2

Anacomp, Inc. and Subsidiaries—Abridged 1982 Annual Report

To Our Shareholders

Fiscal 1982 marked the beginning of one era and the end of another for Anacomp.

A new era began with five events having tremendous long-term significance for Anacomp: the purchase of two major software products, the completion of our most significant acquisition, an offering of $50 million in convertible debentures, the formation of history's largest software research and development partnership and Anacomp's listing on the New York Stock Exchange. Thus, despite a difficult fourth quarter which was affected by several non-recurring items and resulted in lower earnings for the year, fiscal 1982 was perhaps the most significant year of achievements in Anacomp's history.

Judged solely by the numbers, of course, 1982 does not seem especially memorable. Although revenues rose slightly over 1981, earnings per share declined due to the impact of fourth quarter results, which reflected several one-time changes and short-term factors. These factors are described in detail in our fourth quarter report.

In terms of positioning the company for future growth, however, 1982 may well be remembered as the most significant year in Anacomp's history.

- In January, Anacomp completed a $50 million offering of 13⅞ percent convertible subordinated debentures which, after an original issue discount, increased the company's working capital position by $41 million.

- Listing on the New York Stock Exchange in April recognized Anacomp's stature in the computer services industry and provided the opportunity for greater visibility as the computer reaches out to new, worldwide markets.

- During June of the year, Anacomp purchased two major retail banking software systems which we had been developing for investment partnerships. CIS, a totally integrated system that we believe will revolutionize retail banking in the 1980s, was purchased for nearly $16 million. CIS has already attracted a financial commitment from nearly 35 banks, seven of which had signed substantial license agreements by the end of the year. BANKSERV® 10000, a system to provide banks with a new level of electronic transaction switching and processing capabilities, was purchased for $2.3 million.

- Also during June, Anacomp signed an agreement with IBM Corporation which gives us the capability to be a primary source of supply for a bank's branch automation requirements.

- The acquisition of 24 micrographic data imaging centers from DSI Corporation and Kalvar Corporation in May provided the ability to deliver Anacomp services to an even broader base of regular, repetitive customers, and the opportunity to offer new services through an expanded delivery system.

- After the close of the fiscal year, funding for the CIBS research and development partnership was completed with the closing of the final portion of $26.25 million in partnership interests. The partnership will contract with Anacomp to develop CIBS, Corporate International Banking System, a complex software system for use by large banks and other financial institutions engaged in international business.

We believe Anacomp's performance in future years will demonstrate that the company is well along in its evolution from a small, explosive-growth firm to a nationally recognized market leader.

Anacomp

To ensure that Anacomp's evolution will result in a stable company, with performance attractive to investors, Anacomp will be placing renewed emphasis in several areas. These areas will include our rate of return, where we anticipate achieving a superior return on investment from the maturation of software projects, existing operations, plus the addition of quality investments.

We also expect to reduce our leverage ratio over the next few years by calling our convertible debt, when this becomes practical, and by taking other appropriate measures. We will continue to employ strategic planning approaches in all our business units. Lastly, we will seek out those acquisitions which blend with our long-term goals.

We have projected record financial results in fiscal 1983 as the company asserts its leadership in bank software and micrographic data imaging. We appreciate the continued support of our stockholders and employees which makes that goal achievable.

Sincerely,

Ronald D. Palamara, Ph.D.
President and Chairman of the Board
September 10, 1982

MANAGEMENT'S DISCUSSION AND ANALYSIS OF FINANCIAL CONDITION AND RESULTS OF OPERATIONS

General

In September 1980, Anacomp completed a public offering of $30,000,000 of 9½% Convertible Subordinated Debentures due 2000. In January 1981, Anacomp completed an offering outside the United States of $12,500,000 of 9% Convertible Subordinated Debentures due 1996, with warrants to purchase a like amount of debentures. In Janu-ary 1982, Anacomp completed the public offering of $50,000,000 of 13⅞% Convertible Subordinated Debentures due 2002. The Debentures were offered at an original issue discount of 15%, with net proceeds of $41,125,000, and carry an effective cost of 16.6%. The cash from these offerings has been used to finance the expansion of receivables and unbilled revenues, to retire long-term debt, to provide funds for acquisitions, and to increase working capital. During the past three years, Anacomp has completed the acquisition of eleven business entities. The acquisitions and the debenture offerings accounted for the major changes in Anacomp's financial condition and results of operations.

Financial Condition and Liquidity

During 1982, working capital increased $1,949,000. The major source of working capital, other than operations, was the increase in long-term debt, primarily the result of the January offering of $50,000,000 of debentures and to a lesser extent the exercise of warrants to purchase $1,289,000 of additional 9% debentures. The major use of working capital was the purchase of computer software systems from limited partnerships. Other major uses of working capital were the purchase of marketable securities held as long-term investments, the retirement of long-term debt, and additions of fixed assets. During the year, cash was used to finance the increase in unbilled revenues, to purchase 92% of the shares of DSI Corporation, and to pay certain software development costs. As a result, the current ratio at June 30, 1982, is 2.40, compared to 3.84 at June 30, 1981. At June 30, 1982, Anacomp had $35,000,000 of available but unused lines of credit that could be used if needed to provide short-term financing. Negotiations are currently being held with a group of banks to establish a revolving credit arrangement which will replace the existing lines of credit.

At the present time, Anacomp has no major commitments to acquire assets or facilities which will require a substantial outlay of working capital. It is anticipated that the current acquisition program will continue in the future as opportunities present themselves.

Anacomp currently expects to incur approximately $6,000,000 during 1983 on enhancements to a computer software system, of which approximately $3,000,000 is expected to be funded by others. The project is being undertaken because the results will yield a product with improved marketability, which at the same time will meet commitments to certain customers.

Operations—Fiscal 1982 Compared to 1981

Revenues for 1982 increased only 3% over fiscal 1981, with the increase being generated primarily by internal growth and the addition of internally generated projects. Software development projects, especially two new projects contracted for by major banks and limited partnerships, and higher levels of sales of minicomputers and microcomputers and related software, contributed the largest portion of the increase. Revenues were also increased by certain data centers. These increases, along with smaller increases in other areas, were largely offset by reduced revenue being generated by other data centers as a result of a consolidation of certain operations.

Total operating costs and expenses increased 10.4% during fiscal 1982. Personnel costs and outside services costs associated with the increased software development activity were the major factors in the increase. Other contributors to the increase were higher supply costs, equipment-related costs, and the cost of computer hardware sales, each caused by higher levels of activity. Also, amortization of purchased software added to the overall increase, along with generally higher prices for all purchased goods and services. These increases were partially offset by cost reductions from the synergism obtained from prior acquisitions, a reduction in costs as a result of consolidating certain administrative functions and, in the third quarter, from the recovery of previously recorded expenses.

Margins for the current periods were substantially lower than the prior year due to the emphasis on completing large systems development projects as opposed to generating new license fees for other products. Margins earned on development work have typically been less than those earned from software licensing and related activities. The reduction in revenue in certain data centers has also tended to reduce margins, as the revenue losses have preceded to some extent the current cost reduction and consolidation efforts.

Interest expense increased in the convertible year as a result of the interest on the 9½% Convertible Subordinated Debentures offered during fiscal 1981 and the 13⅞% Convertible Subordinated Debentures offered in January 1982. Interest income was derived from investing the proceeds from these offerings not otherwise utilized. Due to the uses of cash mentioned previously and a lowering of interest rates on investments, interest income decreased throughout the current period.

The extraordinary credit arose from the sale of a branch office which had been acquired in 1981 in a transaction accounted for as a pooling of interests. The amount of the credit is the gain realized, net of related income taxes.

The provision for income taxes reflects the normal tax relating to the income reported for financial statement purpose4 after recognizing the impact of investment tax credits, non-deductible expenses, and the effect of interest due from the under-depositing of tax payments as a result of the denial of a request for a change in certain reporting policies for tax purposes.

Fiscal 1981 Compared to 1980

Of the $34,725,000 increase in revenue, the major portion was attributable to acquisitions included for the first time in 1981, or for the full period in 1981, plus internal growth generated by those acquisitions. Other changes in revenue for the year resulted primarily from new software development sales and non-recurring licensing agreements (especially from new software systems for banks, financed in part by limited partnerships), offset in part by reduced revenues due to declining activity in certain data centers and the completion of certain non-repetitive software projects.

Direct costs of service and equipment increased 54%, primarily from the costs associated with the recent acquisitions plus increased expenses required to support increased software development, and rising costs for personnel and other services. Selling, general and administrative expenses increased 17% from the costs associated with the recent acquisitions plus the expenses necessary to manage the rapidly growing company and from rising personnel costs. The increases in other direct operating and selling, general and administrative costs were offset in part by a savings of approximately $1,255,000 being realized during 1981 due to a change in the funding of Anacomp's contribution to the Thrift Plan for Employees.

Interest income increased from interest earned by cash investment programs and from the interest earned on notes receivable.

Interest expense increased primarily from the interest on the recently issued 9% and 9½% Convertible Subordinated Debentures, with other increases from debt incurred to finance acquisitions and interest on short-term borrowings, offset somewhat by lower interest on the 10% Convertible Subordinated Debentures due to conversions to equity.

Other income included the gain from a transaction with Kalvar which resulted from an agreement whereby Anacomp sold to Kalvar its Kalvar preferred stock for Kalvar common stock and sold its option to acquire additional Kalvar common stock in exchange for a promissory note from Kalvar.

The provision for income taxes reflects the normal tax relating to the income reported for financial statement purposes after giving effect to the benefits obtained from investment tax credits and from the exclusion of dividend income. The expected tax rate for fiscal 1981 was revised downward during the fourth quarter as a result of a large capital gain arising primarily from the transaction with Kalvar.

Anacomp

SELECTED FINANCIAL DATA

(dollars in thousands, except per share amounts)	1982	1981	1980	1979	1978
For the year ended June 30					
Revenues	$109,599	$106,368	$71,643	$41,662	$23,433
Income before provision for income taxes and extraordinary credit	3,622	13,997	7,787	5,045	3,154
Income before extraordinary credit	2,779	7,938	4,627	2,704	1,542
Net income	4,609	7,938	4,627	2,704	1,542
Earnings per common and common equivalent share:					
Income before extraordinary credit	$.30	$.87	$.70	$.57	$.39
Net income	.50	.87	.70	.57	.39
Earnings per common share assuming full dilution:					
Income before extraordinary credit	$.29	$.83	$.66	$.51	$.32
Net income	.48	.83	.66	.51	.32
Cash dividends declared per common share	.12	.11	.10	.09	.06
As of June 30					
Current assets	$ 99,044	$ 75,453	$33,453	$16,200	$ 9,869
Current liabilities	41,276	19,634	22,079	11,452	3,561
Working capital	7,768	55,819	11,374	4,748	6,308
Total assets	211,660	130,798	76,950	30,069	14,182
Long-term debt	105,208	50,591	10,608	8,162	3,993
Stockholders' equity	61,035	55,891	44,077	10,211	6,639
Book value per common share	$6.59	$6.18	$5.56	$2.14	$1.55
Number of employees	2,300	2,000	1,800	895	430
Number of holders of common stock	7,930	5,575	3,810	1,955	1,225

Anacomp

CONSOLIDATED BALANCE SHEET

	June 30	
(dollars in thousands, except per share amounts)	1982	1981

ASSETS

Current assets:		
Cash (including temporary investments)	$ 34,519	$ 29,392
Accounts and notes receivable, less allowances for doubtful accounts of $1,915 and $1,210, respectively	25,284	23,216
Unbilled revenues	18,534	15,863
Inventories	4,469	3,014
Deferred CIBS development costs (Note 3)	5,647	—
Prepaid expenses (including income taxes of $3,018 and $1,242, respectively)	10,591	3,968
Total current assets	99,044	75,453
Property and equipment, at cost less accumulated depreciation and amortization of $10,189 and $8,660, respectively	25,112	14,930
Cost of computer software systems purchased, less accumulated depreciation of $1,584 and $186, respectively	20,363	1,747
Excess of purchase price over net assets of businesses acquired, less accumulated amortization of $2,319 and $1,285, respectively	42,646	24,291
Other assets	24,495	14,377
	$211,660	$130,798

LIABILITIES AND STOCKHOLDERS' EQUITY

Current liabilities:		
Notes payable, banks	$ 14,000	$ —
Current portion of long-term debt	2,907	2,359
Accounts payable	8,151	8,787
Accrued salaries, wages and bonuses	4,604	3,863
Accrued interest payable	5,129	1,747
Income taxes	—	419
Other accrued liabilities	6,485	2,459
Total current liabilities	41,276	19,634
Long-term debt, net of current portion:		
Convertible subordinated debentures	86,274	43,340
Other long-term debt	18,934	7,251
Total long-term debt	105,208	50,591
Deferred income taxes	3,177	4,015
Minority interest	964	667
Stockholder's equity:		
Preferred stock—$1 par value, authorized 1,000,000 shares, none issued	—	—
Common stock—$1 par value, authorized 25,000,000 shares, 9,256,544 and 9,042,722 issued, respectively	9,257	9,043
Capital in excess of par value of common stock	37,305	35,207
Unrealized losses on marketable securities	(899)	(233)
Retained earnings	15,372	11,874
Total stockholders' equity	61,035	55,891
	$211,660	$130,798

Anacomp

CONSOLIDATED STATEMENT OF INCOME

(dollars in thousands, except per share amounts)	Year Ended June 30		
	1982	1981	1980
Revenues			
Services provided	$88,045	$87,304	$58,781
Equipment sold	21,554	19,064	12,862
	109,599	106,368	71,643
Operating costs and expenses			
Costs of services provided	67,302	62,464	40,342
Costs of equipment sold	16,764	13,900	9,172
Selling, general and administrative expenses	19,888	17,821	15,284
	103,954	94,185	64,798
	5,645	12,183	6,845
Interest income	5,525	3,204	485
Interest expense	(8,158)	(4,090)	(1,381)
Other, net	610	2,700	1,838
	(2,023)	1,814	942
Income before provision for income taxes and extra-ordinary credit	3,622	13,997	7,787
Provision for income taxes	843	6,059	3,160
Income before extraordinary credit	2,779	7,938	4,627
Extraordinary credit, net of related tax	1,830	—	—
Net income	$ 4,609	$ 7,938	$ 4,627
Earnings per common and common equivalent share			
Income before extraordinary credit	$.30	$.87	$.70
Extraordinary credit	.20	—	—
Net income	$.50	$.87	$.70
Earnings per common share assuming full dilution			
Income before extraordinary credit	$.29	$.83	$.66
Extraordinary credit	.19	—	—
Net income	$.48	$.83	$.66
Cash dividends declared per share	$.12	$.11	$.10

Anacomp

CONSOLIDATED STATEMENT OF CHANGES IN FINANCIAL POSITION

	Year Ended June 30		
(dollars in thousands)	1982	1981	1980
Working capital was provided by:			
Income before extraordinary credit	$ 2,779	$ 7,938	$ 4,627
Charges to income not requiring an outlay of working capital:			
Depreciation and amortization	6,708	4,368	3,026
Deferred income taxes	(1,314)	3,951	2
Other	143	416	331
Working capital provided by operations	8,316	16,673	7,986
Working capital provided by extraordinary credit	742	—	—
Dispositions of property and equipment	702	218	2,001
Decrease in investment in Computer Micrographics, Inc.	—	—	1,733
Long-term debt incurred	55,680	43,636	7,158
Issuances of common stock	2,236	4,813	28,371
Other	3,224	1,024	(84)
	70,900	66,364	47,165
Working capital was applied to:			
Additions to property and equipment	11,172	3,533	5,171
Excess of purchase price over net assets of businesses acquired	19,791	4,172	18,900
Noncurrent assets of companies acquired in purchase transactions	5,315	1,088	4,593
Noncurrent liabilities of businesses acquired in purchase transactions	(2,892)	(1,040)	(2,199)
Purchase of computer software systems	20,014	1,734	—
Increase in investments	6,099	4,806	2,027
Increase in other assets	4,441	1,977	4,443
Reduction of long-term debt	3,900	4,693	6,911
Cash dividends declared	1,111	956	693
	68,951	21,919	40,539
	$ 1,949	$44,445	$ 6,626

(continued)

Anacomp

CONSOLIDATED STATEMENT OF CHANGES IN FINANCIAL POSITION (continued)

	Year Ended June 30		
(dollars in thousands)	1982	1981	1980
Increase in working capital represented by:			
Increase (decrease) in current assets:			
Cash (including temporary investments)	$ 5,127	$24,649	$ 1,484
Accounts and notes receivable	2,068	6,841	8,333
Unbilled revenues	2,671	7,283	5,605
Inventories	1,455	513	1,383
Deferred CIBS development costs	5,647	—	—
Prepaid expenses	6,623	2,714	448
Decrease (increase) in current liabilities:			
Notes payable	(14,000)	4,000	(3,250)
Current portion of long-term debt	(548)	791	(315)
Accounts payable	636	(1,022)	(4,716)
Accrued salaries, wages and bonuses	(741)	(1,185)	(683)
Accrued interest payable	(3,382)	(1,639)	(48)
Income taxes	419	1,162	286
Other accrued liabilities	(4,026)	338	(1,901)
Increase in working capital	$ 1,949	$44,445	$ 6,626

The accompanying notes are an integral part of the consolidated financial statements.

NOTES TO CONSOLIDATED FINANCIAL STATEMENTS

Anacomp, Inc. and Subsidiaries
(dollars in thousands, except per share amounts)

Note 1. Summary of Significant Accounting Policies

Consolidation

The consolidated financial statements include the accounts of Anacomp, Inc. ("Anacomp") and its majority-owned subsidiaries except Anacomp Leasing Company, Inc., an immaterial wholly-owned subsidiary, which is reflected in the equity method in the accompanying financial statements. Intercompany transactions have been eliminated. Certain amounts in the 1981 and 1980 financial statements have been reclassified to conform to the 1982 presentation.

Revenue Recognition

Revenues are generally recognized as follows:

(1) Data preparation, data processing, facility management and computer output microfilm ("COM") services and sales are recognized as the services are performed or products are shipped.

(2) Revenues from granting perpetual licenses of existing software systems which do not require substantial modification are recognized at the time the license agreement is executed, if collectibility is reasonably assured and the software system is delivered to the customer.

(3) Revenues from contracts for development and/or modifications to existing software systems are recognized under methods which approximate the percentage-of-completion method, except for revenues from development contracts with certain limited partnerships which are reported on the completed contract method, other than immaterial amounts reported for 1980 (see Note 3). Losses on such contracts are recognized when identified.

Revenue recognized under items (2) and (3) may precede the date at which the customer may be billed pursuant to the contract terms. Substantially all unbilled revenue is collected in the year subsequent to the year revenue is recognized.

The subject of revenue recognition for development contracts with limited partnerships including certain arrangements described in (3) above is presently under review by the Financial Accounting Standards Board (FASB). Anacomp will comply with any Statement of Financial Standards issued by the FASB. In April, 1982, the FASB issued an exposure draft entitled "Research and Development Arrangements." Anacomp believes that it is in substantial compliance with the exposure draft, and that approval of the draft by the FASB would not result in an adjustment to the amounts presented in the financial statements.

Inventories

Inventories are stated at the lower of cost or market, cost being determined primarily on the specific identification basis. The cost of the inventories is distributed as follows:

	June 30		
	1982	1981	1980
Equipment held for resale	$3,084	$1,899	$1,315
Operating supplies	1,385	1,115	1,186
	$4,469	$3,014	$2,501

Purchased Computer Software Systems

Purchased computer software systems held for licensing to others are earned at cost less accumulated depreciation. Depreciation is recorded over the estimated marketing lives of the software, and is computed based on the greater of the amount calculated using either a percent-of-revenue or the straight-line method. The percent-of-revenue method is based on the total estimated future revenues expected to be derived from sales of the software, while straight-line depreciation is provided using estimated marketing lives of five to ten years.

Amortization of Excess Purchase Price over Net Assets

Excess of purchase price over net assets of business acquired is amortized on the straight-line method over the estimated useful life, currently ranging from five to twenty years, if determined, and over 40 years if life is indeterminate.

Earnings per Share

The computation of earnings per common and common equivalent share is based upon the weighted average number of common shares outstanding during the year plus (in years in which they have a dilutive effect) the effect of common shares contingently issuable, primarily from stock options, conversion of subordinated debentures issued during fiscal 1981 and, for 1980, common shares purchased in July 1980, in connection with an employment agreement (see Note 13). Interest expense, net of taxes, on the subordinated debentures is added to net income in the computation of earnings per common and common equivalent share.

The fully diluted per share computation reflects the effect of common shares contingently issuable upon conversion of each convertible subordinated debenture outstanding in years in which such conversions would cause dilution. Interest expense, net of income taxes, on the debentures assumed to be converted is added to net income in the computation of fully diluted earnings per share. Fully diluted earnings per share also reflects additional dilution related to stock options due to the use of the year-end market price, when higher than the average price for the year.

The weighted average number of common and common equivalent shares used to compute earnings per share is 9,281,640, 9,425,788 and 6,624,955 for 1982, 1981 and 1980, respectively. The average number of shares used to compute earnings per common share assuming full dilution is 9,667,794, 11,457,335 and 7,149,132 for the respective years. The numbers of shares for all years are adjusted for all stock splits and stock dividends declared.

Vacation Pay

In November 1980, the Financial Accounting Standards Board issued Statement of Financial Accounting Standards No. 43 (SFAS No. 43), "Accounting for Compensated Absences," which requires the accrual of vacation pay earned but not taken. The provisions of SFAS No. 43 require the restatement of prior periods and therefore the cumulative effect as of July 1, 1979, is shown as an adjustment to retained earnings at that date. The effect of this change was to reduce net income by $97 ($.01 per share) in 1982, $72 ($.01 per share) in 1981 and $273 ($.03 per share) in 1980.

Note 3. Major Software Products and Related Party Transactions

CIS

In June 1982, Anacomp purchased for $16,000 a major new computer software system called CIS (Continuous Integrated System) developed by Anacomp for RTS Associates ("RTS"), a limited partnership formed in 1979. Several officers and directors of Anacomp who are affiliated with RTS's general partner are also investors in RTS, aggregating approximately 39% of the combined general and limited partnership units. The remaining partnership interests are owned by persons not affiliated with Anacomp. Anacomp contracted to develop the system on a best-efforts basis, and RTS agreed to pay a development fee of $6,000, of which $4,750 was paid through 1981, and an additional $1,250 during 1982. RTS paid Anacomp an additional $1,500 after actual costs to Anacomp exceeded $6,000. Anacomp had previously loaned $2,200 to RTS, personally guaranteed by the limited partners, and loaned the additional $1,500 as provided for in the development agreement. RTS paid all such loans in full out of the proceeds of the sale of the CIS system.

Concurrent with the development of CIS for the RTS partnership, a complimentary project was being developed for four CIS Primary Development Banks. Each bank committed $1,500 to fund modifications of the CIS project to conform to their specific requirements and thereby obtained a nonexclusive license to CIS as so modified. Under the terms of the Primary Development Bank agreements, 10% of any revenue from licensing CIS to others will accrue to each of the banks until such time as their entire $1,500 development fee has been recovered. At June 30, 1982, seven other banks had entered into, or committed to enter into, license agreements for CIS.

During 1981 and 1982, twenty major banks contracted with Anacomp to participate as Advisory Development Banks on the CIS project for a nonrefundable fee of $150. The fee permits each bank to review the project during development and provide input, which is not binding to Anacomp, regarding changes which would enhance the marketability of CIS. Anacomp defers a portion of this fee which will be recognized as services are provided to the participating banks throughout the terms of their contracts.

Anacomp

EFT

During fiscal 1981, Anacomp initiated and completed development of a new computer software switching system called H-10000 to be marketed to major financial institutions. Anacomp entered into an agreement with EFT Partners, Ltd. ("EFT"), a limited partnership formed in the fall of 1980. Several officers and directors of Anacomp purchased limited partnership units in EFT, aggregating approximately 31% of the partnership units, and Kranzley & Co., a wholly-owned subsidiary of Anacomp, was the general partner. The remaining limited partnership interests were owned by persons not affiliated with Anacomp. Anacomp agreed to develop and market the system, and EFT agreed to pay a development fee of $1,000, of which $910 was paid during 1981 and an additional $90 during 1982. The contract was reported on the completed contract basis; revenue and profits were recognized upon completion during the fourth quarter of 1981. In June 1982, Kranzley & Co. exercised its right under the purchase option to buy the interests of the limited partners at the appraised fair market value for the H-10000 system of $2,300.

CEFT

During fiscal 1981, Anacomp entered into an agreement with CEFT Partners, Ltd. ("CEFT"), a limited partnership formed in December 1980, and primary development banks to jointly develop a new computer funds transfer software system to be marketed to major financial institutions. Certain officers, directors and employees of Anacomp purchased limited partnership units in CEFT aggregating approximately 9% of the limited partnership units. The remaining partnership interest and the general partnership interest are owned by persons not affiliated with Anacomp.

Under the development agreement, Anacomp agreed to develop the new system on a best-effort basis. The agreement permits Anacomp to contract with primary development banks to provide development fees up to $1,000 in addition to the $2,100 development fee to be paid by the partnership. In June 1981, the general partner agreed to permit Anacomp to increase the bank fees allowable to $2,000 on this project. Contracts with five banks aggregating $2,000 have been completed.

Anacomp has acquired rights to a system owned by a major bank at a cost of $500 to assist and expedite the completion of the system. A portion of this cost has been charged to expense as a system development cost and the remainder is being amortized over the expected marketing life of the purchased system in its unmodified form.

The system was certified as being complete in July 1982, and Anacomp has agreed to market it for seven years on an exclusive commission basis. Anacomp has the option to acquire all rights to the system at the greater of (a) fair market value or (b) $3,000 to $5,000, depending on the date the option is exercised. Revenues earned on this software development project were $3,150 and $942 during fiscal 1981 and 1982.

CBS

During fiscal 1981, Anacomp entered into an agreement with CBS Partners, Ltd. ("CBS"), a limited partnership formed in April 1981, and primary development banks to jointly develop a wholesale banking computer software system to be marketed to major financial institutions. Certain officers, directors and employees of Anacomp purchased limited partnership units in the partnership aggregating approximately 20% of the limited partnership units. The remaining limited partnership interest and the general partnership interest are owned by persons not affiliated with Anacomp. Under the development agreement, Anacomp agreed to develop the new system on a best-efforts basis. The agreement permits Anacomp to contract with primary development banks to provide development fees up to $3,750 in addition to the $4,500 development fee to be paid by the partnership. Contracts with three banks aggregating $3,750 have been completed.

Anacomp has acquired rights to a wholesale banking system owned by a major bank at a cost of $1,350 to assist and expedite the completion of the system. A portion of this cost is being charged to expense as a system development cost and the remainder is being amortized over the expected marketing life of the purchased system in its unmodified form.

Upon completion of the system, Anacomp has agreed to market it for seven years on an exclusive commission basis. Anacomp has the option to acquire all rights to CBS at the greater of (a) fair market value or (b) $7,000 to $9,000, depending on the date the option is exercised. Revenues earned on this software development project were $2,620 and $4,319 during 1981 and 1982.

CIBS

Subsequent to June 30, 1982, Anacomp entered into an agreement with CIBS Partners, Limited ("CIBS"), a limited partnership formed in April 1981, to develop new software systems for large banks engaged in international business. Certain officers, directors and employees of Anacomp purchased limited partnership units in CIBS aggregating approximately 6.5% of the limited partnership units. The remaining limited partnership interests are owned by persons not affiliated with Anacomp. Anacomp is the sole holder of $400 of the non-voting preferred stock of the corporate general partner. The partnership payments under the development agreements are to be funded with $26,250 of partners' capital investment.

Under the development agreement, Anacomp has agreed to develop the new systems on a best-efforts basis. The agreement permits Anacomp to contract with primary development banks to provide development fees up to $12,000 in addition to the $23,000 development fee to be paid by the partnership. A contract with one bank for $500 has been completed.

Upon completion of the systems, Anacomp has agreed to lease the systems for five years on an exclusive basis at rental based on a percentage of license fees generated. Anacomp has the option to acquire all rights to the systems during the three-year period commencing one year after completion of the systems at total prices ranging from $46,400 to $59,700, plus a share of licensing fees generated thereafter, depending on the year in which the option is exercised.

At June 30, 1982, the Company considered the funding for this project to be imminent. Accordingly, costs of $5,647, including $2,750 to acquire rights to certain software incurred in commencing the development of CIBS, were deferred until such time as project funding became available in August 1982. Such costs will be charged to operations in fiscal 1983.

Other

During fiscal 1980, a group of officers and directors of Anacomp formed a limited partnership which purchased a computer system and leased it to Anacomp at a competitive rental rate. In May 1982, the Company purchased the computer equipment from the partnership for $1,167, which was its appraised value.

Note 5. Cash, Cash Investments and Short-Term Borrowings

Cash balances at June 30, 1982 and 1981, include temporary investments of $34,380 and $26,550, respectively, at costs which approximate market value. Of the amounts invested at June 20, 1982, $10,000 is pledged as collateral for the short-term borrowings from banks of $10,000 and is restricted as to withdrawal.

At June 20, 1982, Anacomp has short-term lines of credit from banks in the amount of $39,000, of which $35,000 is unused. Anacomp has agreed to maintain compensating balances, not restricted as to withdrawal, on certain of these lines. The average of compensating balances on these lines was approximately 5% of the available lines during fiscal 1982.

Anacomp

Note 7. Other Assets

The following comprise other assets:

	June 30	
	1982	1981
Investment in Kalvar Corporation, including $1,028 note receivable in both years and income bond and preferred stock in 1982	$ 6,428	$ 3,398
Marketable securities valued at the lower of cost or market	6,068	3,665
Notes receivable, RTS Associates	—	2,095
Notes receivable, other	4,132	400
Employment and non-compete agreements, less accumulated amortization of $1,297 and $848, respectively	491	737
Deferred debenture costs, less accumulated amortization of $313 and $152, respectively	3,470	2,026
Deferred charges, other	3,906	2,056
	$24,495	$14,377

Note 8. Long-Term Debt

Long-term debt is comprised of the following:

	June 30	
	1982	1981
10% Convertible Subordinated Debentures due November 1, 1988	$ 758	$ 915
9½% Convertible Subordinated Debentures due September 1, 2000	29,925	29,925
9% Convertible Subordinated Debentures due January 15, 1996	13,789	12,500
13⅞% Convertible Subordinated Debentures due January 15, 2002 (net of unamortized original issue discount of $7,440	42,560	—
Notes payable to banks at an average rate of 15.5% at June 30, 1982, due in installments to 1985	12,880	1,436
Other	8,203	8,174
	108,115	52,950
Less current portion	2,907	2,359
	$105,208	$50,591

Other debt includes equipment purchase notes, debtor to finance acquisitions, mortgages and obligations under capitalized financial leases. These items have effective costs of 9¾% to 15% and are payable in installments over varying periods extending to 2006. Shares representing substantially all of the operations of DSI are pledged as collateral for a note with a discounted balance of $2,793 at June 30, 1982. At June 30, 1982, processing equipment with an aggregate book value of approximately $3,600 is pledged as collateral under certain of the debt agreements.

Anacomp is guarantor of a bank loan to Anacomp's wholly-owned leasing subsidiary. At June 30, 1982, the balance of the debt being guaranteed is $480.

At June 30, 1982, the aggregate maturities of long-term debt through fiscal year 1987 are: 1983, $2,907; 1984, $12,972; 1985, $3,482; 1986, $347; and 1987, $219.

Note 9. Capital Stock

Stock Dividends and Stock Splits

The Board of Directors declared the following stock dividends and stock splits during the three years ended June 30, 1982:

January, 1980—five-for-four stock split
March, 1981—five-for-four stock split

All applicable share and per share amounts have been restated to reflect the stock dividends and stock splits. All conversion prices and stock option data have also been adjusted to give effect to the stock dividends and stock split.

Note 10. Segment Information

Anacomp operates in two business segments—data center services and computer services. Data center services consist of providing computer output microfilm ("COM") and computer processing for banks and credit unions through a network of branch offices, where Anacomp's equipment and personnel process data for numerous customers at each branch site. Computer services consist of providing computer software, primarily to large financial institutions, and managing computer facilities for large customers, primarily state and local governments.

	Year Ended June 30, 1982			Year Ended June 30, 1981		
	Consolidated	Data Center Services	Computer Services	Consolidated	Data Center Services	Computer Services
Revenues	$109,599	$67,418	$42,181	$106,368	$67,899	$38,469
Operating profit	12,451	8,504	3,947	18,191	7,294	10,897
Income before taxes	3,622			13,997		
Depreciation and amortization	6,054	3,636	2,418	3,859	2,527	1,332
Corporate depreciation and amortization	654			509		

	June 30, 1982			June 30, 1981		
Identifiable assets	$155,039	$84,785	$70,254	$93,737	$57,332	$36,405
Corporate assets	56,621			37,061		
	$211,660			$130,798		

Approximately 19% of Anacomp's fiscal 1982 consolidated revenues were provided by major computer services contracts which extend beyond one year, including those contracts in process discussed in Note 3. Contracts of this type provided 18% of the 1981 and 20% of the 1980 revenue. This included system licensing and modification contracts, which accounted for 13% of revenues in 1982, 11% in 1981 and 1980, and facility management arrangements, which accounted for 6% of revenue in 1982, 7% in 1981 and 9% in 1980.

Revenues from various federal, state and local government agencies amounted to approximately 11% of revenue in 1982 and 1981, and 14% in 1980.

Note 11. Income Taxes

Deferred taxes are provided where differences exist between the period in which transactions affect taxable income and the period in which they enter into the determination of income for financial reporting purposes. Investment tax credits are reflected in income in the year realized by reducing the current provision for federal taxes on income.

The following table sets forth the components of the provision for income taxes:

Year ended June 30,	1982	1981	1980
Charge equivalent to realized tax benefits of preacquisition losses of acquired companies	$ 67	$ 164	$ 250
Charge equivalent to realized tax benefits from early disposition of shares issued under qualified stock option and stock purchase plans	76	252	81
Charge equivalent to realized tax benefits from certain acquisition expenditures	276	—	—
Taxes currently payable:			
Federal	2,536	1,034	2,263
State	889	602	377
Deferred	(3,001)	4,007	189
	$ 843	$6,059	$3,160

The deferred income tax effects of timing differences are as follows:

Year ended June 30,	1982	1981	1980
Excess of tax over book depreciation	$ 1,906	$ 265	$189
Use of cash basis accounting for tax purposes	(3,830)	3,830	—
Accrued interest on convertible debentures	(1,282)	(436)	—
Election of installment sale for tax purposes	506	(8)	—
Deferred income of foreign subsidiary	109	187	—
Deferred income of DISC	(156)	140	—
Transfer from deferred to currently payable	(264)	—	—
Other	10	29	—
	$(3,001)	$4,007	$189

The following is a reconciliation of income taxes calculated at the United States federal statutory rate to the provision for income taxes:

Year ended June 30,	1982	1981	1980
Provision for taxes on income at statutory rate	$1,666	$6,439	$3,582
Investment tax credit	(1,950)	(333)	(377)
State income taxes, net of federal income tax benefit	569	325	204
Nondeductible amortization of intangible assets	474	332	169
Difference between capital gain and statutory tax rates	—	(316)	(269)
Dividend deduction of 85% of dividend income	(119)	(179)	—
Interest on tax deposits, net of federal income tax benefit	302	—	—
Other	(99)	(209)	(149)
	$ 843	$6,059	$3,160

At June 30, 1982, certain subsidiaries of Anacomp have net operating loss carryforwards of approximately $1,997. The carryforwards pertain to preacquisition losses of the subsidiaries and therefore can be utilized only to the extent that the subsidiaries produce taxable income in the future. Any tax benefit resulting from the utilization of these carryforwards will reduce the intangible assets recorded at the time of purchase of the subsidiaries. The carryforwards expire in the following fiscal years: 1992, $357; 1993, $774; 1994, $514; and 1995, $352.

Note 12. Other Income and Extraordinary Credit

Year ended June 30,	1982	1981	1980
Gain (loss) on transaction with Kalvar	$(725)	$ 898	$1,567
Gain on sale of certain assets	630	855	25
Other	705	947	246
	$610	$2,700	$1,838

The extraordinary credit in 1982 arose from the sale of a branch office which had been acquired in 1981 as part of an acquisition accounted for as a pooling of interests. The gain was $2,541 before income taxes, determined at the capital gains rate of $711.

Note 13. Lease and Other Commitments

Anacomp has commitments under long-term operating leases, principally for building space, covering periods generally up to five years. The following summarizes by year the future minimum lease payments due within the next five years and under all noncancellable operating lease obligations which extend beyond one year.

Fiscal	As of June 30
1983	$3,933
1984	3,159
1985	2,362
1986	1,605
1987	565
1988 and thereafter	626
Total minimum payments required	$12,250

Anacomp

Anacomp

Anacomp and Dr. Ronald D. Palamara, president and chairman of Anacomp, are parties to a March 27, 1980, employment and noncompetition agreement pursuant to which Anacomp agreed (a) to pay Dr. Palamara commencing July 1, 1980, a base annual salary of $125 plus an amount equal to 3.54% of Anacomp's annual income before income taxes in excess of $1,000, (b) to make a one-time payment of $430 in July, 1980, to Dr. Palamara for his agreement not to compete with Anacomp for three years following any termination of service with Anacomp and (c) to sell Dr. Palamara, in July, 1980, 428,688 shares of Anacomp common stock for a consideration of $6.08 per share, that being the per share market price on the date of the agreement. Of the $6.08 per share consideration, Dr. Palamara agreed to pay $1.22 per share and granted Anacomp a right of first refusal to purchase such shares upon any resale by Dr. Palamara or subsequent holders at $4.86 below the sale price, $4.86 being the balance of the $6.08 per share consideration.

Note 15. Supplementary Income Statement Information

Supplementary income statement information follows.

Year ended June 30,	1982	1981	1980
Maintenance and repairs	$4,475	$3,738	$2,271
Depreciation and amortization of property, equipment and purchased computer software systems	$4,789	$2,938	$2,246
Amortization of intangible assets	$1,919	$1,430	$780
Taxes other than payroll and income taxes	$1,000	$507	$410
Rents	$7,503	$8,084	$4,819

REPORT OF INDEPENDENT ACCOUNTANTS

To the Board of Directors and Stockholders of Anacomp, Inc.:

We have examined the consolidated balance sheet of Anacomp, Inc. and Subsidiaries as of June 30, 1982 and 1981, and the related consolidated statements of income, stockholders' equity, and changes in financial position for each of the three years in the period ended June 30, 1982. Our examinations were made in accordance with generally accepted auditing standards and, accordingly, included such tests of the accounting records and such other auditing procedures as we considered necessary in the circumstances.

In our opinion, the financial statements referred to above present fairly the consolidated financial position of Anacomp, Inc. and Subsidiaries as of June 30, 1982 and 1981, and the consolidated results of their operations and changes in financial position for each of the three years in the period ended June 30, 1982, in conformity with generally accepted accounting principles applied on a consistent basis, after restatement for the change, with which we concur, in the method of accounting for vacation pay as described in Note 1 to the financial statements.

Coopers & Lybrand

Indianapolis, Indiana
September 1982

Arch Communications Group Inc.

There are some great bargains to be had in paging stocks, analysts say. The sector, bruised repeatedly since the start of the year, got kicked again when technology stocks plummeted recently, and for no good reason. . . . One stock—Arch Communications—is an absolute bargain. "One of the most beaten up stocks is Arch, and there is no reason for it," said Christopher Larsen of NatWest Securities.

The paging industry has been deluged with bad news in the last six months, from management turmoil and broken bank covenants to broad worries of a rise in interest rates and of paging being eclipsed by a new generation of mobile phones. . . . Arch stock has fallen from a trading range of $22–$26 early in the year to as low as $12 in recent sessions . . . but analysts are adamant the sector has a bright future.

Reuters Financial Service, July 29, 1996[1]

COMPANY BACKGROUND

Founded in 1986, Arch Communications Group Inc. was the third largest paging company in the U.S., serving nearly three million subscribers. Arch offered paging services and equipment on local, regional, and nationwide (40 states) bases, and in 180 of the 200 largest U.S. cities.

Arch followed a strategy that consisted of three primary elements: low prices, standard and reliable technologies, and prompt and efficient service delivery. Arch offered competitively priced messaging services and was able to do so because of its own low cost structure. Arch's low costs were drawn from economies of scale in its operations and the size of its subscriber base. Second, for the majority of its paging services, Arch avoided using experimental paging technologies. Rather, Arch endorsed paging technologies that might not be the latest or most advanced but were consistently predictable and dependable. When it came to pioneering new technologies, Arch preferred to let other companies lead and take the risks. Finally, Arch strove to consistently deliver reliable and immediate service by its choice of technologies and protocols,[2] and by expanding its networks and their capacities to accommodate and expedite message flow. Arch believed that fast, reliable, and efficient message delivery was the core objective of paging and critical to generating and retaining customers.

Arch was one of the industry's fastest growing paging providers, seeking growth through a blend of strategic acquisitions and internal additions. The firm had grown from a local provider to a national one, traditionally concentrating on serving small and medium sized markets with low pager penetration rates. Now Arch was also entering major metropolitan markets, in an effort to establish a nationwide footprint.

In Arch's industry, financial performance was commonly assessed by analyzing operating cash flows or EBITDA. Most paging companies were not able to show positive earnings, and net losses were considered an ordinary near-term industry phenomenon.

Research Associate Sarayu Srinivasan prepared this case under the supervision of Professor Krishna G. Palepu. The case is intended solely as the basis for class discussion and is not intended to serve as an endorsement, source of primary data, or illustration of effective or ineffective management. Copyright © 1996 by the President and Fellows of Harvard College. HBS Case 9-197-047.

1. Nick Louth, "Talking Point—Bargains Shine in Paging Stocks," *Reuters Financial Service*, July 29, 1996.
2. *Pager protocol is the set of rules defining a network's capacity and the rate at which data travels through it.*

These losses in part resulted from the large capital expenditures, heavy debt financing, and high depreciation rates common to the sector. Analysts expected earnings to turn positive when networks matured and infrastructure spending slowed. Performance evaluation for the present was, therefore, based on EBITDA.[3] Arch's EBITDA grew 162.6 percent from $18 million in 1994 to $47.2 million in 1995. Net revenues also grew: 124.7 percent from $63.1 million in 1994 to $141.8 million in 1995. Subscriber numbers grew from 538,000 in 1994 to 2,006,000 in 1995. (Exhibit 4 shows Arch's financial statements.)

On November 13, 1995, Arch stock was trading at $29.62. Five months later, in March 1996, the stock had fallen to $23. By July 1996 Arch's stock price had dropped to $12.50 per share. The plunge in the stock's value had paralleled the falls in prices of most paging sector stocks. Analysts, however, felt Arch was still a sound investment, suffering from "guilt by association" due to the poor performance of fellow companies in its sector, and investor misunderstanding of industry dynamics. Despite the falls in price, analysts continued to recommend investing in Arch stock, rating it a "buy."

THE U.S. PAGING INDUSTRY

Introduced in the 1950s, pagers were compact, portable, one-way wireless messaging devices used for mobile communication. Pagers were first used almost exclusively by the business sector and time sensitive professionals such as doctors and law enforcement personnel. But by 1995, the paging industry had revenues over $4.1 billion, 34.5 million paging subscribers (eight million units added in 1995), and a 13 percent pager penetration rate of the population.

Most pagers worked on the same basic technology. Each pager had an identification number and was basically a receiver always tuned to a specific radio frequency listening for messages directed to its number among a constant broadcast of messages. To page a user, a caller dialed the pager's identification number by phone and left a voice[4] or text message with either an operator or an automated system. The pager user was then alerted to message receipt by the broadcast of a paging signal (tone) to the pager. Users then called the operator or checked the pager to retrieve the message.

There were four pager types:

Tone   The simplest type alerted by tone. Users called an answering service for messages.

Digital/Numeric   Digitals displayed numeric messages, usually a phone number where the caller could be reached. Digitals alerted by tone or vibration (for loud or quiet alerts), and screened and stored numbers. In 1995, digitals accounted for 85 percent of all pagers in use.

Alphanumeric   These pagers had both numeric and text messaging, eliminating message retrieval. The pagers' text capability allowed for immediate user action. These accounted for only 10 percent of the market but were the fastest growing segment.

Tone/Voice   These pagers delivered voice messages after tone alerts, and made up 3 percent of the market. Average retail price per pager was $57 for tone, $77 for digital, $138 for alphanumeric, and $189 for tone/voice.[5] Pagers had an estimated 4–5-year life.

3. EBITDA (Earnings Before Interest, Taxes, Depreciation, & Amortization) is the paging industry's measure of financial performance. This metric is the basis for a firms's valuation by industry equity analysts and is important in a company's ability to secure financing.

4. Voice messages, while easy to use, occupy large airtime on a provider's limited frequency.

5. State of the U.S. Paging Industry: 1996, MTA-EMCI.

The two main industry participants were pager manufacturers and paging service providers (paging companies). Most pagers were made by one of a few major manufacturers. In 1994 Motorola had produced 83 percent of all pagers in service, while NEC (another manufacturer) had produced 12 percent.[6] Motorola's dominance was based on its ability to consistently meet service providers' delivery schedules, its reliable equipment, and strong brand. Most equipment was distributed and activated by service providers, and most service providers sourced equipment mainly from a major maker.

Paging companies provided paging service and also leased and sold pagers. In 1995–1996 the three largest service providers, PageNet, MobileComm, and Arch, together served 45 percent of the total paging market. Over half the market was served by the 8–10 largest companies, while the rest of the market was served by small local providers. While most paging was regional, nationwide service was also available. Rarely, companies had "roaming" agreements, fee-based contracts between providers to serve users that entered areas not covered by their provider, as was common practice in the cellular industry. On average, it cost $11.00 per month to use a service. Users were charged fixed periodic fees, regardless of usage, that included pager rental but not special fees such as excess use charges. The most costly service was alphanumeric, followed by tone/voice, digital, and tone only.

In 1995 only three companies offered nationwide service as it consumed a lot of bandwidth,[7] was not widely demanded, and might require market frequency compatibility if the provider did not have a nationwide license. Nationwide licenses, because they operated on one frequency, were useful to large providers that had many resellers because they eliminated the need to coordinate equipment, infrastructure, and frequencies from market to market. Nationwide service was used mostly by business travelers. Providers also offered nationwide service to differentiate themselves.

Distribution

There were three distribution channels: direct, retail, and reseller. Retail and resellers were indirect channels and were becoming very important as consumers became a growing market segment. In 1994 30 percent of all new pagers added were through resellers.

Direct Distribution

Equipment and service were acquired by subscribers directly from service providers. Providers bought pagers from the manufacturer and leased or sold pagers to subscribers, more commonly leasing, in addition to providing service. Leasing contributed to the large costs borne by providers: equipment, maintenance, and replacement tied up large sums of cash as 25 percent of a company's pagers were replaced each year. Increasingly, however, subscribers opted to own their pagers (28 percent owned pagers in 1989; 52 percent by 1994). "Churn"[8] in this channel was the lowest across channels, roughly 3 percent per month. The providers bore all expenses, but produced the highest average revenue per unit (ARPU) because it sold direct. This channel had the highest cash flow per subscriber and was the most profitable channel for providers.

....

6. Telecommunications Market Review and Forecast, 1995 NATA.

7. Bandwidth is the volume of information per unit time that a transmission medium can handle. Larger bandwidth means more information can be transmitted in a given time period and at a faster speed.

8. Churn is the rate at which subscribers leave service providers by switching providers, subscribing at introductory costs and then dumping the provider at the end of the promotion, skipping payments, and other voluntary or involuntary service deactivation. Churn is higher among consumers than business users.

Retail

Equipment and service acquired through retailers were usually subject to mark-ups to compensate the retailer who did not work for the equipment maker or service provider. After the sale, the subscriber became the service provider's client and had no further contact with the retailer. Provider ARPU was equal to that from the direct channel, but churn was the highest among channels.

Resellers

Resellers purchased equipment and service directly from the provider and resold to their own clients. Resellers bore the full costs of service and equipment and supplied providers with the lowest ARPU. Low revenue, however, was accompanied by low costs, and thus higher cash flow margins for the providers. Churn was zero, because the provider only focused on net additions.

Substitute Products

Cellular Phones

Two-way cell phone communication had analysts continually predicting the demise of paging, yet in 1995 pagers had 34.5 million subscribers to the 32 million cellular subscribers. Several factors explained pager dominance. First, $56 per month for cell service made $11 per month paging service the lowest cost form of wireless messaging. Cell users were also charged per incoming or outgoing call, and if they went out of their service area. Second, cell phones had a shorter battery life (a few hours) than the multiple-month pager battery life. Third, pagers were also cell complements, used as screening devices for the phones. Fourth, pagers helped manage cell costs. Cell users generally made rather than received calls (over 85 percent of all cell calls were outbound), and left phones off to conserve batteries and control costs, using pagers to get messages. Cell phones were, however, becoming smaller, less costly, and more feature laden (including longer battery lives and silent alerts). Cell phones also had a unique value as emergency situation devices.

Personal Communication Services (PCS)

PCS was a generic term used for a range of advanced mobile communication technologies. PCS used a larger spectrum (range of sound wave frequencies) that could be either narrowband (NPCS) for advanced paging technologies like two-way paging, or broadband (BPCS), which supported the more costly, spectrum consumptive technologies cell service was based on. Narrowband providers could offer advanced services and have more reliable networks. NPCS and BPCS offerings were feared to cannibalize or destroy current paging networks.

Mobile Satellite Communications

Satellites served subscribers not served by land or cellular systems, and nonconsumer markets. Satellites offered wireless services over vast geographic areas with minimal ongoing capital costs for the provider. Profitable satellite-based global wireless services could be developed, and already satellite providers had started to eye the consumer market.

Paging subscribers had grown 27 percent per year from 1990–1995. Large paging companies had even higher subscriber growth rates. This growth was fueled by the market shift from business to consumer, changing user perceptions of pagers, falling product and service prices, and an expanding variety of product and service options. The historical images of pagers as costly professional items or illegal drug trade tools were fading: nearly

65 percent of new owners used pagers as personal "lifestyle management" tools. Increasingly time constrained and busy consumers demanding both accessibility and mobility relied on pagers as integrative tools. But, despite such high growth, service providers had slim margins. Paging was capital intensive and companies needed large recurrent capital injections. Infrastructure and equipment accounted for the two largest capital outlays.

COMPETITION IN THE PAGING INDUSTRY IN THE 1990s

From 1994 to 1996 the Federal Communications Commission (FCC), the regulatory authority over the airwaves, allocated limited radio spectrum to be auctioned off by license for various wireless services. The auctions debuted licenses for bandwidth supporting advanced services, such as PCS. Bidders for and winners of the new licenses were subject to FCC determined regulations meant to limit bidding to only serious investors, promote rigorous competition, and ensure effective use of spectrum. These rules included limiting the number of different PCS channels a provider could own to three, restricting license transfers, and requiring providers to show pro forma construction plans.

For auctioning purposes, spectrum suitable for paging was divided into four geographic service areas: nationwide, regional (comprised of five regions each with 20 percent of the U.S. population), MTAs (51 major trading areas), and BTAs (493 basic trading areas). Each service area was allotted channels of frequency requiring operating licenses. A total of 7 MHz of spectrum[9] was available or already being used by paging companies, approximately 4 MHz of which was for advanced paging. Commonly, 25 kHz of one-way frequency supported numerous local and regional providers using a variety of protocols. The same channel in different markets could be occupied by many providers.

By 1995 the nationwide and regional auctions had taken place. (MTA and BTA licenses were to be auctioned in 1996.) The auctions sold licenses for eleven nationwide channels and 30 regional channels (six channels in each region). Channels two and four of the six channels were identical in each region so that a provider could acquire the same channel in each of the five regions and thus have the coverage of a nationwide license without actually bidding on one. MTAs would have a total of 561 licenses available (51 MTAs × 11 licenses) and BTAs, 2,958 licenses (493 BTAs × 6 licenses).

The number of providers in a market was technically limited by the number of operating licenses issued for that market. But since license holders could sell portions of their spectrum to resellers, the number of providers a market could physically accommodate and the spectrum's capacity defined the true number of firms operating in a market. Licenses could also be bought by a group of companies, so that multiple providers could operate on the same license in the same area.

The minimum provider investment necessary to start a paging company varied by the technology, protocols, and licenses used. In 1996 the minimum outlay for a simple one-way nationwide network was approximately $200 million dollars.[10] A nationwide license would cost an additional $25 million dollars. A regional network of the same specifications, with licenses, would cost approximately $40 million. Larger, better capitalized providers, therefore, had advantages.

While the six largest providers served over 60 percent of the market, the remainder of the industry was highly fragmented. Competition was intense at all levels, and since

....

9. MHz (megahertz) is a unit of frequency comprised of a million hertz. 1 hertz = 1 cycle per second. 1 MHz = 1,000 kHz (kilohertz).

10. This scenario assumed the network used FLEX protocol and 1,000 radio transmitters to broadcast messages.

service was hard to differentiate, it rested on the linked elements of cost, data delivery, and price. Low costs, in a high fixed cost industry, were achieved by "loading" infrastructure, that is, piling as many subscribers as possible onto an existing network. Allocating costs over a large subscriber base lowered per-unit costs and could be reflected in pricing. Loading, however, swelled the number of messages that had to travel the network, increased transmission time, and delayed messages to the end user. In paging, rapid message delivery was critical. Low prices drew subscribers, but long term loyalty was a function of the ability to deliver data immediately. Providers could manage these components by upgrading to faster protocols or adding spectrum.

In the pursuit of scale and spectrum, a pan-industry rush of mergers took place in the 1980s and 1990s. In one decade, providers consolidated from 1,000 to 500 with 8–10 large regional or national companies. By 1996, however, merging pains, management mismatches, concern over the merger wave ending, delays in deployment of NPCS networks, and fears that PCS would cannibalize paging and that no room was left for internal growth, caused sector morale to go down.

Arch's Largest Competitors, 1990s

PageNet

Founded in 1981, PageNet was the largest and fastest growing provider in the U.S., with service in all 50 states, the U.S. Virgin Islands, and Puerto Rico. PageNet was considered a trend setter (first to add a million units via internal growth), the low cost leader, and the most successful company in the industry (160 percent the size of its closest competitor). PageNet had 7.8 million subscribers (20 percent of the industry base), adding 2.3 million subscribers in 1995 (350,000 by acquisition).

PageNet's growth strategy focused primarily on addition through internal growth. Due to this strategy, PageNet did not have the acquisition problem of consolidating networks of different frequencies or back office systems. PageNet's strategy of aggressive pricing policies, reliable service, and emphasis on direct sales (largest industry sales force with 1,000 people and 6,000 resellers) was executed by decentralized management. PageNet owned the most spectrum of any provider. The company built a 24-hour support/distribution center and a National Accounts Division to provide one contact point to large, national clients and to forge and manage such alliances.

PageNet regularly entered partnership and distribution agreements to expand its client base. Sprint, MCI, and GTE were PageNet clients who resold services to their own clients. Partners could market services under their own or PageNet's brand and could customize agreements. With Sprint and MCI, PageNet handled shipping, customer service, and pager leasing. Sprint and MCI oversaw advertising, billing, and marketing. Subscribers were unaware they were dealing with PageNet at all. GTE was a typical reseller, owning its pagers and handling its own customer service and billing. Reseller churn impacted PageNet's subscriber numbers but not its revenues.

PageNet's future projects included the first commercial wireless pocket answering machine, dubbed VoiceNow, which was in its final testing stages. PageNet was also expanding its business overseas through its recently formed international division.

MobileComm

MobileComm was the second largest provider of paging services (4.4 million subscribers) with local, regional, and national service in the 50 states, Canada, and the Caribbean.

MobileComm served 97 of the top 100 largest metropolitan markets. In 1996 MobileMedia acquired (and renamed itself) MobileComm for $930 million (the largest industry acquisition), netting 1.8 million subscribers and consolidating revenues of $323 million.

MobileComm's acquisitions aimed at establishing national presence in one-way and two-way networks (it had two nationwide PCS licenses), growing sales distribution capability to retail channels, and adding spectrum. MobileComm's internal growth plan emphasized high sales productivity and strategic alliances. After the MobileMedia merger, MobileComm began centralizing back office functions (all credit and collection tasks in one place) and building two service centers (in Texas and Maryland) that provided 24-hour customer service and billing support.

By mid-1996 MobileComm was the victim of high churn: 3.8 percent (industry average: 2–3 percent). This was due to network congestion[11] that delayed message delivery during peak hours in major markets and a rise in resellers on its networks. MobileComm was also still trying to cut duplicate back office/support expenses from the merger. In late 1996 MobileComm changed its entire upper management. The restructuring slowed the already troubled integration and Texas center project. Standard & Poor's downgraded its rating on MobileComm's $460 million debt. MobileComm was bound by its creditors to raise $100 million in equity capital by year's end.

Other Providers

The fourth largest provider, Metrocall, gained scale by a series of fast acquisitions, but would expend considerable resources to mold the various parts into one entity, while also attempting to integrate new management. American Paging, the seventh largest player, was undergoing a large restructuring which included a management turnover. The restructuring was blamed for the drop in subscriber additions and weak operating performance the firm experienced.

The fifth largest provider, ProNet, had followed a fast growth strategy that focused on dense urban markets. Despite acquisitions, doubling subscribers in one year, creating reseller programs to drive long-term internal growth, and one of the lowest cost structures, ProNet announced mid-1996 that, due to price concessions to resellers, it would be unable to grow cash flow for several quarters. Standard & Poor's lowered ProNet's credit rating. Consequently, ProNet saw its stock dumped.

ARCH'S PERFORMANCE, POSITION, AND FUTURE

Arch offered local, regional, and nationwide service, every pager type, and also special services such as voice mail. In 1995 87 percent of Arch's in-service pagers were digital display, 7 percent were alphanumeric, 2 percent tone only, and 2 percent tone/voice. Arch owned, leased, and provided service to 45 percent of its in-service pagers and provided service only to the remainder (30 percent of which were subscriber owned pagers, 25 percent reseller owned).

Arch owned and was developing two nationwide channels (acquired primarily to expand its regional services) but had followed a unique service strategy of offering nationwide paging through a network of affiliates. When a subscriber using Arch's nationwide paging left one affiliate's market and entered another, he/she called a toll-free

Arch Communications Group

---

11. *MobileComm had the industry's largest alphanumeric subscriber base (14 percent of its subscribers used alphanumerics). High revenue alphanumeric paging, however, uses four to five times the capacity of numeric paging, congesting and over-trafficking the paging networks they occupy.*

number that would prompt the user's pager to become active and receive messages (on the affiliate's channel) in the new market.

Arch acquired 60 percent of its subscribers through direct distribution (direct sales and firm owned stores). Direct distribution was a more expensive channel by which to add subscribers, but it gave Arch an ARPU higher than the industry average. The indirect channel (comprised of low cost, low ARPU resellers and high ARPU retailers) contributed the remaining 40 percent of subscribers.

Over the past few years, Arch had shown a decline in monthly ARPU. This was because the number of subscriber or reseller owned pagers for which Arch received no recurring rental fee had increased more than 25 percent over the past few years. Secondly, over the same period, the percentage of new pagers in service added through indirect channels (mostly resellers who purchased bulk airtime at discount) had increased. Finally, the decline in paging service retail prices, resulting from pressure on pricing due to increased competition and growth, also drove revenues down. Arch's revenue decline mirrored an industry-wide decline. While some observers were alarmed by the sustained declines, others measured operating performance by EBITDA rather than revenues and paid little attention to the drop. Revenue declines ignored both the differences in operating margins from different distribution channels and the fact that paging was a volume driven, fixed cost business and that spreading those costs over a large base had a positive impact on margins.

Arch generated most of its revenues by charging subscribers fixed periodic fees. As long as subscribers remained in service, the recurring payments constituted an income stream free of additional selling expenses. Arch's net losses were mostly due to the interest on debt incurred to finance growth, and the large depreciation and amortization charges related to assets. Arch required considerable funds to service debt, finance acquisitions, fund expansion and upkeep of existing operations, and cover pager and paging system expenditures. The company's capital expenditures had increased from $10.5 million in 1992 to over $60.6 million in 1995 and were expected to reach the $100 million mark in 1996. These expenditures were supported by cash from operations, equity issues, and debt. At the end of 1995 Arch had assets totaling $785.3 million. The company expected to generate positive cash flow by 1998.

During 1995 Arch had several important accomplishments: it made six acquisitions of which the $540 million USA Mobile (second largest industry acquisition) and Westlink (substantially adding to Arch's nationwide presence) helped push it from the industry's tenth to third largest company; added 1.1 million subscribers (acquisition) and 366,000 subscribers (internal growth—tripling quarterly internal growth); expanded service from 13 to 40 states; grew EBITDA from $18 million in 1994 to $47.2 million; grew total revenues 114.2 percent to $141.8 million (and grew net revenue by 124.7 percent); and raised over $300 million in new debt and equity capital. These results crowned 17 consecutive quarters of net revenue and cash flow increases in an industry where such measures were expected to remain weak for the foreseeable future. Table A shows selected Arch financial highlights.

Strategy

Arch followed a strategy that emphasized low prices, proven technologies, and reliable delivery of service. Arch's management team, headed by CEO C. Edward Baker Jr., was considered to have the longest successful management track record in the public paging industry. Arch's decentralized management structure allowed it to control costs, smoothly consolidate acquisitions, and respond to subscriber needs quickly.

Table A Arch Financial Highlights

	Year Ended 12/31/95	Year Ended 12/31/94	Year Ended 12/31/93
Net revenues	$141,809,000	$63,116,000	$41,277,000
Earnings before interest, taxes, depreciation and amortization (EBITDA)	47,186,000	17,969,000	11,315,000
Net income (loss)	(36,602,000)	(6,462,000)	(5,725,000)
Per share data:			
Weighted average shares	13,498,000	7,183,000	7,125,000
EBITDA	$ 3.50	$ 2.50	$ 1.59
Net Income (loss)	$(2.72)	$(0.90)	$(0.80)
Ending subscriber units in service	2,006,000	538,000	254,000

Source: Arch 1995 Annual Report.

As one of the industry's lowest cost providers, Arch was able to price competitively, sustaining its cost structure by consolidating operating functions, using fast transmission systems, and spreading costs by taking advantage of economies of scale arising from pursuing large scale.

Arch offered its subscribers no frills paging services based on standard and tested technologies that could be depended upon to deliver messages reliably and quickly with none of the potential hiccups that services based on new or experimental technologies might present. Arch did, however, keep up with emerging paging technologies by investing in a consortium that was developing advanced paging services. Scott Hoyt, Arch Marketing V.P., explained, "This industry will eat you alive if you're wrong as a technology innovator. We prefer to take advantage of other people's mistakes." Hoyt added that Arch considered itself a "fast follower."[12]

While Arch's subscriber numbers seemed to attest to reliable and timely message delivery, some of Arch's clients did not agree. In August 1996, Arch had a 2½ hour service outage in Portland, Maine. Further, due to a computer glitch, many serviceless subscribers failed to receive notification from Arch that their pagers were down. Portland Police Chief Michael Chitwood, whose department used eighteen Arch pagers for emergency pagers, said, "To be down for two and a half hours without being notified is crazy. We are talking about public safety here."[13]

Growth

Arch's growth strategy combined internal growth (developing markets and extending out into adjacent or existing markets) and a series of acquisitions. The acquired companies were all characterized by what were considered sound operating performance track records. By 1996 Arch had the second highest absolute subscriber growth rate in the industry and had felt few growing pains.

Internal growth, which was over 40 percent in 1995 (higher than industry growth), was driven by market development and penetration, and expanding marketing activities and

12. Audrey Choi, "Arch Builds Strong Paging Business Slowly But Surely," Wall Street Journal, August 22, 1996.
13. Ibid.

Arch Communications Group

sales. Arch had traditionally entered small and medium sized markets with lower rates of pager penetration because of the greater growth opportunities these markets offered. Increasingly, however, Arch also concentrated on strengthening its nationwide presence, entering and establishing itself in major metropolitan areas and larger markets by both using service agreements with other paging carriers and extending its national footprint through acquisitions (bypassing buying a nationwide license).

Arch's acquisitions were made to expand subscriber base, geographic operations, and spectrum without deploying new networks. Most of Arch's acquisitions fell into one of three groups: (1) acquisitions that primarily expanded geographic reach and were likely to be in adjoining markets, (2) acquisitions that operated in Arch's markets and would be folded into Arch, and (3) acquisitions, mostly in nonadjacent markets, made for strategic purposes that extended Arch's physical reach and added new markets. The company had experienced few of the acquisition integration difficulties that had plagued its competitors and the industry. Arch CEO Baker tried to explain their success:

> We've certainly learned a great deal as we've done thirty-two acquisitions. . . We've put in place a program called the SOAP [Standard Operating and Accounting Practices] package, so that every time we make an acquisition, we put a team together that very rapidly and efficiently implements this package at all of our acquired targets. It's really a proven methodology for quickly and efficiently integrating these acquired properties. Arch was very fortunate with our latest and largest acquisitions, because the most difficult thing that you encounter when you integrate companies is integrating the backroom operations—your accounting, your customer support, and your operating systems. We were fortunate enough in those two most recent acquisitions to have bought companies who were using the same billing, customer support, and operating packages that we were.[14]

Arch also actively attempted to increase the capacity of its existing infrastructure and network by upgrading to faster protocols. Protocol upgrades allowed messages to travel the network faster, increasing the network's subscriber carrying capacity. Faster protocols eliminated the need to purchase additional spectrum or invest in dispatching new networks. One past example was the company's upgrade to a protocol called FLEX. The upgrade doubled capacity without the substantial capital outlay acquiring new spectrum would entail. Future upgrade plans included acquiring a protocol called ReFLEX25, a two-way messaging protocol being developed by Motorola.

Competitive Position

Arch faced competition from at least one other paging company in every market it operated in. Although no single company competed with Arch in all its markets, some competitors held nationwide licenses so that they could potentially enter all of Arch's markets.

Arch believed that competition for subscribers rested on quality of service, geographic coverage, and price, and felt itself competitive on these dimensions. In response to the competitive threat of cellular technology, Arch CEO Baker had this to say:

> Broadband PCS [cellular] is not going to affect our growth. . . . We have people on the street utilizing APC's [a cellular/PCS firm operating in Arch markets] BPCS network for messaging, and it doesn't work well. . . . And there is absolutely no way, in our view, that it is going to affect the growth of messaging. It doesn't perform well;

14. Sarah E. Reynolds, "Staying True to the Company's Vision," Worcester Business Journal, April 29, 1996.

you've got coverage problems; there are penetration problems; you've got battery life issues. All the things that we've talked about, and others have written about, are proving themselves to be true with respect to how messaging will perform over broadband PCS networks. . . . Metrocall [a paging provider in APC's market] posted record growth and has not experienced a single customer loss to APC.[15]

Arch invested in new wireless technologies such as wireless data delivery, two-way messaging, voice paging, and narrowband PCS by acquiring shares in a consortium of companies that owned five regional NPCS licenses. In this way Arch would have a stake in emerging technologies with comparatively small capital investments and risk. Despite such forays into emanating technologies, Arch remained loyal to its proven technology strategy.

Future

To maintain a competitive edge, Arch intended to pursue several future strategic initiatives, including strengthening distribution channels, increasing the capacity to serve more customers through expansion of its two national paging channels, building more efficient support infrastructure by expanding the national sales and customer service operations, and continued investment into select technologies.[16] Arch also planned to use the extra capacity it would acquire from its protocol upgrades to build up its alphanumeric subscriber base.

Arch's acquisitions to date had been free of the troubles that had traditionally accrued to acquiring companies. Arch intended to continue its acquisitions, but there was no guarantee that the pattern of smooth integration would be sustainable. Future acquisitions could be difficult to identify, troublesome to integrate, and demand excessive financial resources and managerial focus. Factors outside the company's control also threatened to affect growth strategies, and included prevailing economic conditions and interest rates, competitive and regulatory environments, technological advances, and the ability to attract and retain professionals.

Despite Arch's stock price of $12.50 per share in July 1996—a drop of more than 100 percent from its trading range at the year's start—analysts remained bullish about the stock (see Exhibit 1 for stock movements). John Adams, an analyst at Wessels, Arnold & Henderson, explained how analysts valued paging companies and might arrive at valuations different from the market's in a report on the paging industry:

When valuing paging companies, analysts do not use P/E multiples on current earnings because there is usually no positive earnings stream from which a multiple can be derived, at least not near-term. Therefore, analysts typically value stock with either a discounted cash flow analysis and/or with an unlevered valuation approach which adjusts the market value of comparative companies for various capital structures (debt and cash in particular) thus permitting an apples-to-apples multiples comparison to operating cash flow or EBITDA.[17]

In his August 1996 report, Adams presented a detailed valuation of Arch using the discounted cash flow analysis (Exhibit 2). For comparison, Exhibit 3 shows Adams's valuation of other paging industry stocks. Based on his analysis, Adams was optimistic about Arch's future:

---

15. "Arch Communications," Lehman Brothers, Analysts Report, August 6, 1996.

16. Arch 1995 Annual Report.

17. John Adams, Wireless Communications Industry Report, Vol. I, Wessels, Arnold & Henderson, September 1995.

We continue to rate Arch's stock Buy-Aggressive Growth. Arch reported an impressive second quarter. . . . As far as we can tell the company has not been plagued with any operating problems in 1996. . . . We believe Arch continues to do an excellent job of managing its business. . . . The company continues to show tremendous momentum in its subscriber base and operating cash. . . . There are absolutely no fundamental problems that we can detect in Arch's operating model.[18]

QUESTIONS

1. Examine the valuation estimates of John Adams in Exhibit 2 and 3. What are the strengths and weaknesses of his detailed forecasts till year 2005? What is your assessment of his terminal value assumption? What is he implicitly assuming about Arch's long-term performance in the terminal period? Is it consistent with Arch's industry structure, competitive position, and its current performance?

2. Do you agree with Adams' conclusion that Arch's stock was undervalued? Which of his assumptions are critical to his conclusion?

3. What is your own estimate of Arch's "intrinsic value" at the time of the case?

18. John Adams, Wireless Communications Industry Report, Wessels, Arnold & Henderson, August 1, 1996.

EXHIBIT I

Arch Communications Stock Price *vs.* S&P 500, November 13, 1995–July 26, 1996

(Both Rebased to 1.00 at 11/13/95)

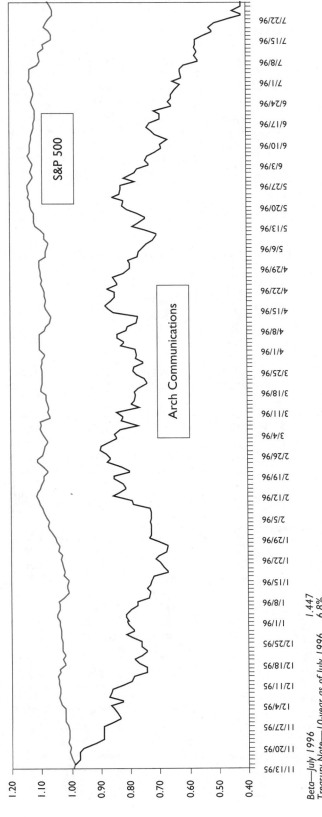

Beta—July 1996	1.447
Treasury Note—10-year as of July 1996	6.8%
Treasury Bill—30-day as of July 1996	4.8%
S&P 500 value as of November 13, 1995	592.3
Arch stock price as of November 13, 1995	$29.63

Source: Adapted from Datastream International by case writer.

Arch Communications Group

Arch Communications Group

EXHIBIT 2

Arch Communications Cash Flow Analysis (in millions, except paging units and per share information)

Fiscal Year: December	1995	1996E	1997E	1998E	1999E	2000E
Subscriber Trends (paging units):						
Beginning pagers	538,000	2,006,000	3,121,000	3,826,000	4,667,720	5,507,910
Net additions	1,468,000	1,115,000	705,000	841,720	840,190	826,186
Ending pagers	2,006,000	3,121,000	3,826,000	4,667,720	5,507,910	6,334,096
% change	272.9	55.6	22.6	22.0	18.0	15.0
Average revenue/unit/month	$11.00	$8.95	$8.29	$7.88	$7.48	$7.19
% change	—	NM	(7.3)	(5.0)	(5.0)	(4.0)
Consolidated Income Statement:						
Net revenues	$141.8	$283.2	$355.6	$444.5	$502.7	$557.7
% change	—	99.7	25.6	25.0	13.1	11.0
EBITDA (operating c.f.)	**47.2**	**102.4**	**135.9**	**171.4**	**198.0**	**225.5**
Cash flow margin (%)	33.3	36.2	38.2	38.6	39.4	40.4
Depreciation and amortization	60.2	155.7	195.6	254.9	269.7	278.7
Operating income	(13.0)	(53.3)	(59.7)	(83.4)	(71.7)	(53.2)
Interest expense	22.5	77.7	96.0	100.8	105.7	108.0
Pretax income	(39.5)	(131.0)	(155.6)	(184.2)	(177.3)	(161.2)
Taxes	(4.6)	0.0	0.0	0.0	0.0	0.0
Net income	(34.9)	(131.0)	(155.6)	(184.2)	(177.3)	(161.2)
EPS ($/share)	($2.59)	($6.51)	($7.60)	($8.82)	($8.32)	($7.42)
Cash Flow Analysis:						
EBITDA	$47.2	$102.4	$135.9	$171.4	$198.0	$225.5
Taxes	(4.6)	0.0	0.0	0.0	0.0	0.0
Capital expenditures	446.8	428.8	111.7	114.9	113.7	114.3
Pre-interest free c.f.	(395.0)	(326.4)	24.2	56.5	84.3	111.2
Interest expense	22.5	77.7	96.0	100.8	105.7	108.0
Free cash flow	(417.6)	(404.1)	(71.8)	(44.2)	(21.4)	3.2
Valuation (discounted cash flow analysis):						
PV (pre-interest free c.f.)	($134.4)	$275.6	$777.3	$948.2	$1,078.5	$1,132.4
PV final year EBITDA (10X)	854.1	972.7	1,107.7	1,261.4	1,436.5	1,635.9
Less net long-term debt	453.4	857.5	929.3	973.5	994.9	991.7
Plus PCS license	6.5	6.5	6.5	6.5	6.5	6.5
Net value	272.8	397.2	962.2	1,242.6	1,526.6	1,783.1
Net value per share	NM	NM	$47.00	$59.50	$71.67	$82.07
Fair price per share	**NM**	**NM**	**$37.60**	**$47.60**	**$57.33**	**$65.65**
Average shares	13.5	20.1	20.5	20.9	21.3	21.7
Net debt per subsidiary	$226	$275	$243	$209	$181	$157

WACC*—13.9%

What Arch's stock is worth in one year ($ per share)

*WACC assumes 7% risk free rate of return, 7% market risk premium, 1.6 Arch beta, 11% borrowing rate, and 40% equity/60% debt mix.

Source: John Adams, Wireless Communications Industry Report, Wessels, Arnold & Henderson, August 6, 1996.

Arch Communications Cash Flow Analysis *(continued)*

Fiscal Year: December	2001E	2002E	2003E	2004E	2005E
Subscriber Trends (paging units):					
Beginning pagers	6,334,096	7,157,529	7,944,857	8,659,894	9,266,086
Net additions	823,432	787,328	715,037	606,193	463,304
Ending pagers	7,157,529	7,944,857	8,659,894	9,266,086	9,729,391
% change	13.0	11.0	9.0	7.0	5.0
Average revenue/unit/month	$6.97	$6.76	$6.63	$6.49	$6.36
% change	(3.0)	(3.0)	(2.0)	(2.0)	(2.0)
Consolidated Income Statement:					
Net revenues	$611.9	$659.4	$704.7	$739.2	$760.7
% change	9.7	7.8	6.9	4.9	2.9
EBITDA (operating c.f.)	**255.2**	**283.9**	**312.7**	**337.5**	**356.8**
Cash flow margin (%)	41.7	43.1	44.4	45.7	46.9
Depreciation and amortization	286.8	217.8	170.8	125.3	118.6
Operating income	(31.6)	66.1	141.9	212.2	238.2
Interest expense	107.7	103.8	95.9	83.1	65.1
Pretax income	(139.3)	(37.7)	46.0	129.1	173.1
Taxes	0.0	0.0	0.0	0.0	0.0
Net income	(139.3)	(37.7)	46.0	129.1	173.1
EPS ($/share)	($6.28)	($1.67)	$1.99	$5.49	$7.22
Cash Flow Analysis:					
EBITDA	$255.2	$283.9	$312.7	$337.5	$356.8
Taxes	0.0	0.0	0.0	0.0	0.0
Capital expenditures	112.5	108.4	100.2	90.4	79.5
Pre-interest free c.f.	142.7	175.5	212.5	247.1	227.3
Interest expense	107.7	103.8	95.9	83.1	65.1
Free cash flow	35.0	71.7	116.4	164.0	212.2
Valuation (discounted cash flow analysis):					
Average shares	22.2	22.6	23.1	23.5	24.0

Arch Communications Group

EXHIBIT 3

Paging Sector Valuations, 1995

March 21, 1996	ACOMᵃ	APGRᵇ	APPᶜ	MBLMᵈ	MCLLᵉ	PAGEᶠ	PNETᵍ	Average
Stock price	$10.75	$23.00	$6.50	$21.00	$19.00	$25.25	$24.25	—
Year-to-date % change	-7%	-4%	6%	-5%	1%	6%	-17%	—
Subscribers:				December Quarter				
Subscriber base	529,450	2,006,000	784,500	2,369,101	944,013	6,737,907	856,302	—
ARPU, paging	$10.85	$9.70	$10.17	$10.26	$8.51	$7.86	$6.40	$9.11
AOCPU, paging	$8.79	$6.13	$8.40	$7.41	$6.41	$4.93	$4.41	$6.64
EBITDA/subscriber	$2.06	$3.57	$1.77	$2.85	$2.10	$2.92	$1.99	$2.47
Selling costs/net addition	NM	$64	NM	$72	$69	$32	$65	$60
Churn	2.9%	2.0%	2.5%	3.4%	2.6%	1.3%	1.6%	2.3%
Reseller base	46%	50%	38%	37%	42%	45%	68%	47%
Direct base	54%	50%	62%	63%	58%	55%	32%	53%
Current Growth Rate:				December Quarter				
Subscriber growth	145%	273%	20%	64%	25%	53%	142%	103%
Revenue growth	47%	224%	14%	53%	26%	38%	76%	68%
EBITDA growth	84%	303%	-5%	82%	-5%	44%	51%	79%
Margin Analysis (total company):				December Quarter				
Net revenues	100%	100%	100%	100%	100%	100%	100%	100%
Service, rental & main. exp.	47%	20%	28%	35%	32%	20%	23%	29%
Selling expense	23%	17%	17%	19%	18%	12%	17%	18%
General and administrative	17%	26%	38%	18%	25%	31%	27%	26%
EBITDA	12%	37%	17%	28%	25%	37%	31%	27%
Depreciation and amortization	34%	55%	28%	29%	43%	27%	44%	37%
Quarter End Ratio and Balance Sheet Analysis:				September Quarter				
Receivable turn (days)	34.9	22.2	43.3	30.9	54.2	19.7	43.4	35.5
Long-term debt/capital	46%	62%	67%	58%	39%	106%	59%	63%
EBITDA/interest ratio	0.9	1.8	4.5	1.5	2.6	2.2	1.8	2.2
Net debt/EBITDA ratio	2.4	5.3	5.0	4.3	0.3	3.8	4.1	3.6
Net debt/subscriber	$39	$226	$106	$144	$7	$133	$104	$108
Quarter end net debt (mil.)	$21	$453	$83	$341	$7	$894	$89	—
Value of PCS license (mil.)	$2	$7	$55	$54	$0	$197	$0	—

(continued)

☐ = strengths

March 21, 1996	ACOM[a]	APGR[b]	APP[c]	MBLM[d]	MCLL[e]	PAGE[f]	PNET[g]	Average
EBITDA Trends:								
EBITDA 1995 ($ mil.)	$4.7	$47.2	$15.7	$61.7	$27.8	$201.1	$18.4	—
EBITDA 1996E ($ mil.)	$15.1	$102.4	$20.3	$177.1	$33.8	$252.3	$27.7	—
EBITDA 1997E ($ mil.)	$22.6	$135.9	$28.5	$207.5	$43.0	$305.7	$34.2	—
Enterprise Value/EBITDA Ratio (adjusted for cash value of PCS licenses):								
1994	19.9	14.3	9.0	14.4	15.8	21.8	9.9	15.0
1995	38.7	18.9	10.6	27.8	11.0	16.6	13.4	19.6
1996E[h]	**15.6**	**12.9**	**10.1**	**11.0**	**11.4**	**13.6**	**10.7**	**12.2**
1997E	**11.2**	**10.3**	**8.8**	**10.0**	**9.3**	**12.0**	**8.9**	**10.1**
YE 1996 Enterprise value/subscriber	$308	$422	$236	$408	$266	$402	$238	$326
Discounted CF Valuation (per share):								
PMV beginning 1996	$24.92	NM	$10.66	$0.00	$29.90	$36.49	$38.62	—
PMV beginning 1997	$32.03	$47.00	$12.26	$39.91	$39.94	$41.98	$55.07	—
Fair price beginning 1996	**$19.93**	**NM**	**$8.53**	**NM**	**$23.92**	**$29.19**	**$30.90**	—
Fair price year-end 1996	**$25.62**	**$37.60**	**$9.81**	**$31.93**	**$31.95**	**$33.59**	**$44.06**	—
Appreciation potential	**138%**	**63%**	**51%**	**52%**	**68%**	**33%**	**82%**	—
Other:								
Subscribers, YE 1996	766,450	3,121,000	864,500	4,774,101	1,446,013	9,129,907	1,244,802	—
Net debt, YE 1995 (mil.)	$85	$453	$91	$920	$28	$952	$90	—
Net debt, YE 1996 (mil.)	$125	$858	$128	$1,015	$103	$1,271	$121	—
Net debt, YE 1997 (mil.)	$141	$929	$172	$1,131	$118	$1,697	$127	—
Net Debt per sub., YE 1996	$163	$275	$148	$213	$71	$139	$98	$158
1996 Cap-X/1997 EBITDA ratio	1.5	3.2	1.8	5.3	2.2	1.3	2.4	2.5
Market cap. (mil.)	$113	$467	$131	$987	$281	$2,598	$175	—
Shares outstanding, YE 1995	9.21	19.38	20.03	40.35	14.63	102.25	6.47	—
Shares outstanding, YE 1996	10.50	20.32	20.10	47.00	14.80	102.90	7.20	—
Shares outstanding, YE 1997	10.59	20.57	20.38	47.44	14.93	104.14	7.30	—
Insider stock ownership (mil. shares)	1.80	1.97	16.54	15.52	5.52	3.96	0.76	—
Insider options (mil. shares)	0.18	0.18	0.34	0.56	0.33	1.42	0.26	—

Source: John Adams, ibid.

Note: In calculating PageNet's enterprise/EBITDA ratio we add back the expected $17 million impact from VoiceNow in 1996.

Ticker Symbols: [a]A+Network. [b]Arch Communications. [c]American Paging Inc. [d]MobileMedia. [e]Metrocall. [f]PageNet. [g]ProNet.

[h]Arch pro forma enterprise multiple 10.9 × 1996 EBITDA.

Arch Communications Group

EXHIBIT 4

Arch Communications Group Abridged 1995 Annual Report

TO OUR SHAREHOLDERS:

Arch Communications Group, Inc. enjoyed unprecedented success in 1995, a year marked by explosive growth which propelled the Company into the top tier of the narrowband wireless communications industry. In this year of extraordinary growth, Arch's subscriber base increased nearly four-fold to more than 2.0 million subscribers from 538,000 at the end of 1994. Arch also produced record financial results in 1995. We now have produced 17 consecutive record quarters of sequential increases in net revenues and cash flows.

To support Arch's rapid growth we raised more than $300 million in new capital including $46 million from a public offering of common stock, and $225 million in a bank credit facility. This capital will be used for acquisitions and capital expenditures. Our ability to raise this amount of capital is a reflection of Arch's past success and future promise.

Unprecedented Growth

Arch's internal growth rate during 1995 was among the highest in the industry. This was the fourth consecutive year in which we produced almost twice as many net new customers from internal distribution channels as we had produced the previous year. During 1995 the Company tripled its quarterly internal growth from approximately 50,000 net new customers per quarter to more than 150,000. We view our 366,000 new subscribers added in 1995 as validation of our strategy for internal growth.

Acquisitions also played a significant role in our growth for the year. We closed six transactions this year which increased our subscribers by over 1.1 million. The most significant acquisition was that of USA Mobile. The $540 million transaction is the second largest in the history of the paging industry and added 959,000 subscribers to Arch.

Record Financial Performance

Financial performance in the wireless communications industry is measured primarily by operating cash flow or "EBITDA" (Earnings Before Interest, Taxes, Depreciation and Amortization). This performance measure is the basis for a company's valuation by the equity markets and an important criterion for a company's ability to secure financing. Arch achieved a record increase of EBITDA from a $20 million annualized rate at year end 1994 to more than $80 million on an annualized basis at year end 1995.

Arch's net revenues in 1995 increased 125% to $141.8 million from the $63.1 million level for 1994. Net revenues are the sum of service and product sales less cost of product sales, which is the standard presentation method in the paging industry. Our shareholder equity base, or market capitalization, increased from $135 million to $500 million.

Industry Consolidation

Arch continues to play a major role in our industry's accelerating consolidation. To date, we have completed 32 acquisitions. These acquisitions have allowed Arch to increase shareholder value by increasing our operating leverage and expanding our access to new geographic markets.

In addition to the major acquisition of USA Mobile, Arch made five other acquisitions in 1995. These consisted of The Beeper Company of America, Inc. with operations in Texas, California, and Georgia; Beta Tele-Page, Inc., with operations in Texas; Data Transmission, Inc., with operations in Georgia; Groome Enterprises, Inc., with operations in Louisiana; and Professional Paging and Radio, Inc. with operations in Florida.

At year end Arch entered into an agreement to acquire Westlink Holdings, Inc. for $340 million. This transaction is expected to close in the second quarter of 1996. Pro forma for the Westlink acquisition, Arch has 2.5 million subscribers, operating in 38 states and is the third largest paging company in the United States. Additionally, we expect our annualized EBITDA to be more than $100 million following the close.

Narrowband Personal Communications Services (NPCS)

We believe that NPCS holds promise as a platform for new narrowband wireless messaging services. Arch is well positioned to participate in this new generation of messaging services as a result of two strategic investments.

Our first investment was made in PCS Development Corporation (PCSD), a company in which Arch played a significant role in its beginnings. PCSD was formed to bid in the Federal Communications Commission 1994 auction for NPCS licenses. PCSD was a successful bidder at the auctions and acquired a national license for paired 50 KHz inbound/50 KHz outbound frequencies. These frequencies are ideally suited for voice paging and wireless data service applications. Through Arch's 10% equity position and its seat on PCSD's Board of Directors, we believe Arch will have the opportunity to offer exciting new NPCS service offerings in the future.

Our second strategic investment results from the upcoming acquisition of Westlink Holdings, Inc. As a part of this transaction, Arch will acquire a 49% equity interest in Benbow PCS Ventures. Benbow is licensed for paired 50 KHz outbound/12.5 KHz inbound frequencies that cover over half of the United States. Benbow's licenses are expected to enhance Arch's ability to be a full participant in the evolving market of NPCS.

Human Resources

As Arch's business has grown significantly in 1995, so has the depth and strength of our management team. With the acquisition of USA Mobile, Stan Sech joined us as president of USA Mobile, now our largest division. Stan brings many years of management experience in paging. Tony Ott was appointed vice president, Information Services. Tony brings to Arch over 20 years of experience in information services and telecommunications. Bob Alperin joined Arch as vice president, Business Development. Bob will be focused on expanding our strategic alliances, developing new distribution partnerships and assisting with future acquisitions. Carol Burns was named director, Human Resources. Carol has over 14 years of experience in the human resources field. We are pleased to welcome these key leaders to the Arch team.

In Conclusion

1995 was the most eventful year in Arch's history. In addition to setting records in all key operating and financial measures, we achieved the size and national geographic presence required for our future success. I want to thank all Arch team members for their dedication, commitment and high performance levels which have been so critical to our track record of operating excellence. And although all of us at Arch are proud of past accomplishments, our motivation comes from our bright prospects for the future.

C.E. Baker, Jr.

Chairman of the Board, President and Chief Executive Officer

March 12, 1996

Arch Communications Group

MANAGEMENT'S DISCUSSION AND ANALYSIS OF FINANCIAL CONDITION AND RESULTS OF OPERATIONS

Overview

Arch is a leading provider of wireless messaging services, primarily paging services, and had 2.0 million pagers in service as of December 31, 1995. From September 1, 1991 through December 31, 1995, Arch's total subscriber base grew at a compound rate on an annualized basis of 89.1% and its compound rate of internal subscriber base growth (excluding pagers added through acquisitions) on an annualized basis was 52.8%.

Arch derives the majority of its revenues from fixed periodic (usually monthly) fees, not dependent on usage, charged to subscribers for paging services. As long as a subscriber remains on service, operating results benefit from the recurring payments of the fixed periodic fees without incurrence of additional selling expenses by Arch. Arch's service, rental and maintenance revenues and the related expenses exhibit substantially similar growth trends. Arch's average paging revenue per subscriber has declined over the past three years for two principal reasons: (i) the percentage of subscriber-owned and reseller-owned pagers for which Arch receives no recurring equipment rental revenues has increased from 29% of pagers in service at August 31, 1992 to 55% of pagers in service at December 31, 1995; and (ii) the percentage of net new pagers in service added to Arch's subscriber base through indirect channels has increased from 3% in the year ended August 31, 1992 to 49% in the year ended December 31, 1995. Most of the indirect channel additions are derived from resellers who purchase air time from Arch at wholesale prices. The reduction in average paging revenue per subscriber resulting from these trends has been more than offset by the elimination of associated expenses so that Arch's margins have improved over such period.

Arch's total revenues have increased from $35.2 million in the year ended August 31, 1992 to $67.2 million in the year ended August 31, 1994, and from

$75.9 million in the year ended December 31, 1994 to $162.6 million in the year ended December 31, 1995. Over the same period, through operating efficiencies and economies of scale, Arch has been able to reduce its per pager operating costs to enhance its competitive position in its markets. Due to the rapid growth in its subscriber base, Arch has incurred significant selling expenses, which are charged to operations in the year incurred. Arch has reported net losses of $6.7 million, $5.7 million, $5.1 million, $3.3 million, $6.5 million, and $36.6 million in the years ended August 31, 1992, 1993, and 1994, the four months ended December 31, 1994 and the years ended December 31, 1994 and 1995, respectively, as a result of significant depreciation and amortization expenses related to acquired and developed assets and interest charges associated with indebtedness. However, as its subscriber base has grown, Arch's operating results have improved, as evidenced by an increase in its EBITDA from $9.8 million in the year ended August 31, 1992 to $16.0 million in the year ended August 31, 1994, and from $18.0 million in the year ended December 31, 1994 to $47.2 million in the year ended December 31, 1995.

EBITDA is a standard measure of financial performance in the paging industry and also is one of the financial measures used to calculate whether Arch and its subsidiaries are in compliance with the covenants under their respective indebtedness, but should not be construed as an alternative to operating income or cash flows from operating activities as determined in accordance with generally accepted accounting principles. Arch's financial objective is to increase its EBITDA, as such earnings are a significant source of funds for servicing indebtedness and for investment in continued growth, including purchase of pagers and paging system equipment construction and expansion of paging systems, and possible acquisitions.

On October 17, 1994, Arch announced that it was changing its fiscal year end from August 31 to December 31. Arch filed a transitional report on Form 10-K with audited financial statements for the period September 1, 1994 through December 31, 1994 and has elected to include herein, for comparative purposes, unaudited financial statements for the period September 1, 1993 through December 31, 1993. Arch's quarterly and annual reporting is now based on its new fiscal year end of December 31.

Results of Operations

The table on the facing page presents certain items from Arch's Consolidated Statements of Operations as a percentage of net revenue (total revenue less cost of products sold) and certain other information for periods indicated.

Year Ended December 31, 1995 Compared with Year Ended December 31, 1994

Total revenue increased $86.7 million, or 114.2%, to $162.6 million in the year ended December 31, 1995 from $75.9 million the year ended December 31, 1994 and net revenues increased $78.7 million, or 124.7%, from $63.1 million to $141.8 million over the same period. Service, rental and maintenance revenues, which consist primarily of recurring revenues associated with the sale or lease of pagers, increased $77.0 million, or 125.2%, to $138.5 million in the year ended December 31, 1995 from $61.5 million in the year ended December 31, 1994. These increases in revenues were due primarily to the increase in the number of pagers in service from 538,000 at December 31, 1994 to 2,006,000 at December 31, 1995. Acquisitions of paging companies added 1,102,000 pagers in service, with the remaining 366,000 pagers added through internal growth. Maintenance revenues represented less than 10% of total service, rental and maintenance revenues in the years ended December 31, 1994 and 1995. Arch does not differentiate between service and rental revenues. Product sales, less cost of products sold, increased 110.7% to $3.3 million in the year ended December 31, 1995 from $1.6 million in the year ended December 31, 1994 as a result of a greater number of pager unit sales.

Service, rental and maintenance expenses, which consist primarily of telephone line and site rental expenses, increased to $29.7 million (20.9% of net revenues) in the year ended December 31, 1995 from $14.4 million (22.8% of net revenues) in the year ended December 31, 1994. The increase in absolute dollars was due primarily to increased expenses associated with system expansions and the provision of paging services to a greater number of subscribers. The decrease as a percentage of revenues resulted from the increase in Arch's subscriber base described above. As existing paging systems became more populated through the addition of new subscribers, the fixed costs of operating these paging systems are spread over a greater subscriber base. Annualized service, rental and maintenance expenses per subscriber decreased to $28 in the year ended December 31, 1995 from $35 in the year ended December 31, 1994.

Selling expenses increased to $24.5 million (17.3% of net revenues) in the year ended December 31, 1995 from $11.5 million (18.3% of net revenues) in the year ended December 31, 1994. The increase in selling expenses was due to the addition of sales personnel to support continued growth in the subscriber base, as the number of net new pagers in service resulting from internal growth increased by 117.9% from the year ended December 31, 1994 to the year ended Decem-

	Year Ended August 31,		Four Months Ended December 31,		Year Ended December 31,	
	1993	1994	1993	1994	1994	1995
Total revenues	109.8%	117.7%	111.7%	120.1%	120.3%	114.7%
Cost of products sold	(9.8)	(17.7)	(11.7)	(20.1)	(20.3)	(14.7)
Net revenues	100.0	100.0	100.0	100.0	100.0	100.0
Operating expenses:						
Service, rental and maintenance	23.1	23.0	22.8	22.4	22.8	20.9
Selling	17.7	17.9	17.6	18.6	18.3	17.3
General and administrative	31.8	31.0	31.8	30.1	30.5	28.5
Depreciation and amortization	33.3	29.8	32.0	29.5	29.0	42.5
Operating income (loss)	(5.9)%	(1.7)%	(4.2)%	(0.6)%	(0.6)%	(9.2)%
Net income (loss)	(13.9)%	(8.9)%	(10.8)%	(14.0)%	(10.2)%	(25.8)%
EBITDA	27.4%	28.1%	27.8%	28.9%	28.5%	33.3%
Annual service, rental and maintenance expenses per pager	$ 48	$41	$44	$33	$35	$28
Selling cost per net new pager in service	$105	$74	$90	$68	$69	$67

ber 31, 1995. Arch's selling cost per net new pager in service decreased to $67 in the year ended December 31, 1995 from $69 in the year ended December 31, 1994. Most selling expenses are directly related to the number of net new subscribers added. Therefore, such expenses may increase in the future if pagers in service are added at a more rapid rate than in the past.

General and administrative expenses increased to $40.4 million (28.5% of net revenues) in the year ended December 31, 1995 from $19.2 million (30.5% of net revenues) in the year ended December 31, 1994. The increase in absolute dollars was due primarily to increased expenses associated with supporting more pagers in service.

Depreciation and amortization expenses increased to $60.2 million (42.5% of net revenues) in the year ended December 31, 1995 from $18.3 million (29.0% of net revenues) in the year ended December 31, 1994. These expenses reflect Arch's acquisitions of paging businesses, accounted for as purchases, and continued investment in pagers and other system expansion equipment to support continued growth. As a result of its September 1995 acquisition of USA Mobile, which also was accounted for under the purchase method of accounting, Arch expects its depreciation and amortization expenses to increase by approximately $70 million annually through the year ending December 31, 2002. Arch's pending acquisition of Westlink, if completed, will result in further significant increases in Arch's future depreciation and amortization expenses.

Operating loss increased to $13.0 million in the year ended December 31, 1995 from $0.4 million in the year ended December 31, 1994 as a result of the factors outlined above.

Net interest expense increased to $22.5 million in the year ended December 31, 1995 from $5.0 million in the year ended December 31, 1994. The increase was attributable to an increase in Arch's outstanding debt and higher interest rates. Arch expects its future interest expense to increase significantly as a result of additional debt incurred in connection with its September 1995 acquisition of USA Mobile, its pending Westlink acquisition, and other acquisitions.

During the year ended December 31, 1995, Arch recognized an income tax benefit of $4.6 million representing the tax benefit of operating losses subsequent to September 7, 1995 which were available to offset previously established deferred tax liabilities arising from Arch's acquisition of USA Mobile. Arch expects to recognize the $28.9 million balance of such tax benefit in the year ending December 31, 1996.

During the year ended December 31, 1995, Arch recognized an extraordinary charge of $1.7 million, representing the write-off of unamortized deferred financing costs associated with the prepayment of indebtedness under a prior credit facility in May 1995. During the year ended December 31, 1994, Arch recognized an extraordinary charge of $1.1 million, representing the write-off of unamortized deferred financing costs associated with the prepayment of indebtedness under a prior credit facility in September 1994.

Net loss increased to $36.6 million in the year ended December 31, 1995 from $6.5 million in the year ended December 31, 1994 as a result of the factors outlined above. Included in the net loss for the year ended December 31, 1995 was a charge of $4.0 million representing Arch's pro rata share of USA Mobile's net loss for the period of time from Arch's acquisition of its initial 37% interest in USA Mobile on

May 16, 1995 through the completion of Arch's acquisition of USA Mobile on September 7, 1995. The increases in depreciation and amortization expenses attributable to Arch's September 1995 acquisition of USA Mobile and its pending acquisition of Westlink, as described above, will increase Arch's future net losses (or decrease its future net income, if any).

EBITDA increased 162.6% to $47.2 million (33.3% of net revenues) in the year ended December 31, 1995 from $18.0 million (28.5% of net revenues) in the year ended December 31, 1994 as a result of the factors outlined above.

Recent and Pending Acquisitions

In September 1995, Arch completed its acquisition of USA Mobile for aggregate consideration of $582.2 million, consisting of $88.9 million in cash (including direct transaction cost), 7,599,493 shares of common stock valued at $209.0 million on the date of completion and the assumption of liabilities of $284.3 million, including $241.2 million of long-term debt. The acquisition was completed in two steps. The first step, Arch acquired an aggregate of 5,450,000 shares of USA Mobile common stock, representing approximately 37% of USA Mobile's then outstanding capital stock, in a tender offer completed in May 1995 for $15.40 per share. On September 7, 1995, Arch completed its acquisition of USA Mobile through the merger of Arch with and into USA Mobile. In accordance with generally accepted accounting principles, Arch was treated as the acquirer in such transaction for accounting and financial reporting purposes. See Note 2 to Consolidated Financial Statements.

During 1995, Arch also completed five additional acquisitions for aggregate consideration of $36.1 million in cash plus the issuance of 395,000 shares of common stock valued at $6.9 million on the date of completion. See Note 2 to Arch's Consolidated Financial Statements.

In December 1995, Arch entered into a definitive agreement to acquire Westlink for approximately $340 million in cash, subject to adjustment by the amount of certain budgeted or approved capital expenditures made by Westlink prior to the closing less the increase in Westlink's bank indebtedness between December 17, 1995 and the closing.

Arch has pursued and intends to continue to pursue acquisitions of paging businesses as part of its growth strategy. As a result, Arch evaluates acquisition opportunities on an ongoing basis and from time to time is engaged in discussions with respect to possible acquisitions. On December 5, 1995, Arch entered into a letter of intent to acquire a paging business for $14.0

million, subject to adjustment, of which $7.5 million would be paid in cash and $6.5 million would be paid through the issuance of unregistered common stock. The acquisition is subject to the execution of a definitive purchase agreement, regulatory approvals and other conditions, and no assurance can be given that the acquisition will be completed.

Sources of Funds

Arch's net cash provided by operating activities was $7.9 million, $8.7 million, $14.8 million, $4.7 million, $14.2 million, and $14.7 million in the years ended August 31, 1992, 1993 and 1994, and four months ended December 31, 1994 and the years ended December 31, 1994 and 1995, respectively.

In February 1995, Arch completed a public offering of 4,600,000 shares of common stock, of which 2,701,296 shares were sold by Arch for net proceeds of $46.2 million and 1,898,704 shares were sold by certain stockholders of Arch (including 1,295,000 shares sold by the former owners of certain paging businesses acquired by Arch). Arch used its proceeds to repay borrowings of $46.2 million under a prior credit facility.

On February 7, 1996, the Company commenced an offer (the "Conversion Offer") to pay a cash premium of $110 for each $1,000 principal amount of the Company's 6-3/4% Convertible Subordinated Debentures due 2003 ("Arch Convertible Debentures") converted into common stock at $16.75 per share. Effective upon the expiration of the Conversion Offer at 12:00 midnight, Eastern Time, on March 6, 1996, the Company accepted for conversion $14,121,000 in principal amount of Arch Convertible Debentures in exchange for an aggregate of approximately 843,000 shares of common stock and $1.6 million in cash.

On March 12, 1996, Arch completed a public offering of 10-7/8% Senior Discount Notes due 2008 (the Senior Discount Notes) in the aggregate principal amount of $467.4 million ($275.0 million initial accreted value). Interest does not accrue on the Senior Discount Notes prior to March 15, 2001. Commencing September 15, 2001, interest on the Senior Discount Notes is payable semi-annually at an annual rate of 10-7/8%. The $266.1 million net proceeds from the issuance of the Senior Discount Notes, after deducting underwriting discounts and commissions and offering expenses, will be used principally to fund a portion of the purchase price of Arch's pending acquisition of Westlink. Pending completion of Westlink acquisition, Arch used $225.0 million of the net proceeds to repay existing indebtedness under Arch's credit facilities, with the remainder primarily invested in short-term, interest-bearing instruments. See Notes 3 and 9 to Arch's Consolidated Financial Statements.

Future Capital Needs

The Company's business strategy requires the availability of substantial funds to finance the continued development and further growth and expansion of its operations, including the Company's pending acquisition of Westlink and other possible acquisitions. The amount of capital required by the Company will depend upon a number of factors, including subscriber growth, technical developments, marketing and sales expenses, competitive conditions, acquisition strategy and acquisition opportunities. No assurance can be given that additional equity or debt financing will be available to the Company on acceptable terms, if at all. The unavailability of sufficient financing when needed would have a material adverse effect on the Company.

Arch Communications Group

CONSOLIDATED BALANCE SHEETS

In 1994 Arch changed its fiscal year end from August 31 to December 31. Included herein are statements covering the period from September 1 to December 31, 1994. Arch's financial reporting is now based on its new fiscal year end of December 31.

December 31, (in thousands, except share amounts)	1994	1995
Assets		
Current assets:		
Cash	$ 2,351	$ 3,643
Accounts receivable (less reserves of $707 and $2,125 in 1994 and 1995, respectively)	4,632	14,278
Inventories	—	11,801
Due from employees	47	41
Prepaid expenses and other	1,453	3,908
Total current assets	8,483	33,671
Property and equipment, at cost:		
Land, buildings, and improvements	3,333	6,813
Paging and computer equipment	73,992	191,461
Furniture, fixtures, and vehicles	2,935	7,362
	80,260	205,636
Less accumulated depreciation and amortization	23,130	36,390
Property and equipment, net	57,130	169,246
Intangible and other assets (less accumulated amortization of $14,255 and $44,915 in 1994 and 1995, respectively)	52,245	582,459
	$117,858	$785,376
Liabilities and Stockholders' Equity		
Current liabilities:		
Current maturities of long-term debt	$ 86	$ 166
Accounts payable	8,567	22,463
Accrued expenses	3,044	8,947
Accrued interest	391	7,845
Customer deposits	1,182	5,258
Deferred revenue	1,800	4,493
Total current liabilities	15,070	49,172
Long-term debt, less current maturities	93,420	457,044
Deferred income taxes	—	28,900
Commitments (Note 6)		
Redeemable preferred stock	—	3,376
Stockholders' equity:		
Preferred stock—$.01 par value, authorized 10,000,000 shares, no shares issued	—	—
Common stock—$.01 par value, authorized 75,000,000 shares, issued and outstanding: 8,058,665, and 19,653,031 shares in 1994 and 1995 respectively	81	197
Additional paid-in capital	60,823	334,825
Accumulated deficit	(51,536)	(88,138)
Total stockholders' equity	9,368	246,884
	$117,858	$785,376

The accompanying notes are an integral part of these consolidated financial statements.

Arch Communications Group

CONSOLIDATED STATEMENT OF OPERATIONS

In 1994 Arch changed its fiscal year end from August 31 to December 31. Included herein are statements covering the period from September 1 to December 31, 1994. Arch's financial reporting is now based on its new fiscal year end of December 31.

(in thousands, except share and per amounts)	Years Ended August 31,		Four Months Ended December 31,		Year Ended December 31,
	1993	1994	1993 (unaudited)	1994	1995
Service, rental and maintenance revenues	$ 39,610	$ 55,139	$ 16,457	$ 22,847	$ 138,466
Product sales	5,698	12,108	2,912	5,178	24,132
Total revenues	45,308	67,247	19,369	28,025	162,598
Cost of products sold	(4,031)	(10,124)	(2,027)	(4,690)	(20,789)
	41,277	57,123	17,342	23,335	141,809
Operating expenses:					
Service, rental and maintenance	9,532	13,123	3,959	5,231	29,673
Selling	7,307	10,243	3,058	4,338	24,502
General and administrative	13,123	17,717	5,510	7,022	40,448
Depreciation and amortization	13,764	16,997	5,549	6,873	60,205
Total operating expenses	43,726	58,080	18,076	23,464	154,828
Operating income (loss)	(2,449)	(957)	(734)	(129)	(13,019)
Interest expense	(3,036)	(4,221)	(1,138)	(2,009)	(22,560)
Interest income	175	109	6	16	38
Equity in loss of affiliate	—	—	—	—	(3,977)
Income (loss) before income tax benefit and extraordinary item	(5,310)	(5,069)	(1,866)	(2,122)	(39,518)
Benefit from income taxes	—	—	—	—	4,600
Income (loss) before extraordinary item	(5,310)	(5,069)	(1,866)	(2,122)	(34,918)
Extraordinary charge from early extinguishment of debt	(415)	—	—	(1,137)	(1,684)
Net income (loss)	(5,725)	(5,069)	(1,866)	(3,259)	(36,602)
Accretion of redeemable preferred stock	—	—	—	—	(102)
Net income (loss) to common stockholders	$ (5,725)	$ (5,069)	$ (1,866)	$ (3,259)	$ (36,704)
Income (loss) per common share before extraordinary item	$ (.74)	$ (.71)	$ (.26)	$ (.29)	$ (2.59)
Extraordinary charge from early extinguishment of debt	(.06)	—	—	(.16)	(.12)
Accretion of redeemable preferred stock	—	—	—	—	(.01)
Net income (loss) per common share	$ (.80)	$ (.71)	$ (.26)	$ (.45)	$ (2.72)
Weighted average number of common shares outstanding	7,125,164	7,153,044	7,149,136	7,238,624	13,497,734

The accompanying notes are an integral part of these consolidated financial statements.

Arch Communications Group

Arch Communications Group

CONSOLIDATED STATEMENT OF CASH FLOWS

In 1994 Arch changed its fiscal year end from August 31 to December 31. Included herein are statements covering the period from September 1 to December 31, 1994. Arch's financial reporting is now based on its new fiscal year end of December 31.

(in thousands)	Years Ended August 31,		Four Months Ended December 31,		Year Ended December 31,
	1993	1994	1993	1994	1995
			(unaudited)		
Cash flows from operating activities:					
Net income (loss)	$ (5,725)	$ (5,069)	$ (1,866)	$ (3,259)	$(36,602)
Adjustments to reconcile net income (loss) to net cash provided by operating activities:					
Depreciation and amortization	13,764	16,997	5,549	6,873	60,205
Deferred tax benefit	—	—	—	—	(4,600)
Extraordinary charge from early extinguishment of debt	415	—	—	1,137	1,684
Equity in loss of affiliate	—	—	—	—	3,977
Accretion of discount on subordinated note	70	—	—	—	—
Accounts receivable loss provision	873	1,239	389	649	3,915
Changes in assets and liabilities, net of effect from acquisitions of paging companies:					
Accounts receivable	(1,296)	(2,683)	(929)	(855)	(9,582)
Inventories	—	—	—	—	(3,176)
Due from employees	8	16	15	2	6
Prepaid expenses and other	(419)	(197)	(164)	(156)	(517)
Accounts payable	23	2,633	2,143	2,338	3,535
Accrued expenses	681	1,093	108	(1,382)	(5,089)
Accrued interest	(143)	523	123	(279)	1,003
Customer deposits	81	248	10	(173)	262
Deferred revenue	389	(19)	(72)	(215)	(272)
Net cash provided by operating activities	8,721	14,781	5,306	4,680	14,749
Cash flows from investing activities:					
Additions to property and equipment, net	(16,607)	(21,506)	(5,340)	(9,438)	(45,331)
Additions to intangible and other assets	(4,246)	(4,151)	(2,146)	(5,841)	(15,137)
Acquisition of paging companies, net of cash acquired	(10,145)	(3,325)	—	(15,085)	(132,081)
Net cash used for investing activities	(30,998)	(28,982)	(7,486)	(30,364)	(192,549)
Cash flows from financing activities:					
Issuance of long-term debt	13,323	40,225	35,225	58,872	191,617
Repayment of long-term debt	(2,061)	(25,791)	(24,125)	(32,776)	(63,705)
Net proceeds from sale of common stock	6	202	190	12	51,180
Net cash provided by financing activities	11,268	14,636	11,290	26,108	179,092
Net increase (decrease) in cash & equivalents	(11,009)	435	9,110	424	1,292
Cash, beginning of period	12,501	1,492	1,492	1,927	2,351
Cash, end of period	$ 1,492	$ 1,927	$ 10,602	$ 2,351	$ 3,643

The accompanying notes are an integral part of these consolidated financial statements.

NOTES TO CONSOLIDATED FINANCIAL STATEMENTS

1. Organizational and Significant Accounting Policies

Organization Arch Communication Group, Inc. (Arch) is a leading provider of wireless messaging services, primarily paging services.

Principles of consolidation The accompanying consolidating financial statements include the accounts of Arch and its wholly-owned subsidiaries. All significant inter-company accounts and transactions have been eliminated.

Revenue recognition Arch recognizes revenue under rental and service agreements with customers as the related services are performed. Maintenance revenues and related costs are recognized ratably over the respective terms of the agreements. Sales of equipment are recognized upon delivery. Commissions are recognized as an expense when incurred.

Inventories Inventories consist of new pagers which are held specifically for resale. Inventories are stated at the lower of cost or market, with cost determined on a first-in, first-out basis.

Property and equipment Effective June 1, 1993, Arch changed its estimate of the useful life of pagers from five years to four years. This change was made to better reflect the estimated period during which pagers will produce equipment rental revenue. The change had the effect of increasing depreciation expense and net loss by approximately $700,000 ($.10 per share) in the quarter ended August 31, 1993.

Effective October 1, 1995, Arch changed its estimate of the useful life of pagers from four years to three years. This change was made to better reflect the estimated period during which pagers will produce equipment rental revenue. The change did not have a material effect on depreciation expense or net loss in the quarter ended December 31, 1995.

Pagers sold or otherwise retired are removed from the accounts at their net book value using the first-in, first-out method.

Arch provides for depreciation and amortization using the straight-line method over the following estimated useful lives:

Asset Classification	Estimated Useful Life
Buildings and improvements	20 Years
Leasehold improvements	Lease Term
Paging and computer equipment	3-8 Years
Furniture and fixtures	5-8 Years
Vehicles	3 Years

Intangible and other assets Intangible and other assets, net of accumulated amortization, are composed of the following at December 31, 1994 and 1995:

(in thousands)	1994	1995
Purchased subscriber lists	$ 5,675	$ 96,686
Purchased FCC licenses	22,886	174,533
Goodwill	12,722	283,814
Non-competition agreements	963	5,321
Deferred financing costs	3,867	6,012
Investment In PCS Development Corporation	1,419	6,500
Other	4,713	9,593
	$52,245	$582,459

Subscriber lists, Federal Communications Commission (FCC) licenses and goodwill are amortized over their estimated useful lives, ranging from five to ten years using the straight-line method. Non-competition agreements are amortized over the terms of the agreements using the straight-line method. Other assets consist of contract rights, organizational and FCC application and development costs, which are amortized using the straight-line method over their estimated useful lives not exceeding ten years. Development costs include non-recurring, direct costs incurred in the development and expansion of paging systems, and are amortized over a two-year period.

Deferred financing costs incurred in connection with Arch's credit agreements (see Note 3) are being amortized over periods not to exceed the terms of the related agreements. As credit agreements are amended or renegotiated, unamortized deferred financing costs are written off as an extraordinary charge. For the four months ended December 31, 1994, a charge of $1,137,000 was recognized, and an additional charge of $1,684,000 was recognized in the second quarter of 1995 in connection with the closing of a new credit facility in May 1995.

On November 8, 1994, PCS Development Corporation (PCSD) was successful in acquiring the rights to a two-way paging license in five designated regions in the United States in the FCC narrowband wireless spectrum auction. Upon completion of the Merger, Arch's equity interest in PCSD became 17.47% but was subsequently diluted to 10.5%. As of December 31, 1995, Arch's investment in PCSD totaled $6.5 million.

Arch evaluates the realizability of goodwill and other intangible assets based on estimated cash flows to be generated from each of such assets as compared to the original estimates used in measuring the assets. To the extent impairment is identified, Arch recognizes a write-down. To date, Arch has not had any such impairments.

Fair value of financial instruments Arch's financial instruments, as defined under Statement of Financial Accounting Standards (SFAS) No. 107, include its cash and its debt financing. The fair value of cash is equal to the carrying value at December 31, 1995.

As discussed in Note 3, Arch's debt financing consists primarily of (1) senior bank debt, (2) fixed rate senior notes, and (3) convertible subordinated debentures. Arch considers the fair value of senior bank debt to be equal to the carrying value since the related facilities bear a current market rate of interest. Arch is unable to determine the fair value of the convertible subordinated debentures due to the specific terms and conversion features available in their respective agreements. These various facilities were negotiated with creditors based on the facts and circumstances available at the time the debt was incurred. Since Arch has undergone significant change over the past year, management is unable to determine what rates and terms would be available currently.

Arch's fixed rate senior notes are traded publicly. The following depicts the fair value of this debt based on the current market quotes as of December 31, 1995:

Description (in thousands)	Carrying Value	Fair Value
9-1/2% Senior Notes due 2004 of USA Mobile II	$125,000	$129,000
14% Senior Notes due 2004 of USA Mobile II	100,000	111,000

Net income (loss) per common share Net income (loss) per common share is based on the weighted average number of common shares outstanding. Shares of stock issuable pursuant to stock options and upon conversion of the subordinated debentures (see Note 3) have not been considered, as their effect would be antidilutive.

Use of estimates The preparation of financial statements in conformity with generally accepted accounting principles requires management to make estimates and assumptions that affect the reported amounts of assets and liabilities and disclosure of contingent assets and liabilities at the date of the financial statements and the reported amounts of revenues and expenses during the reported period. Actual results could differ from those estimates.

Unaudited interim consolidated financial statements The consolidated statements of operations and cash flows for the four months ended December 31, 1993 are unaudited and, in the opinion of Arch's management, include all adjustments, consisting of normal, recurring adjustments, necessary for a fair presentation of Arch's consolidated financial position, results of operations, and cash flows. The results of operations for the four months ended December 31, 1993 are not necessarily indicative of the results of any other period.

Change in year end In October 1994, Arch changed its fiscal year end from August 31 to December 31. Arch's quarterly and annual reporting is now based on Arch's new fiscal year end.

Reclassifications Certain amounts of prior periods were reclassified to conform to the 1995 presentation.

2. Acquisitions

During the year ended August 31, 1993, Arch acquired, in separate transactions, four paging systems located in New York, New Hampshire, and Maine for an aggregate purchase price of approximately $10,100,000.

During the year ended August 31, 1994, Arch acquired a paging system located in Rhode Island for approximately $3,325,000.

During the four months ended December 31, 1994, Arch acquired in separate transactions the paging assets of a system located in Florida and the stock of a paging company located in Illinois and Wisconsin for an aggregate purchase price of approximately $31 million including 900,000 shares of Arch common stock valued at $15.9 million. In connection with the stock acquisition, the fair value of assets acquired was approximately $33 million less liabilities assumed of approximately $2 million. In December 1994, Arch purchased certain paging system assets and frequencies from BellSouth Telecommunications, Inc. for approximately $500,000 in cash.

On September 7, 1995, Arch completed its acquisition of USA Mobile Communications Holdings, Inc. (USA Mobile). The acquisition was completed in two steps. First, in May 1995, Arch acquired approximately 37%, or 5,450,000 shares, of USA Mobile's then outstanding common stock for $83.9 million in cash, funded by borrowings under the Arch Enterprises Credit Facility (see Note 3). Second, on September 7, 1995, the acquisition was completed through the merger of Arch with and into USA Mobile (the Merger). Upon consummation of the Merger, USA Mobile was renamed Arch Communications Group, Inc. In the Merger, each share of USA Mobile's outstanding common stock was exchanged for Arch common stock on a .8020-for-one-basis (an aggregate of 7,599,493 shares of Arch common stock) and the

5,450,000 USA Mobile shares purchased by Arch in May 1995 were retired. Outstanding shares of USA Mobile's Series A Redeemable Preferred Stock remained outstanding and were not otherwise affected by the Merger (see Note 4).

Arch is treated as the acquirer in the Merger for accounting and financial reporting purposes. The aggregate consideration paid or exchanged in the Merger was $582.2 million, consisting of cash paid of $88.9 million, including direct transaction costs, 7,599,493 shares of Arch common stock valued at $209.0 million and the assumption of liabilities of $284.3 million, including $241.2 million long-term debt.

During the year ended December 31, 1995, Arch completed five acquisitions of paging companies, in addition to the Merger, for purchase prices aggregating approximately $43.0 million, consisting of cash of $36.1 million and 395,000 shares of Arch common stock valued at $6.9 million. Goodwill resulting from the acquisitions and the Merger is being amortized over a ten-year period using the straight-line method.

These acquisitions have been accounted for as purchases, and the results of their operations have been included in the consolidated financial statements from the dates of the respective acquisitions. The following unaudited pro forma summary presents the consolidated results of operations as if the acquisitions had occurred at the beginning of the periods presented, after giving effect to certain adjustments, including depreciation and amortization of acquired assets and interest expense on acquisition debt. These pro forma results have been prepared for comparative purposes only and do not purport to be indicative of what would have occurred had the acquisitions been made at the beginning of the period presented, or of results that may occur in the future.

3. Long-Term Debt

Long-term debt consisted of the following at December 31, 1994 and 1995:

(in thousands)	1994	1995
Senior bank debt	$58,872	$204,500
9-1/2% Senior Notes due 2004 of USA Mobile II	—	125,000
14% Senior Notes due 2004 of USA Mobile II	—	100,000
Convertible subordinated debentures	34,475	27,485
Non-competition agreement obligations	135	210
Capital lease obligations	24	15
	93,506	457,210
Less-current maturities	86	166
Long-term debt	$93,420	$457,044

9. Subsequent Events

On March 6, 1996, the holders of $14.1 million principal amount of Arch Convertible Debentures (see Note 3) elected to convert their Arch Convertible Debentures into Arch common stock at a conversion price of $16.75 per share and received approximately 843,000 shares of Arch common stock, together with a $1.6 million cash premium.

On March 12, 1996, Arch completed a public offering of 10-7/8% Senior Discount Notes due 2008 (the Senior Discount Notes) in the aggregate principal amount of $467.4 million ($275.0 million initial accreted value). Interest does not accrue on the Senior Discount Notes prior to March 15, 2001. Commencing September 15, 2001, interest on the Senior Discount Notes is payable semi-annually at an annual rate of 10-7/8%. The $266.1 million net proceeds from the issuance of the Senior Discount Notes, after deducting underwriting discounts and commissions

(unaudited)	Year Ended August 31,	Four Months Ended December 31,		Year Ended December 31,
	1994	1993	1994	1995
Revenues	$155,566	$42,093	$67,512	$249,507
Income (loss) before extraordinary item	(75,523)	(25,161)	(25,188)	(71,806)
Net income (loss)	(75,523)	(25,161)	(26,325)	(73,490)
Net income (loss) per common share	(4.71)	(1.57)	(1.64)	(3.93)

On December 17, 1995, Arch entered into a definitive stock purchase agreement to acquire Westlink Holdings, Inc. for approximately $340 million in cash subject to adjustment by the amount of certain budgeted or approved capital expenditures made by Westlink prior to the closing less the increase in Westlink's bank indebtedness between December 17, 1995 and the closing. This acquisition is subject to closing conditions, including FCC approval.

and offering expenses, principally will be used to fund a portion of the purchase price of Arch's pending acquisition of Westlink (see Note 2). Pending completion of the Westlink acquisition, Arch used $225.0 million of the net proceeds to repay existing indebtedness under Arch's credit facilities, with the remainder primarily invested in short-term, interest-bearing instruments.

Arch Communications Group

Arch Communications Group

REPORT OF INDEPENDENT PUBLIC ACCOUNTS

To Arch Communications Group, Inc.:

We have audited the accompanying consolidated balance sheets of Arch Communications Group, Inc. (a Delaware corporation) and subsidiaries as of December 31, 1994 and 1995 and the related consolidated statements of operations, stockholders' equity (deficit) and cash flows for each of the two years in the period ended August 31, 1994, for the four months ended December 31, 1994 and the year ended December 31, 1995. These financial statements are the responsibility of Arch's management. Our responsibility is to express an opinion on these financial statements based on our audit.

We conducted our audit in accordance with generally accepted accounting standards. Those standards require that we plan and perform the audit to obtain reasonable assurance about whether the financial statements are free of material misstatement. An audit includes examining, on a test basis, evidence supporting the amounts and disclosures in the financial statements. An audit also includes assessing the accounting principles used and significant estimates made by management, as well as evaluating the overall financial statement presentation. We believe that our audits provide a reasonable basis for our opinion.

In our opinion, the financial statements referred to above present fairly, in all material respects, the financial position of Arch Communications Group, Inc. and subsidiaries as of December 31, 1994 and 1995 and the results of their operations and their cash flows for each of the two years in the period ended August 31, 1994, for the four months ended December 31, 1994 and the year ended December 31, 1995, in conformity with generally accepted accounting principals.

Arthur Andersen LLP

Boston, Massachusetts
February 15, 1996 (except with respect to Note 9 as to which the date is March 12, 1996)

Boston Chicken, Inc.

Perhaps no company better captures the spirit of the new economy than Boston Chicken Inc., which aims to do for the rotisserie what Colonel Sanders did for the deep fryer. . . . There is nothing particularly new about rotisserie chicken—those birds have been turning succulently in delicatessen windows for generations. But Boston Chicken is not really about poultry—it is about developing a market-winning formula for picking real estate, designing stores, organizing a franchise operation and analyzing data. These are Boston Chicken's innovations—trade secrets that can be every bit as valuable as a new drug or computer chip design. With them, Boston Chicken has not only developed the secret for delivering generous quantities of home-cooking at affordable prices, but also transformed what had been a mom-and-pop business into a new national category—take-out home-cooked food—that potentially can draw business away from both supermarkets and restaurants.

The Washington Post, July 4, 1994

Boston Chicken was founded in 1989 by Scott Beck to operate and franchise food service stores that sold meals featuring rotisserie-cooked chicken, fresh vegetables, salads, and other side dishes. The firm's concept was to combine fresh, flavorful, and appealing meals associated with traditional home cooking with a high level of convenience and value. Meals cost less than $5 per person, were sold in bright, inviting retail stores, and were available for take-out or for on-site consumption. "Our strategy," Beck noted, "is to be a home meal replacement. Our number one competitor is pizza."[1]

To help operationalize his vision, Beck assembled a management team with considerable prior experience in both the fast-food business and franchising operations. Beck himself became one of the first and largest franchisees for Blockbuster Video while still in his twenties. He later sold his franchises back to the parent company for $120 million. Other top executives included the former president of Kentucky Fried Chicken, and former vice-presidents of Bennigan's, Taco Bell, Red Lobster, Chili's, and Baker's Square.

COMPANY STRUCTURE AND GROWTH STRATEGY

By the end of 1994, the Boston Chicken system operated 534 stores, compared to only 34 stores at the end of 1991. This translated to an annual rate of growth of almost 500 percent per year, with a new store being opened on average every two days. As reported in the financial statements presented in Exhibit 1, revenues for this period increased dramatically, from $5.2 million in 1991 to $96.2 million in 1994 and net income rose to $16.2 million (from a loss of $2.6 million). This growth continued throughout 1995; by the third quarter there were more than 750 stores in operation and quarterly sales had reached $38 million (see Exhibit 2 for a summary of quarterly results). The company was voted "America's Favorite Chicken Chain" in a 1995 survey published by *Restaurant and Institutions* magazine.

Professor Paul M. Healy prepared this case. The case is intended solely as the basis for class discussion and is not intended to serve as an endorsement, source of primary data, or illustration of effective or ineffective management. Copyright © 1997 by the President and Fellows of Harvard College. HBS Case 9-198-032.

1. The Washington Post, *July 4, 1994.*

To provide financing for its rapid growth, Boston Chicken went public in November 1993. The offering, for 1.9 million shares, was highly successful, as the stock price soared from the initial offering price of $10 to a high of $26.50. However, within months of the offer the stock had fallen back to $18. Nonetheless, a second offering for two million shares at $18.50 in August 1994 was oversubscribed. The company responded by increasing the offer to six million shares, raising $105 million of new capital (after issue costs).

Competition in the $200 billion restaurant industry was fierce, and several other companies were quick to take advantage of Boston Chicken's success. For example, in mid-1993 Pepsico's Kentucky Fried Chicken (KFC) introduced "rotisserie-gold" roasted chicken in most of its 5,100 restaurants. Within four months KFC reported that sales of the new chicken had topped $160 million, making KFC the world's largest rotisserie chicken chain. KFC spent $100 million to launch the new product, including a national network advertising campaign. However, some analysts believed that Boston Chicken's biggest challenge would not come from other competitors, but on how well the company met its goals.[2]

In its 1994 Annual Report, Boston Chicken described its main goals as strengthening its area developer organizations, creating communications infrastructure to support area developers, building an organization to continue new market development, and continuing operational improvements to ensure that the retail concept kept pace with changes in consumer tastes.

Area Developer Organizations

The company's franchising strategy was different from that of most other successful franchisers. Instead of selling store franchises to a large number of small franchisees, Boston Chicken focused on franchising to large regional developers. It established a network of 22 regional franchises, which targeted the 60 largest U.S. metropolitan markets. Each franchise was expected to have the scale necessary to ensure operational efficiency and marketing clout. The typical franchisee was an independent businessman with 15–20 years of relevant management experience, strong financial resources, and a mandate to open 50 to 100 new stores in the region. This structure was intended to provide the entrepreneurial energy of a franchise operation with the control and economies of scale of company-owned operations.

Under typical franchise agreements, developers paid Boston Chicken a one-time $35,000 per store franchise fee, a $10,000 fee to cover grand opening expenses, and an annual 5 percent royalty on gross revenues. In addition, franchisees contributed 2 percent and 3.75 percent of sales per year, respectively, for national and local advertising campaigns. In 1994 royalties from these agreements amounted to $17.4 million, and initial franchise fees for new stores were $13 million. The company also earned interest income from franchise developers, since it provided a line of credit to assist them in new store development. This source of revenue grew rapidly in 1994 to $11.6 million. Other revenue sources included income from leasing some of its stores to franchise operators, and fees for software services provided to developers.

Area developer financing was provided to qualifying developers to assist them in expanding their operations. Under these arrangements, Boston Chicken provided the developer with a revolving line of credit which became available once at least 75 percent of the developer's equity capital had been spent on developing stores. The agreement provided limits on the amount that the developer could draw over time, primarily as a function of developers' equity capital. Once the drawing period expired, the loan converted to an amortizing four- to five-year term loan, with a variable interest rate set at 1 percent over the Bank of America Illinois "reference rate." Some loans also included a conversion option, permitting Boston Chicken to convert the loan into equity in the developer after two years, usually at a 12–15 percent premium over the equity price at the loan's inception.

Communications Infrastructure

The company invested $8–10 million to build computer software that provided support for its network of stores, and linked headquarters to developer stores. This software used information entered at the checkout counter to advise store managers when to put on another rack of chickens or to heat up another tray of mashed potatoes. It made appropriate adjustments for the day of the week, the season, and customer preferences at a particular store in making its recommendations. The software also provided information on employee work schedules to match daily peaks in customer purchases, automatically reordered food supplies from approved vendors, and updated the store's financial performance on an hourly basis.

New Market Development

New store site selection was critical to the company's future success. In 1995 it employed more than 180 real estate and construction professionals to ensure that the pace of development was sustained and that site standards were maintained. Given these resources the company was optimistic that it could open at least 325 new stores per year in the foreseeable future.

Operating Improvements

In 1994 the company implemented a number of plans to improve operating efficiency and reduce store-level costs. These included long-term agreements with key suppliers, the introduction of flagship stores, expanded menus, in-store computer feedback from customers, and drive-thru lanes. Long-term agreements with suppliers provided opportunities to lock in prices for key inputs. For example, in October 1994 the firm reached a five-year cost-plus agreement with Hudson Foods to purchase the entire capacity from two Hudson poultry processing plants.

Flagship stores included a retail store and a kitchen facility with enough space and equipment to perform the initial stages of food preparation, such as washing and chopping vegetables, for up to 20 "satellite" stores. Prepared food was then sent to satellite stores, which completed the cooking process and served the products. This concept increased the quality and freshness of the side items, because a flagship had more frequent delivery of fresh ingredients. It also led to greater consistency in food taste, facilitated increased innovation in menu items (since there were fewer production people to train), and utilized facilities more effectively.

In fall 1994 the company added vegetable pot pies, Caesar salad, and cinnamon apples to its menu to satisfy customer demand for more variety in food offerings. Rotisserie-roasted turkey, ham, and meat loaf entrees were added in mid-1995. Stores offering these new products showed double-digit sales gains without any significant new advertising campaign. A new line of deli-type sandwiches featuring turkey, ham, and meat loaf on fresh-baked bread was also added to boost lunch sales. In 1995 the firm invested $20 million in Progressive Bagels (PBCI), a retailer of fresh gourmet bagels. Under this agreement, Boston Chicken provided an eight-year senior secured loan to Progressive Bagels, as well as providing administrative, real estate, and systems support services. Management argued that this investment provided the firm with the opportunity to learn more about the potential of morning service, which could further increase store productivity. By late 1995 this investment was increased to $80 million, and PBCI had grown to 53 stores (from a base of 20 units), with plans to open 200–225 stores in 1996. Finally, in an attempt to increase sales in the traditionally weak fourth quarter, the company began offering whole hams and turkeys for Thanksgiving and Christmas meals. As a result of these expanded product offerings, Boston Chicken decided to change its name to Boston Market.

In 1995 the company began using technology to keep in better touch with store customers. Touch-activated computer terminals were added to some stores, enabling customers to rate the quality of food and service. Blaine Hurst, the former Ernst & Young partner who headed Boston Chicken's computer operations, pointed out, "If I can save half a percentage point on food costs, that's a lot of money. But if I can know almost instantaneously that customers don't like the drink selection and I can have that changed within a week— that's worth a lot more money."

Finally, to improve convenience for customers, the company decided to add drive-thru lanes to its stores. By late 1994, 62 stores in eighteen states had drive-thru windows. In some cases, as much as 30 percent of store sales came from these windows. The company's market research indicates that as many as two-thirds of these customers would not have visited the stores had this convenience not been available. Drive-thrus were planned for a further 65 stores in 1995, and ultimately 70 percent of the stores were expected to be converted to drive-thru.

EXPECTED FUTURE PERFORMANCE

In late 1995, most restaurant analysts were bullish about Boston Chicken's future performance. For example, Michael Moe of Lehman Brothers noted: "Boston Chicken is truly the leader in the home meal replacement market. . . . Dual-income families are searching for an affordable alternative to preparing meals at home. Boston Chicken satisfies this need by preparing food that customers view as high quality, healthy and convenient. This home meal replacement is a hit with value-minded consumers. The bagel industry is another hot area of opportunity for Boston Chicken. Presently the bagel industry is one of the hottest growth areas in America."[3] Moe rated the stock to be a strong buy, and projected that EPS would be $0.63 in 1995, $0.90 in 1996, and would continue to grow by 45 percent per year from 1997 to 2001.

However, not everyone was impressed. Roger Lipton of Lipton Financial Services contended that Boston Chicken's franchisees had actually lost money. Lipton Financial Services is an affiliate of Axiom Capital Management, which had shorted the stock. He estimated that sales at a franchised store had to average $23,000 a week (net of promotional discounts) to cover labor, cost of sales, and other expenses. Actual average weekly sales, Lipton claimed, were only $18,900 per store, implying that franchisees were losing money. Lipton pointed out that "the quality of earnings is very low, since all of Boston Chicken's income comes from fees, royalties, and interest payments from franchisees, most of whom were financed by the franchiser."[4]

....

3. *Michael Moe, Lehman Brothers, October 25, 1995.*
4. *"Inside Wall Street," Business Week, June 12, 1995.*

Management responded to concerns about the economics of franchisees by reporting that average weekly store sales were $23,388 for the third quarter of 1995, versus $22,227 for the second quarter, and that EBITDA store margins were running at about 15–16 percent. On December 1, 1995, the stock closed at $33.75, up more than 100 percent over the beginning of the year price (versus a 56 percent increase for the S&P 500).[5] But uncertainty about the company persisted. Short interest positions in the stock were at an all-time high of 10 million shares, more than 20 percent of the shares outstanding and double the short interest position at the beginning of 1995.

QUESTIONS

1. Assess Boston Chicken's business strategy. What are its critical success factors and risks?

2. How is the company reporting on its performance and risks? What are the key assumptions behind these policies? Do you think that its accounting policies reflect the risks?

3. What adjustments, if any, would you make to the firm's accounting policies?

4. What questions would you ask management about the company's performance?

5. How is Boston Chicken performing?

6. What assumptions is the market making about the company's future performance and risks? Do you agree with those assessments?

EXHIBIT I

Boston Chicken, Inc., Abridged 1994 Annual Report

FINANCIAL HIGHLIGHTS

| | Fiscal Years Ended | |
| | December 25, | December 26, |
(dollars in thousands, except per share data)	1994	1993
Systemwide store revenue	$383,691	$152,056
Company revenue	96,151	42,530
Net income	16,173	1,647
Net income per share	$0.38	$0.06
Shareholders' equity	$259,815	$94,906
Weighted average number of shares outstanding	42,861	32,667

---

5. The equity beta for Boston Chicken was 1.50, and at December 1, 1995, the 30-year U.S. Government Treasuries yielded 6.04%.

MANAGEMENT'S DISCUSSION AND ANALYSIS

General

The total number of stores in the Boston Market system increased from 34 at the year ended December 29, 1991, to 534 at the year ended December 25, 1994. This rapid expansion significantly affects the comparability of results of operations from year to year as well as the Company's liquidity and capital resources. The following table sets forth information regarding store development activity for the years indicated.

	Stores at Beginning of Year	Net Stores Opened in Year	Net Stores Transferred in Year[a]	Stores at End of Year
Year Ended December 27, 1992:				
Company-operated	5	15	(1)	19
Financed area developers	0	3	0	3
Non-financed area developers and other	29	31	1	61
Total	34	49	0	83
Year Ended December 26, 1993:				
Company-operated	19	28	(9)	38
Financed area developers	3	66	9	78
Non-financed area developers and other	61	40	0	101
Total	83	134	0	217
Year Ended December 25, 1994:				
Company-operated	38	49	(46)	41
Financed area developers	78	168	68	314
Non-financed area developers and other	101	100	(22)	179
Total	217	317	0	534

[a]*Stores transferred during the year primarily reflect the Company's practice of opening new Company-operating stores to seed development in targeted markets prior to execution of area development agreements relating to such markets. At the time such agreements are executed, the Company typically sells Company-operating stores located in the market to the area developer in that market. Stores transferred also reflect the purchase and/or sale of Boston Market stores in markets with multiple area developers in order to facilitate consolidation of such markets.*

Results of Operations

Fiscal Year 1994 Compared to Fiscal Year 1993

Revenue

Total revenue increased $53.7 million (126%) from $42.5 million for 1993 to $96.2 million for 1994. Royalty and franchise-related fees increased $42.5 million (335%) to $55.2 million for 1994, from $12.7 million for 1993. This increase was primarily due to an increase in royalties attributable to the larger base of franchise stores operating systemwide, from 179 stores at December 16, 1993 to 493 stores at December 5, 1994, an increase in franchise fees related to the increase in the number of stores that commenced operation as franchised stores during the year, and higher interest income generated on increased loans made to certain area developers. Additional factors contributing to the increase in revenue from royalty and franchise-related fees include an increase in lease income due to a higher number of store sites which the Company owns and leases to area developers, and recognition of software license and maintenance fees for store-level computer software systems developed by the Company for use by franchisees. No software-related fees were earned in 1993.

Revenue from Company-operated stores increased $11.1 million (37%) from $29.8 million for 1993 to $40.9 million for 1994. This increase was due to a higher average number of Company-operated stores open during the year. The Company had 38 Company-operated stores at December 26, 1993, compared to 41 at December 25, 1994. During 1994, the Company sold 54 Company-operated stores which it had opened to seed new markets.

Cost of Products Sold

Cost of products sold increased $4.6 million (41%), to $15.9 million for 1994 compared with $11.3 million for 1993. This increase was primarily due to an increase in the number of Company-operated stores open during the periods. Management does not believe that the cost of products sold as a percentage of store revenue at Company-operated stores is indicative of cost of products sold as a percentage of store revenue at franchise stores due to the Company's practice of opening new stores primarily to seed new markets. These newer stores, which constitute the majority of the Company-operated store base, tend to have higher food and paper costs as a result of increased food usage for free tasting, inefficiencies resulting from employee inexperience, and a lack of store-specific operating history to assist in forecasting daily food production needs.

Salaries and Benefits

Salaries and benefits increased $7.2 million (47%), from $15.4 million in 1993 to $22.6 million in 1994. The increase resulted from an increase in the number of employees at the Company's support center necessary to support systemwide expansion and an increase in the number of employees at Company-operated stores due to a higher average number of Company-operated stores open during the year.

General and Administrative

General and administrative expenses increased $14.0 million (101%) to $27.9 million for 1994 from $13.9 million for 1993. The increase is attributable to the development of the Company's support center infrastructure necessary to support systemwide expansion and higher general and administrative expenses at Company-operated stores resulting from a higher average number of Company-operated stores open during the year. Included in general and administrative expenses were depreciation and amortization charges of $6.1 million in 1994 and $2.0 million in 1993. The increase in depreciation and amortization expense is primarily attributable to a substantially higher fixed asset base reflecting the Company's investment in its infrastructure.

Provision for Relocation

In September 1994, the Company consolidated its four Chicago-based support center facilities into a single facility and relocated to Golden, Colorado. The total cost of relocation was $5.1 million.

Other Expense

The Company incurred other expense of $4.2 million in 1994, compared with other expense of $0.3 million in 1993. This increase reflects higher interest expense, primarily attributable to the $130.0 million of convertible subordinated debt and short-term borrowings under its unsecured credit facility, partially offset by higher interest income.

Income Taxes

Included in income taxes in 1994 is a $3.5 million benefit reflecting the realization of deferred tax assets attributable to the increased level of operating income, offset by a current provision for income taxes.

Liquidity and Capital Resources

Liquidity

The Company's primary capital requirements are for store development, including providing partial financing for certain of its area developers, purchasing real estate which is then leased to its area developers, and opening Company-operated stores. The remainder of the Company's capital requirements related primarily to investments in corporate infrastructure, including property and equipment and software development, which are necessary to support the increase in the number of stores in operation systemwide. For the year ended December 25, 1994, the Company expended approximately $268.1 million on store development, including financing area developers, purchasing real estate and opening Company-operated stores. The Company also expended approximately $52.3 million on corporate infrastructure, including its new support center facility.

The Company has entered into secured loan agreements with certain of its area developers whereby the area developers may draw on a line of credit, with certain limitations, in order to provide partial funding for expansion of their operations. In connection with certain of these loans, after a specified moratorium period, the Company has the right to convert the loan which typically results in a controlling equity interest in the area developer. As of December 25, 1994, The Company had secured loan commitments aggregating approximately $332.5 million, of which approximately $201.3 million had been advanced. The Company anticipates fully funding its commitments pursuant to its loan agreements with these area developers, and anticipates increasing such loan commitments and entering into additional loan commitments with other area developers in targeted market areas. In connection with entering into new area development agreements, the Company intends to sell Company-operated stores located in any such areas to the respective area developer. The Company is currently negotiating such agreements for a number of metropolitan areas, including Kansas City, Minneapolis, Omaha, New York, and San Francisco/San Jose. The timing of such transactions will have significant effect on the size and timing of the Company's capital requirements.

In 1994, the Company sold 54 Company-operated stores to its area developers in the Philadelphia, Detroit, Denver, Colorado Springs, Phoenix, Tucson, Las Vegas, Albuquerque, Salt Lake City, Southern New Jersey, and Boston metropolitan areas. In addition to opening stores to seed development in new markets and subsequently selling such stores to the new area developer for such market, the Company purchases and resells Boston Market stores in markets with multiple area developers in order to facilitate consolidation of such markets. In connection with these consolidation activities, the Company has issued a total of 1,112,436 shares of common stock pursuant to its shelf registration statement for the acquisition of 32 Boston Market stores and paid cash for 2 Boston Market stores. Of the 34 stores purchased, 26 stores were subsequently sold. The Company believes that all of the shares issued in connection with these consolidation activities have been sold by the recipients pursuant to Rule 145 (d) under the Securities Act of 1933, as amended. The aggregate proceeds from the sale of Company-operated stores to seed new markets and from the sale of stores which were acquired to consolidate markets were approximately $62.3 million. There were no material gains recognized as a result of these sales.

In March 1995, the Company entered into a secured loan agreement providing $20 million of convertible debt financing to Progressive Bagel Concepts, Inc. ("PBCI"). The Company has agreed to increase the amount available to PBCI under the loan agreement subject to PBCI's ability to meet certain conditions.

Capital Resources

For the year ended December 25, 1994, the Company's primary sources of capital included $35.9 million generated from operating activities, $130.0 million from the issuance of 4½% convertible subordinated debentures maturing February 1, 2004 (the "Debentures"), and $125.7 million from the sale of shares of common stock. The Debentures are convertible at any time prior to maturity into shares of the Company's common stock at a conversion rate of $27.969 per share, subject to adjustment under certain conditions. Beginning February 1, 1996, the Debentures may be reduced at the option of the Company, provided that until February 1, 1997, the Debentures cannot be redeemed unless the closing price of the Company's common stock equals or exceeds $39.16 per share for at least 20 out of 30 consecutive trading days. The Debentures are redeemable initially at 103.6% of their principal amount and at declining prices thereafter, plus accrued interest. Interest is payable semi-annually on February 1 and August 1 of each year.

In 1994, the Company entered into a $75.9 million master lease agreement to provide equipment financing for stores owned by certain of its area developers and certain Company-operated stores. The lease bears interest at LIBOR plus an applicable margin and, including renewal terms, expires in December 1998. As of December 25, 1994, the Company had utilized $66.1 million of the facility.

As of December 25, 1994, the Company had $25.3 million available in cash and cash equivalents, $75.0 million available under its unsecured revolving credit facility, and $8.9 million available under its master lease agreement.

The Company anticipates that it and its area developers will have need for additional financing during the 1995 fiscal year. The timing of the Company's capital requirements will be affected by the number of Company-operated and franchise stores opened, operational results of stores, the number of real estate sites purchased by the Company for Company use and for leasing by the Company to franchisees, and the amount and timing of borrowings under the loan agreements between the Company and certain of its existing or future area developers and by PBCI. As the Company's capital requirements increase, the Company will seek additional funds from future public or private offerings of debt or equity securities. There can be no assurance that the Company will be able to raise such capital on satisfactory terms when needed.

Seasonality

Historically, the Company has experienced lower average store revenue in the months of November, December, January, and February as a result of the holiday season and inclement weather. The Company's business in general, as well as the revenue of Company-operated stores, may be affected by a variety of other factors, including, but not limited to, general economic trends, competition, marketing programs, and special or unusual events. Such effects, however, may not be apparent in the Company's operating results during a period of significant expansion.

Boston Chicken

CONSOLIDATED BALANCE SHEETS

Boston Chicken

	1994	1993
Assets		
Current assets		
Cash	$25,304	$ 4,537
Accounts receivable, net	6,540	2,076
Due from affiliates	6,462	3,126
Notes receivable	16,906	1,512
Prepaid expenses & other current assets	2,282	1,843
Deferred income taxes	1,835	
Total current assets	59,329	13,094
Property & equipment, net	163,314	51,331
Notes receivable	185,594	44,204
Deferred financing costs	8,346	358
Other assets	10,399	1,077
Total assets	$426,982	$110,064
Liabilities & Stockholders' Equity		
Current liabilities		
Accounts payable	$15,188	$6,216
Accrued expenses	6,587	1,835
Deferred franchise revenue	5,505	2,255
Total current liabilities	27,280	10,306
Deferred franchise revenue	5,815	3,139
Convertible subordinated debt	130,000	
Other noncurrent liabilities	1,061	1,713
Deferred income taxes	3,011	
Stockholders' Equity		
Common stock	447	347
Additional paid-in capital	252,298	103,662
Retained earnings (deficit)	7,070	(9,103)
	259,815	94,906
Total liabilities and stockholders' equity	$426,982	$110,064

CONSOLIDATED STATEMENTS OF OPERATIONS

	1994	1993	1992
Revenue			
Royalties & franchise-related fees	$55,235	$12,681	$2,627
Company-operated stores	40,916	29,849	5,656
Total revenues	96,151	42,530	8,283
Costs and expenses			
Cost of products sold	15,876	11,287	2,241
Salaries and benefits	22,637	15,437	7,110
General and administrative	27,930	13,879	5,241
Provision for relocation	5,097	—	—
Total costs and expenses	71,540	41,603	14,592
Income (loss) from operations	24,611	927	(6,309)
Other income (expense)			
Interest income (expense), net	(4,235)	(440)	270
Other income, net	74	160	189
Total other income (expense)	(4,161)	(280)	459
Income (loss) before income taxes	20,450	647	(5,850)
Income taxes	4,277	—	—
Net income (loss)	$16,173	$ 647	$(5,850)
Net income (loss) per share common and equivalent share	$0.38	$0.06	$ (0.21)
Number of shares	42,861	32,667	28,495

Boston Chicken

CONSOLIDATED STATEMENTS OF CASH FLOWS (in thousands)

	Fiscal Years Ended		
	Dec. 25, 1994	Dec. 26, 1993	Dec. 27, 1992
Cash from operating activities			
Net income (loss)	$ 16,173	$ 1,647	$ (5,850)
Adjustments to reconcile income (loss) to net cash provided by (used in) operating activities			
Depreciation and amortization	6,074	1,970	260
Deferred income taxes	4,277		
Vesting of common stock for services rendered			39
Gain on disposal of assets	(368)	(150)	(29)
Changes in assets and liabilities			
Accounts receivable and due from affiliates	(7,800)	(4,343)	(689)
Accounts payable and accrued expenses	13,724	6,247	1,102
Deferred franchise revenue	5,926	3,236	1,223
Other assets and liabilities	(2,088)	(561)	332
Net cash from (used in) operations	35,198	8,046	(3,612)
Cash from investing activities			
Purchase of plant, property & equipment	(163,622)	(49,151)	(8,453)
Proceeds from sale of assets	62,342	6,161	385
Acquisition of other assets	(12,790)	(1,093)	(273)
Issuance of notes receivable	(225,282)	(45,690)	(773)
Repayment of notes receivable	68,498	747	—
Net cash used in investing activities	(270,854)	(89,026)	(9,114)
Cash from financing activities			
Proceeds from issue common stock	125,703	66,150	19,843
Proceeds from convertible subordinate notes	130,000	9,658	
Borrowings under credit facility	96,130	32,275	
Repayments under credit facility	(96,130)	(32,275)	
Payment of capital lease obligation	—	—	(300)
Net cash from financing activities	255,703	75,808	19,543
Net increase (decrease) in cash	20,767	(5,172)	6,817
Cash, beginning of year	4,537	9,709	2,892
Cash, end of year	$ 25,304	$ 4,537	$ 9,709
Supplemental cash flow information			
Interest paid	$ 3,395	$ 226	$ 29
Noncash transactions			
Conversion of convt. subord. notes into common stock	$ —	$ 10,072	$ —
Issuance of common stock for assets	$ 19,931	$ —	$ —

The accompanying notes to the consolidated financial statements are an integral part of these statements.

Boston Chicken

OTHER INFORMATION

	1994	1993	1992	1991
Store Information				
Company operated	41	38	19	5
Finance area developers	314	78	3	0
Nonfinanced area developers	179	101	61	29
Total	534	217	83	34
Systematic store revenue	383.7	152.1	42.7	20.8
Quarterly Data Revenue				
1st quarter	23,449			
2nd quarter	20,360			
3rd quarter	25,186			
4th quarter	27,165			
Net Income				
1st quarter	2,561			
2nd quarter	3,383			
3rd quarter	4,679			
4th quarter	5,550			

Boston Chicken

NOTES TO CONSOLIDATED FINANCIAL STATEMENTS

1. Description of Business

Boston Chicken, Inc., and Subsidiary (the "Company") operate and franchise food service stores that specialize in complete meals featuring home style entrees, fresh vegetables, salads, and other side items. At December 26, 1993, there were 217 stores systemwide, consisting of 38 Company-operated stores and 179 franchise stores. At December 25, 1994, there were 534 stores systemwide, consisting of 41 Company-operated stores and 493 franchise stores. In 1992, 1993, and 1994, in connection with its practice of opening new stores to seed development in targeted markets, the Company sold 1, 13, and 54 Company-operated stores, respectively, to new formed area developers or franchisees of the Company. During 1994, in connection with its practice of acquiring stores in markets with multiple area developers in order to facilitate consolidation of such markets, the Company purchased 34 stores and resold 26 of them.

2. Summary of Significant Accounting Policies

Principles of Consolidation

The accompanying consolidated financial statements include the accounts of the Company and its subsidiary. All material intercompany accounts and transactions have been eliminated in consolidation.

Fiscal Year

The Company's fiscal year is the 52/53-week period ending on the last Sunday in December. Fiscal years 1992, 1993, and 1994 each contained 52 weeks, or thirteen four-week periods. The first quarter consists of four periods and each of the remaining three quarters consists of three periods, with the first, second, and third quarters ending 16 weeks, 28 weeks, and 40 weeks, respectively, into the fiscal year.

Cash and Cash Equivalents

Cash and cash equivalents consist of cash on hand and on deposit, and highly liquid instruments purchased with maturities of three months or less.

Inventories

Inventories, which are classified in prepaid expenses and other current assets, are stated at the lower of cost (first-in, first-out) or market and consist of food, paper products, and supplies.

Property and Equipment

Property and equipment is stated at cost, less accumulated depreciation and amortization. The provision for depreciation and amortization has been calculated using the straight-line method. The following represent the useful lives over which the assets are depreciated and amortized:

Buildings and improvements	15–30 years
Leasehold improvements	15 years
Furniture, fixtures, equipment and computer software	6–8 years
Pre-Opening costs	1 year

Property and equipment additions include acquisitions of property and equipment, costs incurred in the development and construction of new stores, major improvements to existing stores, and costs incurred in the development and purchase of computer software. Pre-opening costs consist primarily of salaries and other direct expenses relating to the set-up, initial stocking, training, and general management activities incurred prior to the opening of new stores. Expenditures for maintenance and repairs are charged to expense as incurred. Development costs for franchised stores are expensed when the store opens.

Deferred Financing Costs

Deferred financing costs are amortized over the period of the related financing, which ranges from two to ten years.

Revenue Recognition

Revenue from Company-operated stores is recognized in the period related food and beverage products are sold. Revenue derived from initial franchise fees and area development fees is recognized when the franchise store opens. Royalties are recognized in the same period related franchise store revenue is generated. The components of royalties and franchise-related fees are comprised of the following:

(In thousands of dollars)	Dec. 25, 1994	Dec. 26, 1993	Dec. 27, 1992
Royalties	$17,421	$5,464	$1,491
Initial franchise and area development	13,057	5,230	1,136
Interest income from area developer financing (See Note 8)	11,632	1,130	—
Lease income	5,361	253	—
Software fees	6,480	—	—
Other	1,284	604	—
Total royalties and franchise-related fees	$55,235	$12,681	$2,627

Subject to the provisions of the applicable franchise agreements, the Company is committed and obligated to allow franchisees to utilize the Company's trademarks, copyrights, recipes, operating procedures, and other elements of the Boston Market system in the operation of franchised Boston Market stores.

Per Share Data

Net income (loss) per common share is computed by dividing net income (loss), adjusted in 1993 for interest related to the conversion of 7% convertible subordinated notes (See Note 9), by the weighted average number of common shares and dilutive common stock equivalent shares outstanding during the year.

Common and equivalent share include any common stock, options, and warrants issued within one year prior to the effective date of the Company's initial public offering, with a price below the initial public offering price. These have been included as common stock equivalents outstanding, reduced by the number of shares of common stock which could be purchased with the proceeds form the assumed exercise of the options and warrants, including tax benefits assumed to be realized.

Employee Benefit Plan

The Company has a 401(k) plan for which employee participation is discretionary and to which the Company makes no contribution.

Reclassification

Certain amounts shown in the 1992 and 1993 financial statements have been reclassified to conform with the current presentation.

4. Debt

The Company has entered into a revolving credit agreement on an unsecured basis providing for borrowings of up to $75 million through June 30, 1997. Borrowings under the agreement may be either floating rate loans with interest at the bank's reference rate of eurodollar loans with interest at the eurodollar rate, plus an applicable margin. In addition, a commitment fee of .25% of the average daily unused portion of the loan is required. The agreement contains various covenants including restricting other borrowings, prohibiting cash dividends, and requiring the Company to maintain interest coverage and cash flow ratios and a minimum net worth. As of December 25, 1994, no borrowings were outstanding.

In February, 1994, the Company issued $130 million of 4.5% convertible subordinated debentures maturing February 1, 2004. Interest is payable semi-annually on February 1 and August 1 of each year. The debentures are convertible at any time prior to maturity into share of common stock at a conversion rate of $27.969 per share, subject to adjustment under certain conditions. Beginning February 1, 1996, the debentures may be redeemed at the option of the Company, provided that through February 1, 1997, the debentures cannot be redeemed unless the closing price of the common stock equals or exceeds $39.16 per share for at least 20 out of 30 consecutive trading days. The debentures are redeemable initially at 103.6% of their principal amount and at declining prices thereafter, plus accrued interest.

5. Income Taxes

As of December 25, 1994, the Company has cumulative Federal and state net tax operating loss carryforwards available to reduce future taxable income of approximately $30.5 million which begin to expire in 2003. The Company has recognized the benefit of the loss carryforwards for financial reporting, but not for income tax purposes. Certain ownership changes which have occurred will result in an annual limitation of the Company's utilization of its net operating losses.

At December 28, 1992, the first day of fiscal 1993, the Company adopted SFAS No. 109 "Accounting for Income Taxes" ("SFAS 109"). Upon adoption of SFAS 109 there was no cumulative effect on the Company's financial statements because the Company's deferred tax assets exceeded its deferred tax liabilities and a valuation allowance was recorded against the net deferred tax assets due to uncertainty regarding realization of the related tax benefits.

The primary components that comprise the deferred tax assets and liabilities at December 26, 1993, and December 25, 1994, are as follows:

(In thousands of dollars)	Dec. 25, 1994	Dec. 26, 1993
Deferred tax assets:		
Accounts payable and accrued expenses	$ 794	$ 78
Deferred franchise revenue	3,469	1,992
Other noncurrent liabilities	262	623
Net operating losses	11,639	4,844
Other	173	52
Total deferred tax assets	16,337	7,589
Less valuation allowance	—	(3,847)
Net deferred taxes	16,337	3,742
Deferred tax liabilities:		
Due from area developers	—	(814)
Property and equipment	(17,047)	(2,807)
Other assets	(466)	(121)
Total deferred tax liabilities	(17,513)	(3,742)
Net deferred tax liability	$ (1,176)	$ —

The decrease in the valuation allowance from December 26, 1993 to December 25, 1994 was $3,847,000 and the decrease in the valuation allowance from December 27, 1992 to December 26, 1993 was $180,000, which was net of a $446,000 increase related to the tax benefit from the exercise of stock options.

The provision for income taxes for the fiscal year ended December 25, 1994, consists of $4,277,000 of deferred income taxes, which is net of an income tax benefit of $3,102,000 pertaining to the exercise of stock options.

The difference between the Company's 1993 and 1994 actual tax provision and the tax provision by applying the statutory Federal income tax rate is attributable to the following:

(In thousands of dollars)	Fiscal Years Ended	
	Dec. 25, 1994	Dec. 26, 1993
Income tax expense at statutory rate	$6,953	$ 560
State taxes, net of Federal benefit	818	66
Other	26	—
Change in valuation allowance	(3,520)	(626)
Provision for income taxes	$4,277	$ —

6. Marketing and Advertising Funds

The Company administers a National Advertising Fund to which Company-operated stores and franchisees make contributions based on individual franchise agreements (currently 2% of base revenue). Collected amounts are spent primarily on developing marketing and advertising materials for use systemwide. Such amounts are not segregated from the cash resources of the Company, but the National Advertising Fund is accounted for separately and not included in the financial statements of the Company.

Boston Chicken

The Company maintains Local Advertising Funds that provide comprehensive advertising and sales promotion support for the Boston Market stores in particular markets. Periodic contributions are made by both Company-operated and franchise stores (currently 3% to 3.75% of base revenue). The Company disburses funds and accounts for all transactions related to such Local Advertising Funds. Such amounts are not segregated from the cash resources of the Company, but are accounted for separately and are not included in the financial statements of the Company.

The National Advertising Fund and certain Local Advertising Funds had accumulated deficits at December 26, 1993, and December 25, 1994, which were funded by advances from the Company. Such advances are reflected in Due from affiliates, net.

8. Area Developer Financing

The Company currently offers partial financing to certain area developers for use in expansion of their operations. Only developers which are developing a significant portion of an area of dominant influence ("ADI") or metropolitan area of a major city and which meet all of the Company's requirements are eligible for such financing. Certain of these financing arrangements permit the Company to obtain an equity interest in the developer at a predetermined price after a moratorium (generally two years) on conversion of the loan into equity. The maximum loan amount is generally established to give the Company majority ownership of the developer upon conversion (or option exercise, as described further below) provided the Company exercises its right to participate in any intervening financing of the developer.

Area developer financing generally requires the developer to expend at least 75% of its equity capital toward developing stores prior to drawing on the revolving loan account, with draws permitted during a two- or three-year draw period in a pre-determined amount, generally equal to two to four times the amount of the developer's equity capital. Upon expiration of the draw period, the loan converts to an amortizing term loan payable over four to five years in periodic installments, sometimes with a final balloon payment. Interest is generally set at 1% over the applicable "reference rate" of Bank of America Illinois from time to time and is payable each period. The loan is secured by a pledge of substantially all of the assets of the area developer and any franchisees under its area development agreement and generally by a pledge of equity of the owners of the developer.

(a) Loan Conversion Option

For loans with a conversion option, all or any portion of the loan amount may be converted at the Company's election (at any time after default of the loan or generally after the second anniversary of the loan and generally up to the later of full repayment of the loan or a specified date in the agreement) into equity in the developer at the conversion price set forth in such loan agreement, generally at a 12% to 15% premium over the per equity unit price paid by the developer for the equity investment made concurrently with the execution of the loan agreement or subsequent amendments thereto. To the extent such loan is not fully drawn or has been drawn and repaid, the Company has a corresponding option to acquire at the loan conversion price the amount of additional equity it could have acquired by conversion of the loan, had it been fully drawn.

There can be no assurance the Company will or will not convert any loan amount or exercise its option at such time as it may be permitted to do so and, if it does convert, that such conversion will constitute a majority interest in the area developer. Absent a default under any such agreement, the Company currently cannot exercise these conversion or option rights.

(b) Commitment to Extend Area Developer Financing

The following table summarizes credit commitments for area developer financing, certain of which are conditional upon additional equity contributions being made by area developers:

(In thousands of dollars, except number of area developers)	Dec. 25, 1994	Dec. 26, 1993
Number of area developers receiving financing	13	5
Loan commitments	$332,531	$ 51,041
Unused loans	(131,265)	(7,243)
Loans outstanding (included in Notes Receivable)	$201,266	$ 43,798
Allowance for loan losses	$ —	$ —

The principal maturities on the aforementioned notes receivable are as follows:

(In thousands of dollars)	
1995	$16,288
1996	4,456
1997	13,132
1998	12,132
1999	15,417
Thereafter	139,841
	$201,266

(c) Credit Risk and Allowance for Loan Losses

The allowance for credit losses is maintained at a level that in management's judgment is adequate to provide for estimated possible loan losses. The amount of the allowance is based on management's review of each area developer's financial condition, store performance, store opening schedules, and other factors, as well as prevailing economic conditions. Based upon this review and analysis, no allowance was required as of December 26, 1993 and December 25, 1994.

11. Relocation

In September 1994, the Company consolidated its four Chicago-based support center facilities into a single facility and relocated to Golden, Colorado. The cost of the relocation, including moving personnel and facilities, severance payments, and the write-off of vacated leasehold improvements was $5.1 million.

12. Subsequent Events

In March 1995, the Company entered into a convertible secured loan agreement providing $20 million of financing to Progressive Bagel Concepts, Inc. ("PBCI"). The Company has agreed to provide PBCI additional convertible secured loans subject to PBCI's ability to meet certain conditions.

In March 1995, PBCI entered into stock purchase agreements with the Company to purchase $19.5 million of common stock. The number of shares to be issued will be based upon the market value of the stock two days prior to the closing date. The Company has granted PBCI registration rights and has provided a price guarantee equal to the per share purchase price on any shares sold within a specified number of days of the registration becoming effective.

REPORT OF INDEPENDENT PUBLIC ACCOUNTANTS

To the Board of Directors and Stockholders of Boston Chicken, Inc.:

We have audited the accompanying consolidated balance sheets of Boston Chicken, Inc. (a Delaware corporation) and Subsidiary as of December 25, 1994 and December 26, 1993, and the related consolidated statements of operations, stockholders' equity, and cash flows for the fiscal years ended December 25, 1994, December 26, 1993, and December 27, 1992. These financial statements are the responsibility of the Company's management. Our responsibility is to express an opinion on these financial statements based on our audits.

We conducted our audits in accordance with generally accepted auditing standards. Those standards require that we plan and perform the audit to obtain reasonable assurance about whether the financial statements are free of material misstatements. An audit includes examining, on a test basis, evidence supporting the amounts and disclosures in the financial statements. An audit also includes assessing the accounting principles used and significant estimates made by management, as well as evaluating the overall financial statement presentation. We believe that our audits provide a reasonable basis for our opinion.

In our opinion, the financial statements referred to above present fairly, in all material respects, the financial position of Boston Chicken, Inc. and Subsidiary as of December 25, 1994 and December 26, 1993, and the results of their operations and their cash flows for the fiscal years ended December 25, 1994, December 26, 1993, and December 27, 1992, in conformity with generally accepted accounting principles.

(Arthur Andersen LLP)

Denver, Colorado

January 31, 1995 (except with respect to the matters discussed in Note 12, as to which the date is March 24, 1995)

Boston Chicken

EXHIBIT 2

Boston Chicken Inc., Summary of 1994–1995 Quarterly Results

	1st Quarter	2nd Quarter	3rd Quarter	4th Quarter
1995				
Revenue ($000)	$40,107	$34,800	$38,671	
Net Income ($000)	7,116	7,420	8,814	
EPS	$0.15	$0.15	$0.17	
1994				
Revenue ($000)	$23,449	$20,360	$25,186	$27,165
Net Income ($000)	2,561[a]	3,383[a]	4,679[a]	5,550
EPS	$0.06	$0.08	$0.11	$0.12

a. *Pre-tax provisions for relocation were $4,708,000 in the second quarter of 1994, and $389,000 in the third quarter of 1994.*

Brierley Investments Limited

In late 1995 Paul Collins, the CEO of Brierley Investments Limited (BIL), was concerned that the company's stock was increasingly being undervalued in the New Zealand market. In a discussion in the 1995 annual report, he stated:

> We have been disappointed with [our] share price. In 1991 I made a prediction that in 1995 the share price would be $2 after having paid $1 billion in cash dividends. While we have been largely successful on the dividend front, the growth in share price has not been achieved. That prediction was based on my confidence of a substantial, sustainable lift in the Company's performance which has been achieved—profits have more than doubled, operating earnings from investments have been significantly increased, debt levels have been slashed and new investments such as Sky City and Sealord provide the foundation for future growth.

Throughout 1995 the company's stock price had steadily climbed from NZ$1.10 at the beginning of the year to a close of NZ$1.20, well below the firm's target of NZ$2. This performance also lagged the New Zealand stock market, which had grown by 20 percent during the same period. BIL had an equity beta of 0.85 and an estimated cost of equity of 13 percent in June 1995.

BUSINESS

BIL was formed in Wellington, New Zealand, in 1961 by Ron Brierley to invest in undervalued assets. The company acquired an Australian subsidiary in 1964 and was first listed on the New Zealand Stock Exchange in 1970. Brierley's grew rapidly throughout the 1960s, 70s and 80s: by 1987 its assets under management were almost NZ$11.3 billion, owners' equity was NZ$1.8 billion, and net income was NZ$342 million. The company was arguably the most successful firm in New Zealand during this period, growing into the nation's third largest publicly traded company.

BIL owed its success to its management's ability to identify companies that were either undervalued or poorly managed. BIL would acquire a stake in these companies, replace poor management, and wait until the market appreciated the real strategic value of the business. Consequently, BIL generated income from two sources: the operations of companies in which it owned stock and the sale of its investments at a price different from purchase. BIL thus performed the same role of corporate investor and takeover specialist in New Zealand as T. Boone Pickens and Carl Icahn performed in the United States, and Sir James Goldsmith and Lord Hanson performed in the United Kingdom.

1990 proved to be a critical turning point for BIL. During that year it embarked on a successful takeover of Mount Charlotte Investments PLC, the UK's second largest hotelier. Mount Charlotte owned 104 hotels under its own name, including 24 located in London, as well as Hospitality Inns and the recently acquired Thistle Hotels. BIL initially acquired an 11 percent stake in Mount Charlotte in 1988, and gradually increased its stake to 30 percent. The Gulf War in 1991 presented the firm with the opportunity to purchase an additional 10 percent from the Kuwait Investment Office. As a result of this holding, BIL

Professor Paul Healy prepared this case. The case is intended solely as the basis for class discussion and is not intended to serve as an endorsement, source of primary data, or illustration of effective or ineffective management. Copyright © 1999 by the President and Fellows of Harvard College. HBS Case 9-100-014.

was required by The City Code on Takeovers and Mergers to make an offer to all remaining shareholders. Upon successful acquisition of the remaining shares outstanding, BIL sold a 30 percent stake in Mount Charlotte to the Government of Singapore. As a result of its acquisition of Mount Charlotte, at the year ended June 30 1991, NZ$5.2 billion of BIL's assets were invested in the U.K. hotelier, a NZ$4.2 billion increase over the prior year.

Almost immediately after the acquisition, performance at Mount Charlotte deteriorated. The Gulf War adversely affected tourism in London, driving down occupancy rates in Mount Charlotte's London hotels from 80 to 62 percent in 1991. A severe recession in the United Kingdom during the early 1990s led to a steady decline in revenues for Mount Charlotte through 1994. Financial information on Mount Charlotte is reported in Exhibit 1. This poor performance acted as a drag on BIL's performance during the same period. Financial information for BIL is presented in Exhibit 2.

Following the Mount Charlotte acquisition, BIL's management vowed to focus the firm's investment activity in Australia and New Zealand, where it had been more consistently successful, and restricted any future investments to no more than 20 percent of shareholders' funds. Its New Zealand investments in the 1990s proved more successful. For example, it acquired stakes in Air New Zealand (the largest domestic and international airline in New Zealand), Sealord Products (New Zealand's largest seafood catching, processing, and marketing company), Carter Holt (the country's largest plantation forest owner), Skellerup (a diversified manufacturing and distribution company), and Sky City (a newly created casino company). Each of these companies showed significant improvements in operating performance and market valuation following their acquisition by BIL. For example, the NZ$326 million investment in Carter Holt was sold for NZ$468 million. The Sky City investment of NZ$152 million generated sale proceeds of NZ$122 and a remaining interest valued at more than NZ$300 million.

NEW ZEALAND ACCOUNTING

The most obvious difference between New Zealand and U.S. financial reports was their format. Income Statements were called Profit and Loss Accounts, and typically did not separately report revenues, cost of sales, and SG&A expenses (even in footnote disclosures). The cash flow statement used the direct method of reporting Cash from Operating Activities, showing cash inflows and outflows rather than the reconciliation of net income and cash from operations (which was reported in a footnote).

New Zealand accounting standards relating to investments were quite similar to those used in the United States. For example, BIL investments of less than 20 percent stakes in publicly traded companies were recorded at market values, similar to U.S. GAAP treatment of securities available for sale. However, in New Zealand any unrealized holding gains or losses were shown on the balance sheet in the liabilities section under the title "Investment Fluctuation" and were only transferred to income when the gains or losses were realized. Under U.S. GAAP, unrealized gains and losses were included as a reserve in owners' equity, and were also included in net income when realized. Investments in associate companies, where ownership is between 20 and 50 percent, were recorded using the equity method. Investments of more than a 50 percent stake were consolidated using the purchase method. Pooling of interests was not permitted in New Zealand. For BIL this implied that the investment in Mount Charlotte was fully consolidated, and the interest of the Government of Singapore was included as a minority interest on both BIL's balance sheet and income statement.

FINANCIAL ANALYSTS' QUESTIONS

Given the lackluster performance of BIL's stock, many analysts were cautious in their recommendations. For example, in October 1995 Raymond Webb of ANZ McCaughan stated:

> As we see it, ultimately the only way for BIL management to end the long period of underperformance is to realign the portfolio by extracting value and then capital from those assets which are underperforming, and by reinvesting in assets with more identifiable growth prospects. . . . We recommend that clients seeking short-term gains look elsewhere and that longer term investors underweight BIL until the company's performance justifies rerating.

By late 1995 many analysts were anticipating that the firm would soon sell all or some of its stake in Mount Charlotte. The key question was what would the firm do with the proceeds. Many analysts advocated a targeted share repurchase program, which would effectively downsize the firm.

MANAGEMENT RESPONSES

In response to the firm's stagnant stock price, in 1995 BIL's management attempted to show how value had been created for stockholders by reporting estimates of intrinsic value of the business. Intrinsic values were estimated by summing the market values of shares owned in listed companies and discounted cash flow estimates of market values of nonlisted shares, and deducting outstanding liabilities. In the firm's 1995 Annual Report, Paul Collins committed that "Over the next three years, BIL's objective is to increase its intrinsic value by NZ$2 billion, equivalent to an 18 percent per annum increase on the June 1995 intrinsic value of NZ$3.7 billion (NZ$1.25 per share)."

Management considered that this goal would be achievable provided the market recognized the value that BIL created in capitalizing on undervalued businesses as an investor and takeover specialist. As Paul Collins considered this challenge, he wondered what tangible actions would best help the market appreciate the firm's operating and trading performance in the New Zealand market during the five preceding years. One approach would be to separate out the financial results for Mount Charlotte from the remainder of the firm's investments, so that analysts could better appreciate its exceptional performance. A second approach would be to undertake a stock repurchase program using the firm's $874 million in cash and marketable securities. Finally, the firm had been approached by a consortium of Malaysian investors interested in acquiring a stake in BIL. Paul Collins wondered whether New Zealand analysts would view such an agreement positively.

QUESTIONS

1. What is the reason for BIL's poor stock performance? Is the company's strategy no longer creating value? Has it been executing its strategy poorly? Or, is there a problem communicating with investors?

2. What changes in strategy, execution, financial reporting and investor communication, and/or governance would you recommend to management to address the problems facing the company? Should BIL sell Mount Charlotte? If not, what should it do? Should it change its strategy? Should it continue reporting under the "intrinsic value method?"

Brierly Investments Limited

Brierly Investments Limited

EXHIBIT I

Mount Charlotte Investments PLC, Five-Year Record from December 25, 1990, to December 25, 1994[a]

(£000)	1994	1993	1992	1991	1990
Revenues	241,215	214,090	217,285	226,128	241,659
Operating profit	74,275	60,352	60,346	72,613	88,427
Profit on sale of properties	—	—	—	—	765
Profit before interest	74,275	60,352	60,346	72,613	89,192
Interest expense	51,119	52,975	59,326	71,075	42,576
Profit before taxes	23,156	7,377	1,020	1,538	46,616
Taxes	3,254	3,008	1,100	—	(3,475)
Profit after taxes	26,410	10,385	2,120	1,538	43,141
Dividends	—	—	—	—	4,673
Retained profit	26,410	10,385	2,120	1,538	38,468
Shareholders' equity	1,184,950	1,158,540	1,148,155	1,126,035	1,101,363
Earnings per share	2.81p	1.11p	0.23p	0.17p	4.89p
Return on sales	30.8%	28.2%	27.8%	32.1%	36.6%

a. BIL and Mount Charlotte have different year ends: BIL is June 30 whereas Mount Charlotte is December 25. Consequently, on June 30 each year BIL consolidates Mount Charlotte results reported for the prior year ended December 25.

EXHIBIT 2

Brierley Investments Limited, Selections from 1995 Annual Report
(all amounts are reported in New Zealand dollars)

CHIEF EXECUTIVE'S REVIEW

It is pleasing to report a record profit of $431.7 million. While only marginally ahead of last year, it nevertheless represents another milestone for the Group. In particular the record results of the last two years underscore the quantum leap which the Group has made since the early 1990s when profits of $212 million, $251 million and $271 million were reported in 1991, 1992 and 1993 respectively. As importantly, the underlying quality of the assets today, in terms of both current and potential earnings and cash flow, has been significantly enhanced, providing a solid platform for future growth in value.

In a review such as this it is easy to dwell on the year's highlights and there have been many. These include the rapid progress on the construction of Sky City casino together with its independent financing and selldown of BIL's holding from 80% to 51%, the continuing improvement in the profitability of Mount Charlotte, an outstanding performance from Air New Zealand and the successful foray into and exit from Wilson & Horton to name but a few. I will comment on these and other highlights in my review of BIL's trading and investment activities.

BIL's financial position continues to strengthen. While total assets of $9.4 billion show little change on last year's $9.1 billion, the underlying profitability of individual assets has materially improved. In addition, the recent sales of shareholdings in Carter Holt Harvey and Wilson & Horton have resulted in the Group being highly liquid with cash deposits at balance date of $874 million. At the same time debt maturing within one year of $922 million has been extended on to a term basis with the average maturity profile for senior debt now exceeding seven years. Overall, net debt to total capitalisation was steady at 32%, which further reduces to 26% if the capital notes of $449 million are treated as quasi-equity rather than debt.

In the early 1990s, the opportunity for BIL to maximise shareholder value was severely constrained due to high debt levels and inadequate profitability. Today the situation is reversed and the Group now has substantial financial flexibility and is well placed to best optimise shareholder value.

The term *shareholder value* is now widely referred to in investor circles and forums. As an investment company, BIL has always been acutely aware of what constitutes value. In our own planning processes we focus not so much on the underlying book net worth of BIL but rather our assessment of BIL's intrinsic value and the strategies required to ensure that there is continuing growth in that value. More recently we have also given considerable thought as to the actions which the Company can take to best ensure that the value which is created is mirrored in tangible shareholder returns—whether it be from higher share prices, cash dividends or share buy backs.

VALUE CREATION

While the notion of value creation is a fundamental underlying business principle, it is particularly relevant in the context of an investment company such as BIL.

In its simplest form, value creation comes back to quality asset management:

- existing assets—increasing returns while at the same time minimising the capital required to achieve these returns;
- new investment—careful evaluation of and commitment to new investment;
- harvesting—where appropriate, selling assets when returns can be maximised and the funds more effectively invested elsewhere;
- minimising risk—by focusing on core management competencies and maximising comparative advantages in the geographic regions in which we invest.

While the financial statements measure the movement in value in an accounting sense, the resultant answer, while in itself a precise number, does not normally represent the underlying intrinsic value of the business or in other words what is today's market value. While assessing the intrinsic value is a more difficult and somewhat imprecise exercise, it is nevertheless highly relevant for an investment company. In BIL's case intrinsic value is established by reference to the underlying market value of listed securities and the discounted earnings and cash flows of unlisted assets. No account is taken of the very real but somewhat more intangible assets such as the Group's tax losses, skilled people resources or its strong balance sheet and resultant capacity to make new investments.

Over the next three years, BIL's objective is to increase its intrinsic value by $2 billion equivalent to an 18% per annum increase on the June 1995 intrinsic value of $3.7 billion ($1.25 per share). In assessing whether this target is credible and achievable it is necessary to review where BIL has come from, its current position and future direction. In this regard during the last decade there have been two watershed events for BIL. The first was the sharemarket crash in October 1987 and the second, the acquisition of Mount Charlotte Investments in late 1990. Each of these events had a fundamental impact on the intrinsic value and external perception of BIL and it is, therefore, relevant to use these periods for comparative purposes:

MOVEMENT IN INTRINSIC VALUE

$ millions	December 1987– June 1991	June 1991– June 1995	June 1995– June 1998
Opening Intrinsic Value	2,045	3,107	3,717
New Capital	422	293	—
	2,467	3,400	3,717
Increase in Intrinsic Value	1,061	1,622	2,000
Foreign Currency Translation	—	(540)	—
	3,528	4,482	5,717
Cash Dividends	(421)	(765)	(717)
Closing Intrinsic Value	$3,107	$3,717	$5,000

$ millions	June 1991	June 1995
Reported Profit	1,185#	1,334*
Book Value	3,231	3,605
Market Capitalisation	2,857	3,335

#3½ years   *4 years

In the 1991 to 1995 period, BIL's intrinsic value grew by $1.62 billion. Adjusted to New Zealand dollars, value grew by $1.08 billion or 9% per annum. This simple statistic hides three key issues:

• With the benefit of hindsight, the June 1991 assessment of BIL's intrinsic value was somewhat flattering given the weak economic activity and capital markets which subsequently eventuated in 1992 and 1993. This is evidenced in the performances of many of the Group companies at that time. By way of example, Mount Charlotte was on course for a virtual break even result (1995: £35 million), Air New Zealand's operating profit was $18 million (1995: $286 million), Skellerup's earnings before interest and tax were $12 million (1995: $64 million) and funding costs and overheads were $378 million (1995: $130 million). There are other similar examples such as Magnum Corporation and Carter Holt Harvey but the simple reality is that the then market capitalisation of BIL gave the Company more credit than it deserved, whereas today the reverse is the case.

- Although Mount Charlotte's operating returns have reflected its continuing outperformance of the UK hotel industry, depressed trading conditions until 1994 and its own high level of indebtedness have resulted in inadequate returns to BIL. While the price paid in 1990 would represent good investment value if made in 1995, it does not compensate for holding costs and foreign currency movements which have denied the Group additional growth in intrinsic value of in excess of $1 billion.
- Foreign exchange—70% of BIL's Parent Company assets are invested internationally which is roughly equivalent to all the Group's shareholders' funds being invested offshore. During the last four years the New Zealand dollar has appreciated by 25% against the currencies of the countries in which we invest. As a consequence BIL's overall returns have been higher in those countries but lower on translation to New Zealand dollars. To put it another way, notwithstanding the strong New Zealand dollar and with 70% of the Group's assets invested offshore, the value of the Company has still grown by over $1 billion in New Zealand dollar terms—a considerable achievement given both the quality of the assets and the financial position of BIL in 1991. In reality the growth in value of $1 billion was largely achieved over the last two years as the weak economic conditions and capital markets which prevailed throughout 1992 and 1993 depressed profits and asset values at that time. Strong economic growth over the last two years and a more robust outlook have contributed to a sharp rise in corporate cash flows and profits. These factors have yet to be fully reflected in asset values and augur well for growth in BIL's intrinsic value.

  Looking to the future we have every confidence that we can continue to create value as we have done in the past. Factors which underpin this confidence include:
- BIL's sustainable profit (after funding costs and overheads but before investment surpluses) is now $225 million per annum and will rise to $300 million per annum in 1997. This compares to $70 million in 1991.
- Over the last eight years in what can best be described as challenging times in equity markets, BIL has achieved investment surpluses (net of ordinary dividends, tax provisions, write-offs and minority interests) of $2,083 million or an average of $260 million per annum. In the first two months of the 1995/96 year, over $80 million in investment surpluses have already been generated.
- BIL is well placed in its core Australia/New Zealand markets with very little competition and a great deal of knowledge and expertise. With its strong financial position BIL is well positioned to take advantage of the relatively static investment markets in these countries.
- BIL's reported earnings for the last two years total $862 million. Assuming a continuation of but no improvement in this trend over the next three years, earnings of $1.3 billion or 65% of the targeted $2 billion would be the outcome. This takes no account of the growth potential in the wider BIL Group or any new investment strategies.
- Intrinsic values at June 1995 have been conservatively assessed. Mount Charlotte achieving its profit forecasts and Air New Zealand being re-rated to 80% of the average market P/E would alone contribute the balance of $700 million or 35% of the $2 billion target.

Obviously, achieving expectations such as these to some degree depends on macro economic factors beyond BIL's control. For the above scenarios it is assumed that inflation, bond yields and economic growth rates in the major economies in which we operate will remain around present levels. It also assumes no major change to BIL's capital structure.

MARKET VALUE

While BIL has a clear raison d'être and a proven ability to create value, it is axiomatic that such value creation be represented in a tangible way in shareholder returns. In 1991 I stated that our objective over the next four years was to make BIL a $2 stock, equivalent to a stock market valuation of $5 billion after paying our shareholders an additional $1 billion in cash dividends.

While we have largely succeeded on the dividend front, we have fallen well short on the share price. While there are various mitigating factors such as the stronger New Zealand dollar and an equity market much weaker than anticipated, BIL's own improved performance, particularly over the last two years, has so far resulted in only a modest re-rating by the market.

In my first year as Chief Executive in 1985/86, the Company's market capitalisation peaked at around $5 billion. At that time shareholders' funds were $939 million and profit $179 million. Notwithstanding BIL's impressive performance at that time, the then market capitalisation assumed an unrealistic growth potential and earning capacity. Today we have the opposite situation. Shareholders' funds (including convertible notes) are $3.6 billion, a record profit of $432 million has been achieved, the Company's growth prospects are sound yet today's market capitalisation is only $3.3 billion.

While some broking houses have moved to a more dynamic basis of valuation for BIL, many still rate the Company on their assessment of BIL's underlying static asset value today and then deduct a discount on the basis that BIL operates in a similar manner to a unit trust.

This valuation approach ignores BIL's active asset management, the very real achievements of the last few years, the substantial improvement in the quality and sustainable earnings mix of the asset base and, in particular, the strength and flexibility now inherent in the Company's overall financial position. In short, BIL is given no premium for future earnings or asset value appreciation which is a fundamental premise in any equity investment. In earlier years these attributes would have resulted in a substantially higher share price. Today's lower share price is perhaps as much a reflection of the implications arising from the Mount Charlotte acquisition five years ago as it is a more restrained view on investment companies generally given the collapse of many of our so termed pretenders in the late 1980s. However, for whatever reason, the share price today is what it is. While BIL's principal objective is to put "runs on the board" and create value, as important an objective is for shareholders to reap the benefit of that enhanced value. In this regard, it is important to understand BIL's view on an optimum level of capital.

OPTIMUM LEVEL OF CAPITAL

In March 1995 the well known investor Warren Buffett, Chairman of Berkshire Hathaway in the United States, commented that:

"... a fat wallet, however, is the enemy of superior investment results ... We now consider a security for purchase only if we can deploy at least US$100 million in it."

BIL's optimum capital requirement is defined by our existing asset base and overall financial position, the opportunities within the regions in which we invest and the people resources available to the Group. While the level of capital required is a somewhat imprecise calculation and will change over time, our present view is that given the Group's current mix of assets and available opportunities, the present level of capital is appropriate. There are two significant factors which could change this view. Firstly, over the next three years we envisage significant growth in the overall value of the Group. To the extent this materialises and there are limited value adding investment opportunities available, the Group could have excess capital.

Secondly, the Group's largest asset is its investment in Mount Charlotte. To put this in context, if Mount Charlotte was sold today at book value for cash, the Parent Company would have $1 billion in cash and no senior debt. Under this scenario the Group could also find itself with excess capital, again the overall level dependent on the extent to which attractive new investment opportunities are available.

Our present view on Mount Charlotte is that it will achieve a significant lift in its earnings in each of the next three years. While Mount Charlotte has detracted from BIL's value over the last four years, its sale in 1995, based on current earnings, would not be in the best interest of BIL shareholders. However, given this investment is too large in the context of one company, one sector and one country, it will be regularly reviewed and, when appropriate, BIL's stake will be reduced.

In the context of an optimum level of capital, an important investment option for BIL will be the ability to buy back and cancel its own shares. The Chairman's Report refers to the adoption of a new Constitution which will provide the Company with the flexibility to undertake share buy backs if and when it is considered in the best interests of all shareholders to do so.

In the introduction to this review I indicated that BIL has two simple objectives:
- to grow the underlying intrinsic value of BIL; and
- to ensure that such growth is reflected in shareholders' hands through increased returns.

Each is important in its own right with the first largely dictating the extent to which the second can be achieved. Management is absolutely committed to both objectives and will take whatever steps are necessary in pursuit of their achievement.

INVESTMENT ACTIVITIES

While investment returns are an important component of BIL's overall profit, the profitable realisation of any specific investment is often not in itself a noteworthy occasion. By the time an investment is sold, its underlying value is usually readily apparent and identifiable, with the marketplace generally having recognised the merits of BIL's original investment decision.

A good case in point was the sale in 1995 of the Group's residual holding in Carter Holt Harvey for $468 million resulting in a surplus of $142 million. The initial investment in Carter Holt Harvey was made in 1990. Around that time its own acquisition strategies had resulted in it becoming heavily indebted and out of favour with the market. While BIL's involvement is well documented and the success of that investment now widely recognised, the reality is that the initial investment was viewed sceptically by the market as, somewhat ironically, was the final selldown—but for quite different reasons.

As a contrarian value-based investor we were delighted with our investment in Carter Holt Harvey which, over time, averaged some $500 million and realised in excess of $1 billion.

The investment highlight of the year was unquestionably the purchase and subsequent sale of a 28% interest in New Zealand's pre-eminent publishing company Wilson & Horton. After an extensive evaluation process BIL acquired its interest in November 1994 at $9.50 per share and a total outlay of $265 million, with the intention of being a long-term shareholder. Subsequent to the acquisition, discussions were held with the company's directors who expressed their preference for a major shareholder to be an existing newspaper industry participant. BIL agreed to work with the company to identify a suitable shareholder and to sell its shareholding, provided the price reflected the strategic value of the shareholding and the real underlying value of the company. The sale process introduced a number of potential buyers who concurred with our view on value and resulted in BIL selling its shareholding for a profit of $65 million. The outcome has already proven to be of significant benefit to all Wilson & Horton shareholders with the company's new dividend policy ensuring that the longer term share price more fully reflects the underlying value of the company.

A more recent outcome and one which will be accounted for in the 1995/96 financial year is the recent completion of the partial selldown of the Group's interest in Auckland casino owner, Sky City. With construction now well advanced and the casino due to open in early 1996, we arranged $300 million in external debt facilities based on equity of $186 million. Having completed this financing, BIL offered 29% of the total capital for sale by way of a private placement. The selldown in July valued Sky City's equity at $425 million and resulted in a profit to BIL of $65 million. BIL retains a 50.6% interest which, based on recent sales, now has a market value of $278 million, which compares favourably to its book value of $95 million.

OUTLOOK

There are three key determinants to BIL's future prospects:
- current investments—a careful review of current investments highlights the opportunity to grow cashflow and earnings and hence enhance value in each of the regions in which the Group operates with the gross trading contribution forecast to rise from $290 million in 1995 to over $400 million in 1997;
- strong financial position—there will always be new investment opportunities available in any market environment. While careful evaluation of, and commitment to, each new investment

Brierly Investments Limited

is a fundamental prerequisite, as important is maintaining a strong financial position which will enable BIL to take advantage of these opportunities; and

• people—the importance of a capable team cannot be underestimated. BIL is appropriately resourced with well motivated, highly skilled people, enabling us to add value to existing investments and create value from new investments.

BIL is well positioned to continue to enhance shareholder value in the future as it has in the past. While the present market capitalisation is a source of disappointment, we nevertheless are committed to ensuring that the value created is represented in a tangible form in the hands of individual shareholders.

FINANCIAL SUMMARY

	BIL Holding	Net Profit 1995 millions	Net Profit 1994 millions	Sales 1995 millions	Sales 1994 millions	Total Assets 1995 millions	Total Assets 1994 millions	Shareholders' Funds 1995 millions	Shareholders' Funds 1994 millions
New Zealand									
Air New Zealand Ltd	42%	$260.2	$190.7	$2,888	$2,598	$3,107	$2,915	$1,274	$1,198
LWR Industries Ltd	66%	$12.6	$13.2	$152	$157	$98	$97	$65	$60
Sealord Products Group	50%	$32.3	$23.5	$307	$301	$325	$320	$158	$128
Skellerup Group Ltd	30%	$44.4	$25.4	$828	$646	$519	$421	$217	$177
Tasman Agriculture Ltd**	52%	$6.1	$5.5	$17	$15	$203	$155	$154	$108
Union Shipping Group Ltd	50%	$14.7	$15.3	$137	$152	$126	$107	$74	$71
Australia									
Australian Consolidated Investments Ltd	96%	A$9.8	A$85.4	A$797	—	A$893	A$440	A$298	A$280
The Austotel Trust	100%	A$7.2	A$5.1	A$351	A$321	A$319	A$391	A$125	A$122
Asia									
Paul Y.—ITC Construction Holdings Ltd*	21%	HK$230.4	HK$201.9	HK$3,965	HK$2,074	HK$3,094	HK$2,039	HK$1,004	HK$611
United States									
Associated Hosts Inc+	100%	US$(5.5)	US$(4.5)	US$58	US$57	US$55	US$62	US$34	US$29
Everest & Jennings International Ltd++	85%	US$(9.7)	US$(55.7)	US$79.4	US$94.5	US$62	US$59	US$(16)	US$(7)
Molokai Ranch Ltd	100%	US$(4.8)	US$(1.0)	US$3	US$5	US$187	US$181	US$175	US$172
United Kingdom									
Mount Charlotte Investments Plc++	70%	£26.4	£10.4	£241	£214	£1,880	£1,853	£1,185	£1,159

BIL holding percentages as at 11 September 1995

* Balance date 31 March
**Balance date 31 May
+ Balance date 30 September
++Balance date 31 December

Brierly Investments Limited

COMPARATIVE FINANCIAL REVIEW

	Consolidated				
	1995 $000	1994 $000	1993 $000	1992 $000	1991 $000
Profits					
Net Operating Surplus	381,356	378,162	222,860	354,829	303,741
Less					
Taxation	1.883	(2,771)	(12,920)	55,392	50,044
Minority Interests	38,786	38,861	23,099	11,696	63,147
Unrealised Reduction in Value of Investment Properties	—	—	18,960	—	—
Add					
Equity Earnings	91,083	88,005	77,623	(36,631)	21,183
Profit Attributable to the Group	431,770	430,077	271,344'	251,110	211,733
Less					
Cash Dividends	226,747	151,988	160,033	225,564	161,676
Profit Retained in the Group	$205,023	$278,089	$111,311	$25,546	$50,057
Capital Funds					
Issued Capital	1,328,701	1,302,882	1,253,135	1,253,135	1,253,135
Reserves and Retained Earnings	2,006,410	1,917,245	1,762,689	2,012,206	1,977,724
Total Shareholders' Funds	3,335,111	3,220,127	3,015,824	3,265,341	3,230,859
Minority Interests in Subsidiary Companies	1,138,725	1,129,278	1,190,180	1,409,895	1,030,091
Capital Notes	449,219	461,838	168,239	—	—
Convertible Notes	269,414	269,414	269,414	—	—
Subordinated Debt	—	74,085	736,575	866,918	372,394
Investment Fluctuation	10,999	252,995	17,155	63,740	21,024
Surplus on Acquisitions	386,568	420.925	454,026	566,178	457,992
Total Capital Funds	$5.590,036	$5,828,662	$5,851,413	$6,172,072	$5,112,260
Represented By					
Fixed Assets	5,712,567	5,938,367	5,991,068	7,502,037	6,320,079
Investments and Intangibles	2,200,187	2,261,430	2,244,149	2,191,372	2,128,494
Current Assets	1,507,710	948,593	1,746,941	1,600,456	3,500,918
Total Assets	9,420,464	9,148,390	9,982,158	11,293,865	11,949,491
Miscellaneous Contingencies	273,849	319,662	334,153	499,808	468,522
Term Liabilities	2,720,263	1,302,619	2,205,993	2,946,632	3,112,251
Current Liabilities	836,316	1,697,447	1,590,599	1,675.353	3,256,458
	$5,590,036	$5,828,662	$5,851,413	$6,172,072	$5,112,260
Statistics					
Adjusted Earnings per 50c Ordinary Share	15.4c	15.8c	10.8c	10.0c	10.5c
Adjusted Dividend per 50c Ordinary Share	9.0c	9.0c	9.0c	9.0c	9.0c
Net Asset Backing per 50c Ordinary Share	$1.26	$1.24	$1.20	$1.30	$1.29
Rate of Net Profit Earned on Year-end Ordinary Capital	32.5%	33.0%	21.7%	20.0%	16.9%
Rate of Net Profit Earned on Average Shareholders' Funds	13.2%	13.8%	8.6%	7.7%	7.1%

Brierly Investments Limited

Brierly Investments Limited

CONSOLIDATED PROFIT AND LOSS ACCOUNT

For the year ended 30 June 1995	1995 $000	1994 $000
Net Operating Surplus (13)	381,356	378,162
Less		
Taxation (14)	1,883	(2,771)
Consolidated Net Profit After Taxation	379,473	380,933
Less		
Share of Profits Applicable to Minority Interests	38,786	38,861
	340,687	342,072
Add		
Equity Earnings (15)	91,083	88,005
Profit Attributable to the Group (4) (16)	$431,770	$430,077

CONSOLIDATED BALANCE SHEET

As at 30 June 1995	**1995** **$000**	1994 $000
Capital Funds		
Authorised Capital (1)	**$2,000,000**	$2,000,000
Issued Capital (1)	**1,328,701**	1,302,882
Reserves (2) (3)	**(31,686)**	129,414
Retained Earnings (4)	**2,038,096**	1,787,831
Total Shareholders' Funds	**3,335,111**	3,220,127
Other Capital Funds		
Minority Interests in Subsidiary Companies	**1,138,725**	1,129,278
Capital Notes (5)	**449,219**	461,838
Convertible Notes (6)	**269,414**	269,414
Subordinated Debt	**—**	74,085
Investment Fluctuation	**10,999**	252,995
Surplus on Acquisitions	**386,568**	420,925
Total Other Capital Funds	**2,254,925**	2,608,535
Total Capital Funds	**5,590,036**	5,828,662
Miscellaneous Contingencies	**273,849**	319,662
Term Liabilities (7)		
Loans and Advances	**2,720,263**	1,302,619
Current Liabilities (8)		
Bank Overdrafts	**126,109**	71,408
Creditors	**563,537**	558,593
Loans and Advances	**144,427**	1,066,362
Provision for Taxation	**2,243**	1,084
	836,316	1,697,447
	$9,420,464	$9,148,390
Fixed Assets (9)		
Land and Buildings	**5,412,658**	5,550,105
Plant, Vehicles and Fittings	**299,909**	388,262
	5,712,567	5,938,367
Investments (10)		
Shares in –		
Public Companies	**535,069**	950,650
Associate Companies	**931,365**	648,620
Other Investments	**733,753**	662,160
	2,200,187	2,261,430
Current Assets (11)		
Cash and Marketable Securities	**874,312**	327,824
Debtors	**364,748**	434,681
Short-term Investments	**27,521**	11,143
Inventories	**241,129**	174,945
	1,507,710	948,593
	$9,420,464	$9,148,390

Brierly Investments Limited

CONSOLIDATED STATEMENT OF CASH FLOWS

For the year ended 30 June 1995	1995 $000	1994 $000
Cash Flows from Operating Activities		
Received from Customers	2,450,876	1,640,717
Interest Received	54,363	111,449
Dividends Received	123,808	52,400
Paid to Suppliers and Employees	(2,256,180)	(1,457,359)
Interest Paid	(275,555)	(363,388)
Tax Paid	(7,074)	20,456
Other	62,991	138,427
Total Operating Cash Flows (21)	153,229	142,702
Cash Flows from Investing Activities (20)		
Sale of Fixed Assets	94,614	13,233
Sale of Investments	941,965	1,154,846
Loans and Advances Repaid	723	2,000
Purchase of Fixed Assets	(278,761)	(230,702)
Interest Paid Capitalised	(14,345)	—
Purchase of Investments	(971,048)	(684,310)
Loans and Advances	(11,069)	—
Other	114,687)	153,902
Total Investing Cash Flows	(123,234)	408,969
Cash Flows from Financing Activities (20)		
Issue of Shares and Capital Notes	58,672	317,517
Borrowings	2,455,015	899,537
Repayment of Borrowings	(1,821,023)	(2,197,576)
Dividends Paid	(178,968)	(138,576)
Other	(28,384)	—
Total Financing Cash Flows	485,312	(1,119,098)
Net Change in Cash	515,307	(567,427)
Opening Cash	256,416	839,798
Effect of Acquisition and Disposal of Subsidiaries	(16,183)	5,232
Effect of Exchange Rate Changes on Cash	(7,337)	(21,187)
Closing Cash	$748,203	$256,416
Closing Cash Comprises		
Cash and Marketable Securities (11)	874,312	327,824
Bank Overdrafts (8)	(126,109)	(71,408)
	$748,203	$256,416

STATEMENT OF ACCOUNTING POLICIES

GENERAL ACCOUNTING POLICIES

The following general accounting policies have been adopted in these financial statements which have been prepared on a going concern basis:

historical cost adjusted by the revaluation of certain assets;

accrual accounting to match expenses with revenues

The financial statements have been prepared under the requirements of the Companies Act 1955 and Financial Reporting Act 1993.

PARTICULAR ACCOUNTING POLICIES

(a) Principles of Consolidation

(i) *Subsidiaries*

The Group financial statements include the financial statements of all subsidiaries, being companies which Brierley Investments Limited control either directly, indirectly or beneficially.

The financial statements of subsidiaries are included in the Group financial statements using the purchase method.

All material inter-company balances and profits resulting from intra-group transactions have been eliminated.

Where subsidiaries are acquired during the year, their results are included from the date of acquisition, while for subsidiaries disposed of during the year, their results are included to the date of disposal.

Date of acquisition is either the date on which the title to the asset passes, or in respect of listed public companies, the date of the last published financial statements, from which the acquisition price is determined.

(ii) *Associate Companies*

An associate company is one in which the Group has an equity interest of between 20% and 50% and has the capacity to significantly influence the policies of that company.

The financial statements of associate companies are included in the Group financial statements using the equity method with the Group's share of associate companies' profits reflected in the consolidated profit and loss account.

(iii) *Details of Subsidiary and Associate Companies*

Details of subsidiary and associate companies are listed in the Group Investments section of the Annual Report. Subsidiary and associate company results are included for the period to the Group balance date except as follows:

	Last Balance Date	Period Included
Paul Y. — ITC Construction Holdings Limited	31 March 1995	Year to 31 March 1995
Steego Corporation	30 April 1995	Year to 30 April 1995
Tasman Agriculture Limited	31 May 1995	Year to 31 May 1995

(iv) *Joint Ventures*

The following joint ventures are included in the Group financial statements on a proportionate basis:

AsiaPower Developments

Sealord Products Group

(b) Balance on Acquisition

On the acquisition of a subsidiary or associate company the fair value of net identifiable assets is ascertained. The difference between the fair value and the cost of investment in the subsidiary or associate company is brought to account either as a surplus or goodwill on acquisition.

Goodwill is amortised by systematic charges against income over the appropriate periods in which benefits are expected to be realised, but not exceeding 20 years. The periods over which the amounts are to be amortised are subject to annual review.

Surplus on acquisitions is included under "Other Capital Funds" on the balance sheet and is released to the profit and loss account as and when the assets to which it relates are disposed of.

(c) Fixed Assets

Fixed assets are recorded at cost of purchase or at adjusted fair values. Investment properties are recorded at their net current value determined by reference to independent valuations. Net changes in the value of investment properties are recorded in the profit and loss account.

(d) Depreciation

Fixed assets are depreciated on a straight-line or diminishing value basis over their estimated economic lives.

Where depreciation is not charged by an overseas subsidiary, its policy has been consistently applied in the preparation of the Group financial statements.

Brierly Investments Limited

Depreciation sales are:

Buildings	1%–5%
Plant, Vehicles and Fittings	4%–33 1/3%

(e) Investments

(i) *Listed Public Securities*

Investments in shares in listed public companies are recorded at market value based on official stock exchange quotations at balance date. The difference between market value and cost is shown in "Investment Fluctuation," which is included in the profit and loss account when realised.

Unrealised losses in the value of investments are taken to the profit and loss account where the diminution is considered to be permanent.

(ii) *Other Investments*

All other investments are included at cost or valuation.

(f) Inventories

Inventories are valued at lower of cost or net realisable value including a share of fixed and variable overheads where appropriate. Cost is determined using various methods including specific identification, average cost, first in first out and standard cost.

(g) Debtors

Debtors are shown at their expected realisable value.

(h) Foreign Currency

Overseas investments and balances payable in foreign currency to and by the Group have been included in the Group financial statements at rates ruling at balance date. Where transactions have been hedged by way of obtaining forward exchange cover over the balances outstanding they are converted at the forward rate.

The assets, liabilities and operating results of overseas subsidiaries are translated at balance date rates. Foreign exchange movements on independent foreign operations, and any offsetting foreign exchange movement on monetary assets or liabilities designated as a hedge of an independent foreign operation, are taken to the Foreign Currency Translation Reserve.

All other exchange differences, including differences arising on the conversion of short-term and long-term monetary items, whether realised or unrealised, are taken directly to the profit and loss account.

Exchange rates used at balance date:

A	$0.94	=	NZ$1.00
SFr	0.77	=	NZ$1.00
HK	$5.16	=	NZ$1.00
US	$0.67	=	NZ$1.00
Stg	£0.42	=	NZ$1.00

(i) Taxation

Taxation has been provided in the financial statements on the basis of the estimated taxation payable on the taxable income by each member company of the Group after taking advantage of all available deductions and concessions.

The deferred tax provision is calculated using the liability method, resulting from short-term differences between profits computed for tax purposes and profits as stated in the financial statements. Provision is not made for timing differences unless a liability is expected to arise in the foreseeable future.

Deferred tax assets of subsidiaries are recognised where the individual subsidiary is able to justify the deferred tax assets. Deferred tax liabilities of individual subsidiaries are recognised if the subsidiary is unable to use Group tax losses available.

(j) Sales

Group sales represent sales to outside parties by the trading subsidiaries and do not include dividends, interest or other investment income. The amount of investment income is disclosed in Note 16 to these financial statements.

(k) Bonus Shares in Lieu of Dividends

The premium on bonus shares issued in lieu of dividends on the election of shareholders has been recognised in the Share Premium Reserve.

(l) Changes in Accounting Policies

There have been no material changes in accounting policies during the year. All policies have been applied on a consistent basis with previous years.

(m) Comparative Figures

Certain comparative figures have been restated to reflect changes in presentation.

12 SEGMENTED ASSETS AND SALES

	Consolidated			
	Assets **$000**	**1995** **Sales** **$000**	Assets $000	1994 Sales $000
By Activity Segment:				
Energy and Oil Royalties	274,335	—	287,990	—
Engineering, Construction and Property	559,591	9,504	572,387	180,987
Food and Beverages	203,419	153,480	326,878	376,658
Hotels	4,540,850	600,406	4,865,027	590,055
Investment	1,059,496	—	1,233,406	—
Manufacturing	309,582	326,114	373,711	157,055
Transport	752,496	136,953	559,466	152,309
Wholesale and Retail	215,929	849,788	11,688	14,315
Other	630,454	500,080	590,013	113,881
	8,546,152	2,576,325	8,820,566	1,585,260
Cash and Marketable Securities	874,312	—	327,824	—
	$9,420,464	$2,576,325	$9,148,390	$1,585,260
By Geographic Segment:				
New Zealand	1,848,934	481,096	1,965,868	724,555
Australia	1,151,317	1,224,339	977,473	—
Asia	294,514	—	222,658	151,028
United States	612,556	270,484	698,535	119,622
United Kingdom	4,638,831	600,406	4,956,032	590,055
	8,546,152	2,576,325	8,820,566	1,585,260
Cash and Marketable Securities	874,312	—	327,824	—
	$9,420,464	$2,576,325	$9,148,390	$1,585,260

The increase in sales in the current year is principally due to the acquisition of Vox Holdings Pty Limited.

Brierly Investments Limited

14 TAXATION

	Consolidated	
	1995 $000	1994 $000
Net Operating Surplus	381,356	378,162
Taxation at 33%	125,847	124,793
Adjusted by the Tax Effect of:		
Non-assessable Dividend Income	(27,918)	(3,660)
Other Non-assessable Revenues	(17,001)	(33,055)
Non-deductible Expenses	109,636	76,257
Deductible Items Carried Forward/(Brought Forward)	(187,283)	(160,162)
Income at Other Tax Rates	(4,546)	(1,765)
Under/(Over) Provisions in Prior Years	(1,470)	(9,870)
Other	4,618	4,691
	$1,883	$(2,771)
Taxation Charged/(Credited)—New Zealand	3,802	6,981
Taxation Charged/(Credited)—Other Countries	(1,919)	(9,752
	$1,883	$(2,771)
Current Taxation	4,050	(2,443)
Deferred Taxation	(2,167)	(328)
	$1,883	$ (2,771)
Deferred Taxation		
Opening Balance	(2,553)	1,501
Deferred Taxation in Profit and Loss Account	(2,167)	(328)
Other Movements	1,248	(3,726)
	$(3,472)	$(2,553)

The Group currently has tax losses available to carry forward and offset against future assessable income in several jurisdictions. The tax benefit of these losses is only recognised to the extent of deferred tax liabilities.

Revenue authorities are currently conducting investigations into the Group which makes the accurate quantification of the unrecognised tax benefit of the tax losses uncertain. The Group considers that there are sufficient tax losses to offset both adjustments arising as a result of these investigations and deferred tax liabilities.

Imputation Credits

Parent Company	4,560	4,560
Subsidiary Companies	47,778	15,863
Minority Interest Share in Subsidiary Companies	(8,385	(12,233)
	$43,953	$8,190

16 Profit Attributable to the Group

			Consolidated	
By Activity Segment:	**Operating Surplus $000**	**Net Interest $000**	**1995 Total $000**	1994 Total $000
Trading Activities				
Energy and Oil Royalties	33,342	—	33,342	120,597
Engineering, Construction and Property	7,867	(627)	7,240	9,363
Food and Beverages	24,853	(8,597)	16,256	20,171
Forestry	—	—	—	27,982
Hotels	192,281	(100,449)	91,832	41,534
Manufacturing	24,971	(7,982)	16,989	19,133
Transport	129,058	(4,230)	124,828	87,179
Wholesale and Retail	(7,938)	1,315	(6,623)	768
Other	20,923	(15,042)	5,881	(8,552)
Trading Contribution	425,357	(135,612)	289,745	318,175
Taxation and Minority Interests			(41,674)	(35,080)
Net Trading Contribution			248,071	283,095
Investment Activities				
Dividend Income			92,711	7,933
Surplus on Sale of Assets and Investments			209,501	269,663
Other Income			13,825	5,252
Investment Contribution			316,037	282,848
Taxation and Minority Interests			1,005	(1,010)
Net Investment Contribution			317,042	281,838

By Geographic Segment:	**New Zealand**	**Australia**	**Asia**	**United States**	**United Kingdom**	**1995 Total $00**	1994 Total $000
Trading Contribution	172,253	34,962	13,665	(22,967)	91,832	289,745	318,175
Investment Contribution	246,094	34,933	15,088	1,838	18,084	316,037	282,848
Total Contribution	418,347	69,895	28,753	(21,129)	109,916	605,782	601,023
Taxation and Minority Interests						(40,669)	(36,090)
Funding Costs and Overheads						(133,343)	(134,856)
Profit Attributable to the Group						$431,770	$430,077

Trading Activities reflects the results of the trading subsidiary and associate companies. Investment Activities reflects the results of the respective holding companies in New Zealand, Australia and Hong Kong.

AUDITORS' REPORT

KPMG Peat Marwick

Chartered Accountants

AUDIT REPORT TO THE SHAREHOLDERS OF BRIERLY INVESTMENTS LIMITED

We have audited the financial statements on pages 61 to 82. The financial statements provide information about the past financial performance and financial position of the Company and Group as at 30 June 1995. This information is stated in accordance with the accounting policies set out on pages 65 and 66.

Directors' Responsibilities

The Directors are responsible for the preparation of financial statements which give a true and fair view of the financial position of the Company and Group as at 30 June 1995 and of the results of the Company and the Group's operations and cash flows for the year ended 30 June 1995.

Auditors' Responsibilities

It is our responsibility to express an independent opinion on the financial statements presented by the Directors and report our opinion to you.

Basis of Opinion

An audit includes examining, on a test basis, evidence relevant to the amounts and disclosures in the financial statements. It also includes assessing:

- the significant estimates and judgements made by the Directors in the preparation of the financial statements; and
- whether the accounting policies are appropriate to the Company and Group's circumstances, consistently applied and adequately disclosed.

We conducted our audit in accordance with generally accepted auditing standards in New Zealand. We planned and performed our audit so as to obtain all the information and explanations which we considered necessary in order to provide us with sufficient evidence to give reasonable assurance that the financial statements are free from material misstatements, whether caused by fraud or error. In forming our opinion we also evaluated the overall adequacy of the presentation of information in the financial statements.

Other than in our capacity as auditors we have no relationship with or interests in the Company or any of its Subsidiaries.

Unqualified Opinion

We have obtained all the information and explanations we have required.

In our opinion:

- proper accounting records have been kept by the Company as far as appears from our examination of those records; and
- the financial statements on pages 61 to 82:
  — comply with generally accepted accounting practice
  — give a true and fair view of the financial position of the Company and Group as at 30 June 1995 and the results of the Company and the Group's operations and cash flows for the year ended on that date.

Our audit was completed on 6 September 1995 and our unqualified opinion is expressed as at that date.

KPMG *Peat Marwick*
Wellington, New Zealand

The City of New York

In July 1996 Moody's Investors Service was reviewing the ratings for the general obligation bonds of the City of New York. With a population of approximately 7.3 million, New York was the largest city in the United States and an international business and cultural center. Its key industries included banking, securities, life insurance, communications, publishing, printing, fashion design, apparel manufacture, retailing, and construction. In addition, the City was the leading tourist destination in the United States.

New York's economy was closely linked to national economic events. Thus, in the early 1990s, it experienced a decline in employment and real gross product. Growth picked up in the period 1992 to 1994, but slowed after 1995. The City's general obligation bonds were rated Baa1, the lowest rated investment grade bonds.

Moody's review included an analysis of the challenges facing U.S. municipalities generally, as well as an examination of the financial performance of New York. At the completion of the review, Moody's had to decide whether to upgrade, downgrade, or maintain the City's current rating.

FINANCIAL CHALLENGES FOR MUNICIPALITIES

Municipal governments typically provided a range of services to local communities, including legislative, executive, and judicial functions. They also offered a range of other services, such as primary and secondary education, public safety (police and fire), public works (streets, sewers, and sanitation), public welfare, public transportation, airports, utilities (water and power), colleges, hospitals, corrections facilities, community development, and parks and recreation facilities. To fund these activities, municipal governments received support from state and federal governments, property and other forms of taxes, charges for various services, and utility revenues.

Municipal governments grew dramatically after World War II, from 2.8 million employees in 1945 to 7.4 million in 1970 and 10 million in 1987. This level of employment exceeded that for the combined state and federal civilian governments.

During the 1990s municipalities faced a number of financial challenges, including deteriorating infrastructure, stagnant revenues accompanied by increasing cost structures, unfunded mandates from federal and state governments to provide additional services, pressures to increase the quality of public services provided (without increasing costs), and competition between municipalities to attract new businesses.

Much of the infrastructure for older U.S. cities such as New York was provided during the Depression. For example, the public works projects of the New Deal provided for the construction of municipal roads, bridges, and some public buildings. The 1970s saw a shift from maintenance and replacement of this infrastructure to increased social services. As a result, infrastructure deteriorated and by the early 1990s often required replacement.

A second financial challenge facing older U.S. municipalities arose from stagnant revenue bases and increased cost structures. Many municipalities in the Northeast and the Midwest had stable or declining populations, and had seen key businesses move to less

Professor Paul M. Healy prepared this case, which has benefited from the comments of Jack Miller and Elizabeth Krahmer. The case is intended solely as the basis for class discussion and is not intended to serve as an endorsement, source of primary data, or illustration of effective or ineffective management. Copyright © 1998 by the President and Fellows of Harvard College. HBS Case 9-198-030.

costly areas of the country. As a result, their revenue base was stagnant. Compounding this problem, their costs had escalated during the 1980s and early 1990s. For example, medical costs increased at rates significantly higher than inflation during this period. This increased significantly the cost of medical benefits for municipal employees, as well as the cost of providing health services to older and poorer residents through public hospital systems.

A third factor affecting municipal governments had been the increase in unfunded state and federal government mandates to provide additional services. For example, state and federal governments required local governments to accept increased responsibility for undertaking such services as police and safety, mass transit, housing for the indigent, and special education, without necessarily providing the full funding for these services.

The 1980s and 1990s also saw increased product and service quality in many areas of the private sector. For example, there were significant product improvements in the computer and auto industries, faster customer response times due to overnight delivery, faxes, and E-mail, as well as opportunities for home shopping and banking. Taxpayers frequently expected the same types of quality improvements in public services, leading to a growing expectations gap between taxpayers and public service providers about the quality and cost of services. As a result, there was widespread pressure on local governments to improve productivity and to make existing resources stretch further.

Finally, there was increased competition among local governments to attract new businesses to their community. In many cases, local governments offered tax incentives and commitments to provide infrastructure to companies considering locating in their communities. For example, in late September 1993, after months of negotiations with at least 30 states and municipalities which were willing to provide attractive location packages, Mercedes-Benz announced that it had decided on Tuscaloosa, Alabama, as the site of its new $300 million plant. The plant, which was expected to open in 1997, would employ 1,500 and manufacture 60,000 sport utility vehicles per year. The city of Tuscaloosa committed as much as $30 million for land acquisition and site preparation; Mercedes would be allowed to buy this package for $100 million, implying that the deal cost local taxpayers roughly $20,000 per new job.

FINANCIAL REPORTING BY MUNICIPALITIES

Financial reporting standards for municipalities were developed by the Government Accounting Standards Board (GASB), as well as by the Financial Accounting Standards Board (FASB) and municipal laws. There were a number of differences between financial reporting for municipalities and reporting by for-profit organizations. Some of these differences were differences in terminology. For example, the income statement was called the Statement of Revenues and Expenditures and Changes in Fund Balances, and owners equity was termed the "fund balance" in government organizations. However, there were also substantive differences, including the use of fund accounting and modifications to accrual accounting.

Fund Accounting

Fund accounting required separate funds reports to be maintained to account and report for many of the different activities of government. For example, separate statements were typically created for the local public hospital, for new capital projects, for debt service, for public employee pension funds, and for general government operations. Each of these activities was viewed as a separate entity or "fund" and received its own allocation of resources. For many funds these resources were restricted, and could only be used for specific purposes. Separate financial reports are therefore prepared for each fund account so that users can monitor whether the resources allocated to the funds were used in the way intended.

For municipalities there are three major classes of funds: governmental funds, proprietary funds, and fiduciary funds.

Governmental funds included the general fund (where resources were unrestricted), special revenue funds (which were restricted to outlays for specific purposes other than major capital projects), capital project funds (where funds were restricted to use for capital expenditures), and debt service funds (used to accumulate funds to pay interest and principal on outstanding debt).

Proprietary funds were for activities that were intended to be operated like a business. They included enterprise funds (such as hospitals and water and sewer operations), which provided goods and services to outside parties and which were intended to be self-supporting. Proprietary funds were also created for operations that provided goods or services for other parts of the government.

Fiduciary funds were assets held by a government unit in trust. They typically included pension funds for government employees.

Financial statements for municipalities presented separate results for all three classes of funds. Also, separate group accounts were reported for debt obligations and fixed assets.

Modifications to Accrual Accounting

For proprietary funds, the traditional accrual accounting system was used. However, for governmental funds several modifications to accrual accounting were made. These modifications (for revenue recognition, accrual of interest, and depreciation), made governmental fund accounting closer to a cash basis of accounting than accrual accounting.

The first key difference between governmental accounting and traditional accrual accounting was that revenues for governmental funds were reported when they become measurable and available, rather than when they were earned. For example, property taxes were recognized as revenue when levied rather than when they were earned. A second major difference was that interest on long-term debt was not recorded until it became due, rather than when it was accrued. Thus, if quarterly interest payments on municipal bonds outstanding were due on January 31, a municipality with a December 31 year-end would not accrue interest owed to bondholders for the months of November and December. Finally, while depreciation was recorded for business-like activities (proprietary funds), for governmental funds new capital outlays were effectively expensed. As a result, the balance sheet for the principal government fund, the general fund, typically included only current assets and liabilities.

THE CITY OF NEW YORK'S FINANCES

New York City had a checkered financial history. In February 1975, the New York Urban Development Corporation was unable to repay a $100 million short-term note to Chase Manhattan Bank. This triggered a crisis that resulted in the City being shut out of the credit market. Its bleak prospects eventually forced bankers, unions, and government to work together to reach an agreement. City management took on three sacred cows (low transit fares, CUNY tuition, and subsidized housing); a special agency, the Municipal Assistance Corporation of the City of New York (MAC) was created as a vehicle to issue new municipal

City of New York

debt; state legislators agreed to provide a 28 percent increase in intergovernmental aid; the banks deferred debt and interest payments and provided additional financing; and municipal employees accepted short-term pay cuts and layoffs (many through attrition) and agreed that their pension fund would invest in new MAC debt.

Subsequent analysis attributed the City's financial collapse to a dramatic increase in short-term debt (from $747 million to $4.5 billion in only six years). The New York State Charter Revision Commission explained:

Since 1970–71 every expense budget has been balanced with an array of gimmicks— revenue accruals, capitalization of expenses, raiding reserves, appropriation of illusory fund balances, suspension of payments, carry-forward of deficits and questionable receivables, and finally, the creation of a public benefit corporation whose purpose is to borrow funds to bail out the expense budget.[1]

As a result of the management and budgetary changes discussed above, by 1981 the City had balanced its budget again, and has since recovered from the financial crisis.

Exhibit 1 presents General Fund Revenues and Expenditures for the City during the period 1992 to 1996, the 1996 budget, footnotes, and management discussion of performance. Revenues were generated from a variety of sources, including real estate taxes, sales taxes, income taxes, as well as funding from the federal and state governments. As reported in Exhibit 2, in 1996 real estate tax rates for the City were 10.37 percent of assessed property values, and 1.88 percent of their market values. This difference reflects the City's practice of assessing property at less than its full market value.[2] The ratio of the assessed value of property to its market value (called the Special Equalization Ratio) had declined steadily from 29.7 percent in 1993 to 22.1 percent in 1996.

Sales taxes arose from the City's 4 percent sales tax as well as the state's 4.25 percent retail sales tax. In addition, the City levied a personal income tax on residents and on earnings made in the City for nonresidents, and a corporate income tax on companies doing business in the city. Other revenues were generated by fees paid to the City for issuing licenses, permits, and franchises; interest income; tuition fees from city-run colleges and universities; and rents collected from city-owned property and airports. In 1995 the City included in Other Revenues $200 million from the recovery of prior year FICA overpayments for Social Security and Medicare, as well as $120 million from the sale of upstate jails to the state. Other revenues in 1996 included one-time receipts of $170 million from the New York City Health and Hospitals Corporation, and $28 million from the New York City Housing Financing Agency.

Most of the federal and state funding provided to the City was in the form of categorical grants, which were earmarked for specific activities. These included expenditures for welfare, education, higher education, health and mental health, community development, job training programs, housing, and criminal justice. The City also received a modest amount of unrestricted federal and state aid, which could be used for general-purpose expenditures. However, this support had been declining.

The City's major General Fund expenditures were for social services, education, public safety, debt service, health, and pensions. As reported in Exhibit 1, the difference between General Fund revenues and expenditures, the General Fund surplus, was $5 million for the three years 1994–1996. However, this surplus did not tell the whole story, since the City was required to balance its budget each year. The reported surplus therefore included

---

1. See R. Herzlinger, Public Sector Accounting (Englewood Cliffs, NJ: Prentice-Hall, 1996, p. 316).

2. Revenues from real estate taxes are limited by the New York State Constitution, which requires real estate revenues to be no more than 2.5 percent of the average market value of real estate for the most recent five years.

discretionary transfers and expenditures used to cover a deficit or to eliminate any surplus. Operating surpluses before discretionary transfers and expenditures were $570 million, $371 million, $72 million, $71 million, and $229 million in the period 1991 to 1996.

New York's financial plan for the period 1997 to 2000, presented in Exhibit 3, shows a steadily growing gap between General Fund revenues and expenditures. By 2000 this gap was projected to be $3.4 billion. To meet this deficit the City had embarked on a series of programs to contain costs and increase revenues. The new programs were expected to provide revenues and cost savings by reducing entitlements, by restructuring City government through consolidating and privatizing operations, by increasing federal and state aid, and by selling assets. In addition, for 1997 the City projected a savings of $150 million in pension fund costs from changing the actuarial assumption on investment earnings.

Other studies, however, suggested that the City's problems may be more serious than official projections. For example, a May 1996 report by the City Comptroller identified between $1.176 billion and $1.546 billion of potential risks for the 1997 forecasts. These included uncertainties about $100 million of assumed state aid, $160 million in proposed revisions to Medicaid benefits, $40 million from changes in entitlement programs, $319 million in airport-related payments which had been the subject of ongoing unsuccessful negotiation, and as much as $400 million from unidentified cuts in education. These concerns were echoed in staff reports from the OSDC and the Control Board. The OSDC report, published in May 1996, concluded that the City had a structural imbalance, and only succeeds in balancing the 1997 budget by including $1.4 billion of one-time items. The study pointed out that the City's structural problems did not appear to have diminished by workforce reductions of more than 20,000 employees, the lowering of public assistance and Medicaid costs, and the scaling back of tax reduction proposals.

In addition to its 1996 operating outlays of $32 billion, the City made capital outlays of $3.8 billion. These were financed through the issuance of bonds by the City and City agencies, as well as by state and federal grants. Exhibit 4 provides a breakdown of Capital Expenditures for the period 1992 to 1996, as well as long-term projections of capital outlays required to maintain and improve the City's infrastructure. These included outlays for mass transit facilities, sewers, bridges and tunnels, and investments to improve the City's operating productivity. The four-year Capital Commitment Plan for the period 1997 to 2000 projected that in 1997 the City would make commitments for capital projects of $4.3 billion, and would have capital expenditures of $3.7 billion.

As required by its charter, the City reported on the condition of fixed assets, and recommended maintenance expenditures and capital outlays needed to ensure assets were in a good state of repair. The report suggested that the City is letting its fixed assets deteriorate. Actual maintenance outlays in the previous five years had been only 33 percent of recommended levels, and the four year Capital Commitment Plan projected a continuance of this pattern for the period 1997 to 2000. In addition, budgeted capital expenditures in the Capital Plan were only 63 percent of those recommended.

Bond Rating Review

As shown in Exhibit 5, at December 31, 1996, the City had $30.3 billion of debt outstanding. This included debt for the City itself, MAC, and City-guaranteed debt. On a per capita basis the City's debt had increased from $2,202 in 1989 to $3,901 in 1995, outpacing the growth in pretax personal income of City residents.

The New York State constitution required that the City's debt outstanding be less than 10 percent of the average market value of taxable real estate for the last five years, and that debt raised to fund low-rent housing, low-income nursing homes, and urban renewal be less than 2 percent of taxable real estate for the previous five years. The City's projections indicated that by 1998 its debt outstanding would exceed the general debt limit. As a result, the City was proposing state legislation to create the new Infrastructure Finance Authority. The Infrastructure Finance Authority would be permitted to issue debt that would not be subject to the constitutional limit.

Throughout 1996 the City's $25.9 billion of general obligation bonds had been rated Baa1 and A– by Moody's and Fitch Investors Service, respectively. However, Standard & Poor's had downgraded their rating from A– to BBB+, and Moody's and Fitch were also contemplating a downgrade. Additional information on Moody's ratings as well as the relation between yields and ratings are presented in Exhibit 6. During 1996 the City issued $5.3 billion of general obligation bonds, using $2.7 billion to refinance outstanding bonds. Yields on 30-year City debt peaked in 1995 at 6.65 percent and declined to 6.18 percent by March 1996. The City's debt traded 53 basis points over the Bond Buyer 20 Bond Index in July 1995, but this spread had declined to 48 basis points by June 1996.

QUESTIONS

1. Who are the key constituents participating in municipal governments? What challenges do they create for New York City?

2. What are the key performance indicators that you would consider in reviewing the performance of The City of New York for Moody's municipal bond ratings? How has The City performed on these dimensions? What concerns, if any, do you have about its recent performance?

3. Given your analysis in question 1, what is your assessment of the reasonableness of the assumptions underlying The City's projections made in its four-year plan?

4. Would you recommend downrating The City's General Obligation bonds?

EXHIBIT I

The City of New York Condensed Financial Statements—General Fund
Revenues and Expenditures, 1992–1996

(in millions)	Adopted Budget 1996	Actual				
		1996	1995	1994	1993	1992
General Fund Revenues						
Taxes (net of refunds):						
Real estate	$7,274	$7,100	$7,474	$7,773	$7,886	$7,818
Sales and use	3,097	3,111	3,013	2,855	2,739	2,621
Income	6,502	6,808	6,015	6,281	5,751	5,389
Other	1,029	1,095	1,184	1,206	1,204	1,221
	17,902	18,114	17,686	18,115	17,580	17,049
Federal, State and Other Aid:						
Categorical	9,891	10,880	10,733	10,143	9,535	8,880
Unrestricted	549	621	603	667	707	826
	10,440	11,501	11,336	10,810	10,242	9,706
Other than Taxes and Aid:						
Charges for services	1,253	1,312	1,298	1,277	1,304	1,195
Other revenues	1,578	1,118	1,244	1,127	961	1,039
OTB transfers	30	26	27	24	29	33
	2,861	2,456	2,569	2,428	2,294	2,267
Total Revenues	31,203	32,071	31,591	31,353	30,116	29,022
General Fund Expenditures						
General government	$811	$855	$853	$875	$862	$853
Public safety and judicial	4,226	4,446	4,121	3,846	3,759	3,586
Board of Education	7,286	7,835	7,863	7,561	7,213	6,626
City University	363	348	348	353	571	459
Social services	7,522	7,901	8,112	8,030	7,430	7,108
Environmental protection	1,096	1,138	1,120	1,156	1,094	989
Transportation services	667	732	933	981	1,023	1,044
Parks, recreation, cultural	239	244	240	238	229	202
Housing	399	455	527	590	516	541
Health (including HHC)	1,544	1,829	1,737	1,620	1,452	1,276
Libraries	176	253	168	172	146	129
Pensions	1,555	1,356	1,273	1,274	1,427	1,370
Judgments and claims	279	309	251	271	231	232
Fringe and other benefits	1,227	1,581	1,444	1,552	1,492	1,378
Other	948	210	307	375	267	257
Transfers for debt service	2,865	2,574	2,289	2,454	2,440	2,968
Total Expenditures	31,203	32,066	31,586	31,348	30,152	29,018
Surplus (deficit)	0	5	5	5	(36)	4

Source: The City of New York, Comprehensive Annual Financial Report of the Comptroller for the Fiscal Year
Ended June 30, 1996.

City of New York

City of New York

FOOTNOTES

Statement of General Fund Revenues and Expenditures

(1) The City's results of operations refer to the City's General Fund revenues and transfers reduced by expenditures and transfers. The revenues and assets of Proprietary Funds included in the City's audited financial statements do not constitute revenues and assets of the City's General Fund, and, accordingly, the revenues of such funds, other than net OTB revenues, are not included in the City's results of operations. Expenditures required to be made by the City with respect to such Proprietary Funds are included in the City's results of operations.

(2) In October 1993, the City reported a General Fund operating surplus of $5,079,000 for the 1993 fiscal year as reported in accordance with then applicable GAAP. The City has been required to restate its fiscal year 1993 financial statements because the City has implemented for the 1994 fiscal year Governmental Accounting Standards Board ("GASB") Statement Number 22, which provides for a change in the method of recognizing certain tax receipts. For purposes of presenting comparative financial statements for the 1994 fiscal year, the City was required to restate the fiscal year 1993 statements as if the Statement were adopted in fiscal year 1993. Accordingly, for purposes of presenting fiscal year 1993 financial statements on a comparative basis, the opening fund balance of fiscal year 1993 was restated from $82,974,000 to $311,435,000 and the surplus for the 1993 fiscal year was restated from $5,079,000 to $(36,025,000).

(3) Real Estate Tax for the 1992, 1993, 1994, 1995 and 1996 fiscal years includes $131 million, $128 million, $147.5 million, and $150 million, respectively, of Criminal Justice fund revenues. Real Estate Tax for fiscal years 1994, 1995 and 1996 also includes $201 million and $223 million from the sale of the City's delinquent tax receivables outstanding as of May 31, 1994 and April 1, 1995, and $182 million from the sale of property tax liens, respectively.

(4) Revenues include amounts paid and expected to be paid to the City Municipal Assistance Corp. (MAC) by the State from sales tax receipts, stock transfer tax receipts and State per capita aid otherwise payable by the State to the City. Pursuant to State statute, these revenues flow directly from the State to MAC, and flow to the City only to the extent not required by MAC for debt service, reserve fund requirements and for operating expenses. The City includes such revenues as City revenues and reports the amount retained by MAC from such revenues as "MAC Debt Service Funding," although the City has no control over the statutory application of such revenues to the extent MAC requires them. Estimates of City "Debt Service" include, and estimates of "MAC Debt Service Funding" are reduced by, payments to the City of debt service on City obligations held by MAC. Other Taxes include transfers of net OTB revenues. Other Taxes for the 1992 fiscal year includes $1.5 million of Criminal Justice Fund revenues from the City lottery.

(5) The General Fund surplus is the surplus after discretionary transfers and expenditures. The City had General Fund operating surpluses of $71 million, $72 million, $371 million and $570 million before discretionary transfers and expenditures for the 1995, 1994, 1993, and 1992 fiscal years, respectively. The Financial Plan projects a discretionary transfer of $243 million for the 1996 fiscal year. The expenditures and discretionary transfers made by the City after the adoption of its fiscal year 1996 and fiscal year 1995 budgets follow:

(in millions)	1996	1995
Transfer to the General Debt Service Fund of real estate taxes collected in excess of the amount needed to finance debt service	$106	$66
Adv. cash subsidiaries to Transit Authority	44	—
Adv. cash subsidiaries to Library System	74	—
Total expenditures and discretionary surplus	224	66
Reported operating surplus	5	5
Total operating surplus	$229	$71

Final results for any given fiscal year may differ greatly from that year's Adopted Budget. The following table shows how actuals for fiscal year 1996 differ from the Adopted Budget:

	Amount (in millions)
Additional Resources:	
Federal categorical aid above budget	$524
State categorical aid above budget	148
Unrestricted federal and state aid above budget	72
Higher revenues from tax collections, excluding property tax refunds	387
Interest income above budget	23
Lower pension contributions	199
Lower subsidy payments to the Health & Hospitals Corporation	88
Release by the Municipal Assistance Corp. of sales tax monies above targets in the Adopted Budget	145
Lower debt service costs due to bond refundings	64
Sale of Mitchell Lama mortgages	265
Higher collection of licenses, permits and privileges revenues	14
Total additional resources	$1929
Enabled the City to:	
Withstand higher than anticipated refunds of property taxes	$174
Withstand reduction of FY95 budgeted surplus to be used to fund FY96 expenditures	129
Provide for future debt service costs	106
Provide for increased overtime costs	81
Provide for increased judgment and claims costs	19
Higher grant costs paid to recipients of the Home Relief program	185
Provide for increased Medicaid expenditures	512
Provide for prepayment of FY97 subsidy to the Library System	74
Provide for prepayment of FY97 subsidy to the Transit Authority	44
Provide for increased subsidy for reduced fares for schoolchildren	45
Withstand lower collection of anticipated federal aid	75
Withstand lower collection of anticipated state aid	50
Withstand lower collection of revenues from firms and forfeitures	40
Withstand higher provision for disallowances of federal and state aid	25
Withstand lower than anticipated transfers from OTB Corp	5
Withstand postponement of the sale of City assets	32

(continued)

City of New York

	Amount (in millions)
Withstand lower than anticipated collection and settlement of back rent from the Port Authority for the Municipal Airports	103
Withstand other overspending and revenue below budget	225
Total	1,924
Reported surplus	$5

MANAGEMENT DISCUSSION: STATEMENT OF GENERAL FUND REVENUES AND EXPENDITURES

Total tax revenue increased by $428 million, or 2.4%, to $18,114 billion in fiscal year 1996. Collections of real estate taxes in fiscal year 1996 were 91.7% of the current fiscal year's tax levy of $7.871 billion. The delinquency rate (an important indicator of fiscal health) was 3.8% in fiscal year 1996, down from 5.0% in fiscal year 1995. Real estate tax collections remained constant at $7.5 billion in fiscal year 1996. The tax levy remained constant as well, $7.9 billion in fiscal years 1995 and 1996.

Revenues from economically sensitive taxes on general sales, personal income, general and financial corporation and unincorporated business income increased 9.6% in fiscal year 1996; these taxes decreased 1.7% in fiscal year 1995. Individually, the taxes changed as follows: general sales tax revenues up 4.6%, the financial corporation tax up 27.6%, unincorporated business income tax up 25.6%, personal income tax up 8.8%, and general corporation tax up 11.4%. The large increase in Financial Corporation Tax is predominantly due to the strength of the City's Wall Street sector and to loan growth stemming from a cut in the Federal Funds rate.

Federal, state and other categorical aid grew $147 million (1.4%) in fiscal year 1996 over 1995. Unrestricted aid increased 3.0% from the fiscal year 1995 level.

General fund expenditures and other financing uses in fiscal year 1996 including transfers for debt service, increased $480 million (1.5%) over fiscal year 1995, to $32.066 billion.

Excluding transfers for debt service, expenditures in fiscal year 1996 increased by 0.7% over fiscal year 1995. Personal service expenditures including pensions and fringes increased 2.1% in fiscal year 1996. Employee salaries and wages in fiscal year 1996 increased 1.9% over fiscal year 1995; health insurance expenditures increased by 9.4% and Social Security increased by 2.9%. Overtime expenditures increased 3.1% to $436 million from $423 million in fiscal year 1995; pension costs increased 2.6% from fiscal 1995, to $1.415 billion. The number of full-time City employees was 236,674 on June 30, 1996, an increase of 2,065 from June 30, 1995. The most significant headcount increases occurred in the Fire Department (3,393), the Police Department (549), the Department of Corrections (288) and the Department of Finance (254). The most significant decreases occurred in the Board of Education (1,407), the Department of Homeless Services (365), and the Department of Housing and Preservation and Development (126). Other than personal services related expenditures excluding Medicaid, Welfare and Debt Service increased 4.8% in fiscal year 1996 over fiscal year 1995.

Transfers for debt service on long-term debt increased by $285 million, or 12.5%, to $2,574 billion in fiscal year 1996.

City of New York

STATEMENT OF SOURCES AND USES OF CASH, 1995–96 (in millions)

	1996	1995
Summary of General Fund Operations		
Revenues	$32,071	$31,591
Expenditures Before Transfers	(29,492)	(29,297)
Surplus Before Debt Service and Other Transfers	2,579	2,294
Transfers for Debt Service and Other Purposes	(2,574)	(2,289)
Surplus from General Fund Operations	5	5
Adjustments to Bring Operations to a Cash Basis		
Increase in Payables	1,659	1,305
Increase in Receivables	(967)	(897)
Provision for Disallowances of Federal and State Aid	40	21
Less Disallowances Paid	(28)	(10)
Cash Provided by Operations	709	424
Other Sources of Cash		
Proceeds from Sale of City Bonds	2,594	2,242
Decrease (Increase) in Amounts Restricted Pending Expenditure	(282)	221
Seasonal Borrowings	2,400	2,200
Total Other Sources of Cash	4,712	4,663
Other Uses of Cash		
Repayment of Seasonal Borrowings	(2,400)	(2,200)
Federal and State Financed Capital Disbursements	(375)	(331)
Less Reimbursements	244	810
City-Financed Capital Construction	(3,421)	(3,344)
Increase in Other	258	427
Total Other Uses of Cash	(5,694)	(4,638)
Net Increase (Decrease) in Cash	(273)	449
Cash, Beginning of Year	748	299
Cash, End of Year	$475	$748

City of New York

EXHIBIT 2

Real Estate Tax Levies, Values, and Tax Collections, The City of New York

Comparison of Real Estate Tax Levies, Tax Limits, and Tax Rates

Fiscal Year	Total Levy	Operating Limit[a]	Rate per $100 of Full Valuation	Average Tax Rate per $100 of Assessed Valuation
1993	$8,392.5	$11,945.0	$1.60	$10.59
1994	8,113.2	13,853.8	1.30	10.37
1995	7,889.8	13,446.5	1.14	10.37
1996	7,871.4	8,633.4	1.88	10.37
1997	7,835.1	7,857.3	2.46	10.37

a. The State Constitution limits the amount of revenue which the City can raise from the real estate tax for operating purposes ("the operating limit") to 2.5% of the average full value of taxable real estate in the City for the current and the last four years less interest on temporary debt and the aggregate amount of business improvement district charges subject to the 2.5% tax limitation. The most recent calculation of the operating limit does not fully reflect the current downturn in the real estate market, which is expected to lower the operating limit in the future.

Billable Assessed and Full Value of Taxable Real Estate

Fiscal Year	Billable Assessed Valuation of Taxable Real Estate (in millions)	÷	Special Equalization Ratio	=	Full Valuation (in millions)
1993	$79,370.6		0.2965		$267,691.6
1994	78,364.6		0.2627		298,304.4
1995	76,202.4		0.2384		319,641.1
1996	76,029.4		0.2209		344,180.3
1997	75,668.5		0.2069		365,724.8

Real Estate Tax Collections and Delinquencies

Fiscal Year	Tax Levy (in millions)	Tax Collections as Percentage of Tax Levy	Delinquent at Fiscal Year End (in millions)	Delinquency as Percentage of Tax Levy
1990	$6,872.4	94.7%	$230.2	3.35%
1991	7,681.3	93.7	315.7	4.11
1992	8,318.8	93.1	370.2	4.45
1993	8,392.5	92.5	411.2	4.90
1994	8,113.2	92.7	403.4	4.97
1995	7,889.8	93.5	381.6	4.84
1996	7,871.4	93.4	288.9	3.67

City of New York

EXHIBIT 3

The City of New York Financial Plan, 1997–2000

(in millions)	Fiscal Year			
	1997	1998	1999	2000
Revenues				
Taxes:				
General property tax	$ 7,088	$ 7,244	$ 7,469	$ 7,752
Other taxes	10,407	10,837	11,352	11,897
Tax audit revenue	659	659	659	659
Tax reduction program	(25)	(188)	(366)	(432)
Miscellaneous revenues	4,468	3,549	3,117	2,894
Unrestricted intergovernmental aid	523	510	509	513
Anticipated state actions	50	—	—	—
Other categorical grants	293	275	281	280
Interfund revenues	260	260	258	256
Less: Intracity revenues	(647)	(647)	(646)	(644)
Disallowances against categorical grants	(15)	(15)	(15)	(15)
Total City Funds	$23,061	$22,484	$22,618	$23,160
Federal categorical grants	3,771	3,600	3,586	3,582
State categorical grants	6,149	6,071	6,106	6,087
Total Revenues	$32,981	$32,155	$32,310	32,829
Expenditures				
Personal service	$16,237	$16,813	$17,612	$18,812
Other than personal service	14,128	14,064	14,256	14,271
Debt service	2,735	3,015	3,124	3,241
MAC debt service funding	328	394	423	370
General reserve	200	200	200	200
Total Expenditures	$33,628	$34,486	$35,615	$36,894
Less: Intracity Expenses	(647)	(647)	(646)	(644)
Net Total Expenditures	$32,981	$33,839	$34,969	$36,250
Deficit	$0	$1,684	$2,959	$3,421

City of New York

EXHIBIT 4

The City of New York Actual and Planned Capital Outlays, 1992–2000

Actual Capital Outlays (in millions)

	1996	1995	1994	1993	1992
Education	$ 812	$ 881	$ 727	$ 758	$ 686
Environmental protection	1,135	819	768	934	1,046
Transportation	554	444	423	341	364
Transit authority	218	150	221	250	330
Housing	246	292	387	431	639
All other	831	1,108	817	903	828
Total Expenditures	$3,796	$3,694	$3,343	$3,617	$3,893

Capital Commitment Plan, 1997–2000 (in millions)

	1997	1998	1999	2000
Education	$ 713	$ 859	$ 799	$1,392
Environmental protection	1,385	1,270	1,488	518
Transportation	760	643	671	590
Transit authority	497	231	231	231
Housing	311	267	317	382
Sanitation	185	604	167	361
City operations/Facilities	1,321	630	650	587
Economic and port development	71	46	35	44
Reserve for unattained commitments	(449)	(107)	(300)	(244)
Total Commitments	$4,793	$4,443	$4,058	$3,861
Total Expenditures	$4,255	$3,958	$4,114	$4,179

City of New York

MANAGEMENT DISCUSSION OF CAPITAL PROJECTS

Capital expenditures increased by $102 million to $3.8 billion in fiscal year 1996, or 2.8% more than in fiscal year 1995 and approximately 2.5% less than just four years ago. Expenditures on the infrastructure component of the Capital Budget were $2.1 billion in fiscal year 1996, $873 million more than in fiscal year 1995. Expenditures for environmental protection (excluding sanitation) accounted for 48.6% of the total spent on infrastructure in fiscal year 1996. Expenditures for mass transit in fiscal year 1996 accounted for 10.6% of the total expenditures on infrastructure. The amount expended on the City's water distribution and sewage collection system in fiscal year 1996 was $1.0 billion.

In October 1990, the City completed a project to inventory the major portions of its physical plant. The first citywide and individual agency report was published in fiscal year 1991, which has been updated yearly. It provides the City with a comprehensive assessment of the condition of its major assets, the projected costs necessary to restore these assets to a state of good repair and schedules detailing the maintenance required to maintain the assets' structural integrity. The City estimates costs for repairs, replacements, and major maintenance for fiscal years 1997 through 2000 to be $4.3 billion.

City of New York

EXHIBIT 5

The City of New York Debt

Combined Net City Debt

(in millions)	1996	1995	1994	1993	1992
Net City debt	$25,052	$23,258	$21,531	$19,424	$17,916
Net MAC debt	3,936	4,033	4,215	4,470	4,657
Net Samurai debt	200	200	200	200	—
Total City, MAC and Samurai Debt	29,188	27,491	25,946	24,094	22,573
City guaranteed debt	1,155	1,104	1,114	733	745
Combined Net City Debt	$30,343	$28,595	$27,060	$24,827	$23,318

City, MAC, and City-Guaranteed Proprietary Corporation Debt Service

Fiscal Years	Principal on City Long-Term Debt	Interest on City Long-Term Debt	City-Guaranteed Debt	Required MAC Funding	Total
1996	$ 22,718	$ 150,987	$ 22,560	$ 425,310	$ 621,575
1997	1,220,995	1,493,357	110,015	570,498	3,394,865
1998	1,206,764	1,401,147	116,997	583,535	3,308,443
1999	1,133,395	1,329,846	125,751	602,079	3,191,071
2000	1,072,079	1,271,698	125,749	537,438	3,006,964
2001	1,072,637	1,218,150	125,634	537,621	2,954,042
2002–2147	19,111,773	11,693,985	1,644,505	3,766,678	36,216,941
Total	$24,817,643	$18,408,183	$2,248,651	$6,597,849	$52,072,326

City, MAC, and City-Guaranteed Proprietary Corporation Debt

Fiscal Year	Debt per Capita	Debt per Capita as Percent of Personal Income per Capita	Debt as Percent of Assessed Value of Taxable Property	Debt as Percent of Full Value of Taxable Property
1989	$2,202	9.96%	25.4%	4.6%
1990	2,490	10.49	26.0	4.5
1991	2,917	11.93	28.0	4.5
1992	3,192	12.14	28.5	4.1
1993	3,389	12.51	31.3	3.9
1994	3,691	n.a.	35.2	4.4
1995	3,901	n.a.	36.9	4.1

City of New York

EXHIBIT 6

Moody's Investor Service, Inc.—Bond Ratings

Rating	Description of Rating	Average Yield, December 20, 1995
Aaa	Best quality or "gilt edge," with the smallest degree of investment risk. Interest payments are protected by large or exceptionally stable margin and principal is secure. Protective elements can be visualized and are most unlikely to impair strong position of such issues.	5.38%
Aa	High quality by all standards. Together with the Aaa group they comprise high grade bonds. They are rated lower than the best bonds because margins of protection may not be as large, fluctuation of protective elements may be of greater amplitude, or risks appear somewhat larger than in Aaa securities.	5.50%
A	Upper medium grade obligations. Security to principal and interest is considered adequate, but are susceptible to impairment sometime in the future.	5.55%
Baa	Medium grade obligations, i.e., they are neither highly protected nor poorly secured. Interest payments and principal security appear adequate for the present but certain protective elements may be lacking or unreliable over any great length of time. Such bonds lack outstanding investment characteristics and have speculative characteristics.	5.70%
Ba	Judged to have speculative elements; their future cannot be considered as well assured. Often the protection of interest and principal payments may be very moderate, and not well safeguarded during good and bad times over the future. Uncertainty of position characterizes bonds in this class.	n.a.
B	Lack characteristics of desirable investment. Assurance of interest and principal payments or maintenance of other terms of the contract over any long period of time may be small.	n.a.
Caa	Poor standing. Such issues may be in default or there may be present elements of danger with respect to principal or interest.	n.a.
Ca	Speculative in a high degree. Such issues are often in default or have other marked shortcomings.	n.a.
C	Lowest rated class of bonds. Issues so rated have extremely poor prospects of ever attaining any real investment standing.	n.a.

Source: *Moody's Bond Record*, Moody's Investors Service, New York.

City of New York

Comdisco, Inc. (A)

Comdisco Inc., the world's leading independent lessor of IBM computers, would seem like a company Wall Street ought to love. Annual revenues are up fourfold since 1978, to an estimated $600 million in the fiscal year that ended September 30. Earnings per share have grown at an even more torrid tempo, and return on shareholders' equity is running at an estimated 35%. Yet at a recent price of $37, the stock was selling at 15 times projected earnings in fiscal 1984—a tepid multiple for a company whose earnings could grow at a 30% clip over the next five years.

.
.
.

Just about the only thing wrong with Comdisco is the tainted reputation that computer-leasing companies acquired as a result of the well-known bankruptcies of OPM Leasing and Itel. Securities analysts, though, see no similarities between Comdisco and those fiascoes. OPM Leasing turned out to be a spectacularly fraudulent operation, and Itel's downfall resulted in large part from overly optimistic accounting assumptions, coupled with a large inventory of obsolete equipment. Comdisco's accounting couldn't be more conservative, analysts say. They add that the company has managed, through the use of ingenious leasing arrangements, to eliminate almost all exposure to equipment obsolescence. Comdisco, asserts John Keefe of Drexel Burnham Lambert, has practically nothing to fear from any future IBM decision.[1]

The quotes above appeared in the Personal Investing Section of *Fortune* magazine in October 1983.

BUSINESS HISTORY AND OPERATIONS

Comdisco, Inc. is a Chicago-based company founded in 1969 by its current chairman of the board and president, Kenneth Pontikes. The company originally began as an IBM computer dealer. As demand for computer leasing started to grow during the late 1970s, the company started emphasizing leasing operations. By 1982, leasing old and new IBM computer equipment constituted the primary business activity of the company, and Comdisco had become the largest computer leasing company. Comdisco's customers were primarily large corporations. In 1982, the company had business relationships with 70 percent of the Fortune 500 companies, including 49 of the 50 largest U.S. companies.

The computer remarketing industry had many participants: small independent operators, larger private organizations, and leasing subsidiaries of conglomerates. Comdisco was one of the few independent public corporations in the industry. The firms in the industry were primarily of two types: broker/dealers or third-party lessors. The broker/dealers obtained for customers computer equipment from either a vendor or current user; third-party lessors provided lease financing. Comdisco engaged in both these activities.

Comdisco achieved its dominance in the computer leasing industry through a strategy of full-service leasing. Under this strategy, the company offered its customers a number

Professor Krishna G. Palepu prepared this case. The case is intended solely as the basis for class discussion and is not intended to serve as an endorsement, source of primary data, or illustration of effective or ineffective management. Copyright © 1986 by the President and Fellows of Harvard College. HBS Case 9-186-299.

1. *Reprinted with permission from* Fortune, *October 31, 1983.*

Comdisco (A)

of services which were not offered by competitors. Comdisco's subsidiaries, Comdisco Technical Services, Inc. and Comdisco Transport, Inc., specialized in equipment refurbishment, delivery, installation, de-installation, and technical planning and site preparation. Comdisco Maintenance Services, another subsidiary, offered a low-cost alternative to IBM's maintenance service. Comdisco Disaster Recovery Services, Inc. was established to provide another valuable service to the company's customers: contingent data processing capacity to be used when a customer's own data center had unavoidable failures. Through this service, Comdisco's customers had access to four fully operational data centers as a backup to their own data centers, to be used in the event of a natural disaster or accident.

Comdisco's broad customer base provided the company with a number of competitive advantages. First, taking advantage of its access to 10,000 important users of IBM equipment in the U.S., the company created a proprietary data base of their computing needs. This data base provided Comdisco's sales force with current and timely information on potential customers and their requirements. Second, being the leading IBM dealer, Comdisco maintained large inventories of a broad range of IBM equipment. Comdisco's personnel closely monitored IBM's new products and pricing policies. This product knowledge combined with large inventories enabled the company to assist customers with their computer acquisition plans and to offer quick deliveries. Finally, using its data base, the company could help its customers sell their old hardware when they acquired new equipment from Comdisco.

While the above strategy enabled Comdisco to establish its dominance over others in the computer leasing industry, the company was still potentially vulnerable to competition from IBM itself since IBM equipment accounted for most of Comdisco's revenues. In 1981, IBM formed a financing subsidiary, IBM Credit Corporation, to provide customer financing. Shortly after that, IBM announced its intention to enter into computer leasing and established a joint venture for this purpose with Merrill Lynch and Metropolitan Life Insurance. A number of industry analysts felt that this might result in increased competition for companies like Comdisco.

Comdisco's management, however, felt that IBM's recent moves did not pose a threat to the company's competitive position because IBM's entry into leasing would enhance the tarnished image of the computer leasing business, a net benefit to the industry. They also believed that, as IBM began to emphasize outright sale of its equipment over short-term rentals, many of IBM's customers might be forced to look for other lessors like Comdisco who offered short-term leases. This was likely to provide additional business opportunities which would offset any loss of long-term lease business to IBM.

While equipment leasing to computer users was Comdisco's primary activity, the company also offered tax-oriented leases to investors who were primarily interested in the tax benefits associated with leasing. In recent years, the financial services income from the tax advantaged transactions accounted for a growing portion of the company's revenues.

ACCOUNTING POLICIES FOR LEASING

Comdisco offered computer equipment to its customers through a variety of lease arrangements. Using the terminology of Financial Accounting Standards Board's Statement No. 3, Comdisco's leases can be classified into one of three types: sales-type leases, direct financing leases, or operating leases.

Classification

Both sales-type and direct financing leases transferred substantially all the benefits and risks inherent in the ownership of the leased property to the lessee. A sales-type lease usually gave rise to a dealer's profit or loss for Comdisco. Therefore, in a sales-type lease, the fair value of the leased equipment (normal selling price) at the inception of the lease differed from the cost or carrying amount. In contrast, in a direct financing lease, the primary service that Comdisco offered was the financing of the equipment's acquisition by a lessee. In such a lease, the fair value of the equipment was equal to the cost or carrying amount. Comdisco earned only a financing income (interest) and no dealer's profit. An operating lease was a simple rental of the equipment, and Comdisco retained ownership of the equipment throughout the lease term.

Under FASB's guidelines, the accounting classification of a lease was based on whether or not it satisfied certain conditions:

1. The lease transfers ownership of the equipment to the lessee by the end of the lease term.
2. The lease contains an option allowing the lessee to purchase the property at a bargain price.
3. The lease term is equal to 75 percent or more of the estimated economic life of the property.
4. The present value of the rental is equal to 90 percent or more of the fair market value of the leased property.
5. Collectibility of the payments from the lessee is reasonably predictable.
6. No important uncertainties surround the amount of cost yet to be incurred by the lessor.

A lease meeting *at least one* of the first four conditions and *both* of the last two conditions was classified as a sales-type lease or direct financing lease. Such a lease was treated as a sales-type lease if the fair value of the leased equipment was different from its carrying amount; otherwise it was classified as a direct financing lease. A lease that did not meet the combination of conditions just described was classified as an operating lease.

Accounting Treatment: Comdisco as Lessor

The accounting treatment in Comdisco's financial statements for the above three types of leases was as follows:

Operating Lease Lease revenue consisted of monthly rentals; the cost of equipment was recorded as leased equipment. The difference between the cost and the estimated residual value at the end of the lease term was depreciated on a straight-line basis over the lease term. Salesmen's commissions and other initial direct costs were capitalized as deferred charges and were amortized on a straight-line basis.

Sales-Type Lease At the inception of the lease, the present value of rentals was treated as sales revenue. Equipment cost less the present value of the residual was recorded as cost of sales. The present value of rentals and of the residual was recorded on the balance sheet as net investment in sales-type lease. As each lease payment was received, the net investment was reduced and interest income was recognized.

Direct Financing Lease At the inception of the lease, the cost of the leased equipment was recorded as net investment in the direct financing lease. As each lease payment was received, the net investment was reduced by the corresponding amount. The difference between the sum of the lease payments and the cost of the leased equipment was unearned profit from the direct financing lease, and it was recognized monthly so as to produce a constant rate of return on the net investment.

Accounting Treatment: Comdisco as Lessee

In addition to the above leases where Comdisco was a lessor, it was also often a lessee: the company acquired equipment from computer vendors and others through leasing arrangements. If such a lease met at least one of the first four conditions listed earlier, it was classified by Comdisco as a capital lease; otherwise, it was classified as an operating lease. The accounting treatment of the leases where Comdisco was a lessee was as follows:

Operating Lease   Monthly rentals were treated as rental expense.

Capital Lease   At the inception of the lease, the present value of lease rentals was recorded as a capital lease asset. An equal amount was also recognized as a liability—an obligation under the capital lease. The capital lease asset was depreciated over the lease term. When a lease payment was made, the obligation under capital lease was reduced and interest expense on the lease obligation was recognized.

NONRECOURSE DISCOUNTING OF LEASE PAYMENTS

In order to finance its investment in leased assets, Comdisco often assigned the stream of lease payments to a financial institution at a fixed interest rate on a nonrecourse basis. In return, Comdisco received from the financial institution a loan equal to the present value of the lease payment stream. The financial institution received the lease payments from the lessee as repayments of the loan. In the event of default by a lessee, the financial institution had a first lien on the underlying leased equipment, with no further recourse against the company.

For operating leases, proceeds from discounting were recorded on the balance sheet as discounted lease rentals liability. As lessees made payments to the financial institutions, discounted lease rentals were reduced by the interest rate method. For sales-type leases and direct financing leases, proceeds from discounting were not included in discounted lease rentals. Instead, future rentals were eliminated from the net investment in sales-type or direct financing leases, and any gain or loss on the financing was immediately recognized in the income statement.

TAX ADVANTAGED TRANSACTIONS

In addition to leasing equipment to computer users, Comdisco undertook leasing transactions with investors who were interested in tax shelters. While the specific terms and conditions of these tax advantaged transactions varied, a typical transaction was as follows:

1. After the inception of the initial user lease and independent of it, Comdisco sold all the leased equipment to a third-party investor. This sale usually occurred three to nine months after the commencement of the initial user lease. The sales price equaled the then current fair market value of the equipment. The payment from the investor to Comdisco consisted of: (a) cash and a negotiable interest-bearing promissory note due within two years for 10–22 percent of the sales price (the "equity payment") and (b) an installment note for the balance payable over an 84-month period.

2. Simultaneously with the sale, Comdisco leased the equipment back from the investors for 84 months. The lease payments under the leaseback obligation were equal to the installment payments receivable by Comdisco from the investor (1.b).

3. As part of the leaseback arrangement, during the 61st through 84th months of the leaseback period, the investor shared in the re-lease proceeds that the company received from subleasing the equipment to a user. Upon the expiration of the leaseback period, the investor had the exclusive right to the equipment.

The net result of the above transaction was that Comdisco gave up the depreciation tax benefit, a portion of the rental revenues for months 61–84, and 100 percent of the equipment value after the 84th month. In return, the company received the nonrefundable equity payment (1.a).

If the equipment sold to the investor was originally under an operating lease, the equity payment was recorded by Comdisco as financial services revenue in the period in which the tax advantaged transaction occurred. From the fourth quarter of 1983, the company began to allocate as cost of financial services a portion of the net book value of the equipment at lease termination. For sales-type and direct financing leases, the equity payment was first applied to reduce a portion of the residual value of the equipment shown in the balance sheet (as investment in sales-type and direct financing leases). This is because the company's ability to recover the residual value was decreased due to the rental sharing under the tax advantaged transaction. The excess of the equity payment over the residual value reduction was recorded as financial services revenue in the period in which the tax advantaged transaction occurred.

RECENT PERFORMANCE

During the ten years ending in 1982, Comdisco's sales and profits grew rapidly. During fiscal 1982 the company reported $29.4 million profits on revenues of $471.6 million, representing an 88 percent increase in profits and 56 percent increase in sales during the year. (See Exhibit 3 for an abridged version of the 1982 annual report.) The company continued its strong growth performance in fiscal 1983. The company's profits and revenues in the first nine months of the fiscal year were $36.1 million and $401.4 million, respectively. (See Exhibit 2 for the company's interim report for this period.)

In Comdisco's second quarterly report for 1983, Kenneth Pontikes commented on the company's future:

> These new activities, along with the continued growth of the company's lease and customer base, enhance the company's long term growth prospects. The company's history of outstanding performance and the recent issuance of $250,000,000 of convertible subordinated debentures, which further strengthened the company's capital base, provide it with the flexibility required for continued growth in today's marketplace.

The company's shares, listed on The New York Stock Exchange, reflected this optimistic outlook: their price appreciated from about $9 in January 1982 to $37 by the end of September 1983. Exhibit 1 shows the movement of Comdisco's stock price and Standard and Poor's 500 index from January 1982 to September 1983. Comdisco's stock price increased by more than 300 percent during this period compared to a roughly 40 percent increase in Standard and Poor's 500 index. However, as the *Fortune* magazine comments indicate, many analysts considered Comdisco's stock to be still undervalued and expected it to continue to outperform the market.

Comdisco (A)

QUESTIONS

1. Evaluate Comdisco's business activities and the company's strategy.

2. Using the information in Comdisco's financial statements and footnotes, fill in the following to the extent possible (use plug figures if necessary):

Account	Balance as of 9/30/81		Increases during fiscal '82		Decreases during fiscal '82		Balance as of 9/30/82
Obligations under capital leases	_____	+	_____	–	_____	=	_____
Discounted lease rentals	_____	+	_____	–	_____	=	_____
Net investment in sales-type and direct financing leases	_____	+	_____	–	_____	=	_____

Identify the business transactions that would have given rise to the changes identified in the above accounts.

3. Analyze the relative contribution of rentals, sales of computer equipment, and financial services to Comdisco's reported profits during fiscal years 1981 and 1982 and the first nine months of fiscal year 1983. What are the reasons for the differences in the profit margins of these three activities? Which activity is contributing most to Comdisco's profits?

4. Evaluate the quality of Comdisco's disclosure in its annual report regarding the company's lease accounting policies. Do you think the disclosure is adequate to evaluate the company's performance?

EXHIBIT 1

Movement of Comdisco's Stock and S&P 500 Index, January 1982–September 1983

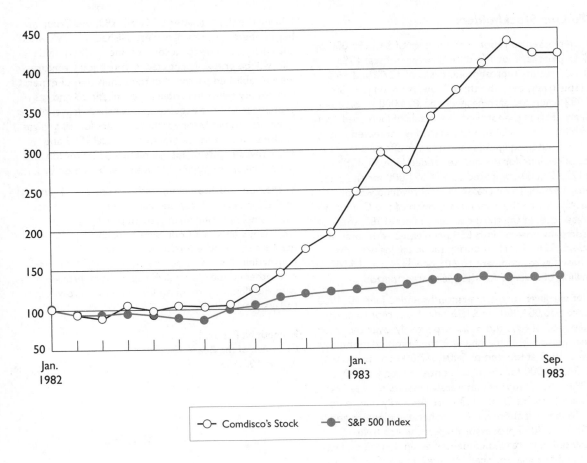

Comdisco (A)

Comdisco (A)

EXHIBIT 2

Comdisco, Inc. Quarterly Report, Third Quarter Ended June 30, 1983

To Our Stockholders

I am pleased to report net earnings of $13,199,000 or $.45 per share for the third quarter of fiscal 1983. These results represent increases of 127% and 96%, respectively, over the three months ended June 30, 1982 when net earnings were $5,824,000 or $.23 per share. Earnings improved as a result of increased profitability of financial services activities, increased leasing of computer equipment and a lower effective tax rate. Total revenue for the quarter ended June 30, 1983 was $127,455,000 compared to $94,691,000 for the prior year period. The increase in total revenue was primarily due to the continued growth of the Company's lease base. In the third quarter of fiscal 1983, the Company entered into 850 new leases with total revenue of $266.1 million during the initial lease terms. These figures compare to 605 new leases and $180.4 million of revenue for the year earlier period.

Net earnings for the nine months ended June 30, 1983 were $36,064,000, or $1.25 per share, representing increases of 69% and 51%, respectively, over the prior year period. Total revenue for the first nine months of fiscal 1983 amounted to $401,367,000 compared to $334,189,000 for the nine months ended June 30, 1982. The Company's impressive results for the first nine months of fiscal 1983 were primarily due to its active participation in the peripheral equipment and 3081 and 3083 processor markets, which have resulted in increased computer equipment sales, leasing and financial services activities. In addition, deliveries by IBM of the 3081 and 3083 processors have stimulated both sale and leasing of displaced IBM 3033 processors.

On July 21, 1983, the Board of Directors declared a cash dividend of $.04 per share to be paid on September 9, 1983 to stockholders of record as of August 19, 1983. This is the twenty-seventh consecutive quarterly cash dividend declared since the Company commenced paying cash dividends in 1977.

In April 1983, the Company announced its Corporate Lease Line Program, an expanded leasing program designed to meet the growing demand for lease financing of office and industrial equipment. The Corporate Lease Line Program expands the Company's array of complementary services and capitalizes on its expertise in providing customers with innovative and cost effective financing options.

During the third quarter of fiscal 1983, the Company began operations of a newly established, wholly owned subsidiary, Comdisco Resources, Inc. ("CRI"). Initially CRI will be primarily engaged, through joint ventures with established partners, in the acquisition of mineral and royalty rights in producing domestic oil and gas properties and the acquisition of onshore leasehold interests, primarily for resale to others for oil and gas exploration and development. For fiscal 1983 and 1984, investments of approximately $32.0 million and $13.0 million, respectively, have been budgeted by CRI.

These new activities, along with the continued growth of the Company's lease and customer base, enhance the Company's long term growth prospects. The Company's history of outstanding financial performance and the recent issuance of $250,000,000 of convertible subordinated debentures, which further strengthened the Company's capital base, provide it with the flexibility required for continued growth in today's marketplace.

Kenneth N. Pontikes
Chairman of the Board and President
August 10, 1983

CONSOLIDATED STATEMENTS OF EARNINGS AND RETAINED EARNINGS
For the Three and Nine Months Ended June 30, 1983 and 1982 (unaudited)

(in thousands except per share data)	Three Months Ended June 30		Nine Months Ended June 30	
	1983	1982	**1983**	1982
Revenue				
Rental	**$ 70,056**	$53,462	**$193,520**	$148,434
Sale of computer equipment	**29,159**	24,113	**129,626**	110,108
Financial services	**15,493**	12,890	**50,073**	62,040
Other	**12,747**	4,226	**28,148**	13,607
Total Revenue	**127,455**	94,691	**401,367**	334,189
Cost and Expenses				
Equipment depreciation, amortization and rental	**56,647**	40,378	**152,586**	115,325
Cost of computer equipment	**26,112**	21,318	**114,631**	99,659
Financial services	**1,524**	1,065	**3,614**	6,641
Selling, general and administrative	**13,938**	10,722	**43,060**	38,074
Interest	**14,035**	12,016	**38,112**	34,560
Total Costs and Expenses	**112,256**	85,499	**352,003**	294,259
Earnings before income taxes	**15,199**	9,192	**49,364**	39,930
Income taxes	**2,000**	3,368	**13,300**	18,568
Net earnings	**$ 13,199**	5,824	**36,064**	21,362
Retained earnings at beginning of period	**$ 92,445**	$58,223	**$71,268**	$43,359
Net earnings	**13,199**	5,824	**36,064**	21,362
Dividends paid	**(1,150)**	(394)	**(2,838)**	(1,068)
Retained earnings at end of period	**$104,494**	$63,653	**$104,494**	$ 63,653
Net earnings per common and common equivalent share	**.45**	.23	**1.25**	.83
Cash dividends per common share	**.04**	.03	**.11**	.09
Common and common equivalent shares outstanding	**29,611**	29,118	**29,234**	28,918

Comdisco (A)

CONSOLIDATED BALANCE SHEET
June 30, 1983 and 1982 (unaudited) and September 30, 1982 (unaudited)

(in thousands except number of shares)	June 30 1983	June 30 1982	September 30 1982
ASSETS			
Cash and marketable securities (at cost which approximates market)	**$175,215**	$ 4,586	$ 39,762
Receivables	**66,430**	38,854	45,055
Inventory of computer equipment	**48,914**	38,716	35,382
Investment in sales-type and direct financing leases	**63,735**	28,541	23,682
Leased and other equipment	**703,759**	532,969	534,611
Less: accumulated depreciation and amortization	**263,401**	174,408	192,714
Net equipment	**440,358**	358,561	341,897
Other assets and deferred charges	**55,925**	43,446	50,901
	$850,577	$512,704	$536,679
LIABILITIES AND STOCKHOLDERS' EQUITY			
Note payable	**$ —**	$ 2,650	$ 2,385
Subordinated debentures	**262,250**	62,250	62,250
Accounts payable	**29,001**	26,982	19,110
Obligations under capital leases	**14,669**	20,122	18,636
Income taxes	**42,817**	31,585	36,197
Other liabilities	**45,139**	39,219	45,265
Discounted lease rentals	**280,976**	247,899	261,780
	674,852	430,707	445,623
Stockholders' equity:			
Common stock $.10 par value Authorized 50,000,000 shares; issued 28,768,366 and 11,757,418 shares at June 30, 1983 and 1982, respectively (11,769,043 at September 30, 1982)	**2,877**	1,176	1,177
Additional paid-in capital	**68,718**	17,657	18,965
Deferred translation adjustment	**(364)**	(489)	(354)
Retained earnings	**104,494**	63,653	71,268
Total stockholders' equity	**175,725**	81,997	91,056
	$850,577	$512,704	$536,679

Comdisco (A)

CONSOLIDATED STATEMENTS OF CHANGES IN FINANCIAL POSITION
For the Nine Months Ended June 30, 1983 and 1982 (unaudited)

(in thousands)	1983	1982
Source of Funds		
Total provided by operations	$123,798	$133,285
Issuance of common stock upon conversion of 13% convertible debentures, net	52,465	—
Proceeds from issuance of subordinated debentures	245,250	—
Discounted lease rentals	141,002	92,535
Other	305	2,624
	562,820	228,444
Application of Funds		
Increase in leased equipment and inventory	238,304	175,193
Decrease in note payable	2,385	795
Redemption of convertible debentures	50,000	—
Reduction of discounted lease rentals and obligations under capital leases	126,332	45,611
Other assets and deferred charges	7,508	11,039
Other	2,838	1,068
	427,367	233,706
Increase (decrease) in cash and marketable securities	135,453	(5,262)
Cash and marketable securities at beginning of period	39,762	9,848
Cash and marketable securities at end of period	$175,215	$4,586

Notes to Consolidated Financial Statements

June 30, 1983 and 1982 (unaudited)

1. Principles of Reporting

The accompanying consolidated financial statements include the accounts of the Company and its wholly-owned subsidiaries after elimination of intercompany accounts and transactions. In the opinion of management, the accompanying consolidated financial statements contain all adjustments necessary for a fair presentation. The Company has a fiscal year that ends September 30.

The balance sheet at September 30, 1982 has been derived from the audited financial statements at that date.

2. Subordinated Debentures

On November 4, 1982, the Board of Directors announced the redemption of all of the Company's 13% Convertible Subordinated Debentures Due 2001 (the "Convertible Debentures") at a redemption price of $1,117 for each $1,000 principal amount of Convertible Debenture, plus accrued and unpaid interest to December 6, 1982. The Convertible Debentures were convertible into shares of common stock of the Company, at the option of the Convertible Debenture holder, at a conversion price of $9.75 per share. Common stock issued upon conversion of $49,839,000 principal amount of the convertible Debentures totaled 5,111,360 shares.

On May 4, 1983, the Company completed the sale of $250,000,000 principal amount of its 8% Convertible Subordinated Debentures Due May 1, 2003 (the "Debentures"). The Debentures are convertible into common stock of the Company at the rate of $36.50 per share. An aggregate of 6,849,315 shares has been reserved for issuance upon conversion of the Debentures. Temporarily, the net proceeds from the Debentures, which amounted to approximately $245,250,000, have been invested in short-term instruments and used to finance an increase in the Company's lease portfolio pending receipt of cash upon discounting of the related lease receivables.

3. Income Taxes

The rates used in computing the provision for federal income taxes at June 30, 1983 and 1982 vary from the statutory tax rate primarily due to investment tax credits generated in the respective years and Domestic International Sales Corporation (DISC) tax benefits. During the third quarter of fiscal 1983, the Company generated substantial investment tax credits resulting from the increase in leasing activity. Accordingly, the Company estimates that the annual effective tax rate will be approximately 27% for fiscal 1983 compared to the estimated rates of 33% and 40% used in the first six months of fiscal 1983 and the first nine months of fiscal 1982, respectively. The reduction in the estimated income tax rate resulted in an increase of approximately $2,100,000 in net earnings or $.07 per share in the third quarter of fiscal 1983. The effective tax rate for the quarter and nine months ended June 30, 1982 varies from the estimated annual rate due to a reinstatement of deferred income taxes resulting from the sale of investment tax credits which had been used to reduce deferred income taxes at September 30, 1981.

4. Common Stock

All references in the financial statements and notes to the number of common shares and per share data have been adjusted for the two-for-one stock split distributed in March 1983.

EXHIBIT 3

Comdisco, Inc. Annual Report for Fiscal Year 1982 (abridged)

To Our Stockholders

In fiscal 1982 Comdisco continued its outstanding performance with record earnings and revenues. Net earnings of $29.4 million, or $2.27 per share, represented increases of 88% and 68%, respectively, over fiscal 1981, while total revenue increased 56% to $471.6 million. These results were achieved despite the recessionary economic environment. The compound annual growth rate in net earnings over the last five years is an exceptional 43%. The primary factors contributing to the record earnings in fiscal 1982 were the increased volume and profitability of financial services activity, the growth of the Company's lease and customer bases, and the ability of the Company to capitalize on the active market for IBM 3033 processors and disk storage devices.

The higher level of financial services activity was the result of tax-advantaged leasing transactions associated with the Company's lease portfolio of used equipment and also the arrangement of "tax benefit transfers" that were structured under the Economic Recovery Tax Act of 1981. Late in fiscal 1982, Congress passed the Tax Equity and Fiscal Responsibility Act of 1982, which included legislation that will eventually eliminate "tax benefit transfers." This will cause the arrangement of traditional leveraged leases to re-emerge as a primary financial services activity of the Company.

The growth of Comdisco's lease base continued on a strong trend in fiscal 1982 as more users committed themselves to the leasing of equipment. The Company significantly increased its activity in the leasing of peripheral equipment. During fiscal 1982 the Company entered into 2,259 new leases with total revenue of $701.6 million during the initial term of these leases. This compares to 1,620 leases and $338.8 million in revenue during fiscal 1981.

The initial deliveries by IBM of its 3081 processor stimulated activity in all Comdisco's businesses. The Company participated in the lease placement of 3081 processors, and in the remarketing of the displaced 3033 processors. The Company's increased marketing efforts led to a 31% increase in its customers, which include most of the largest corporations in the United States. In fiscal 1981 Comdisco set up a "mid-range" marketing force that has successfully expanded the Company's customer base among medium-sized corporations. Comdisco's foreign subsidiaries continued to increase their marketing presence and also produced record results in the twelve months ended September 30, 1982. Fiscal 1982 also saw the continued refinement of Comdisco's computerized marketing data base that tracks user information for virtually all large IBM systems installed in the United States.

Two of Comdisco's newer subsidiaries, Comdisco Disaster Recovery Services and Comdisco Technical Services, made significant progress in fiscal 1982. The addition of the Texas Disaster Recovery Center by December 31, 1982 will bring the number of centers to four, providing further evidence that Comdisco Disaster Recovery Services can provide its customers with the most comprehensive disaster back-up services available. Comdisco Technical Services expanded its equipment installation and facilities planning operations and showed increased profitability.

Probably as significant as the record earnings results achieved in fiscal 1982, was the strengthening of Comdisco's financial position. Total assets increased 33% to $536.7 million, while stockholders' equity increased 55% to $9.1 million. The announcement in early November 1982 of the redemption of the Company's $50 million convertible debentures is anticipated to increase stockholders' equity to approximately $140 million and will reduce the Company's interest expense by $6.5 million per year. In addition, the Company had nearly $40 million in cash and marketable securities at September 30, 1982 while borrowing under various revolving credit agreements was zero. Because of its improved financial position, Comdisco is ideally situated to capitalize on opportunities in its traditional marketplace as well as those that arise in other areas.

In September 1982 Raymond F. Sebastian, formerly President of Comdisco Financial Services (CFS), was appointed to the position of Senior Vice President/ Corporate Development of Comdisco and will devote full time to the analysis of various investment opportunities available to the Company. He was replaced as President of CFS by Basil R. Twist, Jr. who, with Mr. Sebastian, has formulated the strategies that have made CFS so successful since its formation in 1976. Michael J. O'Connell has resigned as Executive Vice President of Comdisco effective January 1, 1983 to pursue other endeavors, but will continue as a Director. Mr. O'Connell has been with Comdisco since 1971 and has made valuable contributions to the Company's success.

In March 1982 Comdisco split its common stock 3-for-2 and paid dividends in fiscal 1982 totaling $.23 per share, an increase of 28% over the prior year, as adjusted. More importantly, return on average stockholders' equity has averaged 34.0% over the last five years. This has occurred over a period of time in which most of the Company's borrowings, other than discounted lease rentals, have been eliminated.

Comdisco begins fiscal 1983 in a strong capital position with high liquidity, a strong, competitive market position and a comprehensive array of complementary services for its customers. The Company provides leasing and other cost-effective services which continue to be attractive despite the current economic outlook. The delivery of more IBM 3081 processors will also increase opportunities for Comdisco in its marketplace.

Perhaps more so than many companies, Comdisco relies on the determination, skill and creative energies of its employees for its past and future success. This is another factor that gives me much optimism for Comdisco's continued success. With the on-going dedication of Comdisco's employees and the support of the Company's customers and stockholders, I am confident that Comdisco's superior growth rates in earnings and revenue can be maintained.

Kenneth N. Pontikes
Chairman of the Board and
President

November 11, 1982

Comdisco (A)

Management's Discussion and Analysis of Financial Condition and Results of Operations

Summary

The Company continued to achieve outstanding growth during fiscal 1982 as total revenue and net earnings increased 56% and 88%, respectively, compared to fiscal 1981. Increases in revenue and net earnings were accomplished despite the recessionary economic climate. Total revenue for fiscal 1982 and 1981 was $471.6 million and $301.5 million respectively. Net earnings increased from $15.6 million, or $1.35 a share, in fiscal 1981 to a record of $29.4 million, or $2.27 a share in fiscal 1982. The primary factors contributing to the record earnings were the increased volume and profitability of financial services activity, the growth of the Company's lease and customer base, and the ability of the Company to capitalize on the active market for 3033 processors and disk storage devices.

Revenue

Total revenue for fiscal 1982 reflected increases in all activities. In fiscal 1981, total revenue increased 19% over fiscal 1980 total revenue, as a result of higher revenue from all activities other than sale of computer equipment. For the five year period ended September 30, 1982, the Company has achieved an annual compound growth rate of 25% for total revenue.

The growth of the Company's lease base continued on a strong trend during fiscal 1982. This growth has been achieved as a result of the increased demand for leasing, broader penetration of the market, and the increase of activity levels created by initial product deliveries by IBM. Leasing offers computer users flexibility through short term commitments and conserves capital in a weak economy. As a result of this growth, rental revenue of $206.6 million in fiscal 1982 and $131.6 million in fiscal 1981 represented increases of 57% and 62%, respectively, over the preceding year.

Revenue from the sale of computer equipment increased during fiscal 1982 as a result of the active market for the IBM 3033 processor. The market for 3033 processors was stimulated by initial deliveries of IBM's 3081 processor and by the impact of IBM purchase price reductions on the 3033, which improved its price/performance ratio. Revenue from the sale of computer equipment declined 16% in fiscal 1981 compared to fiscal 1980, primarily due to computer users' increased preference for leasing.

Financial services revenue totaled $73.9 million in fiscal 1982 in comparison to $30.8 million in fiscal 1981. The increase in financial services revenue was primarily the result of tax-advantaged computer leasing transactions associated with a portion of the Company's lease portfolio of used equipment and also tax benefit transfers that were structured under the Economic Recovery Tax Act of 1981. Fiscal 1981 financial services revenue increased 119% over fiscal 1980 due to higher revenue from tax leveraged leases with third-party investors.

Costs and Expenses

Total costs and expenses of $417.8 million for fiscal 1982 increased 49% over total costs and expenses of $280.2 million in fiscal 1981. Fiscal 1981 total costs and expenses were 15% higher than fiscal 1980. The increases were the result of the growth in the Company's lease portfolio and customer base and the continuing expansion in marketing of the Company's services.

Selling, general and administrative expenses were $51.8 million in fiscal 1982, $28.5 million in fiscal 1981 and $19.3 million in fiscal 1980. The increases were primarily due to costs associated with the Company's expanding marketing activities, including higher commissions and administrative expenses.

The increases in interest expense in fiscal 1982 and fiscal 1981 were due to increased discounted lease rentals as a result of the growth in the Company's leasing activity. Interest expense on discounted leases, which is a non-cash expense, is the largest component of total interest expense (69% and 46% of total interest expense in fiscal 1982 and 1981, respectively). The Company finances leases by assigning the noncancellable rentals to financial institutions on a nonrecourse basis at a fixed interest rate and receives from the lender the present value of the rental payments (the discounted amount). As rental payments are made directly to the lender, the Company recognizes interest expense.

Income Taxes

Income taxes as a percentage of earnings before income taxes were 45.4% in fiscal 1982 compared to 26.8% in fiscal 1981 and 20.8% in fiscal 1980. Note 7 of Notes to Consolidated Financial Statements provides details about the Company's income tax provisions and effective tax rates. The higher effective tax rate in fiscal 1982 was attributable to lower investment tax credits due to the sale of such benefits by the Company as permitted under the Economic Recovery Tax Act of 1981 (the "Act"). The Act liberalized the leasing provisions of the tax law and made it possible for corporations which cannot use all their current year tax deductions and credits to transfer them to other corporations. The tax benefit transfers completed by the Company in fiscal 1982 provided cash flow benefits which otherwise would not have been available until future years.

International Operations

The Company operated principally in three geographic areas during fiscal 1982 and 1981; United States, Europe and Canada. The Company has subsidiaries in Belgium, Germany, Switzerland, the Netherlands, France, the United Kingdom and Canada. These subsidiaries offer services similar to those offered in the United States.

A more favorable environment in fiscal 1982 resulted in an increase in revenue from international operations of 42% from $55.9 million in fiscal 1981 to $79.6 million in fiscal 1982. The prior year's results had been depressed as a result of computer users deferring action pending shipment of new products. International revenues represented 17% of the Company's total revenue in fiscal 1982, and 18% in fiscal 1981.

Market and Dividend Information

The Company's common stock is traded on the New York Stock Exchange under the symbol CDO. The following table shows the quarterly price range and dividends paid for fiscal years 1982 and 1981, adjusted to reflect the three-for-two and five-for-four common stock splits effected in March 1982 and 1981, respectively.

	1982			1981		
Qtr.	High	Low	Div.	High	Low	Div.
1st	$18.00	$11.75	$.05	$13.27	$ 7.87	$.04
2nd	18.00	13.50	.06	15.50	11.50	.05
3rd	19.25	15.50	.06	16.09	13.17	.05
4th	23.00	15.00	.06	15.33	10.67	.05

At September 30, 1982, there were approximately 2,900 record holders of common stock.

Financial Position

During fiscal 1982, the Company's financial position and liquidity improved significantly, with cash and marketable securities amounting to $39.8 million at September 30, 1982 compared to $9.8 million at September 30, 1981. These improvements were due to an increased earnings level and continued emphasis on effective asset management. Major sources and uses of funds are set forth in the Consolidated Statements of Changes in Financial Position.

At September 30, 1982, the Company had $45 million of available borrowing capacity under various lines of credit from commercial banks. During fiscal 1982, the Company entered into agreements for the purpose of issuing commercial paper which may be used from time to time to meet some of the Company's short term debt requirements. These facilities ensure the availability of significant funds to finance additional growth.

The trend of computer users toward leasing rather than purchasing computer equipment is expected to continue due to economic conditions, IBM pricing policies, and new product announcements. The major portion of funds required by the Company to finance the purchase of equipment acquired for leasing is generated by assigning the noncancelable rentals to various financial institutions at fixed interest rates on a nonrecourse basis.

In June 1981, the Company sold $50 million of 13% convertible subordinated debentures. The proceeds of the lower cost, fixed-rate long term debt were used to replace bank borrowings. The Company had no short term debt at September 30, 1982.

Total notes and debentures as a percentage of total capital (the sum of notes and debentures payable, discounted lease rentals and stockholders' equity) has declined in each of the last three fiscal years, to 16% at September 30, 1982, compared to 29% at September 30, 1980. Improved earnings have contributed to the high returns on average stockholders' equity. This key financial measure of performance reached 39.2% in fiscal 1982, compared with 30.6% in fiscal 1981. The Company's strong financial position and history of earnings growth provide a solid base for obtaining the necessary financial resources to finance additional growth and for investment opportunities.

Ratios

The following table presents ratios which illustrate the changes and trends for the last three fiscal years:

	1982	1981	1980
Return on average stockholders' equity	39.2%	30.6%	18.0%
Return on average assets	6.2%	4.9%	3.5%
Earnings before income taxes (as a percentage of revenue)	11.4%	7.1%	3.5%
Net earnings (as a percentage of revenue)	6.2%	5.2%	2.8%

Comdisco (A)

Comdisco (A)

CONSOLIDATED FINANCIAL STATEMENTS

FIVE YEAR SELECTED FINANCIAL DATA

Years Ended September 30,	1982	1981	1980	1979	1978
Consolidated Summary of Earnings (in thousands):					
Revenue					
Rental	$206,592	$131,571	$ 80,979	$ 60,947	$ 42,524
Sale of computer equipment	166,705	125,384	149,708	149,983	103,995
Financial services	73,879	30,837	14,079	9,991	4,046
Other	24,454	13,746	8,348	4,355	2,717
Total Revenue	471,630	301,538	253,114	225,276	153,282
Cost and expenses					
Equipment depreciation, amortization and rental	160,523	99,413	68,328	47,698	32,260
Cost of computer equipment	149,654	111,784	134,595	128,470	93,176
Financial services	8,617	6,784	4,878	5,108	1,768
Selling, general and administrative	51,785	28,529	19,341	16,176	9,246
Interest	47,242	33,657	16,988	13,319	10,360
Total cost and expenses	417,821	280,167	244,130	210,771	146,810
Earnings before income taxes	53,809	21,371	8,984	14,505	6,472
Income taxes	24,432	5,730	1,870	3,900	1,550
Net earnings	$ 29,377	$ 15,641	$ 7,114	$ 10,605	$ 4,922
Common and Common Equivalent Share Data:					
Net earnings	$ 2.27	$ 1.35	$ .65	$ 1.07	$ .53
Stockholders' equity	$ 7.74	$ 5.17	$ 3.95	$ 3.50	$ 1.77
Average shares outstanding (in thousands)	14,487	12,270	11,051	9,929	9,222
Cash dividends paid	$ .23	$ .18	$ .15	$ .12	$ .06
Financial Position (in thousands):					
Total assets	$536,679	$404,507	$229,170	$173,950	$144,223
Total long-term debt	83,271	84,945	29,055	25,573	25,447
Discounted lease rentals	261,780	197,672	85,612	74,569	61,703
Stockholders' equity	91,056	58,746	43,565	35,508	14,994

Common and common equivalent share data have been adjusted to reflect a three-for-two stock split effected in February 1978, a two-for-one common stock split effected July 1978, a three-for-two common stock split effected in February 1979, a five-for-four common stock split effected in March 1981, and a three-for-two common stock split effected in March 1982.

CONSOLIDATED BALANCE SHEETS
(in thousands except number of shares)

September 30,	1982	1981
ASSETS		
Cash and marketable securities (at cost of $3,909 in 1982 and $1,883 in 1981 which approximates market)	$ 39,762	$ 9,848
Receivables:		
Accounts and notes (Net of allowance for doubtful accounts of $628 in 1982 and $528 in 1981)	41,368	28,379
Other	3,687	3,827
Inventory of computer equipment	35,382	25,036
Net investment in sales-type and direct financing leases	23,682	17,890
Leased and other equipment:		
Leased computer equipment	502,494	374,044
Capitalized leases—computer equipment	24,158	23,225
Buildings, furniture and other	7,959	4,184
Total equipment	534,611	401,453
Less: accumulated depreciation and amortization	192,714	115,073
Net equipment	341,897	286,380
Other assets and deferred charges	50,901	33,147
	$536,679	$404,507
LIABILITIES AND STOCKHOLDERS' EQUITY		
Note payable to bank	$ 2,385	$ 3,445
Convertible subordinated debentures	50,000	50,000
Subordinated debentures	12,250	12,250
Accounts payable	19,110	27,492
Obligations under capital leases	18,636	19,250
Income taxes:		
Current	6,076	—
Deferred	30,121	13,017
Other liabilities	45,265	22,635
Discounted lease rentals	261,780	197,672
	445,623	345,761
Stockholders' equity:		
Common stock $.10 par value. Authorized 50,000,000 shares in 1982 and 15,000,000 shares in 1981; issued 11,769,043 shares (7,571,151 in 1981)	1,177	757
Additional paid-in capital	18,965	14,630
Deferred translation adjustment	(354)	—
Retained earnings	71,268	43,359
Total stockholders' equity	91,056	58,746
	$536,679	$404,507

See accompanying notes to consolidated financial statements.

Comdisco (A)

CONSOLIDATED STATEMENTS OF EARNINGS
(in thousands except per share data)

Years Ended September 30,	1982	1981	1980
Revenue			
Rental	$206,592	$131,571	$ 80,979
Sale of computer equipment	166,705	125,384	149,708
Financial services	73,879	30,837	14,079
Other	24,454	13,746	8,348
Total revenue	471,630	301,538	253,114
Cost and Expenses			
Equipment depreciation, amortization and rental	160,523	99,413	68,328
Cost of computer equipment	149,654	111,784	134,595
Financial services	8,617	6,784	4,878
Selling, general and administrative	51,785	28,529	19,341
Interest	47,242	33,657	16,988
Total costs and expenses	417,821	280,167	244,130
Earnings before income taxes	53,809	21,371	8,984
Income taxes	24,432	5,730	1,870
Net Earnings	$ 29,377	$ 15,641	$ 7,114
Net Earnings Per Common and Common Equivalent Share	$ 2.27	$ 1.35	$ .65

See accompanying notes to consolidated financial statements.

Comdisco (A)

CONSOLIDATED STATEMENTS OF STOCKHOLDERS' EQUITY
(in thousands)

Years Ended September 30, 1982, 1981 and 1980

	Common Stock $.10 Par Value	Additional Paid-in Capital	Retained Earnings	Deferred Translation Adjustment
Balance at September 30, 1979	$ 541	$12,405	$22,56	$ —
Net earnings	—	—	7,114	—
Dividends paid	—	—	(865)	—
Stock options exercised	46	639	—	—
Income tax benefits resulting from exercise of non-qualified stock options	—	1,123	—	—
Balance at September 30, 1980	587	14,167	28,811	—
Net earnings	—	—	15,641	—
Dividends paid	—	—	(1,093)	—
Stock split	148	(148)	—	—
Stock options exercised	22	611	—	—
Balance at September 30, 1981	757	14,630	43,359	—
Cumulative amount as of September 30, 1981	—	—	—	(232)
Net earnings	—	—	29,377	—
Dividends paid	—	—	(1,468)	—
Stock split	391	(400)	—	—
Stock options exercised	14	835	—	—
Common stock issued	15	2,648	—	—
Translation adjustment	—	—	—	(122)
Income tax benefits resulting from exercise of non-qualified stock options	—	1,252	—	—
Balance at September 30, 1982	$1,177	$18,965	$71,26	$(354)

See accompanying notes to consolidated financial statements.

Comdisco (A)

CONSOLIDATED STATEMENTS OF CHANGES IN FINANCIAL POSITION
(in thousands)

Years Ended September 30,	1982	1981	1980
Source of Funds:			
From operations			
Net earnings	$ 29,377	$ 15,641	$ 7,114
Noncash charges (credits) to operations:			
Depreciation and amortization	133,902	77,528	46,212
Increase in receivables	(12,849)	(5,531)	(12,278)
Investment in sales-type and direct financing leases	(5,792)	(11,732)	323
Income taxes	23,180	5,730	747
Increase in accounts payable and accrued liabilities	14,248	18,611	11,322
Other, net	474	(1,233)	2,490
Total provided from operations	182,540	99,014	55,930
Proceeds from issuance of subordinated debentures	—	48,560	—
Increase (decrease) in notes payable	(1,060)	(33,460)	25,339
Obligations under capital leases	5,663	14,249	2,885
Discounted lease rentals	145,626	183,557	62,786
Other	4,201	924	766
	336,970	312,844	147,706
Application of Funds:			
Increase in leased equipment and inventory	190,180	202,002	75,361
Reduction of discounted lease rentals and obligations under capital leases	87,795	75,781	55,916
Purchase of subordinated debentures	—	2,162	—
Capitalized leases—computer equipment	5,663	14,249	2,885
Other assets and deferred charges	21,950	12,343	13,555
Cash dividends	1,468	1,093	865
	307,056	307,630	148,582
Increase (decrease) in cash and marketable securities	29,914	5,214	(876)
Cash and marketable securities at beginning of year	9,848	4,634	5,510
Cash and marketable securities at end of year	$ 39,762	$ 9,848	$ 4,634

See accompanying notes to consolidated financial statements.

Comdisco (A)

NOTES TO CONSOLIDATED FINANCIAL STATEMENTS

1. Summary of Significant Accounting Policies

Principles of Consolidation: The accompanying consolidated financial statements include the accounts of the Company and its wholly-owned subsidiaries after elimination of intercompany accounts and transactions.

Revenue Recognition: Leases are accounted for either as sales-type, direct financing or operating leases. Lease terms generally range from four months to five years. Revenue from sales-type leases is recorded upon acceptance of the equipment by the customer and is reflected as sale of computer equipment. Revenue from direct financing leases is recorded over the term of the lease as interest income calculated using the interest method. Rental revenue from operating leases is recognized in equal monthly amounts over the term of the lease.

Revenue from the sale of computer equipment and the related cost of equipment is reflected in earnings at the time of acceptance of the equipment by the customer.

Revenue from the sale of equipment subject to operating leases is recognized at the closing of the transactions and is included as sale of computer equipment in fiscal 1981 and 1980. In addition to this revenue, the Company is also entitled to the use of such equipment subsequent to the lease expiration date for periods ranging generally from six months to four years. Revenue, if any, from the re-leasing of such equipment during this period is recognized upon acceptance of the equipment by the customer and is reflected as other revenue.

Under the provisions of the Economic Recovery Tax Act of 1981, the Company sold the tax benefits (investment tax credits and cost recovery allowances) on new equipment purchased for the Company's lease portfolio. The proceeds from the sale of tax benefits are recorded as financial services revenue. Also included as financial services revenue are fees for arranging tax benefit transfer agreements with third parties.

Fees from the sale of equipment included in the Company's lease portfolio of used equipment are recognized at the closing of the transactions and included as financial services revenue. Such transactions, which are structured as tax advantaged leases, entitle the Company to the use of such equipment for periods ranging generally from one to six years subsequent to the initial lease expiration date.

The Company, through its CFS subsidiary, has entered into certain computer equipment transactions in which it has leased equipment (the "Lease") and in turn has subleased such equipment (the "Sublease"). In substantially all of these transactions, the Lease term exceeds the Sublease term. Monthly Sublease rentals are greater than the monthly Lease rentals; however, the present value of the total Sublease rentals ("Sublease Proceeds") may be less than the present value of the total Lease rentals ("Lease Obligations") due to the difference in lease terms. Rentals from the sublease are discounted by the Company with a financial institution on a nonrecourse basis. An escrow account is established to fund the Company's obligations under the lease for the period after the expiration of the Sublease. In the event the Sublease Proceeds exceed the Lease Obligations, the Company recognizes profit. When Lease Obligations exceed the Sublease Proceeds, no profit is recognized and the next excess Lease Obligation is deferred to be recovered from the Company's right to future rentals during the remaining term of the Lease. At September 30, 1982 and 1981, $21,258,000 and $10,148,000, respectively, of costs were deferred in connection with such transactions and are included in the balance sheet caption "Other assets and deferred charges." The Company recognized $3,113,000, $4,286,000, and $1,890,000 of interest income on investments held in escrow during the years ended September 30, 1982, 1981 and 1980, respectively.

Inventory of Computer Equipment: Inventory of computer equipment is stated at the lower of cost or market.

Equipment, Depreciation and Amortization: Leased equipment owned by the Company is generally recorded at cost. Depreciation and amortization of leased equipment are computed on the straight-line method for financial reporting purposes to estimated fair market value at lease termination (See Note 2).

Deferred Lease Costs: Salesmen's commissions and other direct expenses related to operating leases are deferred and amortized over the lease term.

Income Taxes and Investment Tax Credits: Deferred income taxes have been provided for income and expenses which are recognized in different periods for income tax purpose than for financial reporting purposes. Investment tax credits are accounted for on a flow-through basis.

Comdisco (A)

Profit Sharing Plan: The Company has a profit sharing plan covering all employees. Company contributions to the plan are based on a percentage of employees' compensation, as defined. Profit sharing payments are based on amounts accumulated on an individual employees basis. Profit sharing expense for the years ended September 30, 1982, 1981 and 1980 amounted to $590,000, $489,000 and $178,000, respectively.

Earnings Per Share: Earnings per common and common equivalent share are computed based on the weighted average number of common and common equivalent shares outstanding during each period including the assumed conversion of the 13% convertible subordinated debentures, after elimination of the related interest expense (net of tax) and after giving retroactive effect to the three-for-two split effected in March 1982 (See Note 9). Dilutive stock options included in the number of common and common equivalent shares are based on the treasury stock method. The number of common and common equivalent shares used in the computation of earnings per share for the years ended September 30, 1982, 1981 and 1980 were 14,486,738, 12,269,703 and 11,050,277, respectively.

Foreign Currency Translation: Fiscal 1982 consolidated financial statements have been prepared in accordance with Financial Accounting Standards Board Statement No. 52, "Foreign Currency Translation," the provisions of which were adopted by the Company on a prospective basis as of October 1, 1981. Previous consolidated financial statements have been prepared in accordance with Statement No. 8, "Accounting for the Translation of Foreign Currency Transactions and Foreign Currency Financial Statements." The effect of the change was not material.

2. Depreciable Lives

Effective October 1, 1980 the Company extended its estimates of depreciable lives of certain IBM peripheral equipment. Effective January 1, 1981 the Company extended its estimates of depreciable lives and salvage values of certain IBM peripheral equipment. Previously, this equipment was depreciated to zero by September 30, 1983. The changes in estimates were made based on revised market conditions and reflect current estimates of the equipment's useful lives and salvage values. The effect of the changes on recorded leased equipment at the effective dates of the changes was an increase in net earnings of $4,488,000 (net of income taxes of $4,142,000), or $.37 per share, for the year ended September 30, 1981.

3. Investment in Sales-Type and Direct Financing Leases

The following table lists the components of the net investment in sales-type and direct financing leases as of September 30:

	1982	1981
	(in thousands)	
Minimum lease payments receivable	$24,142	$18,504
Estimated residual values of leased property	12,324	9,160
Less unearned income	12,784	9,774
Net investment in sales-type and direct financing leases	$23,682	$17,890

Future minimum lease payments to be received under the above lease agreements are as follows:

Years ending September 30	Sales-type and direct financing leases
	(in thousands)
1983	$ 7,306
1984	7,416
1985	5,534
1986	2,637
1987	1,249
	$24,142

The Company finances most sales-type and direct financing leases by assigning the non-cancellable rentals on a non-recourse basis. The proceeds from the assignment reduce the investment in sales-type and direct financing leases. Any gain or loss on the assignment is recognized at the time of such assignment.

4. Capitalized Leases

Capitalized leases – computer equipment at September 30 is comprised of the following:

	1982	1981
	(in thousands)	
Capitalized leases – computer equipment	$24,158	$23,225
Less accumulated amortization	15,354	12,099
Net capitalized leases – computer equipment	$ 8,804	$11,126

At September 30, 1982, the Company, as lessee, was obligated to pay rentals under capitalized leases. The related equipment has been subleased and accounted for either as operating leases or as direct financing leases. The following table summarizes minimum rentals payable by the Company as lessee under capitalized leases:

Years ending September 30	Capitalized Leases
	(in thousands)
1983	$ 8,196
1984	6,987
1985	4,801
1986	2,618
1987	1,810
Later years	521
Total minimum lease payments	24,933
Less imputed interest (9% to 17%)	6,297
Present value of net minimum lease payments	$18,636

Total minimum lease payments for capitalized leases have not been reduced by minimum non-cancelable sublease rentals of $16,094,000 due the Company in the future.

5. Bank Borrowings and Compensating Balances

The Company has a revolving credit agreement which entitles the Company to borrow up to $25,000,000 on an unsecured basis. The agreement, which expires March 31, 1983, carries an interest cost of prime rate (13.5% at September 30, 1982) and includes a fee of 3/8% per annum of the average daily unused amount. If the Company or the bank elects not to renew the agreement, the loan becomes a two-year term loan payable in equal quarterly installments with an interest cost of prime rate plus 1%. Under the agreement, the Company is required to maintain a defined debt to net worth ratio and dividend payments cannot exceed 20% of consolidated net earnings subsequent to September 30, 1980. At September 30, 1982, approximately $4,280,000 of retained earnings were available for payment of dividends.

In accordance with the terms of the agreement, the Company is required to maintain average cash balances with the bank equal to 5% of the $25,000,000 loan commitment. The amount of unused available borrowings under the agreement was $25,000,000 at September 30, 1982.

At September 30, 1982, the Company had additional unused lines of credit totaling $20,000,000 under which borrowings would bear interest at the prime rate. Under the agreements, the Company is required to maintain compensating balances equal to 5% of the outstanding borrowings.

6. Note Payable to Bank and Subordinated Debentures

Note Payable to Bank: The note payable to bank at September 30, 1982 and 1981 was an 11¾% term note payable in quarterly installments through December, 1984.

13% Convertible Subordinated Debentures: In June 1981, the Company issued $50,000,000 of 13% convertible subordinated debentures ("Convertible Debentures") due in 2001. Issue costs of $1,440,000 relating to the Convertible Debenture may be converted into shares of common stock of the Company, prior to maturity, at the option of the convertible Debenture holder at a conversion price of $19.50 per share.

The Convertible Debentures are redeemable in full or in part at the option of the company beginning in 1981 at an amount equal to 113.0% of the principal amount of the Convertible Debentures, the premium on redemption declining 1.3% per annum commencing in 1982 through 1991, and redeemable thereafter at par.

11½% Subordinated Debentures: At September 30, 1982, $12,250,000 of 11½% subordinated debentures (the "Debentures") due December 1, 1992, were outstanding. Annual sinking fund payments of $1,350,000 (9% of the aggregate original principal amount) commence December 1, 1982, and are calculated to retire 90% of the issue prior to maturity. During fiscal 1981, the Company, in connection with future sinking fund requirements, acquired $2,750,000 principal amount of the outstanding debentures which resulted in a gain of $318,000 (net of income taxes of $270,000).

Both the Debentures and the Convertible Debentures are subordinated to all senior indebtedness as defined in the indenture agreements. At September 30, 1982, the Company's senior indebtedness was approximately $2,473,000.

The annual maturities and sinking fund requirements of the note payable and subordinated debentures for the next five years are as follows:

Years ending September 30	Aggregate Maturities
	(in thousands)
1983	$1,060
1984	1,060
1985	1,565
1986	1,350
1987	1,350

7. Income Taxes

The following data relate to the provision for income taxes for the years ended September 30:

	1982	1981	1980
Provision in lieu of income taxes	$ 1,252	—	$1,123
Current:			
Federal	5,000	—	—
State	1,076	—	—
	6,076	—	—
Deferred:			
Federal	16,281	4,216	147
State	273	553	220
Foreign	550	961	380
	17,104	5,730	747
Total tax provision	$24,432	$5,730	$1,870
Earnings before income taxes:			
Domestic	$51,166	$18,992	$8,203
Foreign	2,643	2,379	781
Total	$53,809	$21,371	$8,984

Income tax benefits of $1,252,000 and $1,123,000 resulting from the exercise of non-qualified stock options were utilized to reduce the current Federal tax provision in fiscal 1982 and 1980, respectively.

The reasons for the difference between the U.S. Federal income tax rate of 46% and the effective income tax rate were as follows:

	Percentage of Pretax Earnings		
Years ended September 30,	1982	1981	1980
U.S. Federal income tax	46.0%	46.0%	46.0%
Increase (reduction) resulting from:			
Domestic International Sales Corporation tax benefit	(.1)	(1.2)	(6.8)
Reduction of deferred income taxes applicable to investment tax credit carryforward	—	(20.4)	(20.1)
Investment tax credit	(2.0)	—	—
State income taxes, net of U.S. tax benefit	1.4	1.2	1.1
Other – net	.1	1.2	.6
	45.4%	26.8%	20.8%

The Company has not provided for income taxes on the unremitted earnings of the Domestic International Sales Corporation (DISC) subsidiary aggregating $4,253,000 through September 30, 1982, since the Company intends to postpone indefinitely the remittance of such earnings.

Deferred income taxes provided for timing differences were as follows:

Years ended September 30,	1982	1981	1980
	(in thousands)		
Sale of tax benefits	$38,661	—	—
Difference between depreciation for tax purposes and financial statement purposes	(18,125)	6,311	570
Deferred compensation expense	754	(754)	—
Deferred leasing income	2,934	(2,093)	—
Deferred leasing costs	1,518	1,164	793
Portion of undistributed earnings in DISC	(178)	(454)	231
Difference between leases accounted for as sales-type leases for financial statement purposes and operating leases for tax purposes	(23,601)	194	2,915
Reinstatement (reduction) of deferred income taxes applicable to:			
Investment tax credit carryforward	12,021	(4,356)	(1,803)
Tax net operating loss realization (carryforward)	—	2,323	(650)
Income tax benefit resulting from exercise of non-qualified stock options	—	1,903	(1,123)
Other – net	3,120	1,492	(186)
	$17,104	$5,730	$747

8. Discounted Lease Rentals

Leased equipment owned by the Company is financed by assigning the noncancellable rentals to various lenders at fixed interest rates on a nonrecourse basis. The proceeds from the assignment of the lease rentals (discounted lease rentals) represent payments due under the lease discounted to their present value at the interest rate charged by the lender, generally ranging from 10% to 19%. The difference between monthly rentals due under discounted leases and the amortization of related discounted lease rentals represents interest expense. This expense amounted to $32,527,000, $15,468,000 and $8,380,000 in 1982, 1981 and 1980, respectively. In the event of default by the lessee, the lender has a first lien against the underlying leased equipment, with no further recourse against the Company.

9. Common Stock and Additional Paid-in Capital

On January 27, 1982, the Board of Directors declared a three-for-two split of the Company's common stock. This distribution was subject to the stockholders approval, which was obtained, amending the Certificate of Incorporation increasing the number of authorized shares from 15,000,000 to 50,000,000 with the par value remaining at $.10 per share. On January 28, 1981, the Board of Directors of the Company declared a five-for-four split of the Company's common stock. All references in the financial statements and notes to the number of shares of common stock and per share amounts have been adjusted for the aforementioned stock splits.

On November 18, 1981, the Board of Directors approved the Settlement Agreement (the "Agreement") between the Company and participants in the Residual Incentive Compensation Plan (the "Plan") related to vested residual computer interests. The Plan provided in part for the allocation of a percentage interest in the residual value of computer equipment to the participants. The Agreement was approved by the stockholders on March 15, 1982, and pursuant to the terms of the Agreement, the Company distributed to participants in accordance with the terms of the Plan, the aggregate sum of $3,000,000 plus 150,000 shares of the Company's common stock.

Dividends on Common Stock: Common stock dividends paid were $.23 per share in 1982 compared with $.18 in 1981 and $.15 in 1980. Certain officers and directors of the Company and their affiliates, owning an aggregate of 5,028,645 shares (43%) of the outstanding common stock at September 30, 1982, have waived their rights to any cash dividends through February 1, 1983, and did not receive any of the previously mentioned cash dividends.

At September 30, 1982, the Company had reserved the following number of common shares for future issuance:

1979 Stock Option Plan	334,438
1981 Stock Option Plan	750,000
Employee Stock Purchase Plan	147,358
Conversion of Convertible Subordinated Debentures	2,564,103
	3,795,899

10. Stock Options and Stock Purchase Plan

On November 18, 1981, the Board of Directors amended the Company's 1979 Stock Option Plan (the "1979 Plan") to qualify the plan as an incentive stock option plan in accordance with the provisions of the Economic Recovery Tax Act of 1981. All outstanding stock options, which retained their original option price, are eligible for treatment as incentive stock options subject to certain limitations as defined in the amended 1979 Plan.

On January 27, 1982, the stockholders approved the 1981 Stock Option Plan (the "1981 Plan"). An aggregate of 750,000 shares were reserved for issuance pursuant to the exercise of options under the 1981 plan.

The Comdisco, Inc. Employee Stock Purchase Plan (the "Stock Plan") was adopted by the Board of Directors on November 17, 1981. An aggregate of 150,000 shares was reserved for issuance under the Stock Plan.

The changes in the number of shares under the option plans during 1982, 1981 and 1980 were as follows:

	1982	1981	1980
	(in thousands except option price range)		
Number of shares:			
Shares under option beginning of the year	512	861	1,119
Options granted	169	—	612
Options exercised	(188)	(349)	(870)
Shares under option end of year	493	512	861
Aggregate option price:			
Shares under option beginning of year	$2,533	$3,257	$480
Options granted	3,284	—	3,187
Options exercised	(850)	(724)	(410)
Shares under option end of the year	$4,967	$2,533	$3,257
Options exercisable at end of year	58	164	12
Aggregate option price of exercisable options outstanding at end of year	$295	$722	$19
Options available for future grant at end of year	591	11	11
Option price range	$4.90– $19.38	$1.35– $7.00	$.12– $7.00

11. Operating Leases

The following table summarizes the Company's future rentals receivable and payable under noncancellable operating leases existing at September 30, 1982 for computer equipment and rentals payable for non-computer equipment and office space:

Years ending Sept. 30	Computer equipment			Other rents payable
	Rents Receivable on Equipment		Rents payable on subleased equipment	
	Owned	Subleased		
1983	$180,581	$21,704	$25,497	$2,033
1984	107,125	13,269	12,197	1,735
1985	43,115	5,799	5,002	1,600
1986	7,237	1,742	792	1,033
1987	352	544	—	233
Later years	11	—	—	77

Comdisco (A)

Total rental income and related expense for the years ended September 30, 1982, 1981 and 1980 applicable to computer sublease activities are as follows:

Years ending September 30	Rental income	Rental expense
	(in thousands)	
1982	$23,633	$27,455
1981	24,152	22,415
1980	22,614	22,455

12. Commitments and Contingent Liabilities

At September 30, 1982, the Company was obligated under the following commitments: (1) to purchase computer equipment in the approximate aggregate amount of $31,768,000, (2) to sell computer equipment in the approximate aggregate amount of $20,926,000, and (3) to lease computer equipment to others with an aggregate initial term rental of approximately $55,107,000.

The Company has arranged for approximately $74,000,000 of letters of credit, primarily as guarantees for certain of the Company's sublease obligations and for future purchases of IBM equipment. The cost of such letters of credit range between ½% and ¾% per annum of the amount outstanding.

ACCOUNTANTS' REPORT

The Stockholders and Board of Directors Comdisco, Inc.:

We have examined the consolidated balance sheets of Comdisco, Inc. and subsidiaries as of September 30, 1982 and 1981 and the related consolidated statements of earnings, stockholders' equity and changes in financial position for each of the years in the three year period ended September 30, 1982. Our examinations were made in accordance with generally accepted auditing standards and, accordingly, included such tests of the accounting records and such other auditing procedures as we considered necessary in the circumstance.

In our opinion, the aforementioned consolidated financial statements present fairly the financial position of Comdisco, Inc. and subsidiaries at September 30, 1982 and 1981 and the results of their operations and the changes in their financial position for each of the years in the three-year period ended September 30, 1982, in conformity with generally accepted accounting principles applied on a consistent basis.

Peat, Marwick, Mitchell & Co.
Chicago, Illinois
November 9, 1982

QUARTERLY FINANCIAL DATA

Summarized Quarterly Financial data for the fiscal years ended September 30, 1982 and 1981, is as follows:

(In thousands of dollars except per share amounts)

Quarter ended:	December 31		March 31		June 30		September 30	
	1981	1980	1982	1981	1982	1981	1982	1981
Total revenue	$121,189	$78,833	$118,309	$64,450	$94,691	$75,722	$137,441	$82,533
Net earnings	9,604	3,285	5,934	3,146	5,824	4,075	8,015	5,135
Net earnings per common and common equivalent share	$.73	$.29	$.47	$.27	$.46	$.35	$.61	$.42

Comdisco (A)

Comdisco, Inc. (B)

A published report implying that the accounting practices of computer leasing giant Comdisco, Inc. could result in overstated earnings has provoked strong rebuttals from the leasing industry while rattling the skeleton of the OPM Leasing Services, Inc. scandal.

The report appeared last week in Barron's financial weekly and suggested that internal and external forces are mixing to create a potential disaster scenario for Comdisco as well as other third-party lessors. Meanwhile, the report stated, company officers, including founder and chairman Kenneth Pontikes, have gone on a Comdisco stock-selling spree in the past two years, getting rich in the process.

After publication of the report, Comdisco's stock lost nearly 37% of its paper value in one frenzied day of trading last Monday, falling from $38 to $24 per share.[1]

The October 17, 1983, issue of *Computerworld* magazine carried the above news about Comdisco, Inc.

BUSINESS HISTORY AND OPERATIONS[2]

Comdisco, Inc. is a Chicago-based company founded in 1969 by its current chairman of the board and president, Kenneth Pontikes. The company originally began as an IBM computer dealer. As demand for computer leasing started to grow during the late 1970s, the company started emphasizing leasing operations. By 1982, leasing old and new IBM computer equipment constituted the primary business activity of the company, and Comdisco had become the largest computer leasing company. Comdisco's customers were primarily large corporations. In 1982, the company had business relationships with 70 percent of the Fortune 500 companies, including 49 of the 50 largest U.S. companies.

The computer remarketing industry had many participants: small independent operators, larger private organizations, and leasing subsidiaries of conglomerates. Comdisco was one of the few independent public corporations in the industry. The firms in the industry were primarily of two types: broker/dealers or third-party lessors. The broker/dealers obtained for customers computer equipment from either a vendor or current user; third-party lessors provided lease financing. Comdisco engaged in both these activities.

Comdisco achieved its dominance in the computer leasing industry through a strategy of full-service leasing. Under this strategy, the company offered its customers a number of services which were not offered by competitors. Comdisco's subsidiaries, Comdisco Technical Services, Inc. and Comdisco Transport, Inc., specialized in equipment refurbishment, delivery, installation, de-installation, and technical planning and site preparation. Comdisco Maintenance Services, another subsidiary, offered a low-cost alternative to IBM's maintenance service. Comdisco Disaster Recovery Services, Inc. was established to provide another valuable service to the company's customers: contingent data processing capacity to be used when a customer's own data center had unavoidable failures. Through

Professor Krishna G. Palepu prepared this case. The case is intended solely as the basis for class discussion and is not intended to serve as an endorsement, source of primary data, or illustration of effective or ineffective management. Copyright © 1987 by the President and Fellows of Harvard College. HBS Case 9-186-299.

1. Reprinted with permission from Computerworld, October 17, 1983.

2. This section and the next, Tax Advantaged Transactions, can be skipped by those who read Comdisco, Inc. (A).

this service, Comdisco's customers had access to four fully operational data centers located as a backup to their own data centers, to be used in the event of a natural disaster or accident.

Comdisco's broad customer base provided the company with a number of competitive advantages. First, taking advantage of its access to 10,000 important users of IBM equipment in the U.S., the company created a proprietary data base of their computing needs. This data base provided Comdisco's sales force with current and timely information on potential customers and their requirements. Second, being the leading IBM dealer, Comdisco maintained large inventories of a broad range of IBM equipment. Comdisco's personnel closely monitored IBM's new products and pricing policies. This product knowledge combined with large inventories enabled the company to assist customers with their computer acquisition plans and to offer quick deliveries. Finally, using its data base, the company could help its customers sell their old hardware when they acquired new equipment from Comdisco.

While the above strategy enabled Comdisco to establish its dominance over others in the computer leasing industry, the company was still potentially vulnerable to competition from IBM itself since IBM equipment accounted for most of Comdisco's revenues. In 1981, IBM formed a financing subsidiary, IBM Credit Corporation, to provide customer financing. Shortly after than, IBM announced its intention to enter into computer leasing and established a joint venture for this purpose with Merrill Lynch and Metropolitan Life Insurance. A number of industry analysts felt that this might result in increased competition for companies like Comdisco.

Comdisco's management, however, felt that IBM's recent moves did not pose a threat to the company's competitive position because IBM's entry into leasing would enhance the tarnished image of the computer leasing business, a net benefit to the industry. They also believed that, as IBM began to emphasize outright sale of its equipment over short-term rentals, many of IBM's customers might be forced to look for other lessors like Comdisco who offered short-term leases. This was likely to provide additional business opportunities which would offset any loss of long-term lease business to IBM.

While equipment leasing to computer users was Comdisco's primary activity, the company also offered tax-oriented leases to investors who were primarily interested in the tax benefits associated with leasing. In recent years, the financial services income from the tax advantaged transactions accounted for a growing portion of the company's revenues.

TAX ADVANTAGED TRANSACTIONS

In addition to leasing equipment to computer users, Comdisco undertook leasing transactions with investors who were interested in tax shelters. While the specific terms and conditions of these tax advantaged transactions varied, a typical transaction was as follows:

1. After the inception of the initial user lease and independent of it, Comdisco sold all the leased equipment to a third party investor. This sale usually occurred three to nine months after the commencement of the initial user lease. The sales price equaled the then current fair market value of the equipment. The payment from the investor to Comdisco consisted of: (a) cash and a negotiable interest-bearing promissory note due within two years for 10–22 percent of the sales price (the "equity payment") and (b) an installment note for the balance payable over an 84-month period.
2. Simultaneously with the sale, Comdisco leased the equipment back from the investors for 84 months. The lease payments under the leaseback obligation were equal to the installment payments receivable by Comdisco from the investor (1. b).

3. As part of the leaseback arrangement, during the 61st through 84th months of the leaseback period, the investor shared in the re-lease proceeds that the company received from subleasing the equipment to a user. Upon the expiration of the leaseback period, the investor had the exclusive right to the equipment.

The net result of the above transaction was that Comdisco gave up the depreciation tax benefit, a portion of the rental revenues for months 61–84, and 100 percent of the equipment value after the 84th month. In return, the company received the nonrefundable equity payment (1.a).

If the equipment sold to the investor was originally under an operating lease, the equity payment was recorded by Comdisco as financial services revenue in the period in which the tax advantaged transaction occurred. From the fourth quarter of 1983, the company began to allocate as cost of financial services a portion of the net book value of the equipment at lease termination. For sales-type and direct financing leases, the equity payment was first applied to reduce a portion of the residual value of the equipment shown in the balance sheet (as investment in sales-type and direct financing leases). This is because the company's ability to recover the residual value was decreased due to the rental sharing under the tax advantaged transaction. The excess of the equity payment over the residual value reduction was recorded as financial services revenue in the period in which the tax advantaged transaction occurred.

THE *BARRON'S* ARTICLE

The October 10, 1983, issue of *Barron's,* a widely circulated financial weekly, carried an article on Comdisco, "Something Doesn't Compute: A Hard Look at Comdisco's Accounting." The article, excerpts from which are given in Exhibit 2, focused on four areas: the company's accounting, competition from IBM Credit Corporation, the company's tax advantaged leasing program, and the sale of company stock by insiders.

The article attracted considerable attention on Wall Street, leading to hectic trading of the company's stock. The company's stock price dropped from $38.250 to $22.875 by the end of the week, representing a loss of about $453.5 million in the market value of the company (see Exhibit 1 for data on Comdisco's stock price).

In response to these events, Kenneth Pontikes, president of Comdisco, issued a letter to shareholders on October 12, 1983. The letter addressed the issues raised in the *Barron's* article and attempted to rebut the charges (see Exhibit 3). Pontikes concluded:

> [Finally,] it is important for you, our stockholders, to understand completely that Comdisco is stronger financially than it has ever been; that we have greater opportunities before us than at any time in our history; and that management is dedicated to retaining stockholder confidence and enhancing stockholder wealth.

Shortly after the above developments, Comdisco released its annual report for fiscal 1983 (Exhibit 4).

QUESTIONS

1. Evaluate *Barron's* criticism of Comdisco's accounting and the company's response. Do you agree with the company or *Barron's?*

2. Compare the level of disclosure in Comdisco's annual reports in the (A) and (B) cases. Do you think the company's poor disclosure prior to 1983 made it vulnerable to the

Comdisco (B)

attack by *Barron's*? Would the market reaction to the *Barron's* article have been different if the company had a better disclosure policy?

3. Do you think Comdisco's stock in November 1983 was a "buy"?

EXHIBIT I

Movement of Comdisco's Stock Price and S&P 500 Index, January 1982–November 1983

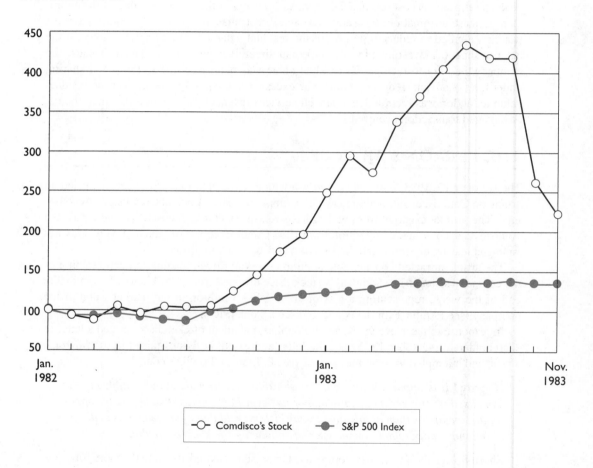

EXHIBIT 2

"Something Doesn't Compute—A Hard Look at Comdisco Accounting Practices"[3]

Rhonda Brammer, *Barron's*, October 10, 1983

Twenty years ago, Ken Pontikes sold computer tapes and tab cards for IBM. He was paid $5,000 a year. When he lit out on his own five years later—starting up a one-man brokerage business in computers—his whole idea, he says "was to make a nice living." That start-up operation today is Chicago-based Comdisco, the biggest computer leasing company in the country. And yes, the 43-year-old Pontikes is making a living. His compensation was $2.4 million last year. So far this year, he's reported stock sales of $2.6 million. And his stake in the company, at the current market price, is worth $200 million plus.

His company could now be ranked an old-timer in the volatile computer leasing business, but its meteoric stock market rise is a recent phenomenon. In 1977, for example, shares could be had for a fraction of a dollar. As late as 1982, investors could have bought the stock under 7. Those same shares now sell at 38, just four points shy of their all-time high.

The spectacular rise in the stock reflects the transformation of the company itself, from a computer brokerage business—one that basically matched up computer buyers and sellers for a fee—into a complex financial service operation. Today, Comdisco not only buys and leases computers, but also re-sells the leased equipment in intricately structured tax shelters. The marketing men of a decade ago have been joined by a cadre of lawyers and accountants—tough, shrewd professionals, paid handsomely to keep one step ahead of the IRS. It's a new emphasis that has done wonders for the bottom line. Since 1980, sales have almost doubled, hitting $472 million in the 1982 fiscal year ended September. More important—thanks to the tax shelters—over the like stretch earnings expanded more than fourfold, to $29 million.

But past is not necessarily prologue. And Comdisco may be running into trouble on several fronts. First, sources close to the IRS say that computer-leasing tax shelters are the object of wrathful scrutiny these days. The very guidelines around which Comdisco structures deals are being rewritten.

Second, IBM is moving into territory where Comdisco had been undisputed king. The IBM Credit Corp. is pushing its way into third-party leasing with partners none other than Merrill Lynch and Metropolitan Life Insurance. By next year, say industry observers, the

Armonk giant will rank No. 1. And with its enormous supplies of cheap capital, IBM already is offering surprisingly aggressive rates. This ominous trend threatens to put an increasing squeeze on the profit margins of computer leasing outfits like Comdisco. To compete they may well have no choice but to take calculated—and dangerous—financial risks.

Finally, there's some controversial accounting. Comdisco's method of accounting for "fees" from tax-advantaged leases is a matter unresolved by the accounting profession—and a potentially explosive issue. Right now, Comdisco has significant latitude in the level of profits it reports and the amount of residual values it carries on the balance sheet. The details are complex, but essentially Comdisco often records what it calls "fees" from tax-advantaged transactions as straight profit—without offsetting such "fees" against the company's investment in the equipment. It thereby keeps on its books a significant investment, recorded in "leased computer equipment" or "net investment in sales and direct financing leases"—an investment it hopes to recoup from the residual value when the equipment is re-leased.

And if there are no residual values when the equipment comes off lease? Well, based on information supplied by the company's financial department, if *all* equipment was considered to have zero residual value, Comdisco's entire net worth, as of the end of fiscal 1982, would vanish.

Obviously, the way residual values are treated affects earnings, too. When Comdisco reasons that it will recoup its net investment after the equipment is released, it books the "fee" from the sale of the tax shelter as pure profit. If, instead, it subtracted its investment in equipment from this fee—recovered the investment and took it off the balance sheet—earnings would be a mere fraction of the substantial sums currently reported.

This method of accounting is thus disturbing on several scores. First, it's possible the residual values simply aren't there. Comdisco insists its assumptions are conservative—and they may well be—but all leasing companies have made such assertions, even the defunct ones. If there's a miscalculation, and the equipment should come off lease and suddenly be worthless, that means Comdisco would face a write-off.

Comdisco (B)

Not to be overlooked, either, is the matter of when profits are recognized by Comdisco. Why should a company be allowed to report earnings today when it won't see the cash for four or five years, if ever? And finally, at the very least, financial statements might reasonably be expected to disclose net investment and assumed residual values, as well as detailed descriptions of how "fees" are booked.

None of this, however, is to say that Comdisco's accounting breaks the rules. Quite the contrary. "The accounting profession hasn't addressed the issue on this type of transaction," John Vosicky, Comdisco's vice president of accounting and financial controls, correctly points out. "One could argue that you could take the entire fee into income right away—on everything. Another could argue you reduce your investment completely, and you don't recognize anything until that investment is covered."

:

To better understand the accounting, consider a typical transaction, which in itself is no simple matter. The "tax-advantaged" leases, in order to get by the IRS, often involve layers of companies. And the shuffling of papers in sale-leaseback transactions can, in short order, obscure the economic realities of the deals.

But here are the basics.

Comdisco finds a user who wants to lease a computer for say, five years, and buys a machine for $100. Comdisco then takes the lease to the bank, and borrows the discounted value of the payments. A typical present value for the lease payments might be $85.

This borrowing from the bank appears on Comdisco's balance sheet as "discounted lease rentals," but the contract is so structured that the risk is essentially transferred to the bank. "These are hell-or-high water agreements," insists one Comdisco executive. If anything goes wrong—if the user fails to make his payments—all the bank can do is confiscate the equipment. It has no recourse to Comdisco. So at this point, Comdisco's investment has effectively been reduced from $100 to $15.

Then comes the "tax advantaged" part of the deal. Comdisco sells the computer to an investor who is looking for a tax shelter. And here things start to get tricky.

Comdisco collects, say, $17 in cash, from the investor and then agrees to take a seven-year note for the remaining $83 of the purchase price of the equipment. At the same time, it signs a seven-year leaseback with the investor, so the rental payments the investor gets are spread over seven years. It's neatly arranged so the

rental payments of this leaseback are precisely enough to cover the payments on the seven-year note. Put another way, Comdisco pays the investor rent, and the investor turns right around and pays this rent back to Comdisco as interest and principal on the note. It's a wash—a paper transaction. It's a nifty tax deal that has no effect on the actual user of the equipment, who continues to make his payments to the bank, which, in turn, reduces Comdisco's discounted lease receivables.

So has Comdisco made money? Well, it has paid $100 for a computer and borrowed $85 from the bank, to be paid off in five years by the user's rental payments. That leaves a $15 net investment. But it's also received $17 cash from the investor, and then shuffled papers so that an $83 note from the investor is exactly offset by lease payables of $83. Comdisco also retains the right to share the proceeds of re-leasing the computer in years six and seven with the investor. The bottom line is this: the $17 in cash offsets the $15 net investment. Comdisco is $2 richer.

So the income statement shows $2?

Not likely. All those high-paid lawyers and accountants on staff argue the $17 cash payment is a "fee"—for, among other things, putting the deal together. Clearly the $17 is theirs; they don't have to give it back. So in many cases Comdisco takes the entire fee as profit. It shows earnings of $17, even though it has only $2 in the cash register.

Where's the other $15? The difference between the reported profits and the actual cash sits quietly on the balance sheet—in "leased computer equipment" or sometimes in "net investment in sales-type and direct finance leases." That's the amount Comdisco hopes to recover from re-leasing the computer in years six and seven. But by booking the entire $17, it has effectively taken this assumed residual value into earnings on day one.

Now if in years six and seven, Comdisco re-leases the computer for, say $20, it can report a $5 profit. If the re-leasing brings in only $15, Comdisco has broken even. It has simply replaced the $15 paper asset on the balance sheet with a more spendable $15 in cash. But what if re-leasing brings in only $5? That presents a nasty problem—indeed, that means that Comdisco is looking at a $10 write-off.

:

Nor is the way "fees" are treated an idle, theoretical matter. It is vitally important to Comdisco's bottom line. For such fees comprise the bulk of the company's "financial services" revenues. And although revenues from computer sales and rentals are two to three times greater, the company's big profit center is clearly financial services. Peter Labe, an analyst at Smith Barney, a firm that has done investment banking for Comdisco, claims in a recent report that financial services "account for the bulk of corporate profits."

Comdisco doesn't dispute it. "No question," says Comdisco's Vosicky, "a large percentage of the profits are attributed to tax-advantaged transactions."

About 80%–90%?

"I wouldn't say 90%," says Vosicky. "It depends on how you want to slice the pie." Profitability, he points out, depends on the allocation of general and administrative expenses. And Comdisco financials do not break out this information.

"I think it would be correct to say," continues Vosicky, "that the primary reason for the earnings increase is because of tax-advantaged transactions or financial services."

The bulk of the increase rather than the bulk of earnings?

"Yes."

In other words, the big leap in pretax earnings from $21 million in 1981 to $53 million in 1982 is primarily because of the tax-advantaged deals?

"Yes. I think that would be fair to say."

And if all fees had been reduced by the amount of investment in the equipment, how much less would financial services revenues have been in 1982?

"A lot of that revenue came from safe harbor leasing transactions where we don't have any investment. . . ."

But if the investment in equipment on all the *other* leases in 1982 was netted out, how much would financial services be reduced?

"It would probably be cut in half," replies Vosicky. "I would think at least cut in half."

And so this year, with no safe harbor leases, netting out all the investment in equipment would cause an even greater drop in financial services?

"Yet, it would."

Insofar as Comdisco reports profits now from the equipment leased—and leaves residual value on the books to be recovered later—it increases its exposure to obsolescence. And as of September 1982, the date of the most recent balance sheet with full footnotes, that exposure was considerable, at least in comparison with the company's net worth.

⋮

Comdisco (B)

EXHIBIT 3

Letter to Comdisco, Inc. Shareholders

October 12, 1983

Dear Stockholders:

As I'm sure most of you know by now, the October 10, 1983 issue of *Barron's* includes an article about our Company. I believe the article and its subsequent impact on the price of the Company's stock entitle our stockholders to a clarification of the facts underlying the key issues raised. The article emphasizes four main areas: (1) The Company's accounting; (2) competition from IBM Credit Corporation; (3) our tax advantaged investment program; and (4) sales by insiders.

Accounting

The article raises questions concerning the Company's accounting policy with respect to the investment risk taken on leased equipment and implies that our policy with respect to payments from tax advantaged leases could result in an overstatement of income. Under the Company's depreciation policy, our leased equipment portfolio as of June 30, 1983 will be depreciated to a net book value at lease termination of $112,000,000. The estimated fair market value of this equipment at lease termination (as provided by independent forecasts from International Data Corporation, a highly regarded equipment valuation expert) was in excess of $279,000,000, a coverage ratio of nearly 2.5 to 1. The facts demonstrate that the Company's policies are conservative, and have created a potential significant source of future earnings. The specific financial implications of our policies are as follows:

(1) Equipment Values

While generally accepted accounting principles require varied accounting treatments for different types of leases, the central issue is the same for all of the Company's leases: Is the Company's depreciation policy reasonable, thus eliminating the likelihood of a future write-off? The answer is that our depreciation policy is reasonable, and, in fact, produced book values of leased equipment which are substantially less than the values estimated by independent industry experts, as shown by the table below:

Total Lease Portfolio at June 30, 1983 (000's omitted)

Lease Type	Net Book Value at Lease Termination	Estimated Fair Market Value at Lease Termination*	IBM List Price
Operating leases	$92,000	$208,000	$876,000
Sales type and direct financing leases	20,000	63,000	847,000
Other	—	8,000	60,000
	$112,000	$279,000	$1,783,000

*Source: International Data Corporation

As shown above, fair market value estimates prepared by International Data Corporation provide a substantial margin over the Company's net book value at lease termination. This is still true even if the equipment is sold under a tax advantaged transaction. Since most tax advantaged transactions are structured so that the equipment will have a zero net book value by the time any tax advantaged investor shares in the fair market value proceeds, this sharing will not have a significant effect on the margin of fair market value available to the Company over the net book value at lease termination.

Another method of evaluating our depreciation policy is to review the operating lease portfolio (which comprises 82% of the total lease portfolio) by comparing, by year of termination, net book value at lease termination to estimated fair market value at lease termination. The following table illustrates this comparison:

Operating Lease Portfolio at June 30, 1983 (000's omitted)

Fiscal Year of Termination	Net Book Value at Lease Termination	Estimated Fair Market Value at Lease Termination	Estimated Excess Fair Market Value
1983	$ 16,000	$ 22,000	$ 6,000
1984	30,000	53,000	23,000
1985	19,000	50,000	31,000
1986	14,000	46,000	32,000
1987	13,000	37,000	24,000
	$ 92,000	$208,000	$116,000

Our auditors, Peat, Marwick, Mitchell & Co., review and agree with the Company's depreciation policies.

Referring to the foregoing table, it should be noted that 71% of the Company's operating lease book value is represented by leases which terminate by September 30, 1985. This short time period increases the reliability of residual value estimates. Equally as important, the Company has historically realized more from the remarketing of leased computer equipment than the value carried on its books, resulting in additional profit at the point of remarketing.

(2) Revenue Recognition

The sale of leased equipment in a tax advantaged transaction is separate from the underlying user lease transaction and results in payments to the Company from the investor. Revenue is recognized from these transactions in accordance with one of two basic methods:

(a) For all equipment where the underlying user lease term is five years or longer, and generally for all 308X mainframe transactions, these investor payments are first applied to reduce the Company's investment in the equipment. Any excess over the investment is recorded in the period in which the tax advantaged transaction occurs. During fiscal 1982 and the nine months ended June 30, 1983, the Company generated $83,160,000 of such payments. The Company's investment in the equipment was reduced by $43,890,000 and the difference, $39,270,000, was recorded as financial services during this period.

(b) For equipment where the underlying user lease term is less than five years (except for 308X mainframe transactions) these investor payments are recognized in the period in which the tax advantaged lease transaction occurs. This accounting treatment is appropriate since the Company's depreciation policy results in net book values at the end of the initial user lease term (typically 2–3 years) that already is less than fair market value estimates. To further reduce the Company's net book value for such equipment would materially understate current income and overstate future income by reducing or eliminating depreciation charges against future rental income.

Competition from IBM Credit Corporation

IBM has been Comdisco's single largest competitor for the entire 14 years Comdisco has been in business. Through its direct lease and rental programs, IBM has always been the dominant force in the computer leasing industry. IBM's increasing emphasis on generating equipment sales, however, is reflected in its withdrawal from the direct leasing business, which has resulted in a greatly expanding third party leasing market.

IBM Credit Corporation's (ICC) entry into the third party leasing business merely replaces part of the parent company's participation in leasing. ICC is participating in the third party

Comdisco (B)

market as a broker in much the same way as Comdisco. Comdisco has access to the same debt and equity markets as ICC, and on terms that will at most be only marginally less attractive to Comdisco than to ICC.

Tax Advantaged Investment Program

Our tax advantaged transactions have been carefully structured and documented. These transactions are bona fide investments with real economic substance and profit potential to the investor. They provide a valuable and effective way for individuals to provide capital for and participate in the equipment leasing industry. We take great pride in our reputation for providing a high quality computer leasing investment.

Like any tax advantaged investment, these transactions have certain tax risks, such as the possibility of IRS challenge and the risk of an adverse change in federal tax laws. We have made every effort to minimize these risks. Our nationally recognized tax counsel have provided their opinion that these transactions qualify as true leases for federal tax purposes under current law. We constantly monitor proposed federal tax changes, and we know of no imminent changes in federal tax laws or regulations affecting tax advantaged "wraparound" leases of computer equipment.

While these transactions have contributed substantially to Comdisco's profitability in recent years, our continued success in the computer equipment marketplace is not dependent on our ability to offer this specific form of transaction to investors. Nor does Comdisco's success depend on continuation of the status quo with respect to federal tax policy. We have employed and continue to employ a variety of transaction structures and have a history of adapting quickly to changes in the federal tax law and the marketplace. In fact, previous changes in federal tax laws and in the marketplace have often created significant opportunities for Comdisco.

Management Stockholdings

Management currently holds approximately 8,950,000 shares or 31% of the outstanding shares of the Company. These shares represent an ownership interest of approximately $240,000,000, based on the closing price on the New York Stock Exchange as of October 11, 1983. Over the years, sales of common stock have been made periodically by management. Tax liabilities created as a result of the exercise of stock options and sales by a retired senior executive who still owns approximately 650,000 shares account for a significant portion of these sales. The remaining sales are not significant when compared to current insider holdings.

Conclusion

In 1969, when we started Comdisco, we committed ourselves to building our business based on the principle of serving our customers with the highest degree of integrity and professionalism. Fortunately, over the years we have attracted talented individuals who share that commitment and who continue to value the principles of service, integrity and professionalism just as we did in 1969. We feel that our reputation and the trust that we have developed with our customers, our equity and debt investors, and our stockholders are our most valuable assets. We have not, and will not, compromise these principles in the conduct of our business.

Finally, it is important for you, our stockholders, to understand completely that Comdisco is stronger financially than it has ever been; that we have greater opportunities before us than at any time in our history; and that management is dedicated to retaining stockholder confidence and enhancing stockholder wealth.

Sincerely,

Kenneth N. Pontikes
(President)

EXHIBIT 4

Comdisco, Inc. Annual Report for Fiscal Year 1983 (abridged)

To Our Stockholders

I am pleased to report that in fiscal 1983 your Company continued its outstanding growth and performance. Net earnings for fiscal 1983 of $51.8 million, or $1.78 per share, represented increases of 76% and 56%, respectively, over fiscal 1982 results. Total revenue increased 15% to $543.2 million. Your Company's continued success in the lease placement of IBM computer equipment, particularly 308X mainframes and 3380 disc storage devices, and in financial services activities were the primary reasons for the record results achieved. Dividends were increased 36% in fiscal 1983 from $.11 to $.15 per share, as adjusted for the 2-for-1 stock split distributed in March, 1983.

Leasing Activity. Leasing activity increased dramatically in fiscal 1983 as Comdisco entered into 3,470 new leases with total rentals in excess of $1 billion during the initial lease terms. This compares to 2,259 leases and over $700 million in total rentals for leases entered into during fiscal 1982. Comdisco leased to its customers 3380 disk storage devices and 3380 disk controllers with an initial cost in excess of $200 million in fiscal 1983. In addition the Company leased 308X mainframes having an aggregate purchase price of $289 million.

The large volume of 308X mainframe lease transactions did not correspondingly increase the Company's total revenue since these leases are required to be accounted for as direct financing leases. Under direct financing lease accounting only the net margins are recorded as revenue, not the gross rentals as under operating lease accounting (see Understanding Comdisco's Accounting for detailed explanation).

Pursuant to the Economic Recovery Tax Act of 1981, Comdisco elected in fiscal 1982 to sell tax benefits, including investment tax credits, to other corporations, and recorded the proceeds as financial services revenue. These "tax benefit transfers" increased both total revenue and earnings before taxes, but the corresponding reduction in investment tax credits increased the effective income tax rate to 45.4%. In fiscal 1983 the large volume of 308X mainframe and 3380 disk storage equipment purchased for its leasing activity increased the amount of investment tax credit available to Comdisco. Because of changes in tax laws in late 1982 effectively eliminating tax benefit transfers, it was no longer attractive for Comdisco to enter into these transactions, so these investment tax credits were utilized for its own account. Investment tax credits of $22 million were earned in fiscal 1983, including $12 million in the fourth quarter, reducing the effective income tax rate to 12%.

Financial Services Activity. In fiscal 1982, proceeds from tax benefit transfers were recorded as financial services revenue. As I mentioned earlier, these tax benefit transfers had the effect of increasing revenue and income tax expense. In fiscal 1983, most of the financial services revenue was generated by the sale of leased equipment in the Company's tax advantaged transactions (see Understanding Comdisco's Accounting). In tax advantaged transactions, Comdisco retains any available investment tax credit. Equipment with a fair market value of $430.2 million was sold under tax advantaged transactions in fiscal 1983 compared to $253.0 million of equipment for the prior year.

Marketplace Perspective. In fiscal 1984, the data processing industry is expected to continue its annual growth rate of 15–25%. IBM Corporation continues to be the dominant factor in the computer leasing industry through its direct lease and rental programs.

However, in recent years IBM has been emphasizing the sale of its equipment, with less emphasis on direct leasing. This is reflected in IBM's pricing strategy which favors the purchase of equipment. For example, during fiscal 1983, IBM reduced lessee purchase option credits to make its leasing program even less attractive. In addition, IBM will eliminate, as of January 1, 1984 its practice of passing through investment tax credits to its lessees. IBM's reduced emphasis on direct leasing has led to increased user demand for third party lease financing, resulting in higher growth in the third party computer leasing marketplace. Your Company is successfully participating in this expanding market.

IBM Credit Corporation has entered the third party leasing market, replacing part of IBM's participation in this market. However, we do not expect this development to adversely affect our competitive position. We believe IBM Credit Corporation to be a reasonable competitor which will not take unacceptable risks nor assume unrealistic residual values. Also, Comdisco has access to the same debt and equity markets as IBM Credit Corporation. Finally, and of critical importance, users of computer equipment need to remarket existing equipment when new equipment is acquired. Because IBM Credit Corporation does not remarket displaced equipment, Comdisco still retains an

Comdisco (B)

advantage by virtue of its ability to remarket used equipment. No company is better situated to handle all of its customers' needs than Comdisco.

Activity in 308X mainframe and 3380 disk drives remains very strong, with your Company continuing to increase its market share. Comdisco's success in an expanding, competitive marketplace is directly attributable to its superior remarketing and lease financing capabilities.

Financial Condition and Liquidity. In fiscal 1983 Comdisco converted its $50 million of 13% convertible debentures into common stock and subsequently issued $250 million of 8% convertible debentures. As a result of these and other factors, Comdisco is in a stronger financial position than it has ever been. Stockholders' equity increased 110% to $91.5 million during fiscal 1983. At September 30, 1983 total assets were nearly $1 billion and cash and marketable securities exceeded $230 million. The continued improvement in your Company's financial condition was recognized by Moody's Investors Service, which raised Comdisco's bond rating for its convertible debentures to BA2 in fiscal 1983.

Personnel Changes. In fiscal 1983, the number of employees increased to 504, enhancing your Company's commitment to full customer service and helping to support continued growth. In November 1983, Raymond F. Sebastian was promoted to Executive Vice President from Senior Vice President- Corporate Development. Mr. Sebastian, an officer of Comdisco for eight years, will continue to over-see corporate development and take on additional administrative duties. In October 1983 Nicholas M. DiBari resigned his positions as Senior Vice President-Marketing and as a Director, for personal reasons. Mr. DiBari made valuable contributions to Comdisco's marketing structure and philosophy. Robert A. Bardagy has replaced Mr. DiBari as Senior Vice President-Marketing and as a Director. For the past six years, Mr. Bardagy has been responsible for the Company's market making and trading programs.

Other Activities. In fiscal 1983, the Company announced its Corporate Lease Line Program. The Corporate

Lease Line Program allows the Company's customers to lease almost all types of capital equipment at attractive lease rates with very little administrative burden. The Company has the ability to administer the program based on the customer's requirements. This program is expected to make a substantial contribution to fiscal 1984 results. Comdisco Disaster Recovery Services has increased its capabilities to meet the growing demands for its services. The contributions of Comdisco Technical Services and Comdisco Maintenance Services assist the Company in providing the whole array of services required by a data processing operation. The Company's international operations continue to contribute significantly to our profitability. Finally, our ability to capitalize on opportunities both inside and outside of our basic industry has never been greater.

A recent misunderstanding of Comdisco has led to lower market prices for our common stock. Accordingly, we expanded this Annual Report to describe our key operations and our accounting policies in greater detail. By any measurement, there are few publicly-held companies that can match Comdisco's performance since its inception in 1969. For the last five years the Company's compound growth rate for net earnings was an outstanding 60%, while net earnings per share and total revenue had growth rates of 46% and 29%, respectively. In fiscal 1983 return on average equity was 37%, with a 5-year average return of 33%. Comdisco's record speaks for itself.

I am proud of Comdisco's performance in fiscal 1983 and even prouder of the efforts and devotion of our employees. Without their outstanding efforts, we would not have achieved the success we have enjoyed. The support of our lenders, customers and you, our shareholders, is particularly gratifying. The first quarter of fiscal 1984 started out as our most active quarter ever, and I am confident that fiscal 1984 will prove to be Comdisco's most successful year to date.

Kenneth N. Pontikes
Chairman of the Board and President
November 28, 1983

Leasing's Four Fundamental Values

Initially, Comdisco was a computer equipment dealer, buying and selling equipment for its own account. Exceptional marketing capability helped make Comdisco the largest dealer in the industry by 1976.

By the late 1970's, market conditions had shifted and demand for computer leasing increased dramatically. Based on its exceptional marketing capability, Comdisco's emerging leasing operation quickly grew to become the Company's most significant business activity. Both dealer activity and the leasing operation—

supported by unmatched remarketing capabilities—now contribute to Comdisco's overall success.

Today, Comdisco's fundamental business, the foundation on which its exceptional pattern of financial performance is based, is leasing—primarily the leasing of new and used IBM computer equipment. And, as business and institutions world-wide become more and more information driven, the demand for data processing systems will continue to grow.

Leasing is widely recognized as the most attractive alternative to purchasing multi-million dollar computer systems. Over the years, Comdisco has achieved leadership in the field, having built a lease portfolio of IBM equipment currently valued at approximately $1 billion.

The leasing business also creates values that enable Comdisco to capitalize on other related sources of revenue and earnings. At the core of Comdisco's business, there are four such fundamental values.

Initial User Lease—Value One

When Comdisco leases its new or used computer equipment to a customer, the customer's rental payments during the original lease term are the primary source of revenue. In fiscal 1983, for example, the Company entered into 3,470 leases having total lease payments of over $1 billion during the initial lease terms.

Lease contracts cannot be canceled, and the customer has full responsibility for maintenance and other expenses. Most leases have terms of two to five years.

These leases also allow Comdisco to finance its leasing growth through "nonrecourse debt." Typically, Comdisco takes an existing lease to a bank and assigns the stream of lease payments to the bank. In return, the bank gives Comdisco cash that is equal to the present value of the lease payment stream at market interest rates. The debt is nonrecourse because the bank looks to the lease payments to repay the loan. This nonrecourse debt for operating leases is recorded as "Discounted Lease Rentals" on Comdisco's Balance Sheet. Interest rates are fixed in this transaction, eliminating Comdisco's exposure to rate fluctuations. Comdisco retains ownership of the computer equipment.

Comdisco's continued success in computer leasing is supported by a variety of factors discussed in greater detail on the following pages of this Annual Report. Among them are a customer relationship with 70% of the *Fortune 500* companies, a proprietary data base containing information on all major data processing installations, a seasoned sales team with offices in key markets throughout the U.S., Canada and Europe, and a complete line of customer support services.

Remarketing Capacity—Value Two

Data processing technology is among the most dynamic in the history of world commerce. The marketplace has a virtually insatiable appetite for increased capacity and a constant stream of new technological advancements.

With change as one of the few constants in the industry, Comdisco's unmatched capacity to remarket equipment is a fundamental component in the Company's formula for success. Indeed, leasing customers place a significant value on Comdisco's market making ability. As new products enter the marketplace, customers know that Comdisco has a unique capacity to remarket existing equipment, making it financially feasible to upgrade systems to a competitive, state-of-the-art level.

Comdisco's ability to capitalize on re-lease values and residual values is directly related to exceptional market penetration, its proprietary data base of marketing information, its professional sales force, and the Company's expertise in computer equipment and that equipment's life cycle.

Tax Benefits—Value Three

Tax benefits are an integral part of any leasing operation. Substantial tax benefits—particularly in the form of investment tax credits and accelerated depreciation deductions—are generated through Comdisco's acquisition of computer equipment.

Comdisco has a number of valuable alternatives concerning these tax benefits. Comdisco can claim the investment tax credits, thus reducing its own income tax. The Company can also choose to pass the investment tax credit through to the lessee in exchange for higher rentals. Or, as a third option, leveraged lease transactions with third party investors can also be arranged. This option has the effect of passing on all benefits of ownership, including tax and residual values. The compensation leasing companies typically receive is a lump sum payment and a share in the residual value of the leased equipment.

The capacity of the Company's basic leasing business, which generates significant tax benefits, allows Comdisco to capitalize on certain favorable tax laws. Such laws can be traced to the Congress' longstanding desire to provide industry with incentives for capital spending. Both investment tax credits and accelerated depreciation deductions are the product of laws that reflect this Congressional intent. Comdisco generates value by structuring transactions which permit the full utilization of the tax benefits associated with its equipment portfolio. Comdisco has demonstrated its ability

Comdisco (B)

Comdisco (B)

to profitably structure transactions in response to changes in tax laws. As long as Congress continues to encourage capital spending, the Company's control of equipment will enable it to continue structuring attractive tax-oriented transactions.

For example, in 1981 Congress devised "Safe Harbor Leasing" of equipment as a method for transferring tax benefits from one corporation to another. Called "tax benefit transfers," compensation for tax benefits was paid in a single lump sum at the beginning of the lease. Tax benefit transfers were, in effect, simply the sale of investment tax credits and depreciation benefits. In 1982, as part of the Tax Equity and Fiscal Responsibility Act of 1982 (TEFRA), Congress effectively eliminated Safe Harbor Leasing. In doing so, Congress did not change its desire to stimulate capital investment through tax incentives, as evidenced by the fact that in 1984 a new type of tax-oriented lease, the finance lease, will be permitted.

Despite the effective elimination of Safe Harbor Leasing, Comdisco continues to be in a position to generate value from significant investment tax credits and ownership rights to substantial amounts of equipment. While the laws have changed, the Congressional philosophy underlying tax-oriented leasing has not.

Tax Advantaged Transactions—Value Four

The fourth fundamental value of Comdisco's leasing activity is the tax advantaged transaction. In this alternative, Comdisco may sell equipment that is under an initial user lease to an independent third party. This is a completely separate transaction having no effect on the equipment user. The buyer is typically an individual or corporate investor who wants to share in the financial rewards of leasing—re-lease values, residual values and tax benefits.

When Comdisco sells computer equipment in a tax advantaged transaction, it receives an equity payment from the buyer in an amount equal to between 10% and 22% of the equipment's fair market value. In return for this equity payment, the new owner receives: (a) the accelerated depreciation benefits on the equipment, (b) a portion of the lease rentals in the sixth and seventh years after the sale is made, and (c) 100% of the equipment's value after the seventh year.

The utilization of tax benefits, either by the Company for its own account or by an investor as a result of a tax advantaged transaction, results in a lower effective cost to the equipment user, which is in accordance with Congress' objective to stimulate capital expenditures.

These four values form the core of Comdisco's business—leasing activity, computer remarketing, tax benefits and tax advantaged transactions. Understanding these values is key to understanding Comdisco's growth potential and how the Company effectively minimizes the business risk in its operations.

Understanding Comdisco's Accounting

Lease Accounting

Comdisco accounts for its lease transactions in accordance with the rules set forth in Accounting for Leases (FASB 13) prescribed by the Financial Accounting Standards Board. FASB 13 contains guidelines for classifying lease transactions as one of the following three types:

- sales-type lease
- direct financing lease
- operating lease

A lease is classified and accounted for as sales-type or direct financing by Comdisco if it meets any one of the following criteria:

a. The lease transfers ownership of the property to the lessee (Comdisco's customer) by the end of the lease term;

b. The lease contains an option allowing the lessee to purchase the property at a bargain price;

c. The lease term is equal to 75% or more of the estimated economic life of the property; or

d. The present value of the rentals is equal to 90% or more of the fair market value of the leased property, less any related investment tax credit retained by Comdisco.

The majority of Comdisco's sales-type and direct financing leases are classified as such because they meet criterion d above.

If the leased equipment is new or purchased from the lessee (purchase/leaseback) and meets one or more of the preceding criteria, the lease is recorded as a direct financing lease; otherwise, the lease is recorded as a sales-type lease. All other leases which do not meet one or more of the preceding criteria are classified and accounted for as operating leases. Operating leases are generally shorter term leases (2–4 years).

Sales-Type Lease. A sales-type lease is recorded in the income statement as "Sale of computer equipment," along with other sales. The amount recorded as a sale is the present value of the lease payments. The cost of the equipment less the present value of estimated residual value at lease termination, if any, is recorded in the income statement as "Cost of computer equipment."

Direct Financing Lease. It is Comdisco's policy to finance all of its direct financing leases on a nonrecourse basis. Therefore, the net margin for a direct financing lease is recorded as "other revenue." The net margin represents the sum of the proceeds from the financing of the lease plus the present value of estimated residual value at lease termination, if any, less the equipment cost.

The present value of the residual values of sales-type and direct financing leases and the present value of the noncancellable lease rentals, prior to their financing, are included in the balance sheets as "Net investment in sales-type and direct financing leases."

Operating Lease. Revenue under an operating lease is recorded as payments accrue, that is, on a monthly basis over the term of the lease. The depreciation expense is also recorded on a monthly basis and the equipment cost is recorded on the Company's balance sheet as "Leased computer equipment."

To summarize, the revenue recognition effects of the three different types of leases is as follows:

- For a sales-type lease, the present value of the lease rentals is recorded as "Sale of computer equipment" at the closing of the transaction.
- For a direct financing lease, the net margin is recorded as "Other revenue."
- For an operating lease, the monthly rentals are recorded as "Rental revenue" over the term of the lease.

Effect of Direct Financing Leases. In fiscal 1983 a substantial portion of leases written by Comdisco were recorded as direct financing leases. Because only the net margins on these leases are recorded, the total leasing volume that Comdisco transacted in fiscal 1983 is understated when compared to prior years when many fewer direct financing leases were recorded. The following table sets forth the cumulative increase in rental revenue that would have been recorded in recent fiscal years if Comdisco had recorded all direct financing leases as operating leases:

	Rental Revenue (in thousands)		
Fiscal Year	As Reported (A)	Increase (B)	Pro Forma
1979	$ 60,947	$ 9,634	$ 70,581
1980	80,979	14,612	95,591
1981	131,571	24,220	155,791
1982	206,592	65,284	271,876
1983	266,628	179,528	446,156

a. Column A represents rentals reported in the Company's income statement for the respective years.

b. Column B represents rentals due under direct financing leases that are not recorded as rental revenue because of the accounting treatment afforded direct financing leases.

As a result, the actual increase in the volume of leasing is not apparent from a review of the Company's income statement.

Residual Values. Residual value is an estimate of the value of the equipment that is expected to be realized at the end of the lease term for sales-type and direct financing leases. Comdisco records the present value of a conservative estimate of residual value.

Depreciation. All of Comdisco's leased equipment under operating leases is depreciated to zero within five years, with a higher rate applicable to the period covered by the initial user lease. Operating leases are depreciated to Comdisco's estimate of fair market value at lease termination. These conservative estimates are supported by forecasts prepared by International Data Corporation (IDC), a recognized expert in residual value projections for computer equipment. In fact, at September 30, 1983 IDC's fair market value projections are 242% of the equipment's net book value at lease termination. As a result of this conservative depreciation policy, the Company has constantly realized substantially more proceeds on the sale or re-lease of its equipment than its recorded book value.

The following table projects the runoff of the Company's September 30, 1983 operating lease portfolio. The table compares the net book value of the equipment to its estimated fair market value in the fiscal year in which the existing leases terminate. Fair market value represents IDC estimates of the equipment value at lease termination.

Comdisco, Inc.—Operating Lease Portfolio Runoff as of September 30, 1983

	Fair Market Value Comparison to Net Book Value (in thousands)		
Fiscal Year of Termination	Net Book Value at Termination	Estimated Fair Market Value at Termination	Estimated Excess Fair Market Value over Net Book Value
1984	$34,725	$70,234	$35,509
1985	15,665	43,682	28,017
1986	18,869	48,868	29,999
1987	13,820	36,525	22,705
1988	1,170	4,191	3,021
Total	**$84,249**	**$203,500**	**$119,251**

Comdisco (B)

Tax Advantaged Transaction

While the specific terms and conditions of tax advantaged transactions vary, the following is a general description of a typical tax advantaged transaction:

1. At a date after the inception of the initial user lease and independent thereof, the Company may sell all or some of the leased equipment to a third party investor ("investor"). If the equipment is sold to an investor, the sale generally occurs three to nine months after the commencement of the initial user lease. The sales price equals the then current fair market value of the equipment and is paid in the form of:

   (a) cash and a negotiable, interest-bearing promissory note (due within two years) for 10–22% of the sales price (the "equity payment"), and

   (b) an installment note for the balance (90–78% of the sales price) payable over an 84-month period.

2. Simultaneously with the sale, the Company leases such equipment back from the investor for 84 months. The lease payments payable under the leaseback obligation generally are equal to the installment payments receivable under the installment note described in 1(b) above.

3. As part of the leaseback arrangement, during the 61st through 84th month of the leaseback period, the investor also shares in the re-lease proceeds that the company receives from subleasing the equipment. Upon the expiration of the leaseback period, the investor has the exclusive right to the equipment.

In summary, the Company has given up the accelerated depreciation benefits on the equipment for tax purposes, a portion of the rentals for months 61–84 and 100% of the equipment value after the 84th month in exchange for the non-refundable equity payment. This equity payment is the only portion of the tax advantaged transaction that is recorded by the Company.

Revenue Recognition. Revenue is recognized, according to the lease classification, in the following manner:

1. For equipment subject to operating leases, the equity payment is recognized as financial services revenue in the period in which the tax advantaged transaction occurs. The Company allocates as a cost a percentage of the net book value at the expiration of the initial user lease to the revenue from the tax advantaged transaction because of its decreased right to re-lease rentals. In all cases, the equipment sold under tax advantaged transactions is fully depreciated prior to the time the investor is entitled to share in re-lease rentals.

2. For sales-type and direct financing leases, the Company may record on its balance sheet an estimated residual value at the inception of the initial user lease. The equity payment is first applied to remove a portion of that residual value. The residual value is decreased because the Company's ability to recover such residual value is reduced by the rental sharing under the tax advantaged transaction. Any excess of the equity payment over the reduction of residual value is recorded as financial services revenue in the period in which the tax advantaged transaction occurs.

Lease accounting and tax advantaged transactions represent two of the more complex areas of Comdisco's accounting. See the footnotes to the Consolidated Financial Statements for additional information.

Management's Discussion and Analysis of Financial Condition and Results of Operations

Summary

Fiscal 1983 was the third consecutive year of record revenue and earnings for the Company. Total revenue for fiscal 1983 and 1982 was $543.2 million and $471.6 million, respectively. Net earnings increased from $29.4 million, or $1.14 per share, in fiscal 1982 to $51.8 million, or $1.78 per share, in fiscal 1983. The Company's continued success in the lease placement of IBM computer equipment, particularly 308X mainframes and 3380 disk storage devices, and in financial services activities were the primary reasons for the record results achieved.

Revenue

Total revenue increased 15% over the prior fiscal year. The increase in total revenue in fiscal 1983 was not as dramatic as the increase in fiscal 1982 despite the substantial increase in the number of lease transactions in fiscal 1983, primarily because of the different mix in lease transactions entered into in fiscal 1983. The lease classification, as determined by FASB Statement No. 13, "Accounting for Leases," has a significant effect on the manner in which revenue is recorded. During fiscal 1983, there was an active market for 308X mainframes, which were recorded as direct financing leases. In fiscal 1982, a larger percentage of leases were accounted for as operating leases. Under operating lease accounting, the gross rental is recognized in equal monthly amounts over the lease term as rental revenue. Since the Company finances most of its direct financing leases on a nonrecourse basis, the net margins are recorded as other revenue. The net margin represents the sum of the present value of the lease rentals, plus the present value of estimated residual value at lease termination, if any, less the equipment.

The growth of the Company's leasing activity continued on a strong upward trend in fiscal 1983. During fiscal 1983, the Company entered into 3,467 new leases with rental payments of $1.1 billion during the initial lease terms. This compared to 2,259 new leases and $702 million of rental payments during the initial lease term for the prior fiscal year. Rental revenue from equipment subject to operating leases increased 29% in comparison to the year earlier. The increase in operating leases in fiscal 1983 was primarily due to the high volume of lease placements of IBM's newest disk storage device, the 3380.

Revenue from the sale of computer equipment increased during fiscal 1983, primarily as a result of an active international market for 308X main-frames.

Financial services revenue for fiscal 1983 totaled $65.6 million, in comparison to $73.9 million in fiscal 1982 and $30.8 million in fiscal 1981. While the total financial services activity increased in volume during 1983, such increase is not reflected in financial services revenue in comparison to 1982. Pursuant to the Economic Recovery Tax Act of 1981, the Company elected in fiscal 1982 to sell tax benefits, including investment tax credits, to other corporations and recorded the proceeds as financial services revenue. In fiscal 1983, most of the financial services revenue was generated by the sales of leased equipment through the Company's tax advantaged transactions with the Company retaining any available investment tax credits on the equipment. In essence, in fiscal 1983, the investment tax credits associated with leasing were reflected in the reduced income tax rate, while in fiscal 1982, the sale of such benefits was reflected in higher financial services revenue. Financial services revenue for fiscal 1983 and 1982 includes $6.0 million and $13.8 million, respectively, of net revenue generated by arranging leases between third parties.

Other revenue for fiscal 1983 totaled $39.8 million in comparison to $24.5 million in fiscal 1982 and $13.7 million in fiscal 1981. The increase in fiscal 1983 is primarily due to higher revenue from direct financing leases, interest income earned on short term investments and higher revenues from the Company's disaster recovery services.

Costs and Expenses

Total costs and expenses of $484.3 million for fiscal 1983 increased 16% over total costs and expenses of $417.8 million in fiscal 1982. Fiscal 1982 total costs and expenses were 49% higher than fiscal 1981. The increases were the result of the growth in the Company's leasing activities and the continuing expansion in the marketing of its services.

Interest expense for fiscal 1983 totaled $53.7 million in comparison to $47.2 million in fiscal 1982 and $33.7 million in fiscal 1981. The primary component is the interest expense associated with the discounting of operating leases. This represented 67%, 69% and 46% of total interest expense in fiscal 1983, 1982 and 1981, respectively. The Company finances leases by assigning the noncancellable rentals to financial institutions on a nonrecourse basis at fixed interest rates and receives from the lender the present value of the rental payments (the discounted amount). For operating leases, the Company recognizes interest expense over the term of the lease. The redemption of the Company's 13% Convertible Debentures Due 2001 reduced the Company's interest expense by approximately $5.3 million in fiscal 1983. Interest expense on the 8% convertible debentures issued May 1, 1983 totaled $8.2 million. The increases in interest expense in fiscal 1982 and fiscal 1981 were due to increased discounted lease rentals as a result of the growth in the Company's leased equipment portfolio.

Income Taxes

Income taxes as a percentage of earnings before income taxes were 11.9% in fiscal 1983 compared to 45.4% in fiscal 1982 and 26.8% in fiscal 1981. The higher effective tax rate in fiscal 1982 was attributable to lower investment tax credits due to the sale of such benefits by the Company as permitted under the Economic Recovery Tax Act of 1981. No significant tax benefit transfer leases were originated by the Company in fiscal 1983 and the Company retained the investment tax credits for its account, thereby reducing the effective tax rate to 11.9% in fiscal 1983. Note 10 of Notes to Consolidated Financial Statements provides details about the Company's income tax provisions and effective tax rates.

International Operations

The Company operates principally in three geographic areas: the United States, Europe and Canada. The Company has subsidiaries in Belgium, West Germany, Switzerland, the Netherlands, France, Sweden, Denmark, the United Kingdom and Canada. These subsidiaries offer services similar to those offered in the

Comdisco (B)

United States. A strong demand for IBM 308X processors, principally in Europe, resulted in an increase in revenue from international operations of 25% from $79.4 million in fiscal 1982 to $98.9 million in fiscal 1983. International revenues represented 18% of the Company's total revenue in fiscal 1983 and 17% in fiscal 1982.

Market and Dividend Information

The Company's common stock is traded on the New York Stock Exchange under the symbol CDO. The quarterly price range and dividends paid for fiscal year 1983 and 1982, adjusted to reflect the two-for-one and three-for-two common stock splits effected in March 1983 and March 1982, respectively, are shown below:

Qtr.	1983			1982		
	High	Low	Dvds.	High	Low	Dvds.
First	$18.38	$10.56	$.03	$ 9.00	$5.88	$.02
Second	27.13	16.56	.04	9.00	6.75	.03
Third	37.88	22.75	.04	9.63	7.75	.03
Fourth	42.00	34.25	.04	11.50	7.50	.03

At September 30, 1983, there were approximately 5,000 record holders of common stock.

Financial Condition

The Company's stockholders' equity increased substantially during fiscal 1983 as a result of the Company's record earnings and the conversion of $50,000,000 of 13% convertible subordinated debentures. Cash and marketable securities totaled $232.6 million at September 30, 1983. In May 1983 the Company sold $250,000,000 of 8% convertible subordinated debentures, the primary reason for the increase in cash and marketable securities. The proceeds of the offering were used to finance the increase in the Company's leasing activities and to invest in short-term marketable securities.

At September 30, 1983, the Company had $40 million of available borrowing capacity under various lines of credit from commercial banks and no short term debt.

The Company's current financial resources and estimated cash flow from operations will be adequate to fund anticipated requirements for fiscal 1984. The major portion of funds required by the Company to finance its leasing operations is provided by assigning the noncancellable rentals to various financial institutions at fixed interest rates on a nonrecourse basis. The Company's liquidity is aided by the maturation of its lease portfolio, since the remarketing of its leased equipment generates substantial funds. For example, the successful remarketing of equipment under leases

which expire in fiscal 1984 is estimated to generate funds in excess of $50 million.

Total notes and debentures as a percentage of total capital (the sum of notes and debentures payable, discounted lease rentals and stockholders' equity) was 32%, 16% and 20% at September 30, 1983, 1982 and 1981, respectively.

Ratios

The following table presents ratios which illustrate the changes and trends in earnings for the last three fiscal years:

	1983	1982	1981
Return on average stockholders' equity	36.7%	39.2%	30.6%
Return on average assets	6.9%	6.2%	4.9%
Earnings before income taxes (as a percentage of revenue)	10.8%	11.4%	7.1%
Net earnings (as a percentage of revenue)	9.5%	6.2%	5.2%

FIVE YEAR SELECTED FINANCIAL DATA

Years ended September 30,	1983	1982	1981	1980	1979
Consolidated Summary of Earnings (in thousands):					
Revenue:					
Rental	$ 266,628	$206,592	$131,571	$ 80,979	$ 60,947
Sale of computer equipment	171,138	166,705	125,384	149,708	149,983
Financial services	65,635	73,879	30,837	14,079	9,991
Other	39,779	24,454	13,746	8,348	4,355
Total revenue	543,180	471,630	301,538	253,114	225,276
Cost and expenses:					
Equipment depreciation, amortization and rental	214,439	160,523	99,413	68,328	47,698
Cost of computer equipment	151,573	149,654	111,784	134,595	128,470
Selling, general and administrative	64,655	60,402	35,313	24,219	21,284
Interest	53,673	47,242	33,657	16,988	13,319
Total costs and expenses	484,340	417,821	280,167	244,130	210,771
Earnings before income taxes	58,840	53,809	21,371	8,984	14,505
Income taxes	7,000	24,432	5,730	1,870	3,900
Net earnings	$ 51,840	$ 29,377	$ 15,641	$ 7,114	$ 10,605
Common and Common Equivalent Share Data					
Net earnings	$1.78	$1.14	$.68	$.33	$.54
Stockholders' equity	6.65	3.87	2.59	1.98	1.75
Average of common and common equivalent shares (in thousands)	29,502	28,973	24,539	22,102	19,858
Cash dividends paid	.15	.11	.09	.07	.06
Stock splits	2 for 1	3 for 2	5 for 4	—	3 for 2
Financial Position (in thousands)					
Total assets	$ 975,004	$536,679	$404,507	$229,170	$173,950
Total long-term debt	276,437	83,271	84,945	29,055	25,573
Discounted lease rentals	356,547	261,780	197,672	85,612	74,569
Stockholders' equity	191,487	91,056	58,746	43,565	35,508
Leasing Data					
Number of new leases	3,467	2,259	1,620	1,083	616
Total firm rents, initial lease term (in thousands)	$1,055,000	$702,000	$339,000	$183,000	$126,000

Comdisco (B)

Comdisco (B)

CONSOLIDATED BALANCE SHEETS
(in thousands except number of shares)

Years Ended September 30,	1983	1982
ASSETS		
Cash and marketable securities (at cost of $205,053 in 1983 and $3,909 in 1982, which approximates market)	**$232,560**	$39,762
Receivables:		
Accounts and notes (net of allowance for doubtful accounts of $1,215 in 1983 and $628 in 1982)	**74,830**	41,368
Other	**9,014**	3,687
Inventory of computer equipment	**59,681**	35,382
Net investment in sales-type and direct financing leases	**96,097**	23,682
Leased computer equipment:		
Owned	**671,697**	502,494
Capitalized leases	**24,353**	24,158
Total leased equipment	**696,050**	526,652
Less accumulated depreciation and amortization	**280,917**	190,817
Net	**415,133**	335,835
Buildings, furniture and other (at cost less accumulated depreciation of $2,764 in 1983 and $1,897 in 1982)	**9,068**	6,062
Other assets and deferred charges	**78,621**	50,901
	$975,004	$536,679
LIABILITIES AND STOCKHOLDERS' EQUITY		
Note payable to bank	**—**	$2,385
Convertible subordinated debentures	**250,000**	50,000
Subordinated debentures	**12,250**	12,250
Accounts payable	**58,963**	19,110
Obligations under capital leases	**14,187**	18,636
Obligations under capital leases income taxes:		
Current	**7,242**	6,076
Deferred	**18,121**	30,121
Other liabilities	**66,207**	45,265
Discounted lease rentals	**356,547**	261,780
	783,517	445,623
Stockholders' equity:		
Common stock $.10 par value. Authorized 50,000,000 shares: issues outstanding 28,808,571 shares in 1983 (11,769,043 in 1982)	**2,881**	1,177
Additional paid-in capital	**69,927**	18,965
Deferred translation adjustment	**(439)**	(354)
Retained earnings	**119,118**	71,268
Total Stockholders' equity	**191,487**	91,056
	$975,004	$536,679

CONSOLIDATED STATEMENTS OF EARNINGS

Years Ended September 30,	1983	1982	1981
Revenue			
Rental	**$266,628**	$206,592	$131,571
Sale of computer equipment	**171,138**	166,705	125,384
Financial services	**65,635**	73,879	30,837
Other	**39,779**	24,454	13,746
Total revenue	543,180	471,630	301,538
Cost and expenses			
Equipment depreciation, amortization and rental	**214,439**	160,523	99,413
Cost of computer equipment	**151,573**	149,654	111,784
Selling, general and administrative	**64,655**	60,402	35,313
Interest	**53,673**	47,242	33,657
Total costs and expenses	484,340	417,821	280,167
Earnings before income taxes	58,840	53,809	21,371
Income taxes	7,000	24,432	5,730
Net Earnings	$ 51,840	$ 29,377	$ 15,641
Net Earnings per Common and Common Equivalent Share	**$1.78**	$ 1.14	$.68

Comdisco (B)

CONSOLIDATED STATEMENT OF STOCKHOLDERS' EQUITY
(in thousands)

Years Ended September 30, 1983, 1982 and 1981	Common stock $.10 par value	Additional paid-in capital	Retained earnings	Deferred translation adjustment
Balance at September 30, 1980	$ 587	$ 14,167	$ 28,811	$ —
Net earnings	—	—	15,641	—
Dividends paid	—	—	(1,093)	—
Stock split	148	(148)	—	—
Stock options exercised	22	611	—	—
Balance at September 30, 1981	757	14,630	43,359	—
Cumulative amount as of September 30, 1981	—	—	—	(232)
Net earnings	—	—	29,377	—
Dividends paid	—	—	(1,468)	—
Stock split	391	(400)	—	—
Stock options exercised	14	835	—	—
Common stock issued	15	2,648	—	—
Translation adjustment	—	—	—	(122)
Income tax benefits resulting from exercise of non-qualified stock options	—	1,252	—	—
Balance at September 30, 1982	1,177	18,965	71,268	(354)
Net earnings	—	—	51,840	—
Dividends paid	—	—	(3,990)	—
Issuance of common stock upon conversion of 13% convertible debentures	256	51,782	—	—
Stock split	1,435	(1,435)	—	—
Stock options exercised	13	582	—	—
Employee Stock Purchase Plan	—	33	—	—
Translation adjustment	—	—	—	(85)
Balance at September 30, 1983	$2,881	$ 69,927	$119,118	$ (439)

Comdisco (B)

CONSOLIDATED STATEMENTS OF CHANGES IN FINANCIAL POSITION
(in thousands)

Years Ended September 30,	1983	1982	1981
Source of Funds			
From operations:			
Net earnings	$ 51,840	$ 29,377	$ 15,641
Noncash changes (credits) to operations:			
Depreciation and amortization	180,676	133,902	77,528
Increase in receivables	(38,789)	(12,849)	(5,531)
Investment in sales-type and direct financing leases	(72,415)	(5,792)	(11,732)
Income taxes	(10,834)	23,180	5,730
Increase in accounts payable and accrued liabilities	60,795	14,248	18,611
Other, net	5,636	474	(1,233)
Total provided from operations	176,909	182,540	99,014
Proceeds from issuance of subordinated debentures	245,250	—	48,560
Issuance of common stock upon conversion of 13% convertible debentures, net	53,365	—	—
Obligations under capital leases	1,984	5,663	14,249
Discounted lease rentals	257,096	145,626	183,557
Other	543	4,201	924
	735,147	338,030	346,304
Application of Funds			
Increase in leased equipment and inventory	282,341	190,180	202,002
Decrease in notes payable	2,385	1,060	33,460
Redemption of convertible debentures	50,000	—	—
Reduction of discounted lease rentals and obligations under capital leases	168,762	87,795	75,781
Purchase of subordinated debentures	—	—	2,162
Capitalized leases—computer equipment	1,984	5,663	14,249
Other assets and deferred charges	32,887	21,950	12,343
Cash dividends	3,990	1,468	1,093
	542,349	308,116	341,090
Increase in cash and marketable securities	192,798	29,914	5,214
Cash and marketable securities at beginning of year	39,762	9,848	4,634
Cash and marketable securities at end of year	$232,560	$ 39,762	$ 9,848

Comdisco (B)

NOTES TO CONSOLIDATED FINANCIAL STATEMENTS

1. Summary of Significant Accounting Policies

Principles of Consolidation: The accompanying consolidated financial statements include the accounts of the Company and its wholly-owned subsidiaries after elimination of inter-company accounts and transactions.

Inventory of Computer Equipment: Inventory of computer equipment is stated at the lower of cost or market.

Initial Direct Costs: Salesmen's commissions and other initial direct costs related to operating leases are deferred and amortized over the lease term.

Investment in Sales-Type and Direct Finance Leases: At lease commencement, the Company records the total lease rentals, estimated residual value of the leased equipment and unearned lease income as investment in sales-type and direct financing leases.

A. Sales-Type Leases

Revenue from sales-type leases is recorded as sale of computer equipment upon acceptance of the equipment by the customer. The amount of the sale is the present value of the lease payment. The carrying value of the equipment less the present value of the estimated residual value at lease termination, if any, is charged to cost of computer equipment. Unearned lease income represents the lease rentals plus the estimated residual value of the equipment less the present value of these amounts.

B. Direct Financing Leases

The total lease rentals plus the estimated residual value of lease termination, if any, less the equipment cost is recorded as unearned lease income.

The Company finances most sales-type and direct financing leases by assigning the noncancellable rentals on a nonrecourse basis. The proceeds from the assignment eliminate the total lease rentals receivable and related unearned income on sales-type and direct financing leases. Any gain or loss on the financing is recognized at the time of such financing. For leases which are not financed, unearned lease income is recognized as other revenue using the interest method over the lease term.

Leased Computer Equipment: Leased computer equipment under operating leases is recorded at cost. During the initial lease term, computer equipment is depreciated to the Company's estimate of fair market value at expiration of the initial lease term. Equipment sold under tax advantaged transactions is fully depreciated within five years. Equipment not sold under tax advantaged transactions is fully depreciated over the next lease term or five years from the date of acquisition, whichever is longer.

Financial Service Transactions: At a date after the inception of an initial user lease and independent thereof, the Company may sell some or all of the equipment to a third party investor. The sales price equals the then current fair market value of the equipment and is paid in the form of cash and a negotiable, interest-bearing promissory note (due within two years) for 10–22% of the sales price (the "equity payment"), and an installment note for the balance (90–78% of the sales price) payable over an 84- to 96-month period. Simultaneously with the sale, the Company leases such equipment back from the investor for 84 to 96 months. The lease payments payable under the leaseback obligation generally are equal to the installment payments receivable under the installment note. As part of the leaseback arrangement, from the 61st month of the leaseback period until the expiration of the leaseback, the investor shares in the release proceeds that the Company receives from subleasing the equipment. Upon the expiration of the leaseback period, the investor has the exclusive right to the equipment.

For equipment subject to sales-type and direct financing leases, the equity payment is first applied to remove a portion of the residual value of the equipment at the expiration of the initial user lease. The residual value is decreased because the Company's right to the full residual has been reduced by the tax advantaged transaction. Any excess of the equity payment over the reduction of residual value is recorded as financial services revenue in the period in which the tax advantaged transaction occurs.

For equipment subject to operating leases, the equity payment is recognized as financial services revenue in the period in which the tax advantaged transaction occurs. Against this revenue, the Company allocates as a cost a percentage of the net book value remaining at termination of the initial user lease. The balance of the net book value remaining at initial lease termination will be fully depreciated within five years from the date of equipment purchase.

In fiscal 1982 and the first quarter of fiscal 1983, the Company sold the tax benefits (investment tax credit and cost recovery allowances) on certain new equipment purchased for the Company's lease portfolio, under the provisions of the Economic Recovery Tax Act of 1981. The proceeds from the sale of tax benefits are recorded as financial services revenue. Also included in financial services revenue are fees for arranging lease transactions between third parties.

Income Taxes and Investment Tax Credit: Deferred income taxes are provided for income and expenses which are recognized in different periods for income tax purposes than for financial reporting purposes. Investment tax credits are accounted for on a flow-through basis.

Earnings Per Share: Earnings per common and common equivalent share are computed based on the weighted average number of common and common equivalent shares outstanding during each period including the effect of conversion of the 13% convertible subordinated debentures, after elimination of the related interest expense (net of tax), and after giving retroactive effect to the two-for-one stock split effected in March 1983. (See Note 11). Dilutive stock options included in the number of common and common equivalent shares are based on the treasury stock method. The number of common and common equivalent shares used in the computation of earnings per share for the years ended September 30, 1983, 1982 and 1981 were 29,501,678, 28,973,476 and 24,539,406, respectively.

2. Investment in Sales-Type and Direct Financing Leases

The following table lists the components of the net investment in sales-type and direct financing leases as of September 30:

	1983	1982
Minimum lease payments	$88,718	$24,142
Estimated residual values of leased equipment	29,863	12,324
Net investment in equipment pending sale to third parties	7,305	—
Less unearned income	29,789	12,784
Net investment in sales-type and direct financing leases	$96,097	$23,682

Future minimum lease payments to be received as of September 30, 1983 are as follows:

Years ending September 30	Minimum lease payments receivable
	(in thousands)
1984	$24,844
1985	22,910
1986	20,696
1987	14,706
1988	5,562
	$88,718

3. Leased Computer Equipment

Leased computer equipment at September 30, 1983 is comprised of the following:

Year lease commenced	Equipment cost	Accumulated depreciation	Net book value
1979	$ 20,357	$ 16,598	$ 3,759
1980	41,718	29,167	12,551
1981	146,118	96,179	49,939
1982	182,301	85,348	96,953
1983	281,203	35,518	245,685
	$671,697	$262,810	$408,887

An analysis of the operating lease portfolio by year the equipment was first available from the manufacturer follows below. This does not represent the year of purchase by the Company. The Company's depreciation policy generally depreciates computer equipment to zero within five years of the date of purchase.

Year of delivery	Net book value
1970	$ 1,816
1973	8,244
1974	21,319
1975	58,656
1976	9,290
1978	58,556
1979	88,338
1980	42,543
1981	31,637
1982	88,488
	$408,887

4. Operating Leases

Rental revenue from operating leases is recognized in equal monthly amounts over the term of the lease. The following table summarizes the Company's future rentals receivable and payable under noncancellable operating leases existing at September 30, 1983 for computer equipment and rents payable for non-computer equipment and office space:

Comdisco (B)

Comdisco (B)

Year ending September 30	Computer equipment			Other rents payable
	Rents receivable on equipment		Rents payable on subleased equipment	
	Owned	Subleased		
	(in thousands)			
1984	$213,012	$28,334	$28,023	$2,430
1985	135,624	17,723	14,118	1,787
1986	63,488	7,309	4,340	831
1987	20,378	2,399	883	435
1988	1,345	275	60	250
	$433,847	$56,040	$47,424	$5,733

Total rental income and related expense for the years ended September 30, 1983, 1982 and 1981 applicable to computer sublease activities were as follows:

Years ended September 30	Rental income	Rental expense
	(in thousands)	
1983	$29,316	$33,694
1982	23,633	27,455
1981	24,152	22,415

5. Discounted Lease Rentals

Leased equipment owned by the Company is financed by assigning the noncancellable rentals to various lenders at fixed interest rates on a nonrecourse basis. The proceeds from the assignment of the lease rentals represent payments due under the lease discounted to their present value at the interest rate charged by the lender. The proceeds from the financing of equipment subject to sales-type and direct financing leases reduce the investment in sales-type and direct financing leases (see Note 1). The proceeds from the financing of equipment subject to operating leases is recorded on the balance sheet as Discounted Lease Rentals. Interest expense under these financings is computed under the interest method and amounted to $36,173,000, $32,527,000 and $15,468,000 in 1983, 1982 and 1981, respectively. In the event of default by the lessee, the lender has a first lien against the underlying leased equipment, with no further recourse against the Company.

The annual maturities of discounted lease rentals for the next five years are as follows:

Year ending September 30	Aggregate maturities
	(in thousands)
1984	$164,193
1985	113,318
1986	56,099
1987	20,528
1988	2,409
	$356,547

6. Capitalized Leases—Computer Equipment

The Company, as lessee, leases computer equipment from other parties which may be recorded as capitalized leases pursuant to FASB Statement No. 13. If the lease qualifies as a capital lease, the Company records as an asset the lesser of the fair market value of the equipment or the present value of the minimum lease payments. The Company amortizes the asset in a manner consistent with its normal depreciation policy for leased equipment.

Capitalized leases of computer equipment at September 30 is comprised of the following:

	1983	1982
	(in thousands)	
Capitalized leases-computer equipment	$24,353	$24,158
Less accumulated computer amortization	18,107	15,354
Net capitalized leases-computer equipment	$ 6,246	$ 8,804

At September 30, 1983, the Company, as lessee, was obligated to pay rentals under those capitalized leases. The following table summarizes minimum rentals payable by the Company as lessee under capitalized leases:

Years ending September 30	Minimum rentals payable
	(in thousands)
1984	$ 7,527
1985	5,244
1986	2,807
1987	1,810
1988	521
Total minimum lease payments	17,909
Less imputed interest (9% to 17%)	3,722
Obligations under capital leases (present value of net minimum lease payments)	$14,187

The Company has subleased equipment under capitalized leases to others resulting in noncancellable sublease rental income of $10,532,000 due to the Company in the future.

7. Other Assets and Deferred Charges

During the third quarter of fiscal 1983, the Company began operations of a newly established, wholly owned subsidiary, Comdisco Resources, Inc. ("CRI"). CRI is primarily engaged, through joint ventures with established partners, in the acquisition of mineral and royalty rights in producing domestic oil and gas properties and in the acquisition of onshore leasehold interests primarily for resale to others for oil and gas exploration and development. At September 30, 1983, included in other assets and deferred charges are $22,959,000 of investments representing primarily onshore leasehold interests in unproved properties held for resale to others. For fiscal 1984, approximately $17,800,000 and $9,000,000, respectively, has been budgeted for investment in proved producing domestic oil and gas properties and unproved onshore leasehold interests for resale to others for oil and gas exploration and development.

The Company, through its CFS subsidiary, has entered into certain computer equipment transactions in which it has leased equipment and in turn has subleased such equipment. In substantially all of these transactions, the lease term exceeds the sublease term. At September 30, 1983 and 1982, $19,336,000 and $21,258,000, respectively, of costs (representing the present value of the excess of lease payments over the initial sublease payments) were deferred in connection with such transactions and are included in other assets and deferred charges. These deferred costs will be recovered from remarketing the equipment after the expiration of the initial sublease. At September 30, 1983, the Company has firm noncancellable rentals under binding contracts totaling $9,102,000 as a result of remarketing a portion of this portfolio. All of these noncancellable rentals will be used to reduce the investment in the period such rentals are received.

8. Bank Borrowings and Compensating Balances

The Company has a revolving credit agreement which entitles it to borrow up to $15,000,000 on an unsecured basis. The agreement, which expires March 31, 1984, carries an interest cost of prime rate (11.0% at September 30, 1983) and includes a fee of $3/8\%$ per annum of the average daily unused amount. If either the Company or the bank elects not to renew the agreement, the loan becomes a two-year term loan payable in equal quarterly installments with an interest cost of prime rate plus 1%. Under the agreement, the Company is required to maintain a defined debt to net worth ratio and dividend payments cannot exceed 20% of consolidated net earnings subsequent to September 30, 1980. At September 30, 1983, approximately $10,658,000 of retained earnings were available for payments of dividends.

In accordance with the terms of the agreement, the Company is required to maintain average cash balances with the bank equal to 5% of the $15,000,000 loan commitment. The amount of unused available borrow-

ings under the agreement was $15,000,000 at September 30, 1983.

At September 30, 1983, the Company had an additional unused line of credit totaling $25,000,000 which bears interest at the prime rate. Under the agreement, the Company is required to maintain compensating balances equal to 5% of the outstanding borrowings.

9. Subordinated Debentures

8% Convertible Subordinated Debentures: In May 1983, the Company issued $250,000,000 of 8% convertible subordinated debentures ("Convertible Debentures") due in 2003. Issue costs of approximately $5,000,000 were deferred and are being amortized over 20 years. Each $1,000 principal amount may be converted into shares of common stock of the Company, prior to maturity, at the option of the Convertible Debenture holder at a conversion price of $36.50 per share.

The Convertible Debentures are not redeemable prior to November 1, 1984 unless the average closing price of the common stock is $51.10 for the twenty consecutive trading days ending on the fifth day preceding the date of notice of redemption. Thereafter, they are redeemable in full or in part at the option of the Company at an amount equal to 108.0% of the principal amount, with the premium on redemption declining 8% per annum commencing in 1984 through 1993, and redeemable thereafter at par.

13% Convertible Subordinated Debentures: On November 4, 1982, the Board of Directors announced the redemption of all of the Company's 13% Convertible Subordinated Debentures Due 2001 at a redemption price of $1,117 for each $1,000 principal amount, plus accrued and unpaid interest to December 6, 1982. Common stock issued upon conversion of $49,839,000 principal amount totaled 5,111,360 shares.

11½% Subordinated Debentures: At September 30, 1983, $12,250,000 of 11½% subordinated debentures due December 1, 1992 were outstanding. Annual sinking fund payments of $1,350,000 (9% of the aggregate original principal amount) commenced December 1, 1982 and are calculated to retire 90% of the issue prior to maturity. During fiscal 1981, the Company, in connection with future sinking fund requirements, acquired $2,750,000 principal amount of the outstanding debentures which resulted in a gain of $318,000 (net of income taxes of $270,000).

The annual maturities and sinking fund requirements of all the subordinated debentures for the next five years are as follows:

Years ending September 30	Aggregate maturities
	(in thousands)
1984	$ —
1985	1,300
1986	1,350
1987	1,350
1988	1,350

10. Income Taxes

The following data related to the provision for income taxes for the years ended September 30:

	1983	1982	1981
Current:			
Federal	$13,000	$ 6,252	$ —
State	6,000	1,076	—
	19,000	7,328	—
Deferred:			
Federal	(12,200)	16,281	4,216
State	(2,200)	273	553
Foreign	2,400	550	961
	(12,000)	17,104	5,730
Total tax provision	$7,000	$24,432	$ 5,730
Earnings before income taxes:			
Domestic	$51,869	$51,166	$18,992
Foreign	6,971	2,643	2,379
Total	$58,840	$53,809	$21,371

Income tax benefits of $900,000 resulting from the redemption of the 13% convertible debentures in fiscal 1983 and $1,252,000 resulting from the exercise of non-qualified stock options in fiscal 1982 were utilized to reduce the current Federal tax liability.

The reasons for the difference between the U.S. Federal income tax rate of 46% and the effective income tax rate were as follows:

	Percentage of Pretax Earnings		
	1983	1982	1981
U.S. Federal income tax	46.0%	46.0%	46.0%
Increase (reduction) resulting from:			
Domestic International Sales Corporation tax benefit	—	(.1)	(1.2)
Reduction of deferred income taxes applicable to investment tax credit carrryforward	—	—	(20.4)
Investment tax credit	(37.9)	(2.0)	—
State income taxes, net of U.S. tax benefit	3.5	1.4	1.2
Other – net	.3	(.1)	1.2
	11.9%	45.4%	26.8%

The Company has not provided for income taxes on the unremitted earnings of the Domestic International Sales Corporation (DISC) subsidiary aggregating $4,253,000 through September 30, 1983, since the Company intends to postpone indefinitely the remittance of such earnings.

Deferred income taxes provided for timing differences were as follows:

	1983	1982	1981
Sale of tax benefits	$(6,172)	$38,661	$ —
Difference between depreciation for tax purposes and financial statement purposes	(6,305)	(18,125)	6,311
Deferred compensation expense	1,264	754	(754)
Deferred leasing income	7,445	2,934	(2,093)
Deferred leasing costs	19	1,518	1,164
Interest income on escrow account bonds not included in book income	(7,972)	—	—
Portion of undistributed earnings in DISC	—	(178)	(454)
Difference between leases accounted for as sales-type leases for financial statement purposes and operating leases for tax purposes	211	(23,601)	194
Reinstatement (reduction) of deferred income taxes applicable to:			
Investment tax credit carryforward	—	12,021	(4,356)
Tax net operating loss realization	—	—	2,323
Income tax benefit resulting from exercise of non-qualified stock options	—	—	1,903
Other – net	(490)	3,120	1,492
	$(12,000)	$17,104	$5,730

The Internal Revenue Service is examining the tax returns for the years 1980, 1981 and 1982. However, no final adjustments have been proposed and no provision for additional taxes is deemed necessary. The Company has settled all tax years through fiscal 1979.

11. Common Stock and Additional Paid-In Capital

On January 20, 1983, the Board of Directors declared a two-for-one split of the Company's common stock effective March 1983. On January 27, 1982 the Board of Directors declared a three-for-two split of the Company's common stock. On January 20, 1981 the Board of Directors of the Company declared a five-for-four split of the Company's common stock. All references in the financial statements and notes to the number of shares of common stock and per share amounts have been adjusted for the aforementioned stock splits.

On November 18, 1981, the Board of Directors approved the Settlement Agreement (the "Agreement") between the Company and participants in the Residual Incentive Compensation Plan (the "Plan") related to vested residual computer interests. The Plan provided in part for the allocation of a percentage interest in the residual value of computer equipment to the participants. The Agreement was approved by the stockholders on March 15, 1982 and, pursuant to the terms of the Agreement, the Company distributed to participants in accordance with the terms of the Plan the aggregate sum of $3,000,000 plus 300,000 shares of the Company's common stock.

Dividends on Common Stock: Common stock dividends paid were $.15 per share in 1983 compared with $.11 in 1982 and $.09 in 1981. Agreements with officers and directors who own approximately 29% (8,358,759 shares) of the outstanding common stock regarding waiver of their rights to certain cash dividends payable prior to February 1, 1983, have expired and have not been renewed.

At September 30, 1983, the Company has reserved the following number of common shares for future issuance:

1979 Stock Option Plan	542,851
1981 Stock Option Plan	1,474,200
Employees Stock Purchase Plan	196,430
Conversion of 8% Convertible Debentures	6,849,315
	9,062,796

12. Employee Benefit Plans

1979 Stock Option Plan: On November 18, 1981, the Board of Directors amended the Company's 1979 Stock Option Plan (the "1979 Plan") to qualify the plan as an incentive stock option plan in accordance with the provisions of the Economic Recovery Tax Act of 1981. All outstanding stock options, which retained their original option price, are eligible for treatment as incentive stock options subject to certain limitations as defined in the amended 1979 Plan.

1981 Stock Option Plan: On January 27, 1982, the stockholders approved the 1981 Stock Option Plan (the "1981 Plan") and 1,500,000 shares were reserved for issuance pursuant to the exercise of options under the 1981 Plan.

Employee Stock Purchase Plan: The Comdisco, Inc. Employee Stock Purchase Plan (the "Plan") was adopted by the Board of Directors on November 17, 1981 and 200,000 shares were reserved for issuance under the Plan.

The changes in the number of shares under the option plans during 1983, 1982 and 1981 were as follows:

	1983	1982	1981
Number of shares:	(in thousands except option price range)		
Shares under option beginning of year	986	1,024	1,722
Options granted	308	338	—
Options exercised	(133)	(376)	(698)
Shares under option end of year	1,161	986	1,024
Aggregate option price:			
Shares under option beginning of year	$4,967	$2,533	$3,257
Options granted	6,739	3,284	—
Option exercised	(596)	(850)	(724)
Shares under option end of year	$11,110	$4,967	$2,533
Options exercisable at end of year	238	116	328
Aggregate option price of exercisable options outstanding at end of year	$1,247	$295	$722
Options available for future grant at end of year	874	1,182	22
Option price range	$2.45–$21.88	$2.45–$9.69	$.68–$3.50

Profit Sharing Plan: The Company has a profit sharing plan covering all employees. Company contributions to the plan are based on a percentage of employees' compensation, as defined. Profit sharing payments are based on amounts accumulated on an individual employee basis. Profit sharing expense for the years ended September 30, 1983, 1982 and 1981 amounted to $834,000, $590,000 and $489,000, respectively.

13. Commitments and Contingent Liabilities

At September 30, 1983, the Company was obligated under the following commitments: (1) to purchase computer equipment in the approximate aggregate amount of $58,782,000, (2) to sell computer equipment in the approximate aggregate amount of $9,370,000, and (3) to lease computer equipment to others with an aggregate initial term rental of approximately $86,133,000.

The Company has arranged for approximately $68,683,000 of letters of credit, primarily as guarantees for certain of the Company's sublease obligations and for future purchases of IBM equipment. The cost of such letters of credit range between ½% and ¾% per annum on the amount outstanding.

Comdisco (B)

ACCOUNTANT REPORT

The Stockholders and Board of Directors, Comdisco, Inc.:

We have examined the consolidated balance sheet of Comdisco, Inc. and subsidiaries as of September 30, 1983 and 1982 and the related consolidated statements of earnings, stockholders' equity and changes in financial position for each of the years in the three-year period ended September 30, 1983. Our examinations were made in accordance with generally accepted auditing standards and, accordingly, included such tests of the accounting records and such other auditing procedures as we considered necessary in the circumstances.

In our opinion, the aforementioned consolidated financial statements present fairly the financial position of Comdisco Inc. and subsidiaries at September 30, 1983 and 1982 and the results of their operations and the changes in their financial position for each of the years in the three-year period ended September 30, 1983, in conformity with generally accepted accounting principles applied on a consistent basis.

Peat, Marwick, Mitchell & Co.
Chicago, Illinois
November 9, 1983

QUARTERLY FINANCIAL DATA

Summarized quarterly financial data for fiscal years ended September 30, 1983 and 1982 is as follows:

(in thousands of dollars except for per share amounts)

Quarter Ended:	December 31		March 31		June 30		September 30	
	1982	1981	1983	1982	1983	1982	1983	1982
Total revenue	$141,011	$121,189	$132,901	$118,309	$127,455	$94,691	$141,813	$137,441
Net earnings	12,531	9,604	10,334	5,934	13,199	5,824	15,776	8,015
Net earnings per common and common equivalent share	$.45	$.37	$.35	$.24	$.45	$.23	$.53	$.31

In the fourth quarter of fiscal 1983, the Company generated substantial investment tax credits, which resulted in an annual effective tax rate of 11.9%. This reduction in the income tax rate resulted in an increase of approximately $7,430,000 in net earnings ($.25 per share) for the fourth quarter of fiscal 1983.

Korea Stock Exchange 1998

In July 1998 Hong In-Kie, Chairman and CEO of the Korea Stock Exchange, was pondering on how best to attract a significant amount of long-term capital into the Korean stock market. Mr. Hong, a graduate of Harvard Business School AMP 85, avid mountain climber, church leader, and accomplished tenor, was aware that there were stiff challenges ahead. At the pinnacle of a successful career as a bureaucrat and as ex-president of a large conglomerate in one of the world's most dynamic economies, he had a unique birds-eye view of Korean society and the economy.

During the past 30 years, the Korean economy had grown at 8.6 percent annually. At the end of 1996, South Korea became the eleventh largest economy in the world and a member of the Organization for Economic Cooperation and Development (OECD). Used to hosannas as a worldwide leader in areas as diverse as shipbuilding, construction, semiconductors, and automobiles, Korea found itself in the unenviable position of having practically depleted its foreign exchange reserves by November of 1997, and having had to seek assistance from the International Monetary Fund (IMF). As a result of the economic crisis, the Korea Composite Stock Price Index (KOSPI) closed at 376.31 by the end of 1997, down 42.2 percent from the closing index of 651.22 in 1996 (see Exhibit 1 for selected economic data).

Mr. Hong described the current situation as follows: "It is like a movie unfolding every day, and we are all watching and on stage at the same time. Events are occurring so fast that the headlines in the evening version of the paper and the morning version of the same paper are often substantially different." Mr. Hong was convinced that finding a way to spur the development of the stock market was a crucial part of the change needed to shepherd Korea out of its current economic predicament.

KOREAN ECONOMIC SYSTEM

Prior to the 1997 economic crisis, the Korean economy was viewed by many, both inside and outside the country, as a dramatic success story. While there were many facets to the export-oriented economic strategy of Korea, two features stood out: a bank-centered financial system that financed the rapid industrial growth, and the chaebol system that created globally competitive enterprises.

Bank-Centered Financial System

Unlike the U.S. and the U.K. economies' reliance on the stock market, the Korean economy relied heavily on the banking system for channeling savings to industrial investments. In this respect, Korea followed the example of Germany and Japan in the development of its financial system. Many commentators, both in Korea and abroad, believed that the bank-centered financial system facilitated long-term investments, largely due to the close relationships between industrial enterprises and financiers. Because stock market investors typically had no

Professors James Jinho Chang (The Wharton School), Tarun Khanna, and Krishna Palepu prepared this case. The case is intended solely as the basis for class discussion and is not intended to serve as an endorsement, source of primary data, or illustration of effective or ineffective management. Copyright © 1998 by the President and Fellows of Harvard College. HBS Case 9-199-033.

Note: All references in this case to the country of Korea mean South Korea.

long-term relationship with the firms that they invested in, the U.S.-style stock market system was alleged to lead to "myopic management."

Even though Korean banks operated in the private sector, the national government had significant influence on the banking industry. Through ownership and the appointment of bank directors, the Korean government could influence banks' lending decisions to further its economic development plans. For example, in the 1970s government policies favored the development of heavy industries, such as construction, machinery, and shipbuilding. The government encouraged companies to expand business in these industries and provided favorable capital related to that expansion through banks.

Business Groups

The Korean economy was dominated by multibusiness organizations known as chaebols. The largest chaebols, such as Samsung, Daewoo, Hyundai, LG, and the SK Group, operated in a wide variety of industries such as construction, shipbuilding, automobiles, consumer electronics, computing, telecommunication, and financial services. The 30 largest chaebols accounted for 51.8 percent of the total industrial output of Korea in 1996. The top four chaebols, Hyundai, Samsung, LG, and Daewoo, accounted for 31.2 percent of the total industrial output of Korea in 1996.

Historically, government policy favored the growth of chaebols. These policies included granting industrial licenses, distributing foreign borrowings, and providing favored access to bank financing.[1] The promotion of chaebols was seen by the Korean government as a way to create domestic industry that could compete in global markets. Indeed, Korean chaebols played a very critical role in the export-led growth of the Korean economy. By 1996 the top seven trading companies of chaebols accounted for 47.7 percent of Korea's total exports.[2]

Chaebol organizational structure conferred several advantages in the early growth stage of the Korean economy by enabling entrepreneurs to overcome the problem of underdeveloped product, labor, and financial markets. At this stage, many of the institutions that underpin the functioning of advanced markets were either missing or underdeveloped in Korea.

In advanced markets, intermediary institutions and legal structures address potential information and incentive problems. These institutions permit individual entrepreneurs to raise capital, access management talent, and earn customer acceptance, and they require all parties to play by the same rules. Entrepreneurs and investors can be sure of the stable legal environment in advanced markets to protect property rights, giving entrepreneurs the confidence that they will reap the fruits of their entrepreneurial activity. In this context found in advanced markets, it is less likely that the entrepreneur will benefit significantly by being associated with a large corporate entity. Hence, the costs of business diversification are likely to exceed any potential benefits.

In an emerging market like Korea, in contrast, there were a variety of market failures, caused by information and incentive problems. For example, the financial markets were characterized by a lack of adequate disclosure and weak corporate governance and control. Intermediaries such as financial analysts, mutual funds, investment bankers, venture capitalists, and the financial press were either absent or not fully evolved. Finally, securities regulations were generally weak, and their enforcement was uncertain. Similar

1. In the early 1970s, the interest rate on foreign borrowing was 5–6 percent, whereas the interest rate on domestic bank debt was 25–30 percent. The interest rate for nonbank borrowing was higher than that from banks. The privilege of using foreign borrowing and bank loans significantly contributed to the accumulation of the chaebols' wealth.

2. The top seven trading companies are Hyundai, Samsung, LG, Daewoo, SK, Ssangyong, and Hyosung.

Korea Stock Exchange

problems abounded in product markets and labor markets, once again because of the absence of intermediaries.

The absence of intermediary institutions made it costly for individual entrepreneurs to acquire necessary inputs like finance, technology, and management talent. Market and legal imperfections also made it costly to establish quality brand images in product markets, and to establish contractual relationships with joint venture partners. As a result, an enterprise could often be more profitably pursued as part of a large diversified business group, a chaebol, which acted as an intermediary between individual entrepreneurs and imperfect markets.

Affiliates of chaebols also enjoyed preferential access to financing from domestic banks because of their strong connections with bankers and government officials. In addition, established companies in a chaebol often provided cross-guarantees on loans to new affiliates, making it easier for new ventures to raise financing from domestic and foreign lenders.

Korean chaebols such as Samsung and Daewoo were also able to use their size and scope to invest in world-class brand names. These brand names enabled new companies promoted by these leading chaebols, even in unrelated fields, to gain instant credibility in export markets and with technology partners.

Chaebols were the preferred employers for students graduating from prestigious Korean universities. Because of their size and scope, chaebols could offer job security in an economy with no safety nets. Further, chaebols such as Samsung and the SK Group made extensive investment in the training and development of their employees, in effect creating their own "business schools." Due to their size, they could hire professors from top business schools around the world to lead their in-house training programs. Because Korea did not have many world-class business schools, the in-house "business schools" of chaebols were in a unique position to develop management talent.

As a result of the above advantages, chaebols were uniquely positioned to launch new ventures in the Korean economy. Chaebols relied extensively on domestic and foreign debt to finance their rapid growth. Reliance on domestic debt arose as a result of the bank-centered nature of the financial system. Further, with a view to keep the control of Korean businesses in Korean hands, government policy restricted foreign direct investment in Korean chaebols. While foreign investors could invest through the stock market, banks and other financial institutions were a more significant channel through which foreign money was invested in Korean companies.[3]

One of the key characteristics of a chaebol is family ownership and cross-holding. In 1995 the average family ownership in the top 30 chaebols was 10.6 percent and the average ownership through cross-holding equity ownership among member firms was 32.8 percent. Cross-holdings increased the founder family's control on large business groups.[4] Traditionally, the voting rights of institutional investors, such as securities firms and insurance companies, were limited by the law and minority shareholders were not active.[5] As a result, the founder or founder's family could effectively control the business group with relatively small direct ownership, and family members took top management positions.[6]

....

3. The details of the institutional investor market in Korea can be found in "The growing financial market importance of institutional investors: the case of Korea," by Yu-Kyung Kim, OECD Proceedings: Institutional Investors in the New Financial Landscape, 1998.

4. Suppose that a family owns 20 percent of Company A and manages it, and Company A has a controlling ownership of Companies B and C, which in turn own 20 percent each of Company A. Through these cross-holdings, the founder's family can effectively own 60 percent of Company A, and control B and C as well.

5. Under these regulations, institutional investors were restricted to so called "shadow voting," which essentially meant that they voted with the management. After the recent crisis, this practice was abolished.

By 1996, prior to the economic crisis, the median debt-to-equity ratio of the top 30 Korean chaebols stood at 420 percent (see Exhibit 2). While each company in a chaebol borrowed money independently, bankers often demanded and received cross-guarantees from the other firms in the chaebol. Since Korean financial accounting rules did not require the disclosure of these cross-guarantees, it was difficult for outsiders to assess the true debt commitments of a given Korean company.

The "IMF Crisis"

The Korean economic crisis in 1997 was part of a broader Asian financial crisis that first started in Thailand, when the baht weakened as foreign investors lost confidence in the Thai economy. Amid the Asian currency crisis, foreign financial institutions, concerned about potential financial distress for Korean firms, started calling in their loans rapidly. Foreign portfolio investors also began to sell their investments and repatriate the sales proceeds for fear of the depreciation of the Korean won.[7]

The outflow of foreign portfolio investment funds continued for four consecutive months, from August to November, bringing Korea close to depleting its foreign exchange reserves. On November 21 the Korean government requested the IMF's assistance to avoid a potential default on its obligations. After frenzied negotiations, the IMF agreed to provide Korea with U.S.$55 billion or more in a bailout package. Exhibit 3 shows the chronology of events surrounding the crisis; the rapid change in the value of Korean won during 1997 and 1998 is shown in Exhibit 4.

The Search for Causes

Many observers, both inside and outside Korea, were stunned by the rapid change of investor sentiment. The darling of foreign investors and economists until then, Korea found itself in the middle of an economic crisis that threatened to wipe out the fruits of hard work of a whole generation. As a sense of gloom enveloped the country, a heated debate focused on the search for the root causes of the crisis.

The nexus of the banking system and the chaebols, once viewed as the means to rapid economic growth, came under increased attack. Influential policy makers, including those at the IMF, believed that the chaebols, with their close connections to politicians and government officials, could get loans without much resistance from banks. As a result, the vaunted "relationship financing" model, meant to facilitate long-term investments, was now viewed more as facilitating "crony capitalism." A consensus began to emerge that, with easy access to financing, a lack of supervision by banks, and the government's emphasis on job creation, chaebols focused excessively on growth and expansion and ignored profitability.

On December 19, 1997, in the middle of the serious economic crisis, Kim Dae-Jung won the election as president of South Korea. Soon after entering office, President Kim noted that big business groups, together with government officials in power in the past, must take responsibility for having brought the economy to near collapse. He proclaimed that it was the collusion between the government and business, the government's control of finance, and widespread corruption that had battered the economy. Kim said, "Unless chaebols implement reform, they would face the recall of existing debts or the suspension

---

6. In 1995, among the top 30 chaebols, only one, KIA Motors, had a CEO who was not related to the founder's family.
7. 1997 Fact Book published by Korea Stock Exchange.

Korea Stock Exchange

of fresh credit. Only profitable enterprises and exporting companies will be regarded as 'patriotic' firms eligible for government supports." [8]

The IMF Program

As a condition for IMF bailout loans, receiving countries must adhere to the economic programs prescribed by the IMF. Michel Camdessus, IMF managing director, stated: "The program comprises strengthened fiscal and monetary policies, far-reaching financial reforms and further liberalization of trade and capital flows, as well as improvement in the structure and governance of Korean corporations." The IMF's Korea program was heavily influenced by the conclusion that it was time for Korea to significantly restructure its financial and industrial sectors (see Exhibit 5 for details of the IMF-supported program of economic reform).

Some Koreans were positive about the IMF program because they felt that it could serve as an opportunity to sharpen Korea's international competitiveness, even though it was to be carried out by the force of outsiders. There were, however, others who expressed concern that the rapid changes proposed under the program were not only unrealistic but could lead to significant layoffs and social instability. In fact, the common reference to the economic crisis as the "IMF crisis" reflected the ambivalence in the Korean reaction to both the causes and the remedies being debated.

ECONOMIC RESTRUCTURING[9]

To implement the IMF program and to restore international confidence in Korea, the newly elected government of President Kim Dae-Jung began to pursue aggressively financial sector reforms and a total restructuring of chaebols. To this end, the Financial Supervisory Commission (FSC) was established on April 1, 1998, under the Prime Minister's jurisdiction to supervise all financial institutions including banks, securities firms, and insurance companies. The restructuring process of the financial industry and the corporate sector was administrated by the FSC. The FSC pursued a strategy of sequential restructuring, beginning with banks and accelerating corporate sector restructuring through bank reform.

Bank Restructuring

The FSC requested twelve banks that fell short of the 8 percent capital adequacy ratio (as of December 1997) set by the Bank for International Settlement (BIS) to submit rehabilitation plans. Bank appraisal committees and accounting firms assessed the size of nonperforming loans through asset due diligence reviews and made full provision and write-offs based on the actual size of nonperforming loans. Based on this review, the FSC conditionally approved the bailout of seven banks and ordered the closure of five nonviable banks. Conditionally approved banks were asked to submit implementation plans which included changes in management, cost reductions, and recapitalization plans such as mergers, joint ventures, or rights issues.

The five banks which were classified as nonviable were to be acquired by healthy banks. To protect acquiring banks from spilled-over problem loans, several measures were taken: only good assets would be sold with a six-month put option; government would

8. Lee Chang-sup, "Kim rules out new currency crisis, Korea Times, September 28, 1998.

9. This section is based on reports published by the Ministry of Finance and Economy (MOFE) and the Financial Supervisory Commission (FSC) in Korea.

inject fresh capital to enhance the acquiring bank's capital adequacy to pre-acquisition level; the acquiring bank's bad assets would be purchased by Korea Asset Management Corporation, funded by public resources; and deposit guarantees would be honored until the completion of all restructuring in order to prevent any bank runs.

One example of bank restructuring was a merger between Commercial Bank of Korea and the Hanil Bank. On July 31, 1998, following the guidelines of the FSC, the two banks announced a one-to-one merger. The newly merged bank proposed that in order for it to succeed, the following actions would be taken: (1) an accountable management system through drastic management improvement; (2) early resolution of nonperforming loans through injection from public resources; and (3) capital injection from international investors.[10]

A key issue in the normalization of the Korean financial sector was to develop a plan to clear nonperforming loans. At the end of March 1998, the nonperforming loans of financial institutions were estimated to be about 120 trillion won, which is about 23.3 percent of Korean financial institutions' entire credit portfolio. The Korean government estimated that the total market value of the nonperforming loans would be equal to 50 percent of their book value. The realized losses borne by financial institutions were therefore estimated to be approximately 60 trillion won.

To finance these losses, the Korean government planned to raise 50 trillion won through government bonds. From this amount, 41 trillion won would be used to purchase nonperforming loans and to recapitalize the affected financial institutions; the remaining nine trillion won would be reserved for the potential new demand for increased deposit protection. The government expected financial institutions to issue new equity worth twenty trillion won, which accounted for as much as one-third of total current capitalization in the Korean stock market.

Corporate Restructuring

In the short term, the Korean government's focus with respect to corporate restructuring was to shut down nonviable enterprises, and to improve the financial condition of the rest. In the long term, the objective was to improve the management and governance of the corporate sector in general, and of the chaebols in particular. To achieve these objectives, the FSC delineated five principles of corporate restructuring: (1) improving the financial structure, (2) eliminating the practice of mutual guarantees of loans among affiliated firms, (3) focusing on "core" business sectors, (4) increasing transparency, and (5) improving corporate governance (e.g., increasing major shareholders' and management's accountability).

In order to direct the restructuring process, the FSC classified all Korean companies into three categories. Companies classified as "viable" would receive full support from financial institutions; those that were classified as "subject to exit" would be sold off or shut down on a timely basis; and those that were classified as "subject to restructuring" would benefit from proactive support toward restructuring from financial institutions. In June 1998, 55 corporations, which represented 17 percent of the total number of corporations subject to the assessment, were classified as nonviable and ordered to exit. Of these 55 corporations, twenty were affiliated companies of the top five chaebols (Hyundai, Samsung, LG, Daewoo, and SK), and 32 were affiliates of the top 6 to 64 business groups.

One of the senior officials at FSC stated: "To reduce excessive reliance on debt financing, the government set a target for reducing Korean companies' debt to equity (D/E) ratio

10. Joint press conference upon announcement of merger between the Commercial Bank of Korea and the Hanil Bank.

from the current level of approximately 500 percent to a level of 200 percent by the end of 1999. To meet this requirement, Korean companies had to raise more equity or sell off some of their assets."

Korean chaebols were directed by the FSC to formulate restructuring plans with a view to identifying core businesses on which they would focus, and to close down or divest the rest. To improve transparency and governance of individual companies in a chaebol, new guidelines curtailed the role of the central corporate office, and prohibited cross-guarantees. The top five chaebols were cajoled into the so-called "Big Deal" swaps of business units in order to boost national competitiveness by cutting out some domestic competition. To expedite the pace of corporate restructuring, government submitted the legislative articles, such as allowing tax benefits to restructuring, simplifying the mergers and acquisitions process, and permitting corporate spin-offs/carve-outs, to the coming session of the National Assembly.

Attracting Foreign Capital

Recognizing the importance of foreign capital for the successful restructuring of Korean banks and chaebols, President Kim Dae-Jung proclaimed his intention to make South Korea a haven for foreign investors. Foreign investors were essential in several ways. First, since all major Korean companies were looking to sell assets and raise new capital, the only viable buyers were foreigner investors. Second, foreign investors brought with them world-class management and governance practices to Korea.

To attract foreign capital, the government proposed several new policies. Under the new policy, foreign firms were allowed to freely establish mutual funds in Korea. At the same time, restrictions on foreign investors were also reduced. Earlier, foreign investors needed the approval of the board of directors of a company to buy more than ten percent of its outstanding shares. On May 25, 1998, under the new rules, the ten percent limit was completely abolished. The government also granted special privileges to domestic companies that attracted foreign investment or sold their assets to foreigners.

While these moves were somewhat effective in increasing foreign investors' interest in Korea, several hurdles remained. Deals for foreign direct investment could not be consummated because of widespread disagreement in valuation estimates of Korean sellers and foreign buyers. These valuation difficulties were exacerbated by the poor quality of accounting information. Further, foreign buyers were uncertain about the ease with which they could lay off employees. Despite the recent agreement between government, industry, and labor unions to cooperate in the restructuring process, the possibility of widespread lay-offs, especially by foreign owners, could be received with hostility.

The popular sentiment towards foreign direct investment was also ambiguous. On the one hand, the Korean government undertook a process of educating Koreans that attracting international investors was critical to economic rebuilding. On the other hand, there was a popular feeling against foreign investment, partly due to the 40-year Japanese rule of the country that ended in 1945. As a result, while many American franchises such as McDonald's and KFC have prospered in Korea, symbolic gestures against foreign investment abounded. When Microsoft attempted to buy a Korean word processing software company in financial distress, there was a fund-raising campaign to save the company and keep it in Korean hands. Even though the amount of foreign investment involved in this deal was only about U.S.$20 million, it was symbolic.

Foreign investors were also wary of the risks involved in investing in Korean companies through the stock market. Even in advanced capital markets, investing in stocks involves taking additional risks relative to investment in bonds or bank deposits. Unlike debt holders, shareholders are not promised a fixed payoff. Finally, when insiders have a controlling stake, they can take actions that are potentially harmful to the minority shareholders. In advanced markets, these potential risks faced by public shareholders are mitigated through a variety of mechanisms such as credible financial reporting, minority shareholder protection laws, the threat of hostile takeovers, scrutiny by an aggressive analyst community, and the supervision of management by an independent board of directors.

In Korea as of early 1998, many of these institutional mechanisms that protect shareholders and reduce their risks were either absent, underdeveloped, or poorly enforced. Relative to international standards, accounting rules and disclosure regulations were lax; there was a widespread belief that external auditors were either unwilling or unable to exercise independence; it was rare for shareholders to sue corporate managers or auditors successfully; boards were viewed as being too close to corporate managers; there was no effective threat of a hostile takeover or a proxy fight to replace a company's management; and the financial analysts themselves often worked for brokerage houses owned by large chaebols. The net result of these institutional voids was a perception among investors, both domestic and foreign, that investing in Korean stocks was very risky.

DEVELOPING THE CAPITAL MARKETS

As Chairman and CEO of the Korea Stock Exchange, Hong In-Kie was committed to leading the development of the Korean capital markets to a truly world-class level. He believed that the long-term prosperity of Korea depended critically on the success of this initiative.

Traditionally, the stock market played a relatively small role in the Korean financial system. The first significant boost to the Korean stock market came in 1976 when the Securities and Exchange Law underwent extensive revision. The main objective of the amendment was to ensure more effective supervision of the securities industry and to reinforce investor protection.

Throughout the latter half of the 1970s, the Korean securities market experienced an unprecedented rush of public offerings. The number of listed corporations, which stood at only 66 in 1972, jumped to 356 by the end of 1978. At the end of 1997, the number of listed companies was 776. During the period from 1972 to 1997, the traded value of listed stocks jumped more than two thousandfold from 71 billion won to 162.3 trillion won and the total market capitalization increased from 246 billion won to 71 trillion won (see Exhibit 6 and Exhibit 7).

Even though the absolute amount of both the traded value of stocks and market capitalization has increased over time, the relative magnitude of market capitalization to GDP declined in recent years. In 1994 and 1995, the market value to GDP ratio was greater than 40 percent, but it declined to 30 percent in 1996 and to 17 percent in 1997 (see Exhibit 8). The significance of equity as a source of financing also decreased over the last decade: The proportion of financing from the stock market relative to all sources of external financing declined from 23 percent in 1989 to 7.87 percent in 1997 (see Exhibit 9 and Exhibit 10).

The KOSPI composite index (100 as of January 4, 1980) rose from 532 on January 1, 1988, to 1007 on April 1, 1989. Many small investors were counting capital gains in excess of 100 percent in a little over a year. However, this 1988–89 upturn in the Korea Stock Exchange was not sustainable. The composite index has since dived and climbed like a roller coaster. On August 21, 1992, the composite index bottomed out at 460. Many small investors became seriously disillusioned with the stock market in 1992, blaming the government for their losses. Indeed, for political reasons the government had repeatedly intervened to prop up share prices by infusing large inflows of cash from various stabilization funds. Hardly anyone approached the market from a long-term perspective of focusing on the fundamental financial soundness of the company, managerial acumen, or on dividend performance.[11]

Recent Developments

After Mr. Hong became the CEO of the stock exchange in 1993, he initiated several efforts to modernize it. In 1996 the stock exchange moved to a new skyscraper with a fully computerized trading floor and a strict computerized surveillance system to monitor trading activity. Under Mr. Hong's leadership, the Korea Stock Exchange introduced derivative products for the first time—KOSPI 200 stock index futures contracts in May 1996, and KOSPI 200 stock index option contracts in July 1997. While Mr. Hong was proud of these innovations, and the investments in improving the physical infrastructure of the exchange, he was aware that the exchange would not become truly world-class without significantly more support of *institutional* infrastructure. Mr. Hong noted with satisfaction some recent developments in this direction.

Recognizing the fact that lack of transparency was one of the weaknesses that contributed to the current crisis, the Korean government proposed major changes in accounting rules. New regulations required the 30 largest conglomerates to prepare certified financial statements which would cover all the affiliated companies on a combined basis beginning in the 1999 fiscal year. The objective of this requirement was to improve the transparency of large conglomerates. There was also a move to make a fundamental change in Korean Generally Accepted Accounting Principles by adopting the more stringent International Accounting Standards.

There was also a change in the process through which accounting standards were set. Earlier, the Korea Securities and Exchange Commissions (KSEC) set accounting standards. When a new accounting standard was proposed, the KSEC would form a temporary board to review that standard. Board members included auditors, accounting professors, and government officials. Starting in April 1998, the KSEC became a part of the Financial Supervisory Board, and the FSC took over the supervision of accounting standard setting.

To improve shareholder rights, the Korean government took a number of steps. For example, in April 1998, to improve minority shareholders' rights, the current requirement of 1 percent ownership to bring suits against management was eased to 0.05 percent; the requirement of 1 percent ownership to request the dismissal of a director or an auditor for an illegal act was relaxed to 0.5 percent; the minimum share-ownership required to examine corporate books was reduced from 3 percent to 1 percent.

New regulations also attempted to ease restrictions that had previously made hostile takeovers of Korean companies very difficult. Earlier, a company or an individual could not acquire more than 25 percent of the outstanding shares of another company unless an open tender offer to purchase more than 50 percent of the outstanding shares was made. However, in February 1998, this provision was abolished. Also, restrictions on institutional investors' voting rights were eliminated.

Public shareholders were also becoming more vocal in demanding management accountability. In May 1998, for the first time, foreign shareholders were beginning to have a voice in the management of Korean companies. The New York-based hedge fund Tiger Management, with the coalition of other foreign funds, staged a successful revolt at SK Telecom, the country's leading cellular phone operator. These outsider shareholders forced the phone company to stop subsidizing its sister companies in the SK Group. SK Telecom, for instance, backed a $50 million loan to its sibling SK Securities, which

11. James M. West, "Korea Stock Exchange," Korea Herald, August 30, 1998.

Korea Stock Exchange

recently suffered heavy losses in derivatives trading. To guard against such maneuvers in the future, minority shareholders demanded—and got—three outside directors on the board of SK Telecom and an independent auditor.[12,13]

Management accountability was also being championed by nongovernmental organizations such as The People's Solidarity for Participatory Democracy (PSPD). The organization was founded in September, 1994, and headed by Professor Chang Ha-sung at Korea University. In July 1998 PSPD successfully won a judgment against the management of the Korea First Bank for failure to exercise due diligence in its lending to a failed company, Hanbo Steel. The court order required four former top managers of Korea First Bank to pay about U.S.$30 million with their personal wealth to the bank (not to the plaintiffs) to make up for the losses caused by their negligence. The Korean press hailed it as the first case where plaintiffs won in a suit against management based on the failure to perform due diligence.

Future Challenges

Mr. Hong was convinced that a lot of progress had been made in the past few months. There was evidence that foreign investors were beginning to come back. Korea was also winning praise from the IMF for following closely its prescriptions. However, he was also aware that much more needed to be done.

Although the new accounting regulations were aimed at improving the quality of information available to investors to monitor corporate managers, there was much skepticism about the rules that had been mandated. The editor of a major Korean newspaper commented, "It's fine for the government and the international investors to demand transparency. However, it's important to realize that the different facets of Korean society are closely tied together—the government, business, and the banks. The entire system will have to be made transparent, not just a part of it."

Mr. Hong also noted that without effective auditing, financial reports were unlikely to be viewed by investors as reliable. One of the senior partners at a Big Five accounting firm in the United States echoed this sentiment: "Foreign investors know that the quality of audits in Korea is suspect; they will not be satisfied unless the financial statements of their Korean companies are signed by reputable international accounting firms."

The recent victory of minority shareholders represented the coming of major changes in Korean financial markets. However, this development was viewed with mixed feelings by several observers. Given the average Korean citizen's lack of sophistication about financial markets, there was a concern that minority shareholder rights would be pushed forward without adequate attention paid to minority shareholder responsibilities. Would the prospect of shareholder lawsuits and second-guessing management decisions by courts hamper the restructuring process?

There was also a debate in Korea and other emerging markets on the appropriate speed of opening capital markets to foreign investors, given the experience of the past few months. One of the major concerns was the instability of the stock market due to speculative hot money. Rapid outflow could significantly damage not only the stock market but also the foreign exchange rate. In order to prevent this, many emerging countries imposed regulations on foreign investment and intervened in their stock markets.

Mr. Hong believed that full liberalization of the stock market was the fundamental solution. He stated, "Government regulations, as in the case of Malaysia, or government

12. Louis Kraar, "Korea's comeback ... Don't expect a miracle," *Forbes*, May 25, 1998, p.120.

13. Starting in 1999, all Korea Stock Exchange listed firms are required to have at least 25 percent of their board members be outside directors.

interventions in the stock market, as in the case of Hong Kong, do not guarantee the long-term development of a stock market. While in the rest of the world the acronym PKO may stand for Peace Keeping Operation, the same term in Asian securities markets is known as Price Keeping Operation, a derogatory term for intervention by the government. As the underlying philosophy of the government is based on democracy and a market economy, stock market participants must not rely on government to implement artificial market-boosting measures. In the short term, the stock market may have difficulty in breaking out of the doldrums, but as the market finds itself free from any sort of intervention, it will grow into a more independent, transparent, predictable, accountable, and self-sustaining market. Korea is following closely the IMF prescription toward a fully open market. The earlier we can get to the open market, the better." However, he wondered whether Korea had the institutional infrastructure necessary to support an open stock market.

As he pondered over these issues, Mr. Hong knew that the stakes were high. A senior editor of one of Korea's leading newspapers summed up the situation: "The newly elected President asked for a year to resolve matters. It has been six months already. If things don't improve, Korean people may not remain patient much longer." Due to the efforts made by government and business, there was a sign of increase in the foreign investment in Korean stocks (see Exhibit 11). However, the level has not met Mr. Hong's expectation. Mr. Hong wondered which of several possible directions the Korean stock market should pursue to attract foreign investment.

QUESTIONS

1. What are the merits and demerits of a stock versus a bank system of financing?

2. To prevent another bad loan problem in the future, what changes should be made in South Korean banks?

3. Is it a good idea for South Korea to rely more on the stock market as a source of corporate finance? Is it a good idea from the perspective of the chaebols?

4. How long do you think it will take South Korea to develop a vibrant stock market? What are the impediments? Are the changes contemplated adequate for the development of a vibrant stock market? What other steps would you recommend?

EXHIBIT 1

Selected Economic Indicators for South Korea

	1995	1996	1997	1998 (estimate)
Korea Composite Stock Price Index (year-end)	882.94	651.22	376.31	
Real GDP growth (percent change)	8.8	5.5	−0.4	−4.0 to −5.5
Consumer prices (percent change)	7.4	4.8	7.7	10.0
Central government balance (% of GDP)	3.0	2.4	−0.9	−2.4
External debt (billion US$)	82.6	90.5	91.8	89.7

Source: International Monetary Fund.

Korea Stock Exchange

EXHIBIT 2

Top 30 Chaebols,[a] 1996 Financial Data

(amounts in billion won)		Assets	Owners' Equity	Debt-to-Equity	Return on Equity
1	Hyundai	52,821	9,842	437%	5.69%
2	Samsung	50,705	13,809	267%	1.71%
3	LG	37,068	8,302	346%	5.64%
4	Daewoo	34,197	7,817	337%	5.90%
5	Sunkyung	22,743	4,703	384%	12.73%
6	Ssangyong	15,802	3,102	409%	−1.90%
7	Hanjin	13,907	2,118	557%	−10.49%
8	Kia	14,121	2,289	517%	−4.70%
9	Hanwha	10,592	1,244	751%	−11.01%
10	Lotte	7,753	2,654	192%	5.34%
11	Kumho	7,399	1,281	478%	−0.58%
12	Halla	6,627	306	2066%	12.89%
13	Dong-Ah	6,289	1,383	355%	4.64%
14	Doosan	6,369	808	688%	−23.33%
15	Daelim	5,849	1,118	423%	6.35%
16	Hansol	4,214	1,075	292%	1.10%
17	Hyosung	4,131	879	370%	7.16%
18	Dongkuk Steel	3,698	1,161	219%	4.75%
19	Jinro	3,826	99	3765%	−169.06%
20	Kolon	3,840	919	318%	4.80%
21	Kohap	3,653	529	591%	7.34%
22	Dongbu	3,423	946	262%	3.00%
23	Tongyang	2,631	646	307%	0.05%
24	Haitai	3,398	448	658%	5.89%
25	New Core	2,796	211	1225%	15.99%
26	Anam	2,638	456	479%	10.22%
27	Hanil	2,599	384	577%	−40.00%
28	Keopyung	2,296	513	348%	−0.04%
29	Miwon	2,233	432	417%	−7.42%
30	Shinho	2,139	362	491%	−2.93%
	Mean	11,325	2,328	617%	−5.01%
	Median	5,032	1,011	420%	3.82%

a. *Excluding financial and insurance industries*
Source: Korea Fair Trade Commissions.

EXHIBIT 3

Chronological Highlights of the Korean Economic Crisis

Date	Events
August 20, 1997	The IMF approves a US$4 billion stand-by credit for Thailand, and releases a disbursement of US$1.6 billion.
October 8, 1997	The IMF announces support for Indonesia's intention to seek support from the IMF and other multilateral institutions.
November 21, 1997	The IMF welcomes Korea's request for IMF assistance.
December 4, 1997	The IMF approves a US$21 billion stand-by credit for Korea, and releases a disbursement of US$5.6 billion.
December 11, 1997	Korean government increases the foreigners' stock ownership ceiling from 26% to 50% (which later changed to 100%).
December 12, 1997	Korean government allows foreigners to invest in short-term financial instruments in domestic market.
December 31, 1997	The Korea Composite Stock Price Index closes the year at 376.31, down 42.2% from the closing index of 651.22 in 1996. Total market capitalization is reduced to about 71 trillion won.
April 1, 1998	Financial Supervisory Commission (FSC) is established to supervise all financial institutions, including banks, securities firms, and insurance companies.
April 9, 1998	The Foreign Exchange Equalization Bonds of US$4 billion are issued successfully and the Korean government shifts its focus from escaping the currency crisis to financial and corporate sector restructuring.
May 25, 1998	The ceiling on foreigners' stock investment is abolished, fully liberalizing the Korean stock market to foreign investors.
June 10, 1998	President Kim Dae-Jung delivers address at the U.S. Chamber of Commerce in Washington, D.C. He promises that Korea will become one of the best countries for international investors to freely and safely do business. Foreign Investment Promotion Act is designed to make Korea hospitable to foreign investors by providing financial concessions and administrative support.
June 18, 1998	The Financial Supervisory Committee (FSC) classified 55 corporations as financially nonviable and ordered them to liquidate.
June 29, 1998	Financial Supervisory Committee (FSC) orders 5 banks to shut down their operation and merge with other banks. FSC requests 7 banks, classified as conditional approval, to submit restructuring implementation plans.
July 24, 1998	Minority shareholders win, for the first time in history, against bank management for their failure to exercise due diligence.
July 31, 1998	Two conditionally approved banks, the Commercial Bank of Korea and the Hanil Bank, announce one-to-one merger.

Korea Stock Exchange

EXHIBIT 4

Bilateral U.S. Dollar–Korean Won Exchange Rate

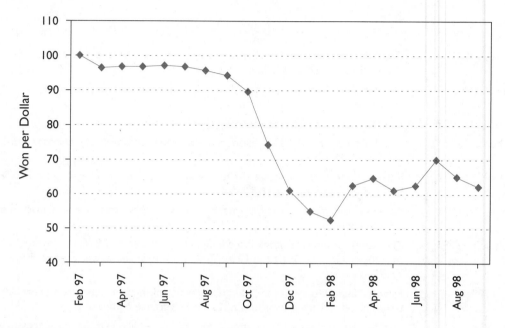

Source: Bank of Korea.

Korea Stock Exchange

EXHIBIT 5

IMF-Supported Program of Economic Reform for South Korea

....

Financial sector restructuring	Comprehensive financial sector restructuring that introduced a clear and firm exit policy for financial institutions, strong market and supervisory discipline, and independence for the central bank.
	Abolishment of regulations prohibiting a foreigner from becoming a director of a commercial bank.
	Requirement that all merchant banks meet their capital adequacy ratios.
Transparency and corporate sector restructuring	Efforts to dismantle the nontransparent and inefficient ties among the government, banks, and businesses, including measures to upgrade accounting, auditing, and disclosure standards. Requirement that corporate financial statements be published every half year, on a consolidated basis, and certified by external auditors according to the international accounting standards.
	Submission of legislation fully liberalizing hostile takeovers of Korean corporations by domestic companies and foreigners.
	Amendment of the Bankruptcy Law to accelerate the corporate bankruptcy procedure.
	Phase-out of the system of cross-guarantees within conglomerates.
Foreign investment	Full liberalization measures to open up the Korean money, bond, and equity markets to capital inflows, and to liberalize foreign direct investment.
	Permission for foreign banks' securities companies to establish subsidiaries in Korea.
Labor market reform	Amendment of layoff-related laws which facilitate the redeployment of labor.
	Increase in the government's financial support for the unemployed.
	Expansion in the number of companies whose employees are eligible for unemployment insurance, and raising the minimum unemployment subsidy.
Trade policy	Trade liberalization measures, including setting a timetable in line with WTO commitments to eliminate trade-related subsidies and the import diversification program, as well as streamlining and improving transparency of import certification procedures.

....

Source: Adapted from reports published by Financial Supervisory Commissions.

Korea Stock Exchange

EXHIBIT 6

Ten-Year History of Korea Composite Stock Price Index (KOSPI)

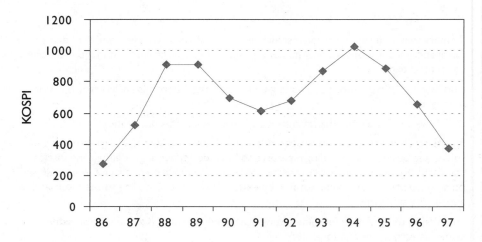

Source: Fact Book published by Korea Stock Exchange.

EXHIBIT 7

Stock Trading Value

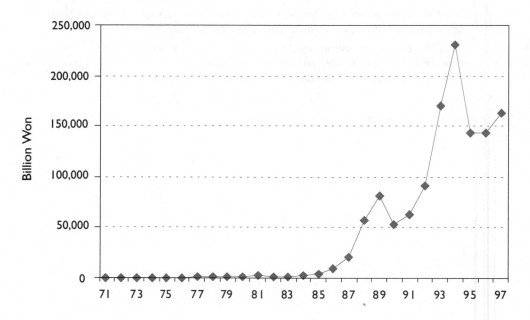

Source: Fact Book published by Korea Stock Exchange.

EXHIBIT 8

Market Value to GDP Ratios

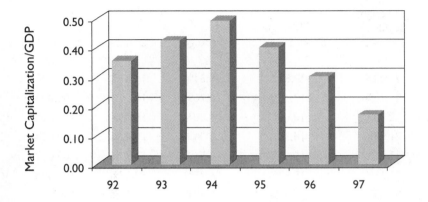

Source: Fact Book published by Korea Stock Exchange.

EXHIBIT 9

Financing of Korean Corporations (in billion won)

| | Through Financial Institutions | | Through Capital Markets | | | | | |
	Bank	Non-Bank	CP	Stock	Bonds	Foreign[a]	Others[b]	Total
1989	5,698	7,963	5,131	8,310	4,932	−185	4,292	36,140
1990	7,995	11,477	1,902	5,987	10,931	3,247	6,517	48,056
1991	11,487	12,686	−2,211	5,555	14,065	2,501	8,002	52,085
1992	8,313	11,599	4,183	7,177	6,616	2,527	9,737	50,152
1993	8,440	11,718	9,017	8,619	9,218	−1,298	9,857	55,571
1994	18,367	20,981	4,405	13,198	13,568	4,037	10,423	84,978
1995	14,991	16,884	16,096	14,445	14,958	5,568	11,656	94,597
1996	18,571	18,424	20,691	13,342	20,265	12,063	13,542	116,899
1997	15,116	28,399	4,773	8,974	27,422	7,162	22,127	113,973

a. Foreign implies funds borrowed from overseas capital markets.
b. Others include letters of credit, loans from government, reserve for retirement allowances, etc.
Source: Bank of Korea.

Korea Stock Exchange

Korea Stock Exchange

EXHIBIT 10

Financing of Korean Corporations (in percent)

	Through Financial Institutions	Through Bond/CP Markets	Through Stock Markets	Foreign	Others	Total
1989	37.80%	27.84%	22.99%	−0.51%	11.87%	100.00%
1990	40.52%	26.70%	12.46%	6.76%	13.56%	100.00%
1991	46.41%	22.76%	10.66%	4.80%	15.36%	100.00%
1992	39.70%	21.53%	14.31%	5.04%	19.42%	100.00%
1993	36.27%	32.81%	15.51%	−2.34%	17.74%	100.00%
1994	46.30%	21.15%	15.53%	4.75%	12.27%	100.00%
1995	33.69%	32.83%	15.27%	5.89%	12.32%	100.00%
1996	31.65%	35.04%	11.41%	10.32%	11.58%	100.00%
1997	38.18%	28.25%	7.87%	6.28%	19.41%	100.00%

Source: Bank of Korea.

EXHIBIT 11

Foreign Investment in Korean Stock

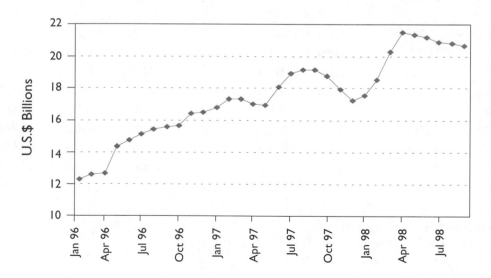

Source: Korea Stock Exchange.

Manufactured Homes, Inc.

This Winston-Salem company sells affordable Southern comfort: fully furnished and carpeted mobile homes for as little as $10,000. Robert Sauls, the 59-year-old founder and chairman, was an orphaned boy who never finished high school. Through acquisitions, Sauls has built the retailer into the industry's largest, with annual sales ballooning to about $180 million in four years. The company sells the homes, built primarily by Fleetwood Enterprises and Redman Industries, to rural blue-collar workers in the Southeast. "Our people buy in good times and bad," says Sauls. If he can raise the capital, he foresees a doubling of sales in four to five years. The stock recently sold at 6.5 times estimated 1988 earnings.

Jane Edwards, Director of Research at a small Boston-based investment management firm specializing in growth stocks, noted the above review of Manufactured Homes in the February 15, 1988 issue of *Fortune* magazine's Companies To Watch column. She knew that attractive growth stocks are hard to find and wondered whether Manufactured Homes would be a good addition to her firm's growth stock portfolio. She checked the recent performance of Manufactured Homes' common stock and noted that the stock performed favorably relative to the stock market (see Exhibit 1). Jane Edwards asked her assistant Peter Herman to gather additional information on the company and to write a report analyzing the company's recent financial statements.

COMPANY BACKGROUND AND MARKETING FOCUS

Herman's preliminary research on Manufactured Homes indicated that the company was founded in 1975 with two retail outlets for mobile homes. The company grew rapidly and by March 31, 1987, had a network of 120 retail outlets located in seven southeastern states. Eighty-five percent of the company's retail centers were located in North Carolina, South Carolina, Alabama, Georgia, and Florida, with the remaining sales centers in Virginia and West Virginia. The company went public in 1983 and was listed on the American Stock Exchange in January 1987.

The southeastern U.S. was the country's fastest growing market for mobile homes due to suitable climate, the easy availability of vacant land for mobile-home parks, and the region's demographics. Potential customers for manufactured homes included individuals seeking a single-family primary residence but lacking the ability to purchase conventional housing, retirees, and those wanting a second home for vacation purposes.

The company targeted individuals in the low income category, which was a segment of the manufactured homes market in the company's seven-state operating area. The company's customers were typically between the ages of 18 and 40, blue-collar workers in manufacturing, service, and agricultural industries, and earned approximately $20,000 per year. Many of them were seeking single-family accommodations for their families and turned to manufactured homes because conventional low-cost housing was becoming increasingly less affordable.

Professor Krishna G. Palepu prepared this case. The case is intended solely as the basis for class discussion and is not intended to serve as an endorsement, source of primary data, or illustration of effective or ineffective management. Copyright © 1989 by the President and Fellows of Harvard College. HBS Case 9-190-090.

Manufactured homes came in a wide variety of styles, including both single and multi-sectional units. They typically had a living room, a kitchen and dining area, and bedrooms and baths, with a wide variety in the size, number, and layout of rooms among the various models. The single-sectional homes ranged in size from 588 to 1008 square feet and retailed at prices between $10,000 and $25,000, with the majority selling below $17,000. The multi-sectional homes were 960–2016 square feet and sold at prices ranging from $17,000 to $40,000. Single-sectional homes represented most of the company's sales. While approximately 30 percent of all unit sales in the industry in 1986 were multi-sectional homes, they represented only about 20 percent of Manufactured Homes' unit volume.

The company believed that its focus on the lower end of the market had two advantages. First, since its customers were seeking to fulfill an essential housing need, sales were less affected by changes in general economic conditions. Second, the company's repossession rates were significantly lower than those of the industry since its customers were likely to work very hard to keep their primary residences even when times were bad.

REVENUES

Most of Manufactured Homes' sales were credit sales where the customer paid a down payment of 5 to 10 percent of the sales price and entered into an installment sales contract with the company to pay the remaining amount over periods ranging from 84 to 180 months. The company generally sold the majority of its retail installment contracts to unrelated financial institutions on a recourse basis. Under this agreement, Manufactured Homes was responsible for payments to the financial institution if the customer failed to make the payments specified in the installment contract.

While the installment sale interest rate that Manufactured Homes charged its customers was limited by competitive conditions, it was typically higher than market interest rates. Therefore, the financial institutions to whom these contracts were sold on a recourse basis usually paid the company the stated principal amount of the contract and a portion of the differential between the stated interest rate and the market rate. (The remainder of the interest rate differential was retained by the financial institutions as a security against credit losses and was paid to the company in proportion to customer payments received. The reserve required varied up to seven percent of the aggregate amount financed, including principal and interest.) The company therefore had two sources of revenue: the sale of homes (sales revenue), and the interest rate "spread" (finance participation income).

Peter Herman noted that Financial Accounting Board's Statement 77 (FASB-77) governs the accounting treatment for installment sales receivables that are transferred by a company to a third party on a recourse basis. Transfers of receivables that are subject to recourse must be reported as sales if the following three conditions are satisfied:

1. The seller unequivocally surrenders the receivable to the buyer.
2. The seller's remaining obligations to the buyer under the recourse provision must be subject to reasonable estimation on the date of the transfer of the receivable. For this purpose, the seller should be able to estimate:
   (a) The amount of bad debts and related costs of collection and repossession, and
   (b) The amount of prepayments. If the seller cannot make these estimates reasonably well, a transfer of the receivable cannot be reported as a sale.
3. The seller cannot be required to repurchase the receivable from the buyer except in accordance with the recourse provision.

If any of the above conditions is not satisfied, the seller of the receivable must report the proceeds from the transfer as a loan against the receivable.

FINANCIAL PERFORMANCE

Manufactured Homes' revenues increased rapidly in recent years, from $11 million in 1983 to $120 million in 1986. In the company's 1986 annual report, Robert Sauls, the CEO, forecasted the company's growth to continue and expected the 1987 revenues to be $140–$145 million. Herman noted that the company's sales for the first nine months of 1987 exceeded this forecast. The company's latest 10-Q statement reported $148 million revenues for the nine months ended September 30, 1987.

Based on the performance in the first nine months of 1987, the *Value Line Investment Survey* forecasted that Manufactured Homes would achieve $180 million revenues and $6 million net income (or $1.65 per share) in 1987, and $210 million revenues and $7.5 million net income (or $2.00 per share) in 1988. *Value Line* commented on the company's near-term prospects as follows:[1]

> We look forward for [per] share net [income] to advance 20% in 1988, despite a difficult selling environment. Industrywide shipments for the company's core Carolina markets were down in the December quarter and are likely to remain soft in the year ahead. We think, however, that Manufactured Homes will nevertheless find growth opportunities. True, the number of retail centers probably won't increase much this year. On the other hand, the rapid expansion of retail centers over the past five years has put in place a large number of dealerships that have plenty of opportunity for increasing volume.
>
> Management is seeking to average 100 units per store as these sales locations mature. At the end of 1986, stores were selling 47 units per year on average, and that figure rose 20% for the first nine months of 1987. Although the market will be very competitive this year, we think the company's special attention to the low-end of the market, to which many large competitors pay less attention, will give Manufactured Homes a solid niche position. Adding in the reduced tax rate, we think full year [per] share net [income] may well reach the $2.00 mark.
>
> Volume buying gives this retailer an edge. Because Manufactured Homes buys in bulk, it can negotiate lower prices from the manufacturers it deals with. And by passing the savings on to customers, the company is able to underprice smaller, "mom and pop" outlets. Furthermore, because of its size, the company is able to more efficiently handle inventory financing and mortgage assistance for its customers.

Before making a final recommendation to Edwards, Herman wanted to take a detailed look at Manufactured Homes' financial statements for the fiscal year 1986 (Exhibit 2) and the interim statements for the first nine months of 1987 (Exhibit 3).

QUESTIONS

1. Identify the accounting policies of Manufactured Homes which have the most significant impact on the company's financial statements. What are the key assumptions behind these policies? Do you think that these assumptions are justified?

....

1. Reprinted with permission from Value Line Investment Survey, February 26, 1988.

2. Evaluate the company's financial and operating performance during 1986 and the first nine months of 1987.

3. Given the company's business strategy, accounting policies, and recent performance, what is your assessment of its current condition and future potential?

EXHIBIT 1

Performance of Manufactured Homes' Common Stock and S&P 500 Stock Index Relative to Their Levels on January 2, 1987

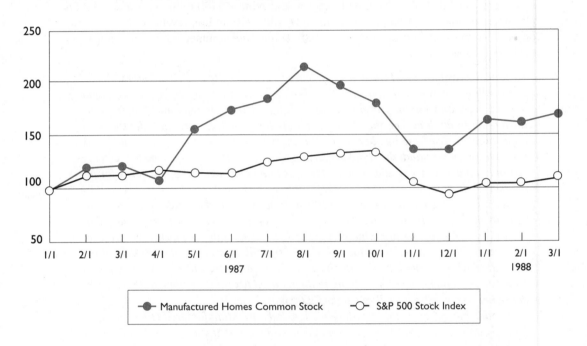

	Manufactured Homes' Stock Price	S&P 500
January 2, 1987	$ 9.000	246.45
March 1, 1988	14.875	267.82
Value Line estimated β	1.05	1.0

EXHIBIT 2

Manufactured Homes, Annual Report for the Year Ended December 31, 1986

Chairman's Letter to Stockholders

The year 1986 was a period of significant accomplishment for your company which served to strengthen our leadership position in the manufactured homes industry. The results achieved were the culmination of a corporate development plan set in motion years ago. For the fourth consecutive year revenues reached record levels, $120 million compared with $80 million in 1985. We are now one of the largest retailers of manufactured, single-family homes in the nation.

As part of our long-term efforts to increase market share, we added 39 retail outlets, bringing the total to 114 at year end. We now have retail outlets in seven states that combined represent approximately 40 percent of the total U.S. market for manufactured homes.

We continue to be primarily a sales and marketing company with manufacturing and retail financing on a limited basis to support the company's growth plan.

We completed a major financing in April 1986 and a second financing in February 1987, both managed by Wertheim Schroder and Company, that totaled $43 million. A portion of the proceeds was used to pay down variable rate debt associated with inventory financing with fixed rate debt and save money in the process. The remainder of the proceeds is to be used for general corporate purposes.

We were pleased at the recognition we received for the growth we have achieved over the last four years as both *Business Week* and *INC. Magazine* included our company in their lists of the fastest growing companies in America. Some describe our growth as explosive. We, however, consider these accomplishments a direct result of a well-structured and carefully executed corporate development plan. Our plans for growth are founded on the basic premise that expansion not exceed our ability to manage our affairs.

From $11 million in revenues in 1983 and a position of near obscurity in the industry, our progress has led us to a position of leadership in the industry. While we are extremely pleased with our revenue performance, we are also mindful that we must operate profitably. Net earnings per share for 1986 were only 53 cents. The sharp decline in 1986 earnings is directly related to a fourth quarter net loss of $1,347,642. Charges against earnings in the fourth quarter for losses on credit sales and other charges totaling more than three million dollars, coupled with the cost of strengthening your company's position in the marketplace, created a temporary setback in earnings while establishing a basis for a strong 1987.

A strategic plan can only be confirmed as correct when tested by adversity; and last year was something of an acid test for our industry. During 1986, many retailers, in hopes of gaining greater market share, or in some cases hoping for survival, engaged in excessive price cutting. In addition, financial institutions in response to concern over the economy in some geographic areas tightened their policies. We not only dealt with the problems that confronted us but turned some into opportunities.

Over the years management has made it a practice to monitor the various retailers of the manufactured homes in our operating area. First, we wanted to understand our competition; and second, we were looking for acquisition candidates. From a large list of companies, we singled out those that best met our standards of performance. We wanted only those firms with superior management and sales teams. We were able to acquire two of these firms on favorable terms and left management in place.

As a result we succeeded in not only enlarging our market penetration in our traditional states of North Carolina, South Carolina, Georgia, Florida and Alabama, but were able to enter new markets with nine retail outlets in Virginia and West Virginia and six additional outlets in Alabama.

Our independent dealer network continues to grow, and now numbers 26 in five states. The independent dealer program offers important advantages and opportunities. Because of the advantages we bring to these small dealers, we continue to receive more requests to join our team.

During the last half of 1986 we sacrificed short-term results to increase market share. We attained that share and as expected it cost us dearly. Selling, general and administrative expense increased from an average of $4.5 million in the first and second quarters to $6 million in the third quarter and to $8 million in the fourth quarter.

As we look to 1987, it is with the knowledge that we are working from a solid foundation. Our financial position is strong. Our debt service requirements are manageable without impairing future earnings performance. Our retail network continues to mature, and sales by location will increase.

Manufactured Homes

Manufactured Homes

Our goal in 1987 is to maintain our market share and show a substantial increase in profit margins. Your Board of Directors has shown confidence in our ability to perform by authorizing me to give you a conservative estimate of our 1987 revenues. Our first quarter revenues are expected to be $32 million with earnings per share of 24 cents. If current economic conditions continue, we expect 1987 revenues to be $140–145 million. The expected significant increase in margins should make this a great year.

I am grateful for the confidence and support of our employees, financial institutions, suppliers and customers; and to you, our shareholders, I would like to say a special "Thanks!"

Robert M. Sauls
Chairman of the Board, President
and Chief Executive Officer

Operating Philosophy

We are convinced that a company is no better than the people selected to manage its affairs. Quality of product and service are vital to any successful enterprise; but again without quality managers and line employees, the business will not succeed. Manufactured Homes has consistently sought and employed only the highest quality individuals at every level within the organization.

It is our practice to provide our employees, at all levels with suitable working conditions and remuneration. We ask only that they perform to the highest level of ability and be innovative in terms of how we can best operate our business.

We believe that the results of the past four years speak for themselves in terms of the invaluable contributions made by our management team and employees.

Industry Profile

The manufactured homes industry is fragmented. At this time there are approximately 10,000 manufactured home retailers throughout the nation, most of which fall into the category of "mom and pop" operations. The industry is presently undergoing a period of transition and consolidation. More and more of the smaller firms, lacking volume buying power and adequate capitalization, are disappearing or becoming a part of a larger company like Manufactured Homes.

The industry has always been competitive but has become more so in recent years. The continuing increases in the average price of conventional housing have forced low income families to seek other alternatives. And more and more are turning to manufactured homes, which have much more to offer than an apartment with the added advantage of equal to lower monthly payments.

In the past, the manufactured home industry suffered from consumer misconceptions created in large part by the use of the term "mobile home." While manufactured homes can be transported from place to place, only five percent are ever relocated once in place. In addition, 60 percent of all homes sold are placed on private property.

Furthermore, the features offered in today's homes are equal to that found in conventional housing but at far less cost.

Industry estimates indicate there are 12 million people living in 6 million manufactured homes. Because of the quality and price advantage, this number is expected to increase on a year-to-year basis for the foreseeable future.

As competition for market share increases, companies like Manufactured Homes will benefit if for no other reason than the financial advantages volume buying affords. This is the primary reason so many independent dealers are actively seeking a working relationship with our company. The same can be said of those companies willing to be acquired.

Retail Operations

During 1986 we sold 6,239 new and used homes, a 61 percent increase over the previous year. These sales generated $113 million in revenues or 46 percent above the previous year. With our enlarged retail network in place, we anticipate that sales will again reach record levels in 1987.

The potential market for manufactured homes includes individuals seeking a single-family residence, but lacking the ability to purchase conventional housing. In addition, these homes are sold to retirees and those wanting a second home for vacation purposes. The latter two groups are increasing in great numbers as our population grows older. However, for our company we have concentrated on a single portion of the marketplace, those individuals in the low income category. This market segment is in great numbers in our seven-state operating area as well as other parts of the nation.

Manufactured Homes had its beginning 11 years ago in Winston-Salem, North Carolina. We began with one retail outlet. Our initial growth took place in North Carolina and eventually South Carolina. These two states accounted for 90 percent of sales in 1985. To continue to market only in these two states eventually could have resulted in corporate stagnation. In 1983, the year we became a publicly-held company, we began to formulate what might be best termed as a geographic expansion plan. The real question was, in which states could we operate most effectively and profitably.

Our initial planning went beyond the southeastern states, which remain the largest single regional source of manufactured home sales. We looked at a number of states including Texas which, at the time, was the number one state in manufactured home sales. After careful evaluation, we concluded that our interests and those of our stockholders would best be served in the southeastern portion of the United States. Texas was the most tempting, but it was obvious to management that the reward was not worth the risk; and as time has proven, Texas has become a graveyard for many manufactured home retail companies.

Like many other retail businesses, presence in the marketplace is critical. After determining to concentrate in the seven states management selected, North Carolina, South Carolina, Georgia, Alabama, Florida, Virginia and West Virginia, we moved aggressively to open new retail outlets and acquire others. In 1983, we had 13 retail outlets; in 1984, the number was 32 and as of March 31, 1987 it's 120.

One of the major keys to success for our company is the insistence that our retail people listen to the customers in terms of interior design and features. When we sense a major trend developing, we go to our suppliers seeking what eventually becomes an entire new line of homes.

We also provide important incentives for our retail managers and sales force. Our base salaries are among the finest in the industry, and we add to that a bonus incentive plan tied directly to margin performance. When times require, we can deal with competitive pricing, but our goal is to maximize sales without sacrificing margins.

Manufacturing

We acquired a manufacturing facility but not as a means of competing with the major manufacturers. In fact, last year we were the largest single retailer of Fleetwood and Redman homes, two of the nation's largest builders of manufactured homes. We acquired the facility to safeguard the company during periods when demand for homes outpaced supply. It also provides the opportunity to manufacture especially designed homes in smaller numbers, thereby eliminat-

ing the major commitment that would be required by unaffiliated suppliers.

The firm we acquired was Craftsman Homes, and we continue to manufacture under this brand name. When we acquired the company in 1985, it was producing one home per day. That operation is now producing ten floors per day. Large numbers of our customers have been asking for more entertainment features in the home. With our manufacturing capabilities, we have responded with a home we call the Entertainment Center, and sales have been most rewarding.

We have no immediate need nor intention to enlarge this facility. As it stands, manufacturing can make important contributions, but we can also put this operation on hold without damage to either revenues or earnings.

Financial Considerations

Believing that interest rates will eventually return to the double digit range, we have been successful in replacing our variable rate debt with fixed rate debt. In April 1986, we completed an $18 million private placement of 9% convertible subordinated notes, due 2001. The notes are convertible into common stock at $17.50 per share. The notes were purchased by Prudential Insurance Company of America and Equity-Linked Investors.

In February 1987, we completed a private placement of $25 million of unsecured senior notes in two series. Series A notes, due 1990, were issued in the amount of $15 million at an interest rate of 8.64%. Series B notes, due 1992, were issued in the amount of $10 million at an interest rate of 9.42%. The entire placement was managed by Wertheim Schroder and Co. and purchased by Prudential Insurance Company of America, and we are gratified with the trust they have placed in the future of Manufactured Homes.

There are four key elements that bear on our financial performance related to the sale of homes. These elements are repossessions, recourse financing, loan losses and finance participation.

In almost all cases mortgages executed by the Company are sold to financial institutions. At this moment all of the elements mentioned come into play. The recourse financing provision requires that the Company reassume ownership of the home when the buyer becomes in default of mortgage payments. We knew this when the company was started 11 years ago, and the actions required to deal with this situation are a part of each year's operating plan.

Manufactured Homes

The possibility of repossessions is another reason for selecting the low income segment of the marketplace. Families in this category will make extreme sacrifices to save their homes. We experience one of the lowest repossession rates in the industry. Of the homes returned, we move quickly to renovate and refurbish them and have them resold, normally within 60 to 90 days, at a price equal to or greater than the loan payoff.

We also make provisions for those instances when loan losses do occur. Based on our historical experience, we now maintain a financial reserve equal to 1.7 percent of total net contingent liability for credit sales. Our annual loan loss provisions have consistently exceeded actual losses by more than 20 percent, even though homes which have been sold for four or more years are seldom repossessed. Finance participation is an important source of income for the Company. Simply, funds derived from finance participation is the "spread" between the finance charges included in the mortgage agreement initiated by the Company and those required by the financial institution. A portion of the "spread" is paid in cash to the Company and the remainder over the life of the mortgage contract.

The portion retained by the financial institution is accounted for by discounting to present value based on the time period, normally 120 to 180 months, required to actually collect the funds.

Financial Services Subsidiary

Plans for our finance operations, MANH Financial Services Corp., are similar in nature to that for our manufacturing division. The company did not enter this business segment to compete with the financial institutions that have historically provided our mortgage banking requirements. This new entity will be employed primarily to facilitate financing agreements with our banks.

Financial Services does have mortgage lending capabilities that will only be employed at those times when our conventional banking arrangements are unable to act on a timely basis. Again, like our manufacturing operations, management has no intention of expanding Financial Services. As it exists now, it provides the Company with the flexibility required to deal quickly with mortgage finance transactions.

Selected Financial Data

Years Ended December 31,	1986	1985	1984	1983	1982
Operating Results:					
Revenues	$120,264,954	$79,525,988	$36,195,802	$10,986,036	$7,477,966
Earnings (loss) before cumulative effect of change in accounting principle[1]	2,033,425	3,718,325	2,694,529	536,881	(59,570)
Earning (loss) per share	.53	.98	.77	.21	(.03)
Net earnings (loss)	2,033,425	3,213,754	2,694,529	536,881	(59,570)
Net earnings (loss) per share	.53	.85	.77	.21	(.03)
Financial Position at Year-End:					
Total assets	$81,377,803	$50,944,924	$17,660,984	$6,836,087	$5,025,130
Long-term debt	18,609,987	1,082,543	400,000	—	491,280
Stockholders' equity	14,167,119	11,052,759	7,633,005	4,938,654	733,195
Working capital	15,111,883	4,820,912	4,819,203	3,699,184	(147,124)

Quarterly Financial Data (unaudited)

Quarter	First	Second	Third	Fourth	Total
1986[1]:					
Revenues	$23,324,633	$29,724,418	$33,295,241	$33,920,662	$120,264,954
Net earnings (loss)	641,702	1,562,205	1,177,160	(1,347,642)	2,033,425
Net earnings (loss) per share	.17	.40	.30	(.36)	.53
Average shares and equivalents	3,850,277	3,944,518	3,922,406	3,733,968	3,864,161
1985:					
Revenues	$10,965,457	$22,103,134	$24,083,556	$22,373,841	$ 79,525,988
Earnings before cumulative effect of change in accounting principle[2]	741,395	1,312,511	1,112,714	551,705	3,718,325
Earnings per share	.21	.34	.29	.14	.98
Net earnings	236,824	1,312,511	1,112,714	551,705	3,213,754
Net earnings per share	.08	.34	.29	.14	.85
Proforma amounts:					
Net earnings	741,395	1,312,511	1,112,714	551,705	3,718,325
Net earnings per share	.21	.34	.29	.14	.98
Average shares and equivalents	3,488,968	3,820,016	3,870,857	3,838,486	3,802,693

1. During the fourth quarter of 1986, the Company provided approximately $3,000,000 for losses on credit sales, primarily due to industry conditions, which are causing unusually high costs relating to the repossession of homes. In addition, the Company incurred abnormal costs in the fourth quarter of approximately $300,000 relating primarily to the write-off of previously recognized finance participation income. The aggregate provision for these items amounted to approximately $3,300,000 in the fourth quarter. The Company cannot determine the extent to which these fourth quarter provisions may be applicable to the first, second and third quarter of 1986.

2. See Note 2 of notes to consolidated financial statements for information regarding a change in accounting principle for finance participation income in 1985.

Common Stock Prices and Dividend Information

The Company's common stock is traded on the American Stock Exchange under the symbol MNH.

	1986		1985	
	High	Low	High	Low
First	15 3/4	10	8 3/4	4 3/8
Second	16 1/2	12 1/4	13 1/4	8 1/4
Third	15	9 3/4	15 3/8	10 1/2
Fourth	12	8 7/8	14	8 3/4

The Company has never paid a cash dividend and does not intend to for the foreseeable future. The weighted average number of shares outstanding for 1986 was 3,660,048 shares, for 1985 and 1984, 3,488,968 shares, for 1983, 2,588,518 shares and for 1982, 2,100,000 shares. The approximate number of stockholders at March 1987 was 2,000.

Manufactured Homes

MANAGEMENT DISCUSSION AND ANALYSIS

Results of Operations

1986 Versus 1985

The Company's net sales in 1986 were $106,095,667 compared with $68,674,779 in 1985, an increase of $37,420,888 or 54%.

The Company's program of managed sales growth resulted in greater penetration due to:

	1986	1985	Increase
An increase of 44% in the number of company-owned and operated sales centers	92	64	28
A 100% expansion of the MANH Independent Retailer network	22	11	11
A total increase of 52% in sales centers for the year	114	75	39

The total number of new and used homes sold in 1986 was 6,239, a 61% increase over the 3,866 homes sold in 1985. New home sales for both years were 87% of total home sales.

A manufactured home sales center usually experiences a five-year growth and development period. The Manufactured Homes (AMEX Symbol: MNH) sales center should develop a sales production level of at least 100 new homes per year at maturity, although this average annual sales volume can vary widely by geographic location. The Company in 1986 averaged 47 new sales per sales center versus 45 in 1985. The average reflects the rapid expansion of new sales centers. Approximately 47% of the average potential capacity per sales center had been achieved, leaving significant growth potential within the Company's current sales center network without the need for significantly increasing the number of sales centers.

New home sales were 80% single-wides in 1986, as compared with 84% in 1985. This reflects a shift to more double-wides resulting from the acquisition of two subsidiaries. In addition, a number of our customers are able to purchase double-wide homes since interest rates are lower. However, the primary emphasis of MNH's marketing plan continues to be towards the less expensive, single-wide home which fits the economic capability of a significant percentage of potential customers within the MNH market area of the five southeastern states, plus Virginia and West Virginia.

The average MNH selling price of new homes by Company sales centers for 1986 was $17,300 versus $17,400 in 1985. The gross profit margins were unchanged for 1985.

Craftsman Manufactured Homes, Inc., a wholly owned subsidiary of MNH, expanded its production capability from one production line to two. Revenues in 1986 were in excess of $15,746,000 of which $7,489,000 were direct sales to non-affiliated dealers with $8,257,000 being sold to Company sales centers for resale. The Company purchased the manufacturing facility in September 1985. The Craftsman manufacturing subsidiary sold 481 homes directly to dealers not associated with MNH in 1986 as compared with 130 homes in 1985.

Repossessions and Early Pay-offs

Manufactured housing, as an industry, has been significantly impacted by the slow economic growth of the economy coupled with an extended period of low interest rates. These factors are reflected by a year-to-year decrease in 1986 of 15% in manufactured homes sold throughout the Company's market area.

Lower interest rates have resulted in two noticeable shifts within the housing industry: (1) certain owners may select conventional homes over manufactured homes; and (2) an intensive marketing effort by financial institutions for mortgage refinancing has resulted in many home owners refinancing their mortgages at lower interest rates, which for MNH usually means a mortgage prepayment.

The Company's experience relative to prepayments of home mortgages, until 1986, had been minor. However, late in 1986, prepayments became a recognized concern. Prepayment of mortgages caused management to reevaluate certain assumptions resulting in a significant increase in the reserve for credit losses related to mortgage prepayments in order to address the prospects of mortgage interest rates continuing to remain at present levels of $8\frac{1}{2}$ to $9\frac{1}{2}$ percent.

Repossessions of homes result primarily from customers' inability to meet their mortgage payment commitment. Approximately 70% of all MNH credit sales are with recourse, which means the Company will buy back from the financial institution holding a customer's mortgage those homes repossessed by the mortgage holder which were originally sold by MNH subsidiaries.

The Company's experience related to repossessions has shown very little change during the past ten years.

However, during the fourth quarter of 1986, approximately $2,000,000 of repossession expense and interest chargebacks were experienced and charged off. Therefore, a charge to earnings, for both prepayments and repossessions, was made and the reserve for credit losses was increased to $3,000,000 at December 31, 1986.

One of the causes of the $2,000,000 charge was the refusal of some unrelated financial institutions to refinance the repossession that occurred in their portfolio, and a second cause was that the Company had to finance them through MANH Financial Services thereby having an immediate charge in finance participation on the pay-off and not recognizing the finance participation income of the resale.

During the first three quarters of 1986, the provision for credit losses was approximately 1% of net sales. Due to the recent fourth quarter charges, management will increase the provision for losses for 1987 to 1½% of net sales as a precautionary measure against future repossession and early pay-off.

Finance Participation

Finance participation was $12,084,108 in 1986 versus $9,715,558 in 1985, a 24.4% increase. As a percentage of net sales, it was 11.4% in 1986 compared with 14.1% in 1985. Several factors caused the percentage of decrease in realized finance participation: (1) increased cash sales; (2) increased non-recourse sales where no finance participation is received; (3) contributions of manufacturing to the sales volume where no finance participation is received; and (4) a decrease in the interest rate spread earned by the Company when the sales contracts are sold to financial institutions. The decreased "spread" was the most important factor in 1986 as two major financial institutions changed their "retail rate" and reduced the "spread" received by the Company by 33%.

Finance participation is an important part of the Company's revenue. This source of revenue is monitored closely and alternative sources of financing are considered for customer mortgage funding on an ongoing basis.

Insurance

The Company earns commissions for writing homeowner insurance policies at the time of sale of the home and from renewal premiums. Income from insurance sales was $721,758 in 1986 compared with $413,282 in 1985, a 75% increase.

Selling, General and Administrative

The Company's selling, general and administrative expense (SG&A) has historically ranged around 17% of revenue. This range varies according to the Company's growth pattern and marketing emphasis.

In 1986, the significant factors affecting the Company's SG&A expense, which was 19% of revenue, were that: (1) the Company initiated a second production line at its manufacturing plant; (2) acquired two additional subsidiaries — Piggy Bank Homes of Alabama and Jeff Brown Homes in Virginia and West Virginia, in mid-September 1986; (3) initiated two additional operating subsidiaries — AAA Mobile Homes (formerly part of MNH), and MANH Independent Retailers Corp. (formerly spread among several subsidiaries for operational purposes); (4) opened 13 new company sales centers; added 11 independent dealers to the retail network; and (5) formed MANH Financial Services Corp. as of October 1986. This expansion and realignment of subsidiaries, which occurred mostly during the fourth quarter, were part of an overall marketing strategy to more effectively penetrate the Company's market. The significant increase in sales over 1985 of 54% resulted from staffing an additional 13 company-owned sales centers, with special emphasis on bonus programs to sell aged inventory and homes received in trade for new sales, as well as improving the percentage of homes which were sold with recourse. This aggressive marketing program was designed to achieve momentum for a strong 1987, but increased SG&A expense significantly at the same time.

Several other cost factors effecting SG&A expense were: (1) An increase in liability insurance rates on policy renewals during 1986 at an annual rate 40% higher than in 1985, or approximately an additional $350,000; and (2) the cost incurred during the year related to the completion of a 15-month standardization of accounting procedures and data processing enhancement program which centralized the Company's management information with on-line capability to each subsidiary. This is a significant step forward in better data management and timely preparation of financial information.

Interest Expense

Interest expense increased $1,543,352 to $3,367,940 in 1986 from $1,824,588 in 1985, or 85%. The increase resulted from a $12,536,000 increase in total inventory and approximately an $8,000,000 increase in total receivables directly related to the expansion of 39 sales centers in 1986.

Manufactured Homes

Income Taxes

The Company's effective income tax rate was 49.8% in 1986 compared to 47.2% in 1985. This increase resulted primarily from the elimination of investment tax credits under the Tax Reform Act of 1986.

Organization

Each of the Company's nine subsidiaries are profit centers. Each subsidiary has its own chief executive officer with total profit and loss responsibility. The Company's long-range plan for growth is by strategic acquisitions, expanding market share, and developing management talent through a newly organized salesperson training program, all to meet the need of providing low-cost housing to the American consumer.

Manufacturing

Craftsman Manufactured Homes, Inc., the MNH manufacturing subsidiary, commenced operations in September 1985. It has grown from virtually a start-up operation to a sales volume in excess of $15,000,000 in 1986. Approximately 57% of the 1,119 homes manufactured were sold to and through Company related sales centers. The balance of the homes were sold to non-related independent retailers. The Craftsman plant operates two production lines with a plant capacity of approximately 3,500 floors (multi-section homes require more than one floor) per year.

Financial Services

MANH Financial Services Corp. was organized on October 14, 1986 to facilitate the marketing of new, repossessed and pre-owned homes. Two major retail financial sources curtailed the purchase of conditional sales contracts which resulted in slow response to contract applications and therefore lost sales. The Company responded with the formation of MANH Financial Services Corp. to operate on a limited basis. The growth of this subsidiary will depend largely on whether or not the unrelated financial institutions continue to service the Company's growth.

1985 Versus 1984

The Company's net sales for 1985 were $68,674,779 compared to $30,480,571 for 1984, an increase of 125%. The majority of this increase was due to the addition of eight retail sales centers during the first quarter and the acquisition of Country Squire Mobile Homes, Inc. on March 22, 1985, with 20 retail sales centers. The Company also opened seven retail sales centers in the second quarter, six in the third quarter, and two in the fourth quarter. Volume increases in

sales centers which were in operation at the end of 1984 also occurred while the average sales price per unit remained fairly constant from 1984 to 1985. The Company's purchase of a manufacturing facility on September 4, 1985, contributed approximately 7% of the 1985 sales increase.

Finance participation income for 1985 was $9,715,558 compared to $5,221,279, an increase of 86%. This was less than the percentage increase in sales due to three factors: (1) The election to discount the unreceived portion of finance participation income to its present value; (2) Country Squire earned significantly less finance participation income than the other retail groups, primarily because of non-recourse sales; and, (3) the inclusion of manufacturing sales which do not earn finance participation income. Insurance commissions, interest and other revenues increased proportionally in relation to the increase in sales.

Cost of sales as a percentage increased approximately 2% in 1985. This increase was due to the substantial increase in sales to independent retailers which traditionally have lower margins, and a slight decrease in margins at Company-owned sales centers. Selling, general and administrative expenses increased in 1985 as a result of increased sales volume and reflect the increase in number of sales centers and additional personnel to support our continued growth. Provision for losses on credit sales remained relatively constant as a percentage of net sales from 1984 to 1985. Interest rates were generally lower in 1985; however, total interest cost increased significantly due to increased inventories to support the added sales centers.

Liquidity and Capital Resources

The Company, in April 1986, sold $18,000,000 of 9% convertible subordinated notes due May 15, 2001. The proceeds were used primarily to reduce floor plan notes payable and to significantly improve the Company's liquidity. During 1986, the Company purchased Jeff Brown Homes, Inc. with nine sales centers and Piggy Bank Homes of Alabama, Inc. with six sales centers, added 13 Company-owned sales centers, formed a finance company subsidiary with an initial capitalization of $500,000, expanded the principal offices of its wholly-owned subsidiary, Tri-County Homes, Inc., and opened a second production line at its manufacturing facility, using funds generated from the sale of the subordinated notes and from operations.

At December 31, 1986, the Company had available $1,000,000 in a bank line of credit and $8,000,000 in unused floor plan lines of credit. On February 13, 1987, the Company sold $25,000,000 of unsecured senior notes due in 1990 and 1992 bearing interest at a blended rate of 8.95%. The proceeds have been partially used to reduce floor plan notes payable.

Although working capital increased significantly in 1986, operations used working capital of $2,956,041 compared to providing working capital of $2,847,026 in 1985 and $2,599,953 in 1984. The use of working capital by operations in 1986 was principally due to the interest rate spread applicable to finance participation and significant reductions in deferred income taxes applicable to the provision for credit losses and finance participation income.

The Tax Reform Act of 1986 will benefit the Company through a reduction of the corporate income tax rate. However, beginning January 1, 1987, the Act will require the Company to accelerate the payment of Federal income taxes. However, the Company believes that funds to be generated by operations, combined with credit lines currently available, will be sufficient to satisfy capital needs for current operations.

Manufactured Homes

Manufactured Homes

CONSOLIDATED BALANCE SHEET

December 31,	1986	1985
ASSETS		
Current Assets		
Cash and cash equivalents:		
Cash and temporary investments	$2,486,024	$2,968,837
Contract proceeds receivable from financial institutions (Note 9)	11,496,078	5,189,535
Total cash and cash equivalents	13,982,102	8,158,372
Finance participation receivable – current portion (Note 2)	2,691,497	2,486,001
Deferred finance participation income	(801,511)	(523,038)
Net finance participation receivable	1,889,986	1,962,963
Other receivables (Note 4)	3,746,863	2,057,674
Refundable income taxes (Note 11)	778,971	—
Inventories (Notes 5 and 9)	38,163,712	25, 628,156
Prepaid expenses	538,419	408,124
Deferred income taxes (Note 11)	761,262	436,496
Total current assets	59,861,315	38,651,785
Finance participation receivable – noncurrent portion		
(Note 2)	16,128,799	10, 269,713
Deferred finance participation income	(3,923,178)	(2,968,629)
Net finance participation receivable	12,205,621	7,301,084
Property, plant and equipment at cost (Notes 6 and 10)	7,504,272	5,467,164
Accumulated depreciation and amortization	(2,410,812)	(1,555,427)
Net property, plant and equipment	5,093,460	3,911,737
Excess of costs over net assets of acquired companies less amortization		
(Note 3)	2,107,874	973, 860
Other assets	2,109,533	106,458
	$81,377,803	$50,944,924
LIABILITIES AND STOCKHOLDERS' EQUITY		
Current Liabilities		
Notes payable	$1,099,971	$ —
Long-term debt – current installments (Note 10)	810,901	1,100,624
Floor plan notes payable (Note 9)	35,207,386	27,468,153
Accounts payable	4,899,250	2,210,560
Income taxes (Note 11)	—	1,828,234
Accrued expenses and other liabilities (Note 8)	2,731,924	1,223,302
Total current liabilities	44,749,432	33,830,873
Long-term debt – noncurrent installments (Note 10)	18,609,987	1,082,543
Reserve for losses on credit sales (Note 7)	3,000,000	1,863,992
Deferred income taxes (Note 11)	851,265	3,114,757
Total liabilities	67,210,684	39,892,165

(continued)

December 31,	1986	1985
Stockholders' Equity (Notes 10 and 12)		
Common stock — $.50 par value per share; authorize 10,000,000 shares; issued and outstanding 3,733,968 shares in 1986 and 3,488,968 shares in 1985	1,866,984	1,744,484
Additional paid-in capital	3,508,351	2,549,916
Retained earnings	8,791,784	6,758,359
Total stockholders' equity	14,167,119	11,052,759
Commitments and contingent liabilities (Notes 3 and 13)		
	$81,377,803	$50,944,924

CONSOLIDATED STATEMENTS OF EARNINGS

Years Ended December 31,	1986	1985	1984
Revenues:			
Net sales	$106,095,667	$68,674,779	$30,480,571
Finance participation income	12,084,108	9,715,558	5,221,279
Insurance commissions	721,758	413,282	231,618
Interest	338,447	163,663	123,564
Other	1,024,974	558,706	138,770
Total revenues	120,264,954	79,525,988	36,195,802
Costs and expenses:			
Cost of sales	86,212,901	56,222,412	24,324,851
Selling, general and administrative	22,852,093	13,639,942	5,895,891
Provision for losses on credit sales (Note 7)	3,777,900	793,497	253,004
Interest	3,367,940	1,824,588	570,527
Total costs and expenses	116,210,834	72,480,439	31,044,273
Earnings before income taxes	4,054,120	7,045,549	5,151,529
Income taxes (Note 11)	2,020,695	3,327,224	2,457,000
Earnings before cumulative effect of change in accounting principle (Note 2)	2,033,425	3,718,325	2,694,529
Cumulative effect on prior years of change in accounting principle for finance participation (Notes 2 and 11)	—	(504,571)	—
Net earnings	$2,033,425	$3,213,754	$2,694,529
Earnings per share:			
Before cumulative effect of change in accounting principle	$.53	$.98	$.77
Cumulative effect on prior years of change in accounting principle for finance participation	—	(.13)	—
Net earnings per share — primary	$.53	$.85	$.77
Net earnings per share — fully diluted	$.53	$.84	$.77
Proforma amounts assuming retroactive application of the change in accounting principle (Note 2):			
Net earnings	$2,033,425	$3,718,325	$2,365,334
Net earnings per share — primary	$.53	$.98	$.68

CONSOLIDATED STATEMENTS OF CHANGES IN FINANCIAL POSITION

Year Ended December 31,	1986	1985	1984
Working capital was provided by			
Operations:			
Net earnings	$2,033,425	$3,213,754	$2,694,529
Adjustments for items not requiring (providing) working capital:			
Depreciation and amortization	946,858	556,23 6	210,699
Noncurrent deferred income taxes	(2,197,061)	78,637	1,412,812
Provision for losses on credit sales, net of actual charges	699,343	(217,402)	134,614
Issuance of nonqualified stock options	142,000	206,000	—
Finance participation income	(12,084,108)	(9,715,558)	(5,221,279)
Collections, current and deferred finance participation income portion of finance participation receivable	7,503,502	8,725,359	3,316,397
Other	—	—	52,181
Working capital provided (used) by operations	(2,956,041)	2,847,026	2, 599,953
Proceeds from long-term debt	18,396,000	1,651,822	400,000
Exercise of stock options	938,935	—	—
Decrease in other assets	—	4,024	—
	16,378,894	4,502,872	2,999,953
Working capital was used for			
Net assets, exclusive of working capital of $806,363 in 1985 and deficits in working capital of $1,109,080 in 1986 and $140,604 in 1984, of acquired companies (Note 3)	1,285,935	422,179	1,220,198
Additions to property, plant and equipment	1,917,489	2,756,178	580,259
Current installments and repayment of long-term debt	1,071,308	1,322,806	70,423
Additions to other assets and excess costs	1,813,191	—	9,054
	6,087,923	4,501,163	1,879,934
Increase in working capital	$10,290,971	$ 1,709	$1,120,019
Changes in working capital, by component			
Cash and cash equivalents	$ 5,823,730	$6,136,129	$ 579,418
Finance participation receivable – current portion	(72,977)	1,193,013	569,838
Other receivables	1,689,189	1,715,543	233,696
Refundable income taxes	778,971	—	—
Inventories	12,535,556	17,448,795	5,616,654
Prepaid expenses	130,295	371,403	25,918
Deferred income taxes	324,766	102,710	203,000
Notes payable	(1,099,971)	—	—
Long-term debt -current installments	289,723	(900,624)	(200,000)
Floor plan notes payable	(7,739,233)	(22,962,163)	(3,986,435)
Accounts payable	(2,688,690)	(1,896,668)	(219,293)
Income taxes	1,828,234	(620,489)	(1,207,745)
Accrued expenses and other liabilities	(1,508,6 22)	(585,940)	(495,032)
Increase in working capital	$10,290,971	$ 1,709	$ 1,120,019

Manufactured Homes

NOTES TO CONSOLIDATED FINANCIAL STATEMENTS

December 31, 1986, 1985 and 1984

Note 1
Summary of Significant Accounting Policies

Principles of Consolidation and Nature of Business

The consolidated financial statements include the accounts of Manufactured Homes, Inc. and all subsidiaries, each wholly-owned, and hereafter referred to collectively as the "Company." All significant intercompany items are eliminated.

The Company is engaged principally in the retail sale of new and used manufactured single-family homes.

Inventories

Inventories are stated at the lower of cost or market, with cost being determined using the specific unit method for new and used manufactured homes and average cost for materials and supplies.

Property, Plant and Equipment

Depreciation of property, plant and equipment is provided principally by the straight-line method over the estimated useful lives of the respective assets. Amortization of leasehold improvements is provided by the straight-line method over the shorter of the lease terms or the estimated useful lives of the improvements.

Income Taxes

Deferred income taxes are recognized for income and expense items that are reported in different periods for financial reporting and income tax purposes.

Income Recognition

A sale is recognized when payment is received or, in the case of credit sales, when a down payment (generally 10% of the sales price) is received and the Company and the customer enter into an installment contract. Installment contracts are normally payable over periods ranging from 120 to 180 months. Credit sales represent the majority of the Company's sales.

Under existing financing arrangements, the majority of installment contracts are sold, with recourse to unrelated financial institutions at an agreed upon rate which is below the contractual interest rate of the installment contract. At the time of sale, the Company receives immediate payment for the stated principal amount of the installment contract and a portion of

the finance participation resulting from the interest rate differential. The remainder of the interest rate differential is retained by the financial institution as security against credit losses and is paid to the Company in proportion to customer payments received by the financial institution. The Company accounts for these transactions as sales in accordance with Statement of Financial Accounting Standards No. 77, "Reporting by Transferors for Transfers of Receivables with Recourse," and recognizes finance participation income equal to the difference between the contractual interest rates of the installment contracts and the agreed upon rates to the financial institutions; the portion retained by the financial institutions is discounted for estimated time of collection and carried at its present value (see Note 2).

Reserve for Losses on Credit Sales

Estimated losses arising from the recourse provisions of the Company's financing arrangements with unrelated financial institutions are provided for currently based on historical loss experience and current economic conditions and consist of estimated future rebates of finance participation income due to prepayment or repossession, estimated future losses on installment contracts repurchased from financial institutions and estimated future losses on installment contracts transferred to new purchasers in lieu of repossession. Actual losses are charged to the reserve when incurred.

Excess of Costs over Net Assets of Acquired Companies

The excess of costs over net assets of acquired companies is being amortized over 30 years on the straight-line method.

Earnings per Share

Primary earnings per share are based on the weighted average number of common and common equivalent shares outstanding. Such average shares are as follows:

Years Ended December 31,	1986	1985	1984
Outstanding shares	3,660,048	3,488,968	3,488,968
Equivalent shares	204,113	313,725	—
	3,864,161	3,802,693	3,488,968

The equivalent shares in 1986 and 1985 represent the shares issuable upon exercise of stock options and warrants after the assumed repurchase of common shares with the related proceeds at the average price during the period. Common equivalent shares were not considered in 1984 as the resulting dilution was insignificant.

Fully diluted earnings per share are based on the weighted average number of common and common equivalent shares outstanding plus the common shares issuable upon the assumed conversion of the convertible subordinated notes and elimination of the applicable interest expense less related income tax benefit. In determining equivalent shares, the assumed repurchase of common shares is at the higher of the average or period-end price.

Note 2
Accounting Change

Prior to 1985, the Company recognized finance participation income without discounting for the estimated time of collection of the portion retained by the unrelated financial institutions as security against credit losses. However, in 1985 the Company adopted the practice whereby the portion of finance participation income retained by the financial institutions is recorded at its present value based upon estimated time of collection. The Company believes the new method is preferable since it more accurately reflects the value of the finance participation receivable at the date the installment contracts are sold to the financial institutions.

As a result of this change, earnings in 1985, before the cumulative effect of the change on prior years, were decreased by $538,466 ($.14 per share). Net earnings were further decreased by $504,571 ($.13 per share), which represents the cumulative effect of the change on prior years. Proforma net earnings and earnings per share amounts reflecting retroactive application of the change are shown in the consolidated statements of earnings.

Note 3
Acquisitions

On January 6, 1984, Manufactured Homes, Inc. acquired the outstanding common stock of Tri-County Homes, Inc., a retailer of manufactured housing located in eastern North Carolina. The purchase agreement required cash payments of $400,000 and potential earn-out payments of $600,000, all earned at December 31, 1984. The acquisition has been accounted for as a purchase and, accordingly, the operations of Tri-County are included in the consolidated financial statements of Manufactured Homes, Inc. beginning in 1984. Effective March 22, 1985, Manufactured Homes, Inc. acquired the outstanding common

stock of Country Squire Mobile Homes, Inc., a retailer of manufactured housing located principally in South Carolina. The purchase agreement required cash payments of $873,000 and includes potential earn-out payments of $1,960,000 over the period 1985 to 1990. The potential earn-out is based on a percentage of Country Squire's pre-tax earnings as defined. At December 31, 1986, $642,947 ($396,000 in 1986 and $246,947 in 1985) of the potential earn-out had been earned and recorded as an adjustment of the purchase price. The acquisition has been accounted for as a purchase and, accordingly, the operations of Country Squire are included in the consolidated financial statements of Manufactured Homes, Inc. since March 22, 1985. The following unaudited proforma data presents the results of operations of the Company and Country Squire as if the acquisition had occurred at January 1, 1984.

Years Ended December 31,	1985	1984
Total revenues	$87,729,677	$59,696,534
Net earnings	3,090,464	2,812,632
Net Earnings per share:		
Primary	$ .81	$ .81
Fully diluted	$ .80	$ .81

In September 1986, Manufactured Homes, Inc. acquired the outstanding common stock of two companies engaged in the retail sale of manufactured homes. The purchase agreements required aggregate cash payments of $151,000 and potential earn-out payments of $874,000 over the period 1987 to 1992. The potential earn-outs are based on a percentage of the respective companies' pre-tax earnings as defined. The acquisitions have been accounted for as purchases and, accordingly, their operations, which are not material, are included in the consolidated financial statements of Manufactured Homes, Inc., since September 1986. At date of acquisition, one company had operating loss carryforwards of $612,049 and to the extent utilized, the income tax reductions will be accounted for as adjustments of the purchase price. At December 31, 1986, $324,510 (tax benefit of $159,226) of the carryforwards had been utilized.

The net assets, exclusive of working capital of $806,363 in 1985 and deficits in working capital of $1,109,080 in 1986 and $140,604 in 1984, of the acquired companies were as follows:

Years Ended December 31,	1986	1985	1984
Finance participation receivable	$ 323,931	$1,337,147	$1,172,853
Property, plant and equipment	169,092	747,092	131,367
Other assets	493,089	23,403	61,016
Long-term debt	(202,752)	(353,527)	(70,423)
Reserve for losses on credit sales	(436,665)	(1,675,000)	(74,615)
Other liabilities	—	(679,524)	—
Excess of costs over net assets of acquired companies	939,240	1,022,588	—
	$1,285,935	$ 422,179	$1,220,198

Note 4
Other Receivables

Other receivables consist of the following:

December 31,	1986	1985
Manufacturers' volume bonuses	$1,979,021	$1,557,029
Sundry	1,767,842	500,645
	$3,746,863	$2,057,674

Note 5
Inventories

Inventories consist of the following:

December 31,	1986	1985
New manufactured homes	$31,920,134	$22,766,030
Used manufactured homes	4,971,040	2,068,099
Materials and supplies	1,272,538	794,027
	$38,163,712	$25,628,156

Note 6
Property, Plant and Equipment

The cost and estimated useful lives of the major classifications of property, plant and equipment are as follows:

	Estimated Useful Life	December 31, 1986	1985
Land	—	$ 735,329	$ 620,083
Buildings	15–20 yrs.	1,660,321	849,427
Manufactured homes— office units	5–7 yrs.	1,048,571	1,013,543
Leasehold improvements	3–5 yrs.	615,319	
Furniture & equipment	3–10 yrs.	1,921,101	1,108,123
Vehicles	3–5 yrs.	1,485,222	1,124,154
Signs	3–7 yrs.	38,409	185,196
		$7,504,272	$5,467,164

Note 7
Reserve for Losses on Credit Sales

An analysis of the reserve for losses on credit sales follows:

Years Ended December 31,	1986	1985	1984
Balance at beginning of year	$1,863,992	$ 406,394	$197,165
Amount at date of acquisition applicable to acquired companies, less actual charges of $69,236 in 1986 and $604,403 in 1985	367,429	1,070,597	74,615
Provision for losses	3,777,900	793,497	253,004
Actual charges	(3,009,321)	(406,496)	(118,390)
Balance at end of year	$3,000,000	$1,863,992	$406,394

Note 8
Accrued Expenses and Other Liabilities

A summary of accrued expenses and other liabilities follows:

December 31,	1986	1985
Payroll and related costs	$1,580,235	$ 697,287
Other	1,151,689	526,015
	$2,731,924	$1,223,302

Manufactured Homes

Note 9
Floor Plan Notes Payable

A substantial portion of the Company's new manufactured home inventories are financed through floor plan arrangements with certain unrelated financial institutions. A summary of floor plan notes payable follows:

December 31,	Rate	Floor Plan Lines	1986	1985
General Electric Credit Corporation	Prime + 1.75 (9.25%)	$27,052,000	**$22,601,520**	$17,183,988
ITT Diversified Credit Corporation	Prime + 2.00 (9.50%)	7,200,000	**5,869,438**	5,224,373
CIT Financial Services	Prime + 2.00 (9.50%)	4,000,000	**3,958,932**	1,761,854
Whirlpool Acceptance Corporation	Prime + 1.50 (9.00%)	1,500,000	**1,210,586**	—
U.S. Home Acceptance	Prime (7.50%)	1,000,000	**36,680**	815,066
Citicorp Acceptance Company, Inc.	Prime + 2.00 (9.50%)	975,000	**—**	1,706,728
Others	Various	1,850,000	**1,530,230**	776,144
		$43,577,000	**$35,207,386**	$27,468,153

The floor plan liability at December 31, 1986 is collateralized by inventories and contract proceeds receivable from financial institutions. The floor plan arrangements generally require periodic partial repayments with the unpaid balance due upon sale of the related collateral.

The weighted average interest rate paid on the outstanding floor plan liability was 10.9%, 11.0%, and 14.7% for 1986, 1985, and 1984, respectively. The maximum amount outstanding at any month end during each year was $35,207,386 for 1986, $27,468,153 for 1985, and $4,508,319 for 1984, with a weighted average balance outstanding for each year of approximately $25,500,000, $16,000,000 and $3,750,000, respectively.

Note 10
Long-Term Debt

A summary of long-term debt follows:

December 31,	1986	1985
9% convertible subordinated notes payable, due in annual installments of $1,800,000 beginning May 15, 1992 through May 15, 2001	**$18,000,000**	—
Note payable, due in monthly installments of $66,667 through October 1, 1987, interest at prime rate (7½% at December 31, 1986) and collateralized by property, plant and equipment with a depreciated cost of $1,160,640	666,670	1,466,667
Obligation payable in January 1988, interest at the prime rate (7½% at December 31, 1986) and collateralized by the common stock of Country Squire Mobile Homes, Inc. (Note 3)	396,000	—
Obligation payable in annual installments of $200,000 through April 15, 1987, repaid in 1986	—	400,000
Various notes payable, due in monthly installments, including interest at rates ranging from 8% to 18%	358,218	316,500
	19,420,888	2,183,167
Less current installments	810,901	1,100,624
	$18,609,987	**$1,082,543**

The aggregate annual maturities of the long-term debt for the five years following December 31, 1986 are: 1987, $810,901; 1988, $508,497; 1989, $53,498; 1990, $33,255; 1991, $14,737.

Pursuant to an agreement dated April 25, 1986 (the "1986 Agreement"), the Company sold its Convertible Subordinated Notes due May 15, 2001, in the amount of $18,000,000 to two lenders. The proceeds from these notes have been used principally to reduce floor plan notes payable. The notes are convertible into shares of the Company's common stock at the conversion price of $17.50 per share. The conversion price is subject to adjustment in the event of stock dividends, stock splits, payment of extraordinary distributions, granting of options or sale of additional shares of common stock. The notes are subject to prepayment at the option of the Company between October 28, 1986 and May 15, 1996 at 100% of par if for a specified period preceding the written notice of prepayment the closing market price per share of the Company's common stock is equal to or greater than a percentage of the conversion price. Such percentage decreases from 200% through May 15, 1989 to 110% at May 15, 2001. The 1986 Agreement contains various restrictive covenants which include, among other things, maintenance of a minimum level of working capital as defined, maintenance of a minimum level of net earnings available for fixed charges as defined, consolidated current assets as defined, equal or greater than senior debt, payment of cash dividends and the creation of additional indebtedness.

Subsequent to December 31, 1986 and pursuant to an agreement dated February 13, 1987 (the "1987 Agreement"), the Company sold the Prudential Insurance Company of America Series A and Series B Senior notes in the aggregate of $25,000,000. The Series A notes in the amount of $15,000,000 bear interest at the rate of 8.64% and are due February 15, 1990. The Series B notes in the amount of $10,000,000 bear interest at the rate of 9.42% and are due February 15, 1992. The proceeds from these notes have been used partially to reduce floor plan notes payable and the remainder added to corporate funds. The 1987 Agreement also contains restrictive financial covenants. The 1987 Agreement financial covenants were changed to reflect more accurately the Company's current financial structure.

Concurrent with the execution of the 1987 Agreement, the financial covenants contained in the 1986 Agreement were amended to conform to the covenants in the 1987 Agreement. At December 31, 1986, the Company was in compliance with the various restrictive covenants in the 1986 Agreement with the exception of the net earnings available for fixed charges covenant. The Company was in compliance with all of the restrictive covenants in the 1986 Agreement, as amended. Retained earnings available for the payment of cash dividends amounted to $1,516,712 at December 31, 1986.

Note 11
Income Taxes

Income taxes are reflected in the consolidated statements of earnings as follows:

Years Ended December 31,	1986	1985	1984
Before cumulative effect of change in accounting principle	$2,020,695	$3,327,224	$2,457,000
Cumulative effect on prior years of change in accounting principle	—	(449,989)	—
	$2,020,695	$2,877,235	$2,457,000

Components of income tax expense (benefit) are as follows:

Years Ended December 31,	1986	1985	1984
Current:			
State	$ 550,653	$ 342,085	$ 166,000
Federal	3,942,668	2,366,685	1,075,000
	4,493,321	2,708,770	1,241,000
Deferred:			
State	(305,198)	20,529	143,000
Federal	(2,167,428)	147,936	1,073,000
	(2,472,626)	168,465	1,216,000
	$2,020,695	$2,877,235	$2,457,000

A reconciliation of the statutory Federal income tax rate with the Company's actual income tax rate follows:

Years Ended December 31,	1986	1985	1984
Statutory Federal income tax rate	46.0%	46.0%	46.0%
State income tax rate less applicable Federal income tax benefit	3.2	3.2	3.2
Investment and jobs tax credit	—	(1.2)	(.4)
Nontaxable items – net	1.1	(.2)	.2
Other – net	(.5)	(.6)	(1.3)
Actual income tax rate	49.8%	47.2%	47.7%

The sources of deferred income tax expenses (benefits) and their tax effects are as follows:

Years Ended December 31,	1986	1985	1984
Provision for losses on credit sales	$(1,622,079)	$743,032	$705,000
Finance participation income	(778,939)	(521,030)	453,000
Operating loss and tax credit carryforwards	—	—	244,000
Manufacturers' volume bonuses	(105,058)	(32,062)	(203,000)
Depreciation	103,519	50,415	17,000
Accrued compensation	63,027	(101,434)	—
Allowance for doubtful accounts	—	29,544	—
Other – net	(133,096)	—	—
	$(2,472,626)	$168,465	$1,216,000

Manufactured Homes

Manufactured Homes

The operating loss and tax credit carryforwards in 1984 represent the reinstatement of deferred tax credit recognized in previous years for financial reporting purposes.

The Tax Reform act of 1986 will benefit the Company through a reduction of the statutory Federal income tax rate.

Note 12
Common Stock

In connection with a public offering of common stock in 1983, the Company sold to the primary underwriter warrants to purchase 142,500 shares of common stock at a price equal to 120% of the public offering price. The warrants are exercisable for a four-year period beginning in 1984 at $3.84 per share. On June 14, 1983, the Board of Directors approved an Incentive Stock Option Plan and reserved 608,900 shares of the Company's authorized common stock for award to officers, directors and key employees. Under the Plan, options are granted at the discretion of a committee appointed by the Board of Directors and may be either incentive stock options or nonqualified stock options. Incentive options must be at a price equal to or greater than fair market value at date of grant. Nonqualified options may be at a price lower than fair market value at date of grant. The Plan expires June 13, 1993.

Activity and price information regarding the plan follows:

	Shares	Option Price Range
Balance December 31, 1983	104,750	$2.40– $3.20
Granted	119,250	$2.40– $3.75
Canceled	(20,500)	$3.20
Balance December 31, 1984	203,500	$2.40– $3.75
Granted	297,600	$4.06–$11.25
Canceled	(5,250)	$2.40– $3.75
Balance December 31, 1985	495,850	$2.40–$11.25
Granted	32,300	$11.00–$17.50
Exercised	(245,000)	$2.40– $4.06
Canceled	(18,250)	$2.70–$10.38
Balance December 31, 1986	264,900	$2.40–$17.50

At December 31, 1986, options for 17,000 shares were currently exercisable. The remaining options become exercisable through the expiration date of the Plan. The excess, if any, of the fair market value at date of grant over the exercise price of nonqualified options is considered compensation and is charged to operations as earned. For 1986 and 1985, the charge to operations was $142,000 and $206,000, respec-

tively. No options were granted at prices lower than fair market value prior to 1985.

At December 31, 1986, 1,534,971 shares of the Company's authorized common stock were reserved for issuance as follows: 142,500 shares for the outstanding warrants, 363,900 shares for the Incentive Stock Option Plan, and 1,028,571 shares for the convertible subordinated notes.

Note 13
Commitments and Contingent Liabilities

The Company leases office space, the majority of its retail sales centers and certain equipment under non-cancellable operating leases that expire over the next five years. Total rental expense under such leases amounted to $1,335,809 in 1986, $888,719 in 1985, and $433,759 in 1984. Approximately 10%, 18%, and 22%, respectively, of such amounts were paid to the Company's majority stockholder and the officers of certain subsidiaries.

Future minimum payments under noncancellable operating leases as of December 31, 1986 follow:

Year Ending December 31,	Minimum Payments
1987	$1,298,346
1988	787,572
1989	498,572
1990	312,510
1991	192,912
	$3,089,912

At December 31, 1986 the Company was contingently liable as guarantor on approximately $180 million (net) of installment sales contracts sold to financial institutions on a recourse basis. [Case writer's note: This contingent liability was $150 million at December 31, 1985, $116 million at December 31, 1984, and $45 million at December 31, 1983.]

Note 14
Supplementary Income Statement Information

Advertising costs amounted to $1,569,658, $1,021,978 and $311,285 in 1986, 1985 and 1984, respectively. Maintenance and repairs, depreciation and amortization of intangible assets, preoperating costs and similar deferrals, taxes, other than payroll and income taxes, and royalties did not exceed 1% of revenues in 1986, 1985 or 1984.

REPORT OF INDEPENDENT CERTIFIED PUBLIC ACCOUNTANTS

THE BOARD OF DIRECTORS AND STOCKHOLDERS MANUFACTURED HOMES, INC.:

We have examined the consolidated balance sheets of Manufactured Homes, Inc. and subsidiaries as of December 31, 1986 and 1985 and the related consolidated statements of earnings, stockholders' equity and changes in financial position for each of the years in the three-year period ended December 31, 1986. Our examinations were made in accordance with generally accepted auditing standards and, accordingly, included such tests of the accounting records and such other auditing procedures as we considered necessary in the circumstances.

In our opinion, the aforementioned consolidated financial statements present fairly the financial position of Manufactured Homes, Inc. and subsidiaries at December 31, 1986 and 1985 and the results of their operations and the changes in their financial position for each of the years in the three-year period ended December 31, 1986, in conformity with generally accepted accounting principles consistently applied during the period except for the change, with which we concur, in the method of recording the uncollected portion of finance participation income as explained in Note 2 to the consolidated financial statements.

PEAT, MARWICK, MITCHELL & CO.
Charlotte, North Carolina
March 10, 1987

Manufactured Homes

EXHIBIT 3

Manufactured Homes, Consolidated Financial Statements for the First Nine Months of 1987

CONSOLIDATED BALANCE SHEETS (unaudited)

	September 30, 1987	December 31, 1986
ASSETS		
Current Assets:		
Cash and cash equivalents:		
Cash and temporary investments (includes) $5,212,849 of restricted cash in 1987	$9,311,240	$2,486,024
Contract proceeds receivable from financial institutions	17,435,191	11,496,098
Total cash and cash equivalents	26,746,431	13,982,102
Finance participation receivable - current portion	4,572,042	2,691,497
Deferred finance participation income	(1,208,275)	(801,511)
Net finance participation receivable	3,363,767	1,889,986
Installment sales contracts held for resale (less unearned interest of $3,648,675)	2,382,573	—
Other receivables	6,343,052	3,746,863
Refundable income taxes	—	778,971
Inventories	41,638,452	38,163,712
Prepaid expenses	587,749	538,419
Deferred income taxes	1,000,262	761,262
Total current assets	82,062,286	59,861,315
Finance participation receivable - noncurrent portion	25,020,194	16,128,799
Deferred finance participation income	(5,984,910)	(3,923,178)
Net finance participation receivable	19,035,284	12,205,621
Property, plant and equipment, at cost	9,248,065	7,504,272
Accumulated depreciation and amortization	(3,166,445)	(2,410,812)
Net property, plant and equipment	6,081,620	5,093,460
Deferred income taxes	1,847,735	—
Excess of costs over net assets of acquired companies, less amortization	2,130,099	2,107,874
Other assets	1,446,657	2,109,533
	$112,603,681	$81,377,803

(continued)

CONSOLIDATED BALANCE SHEETS (unaudited) *(continued)*

	September 30, 1987	December 31, 1986
LIABILITIES AND STOCKHOLDERS' EQUITY		
Current liabilities:		
Notes payable	$ —	$ 1,099,971
Long-term debt—current installments	90,038	810,901
Floor plan notes payable.	28,306,796	35,207,386
Accounts payable	8,181,736	4,899,250
Income taxes	2,469,015	—
Accrued expenses and other liabilities	5,351,963	2,731,924
Total current liabilities	44,399,548	44,749,432
Long-term debt - noncurrent installments	43,000,000	18,609,987
Reserve for losses on credit sales	4,850,000	3,000,000
Deferred income taxes	—	851,265
Total liabilities	92,249,548	67,210,684
Stockholder's equity:		
Common stock—$.50 par value per share; authorized 10,000 shares; issued and outstanding 3,777,168 shares in 1987 and 3,733,968 in 1986	1,888,584	1,866,984
Additional paid-in capital	3,830,314	3,508,351
Retained earnings	14,635,235	8,791,784
Total stockholders' equity	20,354,133	14,167,119
	$112,603,681	$81,377,803

Manufactured Homes

Manufactured Homes

CONSOLIDATED STATEMENTS OF EARNINGS (unaudited)

	Three Months Ended September 30,		Nine Months Ended September 30,	
	1987	1986	1987	1986
Revenues:				
Net sales	$44,590,244	$29,464,161	$126,599,392	$76,396,868
Finance participation income	8,439,473	3,277,085	18,895,975	8,629,223
Insurance commissions	291,868	180,870	976,128	465,577
Interest	373,415	98,327	925,116	230,602
Other	534,916	121,378	786,971	221,448
Total revenues	54,229,916	33,141,821	148,183,582	85,943,718
Costs and expenses:				
Cost of sales	36,325,647	23,741,484	101,997,757	61,554,367
Selling, general and administrative	10,806,534	5,905,930	27,973,865	14,823,385
Provision for losses on credit sales	1,096,027	294,716	3,203,913	772,417
Interest	1,568,906	877,531	4,416,596	2,303,482
Total costs and expenses	49,797,114	30,819,661	137,592,131	79,453,651
Earnings before income taxes	4,432,802	2,322,160	10,591,451	6,490,067
Income taxes	2,038,000	1,145,000	4,748,000	3,109,000
Net earnings	$2,394,302	$1,177,160	$5,843,451	$3,381,067
Net earnings per share:				
Primary	$ .60	$ .30	$ 1.48	$ .87
Fully diluted	$ .53	$ .28	$ 1.31	$ .83

CONSOLIDATED STATEMENTS OF CHANGES IN FINANCIAL POSITION (unaudited)

	Nine Months Ended September 30	
	1987	1986
Working capital was provided by:		
Operations:		
Net earnings	$ 5,843,451	$ 3,381,067
Adjustments for items not requiring (providing) working capital:		
Depreciation and amortization	921,388	664,769
Noncurrent deferred income taxes	(2,699,000)	(345,000)
Provision for losses on credit sales, net of actual changes	1,850,000	(318,539)
Issuance of nonqualified stock options	39,000	106,500
Finance participation income	(18,895,975)	(8,629,223)
Collections and net change in noncurrent portion of finance participation receivable	12,066,312	5,019,381
Working capital used by operations	(874,824)	(121,045)
Proceeds from long-term debt	25,000,000	18,000,000
Exercise of stock options	304,563	1,060,805
Decrease in other assets	662,876	—
	25,092,615	18,939,760
Working capital was used for:		
Net assets, exclusive of working capital, of acquired companies:		
Finance participation receivable	—	349,749
Property and equipment	—	212,716
Other assets	—	509,514
Long-term debt	—	(257,571)
Reserve for losses on credit sales	—	(436,664)
Deferred income taxes	—	78,486
Excess of costs over net assets of acquired companies	—	867,849
	—	1,324,079
Additions to property, plant and equipment	1,851,773	1,365,703
Current installments and repayment of long-term debt	609,987	1,015,876
Additions to other assets and excess costs	80,000	879,665
	2,541,760	4,585,323
Increase in working capital	$22,550,855	$14,354,437
Changes in working capital, by component:		
Cash and cash equivalents	$12,764,329	$ 6,425,144
Finance participation receivable - current portion	1,473,781	239,967
Installment sales contracts held for resale	2,382,573	—
Other receivables	2,596,189	2,818,093
Refundable income taxes	(778,971)	—
Inventories	3,474,740	6,923,301
Prepaid expenses	49,330	59,791
Deferred income taxes	239,000	52,001
Notes payable	1,099,971	(1,391,500)
Long-term debt - current installments	720,863	167,046
Floor plan notes payable	6,900,590	1,424,866
Accounts payable	3,282,486)	(2,811,331)
Income taxes	(2,469,015)	1,820,226
Accrued expenses and other liabilities	(2,620,039)	(1,373,167)
Increase in working capital	$22,550,855	$14,354,437

Manufactured Homes

Notes to Consolidated Financial Statements

1. Pursuant to an agreement dated February 13, 1987, the Company sold to Prudential Insurance Company of America Series A and Series B Senior notes in the aggregate of $25,000,000. The Series A notes in the amount of $15,000,000 bear interest at the rate of 8.64% and are due February 15, 1990. The Series B notes in the amount of $10,000,000 bear interest at the rate of 9.42% and are due February 15, 1992. The proceeds from these notes have been used partially to reduce floor plan notes payable and to fund the Company's finance subsidiary with the remainder added to working capital.

2. On August 18, 1987, the Company's finance subsidiary sold, with recourse, a portfolio of retail installment sales contracts with a principal balance of approximately $8,300,000 to an unrelated financial institution. As a result, the Company recognized, in the third quarter, finance participation income, net of discounts and estimated future servicing costs, of $1,688,690. The terms of the sale required the Company to provide to the unrelated financial institution as security against credit losses, an irrevocable reducing letter of credit in the amount of $3,000,000 secured by a six-month renewable certificate of deposit equal in amount to the letter of credit. At September 30, 1987, approximately $2,200,000 of the proceeds from the sale was held in an escrow account pending receipt, from the appropriate state agencies, of the titles to certain of the new and pre-owned homes securing the retail installment sales contracts in accordance with the terms of the sale.

3. Primary earnings per share are based on the weighted average number of common and common equivalent shares outstanding. Such average shares are as follows:

	Three Months Ended September 30,		Nine Months Ended September 30,	
	1987	1986	1987	1986
Outstanding shares	3,773,894	3,726,427	3,758,245	3,635,137
Equivalent shares	205,159	195,979	187,848	272,150
	3,979,053	3,922,406	3,946,093	3,907,287

The equivalent shares represent shares issuable upon exercise of stock options and warrants after the assumed repurchase of common shares with the related proceeds at the average price during the period.

Fully diluted earnings per share are based on the weighted average number of common and common equivalent shares outstanding plus the common shares issuable upon the assumed conversion of the convertible subordinated notes and elimination of the applicable interest expense less related income tax benefit. In determining equivalent shares, the assumed repurchase of common shares is at the higher of the average or period-end price.

4. Certain amounts in the 1986 financial statements have been reclassified to conform to the presentation adopted in 1987.

5. In the opinion of management, all adjustments which are necessary for a fair presentation of operating results are reflected in the accompanying interim financial statements. All such adjustments are considered to be of a normal recurring nature.

MANAGEMENT'S DISCUSSION AND ANALYSIS OF FINANCIAL CONDITION AND RESULTS OF OPERATIONS

Results of Operations

The Company's net sales for the three-month period ended September 30, 1987 were $44,590,244 compared to $29,464,161 for the comparable period of 1986, an increase of 51%. Net sales for the nine-month period ended September 30, 1987 were $126,599,392 compared to $76,396,868 for the comparable period of 1986, an increase of 66%. These increases are due primarily to the acquisitions in September 1986 of Jeff Brown Homes, Inc., with nine retail sales centers, and Piggy Bank Homes of Alabama, Inc., with six retail sales centers, and the opening of 24 additional retail centers between September 30, 1986 and September 30, 1987. In addition, the average number of homes sold per retail sales center for the three-month and the nine-month periods ended September 30, 1987 increased by 28% and 20% respectively, over the corresponding periods of 1986.

Finance participation income for both the three-month and the nine-month periods ended September 30, 1987 was greater as a percentage of net sales than in the comparable periods of 1986 due primarily to improved financing terms from third-party finance sources and the sale in August 1987 of a portfolio of retail installment sales contracts with a principal balance of approximately $8,300,000, which resulted in finance participation income of $1,688,690 net of discounts and estimated future servicing costs. This portfolio consisted of retail installment sales contracts originated during 1987 and the fourth quarter of 1986. Insurance commissions increased as a percentage of net sales due to added emphasis being placed on this revenue source. Interest income increased significantly due to an improved cash position in 1987 and the interest earned on retail installment sales contracts while held in the Company's finance subsidiary. Other income increased primarily due to a gain of $400,000 recognized in September 1987 on the cancellation of a lease on one of the Company's sales centers.

Cost of sales increased as a percentage of net sales for the three-month period ended September 30, 1987 as compared to the corresponding period of 1986 primarily as a result of extremely competitive market conditions. For the nine-month period ended September 30, 1987, cost of sales as a percentage of net sales was unchanged from the comparable period of 1986. Selling, general and administrative expenses were higher, as a percentage of total revenues, for both the three-month and nine-month periods ended September 30, 1987 as a result of expenses incurred for the following activities: the acquisitions in September 1986 of Piggy Bank Homes of Alabama, Inc. and Jeff Brown Homes, Inc.; the segregation and expanded operations of MANH Independent Retailers Corp. and AAA Mobile Homes, Inc. as separate subsidiaries of the Company; the increased number of retail sales centers; and the establishment in October 1986 of the Company's finance subsidiary.

The provision for losses on credit sales, as a percentage of total revenues, increased significantly for both the three-month and nine-month periods ended September 30, 1987 as compared to the corresponding periods of 1986, primarily as a result of industry-wide problems which became evident in the second half of 1986 and which caused the Company to incur increased costs relating to the prepayment of retail installment sales contracts, the repossession of homes and the resale of repossessed homes.

Interest rates were generally lower in 1987; however, total interest expense increased significantly in 1987 due to increased borrowings to support additional retail sales centers and to fund the activities of the Company's finance subsidiary.

Liquidity and Capital Resources

Liquidity and capital resources were greater at September 30, 1987 than at September 30, 1986 due to the sale in February 1987 of $25,000,000 of unsecured senior notes due in 1990 and 1992 bearing interest at a blended rate of 8.95% and to increased floor plan lines of credit.

Manufactured Homes

At September 30, 1987, the Company had available $3,000,000 in a bank line of credit and approximately $18,500,000 in unused floor plan lines of credit. In addition, the Company filed a registration statement with the Securities and Exchange Commission on September 22, 1987 for the proposed sale by the Company of 1,200,000 shares of its previously unissued common stock. Due to recent events in the financial market place, the status of this proposed sale is now uncertain.

The Tax Reform Act of 1986 is benefiting the Company through a reduction of the corporate income tax rate. However, beginning January 1, 1987, the Act required the Company to change from the reserve method to the direct write-off method for providing for losses on credit sales, which is requiring the Company to accelerate the payment of federal income taxes. However, the Company believes that funds to be generated by operations, combined with financial resources and credit lines currently available, will be sufficient to satisfy capital needs for current operations.

Maxwell Shoe Company, Inc.

Ina McKinsey, an active investor in the stock market, was intrigued by the following brokerage report recommendation of Maxwell Shoe Company:

> *Maxwell Shoe reported fourth quarter earnings per share on an operating basis of $0.33, slightly above our estimate of $0.32. Operating EPS for fiscal 1998 was $1.37. Including the final one-time tax benefit related to the company's secondary offering, net EPS was $0.36 for the fourth quarter and $1.44 for the year.*
>
> *The company's backlog was up 10.4%, lower than previous quarters but still very solid given the tough retail conditions. . . . We remain very positive toward Maxwell Shoe given the brand's performance in a challenging retail environment, management's execution, and its low-cost sourcing capabilities.*
>
> *We are adjusting our 1999 EPS estimate to $1.50 from $1.55 due mostly to higher tax rate and weighted average share count assumptions. Additionally, we are increasing our revenue estimates to $188 million from $182 million. The company is trading at only 8.0 times our fiscal 1999 estimate, which is a discount to the industry. Additionally, the company has no debt and has about $2.00 per share of cash on its balance sheet. We reiterate our Strong Buy rating.*
>
> S. A. Richter et al., of Tucker Anthony
> & R. L. Day, December 18, 1998

This analyst report reminded McKinsey of another equally bullish evaluation of Maxwell she read a few months ago in *Barron's* (see Exhibit 1). As it was becoming increasingly difficult to find undervalued stocks in the current bull market, McKinsey decided to investigate Maxwell Shoe further.

COMPANY BACKGROUND[1]

Maxwell Shoe was originally a closeout footwear business founded in 1949. It was incorporated as Maxwell Shoe Company, Inc. in 1976. During the late 1980s, the company began focusing on designing, developing, and marketing full lines of branded women's footwear. The company went public with a listing on the NASD in 1994.

In 1998 the company offered casual and dress footwear for women in the moderately priced market segment ($20 to $90 price range) under Mootsies Tootsies, Sam & Libby, and Jones New York brand names. The company also designed and developed private label footwear for selected retailers under their own brand name, or under the names of J.G. Hook or Dockers. Substantially all of the company's products were manufactured overseas by independent factories in low-cost locations such as China.

Maxwell sold its footwear primarily to department stores, specialty stores, catalog retailers, and cable television shopping channels. In April 1997 the company entered into a joint venture with Butler Group LLC, a wholly owned subsidiary of General Electric Capital Corporation, to operate approximately 130 retail Sam & Libby and Jones New York

....

Professor Krishna G. Palepu prepared this case. The case is intended solely as the basis for class discussion and is not intended to serve as an endorsement, source of primary data, or illustration of effective or ineffective management. Copyright © 1999 by the President and Fellows of Harvard College. HBS Case 9-100-038.

1. Material in this section is drawn from Maxwell's 1998 10-K report.

women's footwear stores through a company called SLJ Retail. Maxwell owned 49 percent of SLJ Retail, the rest being owned by GE Capital.

Since 1987, when Maxwell first focused on its branded footwear strategy, it has reported sales and profit increases every year. The company attributed this financial success to the following strengths: established brand recognition by consumers, strong manufacturing relationships with overseas manufacturers and buying agents, emphasis on high volume, moderately priced footwear, and comprehensive customer relationships enhanced through electronic data interchange (EDI) systems.

The company expected to build on this competitive advantage, and grow in future by enhancing its current brands, by increasing its private label business, and by acquiring new brands as consolidation in the fragmented footwear industry continued.

FINANCIAL PERFORMANCE

Maxwell reported for the year ending October 21, 1998, $165.6 million in revenues and 13.3 million in profits (see Exhibit 2 for the company's balance sheet, income statement, and cash flow statement for the year). The company's revenues and profits grew at average rates of 16 percent and 24 percent during the previous three years. The corresponding five-year sales and profit growth rates for the footwear industry as a whole were 17 percent and 9 percent.

Until the middle of July 1998, Maxwell's financial performance was mirrored by the company's stock price performance (see Exhibit 3). The company's share price increased from about $5 in 1995 to a peak of $19 by July 1998. However, in the subsequent months, the company's share price began to drop, ending at $11 by December 1998. Analysts attributed this share price decline to overall concerns with the footwear industry, which was expected to grow at a relatively modest rate in future because of cheap imports from Asia and relatively flat consumption patterns. Analysts, however, expected Maxwell to do better than the industry because of its focus on the moderate price segment and its heavy reliance on low-cost overseas manufacturing. For example, Tucker Anthony's analysts stated:

> *Investors' concerns rest with the challenging footwear industry, tough retail environment and overall inventory concerns. While we believe the footwear sector will continue to underperform as a group, we believe Maxwell's shares currently discount investor's concerns. If the company continues to perform as we estimate, we believe the risk/reward ratio is very attractive at the current levels.*[2]

Ina McKinsey was wondering how she should go about evaluating the analysts' view that Maxwell is an undervalued stock.

QUESTIONS

1. Evaluate Maxwell Shoe's strategy. Do you believe that it will enable the firm to sustain its current level of performance? Why (or why not)?

2. Use the BAV Tool to build forecasted income statements and balance sheets for Maxwell Shoe. How long will it take for the company's performance to stabilize?

3. Given your assumptions, what is the value of the company's stock?

....

2. *"Maxwell Shoe Company,"* by S. A. Richter et al., of Tucker Anthony & R. L. Day, December 18, 1998.

EXHIBIT 1

"Best Foot Forward"

Rhonda Brammer, *Barron's*, September 28, 1998

As somebody or other once said, Trouble is only opportunity in work clothes. Which could be a motto of our pal Scott Black, who runs Delphi Management up in Boston. A shrewd contrarian and first-rate value manager of the old school (yes, book and p/e do matter), Scott talks a mile a minute, can recite vital statistics on over 100 names in his portfolio (without crib sheets) and, here's the amazing part, he actually gets the numbers right.

These days, many a small-cap manager is pretty glum—and no wonder, with the Russell 2000 off 15% for the year, compared with an 8% gain for the S&P 500. But, we're happy to report, when we checked in with Scott, he was positively upbeat.

Sure, small stocks have been "annihilated," he concedes. Worse still, in his eyes at least, Delphi is down 4% for the year (he hates to lose money). But the definite bright spot: "We're buying companies—and I am talking about decent companies—at 10 and 11 times earnings."

Which is how we got to talking about Maxwell Shoe.

Founded half a century ago, when Maxwell Blum started a closeout footwear business, Maxwell Shoe today boasts sales of over $160 million. The company designs and markets casual and dress shoes for women—and to a lesser extent, kids—under several brand names, carefully targeting each brand to a specific segment of the market.

Shoes in the Mootsies Tootsies line, for example, which chips in almost half of revenue, are designed to appeal to women 18 to 34. They sell for $25 to $40 a pair and might be found at Kohl's or Mercantile Stores. The slightly pricier Sam & Libby line—about 10% of sales—are targeted at women 21 to 35, sell for $35–$50 a pair, and might wind up at Rich's or Robinson-May. The relatively upscale Jones New York brand—some 25% of revenue—are designed for women over 30. A pair fetches $65 to $90 and you might see them in the window at Macy's or Lord & Taylor.

Most of Maxwell's shoes are made in China, though some of the Jones New York Line are manufactured in Spain and Italy. To leverage its offshore experience, Maxwell makes private label shoes for others, which account for roughly the balance of sales.

Now there's no denying, footwear is a slow-growing, fiercely competitive business—one that isn't likely to prosper in a sluggish economy. Global players, like Nike and Reebok, moreover, have already been hard hit by weakness in Asia.

But there's no reason, Black argues, that shares of Maxwell Shoe, which recently traded over 23, should have been hammered to 12.

"People group them all together," he shrugs. "But this is no Nike where, at the margin, they were dependent on Japan and the Far East for their growth."

Indeed, Maxwell's results sparkle.

In fiscal '97, ending October, sales grew by 28% to 134 million, while net rose over 50%, to $9 million, or $1.09 a share. In the first nine months, ended July, sales advanced 27%, while net climbed 44%, to $9.8 million, or $1.08 a share. For all of fiscal '98, Black's looking for $1.35–$1.40 a share.

Book value is over $8 and the company is debt-free—something Black likes. "If the economy turns south," he quips, "at least they live to fight another day."

Maxwell Shoe Company

....

Worth noting, too—at least for those who remember Maxwell from years back—is that the Class B voting stock, controlled by the Blum family, was eliminated via a stock offering this spring.

Looking ahead to fiscal 1999 (and assuming a 33% tax rate), Black sees Maxwell earning $1.65 a share. Which works out to P/E of 7.3.

"That's one third of the market multiple," he stresses, "and for a company with a legitimate 20 percent growth rate."

Of course, shoe companies rarely command sexy multiples. But even putting a humble P/E of 12 on Black's estimate translates into a stock price of $20.

EXHIBIT 2

Maxwell's Abridged Financial Statements

MAXWELL SHOE COMPANY, INC.—BALANCE SHEET ($ millions)

	31-Oct-98	31-Oct-97	31-Oct-96
Assets			
Cash and cash equivalents	18.7	3.1	10.4
Accounts receivable, net	35.7	28.6	16.9
Inventory	22.9	20.1	12.2
Prepaid expenses	1.6	0.3	0.1
Deferred income taxes	1.1	1.5	0.8
Total Current Assets	**80.0**	**53.6**	**40.4**
Property, plant and equipment	8.7	3.0	2.5
Accumulated depreciation and amortization	−2.5	−1.7	−1.5
Property plant and equipment, net	6.2	1.3	1.0
Trademarks and other assets, net	4.8	5.1	5.5
Total Assets	**91.0**	**60.1**	**46.9**
Liabilities			
Accounts payable	3.8	2.2	0.9
Current portion of capital leases	0.1	0.1	0.1
Accrued expenses and other current liabilities	6.2	6.9	3.8
Total Current Liabilities	**10.2**	**9.2**	**4.8**
Capitalized lease obligations	0.2	0.3	0.5
Deferred taxes	1.3	0.0	0.0
Total Liabilities	**11.7**	**9.5**	**5.3**
Stockholders' Equity			
Common stock	0.1	0.1	0.1
Additional paid-in capital	43.0	27.3	27.3
Retained earnings	36.5	23.2	14.2
Deferred compensation	−0.3	0.0	0.0
Total Shareholders' Equity	**79.3**	**50.6**	**41.6**
Total Liabilities and Shareholders' Equity	**91.0**	**60.1**	**46.9**
Shares outstanding	8.8	2.5	2.5

Note: some numbers may not add up because of rounding errors.

MAXWELL SHOE COMPANY, INC.—ANNUAL INCOME STATEMENT ($ millions)

	31-Oct-98	31-Oct-97	31-Oct-96
Total sales	165.9	134.2	104.3
Cost of goods sold	121.0	98.2	79.9
Gross profit	**44.9**	**36.0**	**24.4**
Selling expense	10.2	7.9	5.6
General and administrative expense	14.9	13.1	9.8
Total operating expenses	**25.1**	**21.0**	**15.4**
Interest expense	–0.0	–0.1	–0.0
Other income-net	0.2	–0.3	0.6
Pretax income	**20.0**	**14.6**	**9.6**
Income taxes	6.6	5.5	3.6
Net income	**13.4**	**9.1**	**6.0**
Basic EPS	**1.61**	**1.19**	**0.78**
Shares to calculate basic EPS (millions)	8.2	7.6	7.6
Diluted EPS	1.44	1.06	0.72
Shares used to calculate diluted EPS (millions)	9.2	8.5	8.3

Note: some numbers may not add up because of rounding errors.

MAXWELL SHOE COMPANY, INC.—STATEMENT OF CASH FLOWS ($ millions)

	31-Oct-98	31-Oct-97	31-Oct-96
Net income	13.3	9.0	5.9
Depreciation	1.2	0.7	0.2
Deferred taxes	1.9	–0.7	0.2
Other noncash items	0.1	0.1	0.1
Changes in operating current assets and liabilities	–9.7	–15.6	3.0
Cash from operations	**6.8**	**–6.5**	**9.4**
Capital expenditures	–5.7	–0.7	–5.6
Cash from investing	**–5.7**	**–0.7**	**–5.6**
Purchase or sale of stock	14.5	0.0	0.0
Payment of capital lease obligations	–0.1	–0.1	–0.2
Cash from financing	**14.4**	**–0.1**	**–0.2**
Net change in cash	**15.5**	**–7.3**	**3.6**
Cash interest paid	0.0	0.1	0.0
Cash taxes paid	4.8	6.8	2.4

Maxwell Shoe Company

Maxwell Shoe Company

EXHIBIT 3

Maxwell Shoe Company, Inc.—Monthly Stock Price History

Month	Month End Closing Price
December 1998	10.938
November 1998	11.875
October 1998	11.750
September 1998	11.875
August 1998	13.125
July 1998	19.375
June 1998	19.875
May 1998	19.625
April 1998	17.750
March 1998	15.813
February 1998	15.750
January 1998	14.125
December 1997	10.750
November 1997	13.625
October 1997	13.125
September 1997	15.000
August 1997	11.000
July 1997	10.500
June 1997	12.250
May 1997	9.250
April 1997	8.250
March 1997	7.875
February 1997	7.625
January 1997	7.375
December 1996	6.625
November 1996	7.250
October 1996	6.625
September 1996	6.313
August 1996	6.125
July 1996	6.000
June 1996	7.750
May 1996	6.500
April 1996	5.000
March 1996	5.000
February 1996	5.000
January 1996	5.250

Source: One Source Information Services, Inc.

Maxwell's equity beta was estimated to be 0.81.

The yield on 30-year treasury bonds in December 1998 was approximately 5%.

The Murray Ohio Manufacturing Company

In March 1985 Dianne Simmons, director of research for the Commonwealth Investment Group, called David McIntosh, a newly joined analyst, into her office and presented a request:

> David, I just received the 1984 annual report and proxy statement of The Murray Ohio Manufacturing Company. A few years ago we bought Murray's stock for our equity income fund. As you know, that fund is marketed to dividend-oriented investors. It's been a good investment so far, thanks to Murray's excellent dividend payment record. I think, though, that it's time for us to take a fresh look at Murray's recent performance and future prospects.
>
> I want you to analyze the company's 1984 annual report [Exhibit 3] and make a recommendation. You may find the information on the company's board reported in the proxy statement useful [Exhibit 2]. I've also collected some information for you on Murray's stock price in recent months [Exhibit 1]. And here's some background information on the company's business.

BUSINESS

Murray Ohio Company was based in Brentwood, a suburb of Nashville, Tennessee. The company's stock was listed on the New York Stock Exchange.

Murray Ohio manufactured and sold power mowers and bicycles. During the 1982–1984 period the shares of these two product lines in the company's sales and operating profits were as follows:

	Sales			Profits		
	1982	1983	1984	1982	1983	1984
Power Mowers	54%	53%	62%	73%	68%	88%
Bicycles	46%	47%	38%	27%	32%	12%

Source: Murray Ohio's 1984 annual report.

Murray produced all its products in a 57-acre manufacturing facility located in Lawrenceburg, Tennessee.

Bicycles

Murray began as a bicycle manufacturer in 1936. The company produced a complete line of bicycles ranging from sidewalk bicycles for small children to lightweight racing bicycles. The bicycles were sold under both the Murray brand name and the private labels of major retailers. Substantially all of the company's bicycles were distributed through department stores, discount stores, toy stores, and other mass merchandise outlets.

Professor Krishna Palepu prepared this case. The case is intended solely as the basis for class discussion and is not intended to serve as an endorsement, source of primary data, or illustration of effective or ineffective management. Copyright © 1987 by the President and Fellows of Harvard College. HBS Case 9-187-178.

In 1984 Murray manufactured approximately one-third of the bicycles made in the United States. The company competed with several domestic bicycle manufacturers including Huffy, Roadmaster, Columbia, and Ross.

Industry Trends   The demand for bicycles was largely dependent on discretionary income. Thus, higher income consumers comprised a major portion of the market. The maturation of the baby boom generation into their peak earning years and the growing incidence of two-income households as a result of more women in the work force had increased this pool of "upscale" consumers in recent years. Another factor that positively affected the demand was migration of the population to the West and the South, where the weather and access to recreational areas are favorable for outdoor activities.

The bicycle industry grew at a compound annual growth rate of 7.8 percent during the ten-year period 1972–1982 and 0.6 percent during the five years 1977–1982. Domestic shipments of bicycles and parts rebounded strongly in 1983 from one of the industry's worst years in more than a decade. Constant dollar shipments increased an estimated 15 percent in 1983, then slowed to a 4 percent increase in 1984. Much of the slowdown in 1984 domestic shipments was attributable to competition from low-priced imports from the Far East. Even though demand remained strong in 1984, a 50 percent rise of imports in 1984 adversely affected the domestic producers of bicycles.

The following table summarizes the total shipment data for the bicycle industry:

	Bicycle and Parts Shipments				
(in millions of dollars)	1980	1981	1982	1983	1984
Domestic	649	733	565	644	683
Imports	281	327	208	329	494

Source: U.S. Department of Commerce, Bureau of the Census.

The long-term demand for bicycles was expected to remain strong. Domestic producers' share of the market would depend on their ability to be cost competitive with foreign producers, particularly those in Taiwan. Import growth would also be influenced by the value of the dollar. In addition, pressure on Taiwanese exporters in the form of proposed tariff legislation and other trade remedies could result in voluntary cutbacks by the exporters. Based on these factors, domestic bicycle shipments were expected to grow at a rate of 3 percent in 1985 and 3.5 percent annually for the five years thereafter.

Power Mowers

Murray entered the power mower market in 1968 and by 1984 had become one of the largest U.S. manufacturers of power mowers. The company had a full line of walk- behind and riding mowers. Some of these models also accepted attachments such as snow blowers, plows, and tillers. Murray also offered a line of tillers to complement its power mower products.

Through 1984 Murray's power mowers were marketed through major national and regional chains, primarily under the Murray label. In early 1985 the company formed a new marketing subsidiary, Sabre Corporation, to sell mowers to outdoor power equipment dealers. These dealers participated in a large share of the higher priced mower market in which Murray was not previously represented.

Industry Trends According to the 1982 Census of Manufacturers, 152 firms produced lawn and garden equipment in the United States. However, many of these producers were small and had fewer than 20 employees. In addition to Murray, the major domestic manu-facturers included Western International, Roper, MTD, and Aircap. Lawn mower producers tended to specialize in one of two distribution markets: the high-volume, low-to-medium price mass merchandisers, which accounted for about two-thirds of industry sales, or the higher priced independent retailers, who serviced equipment in addition to selling it. Sales through national department stores had been declining since 1978 as specialty retailers and hardware stores were handling a greater share of the market.

Demand for lawn and garden equipment, like demand for other household durables, was closely related to the level of real disposable income and to the health of the housing market. Between 1972 and 1979, constant dollar shipments of lawn and garden equipment increased at a compound annual rate of 5.5 percent. Record high interest rates from 1979 through 1982 severely depressed the housing market, and constant dollar shipments of lawn and garden equipment declined 31 percent to their lowest level since 1972. The recovery began in 1983 as real disposable income and housing starts rebounded. The expansion continued in 1984 with an estimated 12 percent increase in lawn and garden equipment shipments.

The balance of trade in lawn and garden equipment was historically very favorable for U.S. producers. In recent years, however, imports began to make inroads into the U.S. market. In 1984, estimated U.S. imports of lawn and garden equipment increased 178 per-cent, continuing a trend begun in 1979 when a Japanese producer, Honda, entered the mar-ket for lawn mowers.

The following table summarizes recent trends in the lawn and garden equipment industry:

Lawn and Garden Equipment Shipments

(in millions of dollars)	1980	1981	1982	1983	1984
Domestic	2419	2270	2387	2536	2956
Imports	26	30	40	66	184

Source: U.S. Department of Commerce, Bureau of the Census.

Constant dollar shipments of lawn and garden equipment were expected to increase at a compound annual growth rate of 4 percent between 1984 and 1989. Growth in housing starts, an increase in real disposable income, and an increase in replacement demand were expected to contribute to this growth. Due to its leading position in the world markets, the U.S. industry was expected to expand exports as world economies recovered and as the value of the dollar dropped. U.S. imports of lawn and garden equipment were also expected to continue to increase, especially in the lower priced models.

FINANCIAL PERFORMANCE

Between 1975 and 1979 Murray's sales grew 158 percent, from $126.6 million to $327.1 million; the company's reported profits grew by 125 percent, from $4.7 million to $10.6 million. During this period, the company had relatively stable profitability, with an average return on sales (ROS) of 3.5 percent, and an average return on equity (ROE) of 13.5 percent.

In contrast to the steady growth during the last half of the 1970s, Murray's performance became erratic beginning in 1980 as foreign competition in its product markets increased significantly. Between 1979 and 1983, the company's sales and profits grew by only 31 percent and 16 percent, respectively. Further, the company's average profitability showed a significant decline. The average ROS and ROE from 1980 to 1983 were 2.6 percent and 10.8 percent, respectively. (See Exhibit 3 for more data on the performance from 1975 to 1983.)

1984 was a challenging year for Murray Ohio. The company's management explained:

The past year, 1984, was a difficult one for our company. While total sales were basically flat with 1983, earnings were down considerably. Two factors primarily accounted for this earnings decline.

First, bicycle imports were up over 55 percent in 1984. This increase, which has been sold almost totally to the mass market merchants, adversely affected our bicycle pricing, production levels, and sales.

Secondly, stronger domestic competition in both our product lines, bicycles and power mowers, increased pressures on our pricing and resulted in a tightening of our profit margins.

The mower segment of Murray's business performed significantly better than the bicycle segment. Following a record sales performance in 1983, Murray's mower sales increased to a new high in 1984, up 15 percent. In contrast, bicycle sales decreased 19 percent in 1984, and operating profits for the year declined by 72 percent.

Murray Ohio's management announced that it would take several steps to improve its future performance: (1) adopting an aggressive bicycle pricing structure to regain market share; (2) improving manufacturing productivity through process modernization, manufacturing resources planning, and better manpower utilization; (3) introducing new and innovative products, including the new Sabre mower line aimed at the power equipment dealers; and (4) working with other domestic producers to lobby the U.S. Congress to increase import tariffs on bicycles.

While these steps were viewed as necessary to prevent further erosion in the company's market share, management realized that profit margin pressure was likely to continue, at least in the short term. Further, the productivity improvement program was expected to require significant capital expenditure outlays. The company increased its capital expenditures in 1984 by 86 percent to $10.9 million, and expected to invest comparable amounts in 1985 as well. Management summed up their view of the future:

We recognize the difficult journey before us. Our past record, however, shows one of success and profitability. With a solid balance sheet and the full commitment of our resources and people, we look forward to the challenges that lie ahead. Our people continue to be our greatest strength. Their innovativeness, team-work, and support provide the company with the impetus it needs. In these times of change, their support and assistance are immeasurable.

DIVIDEND POLICY

David McIntosh knew that the Commonwealth Investment Group had found Murray Ohio's stock attractive for Commonwealth's equity income fund because of its reliable dividend policy. Murray's dividend per share grew steadily from $0.67 in 1975 to $1.20 in 1980. Despite the company's mixed performance between 1980 and 1984, dividends remained constant. As the company's annual report stated, Murray's management was proud of the company's dividend history—it had paid them quarterly without a reduction for the past 49 consecutive years. McIntosh wondered whether Murray Ohio would be able to maintain this record given the company's changed business circumstances. Has the nature of Murray's business changed enough to warrant a reevaluation of its dividend policy? If the company decided to change its longstanding policy, how would investors react?

QUESTIONS

1. Analyze Murray Ohio's recent financial performance and cash flows. Can the company afford to maintain its current dividend if operating conditions remain about the same?

2. Evaluate management's business strategy for the future. What does this strategy imply for the company's future cash requirements? Given this new strategy, is the company more or less likely to maintain its current dividend policy?

3. Is there an alternative strategy that is better than management's proposed strategy for increasing shareholders' value? Is the company's current management likely to pursue this alternative strategy? If not, is the company an attractive takeover target?

4. What are the implications for current stockholders of Murray Ohio? What should the Commonwealth Investment Group do?

EXHIBIT I

The Murray Ohio Manufacturing Company—Stock Prices, January 1984–March 1985

Month	Murray Ohio's Stock Price at Month End	Standard and Poor's 400 Industrial Index at Month End
1984		
January	21 6/8	184
February	21 4/8	177
March	22 4/8	180
April	22 5/8	182
May	21 5/8	171
June	23 2/8	175
July	20 2/8	171
August	20 7/8	189
September	21 2/8	187
October	20 2/8	187
November	19 2/8	183
December	19 4/8	186
1985		
January	20 5/8	201
February	20 5/8	203
March	20 3/8	202

Murray Ohio's Common Stock ß = 0.8 (Value Line estimate).
Interest rates at the beginning of 1985:
3-month Treasury bills: 8.8%
20-year Treasury bonds: 11.7%

Murray Ohio Manufacturing Company

EXHIBIT 2

The Murray Ohio Manufacturing Company—Board of Directors, 1984

Name	Principal Occupation, Business Experience, and Other Directorships in Public Companies (1)	Age on April 2, 1985	Beginning Year, Period of Service
John N. Anderson	President and Chief Executive Officer of the Company. Director of Third National Bank, Nashville, Tennessee.	60	1979
Lovic A. Brooks, Jr.	Senior Partner in the firm of Constangy, Brooks & Smith, Atlanta, Georgia (attorneys). Constangy, Brooks & Smith has performed legal services for the Company for many years and is expected to continue to do so.	57	1972
Sam M. Fleming	Retired. Former Chairman of the Board, Third National Bank, Nashville, Tennessee. Director of Hillsboro Enterprises, Inc., Nashville, Tennessee.	76	1965
Robert A. Flesher	Retired. Former Vice Chairman of the Board of the Company.	66	1966
Charles W. Geny	Vice President, Alexander & Alexander, Incorporated, Nashville, Tennessee (insurance and bonds).	71	1972
William M. Hannon	Chairman of the Board and retired Chief Executive Officer of the Company. Director of Third National Bank, Nashville, Tennessee.	65	1955
Thomas M. Hudson	Investments. Retired Senior Vice President of the The Robinson-Humphrey Company, Inc. (an investment banking firm). The Robinson-Humphrey Company, Inc. has performed investment banking services for the Company for many years and is expected to continue to do so. Director of the United Cities Gas Company, Nashville, Tennessee.	63	1980
William C. Keyes	Retired. Former Senior Executive Vice President of the Company. Director of Commerce Union Bank, Nashville, Tennessee.	65	1966
H. Theodore Meyer	Partner in the firm of Jones, Day, Reavis & Pogue, which has performed legal services for the Company for many years and is expected to continue to do so.	49	1985
Gerald E. Sheridan	President, Sheridan Construction Co., Nashville, Tennessee.	60	1983
G. Cromer Smotherman	Executive Vice President and Chief Operating Officer of the Company. Director of First National Bank of Lawrenceburg, Lawrenceburg, Tennessee.	59	1971
David K. Wilson	President, Cherokee Equity Corporation, Nashville, Tennessee (holding company). Director of First American National Bank, Winners Corporation, and Genesco, Inc., all located in Nashville, Tennessee, and Torchmark Corporation, Birmingham, Alabama.	65	1983

All directors and officers of the company as a group (26 persons, including those named above) own 10.4 percent of the company's common stock.

EXHIBIT 3

The Murray Ohio Manufacturing Company—1984 Annual Report (abridged)

LETTER TO SHAREHOLDERS

March 4, 1985

The past year, 1984, was a difficult one for our Company. While total sales were basically flat with 1983, earnings were down considerably. Two factors primarily accounted for this earnings decline.

First, bicycle imports were up over 55% in 1984. This increase, which has been sold almost totally to the mass market merchants, adversely affected our bicycle pricing, production levels, and sales.

Secondly, stronger domestic competition in both our product lines, bicycles and power mowers, increased pressures on our pricing and resulted in a tightening of our profit margins.

Net sales for the year were $383,589,000, a 1% decrease from 1983. Power mower sales, however, were up 15%, with bicycle sales down 19%.

Earnings, after nonrecurring adjustments for 1984, were $7,826,000, a 37% decrease from 1983. The majority of this decrease, as stated above, was due to the bicycle segment of our business. Earnings per share, after nonrecurring adjustments, decreased 43% to $2.01 from $3.53 in 1983. The difference between the percent change in earnings and earnings per share is a result of the June, 1983 equity offering of 770,000 shares of common stock.

The 1984 nonrecurring adjustments are benefits arising from the elimination of a provision for deferred taxes of our international sales operations (DISC) and an accounting change in the method for recognizing investment tax credits. These benefits resulted in earnings of $920,000 and $1,404,000, respectively, or $.24 and $.36 per share.

The declining profitability experienced in 1984 presented Murray with a difficult challenge that we are determined to face. In the third quarter report, we announced the first step in our program to improve profitability. This step involves an aggressive bicycle pricing structure aimed at maintaining our necessary production levels and at regaining market share lost to imports. Our pricing stance has shown success and will help Murray regain lost market share in 1985.

Productivity and Marketing—Steps for the Future

While putting a pricing structure in place to regain bicycle market share, we began major programs in two areas—productivity and marketing—to improve our profitability in both of our product lines. Neither program will create overnight success, but both will help keep Murray on solid ground and a strong course for the future.

Murray's productivity program involves several facets—process modernization, Manufacturing Resources Planning (MRP), and improved manpower productivity.

Our 1984 capital expenditures amounted to $10,878,000, an 86% increase over 1983. This increase strengthened our continuing program of process modernization. Major investments included the installation of modern tube cutting equipment, robot welders, a computer aided design system, and the initial phase of a state of the art press room. The commitment to the modernization of our facilities is one that will continue, and we are projecting comparable expenditures in 1985.

In 1984, we also began installation of a Manufacturing Resources Planning (MRP) System. The MRP System will lead to reduced inventory levels and better control and utilization of our manufacturing facility and processes. Such efficiency will improve our cost of operations.

With regards to marketing, Murray has always been innovative in product introductions. We have been successful in introducing BMX, mountain bikes, and freestyle bicycles into the mass market. Murray revolutionized the riding mower market when we entered this industry in 1968 in both performance and design, and we have continued as an innovator in this industry. In 1984, we reaffirmed our commitment to this type of innovation.

Bicycles and power mowers continue to be viable products for the consumer. We recognize the need to intensify our efforts to compete in these markets. At the same time, we are analyzing our present and related markets for expansion opportunities. This effort is continuing, and its benefits are beginning to show in our marketing plans.

Murray Ohio Manufacturing Company

One result of this market analysis was the introduction of our Sabre mower line for the spring of 1985. The Sabre line will target the outdoor power equipment dealer who participates in a large share of the mower market in which Murray is not currently represented. This new line, which will be sold directly to the dealer, offers him high quality merchandise with the ability to improve profit margins. Murray will continue such expansion or diversification moves as prove correct for our business future.

Our power mower products continue to meet with great success. The 1985 Murray line has been well received by our customers, and we expect the momentum created by our steady mower sales rise over the past 15 years to be maintained.

This year again, we were pleased to be selected to receive the Sears "Partners in Progress Award." We were one of only 23 suppliers to receive this award for the third consecutive year. The award is presented for overall excellence as a manufacturer of products for Sears. Sears has a total of over 12,000 suppliers.

We and our industry continue to make every effort in Washington to draw attention to the unfair competition we face from imported bicycles. The industry was successful in May with having H.R. 5754 introduced in the House of Representatives. This Bill provides for a 24% duty on imported bicycles and bicycle parts, a duty comparable to that in foreign markets. No action was taken on this Bill, and it will be reintroduced in the new session of Congress. It is the aim of the domestic industry to have our Government recognize and control the flood of unfairly traded import bicycles coming into this country.

If the economy continues on its present course, our sales for 1985 should improve. While our plans for 1985 and the future will help offset our 1985 pricing structure, we expect continued profit margin pressure.

Board of Director Changes

At the February 1985 Board Meeting, we regretfully accepted the resignation of Eugene T. Kinder, a recently retired partner in the law firm of Jones, Day, Reavis & Pogue. Though leaving our Board, Mr. Kinder will continue to be available as requested to render the excellent counsel that he has given Murray in his 12 years on the Board.

H. Theodore Meyer, also a partner of Jones, Day, Reavis & Pogue and currently Secretary of Murray Ohio, was elected to fill the vacant position. His elec-

tion continues the tradition since 1925 of having a member of this firm on our Board.

Solid Record for the Future

We recognize the difficulty of the journey before us. Our past record, however, shows one of success and profitability. With a solid balance sheet and the full commitment of our resources and people we look forward to the challenges that lie ahead.

Our people continue to be our greatest source of strength. Their innovativeness, team-work, and support provide the Company with the impetus that it needs. In these times of change, their support and assistance are unmeasurable.

Very truly yours,

W. M. Hannon
Chairman of the Board

John N. Anderson
President and Chief Executive Officer

G. Cromer Smotherman
Executive Vice President and
Chief Operating Officer

FINANCIAL REVIEW

Sales in 1984 were $384 million, which was within 1% of the company's all-time record sales year of 1983. This included an increase of over 15% from the company's previous record for its power mower line, while bicycle sales were adversely impacted by import competition to record a 19% decrease from 1983.

Net income and earnings per common share were $7.8 million and $2.01, respectively, each after nonrecurring adjustments. This resulted in profit margins of 2.04% and return on average shareholders' equity of 7.05%.

Murray Ohio has spent approximately $59 million during the past ten years to modernize and automate its facilities, to increase the productive efficiency and to expand the plant capacity. This included a significant increase in 1984 to further pursue the goals stated above.

During this ten-year period, the company has significantly expanded both its power mower and bicycle production capacities at Lawrenceburg, including additions of 600,000 square feet. Other expenditures were for research and development facilities, and an expansion to the corporate office. Another $9.7 million is budgeted for capital expenditures in 1985.

Total long-term debt at the end of 1984 was $23.0 million or 16.9% of total capitalization. This compares to $26.0 million and 19.2% for 1983. Working capital stands at $86.5 million at December 31, 1984, resulting in a current ratio of 2.2 to 1.

Shareholders' equity per share has increased every year for the last ten years to $28.93 at December 31, 1984, an increase of 91% for the ten-year period.

Murray Ohio paid cash dividends of $1.20 per common share in 1984. Murray is proud of its history of paying regular quarterly dividends without a reduction for the past 49 consecutive years. During this period Murray's stock became listed on the New York Stock Exchange and the Midwest Stock Exchange in 1969 and 1971, respectively, and continues to be so listed. Prior to 1969 Murray was listed on the American Stock Exchange.

Murray Ohio's cash payout over the past ten-year period has averaged 43% of net income. At year end, 3,896,670 shares of the company's common stock were outstanding. Of this total, 1,113,041 shares (29%), were owned by directors, officers, and current employees.

Murray Ohio Manufacturing Company

TEN YEARS OF GROWTH

Summary of Operations	1984	1983	1982	1981
Net Sales	$383,589,105	$386,493,993	$288,642,358	$332,278,451
Power Mowers and Accessories	236,421,047	205,036,387	155,415,363	161,076,211
Bicycles and Accessories	147,079,185	181,377,604	133,138,347	170,619,908
Other Products	88,873	80,002	88,648	582,332
Cost of Products Sold	335,374,269	327,134,491	245,394,295	283,353,873
Depreciation and Amortization	3,635,096	3,361,666	3,253,897	2,876,664
Interest Expense	4,689,476	4,336,223	6,847,499	7,217,509
Income Before Income Taxes	9,129,558	22,527,621	9,429,651	17,180,728
Federal and State Income Taxes	2,708,000(b)	10,153,000	4,337,000	8,090,000
Income Before Cumulative Effect of Change in Accounting Principle	6,421,558	12,374,621	5,092,651	9,090,728(d)
Cumulative Effect of Change in Accounting Principle for Investment Tax Credit	1,404,000	—	—	—
Net Income (a)	7,825,558(b)	12,374,621	5,092,651	9,090,728(d)
Percent of Net Income to Net Sales	2.04%	3.20%	1.76%	2.74%
Return on Average Shareholder's Equity	7.05%	13.02%	6.39%	11.96%
Earnings per Common Share Before Cumulative Effect of Change in Accounting Principle	1.65	3.53	1.63	2.93(d)
Cumulative Effect of Change in Accounting Principle for Investment Tax Credit	.36	—	—	—
Earnings per Common Share (a, c, e)	2.01(b)	3.53	1.63	2.93(d)
Cash Dividends Paid	4,649,740	4,118,992	3,701,465	3,674,103
Cash Dividends Declared and Paid per Common Share (e)	1.20	1.20	1.20	1.20
Common Shares Outstanding at Year End (net of Treasury Shares) (c, e)	3,896,670	3,873,748	3,134,565	3,099,527
Number of Shareholders (h)	4,813	4,802	5,203	4,711
Average Number of Employees	3,500	3,403	2,868	3,534

Financial Condition at Year End				
Total Assets	$209,777,365	$188,845,331	$171,732,458	$173,521,388
Current Assets	157,938,259	142,782,974	127,822,330	132,297,984
Current Liabilities	71,395,177	48,140,763	58,037,639	62,352,490
Current Ratio	2.2 to 1	3.0 to 1	2.2 to 1	2.1 to 1
Working Capital	86,543,082	94,642,211	69,784,691	69,945,494
Shareholders' Equity	112,721,223	109,368,410	80,741,336	78,713,813
Shareholders' Equity per Common Share (e)	28.93	28.23	25.76	25.40
Property, Plant and Equipment (net)	50,794,929	44,778,715	42,628,946	39,721,024
Capital Expenditures	10,878,234	5,862,985	6,277,156	6,104,077
Total Amount of Long-Term Debt	22,978,225	26,014,300	29,075,375	30,131,450
Long-Term Debt as a Percentage of Total Capitalization	16.9%	19.2%	26.5%	27.7%

(a) Pro forma based on revised method of accounting for investment tax credit, applied retroactively:

	1984	1983	1982	1981	1980	1979	1978	1977	1976	1975
Net Income (000's)	6,422	12,521	5,184	9,242	8,566	10,704	7,936	8,435	5,768	4,850
Earning per Common Share	1.65	3.57	1.66	2.98	2.76	3.46	2.56	2.73	1.86	1.57

(b) Income taxes, net income, and earnings per common share for 1984 include the nonrecurring effect of the reversal of certain deferred taxes. Refer to the financial statements and management's discussion and analysis for further explanation.

(c) Earnings per common share are computed based on the average common shares outstanding each year. The average common shares for 1983 (3,505,567) were significantly different from the common shares outstanding at year end due to the issuance in June 1983 of 770,000 common shares.

1980	1979	1978	1977	1976	1975
$294,745,956	$327,137,268	$254,113,710	$212,773,180	$150,815,365	$126,655,353
153,706,766	165,313,297	136,748,819	100,660,828	63,342,453	46,862,481
139,178,541	161,823,971	117,364,891	112,112,352	87,472,912	79,792,872
1,860,649	—	—	—	—	—
251,746,135	283,699,952	220,067,742	181,971,227	127,930,166	106,560,985
2,742,559	2,668,797	2,453,631	1,643,479	1,577,229	1,440,611
7,534,174	4,979,286	3,875,387	1,787,587	1,549,272	1,878,782
15,878,660	20,108,133	15,264,403	16,155,618	11,164,297	9,272,287
7,405,000	9,480,000	7,464,000	7,916,000	5,425,000	4,544,000
8,473,660	10,628,133	7,800,403	8,239,618	5,739,297	4,728,287
—	—	—	—	—	—
8,473,660	10,628,133	7,800,403	8,239,618	5,739,297	4,728,287
2.87%	3.25%	3.07%	3.87%	3.81%	3.73%
11.95%	16.42%	13.33%	15.46%	11.79%	10.41%
2.73	3.43	2.52	2.66	1.85	1.53
—	—	—		1.85	1.53
2.73	3.43	2.52	2.66		
3,643,351	3,185,688	3,071,258	2,777,681	2,252,703	2,041,374
1.20	1.05	1.00	.90	.73	.67
3,099,527	3,099,527	3,094,563	3,094,563	3,093,154	3,093,079
5,002	4,874	4,872	4,728	4,663	4,713
3,106	3,676	3,350	3,050	2,423	2,212
$162,593,699(f)	$165,676,630(f)	$137,954,695(f)	$118,184,974(f)	$96,521,505(f)	$77,703,626(g)
123,774,401(f)	128,536,269(f)	104,553,999(f)	92,158,408(f)	74,098,444(f)	56,496,582(g)
56,045,182	62,951,762	41,929,128	47,978,918	31,202,317	15,060,145
2.2 to 1	2.0 to 1	2.5 to 1	1.9 to 1	2.4 to 1	3.8 to 1
67,729,219(f)	65,584,507(f)	62,624,871(f)	44,179,490(f)	42,896,127(f)	41,436,437(g)
73,271,961	68,498,679	60,922,713	56,087,652	50,497,987	46,894,095
23.64	22.10	19.69	18.12	16.32	15.16
36,563,771	34,071,357	30,560,878	24,692,169	20,408,767	19,747,300
5,322,612	6,891,287	7,648,408	5,962,610	2,335,131	1,600,299
31,177,525(f)	32,213,600(f)	33,249,675(f)	12,470,000(f)	13,480,000(f)	14,485,000(g)
29.9%	32.0%	35.3%	18.2%	21.1%	23.6%

(d) Net income in 1981 was reduced by $3,047,000 ($.98 per common share) due to the change to the LIFO, from the FIFO, method of accounting for inventories.

(e) Adjusted for the 3-for-2 stock split distributed August 31, 1977.

(f) Includes a long-term loan of $20,000,000 at 9¼% annual interest.

(g) Includes a long-term loan of $5,000,000 at 10¼% annual interest.

(h) Represents the number of shareholders of record as of the approximate December 15, dividend record date of each respective year.

Murray Ohio Manufacturing Company

Murray Ohio Manufacturing Company

QUARTERLY RESULTS OF OPERATIONS
In Thousands of Dollars (except for per share data)

Comparison of Quarterly Results for Years Ended December 31, 1984, and December 31, 1983

| | Net Sales | | | | | | | |
| | Power Mowers and Accessories | | Bicycles and Accessories | | Other Products | | Total | |
Quarter	1984	1983	1984	1983	1984	1983	1984	1983
1st	$114,820	$104,446	$ 40,664	$33,918	$22	$ 6	$155,506	$138,370
2nd	94,213	70,445	39,775	48,387	50	16	134,038	118,848
3rd	12,641	11,561	32,908	48,759	11	46	45,560	60,366
4th	14,747	18,584	33,732	50,314	6	12	48,485	68,910
Total	$236,421	$205,036	$147,079	$181,378	$89	$80	$383,589	$386,494

| | Income | | | | | | | | | |
| | Gross Profit[1] | | Income (Loss) Before Cumulative Effect of Accounting Change | | Net Income (Loss) | | Earnings (Loss) per Common Share Before Cumulative Effect of Accounting Change | | Earnings (Loss) per Common Share | |
Quarter	1984	1983	1984[3]	1983	1984[3]	1983	1984[3]	1983[2,3]	1984[3]	1983[2,3]
1st	$18,688	$17,625	$4,340	$4,953	$5,744	$4,953	$1.12	$1.58	$1.48	$1.58
2nd	15,147	16,943	2,460	4,296	2,460	4,296	.63	1.37	.63	1.37
3rd	4,782	10,146	285	1,693	285	1,693	.07	.44	.07	.44
4th	6,300	11,570	(663)	1,433	(663)	1,433	(.17)	.37	(.17)	.37
Total	$44,917	$56,284	$6,422	$12,375	$7,826	$12,375	$1.65	$3.53	$2.01	$3.53

(1) Gross Profit represents net sales less those costs directly related to the manufacturing process (i.e. labor, and over-head costs consumed within the factory).

(2) Due to the sale of the Common Shares (See Note J), average common shares outstanding for the year differed from the average common shares outstanding for each quarterly period. Earnings per common share for each period is computed by dividing total net income by the period's average common shares outstanding. As a result, the sum of earnings per common share for the individual quarters will not equal the per share amount for the year. The additional shares caused earnings per share to increase by a smaller percentage than total net income.

(3) Net income for the third quarter ended September 30, 1984 and for the year ended December 31, 1984 reflects the reversal of $920,000, or $.24 per common share, (after deductions of expenses relating to employee fringe benefits) of deferred taxes provided in prior years for the company's export sales through its Domestic International Sales Corporation (DISC).

The company changed its method of accounting for investment tax credit effective January 1, 1984. The cumulative effect of the accounting change increased 1984 first quarter earnings per common share by $.36. Other than the cumulative effect, there was no material impact on net income and earnings per common share in any quarter of 1984.

Refer to the Financial Statements and Management's Discussion and Analysis for further explanation.

Common Stock: Market and Dividend Information

Quarter	1984 Price Range High	1984 Price Range Low	1984 Dividends Paid	1983 Price Range High	1983 Price Range Low	1983 Dividends Paid
1st	24 5/8	20 3/8	$ .30	$23 3/4	$20	$ .30
2nd	23 3/8	21 1/8	.30	30 1/2	23 1/4	.30
3rd	23 3/4	20	.30	31 1/4	26 1/8	.30
4th	21 5/8	18 3/8	.30	29 3/8	22	.30
Total	24 5/8	18 3/8	$1.20	$31 1/4	$20	$1.20

The most restrictive provisions of the company's long-term debt agreements place certain restrictions (which do not currently limit any existing or presently contemplated company policies) on the payment of dividends and the purchase or redemption of the company's Common Shares.

CONSOLIDATED FINANCIAL STATEMENTS

STATEMENT OF FINANCIAL POSITION

	December 31 1984	1983
ASSETS		
Current Assets		
Cash	$ 1,424,761	$ 1,318,101
Trade accounts receivable, less allowance of $300,000	28,339,695	41,974,966
Other accounts receivable	501,387	764,285
Inventories	123,360,661	95,673,256
Company Common Shares acquired for employees' stock plans, at cost	767,737	777,518
Prepaid expenses	796,138	1,142,561
Deferred federal income tax benefits	1,163,467	1,132,287
Refundable federal income taxes	1,584,413	—
Total Current Assets	157,938,259	142,782,974
Property, Plant and Equipment		
Land	758,122	708,121
Buildings	31,054,300	27,619,109
Machinery and equipment	53,154,907	47,477,011
Allowances for depreciation and amortization (deduction)	(34,172,400)	(31,025,526)
	50,794,929	44,778,715
Deferred Charges, Investments and Other Assets	1,044,177	1,283,642
	$209,777,365	$188,845,331

(continued)

Murray Ohio Manufacturing Company

STATEMENT OF FINANCIAL POSITION *(continued)*

	December 31	
	1984	1983
LIABILITIES AND SHAREHOLDERS' EQUITY		
Current Liabilities		
Notes payable to banks	**$ 32,348,675**	$ 1,190,454
Accounts payable and other liabilities	**24,015,784**	25,459,837
Reserves for product warranty and product liability	**1,400,000**	1,300,000
Accrued payroll, commissions, and other compensation	**8,722,810**	12,803,699
Accrued interest, payroll taxes and other taxes	**1,387,602**	1,494,495
Federal and state income taxes	**444,231**	2,831,203
Portion of long-term debt due within one year	**3,076,075**	3,061,075
Total Current Liabilities	**71,395,177**	48,140,763
Long-Term Debt—less portion shown as current liability		
Notes payable to insurance companies:		
10 1/4% notes	**2,075,000**	2,400,000
9 1/4% notes	**16,000,000**	18,000,000
8% notes	**1,750,000**	2,000,000
6 1/4% notes	**750,000**	1,125,000
Other notes payable	**93,225**	84,300
Lease obligations	**2,310,000**	2,405,000
	22,978,225	26,014,300
Deferred Credits		
Investment tax credit	**—**	2,121,877
Obligations under deferred compensation plans and other deferred credits	**705,685**	747,427
Deferred federal income taxes	**1,977,055**	2,452,554
	2,682,740	5,321,858
Shareholders' Equity		
Serial Preferred Shares, no par value: Authorized 500,000 shares; issued—none		
Common Shares, par value $2.50 a share: Authorized 8,000,000 shares; Issued—3,904,565 shares in 1984 and 1983	**9,761,413**	9,761,413
Additional paid-in capital	**42,292,504**	42,804,155
Retained earnings	**60,848,757**	57,672,939
	112,902,674	110,238,507
Less cost of Common Shares held in treasury (7,895 shares in 1984 and 30,817 shares in 1983)	**(181,451)**	(870,097)
	112,721,223	109,368,410
	$209,777,365	$188,845,331

See notes to financial statements.

Murray Ohio Manufacturing Company

STATEMENT OF INCOME

	Year Ended December 31		
	1984	1983	1982
Net sales	**$383,589,105**	$386,493,993	$288,642,358
Deductions from (additions to) income			
Cost of product sold (exclusive of depreciation and amortization)	**335,374,269**	327,134,491	245,394,295
Provision for depreciation and amortization	**3,635,096**	3,361,666	3,253,897
Selling, general and administrative expenses	**30,941,548**	30,070,404	23,729,181
Interest on long-term debt	**2,438,759**	2,627,100	2,711,077
Interest on short-term borrowings	**2,250,717**	1,709,123	4,136,422
Interest income	**(180,842)**	(936,412)	(12,165)
	374,459,547	363,966,372	279,212,707
Income before income taxes	**9,129,558**	22,527,621	9,429,651
Federal and state income taxes	**3,628,000**	10,153,000	4,337,000
Reversal of deferred taxes	**(920,000)**	—	—
Net income taxes	**2,708,000**	10,153,000	4,337,000
Income before cumulative effect of change in accounting principle	**6,421,558**	12,374,621	5,092,651
Cumulative effect of change in accounting principle for investment tax credit	**1,404,000**	—	—
Net income	**7,825,558**	12,374,621	5,092,651
Earnings per common share:			
Before cumulative effect of change in accounting principle	**$1.65**	$3.53	$1.63
Cumulative effect of change in accounting principle for investment tax credit	**.36**	—	—
Earnings per common share	**$2.01**	$3.53	$1.63
Pro forma based on revised method of accounting for investment tax credit, applied respectively:			
Net income	**$ 6,421,558**	$12,520,798	$5,184,024
Earnings per common share	**$1.65**	$3.57	$1.66
Average common shares outstanding	**3,889,345**	3,505,567	3,115,750
Retained earnings at beginning of year	**$ 57,672,939**	$ 49,417,310	$ 48,026,124
Add:			
Net income	**7,825,558**	12,374,621	5,092,651
Deduct:			
Cash dividends paid, $1.20 per common share each year	**4,649,740**	4,118,992	3,701,465
Retained earnings at end of year	**$ 60,848,757**	$ 57,672,939	$ 49,417,310

See notes to financial statements.

Murray Ohio Manufacturing Company

Murray Ohio Manufacturing Company

STATEMENT OF CHANGES IN WORKING CAPITAL

	Year Ended December 31		
	1984	1983	1982
Source of working capital			
From operations:			
Net income	$ 7,825,558	$12,374,621	$ 5,092,651
Non-cash charges (credits):			
Cumulative effect of change in accounting principle for investment tax credit	(1,404,000)	—	—
Provision for depreciation and amortization	3,635,096	3,361,666	3,253,897
Deferred income taxes, non-current	(118,474)	1,364,331	1,782,871
Other	88,084	243,269	97,787
Total from operations	10,026,264	17,343,887	10,227,206
Net book value of property, plant and equipment disposals	1,226,924	351,550	115,337
Decrease (increase) in investments	239,735	(15,711)	51,496
Increase in long-term debt	40,000	—	—
Issuance of common stock	—	21,270,179	603,205
Tax benefits for non-qualified stock options exercised	308,105	—	—
Treasury shares reissued under stock option plans	688,646	—	—
Other	37,675	15,907	—
	12,567,349	38,965,812	10,997,244
Application of working capital			
Additions to property, plant and equipment	10,878,234	5,862,985	6,277,156
Decrease in long-term debt	3,076,075	3,061,075	1,056,075
Cash dividends	4,649,740	4,118,992	3,701,465
Stock options exercised from repurchased stock	181,202	71,445	—
Stock options exercised from treasury shares	668,407	—	—
Treasury shares acquired	—	870,097	—
Reclassification of deferred investment tax credit	717,877	—	—
Reclassification of deferred taxes	357,025	—	—
Other	137,918	123,698	123,351
	20,666,478	14,108,292	11,158,047
Increase (decrease) in working capital	(8,099,129)	24,857,520	(160,803)
Working capital at beginning of year	94,642,211	69,784,691	69,945,494
Working capital at end of year	$86,543,082	$94,642,211	$69,784,691
Changes in components of working capital			
Increase (decrease) in working capital assets:			
Cash	$ 106,660	$ (134,612)	$ (148,491)
Accounts receivable	(13,898,169)	16,175,577	3,312,330
Inventories	27,687,405	(723,170)	(8,896,653)
Refundable federal income taxes	1,584,413	—	—
Other	(325,024)	(357,151)	1,257,160
	15,155,285	14,960,644	(4,475,654)
Increase (decrease) in working capital liabilities:			
Notes payable to banks	31,158,221	(27,104,946)	1,748,236
Accounts payable and other liabilities	(1,444,053)	6,708,503	(1,366,321)
Reserves for product warranty and product liability	100,000	200,000	—
Accrued payroll, commissions, and other compensation	(4,080,889)	6,239,607	(3,481,353)
Accrued interest, payroll taxes, and other taxes	(106,893)	126,068	(500,166)
Federal and state income taxes	(2,386,972)	1,928,892	(725,247)
Portion of long-term debt due within one year	15,000	2,005,000	10,000
	23,254,414	(9,896,876)	(4,314,851)
Increase (decrease) in working capital	$(8,099,129)	$24,857,520	$ (160,803)

See notes to financial statements.

NOTES TO FINANCIAL STATEMENTS

Note A—Accounting Policies

The accounting policies that affect the more significant elements of the company's financial statements are summarized below. Certain reclassifications have been made in the financial statements to conform to the 1984 presentation.

Inventories—Inventories are stated at the lower of cost (last-in, first-out method) or market. The company adjusts the carrying value on a current basis for potential losses from obsolete or slow-moving inventories.

Property, Plant and Equipment—Property, plant and equipment are carried at cost. The company provides for depreciation of property, plant and equipment on annual rates, applied generally by the straight-line method, designed to amortize the cost of the respective assets over the period of their estimated useful lives (buildings—20 to 40 years; machinery and equipment—15 years). Structural die costs are capitalized and amortized up to 3 years. When properties are disposed of, the related costs and accumulated depreciation are removed from the accounts at the time of disposal, and the resulting gain or loss is reflected in income.

Product Warranty and Product Liability—These costs are expensed in the year in which they are incurred. The related reserves are reviewed at each year end for reasonableness of possible future costs applicable to the current year's products.

Federal Income Taxes—Deferred taxes are provided with respect to timing differences resulting from those items for which the period of reporting for income tax purposes is different from the period of reporting for financial statement purposes. Effective for 1984, the company adopted the flow-through method of accounting for investment tax credits. In prior years investment credit had been amortized over a ten-year period for financial reporting, but taken for the full amount of the credit in the year in which the credits were available for tax purposes.

Earnings per Common Share—Earnings per Common Share is calculated by dividing net income by the weighted average number of Common Shares outstanding during the year. The only Common Share equivalents are stock options which have no material dilutive effect on earnings per common share.

Note B—Federal and State Income Taxes

Federal income tax returns filed by the company have been examined and approved by the Internal Revenue Service through the year ended December 31, 1979.

The provision for federal and state income taxes is composed of the following:

	1984	1983	1982
Federal income tax currently payable:			
Gross	$3,405,740	$ 8,866,388	$2,409,611
Investment and other credits	(976,220)	(847,365)	(451,788)
Net	2,429,520	8,019,023	1,957,823
Reversal of DISC deferred taxes	(920,000)	—	—
State income tax currently payable	502,150	1,002,000	325,000
Deferred federal income tax	696,330*	1,131,977*	2,054,177*
	$2,708,000	$10,153,000	$4,337,000

*Accelerated depreciation methods resulted in $1,027,943, $976,510 and $820,609 of deferred tax for the years 1984, 1983 and 1982, respectively. Tool and die amortization methods resulted in deferred tax of $365,811 for 1984. The DISC resulted in $406,275 of deferred tax in 1982.

Reconciliation of U.S. statutory tax rate to effective rate:

	1984
Statutory tax rate	46.0%
Investment tax credits (net of recapture)	(6.0)
PAYSOP tax credit	(4.1)
State income taxes (net of federal tax benefit)	3.0
Other (net)	.8
Subtotal	39.7
Reversal of DISC deferred taxes	(10.0)
Effective tax rate	29.7

The effective tax rate for 1983 and 1982 was not significantly different from the statutory rate.

Net income for the third quarter ended September 30, 1984 and for the year ended December 31, 1984 reflects the reversal of $920,000, or $.24 per common share, (after deductions of expenses relating to employee fringe benefits and related tax effects) of deferred taxes provided in prior years for the company's export sales through its Domestic International Sales Corporation (DISC). As a result of tax legislation enacted in 1984, the potential payment of these taxes has been eliminated. In accordance with a pronouncement of the Financial

Murray Ohio Manufacturing Company

Accounting Standards Board, the entire reversal is reflected in the third quarter results.

Note C—Accounting Change (Investment Tax Credit)

Effective January 1, 1984, the company changed to the flow-through method of accounting for investment tax credits. The deferred method had been used in prior years. The change was made to conform to predominant U.S. industry practice. The flow-through method includes these credits in income in the year earned, while the deferred method amortized the credits over a ten-year period. This change in accounting method (after deductions of expenses relating to fringe benefits and related tax effects) increased 1984 net income by approximately $103,000 for credits earned during the year, and by $1,404,000 for the cumulative effect of the change; earnings per common share was increased by $.03 and $.36, respectively. Pro forma net income and earnings per common share amounts reflecting retroactive application of this change are shown on the Statement of Income.

Note D—Long-Term Debt

The company negotiated long-term loans of $6,000,000 at 6¼% annual interest during 1967, $5,000,000 at 8% during 1972, $5,000,000 at 10¼% during 1975, and $20,000,000 at 9¼% during 1978, with groups of insurance companies. Under the provisions of the loan agreements, the company is required to maintain current assets of not less than 150% of current liabilities.

The 6¼% notes mature in equal annual installments from September 1972 to September 1987. The 8% notes mature in equal annual installments from December 1973 to December 1992. The 10¼% notes mature in equal annual installments from April 1977 to April 1991. The 9¼% notes mature in equal annual installments from June 1984 to June 1993.

Capitalized Lease Agreements—During 1971 and 1978, the company entered into lease obligations with the Industrial Development Board of the Town of Franklin, Tennessee, for the lease of its office building and an addition thereto. The lease obligation, in an original amount of $1,600,000, will be repaid over a twenty-year term ending in 1991. The second lease obligation, also in the amount of $1,600,000, will be repaid in total in 1998. The company will own the buildings at the expiration of the lease, and has the option to purchase the underlying land at its market value after July 31, 1992.

Future maturities of long-term debt are as follows:

	Notes	Lease Obligations	Total
1985	$2,981,075	$95,000	$3,076,075
1986	2,981,075	100,000	3,081,075
1987	2,981,075	105,000	3,086,075
1988	2,606,075	115,000	2,721,075
1989	2,575,000	120,000	2,695,000
1990 and later	9,525,000	1,870,000	11,395,000

Rental expense and other future lease commitments are not considered to be material.

In early 1985, the company entered into a lease obligation with the Industrial Development Board of the City of Lawrenceburg, Tennessee, for the lease of environmental control facilities at its factory. This lease obligation, in an original amount of $2,500,000, will be repaid over a fifteen-year term ending in 2000. The bondholder has the option to redeem the bonds after the tenth year. The company will own the facility upon the redemption of the bonds. This lease obligation is not included in the above maturity schedule.

Note E—Company Stock Plans

Eligible employees may contribute up to 5% of their base compensation to the company's stock purchase plan. The company may contribute an additional 50% of the employees' contributions. The company made such contributions for portions of 1982 and 1983, and for all of 1984. At December 31, 1984, 1,092 of the 2,220 employees eligible to participate in this plan were participants. There were 35,669 and 37,357 Common Shares held for this purpose at December 31, 1984 and 1983, respectively.

Unissued Common Shares of the company are reserved for issuance under stock option plans authorized by the shareholders during 1969, 1973, 1979 and 1984. The terms of the plans provide that qualified or non-qualified options may be issued to key employees, including officers, of the company at a price not less than the market value of the shares at the date of grant. The options generally become exercisable one year from the date of grant ratably over the succeeding four years and expire not later than ten years from the date of grant. The qualified options must be exercised in order of grant dates. The company makes no charges to income in connection with these options.

A summary of option activity follows.

Options	Shares	Option Prices
Outstanding January 1, 1984	283,982	$9.33–28.00
Exercised during 1984	(65,237)	$9.33–12.25
Expired during 1984	(9,422)	$11.50–28.00
Outstanding December 31, 1984	209,323	$9.33–28.00
Exercisable:		
December 31, 1984	167,193	
December 31, 1983	204,107	
December 31, 1982	190,731	
Exercised during 1983	8,374	$9.33–20.88
Exercised during 1982	-0-	

There were 513,369 and 203,947 unoptioned shares at December 31, 1984 and 1983, respectively.

Stock appreciation rights may be granted in tandem with options granted under the company's stock option plans. The amounts recorded each year by the company as income or expense attributable to these stock appreciation rights are insignificant.

The company has maintained since 1970 a Contingent Supplemental Retirement Benefit Plan pursuant to which additional retirement benefits may be awarded on an annual basis in amounts and to key employees of the company as designated by the Compensation Committee of the Board of Directors. Payment of such benefits is contingent upon certain employment conditions.

Note F—Pension Plans

The company has noncontributory pension plans which cover substantially all of its employees. The company makes annual contributions to the plans equal to the amounts accrued for pension expense in the prior year.

The total pension expense was $1,654,100, $2,417,400 and $2,552,900 for 1984, 1983 and 1982, respectively. The decreases in pension expense have resulted principally from the increased assumed rate of return and changes in the employment levels. The company's consulting actuary has estimated certain information for the 1984 and 1983 plan years as follows:

	1984	1983
Date of actuarial valuation:		
Hourly Plan	January 1, 1984	January 1, 1983
Salary Plan	December 1, 1983	December 1, 1982
Net assets available for plan benefits	$47,151,444	$41,586,931
Actuarial present value of plan benefits:		
Vested	27,463,800	27,411,600
Non-Vested	4,496,200	4,362,600
Assumed rate of return*:		
Hourly Plan	8.0%	7.0%
Salary Plan	8.5%	7.0%

*Used in determining the actuarial present value of plan benefits, which would have been approximately $5,900,000 higher had the rate remained at 7%. Actual plan benefits were not affected.

In addition to providing pension benefits, the company provided certain health care and life insurance benefits for retired employees and their dependents. Substantially all of the company's employees who retire under the company's retirement plans may become eligible for these benefits. The cost of retiree health care and life insurance benefits is recognized as an expense as incurred. For 1984, these costs totaled approximately $261,000.

Note G—Short-Term Credit Arrangements

Under lines of credit arrangements for short-term debt with eleven financial institutions, the company may borrow up to $111,100,000 on such terms as may be mutually agreeable. These arrangements do not have termination dates but are reviewed annually for renewal. At December 31, 1984, the unused portion of the credit lines was $78,751,325.

Under various informal and unrestricted arrangements with the financial institutions, compensating balances are maintained at varying terms against credit lines and related borrowings. During 1984, such compensating balances averaged approximately $2,830,000 and were satisfied substantially by float.

Murray Ohio Manufacturing Company

Note I—Business Segment Information

The components of revenue, operating profit and other data by business segments are set forth within the following table for the years ended:

December 31, 1984	Power Mowers and Accessories	Bicycles and Accessories	Other Products	Total
Net Sales	$236,421,047	$147,079,185	$88,873	$383,589,105
Operating Profit (loss)	24,533,300	3,352,581	(27,349)	27,858,532
General and Administrative Expense (1)	8,721,454	5,316,076	1,968	14,039,498
Interest (2)	3,222,125	1,467,173	178	4,689,476
Income (Loss) Before Taxes	$12,589,721	$(3,430,668)	$(29,495)	$9,129,558
Identifiable Assets (3)	$119,534,386	$49,353,639	$54,766	$168,942,791
General Corporate Assets				40,834,574
				$209,777,365
Depreciation and Amortization Expense	$1,797,348	$1,613,597	$-0-	$3,410,945
General Depreciation Expense				224,151
				$3,635,096
Identifiable Capital Expenditures	$5,792,543	$4,246,449	$-0-	$10,038,992
General Capital Expenditures				839,242
				$10,878,234
December 31, 1983				
Net Sales	$205,036,387	$181,377,604	$80,002	$386,493,993
Operating Profit (Loss)	25,057,921	12,000,318	(4,639)	37,053,600
General and Administrative Expense (1)	6,505,761	3,682,691	1,304	10,189,756
Interest (2)	2,595,403	1,740,577	243	4,336,223
Income (Loss) Before Taxes	$15,956,757	$6,577,050	$(6,186)	$22,527,621
Identifiable Assets (3)	$84,424,799	$51,061,136	$305,592	$135,791,527
General Corporate Assets				53,053,804
				$188,845,331
Depreciation and Amortization Expense	$1,632,805	$1,537,759	$4,027	$3,174,591
General Depreciation Expense				187,075
				$3,361,666
Identifiable Capital Expenditures	$2,682,958	$2,954,450	$-0-	$5,637,408
General Capital Expenditures				225,577
				$5,862,985
December 31, 1982				
Net Sales	$155,415,363	$133,138,347	$88,648	$288,642,358
Operating Profit (Loss)	18,603,595	7,086,836	(230,795)	25,459,636
General and Administrative Expense (1)	5,815,558	3,365,070	1,858	9,182,486
Interest (2)	4,577,197	2,269,850	452	6,847,499
Income (Loss) Before Taxes	$8,210,840	$1,451,916	$(233,105)	$9,429,651
Identifiable Assets (3)	$94,912,121	$39,142,707	$348,421	$134,403,249
General Corporate Assets				37,329,209
				$171,732,458

(continued)

December 31, 1984	Power Mowers and Accessories	Bicycles and Accessories	Other Products	Total
Depreciation and Amortization Expense	$1,643,064	$1,426,993	$3,811	$3,073,868
General Depreciation Expense				180,029
				$3,253,897
Identifiable Capital Expenditures	$2,099,488	$4,115,209	$-0-	$6,214,697
General Capital Expenditures				62,459
				$6,277,156

(1) General and administrative expenses were directly allocated by segment where reasonable bases existed with the remainder of these expenses allocated based upon the ration of the segment's net sales to total net sales. Interest income, receipts from an antitrust settlement and losses on capital disposals are included in general and administrative expenses. The combination of these items increased general and administrative expenses by $806,000 in 1984, while the same items decreased this category by $1,466,000 in 1983, resulting in $2,272,000 of the total change in general and administrative expenses between the two years. The balance of the increase was composed of a number of different items. The above mentioned items were insignificant in 1982.

(2) Interest expense was partially allocated using the ratio of the segment's identifiable assets to total assets with the portion of interest related to general assets allocated based upon the ratio of the segment's net sales to total net sales.

(3) Identifiable assets by segment includes both assets directly identified with those operations including finished and in-process inventories and an allocable share of jointly used assets. General assets consist of cash, receivables and other unallocable assets.

Of the company's total revenue, its three largest customers provided $69 million, $43 million and $43 million, respectively in 1984, while one customer provided $79 million and $68 million in 1983 and 1982, respectively, from purchases of both power mowers and bicycles.

Note J—Change in Capital Accounts

A summary of changes in capital accounts for 1984, 1983 and 1982 follows.

	Common Shares Outstanding		Additional Paid-In Capital	Treasury Shares
	Number	Amount		
Balance at January 1, 1982	3,099,527	$7,748,818	$22,938,871	—
Stock issued to Stock Purchase Plan	35,038	87,595	515,610	
Credit attributable to deferred compensation			33,132	
Balance at December 31, 1982	3,134,565	7,836,413	23,487,613	—
Stock options exercised from repurchased stock			(71,445)	
Additional common stock issued less cost of issue	770,000	1,925,000	19,345,179	
Treasury shares acquired	(30,817)			(870,097)
Credit attributable to deferred compensation			42,808	
Balance at December 31, 1983	3,873,748	9,761,413	42,804,155	(870,097)
Stock options exercised from repurchased stock			(181,202)	
Treasury shares reissued under stock options plans	22,922		(668,407)	688,646
Tax benefits of non-qualified stock options exercised			308,105	
Credit attributable to deferred compensation			29,853	
Balance at December 31, 1984	3,896,670	$9,761,413	$42,292,504	(181,451)

The company sold 770,000 Common Shares in a public offering during June 1983. The company's net proceeds from this sale totaled $21,270,179. Had these shares been issued at the beginning of 1983 and the proceeds applied to short-term debt at that time, earnings per common share for 1983 would have been $3.31 as compared to the reported amount of $3.53.

Murray Ohio Manufacturing Company

Murray Ohio Manufacturing Company

Note K—Inventories and Cost of Sales

The inventory components are as follows:

	1984	1983
Finished and in-process products	$121,931,069	$ 90,822,673
Raw materials	6,695,859	8,859,494
Manufacturing supplies	1,582,733	1,392,089
	130,209,661	101,074,256
Less allowance to reduce carrying value to LIFO basis	(6,849,000)	(5,401,000)
Inventory at LIFO	$123,360,661	$ 95,673,256

During 1982, certain inventory quantities were reduced, resulting in a liquidation of LIFO quantities carried at the cost prevailing in the prior year. The effect was to increase 1982 net profit by approximately $130,000.

Note L—Non-Monetary Transactions

During 1983 and 1982 the company exchanged certain inventory for advertising services to be received. These transactions resulted in no significant gain or loss. At December 31, 1984, 1983 and 1982, the unused amounts of $577,000, $935,000 and $1,321,000, respectively, were classified as prepaid expenses.

Note M—Miscellaneous Receipts and Charges

Selling, general and administrative expenses include miscellaneous receipts and charges which normally are insignificant. However, in the second quarter of 1984 and the first quarter of 1983 the company received approximately $85,000 and $628,000, respectively, for distributions from a class action antitrust settlement involving certain members of the corrugated container industry. In the fourth quarter of 1984, the company recorded an expense of $998,000 due to the write-off of an inoperative machine.

REPORTS OF INDEPENDENT ACCOUNTANTS AND MANAGEMENT

Report of Independent Accountants

Board of Directors and Shareholders
The Murray Ohio Manufacturing Company
Brentwood, Tennessee

We have examined the statement of financial position of The Murray Ohio Manufacturing Company as of December 31, 1984 and 1983, and the related statement of income, retained earnings and changes in working capital for each of the three years in the period ended December 31, 1984. Our examinations were made in accordance with generally accepted auditing standards and, accordingly, included such tests of the accounting records and such other auditing procedures as we considered necessary in the circumstances.

In our opinion, the financial statements referred to above present fairly the financial position of The Murray Ohio Manufacturing Company at December 31, 1984 and 1983, and the results of its operations and changes in working capital for each of the three years in the period ended December 31, 1984, in conformity with generally accepted accounting principles applied on a consistent basis, except for the change, with which we concur, in the method of accounting for investment tax credits as described in Note C of Notes to Financial Statements.

Ernst and Whinney
Nashville, Tennessee
January 28, 1985

Report of Management

The management of The Murray Ohio Manufacturing Company is responsible for the integrity of all information and representation contained in the financial statements and other sections of this Annual Report.

The Company's financial statements are based on generally accepted accounting principles and as such include amounts based on management's judgment and estimates.

The company has a system of internal accounting controls which is designed to provide reasonable assurance that assets are safeguarded, transactions are executed in accordance with management's authorization and financial records are reliable as a basis for preparation of financial statements. The system includes the selection and training of qualified personnel, an organizational structure which permits the delegation of authority and responsibility, the establishing and disseminating of accounting and business policies and procedures and an extensive internal audit program. There are limits inherent in all systems of internal control and a recognition that the cost of such systems should not exceed the benefits to be derived. We believe the company's systems provide this appropriate balance.

The company's independent accountants, Ernst & Whinney, have examined the financial statements. As independent accountants, they also provide an objective review of management's discharge of its responsibility to report operating results and financial condition. They obtain and maintain an understanding of the company's systems and procedures and perform such tests and other procedures, including tests of the internal accounting controls, as they deem necessary to enable them to express an opinion on the fairness of the financial statements.

The Board of Directors pursues its oversight role for the financial statements through its Audit Committee composed of three outside directors. The Audit Committee meets as necessary with management, the internal auditors and the independent accountants. The independent accountants and internal auditors have free access to the Audit Committee without the presence of management representatives to discuss internal accounting controls, auditing and financial reporting matters.

MANAGEMENT'S DISCUSSION AND ANALYSIS OF THE SUMMARY OF OPERATIONS

Sales for 1984 remained basically constant with 1983 as a result of a 15% increase in power mower sales which represented 62% of total sales and a 19% decrease in bicycle sales which represented the remaining 38% of total sales. In 1983 power mower sales represented 53% and bicycle sales represented 47% of total sales. The increase in 1984 power mower sales was attributable to increased volume. The company's bicycle pricing, production levels and sales have been adversely affected by increased bicycle imports

and heightened domestic bicycle competition. Net income as a percentage of sales decreased to 2.0% in 1984 from 3.2% in 1983.

Net income for 1984 was down 37% reflecting narrower operating margins than were experienced in 1983 and 1982 for power mowers and especially bicycles. Operating profit as a percentage of sales for power mowers was 10.4%, 12.2% and 12.0% for 1984, 1983 and 1982, respectively. Bicycle operating profit as a percentage of sales was 2.3%, 6.6% and 5.3% for 1984, 1983 and 1982, respectively. Increased domestic competition in both product lines contributed to the narrower operating margins. However, the increasing volume of imports, principally from Taiwan, had an added impact upon the bicycle operating profit for 1984. The decrease in earnings per common share was greater than the corresponding decrease in net income for 1983 to 1984 due to the increase in the average number of common shares outstanding resulting from the sale of additional common shares in June 1983.

Net income for 1984 reflects the reversal of $920,000, or $.24 per common share (after deductions of expenses relating to employee fringe benefits and related tax effects), of deferred taxes provided in prior years for the company's export sales through its Domestic International Sales Corporation (DISC). As a result of tax legislation enacted in 1984, the liability for potential payment of these taxes has been eliminated. For further explanation refer to Note B of Notes to Financial Statements.

Effective January 1, 1984, the company changed to the flow-through method of accounting for investment tax credits. The deferred method had been used in prior years. This change in accounting method (after deductions of expenses relating to employee fringe benefits and related tax effects) increased 1984 net income by approximately $103,000 ($.03 per common share) for credits earned during the year, and by approximately $1,404,000 ($.36 per common share) for the cumulative effect of the change. For further information refer to the Statement of Income and Note C of Notes to Financial Statements.

The company experienced an exceptional year in both sales and net income for 1983. The sales and net income increases in 1983 from 1982 were attributable primarily to increased sales volume resulting from the general improvement in the economy. Both the bicycle and power mower product lines contributed to the increased sales and net income in 1983. Net income as a percentage of sales increased to 3.2% in 1983 from 1.8% in 1982.

Murray Ohio Manufacturing Company

Selling, general and administrative expenses for 1984 remained relatively constant compared to 1983. Selling, general and administrative expenses for 1984 and 1983 were reduced by approximately $85,000 and $628,000, respectively, for distributions received from a class action antitrust settlement involving certain members of the corrugated container industry. In 1984 an expense of $998,000 was recorded due to the write-off of an inoperative machine. Increased advertising expenditures along with increased costs associated with increased sales caused the company's 1983 selling, general and administrative expenses to increase $6.3 million (26.7%) from 1982.

Interest expense on short-term borrowings reflects an increase for 1984 as compared to 1983 as a result of higher levels of average borrowing at higher interest rates. Short-term borrowings increased in 1984 from 1983 due to higher average inventory levels experienced during 1984 and the use of the proceeds from the common stock offering to repay short-term borrowings in 1983 as later discussed.

Inventories at December 31, 1984 are considerably higher than at December 31, 1983, primarily due to power mower inventory levels reflecting an expectation of increased orders for the 1985 riding mower lines. Notes payable have correspondingly increased due to the increased inventory levels.

Accounts receivable outstanding at year-end decreased in 1984 compared to 1983 primarily due to decreased sales experienced in the fourth quarter in 1984. Traditionally, sales in the last 45 days of the year cause receivables to be correspondingly higher.

Accrued payroll, commissions and other compensation decreased from $12.8 million in 1983 to $8.7 million in 1984. This decrease principally resulted from decreased net income, year-end employment levels and related employee fringe benefits.

The effective income tax rate of 29.7% was significantly lower that the effective rates of 45.1% for 1983 and 46% for 1982. The effective tax rate for 1984 differs from the statutory rate principally because of tax credits and the impact of the reversal of DISC taxes. The company continues to review, and adopt where appropriate, methods of tax accounting, all within tax regulations, which allow the company to defer payment of tax and thus increase its cash flow.

The company's business cycle imposes fluctuating demands on its cash flow, due to the temporary buildup of inventory in anticipation of, and receivables subsequent to, shipping during the peak seasonal periods. The company has in the past used lines of credit arrangements for short-term debt to meet its cash flow demands. These arrangements, the details of which are further discussed in Note G of Notes to Financial Statements, provide the company with immediate and continued sources of liquidity.

During June 1983, the company sold an additional 770,000 shares of Common Stock in a public offering at $29.25 per share. The net proceeds to the company, totaling approximately $21 million were used to repay outstanding short-term instruments pending application to the company's working capital requirements. Decreased interest expense on short-term borrowings and increased interest income for 1983 reflect the use of the proceeds from the sale of Common Stock.

In addition to cash flow and existing lines of credit, management believes that alternatives are available to the company to meet future cash needs. These may include additional short-term debt, commercial paper, or equity securities. The company's strong debt to equity ratio should place it in a favorable position to issue new debt or equity securities. The company reviews these alternatives relative to current market and economic conditions on a continuing basis.

Capital expenditures for 1984 amounted to $10.9 million as compared to $5.9 million in 1983. Major expenditures included modern tube cutting equipment, robot welders, a computer aided design system and the initial phase of a state of the art press room. The company has budgeted $9.7 million for its 1985 capital expenditures. This budget is based on current economic conditions, and is subject to change in the event of significant changes in the general economy and/or the company's performance. This budget includes projects for further modernization and automation of production processes, and for continued vertical integration. These projects are anticipated to be financed principally from working capital sources. In early 1985, the company entered into a 2.5 million Industrial Development Revenue Bond financing for environmental control facilities at its factory. Refer to Note D of Notes to Financial Statements for further information.

Virtually all costs and expenses are subject to normal inflationary pressures and the company is continually seeking ways to cope with its impact. The effects of inflation on the company's operations are summarized and discussed in Note H of Notes to Financial Statements.

Oracle Systems Corporation

In August 1990 Lawrence J. Ellison, CEO of Oracle Systems Corporation, was facing increasing pressure from analysts about the method the company used to recognize revenue in its financial reports. Analysts' major concerns were clearly articulated by a senior technology analyst at Hambrecht & Quist, Inc. in San Francisco:

> *Under Oracle's current set of accounting rules, Oracle can recognize any revenue they believe will be shipped within the next twelve months. . . . Many other software firms have moved to booking only the revenue that has been shipped.*

Given its aggressive revenue-recognition policy and relatively high amount of accounts receivable, many analysts argued that Oracle's stock was a risky buy. As a result, the company's stock price had plummeted from a high of $56 in March to around $27 in mid-August. This poor stock performance concerned Larry Ellison for two reasons. First, he worried that the firm might become a takeover candidate, and second that the low price made it expensive for the firm to raise new equity capital to finance its future growth.

ORACLE'S BUSINESS AND PERFORMANCE

Since its formation in California in June 1977, Oracle Systems Corporation has grown rapidly to become the world's largest supplier of database management software. Its principal product is the ORACLE relational database management system, which runs on a broad range of computers, including mainframes, minicomputers, microcomputers, and personal computers. The company also develops and distributes a wide array of products to interface with its database system, including applications in financial reporting, manufacturing management, computer aided systems engineering, computer network communications, and office automation. Finally, Oracle offers extensive maintenance, consulting, training, and systems integration services to support its products.

Oracle's leadership in developing software for database management has enabled it to achieve impressive financial growth. As reported in Exhibit 1, the company's sales grew from $282 million in 1988 to $971 million two years later. Larry Ellison was proud of this rapid growth and committed to its continuance. He often referred to Genghis Khan as his inspiration in crushing competitors and achieving growth.

The primary factors underlying Oracle's strong performance have been its successes in R&D and its committed sales force. The firm's R&D triumphs are proudly noted in the 1990 annual report:

> *In 1979, we delivered ORACLE, the world's first relational database management system and the first product based on SQL. In 1983, ORACLE was the first database management system to run on mainframes, minicomputers, and PCs. In 1986, ORACLE was the first database management system with distributed capability, making access to data on a network of computers as easy as access on a single computer.*
>
> *We continued our tradition of technology leadership in 1990, with three key achievements in the area of client-server computing. First, we delivered software that*

....

Cholthicha Srivisal and Professor Paul M. Healy prepared this case at the MIT Sloan School of Management. The case is intended solely as the basis for class discussion and is not intended to serve as an endorsement, source of primary data, or illustration of effective or ineffective management.

*allows client programs to automatically adapt to the different graphical user inter-
faces on PCs, Macintoshes, and workstations. Second, we delivered our complete
family of accounting applications running as client programs networked to an ORA-
CLE database server. Third, the ORACLE database server set performance records of
over 400 transactions per second on mainframes, 200 transactions per second on
minicomputers, and 20 transactions per second on PCs.*

Oracle's sales force has also been responsible for its success. The sales force is compensated on the basis of sales, giving it a strong incentive to aggressively court large corporate customers. In some cases salespeople even have been known to offer extended
payment terms to a potentially valuable customer to close a sale.

Oracle's growth slowed in early 1990. In March the firm announced a 54 percent jump
in quarterly revenues (relative to 1989's results)—but only a 1 percent rise in earnings (see
Exhibit 2 for quarterly results for 1989 and 1990). Management explained that several factors contributed to this poor performance. First, the company had recently redrawn its
sales territories and, as a result, for several months salespeople had become unsure of their
new responsibilities, leaving some customers dissatisfied. Second, there were problems
with a number of new products, such as Oracle Financials, which were released before all
major bugs could be fixed. However, the stock market was unimpressed by these explanations, and the firm's stock price dropped by 31 percent with the earnings announcement.

REVENUE RECOGNITION

The deterioration in its financial performance prompted analysts to question Oracle's method of recognizing revenues. For example, one analyst commented:

*Oracle's accounting practices might have played a role in the low net income results.
The top line went up over 50%, though the net bottom line did not do so well, because
Oracle's running more cash than it should be as a result of financial mismanagement.
The company's aggressive revenue-recognition policy and relatively high amount of
accounts receivables make the stock risky.*

Oracle's major revenues come from licensing software products to end users, and from
sublicensing agreements with original equipment manufacturers (OEMs) and software
value-added relicensors (VARs). Initial license fees for the ORACLE database management
system range from $199 to over $5,500 on micro- and personal computers, and from
$5,100 to approximately $342,000 on mini- and mainframe computers. License fees for
Oracle Financial and Oracle Government Financial products range from $20,000 to
$513,000, depending on the platform and number of users. A customer may obtain addi-
tional licenses at the same site at a discount. Oracle recognizes revenues from these
licenses when a contract has been signed with a financially sound customer, even though
shipment of products has not occurred.

OEM agreements are negotiated on a case-by-case basis. However, under a typical contract Oracle receives an initial nonrefundable fee (payable either upon signing the contract
or within 30 days of signing) and sublicense fees based on the number of copies distributed. Under VAR agreements the company charges a development license fee on top of the
initial nonrefundable fee, and it receives sublicense fees based on the number of copies
distributed. Sublicense fees are usually a percentage of Oracle's list price. The initial nonrefundable payments and development license fees under these arrangements are recorded
as revenue when the contracts are signed. Sublicense fees are recorded when they are
received from the OEM or VAR.

Oracle also receives revenues from maintenance agreements under which it provides technical support and telephone consultation on the use of the products and problem resolution, system updates for software products, and user documentation. Maintenance fees generally run for one year and are payable at the end of the maintenance period. They range from 7.5 percent to 22 percent of the current list price of the appropriate license. These fees are recorded as unearned revenue when the maintenance contract is signed and are reflected as revenue ratably over the contract period.

The major questions about Oracle's revenue recognition concern the way the firm recognizes revenues on license fees. There is no currently accepted standard for accounting for these types of revenues.[1] However, Oracle tends to be one of the more aggressive reporters. The firm's days receivable exceeds 160 days, substantially higher than the average of 62 days receivable for other software developers (see Exhibit 3 for a summary of days receivable for other major software developers in 1989 and 1990). As a result, some analysts argue that the firm should recognize revenue when software is delivered rather than when a contract is signed, consistent with the accounting treatment for the sale of products. In addition, the collectibility of license fees is considered questionable by some analysts, who have urged the firm to recognize revenue only when there is a reasonable basis for estimating the degree of collectibility of a receivable. Estimates by Oracle's controller indicate that if Oracle were to change to a more conservative revenue recognition policy, the firm's days receivable would fall to about 120 days.

MANAGEMENT'S CONCERNS

Oracle's management was concerned about analysts' opinions and the downturn in the firm's stock. The company had lost credibility with investors and customers due to its recent poor performance and its controversial accounting policies.

One of the items on the agenda at the upcoming board meeting was to consider proposals for changing the firm's revenue recognition method and for dealing with its communication challenge. Ellison knew that his opinion on this question would be influential. As he saw it, the company had three alternatives. One was to modify the recognition of license fees so that revenue would be recognized only when substantially all the company's contractual obligations had been performed. However, he worried that such a change would have a negative impact on the firm's bottom line and further depress the stock price. A second possibility was to wait until the FASB announced its position on software revenue recognition before making any changes. Finally, the company could make no change and vigorously defend its current accounting method. Ellison carefully considered which alternative made the most sense for the firm.

QUESTIONS

1. What factors might have led analysts to question Oracle Systems' method of revenue recognition in mid-1990? Are these legitimate concerns?

2. Estimate the earnings impact for Oracle from recognizing revenue at delivery, rather than when a contract is signed.

3. What accounting or communication changes would you recommend to Oracle's Board of Directors?

....

1. The Financial Accounting Standards Board was considering the issue of revenue recognition for software developers at this time. It was widely expected that the Board would make a pronouncement on the topic early in 1991.

Oracle Systems Corporation

EXHIBIT I

Oracle Systems Corporation – Consolidated Financial Statements

CONSOLIDATED BALANCE SHEETS
As of May 31, 1990 and 1989 (in $000, except per share data)

	1990	1989
ASSETS		
CURRENT ASSETS:		
Cash and cash equivalents	$ 44,848	$ 44,848
Short-term investments	4,980	4,500
Receivables		
Trade, net of allowance for doubtful accounts of $28,445 in 1990 and $16,829 in 1989	468,071	261,989
Other	28,899	16,175
Prepaid expenses and supplies	22,459	9,376
Total current assets	569,257	336,933
PROPERTY, net	171,945	94,455
COMPUTER SOFTWARE DEVELOPMENT COSTS, net of accumulated amortization of $14,365 in 1990 and $6,180 in 1989	33,396	13,942
OTHER ASSETS	12,649	14,879
TOTAL ASSETS	$787,247	$460,209
LIABILITIES AND STOCKHOLDERS' EQUITY		
CURRENT LIABILITIES:		
Notes payable to banks	$ 31,236	$ 9,747
Current maturities of long-term debt	11,265	13,587
Accounts payable	64,922	51,582
Income taxes payable	18,254	14,836
Accrued compensation and related benefits	61,164	39,063
Customer advances and unearned revenues	42,121	15,403
Other accrued liabilities	32,417	23,400
Sales tax payable	22,193	8,608
Deferred income taxes	—	2,107
Total current liabilities	283,572	178,333
LONG-TERM DEBT	89,129	33,506
OTHER LONG-TERM LIABILITIES	4,936	5,702
DEFERRED INCOME TAXES	22,025	12,114
STOCKHOLDERS' EQUITY:		
Common stock, $.01 par value-authorized, 200,000,000 shares; outstanding: 131,138,302 shares in 1990 and 126,933,288 shares in 1989	388	346
Additional paid-in capital	118,715	84,931
Retained earnings	267,475	150,065
Accumulated foreign currency translation adjustments	1,007	(4,788)
Total stockholders' equity	387,585	230,554
TOTAL LIABILITIES AND STOCKHOLDERS' EQUITY	$787,247	$460,209

CONSOLIDATED STATEMENTS OF INCOME
For the Years Ended May 31, 1990 to 1988 (in $000, except per share data)

	1990	1989	1988
REVENUES			
Licenses	$689,898	$417,825	$205,435
Services	280,946	165,848	76,678
Total revenues	970,844	583,673	282,113
OPERATING EXPENSES			
Sales and marketing	465,074	272,812	124,148
Cost of services	160,426	100,987	51,241
Research and development	88,291	52,570	25,708
General and administrative	67,258	34,344	17,121
Total operating expenses	781,049	460,713	218,218
OPERATING INCOME	189,795	122,960	63,895
OTHER INCOME (EXPENSE):			
Interest income	3,772	2,724	2,472
Interest expense	(12,096)	(4,318)	(1,540)
Other income (expense)	(8,811)	(1,121)	152
Total other income (expense)	(17,135)	(2,715)	1,084
INCOME BEFORE PROVISION FOR INCOME TAXES	172,660	120,245	64,979
PROVISION FOR INCOME TAXES	55,250	38,479	22,093
NET INCOME	$117,410	$81,766	$42,886
EARNINGS PER SHARE	$ .86	$ .61	$ .32
NUMBER OF COMMON AND COMMON EQUIVALENT SHARES OUTSTANDING	136,826	135,066	132,950

Oracle Systems Corporation

Oracle Systems Corporation

CONSOLIDATED STATEMENTS OF CASH FLOWS
For the Years Ended May 31, 1990 to 1988 (in $000)

	1990	1989	1988
CASH FLOWS FROM OPERATING ACTIVITIES			
Net income	$117,410	$81,766	$42,886
Adjustments to reconcile net income to net cash provided by operating activities:			
Depreciation and amortization	44,078	23,156	12,973
Provision for doubtful accounts	16,625	9,211	4,839
Increase in receivables	(227,046)	(149,900)	(74,777)
Increase in prepaid expenses & supplies	(12,834)	(5,684)	(1,458)
Increase in accounts payable	12,491	25,236	12,854
Increase income taxes payable	3,002	6,821	7,940
Increase in other accrued liabilities	42,166	38,057	21,420
Increase in customer advances and unearned revenues	25,786	6,496	5,682
Increase (decrease) in deferred taxes	7,728	(10,857)	8,170
Increase (decrease) in other non-current liabilities	(766)	1,938	—
Net cash provided by operating activities	28,640	26,240	40,529
CASH FLOWS FROM INVESTING ACTIVITIES			
Increase in short-term investments	(480)	2,998	(7,498)
Capital expenditures	(89,275)	(68,428)	(30,959)
Capitalization of computer software development costs	(27,639)	(10,526)	(4,447)
Increase in other assets	(1,116)	(2,084)	(481)
Purchase of a business	—	(6,650)	—
Net cash used for investing activities	(118,510)	(84,690)	(43,385)
CASH FLOWS FROM FINANCING ACTIVITIES			
Notes payable to banks	21,156	10,305	(169)
Proceeds from issuance of long-term debt	68,530	37,539	1,445
Payments of long-term debt	(34,239)	(6,205)	(3,638)
Proceeds from common stock issued	18,460	11,060	4,712
Tax benefits from stock options	15,366	10,593	3,992
Net cash provided by financing activities	89,273	63,292	6,342
EFFECT OF EXCHANGE RATE CHANGES ON CASH	552	(1,061)	69
NET INCREASE (DECREASE) IN CASH	**(45)**	**3,781**	3,555
CASH: BEGINNING OF YEAR	44,893	41,112	37,557
Cash: end of year	**$44,848**	**$44,893**	**$41,112**

EXCERPTS FROM NOTES TO CONSOLIDATED FINANCIAL STATEMENTS

1. Organization and Significant Accounting Policies

Organization

Oracle Systems Corporation (the Company) develops and markets computer software products used for database management, applications development, decision support, programmer tools, computer network communication, end user applications, and office automation. The Company offers maintenance, consulting, and training services in support of its clients' use of its software products.

Basis of Financial Statements

The consolidated financial statements include the Company and its subsidiaries. All transactions and balances between the companies are eliminated.

Business Combination

In November 1988, the Company's subsidiary, Oracle Complex Systems Corporation, acquired all of the outstanding shares of Falcon Systems, Inc., a systems integrator, for $13,714,000 in cash and $4,600,000 in notes which become due November 1, 1991. The acquisition was accounted for as a purchase and the excess of the cost over the fair value of assets acquired was $5,648,000, which is being amortized over 5 years on a straight-line method. Pro forma results of operations, assuming the acquisition had taken place June 1, 1987, would not differ materially from the Company's actual results of operations.

Software Development Costs

Effective June 1, 1986, the Company began capitalizing internally generated software development costs in compliance with Statement of Financial Accounting Standards No. 86, "Accounting for the Costs of Computer Software to be Sold, Leased or Otherwise Marketed." Capitalization of computer software development costs begins upon the establishment of technological feasibility for the product. Capitalized software development costs amounted to $27,639,000, $10,526,000, and $4,447,000 in fiscal 1990, 1989, and 1988, respectively.

Amortization of capitalized computer software development costs begins when the products are available for general release to customers, and is computed product by product as the greater of: (a) the ratio of current gross revenues for a product to the total of current and anticipated future gross revenues for the product, or (b) the straight-line method over the remaining estimated economic life of the product. Currently, estimated economic lives of 24 months are used in the calculation of amortization of these capitalized costs. Amortization amounted to $8,185,000, $3,504,000, and $2,345,000 for fiscal years ended May 31, 1990, 1989, and 1988, respectively, and is included in sales and marketing expenses.

Statements of Cash Flows

The Company paid income taxes in the amount of $33,731,000, $29,006,000, and $711,000 and interest expense of $8,026,000, $4,274,000 and $1,540,000 during the fiscal years ended 1990, 1989, and 1988, respectively. The Company purchased equipment under capital lease obligations in the amount of $17,616,000, $4,692,000, and $4,108,000 in fiscal 1990, 1989 and 1988, respectively.

Revenue Recognition

The Company generates several types of revenue including the following:

License and Sublicense fees. The Company licenses ORACLE products to end users under license agreements. The Company also has entered into agreements whereby the Company licenses Oracle products and receives license and sublicense fees from original equipment manufacturers (OEMs) and software value-added relicensors (VARs). The minimum amount of license and sublicense fees specified in the agreements is recognized either upon shipment of the product or at the time such agreements are effective (which in most instances is the date of the agreement) if the customer is creditworthy and the terms of the agreement are such that the amounts are due within one year and are nonrefundable, and the agreements are noncancellable. The Company recognizes revenue at such time as it has substantially performed all of its contractual obligations. Additional sublicense fees are subsequently recognized as revenue at the time such fees are reported to the Company by the OEMs and VARs.

Maintenance Agreements. Maintenance agreements generally call for the Company to provide technical support and certain systems updates to customers. Revenue related to providing technical support is recognized proportionately over the maintenance period, which in most instances is one year, while the revenue related to systems updates is recognized at the beginning of each maintenance period.

Consulting, Training, and Other Services. The Company provides consulting services to its customers; revenue from such services is generally recognized under the percentage of completion method.

2. Short-Term Debt

Short term debt (in $000) consists of:	Year Ended May 31	
	1990	1989
Unsecured revolving lines of credit	$18,198	$5,955
Other	13,038	3,792
Total	$31,236	$9,747

At May 31, 1990, the Company had short-term unsecured revolving lines of credit with two banks providing for borrowings aggregating $42,000,000, of which $18,198,000 was outstanding. These lines expire in September 1990 ($2,000,000), November 1990 ($10,000,000), and January 1991 ($30,000,000). Interest on these borrowings is based on varying rates pegged to the banks' prime rate, cost of funds, or LIBOR. The Company also had other unsecured short-term indebtedness to banks of $13,038,000 at May 31, 1990, payable upon demand. The average interest rate on short-term borrowings was 9.4% at May 31, 1990.

The Company is required to maintain certain financial ratios under the line of credit agreements. The Company was in compliance with these financial covenants at May 31, 1990.

3. Long-Term Debt

At May 31, 1990, the Company had long-term unsecured revolving lines of credit with four banks providing for borrowings aggregating $135,000,000, of which $61,460,000 was outstanding. Of the $61,460,000 outstanding, $58,210,000 was classified as long-term debt and $3,250,000 was classified as current maturities of long-term debt. These lines of credit expire in December 1991 ($60,000,000), March 1992 ($15,000,000), July 1992 ($20,000,000), January 1991 ($20,000,000), and March 1991 ($20,000,000). The Company has the option to convert $20,000,000 of its line expiring in January of 1991 and $8,000,000 of that expiring in March of 1991 into two term loans which would mature in 1993. Interest on these borrowings vary based on the banks' cost of funds rates. At May 31, 1990 the interest rate on outstanding domestic and foreign currency borrowings ranged from 8.6% to 15.6%. The aggregate amount available under these lines of credit at May 31, 1990 was $73,540,000.

Under the line-of-credit agreements, the Company is required to maintain certain financial ratios. At May 31, 1990 the Company was in compliance with these financial covenants.

Subsequent to May 31, 1990, the Company obtained two additional unsecured revolving lines of credit, one which expires May 1992 ($20,000,000) and one which expires January 1991 ($20,000,000).

4. Stockholders' Equity

Stock Option Plan

The Company's stock option plan provides for the issuance of incentives stock options to employees of the Company and nonqualified options to employees, directors, consultants, and independent contractors of the Company. Under the terms of this plan, options to purchase up to 23,335,624 shares of Common Stock may be granted at not less than fair market value, are immediately exercisable, become vested as established by the Board (generally ratably over four to five years), and generally expire ten years from the date of grant. The Company has the right to repurchase shares issued upon the exercise of unvested options at the exercise price paid by the stockholder should the stockholder leave the Company prior to the scheduled vesting date. At May 31, 1990, 271,300 shares of Common Stock outstanding were subject to such repurchase rights. Options to purchase 5,005,720 common shares were vested at May 31, 1990.

Non-Plan Options

In addition to the above option plan, nonqualified stock options to purchase a total of 5,712,000 common shares have been granted to employees and directors of the Company. These options were granted at the fair market value as determined by the Board of Directors, became exercisable immediately, vest either immediately (for directors) or ratably over a period of up to five years (for individuals other than directors) and generally expire ten years from the date of grant. The Company has the right to repurchase shares issued upon the exercise of unvested options at the exercise price paid by the stockholder should the stockholder leave the Company prior to the scheduled vesting date. Options to purchase 160,000 common shares were vested as of May 31, 1990.

As of May 31, 1990, the Company had reserved 11,135,194 shares of Common Stock for exercise of options.

Stock Purchase Plan

In October 1987, the Company adopted an Employee Stock Purchase Plan and reserved 8,000,000 shares of Common Stock for issuance thereunder. Under this plan, the Company's employees may purchase shares of Common Stock at a price per share that is 85% of the lesser of the fair market value as of the beginning or the end of the semi-annual option period. Through May 31, 1990, 2,326,772 shares have been issued and 5,673,228 shares are reserved for future issuances under this plan.

Oracle Systems Corporation

Oracle Systems Corporation

REPORT OF INDEPENDENT PUBLIC ACCOUNTANTS

To Oracle Systems Corporation:

We have audited the accompanying consolidated balance sheets of Oracle Systems Corporation (a Delaware corporation) and subsidiaries as of May 31, 1990 and 1989 and the related consolidated statements of income, stockholders' equity, and cash flows for each of the three years in the period ended May 31, 1990. These financial statements are the responsibility of the company's management. Our responsibility is to express an opinion on these financial statements based on our audits. We conducted our audits in accordance with generally accepted auditing standards. Those standards require that we plan and perform the audit to obtain reasonable assurance about whether the financial statements are free of material misstatement. An audit includes examining, on a test basis, evidence supporting the amounts and disclosures in the financial statements. An audit also includes assessing the accounting principles used and significant estimates made by management, as well as evaluating the overall financial statement presentation. We believe that our audits provide a reasonable basis for our opinion.

In our opinion, the financial statements referred to above present fairly, in all material respects, the financial position of Oracle Systems Corporation and subsidiaries as of May 31, 1990 and 1989 and the results of their operations and their cash flows for each of the three years in the period ended May 31, 1990, in conformity with generally accepted accounting principles.

Our audits were made for the purpose of forming an opinion on the basic financial statements taken as a whole. The schedules listed under Item 14(a)2. are presented for purposes of complying with the Securities and Exchange Commission's rules and are not part of the basic financial statements. These schedules have been subjected to the auditing procedures applied in the audit of the basic financial statements and, in our opinion, fairly state in all material respects the financial data required to be set forth therein in relation to the basic financial statements taken as a whole

ARTHUR ANDERSEN & CO.
SAN JOSE, CALIFORNIA
JULY 9, 1990

EXHIBIT 2

Oracle Systems Corporation – Review of Quarterly Results in Fiscal
1989 and 1990 (in $000 except per share data)

	Fiscal 1990 Quarter Ended			
	Aug. 31 1989	Nov. 30 1989	Feb. 28 1990	May 31 1990
Revenues	$175,490	$209,023	$236,165	$350,166
Net income	11,679	28,491	24,282	52,958
Earnings per share[a]	$ .09	$ .21	$ .18	$ .39

	Fiscal 1989 Quarter Ended			
	Aug. 31 1988	Nov. 30 1988	Feb. 28 1989	May 31 1989
Revenues	$90,639	$123,745	$153,354	$215,935
Net income	7,067	17,189	23,964	33,546
Earnings per share[a]	$ .05	$ .13	$ .18	$ .25

a. Adjusted to reflect the two-for-one stock splits in the third quarter of fiscal 1988 and the first quarter
of fiscal 1990.

EXHIBIT 3

Days' Receivable for Selected Companies in the Software
Industry for 1989–1990

Company	1989	1990
Borland International Corp.	49	45
Lotus Development Corp.	64	64
Microsoft Corp.	51	56
Novell Corp.	85	81
Average	62	62

Sensormatic Electronics Corporation—1995

On July 7, 1995, Sensormatic said earnings would be substantially below expectations and below last year's fourth quarter. Also troublesome was an August 31 announcement that the release of 1995 results would be delayed, pending an extended audit by Ernst & Young that is to be completed by mid-September. [Sensormatic] says it doesn't believe there will be any "major write-offs." [However], Wall Street short-sellers, who thrive on signs of accounting shenanigans, have targeted the company. [They argued that] Sensormatic's revenue accounting, while permissible under generally accepted accounting principles, was "overly aggressive." While that put pressure on the stock, it was the July 7 announcement that caused the stock to fall to $23 from a high of $36 two days earlier.[1]

Business Week, 9/18/95

BUSINESS HISTORY AND OPERATIONS

Overview

Ronald Assaf, CEO of Sensormatic, founded Sensormatic in 1965 after a burglary in his grocery store in Akron, Ohio. His idea was a security device that would deter shoplifting. With the help of two scientists, Assaf developed a semiconductor device encased in a plastic tag that could be attached to clothing. The tag, which must be removed with a special tool, operates in conjunction with a transmitter of microwave signals near the store exit. When the thief tries to leave the store, the microwave signal sets off an alarm.

Incorporated in 1968, Sensormatic grew steadily. For 39 consecutive quarters prior to July 1995 Sensormatic reported revenue and earnings growth of 20 percent or more. In 1995 Sensormatic reported sales of $860 million and net income of $73 million. Sensormatic's tags guarded everything from stereos at Macy's department stores to shampoo at CVS drugstores and lumber at the Home Depot. Hospitals used Sensormatic's equipment to prevent babies from being snatched from nurseries.

With diversification through acquisition, Sensormatic became an integrated supplier of electronic security systems to retail, commercial, industrial, and governmental markets. Sensormatic manufactured and marketed electronic article surveillance (EAS), closed circuit television (CCTV) systems, and Access Control systems. In fiscal 1995, revenues from EAS accounted for 57 percent of Sensormatic's total revenues and revenues from CCTV and Access Control accounted for 34 percent of total revenues. Sensormatic's products were marketed by a worldwide sales and service organization complemented by a broad network of business partners, independent distributors, and dealers. Sensormatic was appointed as an electronic security supplier for the 1996 Olympics.

Doctoral Candidate James Jinho Chang prepared this case under the supervision of Professor Krishna G. Palepu. The case is intended solely as the basis for class discussion and is not intended to serve as an endorsement, source of primary data, or illustration of effective or ineffective management. Copyright © 1997 by the President and Fellows of Harvard College. HBS Case 9-197-041.

1. Excerpts from "This anti-theft company is feeling insecure," *Business Week*, September 18, 1995.

Electronic Security Industry[2]

There were two theft-prevention methods: to monitor articles and to monitor people. The electronic security industry, based on EAS, monitored articles, and CCTV/Access Control systems monitored people. EAS, CCTV, and Access Control systems were used by retailers to deter shoplifting and internal theft. Inventory shrinkage was often the second largest variable operating expense of retailers, after payroll costs, and normally ranged from 1 to 5 percent of sales.

EAS systems consisted of two components: detectable security circuits embedded in tags, which were attached to the articles to be protected; and electronic detection equipment, referred to as sensors, usually located in the exit path. By 1995 the EAS market reported about $1 billion sales and was estimated to grow at 20 percent annually. The ultimate market size of EAS was estimated to be $2.5 billion. The fast industry growth was due to several factors: improved technology capabilities of loss prevention devices, lower costs of electronic security systems, the rising cost of security staff labor, and an increased need for open display of product. Major players in the EAS industry included Sensormatic, Checkpoint Systems, and 3M in the U.S. as well as Esselte Meto and Nedap B.V. in Europe. In 1995 Sensormatic was the world's largest provider of electronic anti-theft technology.

EAS products were first used by retailers to protect soft goods (e.g., apparel merchandise). Due to subsequent technological advances, applications for hard goods merchandise, which was generally packaged, also became economical and effective. Hard goods retailers such as drugstores, supermarkets, home improvements centers, and video stores increasingly became users of EAS products.

Sensormatic and Checkpoint competed primarily in the hard goods market, which accounted for 40 percent of Sensormatic's total revenues. Even though Sensormatic and Checkpoint had expanded the installation of EAS substantially, EAS penetration into hard goods stores was still low in 1995. The drugstore penetration by EAS was only 41 percent of the 38,150 drugstores in the U.S. Penetration in the supermarket industry (five times the size of the drugstore market) was just beginning. Only 4 percent of a total of 125,000 stores in the U.S. supermarket industry used EAS in 1995. Currently Sensormatic and Checkpoint split the EAS market in the supermarket industry evenly.

EAS sales are comprised of one-time sales and recurring revenues. Installation of an EAS sensor in the exit path (one-time sale) was charged at $40,000 per store with a 50 percent gross margin. Recurring revenues included disposable tags used by hard goods retailers. Each supermarket was expected to use 175,000 antitheft tags annually. Each antitheft tag was sold at $0.035 with gross margin approximately 70 percent. The recurring revenues from tags could grow from 25 to 50 percent of total revenues within the next three years.[3]

Checkpoint Systems, Sensormatic's main domestic competitor, was a popular supplier to the drugstore industry for many years (71 percent market share in 1995) because it was a first mover and a low cost provider. With revenues of approximately $204 million in 1995, Checkpoint had less resources than Sensormatic did. However, Checkpoint's competitive position was supported by its manufacturing know-how and, to a lesser degree, its technology and patents. Checkpoint believed that its manufacturing efficiencies gave it a significant cost advantage over its competitors. Checkpoint expected that volume

2. *Some of the material in this section is drawn from a report on checkpoint systems by Barry J. Peter, Deutsche Morgan Grenfell Inc., October 24, 1996.*

3. *Excerpts from Deutsche Morgan Grenfell Analyst Report.*

increases would result in a further decrease of product cost. Checkpoint's strategy was to continue to increase its sales penetration in existing markets and to develop a significant presence in new geographic markets.

Checkpoint's current technology advantage was its reliable scan-deactivation of hidden tags. This technology deactivates hidden tags as salespeople check out customers' shopping items. Sensormatic was offering a different technology, a pass-around system that did not have the deactivation process. Under the pass-around system, merchandise is passed around a pair of sensors located at the checkout lane and only the customers go through the sensors. Problems of the pass-around system were tag pollution (tags which were not deactivated might cause false alarms at other stores) and higher capital costs (one pair of sensors per checkout lane rather than one per store). However, Checkpoint's scan-deactivation technology was not likely to be a sustainable advantage because Sensormatic was expected to develop the same technology in the near future.

The new trend in the EAS industry was source tagging, where disposable tags were packaged into consumer products at the point of manufacturing. The application of tags in an automated factory rather than at retailers' stores reduced labor costs. Source tagging increased tagging compliance and its feature of being hidden inside the package improved effectiveness. The ultimate market size for source tagging was believed to be in the neighborhood of 20–30 billion tags annually.

Most companies producing EAS expanded not only domestically but also internationally. EAS sales in Europe and Latin America had increased substantially. Industry experts forecasted that there was a great growth opportunity for EAS sales in the Asia/Pacific market.

CCTV products were used to protect against inventory shrinkage in retail businesses, and for the protection and monitoring of personnel and assets in office and manufacturing complexes. CCTV systems could be used alone or in combination with EAS and Access Control. The electronic door lock Access Control systems allowed employees with clearance to have free access and movement around the plant and offices without the need for constant checks or locked doors.

CCTV and Access Control markets were estimated to have $2–$3 billion combined annual sales. These businesses were also benefiting from the increasing costs of labor intensive methods (such as hiring security guards). The companies in CCTV and Access Control systems competed on the basis of product performance, multiple technologies, service, and price. CCTV and Access Control systems markets were highly fragmented with numerous providers, including Philips, Panasonic, CardKey, and Westinghouse Electronic Corporation, and there were few significant entry barriers. Firms with greater financial and other resources could enter into direct competition with existing companies.

Sensormatic's Strategies

Growth Strategy Sensormatic's key element for growth was to expand its product line and geographic market presence through acquisitions. Acquisitions were intended to strengthen Sensormatic's core business by increasing its ability to distribute its products and achieving synergy in the combined companies. In fiscal 1993, Sensormatic acquired Automated Loss Prevention Systems (ALPS), a large European distributor of EAS, and Security Tag Systems, Inc. (Security Tag), a U.S. manufacturer and distributor of loss prevention products. In 1995 Sensormatic acquired Knogo's overseas operations through a stock exchange.

The acquisitions of ALPS, Security Tag, and Knogo resulted in goodwill of approximately $223 million, $47 million, and $114 million, respectively, which were being amortized over 40 years. Sensormatic believed that this goodwill at the end of fiscal 1995 would be fully recoverable because the acquisitions were made to enhance the revenue and profit potential for the indefinite future of these companies by increasing efficiencies, and realizing synergies with Sensormatic's own core businesses.

The acquisition of direct and indirect distribution channels helped Sensormatic to reach a wide range of potential customers worldwide. Sensormatic applied the same approach used in penetrating the U.S. commercial/industrial market to developing a presence in this market in Europe. The company felt that not only its wide geographical presence but also its broad product portfolio provided it with a competitive advantage; if a company used an EAS from Sensormatic, it was also likely to choose Sensormatic for other related security products such as CCTV and Access Control since compatibility was an issue. Honeywell, Toshiba, Panasonic, Lux Products, Monsanto, and GTE were companies that had used Sensormatic's EAS and chose CCTV/Access Control systems from Sensormatic.

However, Sensormatic's management felt that the company had grown faster than its management and organization. The integration of the Knogo European operations was slower and costlier than planned. The rapid growth in sales, product diversity, and the demands of integrating acquired businesses outpaced the growth in corporate infrastructure and systems, resulting in adverse bottom-line figures in 1995 as expenses grew significantly faster than revenues.

Marketing Strategy Sensormatic's major retail customers included Blockbuster Video, Sears Roebuck, Kmart, Wal-Mart, J.C. Penney, CVS, and Crown Books. Retail customers did not want to pay cash for the purchase of anti-theft systems until they achieved the benefits (payback period for the typical installation was six months).

A key element of Sensormatic's marketing strategy was to increase market penetration by providing alternative financing options to its retail customers (i.e., vendor financing). Sensormatic's management believed that this strategy gave the company a significant competitive advantage and helped it rapidly penetrate markets and increase customer loyalty. The longer-term financing arrangements were limited to products which had long useful lives (i.e., not offered with the sale of products such as disposable tags).

In order to finance customer receivables, Sensormatic entered into an agreement with a third-party financing institution whereby it could sell (with recourse) or assign (without recourse) certain pre-approved U.S. accounts receivables. This program also provided Sensormatic with the expertise of outside parties who were fully dedicated to the business of collecting receivables.

Checkpoint, a main competitor of Sensormatic, did not depend much on long-term financing arrangements, such as installment sales and deferred payment sales, to increase revenue. At Checkpoint, the only sales transactions made under long-term financing arrangements were sales-type leases, which accounted for a minor percentage of total sales in 1995. However, Sensormatic believed that Checkpoint would build up long-term receivables over time as Checkpoint received large orders from discount stores.

ACCOUNTING CONTROVERSY

Accounting Policy

Sales Under Long-Term Financing Arrangements

Sensormatic recognized revenue when a customer took title of the product, even though payments were sometimes not received for a considerable period of time thereafter. The longer term financing arrangements offered by the company included the following (see Exhibit 1 for the accounting method of alternative financing options, as reported by Sensormatic):

Installment sales   One financing option offered by Sensormatic, primarily to U.S. retail customers, was installment sales. Under this option, the purchase price was payable in equal installments, normally monthly, over the period of the sales contract, from one to five years. The stream of scheduled payments was discounted to its present value, using a market rate of interest. This amount was recognized as sales revenue at the date of shipment. Legal title to the equipment passed to the customer upon shipment, but Sensormatic normally retained a security interest in the equipment to secure the receivable. The total amount of installment sales receivables on Sensormatic's balance sheet represented total outstanding installment sales receivables less unearned interest income, unearned maintenance fees, and an allowance for doubtful accounts.

Deferred payment sales (extended credit terms)   A second financing option offered primarily to U.S. retail customers was deferred payment sales, under which the payment date was delayed for a specific period, more than 90 days but not more than 365 days after the product shipment date. The accounting treatment was the same as was used with installment sales—the sales revenue was discounted, using a market rate of interest, to its present value at the date of shipment. The deferred receivables on the balance sheet represented the gross receivable less unearned interest income and an allowance for doubtful accounts.

Sales-type leases   A third alternative was sales-type leases, offered primarily to European retail customers. Under this option, the Company's equipment was leased to the customer for a period generally running between 60 and 72 months. During the term of these leases, which were noncancelable, all of the benefits and risks of ownership were effectively transferred from Sensormatic to the lessee. The sales revenue recognized on sales-type leases was the present value of the stream of scheduled payments, using a market rate of interest. The amount reported on Sensormatic's balance sheet as "net investment in sales-type leases" represents total lease payments less unearned interest income, unearned maintenance fees, and an allowance for doubtful accounts.[4]

Sales of Receivables to Financial Institutions

Sensormatic financed its investments in receivables and leases by transferring them to financing institutions. These receivables and leases were *sold with recourse* or *assigned without recourse*.

Sales of Receivables with Recourse   When receivables and leases were sold with recourse, Sensormatic was obligated to repurchase the receivables and leases, if customers were delinquent in their scheduled payments beyond a defined period of time. Once receivables were sold (with recourse) to a third party, these receivables were removed from Sensormatic's balance sheet.

Related to the receivables sold with recourse, Sensormatic accrued a liability for estimated future losses due to the default of customer payments and the repurchase of receivables from financial institutions. At June 30, 1994, the company accrued loss contingencies of $1.3 million related to $199.8 million of receivables and leases sold to and

---

4. Excerpts from White Paper, Sensormatic Electronics Corporation, September 1995.

outstanding with the financing institutions which were subject to repurchase.[5] In fiscal 1995, Sensormatic repurchased approximately $13 million of receivables/leases sold with recourse to financing institutions, of which approximately $8.6 million was outstanding on Sensormatic's balance sheet at June 30, 1995. Upon repurchase, these receivables were accounted for by recording the specific receivables or sales-type leases on the balance sheet and an allowance for doubtful accounts, if necessary.

Sales of Receivables Without Recourse   Sensormatic also had agreements with third-party financing institutions whereby the company assigned receivables without recourse. Under this agreement, Sensormatic did not have an obligation to repurchase the receivables assigned, even if customers were delinquent in scheduled payments. When Sensormatic assigned receivables (without recourse) to a third party, these receivables were eliminated from Sensormatic's balance sheet. No liability was accrued with respect to the receivables assigned, because Sensormatic would not incur any loss even if there was a default.

The receivables sold or assigned usually carried fixed interest rates. However, Sensormatic sold them to the financing institution at a floating rate indexed to one month LIBOR. Any differential in interest (fixed vs. floating) was either paid or received by Sensormatic. In order to manage the interest rate risk associated with the receivables sold, Sensormatic entered into interest rate instruments such as floating to fixed interest rate swaps. This resulted in offsetting interest rate differential payments or receipts.

Barron's Criticism

In March 1995 *Barron's*, a widely circulated financial weekly, issued an article criticizing Sensormatic's accounting policies as aggressive. The article explained[6]:

> . . . *while the 35% gain in revenues and 33% increase in net income that Sensormatic reported for its fiscal first half are right on the pace it maintained for all of fiscal 1994, a close reading of its financials raises the suspicion that it has had to make increasingly aggressive accounting assumptions to stay on that track.*
>
> . . . *Sensormatic's stated policy is to use its balance-sheet heft as a marketing tool by offering new customers a variety of flexible deferred payment arrangements. Thus, it carries a big chunk of receivables on its balance sheet, as well as sales-type lease arrangements. And, to turn some of that business into cash, it sells part of its receivables, generally with recourse, to third parties.*
>
> *What's notable is that while the receivables on its books increased roughly in line with sales, to $174.5 million [2ⁿᵈ quarter of fiscal year 1995] from $127.6 million [4ᵗʰ quarter of fiscal year 1994] between June and December, the amount it expensed as a reserve for doubtful accounts stayed flat at $10.4 million and thus dropped, in percentage terms, to 6% from 8% of receivables. A back-of-the-envelope calculation is that, had the reserve stayed at 8%, pretax charges against Sensormatic's income would have risen by roughly $3.5 million . . .*
>
> *Moreover, the receivables and leases it had sold to and outstanding with third parties climbed over that stretch to $273.5 million [2ⁿᵈ quarter of fiscal year 1995] from $199.9 million [4ᵗʰ quarter of fiscal year 1994]. Yet the loss contingencies Sensormatic*

5. Sensormatic disclosed the amount of accrued loss contingencies in 1994 but did not disclose it in the 1995 Annual Report.

6. Excerpts from Barron's Financial Weekly, March 20, 1995.

accrued on those grew by all of $500,000 to $1.8 million [2nd quarter of fiscal year 1995]. That amounted to 1% of outstandings, a puny percentage under any circumstances. But it seems downright skimpy considering the seemingly endless chain of store closings, restructurings and bankruptcies that shapes the history of the industry from which Sensormatic draws most of its customers. Not to mention the fact that last fiscal year, it ended up repaying nearly $13 million, or 5%, of the funds it was advanced for receivables—mostly because customers turned out to be deadbeats.

. . . If Sensormatic's business and prospects are as good as it would have the Street believe, why push the numbers?

It's worth noting, in that context, that while Sensormatic insiders still own well over a million of its shares, they've blown out all 157,500 shares that they've acquired through the exercise of options over the past year. And they've sold an additional 115,600 shares, at prices ranging from 28 and a fraction all the way up to the stock's all-time high of 39. . . .

Sensormatic's Response

In response to the criticism by *Barron's*, Sensormatic's management argued that the company followed U.S. GAAP and that their accounting policies were consistent with the practice of many companies in the EAS industry. Also, Sensormatic issued a "white paper" which explained its accounting policies in detail (see Exhibit 1).

The White Paper tried to answer why the allowance for doubtful accounts did not increase proportionately with revenue growth. Sensormatic's management explained[7]:

The Company as well as many financial analysts believe that the ratio of allowance for doubtful accounts to revenue is far less meaningful than 1) the ratio of the provision for doubtful accounts to total revenues (expense to revenue) and 2) the ratio of allowance for doubtful accounts to outstanding receivables and sales-type leases. The Company routinely reviews the credit quality of each customer before an order is accepted. Thereafter, the Company continues to evaluate the collectibility of the accounts and provides for estimated uncollectible amounts. At such time, an expense is recorded which reflects the Company's best estimate of the amount which will not be collected. As shown in Exhibit 2, the bad debt expense as a percentage of revenue has remained fairly constant from fiscal 1993 to fiscal 1995, at approximately 1.9 percent.

The Company evaluates the total allowance for doubtful accounts on a quarterly basis to ensure that it is adequate, based on recent payment patterns, write-off amounts, etc., and records additional bad debt expense, if necessary. As shown in Exhibit 3, the allowance for doubtful accounts from fiscal 1993 to fiscal 1995 has remained constantly between five and six percent of receivables outstanding.

The Company's evaluation of the allowance for doubtful accounts is influenced by several factors. First, the aging profile of the accounts receivable outstanding — amounts past due for more than 30, 60, 90 days, etc.—at quarter-end is somewhat longer in the Company's presentation and appears to give more cause for concern about aging and ultimate collection than is warranted. While the aging profile may show amounts that are technically 30, 60 or even 90 days past due, internal approvals and processing of accounts payable for many retailers normally take between 30 and

7. *Excerpts from White Paper, Sensormatic Electronics Corporation, September 1995.*

90 days, resulting in more aged accounts receivables outstanding. In addition, like many other companies which do business with retailers, the Company has experienced a historical pattern of longer payment cycles by major retail customers. Delayed payments are often a business practice by large retailers, and not an indication of credit unworthiness. Through working to accelerate collection of receivables, the Company historically has accepted the longer collection cycles as part of its strategy to maintain and further penetrate this important market segment. The lost interest income due to the delayed payment is just another cost factor that is considered by the Company in the pricing of its products.

Second, as Sensormatic's sales to larger, relatively high creditworthy customers have increased, the required allowance for doubtful accounts, as a percentage of total sales, has decreased. In addition, a number of European customers have agreed to a payment arrangement on sales-type leases whereby a direct debit is made to the customer's bank account on scheduled dates. This is a common practice in Europe.

A third factor relates to acquisitions. Receivables acquired through acquisitions, such as those of Knogo in the most recent fiscal year, are initially recorded net of allowance for doubtful accounts, as is required by U.S. GAAP. This lowers the percentage relationship between the allowance for doubtful accounts and receivables in the year of the acquisition relative to prior years.

Finally, the Company normally retains a security interest in most underlying equipment for which a deferred or installment receivable is outstanding, and it retains legal title to equipment under a sales-type lease agreement. In either case, if necessary, the Company can repossess, refurbish and resell the equipment. The high resale value of used equipment enables Sensormatic to resell the repossessed equipment and substantially reduce its ultimate loss on the receivable or lease.

With respect to the risks of repurchasing receivables and leases, Sensormatic argued that, based on its experiences, some form of payment program could be worked out with the customer. Sensormatic's management explained[8]:

The Company establishes a liability, reported in Accrued Liabilities, for estimated future losses attributable to a risk of default. This liability is generally based on a portfolio basis rather than on a specific identification approach and is, as a percentage of outstanding receivables and leases, much lower than allowances for doubtful accounts relating to receivables and leases on the balance sheet. Even if the receivable or lease is repurchased, the Company's experience is that in many cases, some form of payment program can be worked out with the customer. An example which illustrates this is the case of Macy's Department Store. When Macy's filed for bankruptcy in early 1992 under Chapter 11 (reorganization), the Company repurchased the Macy's installment sales receivable it had sold to a financing institution (approximately $7 million). The Company recorded the receivable on its balance sheet and an allowance for doubtful account based on its best estimate of the potential ultimate loss from default. Ultimately, the Company did not incur any such loss. Even while under Chapter 11, Macy's was allowed to continue making scheduled payments to Sensormatic and recently paid off its obligation ahead of schedule. In addition, Macy's made a number of additional purchases of Sensormatic EAS equipment while still in bankruptcy.

8. *Ibid.*

Sensormatic Electronics Corporation

RECENT DEVELOPMENTS

Since *Barron's* criticism of Sensormatic's accounting policy in March 1995, short interest in Sensormatic shares increased to 4 million shares (out of 73 million shares outstanding) at the end of June 1995 (see Exhibit 5 for the trend of Sensormatic shares sold short). On July 7, 1995, with the pressure of short-sellers' criticism in the background, Sensormatic announced that its fourth-quarter earnings would be substantially lower than analysts' earnings forecast. Sensormatic never had a down quarter in the prior ten years. Sensormatic's management stated that costs related to higher expenses and Sensormatic's acquisition of rival Knogo Corporation's overseas electronics security business for $103 million in stock in January 1995 contributed to lower earnings. On the day of this announcement, Sensormatic shares fell $12 3/8 to close at $23. The 35 percent drop was the biggest percentage decline among U.S. stocks on that day.

A few weeks later, on August 31, Sensormatic announced that its fiscal 1995 result would be delayed pending an extended audit by Ernst & Young. The expanded audit focused on two specific accounting issues: (1) shifting revenue between reporting periods and (2) one-time expenses related to the Knogo acquisition. Upon the announcement of extended audit, Sensormatic share price dropped by a further 17 percent.

Sandwiched between the bad news in early July and the bad news in late August, moreover, was the disclosure of shareholder class-action lawsuits. Three shareholders filed lawsuits after the stock drop in July, claiming the company lowered reserves for risky accounts while its revenues and receivables increased dramatically. According to these lawsuits, Sensormatic made earnings look better by lowering reserves for doubtful accounts.

However, some investors believed that the bad news could not overshadow the underlying strengths of Sensormatic's business. On September 15, 1995, billionaire investor George Soros filed forms with the Securities and Exchange Commission disclosing his 6 percent stake, valued at about $104 million, in Sensormatic.

On October 3, 1995, Sensormatic released financial results for the fourth quarter and fiscal year 1995, following the completion of an expanded audit. The expanded audit identified two accounting problems. First, in certain instances, the company booked sales in a quarter for products that were physically shipped several days following the quarter's end. Correcting for this error would shift $35 million in revenues from fiscal 1995 to 1996. Second, related to Sensormatic's acquisition of Knogo Corporation's international operations, the company capitalized items that should have been expensed. The company was estimated to take a one-time nonrecurring charge of about $8 million in fiscal 1995 to correct for this error.

Sensormatic's management stated that the extended audit results suggested that improper accounting was not material to Sensormatic. One analyst said, "It is definitely a sigh of relief that this accounting issue is behind us. The disaster many feared—and some hoped for—didn't occur."[9] With no major surprises, on October 3, 1995, Sensormatic's share slipped 12 cents to $22.88 in normal trading volume.

After this audit was over, Assaf, the CEO and chairman of Sensormatic, stated:

The fourth-quarter earnings disappointment, the audit adjustments, and the third-quarter restatement demonstrate a need to better assure compliance with our financial and administrative controls. However, the accounting issues related to extended audit are different from the attack made by short-sellers. [Short-sellers] have been

9. Excerpts from the Wall Street Journal, October 3, 1995.

attacking our accounting for a year, and there is nothing wrong with our accounting [related to short-sellers' arguments].[10]

On October 5, 1995, Sensormatic issued a 20-page White Paper as a response to allegations that its accounting methods did not give an accurate picture of the company's financial position. At the end of October, 1995, Sensormatic's share price remained at $21 and had a short position of 6 million shares (see Exhibits 4 and 5).

QUESTIONS

1. Customer financing is a key element of Sensormatic's business strategy. What are the benefits and risks of this strategy? What is your assessment of how the company is managing the associated risks?

2. Sensormatic's management provided a partial description of the accounting consequences of its customer financing strategy in Exhibit 1. Identify all the transactions Sensormatic undertakes in association with this strategy. Estimate, in as much detail as possible, the effects of this strategy on Sensormatic's income statement, balance sheet, and cash flow statement in 1995.

3. Do you consider Sensormatic's accounting estimates for potential customer defaults appropriate? Evaluate the relative merits of Barron's concerns about this accounting, and the company's response? What else should the management do?

4. At the end of October 1995, while short sellers were betting that Sensormatic's stock was overvalued, George Soros seemed to view the stock as a good investment. Based on the company's fundamentals, what is your assessment?

----

10. *Short-sellers sell borrowed shares of stock, betting the price will fall so they can profit when they buy the shares back later. Short-selling is inherently riskier than ordinary investing. If you sell a stock short, the share price can rise an unlimited amount, allowing the potential for unlimited losses. If you buy a stock "long"—betting the price will go up—you can only lose what you invested.*

EXHIBIT 1

Sensormatic Electronics Corporation: Example of Accounting Treatment of Alternative Revenue Transactions

Contract Terms

Date of Contract: 1/1/95   Date of Shipment: 1/15/95   Date of Installation: 2/15/95

	Accounts Receivable	Deferred Receivable	Installment Receivable	Sales-Type Leases
Contract Price:				
Sales Price	$1,000	$1,000	$1,000	n/a
Monthly Payments	n/a	n/a	$20.50	$21.00
Stated Interest Rate	n/a	n/a	8.50%	none
Payment Terms:				
Single Payment due	3/15/95	7/15/95	n/a	n/a
Monthly Payments due:				
# of months	n/a	n/a	60	60
Final payment due	n/a	n/a	1/15/00	1/15/00
Market Interest Rate				
(based on length of contract)	n/a	6%	9.50%	9.50%

Income Statement Recognition (for quarter ended 3/31/95)

Revenue	$1,000	$971	$976	$1,000
Cost	450	450	450	450
Gross Profit	$550	$521	$526	$550

Balance Sheet Recognition (at June 30, 1995)

Account Receivable	$1,000			
Deferred Receivable		$971		
Installment Receivable			$976	
Net Investment in Sales-Type Lease				$1,000

Source: White Paper, Sensormatic Electronics Corp., September 1995.

Sensormatic Electronics Corporation

Sensormatic Electronics Corporation

EXHIBIT 2

Bad Debt Expense as a Percent of Revenues

% of Revenues

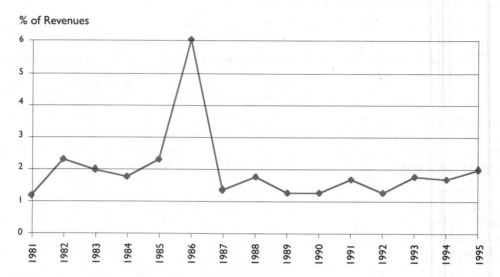

Source: White Paper, Sensormatic Electronics Corp., September 1995.

EXHIBIT 3

Year-End Allowance as a Percent of Gross Receivables

% of Gross
Receivables

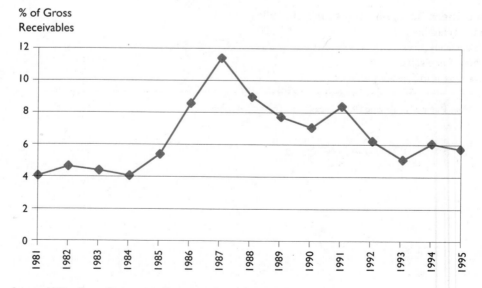

Source: White Paper, Sensormatic Electronics Corp., September 1995.

EXHIBIT 4

Sensormatic's Share Price from October 1994 to October 1995

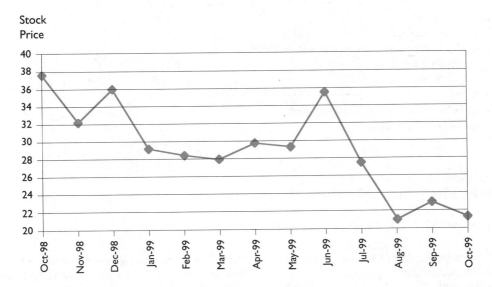

Source: White Paper, Sensormatic Electronics Corp., September 1995.

EXHIBIT 5

Sensormatic Shares Sold Short from October 1994 to October 1995

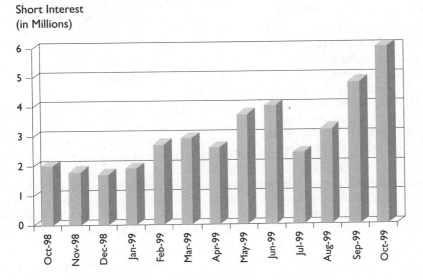

Source: White Paper, Sensormatic Electronics Corp., September 1995.

Sensormatic Electronics Corporation

EXHIBIT 6

Data for Valuation

Sensormatic equity beta*	1.10
Treasury bill rate in December 1995 (3 months)**	5.08%
Government 30-year treasuries rate in December 1995**	6.75%
Sensormatic corporate bond average yield**	8.21%
US federal statutory tax rate in 1995	34%

* Source: Value Line Investment Survey, October 20, 1995.

** Source: Bloomberg Financial Analysis.

EXHIBIT 7

Sensormatic Electronics 1995 Annual Report - Edited

LETTER TO SHAREHOLDERS, CUSTOMERS AND EMPLOYEES:

Fiscal 1995 was a year of both successes and disappointments for Sensormatic. The successes we achieved were significant, and provide us with great confidence for the future. Revenue grew 36 percent, with increases across the board—18 percent for U.S. retail, 53 percent for Asia/Pacific, 40 percent for Europe and 36 percent for exports to Latin America, Eastern Europe and the Middle East. Most impressively, revenues for our commercial/industrial business grew 73 percent to $213 million worldwide and now account for approximately one-fourth of our businesses, compared with just 3 percent five years ago.

This revenue growth clearly demonstrates the strength of our business in all segments of the electronic security industry. We have almost doubled our business over the past two years and before that, doubled it more than two times in nine years. We have grown from a single-focus retail loss prevention company to a large, diversified operation providing turnkey, integrated electronic security systems for retail and commercial/industrial establishments across the globe.

In 1995 we continued to make the investments required of a leader. We strengthened our product and market breadth with strategic acquisitions, including the operations of Knogo Corporation outside North America; Software House, Inc., a leading supplier of high-end Access Control systems; Case Security Limited, a leading supplier of security systems to the U.K. financial industry; and Glen Industrial Communications, Inc., one of the leading U.S. systems integrators.

We introduced new products using innovative technology, including Rapid Pad II, an improved, lower-cost

Ultra-Max deactivator; a new line of Video Managers that can integrate CCTV systems with any PC or software system; and SensorStrip, a new electromagnetic label designed for source tagging in Europe.

To better serve our customers, we implemented a "Customer Care" program company wide. In the U.S., this includes a fully computerized Customer Response Center, providing 24-hour access to Sensormatic's sales and service organizations; a "Help Desk," providing expert technical and product information to Sensormatic representatives; and a national Operations Group to service customers when product installations extend beyond regional lines. We are undertaking similar initiatives internationally. In addition, we increased the number of customer service engineers supporting our global customer base to over 1,600 worldwide.

To continue building our commercial/industrial business, we restructured our product companies—Robot Research, American Dynamics, Software House and Continental Instruments—into the Security Product Division (SPD). With a single organization, we will be better able to coordinate, control and expand our product offerings to our dealers. In April, we established the first non-U.S. office of SPD in Paris, which will serve as the headquarters of SPD's European operations.

Despite our customer and product successes, which generated impressive revenue growth, we failed to meet our earnings targets this year. Our fourth quarter earnings shortfall and an extensive year-end examination by our auditors graphically demonstrated that in focusing on revenue growth, we have grown the Company faster than the management organization. As a consequence, we stretched our management resources—with adverse bottom-line results.

Contributing to our disappointing results were the following:

Expenses grew significantly faster than revenues, particularly in the second half of the fiscal year.

The integration of the Knogo European operations was slower and more costly than anticipated.

Revenues from three of our four international units were below forecast, impacting overall margins.

A downward restatement of our third quarter results was required primarily due to the premature recognition of revenue on certain shipments made after quarter-end and on certain shipments subject to non-standard contractual terms.

As a result of these problems, we initiated immediate corrective action.

We centralized all financial activities that formerly reported to the individual Business Units. This will provide for closer corporate control, as well as improve the speed of reporting.

We are implementing a company-wide expense reduction program, intended to reduce corporate operating expenses by 10 percent.

We are increasing throughput at our Irish production plant to increase margins.

We initiated programs to improve inventory turns and accelerated the collection of receivables. Improving our cash flow and reducing debt and related interest expense is a key priority.

Most importantly, we are pleased to announce the appointment of Bob Vanourek as President and Chief Operating Officer. Previously, Bob was President and Chief Executive Officer of Recognition International, Inc., an international provider of document processing hardware, software and services. He has more than 25 years' experience in marketing and general management, including eight years at Pitney Bowes and several years' experience in our industry. We welcome Bob and look forward to his contributions to Sensormatic's continued growth in the months and years to come.

Despite the disappointments of the past year, the fundamentals of our business remain strong. Our market is large and growing. Our leadership position is intact. As we address the financial and administrative issues described above, we will continue to pursue our many growth opportunities by:

- Increasing global market penetration;
- Accelerating source tagging;
- Building and marketing our systems integration capabilities for both retail and commercial/industrial customers.

And finally, to help shareholders better understand the uniqueness of our business and measure our progress against the objectives outlined above, with this annual report, we have expanded the discussion of our lines of business and the presentation of our financial results. We are committed to achieving and maintaining the highest standards of performance in all aspects of our business—for employees, customers, and fellow investors.

Ronald G. Assaf
Chairman of the Board and Chief Executive Officer

October 16, 1995

MANAGEMENT'S DISCUSSION AND ANALYSIS OF FINANCIAL CONDITION AND RESULTS OF OPERATIONS (edited by the case writers)

The Company's consolidated financial statements present a consolidation of its worldwide operations. This discussion supplements the detailed information presented in the Consolidated Financial Statements and Notes thereto and is intended to assist the reader in understanding the financial results and condition of the Company.

Overview

Consolidated revenues increased 36% in fiscal 1995 compared to fiscal 1994, and 35% and 57% in fiscal 1994 and 1993, respectively, over the prior years, rep-

resenting an annual compounded growth rate of 42% over the last three fiscal years. This growth rate is largely attributable to successfully implementing a strategy of product, customer and geographic market diversification. More than 52% of fiscal 1995 revenues were generated from outside of the United States.

The Company's increased internal product research, development and engineering activities resulting in a broad array of new proprietary products, as well as selected strategic acquisitions over the last several years, have been a key element in the diversification strategy. The Company invested $25.5 million in fiscal

1995, and anticipates investing approximately $31.0 million in fiscal 1996, in research and product development and engineering support. These activities will contribute to broadening product lines and expanding product applications. Introduction of new products into the market place will be made in accordance with its strategic marketing plans.

Additionally, the Company has made a number of strategic acquisitions over the last several years including Security Tag Systems, Inc. (Security Tag), a U.S.-based manufacturer and marketer of loss prevention products, Software House, Inc. (Software House), a premier U.S.-based developer of high-end Access Control and integrated security systems, Robot Research Inc. (Robot Research), a U.S. manufacturer of sophisticated CCTV equipment, and Case Security Limited (Case Security), a distributor of visual security systems, and Automated Loss Prevention Systems (ALPS), as well as the merger with Knogo Corporation's operations outside of the U.S., Puerto Rico and Canada (Knogo), all under the diversification strategy (see Note 11 to Notes to Consolidated Financial Statements).

The acquisitions of Knogo and ALPS significantly broadened the Company's presence and direct distribution capacity in Europe. The acquisitions of Software House, Robot Research and Case Security, as well as American Dynamics and Continental Instruments Corporation in fiscal 1991 and 1990, respectively, broadened the Company's customer base by adding new proprietary products and distribution channels aimed at commercial, industrial and other non-retail customers.

Another strategy is to focus on expanding the Company's base of recurring revenues. Recurring revenues are generated from sales of disposable labels to the hard goods retailers, maintenance agreements entered into in connection with the sale or lease of systems, and rental revenues from operating leases. The latter is a particular focus of the marketing efforts of certain European and Asia/Pacific subsidiaries. In fiscal 1995, recurring revenues were approximately $152 million compared to approximately $120 million and $106 million in fiscal 1994 and 1993, respectively. The sale of disposable labels to the hard goods retailers is the fastest growing component of the recurring revenue stream, growing from less than $4 million in fiscal 1988 to approximately $76 million in fiscal 1995, an annual compounded growth rate of over 52%.

In fiscal 1993, the Company took a major step in its efforts to increase future recurring label revenues through the introduction of its Universal Product Protection (UPPSM) program. Under this program (also referred to as source labeling), EAS labels are incorporated into or affixed to the merchandise to be protected during the process of manufacturing, packaging or distribution rather than at the retail store. At June 30, 1995, over 500 manufacturers and suppliers located worldwide applied the Company's labels to merchandise delivered to retailers' stores. The Company has been working with a number of its retailer customers around the world, from various segments of the soft and hard goods retail marketplace (including retailers from the music, home improvement centers and discount industries), as well as strategic suppliers and manufacturers, to accelerate this initiative.

Operating income in fiscal 1995 decreased 7% from fiscal 1994. This was primarily a result of a 51% increase in selling, customer service and administrative and research, development and engineering expenses (increasing as a percentage of revenue to 46% in fiscal 1995 from 41% in fiscal 1994), including approximately $6.0 million of expenses related to acquisitions, primarily the merger with Knogo. This was partially offset by a 36% increase in product sales earning gross margins of 54% (consistent with fiscal 1994). Operating income as a percentage of total revenues decreased to 11% compared to 16% in fiscal 1994. Operating income in fiscal 1994 increased 48% over fiscal 1993. Growth in operating income outpaced the revenue growth as a result of improved gross margins and a reduction in operating expenses.

Income from continuing operations decreased 3% in fiscal 1995 and increased 33% in fiscal 1994 as a result of the matters discussed above. In addition net income was $74 million for fiscal 1995 compared to $72 million for fiscal 1994. Fiscal 1995 net income included the effects of a $4.1 million reduction of income taxes payable relating to a previously discontinued business, which reserve was no longer required.

Financial Condition

During fiscal 1995, cash and marketable securities increased $16 million primarily due to: (a) increased short-term borrowings ($105 million); (b) proceeds from issuance of Common Stock pursuant to employee benefit plans ($13 million); and (c) a net decrease in deferred and installment receivables and sales-type leases ($14 million). These were offset in part by (a) increased inventory available for sale ($63 million); (b) capital expenditures ($63 million); and (c) the payment of dividends on Common Stock ($16 million).

Total receivables and sales-type leases increased from $309 million at June 30, 1994 to $401 million at June 30, 1995 principally as a result of the higher level of business in fiscal 1995 and from the acquisition of Knogo (approximately $37 million acquired at December 29, 1994); offset in part by an increase in sales of receivables and sales-type leases to third party financing institutions (described further below).

The Company has historically had a high level of receivables and sales-type leases outstanding, measured as a percentage of revenues. This results in part from a key element of the Company's marketing strategy, based on its size and financial strength, to increase market penetration by providing alternative financing options to its retail customers (i.e., vendor financing). This strategy has given the Company a significant competitive advantage and has helped the Company penetrate markets and increase customer loyalty and commitment to Sensormatic. The ability to pursue such a strategy results from the Company's relatively high profit margins, strong balance sheet, and its ability to sell receivables and leases to financing institutions.

Additionally, like other companies which do business with retailers, the Company has experienced an historical pattern of delayed payments by certain major retail customers which has extended the Company's receivables aging profile. Internal approvals and processing of accounts payable for many retailers normally take between 30 and 90 days, which has extended its receivables aging profile. In addition, further delays in payments are often a business practice by large retailers, and not an indication of credit unworthiness. Though working to accelerate collection of receivables, the Company historically has accepted the longer collection cycles as part of its strategy to maintain and further penetrate this important market segment. The lost interest income due to the delayed payment is another cost factor that is considered by the Company in the pricing of the product.

The Company continues to manage its receivables and sales-type leases by, among other things, using third-party servicing agents to enhance the efficiency of its billing and collection practices and expanding the number and use of relationships with third-party financing institutions to sell or assign receivables and sales-type leases (see Note 2. of Notes to Consolidated Financial Statements). The results of these ongoing efforts have been to reduce the average collection time and to provide the Company with the flexibility to convert its receivables and sales-type leases into cash as needed. The Company received proceeds of $458 million and $271 million from the sale and assignment of receivables and sales-type leases in fiscal 1995 and 1994, respectively (net of repurchases due to customer non-payment of approximately $14 million and $13 million, respectively).

Finally, short-term receivables from the Company's slower paying retail customers are becoming a relatively smaller part of its overall business as a result of 1) the expansion of the Company's source labeling program, whereby Sensormatic sells labels to vendors and manufacturers who apply the labels prior to shipment to the retailer; and 2) the continued growth of the commercial/ industrial customer base which is made up of customers which (i) tend to be the higher end commercial/industrial users with higher credit ratings than many retailers and (ii) a closely monitored network of third-party dealers and distributors. In adding this new commercial/industrial customer base to the Company's historical retail customer base, the Company has developed a base of generally faster paying customers.

The Company believes its total allowance for doubtful accounts for receivables and sales-type leases, and its related reserve for receivables and sales-type leases sold to financing institutions which are subject to full or partial recourse, are adequate after taking into account, among other things: (a) the aging of its receivables and sales-type leases (including those repurchased or subject to repurchase from financing institutions); (b) the payment history of its customers; (c) the Company's security interest in equipment financed under deferred and installment sales contracts and the Company's retention of title in equipment under sales-type leases; (d) its ability to re-market such equipment if needed; (e) the prospects of its collection efforts; and (f) its relationship with major retail customers. Additionally, with the broadening of the Company's customer base both geographically and to include hard goods retailers, and commercial and industrial customers, the Company's historical concentration in soft goods retailers is being reduced.

Inventories at June 30, 1995 increased $77 million over June 30, 1994 to meet increased forecasted production and sales levels and reduce the risk of inventory shortages resulting from the rapid growth in market demand. Other property, plant and equipment increased $44 million primarily due to the purchases of additional production equipment in Florida and Puerto Rico and the start-up of the manufacturing facility in Ireland. Deferred income taxes, patents and other assets increased $42 million primarily as a result of increased deferred income taxes and other assets principally related to companies acquired in fiscal 1995.

Total stockholders' equity at June 30, 1995 increased $225 million over the June 30, 1994 balance, to $953 million, principally as a result of the issuance of 4.6 million shares of Common Stock (aggregating $149 million) in connection with acquisitions, and net income.

Total debt increased $108 million over the June 30, 1994 balance, to $327 million, primarily as a result of an increase in short-term credit line borrowings and other debt (approximately $23 million of Knogo debt was incurred as part of the merger). The debt-to-total capitalization ratio was .26 to 1 at June 30, 1995 compared to .23 to 1 at June 30, 1994.

The Company estimates capital requirements for fiscal 1996 to include capital expenditures for new production equipment and a facility to consolidate the Company's research and product development, engineering support, and certain corporate marketing and administrative personnel and equipment at approximately $30 million, and expenditures for research and product development and engineering support at approximately $31 million. Such capital requirements and other expenditures will be funded through operating activities (including sale of receivables and sales-type leases), existing cash and marketable securities and worldwide credit lines (see Note 6. of Notes to Consolidated Financial Statements).

Additionally, future niche acquisitions, a fundamental element of the Company's diversification and growth strategy, may be funded, when deemed appropriate, through the issuance of shares of Sensormatic Common Stock. The Company maintains a shelf registration statement filed with the Securities and Exchange Commission under which the Company is able to issue up to 4.5 million shares of its Common Stock (approximately 2.5 million shares remain available).

Results from Continuing Operations

Revenues. Consolidated revenues for fiscal 1995 were $889 million, a 36% increase from $656 million in fiscal 1994. The revenue growth in 1995 resulted principally from: (a) increased EAS revenues, particularly from the Ultra-Max product line, primarily for hard goods retail customers and used in source labeling programs; (b) increased CCTV product volume from retailers; (c) increased volume from the U.S.-based Commercial/Industrial Group; and (d) the foreign exchange effect on the international subsidiaries' local currency revenues when translated into U.S. dollars for financial statement purposes caused by the weaker average U.S. dollar (relative to the international subsidiaries' local currencies, in the aggregate) throughout fiscal 1995 compared to fiscal 1994 (approximately $3 million).

Consolidated revenues from the EAS product lines for retail customers increased 25% to $511 million in fiscal 1995 compared to $406 million in fiscal 1994. This increase resulted principally from a 47% volume increase from the Ultra-Max product line and the inclusion in the last six months of fiscal 1995 of reve-

nues from the Knogo product line ($29 million). Revenues from the CCTV product lines for retailers exceeded $112 million compared to $72 million in fiscal 1994. Revenues from the Commercial/Industrial Group (including installation revenues) increased 83%, to $143 million compared to $78 million in fiscal 1994, due primarily to the sale of CCTV and Access Control products to non-retail customers, and incremental revenue from recent acquisitions. Revenues from the Company's CamEra™ systems increased 38% to $66 million in fiscal 1995 compared to $48 million in fiscal 1994. The Company generated $256 million of revenue in fiscal 1995 from all of its CCTV products and systems combined, worldwide.

International revenues were $468 million, $333 million and $267 million in fiscal 1995, 1994 and 1993, respectively, and included revenues of the European subsidiaries of $386 million, $275 million and $232 million, respectively.

In fiscal 1994, consolidated revenues increased $169 million (35%) compared to fiscal 1993 principally as a result of increased revenue from the Ultra-Max product line, inclusion of revenue from the Security Tag EAS and Ink Tag® product lines, increased revenues from the sale of CCTV products to retailers, and increased revenues from the Commercial/ Industrial Group; offset in part by the foreign exchange effect caused by the stronger average U.S. dollar (approximately $34 million).

In fiscal 1993, consolidated revenues increased $177 million (57%) compared to fiscal 1992 principally as a result of the inclusion of revenues generated from ALPS products, increased worldwide revenues in every EAS product line for the hard goods retailers, increased revenues from the sale of CCTV products to retailers and increased revenues from the Commercial/Industrial Group.

Operating Costs and Expenses. Operating costs and expenses in fiscal 1995 increased to 89% of consolidated revenues, compared with 84% in fiscal 1994 and 85% in fiscal 1993. The reduced operating margin in fiscal 1995 was due primarily to: 1) higher than budgeted selling and customer service expenses (in part due to the opening of a distribution center and a customer response center in the U.S., and activities associated with the expansion of the source labeling program); 2) significant integration costs and expenses related to acquisitions, primarily Knogo (approximately $6 million); 3) costs associated with the opening of the manufacturing facility in Ireland; and 4) expenses associated with the Company's sponsorship of the 1996 Summer Olympics.

Gross margin on product sales in fiscal 1995 remained at 54% compared to fiscal 1994. Gross margin on product sales in fiscal 1994 increased to 54% from 53% in fiscal 1993, primarily from improved gross margins on certain EAS and CCTV product lines (resulting from improved manufacturing efficiencies) and the inclusion of the manufacturer's gross margin (as a result of the acquisition of Security Tag) on the Security Tag product line; offset in part by a relative increase in sales of lower margin products (such as CCTV products and labels) compared to fiscal 1993.

Total selling and customer service, administrative, research, development and engineering expenses (operating expenses) for fiscal 1995 increased to 46%, as a percentage of total consolidated revenues, from 41% in fiscal 1994, and increased 51% over fiscal 1994, primarily as a result of higher selling and customer service expenses including significant integration costs of the Knogo operations in Europe. The increases in operating expenses include the foreign exchange effect caused by the weaker average U.S. dollar (approximately $15 million). Operating expenses in fiscal 1994 and 1993 increased 31% and 62% over the respective prior fiscal year primarily as a result of the higher levels of business (including the effect of the ALPS acquisition in fiscal 1993) and an increase in research, development and engineering expenses of 31% and 20% over the respective prior years; offset in part by the foreign exchange effect caused by the stronger average U.S. dollar in fiscal 1994 compared to 1993 ($14 million).

Other Income (Expenses). Interest income increased by $3 million in fiscal 1995 principally due to higher amounts of sales-type leases and deferred and installment receivables outstanding throughout fiscal 1995 compared to fiscal 1994. Interest income declined by $3 million in fiscal 1994 due primarily to a decline in long-term interest rates throughout the year earned on higher amounts of sales-type leases and deferred and installment receivables. In fiscal 1993 interest income increased by $10 million principally due to interest income earned on sales-type leases acquired in connection with the ALPS acquisition and higher amounts of deferred and installment receivables.

Interest expense increased by $6 million, $4 million and $7 million in fiscal 1995, 1994 and 1993, respectively, due to higher levels of net short-term bank borrowings used to fund (i) increases in the Company's working capital (including the longer-term receivables and sales-type leases) and (ii) in fiscal 1995, debt assumed as part of the acquisition of Knogo and increased long-term debt in fiscal 1993, incurred with respect to the acquisition of ALPS. As previously mentioned, the Company

entered into three-year interest rate swaps in fiscal 1993 to lower its current interest expense on the $135 million 8.21% Senior Notes by exchanging their fixed interest rate for a floating interest rate based on six month LIBOR rates (throughout the term of the swap agreements) in order to take advantage of the then lower prevailing short-term interest rates. The effective rate on the Senior Notes was approximately 9.2%, 6.8% and 6.8% in fiscal 1995, 1994 and 1993 through the use of these swap agreements.

Income Taxes

The effective consolidated tax rate on income from continuing operations was 22% for fiscal 1995, and 25% for both fiscal 1994 and 1993. The fiscal 1995 effective tax rate was negatively affected by (i) earnings of the Company's international subsidiaries which are subject to statutory tax rates generally higher than the U.S. effective rate, (ii) increases in U.S. earnings not qualifying for U.S./Puerto Rico "Section 936" tax benefits (see Note 5. Of Notes to Consolidated Financial Statements) and (iii) increases in amortization of costs in excess of net assets acquired (substantially all of which are non-deductible for income tax purposes). However, these effects were offset by an adjustment of prior years' tax accruals which were no longer required. In addition to the items above, changes in U.S. and Puerto Rico tax law related to the Company's operations in Puerto Rico (effective for fiscal 1995), as well as potentially more adverse changes presently being considered by the U.S. Congress, will continue to exert upward pressure on the Company's effective tax rate. Legislation proposals in the U.S. Congress in recent years have sought to limit or phase out the favorable tax status in Puerto Rico. The potential effect of these items is continually being examined by the Company in order to develop strategies to minimize their effect.

Discontinued Operations

In fiscal 1995, the Company recorded a $4.1 million reduction in income tax liabilities related to a previously discontinued business which was no longer required.

Net Income

Consolidated net income for fiscal 1995, 1994 and 1993 increased $2 million, $18 million and $23 million compared to their respective prior years, representing an annual compounded rate of growth of 33% over the last three fiscal years, due principally to the factors discussed above.

Sensormatic Electronics Corporation

Sensormatic Electronics Corporation

CONSOLIDATED BALANCE SHEETS
June 30, 1995 and 1994 (In thousands, except par value amounts)

	1995	1994
ASSETS		
Cash and marketable securities (including marketable securities of $26,727 in 1995 and $33,618 in 1994)	$ 70,307	$ 54,542
Accounts receivable, net	221,873	134,517
Deferred and installment receivables, net	67,843	64,375
Net investment in sales-type leases	110,942	109,607
Inventories, net	240,807	163,906
Revenue equipment, less accumulated depreciation of $46,439 in 1995 and $36,183 in 1994	49,920	58,326
Other property, plant and equipment, net	150,957	107,152
Deferred income taxes, patents and other assets, less accumulated amortization of $17,685 in 1995 and $13,114 in 1994	161,614	120,061
Costs in excess of net assets acquired, less accumulated amortization of $29,863 in 1995 and $17,930 in 1994	496,641	343,017
	$1,570,904	$1,155,503
LIABILITIES AND STOCKHOLDERS' EQUITY		
Accounts payable	$ 63,314	$ 40,884
Accrued liabilities	209,091	143,067
Accrued and deferred income taxes payable	19,059	24,687
Debt	326,710	219,173
Commitments and contingencies		
Stockholders' equity:		
Preferred stock, $.01 par value, 10,000 shares authorized, none issued; Common stock, $.01 par value, 125,000 shares authorized, 73,023 and 67,612 shares outstanding in 1995 and 1994, respectively	713,866	546,577
Retained earnings	295,680	237,553
Treasury stock at cost and other, 1,095 shares in 1995 and 1,162 shares in 1994	(13,222)	(10,835)
Currency translation adjustments	(43,594)	(45,603)
Total stockholders' equity	952,730	727,692
	$1,570,904	$1,155,503

CONSOLIDATED STATEMENTS OF INCOME
June 30, 1995, 1994 and 1993 (In thousands, except par value amounts)

	1995	1994	1993
Revenues:			
Sales	$762,375	$557,393	$398,122
Rentals	50,601	46,566	46,021
Other	76,107	52,007	43,176
Total revenues	889,083	655,966	487,319
Operating costs and expenses:			
Costs of sales	353,990	256,003	188,138
Depreciation on revenue equipment	16,327	14,974	15,394
Selling, customer service & administrative	383,583	251,933	192,077
Research, development and engineering	22,666	18,023	13,739
Amortization of intangible assets	14,598	10,246	6,963
Total operating costs and expenses	791,164	551,179	416,311
Operating income	97,919	104,787	71,008
Other income (expenses):			
Interest income	17,221	14,262	17,114
Interest expense	(28,989)	(22,711)	(18,656)
Other, net	2,900	(373)	2,518
Total other income (expenses)	(8,868)	(8,822)	976
Income from continuing operations before income taxes	89,051	95,965	71,984
Provision for income taxes	19,500	23,900	17,900
Income from continuing operations	69,551	72,065	54,084
Discontinued operations - adjustment of prior year amounts (Note 5)	4,100	—	—
Net income	$ 73,651	$ 72,065	$ 54,084
Primary earnings per common share:			
Continuing operations	$ .97	$1.16	$ .97
Discontinued operations	.05	—	—
Net income	$1.02	$1.16	$ .97
Fully diluted earnings per common share:			
Continuing operations	$ .97	$1.13	$ .93
Discontinued operations	.05	—	—
Net income	$1.02	$1.13	$ .93

Sensormatic Electronics Corporation

CONSOLIDATED STATEMENTS OF CASH FLOWS
June 30, 1995, 1994 and 1993 (In thousands, except par value amounts)

Sensormatic Electronics Corporation

	1995	1994	1993
Cash flows from operating activities:			
Income from continuing operations	$69,551	$72,065	$54,084
Adjustments to reconcile income from continuing operations to net cash provided by (used in) operating activities:			
Depreciation	26,705	22,603	21,446
Amortization	14,615	11,681	7,917
Other non-cash charges to operations, net	19,993	11,502	9,508
Net changes in operating assets and liabilities, net of effects of acquisitions:			
Inventories	(63,589)	(56,333)	(6,299)
Net investment in sales-type leases	17,194	(42,269)	(9,824)
Accounts receivable and receivables from financing institutions	(77,294)	(23,858)	(52,742)
Deferred and installment receivables	(3,099)	(9,268)	12,277
Other assets	(9,497)	(31,345)	1,541
Accrued liabilities	3,197	13,506	14,320
Accounts payable	15,108	10,801	(2,778)
Income taxes	(3,830)	7,473	12,631
Net cash provided by (used in) operating activities	9,054	(13,442)	62,081
Cash flows from investing activities:			
Capital expenditures	(62,972)	(51,835)	(26,735)
Purchases of marketable securities	(843)	(18,178)	(8,921)
Maturities of marketable securities	7,717	13,294	24,262
Increase in revenue equipment and available for lease	(3,959)	(17,033)	(35,177)
Acquisitions (net of cash acquired of $6,687 in 1995, $1,135 in 1994 and $8,223 in 1993)	(9,587)	(11,467)	(299,342)
Other, net	5,696	5,676	2,837
Net cash used in investing activities	(63,948)	(79,543)	(343,076)
Cash flows from financing activities:			
Bank borrowings and other debt	105,370	30,500	128,271
Proceeds from issuances of common stock under employee benefit plans and for acquisitions	12,902	17,167	212,154
Cash dividends	(15,524)	(12,530)	(10,588)
Repayments of bank borrowings and other debt	(25,198)	(10,329)	(109,934)
Issuance of Senior Notes, net	—	—	134,111
Net cash provided by financing activities	77,550	24,808	354,014
Net increase (decrease) in cash	22,656	(68,177)	73,019
Cash at beginning of year	20,924	89,101	16,082
Cash at end of period	43,580	20,924	89,101
Marketable securities at end of year	26,727	33,618	28,798
Cash and marketable securities at end of year	$70,307	$54,542	$117,899

NOTES TO CONSOLIDATED FINANCIAL STATEMENTS

Note 1. Summary of significant accounting policies

a. Basis of presentation. The Consolidated Financial Statements include the accounts of Sensormatic Electronics Corporation and all of its subsidiaries (the Company). All significant intercompany balances and transactions have been eliminated.

The accompanying Consolidated Balance Sheets are presented in a format which does not segregate current assets and current liabilities. As a result of the constantly changing mix of inventories and revenue equipment sold and leased, including sales of equipment originally installed under lease contracts, it is not possible to accurately determine the amount of revenue equipment that will be sold and thus realized currently. The Company believes presentation of its financial position in the non-classified format avoids misunderstandings as to the relationships of current and non-current assets and liabilities. However, information with respect to the current and non-current nature of certain assets and liabilities is included in Notes below.

b. Cash and marketable securities. The Company classifies cash equivalents (highly liquid investments with a maturity of three months or less when acquired) as cash. Effective July 1, 1994, the Company adopted FASB Statement No. 115 "Accounting for Certain Investments in Debt and Equity Securities." In accordance with FASB 115, the Company has classified certain of its non-equity investments as available-for-sale securities which are carried at market value (versus cost or amortized cost prior to the adoption of FASB 115). Unrealized gains and losses are recorded, net of tax, in Stockholders' equity ($0.3 million loss at June 30, 1995).

c. Inventories. Inventories are stated at the lower of cost (first-in, first-out) or market.

d. Revenue equipment and other property, plant and equipment. Revenue equipment (principally equipment on lease) and other property, plant and equipment (including assets acquired under capital leases) are recorded at cost and depreciated using the straight-line method over their estimated useful lives (4 years and 6 years for revenue equipment, 10 years through 40 years for buildings and improvements and 3 years through 10 years for other property, plant and equipment).

e. Revenue recognition. Revenue from sales of equipment is recognized when a customer takes title to the product, in accordance with the terms agreed upon by the parties (i.e. "FOB Shipping Point," "FOB Destination," acceptance of a customer order to purchase presently installed equipment or acceptance by a third party leasing company of an operating lease and the related equipment). Payment terms are either cash and/or acceptance of deferred term (i.e., extended payment terms normally not greater than 365 days) or installment obligations (generally with terms of 60 months) subject to stated or imputed interest, and are generally secured. Revenue from sales-type leases (primarily with terms of 60 months or greater) is recognized as a "sale" upon receipt of a customer order and shipment in an amount equal to the present value of the minimum rental payments under the fixed non-cancelable lease term. Interest income on deferred and installment obligations and net investment in sales-type leases is recognized over the term of the contract using the effective interest method.

The Company also leases equipment under long-term operating leases (primarily leases with terms of 36 to 54 months) which are generally non-cancelable. Rental revenues are recognized as earned over the term of the lease. Minimum future rentals on non-cancelable operating leases at June 30, 1995 aggregated (in millions) $107.2 and are due as follows: 1996 - $32.4; 1997 - $25.8; 1998 - $22.0; 1999 - $15.5 and 2000 - $11.5.

Service revenues are recognized as earned and maintenance revenues are recognized ratably over the service contract term.

f. Research, development and engineering. In fiscal 1995, 1994 and 1993 "Research, development and engineering" included research and development expenses of $18.2 million, $14.7 million and $11.9 million, respectively.

g. Accounting for currency translation and transactions. The Company's international subsidiaries' assets and liabilities are translated into U.S. dollars at the rate of exchange in effect at their balance sheet dates and their revenues, costs and expenses are translated into U.S. dollars at the average rate of exchange in effect during their respective fiscal years. Translation adjustments resulting therefrom and transaction gains or losses attributable to certain intercompany transactions are excluded from results of operations and accumulated in a separate component of consolidated stockholders' equity. Gains and losses attributable to other intercompany transactions are included in results of operations.

Sensormatic Electronics Corporation

The Company has a policy of not hedging its investment in the net assets of its international subsidiaries (aggregating $370 million and $250 million at June 30, 1995 and 1994, respectively, primarily located in 15 countries in Europe) against exchange rate fluctuations due to the high economic costs of such a program and the long-term nature of its investments. The gains and losses resulting from these exchange rate fluctuations ($2.0 million and $15.9 million net gain in fiscal 1995 and fiscal 1994, respectively) are excluded from results of operations and accumulated in a separate component of consolidated stockholders' equity.

The Company has a policy of purchasing forward exchange contracts (forward contracts) and options designated to hedge certain identifiable, foreign currency anticipatory, intercompany commitments. Forward contracts and options are stated at cost, if any. Market value gains or losses resulting from such forward contracts and options, and from the related hedged commitments, occurring in periods prior to the period in which they are settled, are deferred, to be recognized in the period when they are settled. Cash flows resulting from the settlement of the forward contracts and options are included in cash provided by operating activities.

Net currency exchange gains (losses) in fiscal 1995, 1994 and 1993 resulting from the settlement of intercompany transfers of products manufactured in Florida and Puerto Rico and sold to certain international subsidiaries were (in millions) $3.0, $0.7 and ($0.1), respectively. Additionally, non-recurring net currency exchange gains of $2.2 million and $1.3 million were recognized in fiscal 1995 and 1993, respectively, after the Knogo and ALPS acquisitions. Net currency exchange gains are included in "Other income (expenses)" in the Consolidated Statements of Income.

h. Intangible assets. Patents, stated at cost, are amortized using the straight-line method over 17 years. Costs in excess of net assets acquired are amortized using the straight-line method over 20 to 40 years. The carrying value of costs in excess of net assets acquired (or goodwill) will be reviewed if the facts and circumstances suggest that it may be impaired. If this review indicates the goodwill will not be fully recoverable over the remaining amortization period, as determined based on the estimated undiscounted cash flows of the assets acquired, the carrying value of the goodwill will be adjusted accordingly. (See Notes 1k. and 11.)

i. Interest rate instruments. The differential to be paid or received on interest rate swap agreements and interest rate cap agreements (interest rate instruments) is accrued as interest rates change and is recognized as an adjustment to interest expense. Premiums paid or received for the early termination of interest rate instruments will be amortized into interest expense over the remaining original term of the instruments should the Company elect to terminate any of the interest rate instruments prior to their expiration date. Interest rate instruments are stated at cost, if any.

j. Primary and fully diluted earnings per common share. Primary earnings per common share is calculated based on the weighted average number of common shares and dilutive common stock equivalents outstanding during the period. Common stock equivalents include stock options issued under employee benefit plans and common stock warrants. Fully diluted earnings per common share in 1993 and 1994 included the if-converted dilutive effect of the 7% Convertible Subordinated Debentures due in 2001 which were fully converted in May 1994.

k. Prospective accounting changes. In March 1995, FASB Statement No. 121 "Accounting for the Impairment of Long-Lived Assets and for Long-Lived Assets to Be Disposed Of" was issued. FASB 121 requires impairment losses to be recorded on long-lived assets (e.g., revenue equipment, property, plant and equipment, patents and costs in excess of net assets acquired related to such assets) used in operations when impairment indicators are present and the undiscounted cash flows estimated to be generated by those assets are less than the assets' carrying amount. FASB 121 also addresses the accounting for long-lived assets that are expected to be disposed of.

The Company will adopt the provisions of FASB 121 in the first quarter of fiscal 1996 and, based on current circumstances, does not believe the effect of adoption will be material.

In July 1995, the Emerging Issues Task Force (EITF) reached a consensus which narrows the scope of intercompany foreign currency commitments which are eligible to be hedged for financial reporting purposes. This applies to transactions arising after July 21, 1995. The Company has not completed the complex analyses and comprehensive study of this matter to either estimate its current or future effect on the Company's operating results or hedging strategy. However, the Company believes it can modify its current hedging practices in order to comply with the new consensus without having a materially adverse effect on its financial condition.

l. Reclassifications. Certain amounts in the prior years' Consolidated Financial Statements have been reclassified to conform to the current fiscal year's presentation.

Sensormatic Electronics Corporation

Note 2. Receivables and net investment in sales-type leases

Accounts receivable are stated net of an allowance for doubtful accounts of $13.5 million and $10.4 million at June 30, 1995 and 1994, respectively.

Net deferred receivables ($24.5 million and $30.5 million outstanding at June 30, 1995 and 1994, respectively) and installment receivables are stated net of the following (at June 30, in millions):

	1995	1994
Allowance for doubtful accounts	$ 5.5	$ 6.4
Unearned interest and maintenance	$24.4	$19.5

The Company leases equipment under sales-type lease agreements expiring in various years through 2002. The net investment in sales-type leases consisted of the following (at June 30, in millions):

	1995	1994
Minimum lease payments receivable	$168.8	$151.6
Allowance for uncollectible minimum lease payments	(7.5)	(3.4)
Unearned interest and maintenance	(50.4)	(38.6)
	$110.9	$109.6

Net receivables and sales-type leases at June 30, 1995 are due as follows (in millions): 1996 - $252.0 and 21.2; 1997 - $12.7 and $22.8; 1998 - $11.8 and $21.8; 1999 - $8.9 and $21.3; 2000 - $4.4 and $18.2, respectively, and with respect to sales-type leases (in millions): $5.6 thereafter.

The Company has agreements with third-party financing institutions whereby certain installment receivables in the United States (U.S.) and sales-type leases in Europe together with certain related rights are sold to the financing institutions. Under such agreements, should certain events occur (principally related to customer non-payment or other customer-related defaults), the Company is obligated to repurchase the specific receivables and sales-type leases.

Under the principal agreement in the U.S., the Company sells fixed interest rate receivables to the financing institution. Under such agreement, the financing institution earns interest throughout the term of the receivables at a floating rate of interest indexed to one month LIBOR. Any resulting differential in interest caused by the varying interest rates (variance amounts) is either paid or received by the Company. In order to manage the risk associated with the variance amounts, the Company enters into interest rate instruments for notional amounts (on a portfolio basis) equal to the outstanding principal amounts of receivables sold. This results in offsetting interest rate differential payments or receipts thereby limiting the variance amounts paid or received by the Company.

Additionally, the Company has an agreement with a third-party financing institution whereby the Company may assign certain pre-approved U.S. accounts receivable. At June 30, 1995 and 1994, receivables assigned and outstanding under such agreement were $79.7 million and $57.9 million, respectively, (substantially all of which were not subject to recourse resulting from the customer's inability to pay) of which the financing institution had advanced in anticipation of their collection $74.6 million and $50 million, respectively, to the Company (bearing interest at fluctuating rates, 6.5% and 4.9% at June 30, 1995 and 1994, respectively).

The Company received proceeds of $458.1 million and $270.5 million upon the sale and assignment of receivables and leases under these agreements in fiscal 1995 and 1994, respectively (net of repurchases due to customer non-payment of approximately $12.6 million and $12.8 million, respectively). The uncollected principal balance of receivables and leases sold which is subject to varying amounts of recourse totaled $333.0 million and 199.8 million at June 30, 1995 and 1994, respectively. Adequate reserves have been provided for receivables and leases sold and are included in accrued liabilities.

At June 30, 1995 balances due from financing institutions under these agreements aggregated $8.2 million, are due within one year and are included in "Deferred income taxes, patents and other assets."

At June 30, 1995 and 1994, there were receivables (including those subject to recourse) due from the following sectors of the U.S. retail market which represented a concentration of credit risk to the Company: department and discount stores 1995 - $48.9 million and 1994 - $40.5 million; supermarkets 1995 - $31.9 million and 1994 - $26.2 million; and specialty stores 1995 - $26.2 million and 1994 - $30.7 million. Assuming the obligors under these receivables were to fail to completely perform according to the terms of the receivables at June 30, 1995, the Company estimates it would have incurred a loss with respect to each retail market of approximately $36.1 million, $21.1 million and $21.2 million, respectively, representing the amount of the receivables less any related allowance for doubtful accounts and the estimated realizable value of the collateralized equipment securing these receivables. The Company minimizes its exposure to credit risk through its credit review procedures, col-

Sensormatic Electronics Corporation

lection practices, and its policy of retaining a security interest in the underlying equipment and ability to re-market such repossessed equipment.

The activity in the allowance for doubtful accounts related to receivables and sales-type leases during fiscal 1995, 1994 and 1993 is as follows (in millions):

	1995	1994	1993
Beginning of year	$20.1	$13.5	$10.6
Additions charged to income	19.6	11.0	8.8
Amounts written off, net	(15.5)	(6.1)	(5.6)
Other (including currency translation)	2.2	1.7	(0.3)
Balance at end of year	$26.4	$20.1	$13.5

Note 5. Income taxes

Effective July 1, 1993, the Company adopted FASB Statement No. 109 "Accounting for Income Taxes" (FASB 109). As permitted by FASB 109, the Company elected not to restate the financial statements of any prior periods. The cumulative effect of the change was not material and therefore no adjustment was separately reported in the Consolidated Statement of Income for the year ended June 30, 1994.

The United States (including Puerto Rico) and international components of income from continuing operations before income taxes are as follows (in millions):

	1995	1994	1993
United States	$62.8	$65.7	$49.8
International	26.2	30.3	22.2
	$89.0	$96.0	$72.0

The components of the provision for income taxes on income from continuing operations before income taxes are as follows (in millions):

	Current	Deferred	Total
1995:			
U.S. Federal	$ 2.0	$ 4.6	$ 6.6
International	3.2	10.0	13.2
Other	—	(0.3)	(0.3)
	$5.2	$14.3	$19.5
1994:			
U.S. Federal	$ 5.6	$ 2.1	$ 7.7
International	12.3	3.1	15.4
Other	1.4	(0.6)	0.8
	$19.3	$ 4.6	$23.9
1993:			
U.S. Federal	$ 8.4	$ (4.1)	$ 4.3
International	11.0	(0.2)	10.8
Other	3.3	(0.5)	2.8
	$22.7	$ (4.8)	$17.9

The deferred provision is presented net of a tax benefit of $20 million for 1995, and $4.1 million for 1994, relating to net operating losses. A reconciliation between the statutory U.S. Federal income tax rate and the consolidated effective tax rate on income from continuing operations before income taxes is as follows:

	1995	1994	1993
Statutory rate	35.0%	35.0%	34.5%
Benefits due to tax exempt earnings and investment income of the Puerto Rico operations	(10.2)	(9.5)	(12.0)
Amortization of costs in excess of net assets acquired	4.6	2.7	2.7
Adjustment of prior years' accruals	(4.9)	(3.4)	—
Other	(2.6)	0.1	(0.3)
	21.9%	24.9%	24.9%

Note 9. Commitments, contingencies and other matters

a. *Commitments.* The Company leases certain operating plant and equipment. The future lease commitments for plant and equipment and other assets at June 30, 1995 aggregated $48.2 million and are due as follows (in millions): 1996 - $12.0; 1997 - $11.7; 1998 - $5.8; 1999 - $3.6; 2000 - $2.3 and $12.8 thereafter. Rent expense was charged to operations as follows (in millions): 1995 - $10.4; 1994 - $10.2 and 1993 - $4.7.

b. *Contingent royalty payments.* In connection with certain acquisitions, the Company pays royalties (ranging from 3% to 10%) on revenues generated by the acquired businesses for periods expiring in 1996 through 2004. Such contingent payments, when incurred, will be recorded as additional cost of the related acquisitions and amortized over the remaining amortization period. Royalty payments in fiscal 1995, 1994 and 1993 were $13.3 million, $7.6 million and $5.6 million, respectively.

c. *Litigation.* In July, August and September 1995, thirteen actions were filed by alleged shareholders of the Company following announcements by the Company that its earnings for the quarter and year ended June 30, 1995, would be substantially below expectations and, in the more recent actions and a complaint amendment, that the scope of the Company's year-end audit had been expanded. The various complaints allege, among other things, that the Company and certain of its directors and officers who are named as defendants issued false and misleading statements about the Company's business prospects, failed to follow appropriate accounting practices, and failed to disclose adverse information. One of the complaints also alleges, among other things, that the Company failed to disclose hazards affecting individuals wearing pacemakers allegedly caused by certain of its products. The claimants are seeking class certification, rescissory damages and/or unspecified compensatory damages, as well as interest, costs and various fees and expenses, on behalf of themselves and other putative class members who purchased the Company's common stock or related securities during the respective class periods alleged by their complaints. In one of the actions, allegedly brought on behalf of Company shareholders who obtained their shares in the Company's merger with Knogo Corporation, the relief sought also includes rescission of the vote on that merger. Also in September 1995, three derivative actions were filed against the Company and its directors for breach of fiduciary duties, mismanagement and waste of corporate assets. Those claimants are seeking, among other relief, restitution and/or damages in favor of the Company and imposition of a constructive trust. The Company intends to vigorously defend against the actions. The ultimate outcome of these actions cannot presently be determined. Accordingly, no provision for any liability that may result has been made in the consolidated financial statements.

d. Restatement of interim financial statements. In fiscal 1995, revenues related to certain shipments that were recorded incorrectly in fiscal 1995 were identified and were reported to the Audit Committee of the Board of Directors by the Company's independent certified public accountants. The Audit Committee authorized an expansion of the scope of the fiscal 1995 audit and retained independent counsel to assist in the investigation of this matter. The results of the investigation concluded that certain accounting irregularities resulted in incorrectly recording revenues and related costs and expenses for certain product shipments in each quarter of 1995, 1994 and 1993. These shipments included both product shipments actually made after the end of each quarter as well as shipments subject to nonstandard contractual terms. In addition, during fiscal 1995, certain expenses were incorrectly capitalized during the third and fourth quarters of fiscal 1995 as an element of the purchase price of Knogo Corporation. After carefully evaluating the findings, the Company concluded the financial statements for the third quarter of fiscal 1995 required restatement. (See Note 13.) Further, the Company concluded the effects of these matters on fiscal 1993, on fiscal 1994 and the quarters therein and on the first and second quarters

of fiscal 1995 were such that restatement of the financial statements of such periods was not required.

Note 11. Acquisitions

On December 29, 1994, the Company acquired the operations outside of the United States, Puerto Rico and Canada of Knogo Corporation ("Knogo") for approximately 3.1 million shares of the Company's Common Stock (with a value of approximately $100 million). Based on the preliminary purchase price allocation, the significant identifiable assets acquired and liabilities assumed and/or incurred in connection with the Knogo acquisition were as follows:

Cash and marketable securities	$ 5.8
Accounts receivable, net	18.7
Net investment in sales-type leases	17.8
Inventories, net	12.5
Deferred income taxes, patents and other assets net	26.0
Accrued liabilities	54.0
Debt	23.5

In fiscal 1993, the Company acquired Automated Loss Prevention Systems (ALPS), a large European distributor of EAS and CCTV products, and Security Tag Systems, Inc. (Security Tag), a U.S.- based manufacturer and marketer of loss prevention products, for an aggregate amount of approximately $323 million consisting of approximately $280 million (funded with net proceeds of approximately $194.8 million from the issuance of 12.6 million shares of its Common Stock and from borrowings under a short-term credit facility) and 1.5 million shares of the Company's Common Stock (with a value of approximately $43 million). The acquisitions of Knogo, ALPS and Security Tag resulted in costs in excess of net assets acquired of approximately $114 million, $223 million and $47 million, respectively (based on a preliminary allocation of the Knogo purchase price), which are being amortized using the straight-line method over 40 years. These acquisitions were accounted for under the purchase method and the respective subsidiaries were consolidated in the Company's financial statements from their respective dates of acquisition.

The Company's unaudited pro forma consolidated condensed statements of income for fiscal 1995, 1994 and 1993, assuming the acquisitions of Knogo (fiscal 1995 and 1994), ALPS (fiscal 1993) and Security Tag (fiscal 1993) were effected at the beginning of each year, are summarized as follows (in millions, except per share data):

	1995	1994	1993
Total revenues	$922.3	$726.1	$510.2
Income from continuing operations before income taxes	89.6	108.7	72.3
Net income	73.7	79.3	53.9
Primary earnings per common share	$1.00	$1.22	$ .91
Fully diluted earnings per common share	$ .99	$1.16	$ .89

This pro forma information does not purport to be indicative of the results which may have been obtained had the acquisitions been consummated at the dates assumed (see the financial statements and other information related to Knogo in the Company's Current Report on Form 8-K filed January 11, 1995, as amended on Form 8-K/A filed January 27, 1995).

In connection with acquisitions during fiscal 1995, 1994 and 1993, the market value of the assets acquired was as follows (in millions):

	1995	1994	1993
Cash paid (net of cash acquired)	$ 9.6	$11.5	$299.3
Liabilities assumed and/or incurred	101.1	13.2	76.6
Common stock	149.3	31.0	43.4
Market value of assets acquired	$260.0	$55.7	$419.3

DIRECTORS OF THE COMPANY

Ronald G. Assaf
Chairman of the Board and Chief Executive Director

Robert A. Vanourek
President and Chief Operating Officer

Thomas V. Buffet*
Vice Chairman of the Board, President, Chipper Investments Retired Chairman of the Board and Chief Executive Officer of Automated Security

Jerome M. LeWine
Partner, Christy & Viener Attorney at Law

James E. Lineberger
Chairman of the Executive Committee
Partner, Lineberger & Co. Private Investment Firm

Dr. Arthur G. Milnes*
Professor Emeritus, Electrical Engineering Department
Carnegie-Mellon University

John T. Ray, Jr.*
Senior Vice President
ASC Division
H.B. Fuller Company

Timothy P. Hartman
Chairman of Nations Bank of Texas, Private Investor

* Member of the Audit Committee

Sensormatic Electronics Corporation

REPORT OF INDEPENDENT CERTIFIED PUBLIC ACCOUNTANTS

The Board of Directors
Sensormatic Electronics Corporation

We have audited the accompanying consolidated balance sheets of Sensormatic Electronics Corporation as of June 30, 1995 and 1994, and the related consolidated statements of income, stockholders' equity, and cash flows for each of the three years in the period ended June 30, 1995. These financial statements are the responsibility of the Company's management. Our responsibility is to express an opinion on these financial statements based on our audits.

We conducted our audits in accordance with generally accepted auditing standards. Those standards require that we plan and perform the audit to obtain reasonable assurance about whether the financial statements are free of material misstatement. An audit includes examining, on a test basis, evidence supporting the amounts and disclosures in the financial statements. An audit also includes assessing the accounting principles used and significant estimates made by management, as well as evaluating the overall financial statement presentation. We believe that our audits provide a reasonable basis for our opinion.

In our opinion, the consolidated financial statements referred to above present fairly, in all material respects, the consolidated financial position of Sensormatic Electronics Corporation at June 30, 1995 and 1994, and the consolidated results of their operations and their cash flows for each of the three years in the period ended June 30, 1995, in conformity with generally accepted accounting principles.

As discussed in Note 9 to the consolidated financial statements, the Company is a defendant in various lawsuits brought by alleged shareholders claiming, among other things, violations of federal securities laws. The Company strongly disputes these charges and intends to vigorously defend against these lawsuits. The ultimate outcome of the litigation cannot presently be determined. Accordingly, no provision for any liability that may result has been made in the consolidated financial statements.

As discussed in Note 5. to the consolidated financial statements, in 1994 the Company changed its method of accounting for income taxes.

ERNST & YOUNG LLP

West Palm Beach, Florida
September 30, 1995

Thermo Electron Corporation

In technology, things that have a high payoff are very risky. You need the ability to pursue risky ventures and yet not risk the company. If that means pursuing a lot of little things instead of one big thing, so be it—especially if the one big thing never panned out.

George Hatsopolous, *Forbes*, 11/16/87

In early July 1994, research analyst John Kolmanoff was considering the recent performance of Thermo Electron (NYSE: TMO), a technology creation company with an impressive track record for capitalizing on internally developed and externally acquired research. In the past, Kolmanoff had strongly recommended Thermo Electron to his clients, and many had profited from its extraordinary price appreciation during the last five years (see Exhibit 1). However, the firm's stock had recently been lagging the S&P 500, declining 19 percent for the six months ended June 30, 1994 (versus only a 10 percent decline for the S&P 500). This decline had been accompanied by an increase in short positions in the stock, and by criticism of the company's accounting. As a result of these developments, Kolmanoff decided that it was time to reconsider the company.

COMPANY BACKGROUND

Dr. George Hatsopolous founded Thermo Electron in 1956 in his Belmont, Massachusetts, garage using a $50,000 loan from his friend Peter Nomikos, heir to a Greek shipping fortune. A graduate student at the Massachusetts Institute of Technology, Hatsopolous hoped to capitalize on his doctoral research by commercializing the process of converting heat directly into electricity without moving parts. Two years later his prototype was completed and was widely acclaimed in the popular press as a breakthrough. One article proclaimed that the invention could be used to power satellites, military equipment, and even motor vehicles. Money flowed in from the venture capital community and the federal government. Although the process subsequently proved to be uneconomical, the research led to several spillover products which were economically viable, and which formed the basis for Thermo Electron's early success.

During the 1960s the company provided contract research for public utilities and government agencies such as NASA, the U.S. Air Force, and the now defunct Atomic Energy Commission. In 1971, when the U.S. Congress required car manufacturers to monitor exhaust emissions, no instruments with the required precision were available. Dr. Hatsopolous saw the opportunity this presented and quickly contacted Ford Motor Company to offer his company's services in developing the new instruments. At the time Ford was skeptical of Thermo Electron's ability to complete the contract, but the instruments were delivered on time, ahead of any competitors. As a result, many other auto companies came to Thermo Electron for the same devices. This infant instruments business grew to become Thermo Instrument Systems, Inc.

Souren G. Ouzounian and Professor Paul M. Healy prepared this case. The case is intended solely as the basis for class discussion and is not intended to serve as an endorsement, source of primary data, or illustration of effective or ineffective management. Copyright © 1998 by the President and Fellows of Harvard College. HBS Case 9-198-033.

The company continued to grow rapidly in the 1980s and early 1990s by developing a wide range of innovative new products. These included a portable device for detecting plastic bombs, a portable drug detector used by customs agents and police, a cardiac assist device to keep patients alive while awaiting transplants, the first commercial detector and analyzer for nitrosamines (carcinogens), a portable remediation system that removes gasoline from contaminated soil, soil-analysis instrumentation for the Environmental Protection Agency, a home-use radon detector kit, and the first commercially practical instrument for monitoring concentrations of NO_2. Other recent innovations included mammography systems, paper-recycling and papermaking equipment, alternative energy systems, industrial process equipment, and a number of other specialized products.

While much of Thermo Electron's research success was internally generated at the company's own research labs, it was not afraid to buy other developers. For example, in 1989 it acquired a San Diego-based laser lab. At the time of the acquisition the lab relied almost exclusively on the shrinking Star Wars budget for funding. Following a remarkable transformation, it developed a painless method to remove unwanted hair using laser technology, and as a result of a spinout in 1991, became ThermoTrex. But not all of the company acquisitions were so successful. A small metal-plate company that had been acquired ended up costing Thermo Electron $18 million, and an environmental engineering company acquired in 1988 cost $6 million.

MANAGEMENT PHILOSOPHY AND CORPORATE STRUCTURE

Thermo Electron mirrored the psyche of its founder, Dr. George Hatsopolous, whose talents spanned many fields—he is an inventor, teacher, self-taught economist, and CEO. He has used the Socratic method to encourage organizational learning and growth, and fostered an open-door policy for employees to discuss problems and ideas.

The almost 9,000-person company was unique in several other ways. First, it had always retained the right to use the technology it developed. This permitted it to use the technology created for one project as a springboard for new ventures. At times this policy was costly, and the firm undertook research at a reduced fee to retain the rights to the technology.

Thermo Electron's corporate structure, designed by Dr. Hatsopolous and his brother John Hatsopolous, the Company's Chief Financial Officer, was also a unique feature of the business. The firm sold a minority interest to the public in subsidiaries that focused on the best ideas and products that came from the parent company's R&D labs. The parent company typically kept between 70 and 80 percent of the stock in these "spinouts," but the units functioned as independent companies with their own management and their own shareholders. As John Hatsopolous explained, "The plan is simple: let employees develop an idea, spend some time and money testing the quality and market potential of the product, then set up a subsidiary and let it grow."[1]

The first unit to be "spun out" was Thermedics, which was sold in August 1983 for $2.51 per share. In March 1994, Thermedic's stock was valued at $12.13. In mid-1994 Thermo Electron had nine "pups," as the spinouts became known on Wall Street. Most had performed well following the initial offering. (See Exhibit 2 for details of stock performance of these units following the spinouts). For example, Thermo Instrument Systems,

---

1. Boston Business Journal 13, November 19, 1993, Sec. 1:3.

Inc., which grew out of the successful instrument project with Ford and which was spun out in 1986, was initially sold for $3.56 per share and in mid-1994 sold for more than $32.

There were several differences between the spinout concept pioneered by Thermo Electron and the more traditional spinoffs. First, under a traditional spinoff all of the subsidiary's equity was distributed to either the parent-company shareholders or to new shareholders through an Initial Public Offering (IPO). In the Thermo spinout the parent company sold off only a minority stake in the division, either through an IPO, a private placement, or both. Second, traditional spinoffs typically arose when the parent wanted to raise cash, to reduce debt obligations, or to rid itself of poor-performing units and focus on its "core" competencies. Consequently, announcements of spinoffs tended to have a negative impact on the parent company stock.[2] In contrast, announcements of spinouts, or "equity carve-outs" as they are sometimes called, usually had a positive 2 to 3 percent effect on the stock of the parent company. Theo Melas-Kyriazi, Thermo's treasurer explained, "We don't sell poor performers, the dogs; we sell our core technologies."[3] The cash generated from these sales was then used to provide working capital for the spun-out units.

Dr. Hatsopolous believed that the company's spinout strategy enabled it to combine the vibrancy of a small high-growth start-up with the financial stability and research strength of an established company. The structure provided strong incentives for management and key researchers, who were rewarded with stock options in the newly created publicly traded subsidiaries. As a result, there was virtually no turnover among key employees at Thermo Electron. In addition, Dr. Hatsopolous was convinced that, by creating a series of "pure plays" on specific technologies, the firm helped investors to better understand its business, and hence lowered its cost of raising capital.

Accounting for Spinouts

One issue that arose from the spinout strategy was how to account for the spinouts. There was no FASB ruling on this accounting practice. However, two options were available to Thermo Electron: (1) record any realized gain or loss on sale of shares in the spun-out unit as an increase or decrease in equity reserves; or (2) report any gain or loss in the income statement. The footnotes in the annual report explained that Thermo Electron followed the second of these options:

> At the time a subsidiary sells its stock to unrelated parties at a price in excess of its book value, the Company's net investment in that subsidiary increases. If at that time the subsidiary is an operating entity and not engaged principally in research and development, the Company records the increase as a gain.
>
> If gains have been recognized on issuance of a subsidiary's stock and shares of the subsidiary are subsequently repurchased by the subsidiary or by the Company, gain recognition does not occur on issuances subsequent to the date of repurchase until such time as shares have been issued in an amount equivalent to the number of repurchased shares.

The impact of this accounting decision was significant. Since the first spinout in 1983, 50 percent or more of the firm's net income arose from gains on spinouts. For example, in 1993 the gain on sale (both before and after tax effects) was $39.9 million, compared to net income of $76.6 million.

---

2. See *Schipper and Smith,* Journal of Financial Economics, *1986: 153–186.*
3. Wall Street Journal, *August 5, 1993: 1.*

Management believed that the accounting policy has been critical in helping the company raise funds, since it enabled the firm to generate smooth earnings growth in its income statement. However, analysts remained concerned about the quality of the firm's earnings.

Recent Financial Performance

In *Fortune* magazine's 1994 ranking of the nation's top 500 industrial companies, Thermo Electron was ranked number one for largest growth in earnings per share from 1983 to 1993. The company also ranked twenty-ninth on the *Fortune* list of firms with the highest total return to investors over for the last ten years. "We attribute our success in large part to our strategy of spinning out promising businesses that serve energy, environmental, and biomedical markets," said Dr. Hatsopolous. "By forming these entities, we are able to tap the capital markets and create an entrepreneurial environment that spurs ingenuity."[4]

For its fiscal year ended January 1, 1994, Thermo Electron reported its ninth consecutive year of record financial performance. Its revenues were $1.2 billion and income before an accounting change was $76.6 million, or $1.75 per share. See Exhibit 3 for a ten-year summary of the company's financial data and Exhibit 4 for its most recent financial statements.

Despite its impressive record, John Kolmanoff was uncertain about whether he should continue to recommend the stock to his clients. Many analysts were forecasting that the company's earnings would grow at a rate of 18 to 22 percent for the next five years. Given the stock price in early July 1994 of $24.75, the company was trading at 1.38 times its book value. However, others were more cautious, and questioned the quality of the firm's earnings, given that much of its income was derived from gains on spinouts. Short sales in the company's stock had grown 21 percent in the previous six months, to approximately 11 percent of its outstanding stock. Given the mixed opinions on the company, Kolmanoff decided that he should undertake a complete review of its business, accounting, and valuation.[5]

QUESTIONS

1. Evaluate how Thermo Electron's strategy for spinning-out its R&D units affects its long-term success. What factors are critical to the success of this strategy, and what are the risks the company faces?

2. Examine Thermo Electron's accounting policies. What is the quality of the firm's earnings?

3. Analyze Thermo Electron's financial performance for 1991, 1992 and 1993 using financial ratio analysis. How is the company managing its cash flows for 1993? Is the company effectively managing its business risks?

4. What is the value of the shares retained by Thermo Electron in spun-out subsidiaries? What is the market value of Thermo Electron itself? What factors explain the difference between these values?

....

4. Wall Street Journal, August 5, 1993: 1.

5. In early July 1994, Thermo Electron's equity beta was 1.1, the 3-month Treasury Bill rate was 4.2%, and the 30-year Government Bond rate was 7.68%.

EXHIBIT I

Five-Year Summary of Stock Performance: Thermo Electron and SPX

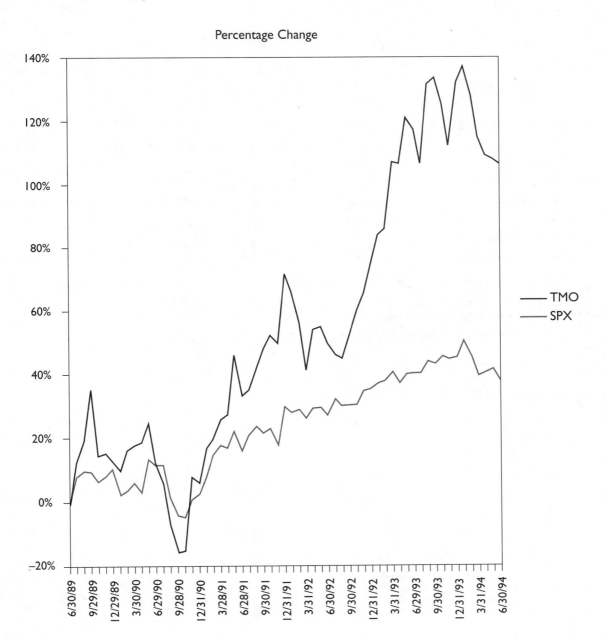

Percentage Change

TMO
SPX

Thermo Electron Corporation

EXHIBIT 2

Stock Performance for Thermo Electron Spinouts

| Company | IPO Date | Split-adjusted IPO Price | 3/3/94 | | CAGR[a] |
			Price	Shares Outstanding	
Thermedics	8/10/83	$2.51	$12.13	31,978	16.1%
Thermo Instrument Systems	8/5/86	3.56	32.25	45,865	33.8
Thermo Process Systems	8/21/86	1.83	9.00	16,041	23.5
Thermo Power	6/26/87	8.50	8.75	12,232	0.4
Thermo Cardiosystems	1/12/89	2.27	19.25	22,878	51.6
Thermo Voltek	3/19/90	2.56	9.00	3,929	37.4
ThermoTrex	7/24/91	7.92	15.50	17,093	29.4
Thermo Fibertek	11/2/92	8.00	14.63	26,832	57.1
Thermo Remediation	12/16/93	12.50	14.13	6,503	77.4

a. CAGR is the Compound Annual Growth Rate from IPO date to 3/4/94. It is calculated as $\left(\frac{End\ Price}{IPO\ Price}\right)^{\frac{1}{n}} - 1$, where n is the number of years from IPO date to 3/3/94.

Source: Centre for Research in Security Prices.

Thermo Electron Corporation

EXHIBIT 3

Thermo Electron Ten-Year Financial Summary

(in millions except per-share amounts)	1993[a]	1992[b]	1991[c]	1990[d]	1989	1988	1987	1986	1985	1984
Revenues	$1,249.7	$ 949.0	$ 805.5	$720.7	$623.0	$540.7	$419.9	$359.1	$286.2	$253.3
Costs and Expenses:										
Cost of revenues	755.5	609.0	533.6	465.3	424.2	359.6	280.3	244.8	194.9	172.6
Expenses for R&D and new lines of business	87.0	62.3	52.6	54.0	46.4	43.2	31.4	26.5	21.5	21.6
Selling, general and administrative expenses	283.6	209.4	177.3	163.1	130.0	113.7	91.5	72.7	56.9	48.2
Costs associated with divisional and product restructuring	8.3	—	3.7	1.0	2.2	0.9	3.5	7.1	4.3	0.1
	1,134.4	880.7	767.2	683.4	602.8	517.4	406.7	351.1	277.6	242.5
Gain on Issuance of Stock by Subsidiaries	39.9	30.2	27.4	20.3	16.8	6.0	16.1	15.9	9.1	—
Other Income (Expense), Net	(24.1)	3.5	13.5	2.3	3.3	4.5	(0.6)	(3.3)	(4.7)	(5.1)
Income Before Income Taxes, Minority Interest, and Cumulative Effect of Change in Accounting Principle	131.1	102.0	79.2	59.9	40.3	33.8	28.7	20.6	13.0	5.7
Provision for Income Taxes	33.4	27.5	24.8	17.8	10.4	9.0	6.0	4.0	2.5	0.1
Minority Interest Expense	21.1	13.9	7.3	7.1	3.3	2.0	1.9	0.5	(0.1)	(0.1)
Income Before Cumulative Effect of Change in Accounting Principle	76.6	60.6	47.1	35.0	26.6	22.8	20.8	16.1	10.6	5.7
Cumulative Effect of Change in Accounting Principle, Net of Tax[e]	—	1.4	—	—	—	—	—	—	—	—
Net Income	$76.6	$59.2	$ 47.1	$ 35.0	$ 26.6	$ 22.8	$ 20.8	$ 16.1	$ 10.6	$ 5.7
Earnings per Share Before Cumulative Effect of Change in Accounting Principle:										
Primary	$ 1.75	$ 1.51	$ 1.31	$1.09	$ .86	$ .77	$ .68	$ .55	$ .42	$ .24
Fully diluted	$ 1.57	$ 1.41	$ 1.23	$1.03	$ .84	$ .75	$ .67	$ .54	$ .41	$ .23
Earnings per Share:										
Primary	$ 1.75	$ .48	$ 1.31	$1.09	$ .86	$ .77	$ .68	$ .55	$ .42	$ .24
Fully diluted	$ 1.57	$ 1.38	$ 1.23	$1.03	$ .84	$ .75	$ .67	$ .54	$ .41	$ .23
Balance Sheet Data:										
Working capital	$ 828.3	$ 503.4	$ 463.5	$241.4	$276.0	$218.8	$210.9	$124.3	$ 79.1	$ 51.3
Total assets	2,473.7	1,818.3	1,199.5	904.4	664.1	524.4	460.8	332.6	240.9	208.0
Net assets related to construction projects	9.4	23.8	29.4	—	—	—	—	—	—	—
Long-term obligations	647.5	494.2	255.0	210.0	176.9	152.7	135.7	61.4	49.1	47.5
Minority interest	277.7	164.3	122.5	83.9	51.8	22.6	25.8	20.1	6.6	1.3
Common stock of subsidiaries subject to redemption	14.5	5.5	5.5	8.7	13.1	—	—	—	—	—
Shareholders' investment	858.5	552.9	480.9	310.2	226.4	194.3	173.5	153.1	106.7	87.8

a. *Reflects the February 1993 acquisition of Spectra-Physics Analytical and the Company's 1993 public offering of common stock for net proceeds of $246.0 million.*

b. *Reflects the August 1992 acquisition of Nicoles Instrument Corporation and the issuance of $260.0 million principal amount of convertible debentures.*

c. *Reflects the issuance of $164.0 million principal amount of convertible debentures.*

d. *Reflects the May 1990 acquisition of Finnigan Corporation.*

e. *Reflects the adoption in fiscal 1992 of Statement of Financial Accounting Standards No. 106, "Accounting for Post-retirement Benefits Other Than Pensions."*

Thermo Electron Corporation

Thermo Electron Corporation

EXHIBIT 4

Thermo Electron Summarized Financial Statements

CONSOLIDATED BALANCE SHEET

(in thousands except per-share amounts)	1993	1992
ASSETS		
Current Assets:		
Cash and cash equivalents	$ 325,744	$ 190,601
Short-term investments, at cost (quoted market value of $377,183 and $180,060)	374,450	178,101
Accounts receivable, less allowances of $14,129 and $11,341	267,377	204,750
Unbilled contract costs and fees	32,574	25,941
Inventories:		
Work in process and finished goods	82,385	60,629
Raw materials and supplies	110,437	106,619
Prepaid income taxes (Note 8)	39,258	54,377
Prepaid expenses	12,318	8,716
	1,244,543	829,734
Assets Related to Projects Under Construction:		
Restricted funds (quoted market value of $34,100 and $95,639)	34,100	95,348
Facilities under construction	128,040	133,876
	162,140	229,224
Property, Plant and Equipment, at Cost:		
Land	40,570	35,729
Buildings	116,895	99,502
Alternative-energy facilities	199,800	30,554
Machinery, equipment and leasehold improvements	224,629	205,508
	581,894	371,293
Less: Accumulated depreciation and amortization	134,423	113,383
	447,471	257,910
Long-term Marketable Securities, at Cost (quoted market value of $45,125 and $45,731)	43,630	44,497
Other Assets	102,347	92,870
Cost in Excess of Net Assets of Acquired Companies (Note 2)	473,579	364,030
	$2,473,710	$1,818,265

(continued)

CONSOLIDATED BALANCE SHEET *(continued)*

(in thousands except per-share amounts)	1993	1992
LIABILITIES AND SHAREHOLDERS' INVESTMENT		
Current Liabilities:		
Notes payable	$ 45,851	$ 22,034
Accounts payable	85,278	69,473
Billings in excess of contract costs and fees	8,564	7,987
Accrued payroll and employee benefits	49,029	45,115
Accrued income taxes (Note 8)	7,713	9,796
Accrued installation and warranty costs	26,049	17,179
Other accrued expenses (Note 2)	193,762	154,786
	416,246	326,370
Deferred Income Taxes (Note 8)	48,387	34,171
Other Deferred Items	58,152	35,500
Liabilities Related to Projects Under Construction (Note 5):		
Payables and accrued expenses	10,680	5,874
Tax-exempt obligations	142,069	199,536
	152,749	205,410
Long-term Obligations (Note 5):		
Senior convertible obligations	275,000	260,000
Subordinated convertible obligations	238,386	199,829
Nonrecourse tax-exempt obligations	108,800	—
Other	25,275	34,323
	647,461	494,152
Minority Interest	277,681	164,293
Commitments and Contingencies (Note 6)		
Common Stock of Subsidiaries Subject to Redemption ($15,390 and $5,468 redemption values)	14,511	5,468
Shareholders' Investment (Notes 3 and 4):		
Preferred stock, $100 par value, 50,000 shares authorized; none issued		
Common stock, $1 par value, 100,000,000 shares authorized; 47,950,580 and 27,099,598 shares issued	47,951	27,100
Capital in excess of par value	467,076	257,105
Retained earnings	362,138	285,505
	877,165	569,710
Treasury stock at cost, 31,898 and 85,342 shares	(1,212)	(3,810)
Cumulative translation adjustment	(13,591)	(7,949)
Deferred compensation (Note 7)	(3,839)	(5,050)
	858,523	552,901
	$2,473,710	$1,818,265

Thermo Electron Corporation

Thermo Electron Corporation

CONSOLIDATED INCOME STATEMENT

(in thousands except per-share amounts)	1993	1992	1991
Revenues:			
Product sales and revenues	$1,103,558	$ 808,928	$ 666,565
Service revenues	121,987	114,268	112,003
Research and development contract revenues	24,173	25,776	26,916
	1,249,718	948,972	805,484
Costs and Expenses:			
Cost of products	664,201	521,668	444,273
Cost of services	91,292	87,307	89,347
Expenses for research and development and new lines of business[a]	87,027	62,343	52,609
Selling, general and administrative expenses	283,390	209,392	177,304
Costs associated with division and product (Note 11)	8,261	—	3,709
	1,134,371	880,710	767,242
Gain on Issuance of Stock by Subsidiaries (Note 9)	39,863	30,212	27,367
Other Income (Expense), Net (Note 10)	(24,091)	3,496	13,564
Income Before Income Taxes, Minority Interest, and Cumulative Effect of Change in Accounting Principle	131,119	101,970	79,173
Provision for Income Taxes (Note 8)	33,400	27,474	24,850
Minority Interest Expense	21,086	13,902	7,269
Income Before Cumulative Effect of Change in Accounting Principle	76,633	60,594	47,054
Cumulative Effect of Change in Accounting Principle, Net of Tax (Note 7)	—	1,438	—
Net Income	$ 76,633	$ 59,156	$ 47,054
Earnings per Share Before Cumulative Effect of Change in Accounting Principle:			
Primary	$ 1.75	$ 1.51	$ 1.31
Fully diluted	$ 1.57	$ 1.41	$ 1.23
Earnings per Share:			
Primary	$ 1.75	$ 1.48	$ 1.31
Fully diluted	$ 1.57	$ 1.38	$ 1.23
Weighted Average Shares:			
Primary	43,779	40,049	35,836
Fully diluted	55,520	47,163	41,711

a. Includes costs of: Research and development contracts	$ 20,435	$ 19,426	$ 21,196
Internally funded research and development	58,943	38,675	26,171
Other expenses for new lines of business	7,649	4,242	5,242
	$ 87,027	$ 62,343	$ 52,609

CONSOLIDATED CASH FLOW STATEMENT

(in thousands)	1993	1992	1991
OPERATING ACTIVITIES:			
Net income	$ 76,633	$ 59,156	$ 47,054
Adjustments to reconcile net income to net cash provided by operating activities:			
Cumulative effect of change in accounting principle (Note 7)	—	1,438	—
Depreciation and amortization	42,356	29,228	23,391
Costs associated with divisional and product restructuring (Note 11)	8,261	—	3,709
Equity in losses of unconsolidated subsidiaries	21,076	3,948	1,663
Provision for losses on accounts receivable	2,675	2,021	3,020
Increase in deferred income taxes	13,888	12,273	169
Gain on sale of investments	(2,469)	(4,968)	(7,622)
Gain on issuance of stock by subsidiaries (Note 9)	(39,863)	(30,212)	(27,367)
Minority interest expense	21,086	13,902	7,269
Other noncash expenses	7,850	11,549	6,804
Changes in current accounts, excluding the effects of acquisitions:			
Accounts receivable	(43,171)	(10,763)	(10,220)
Inventories	(6,525)	(4,753)	8,224
Other current assets	(230)	(9,860)	5,276
Accounts payable	10,014	(2,479)	(10,140)
Other current liabilities	15,355	(15,363)	(11,684)
Other	(198)	(175)	(142)
Net cash provided by operating activities	126,738	54,942	39,404
INVESTING ACTIVITIES:			
Acquisitions, net of cash acquired (Note 2)	(142,962)	(251,738)	(7,552)
Purchases of property, plant and equipment	(56,580)	(60,007)	(33,469)
Purchases of long-term investments	(20,573)	(70,340)	(21,278)
Proceeds from sale of short-term investments	16,651	35,899	15,814
(Increase) decrease in short-term investments	(193,894)	68,260	(175,701)
Increase in assets related to construction projects	(3,781)	(132,971)	(67,790)
Other	1,848	313	(4,834)
Net cash used in investment activities	(399,291)	(410,584)	(294,810)
FINANCING ACTIVITIES:			
Proceeds from issuance of long-term obligations	102,151	255,694	162,273
Repayment and repurchase of long-term obligations	(11,732)	(27,415)	(10,493)
Proceeds from issuance of tax-exempt obligations	—	133,536	66,000
Proceeds from issuance of Company and subsidiary common stock	378,790	100,749	64,947
Purchases of Company and subsidiary common stock	(57,198)	(45,334)	(11,663)
Other	(941)	485	(430)
Net cash provided by financing activities	411,070	417,715	270,634
Exchange Rate Effect on Cash	(3,374)	(2,424)	(2,499)
Increase in Cash and Cash Equivalents	135,143	59,649	12,729
Cash and Cash Equivalents at Beginning of Year	190,601	130,952	118,223
Cash and Cash Equivalents at End of Year	$325,744	$190,601	$130,952
CASH PAID FOR:			
Interest	$ 29,438	$ 18,287	$ 15,426
Income taxes	$ 9,699	$ 16,593	$ 15,723
NONCASH ACTIVITIES:			
Conversions of convertible obligations	$ 50,403	$ 13,863	$109,865
Subsidiary stock issued for acquired business (Note 2)	$ —	$ 9,673	$ 1,026
Purchase of electric-generating facility through assumption of debt	$ 66,900	$ —	$ —

Thermo Electron Corporation

SELECTED NOTES TO CONSOLIDATED FINANCIAL STATEMENTS

1. SIGNIFICANT ACCOUNTING POLICIES

Principles of Consolidation

The accompanying consolidated financial statements include the accounts of Thermo Electron Corporation and its majority- and wholly owned subsidiaries (the Company). All material intercompany accounts and transactions have been eliminated. Majority-owned public subsidiaries include Thermedics, Inc., Thermo Instrument Systems, Inc., Thermo Process Systems Inc., Thermo Power Corporation, ThermoTrex Corporation, and Thermo Fibertek Inc. Thermo Cardiosystems Inc. and Thermo Voltek Corp. are majority-owned public subsidiaries of Thermedics. Thermo Remediation Inc. is a majority-owned public subsidiary of Thermo Process. Thermo Energy Systems Corporation is a majority-owned, privately held subsidiary of the Company; ThermoLase Inc. is a majority-owned, privately held subsidiary of TherTrex; and J. Amerika N.V. is a majority-owned, privately held subsidiary of Thermo Process. The Company accounts for investments in businesses in which it owns between 20% and 50% under the equity method.

Fiscal Year

The Company has adopted a fiscal year ending the Saturday nearest December 31. References to 1993, 1992, and 1991 are for the fiscal years ended January 1, 1994, January 1, 1992, and December 28, 1991, respectively. Fiscal years 1993 and 1991 each included 52 weeks; 1992 included 53 weeks.

Revenue Recognition

For the majority of its operations, the Company recognizes revenues based upon shipment of its products or completion of services rendered. The Company provides a reserve for its estimate of warranty and installation costs at the time of shipment. Revenues and profits on substantially all contracts are recognized using the percentage-of-completion method. Revenues recorded under the percentage-of-completion method were $176,727,000 in 1993, $186,407,000 in 1992, and $173,210,000 in 1991. The percentage of completion is determined by relating either the actual costs or actual labor, respectively, to be incurred on each other. If a loss is indicated on any contract in process, a provision is made currently for the entire loss. The Company's contracts generally provide for billing of customers upon attainment of certain milestones specified in each contract. Revenues earned on contracts in process in excess of billings are classified as "Unbilled contract costs and fees," and amounts billed in excess of revenues earned are classified as "Billings

in excess of contract costs and fees" in the accompanying balance sheet. There are no significant amounts included in the accompanying balance sheet that are not expected to be recovered from existing contracts at current contract values or that are not expected to be collected within one year, including amounts that are billed but not paid under retainage provisions.

Gain on Issuance of Stock by Subsidiaries

At the time a subsidiary sells its stock to unrelated parties at a price in excess of its book value, the Company's net investment in that subsidiary increases. If at that time the subsidiary is an operating entity and not engaged principally in research and development, the Company records the increase as a gain.

If gains have been recognized on issuances of a subsidiary's stock and shares of the subsidiary are subsequently repurchased by the subsidiary or the Company, gain recognition does not occur on issuances subsequent to the date of a repurchase until such time as shares have been issued in an amount equivalent to the number of repurchased shares. Such transactions are reflected as equity transactions and the net effect of these transactions is reflected in the accompanying statement of shareholders' investment as "Effect of majority-owned subsidiaries' common stock transactions."

Income Taxes

The Company adopted Statement of Financial Accounting Standards (SFAS) No. 109, "Accounting for Income Taxes," as of the beginning of 1992. Under SFAS No. 109, deferred income taxes are recognized based on the expected future tax consequences of differences between the financial statement basis and the tax basis of assets and liabilities calculated using enacted tax rates in effect for the year in which the differences are expected to be reflected in the tax return. Prior to 1992, the Company recorded income taxes on timing differences between financial statement and tax treatment of income and expenses under Accounting Principles Board Opinion No. 11. The implementation of SFAS No. 109 and the effect of adoption were not material to the Company's financial statements.

Earnings per Share

Primary earnings per share have been computed based on the weighted average number of common shares outstanding during the year. Because the effect of common stock equivalents was not material, they have been excluded from the primary earnings per share calculation. Fully diluted earnings per share assumes the effect of the conversion of the Company's dilutive convertible obligations and elimination of the related interest expense, the exercise of stock options, and their related income tax effects.

Stock Splits

All share and per share information has been restated to reflect a three-for-two stock split, effected in the form of a 50% stock dividend that was distributed in October 1993.

In addition, all share and per share information pertaining to Thermedics, Thermo Instrument, ThermoTrex, and Thermo Voltek has been restated to reflect three-for-two stock splits, effected in the form of 50% stock dividends, that were distributed in 1993. All share and per share information pertaining to Thermo Cardiosystems and ThermoLase has been restated to reflect two-for-one stock splits, effected in the form of 100% stock dividends, that was distributed for Thermo Cardiosystems in 1993 and will be effected for ThermoLase on March 15, 1994.

Cash and Cash Equivalents

Cash equivalents consist principally of U.S. government agency securities, bank time deposits, and commercial paper purchased with an original maturity of three months or less. These investments are carried at cost. The fair market value of cash and cash equivalents was $325,823,000 and $191,004,000 at January 1, 1994 and January 2, 1993, respectively.

Short- and Long-Term Investments

Short- and long-term investments consist principally of corporate notes and U.S. government agency securities. Securities with an original maturity of greater than three months, which the Company intends to hold for less than one year, are classified as short-term. Securities that are intended to be held for more than one year are classified as long-term. These investments are carried at the lower of cost or market value.

In May 1993, the Financial Accounting Standards Board issued SFAS No. 115, "Accounting for Certain Investments in Debt and Equity Securities." SFAS No. 115 requires that marketable equity and debt securities considered trading securities be accounted for at market value with the difference between cost and market value recorded currently in the statement of income; that securities considered available for sale be accounted for at market value, with the difference between cost and market value, net of related tax effects, recorded currently as a component of shareholders' investment; and that debt securities considered held-to-maturity be recorded at amortized cost. The Company is required to adopt SFAS No. 115 at the beginning of fiscal 1994. Management believes that the

marketable equity and debt securities in the accompanying balance sheet will be considered available-for-sale and that the adoption of SFAS No. 115 will result in a total increase to shareholders' investment of approximately $2,600,000.

Inventories

Inventories are stated at the lower of cost (on a first-in, first-out or weighted average basis) or market value and include materials, labor, and manufacturing overhead.

Property, Plant and Equipment

The costs of additions and improvements are capitalized, while maintenance and repairs are charged to expense as incurred. The Company provides for depreciation and amortization using the straight-line method over the estimated useful lives of the property as follows: buildings and improvements—10 to 40 years; alternative-energy facilities—25 years, machinery and equipment—3 to 20 years; and lease-hold improvements—the shorter of the term of the lease or the life of the asset.

Assets Related to Projects Under Construction

"Facilities under construction" in the accompanying 1992 balance sheet included an alternative-energy facility that was under construction in Delano, California. This facility was completed in 1993 and is included in "Alternative-energy facilities" in the accompanying 1993 balance sheet. "Facilities under construction" in fiscal 1993 and 1992 include a waste-recycling facility located in San Diego County, California. Construction costs for this facility were capitalized as incurred. Construction was completed in early 1994.

"Restricted funds" in the accompanying balance sheet represents unexpended proceeds from the issuance of tax-exempt obligations (Note 5), which are invested principally in U.S. government agency securities and municipal tax-exempt obligations. These investments are carried at the lower of cost or market value.

In August 1993, the Company agreed, in exchange for a cash settlement, to terminate a power sales agreement between a subsidiary of the Company and a utility. The power sales agreement required the utility to purchase the power to be generated by the Company's 55-megawatt natural gas cogeneration facility under development on Staten Island, New York. Under the termination agreement, the Company received $9.0 million in August 1993, with subsequent payments to be made as follows: $3.6 million in 1994; $2.7 million in 1995; $1.8 million in 1996; and $0.9 million in 1997. The Company will be obligated to return $8.2 million of this settlement if the Company elects to proceed with the Staten Island facility and it achieves commercial operation before January 1, 2000. Accordingly, the Company has deferred recognition of $8.2 million of revenues, pending final determination of the project's status. During 1993, the Company recorded revenues of $9.8 million and segment income of $5.4 million from the termination of the power sales agreement.

Other Assets

"Other assets" in the accompanying balance sheet include capitalized costs associated with the Company's operation of certain alternative-energy power plants, as well as the cost of acquired trademarks, patents, and other identifiable intangible assets. These assets are being amortized using the straight-line method over their estimated useful lives, which range from 4 to 20 years. These assets were $41,252,000 and $49,646,000, net of accumulated amortization of $16,699,000 and $11,002,000, at year-end 1993 and 1992, respectively.

Cost in Excess of Net Assets of Acquired Companies

The excess of cost over the fair value of net assets of acquired businesses is amortized using the straight-line method principally over 40 years. Accumulated amortization was $32,439,000 and $20,954,000 at year-end 1993 and 1992, respectively. The Company continually assesses whether a change in circumstances has occurred subsequent to an acquisition that would indicate that the future useful life of the asset should be revised. The Company considers the future earnings potential of the acquired business in assessing the recoverability of this asset.

Common Stock of Subsidiaries Subject to Redemption

In March 1993, ThermoLase sold 3,078,000 units at $5 per unit, each unit consisting of one share of Thermo-Lase common stock and one redemption right. A redemption right allows holders to redeem Thermo-Lase common stock for $5 per share, and is exercisable in December 1996 and 1997. The redemption rights are guaranteed on a subordinated basis by the Company.

"Common stock of subsidiaries subject to redemption" in the accompanying 1992 balance sheet represents amounts associated with redemption rights outstanding that were issued in connection with the Thermo Cardiosystms 1989 initial public offering and were guaranteed on a subordinated basis by the Company. These redemption rights expired at the end of 1993 and, as a result, the Company transferred $5,468,000 of "Common stock of subsidiary subject to redemption" to "Minority interest" and "Capital in excess of par value."

Foreign Currency

All assets and liabilities of the Company's foreign subsidiaries are translated at year-end exchange rates, and revenues and expenses are translated at average exchange rates for the year in accordance with SFAS No. 52, "Foreign Currency Translation." Resulting translation adjustments are reflected as a separate component of shareholders' investment titled "Cumulative translation adjustment." Foreign currency transaction gains and losses are included in the accompanying statement of income and are not material for the three years presented.

Presentation

Certain amounts in 1992 and 1991 have been reclassified to conform to the 1993 financial statement presentation.

---

2. ACQUISITIONS

In February 1993, Thermo Instrument acquired Spectra-Physics Analytical, a manufacturer of liquid chromatography and capillary electrophoresis analytical instruments, for $6.7 million in cash. In 1993, the Company's majority-owned subsidiaries made several other acquisitions for $76.5 million in cash.

In 1992, Thermo Instruments acquired Nicolet Instrument Corporation. The total purchase price to the Company was approximately $175 million. Nicolet designs, manufactures, and markets instrumentation for a broad range of analytical chemistry, neurodiagnostic, and electronic engineering problem-solving applications in science and industry.

In 1992, the Company's majority-owned subsidiaries made several other acquisitions for $77.7 million in cash, assumption of debt in the amount of $7.3 million, prepayment of debt in the amount of $1.5 million, and issuance of common stock and stock options of a majority-owned subsidiary valued at approximately $12.3 million.

These acquisitions have been accounted for as purchases and their results of operations have been included in the accompanying financial statements from their respective dates of acquisition. The aggregate cost of these acquisitions exceeded the estimated fair value of the acquired net assets by $325 million, which is being amortized principally over 40 years. Allocation of the purchase price was based on the fair value of the net assets acquired and, for acquisitions completed in fiscal 1993, is subject to adjustment.

Based on unaudited data, the following table presents selected financial information for the Company, Spectra-Physics Analytical, and Nicolet on a pro forma basis, assuming the companies had been combined since the beginning of 1992. Net income and earnings per share are shown before Nicolet's discontinued operations, which occurred in fiscal 1992. The effect on the Company's financial statements of the acquisi-

tions not included in the pro forma data was not significant.

(In thousands, except per share amounts)	1993	1992
Revenues	$1,257,523	$1,105,907
Earnings per share before cumulative effect of change in accounting principal:	75,631	43,016
Primary	1.73	1.07
Fully diluted	1.55	1.04

9. Transactions in Stock of Subsidiaries

"Gain on issuance of stock by subsidiaries" in the accompanying statement of income results primarily from the following transactions:

1993

Public offering of 3,225,000 shares of Thermedics common stock at $10.00 per share for net proceeds of $29,980,000 resulted in a gain of $10,707,000. Public offering of 4,312,500 shares of Thermo Power common stock at $9.00 per share for net proceeds of $35,998,000 resulted in a gain of $10,578,000.

Private placements of 2,062,500 shares of ThermoTrex common stock at $11.17 and $14.50 per share for net proceeds of $27,463,000 resulted in a gain of $11,400,000.

Private placement of 200,000 shares and initial public offering of 1,100,000 shares of Thermo Remediation at $9.89 and $12.50 per share, respectively, for net proceeds of $14,554,000 resulted in a gain of $4,239,000.

Conversion of $7,270,000 of Thermedics 6½% subordinated convertible debentures convertible at $10.42 per share into 697.919 shares of Thermedics common stock resulted in a gain of $2,506,000.

1992

Private placement of 2,709,356 shares and initial public offering of 3,000,000 shares of Thermo Fibertek common stock at $6.70 to $8.00 per share in net proceeds at $39,748,000 resulted in a gain of $34,303,000.

Issuance of 1,566,480 restricted shares of ThermoTrex common stock valued at $6.17 per share, or $9,673,000 to acquire Lorad Corporation resulted in a gain of $3,081,000.

Private placement of 375,000 shares of ThermoTrex common stock at $10.67 per share for net proceeds of $3,556,000 resulted in a gain of $1,745,000.

1991

Conversion of $9,099,000 of Thermo Instrument 6% and 6½% subordinated convertible debentures convertible at $12.19 and $10.83 per share, respectively, into 766.786 shares of Thermo Instrument common stock resulted in a gain of $3,707,000.

Conversion of $6,200,000 of Thermo Process 6½% subordinated convertible debentures convertible at $10.33 per share into 600.191 shares of Thermo Process common stock resulted in a gain of $3,043,000.

Repurchases of $3,700,000 of Thermedics 6½% subordinated convertible debentures convertible at $10.42 per share for $941,000 in cash and 367,500 shares of Thermedics common stock valued at $7.14 per share, or $2,623,000, resulted in a gain of $1,010,000.

Private placement of 1,660,197 shares and initial public offering of 2,250,000 shares of ThermoTrex common stock at $5.55 and $8.00 per share, respectively, for net proceeds of $24,764,000 resulted in a gain of $13,958,000.

Private placement of 1,591,549 shares of common stock of J. Amerika N.V. at 6.00 Dutch guilders per share for net proceeds of $4,573,000 resulted in a gain of $2,148,000.

Sale of 244,200 shares of Thermo Cardiosystems common stock by Thermedics at an average price of $8.43 per share for net proceeds of $2,040,000 resulted in a taxable gain of $1,958,000.

The Company's ownership percentage in these subsidiaries changed primarily as a result of the transactions listed above, as well as the Company's purchases of shares of majority-owned subsidiary stock, the subsidiaries' purchases of their own stock, the sale of subsidiaries' stock by the Company or by the subsidiaries under employees' and directors' stock plans or in other transactions, and the conversion of convertible obligations held by the Company, its subsidiaries, or by third parties.

Thermo Electron Corporation

Thermo Electron Corporation

The Company's ownership percentages at year-end were as follows:

	1993	1992	1991
Thermo Instrument	81%	81%	80%
Thermo Fibertek	80%	80%	100%
Thermedics	52%	59%	59%
Thermo Power	52%	81%	81%
ThermoTrex	55%	62%	70%
Thermo Process	72%	71%	71%
Thermo Energy Systems	88%	87%	87%
Thermo Cardiosystems (a)	57%	58%	55%
Thermo Voltek (a)	67%	57%	52%
Thermo Remediation (b)	67%	85%	93%
ThermoLase (c)	81%	100%	100%

(a) Reflects combined ownership by Thermo Electron and Thermedics.

(b) Reflects ownership by Thermo Process.

(c) Reflects ownership by ThermoTrex.

REPORT OF INDEPENDENT AUDITORS

To the Shareholders and Board of Directors of Thermo Electron Corporation:

We have audited the accompanying consolidated balance sheet of Thermo Electron Corporation (a Delaware corporation) and subsidiaries as of January 1, 1994 and January 2, 1993, and the related consolidated statements of income, shareholders, investment, and cash flows for each of the three years in the period ended January 1, 1994. These consolidated financial statements are the responsibility of the Company's management. Our responsibility is to express an opinion on these consolidated financial statements based on our audits.

We conducted our audits in accordance with generally accepted auditing standards. Those standards require that we plan and perform the audit to obtain reasonable assurance about whether the financial statements are free of material misstatement. An audit includes examining, on a test basis, evidence supporting the amounts and disclosures in the financial statements. An audit also includes assessing the accounting principles used and significant estimates made by management, as well as evaluating the overall financial statement presentation. We believe that our audits provide a reasonable basis for our opinion.

In our opinion, the consolidated financial statements referred to above present fairly, in all material aspects, the financial position of Thermo Electron Corporation and subsidiaries as of January 1, 1994 and January 2, 1993, and the results of their operations and their cash flows for each of the three years in the period ended January 1, 1994, in conformity with generally accepted accounting principles.

As discussed in Note 7 to the consolidated financial statements, effective December 29, 1991, the Company has changed its method of accounting for postretirement benefits other than pensions.

Arthur Andersen & Co.

Boston, Massachusetts
February 17, 1994

MANAGEMENT DISCUSSION AND ANALYSIS

OVERVIEW

The Company develops and manufactures a broad range of products that are sold worldwide. The Company expands its products and services by developing and commercializing its own core technologies and by making strategic acquisitions of complementary businesses. The majority of the Company's businesses fall into three broad market segments: environmental, energy, and selected health and safety instrumentation.

An important component of the Company's strategy is to establish leading positions in its markets through the application of proprietary technology, whether developed internally or acquired. A key contributor to the growth of the Company's segment income (as defined in the results of operations below), particularly over the last two years, has been the ability to identify attractive acquisition opportunities, complete those acquisitions, and derive a growing income contribution from these newly acquired businesses as they are integrated into the Company's business segments.

The Company seeks to minimize its dependence on any specific product or market by maintaining and diversifying its portfolio of businesses and technologies. Similarly, the Company's goal is to maintain a balance in its businesses between those affected by various regulatory cycles and those more dependent on the general level of economic activity. To date, the Company's overall financial performance has been relatively unaffected by the recession in the U.S. economy in 1991 and 1992 and the general economic weakness in Europe and Japan in 1992 and 1993. This is due in large part to strong contributions from newly acquired businesses and the continued strength of businesses primarily driven by environmental regulation. Although the Company is diversified in terms of technology, product offerings, and geographic markets served, the future financial performance of the Company as a whole depends upon, among other factors, the strength of worldwide economies and the continued adoption and diligent enforcement of environmental regulations.

The Company believes that maintaining an entrepreneurial atmosphere is essential to its continued growth and development. In order to preserve this atmosphere, the Company adopted in 1983 a strategy of spinning out certain of its businesses into separate subsidiaries and having these subsidiaries sell a minority interest to outside investors. The Company believes that this strategy provides additional motivation and incentives for the management of the subsidiaries through the establishment of subsidiary-level stock option incentive programs, as well as capital to support the subsidiaries' growth. As a result of the sale of stock by subsidiaries, the issuance of shares by subsidiaries upon conversion of indebtedness, and similar

transactions, the Company records gains that represent the increase in the Company's net investment in the subsidiaries and are classified as "Gain on issuance of stock by subsidiaries" in the accompanying statement of income. These gains have represented a substantial portion of the net income reported by the Company in recent years. Although the Company expects to continue this strategy in the future, its goal is to continue increasing segment income over the next few years so that gains generated by sales of stock by its subsidiaries will represent a decreasing portion of net income. The size and timing of these transactions are dependent on market and other conditions that are beyond the Company's control. Accordingly, there can be no assurance that the Company will be able to generate gains from such transactions in the future.

Thermo Electron Corporation

OTHER INFORMATION

(In thousands)	1993	1992	1991
Revenues:			
Thermo Instrument Systems, Inc.	$ 584,176	$ 423,199	$ 338,747
Thermo Fibertek Inc.	137,088	125,577	124,731
Thermedics Inc. (a)	80,220	45,778	32,295
Thermo Power Corporation	77,360	43,904	29,131
ThermoTrex Corporation	54,329	19,843	16,801
Thermo Process Systems Inc. (b)	53,839	47,082	50,632
	987,012	705,383	592,337
Wholly and majority-owned nonpublic companies	262,706	243,589	213,147
	$1,249,718	$ 948,972	$ 805,484
Segment Income (c):			
Thermo Instrument Systems Inc.	$ 96,786	$ 63,373	$ 49,742
Thermo Fibertek Inc.	15,902	15,716	14,652
Thermedics Inc. (a)	8,292	841	(3,048)
Thermo Power Corporation	2,707	715	(3,158)
ThermoTrex Corporation	485	(1,185)	(113)
Thermo Process Systems Inc. (b)	1,338	371	(1,487)
	125,510	79,831	56,588
Wholly and majority-owned nonpublic companies	17,122	7,237	7,315
	142,632	87,068	63,903
Equity in Losses of Unconsolidated Subsidiaries	(21,076)	(3,948)	(1,663)
Corporate	9,563	18,850	16,933
Income Before Income Taxes, Minority Interest, and Cumulative Effect of Change in Accounting Principle	$131,119	$101,970	$ 79,173

(a) Includes Thermo Cardiosystems Inc. and Thermo Voltek Corp.

(b) Includes Thermo Remediation Inc.

(c) Segment income is income before corporate general and administrative expenses, costs associated with divisional and product restructuring, other income and expense, minority interest expense, and income taxes.

COMMON STOCK MARKET INFORMATION

The following table shows the market range for the Company's common stock based on reported sales prices on the New York Stock Exchange (symbol TMO) for 1993 and 1992. Prices have been restated to reflect a three-for-two stock split distributed in October 1993.

Quarter	1993		1992	
	High	Low	High	Low
First	$38	$31⅓	$31⅔	$26¼
Second	41⅙	36⅓	29¹/₁₂	25⅙
Third	43¼	37¼	28⅓	25
Fourth	43	38⅛	31½	26½

DIVIDEND POLICY

The Company has never paid cash dividends and does not expect to pay cash dividends in the foreseeable future because its policy has been to use earnings to finance expansion and growth. Payments of dividends will rest within the discretion of the Board of Directors and will depend upon, among other factors, the Company's earnings, capital requirements, and financial condition.

The closing market price on the New York Stock Exchange for the Company's common stock on February 25, 1994, was 39½ per share.

As of February 25, 1994, the Company had 6,406 holders of record of its common stock. This does not include holdings in street or nominee names.

Common stock of the following majority-owned public subsidiaries is traded on the American Stock Exchange: Thermedics Inc. (TMD; Thermo Instrument Systems Inc. (THI); Thermo Power Corporation (THP); Thermo Process Systems Inc. (TPI); Thermo Voltek Corp. (TVL); ThermoTrex Corporation (TKN); Thermo Fibertek Inc. (TFT); and Thermo Remediation Inc. (THN).

The Upjohn Company:
The Upjohn – Pharmacia Merger

Pharmacia & Upjohn will be a powerful new competitor in the global pharmaceutical industry. For both Pharmacia and Upjohn, this merger is a bold strategic move to build a highly competitive company as the worldwide pharmaceutical industry continues to consolidate. The new company will be positioned to attain its goals of revenue growth above the industry average and operating margins exceeding 25% by 1998.

Jan Ekberg, President and CEO of Pharmacia
Proposed Chairman of Pharmacia & Upjohn

This is a merger that truly constitutes far more than the sum of the parts. The new company will be able to take full advantage of uniquely complementary geographic reach, product portfolio, pipeline and R&D strengths. As a result of the merger, Pharmacia & Upjohn will have extensive financial and operating resources, market scope and earnings potential. Consequently, we fully expect the new company to achieve additional growth in expected 1996 EPS as well as acceleration of future earnings growth. Above all, Pharmacia & Upjohn is expected to generate significantly enhanced value for shareholders.

John L. Zabriskie, Ph.D., Chairman and CEO of Upjohn
Proposed President and CEO of Pharmacia & Upjohn

On August 20, 1995, The Upjohn Company and Pharmacia AB, two pharmaceutical companies incorporated in the U.S. and Sweden, respectively, announced that they were forming a "merger of equals." With combined sales of nearly $7 billion, the new company would be the ninth largest pharmaceutical company in the world. Management and major shareholders alike seemed excited by the deal. William U. Parfet, great-grandson of founder W. E. Upjohn and a company director, stated, "We recognize we're being distanced from our heritage, and that tugs at you, but this is absolutely the right thing for Upjohn to do in today's environment, and John Zabriskie is really the key."[1]

THE UPJOHN COMPANY

The Upjohn Company, founded in 1886, developed, manufactured, and sold prescription and nonprescription pharmaceuticals (68 percent of sales), animal health products (10 percent), and bulk pharmaceutical chemicals and other products (22 percent). Upjohn maintained headquarters in Kalamazoo, Michigan, and owned research, manufacturing, and distribution facilities throughout the world. In 1994 Upjohn had sales of $3.3 billion of which 59 percent were U.S. sales, 20 percent European, 13 percent Japanese and Pacific Rim, and 8 percent in other countries. Sales were down 2 percent from the previous

Research Associate James Weber prepared this case under the supervision of Professors Amy Patricia Hutton and Krishna Palepu. The case is intended solely as the basis for class discussion and is not intended to serve as an endorsement, source of primary data, or illustration of effective or ineffective management. Copyright © 1996 by the President and Fellows of Harvard College. HBS Case 9-197-034.

1. Keith Naughton and Heidi Dawley, "Upjohn Finally Makes It to The Big Leagues," Business Week, September 4, 1995.

year while net income, at $491 million, was up 25 percent. Upjohn employed 16,900 worldwide.[2]

The proposed merger with Pharmacia was an attempt by Upjohn to address a number of the strategic problems it faced. While some of these problems affected the industry as a whole, others were specific to Upjohn. For the industry, the increasing strength of cost-conscious buyers such as hospital networks, Health Maintenance Organizations (HMOs), and insurers, was putting downward pressure on pharmaceutical companies' margins. In an effort to maintain margins, drug companies were consolidating in order to reduce costs and obtain economies of scale. For Upjohn, a number of its patents had expired on key products resulting in stiff competition from lower priced generic drugs. Upjohn had fewer products than it would have liked in its product development pipeline with which to replace these older drugs. Further, Upjohn was weak in foreign sales, a market segment that made up approximately two-thirds of the world market for pharmaceutical products. Finally, Upjohn's stock price had been stagnant over the six months preceding the merger announcement and the company was rumored to be a potential takeover target.

THE PHARMACEUTICAL INDUSTRY

The worldwide prescription drug market was estimated at $252 billion in 1994 and was expected to grow by 6 percent in 1995. North America was the largest segment ($79 billion), followed by Europe ($77 billion) and Japan ($49 billion). Even with the ongoing consolidation among pharmaceutical firms, the industry was still highly fragmented with many competitors. Glaxo Wellcome, the largest firm in the industry in mid-1995, had pharmaceutical sales of just under $12 billion, while the top ten firms in pharmaceutical sales had a 28 percent market share and the top 50 firms had just over 60 percent.[3] Further, in an industry where companies needed large markets to cover high development costs, the sales of many companies were concentrated in one or two markets.

Prior to the late 1980s, drug companies had greater power in relation to drug buyers. Drug company salespeople contacted doctors directly and sold them on the superior benefits of their company's products. Doctors were largely free to prescribe medications of their choosing and they frequently chose the branded products that were developed by the major pharmaceutical companies and with which they were most familiar. Payers—mostly insurance companies, employers, and governments—had little choice other than to pay for what doctors prescribed. In this market, drug companies continuously raised prices on their products and most companies were able to increase earnings over 10 percent yearly. Some observers felt that this high historical profitability in the industry had led to significant excess capacity in production and bloated administration staffing.

Since the late 1980s, significant change had been occurring in the pharmaceutical industry. Most of this change was a direct result of pressures from buyers to reduce the costs of health care. The high prices charged by the pharmaceutical companies for prescription drugs made them an obvious target. Buyers of pharmaceutical products were consolidating into increasingly larger entities and gaining power relative to suppliers. Drug purchasing decisions were increasingly being made by plan administrators and pharmaceutical benefit management (PBM) firms, with a strong eye on cost, rather than by individual doctors.

2. *The Upjohn Company 1994 Annual Report.*
3. Medical & Healthcare Marketplace Guide, 11th Edition, p. 55.

PBM companies served as intermediaries between pharmaceutical companies and large drug purchasers such as HMOs, hospital networks, and insurance companies. Both PBMs and individual plan administrators were able to negotiate lower prices through bulk purchases. These bulk purchases were made possible by the large numbers of patients they were buying for, and by the ability to limit the number of different drugs purchased by requiring doctors to prescribe only drugs that appeared on approved lists called formularies. The large drug buyers also sought to limit the number of suppliers they purchased from by purchasing from large suppliers that could provide many different drug products.

Generic Drugs and Patents

The new pharmaceutical environment opened the door for producers of generic drugs. Under the old system, doctors and patients tended to select well-known branded drugs even when generic drugs were available. By the mid-1990s, drug buyers were requiring the use of lower cost drugs wherever possible and doctors were required to justify their use of higher cost drugs whenever lower cost alternatives were available. Further, doctors working for HMOs and other medical plans often had financial incentives to prescribe generic products.

The development and use of generic drugs became possible once patent protection had expired on the branded product that had opened the market. While some branded products seemed to have unreasonably high prices, the pharmaceutical companies that developed the branded products argued that the high cost of R&D and the long regulatory approval process justified such prices. Bringing a new drug to the market could take fifteen years and cost between $350 million and $600 million.[4] Generic producers did not have these costs, nor did they have the advertising expenditures associated with branded drugs; thus, generic drugs typically were priced at one-half the price of their branded equivalents. In 1995 generic drug makers had a 40 percent U.S. market share, up from 23 percent in 1980. By the late 1990s, it was estimated that generics would control two-thirds of the market.[5] In an effort to limit lost sales, some branded drug producers, including Upjohn, had begun selling generic drugs that copied their own branded products.

Drugs coming off patent were a significant issue in the pharmaceutical industry. Between 1996 and 2000, drugs generating $15 billion in sales would lose patent protection and become open to generic competition.[6] The concern for the branded producers was that there were few blockbuster drugs, those with expected sales of over $500 million, in the development pipeline to replace the lost sales due to generics. A key reason for this was that the chronic diseases that had yet to be solved, and that affected large numbers of people, were only poorly understood. Thus, breakthrough drugs for chronic diseases were not expected until perhaps early in the next century. There were few diseases such as diabetes where an individual could be successfully treated by pharmaceuticals for a lifetime. The difficulty in developing new drugs had led to industry R&D expenditures of nearly 19 percent of sales in 1994, up from less than 16 percent in 1990.[7]

The Industry's Response to the New Environment

In the face of the economic changes occurring in the industry, pharmaceutical companies began making significant changes in their operations, strategies, and organizations. The

4. Eric Reguly, "Drug Firms Take the Merger Treatment to Stay Healthy," Times Newspapers, Ltd., August 22, 1995.

5. Health Care Products & Services, Standard & Poor's Industry Surveys, 1995, p. 26.

6. Ibid.

7. Marketplace Guide, 11th Edition, p. 66.

The Upjohn Company

first step that many companies took was to rationalize their operations in search of efficiency gains. Downsizing, restructuring, and the closing of plants had been the order of the day. Further, companies were selling off their nonpharmaceutical businesses to focus on their core activities. The use of a "disease management" approach to health care was growing. Disease management involved focusing on all facets of an illness from prevention to diagnostics and treatment in an effort to offer a complete care package that was of higher quality and lower cost than a piecemeal approach. For drug companies, this often meant joint ventures with medical device companies and even medical care providers.

The most dramatic change in the industry, however, was the ongoing consolidation. Nearly $70 billion in mergers and acquisitions occurred in the two years prior to the Upjohn-Pharmacia announcement. Further, while the top ten companies had less than a 30 percent market share in 1995, they were expected to have a near 50 percent market share by the turn of the century. Between 1993 and 1994, the consolidation trend, along with company downsizing efforts, had led to the elimination of over 60,000 jobs in the industry worldwide.[8]

Pharmaceutical companies were consolidating through both vertical and horizontal integration. The vertical integration was an attempt to move closer to the patients by merging with or acquiring major drug buyers, PBMs, HMOs, and other large networks. By integrating vertically, drug companies were seeking access to patients and inclusion on drug formularies.

The horizontal integration of drug companies was being driven by a number of factors. First, buyer strength was increasing through consolidation in this segment of the market as well. Second, the cost to develop new drugs was rising, making it difficult for many companies to go it alone. Third, pharmaceutical markets were becoming increasingly worldwide as more countries sought to improve their health care systems, and as drug companies looked for larger markets over which to spread their costs. Companies weaker in some markets than in others were seeking to join with companies in a similar situation, but with different markets so that the combined company would be strong in all markets. Fourth, under pressure to reduce costs, drug companies were seeking efficiency gains through economies of scale. And last, companies with weak product development pipelines were looking for new products to sell.

Examples of horizontal integration were both more numerous and larger in size than those of vertical integration. Further, horizontal integration was the more "proven" strategy. However, some analysts believed that vertical integration was the more significant trend for the longer term structure of the industry.

The Industry's Future

Despite the increasing competitive pressures faced by individual companies, the long-term economic factors appeared positive for the industry as a whole. Several of these factors pointed towards a growing industry and the increased use of pharmaceuticals: the population had been aging, particularly in the U.S.; an increasing number of health insurance plans covered prescription drugs; the use of pharmaceutical products tended to be more cost effective than hospitalization; an increasing number of countries were attempting to improve their health care systems; and finally, the pharmaceutical industry was relatively recession proof.

8. Health Care Products 1995, p. 4.

UPJOHN'S POSITION

Upjohn operated in several market segments. Its pharmaceutical product sales were divided into six areas: central nervous system; steroids, anti-inflammatory, and analgesic; reproductive and women's health; critical care, transplant, and cancer; infectious disease; and metabolic. Although primarily in human prescription and nonprescription drugs, Upjohn was the world's ninth largest producer of animal pharmaceuticals. The company also had significant bulk pharmaceutical chemical sales and had spent some $100 million on two new production facilities in 1994. Upjohn's top ten human pharmaceutical products accounted for approximately 56 percent of company sales (see Table A).

To a certain extent, Upjohn's problems were not unique: the problems it faced were those typical to many companies in the industry. As the world's nineteenth largest pharmaceutical company, Upjohn was a mid-sized company in an industry where success was increasingly characterized by larger companies and by small innovative companies. Middle tier companies such as Upjohn were at a disadvantage to their larger competitors in dealing with major buyers. Upjohn was particularly hard hit by the loss of patent protection on four key drugs and the ensuing generic competition that led to a $400 million decline in sales on these products. For one of these drugs, Xanax, Upjohn's highest selling product, generics were selling at 20 percent of Xanax's price prior to patent expiration. Despite the loss of Xanax sales dollars, Upjohn was able to maintain approximately 80 percent of its Xanax unit volume sales by the introduction of its own generic equivalent. Upjohn was also weak in international sales. This was particularly true in Europe, a market approximately the same size as the U.S. market but where Upjohn had sales of only one-third its U.S. sales. Further, there were significantly better opportunities for sales growth in overseas markets than in the more highly competitive U.S. market.

Another problem faced by Upjohn was a weak product development pipeline. While the company claimed its pipeline was "one of the strongest in Upjohn's history, with ten

Table A Upjohn's 1994 Top Selling Human Pharmaceutical Products

Product	Description	1994 Sales ($ millions)	Percent Increase (Decrease) 1994 over 1993
Xanax	Anti-Anxiety/Panic Disorder	$ 342	(45.2)%
Micronase	Oral Anti-Diabetes	271	(4.2)
Cleocin	Antibiotic	248	6.4
Provera	Sex Hormone	211	2.4
Solu-Medrol	Injectable Steroid	153	7.7
Depo-Provera	Injectable Contraceptive	134	86.1
Ibuprofen	Analgesic, Anti-Inflammatory	129	3.2
Rogaine	Hair Loss Treatment	122	10.9
Ansaid	Anti-Inflammatory	105	(14.6)
Halcion	Hypnotic Sleep Induction	104	(14.0)
Total Top 10		1819	(10.8)
Other Products	Various	1456	11.9
Total All Products		$3275	(1.9)%

Sources: Pharmacia & Upjohn Merger Prospectus, September 15, 1995; Upjohn's 1994 Annual Report; and Joseph P. Riccardo and Scott J. Shevick, *The Merger: Upjohn Co., Pharmacia AB,* Analyst Report, Bear Stearns & Co. Inc., September 18, 1995.

The Upjohn Company

compounds in late-stage development,"[9] analysts noted that none of these new drugs were expected to be blockbusters. The weak pipeline remained despite Upjohn spending 18.5 percent of sales or $607 million on R&D in 1994. On the positive side, 25 percent of 1994 sales were from products introduced since 1992, and between 1990 and 1994, Upjohn had cut in half the time necessary to move a product through its R&D pipeline.

In January 1993, Upjohn hired John Zabriskie as its new CEO. Zabriskie, who arrived at Upjohn after nearly 30 years at Merck, then the industry's largest company, began a number of initiatives aimed at improving Upjohn's performance. These initiatives included cutting costs, particularly in marketing and administration, reducing the workforce by some 1,300 people,[10] selling off non-core activities, such as the Asgrow Seed Company and part interest in a chicken breeding venture, and consolidating sixteen divisions into three—R&D, manufacturing, and marketing. (For more details, see Exhibit 1: Upjohn Company – 1994 Letter to Shareholders and Financial Review.)

THE PHARMACIA MERGER

Given the strategic problems Upjohn faced in the changing pharmaceuticals market, and the general belief that size was an important factor in determining success, the company's announcement of the proposed merger was of little surprise.

Details of the Merger

The proposed merger had Upjohn and Pharmacia executing a tax-free exchange of shares (pooling of interests) to create a new company named Pharmacia & Upjohn, Inc. One Upjohn share would be exchanged for 1.45 shares in the new company, while Pharmacia shares would be exchanged one-for-one. (See Exhibit 2: Abridged Merger Prospectus.) The new company would have 504 million shares outstanding, with 248 million held by Upjohn shareholders and 255 million held by Pharmacia owners. In the new company, Upjohn's Zabriskie would be the President and CEO while Pharmacia's Jan Ekberg would serve as Nonexecutive Chairman. An Upjohn executive would serve as CFO. Pharmacia & Upjohn's board of directors would be formed from an equal number of current Upjohn and Pharmacia board members. Pharmacia & Upjohn would have corporate headquarters in London and operational headquarters in Kalamazoo, Michigan; Stockholm/Uppsala, Sweden; and Milan, Italy. A special meeting of Upjohn stockholders was to be held on October 17, 1995, to vote on the proposed merger. The merger had the unanimous support of Upjohn's board of directors. Exhibit 3 shows data on the stock prices of Upjohn and Pharmacia around the date of the merger announcement.

Pharmacia

Pharmacia was the world's eighteenth largest pharmaceutical company, with 1994 sales of $3.4 billion. Headquartered in Sweden, the firm's predecessor, Procordia AB, was part of a state holding company along with a number of unrelated businesses until the late 1980s. Between 1989 and 1993, the company evolved through a series of mergers and acquisitions to become primarily an international health care company focused in pharmaceutical products. During this period, Procordia also divested a significant portion of its lines of branded

9. *The Upjohn Company 1994 Annual Report*, p. 4.

10. Between 1988 and 1994, Upjohn had eliminated 4,600 jobs.

The Upjohn Company

consumer products and changed its name to Pharmacia. Following the 1993 acquisition of the Italian firm FICE, with its approximately $900 million in sales, Pharmacia sales were 59 percent in Europe, 16 percent in each of North America and Japan, and 9 percent in the rest of the world. Only 8 percent of Pharmacia sales were in their home country. At the end of 1994, Pharmacia employed 18,600 individuals worldwide.

Pharmacia was a market leader in several product areas including cancer treatment, growth hormones, cataract surgery products, intravenous nutrition, allergy diagnostics, smoking cessation, and chemicals for biotechnology R&D. See Table B for information on Pharmacia's top selling products, which accounted for 44 percent of company sales.

In an effort to combine the several companies that had formed Pharmacia, and to better meet the increased competition in the pharmaceuticals industry, Pharmacia had undergone significant restructuring between 1993 and 1995. This restructuring included: a consolidation and reduction in the size of the combined sales and marketing organizations; rationalizing production facilities, including a reduction from 52 to 43 plants and the planned reduction in plants to 22 by 1998; the elimination of some 1,300 jobs, mainly from the middle management ranks; and a refocusing of R&D onto fewer projects in fewer areas.

Pharmacia's business strategy was somewhat different than the typical pharmaceutical company. The industry in general pursued the broad general practitioner market segment while Pharmacia focused on the smaller segment of hospitals and specialists. Pharmacia had no blockbuster drugs in its product development pipeline, partly as a result of this niche-market strategy, but rather relied on a larger number of products with smaller potential sales. Further, at least one analyst believed that Pharmacia stock was somewhat undervalued because of the lack of a high-profile blockbuster drug in the pipeline.[11]

Table B Pharmacia's 1994 Top Selling Human Pharmaceutical Products

Product	Description	1994 Sales ($ millions)	Percent Increase (Decrease) 1994 over 1993
Genotropin	Growth Hormone	$ 335	1.2%
Healon	Cataract Surgery Aid	208	(1.9)
Farmorubicin	Anticancer	191	11.7
Allergy Diagnostics	Blood Tests for Allergies	175	8.7
Adriamycin	Anticancer	140	6.1
Sermion	Senility Disorders	105	(2.8)
Nicorette	Smoking Cessation	105	1.9
Fragmin	Blood Clot Treatments	100	(8.3)
Intralipid	Intravenous Nutrition	88	1.1
Salazopyrin	Inflammatory Bowel Disease	84	9.1
Total Top 10		1531	2.7
Other Products	Various	1921	(3.4)
Total All Products		$3452	(0.7)%

Sources: Pharmacia & Upjohn Merger Prospectus, September 15, 1995; Pharmacia's 1994 Annual Report; and Joseph P. Riccardo and Scott J. Shevick, *The Merger: Upjohn Co., Pharmacia AB*, Analyst Report, Bear Stearns & Co. Inc., September 18, 1995.

11. Pharmacia, *Analysts Report, Auerbach Grayson & Company, July 7, 1995.*

The Combined Companies

The August 20 merger announcement described the combined company as follows:

> *The company, named Pharmacia & Upjohn, Inc., would have had combined 1994 sales of nearly $7 billion, with prescription pharmaceutical sales placing it in the top ten in the worldwide industry. Annual research and development expenditures will exceed $1 billion, also in the top tier of the pharmaceutical industry. The complementary geographical strengths of the two companies will give Pharmacia & Upjohn sales ranking among the top five pharmaceutical companies in Europe, top 15 in North America, and top 20 in Japan (also among the top two or three non-Japanese companies in Japan). Pharmacia & Upjohn will have a broad product portfolio with sales exceeding $500 million in six key therapeutic areas. Sales growth in Pharmacia & Upjohn, led by 28 product introduction and line extensions in the next three years and deeper penetration of existing markets, is expected to exceed industry averages. Projected annual operating cost synergies of over $500 million, more than 85% of which are expected to be in effect by the end of 1996, are anticipated to further contribute to increased earnings and a strong balance sheet as well as provide flexibility to take advantage of further growth opportunities.*

According to company management, the combination of Upjohn and Pharmacia would create a company better prepared to compete in the changing environment of the pharmaceuticals industry. Specifically, a merger with Pharmacia would strengthen Upjohn in terms of market presence, R&D, geographic reach, product portfolio, cost synergies, financial position and growth, and provide the management experience necessary to succeed. (See Exhibit 3 for the stock market reaction to the merger announcement.)

Market Presence   Pharmacia & Upjohn would become the world's ninth largest pharmaceutical company. In a world increasingly dominated by large buyers looking to deal with fewer suppliers, the general belief in the industry was "bigger is better."

R&D   The increasing cost of developing new pharmaceutical products was making it more difficult for smaller companies. Some analysts believed that $1 billion in yearly R&D expenditures was becoming a minimum threshold for continued long-term success. Upjohn alone had been spending above the industry average for R&D, but was still significantly short of this threshold. The addition of Pharmacia would enable Upjohn to reach this level. Further, although Pharmacia's pipeline was not in the industry's top tier and did not contain potential blockbusters, it did have several products expected to begin making moderate contributions to sales growth in the 1995 to 1997 period, and had several more potential products further back in the pipeline.

Geographic Reach   Upjohn alone was weak in the world's second and third largest markets, Europe and Japan. While some drugs were tailored to specific markets, most could be used worldwide, and particularly in the top three markets. Thus, as the cost of developing drugs rose, it became increasingly important to be able to access the world market. Improving Upjohn's position outside of the U.S. would require market specific drugs, but more important it required a developed sales and marketing organization with good contacts among the many buyers in these markets. Pharmacia provided both, particularly since Europe, which was Upjohn's weakness, was Pharmacia's strongest market.

Product Portfolio   One of the key benefits of the merger for Upjohn was the addition of Pharmacia's products. The combined companies would have sales of over $500 million in each of six areas. In five of Upjohn's top selling product areas (central nervous system;

reproductive and women's health; critical care, transplant, and cancer; infectious disease; and metabolics) Pharmacia added strong products of their own, potential products to be introduced within a few years, or better access to key markets. Further, the addition of Pharmacia's over-the-counter products, such as Nicorette and Nicotrol for smoking cessation, the laxative Microlax, and various dietary supplements, to Upjohn's Motrin IB pain reliever, Kaopectate for diarrhea, Dramamine for motion sickness, and Unicap vitamins, may give this area a critical mass that it lacked at both companies individually. Also, Pharmacia added additional experience in moving products from being prescription drugs to over-the-counter products. This could prove useful as Upjohn attempted to make this switch with several of their products in various world markets.

Cost Synergies   The combined companies had announced $500 million in expected operating cost synergies as a result of the merger with some 85 percent of the reductions in place by the end of 1996. One analyst estimated that one-half of the savings would come from Selling, General, and Administrative expenses and one-quarter each from manufacturing expenses and R&D expenses.[12] A part of these savings was to be the reduction of over 4,000 jobs.

Financial Position   The combined company would have a strong balance sheet. Because this was a pooling of interests merger financed by stock, there would be no acquisition-related interest costs or amortization of goodwill. Further, because it was one of the least leveraged companies in the industry, Pharmacia & Upjohn would be able to pursue future growth opportunities without severe financial constraints.

Growth   In addition to growth by acquisition, management expected the addition of Pharmacia would increase the growth of the existing company. Although in mid-1995 Pharmacia was growing faster than Upjohn, both companies were growing at below industry average rates. However, management believed that because Pharmacia's sales organization was strong where Upjohn's was weak, the combined companies would grow faster than either would separately—even faster than the industry average.

Management Experience   While Upjohn had management skilled in rationalizing operations, Pharmacia management brought critical skills in terms of integrating merged or acquired companies, having done so several times since the late 1980s. In particular, with the 1993 acquisition of FICE, Pharmacia had to restructure the company and combine and reduce its manufacturing, sales, and marketing organizations, as would be necessary with the proposed merger. The potential of the new company could not fully be realized unless it was successful in combining different operations and cultures to create effective and efficient functional units.

The Decision

As the date of the shareholders meeting approached, Upjohn's shareholders were trying to decide whether to approve the proposed merger with Pharmacia. Many observers saw the merger as a significant step toward addressing Upjohn's strategic problems, and in the days following the announcement several investment firms raised their recommendations on Upjohn stock from neutral to outperform. However, it was not clear that the proposed deal was the best one available for the shareholders. Difficult questions remained to be answered.

....

12. Joseph P. Riccardo and Scott J. Shevick, The Merger: Upjohn Co., Pharmacia AB, *Analyst Report*, Bear Stearns & Co. Inc., September 18, 1995.

A merger with Pharmacia appeared to make Upjohn a top tier firm. However, merging two companies of this size from different countries and with different cultures might be more complex than management believed. Was $500 million in cost synergies obtainable by the merger of two companies that had already achieved significant improvements in margins through rationalization efforts over the preceding few years? Even though Pharmacia's sales force was strong in Europe and Japan, there were questions about whether that sales force had the right contacts to achieve the sales increase that Upjohn was expecting. Further, Upjohn's product development pipeline had no blockbuster products and the addition of Pharmacia did not solve this problem. Were blockbuster drugs necessary for success, or was a relatively large number of lower potential products sufficient? Was Pharmacia the right partner with which to merge? Might Upjohn be better off acquiring rather than merging? Or perhaps shareholders would receive a higher premium by having Upjohn be acquired by some other firm. Finally, assuming Pharmacia was a good merger partner, was the stock exchange ratio a fair one for shareholders?

These questions were complicated by the fact that this might very well be an interim step for Upjohn if they hoped to remain a top tier player in the industry. The proposed merger would make Pharmacia & Upjohn a top ten company in 1995, but they might not be able to hold that position because other top companies were likely to merge and/or had potential blockbuster drugs in their pipelines.

QUESTIONS

1. Evaluate the strategic reasoning behind the proposed merger of Upjohn and Pharmacia. Will the merger effectively address the strategic challenges faced by Upjohn?

2. What is your interpretation of the stock market reaction to the announcement of the deal? What is the magnitude of performance improvements the market is expecting from the merger? Are these expectations realistic?

3. Can you think of an alternative restructuring strategy that might address the strategic challenges of Upjohn better? What are the likely risks and benefits from this strategy?

4. If you were a shareholder of Upjohn, would you support this merger proposal?

EXHIBIT I

Upjohn Company - 1994 Letter to Shareholders and Financial Review

To Our Shareholders:

In 1994, The Upjohn Company sharpened its focus and directed its resources toward a long-range strategy for growth. We began re-examining everything we do to find ways to do things better. We sold non-core businesses and initiated the re-engineering of our supply (manufacturing), sales and marketing and research and development operations. We redirected our sales and marketing efforts to exploit growth opportunities around the world. We continued to concentrate our research and development on major unmet medical needs. Through these key initiatives, we have strengthened our prospects for increasing the company's long-term performance and value.

We pursued these initiatives during one of the most challenging years in our company's history, balancing our efforts to establish long-term programs and priorities and the need to achieve a respectable financial performance today. Our sales for 1994 reached $3.3 billion, slightly below 1993 levels. Net earnings were $491 million in 1994, compared to $392 million in 1993. Earnings from continuing operations (before restructuring and unusual items and the cumulative effect of accounting changes) were $489 million, compared to $575 million in 1993. These results met our goal and exceeded external expectations.

Four of our largest-selling products—XANAX, HALCION, MICRONASE and ANSAID—lost U.S. patent protection, resulting in a $400 million decline in sales from intense generic competition. We offset substantially all of this loss in revenue with new-product sales, strong growth in international markets and a generics effort of our own. Our generics strategy helped us retain 83 percent of the dispensed new prescriptions for XANAX and alprazolam in the U.S. anti-anxiety market in 1994. While this competition will continue, we have a unique array of products in our pipeline aimed at penetrating new, specialized markets.

As we strengthen our product portfolio, we are rationalizing and consolidating our manufacturing sites worldwide to reduce excess capacity and operating costs in the years ahead. We also sold Asgrow Seed Company and our chicken-breeding joint venture, enabling us to focus on our core human and animal health pharmaceutical businesses. Our re-engineering and cost-containment efforts, including work-force reductions, contributed $75 million to operating earnings in 1994.

We are accelerating growth of our international business, which now contributes 44 percent of our total sales. We received 199 international product registrations in 1994. A joint venture in China, a growing presence in Central and Eastern Europe, and a return to Argentina and Brazil positions Upjohn to take maximum advantage of some of the world's fastest-growing markets.

We restructured our U.S. pharmaceutical sales and marketing operations to focus on integrated health care systems, HMOs, business coalitions, insurance providers and other emerging large customers in medical specialty areas. We formed Greenstone Healthcare Solutions to add the dimension of comprehensive disease management and analysis services to our traditional role of researcher, manufacturer and marketer of health care products.

Of course, the key to our company's long-term performance remains research and development. Our 1994 investment in R&D was $607 million, or 18.5 percent of sales, a rate above the industry average. This investment, along with a relentless discovery focus and accelerated development pace, comprises our commitment to create new products with high value and line extensions that maximize the value of our existing products.

Our current R&D pipeline is one of the strongest in Upjohn's history, with 10 compounds in late-stage development. We expect to file 10 New Drug Applications in the U.S. between 1994 and 1996. Over the last five years, we have reduced by more than 50 percent the time it takes to move a product through the R&D pipeline. Our R&D strategy is sharply focused, concentrating on 30 high-potential projects.

We are seeking unique products targeted at conditions for which adequate treatment is unavailable. Our pipeline includes promising compounds in late-stage development for cancer, certain types of stroke, head and spinal cord injuries and AIDS.

Upjohn's plan for dramatically improving its performance in the short-term and eventually moving into an industry leadership position is clear. By controlling costs and re-engineering our processes, we are finding better, more efficient ways to operate our business. By focusing on our customers and taking advantage of global opportunities in emerging markets, we are effectively adapting to the changing marketplace. By targeting our R&D efforts on major unmet medical

The Upjohn Company

needs and accelerating product development on a glo-bal scale, we are creating opportunities for the decades ahead. We are a company on the move. We are confident that these strategic initiatives in every area of the company have positioned us to take advantage of future opportunities.

I would like to thank our 16,900 employees worldwide for their hard work and dedication. Together, we demonstrated in 1994 what our employees can do when we believe in ourselves. I am proud of what our

employees have accomplished and look forward to working with them to achieve our vision for growth in the years ahead.

John L. Zabriskie, Ph.D.
Chairman of the Board and
Chief Executive Officer

March 3, 1995

Overview of Consolidated Results

Dollars in millions, except per-share data	1994	% Change	1993	% Change	1992
Total revenue	$3,344.5	(1)%	$3,380.5	3%	$3,284.7
Operating income	599.4	30	459.5	(31)	662.7
Earnings from continuing operations before income taxes and minority equity	643.3	34	480.0	(29)	671.9
Earnings from continuing operations	489.1	23	396.4	(25)	527.0
Net earnings	490.8	25	392.4	21	324.3
Net earnings per common share:					
Primary	$2.76	27	$2.18	22	$1.78
Fully diluted	$2.68	26	$2.13	22	$1.74

When comparing year-to-year earnings, accounting changes and restructuring recorded in each of the prior two years should be considered. In 1993, the company made two accounting changes: the adoption of calendar-year reporting for subsidiaries formerly reporting on a fiscal year and the adoption of Statement of Financial Accounting Standards (SFAS) No. 112 relating to postemployement benefits. The cumulative effect of these changes reduced 1993 net earnings by $18.9 million ($.11 per share). In 1992, the company adopted SFAS No. 106 relating to the postretirement benefit costs other than pensions and SFAS No. 109 relating to accounting for income taxes. The cumulative effect of these accounting changes reduced net earnings by $223 million ($1.26 per share).

In 1993, the company recorded restructuring charges that reduced operating income by $209 million ($155 million, or $.89 per share after tax), primarily associated with a worldwide work-force reduction, the write-down of certain assets and the reduction of excess manufacturing capacity. In 1992, restructuring charges of $22 million ($13.4 million, or $.08 per share after tax) were made to reflect the cost of a special voluntary early retirement program.

Several actions were taken to increase the company's focus on its core pharmaceutical business, including the 1994 divestitures of the Asgrow Seed Company and the company's interest in a chicken-breeding joint venture and the 1993 divestiture of Asgrow Florida Company. Both the sales of the Asgrow Seed Company and Asgrow Florida Company have been reported as discontinued operations. Accordingly, certain prior-period financial data have been restated to reflect only the continuing operations of the company.

With the sale of three agricultural segment operations identified above, the company has elected to report its business operations as a single industry segment—Pharmaceutical Products. This industry designation more accurately reflects the ongoing operations of the company. Prior-year data presented in this review also reflect the single Pharmaceutical Products industry segment.

Product Sales

The table below provides a year-to-year comparison of consolidated net sales by major pharmaceutical product group:

Dollars in millions	1994	% Change	1993	% Change	1992
Central nervous system	$ 455.3	(39)%	$ 749.7	(4)%	$ 783.3
Steroids, anti-inflammatory and analgesic	413.4	2	406.5	(4)	422.1
Reproductive and women's health	511.1	41	362.5	24	292.6
Critical care, transplant and cancer	412.1	8	383.1	11	344.3
Infectious disease	439.0	11	394.0	14	346.4
Animal health	336.2	1	332.6	4	320.7
Other products and materials	707.9	(1)	711.6	(5)	746.8
Consolidated net sales	$3,275.0	(2)	$3,340.0	3	$3,256.2

Prior-year data have been conformed to current year product group classification.

Consolidated domestic sales of pharmaceutical products in 1994 decreased 10 percent to $1,847 million from $2,046 million in 1993, and compared to $2,003 million in 1992. Domestic sales in 1994 were 56 percent of total consolidated sales, down from 61 and 62 percent in 1993 and 1992, respectively. International sales in 1994 were $1,428 million, up 10 percent from $1,294 million in 1993 and compared to $1,253 million in 1992. Consolidated sales for 1994 were down as the result of a 3 percent decline in price, offset in part by a 1 percent benefit from foreign exchange. Volume was unchanged.

The current year decline in worldwide sales of central nervous system agents was the result of intense generic competition against XANAX, the anti-anxiety agent, which lost U.S. patent protection in October 1993. The U.S. decline in sales of XANAX was offset somewhat by sales of the company's generic anti-anxiety agent alprazolam. In international markets, XANAX continued to record good growth. Sales of HALCION Tablets (triazolam), the sleep inducing agents, were also down in the U.S. largely due to the loss of U.S. patent protection in October 1993. Sales of HALCION in international markets were up in 1994, reversing the trend of decline encountered over the past few years. The decline in sales of central nervous system agents is expected to continue in 1995. The 1993 decrease from 1992 sales levels also resulted from the loss of U.S. patent protections, offset somewhat by the launch of generic versions of XANAX and HALCION.

The 1994 growth in steroids, anti-inflammatory and analgesic product group was let by MOTRIN IB, the over-the-counter nonsteroidal analgesic agent, which continued to perform well in a very competitive market. This performance resulted in part from a 1993 agreement that provided access to new-product technology and product-line extensions. This and other products sales gains offset the decline in U.S. sales of ANSAID Tablets (flurbiprofen), which resulted from

generic competition encountered in late 1994. U.S. patent protection for ANSAID was lost in February 1993.

Sales of reproductive and women's health products recorded strong, benefiting from the addition of OGEN, the estrogen replacement therapy acquired in late 1993. Sales of DEPO-PROVERA, the injectable contraceptive, continued to record strong increases in both U.S. and international markets. Combined worldwide sales of PROVERA Products (medroxy-progesterone), the progestational agents, were up for the year in spite of a moderate decline in the U.S. due to increasing generic competition. CAVERJECT, for erectile dysfunction, was approved for sale in 12 countries in 1994 and also contributed to sales.

International sales of SOLU-MEDROL, the injectable steroid, and other MEDROL Products led the growth in the critical care, transplant and cancer product group. Sales of ATGAM, the immunosuppressant, were up slightly for the year. In 1994, the company completed a series of agreements with Yakult Honsha Co. Ltd. for the rights to develop and market the anti-cancer compound irinotecan for several indications in the U.S., Canada, and Latin America. Clinical development of this compound is currently in process.

VANTIN, the broad-spectrum oral antibiotic sold primarily in the U.S., led the growth in the infectious disease product group. Sales of CLEOCIN (DALACIN in international markets), the family of antibiotic products, demonstrated good growth in international markets but declined in the U.S. Sales of CLEOCIN T Products (clindamycin topical) were down for the year due to U.S. generic competition.

In the animal health product group, PIRSUE, introduced late in 1993 for the treatment of mastitis, and LUTALYSE, the fertility-control agent, both provided 1994 sales growth. Sales of MGA, the feed additive, were flat. Sales of NAXCEL (EXCENEL in international markets), the antibiotic, were up in international markets and down slightly in the U.S. due to a lower-than-average cattle population. Sales of lincomycin and companion animal products were down in 1994.

In other products and materials category, GLYNASE Press Tab, the oral anti-diabetes agent, continued to record good growth in the U.S. Sales of MICRONASE Tablets (glyburide), the oral anti-diabetes agents, were down significantly from 1993 levels as a result of the loss of U.S. market exclusivity in the second quarter of 1994. While the company will continue to sell its generic glyburide to minimize the effect of third-party generic competition, it is anticipated that combined sales of MICRONASE and glyburide will decline in 1995. Sales of ROGAINE, the treatment for hair loss, were up for the year. The consumer products COR-TAID, the anti-itch medication; DOXIDAN and SURFAK, the treatments for constipation; and DRA-MAMINE, the treatment for motion sickness, all demonstrated good growth, while sales of KAOPECTATE, the treatment for diarrhea, were down for the year.

Other Operating Revenue

Operating income for 1994 benefited from marketing alliance agreements with Burroughs-Wellcome Co. for the promotion of their product ZOVIRAX, and with Hoechst-Roussel Pharmaceuticals Inc. (HRPI) to market and detail their product ALTACE. The agreement with Burroughs-Wellcome expires at the end of 1995. An agreement has been reached with HRPI to sell the company's rights relating to ALTACE effective January 1, 1995.

Cost and Expenses

Consolidated operating expenses, stated as a percent of sales, were as follows:

	1994	1993	1992
Cost of products sold	25.7%	23.5%	23.2%
Research and development	18.5	18.3	17.0
Marketing and administrative	39.5	39.4	39.7
Restructuring		6.3	0.7
Operating income	18.3	13.8	20.4

The rise in 1994 cost of products sold compared to that of the prior two years is the result of a change in product mix, which is primarily due to U.S. generic competition encountered with the major products identified previously. Compared to the products that lost patent protection, the company's generic equivalents and other products have lower gross margins. The decline is also due to a higher percentage of total worldwide pharmaceutical product sales in international markets where the company's products generally carry lower gross margins.

Expenditures for research and development in 1994 were up slightly as a percent of sales from 1993 due primarily to the timing of expenses related to large clinical programs. Both 1994 and 1993 research and development expenditures are significantly higher than in 1992 due to the continuing costs associated with accelerated development of FREEDOX IV Solution (tirilazad mesylate) and other compounds.

In December 1994, further enrollment in the North American clinical trial of FREEDOX for severe to moderate head injury was suspended pending further analysis of an unexplained difference in mortality rates. At the time of suspension, enrollment in this trial was 98 percent complete. The results were unexpected because a fully-enrolled study in Europe showed no signs of the effects encountered in the North American trial. The company will continue to medically evaluate patients in both the North American and European trials for six months following treatment. The data from both trials will be analyzed to assess the therapeutic benefit of FREEDOX in the treatment of severe to moderate head injury and to determine the reason for the difference in mortality encountered in the North American trial. Analysis of the results of other clinical trials of FREEDOX for subarachnoid hemorrhage, spinal cord injury and stroke has not identified any safety concerns and these trials will continue.

Marketing and administrative expense as a percent of sales in 1994 was comparable to both 1993 and 1992. Savings from the 1993 and 1992 restructurings realized in this expense category were offset by increases in other costs related to various marketing programs and by other expenses. A portion of the increased costs in 1994 resulted from new-product marketing expenses related to LUVOX, the treatment for obsessive-compulsive disorder, which will be sold in the U.S. LUVOX is a product of Solvay Pharmaceuticals Inc. Unfavorable foreign exchange comparisons in certain international markets also added to this expense category in 1994.

The restructuring plan announced in October 1993 was in the process of being implemented during 1994. At the beginning of 1994, approximately 400 employees had left the company under the 1993 restructuring, while at the end of 1994 that number had increased to approximately 1,100. Certain elements of the 1993 plan are still in the process of implementation. All aspects of the 1992 plan had been implemented by the end of 1993. The gross combined benefit to 1995 earnings from the 1992 and 1993 restructurings is expected to be approximately $120 million. The benefit is expected to increase moderately after 1995 when all aspects of the 1993 restructuring plan are fully implemented.

Earnings before taxes and minority equity from the company's operation in Europe of $44 million were up significantly in 1994 from a loss of $39 million and earnings of $11 million in 1993 and 1992, respectively. This improvement is the result of increased sales volume, a net favorable effect from exchange and savings from expense reductions. The 1993 European measure was depressed largely due to unfavorable exchange and the costs of restructuring. Sales increased in Japan largely as the result of favorable exchange, which was partially offset by continuing price erosion in that market. Restructuring did not have a significant adverse effect on earnings in the Japan and Pacific geographic area in 1993. In other international markets, increases in sales volume, which were offset somewhat by exchange, and expense savings led to the significant increase in earnings before taxes from 1993 levels. The cost of restructuring reduced earnings in other international markets in 1993.

Nonoperating Income and Expense

The favorable interest income to interest expense relationships have increased in each of the years 1992 through 1994. Nonoperating income in 1994 also benefited from the favorable resolution of a coverage dispute with an insurance carrier and the gain on the sale of a joint venture. The 1993 measure includes a nonoperating gain on the sale of a cough/cold medicine trademark. There were no such gains in 1992.

Income Taxes

The effective tax rate for 1994 was 24 percent, compared to 17.5 percent and 21.7 percent in 1993 and 1992, respectively. When the tax benefits related to restructuring are excluded, the 1993 rate would have been 22 percent. The increase in 1994 is the result of a higher proportion of earnings from international operations, which are taxed at relatively higher rates, and a lower proportion of total earnings from operations in Puerto Rico. The major products encountering U.S. generic competition are manufactured in Puerto Rico.

The Omnibus Budget Reconciliation Act of 1993 will have a significant impact on the company's net earnings beginning in 1995. The Act ultimately reduces tax benefits from operations in Puerto Rico under Section 936 of the Internal Revenue Code by 60 percent. The change had little effect on the tax rate for 1994.

SFAS No. 109 was adopted effective January 1, 1992. The cumulative effect of this accounting change was a favorable adjustment to 1992 net earnings of $13 million, resulting primarily from adjusting deferred tax balances to reflect current tax rates.

Financial Condition

	1994	1993	1992
Working capital (millions)	$1,011	$678	$582
Current ratio	1.9	1.7	1.5
Debt to total capitalization	26.0%	28.1%	30.3%
Return on average equity-continuing operations before accounting changes	21.9%	19.3%	26.2%

The significant increase in working capital and the corresponding improvement in the current ratio were largely the result of the year-end 1994 receipt of the proceeds from the sale of the Asgrow Seed Company which were temporarily invested in cash equivalents. Also contributing to the improvement in these measures was the increase in short-term investments, which were classified on the balance sheet as other current assets. The company recently announced a common stock repurchase program, to be completed in 1995, which will utilize approximately $300 million. The working capital increase and improvement in the current ratio realized at the end of 1993 was because the proceeds of medium-term notes had been used during the year to reduce outstanding commercial paper.

The 1994 ratio of debt to total capitalization benefited from the increase in total shareholders' equity when compared to a consistent level of year-to-year total borrowing. The improvement in 1993 when compared to 1992, resulted from lower total debt.

The 1994 improvement in return on average equity before accounting changes was due to the favorable earnings comparison. Net earnings in 1993 and 1992 were reduced by the after-tax expense associated with restructuring, totaling $154.6 and $13.4 million, respectively. Excluding the cost of restructurings, return on average equity would have been 27.5 percent in 1993 and 27.9 percent in 1992.

Net cash provided by operations was $710 million in 1994 compared to $780 million and $597 million in 1993 and 1992, respectively. Significant adjustments were made to 1993 cash provided by net earnings to reflect the non-cash effects of restructuring charges. Spending against the related restructuring reserves reduced the 1994 measure by $72 million. This spending was primarily the result of the reduction in personnel and is expected to be less than $35 million in 1995. Cash provided by 1992 net earnings was adjusted to reflect the non-cash effects of a restructuring and a

The Upjohn Company

significant accounting change. Nonoperating uses of cash in 1994 included purchase of investments; the addition of property, plant and equipment; the payment of dividends to shareholders; and the purchase of treasury stock. The largest source of cash from nonoperating activities was realized from the sale of the Asgrow Seed Company.

In 1993, proceeds of a $200 million 5.875% debt issue under a 1993 shelf registration were utilized to redeem $200 million 8% notes that were called at par on July 1, 1993. Medium-term borrowing at the end of 1994 was unchanged from 1993 at $466 million and compared to $138 million in 1992. The company had $134 million available for future borrowing under the 1993 and 1991 shelf registrations at the end of 1994.

The company utilizes derivative financial instruments in conjunction with its foreign currency risk management programs. These programs employ over-the-counter forward exchange contracts and purchased foreign currency options to hedge existing net transaction exposure and certain existing obligations in several subsidiary locations. These exposures arise both from intercompany and third-party transactions. Foreign currency options are occasionally utilized to hedge anticipated transactions. Risk of loss in the hedging of anticipated transactions is minimized through the exclusive use of purchased foreign currency options.

The hedging activities seek to protect operating results and cash flows from the potential adverse effects of foreign currency fluctuations. This is done by offsetting the gains or losses on the underlying exposures with losses and gains on the instruments utilized to create the hedge. The company does not utilize derivative financial instruments for trading purposes.

The company is obligated to make contributions to certain employee benefit programs and may elect to continue funding one other program. The company's cash flow requirements under the Employee Stock Ownership Plan will begin to accelerate in 1996 from current levels, and there will be a minimum contribution required for the U.S. pension plan of approximately $25 million. In each of the years 1992 through 1994, the company has made contributions to a Voluntary Employee Benefit Association to partially prefund postretirement benefit obligations. Future contributions are discretionary.

The company has committed to make a series of investments in a company that intends to manufacture a hemoglobin-based oxygen carrier as certain progress goals are met.

The company's future cash provided by operations and borrowing capacity are expected to cover normal cash flow needs and planned capital additions for the foreseeable future, despite the adverse effects of the expiration of patents and other product protection discussed below.

Patent Expirations

A U.S. Food and Drug Administration (FDA) moratorium on the approval of Abbreviated New Drug Applications (ANDAs) for products containing glyburide, the generic name for MICRONASE, expired in May 1994. Patent protection of ANSAID, CLEOCIN T, XANAX, and HALCION expired in 1993. No significant patent protection remains on PROVERA. The company began marketing generic equivalents for most of these products in 1993 and 1994. U.S. sales of these six products, including that of the generic equivalents, declined from $1,068 million in 1993 to $672 million in 1994. While it is anticipated that sales of these products will continue to decrease over the next several years, the decline is expected to be lower than that experienced in 1994.

FDA moratoriums on the approval of ANDAs protect exclusivity for GLYNASE until March 1995 and for DEPO-PROVERA until November 1995. U.S. patent protection for ROGAINE will expire in February 1996.

Sales growth of other existing products, the acquisition and development of new products, the marketing of generic equivalents, and efforts to control costs and enhance revenues are expected to offset much of the effects of the loss of patent and ANDA protection. Therefore, the combined earnings impact of the patent expirations, offset by these strategies and actions, are not expected to be as severe in 1995 as in 1994. Earnings in years subsequent to 1995 depend on the success of new products and the strategies noted above.

Other Items

The company is subject to environmental legislation and regulation. Environmental compliance costs, including capital expenditures related to future productions, have been increasing each year. Spending at the Kalamazoo, Mich., production site is expected in the near future related to groundwater remediation and improved control of surface water discharges.

Other projects related to the prevention, mitigation and elimination of environmental effects are being planned and implemented worldwide.

The company is involved in several administrative and judicial proceedings relating to environmental matters, including actions brought by the U.S. Environmental

Protection Agency (EPA) and state environmental agencies for cleanup at approximately 40 "Superfund" or comparable sites, including the West KL Avenue Landfill in Kalamazoo County, Mich. The company's estimate of the ultimate cost to be incurred in connection with these environmental situations could change due to the potential existence of joint and several liability, possible recovery from other potentially responsible parties, the levels of cleanup to be required and the technologies to be employed. An accrual has been recorded, but added costs could be incurred in connection with the various remedial actions. Although the company cannot predict the outcome of these matters, the ultimate liability should not have a material effect on the company's consolidated financial position; and unless there is a significant deviation from the historical patterns of resolution of such issues, the ulti-

mate liability should not have a material adverse effect on the company's results of operations or liquidity.

Studies directed toward a final remediation plan for the site of the company's discontinued industrial chemical operations in North Haven, Conn., are in process. Issues related to removal of a sludge pile located on the site due to zoning violations have been resolved with the town. The final plan of remediation of the pile will be worked out among the company, the Connecticut Department of Environmental Protection and the U.S. EPA with input from the public. The company cannot at the present time predict the final resolution of the sludge pile issue and has not established any reserves for the cost of off-site disposal. The company believes that it has established sufficient reserves to cover the costs of other remedial activities that may be required.

The Upjohn Company

Selected Financial Data (Dollar amounts in millions, except per-share data)

Years ended December 31	1994	1993	1992	1991	1990
Operating revenue	$3,344.5	$3,380.5	$3,284.7	$3,057.9	$2,675.3
Earnings from continuing operations before cumulative effect of accounting changes[a]	489.1	396.4	527.0	521.5	435.9
Earnings per share from continuing operations before cumulative effect of accounting changes[a]	2.75	2.20	2.92	2.87	2.36
Dividends declared per share	1.48	1.48	1.42	1.26	1.04
Total assets	5,162.5	4,811.9	4,513.1	4,053.9	3,578.8
Long-term debt	521.0	526.8	402.9	295.5	274.6

(a) Relating to January 1, 1993 accounting changes resulting in a net charge of $18.9 or $.11 per share and to January 1, 1992 accounting changes resulting in a net charge of $222.9 or $1.26 per share.

The Upjohn Company

EXHIBIT 2

Abridged Merger Prospectus

UNAUDITED CONDENSED PRO FORMA COMBINED FINANCIAL STATEMENTS

The following unaudited condensed pro forma combined balance sheet as of June 30, 1995, and the unaudited condensed pro forma combined statements of earnings for the years ended December 31, 1994, 1993, and 1992 and the six-month periods ended June 30, 1995 and 1994 have been prepared to illustrate the estimated effects of the proposed combination of Pharmacia and Upjohn in accordance with U.S. GAAP under the "pooling of interests" method of accounting. A condition in order to account for the merger as a "pooling of interests" under U.S. GAAP is that there must at a minimum be an exchange of at least 90% of the outstanding common stock of each of Upjohn and Pharmacia. The Combination will occur through the formation of the company which will issue an assumed 503,722,558 shares of New Common Stock and an assumed 7,263 shares of New Preferred Stock, which will be exchanged for all of the outstanding Pharmacia Securities and shares of Upjohn Common Stock and Upjohn Preferred Stock. The Unaudited Condensed Pro Forma Combined Balance Sheet as of June 30, 1995 was prepared as if the Combination was consummated at June 30, 1995. The Unaudited Condensed Pro Forma Combined Statements of Earnings for the years ended December 31, 1994, 1993 and 1992 and the six-month periods ended June 30, 1995 and 1994 were prepared as if the Combination was consummated as of January 1, 1992. The unaudited condensed pro forma combined financial statements are based on the historical consolidated financial statements of Pharmacia and Upjohn giving effect to the Combination under the assumptions and adjustments outlined in the accompanying Notes to Unaudited Condensed Pro Forma Combined Financial Statements.

The unaudited condensed pro forma combined financial statements have been prepared in accordance with U.S. GAAP. The financial statements of Pharmacia have been converted from Swedish GAAP to U.S. GAAP and translated into U.S. dollars for purposes of this presentation (see Note 1 of the Notes to unaudited condensed pro forma combined financial statements.) Swedish GAAP differs in certain significant respects from U.S. GAAP. A reconciliation of net income and shareholders' equity of Pharmacia from Swedish GAAP to U.S. GAAP is presented in Note 25 to the Consolidated Financial Statements of Pharmacia.

The unaudited condensed pro forma combined financial statements do not give effect to certain restructuring and rationalization costs expected to be incurred following the Combination. The management of the company presently is considering the nature and extent of the charges to be so incurred. Such costs presently cannot be reasonably predicted in a manner sufficient to quantify the amount and timing of such charges under U.S. GAAP. Upon final determination, a substantial charge or charges will be recorded during 1995 and/or 1996 and be reflected in the company's statement of earnings as a non-recurring charge or charges to operations in accordance with the U.S. GAAP. The actual payments to implement the restructuring and rationalization are expected to be made over a two- to three-year period. In addition, although the company expects to realize cost reductions from the Combination and the restructuring and rationalization, no effect has been given in the company's unaudited condensed pro forma combined financial statements to any such benefits.

The unaudited condensed pro forma combined financial statements are provided for illustrative purposes only and do not purport to represent what the financial position or results of operations of the company would actually have been if the Combination had in fact occurred on the dates indicated or to project the financial position or results of operations for any future date or period. The unaudited pro forma combined financial statements should be read in conjunction with the notes thereto and the consolidated financial statements of Pharmacia and Upjohn and the related notes thereto contained elsewhere herein.

The Combination Agreement provides that each outstanding Pharmacia Class A Common Share, Pharmacia Class B Common Share and ADS representing one Pharmacia Class A Common Share will be exchanged for one share of New Common Stock or SDS, each outstanding share of Upjohn Common Stock will be exchanged for 1.45 shares of New Common Stock and each outstanding share of Upjohn Preferred Stock will be exchanged for one share of New Preferred Stock. The precise number of outstanding shares cannot be determined until the Effective Date. For purposes of the unaudited condensed pro forma financial statements, the actual number of shares of capital stock of Pharmacia and Upjohn issued and outstanding at June 30, 1995 has been used to calculate the issuance of shares of New Common Stock and New Preferred Stock pursuant to the Offer and the Merger.

UNAUDITED CONDENSED PRO FORMA COMBINED BALANCE SHEET, JUNE 30, 1995

	Historical	
(dollar amounts in thousands)	Pharmacia (Note 1)	Upjohn
Current assets:		
Cash and cash equivalents	$ 198,141	$ 303,914
Short-term investments	900,929	328,443
Trade accounts receivable (net)	913,046	671,767
Inventories	500,379	502,172
Deferred income taxes and other	286,541	335,584
Total current assets	2,799,036	2,141,880
Investments	127,367	598,254
Property, plant and equipment, at cost	2,359,380	3,203,532
Less allowance for depreciation	(1,035,456)	(1,351,189)
Net property, plant and equipment	1,323,924	1,852,343
Other noncurrent assets	119,656	426,390
Intangibles (net)	1,592,702	224,719
Total assets	$5,962,685	$5,243,586
Current liabilities:		
Accounts payable, accrued liabilities and dividends payable	$ 732,392	$ 297,119
Short-term borrowings, including current maturities of long-term debt	700,034	60,285
Income taxes payable	180,103	226,702
Other	179,140	494,967
Total current liabilities	1,791,669	1,079,073
Long-term debt	85,508	515,005
Guaranteed of ESOP debt		267,200
Postretirement benefit cost	15,040	374,607
Deferred income taxes and other noncurrent liabilities	609,401	505,322
Shareholders' equity:		
Preferred stock	—	292,719
Common stock	880,413	190,590
Capital in excess of par value, statutory reserves and other	1,755,034	97,291
Retained earnings	825,620	2,891,048
ESOP deferred compensation and note receivable from ESOP trust		(273,430)
Treasury stock, at cost	—	(695,839)
Total shareholders' equity	3,461,067	2,502,379
Total liabilities and shareholders' equity	$5,962,685	$5,243,586

(continued)

The Upjohn Company

UNAUDITED CONDENSED PRO FORMA COMBINED BALANCE SHEET, JUNE 30, 1995 *(cont.)*

(dollar amounts in thousands)	Pro Forma Adjustments	Combined
Current assets:		
Cash and cash equivalents (Note 2)	$ (69,000)	$ 433,055
Short-term investments		1,229,372
Trade accounts receivable (net)		1,584,813
Inventories		1,002,551
Deferred income taxes and other		622,125
Total current assets	(69,000)	4,871,916
Investments		725,621
Property, plant and equipment, at cost		5,562,912
Less allowance for depreciation		(2,386,645)
Net property, plant and equipment		3,176,267
Other noncurrent assets		546,046
Intangibles (net)		1,817,421
Total assets	$ (69,000)	$11,137,271
Current liabilities:		
Accounts payable, accrued liabilities and dividends payable		$1,029,511
Short-term borrowings, including current maturities of long-term debt		760,319
Income taxes payable		406,805
Other		674,107
Total current liabilities		2,870,742
Long-term debt		600,513
Guaranteed of ESOP debt		267,200
Postretirement benefit cost		389,647
Deferred income taxes and other noncurrent liabilities		1,114,723
Shareholders' equity:		
Preferred stock (Note 3d)	$(292,719)	292,719
(Note 3d)	292,719	
Common stock (Note 3a)	(880,413)	5,038
(Note 3a)	2,558	
(Note 3b)	(190,590)	
(Note 3b)	2,480	
Capital in excess of par value, statutory reserves and other		
(Note 3a)	877,855	2,222,451
(Note 3b)	188,110	
(Note 3c)	(695,839)	
Retained earnings (Note 2)	(69,000)	3,647,668
ESOP deferred compensation and note receivable from ESOP trust		(273,430)
Treasury stock, at cost (Note 3c)	695,839	
Total shareholders' equity	(69,000)	5,894,446
Total liabilities and shareholders' equity	$ (69,000)	$11,137,271

The accompanying notes are an integral part of the unaudited condensed pro forma combined financial statements.

The Upjohn Company

UNAUDITED CONDENSED PRO FORMA COMBINED STATEMENT OF EARNINGS
FOR THE SIX MONTHS ENDED JUNE 30, 1995

(dollar amounts in thousands, except per share amounts)	Historical		Pro Forma Combined
	Pharmacia (Note 1)	Upjohn	
Operating revenue:			
Net sales	$1,808,125	$1,643,446	$3,451,571
Other revenue	21,117	74,123	95,240
Total	1,829,242	1,717,569	3,546,811
Operating costs and expenses:			
Cost of products sold	525,735	446,828	972,563
Research and development	289,324	290,809	580,133
Marketing and administrative	681,085	628,153	1,309,238
Restructuring, rationalization and merger-related costs	11,853		11,853
Total	1,507,997	1,365,790	2,873,787
Operating income	321,245	351,779	673,024
Interest income	57,900	40,690	98,590
Interest expense	(32,015)	(12,988)	(45,003)
Foreign exchange	(23,160)	(1,147)	(24,307)
Other (net)	—	(1,557)	(1,557)
Earnings from continuing operations before income taxes	323,970	376,777	700,747
Provision for income taxes	131,740	109,300	241,040
Earnings from continuing operations	192,230	267,477	459,707
Dividends on preferred stock (net of tax)	—	6,186	6,186
Earnings from continuing operations available for common shareholders	$192,230	$261,291	$453,521
Primary earnings from continuing operations per common share (Note 4)			$0.90
Fully diluted earnings from continuing operations per common share (Note 4)			$0.88
Weighted average equivalent shares used in primary per-share calculation (Note 4)			506,277
Weighted average equivalent shares used in fully diluted per share calculation (Note 4)			519,694

The accompanying notes are an integral part of the unaudited condensed pro forma combined financial statements.

The Upjohn Company

UNAUDITED CONDENSED PRO FORMA COMBINED STATEMENT OF EARNINGS
FOR THE SIX MONTHS ENDED JUNE 30, 1994

(dollar amounts in thousands, except per share amounts)	Historical		Pro Forma Combined
	Pharmacia (Note 1)	Upjohn	
Operating revenue:			
Net sales	$1,730,358	$1,619,350	$3,349,708
Other revenue	23,276	24,507	47,783
Total	1,753,634	1,643,857	3,397,491
Operating costs and expenses:			
Cost of products sold	507,002	420,558	927,560
Research and development	233,995	303,091	537,086
Marketing and administrative	692,472	617,982	1,310,454
Total	1,433,469	1,341,631	2,775,100
Operating income	320,165	302,226	622,391
Interest income	45,286	27,356	72,642
Interest expense	(46,045)	(12,671)	(58,716)
Foreign exchange	4,933	(2,079)	2,854
Other (net)	(126)	(374)	(500)
Earnings from continuing operations before income taxes	324,213	314,458	638,671
Provision for income taxes	137,629	72,500	210,129
Earnings from continuing operations	186,584	241,958	428,542
Dividends on preferred stock (net of tax)	—	6,126	6,126
Earnings from continuing operations available for common shareholders	$186,584	$235,832	$422,416
Primary earnings from continuing operations per common share (Note 4)			$0.84
Fully diluted earnings from continuing operations per common share (Note 4)			$0.82
Weighted average equivalent shares used in primary share calculation (Note 4)			505,360
Weighted average equivalent shares used in fully diluted per share calculation (Note 4)			518,197

The accompanying notes are an integral part of the unaudited condensed pro forma combined financial statements.

UNAUDITED CONDENSED PRO FORMA COMBINED STATEMENT OF EARNINGS
FOR THE YEAR ENDED DECEMBER 31, 1994

(dollar amounts in thousands, except per share amounts)	Historical		Pro Forma Combined
	Pharmacia (Note 1)	Upjohn	
Operating revenue:			
Net sales	$3,429,364	$3,274,996	$6,704,360
Other revenue	48,880	69,542	118,422
Total	3,478,244	3,344,538	6,822,782
Operating costs and expenses:			
Cost of products sold	1,046,702	843,152	1,889,854
Research and development	490,081	607,187	1,097,268
Marketing and administrative	1,357,367	1,294,752	2,652,119
Restructuring, rationalization and merger-related costs	19,837		19,837
Total	2,913,987	2,745,091	5,659,078
Operating income	564,257	599,447	1,163,704
Interest income	97,630	59,624	157,254
Interest expense	(87,517)	(24,600)	(112,117)
Foreign exchange	23,208	(1,087)	22,121
Other (net)	30,210	10,104	40,314
Earnings from continuing operations before income taxes	627,788	643,488	1,271,276
Provision for income taxes	283,425	154,400	437,825
Earnings from continuing operations	344,363	489,088	833,451
Dividends on preferred stock (net of tax)	—	12,291	12,291
Earnings from continuing operations available for common shareholders	$344,363	$476,797	$821,160
Primary earnings from continuing operations per common share (Note 4)			$1.62
Fully diluted earnings from continuing operations per common share (Note 4)			$1.60
Weighted average equivalent shares used in primary share calculation (Note 4)			505,432
Weighted average equivalent shares used in fully diluted per share calculation (Note 4)			518,363

The accompanying notes are an integral part of the unaudited condensed pro forma combined financial statements.

The Upjohn Company

UNAUDITED CONDENSED PRO FORMA COMBINED STATEMENT OF EARNINGS
FOR THE YEAR ENDED DECEMBER 31, 1993

	Historical		Pro Forma
(dollar amounts in thousands, except per share amounts)	Pharmacia (Note 1)	Upjohn	Combined
Operating revenue:			
Net sales	$3,167,530	$3,339,957	$6,507,487
Other revenue	12,692	40,579	53,271
Total	3,180,222	3,380,536	6,560,758
Operating costs and expenses:			
Cost of products sold	1,038,665	783,590	1,822,255
Research and development	481,591	612,490	1,094,081
Marketing and administrative	1,330,111	1,316,138	2,646,249
Restructuring, rationalization and merger-related costs	59,869	208,789	268,658
Total	2,910,236	2,921,007	5,831,243
Operating income	269,986	459,529	729,515
Interest income	176,529	50,789	227,318
Interest expense	(151,018)	(31,496)	(182,514)
Foreign exchange	2,308	(4,556)	(2,248)
Other (net)	(641)	6,306	5,665
Earnings from continuing operations before income taxes	297,164	480,572	777,736
Provision for income taxes	132,942	84,201	217,143
Earnings from continuing operations	164,222	396,371	560,593
Dividends on preferred stock (net of tax)	—	12,125	12,125
Earnings from continuing operations available for common shareholders	$164,222	$384,246	$548,468
Primary earnings from continuing operations per common share (Note 4)			$1.08
Fully diluted earnings from continuing operations per common share (Note 4)			$1.07
Weighted average equivalent shares used in primary share calculation (Note 4)			506,414
Weighted average equivalent shares used in fully diluted per share calculation (Note 4)			519,256

The accompanying notes are an integral part of the unaudited condensed pro forma combined financial statements.

The Upjohn Company

UNAUDITED CONDENSED PRO FORMA COMBINED STATEMENT OF EARNINGS
FOR THE YEAR ENDED DECEMBER 31, 1992

(dollar amounts in thousands, except per share amounts)	Historical		Pro Forma Combined
	Pharmacia (Note 1)	Upjohn	
Operating revenue:			
Net sales	$2,653,657	$3,256,188	$5,909,845
Other revenue	—	28,560	28,560
Total	2,653,657	3,284,748	5,938,405
Operating costs and expenses:			
Cost of products sold	868,863	754,483	1,623,346
Research and development	344,367	553,297	897,664
Marketing and administrative	1,142,560	1,292,204	2,434,764
Restructuring, rationalization and merger-related costs	24,221	22,055	46,276
Total	2,380,011	2,622,039	5,002,050
Operating income	273,646	662,709	936,355
Interest income	197,547	50,054	247,601
Interest expense	(104,270)	(31,253)	(135,523)
Foreign exchange	(95,166)	(3,397)	(98,563)
Other (net)	2,748	(5,223)	(2,475)
Earnings from continuing operations before income taxes	274,505	672,890	947,395
Provision for income taxes	97,743	145,900	243,643
Earnings from continuing operations	176,762	526,990	703,752
Dividends on preferred stock (net of tax)	—	12,084	12,084
Earnings from continuing operations available for common shareholders	$176,762	$514,906	$691,668
Primary earnings from continuing operations per common share (Note 4)			$1.36
Fully diluted earnings from continuing operations per common share (Note 4)			$1.34
Weighted average equivalent shares used in primary share calculation (Note 4)			508,565
Weighted average equivalent shares used in fully diluted per share calculation (Note 4)			521,446

The accompanying notes are an integral part of the unaudited condensed pro forma combined financial statements.

The Upjohn Company

PHARMACIA AND UPJOHN, INC.—NOTES TO UNAUDITED CONDENSED PRO FORMA COMBINED FINANCIAL STATEMENTS
(dollar amounts in thousands, except per share data)

The unaudited condensed pro forma combined financial statements have been prepared to reflect the Combination of Pharmacia and Upjohn through the formation of the company which will issue an assumed 503,722,558 shares of New Common Stock and an assumed 7,263 shares of New Preferred Stock, which will be exchanged for all of the outstanding Pharmacia Securities and shares of Upjohn Common Stock and the Upjohn Preferred Stock. The Combination is accounted for under the pooling-of-interests method of accounting in accordance with U.S. GAAP.

Note 1

The historical Pharmacia consolidated financial statements included elsewhere herein have been prepared in accordance with Swedish GAAP and denominated in Swedish kroner with a reconciliation of net income and stockholders' equity to U.S. GAAP included in the Notes to the consolidated financial statements. See "Note 25 to the Consolidated Financial Statements of Pharmacia." The Pharmacia historical financial information included in these unaudited condensed pro forma combined financial statements has been presented in accordance with U.S. GAAP and translated into U.S. dollars at a rate of $1 = SEK 7.2625 as of June 30, 1995 and using the weighted average rate of exchange for the six-month periods ended June 30, 1995 and 1994, and for the years ended December 31, 1994, 1993 and 1992 of $1 = SEK 7.3402.

Note 2

To record estimated expenses associated with the Combination, which include, without limitation, fees and expenses of investment bankers, legal counsel, accountants and consultants incurred by Pharmacia and Upjohn in connection with or related to the authorization, preparation, negotiation and execution of the Combination Agreement and the preparation, printing, filing and mailing of this Prospectus including solicitation of stockholder approvals and all other matters related to closing the Transactions.

Note 3

To record the issuance of shares of New Common Stock, and 7,263 shares of New Preferred Stock in exchange for the outstanding Pharmacia Securities, the outstanding shares of Upjohn Common Stock (at an exchange ratio of 1.45 to 1) as set forth below, and 7,263 outstanding shares of Upjohn Preferred Stock.

	Pharmacia
Pharmacia Class A Common Shares outstanding (par value SEK 25)	164,724,715
Pharmacia Class B Common Shares outstanding (par value SEK 25)	91,027,398
Upjohn Common Stock outstanding (par value $1.00)	—
	255,752,113
Exchange ratio to New Common Stock (par value $.01)	1.00
	255,752,113

(continued)

	Upjohn
Pharmacia Class A Common Shares outstanding (par value SEK 25)	—
Pharmacia Class B Common Shares outstanding (par value SEK 25)	—
Upjohn Common Stock outstanding (par value $1.00)	171,014,100
	171,014,100
Exchange ratio to New Common Stock (par value $.01)	1.45
	247,970,445
New Common Stock to be issued	503,722,558

Note 3a

Record issuance of New Common Stock to Pharmacia stockholders.

Note 3b

Record issuance of new Common Stock to Upjohn stockholders.

Note 3c

Record cancellation of Upjohn treasury stock pursuant to the Combination Agreement.

Note 3d

Record exchange of Upjohn's Preferred Stock for New Preferred Stock (an exchange ratio of 1:1) pursuant to the Combination Agreement.

Note 4

Primary earnings from continuing operations per share are computed by dividing earnings from continuing operations available to holders of New Common Stock by the weighted average of common shares outstanding based on the share exchange ratio (including common share equivalents, principally stock options). Fully diluted earnings from continuing operations per share have been computed assuming that all of the convertible preferred stock and convertible debenture loans are converted into common shares.

The Upjohn Company

EXHIBIT 3

Upjohn–Pharmacia Merger Announcement—August 20, 1995

A Upjohn Stock Price and Trading Volume

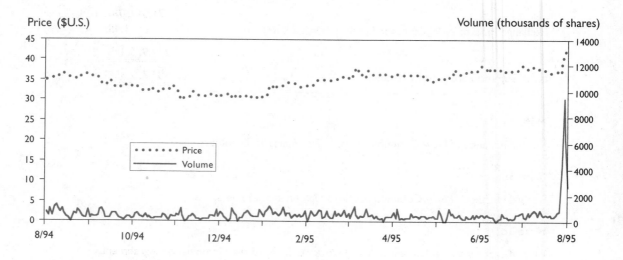

B Pharmacia Stock Price and Trading Volume

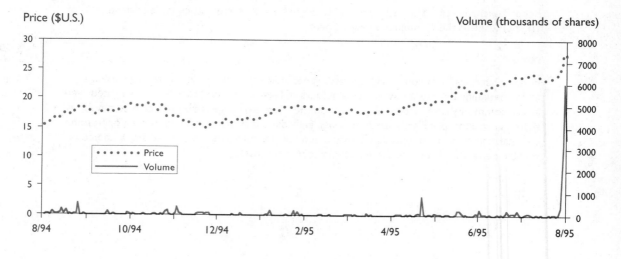

The Upjohn Company

C Upjohn and Pharmacia Daily Stock Returns on Trading Days Surrounding the Merger Announcement

	Upjohn	Pharmacia
3 days prior to announcement	+0.34%	+1.54%
2 days prior to announcement	−2.36	+1.08
1 day prior to announcement	+9.31	+4.63
1 day after announcement	+2.84	+4.43
2 days after announcement	+5.52	+5.21
3 days after announcement	−2.33	−2.23

Source: Datastream International.

D Valuation Data at Announcement

Upjohn's share price on August 18, 1995	$39.63
Pharmacia's share price on August 18, 1995	$25.38
Upjohn's Beta	0.95
Pharmacia's Beta	0.91
US T-Bills, 30 day, August 1995	5.3%
30-Year US Treasury Bonds	6.9%

The Upjohn Company

INDEX

AUTHOR INDEX